ISBN 978-1-330-25841-5
PIBN 10004077

THE FARMER'S MAGAZINE.

VOLUME THE SEVENTH.

(SECOND SERIES.)

JANUARY TO JUNE, MDCCCXLIII.

LONDON:

OFFICE, 24, NORFOLK STREET, STRAND.

MAY BE HAD BY ORDER THROUGH ALL BOOKSELLERS.

LONDON:
PRINTED BY JOSEPH ROGERSON,
24, NORFOLK-STREET, STRAND.

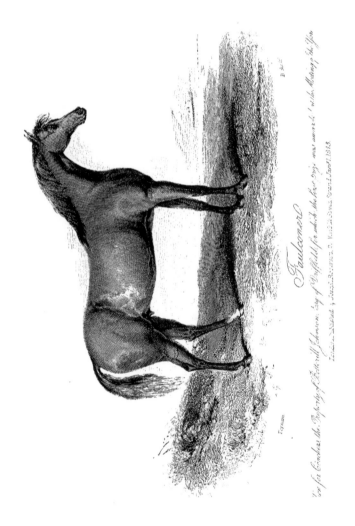

Falconer

Drawn for Cumpher, the Property of R. H. and J. Solomon, Esq. of Sheffield, for which the bay was won 1 with Mathey's Sol 5 lbs

Painted by W. J. Nicholson ......

Engraved by Hall & Son from Green & Sept. 1818.

THE FARMER'S MAGAZINE.

JANUARY, 1843.

No. 1.—Vol. VII.]   [Second Series.

PLATE I.

PORTRAIT OF THE LATE EARL OF LEICESTER.

PLATE II.

FAULCONER.

Faulconer is the property of Mr. Botterill Johnson, of Frodinghambridge, near Driffield, Yorkshire ; he is a beautiful grey, rising five years old, stands full sixteen hands high, with superior action, and was got by Falcon, dam by Admiral, grandam by Peerless, great grandam by Greek, great great grandam by Mr. Pickering s noted yellow Horse, of Willerby. Falcon was by Interpreter, dam Miss Newton, the dam of Merlin, Buzzard, &c., by Delphini ; her dam Tipple Cyder, by King Fergus, Sylvia, by Young Marsk ; out of Ferret, by a brother to Silvio, Regulus, &c. Admiral was got by General Benefit, his dam by Mr. Goodlass's noted horse Old Turk, grandam Mr. Lamplugh's Old Volunteer, great grandam Mr. Sawden's old horse, of Lund ; great great grandam by Mr. Dunsley's celebrated Horse. In 1837, Faulconer's dam won the prize and sweepstakes at Beverley, as the best coaching mare, and within the last three months her worthy owner, Mr. Windass, of Beverley Park, refused a large sum for her. In 1838, Faulconer obtained the premium at Beverley, as the best coaching foal, and in 1841, at Burlington, for the best coaching stallion, with a sweepstakes at Beverley. In the same year, at the Yorkshire show, which was open to all England, he carried off the first prize in his class, although he had numerous competitors of great merit.

MEMOIR OF THE LATE EARL OF LEICESTER.

BY CUTHBERT W. JOHNSON, ESQ., F.R.S.

It is a good sign of the present day, and indeed it has almost universally been so in the best and brightest periods of England's eventful history, that her children are ever ready to do impartial justice to the dead. The grave with them closes over all strife ; the breath of party violence, of envy, and of ambition is heard no more; the good actions of the departed are then chiefly and gratefully remembered. And this meed of approbation has in all ages been with more than ordinary readiness awarded to those who have in any way contributed to the better, the more profitable, cultivation of the earth.

Of the first of such a class of England's benefactors, must ever be placed the name of the subject of this memoir; a beautifully engraved

OLD SERIES.]

portrait of whom, by W. H. Davis, embellishes the first page of our magazine for the present month.

The Right Honourable Thomas William Coke, Earl of Leicester, of Holkham, in the county of Norfolk, and Viscount Coke, was born on the 4th of May, 1752 ; the son of Wenman Roberts, Esq., who assumed the name and arms of the Coke family on succeeding to their estates, by the death of his maternal uncle, Thomas Coke, Earl of Leicester.

Of the ancestors of such a man, the farmer will be glad to hear all that diligent research can discover. He was descended from the great lawyer, Sir Edward Coke, who was twice married, and had by his first wife, Bridget Paston, of Huntingfield, in Suffolk, ten children—seven sons and three daughters. Of the daughters : 1st.—Elizabeth*, died

* "Here lyethe the Bodye of Elizabeth Cooke, Daughter to Edward Cooke and Bridget his Wyfe,

B   [No. 1.—VOL. XVIII.

in her infancy 2nd.—Ann, who was baptised at Huntingfield, March 7th, 1584, married Ralph, son and heir of Sir Thomas Sadler, the grandson of Sir Ralph Sadler, chancellor of the duchy of Lancaster; she died without issue (*Chauncey's Hertfordshire, vol. 2. p. 180).* 3rd.—Bridget, married William, son and heir of Sir Vincent Skinner (*Collins, vol. 4, p. 353).* Of the sons: 1st.—Edward, baptized at Huntingfield, Dec. 5, 1583, died an infant. 2nd.—Robert, baptized at Huntingfield, Oct. 3, 1587; received the honour of knighthood; he married Theophila, daughter of Thomas Lord Berkeley, by whom he had no issue. He died July 19, 1658, aged 67 (*Monument in Epsom Church*). Through this Robert Coke, the London library of Sir Edward Coke came into the possession of the Berkeley family; and was by George, the fourteenth Earl Berkeley, presented, in 1680, to the corporation of Sion College, in London. 3rd.—Arthur, baptized at Huntingfield, March 7th, 1588, who married Elizabeth, daughter and heiress of Sir George Walgrave, by whom he had four daughters.* 4th.—John, baptized at Huntingfield, March 4, 1590, who was seated at Holkham; he married Meriel, the daughter of Anthony Wheateley, Esq., by whom he had six sons and nine daughters.† The estate, however, descended to his youngest son John, and he dying unmarried, the property descended to the heirs of Henry Coke (*Collins, vol. 4, p. 155).* 5th.—Henry, who was baptized at Huntingfield, August 30, 1592, was seated at Thurrington, in Norfolk. He was elected member of Parliament in 1623 for Wycomb, twice in 1625 for the same borough, and in 1640 for Dunwich (*Willis Not. Parl. vol. 2, p. 187, 198, 208, 286).* He married Margaret, daughter to and heiress of Edward Lovelace, Esq., by whom he had a son, Richard, who espoused Mary, daughter of Sir John Rous, Bart., by whom he had a son, Robert, who succeeded, on the death of John Coke, to the Holkham estates, and the greatest part of Sir Edward Coke's property (*Monument in Titleshall Church*). This Robert Coke married Lady Ann Osborn, daughter of Thomas Duke of Leeds, by whom he had only one son, Edward. Robert Coke died January 16, 1679, in the twenty-ninth year of his age; and

---

who deceased the 11 Daye of November, in the yeare of our Lord 1586"—is inscribed on a flat stone with a brass plate, before the altar of Huntingfield Church, in Suffolk.
* Epitaph in Bramfield Church, in Suffolk.
† In the chapel on the south side of Holkham Church is a marble monument, on which is inscribed—"To the reviving memory of William Wheateley, Esq., and Martha Skinner, his wife; and Anthony Wheateley, Esq., and Ann Armiger, his wife; and also of Meriel Coke, late wife of John Coke, of Holkham, in the county of Norfolk, Esq., the fourth son of the Right Honourable Sir Edward Coke, Knight, late chief judge of the court of Common Pleas, and afterwards Chief Judge of the King's Bench, &c., &c., &c. Her loving husband, John Coke, Esq., to whom she bore six sons and nine daughters, and lyeth here buried, erected this to her memory. She died the fourth of July, 1636.
In the chancel of the same church is a grave-stone, on which is engraved—"In memory of John Coke, Esq., fourth son of Sir Edward Coke, &c., &c., who married Meriel, daughter of Anthony Wheateley, Esq., of Hill Hall, in Norfolk (*Blomfield's History of Norfolk, vol. 5, p. 810).*

was buried at Titleshall, where there is a monument to his memory. His son Edward married Carey, daughter of Sir John Newton, of Gloucestershire; he died on the 13th of April, 1707, and his widow soon afterwards; they had three sons and two daughters—1, Thomas; 2, Edward, who died at his seat at Longford in August, 1733, unmarried.
It was on this Mr. Edward Coke's behalf, that the celebrated Sarah Duchess of Marlborough pretended to have been offered six thousand pounds for a peerage, "And how easy and inoffensive a thing," says the Duchess, "would that have been at that time! for he was a gentleman, of an estate equal to the title desired, and was grandson to the Duke of Leeds, and in that interest which hitherto carried all before it at court (*Account of her own conduct,* 346)." But dying, as before stated, unmarried, he left his estate to his youngest brother Robert.
This Robert Coke was Vice Chamberlain to Queen Caroline, and married in June, 1733, Lady Jane, daughter and co-heir of Philip Duke of Wharton, and relict of John Holt, Esq., of Redgrave, in Suffolk.
The daughters were: 1st.—Carey, who married Sir Marmaduke Wyville, Bart., of Burton Constable, in Yorkshire; and 2nd., Anne, married to Major Philip Roberts, of the second Life Guards.
Thomas Coke, Esq., however, their elder brother, succeeded to the family estates; he was made Knight of the Bath in May, 1725; in 1728, Lord Lovel, of Minster Lovel, in Oxfordshire; and in 1747, Viscount Coke, and Earl of Leicester.
He married in July, 1718, Lady Margaret Tufton, one of the daughters and co-heiresses of Thomas Earl of Thanet, to whom George the II. confirmed her right of descent to the Barony of Clifford; by this lady he had a son, Edward, who married Lady Mary Campbell, daughter of Field Marshal the Duke of Argyle, and died at Greenwich, in the life time of his parents, without issue.
The magnificent seat of Holkham, by far the finest mansion in the East of England, was erected under the direction of this Lord Leicester; who, when he had finished his work, placed an inscription over the hall door, where it still remains, to inform the spectator that the ground on which he erected the house, he had found a barren waste.
6th.—*Clement,* the sixth son of Sir Edward Coke, who was baptized at Huntingfield, September 4, 1594, married Sarah, daughter of Alexander Reddicke, by whom he had two sons and two daughters; his descendants were all extinct in 1727.
He represented the borough of Heydon, in 1614 (*Willis Not. Parl., vol. 2, p. 169, 170),* and committed himself by using some rather rash expressions, which the Government of Charles the First sorely resented.*

---

* His monument is in the Temple Church, with this inscription:—"Here resteth the body of Clement Coke, of Langford, in the county of Derby, Esq., youngest son of Sir Edward Coke, Knight, late Chief Justice of England; and of Bridget his wife, daughter and co-heir of John Paston, of Paston, in the county of Norfolk, Esquire.—This Clement married Sarah, daughter and co-heir of Alexander Redicke, of Redicke, in the county of Lancaster; and of Catherine, his wife, sole daughter and heir of Humphry Dethick, of Newal, in the county of Derby, Esq.; and had issue by the said Sarah, living at his death, Edward, Robert, Bridget, and Avise. He in the Inner Temple,

7th.—Thomas, the youngest son of Sir Edward Coke, died young.

By his second wife, Lady Hatton, Sir Edward Coke had two daughters. 1st.—Elizabeth, who died unmarried. 2nd.—Frances, who married Sir John Villiers, brother of Villiers Duke of Buckingham, anti afterwards created Viscount Parbeck, but by whom, according to a decision of the House of Lords, she had no children.

On the death of Lord Leicester, in 1759, the Earldom of Leicester, &c., became extinct, but his estates devolved upon his nephew, Wenman Roberts, Esq. (the son of Lord Leicester's sister Ann), who, as we have before observed, assumed the name of Coke, and died in 1776. He married Elizabeth Chamberlayne, and had by her—1st, Thomas William, his heir ; 2nd, Edward ; and two daughters.

On his death, in 1776, he was succeeded by the subject of this paper, Thomas William Coke, afterwards, as we have already seen, created Earl of Leicester ; who married first, Jane, daughter of James Dutton, Esq., of the county of Dorset, by whom, who died in June, 1800, he had three daughters, viz. :—1st, Jane Elizabeth, who married first in 1796, to Charles Nevison Viscount Andover, who was killed by the bursting of a fowling piece, in 1800 ; secondly, in 1806, to Vice-Admiral Sir Henry Digby, by whom she had issue —1st, Edward ; 2nd, Kenelm ; 3rd, Jane, married in 1824, to Lord Ellenborough, but which marriage was dissolved in 1830. 2nd.—Ann Margaret, married in 1794 to Viscount Anson, by whom she had, with several other children, the present Earl of Lichfield. 3rd.—Elizabeth Wilhelmina, married in 1822 to John Spencer Stanhope, Esq., of Cannon Hall, in Yorkshire.

Mrs. Coke died June 2, 1800 ; and after remaining a widower for more than twenty-one years, Mr. Coke, in February, 1822, married secondly, Lady Ann Amelia Keppel, daughter of the present Earl of Albemarle, and had issue—Thomas William, now Earl of Leicester, born December 26th, 1822 ; Edward Keppel, born August 20th, 1824 ; Henry John, born January 3rd, 1827 ; Wenman Clarence Walpole, born July 13th, 1828 ; Margaret Sophia, March 7th. 1832.

Thomas William Coke, the subject of this memoir, upon losing his father in 1776, was immediately chosen to succeed him as the representative in Parliament for the county of Norfolk ; again elected in 1780, he was an unsuccessful candidate in 1784, but was again returned in 1790, 1796, and 1802 ; was declared not duly elected by a committee of the House of Commons, after the general election of 1806, but was again returned in 1807, and in every succeeding election until 1832, when he declined to offer himself again. In 1837 he was created a peer. With his political history we have little to do in this work ; he never suffered political feeling to interfere with either his personal friendship, or his noble agricultural pursuits, and we have no intention of departing from so excellent an example. He spoke himself of his own Parliamentary career, when in 1833 he had retired from the representation of his native county, without self-flattery or bitterness, and with no attempts at an eloquence which he never

being a Fellow of the House, christianly and comfortably in his flourishing age yielded up his soul to the Almighty, the three and twentieth of May, A.D. 1629."—*Stowe's London*, 763.

possessed ; when he said, "When I first offered myself for this county, I did so with great reluctance, for I had no wish to come into Parliament. I was no orator, no politician. I was young, and just returned from abroad, and my own pursuits (if I could appeal to the ladies), were much more congenial to my feelings. But I was much solicited by Sir Harbord Harbord, Sir E. Astley, and Mr. Fellowes, of Shottisham, who said, and said truly, that I owed it to my father's memory, to Sir E. Astley, who had just stood a severe contest, and that if I did not stand a tory would come in. At the mention of a tory coming in, gentlemen, my blood chilled all over me from head to foot, and I came forward. I was desired to write one letter to George Earl of Orford, which I did, and I well remember the answer : ' Houghton and Holkham have always been united in the bonds of friendship, let it ever be so.' Soon after I met the noble Earl, who said, ' I can never support you again, you always clog the wheels of Government.' This was not very pleasant. I had not been in the House of Commons more than two months, when Charles Tompson said to me one day, ' If Mr. Coke is inclined for a Peerage, I will mention it.' Soon after this the Duke of Portland wrote to me, and said that the King allowed them to make three Peers, and I should be the first if I liked.' I immediately went to London, to Burlington House, and called on the noble Duke, and told him I was astonished that he should think I would desert Mr. Fox, and that so great was my regard for him, that so long as I lived I would ever support him." This will give the reader a fair idea of the late Lord Leicester's politics. He seemed to be in that respect ever straightforward and uncompromising, and if he did now and then, in some of his after-dinner addresses, betray a want of taste in culling his expressions of contempt, he did it without intending to hurt the feelings of any one. Leaving, therefore, the reader to judge of Lord Leicester's political tenets by his own feelings, we turn to his great and successful agricultural efforts, which have redounded so much to his honour, and which will in all probability be remembered with gratitude by all the cultivators of England as long as farming shall be held to be the best and noblest support of the land of our birth. Some of the chief results of the late Lord Leicester's attempts to improve his extensive Norfolk estates has been sketched by Lord Spencer (*Journ. Roy. Ag. Soc. v. II. p.* 1) ; and what he has done so well, it is needless to attempt to give in other language. From that paper we learn that at the time Lord Leicester came into the possession of his estates, in 1776, " the whole district around Holkham was unenclosed, and the cultivation of the most miserable description : the course of cropping, as long as the land would produce anything, was three white crops in succession, and then broadcast turnips ; no manure was purchased, and very little, and that of no value, was produced on the farm. The sheep were of the old Norfolk breed, and, with the exception of a few milch cows, there were no cattle kept upon any of the farms." Chance, which has often paid to it honours very undeserved, had, however, it seems, much influence in making Lord Leicester a farmer. It is, it seems, entirely to the obstinacy of a farmer of the old school that England is indebted for the improvements which emanated from the great agricultural school of Holkham. " It happened," continues Lord Spencer, " that the lease of a large part of the land which now forms

Holkham Park was within two years of its expiration. In the lease previous to the one then current this land had been let at 1s. 6d. per acre; in the then current lease it had been raised to 3s. Lord Leicester offered to the tenant to renew it at 5s.; but Mr. Brett, the tenant, who deserves to have his name recorded for the great good he unintentionally did to his country, refused to give so much for the land ; upon which Lord Leicester determined to take it into his own hands. The real origin, therefore, of the great improvement of this district was, that Mr. Brett refused to give 5s. an acre for land which now, under an improved system of cultivation, usually produces nearly four quarters of wheat per acre; for nothing would have been much more improbable than that Lord Leicester—then an extremely young man, fond of and excelling in field sports, with a princely fortune—should have applied himself to the detailed management of a farm, had he not been compelled to take this tract of land into his own hands by the refusal of Mr. Brett to accept the terms which were offered to him. But, having taken the farm into his own hands, he soon found, as every man who applies himself to agriculture will find, the high interest of the pursuit : his taste was formed, the habits of his life accommodated themselves to it, and, applying the whole energy of his mind to the collection and dissemination of all the knowledge which he could derive from practical and scientific farmers, he at length effected the great improvements which, while they were a source of continual happiness to himself, produced the most incalculable benefits to his country.

The lease having thus expired in 1778, Lord Leicester commenced farming. He was, however, necessarily ignorant of any of the knowledge necessary to conduct the management of a farm ; but he took the only means which could give him the information he required—he began at once to collect around him practical men, and invited to his house annually a party of farmers, at first only from the neighbouring districts. At these meetings agricultural subjects were discussed ; Lord Leicester's farm was examined, and his management of it either criticised or approved ; and, by thus receiving information, and again communicating to others, not only did Lord Leicester himself arrive at the knowledge of agricultural management, but the practical men who attended these meetings left them better informed than they came. In the course of time, the friends of Lord Leicester came from a distance to attend them, and ultimately, from such a small beginning, came the far-famed Holkham Sheep-shearing, which was annually long the great centre of agricultural attraction ; until at last they became too great and too expensive to be longer continued. They had, besides, accomplished all the benefits that Lord Leicester originally anticipated from the repeated visits to one district of so great an assemblage of accomplished practical farmers.

But he did not confine his researches to his own immediate neighbourhood : he was the friend and correspondent of all the great farmers of his time— of such men as Francis Duke of Bedford, Sir John Sinclair, Robert Bakewell, Matthew and George Culley, and Arthur Young. In 1784, Young visited Holkham, and published some of his observations (*Annals of Agriculture, v.* II *, p.* 355*)*. Lord Leicester's farm then consisted, it seems, of about 3,000 acres—£2,000 rent.

400	Acres of	Platation.
400	"	Sainfoin.
500	"	Turnips.
300	"	Barley.
130	"	Oats.
30	"	Wheat.
40	"	Peas.
800	Norfolk Ewes.	
100	of Bakewell's breed of Sheep.	
600	Wethers.	
120	Fat Oxen.	
12	Working Oxen.	
30	Cows.	
8	Carters and Servants.	
40	Labourers.	

It is evident that Lord Leicester had already succeeded in improving the enterprise and skill of the old race of Norfolk farmers ; for Young adds, " Mr. Coke resides in the midst of the best husbandry in Norfolk." Young was again in Holkham October 29, 1792. *(Annals, v.* XIX. *p.* 441.*)* Lord Leicester communicated to Young *(Annals, v.* XV. *p.* 586*)* an account of the ponds he had caused to be made at Holkham, for the convenience of watering sheep and cattle.

The celebrated farmer, J. Boys, of Betshanger, in Kent, and J. Ellman, of Glynde, in Sussex, were at Holkham in July, 1792 ; and Boys describes, in a very laudatory way, in his published " Minutes," all that he saw there. *(Annals, vol.* XIX*, p.* 118.*)*

The first Mrs. Coke was evidently also very partial to farming ; for Boys observes, " While Mr. Coke attended to receive his rents from a great number of tenants, it being audit day, Mrs. Coke rode with us nearly thirty miles. It is impossible to describe either the pleasure we enjoyed in this morning's ride, or the agreeable surprise in meeting with an amiable lady in high life so well acquainted with agriculture, and so condescending as to attend two farmers out of Kent and Sussex a whole morning, to show them some Norfolk farms. What improvements," he adds, " would be made in this country if one-half of the gentry of landed property understood and delighted in agriculture like this worthy family !" Boys noticed, with the quick eye of a farmer, the advantages of the Holkham agriculture, and speaks with pleasure of " immense fields of barley," " very great crops, and perfectly clean, on land naturally poor ;" " the house, a palace of the first rate."

Young describes very briefly *(Annals, v.* XXIX. *p.* 140) the Annual Sheep-shearing at Holkham, in 1797. And more at length, that of June 20, 1803 *(Annals, v.* XL. *p.* 604), he says—" The district, though long famous for its husbandry, has been greatly improved in the last ten or twelve years ; and it is much deserving of notice, that this is also the period of the existence of Holkham Sheep-shearings, affording reason for the obvious conclusion, that the spirit of improvement, so nearly allied to the renunciation of prejudices, has arisen in consequence of the conversation promoted at these meetings, of the emulation excited by premiums, and of the certainty that no exertions in experimental agriculture made by the tenantry of an extensive county, will be overlooked by the pervading eye, or neglected by the munificence, of the great patron of Norfolk improvements."

At this meeting there attended, amongst others, the Duke of Bedford, Sir Joseph Banks, Sir Humphrey Davy, John Culley, Arthur Young, Edmund Cartwright, and about three or four hundred other gentlemen. " As one of the first consequences," continues Lord Spencer," of the discussions at these meetings, Lord Leicester adopted a somewhat improved course of cropping ; instead of growing three white crops in succession, he only grew two, and kept the land in pasture for two years in every course. This change appears gradually to have improved the land ; and I find, from the old accounts of the farm, that wheat was first sown upon it in 1787 (according to Arthur Young, ante it was grown in 1784). This improved course of cropping, though quite essential, was not of itself sufficient to enable him to grow wheat. The land, naturally very weak, was still more impoverished by the exhausting treatment it had received. In order to get it into better condition, it was absolutely necessary greatly to increase the number of live stock which had hitherto been kept upon it ; but the production for them was so small, that it was impossible at first to adopt this mode of improvement to any great degree. The first thing to be done was the purchase of manure. Another much more effective source of fertility was adopted, and to a much greater degree than it had been hitherto. The surface soil of the whole district is a very light sand, but nearly throughout it, at various depths, there is a stratum of rich marl. Pits were opened, and the marl dug out and laid upon the surface ; this not only increased its fertility, but gave to the soil the solidity which is essential to the growth of wheat. By such means, clover and other artificial grasses were raised, and the power obtained of keeping more live stock. The only live stock then kept were the Norfolk sheep—there were no cattle. At first, Lord Leicester made no alteration ; but he adopted Mr. Bakewell's Leicester breed of longhorned cattle. When, however, some time afterwards, he found that the Norfolk sheep were a very unprofitable sort, he tried the new Leicesters—a variety of sheep but ill calculated to succeed on the soils of Holkham. He at last found that the Southdowns were the best breed of sheep he could adopt. He made, however, many careful, long-continued comparative trials before he finally resolved upon the change. So late as the Sheep shearing of 1812, Leicester and Norfolk sheep were kept at Holkham ; since then, only the Southdowns have been kept. He tried, but only for a short period, the Merinos. He was a decided friend to the Devon breed of cattle, with which he replaced the longhorned variety."

When Lord Leicester had proved, by his own practice, that wheat might be profitably grown, he endeavoured to persuade the neighbouring farmers to follow his example ; but it was nine years before any of them did so. At last the late Mr. Overman, whose skill and ability are well known, made the attempt with perfect success ; and from that time the old system fell into disrepute, and the present Norfolk agriculture gradually replaced it.

But many difficulties and contentions, many arguments and restraining covenants, had to be employed before this very desirable consummation could be effected—although at first the tenantry were only restrained from taking more than two white crops in succession. At last, however, he succeeded. " The effect of even this alteration," continues Lord Spencer, " was such that it proved how disadvantageous to all parties the old system had been ; and upon the late Mr. Overman taking a farm of Lord Leicester, he was allowed to draw the covenants of his own lease himself ; he then inserted the modern improved course of cropping, well known as the best adapted to light turnip lands. This lease has been the model on which Lord Leicester's leases have since been drawn—making, of course, any changes which the peculiar nature of each farm may require. The tenants make no difficulty now about agreeing to adopt the covenants inserted in their leases, for the able and skilful farmers of his estates know full well that the course of husbandry thus enforced, whilst it is the most advantageous for the improvement of the property of their landlord, is the most profitable for themselves."

Such, then, is a very rapid sketch of the great agricultural efforts of the late Thomas William Coke, Earl of Leicester—such were his enlightened views — such the labours he encountered in the service of agriculture : works which were only closed by his death, which happened on the 30th of June, 1842, when he was in the 91st year of his age.[*] And, as it has been truly remarked in another place (and with this summary of the efforts of the great " Coke of Norfolk" we conclude this brief review of his life), it is impossible for such a man as this to depart, as he has recently done, full of years and honour, without carrying with him the farmers' grateful remembrance ; for the benefit of his oj first unaided exertions—his triumphs over the poor drifting sands of Norfolk—were not confined to the tenants of his own princely estates, but they were felt to the remotest corners of the island. He, too, was not the farmer who confined his views to the immediate profits which even bad farming, the most execrable rotation of crops, at first affords ; he took a wider, a nobler position—he laboured, and he exerted himself successfully too, to increase the permanent fertility of the soil ; he effected this excellent object, not only by improved rotations of crops, but by the application of marl and clay, by the judicious use of artificial organic manures ; and by the adoption of a more numerous and a more profitable description of live stock, he banished the old race of profitless Norfolk sheep. He excited the more general use of the drill ; and, by such and other improvements, he at last succeeded in growing the wheat crop in an extensive portion of Norfolk, where wheat had never before been grown. Lord Leicester, too, had the wisdom to conclude that the interest of the landlord and the tenant were too closely united to be readily separated. He granted, therefore, leases of a liberal nature and extent, and burthened the cultivators of his estates with but few restraining covenants ; for these, he well knew, while they retard the exertions of the good farmer, but seldom improve the farming of

[*] We have not attempted to follow in detail all the great agricultural improvements which Lord Leicester either originated or supported. The use of artificial manures, such as bones, gypsum, rape cake, the use of dung in a fresher state (Com. to Board of Agriculture, vol. vi. p. 366); the use of the drill, and the manure drill also ; the drilling turnips on ridges ; the use of mangel-wurzel ; the more genera introduction of green crops—of improved agricultural implements; and of many other modern improvements, were all supported by Lord Leicester's influence and example. He infused, too, into the minds of all those with whom he associated the advantages to be derived by the farmers from coming into collision with men of science, and with the cultivators of distant districts ; and on all occasions endeavoured to acquire and diffuse knowledge.

the bigotted and the indolent.* That his noble agricultural efforts were appreciated in his lifetime, both at home and abroad, the crowds who annually attended his great sheep-shearings sufficiently attested; and now that he has departed, in his good old age and full of honour, we rejoice to see, by the just and graceful tribute which the agriculturists of his country are about erecting to his memory, that they are not willing that his great services, or the gratitude of his brother farmers, should be allowed long to remain unrecorded.—*Johnson's Life of Sir Edward Coke, Gentleman's Magazine, Lord Spencer's Sketch, Johnson and Shaw's Farmers' Almanac for* 1843.

ON THE PRINCIPLES OF DRAINING, AND THEIR PRACTICAL APPLICATION.

TO THE EDITOR OF THE FARMER'S MAGAZINE.

Sir,—In a letter on this subject, inserted, in your journal for May last, I dwelt on the necessity of examining the subsoil before we determine on the plan to be followed; and on reading again the former letter to which I then referred, am inclined, under the impression that good may come by drawing the attention of others at this period, to explain more fully my opinions on the theory of draining. In the several treatises it has fallen to my lot to read (and I have read but few for some years, except the different articles that have appeared in your journal,) I have seen little analysis of its principles, or search into the physical laws of nature as they act on and control our operations. In attempting the following discussion, I am aware of the difficulty of the task; aware that when we enter into an examination of one of the principles of nature, we find a wonderful combination of matter acting in the universal scheme, that should occupy our attention ere we arrive at any conclusion. But this is not perhaps strictly applicable to the comparatively confined view I purpose taking of the subject; and did I enter on it with an idea of embracing one half of the argument necessary for the development of the properties relating to it, I should have a very false view of my own powers. In short, as opportunities have occurred of dispelling a doubt, or correcting an error, by seeking aid from a few popular works on science that have come to hand, I have availed myself of them—of the pleasure of comparing practice with theory; hence emanate the following observations, and without such confirmation I should not be sanguine enough to make the attempt. With me, the general mode has been reversed—the theory has been subsequent to the practice; and when we can bring the known natural laws to bear on, to justify the plans we follow, we have reason to feel convinced of their correctness. We have sought

the only test, the only guide by which we can hope to arrive at the truth; and if we err, the inference drawn from effects, the judgment is in fault; deprived of such guide, whatever be the pursuit, though by experience we may hit the right mode, we shall ever be liable to err : and surely if there is one agricultural question more worthy than another of our labour to establish a system based on unerring principles, it is this. However much the method may require changing as circumstances may change, it needs no demonstration that as certain natural laws are ever in action, certain plans of draining modelled by, and adapted to those laws, must constitute a true system. On any given soil there can be but one perfect mode of operation. Although, as mentioned in my last letter, I am convinced there is no chance of arriving at any definite plan on a subject giving so wide a scope for the differences of opinion, yet the more we can bring into question the principles as a point on which we can rest our views, the nearer we are likely to attain to it.

As the following remarks will more exclusively apply to the draining of those lands where the water does not rise in the form of springs, but is diffused through a considerable extent of soil—and we are well aware that water is constantly passing through the deeper strata of the earth, connected with, and flowing from and to the surface—it seems sufficient for my purpose that I only take a superficial view of the soil, noticing the effects of gravitation and capillary attraction on the water passing through it. I will first then briefly examine the nature and properties of water, and its action subservient to the above powers, leaving the consideration of the soil, the physical properties of which it will be necessary to notice when I come to the application.

Water is to all so well known that it seems superfluous to describe it, but it is requisite some of its properties should be well considered. It is a perfectly homogeneous fluid, and so small are the particles of which it is composed, that no one has, even with the best microscope, been able to discover the least variation of structure. "It is equally divisible in all directions, and it offers no resistance but the resistance of gravity, unless in consequence of the action of something else." The hardness and minuteness of its particles, and its nearly incompressible nature, have been beautifully shewn. "A globe made of gold was filled with water, and closed so accurately that none of it could escape : the globe was then put into a press and a little flattened at the sides, the consequence of which was that the water came through the fine pores of the golden globe, and stood upon its surface like drops of dew." In steam, when by heat the particles have become more divided, we can form some idea of their minuteness. "Steam is an invisible elastic fluid, like common air, and possessed of similar mechanical properties. We are, it is true, in the habit of associating a smoky appearance with steam, because we generally observe it when it is beginning to be condensed, as when it escapes, for instance, from the spout of a teakettle; but when perfectly formed it is quite invisible, and it only becomes visible when it escapes into the air, and suffers incipient condensation." Water is about 815 times heavier than common air.

We have perpetual instances of the *attraction of gravitation or gravity* in the falling of bodies to the earth; but when we apply this term to water rising to the surface of the earth, we seemingly utter a

---

* He was nobly consistent, even to the last; for, a short time before his decease, he called around him his numerous tenantry, and offered to renew all their then running leases for twenty-one years.—As it is very probable that this imperfect memoir may be published in a separate and enlarged form, its author would be obliged by suggestions and corrections.

paradox; yet it is strictly correct, as "fluids press equally in all directions—upwards, downwards, aslant, or laterally."

"The descent of a solid by gravitation is a power to the full extent of its weight or quantity of matter, the same as the descent of a liquid; but the solid is a dead power; the liquid in a certain sense a living one;" never resting till the whole of its upper surface exposed to the air is horizontal. Hence we have what is termed the hydrostatical paradox, "that any quantity of water, however small, may be made to balance and support any quantity, however large." "For instance, if a narrow vessel, say only one inch in section, is connected with one ever so wide, by means of a pipe at the bottom of both, water will stand at an equal height in the two vessels; and if an additional pound of water is poured into the narrow one, it will raise as many pounds in the wide as there are inches in its section, until the water again comes to the same height in both. This is not only true, but if a tube which admits a liquid to pass freely be made strong enough and of sufficient height, and the lower end of it communicate with the under part of a vessel full of the same, or any other liquid, and having no means of escape, a very small quantity of liquid poured into the tube will exert so much pressure as to burst the vessel. Thus a pipe an inch in diameter, and a mile high, contains about 36 cubic feet, or nearly a ton of water, and this water presses on the inch of base with the force of a ton. Now if such a pipe is supposed to be a perpendicular fissure in a mountain, and to terminate below in a cavern which has no outlet, and which presents towards the weak side of the mountain an extent of thirty yards in length and ten yards in height, the pressure tending to burst the mountain will be very great—namely, 259,000 tons; a pressure which it would take a strong mass of mountain to resist.[*] The pressure then of water and other fluids differs from their weight; the weight is according to the quantity, but the pressure is according to the perpendicular height."

Water and all liquids that wet the surfaces of solids rise in the openings of them by what is called *capillary attraction*, so called from its causing the visible rise of fluids in tubes of very small bore. "Thus, if a tube with a capillary bore of one-fiftieth of an inch, be dipped at one end into a glass of water, the water rises to about two inches and a half. It also takes place between flat surfaces of any extent, so that they are near to each other and the edges of both in the liquid; and the rise is great in proportion to the smallness of the aperture, for it ascends in all instances till the

* I am indebted for this and several other quotations to a very useful little book, "Readings in Science," published by the Society for Promoting Christian Knowledge; indeed, the greater part of the above observations under the head of hydrostatics may be considered as extracts either from that book, or from the works of Dr. Olinthus Gregory and Mr. Brande; and I have affixed the usual marks to all passages copied *verbatim*, or nearly so, as a confirmation of their correctness. I might perhaps have made a more indiscriminate use of these known truths without confining myself to the words of others, but I should then have deprived them of their influence. What I have sought is to place them in a plain unvarnished manner before your readers, with all the authority the names mentioned must necessarily confer on them.

weight of the quantity of liquid in the opening balances, or is equal to the attraction of the surface to which it adheres." If two plates of glass are so held that on one side their edges touch, leaving them a little open at the other, so as to form an acute angle with each other, and the lower edges dipped into coloured water, it will be seen to rise between them in the form of a curve (a hyperbola), rising highest where the space between them is least. The rising of fluids in sponges and many species of stones, "clay stones that appear perfectly solid," and the distribution of the juices of plants, are familiar instances. "Capillary attraction as it acts only between surface and surface, cannot act further than those surfaces extend; it does not produce a current through a tube even under the most favourable circumstances, unless it is assisted by gravitation, and as when it acts upwards it acts contrary to gravitation, and overcomes, but does not destroy the tendency in the liquid to gravitate, it must then act at some disadvantage. Thus whatever effect it may have in raising moisture within the earth as high as the surface, it never can make that moisture flow out in a spring or rise in a jet. These must always be produced by hydrostatical pressure; either the pressure of a "head" of water above the orifice, or the pressure of strata heavier than water upon the yielding stratum in which the water is contained." To those who may think I have thus far treated the subject too scientifically, dwelt longer on the above properties of water than was requisite, I would repeat, unless these properties are known (and they are very simple), we want our guide in draining, and our operations must to a certain extent be without foundation; we shall have experience alone to direct us, which must be extensive indeed to embrace all soils and circumstances without some theoretical knowledge. My fear is that I have taken too wide a view to be able to do it justice; that in catching at the leading points for the sake of conciseness, I have left out much that should be inserted.

If in a wet piece of land we dig a drain[*] or ditch from three to four feet deep, we invariably find the water flowing from the sides and bottom of our cut, varying in proportion and generally increasing in the size and diminishing in the frequency of the jets, as we increase the depth; the upper portion of the soil being more divided from cultivation, atmospheric influence, and the effects of animal and vegetable life, the water passes as through a filter; but when from changes in the subsoil, which are more or less generally present, and the continual flowing of water through the same channels as we get deeper the tubular cavities are frequently very evident, the water appearing in undulating lines according to the variation of the subsoil. We may, I believe, to a certain extent apply this to the most adhesive soils, as well as to those of a light nature; for although there are some lands in their natural state so extremely retentive as to be almost impervious to water, they will become pervious when thoroughly drained. The soil, if it is of an adhesive description, is too often looked upon as a mass impenetrable by water. When undrained

* In this letter a drain is supposed to be a conduit or pipe; the earth moved in digging it being returned and laid closely on the materials used, the water being only allowed to reach it by filtering through the soil.

heavy land is viewed, from which, at least in wet times, all the water that falls on it runs off, or in walking across it one is nearly mired, or after digging a hole the water stands in it level or nearly with the surface, it is at once concluded the soil is so close that no water can penetrate it; but this is certainly an erroneous conclusion, it is already saturated, and every drop that is added is more than it can contain. What are the different gradations of hardness, softness and mire caused by? every one is aware they are but the different degrees of wetness. Do we find a soil except the most porous that does not partake of these changes? No clod is so hard and close but the water will enter; and the reason is obvious. Soils are formed of numberless minute particles, which vary in size (and not to enter into an analysis it will be sufficient for my purpose to say), the coarser constitute the sandy, and the finer the adhesive and clays. These particles are kept together by adhesive attraction, water, their own weight, and atmospheric pressure, thus forming a mass the union of which is affected by every change; heat, air, and water, have the power of dividing them, of breaking their adhesion, their solidity being but a closer contact. But admitting the most adhesive clays would be from the fineness of their particles, their power of absorbing and retaining water, impervious; and that the atmospheric influence would be too superficial to materially affect their porosity, we have—to which I have already alluded—animals and vegetables in action creating tubular cavities in every direction. It is true the one cannot act in a soil thoroughly saturated with water, before it is drained, but the other does; however wet it may be, some plants will vegetate and strike their roots deeper into the soil than many perhaps are aware of. In very dry times, even the wettest undrained land (of the description here referred to), cleaves to a considerable depth from the loss of moisture, admitting the roots in seeking water to penetrate with little obstruction. Here then we have cavities formed which in arable land, from the constant change of plants and the consequent decay of the roots, become perpetual—as one is abstracted by the new root, another is opened by the decay of the old; but if these changes of plants did not take place, from what we see of the nature of water we cannot think when the root has penetrated the water will be obstructed. Again, supposing on some of the most stiff clays the above causes do not act to a sufficient depth to cause filtration; that from its extreme retentive power, its position to receive a supply of water, the want of tillage &c., the soil is never in a state to admit their action, yet as soon as we have drained and tilled it will be, at least I never saw a soil that would not. The radical change effected in the texture of the soil by draining and cultivation is far too little regarded in general. On well drained clays or heavy lands the first drought will cause numberless fissures to open, which, to a certain extent, I believe, remain permanently efficient for the admission of water to the drains. If we dig into such land after being once thoroughly dried, we shall be able to trace the fissures, which, if not still partially open, will, on arable land, be found lined with a sediment brought down from the surface. When the earth is again wetted by rain the clefts are filled with water, the weight of which counteracts the expansion of the earth, the water being nearly or quite half as heavy as the earth; and we must bear in mind that the pressure, particularly if in contact with a body of water in the drain, will be very different from its weight, and no doubt from the friction of its motion from permanent filtrating tubes into the drain: of this, those who have witnessed the effects, who have seen how quickly the water passes into a deep drain after heavy rains, can have, I think, little doubt. * And further, in all the above suppositions I have not availed myself of the courses for the water formed by the change of the layers, which will generally be found present to a greater or less extent even in the stiffest clays, formed perhaps in some instances by the agency of water. This, though placed last, is one of the facts that I principally rely on for the support of my argument on clays; were these changes wanting, the drainage of some of these soils would be very difficult.†

Assuming, then, that every soil is or will become permeable to water, and that the interstices passing in every direction, branching into and from each other, form a set of tubes, only being disunited by any change that may be present in the soil, the object must be to place our drains at such a depth as to prevent the earth being filled with water sufficiently high to injure vegetation.

In the general views taken of draining, the tendency of water to rise to the surface either by gravitation or capillary attraction has been too little regarded, and a want of attention to this fact has, I believe, been the cause of many errors with respect to depth, equally apparent in the very deep as in the shallow drain. In the deep drain (of from 4½ to 5½ or 6 feet) the view has been to cut off and sink to that depth the whole of the superfluous water in the soil; and this in many soils, from their porosity, has answered the purpose, though even then most probably not necessary, and if less deep would have answered better; but in other soils the change of measures between the drains has completely frustrated the object. In the case of a drain being placed in a wrong direction, it is not unusual to see the surface wet within a few feet of the drain, and that directly over it perfectly dry, the water in the soil being divided by some retentive measure that runs parallel with the drain.‡ In the shallow drain (of from

---

* I walked across a field in July last, which a few years since was, from being always saturated with water, quite worthless. It is a heavy alluvial soil on a mixed subsoil; it was cleft from the dry weather to the depth of at least 18 inches. This field is now one of the best on the farm. It has been frequently flooded since it was drained, but the water will not remain on it any length of time, so completely is the filtering property of the soil brought into action by drainage.

† I have seen some deep blue alluvial clay in which these changes of soil have not been present, that when drained cleft to such an extent as to form permanent fissures; the land being pasture they were not filled up by cultivation. I have not seen the field I allude to for some years, but the fissures no doubt are very evident now. They remained for many years through the wettest times, only contracting and expanding with any extreme changes.

‡ This, to prevent misconstruction, requires perhaps a little explanation. I here deem the measures of clay as bars to the circulation of the water in the soil, although I have before assumed clayey lands to

18 to 24 inches) we do not cut at a sufficient depth the interstices of the soil to prevent its flowing to the surface between our drains, unless they are very closely laid : we lose the effect of gravity in its downward course, and leave it an unimpeded action, as before, towards the surface. Many are advocates for the shallow drain on heavy land, under the impression that on such land it is "top water" alone they have to contend with—that, from the course of the soil, no water can pass from below to the surface. But it should be borne in mind, the smaller the cavities of the soil are, the higher the water will rise unassisted by gravitation ; the greater the apparent impediment (until the soil is quite impervious), the easier the passage. It is worthy of notice, too, that the more tenacious the soil is, the greater is its affinity for water, which, until it is saturated, will probably materially affect the passing of water through its pores. The arguments I have already used perhaps sufficiently explain my opinion on this head ; but believing it to be one of the errors most fatal to the efficient drainage of the country, I wish to be explicit. That there may be instances of "top water" only before the soil is opened, I admit ; but, as before mentioned, I have never yet seen a soil that would remain impervious. Looking at the fluidity and the weight of water, the extreme minuteness of its particles, their attraction for each other and for the soil, it is not probable that the surface can be long wet if the subsoil be not also wet, or that the surface should be dry if the subsoil be saturated, unless there is a "pan" or bed of closely cohering earth betwixt the surface and the subsoil, produced by constantly ploughing at one depth in wet seasons ; and this is, I think, one of the greatest and most common evils on stiff soils : it does not, of course, affect my argument, as it is remediable by the subsoil plough, which always should be used on these soils after draining. This forms a strong argument in favour of the deeper drain ; the shallow drain can never be safe for any length of time where subsoiling is practised. However much it may differ from what either practice or theory yield to my perception, I do not seek to depreciate the value of the shallow drain, for I have seen much good produced by it ; but to represent its inferiority to the deeper drain, both as regards the effect produced and its durability—to assert my conviction that we have the means of depriving the whole soil to a greater depth of the superabundant water, and giving it the power of filtration necessary for vegetation, for the proper and sufficient reception and nourishment of the roots of plants. If we dig up a plant of corn (either wheat or beans) growing on an open soil conge-

be pervious. This may seem paradoxical, but in this case practice has been my guide : and if we compare the one with the other, I think we shall find less analogy existing between them than at first sight may appear. In both cases I have allowed them to be impervious before draining, and as regards clayey soils, I have not considered them as formed entirely of clay, having—with the exception of now and then a peculiar instance—always found a change of soil as observed. The chief difference I believe to be this : the clay land properly drained is deprived of its surplus water ; whilst the clay bars, in the case of a drain being placed in a wrong direction, are still supplied, remaining exactly in the same state as before.

nial to its growth, we shall find its roots, if we cautiously trace them, very deep. But on this point it is needless to dwell, every one being aware that the deeper the soil is unclosed the better, if it have a sufficient supply of water ; and this must always be the case on all land requiring draining, unless it is carried to an extreme and useless extent. It affords a reason for the productive nature of many soils after being drained—by the constant admission of air through the drains the soil is gradually and permanently opened, if properly treated afterwards. The percolation of water from the surface carrying down the minute nutritive matter to the roots of plants after showers, the capillary action of the water in the soil toward the surface in very dry weather, are benefits of great moment ; with their aid, any tillage, any manure we may apply, will not fail to have its full effect, and without their existence in some degree it is almost superfluous to add its action will be always doubtful. In the frequent shallow drain system, these benefits are in a great measure lost ; there is no difficulty by the frequency of the drains in drying the surface, but the results are undoubtedly very different, and will generally be evident to the experienced eye during any extreme changes. We make the soil immediately in contact with the drains too dry, and deprive it of the power of obtaining sufficient moisture during great droughts by capillary attraction ; any corn growing directly over them will, from their unnatural dryness, be in danger, or the roots may penetrate them in search of water forming obstructions. The mole too, as these drains will always cease running in very dry weather, will be found a troublesome enemy, from which the deeper drain is quite free.* It may be supposed, looking to the power of

* It may form an objection with some against my deductions that I have failed to prove any particular depth to be the best. These observations may be looked on as mere generalizing, without any directly practical application. I have sought to make them as much so as the light in which the subject is viewed would allow. It is but an endeavour to illustrate principles on which our operations in practice must depend. In a former letter, when my remarks were confined to the draining of a particular description of soil, I named 3 and 3½ feet, having found those depths answer well ; the latter, I believe, is generally preferable. Taking a wider scope, I should say from 3 to 4 feet ; that as the operative causes of wetness and their remedies are in obedience to the laws of matter, our operations to obtain their full effect must, of course, vary with the nature of the soil and the changes of the strata that may be present in the subsoil. Every drainer has probably his nostrum—his vision becomes contracted to one particular focus, and it is not easy to change his sight ; for this, as regards the depth of the drain, I think there is some reason, having found the depths named effectual. But it would be presumptive, without taking into consideration every point bearing on the question, to say they are under all circumstances the best. Still I flatter myself the deductions drawn, or that may be drawn from a more close and searching examination, will be found in favour of those depths—will tend to prove the necessity of all soils being unclosed to the depth of from three to four feet, and that any greater depth is not needful for the perfect growth of any of our agricultural productions ; and farther, that a much greater depth will on some soils be found ineffectual, and on others injurious.

capillary attraction, we cannot reduce the water in the soil to the level of our drains, and this is in part no doubt correct; but it is equally true that we prevent the power of gravitation acting above that depth, and capillary attraction alone will not create much superabundant surface water; the particles of water, as before shown, must be first set in motion by gravitation from below; at any rate there must be a continual supply, either stagnant or in motion. When we have cut our drain we have severed the orifices of the soil, and as those orifices are parts of a series of cavities running in every direction, perpendicular, horizontal, and oblique, we give the water to the distance at which the drain acts a fresh action; we inverse it so long as there is sufficient left in the soil to act by its gravity, or until the superfluous water is carried off. The drain may be considered the nucleus around which as a centre the drained portions of earth extend in semicircles, until from the distance at which the water in the cavaties is acted on by the drain the effect ceases, each circle becoming less affected as they diverge from the centre, dependant on the resisting tenacity of the soil.

To many whose views differ from mine these observations may seem positive and dictatorial; in inferring causes from effects I have confidently expressed my opinions, but I would not be understood to assume that my inferences are infallible. I hope some of your readers may be induced to look more closely to the subject, to scrutinize these conclusions; and if they differ from their own, unless they can confute them, to give them the only true test—a practical trial: when, I am convinced, if judiciously done, they will have added a main link to the chain of operation, by which they can hope to contend against these trying times.   I am, Sir, your obedient servant,

Dec. 8.   AGRICULTOR.

ROYAL AGRICULTURAL SOCIETY OF ENGLAND.

DR. L. PLAYFAIR'S LECTURES ON THE APPLICATION OF THE PRINCIPLES OF PHYSIOLOGY TO THE GRAZING AND FATTENING OF CATTLE.

(FROM THE GARDENERS' CHRONICLE.)

EVENING MEETING, Dec. 7th.—The Duke of Richmond having briefly introduced Dr. Lyon Playfair, the latter gentleman commenced his lecture. He stated that the object of the lecture was to point out in what manner the principles of physiology, especially those which had been lately developed by the chemical researches of Liebig, might be applied to the grazing and fattening of cattle. In the first place, he should endeavour to give a clear conception of what the principles of physiology were, that were involved in the feeding and growth of animals. Vegetables, in their growth, derive all their food from the mineral kingdom, principally from the air, which had been called a gaseous mineral; whilst animals derived their principal nutriment directly from the vegetable kingdom. Vegetables effected many chemical changes in the food they took up, animals few. Gluten and albumen are the nutrient principles of plants, and in chemical composition they are identical with the albumen of the white of an egg, of the muscle of an ox, or the blood of a sheep. By identity was not meant similarity, but positively the same thing. The

albumen of blood, of muscle, and of an egg differed in physical but not in chemical characters. The composition of these substances, as analysed by various chemists from the animal and vegetable kingdom, as seen in the following table, prove their identity.

	Gluten. Boussin-gault.	Casein Scherer.	Albumen. Jones.	Ox blood Playfair.	Ox-flesh. Playfair.
Carbon	54·2	54·	55·	54·10	54·12
Hydrogen	7·5	7·1	7·	7·5	7·89
Nitrogen	14·	15·6	15·9	15·72	15·72
Oxygen	24·4	23·2	22·1	22·50	22·3

These analysis do not differ more than the analysis of the same substance. Plants, in fact, contain within them the flesh of animals, and all the animal organization does in nutrition, is to put this flesh in the right place. But animals take up with their food other constituents of plants, which contain no nitrogen; such are starch, sugar, gum, &c. These are not nutritive principles; they do not assist in making the flesh of animals; and when animals are fed on these alone, they die. But animals possess a certain degree of heat, and their bodies have generally a temperature above that of the atmosphere—about 100° of Fahrenheit's thermometer. Whence then comes the heat? From the burning of the sugar, starch, gum, &c. The air that animals expire is carbonic acid, the very gas that is produced by the burning of wood or charcoal in a fire. Charcoal is carbon, and animals take in daily a large quantity of carbon in their food. It is the burning or combustion of this substance in the body that produces animal heat. In hot countries, animals on this account take less carbon. The food of the East Indian contains only about 12 per cent. of carbon; whilst that of the Greenlander contains 70 per cent. The depraved taste of the Greenlander, who drinks train-oil and eats tallow-candles by the dozen, might be pitied or wondered at; but it is necessary to his healthy existence. Another reason for animals acquiring carbonaceous food in cold climates is, that the air is more condensed, and the same measure contained a greater quantity of oxygen; that gas being the agent which, by uniting with the carbon and forming carbonic acid, gave out the heat. Strong exercise also demands a large supply of carbonaceous food, on account of the oxygen taken in during the hard breathing thus produced. Oxygen, when once taken in to the system, never escapes uncombined, and would destroy the whole fabric of the body unless a fresh supply of material was given. Clothes, by keeping in animal heat, rendered less carbonaceous food necessary, in order to keep the body up to its proper temperature. The following table exhibits the principles of food necessary for the two great processes of life—nutrition and respiration:—

Elements of Nutrition.	Elements of Respiration.
Vegetable Fibrine	Fat
,, Albumen	Starch
,, Casein	Gum
Animal Flesh	Sugar
,, Blood	Wine
	Spirits
	Beer

If it were not for some power or force within the animal fabric, it would soon become a prey to the chemical action of oxygen. The force that withstands this action is vitality—a principle independent of the mind, and which constantly opposes the destructive chemical laws to which the body is subject. Disease is the temporary ascendancy of the chemical over the vital force. Death is the victory of the chemical force. A dead body exposed to the action of oxygen is soon resolved into its primitive elements—carbon, hydrogen, and nitrogen, in the form of carbonic acid, ammonia, and water; and these are the elements from which plants again prepare materials for the living body. These remarks will explain many facts known to the agriculturist, and will assist him in insuring more certainly many of the objects of his labours. It is very well known that cattle do not fatten so well in cold weather as in hot. The reason is this:—The fat is a highly-carbonised substance, formed by the animal from its carbonaceous food. In cold weather, the carbon in this food is consumed in keeping up the heat of the animal, which is at that season more rapidly carried off. This is also illustrated in an experiment made by Lord Ducie at Whitfield. One hundred sheep were placed in a shed, and ate 20lbs. of Swedes each per day; another hundred were placed in the open air, and ate 25 lbs. of Swedes per day—yet at the end of a certain period the sheep which were protected, although they had a fifth less food, weighed 3 lbs. a head more than the unprotected sheep. The reason of this is obvious: the exposed sheep had their carbonaceous food consumed in keeping up their animal heat. Warmth is thus seen to be an equivalent for food. This is also illustrated by the fact, that two hives of bees do not consume so much honey when together as when separate, on account of the warmth being greater; and they have less occasion for consuming the honey, which is their fuel. Cattle, for the same reason, thrive much better when kept warm, than when exposed to the cold. The cause of animals getting fat is, that they take in more carbonaceous food than they require for producing animal heat; the consequence is, that it is deposited in the cellular tissue in the form of fat. Fat is an unnatural production, and its accumulation is not necessary for securing the health of the body. When stored up, however, it will serve the body for keeping up its animal heat, and by this means its life, till it is all consumed. An instance is related of a fat pig having been kept without food for 160 days, having been kept alive by its own fat. Another element necessary to be taken into consideration in the fattening of animals is motion or exercise. Every action of the body—nay, every thought of the mind, is attended with chemical change; a portion of the deposited tissues are thus being constantly consumed. It is on this account that when animals are fattened, they are kept quiet and still. The cruel practice of fatteuing geese by nailing their feet to the floor, and of cooping pigeons and chickens before they are killed, arises from a knowledge of this fact. When prizes were given by our agricultural societies for fat, and not for symmetry, animals were strictly prevented from taking any exercise at all. Mr. Childers found that sheep which were kept warm and quiet fattened much faster than those that were allowed the open air and action. It is very difficult to fatten sheep and oxen in July, on account of the flies, which stinging them, keep them in a state of constant motion. The Cornish miners, on account of the laborious nature of their occupations, consume more food than labourers with lighter work. During the late riots in Lancashire the poor unemployed operatives found out that exercise and cold made them hungry; accordingly, they kept quiet in bed, and heaped upon themselves all the covering they could find. Englishmen in the East Indies are obliged to take a great deal of exercise, because they will insist on eating and drinking highly-carbonized foods; and the heat of

the climate not allowing the escape of much heat from the body, they are obliged to take in by exercise the oxygen of the air, in order to destroy the carbon which would otherwise accumulate in the system, and produce liver disease. In the Scotch prisons, the quantity of food given to the prisoners is regulated by the kind of work on which the prisoners are engaged, the hardest workers having the most food. The reason of the flesh of the stag becoming putrid shortly after its death arises from the quantity of oxygen which it takes into its system during the hard breathing of the chase. A hunted hare, for the same reason, is as tender as one that has been kept for a fortnight after being shot. The reason is the same. In both cases, the action of the oxygen on the flesh produces decomposition—in the one quickly, in the other slowly. Bacon, on the same principle, was at one time rendered more delicate by whipping the pig to death. Epileptic fits produce great emaciation, on account of the violent action to which they expose the body. Lord Ducie has performed some experiments highly illustrative of the foregoing general principles, and which also indicated what might be expected from their application to the practice of grazing, 1st experiment.—Five sheep were fed in the open air between the 21st of November and the 1st of December; they consumed 90lbs. of food per day, the temperature of the atmosphere being about 44°. At the end of this time they weighed 2lbs. less than when first exposed. 2nd experiment.—Five sheep were placed under a shed and allowed to run about, at a temperature of 49°; they consumed at first 82lbs. of food per day, then 70lbs., and at the end of the time had increased in weight 23lbs. 3rd experiment.—Five sheep were placed in same shed as in the last experiment, but not allowed to take any exercise; they ate at first 64lbs. of food per day, then 58lbs., and increased in weight 30lbs. 4th experiment.—Five sheep were kept quiet and covered, and in the dark; they ate 35lbs. a day, and were increased 8lbs. These experiments prove very satisfactorily the influence of warmth and motion on the fattening of cattle, and are still going on.

Dr. Playfair then stated that he should proceed to examine the different kinds of food of cattle. The food of cattle is of two kinds—azotised and unazotised—with or without nitrogen. The following table gives the analysis of various kinds of food of cattle in their fresh state:—

lbs.	Water.	Organic Matters.	Ashes.
100 Peas	16	80½	3½
,, Beans	14	82½	3½
,, Lentels	16	81	3
,, Oats	18	79	3
,, Oatmeal......	9	89	2
,, Barley Meal..	15½	82½	2
,, Hay	16	76½	7½
,, Wheat Straw..	18	79	3
,, Turnips	89	10	1
,, Swedes	85	14	1
,, Mangel Wurzel	89	10	1
,, White Carrot	87	12	1
,, Potatoes	72	27	1
,, Red Beet	89	10	1
,, Linseed Cake .	17	75½	7½
,, Bran	14½	80½	5

A glance at this table would enable a person to estimate the value of the articles as diet. Thus every 100 tons of turnips contained 90 tons of water. But the value of the inorganic and organic matters which these foods contained differed. Thus Mr. Rham states that 100 lbs. of hay were equal to 339 lbs. of mangel wurzel. It would be seen by the table that that quantity of hay contained 76 lbs. of organic matter, whilst the mangel wurzel contained only 34 lbs. One result of feeding animals on foods containing much water is, that the water abstracts from the animal a large quantity of heat for the purpose of bringing it up to the temperature of the body, and in this way a loss of material took place. The mode proposed by Sir Humphrey Davy of ascertaining the nutritive properties of plants, by mechanically separating the gluten, is unsusceptible of accuracy. The more accurate way is to ascertain the quantity of nitrogen, which being multiplied by 6·2, will give the quantity or albumen contained in any given specimen of food. The following is a table of the equivalent value of several kinds of food, with reference to the formation of muscle and fat; the albumen indicating the muscle-forming principle ; the unazotised matters indicating the fat forming principle :—

lbs.		Albumen.	Unazotised matter.
100	Flesh	25	0
,,	Blood	20	0
,,	Peas	29	51½
,,	Beans	31	52
,,	Lentils	33	48
,,	Potatoes	2	24½
,,	Oats	10½	68
,,	Barley Meal	14	68
,,	Hay....	8	68¾
,,	Turnips	1	9
,,	Carrots	2	10
,,	Red Beet ..	1½	8½

The analysis in this table are partly the result of Dr. Playfair and Boussingault's analysis, and partly Dr. Playfair's own analysis. The albumen series indicate the flesh-forming principles, and the unazotised series indicate the fat-forming principles. By comparing this table with the former, it will at once be seen which foods contain not only the greatest quantity of organic matter, but what proportion of this organic matter is nutritive and which is fattening ; or that which furnishes living tissue and that which furnishes combustible material. In cold weather those foods should be given which contained the largest production of unazotised matters, in order to sustain the heat of the body. Thus it will be seen that potatoes are good for fattening, but bad for flesh-ening. Linseed cake contains a great deal of fattening matter, and but little nutritive matter ; hence, barley-meal, which contains a good deal of albumen, may be advantageously mixed with it. Dumas a French chemist, states that the principle of fat exist in vegetables, as in hay and maize, and that like albumen, it is deposited in the tissues unchanged. But Liebig regards fat as transformed sugar, starch, gum, &c., which has undergone a change in the process of digestion. This is why linseed cake is fattening: all the oil is squeezed out of the seed, but the seed-coat, which contains a great deal of gum, and the starch of the seed is left, and these are fattening principles. The oxygen introduced by respiration into the lungs is destined for the destruction of carbonaceous matter, but there is a provision made for taking it into the stomach with the food, and this is done with the saliva. The saliva is always full of bubbles, which are air-bubbles, which carry the oxygen of the atmosphere into the stomach with the food. The object of rumination in animals is the more perfect mixing of the food with the oxygen of the air. This is why chaff should not be cut so short for ruminating as for non-ruminating animals, as the shorter the chaff is the less it is ruminated, and the less oxygen it gets. Chaff is cut one inch for the ox, half an inch for the sheep, and a quarter for the horse. Some might, in consequence of this, suppose that cutting food is, then, of little use ; but when it is considered that rumination is a strong exercise, or that an animal will not be eating more food that is ruminating, it will easily be seen how cutting facilitates fattening. In order that food may be properly ruminated, it requires a certain amount of consistency and bulk : hence all watery foods, as turnips and mangel wurzel, should be mixed with straw. The opinion is very correct, that an animal " cannot chew its food without straw." An important inorganic constituent of the food is salt, it is a chloride of sodium. Whilst the chlorine goes to form the gastric juice, which is so important an agent in digestion, the soda goes to form the bile, which is a compound of soda. The bile is, in fact, a secondary combination, by which the carbonaceous matter is brought in contact with the oxygen, in order to be burnt. It is thus that common salt becomes so important and necessary an article of diet. In the series of changes by which the oxygen of the air is brought in contact with the carbonaceous matters in the body, iron plays an important part, and is hence one of the necessary ingredients of animal food. There are two oxides of iron, the peroxide, and the protoxide ; the first containing a large quantity of oxygen, the second a smaller quantity ; the first, on being introduced into the blood, gives up a portion of its oxygen to the carbonaceous material of the bile, carbonic acid and protoxide of iron being formed ; these two unite, forming a carbonate of the protoxide of iron, which, on being carried to the lungs, gives off its carbonic acid, and the protoxide of iron absorbing the oxygen brought into the lungs by respiration, forms again a peroxide, which again goes into the circulation, and meeting with carbonaceous matters of the bile, unites with them and produces again and again the same series of changes. The small quantity, then, of inorganic ingredients in the food performs very important functions; and in the absence of them, animals would die. In the next lecture the various conditions of fattening cattle will be more fully considered. The Duke of Richmond proposed a vote of thanks to Dr. Playfair for his very able lecture, which was seconded by Earl Spencer, and was warmly responded to by the meeting.

EVENING MEETING, Dec. 8th.—The Duke of Richmond in the Chair.—Dr. Lyon Playfair commenced his second lecture. He stated that in the last lecture he had examined the nature of the food of animals ; in this evening's lecture the process of growth and fattening in animals would be more particularly considered. The health of an animal depends on the supply of nutriment being equal to the waste that is going on in the body. Healthy adult animals weigh as much at the end as at the beginning of the year, and this depended on their having had enough food to supply the waste going on in the system. In young and growing animals it is somewhat different ; they require more supply than there is waste, because their bodies are constantly increasing in size. When animals are first born, the functions of organic life are chiefly performed. Respiration is at this time more active than in the adult. Nutrition is also more active.

The food that nature supplies animals with at this period of their life is well adapted to assist those functions. In the milk of animals is found nitrogenised matter for developing the system, and carbonised matter for supplying animal heat. The following is an analysis of the milk of a woman, a cow, and an ass, made by Dr. Playfair.

	Woman.	Cow.	Ass.
Casein . . .	1·5	4·0	1·9
Butter . . .	4·4	4·6	1·3
Sugar . . .	5·7	3·8	6·3
Ashes , . .	0·5	0·6	—
Water . . .	88·0	89·0	90 5

The casein is the nitrogenised principle which affords nutriment to the muscular and other tissues. This is in greatest quantity in the cow. The butter and sugar are the combustible materials which by their combustion supply heat to the body. The ashes consist of phosphate of lime and common salt, both of which materials are necessary for the healthy function of the body. Thus, in milk we have all that is necessary for the growth of the body, and it is the type and representative of all food ; for unless food contain the principles of milk, it is not fitted for the purposes of the body. Casein is the principle of cheese. In its ordinary state, as made for the food of man, cheese contains both casein and butter. The stomachs of young animals are not adapted for separating the nitrogenous principles from food, and the casein of milk is supplied to them ready separated. In the young ruminant, as the calf, the three first stomachs into which the food of the adult animals enter before it is digested are not used at all. The milk passes at once into the fourth stomach. Hence the necessity of weaning these animals gradually, in order that their stomachs may be fully able to prepare the raw food for digestion. All food for weaning children, also, should be prepared on the model of milk, changing the relations of the nitrogenised to the carbonaceous materials only as circumstances require. In the milk of the cow the carbonised materials are as two to one, but in the food of adult animals they are as six to one. The large quantity of casein in milk is required for the rapid development of the body ; the butter, a highly-carbonised material, is required for supporting a large amount of animal heat. It is, consequently, a bad thing to feed calves on skim-milk, as the butter and casein have been removed, in the shape of cream. Earl Spencer, who is very successful in weaning his calves, feeds them first with new milk, then with skim-milk and meal, the meal supplying the necessary azotised and unazotised materials (azote and azotised are synonymous terms with nitrogen and nitrogenised). In feeding young animals, as well as young children, they should have good food, and there should be no stinting them as to quantity. That farmer will lose in the end who thinks to save his milk by stinting his calves. Artificial food is sometimes made and used as a substitute for milk. The Duke of Northumberland employs a mixture of treacle and oil-cake, bruised flax, and hay. The fruit of Leguminosæ contains casein ; hence we may infer that peas and beans would be good food for calves. The difference between casein and albumen is, that the former is much more soluble than the latter, and probably on that account more adapted for young animals. Beans and peas are known to be good things for growing pigs, whilst barley-meal is good for fattening them. In the growth of young

animals, as well as the fattening of adult ones, all exposure to cold should be as much as possible avoided. Cold diminishes the vitality of the body, and whatever diminishes vitality gives a preponderance to chemical action in the body, and injury of some kind is the result. Exercise is also necessary for the rearing of young animals, although it should be avoided in fattening. In order to develop the calf and the lamb, they should be allowed plenty of exercise ; but in fattening another object is to be gained. All motion consumes something in the body, therefore motion is so much loss of material in the fattening an animal. In the same manner, exposure to cold, as was proved by the experiments repeated in the last lecture, was a positive loss in the fattening of animals. Stall-feeding is beneficial, both on account of warmth and quietude. The primary cause of all this waste is the supply of oxygen ; whatever increases the supply of oxygen increases the waste of the body, and the necessity for supply. Fatting animals are often kept in the dark. Darkness favours sleep, and sleep quietude. It was thus that darkness was favourable to fattening. A case was related of a pig that was placed in a box in the dark, and the sides stuck full of pins, to prevent the animal moving in any manner, and the animal quickly got fat. The fattening of ortolans in Italy illustrated this point. The ortolan is a bird that takes its food at dawn of day, and the breeders of these birds take advantage of this, and shutting them up in a dark room, they contrive to let in the light four or five times a day, and to supply the birds with plenty of food. The birds, at every admission of light, thinking the time is come to eat, take their usual quantity of food, and on the light being withdrawn they fall asleep, and in this manner they rapidly get very fat. Sleepy, good-natured pigs fatten fast ; but active pigs, as the Irish, never get fat at all. A question may still arise as to whether it is better to feed animals in stables or small yards. The manure of the latter is stated to be better, and there is no doubt of this, but then the gain of the manure is lost in the fattening of the animal. Manures will also vary in value, according to the food animals take. The manure furnished from cattle eating turnips was nothing like the value of the manure furnished by cattle eating linseed-cake. Feeding cows for the dairy was a subject worthy great attention. In the first place, it seemed necessary to supply cows with food containing potassa. Potassa converted albumen into casein—that is, it made it soluble—and soluble albumen is casein, and casein is the most important constituent of milk. It might be a question as to whether casein was introduced directly into the blood from the food, or whether it might not be the result of the destruction of the already formed tissues. Animals fed in the open air gave milk with more casein than animals fed in close places. The lecturer found more casein in the milk given in the evening after the cows were out all day, than in milk given in the morning after the cows had been standing all night. The tissues are consumed by exercise, and thus yield the casein. Parturition makes a great demand on the powers of the system, and Braconnot found that the milk of a cow directly after calving contained 15 per cent. of casein—a much larger proportion than ordinary. The alkalies, set free by motion, convert the albumen into casein. The butter in milk is not introduced, as Dumas asserts, with the food. It is formed from the starch that exists in the food. The only change necessary to convert starch into fat is the abstraction of oxygen. The sugar of milk is a peculiar compound ; it consists of starch, with two proportions of water. The state of the mind affects the secretion of milk. In women, anger, sorrow, and anxiety affect their milk so much, that children suffer very much, or even die, from the effects of partaking of it. For the same reasons, cows should be kept free from all kinds of irritation. When at a distance, they should be allowed to walk to the milking-place at their own pace, and never be driven. Exercise is bad for the butter. Where much exercise is allowed, the produce of butter is small ; this arises from the oxygen consuming the carbonaceous material that would otherwise be secreted in the milk in the form of butter. In summer, flies torment cows in the day, and they do not yield so much butter. This may be remedied by sending the cows into the field at night, and keeping them at home in the day ; but this must only be done in summer, as it would be a bad system during cold nights. Stall-fed cows produce most butter ; and where butter is the object, cows should be turned into the richest pastures. With regard to the pastures for producing casein, or cheese, there is a very general impression that poor land is best adapted for producing cheese. In general, in cheese districts the pastures are poor. It is, perhaps, the exercise which the animals take on poor land, in order to obtain food, that (for reasons before stated) developes the casein in the milk. Stall-fed cows yield much less casein than those fed in pastures. Cows that are required to yield cheese should not be kept poor, but it is desirable that they should have to travel some way for their food. Some foods that animals eat flavour their milk, as Swedish turnips : buttercups colour it. Many plants may affect cows when taken with their food. The lecturer, a short time since, was in company with Dr. Daubeney and Dr. Buckland, in Somersetshire, where they met with a farmer, who stated, as a singular fact, that he had two pastures, the one of which, when he turned his cows in, they became purged ; and the other, when he turned them in, produced constipation. The farmer could not account for this ; but Dr. Daubeney, on examining the fields, found that the one which purged the cows contained a large quantity of purging flax (Linum catharticum) with the grass, whilst the other contained an equal abundance of the common tormentil, or septfoil (Potentilla Tormentilla), a very astringent plant, which at once accounted for their peculiar action. In Scotland, they procure good milk from stall-fed cows, by feeding them upon malt refuse and bean and pea meal, and giving them beer to drink. The malt refuse supplies the materials for butter and sugar, the beans and peas the casein, whilst the beer keeps up the animal heat. Water would carry off the heat, besides acting injuriously by dissolving the blood globules.

The principles of chemistry will also enable us to assign the causes, and in some measure to prevent the occurrence, of diseases among cattle. What is called consumption, rot, foot-rot, &c., in cattle, arises from a slow combustion or destruction of their tissues, by the agency of oxygen. The same process goes on in vegetables ; and it is well known that this process can be communicated from one vegetable to another, as from an apple to an orange, &c., and decaying vegetable matter will communicate this process to an animal. These diseases always occur amongst animals closely kept where there is much decaying vegetable matter about. Animals exposed to draughts do not take these diseases ; the draught carries off the decaying ferment. When this process is established in the intestines, it produces diarrhœa, and this probably arises from animals consuming bad food. Red water and black water arise from the same disease extending to the kidneys. Rot in the feet comes on from the same cause. It always occurs at that season of the year when vegetable decomposition is greatest, and occurs to the greatest extent where animals are obliged to tread on decaying vegetable matter. The treatment of these diseases should be by antiputrescent materials, such as chlorine and the empyreumatic oils, &c. These will disinfect the stalls or sheds where animals are kept.

Dr. Playfair then stated that he had a few observations to make on the character of the internal and external structure of the organs of animals, in order to arrive at a knowledge of them as indications of their capacity for fattening and reaching an early maturity. These observations he wished to be put to the test of experiment, as he was aware that some of them were opposed to generally received views. First, with regard to internal structure, which was the most important. It was generally considered that animals with large chests fattened best, and it was supposed that all animals with broad round chests had large lungs. But this is not the case. Sheep have round chests and small lungs. Horses have narrow chests and large lungs. Southdown sheep have narrower chests than Leicester sheep, yet they have the largest lungs. The Leicester sheep are known to fatten soonest. He spoke here of the aboriginal breeds of these animals. He had asked butchers, and they were unanimously of opinion that the fattest cattle had small lungs and small livers. Now this was a necessary consequence of the preceding principles. Where most oxygen was taken into the system, there would there be the greatest destruction of carbon, and consequently less carbonaceous material deposited in the form of fat. If two pigs had the same quantity of food, and one had lungs of double the capacity of the other, that pig would only appropriate half as much of its food in the form of fat. Milk with much butter in it was known to be produced by cows with small lungs. The same held good with regard to the liver ; where there was a large liver, there would be a large secretion of bile, and a large destruction of carbonaceous matter. If two animals ate 60lbs. of food, and one secreted 37lbs. of bile, and the other only 30lbs., the food that was not formed into bile would be converted into fat ; hence the gain on the animal with a small liver. With regard to external signs, small bones indicated a delicacy of constitution, smallness of lungs and liver, and a tendency to fatten rapidly ; whilst large bones indicated just the contrary. The " mellow" feel of an animal depended on the resiliency of the cellular tissue of the animal, the tissue in which the fat is deposited. When there is much mellowness, it arises from the blood being easily pressed from one part of the cellular tissue to another, and indicates a susceptibility to fattening. The reason why animals get more rapidly fat at the end of their feeding-season is, that the fat accumulating in the abdomen presses upon the diaphragm and abdominal muscles, and thus prevents the more complete action of the lungs, and consequently the destruction of the carbonaceous material by the inhalation of oxygen. The fat also prevents the oxygen being absorbed by the skin, and diminishes by its pressure the capacity also of the liver, and thus also adds to the fattening process. Large ears indicate a general coarseness of bone and muscle, and the same condition of lungs and liver, and are thus indicative of a small capacity for fattening, There were other indications which might be referred to, but the lecturer hoped these hints would be sufficient to set enquiry afloat on a very important subject. He apologised for what he considered the incomplete evidence he had brought forward to establish some of his views, but stated he had experiments in progress which he hoped would throw more light on many of the more obscure points to which he had alluded. Lord Spencer proposed a vote of thanks to Dr. Playfair for his lectures, and stated how much gratified he had been in listening to them. He hoped agriculturists would see from these lectures the great benefit likely to accrue to them from a knowledge of the principles of the science of physiology and chemistry. Mr. Pusey seconded the motion. Dr. Playfair, in returning thanks, stated that he had drawn up a series of statistical tables for circulation amongst butchers, for the purpose of gaining information on the internal structure of the animals which they slaughtered.

SCOTCH AND ENGLISH FARMING.

TO THE EDITOR OF THE FARMER'S MAGAZINE.

Sir,—Having in the last number of your magazine published a letter of mine, which had appeared in the *Manchester Guardian*, you will perhaps do me the favour of inserting the following as a sequel to the last, in your next number.

In my last letter, on Scotch and English farming, there was one circumstance which I only glanced at, I now wish to put that part of the subject in its proper light, as Mr. Greg in his letter has not said a word upon it, in speaking of the rents paid by the Lothian farmers; and yet it is of great importance in making a comparison. The *quality of soil*, and the *nature* of the *climate*, must be taken into account; also the *public burdens* upon the land, of which the Scotch farmers are exempt.

In this parish, sixteen miles from Liverpool and Manchester, there are very few acres equal in quality to thousands I have seen in the Lothians. The rent here, for land of average quality, will be 50s. per Scotch acre : and in addition to this, the tenant would have to pay for land-tax, 8d.; church-rate, 5d.; poor-rate, 5s.; highway-rate, 2s.; tithe, 4s. 8d. per Scotch acre—total, including rent 3l. 2s. 9d. per acre. Now, I will venture to say, that such land would not let in the Lothians, sixteen miles from Edinburgh, for more than 3l. per acre. I will give the case of a farm seven miles from Manchester; part of it was a bog not many years ago, the remainder is a light blackish soil. The rent is 65s. per Scotch acre ; the tithe and other burdens on an average, 15s.—total 80s. per acre ; soil nothing to compare with the average of the Lothians, but is in a good climate for Lancashire. Tenant cultivates 30 acres of potatoes every year, average produce, 15 tons ; last year

it was 16 tons, and this year will be nearer 18 tons per Scotch acre. Wheat averages at · least six quarters. His expences will be *more than 47 per cent.*, on account of the quantity of dung he purchases, which he has to cart seven miles. He also gives the land a light dressing of marl once in seven years. I feel very much surprised that a man of Mr. Greg's penetration and business habits, should, in giving the rent of land in a district, entirely overlook the *quality* of the soil, the *climate*, and the *burdens upon it*. I know little of either the rent of land or public burdens in the South of England, I am comparing Lancashire and Cheshire with the Lothians.

It will be seen that when all things are considered, we Lancashire farmers pay *as respectable rents* as the Lothian farmers; but in profits, and *irregularity of living*, it seems we fall short of them. I have said we have much to learn, and I hope we shall continue to learn. My object in writing is, fair play, because greater credit is given to our Northern brethren for their management than is due to them. I do not know that there has been one who has come to farm upon his own account in Lancashire, but who has had to give up; and nearly all those who have come to farm for gentlemen, have at the commencement of their undertaking, ploughed up *fine old meadow and pasture*, which have given them fine crops, and by this means, got their names agoing for good farmers with all *superficial thinkers*, and those *ignorant* of agriculture. If an Englishman had done the same, in several instances I am aware of, their masters would have discharged them, and perhaps sent them to the lunatic asylum. Now, I am no advocate for great breadths of old meadows or pastures, where arable cultivation is carried on to a considerable extent. I do not, therefore, blame the Scotch bailiffs for this, I only wish to show that this has been the means of getting them a name for raising *good crops* at less expence than we Lancashire farmers; but I shall say this, that a very considerable portion of this county (Lancashire) will never, from *soil*, *climate*, and other *local circumstances*, raise so much *clear money* as when under grass from one-third to three-fourths of its time, and in some situations in *permanent grass*. To be constantly under the plough, like the Lothians, would neither answer for the *land*, the *landlord*, nor the *tenant*, particularly in the Eastern division of the county. The Lothian farmers, who have gone into Ayrshire, have found that the same system could not answer there.

I am, Sir, yours respectfully,

Winwick, Dec. 16th.　　　　W. Rothwell.

We are informed that the trial of implements made at the meeting of the Richmond Agricultural Society, although not so complete as could be wished, has nevertheless been so successful as to induce the President, Mr. Jaques, to make arrangements for a trial at the meeting next year, to last a week or eight days. In order to enable the Committee of the Society to make the necessary provision of horses and other matters, it will be highly desirable that the manufacturers and exhibitors intending to send implements for trial at the next meeting of the Society should give timely notice to Mr. Jaques.

BATH AND WEST OF ENGLAND AGRICULTURAL SOCIETY.

The Bath Agricultural Society held their annual exhibition and meeting on Tuesday, Dec. 13.

The Marquis of LANSDOWNE, the president of the society, having been called to the chair, the ordinary business of the meeting was then gone through—the election of officers, &c. The premiums for the various descriptions of stock, &c., were also awarded. The most important business of the meeting then ensued, which was the report of the committee appointed to experimentalize upon Daniell's patent manure.

The report stated, that having been appointed to inspect and report on the effects produced by Daniell's patent manure upon a piece of arable land belonging to Mr. William Miles, M. P., at Kingsweston, and also upon some meadow lands at High Lyttleton, on Captain Scobell's farm, they had obtained from those gentlemen the manner in which they had applied the manure. In June last the committee were convened to examine the meadow the property of Captain Scobell, upon which Daniell's and various other manures had been used. They first saw that marked A. on the paper appended to the report. A few swaths had been cut across it, so that the several compartments were intersected, but the greater portion of the grass was then standing. The crop generally on the parts not manured, as well as on those that were, was above the average crops for the season. On No. 2, which was covered with earth only, they could perceive but slight improvement as compared with No. 3, which had no manure of any sort upon it. The increase of crop was somewhat larger on No. 8, which had been manured with lime and earth; and a still greater improvement was produced on No. 7, which had been manured with stable dung; but, either from the season or some other cause, neither of the three mentioned manures had effected the decided improvement which might have been expected. Perhaps this might in part have arisen from their having been put on late in the season. In No. 4 and 6, on which the patent manure had been applied, there was no perceptible difference from Nos. 3 and 5, on which no manure had been put. In the field marked C, the crop of hay was cut, and in swaths, but there did not appear any difference in those parts which had had Daniell's patent manure applied and those which had not. The grass field B, which was all clay land, was then standing, but Daniell's manure had produced no visible effect, and it was impossible to judge which was the part that had been covered by it. The committee reported that they had several times since seen the fields, and could not mark any improvement from the patent manure. The last time they saw them was on the 12th instant, and the part on which earth and lime had been applied appeared most green and closest fed.

G. T. SCOBELL,
T. HOLLOWAY,
J. GRAY,
WILLIAM S. WAITE.

The committee also reported that, in July last, they proceeded to inspect the arable land of Mr. Miles, of Kingsweston-park, on which Daniell's patent manure had been used. It was a field of 14 acres, and had been sown with wheat, about two acres only of which remained, the rest having been ploughed up. The crop was deficient. The wheat on that part not ploughed up was very inferior, and so much so, that judging from it they thought Mr. Miles was justified in destroying the wheat. He had sown carrots, mangel-wurzel, &c., which did not appear in luxuriant growth, except a root here and there. In the field next adjoining, separated by a hedge, a crop of wheat was standing, thick, well-eared, and a good average crop. In concluding their report the committee stated their unanimous opinion that Daniell's manure had failed to produce those beneficial results they expected to have witnessed; but whether any peculiarity of the season, the nature of the soil, or other causes of which they had no knowledge, had counteracted its fertilizing quality, they could not tell. They recommended that a trial should be made in the ensuing year upon soils and in situations different. it remained, too, to be proved, now that the land on which the committee reported was more fully impregnated with the manure, whether it would not produce more favourable results next year.

The committee added that a ridge in the field at Mr. Miles's was sown without manure, and did not produce a better crop.

After the report had been read, Mr. Miles addressed the meeting in support of it.

Mr. BLAKE, of Warminster, a practical and well-known agriculturist, stated that a friend of his had tried 100 bushels of the patent manure on a field of turnips, upon a part of which also he had tried bone-dust, and the result was, that he gave the greatest preference to the patent manure. He had himself tried it on a field of wheat, a part of which was manured with other manure; finding some part of the wheat looking very unhealthy, he had used some of the patent manure, and the result had been most beneficial, as, although that part of the wheat had been sown five weeks after the other, it was ripe within three or four days of the other. Mr. Bennett, also, than whom no man was more accurate and careful in his mode of agriculture, had tried 150 bushels of it on Swedes, a portion of which same field was manured with bone-dust, guano, and other manures, and he expressed himself highly satisfied with the effects of the bone dust and the patent manure, and that he firmly believed them to be far superior to all other manures. Indeed, he (Mr. Blake) thought that its being a vegetable and bituminous composition must prove its being highly calculated for manure. Soot, which was a manure that had never failed, owed its results entirely to its bituminous composition, and every body knew that vegetable matter in a state of decay was equally excellent. This manure, therefore, being composed of decayed wood and gas-tar, united both those properties. He must, however, at the same time say that, although he had known it to be most successful in many instances, there were also instances of failure.

Captain SCOBELL also stated many instances of the results of the manure, some of which were successful, and others not.

Mr. G. WEBB HALL could bear testimony to its effects, having tried 500 bushels of it in various ways, and sometimes under the most unfavourable circumstances. He had ever found it successful, and thought the instances of failure were to be attributed to its not having been sufficiently diffused over the land, as it was of too caustic a nature to be applied in a concentrated state. Last year had been a season of drought, which accounted for its failure on grass lands, as it was of that volatile character, that unless washed in by rain its volatile parts were swept away. It was a manure which was intended to be diffused, and not applied to the land by means of the drill.

After various other observations, the report was ordered to be received, printed, and circulated throughout England.

The meeting then broke up.

KEEPING BONE - DUST AND RAPE - CAKE.

BY MR. JAMES HALKETT, MANAGER OF THE PERTH-SHIRE AGRICULTURAL COMPANY, PERTH.

(From the Quarterly Journal of Agriculture.)

If bones are crushed, either in a green or damp state, and the dust allowed to lie in a heap together, it is certain to heat, and a violent fermentation will take place, in a shorter or longer term, according to the quantity of moisture and the temperature at the time; but, in general, it will be at the hottest from the fifth to the eighth day, after which it will cool gradually. On this being the case, a diminution of bulk takes place; but this does not appear very perceptible until the mass is measured over, when, if measured before, it will now be found to come far short. This is well known; but as I find there is much misapprehension amongst farmers in regard to this phenomenon, and the proper manner of keeping both bone-dust and rape-dust, I think a few words on the subject may not be unacceptable.

That bone dust, however dry, will heat more or less immediately after crushing. is a fact, which every one at all conversant with its nature will readily allow; but I find that the effects of the heating on the quality of the manure, is looked upon in very different lights by different people. Some request me to send them the newest ground bone-dust we have. From this I infer, they are of the opinion, that the dust which has been some time crushed is deteriorated in quality, or, in other words, is not so strong, and has lost part of its strength. Others, again ask the very oldest we have, and in some cases, come themselves to see if they can discover any old stock about the premises to be supplied from. The former of these customers state, that they never have good turnips but from fresh bone-dust; the other, that the best turnips they ever had were with old bone-dust. Both instances may be true; but, at the same time, it may also be true, that both from season and management, may have the best crop of turnips they ever had with the worst bone-dust they ever used. As far as such experience goes, it asserts nothing in solving the question, which is its best state for raising a crop? but I have found them so wedded to their opinions, that it was vain to urge them to make a trial of any other.

That a change does take place in the value of the commodity on being heated, I shall endeavour to show, as also that after being heated, it is a better bargain for the buyer than the seller. Suppose, then, from a parcel of good bones, although a lit-tle damp, 1000 bushels of bone-dust are made in February, and put past by the crusher, the weight of the same being 47lb. per bushel. This is allowed to lie and heat, and cool again, until the middle of May, when another 1000 bushels are crushed from the same parcel, and the weight of this is also found to be 47lb.; thus, the two parcels were equal when crushed. May being sowing time, both are sold to the consumers as they are; but, on the first being reweighed, it will be found to be about 49lb. per bushel; and consequently, instead of 1000 bushels in the heap, there will only be about 960. I have here made but little allowance for evaporation, for although it will be considerable, it is not the principal cause of the dust increasing in weight per bushel, and decreasing in measure; but by the heating it has become more friable, and

the sharp points breaking off have allowed it to come closer together in the bushel. From this it is obvious that the buyer of the old crushed dust gets 49lb. for the same money the buyer of the fresh dust gets 47lb. for, being 4 per cent., and it will often be found much more. And I cannot allow that heating deteriorates the dust; for being an active agent in decomposition, it has already partly prepared the manure as food of the plants to which it is to be applied, and on its being incorporated with the soil it will consequently act more promptly. From this, I think, it will appear that old crushed dust is the best bargain for the consumer; but the crusher, if he crushes before it is wanted, will lose in a corresponding degree, unless he charges more for it.

However, it often happens that it is in the pur-chaser's power to procure old dust, that has remained unsold on the previous season; which, if it have been long crushed and heated, will appear either of a blue or yellow tint, and, on examining it with a microscope, will be found full of mites. It may also be possible to purchase dust imme-diately after the season is over at such a price as will more than remunerate him for the outlay of cash before next season. In either case it may be necessary to keep it by him for a length of time. On this being the case, when he gets it, he should put it on a dry floor, as a damp one rots it away very fast; it will heat again, but not so hot as at first, and every time it is turned about it will re-heat, which is occasioned by the re-arrangement of the particles and the admission of air into the mass. It should never be kept in bags, as it wil destroy them in a very short time. It is injurious to boarded floors, both above and below it, but especially to the one above it, as the heat going off at the top condenses on the under side of the floor and rots it. When spread thin on the floor it will not heat so much as when thick; but it should never be kept near horses nor cattle, especially the former, as they evince great dislike to its smell, for it will be found that, otherwise a quiet horse, if brought near it, becomes restive and troublesome.

If dust be got new from the mill in the sowing season, and in a fresh state, and it be desirable to give it a good heat (which I would strongly re-commend,) that can be easily done in a very short time. Take either sifted coal ashes, or the best earth you can get, a bushel for every two of bones, and mix them together, adding as much water as will make the whole damp. Turn the mass several times over until well incorporated, then leave it in a heap, and in forty-eight hours you will have it as hot as you cannot hold your hand in it. But in fol-lowing the foregoing receipt, take care not to put more water than makes the heap merely damp, for if it is saturated, you will defeat your purpose for a length of time; and although it will heat with much more ashes or earth amongst it, I would not recommend more, as it will then not dry effectually, and great difficulty will be experienced in getting it to pass through the sowing-machine.

I shall now make a few observations on keeping rape-cakes and dust. There are no rape-cakes made in the quarter from which I write—all being imported from the Continent. There is great va-riety in the appearance of the cakes imported into this country. What we consider the best is of a yellowish green colour when new made, but they become darker on being long kept. On the receipt of a cargo of cakes they should be put into a ware-house in a dry day, on a dry clay or strong deal

C

floor (for except by their weight they will do wood no harm,) and neatly built close up, clear of the walls, in case they should draw damp from them; and, as little, and especially damp, air as possible should be admitted into the apartment, as it is the cause of their becoming mouldy and losing their light colour. Should the cakes have been new made they will heat a little; but in general, after the sweat they have had in the ship this will not be great, and if there is any apprehension of heat, the small dust of the cargo which has the strongest tendency to occasion it should be kept by itself.

It is always necessary for the dealer, and often for the consumer, to have a quantity of rape in the shape of dust by them, in which case I would here reprobate a practice I have seen of flinging it down in a corner of a cart or turnip shed, where pigs dig and fowls scratch amongst it, and where it is exposed to the moisture of the air. However dry it may appear, and however dry it may be kept, on its being put somewhat thick together, sooner or later it will heat. When very dry I have known it three weeks, or even a month, before it would heat; but if damp, it will do so in a short time, and then it will get hotter and hotter, until in the middle of the heap will be found large lumps actually burnt as black as soot, and which, on being broken down, are not easily distinguishable from coal cinders. This is a state in which carelessness may easily put it, and it should be avoided, for although I am not chemist enough to state what change has taken place in it, I am afraid its utility is much impaired. To avoid this, it ought to be examined now and then, not merely on the outside, but by digging a hole into the middle, and when heat is discovered the heap should be turned carefully over, and this should be repeated now and then; and although you may not manage to keep heat entirely away, you will prevent it being to strong as to burn the dust into the state I have described.

From what has been said, it will appear that my views are, that those who buy old bone-dust get a better bargain than those who buy new; that heating improves bone-dust, and therefore what is fresh ground ought to be heated before being used; that those who buy rape-dust should have it new crushed, and that heating impairs its qualities.

MANURES.

At the Preston Agricultural Meeting, on the 1st of October, the Chairman, R. TOWNLEY PARKER, Esq., in the course of the evening, said—" He had himself made some experiments with the guano manure, which had been strongly recommended to him, a portion of which he had used on pasture, and another on meadow land. The guano was applied on April 28, and the land was of a stiff nature. The quantity of land was eight acres, and the guano was used after the rate of 3 cwt. to the statute acre. The effect of the application was almost immediately perceptible in the altered appearance of the land, and the fondness of the cattle for the grass was astonishing; indeed it was almost impossible to keep them from it. He had also made an experiment on five acres, by using guano mixed with charcoal dust, after the rate of 2½ cwt. to the statute acre, which seemed to give an impulse to nature, and caused the grass to be very forward. The cost of the guano was 16s. per

cwt., carriage 1s. 6d., spreading it 1s., making it altogether £2 10s. 6d. for the quantity applied to each statute acre. The crop answered every expectation, both in quantity and quality; indeed it exceeded all that the mowers had ever before witnessed. He had made an experiment in the same field with well-rotted farm-yard manure, of which he had used 30 tons per statute acre, but he found that the result of the guano application was the more satisfactory one. He must, however, observe, that as the grasses raised by guano were evidently of a much more succulent nature than those produced from farm-yard manure, so it is essentially necessary that the greater pains should be taken in making the hay, and a somewhat longer period allowed for the operation, otherwise great danger will exist of the stack firing, as he had found by experience in his own case. The effect of guano on pasture land seemed equally beneficial as to meadows. With respect to the use of guano for other descriptions of crops, he had heard it spoken of and recommended; but not having tested, he was not able to acquaint the meeting with any results from his own experience."

Mr. OUTHWAITE, then at the request of the Chairman, made a few observations on the satisfactory results he had witnessed from the use of rape dust as a manure, especially for corn. He had also derived great advantage from the bone manure for turnip crops, and he had likewise tried the nitrate of soda. He, however, preferred the rape dust before the nitrate of soda for corn, for he found that the latter, although a very active stimulant, was evidently not so permanent in its effects as the former.

Mr. WILSON FRANCE begged to say that he could confirm Mr. O.'s statement, as to the utility of rape dust, from his own experience. He had procured two tons of it, which he put upon black land for potatoes. The field was before a very poor one, and would not have yielded more than two loads from the statute acre, but after applying a manuring of rape dust, at the rate of 14 cwt. to the statute acre, it produced a most magnificent crop, amounting to 150 loads, from the customary acre of seven yards to the rood. This was followed with spring wheat and clover, without additional manure, and the crop was a beautiful one—24 bushels on an acre. He got 4 tons of this manure for potatoes and turnips, and he had also used guano and farm-yard manure; and he felt, that although the advantages of rape dust were great, as he had experienced, he must be allowed to say, that both it and farm-yard manure were surpassed by guano, as applied to turnips, for it forced the growth more rapidly, and enabled them to take the mildew the sooner. The cost of the rape dust was £7 10s. per ton, of which he used 14 cwt. to the acre, so that the whole cost would not be much less than £6 per acre. Of guano he applied 3 cwt. to the acre, the cost of which was 16s. per cwt., and carriage 4s., making together 20s., from which it appeared that guano manure could be used at one half the cost of rape dust.

Mr. THRELFALL next rose to address the meeting, in order to answer an observation made by Mr. Outhwaite, on the questionable advantage of adopting spade labour, especially in its inapplicability to large farms, and proceeded by saying,— I think it a fortunate circumstance that I happened to be in the room when our friend from a distance made his remarks respecting a neighbour of his having dug some land as an experiment for growing corn, and found the results so very unsatisfactory. I am not acquainted with the neighbourhood from whence he comes, nor has he told us the nature of the soil upon which the experiment was made—it might be very different from that upon which mine was made, the particulars of which I gave at Lytham; but in addition to that case, I am prepared to prove that there is great advantage in amount of produce for succeeding years, where the spade has been employed in clay soil. For instance, in the year 1839, I dug part of a field which had been oats from ley, and planted it with potatoes, which were taken early to market, and replanted with Swedish turnips; after which it was, in the same year, sown with wheat. I prepared a part of the same field for Swedish turnips in drill with the plough, and the remainder of the field was ploughed in the ordinary way for oats. In 1840 the drill turnip ground was sown with oats, and also with clover and rye-grass, along with the dug ground in wheat. In 1841 the dug ground bore a much heavier crop of clover, &c., than the other. In 1842 both lots were sown with oats, prepared by the plough, but the land which had been dug in 1839 had, in appearance, at least a third heavier crop. That portion which was sown with oats in 1839, was dug for Swedish turnips in 1840; in 1841 planted with potatoes by once ploughing, without manure, and in 1842 sown with oats without manure, and the produce from appearance was twice as much as that part which had never been dug. These are the results of my experiments upon a clay soil, and I have no reason to suppose but that the same results would follow the efforts of any other person upon a similar soil (Cheers).

Mr. WILSON FFRANCE made a few observations preparatory to introducing to the meeting the following letter, the subject of which he deemed of much importance to agriculturists.

SUBSOILING.

IMPORTANT TO THE FARMERS OF KERRY.

To the Editor of the Kerry Evening Post.

Dear Sir,—I hasten to lay before the farmers of this county, through the medium of your journal, the following important details in connection with the subject of subsoiling, to which my attention was directed, during our assizes, by David T. Wilson, Esq., of Belvoir; and in doing so I shall freely make use of the published account of that gentleman's very satisfactory experiment, which is in some places fuller than the memoranda with which he had the kindess to furnish me.

It is a well known axiom in agriculture, that the deeper the soil is the more favourable will it be for the purposes of cultivation. To produce this desideratum, several plans have been adopted either by the thorough trenching with the spade, or by the use of the subsoil plough.

Now, the subsoil plough requires, in the first place, capital to try it—great skill to guide it—at least four horses to work it, and a soil not greatly obstructed by stones in which to use it. If used in winter, you work it in short days and bad weather. If in summer, your land is idle during the process. You loosen the subsoil, but it is not exposed to the atmosphere for a sufficient time to reap any benefit from its influence. Lastly, whatever the advantages of the subsoil plough, it is altogether beyond the reach of the cottier, and

within that of very few of our ordinary classes of farmers.

As to trenching, unless when the land is idle, it cannot be resorted to. Winter is, therefore, the time generally chosen for the operation, and little can be done in short wet days. It is a tedious and expensive process, especially if performed in winter, and it must be finished off at once. The cost of labour is consequently spread over a number of years, and, of course, is felt to press more heavily on the pocket of the farmer. For these reasons, but very few of our cottiers, or even of our gentry and farmers, have courage enough to begin to trench.

It occurred to Mr. Wilson that the deepening of the soil, which is the object contemplated in the use of the subsoil plough, and in that of trenching, could be more easily and more cheaply effected, particularly in those moist mountain lands, where it has been customary to till the ground in the way of ridge or furrows, to take off the superabundant moisture. Mr. Wilson's plan then is this :—

He proposes by means of *wide, diagonal,* and *sloping furrows,* to loosen subsoil—without capital, without skill, and with very little labour.

1st.—As to the saving of capital, states Mr. Wilson, I only use a light crowbar and spade.

2ndly.—As to skill, the use of those implements require none, or but very little.

Next.—As to labour; I form my ridges diagonally, sloping along at one side, and not down the incline of each field. I make them four feet wide, and the furrows two feet inside (they may be made even two feet and a half where the soil is very thin). In the process of tilling, whether for potatoes or corn, every particle of good soil being taken from the furrow in order to deepen it as much as possible, as well as to increase the depth of surface on the ridge, I commence loosening the subsoil in the furrows to the depth of from eight to ten inches. The spade performs the work admirably well in the ordinary description of stiff, white, or yellow clay ; but the crowbar is required for hard, adhesive gravel, and the operation is somewhat slow.

The second year, split the ridge, running the two-foot furrow in the centre, the furrow of the first year forming the centre of the ridge of the second year. The same process is followed as before, and thus the subsoil of two-thirds of a field is loosened in two years ; the remaining third, consisting of *bars* (if I may so term them) of only one foot in breath.

The third year, I opened furrow drains, of 15 or 20 feet apart, 30 inches deep, and running directly down the incline ; *the furrows which I had previously loosened inclining towards them, the bars or portions not loosened, acting as conductors in drawing off the water.*

The advantages of this system, in addition to those already stated, are that of loosening the subsoil while the land is bearing me a crop. That crop, though covering a lesser space of ground than it would cover according to the usual mode of culture, giving a decided increase in produce, in consequence of the increased depth of surface.

I spread the period of operation over. two or three years, during which time the furrows answer the purpose of drains.

The work is performed in long days, at the idle time of the year, after the potatoes are tilled, and till hay-making commences, on the mornings of hay-making, and after harvest, before the potato-digging commences.

The subsoil, taking the time before and after loosening, is exposed to the atmosphere altogether for a period of six or seven months. Several acres will be in process at the same time. And, above all, the plan is so simple and attended with so little expence, that it comes within the power of the poorest cottier to carry it into effect.

In order to explain more fully the practical working of the system, and to show its cost, writes the very intelligent gentleman who drew up the narrative of the experiment lately tried at Belvoir, the assembled gentlemen and agriculturists (and many of the latter were scientific Scotchmen, connected with the different estates in the eastern division of the county Clare) were brought to a field which had been tilled diagonally, and compartments of four statute perches each were marked off, and men drawn indiscriminately from other work, were formed into squads of four each—each squad being supplied respectively with either spades, crowbars, or picks, and they were set to loosen the subsoil of the furrows, being directed at the same time to use no greater exertion than they were accustomed to use on ordinary occasions. The first set of four men, with their spades, furnished their compartment in 26 minutes. Those with the crowbars were next done, and lastly, those with the picks, but the difference of time was not material. A second trial was made, in a different part of the demesne, where it was supposed that the subsoil was more tenacious. Here, the spades took 33 minutes, the crowbars 36 minutes, and the picks 45 minutes. In this trial it was evident that on such land the picks were unsuited for this kind of work; and besides, the men, in using these tools, had to trample down the moved ground as they proceeded backwards with their work. The superiority of the spades being fully admitted, it was then suggested that a third trial should be made with the spades alone; and as some of the agriculturists thought that the bottom of the furrow was not left sufficiently even, in the former trials, to allow the water to pass freely into the drains. This squad of men, four in number, were directed to dig out the subsoil with an even bottom, and they completed the two perches allotted to them in 13 minutes; an evident improvement on the first and second trials, which could only be attributed to the experience they had now acquired. The two gentlemen who remained to watch the execution of this last work, had no hesitation in giving their opinion that it could have been done by task work in nearly half the time. But suppose the average to be 15 minutes, in a subsoil with a hard indurated crust it might take longer. This would be 2 perches per hour for one man, or 20 perches for the day of 10 hours. Twenty perches being half a rood, multiplied by eight, will give 160 perches or 1 statute acre. Thus, it will take eight days for one man to finish one acre of the first year's subsoiling, which, at 8d. a day, the wages of the locality, will come to 5s. 4d.; and the price of executing the furrows of the second year being 5s. 4d. more, will make a total of 10s. 8d, as the expence of subsoiling one statute acre. In Scotland this operation costs about 30s. per acre; so that, between the expence of a subsoil plough, and the cost of a team of from four to six horses to draw it, which horses and ploughmen must have had previous training to enable them to accomplish

this species of work, few, even opulent farmers, in this country, could be induced to try this improvement.

With respect to the upright drains, Mr. Wilson prefers that they should be made of stone, with flat covering, as affording a more easy entrance to the water from the diagonal furrows; and he recommends that they should not be closed up till the water shall have had time to filter clearly through the bottoms of the furrows, to prevent any deposit of mould in the drains. During the deepening of the furrows, all stones that may present themselves are collected and placed in heaps at the top or bottom of the field, exactly opposite the lines marked out for the drains.

Mr. Wilson did not make any estimate of the expence of those drains, but in a late account of some subsoil draining in Scotland, the total expenditure was set down at 30s.; so that when it is taken into account that manual labour is so much cheaper in this country, we may set down the cost of the drains under the Wilson system at little more than half.

Trusting that these compilations will be found sufficiently explicit, I have only to observe in conclusion, that a diagram of Mr. Wilson's plan, which that intelligent and benevolent gentleman permitted me to copy, is at present in the hands of Mr. John M'Gowan, Nelson-street, the very eminent engineer.

I am, dear Sir, faithfully yours,
JAMES R. EAGAR.

Tralee, Strand-street, Aug. 5, 1842.

At the meeting of the East Norfolk Agricultural Society, on the 13th of September, Lord WODE-HOUSE, in an excellent speech, remarked that, proud as he was to see the exhibition of that day, yet it should be recollected that fine as those animals were, they were kept more as vehicles of manure—the sheep were nothing more than a dung cart, and were as economical, in fact cheaper than having to purchase manure. But then every one present knew that what was produced from the farm-yard was the best; and, although many discoveries had been made, still nothing was equal to the manure from the yard. It was, however, not to be denied, that some assistance was wanted. He remembered an anecdote of an old farmer, who, upon being told of the great improvements made by Mr. Coke, said, " give me muck; I do not care about squire Coke:" and Mr. Coke was I believe of the same opinion. There was no doubt that muck was the main ingredient, but under the present state it was necessary to obtain a great addition: if their object was to produce greater crops, and exclude the foreigners, which he feared they never should be able to do, their land must be much better farmed. With regard to additional manure, for that they must look to the great chemists of the day, who had done their part; they must look to Sir. H. Davy, and read with careful attention the work of Professor Liebig. If they followed the instructions of these great men, they could not fail to increase their produce. He did not pretend to be an experienced agriculturist, but from the experience he had, he thought that next to the produce of the yard, came bone manure. But Professor Leibig had recommended a mixture of sulphuric acid and bone manure. He had tried this, and was trying it at this moment, but he could not see any difference between that and the common manure; and if the crop comes to perfection, the bone manure and sulphuric acid will not be less expensive and more economical. There were two descriptions of agriculturists—one who are by their skill and industry daily increasing their great wealth, and will ultimately arrive at the highest position; and others who like myself, left-shoulder farmers. The industrious farmer is a far different person— he labours incessantly from morn till eve, and passes many a sleepless night in considering his plans. We left-shoulder men make the experiments. If they succeed, they are adopted ; if not, they laugh at us. But it was important to have such experiments tried.

At the Liverpool meeting, SAMUEL SANDASH, Esq., one of the Vice-presidents, observed that the Secretary had said something about guano, and if any gentleman here would give the results of some experiments, he would be glad to hear him. He had tried it himself, and had made notes of the results, which he would give if required, although they might appear insignificant as compared with others in the room. The first time he made use of guano was in rows of peas, but very few appeared above ground. He tried the same in three rows of carrots. He put one pound of it in one row, two pounds in another, and three pounds in the third. The carrots with one pound came up very well, those with two pounds still less, and with the three pounds none at all. He also tried it with turnips. He put in the first four drills 90 yards by each ten pounds of guano at the bottom of the drill, without manure. He then covered it over and sowed the turnips, and it appeared to be a very promising good crop. In the second four drills he put the manure on the top of the drill, and mixed the seed with it. It nearly destroyed the seed. On the third four drills he put five pounds of guano at the bottom of the drills along with some manure, and that was the best crop of all. After giving some results with respect to potatoes, which were inaudible, he said that he had tried it for wheat, and the ground on which guano was used produced 343lbs., whilst the same quantity of land manured in the ordinary way produced only 324lbs. He said guano was a very valuable manure, if properly understood and properly applied, but it required great caution.

The Chairman asked if there was any gentleman present who would give the results of guano. He was sure the company would be glad to hear him.

R. NEILSON, Esq., said he was induced to try guano for wheat. He had a piece of land of ten statute acres, which he worked up with guano. Out of the ten acres seven were entirely destroyed by the strength of the manure, and the other three were preserved in consequence of his not putting so much of the manure on. These had produced a very fine crop, some of which had been shown that day, and that from a wheat that was not large in the head. He tried the guano with mangel wurzel, and found that four or five cwt. of it were as good as twenty tons of the farm-yard manure. It was decidedly an advantageous manure for cheapness, if it were properly introduced into the soil, but he did not think it would answer well for top dressing. It ought to be mixed up with the manure and harrowed in. With turnips it had the same effect. Wherever the seed was in contact with the guano, or put into the drill where the guano was sprinkled on it, it destroyed it. The heat of the manure was so powerful that it ought

to be harrowed into the land, and remain some short time for the soil to absorb the virus of the manure before the seed went in. He had made a mixture of charcoal guano and farm-yard manure, and he found that answered the best. He believed guano was a decidedly valuable introduction into this country, and of great benefit to the farmer, even if he was obliged to repeat it year after year. The expense was slight, and the convenience of putting it in was obvious. It had only to be more generally tried to be more generally used (*Applause*).

Mr. CRACKENTHORPE, as an instance of bigoted prejudice, remarked that he might as well attempt to persuade his neighbours at Eastham, to manure their ground with turtle soup as with guano (*much laughter*). They say their fathers and grandfathers never did so, nor would they; but he had seen some fields of turnips in his neighbourhood sprinkled with it, and they were not equal to his own (*hear, hear*). Forty tons to the acre had been spoken of by the Chairman as an extraordinary quantity, but he had never had less than from thirty-five to forty (*hear*). For this he had to show a silver tea-pot, a silver sugar basin, a silver cream jug, and prizes of 5l., 6l., and 2l.; therefore he thought that he was no loser, and that his example might encourage others to do the same (*hear*).

At the West Suffolk Agricultural Association Meeting, on the 30th of September, Mr. SHILLITO said the agriculturists present had been called upon to state, as far as they could, what they considered to be the best mode of cultivating their lands, and he would touch upon the question of manure. He would begin by stating what he had done on the farm he occupied under the Marquess of Bristol. If he were asked what natural manure was best for land, he believed he should be borne out by the opinion of men of the first ability and practice in his reply, that no manure was so substantial and sound as that made from fat animals ; but if he were asked what was best as an artificial manure, he must answer that in his idea that would depend principally on the soils. On his Barrow soil he had never found from bones the advantage there should be for the outlay and expense; he thought there was not the staple in the land to make them beneficial. He was induced to use it in consequence of some observations of a practical farmer from Lincolnshire, who thought it would suit his land, as it had been found very advantageous on the Wolds of that county. He boned 50 acres last year, but it failed in producing the result he expected, and he had since tried it on various parts of the farm with no better success. With oil and rape cake he had been more fortunate both on turnips and wheat. If he were asked which was the best crop to apply it to, he should say he would sooner use it to wheat than turnips, and his reason was this :—At the time the wheat was put in the earth was moist, and the rape-cake had better effect at that season of the year than when applied to turnip land, if it happened to be dry. He was not going to destroy the bone crusher, for he had tried bones on a different sort of occupation, peat fen land ; and he had also observed the result of them when applied by his neighbours on such land, particularly on that farmed by Mr. Paine, of Risby. That gentleman used it for coleseed, and had as fine a piece of coleseed as he could wish to see. He tried it himself, and boned on his Fen Farm 33 acres for coleseed, using 10 bushels per acre, in rows 15 inches asunder, and he thought he might challenge the county to produce 33 such acres of coleseed on land which 40 years ago did not cost 5*l.* per acre ; indeed he did not know if it was not better than he wished, for he thought he should have to mow off the top before it was fed off. Next year, instead of ten bushels, he should put on only seven, and he then thought it would be sufficient to feed off.

Mr. GEDNEY condemned the use of artificial manures, as when a man bought them he was apt to become a lazy farmer, and to forget what he had at home which would do much better. He was not much of a light-land farmer, but if bones answered anywhere he was sure they answered on a light soil. His friend, Mr: Shillito, thought ten bushels too much, and that seven were enough ; he (Mr. Gedney) was sure that none at all were sufficient for that land for profit—the very small quantity applied, 7 bushels per acre, could not avail in producing any great return. He believed that in this country, if they wished to benefit the soil, it must be done at great cost—with a little they could not do a great deal, but with a great deal they might do a little.

Mr. SHILLITO said he should be happy to shew Mr. Gedney the result of the coleseed being boned, and this he could easily do, as he desired his men to leave a stetch without any, and it could be plainly perceived where it was put on. Where it was boned, the coleseed was two feet and a half high, where no bones were it was not a foot high. He thought therefore that he had good grounds for his calculation, that if he put the coleseed at 18 inches and 7 bushels per acre it would be sufficient.

At the recent meeting of the Essex Agricultural Society, Mr. PALMER, M.P., in acknowledging his health which had been drank, observed that he had done what little he could to promote the interest of agriculture in this district, and he would appeal to Mr. Philby and other gentlemen to whom he had stated some little experiments he made, 18 months ago, as to the effect of different kinds of manure and stimulants on the land. He tried different sorts of manure on a piece of grass land, and a piece of arable. On the arable land he put stimulants, such as saltpetre, soda, and such like things ; and the first year it appeared to have a great effect on the crop, but in the following year he could find no benefit from it. His land was of a strong description, and when he applied chalk or lime, whether on arable or pasture, he saw no benefit arising from it the first year, but the second year both arable and pasture so treated showed a great advantage over every other part. He took the same average value per acre, viz., 25s. for salt-petre and soda, and the cartage of chalk being heavy, the same for that.

At the Waltham meeting, on the 26th of September, Mr. T. BEASLEY, Vice-president, made the following observations :—In the system of agriculture that prevailed, he always experienced surprise at the waste of manure which he observed in almost every quarter ; the waste of this ingredient he felt convinced was equal to the amount of the artificial manure that they purchased at such expence. In riding through villages after heavy showers, they must have perceived that every gutter was filled with liquid manure. He thought that no farmer

alive to his own interests, and sensible of his responsibility, ought to delay a week in constructing a reservoir for the collection of liquid manure. He was about to hazard a bold saying ; but in his opinion what might be produced by the wasted manure, if it was only properly taken care of and judiciously applied, would pay the interest of the national debt. Mr. Beasley added, that he did not allude to the waste in farm-yards only ; but to that in large towns, in addition thereto. He had another observation to make respecting lime. It was frequently lying two or three months in small heaps, to be saturated with wet, and lose all its stimulating qualities ; he would urge them to use it as soon as possible after it was brought from the kiln. He mentioned these things for their consideration, because every farmer was bound not to leave a stone unturned in order to make the soil yield as much as it possibly could ; to make two blades of grass and two ears of corn grow where but one grew before, and two oxen be bred where but one was previously fattened. This was a duty incumbent upon all.

NEW KIND OF MANURE.—Count Hompesch, a Belgian gentleman, has taken out a patent for the preparation of a manure more powerful and cheaper than any yet invented. His plan is said to consist in fixing all the volatile parts of night-soil and other such substances by means of the ashes of the oolitic shale of 'Portland. The shale is employed, in the first place, as a source from which oil, turpentine, and other substances are extracted ; the residue goes to the preparation of the manure, which is said to be converted somewhere on the Isle of Dogs, and sold in a dry state, in the form of bricks. As the materials to be thus employed are inexhaustible, and at present almost valueless, it is expected that the preparation of the fertilizer in question will become a matter of great national importance. As people have become too wise to wonder at sugar being made from old rags, so will they be equally prepared to hear that oil, and tallow, and soap, are to be fabricated from the hardened mud of the coal mines ; for such is " shale."

ROSS FARMERS' CLUB.

The usual annual meeting of this society took place on Thursday , the 27th Oct., on which occasion their ploughing match came off in a field of clover ley on the Bollin estate, within a mile of the town.

Twenty-one competitors made their appearance on the ground by half-past nine o'clock, all appearing like true and sturdy ploughmen resolved to win the several prizes offered by the society. Mr. Price, the hon. secretary, having previously allotted out the half-acre quantities, which they were to plough in three hours, and having assembled the competitors, each drew his number, which being placed on his hat, he proceeded with his plough and pair of horses to the corresponding number marked on pegs placed in the ground against each lot. The signal having been given for starting, away they went, " whistling o'er the lea." The sun shining forth in its autumnal glory, with the numerous assemblage of spectators, presented a most lively and interesting scene.

The judges, Messrs. Rudge, Marfell, and Merrick, having arrived on the ground on the completion of the work, and carefully examining the several performances, ultimately awarded the society's premiums as under:—

No. 6.—Mr. A. Dowle, Llangarren, owner ; T. Matthews, ploughman, 2h. 34m., 2l. 10s.

No. 10.—Mr. H. Higgins, Fawley, owner ; W. Howells, ploughman, 2h. 57m., 1l. 10s.

No. 13.—Mr. T. Phelps, Sellack, owner ; J. Lewis, ploughman, 2h. 25m:, 1l.

No. 1.—Mr. B. Street, Llangarren, owner ; W. Phillips, ploughman, 2h. 30m., 15s.

No. 11.—Mr. T. Woodhall, The Bollin, owner ; H. Rudge, ploughman, 2h. 12m., 10s.

And to the unsuccessful candidates, 2s. 6d. each.

An iron two-wheel plough, of modern construction, belonging to Mr. Higgins, of Fawley, and a single wheel DP plough, peculiar for its construction, and for which the makers (Barrett and Co., of Reading) received the Royal English Agricultural Society's prize at Liverpool, as the "lightest in draught," belonging to Mr. Price, of Benhall, were much admired on the ground.

The society afterwards sat down to an excellent dinner, laid out in their room at the New Inn, the display of which, and the excellent wines, were much admired by about 45 or 50 of the most influential agriculturists of the neighbourhood, including a fair sprinkling of the respectable inhabitants of the town. Henry Chillingworth, Esq., of Grendon Court, the president of the year, assisted by Thomas Woodhall, Esq., as vice-president, conducted the routine of toasts in the most able and eloquent manner.

After the usual toasts of "The Queen," "Prince Albert and the Prince of Wales," "The Queen Dowager and the rest of the Royal Family," the PRESIDENT gave, amidst much applause, "Lord Ashburton, the Patron of the Society;" "The Members of the County, who had so handsomely come forward to render the society their countenance and support ;" "The Royal English Agricultural Society ;" "The Herefordshire Agricultural Society." Among the toasts given of several gentlemen residing in the neighbourhood of Ross, who had lent their aid and support in furthering the objects of the society, we noticed those of "K. Evans, Esq., of the Hill ;" "S. W. Compton, Esq., of Walford ;" "Thomas Brooke, Esq., of Pencraig Court ;" "William Bridgman, jun., Esq., of Weston;" "John S. Collins, Esq.;" "William Hooper, Esq.;" "The Rev. T. P. Symonds, of Pengethley," as well as other members of the club.

The PRESIDENT gave the following toast :— "Success and utility to the Ross Farmers' Club," introducing it and enlarging on it in the most able and enlightened manner, and which was received with the most deafening applause. The next toast drunk, "Henry Chillingworth, Esq., the President," was received with the warmest plaudits, who fully responded to it, assuring the society of his earnest and hearty desire for the well-being and prosperity of the institution, in whose power it was, if properly supported, of conferring the greatest advantage on the agricultural community of the neighbourhood, and particularly on the deserving, sober, and industrious labourers. The PRESIDENT then gave "Earl Somers, the Friend and Supporter of Agriculture," after which he read the award of the committee, of the premiums to agricultural labourers, &c., as follows :—

"To the married labourer in husbandry who has brought up the greatest number of children without parochial assistance, with a general good character." A premium to Edward Morgan, recommended by the Rev. T. P. Symonds, as having reared nine children, and worked on his farm for ten and a half years, 1l.

To the second in this class. A premium of 15s., awarded to John Burford, recommended by Mr. Wm. Jones of Baysham, for having reared a family of eight children, and living in his service thirty-five years.

To the third in this class. A premium of 10s. to Richard Davies, recommended by Mr Thomas Woodhall, of the Bollin, for having reared six children, and having been in his employ twelve years.

"To the farm labourer who has been employed by his master the longest period." A premium of 1l. was awarded to Michael Cole, recommended by Mr. W. Jones of Baysham, for having lived in his father's service and his own for a period of fifty-one years without interruption.

To the second in this class. A premium of 1l. was awarded to Thos. Matthews, recommended by Mr. F. Rootes, of Weston, for having lived without intermission in his grandfather's and his own service for twenty-five years.

To the third in this class. A premium of 10s. to Thomas Taylor, recommended by Mr. Timothy Marfell, as having lived in his service thirty-seven years. This premium would have been greater, but Mr. Marfell not being a member of the club, the committee could not consistently allow the man to become a competitor.

"To the waggoner who has lived the longest period in his present service." A premium of 2l. was awarded to Thomas Roberts, recommended by Mr. Wm. Jones of Baysham, for a servitude in that capacity of twenty-five years.

To the second in this class. A premium of 1l. was awarded to Wm. Caton, recommended also by Mr. Wm. Jones, for having lived in his employ on another farm a period of thirteen years.

To the third in this class. A premium of 10s. to Joseph Williams, recommended by Mr. Thomas Williams, of Llangarren, for a servitude of thirty-three years. The latter premium would have been higher had Mr. Thomas Williams been a member of the club, but the excellent character given to the candidate induced the committee to notice it.

"To the woman who has done the most out-door work on any farm annually, and is still employed." A premium of 1l. was awarded to Elizabeth Husbands, recommended by Henry Chillingworth, Esq., for having worked on his farm ten years.

To the second in this class. A premium of 10s. was awarded to Jane Morgan, recommended by Mr. Wm. Price, of Benhall, for having worked on his farm, in the employ of his predecessor and himself, a period of twelve years.

"To the female servant in husbandry who can produce the most satisfactory character for long servitude, and general good conduct. No candidates.

To the second in this class. No candidates.

"To the shepherd who has reared the greatest number of lambs, &c." Lord Ashburton's premium of 3l.; T. B. M. Baskerville, Esq's. premium of 2l.; and the society's premium of 1l. to the third best in this class, will be awarded at Midsummer next.

The CHAIRMAN then gave, "The owners of the teams whose ploughmen had gained the premiums," which was followed by the toast of "The honest and industrious Labourers." Then succeeded the toast of "Thomas Woodhall, Esq., the excellent Vice-president, and thanks to him for his ground for the ploughing match, and also for the unbounded hospitality shown by him on the occasion." "Mr. Price, of Benhall, the indefatigable Secretary and Treasurer to the society; and thanks to him for his unabated zeal and unwearied exertions for the welfare of the society;" both of which toasts were warmly greeted, and were responded to at some length by those gentlemen.

Next followed "The Judges of the Ploughing;" "Henry Burgum, Esq.," "Mr. Henry Higgins," "and Mr. Thomas Phelps," who proposed to offer a sovereign each, as a joint premium, to be awarded at the next meeting to the maker of the best constructed plough. "The Committee," one of whom announced that the society would give a second premium in this class. "Mr. Samuel Edwards, of Foxhall;" "Mr. John Jones, of Pennoxton;" "Mr. Carey Cocks, and the other gentlemen who gave premiums at the last annual meeting;" "The Ladies," &c., &c.

The remarks and observations made by the several speakers during the evening, evinced the great practical utility of these societies; and we have no doubt that the most eminent success will attend their useful labours. After having enjoyed an evening of the most friendly intercourse and social feeling, the party separated delighted with the pleasures of the day.

PROBUS FARMERS' CLUB.

HORSES AND OXEN.

At a meeting of the members of this Society, on Saturday, November 19, an interesting paper, *on the comparative advantages in the employment of horses and oxen in farming work*, was brought before their notice. The importance of this subject occasioned a large attendance of members, it being obvious to every practical farmer, that the cost of labour in an arable farm amounts to a much more considerable sum than the rent, and any improvement that might be suggested by the lecturer would be deemed of considerable importance. He first alluded to the antiquity of the ox as a beast of burden, and shewed by reference to ancient history, that he was employed long before the horse. The earliest record we have of the ox is in the sacred volume—where we are informed, that "Jubal son of Lemech, was the father of such as dwell in tents and of such as have cattle. The inference to be drawn from this is, that the ox was early domesticated, and that until that took place, all efforts of tillage must have been insignificant. Alluding to the comparative merits of the ox and horse, as beasts of labour for agricultural purposes, he said, that this was a disputed subject, and the opinions on either side were conflicting—one party contending that horses are getting too much into use, to the exclusion of the ox, and that the farmers are injuring themselves by employing them, as they would by the by discover, when they find

a lot of old horses on their farms fit only for the kennel; whilst the opposite party affirm, that oxen should never be worked, and only kept for the purpose of feeding, and that the horse was better adapted for all agricultural purposes, and would accomplish the requisite work faster and cheaper.

To arrive at something like the truth between these conflicting opinions, the author submitted the following calculations to the club, by which it will be perceived that the advantage is considerable on the side of horses.—He first considered the difference between the cost of two horses and four oxen, as proposed at the Gloucester Farmers' Club, by Mr. Stokes—thus supposing 4 oxen equal to the work of 2 well fed horses. Each ox to have per day for the winter half-year 1½ cwt. of Swede turnips at 6d. per cwt—9d.; 2 quarts of corn, 2d.; straw, 1d.; which would make 1s. per day. The summer half-year, the cattle to have good grass, and 2 quarts of corn each, at the cost of 6s. per week.

	£. s. d.	£. s. d.
Thus: Keep of 4 oxen for 26 weeks, at 1s. per day each, in winter	36 8 0	
Keep of ditto during the summer, for 26 weeks, at 6s. per week	31 4 0	
Amount of 1 year's interest on 4 oxen, at 13l. each	2 12 0	
	70 4 0	
Deduct for the improvement on 4 oxen, for 1 year, 2l. each	8 0 0—62 4 0	
Keep of 2 horses		52 16 0
		9 8 0

This method of keeping oxen the Lecturer disapproved of, and besides, he questioned very much the capability of four oxen, even with the high keep, to do the work of two good horses; and the plan he proposed as a fair trial between horses and oxen, would be, to match 6 oxen against 2 horses kept in the following manner. In the winter weeks to be allowed 1 cwt. of Swede turnips each per day, at 6d.; 2 quarts of corn, 2d.; straw, 2d.; which would amount to 10d. per day each, and in summer good grass at 5s. per week.

	£. s. d.
Thus: Keep 6 oxen 26 weeks in winter, at 10d. per day each	45 10 0
Keep of ditto 26 summer weeks, each 5s. per week	39 0 0
One year's interest on 6 oxen, at 13l. each	3 18 0
	88 8 0
Deduct for the improvement of the Cattle 2l. 10s. each, during the year	15 0 0
	73 8 0

	£. s. d.
The horses, he calculates, would cost to keep in good working condition 9s. per week each, throughout the year, which would amount to	46 16 0
The year's interest on two horses, valuing them at 20l. each	2 0 0
To wear and tear of the two horses at 2l. per each	4 0 0
	52 16 0
Balance in favour of horses	£20 12 0

But even taking the extreme case of the Glon-cester Farmers' Club, that of matching 4 oxen against 2 horses, the difference would still be in favour of horses, amounting to 9*l*. 8*s*. per year. Although he said the balance from the above accounts is so much in favour of horses, he would by no means exclude oxen altogether from farms where more than one team is kept. In busy seasons they are a most desirable auxiliary to the horse team, and when no longer wanted might be fettened, and sold to the butcher.

This opinion was coincided in by the members of the club. In the course of the debate which ensued after the paper was read, the age and breed of both horses and oxen, the cost of maintenance, and the presumed value of horses and oxen, with their gear when put to work, and their value at the close of the comparison, as well as the comparative number of oxen or horses which would be required to do the same work, were each separately discussed.

[As truth is best struck out by the collision of opposite opinions, and advocates are generally disposed to give undue weight to their arguments, and to strain their conclusions, we give as an opposite view of the same subject, the substance of a discussion which took place last week, at the Westfirle Farmers' Club, in Sussex, at which John Ellman, Esq., a member of the Smithfield club, presided. At this meeting the following estimate was given of the comparative cost of the ox and the horse, furnished, as it was stated, by a farmer of great experience.

Cost of one horse per year. £. s. d.

Prime cost of a horse three years old.... 30 0 0
Keep, shoeing, attendance, harness, &c., for 10 years, at 25*l*. per year 250 0 0

280 0 0
Deduct value of horse at 13 years of age 10 0 0

270 0 0
Cost of one horse annually 27 0 0

Cost of one pair of oxen per year.

Prime cost of one pair of three-year old oxen 30 0
Keep, &c., five years, at 16*l*. per year.... 80 0 0

110 0 0
Deduct value of oxen at eight years old .. 40 0 0

70 0 0
Cost of one pair of oxen annually 14 0 0

Thus it will be seen that there is a decided advantage of 13*l*. per annum, in favour of a pair of oxen. It should be remarked that it is a general calculation in Sussex, that the labour of one horse is equal to that of a pair of oxen, although for heavy draughts experience has proved that the power of one horse is very inferior to two oxen ; and the author of the " Annals of Agriculture," has given evidence that one ox for a steady draught is equal to a horse. An instance was quoted at this meeting of a bull having shown superior strength to three horses, and it was maintained by the meeting that pairs of oxen from four to seven years old were more than equal to single horses.

It was complained at this meeting, and the

Chairman joined in the complaint, that the Smith-field committee excluded working oxen from competition, by offering no prize for oxen above five years old. This regulation, it was stated, was framed by the breeders of short-horns. On some farms, it was observed, it is better to keep horses ; on others, both horses and oxen ; and on some, oxen alone can profitably do the work. The beef of the working oxen was said to be superior to any other : at eight years old it was at perfection.

A member stated that the light soils in his parish could not be cultivated without oxen. He used 14 oxen, and the keep to support them last winter was only two acres of cabbage, one acre of Swedes, four tons of hay, with oat straw, and he worked 12 of them daily to the end of the year. The manure from them was sufficient for 11 acres.

Another member stated, that on heavy soils oxen ought to be used as an auxiliary force for the preparation of the barley season, carrying out dung, and upon any emergency when extra power was required. His experience showed him that a pair of oxen could draw heavier weights than one horse ; and in ploughing they were steadier at the draught. By using oxen as an auxiliary force, a farmer was enabled to avail himself of the proper seasons, and when he no longer needed his yokes, the cattle were improving in value, and adding largely to the manure heap. In all these considerations they are more valuable than horses.

It was stated that stall-feeding in summer was advantageous. The gentleman making this statement said he had kept his oxen last summer upon cut lucerne and grass, as also his dairy of 13 cows, and he did not think they had eaten ten tons of hay for the past three years. Of the capabilities of oxen, it was satisfactorily proved that steady draught oxen were superior to horses, and that six oxen would, if carefully driven at first, plough an acre of ground as quickly as three horses. Instances were mentioned of such a yoke having ploughed an acre in 3h. 20m., and two yokes of oxen having done their acre each day ; but it was shown that to work oxen in the same manner as horses constantly would be unprofitable, as the loss of flesh would be considerable. Several other points pertaining to the subject engaged the attention of the meeting some time longer, and after having canvassed the whole, it came to the following resolutions :—

" That it is the opinion of this meeting that the working of oxen on most soils is advantageous, and on light soils far preferable to that of horses. That copies of the calculations of the relative expence of horses and oxen be sent to the secretary of the Smithfield Club."

We think it right to assist the judgment of our agricultural readers, by placing, the opinions of the Cornish and Sussex, the Probus and Westfirle farmers, thus in opposition.]

CARROTS IN A SANDY SOIL.

TO THE EDITOR OF THE DUMFRIES-SHIRE AND GALLO-WAY HERALD.

SIR,—A " Dumfries-shire Farmer," some weeks ago, complained in the *Mark-Lane Express* that, " for culinary purposes, he has, for several successive years," attempted to grow carrots in his garden, in "a fine sandy soil," without success; that " at first they grow very rapidly, till they have attained the thickness of a goose quill, and then the leaves begin to droop," and he finds " the root all run through with a small white worm, about the thickness of a common pin." He desires to be informed of the best way to prevent this " worming."

As no answer has appeared in the *Mark-Lane*, as I feel for my neighbour in his long want of good *hotch potch*, and think it unnecessary to write him by the London post while your columns are open to every subject connected with agricultural science, you will favour me by offering him a few hints.

He states a strong case, yet I have occasion to know that it is not uncommon, and I deem it connected with some very important questions in the science of vegetation. If what he complains of can be obviated, an important stage will be gained not only in the growth of carrots, but also in the successful culture of other culinary vegetables, and even of some field crops.

The soil of his garden is a fine sand (a soil unfavourable to the retention of ammonia), and it has probably been often manured with dung, limed, and long used only for green crops. Such a soil, so treated, especially in a low or sheltered situation, is extremely apt to have an excess of nitrogenous matter which genders worms, gives a strong and bad flavour to cabbages, colewort, turnips, and most vegetables, and either injures the flavour and tenderness of carrots, or leaves them a prey to vermin.

Nitrogenous matter in a sandy soil yields chiefly nitrates; and as far as observations have been made, nitrates tend chiefly to the formation of woody-fibre. They rapidly stimulate growth for a time, but as they are unfavourable to the production of sugar, they bring forward carrots or red-beet in an unhealthy state, and soon leave them a prey to worms. Such plants, if not destroyed by vermin, will be found to have cleft roots, and to be hard, woody, and ill-flavoured.

Hence, to give my neighbour good carrots from his garden, two objects require attention; the vermin must be got rid of, and the soil needs to be improved, either by removing the excess of nitrates, or by supplying what their excess renders deficient in a sandy soil.

Fortunately, the substance chiefly wanting in the soil is the best agent for destroying worms; I mean ammonia. If my neighbour has access to the ammoniacal liquor of the gas works, he will find its repeated use in spring of much value; if he has not, the urine either of the stable or of the chamber will in part supply its place. It must be used stale, and either diluted with water, or put on during rain. Besides carbonate of ammonia, urine contains various other salts of high value in vegetation.

But the continued use of urine alone will, after a few seasons, aggravate the evil which it at first remedied; nitrates and vermin will abound more than ever. Substances must be used which act upon and retard the formation of nitric acid. Of these I know none equal to soot. It contains creosote, capnomone, and other substances, which at once check the formation of nitrates, and banish vermes from the soil. It also contains sulphate of ammonia and gypsum. Hence gardeners have found it a very valuable manure.

The spirit of tar has been found effectually to remove the worms; and perhaps a compost of common wood-tar, carefully mixed in soil, would both remove the worms, and, by its absorbent power, improve the flavour of the carrots. Tar is more antiseptic than soot is, and I have found that it powerfully absorbs the gases given off in putrefaction, and *holds* them till brought in contact with caustic alkalies. In absorbent power it seems much to resemble carbon, and, as it is cheap, I have often thought it may become a valuable auxiliary to our manures. There can be little doubt of its absorbing those gases which give a bad flavour to many culinary vegetables on sandy soils. There is no risk of its being taken up by the roots; and if it were, it would only give them the virtues of tar-water, a medicine deservedly extolled by the Bishop of Cloyne and others.

But all this is only doctoring a bad subject. The soil is radically deficient. There is little hope of raising an uninterrupted succession of healthy well-flavoured green crops from a fine sandy soil. Carrots, indeed, prefer a sandy soil; but then it is only while the soil is *fresh*, not after it has been converted into a nitre-bed. Hence gardeners find the value of bringing up an inch of fresh subsoil as often as the plot is trenched. But I have never seen culinary vegetables long cultivated with success in soils where *clay* was not present. A portion of red clay is indispensable. One inch will do more for my neighbour's soil than all the drugs in the pharmacopœia. Red clay, after sufficient exposure to the air, first absorbs ammonia, and then gradually combines with it, forming salts little washed off by rain, as they are but sparingly soluble in water. The effect of this is pointed out in the popular phrases, " *a rich clay*," and " *a hungry sand.*" The former retains ammonia and other manures, and slowly gives them off as needed by plants; hence clay soils, in field-labour, gradually accumulate riches, and require lime occasionally to aid in the evolution of their ammonia. Sandy soils, on the contrary, cannot retain ammonia; it is washed from them by rain; hence they are poor and hungry, and, in the farmer's phrase, " can stand but little lime."

The successful use of clay requires a little management, as I knew a farmer who lost four crops by laying a heavy dose, just dug from the pit, on sandy soil *in spring*, and working it in immediately. The clay should be laid on in October or November, equally, spread and broken into small lumps by the spade. The dressing should be only about an inch thick. Thus exposed to the rains and frosts of winter, it gradually falls into a fine powder, which will have been partly washed into the sandy soil by Candlemas. It should then be dug in and well mixed when the soil and clay are damp, but not wet. The iron in the clay strongly attracts oxygen, and by this procedure it will soon be peroxidated. The soil will now be in a much better state for retaining the ammonia, and quality of culinary vegetables will be much improved. Where the subsoil is open, this dressing should be renewed in seven or ten years, as the clay is gradually washed down.

For carrots it probably requires no other manures except the urine. Potash and phosphoric acid are, most likely, deficient in the soil; if so, the ashes of burnt couch (especially from a clayey soil), or wood-ashes, are suitable. Neither farm nor street manure, nor coal ashes, should be used; either of these will increase the disease complained of. A weak solution of common black soap, or even " soap-suds," may be valuable; or the beautiful gem—guano.

My scroll is not finished, but Homer sleeps, and I shall close. Sir, your obedient servant,   G.

Dumfries-shire, 21st October, 1842.

ON LEASES.

TO THE EDITOR OF THE MARK LANE EXPRESS.

SIR,—My attention having been directed to the appeal you made to your Scottish readers in your journal of the 10th October last, I have thrown together a few facts on the subject of leases and rents, being such as have passed under my own observation, or have obtained on authentic information ; and if you judge them worthy of insertion, they are quite at your service.

Farms in Scotland have from time immemorial been held on leases ; and a tenant at will is an anomaly quite unknown.

Leases were formerly granted for a much longer period than they are at present—many being for fifty-seven years, with continuation of the contingency of a life selected towards the close of the fifty-seven years ; so that in some instances leases have extended to a full century. Several of these leases are yet unterminated. At present, however, leases are granted for nineteen years, but these nineteen years leases are frequently renewed, so that the same farm is often held by one family for several successive generations.

The renewal of these leases is effected in this way : —sometime before the expiry of the lease, the tenant is requested to make an offer for a new one ; and should his offer prove nearly equal to the ascertained value of the farm, the lease is at once renewed. Should the tenant's offer be considered below the value of the land, he receives notice that the farm is to be advertised. This does not, however, exclude him from again making an offer, even the same offer as before ; and it not unfrequently turns out to be the preferable one. and his lease is renewed. We know individuals who in this way have held successively three such leases, and have entered upon a fourth. The following are the most common courses in which farms fall to be advertised to be let by tender, namely —the insolvency of a tenant ; the death of a tenant, who leaves no family to mourn him, or whose family are settled in other farms, or in another line ; the advanced age of a tenant, who is circumstanced as to family as in the last case, who therefore declines to enter upon a new lease ; when a tenant has been so successful as to have been able to purchase a farm, and wishing to occupy his own land, therefore declines renewing his lease, a circumstance that has sometimes occurred in Scotland ; and when the landlord is a ward, his guardians sometimes feel it their duty, for their own protection, to advertize what farms may fall to be let. When from any of these causes a farm is to be let by tender, a day is fixed for receiving tenders.

In the meanwhile, intending competitors—for in such cases there is always a keen competition—inspect the farm, examine its capability of improvement, calculate the expense of these improvements, and the probability of a return for the outlay ; correspond with the landlord or his land-agent regarding the sum to be allowed at commencement of the lease for improvement or erection of farm house and offices, draining and fences, regarding the rotation of crops, the quantity of land for turnips, the old and young grass to be obtained at entry, and left at the expiry of the lease. On the day appointed, the tenders are opened, examined, and compared, the character and qualifications of the competitors carefully considered. The highest tender is frequently not accepted. So much for the practice of letting farms by tender.

The only cases that have come under our own observation, or that we can learn, in which farms have been put up to public auction, either in the Lothians or in any cultivated district in Scotland , are corporation lands, farms, or entailed estates when under the management of assignees, and particularly farms on lease, with a power of granting sub-leases. Occasionally too old rich pasture lands, in the landlord's enclosures, when he himself does not keep an agricultural establishment, are let by public auction for two or more crops, to be again laid down in grass.

Rents were long ago always paid in produce, of which there are in many parts of Scotland monuments still standing in the shape of huge old granaries, in which the produce was stored till the landlords could find a market for it.

In some districts the landlord, when he let a farm, also let the rent produce to other parties at a fixed price during the currency of the lease. It is easy to see that this was a cumbrous mode of proceeding, and about a century ago it began to fall into disuse, and a fixed money rent became the general rule, and continued so down to the year 1819 or thereabout. Farmers who had taken leases toward the conclusion of the French war and the downfall of Bonaparte, began to grumble at their high rents, when they found, with all the bolstering up of corn laws the war prices could not be realised, and as a remedy proposed a corn rent—to meet their views. The existing leases were very generally converted into a corn rent, part wheat, barley, and oats, but chiefly wheat, and new leases began to be granted in the same way. The corn was not, however, as in olden times paid in kind, but at the average price of the respective county for the year. Even this mode has not proved so satisfactory to the tenant as was at first expected ; for he now finds that in these years when the crop is deficient and prices consequently high, he has the highest rent to pay, while he has the least produce to pay it with. A new mode of paying rent has, therefore, lately been gradually coming into use, being partly a money rent and partly grain—and a new element has recently been introduced even into this mode, namely—so much money and so much grain, not at the average price of the year, but as ascertained by the average of seven or some other number of years previous to the commencement of the lease. Now it is easy to see that this mode, while nominally in part a corn rent, is in reality a fixed money rent—evidently admitting that a money rent is after all the best rent for the tenant.

As to the propriety of granting leases, our opinion, or that of any individual however distinguished, would in Scotland have no influence in abolishing the practice. Tenants at will is, as already stated, an anomaly altogether unknown in the Lothians or any cultivated district of Scotland ; and the state of agriculture, at followed on those farms held under the contingency of a life, is sufficient to satisfy any proprietor of the folly of tenants holding land without a lease. Nor would any tenant enter upon a farm without the security of a lease. The large capital he must lay out in improving and stocking a farm, amounting in many instances to thousands of pounds, entirely forbids the practice. The only wonder in Scotland is, *that tenants can be found to farm land without leases.* Had it not been for the practice of granting leases, and even long leases, Scotland had still been a tangled wilderness or a stagnant morass. I remain, Sir,

Nov. 8. A LOOKER-ON IN THE LOTHIANS.

AGRICULTURAL IMPROVEMENTS.

ON LEASES AND LETTING OF FARMS IN SCOTLAND.

(FROM THE BANNER OF ULSTER).

It is calculated that the imports of wheat during 1842 will reach to *three millions* of quarters, and the cost at the ports of shipment will not be under *six million* pounds. There is every probability that other grains will be imported to the value of *two million* pounds, and the cost of foreign cattle and provisions brought in under the new tariff will not be less than *one million*. A sum of money amounting to *nine million*, and equivalent to nearly one-fifth of our exports, is thus paid for produce that might have been, with good management, raised at home. This fact alone suffices to explain the paralysed state of industry and commerce. Under the law, as it exists at present, we have not the slightest reason to expect that our manufactures will be taken in exchange for the corn required; and if that were certain, it would still be foolish to exchange linens for corn that could be produced at home. We entirely coincide with those who consider freedom of trade a most desirable object; but the Government have done nothing to secure it, and Parliament did not offer them any powers on that subject. Until our diplomatists are enabled at once to offer discriminating duties in favour of the produce of nations whose rulers are willing to deal with us, it is unnecessary to expect any realization of those dreams of future activity and prosperity that were based on "free trade."

The exports of gold for foreign grain might ere now have turned the attention of agriculturists to the necessity of active measures to increase their produce. The wheat districts of England and Ireland yield a less return per acre than those of Scotland. This fact can only be accounted for on the supposition that the farms in Scotland are better managed than those of England or Ireland; and the question immediately arises, from what cause springs this superiority of management? The answer, we believe, will be found in the nature and length of leases. The Scottish farmers have been deeply indebted to the example set them by many landowners in that country, and to the information afforded by the Highland Society, but infinitely more to the encouragement afforded by long leases. The class of farmers who will improve a district must be prudent men, and no prudent man will lay out money on the fields of another person, without an opportunity being secured him of drawing it in again. Several landowners seem to consider it an imputation on their personal honour, or the honour of their family, to require leases. They are men evidently misplaced in the world. They live beyond their times by a generation or two. Men require security at every step they take in these degenerate commercial days—that is, at every step affecting so intimately their own comfort, and that of their family, as the investment of their entire capital. There is certainly no reflection cast upon the honour and integrity of any man, or of any family, in requiring a lease. If it were possible that landlords could live for an assured period, or that estates would continually remain in the same family, there might be some pretext for the insinuation. That, however, is impossible; and if it were not, there are few men so wedded to their "family

honour" as to speak positively for posterity, although they may stand firm on the ancestral portion of the matter.

There are really no means of improving the agriculture of England and Ireland to that extent which is necessary to enable them to produce an amount of grain equivalent to the demands of the population, that do not include "fixed tenures" as indispensable to their operation. We are, therefore, glad to observe that the leading agricultural journals advocate this change with great earnestness. There have recently appeared several very able articles on this subject in the *Mark-lane Express*, which is probably the highest authority on agricultural subjects. In one of these articles we find the following extract from a speech at an agricultural dinner by the Marquis of Salisbury :—

"The Marquis of Salisbury, who presided at the meeting of the Herts Agricultural Society, said—The idea of nineteen years' leases had been particularly pressed on the attention of those present. He could inform them that, though it was the case to grant leases for this period in Mid-Lothian, no sooner had the leases expired than they were put up by auction, to fetch the highest price, or by public tender to the highest bidder. If this plan suited any one as a tenant, it did not suit his ideas as a landlord."

Upon this the editor of the *Express* has the following remarks :—

"Now, upon this point, we will not contradict the statement of the noble earl, although we feel confident we might do so with propriety, as we are convinced that he is mistaken; but we shall feel extremely obliged if some of our Scottish readers will inform us if it be true that it is the general practice in Mid-Lothian to let farms by auction or tender to the highest bidder. We know that in this country charity lands, corporation lands, and in some instances private estates, are let by auction; and the consequence is, that they are uniformly the worst cultivated in the district in which they may happen to be."

We can give the *Express* some information on this subject. A very considerable number of the farms in the Lothians, and elsewhere in Scotland, are let in the manner described. The proportion is probably equal to one-third of the entire number; and we should think it is increasing. Some of the English landlords might object to this plan of forming agreements regarding the cultivation of their land; but their neighbours in Scotland find it very convenient, and we cannot suppose that a better plan could be devised. The terms, with regard to cropping, on which the lease will be given, are fully described; and the tenant contracts to fulfil them, in addition to the payment of a given rent. The system, indeed, is very extensively adopted in this country, and no inconvenience arises from it. A holder is not bound to accept the highest offer made to him; and, practically, we believe, he very rarely closes with the person offering the highest rent, but, more frequently with the man from whose skill and capital there is reason to anticipate that his farm will be fairly treated. We do not, however, perceive that the slightest weight is attached to the objection made by the noble marquis. He would not be bound to bring his farm into the market at the expiry of a lease. He might renew it without informing the public that there had ever been a break in the agreement. It is necessarily no part of this system that farms should be brought into the market. In Scotland, if a person is desirous of renewing his lease, unless political considerations interfere—and that in late years has been too frequently the case—he generally experiences no difficulty. It is supposed by others that he is the best judge of its value, and many landlords are beginning to perceive that the most profitable tenants do not always offer the highest rent.

There will be found much difficulty in altering existing practices in this respect ; but, if the farming societies would take the subject under their consideration, we have little doubt that they would ultimately be successful. They will be materially assisted by the fact that, without some immediate improvements in agriculture, the rents of many districts must be reduced. Notwithstanding many statements to the contrary, there can be no doubt that the value of stock, under the operation of the new tariff, will be gradually lowered. Some persons state that the quantity hitherto imported is very small; but they forget that a small quantity of extra goods thrown upon the market may cause a very great reduction in the value of any article. It has yet, however, to be proved that the quantity of cattle and cured provisions imported from foreign countries will be small. In the spring months of this season it was not anticipated that the British market would be opened for foreign cattle ; and it cannot be reasonably supposed that any preparation was made to meet the autumnal demand. The business of 1843 and 1844 will very probably find the foreign dealers more prepared to meet it, and we observe that several new steamers are to be placed upon the passage betwixt Hull or London and Denmark, by which it may be inferred that the shipowners anticipate importations from that quarter.

ON SEED WHEAT, AS AFFECTED BY SOIL AND RIPENESS.

TO THE EDITOR OF THE WEST BRITON.

Sir,—An author can gain but little attention without a critic,—and a poor critic is better than none ; and whether he praise or blame, the result is just the same, because people thus judge,—if a work is worth criticism, it is worth reading. And in these days of diffused knowledge, all people read and judge for themselves, except, indeed, party religionists, and party politicians, who, of course, read nothing but what is stamped with the *probatum est* of their leaders.

But what has all this to do with seed wheat? Let us just see. Mr. J. Prideaux has written about it, and I am very desirous that farmers should read and understand what he writes. I have, myself, paid some attention to seed corn and seed potatoes in my day, and have always found a change from one district to another advantageous, especially from worse soil to better. I have also observed what Mr. P. fetches out of "*Sprengel*," that ', *Seed corn should contain much starch and little gluten.*" Glutinous wheat is not so good for seed as starchy wheat. The latter is fair and white] to the eye ; the former brownish and waxy. Perhaps the difference is attributable to different degrees of ripeness, rather than diversity of soil. In light dry wheat soils, and in warm situations, the grain ripens sooner and more rapidly than on heavier and richer soils more elevated and exposed. Observant farmers have ascertained that it is for their profit to reap wheat in its mood, because, if left to get dead ripe, it does not weigh so well. It gains in starch and whiteness, but loses in gluten.

The fact is now well known, that the riper the corn is, the quicker it will vegetate. There is great risk, therefore, attending very ripe corn in wet harvests ; such corn sprouts, while, corn nearly ripe, but not quite so, remains sound and good. Soil, no doubt, has something to do in the matter ; but how can farmers know anything about "*phosphates*" and "*sulphates*'?" This is to them unintelligible Greek. They know something about lime, it is true, but not half so much as they ought to know, for they now use it indiscriminately on all sorts of soils.

I wish all chemists who write on these subjects were practical farmers, for then they would be able to explain their hard words in such terms as farmers understand ; and it is also much to be wished that all farmers were chemists to a certain extent, because a little chemical knowledge is of great practical advantage to a farmer. A little, or even a good deal of what is often called learning and scholarship, may be dangerous and vain ; but not so knowledge—ever so little of sound, useful knowledge, is beneficial to the lowest and meanest of the people.

I know an inquisitive and reading farmer, who took it into his head that sand, which he and his neighbours had been in the habit of using for manure, especially for wheat, was useless, and therefore the carriage of it labour thrown away. But he was not so rash and foolish as to discontinue its use before he had convinced himself by a fair trial. And this he did. He had a very poor piece of land, about four or five acres, spaded and burnt for wheat. The field was oblong in shape. The greater part of it he sanded at the rate of ten cart-loads an acre. On one broad stripe across the middle he put no sand ; and on another such stripe adjoining he put a double quantity, that is to say, he sanded it at the rate of twenty cart-loads an acre. Hear the result :—

There was scarcely any wheat at all on the part without sand ; on all the rest of the down-park—for such it was—there was a very fair crop of red wheat. But it was not better where sanded at the rate of twenty loads an acre, than where it had only ten. The unsanded spot is visible to this day, (after a lapse of seven years,) being almost bare of grass.

Perhaps Mr. P. will have the kindness to explain this phenomenon, and tell how it is that the beautiful yellow shelly sand, beyond a given quantity, was thrown away. I believe it is very much the same with lime as with shelly sand. We farmers, who have "practice" without "science," want to know something about "*potass, magnesia, sulphates,* and *phosphates,*" but these words convey little or no meaning or information to our minds. A knowledge of mere hard words can avail us but little ; what we want is a knowledge of the things which they signify. I hope Mr. P. will still go on writing about these interesting matters, explaining them in vulgar phrase as well as can be—and none can do this better than he—and I will come along after him, calling attention to his valuable labours, and, if need be, pointing out his faults. The worst is, sir, there are no fees for either of us, we can hope to get nothing but our labour for our pains. But I am reminded that man was not born to live entirely for himself, but for the good of the public—the community in which his lot is cast ; and besides this, there is a pleasure in communicating to others the little knowledge which we ourselves have acquired.

I remain, Sir, yours, &c.

November 1st, 1842,   An Old Farmer.

CULTIVATION OF TURNIPS.

TO THE EDITOR OF THE MARK LANE EXPRESS.

SIR,—In your paper of the 7th inst., I observe one of your correspondents putting certain queries in reference to Mr. Scougall's mode of raising turnips. It so happens that although I know nothing of Mr. S., and until a late publication of yours heard no more of his experiment than if he had lived in the planet Jupiter; but that as I have been raising turnips on the same plan (not upon first-rate turnip soil, but upon land the very opposite) I deem it not out of place to give you an account of my experiment—not in opposition to Mr. S., but in confirmation of the advantages to be derived in certain situations from this new method of working.

I would beg, then, to state that the greater part of the land 1 farm is a stiff retentive loam upon a clay subsoil, not at all adapted for raising green crops when wrought in the old way, as the herculean labour which such land requires to bring it to a proper state of pulverisation, either for potatoes or turnips, exhausts the moisture so much in dry seasons that there can be no vegetation; at least, this is my experience during the 10 years I have been tenant of Piffer Mill, and half crops don't do well when rents are so high as in our neighbourhood.

After the experience I have had, and the difficulties I had to contend with in working such land—evidently not adapted for green crop, particularly for turnip husbandry, when wrought in the old way—I resolved to try if nature would not help me if wrought in some other way.

The crop upon the field (one of the stiffest I have) I experimented upon was tares, which were cut green; so soon as they were removed from the ground, I cross-ploughed the field with deep furrow. It was then well wrought with the grubber and harrows, and early in the month of October the field was single-drilled at twenty-eight inches apart, but owing to the season, was prevented putting in the dung until the end of December and beginning of January, at which time we carted it into the drills.

The manure was nearly of the same kind as our police manure, which principally consists of ashes from coal, with a proportion of night soil, &c., &c., of which we gave about forty single horse carts per Scotch acre; it (i.e. the manure) was then covered in by splitting the drills with the common plough, and in this state, rough as it was, it lay until the end of March, when the drills were found almost as soft and fine as a piece of garden ground from the action of the frost. The field was rather foul, and at this period we gave the drills a double turn of the harrows, gathered off the weeds with the hand, run down between the drills with a single horse-grubber, and again set up the drills with the double-moulded plough; the same operation was performed just before sowing, for the purpose of keeping the annuals, with which we are troubled, in check. The field was then sown on the 15th May with green top yellow, and the remainder with white globe on the 25th and 26th of same month.

This is therefore the way in which I went to work, and which I found mere child's play compared with the old way. But what is of far more importance, in the month of September I found the crop infinitely better than any crop I have raised in former years, and quite superior to some I had

wrought in spring this year, weighing about forty tons per Scotch acre, including tops; and while, almost without exception, the whole turnips in the neighbourhood were much injured by mildew, these were nearly free, although sown much earlier than we are accustomed to sow.

The field was dunged 5 years back, but has been twice top-dressed with soot to the extent of 10 bags of 4 bushels each per acre since it was changed.

I may add, in conclusion, that although the plan was never heard of in this neighbourhood until this year, a number of our best farmers are adopting it to some extent; and I am making ten acres this year instead of seven acres, which I had last year.

I have thus, Sir, stated at greater length than I intended when I sat down to write you my views of the plan I have adopted; and if it shall meet with your approbation, and be found of as much balm to the country as I think it is, I shall rejoice in subscribing myself,

Your most humble servant,
PETER THOMPSON.

Piffer Mill, Liberton, Mid Lothian, Nov. 10.

ARTIFICIAL, OR STRONG PORTABLE MANURES.

TO THE EDITOR OF THE WEST BRITON.

SIR,—I have many times been gratified in observing Mr. J. Prideaux's endeavours to instruct farmers; but the great difficulty is to induce them to read and learn. In some things, they are regular Tories. They like old customs, however absurd, and, consequently, have great aversion to change; and their veneration for the wisdom of their ancestors is such, that as their fathers and grandfathers did, so do they. They all profess to know the value of dung as manure, and yet take little or no care to make the most of it. To be sure, the farm-yards are in general miserably constructed, with the cattle houses so scattered and inconveniently placed, that it is most difficult to bring all the dung together into one common saucerlike pit, according to Mr.P.'s excellent plan. The waste occasioned by having a little heap of dung here, and another there, is incalculable. If Mr. P.'s simple plan, involving only a little more than ordinary labour, were adopted and carefully acted upon, farmers' dung heaps would be bigger and better than they usually are.

Having said this much in commendation of Mr. P.'s laudable aim, I must now notice one little sentence, which has an evident tendency to cherish a prejudice already too prevalent among our west country farmers. Strong artificial manures are with many of them in low repute; and yet there are numberless farms that never can be improved to any considerable extent without the use of them. It is with regret, therefore, that I find Mr. P. writing this sentence :—" *They generally force or forward the crop, without doing much to enrich the soil with humus;*" and marking it, too, with italics, to indicate, as it would seem, that be attached to it more than ordinary importance. Why, prejudiced and ignorant farmers have said the same thing, after their fashion, over and over. " How," say they, " ken a leetle crame o' bone dest, or ziche leek trade theek'n and improve the land?" And thus they despise what they ought to test by experiment.

Farmers are proverbially a prejudiced and unreasoning race; reflecting but ltttle on the connexion of causes and effects, so that it is no great wonder that they overlook the advantages of a large crop produced by the application of a very small quantity of strong manure. But it is strange that your scientific correspondent should not perceive them, seeing there are few more shrewd and acute reasoners than he. "It produces a good crop, but does not do much to enrich the soil." This is little better than nonsense, and, therefore, utterly unworthy of Mr. J. Prideaux. This logic must be tried a little. A good crop of vegetable matter, turnips to wit, if properly managed, does much to enrich the soil upon which it grows. A very small quantity of strong artificial manure will produce a good crop of turnips; therefore, a small quantity of strong artificial manure will enrich the soil. No deduction can be clearer than this. It is true, the artificial manure itself does not directly enrich the land, but it produces that which does enrich it, namely, a good crop of turnips; and, according to a good old maxim, "the cause of the cause, is the cause of the thing caused." Once more. The land is enriched, the turnips make the dung for enriching it, and the artificial manure produces the turnips. How this view of the matter escaped Mr. P. I know not; however, some good will probably result from it, in that it has afforded me an opportunity and a motive to excite attention to his instructive and useful writings. And I trust it may also put him more on his guard against setting down anything having the slightest tendency to encourage the prejudices of a notoriously prejudiced class.

Artificial manures have already done much, and there is no doubt that in conjunction with thorough draining they will yet effect much more. Ladies apply bone dust to their flower pots—they are covered with flowers. Gardeners apply it to their onion beds—they are covered with onions. Farmers apply it to their arish fallows, and, lo! they are covered with turnips. And turnips so cultivated are hoed and kept clean from weeds at half the ordinary expense. Stall-dung begets weeds, especially in wet seasons. Besides, the dung may be applied to the thin land for corn with much advantage, improving the grain, and at the same time enriching the soil. Whatever a farmer forgets, he ought to bear this always in mind—that whatever manure increases the weight of his crops, must ultimately, with good management, improve his land. The dropping and rotting of the leaves of a good crop of turnips adds to the humus of the soil, and thereby improves its condition. A heavy crop of turnips is generally followed by a good crop of barley and seeds; and these being consumed on the land by all sorts of stock, will still further increase the humus by which the soil is enriched.

Humus is *rotten*, or, as chemists call it, *decomposed* vegetable substance, and the more of this is applied to the soil the richer it will become. But Mr. P. can treat this subject scientifically (which I cannot) and otherwise much more ably than I, who am but an old farmer; and I therefore cheerfully leave it to him, apologizing for presuming to criticise, and at the same time thanking him heartily for his able writings for the instruction of farmers, for we all need it more or less, whether great or small; and

I am, Sir, your obedient servant,
Oct. 1, 1842. An Old Farmer.

REPORT

OF THE INSPECTORS OF FARMS AND CROPS TO THE LIVERPOOL AGRICULTURAL SOCIETY AT THEIR RECENT MEETING.

The following is the substance of the report made to the committee by Messrs. Robertson and Pemberton, the inspectors of farms and crops :—

Having already reported to the committee and other members of the society who have attended this meeting, the various particulars required from us as to the crops and cultivations of those farms, the occupiers of which are candidates for the society's prizes, it now remains to us to make a few remarks upon the state and progress of agriculture in the district generally. In doing so, we would first acknowledge the goodness of Divine Providence in graciously giving us a season so favourable for all the operations of the farmer, and such as we do not remember to have had for the last sixteen years. Corn has been better ripened than usual, and the gathering accomplished earlier, the harvest being, with few exceptions, completed by the second week in September. The prospect of having *good bread* must be a subject of thankfulness, not only to the farmer, but to every member of the community.

Your inspectors have pleasure in stating that the *under-draining* of land continues on the increase, and although much has already been done, and is now doing, very much still remains to be done. The establishment of draining tile manufactories in various parts of the district, and the moderate price at which tiles may now be purchased, are great inducements both to landowners and occupiers to continue this system of improvement. Draining with broken stones, and with cinders, is also carried on to a great extent, more particularly in situations where these materials are easily obtained, and answers remarkably well. The advantage of draining is felt in another way. Being generally done during the winter months, it affords employment for labourers at a time when the farmer would probably have nothing else for them to do, thereby rendering a great service to the poor man's family, and probably keeping them from the parish. Men of experience are engaged upon some estates solely for the purpose of superintending the draining. The landlord in these cases pays the whole expence, and charges the tenants what he considers a fair per centage on the outlay. The practice is much to be commended. We believe the noble patron of this society was the first to begin it in this neighbourhood. The new system of cutting the drains in a longitudinal direction, as recommended by Mr. Smith, of Deanston, in Scotland, seems to be obtaining favour. A portion of the work of excavating can be performed by the plough, and a consequent saving of expense effected.

The *subsoil-plough* has been so little used in the district of this society, that your inspectors cannot report either favourably or otherwise of its effects at present.

The claimants upon large farms are more numerous this year than usual, and the management and cultivation of the land is of a very superior order; very different, indeed, to what it was when the Liverpool Agricultural Society was first established.

The *marling* of land is less frequently met with than formerly, other manures of a lighter character being preferred. An objection has also been started in some places, and not without good ground, that the permanent damage done by making pits is, in some instances, equal to the temporary benefit conferred on the soil by the application of marl.

In the *laying down of land* to grass we observe great improvement, both in the ploughing and preparation of the surface, and also in the description of the seeds sown.

Reservoirs for the reception of dung water are becoming more general, and many of them are proving useful adjuncts to the farmer's other means of improvement.

In the *planting of new hedges* your inspectors regret to say little progress is making—at the same time they are well aware there are many places in the district where they are much required, and would, if made, prove a great convenience, if not an ultimate saving. One great obstacle to the farmer undertaking much of this work is, the expence of protecting the young quicksets, which require to be fenced with rails or hurdles for at least four or five years after planting.

The *cutting and laying of hedges* is not so much practised, nor so well done, as might be wished. The prize given by the Right Honourable Lord Lilford, to whom the society is much indebted, has not always been claimed; and when it has, the competitors have never been numerous. His lordship's agent, Mr. Selby, of Atherton, having a desire to see the work performed more scientifically, has sent for an experienced man from Northamptonshire, who has already cut and laid a considerable length of fencing in a first-rate manner.

The *crops of wheat* have generally proved thin upon the ground this year, which is chiefly attributable to the unfavourable weather in October and November when the seed was sown: the grain, however, is finer and better than usual, and, we think, upon the whole, the yield will not be less than what is generally described as *an average crop*. *Oats* are also a good sample, but we do not calculate on more than an average quantity. *Barley* we consider much better, although but little is grown in this district. *Beans* are moderately well podded and a fair average crop.

The *second crop of clover* is good, and the weather has, fortunately, proved fine for gathering it, which has rarely been the case of late years. It is hoped this crop will make up in some measure for the farmer's deficient hay crop.

Potatoes have grown very luxuriantly this year and are likely to prove better in quality and greater in quantity than usual; yet some little rot is preceptible.

From what your inspectors have seen this season *mangel wurzel* is becoming less cultivated, and yet it must be acknowledged there is no green crop succeeds better upon peat soils.

The growth of *Swedish turnips* is very much on the increase; nearly all the early potatoe ground is now planted with this valuable root as a second crop, the greatest part of which have been transplanted from the seed bed.

An unusual quantity of land is also sown with this and other kinds of turnips, and we think the quantity produced in the district of this society is more than quadrupled since the establishment of the society in 1830. The mildew has, unfortunately, made its appearance, and the crops will consequently, be more or less deteriorated.

Having only met with the application of the new manure Guano, in a few instances, and that only in this year, your inspectors are not able to speak decidedly of the permanent good which is likely to be effected by it. Appearances are at present in its favour. It is doubtful, however, whether it will ever be extensively used, unless it can be obtained at a more moderate price than what it has hitherto been sold at.

LIME AS A FERTILISER.

(TO THE EDITOR OF THE WEST BRITON.)

SIR,—I omitted in my last on bone-dust, the reaction of the ammonia produced, on the phosphate of lime : this produces, in the damp soil, carbonate of lime and phosphate of ammonia — the latter a very soluble salt, entering readily into the sap, and acting both by its acid and alkali.

"A young farmer" will allow for my hesitating to send this last week, after occupying so much of your previous number. The use of lime is perhaps the most important problem of agricultural chemistry. That it is not yet clearly explained, even by the multitude of known facts and experiments relating to it, will be a reason for diffidence in our conclusions ; but by no means for discouragement in our research. On the contrary, the more obscure and the more important to understand, the greater the call for diligent investigation.

The arguments, *pro.* and *con.*, are of course too extensive for communications of this kind, and may exercise the logic of your correspondent and his associates : the leading facts and inferences concisely stated will be quite long enough for your columns, and give the reader a more perspicuous view of the question.

The first step of the enquiry *how* lime acts, is to ascertain *what* it does.

A. It enters into the composition of plants, and of course of the soils on which they grow.

Lime in 1000lb. each of

	wheat.	Barley.	Oats.	Potatoes.	Turnips.
Straw and Tops }	1	1·1	0·9	0·3	0·8lbs.
	2	5	1·5	13	6
Or per Acre } average	8·6	14·9	7·6	40	80

whilst we add to the soil 100 to 200 imperial hushels per acre, or more, with evident advantage. See below (1).

B. It tends to loosen clays, and render them drier ; whilst on light sandy soils, it produces a binding and moistening effect (9). Wet, stiff, and humus soils requiring much larger quantities than light soils containing little humus (2).

C. It corrects acid and hurtful ingredients in the soil ; kills worms, insects, and some weeds and germs (7); must not, therefore, be brought into *contact* with corn and other seeds in quantity sufficient to endanger their germination. Limewater is said to kill grass (7), and it acts wastefully (2) upon dung, unless first well mixed in with the soil.

D. It converts heath and moss into pasture ; renders herbage closer, firmer, more palatable and nutritious ; and is said to prevent the rot and foot rot in sheep feeding on such herbage (1, 2, 3, 7).

E. In arable, it increases the crops (1, 2, 3, 5), and ripens them earlier (8).

F. Produces heavy crops in some cases where

dung will not (1, 2, 8), but not many such crops in succession (4).

G. Gives better ear and grain than dung alone, and never lays the corn (10).

H. In too large proportion to mould or dung reduces fertility, drying up the plant; lime and dung must be applied alternately (4).

I. Renders humus, &c., soluble and effective, thus exciting rich soils and exhausting poor ones (2, 3, 4).

K. Excites heavy clays and sour moulds, producing better crops, as well in quality as in quantity (6, 7, 8).

Besides many effects of less importance, referable to the same principles, and perhaps others which I may have failed to recollect or refer to.

From these observations, compared with its known chemical properties, we infer that lime

FEEDS THE PLANT.

1. *Directly* in supplying the quantity of lime necessary for its healthy growth; which, however, is so small a proportion (see A) of the quantity beneficially employed, that we must look for other more extensive effects.

2. *Indirectly* by acidifying humus (5), and rendering it soluble; and by promoting the decomposition of dead roots, and other organic matters (F) generating soluble compounds, and fertilizing gases (C) as carbonic acid, ammonia, and some others, most of which are taken up by the moisture of the soil, and enter the sap by the roots, with the humate of lime and other soluble organic matters produced; thus supplying the plant with *organic* ingredients.

3. Also *indirectly*, by decomposing the insoluble alkaline silicates, and some other salts; thus giving them the solubility requisite for being taken up by the roots, and supplying the sap with alkalies and other requisite inorganic matters.

4. Of course, by thus bringing all these substances into use, it must gradually exhaust them, unless replaced; hence the danger of overliming. Without humus, and probably nitrogen, lime seems to dry up the plant.

5. Further *indirectly*, its alkalescent property, disposing the soil to absorb oxygen, thus acidifies, besides the humus and carbonaceous matters; also nitrogen (producing nitrates), which not only enters into the plant, but powerfully promotes its appropriation of other organic elements, both from the sap and from the air. This effect of lime is, however, very slow, unless under particular circumstances.

ACTS ON THE SOIL.

6. Thoroughly pervading it (when properly applied), its slaking quality making it easy to spread and mix, and its solubility in water diffusing it generally. Even the carbonate of lime is soluble in the water of the soil, by aid of the carbonic acid generated there, or brought down by the rain and dew. By this solubility it is gradually washed down by the rains, &c., and of course lost to the soil in course of years.

7. Its alkalescent property destroys hurtful ingredients, neutralising acids, and decomposing salts of iron, manganese, and alumina (C), rendering the oxides insoluble, and subjecting them to peroxidation, when they are rather useful than otherwise; while the acids, generally sulphuric, phosphoric, or humic, combining with the lime, produce well known fertilisers, gypsum, bone earth, &c. Its solubility also enables it to follow and kill

some worms, insects, weeds, and germs; of course it may also kill or damage our seeds and young plants, if incautiously applied.

8. Its strong chemical affinities thus inducing a variety of combinations and decompositions, liable again to changes from wet and dry, heat and cold, keep the soil in continual chemical activity, evolving electricity, one of the most active promoters of vegetation. The rich verdure following a thunder storm is well known. These electrical re actions of the soil probably contribute, with the drying tendency of the lime (H) to forward the ripening.

9. All these results are produced the most effectively by lime in its caustic state: its activity diminishing in proportion as it absorbs carbonic acid, but the property of loosening stiff soils (B) continues when it is quite saturated and mild.

10. Lime is said to increase the ear, and never to lay the corn (G), but it appears to dry it up where organic manures are deficient (H); this is a remarkable distinction from the *nitrogenous* fertilisers, which, in excess, produce a deep green, rank vegetation, running to leaf and straw, producing little ear, and laying before harvest. Thus they appear to correct each other. The examination of this difference is not the least interesting part of our present enquiry.

Nitrogen (in its general fertilizing compound—ammonia) promotes *vital* transformations in the *sap*; hence rapid appropriation of organic elements, and secretion of vegetable constituents; the plant becomes deep green, and grows luxuriantly.

Lime seems to produce re-actions in the *soil*—supplying the sap with inorganic as well as organic ingredients where it enters the *root*; but not exciting the *vital* transformations in the leaf, &c. Hence it will not produce rank vegetation, but hardens the straw, and sends up materials for the rain.

Hence, if the ammonia (or nitrogen) is in excess, the straw runs up deep green and soft—if the lime be in excess, pale and hard, or even dry, from over dosing with mineral constituents. But when both are present in due proportions, with the other requisite ingredients, luxuriance in growth, and firmness of texture are cowned with heavy ears. This brings us back to the question in my last—*What is it to limit the quantity of our manures, and the consequent production, when they are applied in due proportions to their respective functions? Twelve quarters of wheat have been grown upon an acre; where lies the improbability of such a produce becoming not extraordinary?* Lime we have plenty, for ages; and thousands of tons of ammoniacal matters are yearly washed away in sewerage.

I am, sir, &c.,

Plymouth, Nov. 9th, 1842.   J. PRIDEAUX.

PRICES OF CATTLE AND LIVE STOCK IN THE OLDEN TIMES.

From Bishop Fleetwood's *Chronicon Preciosum,* we draw the following curious particulars as to the prices of stock, &c., in England in the olden time: —In King Ina's laws, which were made betwixt 712 and 727 (A. D.), it is said that an ewe with her lamb, is worth 1s. till thirteen nights after Eas.

ter. About the year 986 a palfrey was sold at 10s: In the *Senatus Consulta de Monticolis*, in the time of King Ethelred, about the year 1000, if a horse be lost, the compensation must be 30s.; a mare or colt of a year old, 20s.; a mule or young ass, at 12s.; an ox at 30d.; a cow, 24d.; a swine, 8d.; a sheep, 1s.; a goat at 11d. (Note, that this is Saxon money, 5d. to the shilling, and 48s. to the pound). In the laws of Henry I., cap. 76, forty sheep are valued at 1l. About the year 1145, the tenants of a place was to pay yearly 20s., or seven oxen each worth 3s. In 1185, the tenant of Shireborn are by custom to pay either 2d. or four hens, which they will. And by the custom of Belesball they are to have a ram or 8d. (In the preface to King Athelstan's laws, a ram was at 4d). In or about 1217, when the king came to Redbourn, the *camerarious* (receiver of rents) of St. Alban's lost three good horses, two asses, and a good new cart; all of which were worth at least 50s. About 1232, the abbot of St. Alban's going a journey, and attended with six esquires on horseback, agrees, that if the horses (hired ones) die on the way, he will give for each horse, 10s.; and the horses are to be strong and handsome. In 1280, a swan was valued at 3s. 4d.; s duck at 1d. In 1298, at Scarborough, Yorkshire, the price of an ox was 6s. 8d.; a cow, 5s.; a heifer, 2s.; and a sheep, 1d. In 1299 was made an act of common council for prices of victuals to be sold at London, by consent of the king and the nobility; and, as to poultry, it was as follows:—A fat cock, 1½d.; two pullets, 1½d.; a fat capon, 2½d.; a goose, 4d.; a mallard, 1½d.; a partridge, 1½d.; a phessant, 4d.; a heron, 6d.; a plover, 1d.; a swan, 3s.; a crane, 1s.; two woodcocks, 1½d. A fat lamb from Christmas to Shrovetide, 1s. 4d.; for all the year after, 4d. In 1302, in London, the price of a bull was 7s. 4d; a cow, 6s.; a " fat muttun," 1s.; a ewe sheep, 8d.; a capon, 2d.; a cock or hen, 1½d.

Amongst other purchases for the feast which Ralph de Borne, prior of St. Augustine's, Canterbury, made on his installation day (in which it appears that he paid very great rates for many portions of his bill of fare, considering the times) we find the following: —30 ox carcases, 27l. or 18s. each; 100 hogs, 16l. or 3s. 2½d. each; 200 " muttons," 30l. or 3s. each; 1000 geese, 16l. or about 3¾d. each; 500 capons and hens, 6l. 5s. or 3d. each; 473 pullets, 3l. 14s. or 1½d. each; 200 pigs, 5l. or 6d. each; 24 swans, 7l. or 5s. 10d. each; 600 rabbits, 15l. or 6d. each (there is some mistake here); 16 shields of brawn, 3l. 5s. or 4s. 0¾d. each; 9,600 eggs, 4l. 10s. or about 9 for a penny.

In 1314, according to Stow, the prices fixed by parliament were :—A stalled, or corn-fed ox, 1l. 4s.; a grass-fed ox, 16s.; a fat stalled cow, 12s.; an ordinary cow, 10s.; a fat mutton, unshorn (corn fed), 1s. 8d.; a fat goose in the city, 3d., but everywhere else, 2½d.; a fat capon in the city, 2½d,, elsewhere, 2d.; a fat hen in the city, 1½d., elsewhere, 1d.; 2 chickens in the city 1½d., elsewhere, 1d.; in the city 3, elsewhere 4, pigeons for 1d.; in the city 20, elsewhere 24, eggs for 1d. But, notwithstanding this act of parliament, things could not be purchased at these rates; for people would not bring them to market (and that is a thing that parliaments cannot remedy), and so the king was fain to revoke the former act, and leave people to sell as they could (for a trade will do as it can, and never be forced one way or ether.)—[Bishop Fleetwood would have made a good free tenant in our days.]

In 1326, 12 hens were sold at 1s. 6d.; the cock and 13 hens, at 1s. 7d. Eight " porkers" and a half,

at 15s.; a cock at 1d. and 3 hens 4½d. In 1336, a fat ox, 6s. 8d.; a fat sheep, 6d. to 8d.; six pigeons for 1d.; a fat goose, 2d.; a pig, 1d. In 1343, oxen, 8s. each; in 1344, a cow, 5s.

In 1348, H. Knighton, who lived at Leicester, says, that in the pestilence things were sold for almost nothing. A horse, worth 40s., was sold for 6s. 8d.; a good fat ox at 4s.; a cow, 1s.; a heifer or steer, 6d.; a fat mutton, 4d.; an ewe, 3d.; a lamb, 2d.; a hog, 5d.; a stone of wool, 9d. In 1349, a fat ox was sold in London for 6s. 8d. In 1361, two hens for a penny; in 1363, a widow is to pay four hens or 4d. in money, and 12 hogs were valued at 18s. or 1s. 6d. each.

In 1407, in a *computus* relating to the prior and canons of Burcester, Oxfordshire, the price paid for a cow is stated at 7s.—for the calf of that cow, 1s. 8d.; for the calf of a cow that was somewhat weak, 1s.; for five calves, 10s. 8d. or nearly 2s. 1½d. each : for a cow and her calf, 7s. 6d.; two oxen, 1l. 6s. 8d.; one ox, 11s. 6d.; a calf, 1s. 7d. In 1473, a ram, 8d. In 1425, a colt, 8s.; five ox hides, 12s.; two cow hides, 2s. 7d.; three cow hides, 4s. 8d.; 16 calf skins, 2s.; 21 lambs, 4s.; 38 sheep skins, of two years old, 9s.; 23 tods of pure wool, 10l. 18s. 6d. or 9s. 6d. the tod; 20 pullets, 1s. 8d.; a quarter of an ox, to salt, 1s. 4d.; for a bay horse, for the prior's stable, 1l. 6s. 8d; two colts, 9s.; eight woodcocks, for a present, 1s. In 1426, five oxen were appraised at 3s. 4d. each; six cows at 2s. 8d. each; three horses at 3s. each. In 1444, six calves, 2s. each; eight porkers, 3s. each without the head; 40 geese, 3d. each : 31 dozen pigeons, at 4½d. per dozen; others at 5½d. and 6d. per dozen; an ox, 1l. 11s. 8d.; eight cygnets or young swans, 3s. each; a flitch of bacon, 1s. 4d.; four oxen (probably young and lean), 13s. each; two plough oxen, 1l. 3s. In 1445, 24 bullocks and heifers, at 5s. per head. In 1449, 15 sheep at 2s. 5½d. each; seven bogs at 1s. 11½d. each.

" In 1533 (says Stow) it was enacted that butchers should sell their beef and mutton by weight; beef for a halfpenny the pound, and mutton for three farthings; which being devised for the great commodity (accommodation) of the realm (as it was thought), has proved far otherwise. For at that time (1553) fat oven were sold for 26s. 8d.; fat wethers for 3s. 4d.; fat calves for the like price; a fat lamb for 12d. The butchers of London sold penny pieces of beef, for the relief of the poor; every piece 2½lb. and sometimes 3lb. for a penny : and 13, sometimes 14 of these pieces for 12d.; mutton, 8d. the qr.; and a cwt. of beef for 4s. 8d. What price it hath grown to since it needeth not to be set down. At this time also, and not before, were foreign butchers (butchers not apprenticed in or living in London) permitted to sell their flesh in Leadenhall market of London." In 1558, a good sheep, 2s. 10d.

In 1574, beef, at Lammas (August), so dear that a stone came to 1s. 10d. In 1595, a hen's egg, 1d.; or at best three eggs for 2d.

OTHER ARTICLES OF FOOD, &c.

In the bill of fare for the installation feast above mentioned, in 1306, we find the following articles and prices:—Malt, 6s. per qr.; wax, 6½d. per lb.; almonds, 1½d. per lb.; salt, nine summas for 10s. In 1315 and 1316, malt was 13s. 4d. per qr.; salt, 1l. 15s. per qr.; good ale per lagenam (flaggon or gallon), 2d. the better sort 3d.—and the best, 4d. The viler ale at 1d. In 1425, for a cade of red herrings, (710 herrings in the cade), 8s.; a frail of figs,

3s. 4d.; 12lb. raisins, 1s. 1d. In 1440, malt, 13s. per qr.; bay salt, 1s. per bush.

In 1444, malt was 4s. per qr.; for 26 warp of ling was paid 1*l.* 10s.4d.; for 100 stock-fish, 17s. 6d.; for a barrel of herrings (*i. e.*, 30 gallons fully packed), 1*l.* In 1445, ale, 1¼d. per gallon; for 3,000 red herrings, 1*l.* 11s In 1448, a cade of red herrings, 5s. 8d.; a barrel of white, 9s. 3d. In 1449, a cade of red herrings, 6s.; a barrel of white herrings, 10s. 3d. In 1451, ale, 1½d. per gallon; a cade of red herrings, 7s. 4d.; a barrel of white herrings, 13s. 6d. In 1453, ale, 1½d. per gallon; cade of red herrings, 7s. 6d.; four score white herrings, 1s. In 1457, ale, 1d. per gallon; a cade of red herrings, 6s. 8d.; 92 white herrings, 1s.

In the 51st year of Henry III. it was determined by authority that, when a quarter of barley was sold at 2s,, then ale might be afforded four quarts for 1d. And when barley was sold at 2s. 6d. per qr., then ale was to be seven quarts for 2d.; and so to increase and decrease after the rate of 6d. per quarter. But no rules can always hold for trade (says Bishop Fleetwood), as you may see by comparing the price of barley and ale in these and other accounts. In 1459, ale 2d. the gallon; red herrings, 7s. 10½d. the cade; 92 white herrings, 1s. In 1460, ale, 1d. the gallon; red herrings, 7s. the cade; 192 white herrings for 2d. In 1416, bay salt, very dear, 24s. the qr.; in 1494, very cheap, 4s. the qr. In 1495, white herrings, 3s. 4d. per barrel. In 1469, bay salt, 2s. 8d. per qr. In 1504, ale of London (per pipe or butt of 126 gallons,) 1*l.* 10s., or nearly 3d. per gallon; ale of Canterbury, 1*l.* 5s.; beer, 1*l* 3s. 4d. In 1531, malt was 3s. 1d. per qr.; from 1553 to 1557, 5s.; but before harvest, in 1557, it had reached the price of 2*l.* 4s. per qr.; after harvest it fell to 6s. 8d. in London, 4s. 8d. in the country. In 1561, it was 5s. again. In 1574, provisions so dear that five herrings sold for 2d., bay salt (never before so dear), 6s. per bushel. In 1595, sweet butter, 7d. per lb. In 1598, pepper, 8s. per lb., raisins, 6d.

REPORT ON THE EXHIBITION OF IMPLEMENTS AT THE BRISTOL MEETING IN 1842.

(FROM THE JOURNAL OF THE ROYAL AGRICULTURAL SOCIETY.)

(Concluded.)

Subsoil pulverizers.—The collections of most of the larger machine-makers contained specimens of subsoil ploughs, efficiently constructed after well known models. Of these it is unnecessary to make particular mention. Three implements of this class were selected for trial, which deserve special notice.

The Honourable M. W. B. Nugent, of Higham Grange, near Hinckley, Leicestershire, exhibited an implement of his own invention, which may be correctly termed a *subsoil pulverizer*, as its object is to undermine, break, and stir the subsoil, without raising it to the surface, which latter is the specific function of the *plough*. These two operations are distinct in their intent and nature; it would appear, therefore, to be more correct to designate the implements used for the two purposes by distinct and appropriate names. Mr.

Nugent's subsoil pulverizer consists of several strong curved coulters or teeth, so fixed to the beam of the implement as to work under the soil at unequal depths, and at distances varying from each other both in length and breadth. Thus, the mass to be broken up is not opposed to the action of a single blade, as in the common subsoil plough, but is cut and disturbed by the successive action of several blades, which penetrate, loosen, and move the soil to the respective depths at which they may be set to act; for which purpose, and to suit various soils, each tine is made adjustable. The implement submitted to trial, which was the first yet constructed, had four blades operating in succession, at six, nine, twelve, and sixteen inches in depth, moving, pulverizing, and incorporating the soil to that depth, and to about twelve inches in the transverse section. It is furnished with two leading, and two hind or trailing wheels, for the following purposes:—First, for assisting in the regulation of the depth stirred; second, to travel the impiement; third, to raise the teeth out of the ground at the end of a bout. Much ingenuity and good workmanship were displayed in bringing about these ends, and in accomplishing, by the hand, and at the will of the holder, an instantaneous change in the working depth of the blades.

Some of the mechanical details of this implement were not in a complete state, and its action, therefore, not so certain and perfect as is desirable; but the judges having had no hesitation in awarding a prize to the inventor, as the quality of the work done seemed to them to justify the correctness of the principles which had guided him in the construction of an important implement; and its defects did not appear to be other than might readily be rectified by a skilful mechanic, aided by the light of further experience in its use.

Mr. Pusey's plough, which has received the name of the *" Charlbury Subsoil,"* was also tried. It is a common wheel plough, having a single tine or stirrer attached to its hinder part, which descends a few inches below the sole, and is intended to loosen the soil in its track, deepening, and to a limited extent pulverizing, the stratum beneath. This modification of a subsoil pulverizer has the advantage of simplicity and cheapness, and the combination may be usefully employed on light soils, and by farmers possessing only a limited command of team.*

Trenching and Subsoil Plough.—To Mr. Law, of Shettleston, near Glasgow, a prize was awarded for a trenching and subsoil plough combined. This implement performed its work very satisfactorily, with a team of six horses, trenching in one direction, and subsoiling in the returning one. A trenching furrow having been cut, the mouldboard or wrest is turned up out of the way, by means of the same simple mechanism as is adapted to Smith's (or Wilkie's) turnwrest plough. The implement is then reversed, put into the furrow, and the operation of subsoiling proceeds without unyoking the team. The trenching or deep ploughing operation is performed on the left-hand side of the implement; and the spur or bar for breaking up the subsoil is placed, in returning, on the right-hand side; consequently, the force is applied on the same side as that on which the furrow-slice has been turned; and it seems rea-

* See a woodcut of this plough in the Journal of the Society, vol. iii., part i., p. 106.

D 2

sonable to conclude that the resistance to be overcome must be less against soil already loosened than if working against the unbroken mass of the land side, as in Armstrong's trenching and subsoil plough. A leading wheel regulates the depth desired, by shifting up or down, so that a furrow may be trenched from eight inches to fourteen inches in depth, and the subsoiling effected, proportionably, to the extent of twenty inches below the surface of the field.

Surface Ploughs.—The following table registers the results of experiments made on a variety of ploughs, at the trial ground, on Mr Webb Hall's farm :—

Experiments on the Draught of Ploughs.

Makers' Names.	Residence.	Number of Horses.	Number of Wheels.	Slice out.		Draught in Stones.	
				Depth, inches.	Width, inches.		
Howard	Bedford	2	2	6	9	22	Prize.
Mason	{ Grafton, near Alcester, Warwickshire }	2	2	6	9	26	Prize.
"	"	2	2	6	9	30	With two knives.
"		2	2	6	9	30	{ Ditto, with skim coulter.
Brayton	Carlisle	2	1	6	9	28	
Sanders & Williams	Bedford	2	2	6	9	30	
Carson..........	Warminster........ ..	2	1	6	9	32	
Mason	Grafton	3	2	6	9	60	Double furrow.
Barrett & Co.....	Reading	3	2	6	9	60	Ditto.
Huckvale	Over Norton, Oxon...	2 { foot or floater }		6	9	36	Turnwrest.
Earl of Ducie....	Uley	2 { swing	}	6	9	26	Prize.
Howard	Bedford	2	"	6	9	26	
Brayton	Carlisle	2	"	6	9	28	
Carson..........	Warminster	2	"	6	9	32	
Merrett	{ Appleadon, near Newent, Gloucestersh. }	2	"	6	9	32	
Law	{ Shettleston, near Glasgow }	2	"	6	9	36	
Wilkie..........	Uddingston, ditto	2	"	6	9	44	Turnwrest.

With respect to the excellence of the work done by these ploughs, as well as lightness of draught, the palm of merit is unquestionably due to Mr. Howards two-wheel implement, the furrow-bottom being left cleaner and flatter, the slice better turned and placed, and the depth more evenly maintained, than by any other of the competing ploughs. The dynamometer exhibited a peculiar steadiness of movement and uniformity of draught in this plough; and the same qualities were distinguishable as belonging, in a superior degree, to all the wheel, compared with the swing, ploughs. The remark made in recording the experiments at Liverpool, viz., that the weight of soil actually raised by the wheel-ploughs was in every case greater than that turned over by the swings, is equally applicable on the present occasion, inasmuch as all the swing-ploughs leaned more or less to the land side, and did not maintain so even and horizontal a bearing on the sole as the wheel-ploughs. The two kinds of plough from the same workshop, of which there were three different pairs in the field, manifested these qualities in every case. Two better ploughs than Mr. Brayton's have rarely been put into the ground, and they were held by an experienced and skilful ploughman of Mr. Falkner's, of Fairfield, near Liverpool; but the work of his one-wheel was decidedly superior to that of his swing plough, though the draught of both was alike. The same may be said of the performance of Mr. Carson's and Mr. Howards implements; and it is worthy of note, that the resistance of Mr. Howard's two-

wheel was less than that of his swing plough by four stones, the latter equaling a new and very elegantly constructed swing plough from the workshop of the Earl of Ducie, to whom the prize was adjudged, as the quality of the work done by the latter was considered to be superior, in a slight degree, to that of the other ploughs of this class.

Surface pulverizing plough.—The judges have to report, in addition to the trials of these well known varieties, the performance of an implement constructed by Mr. Mason, of Grafton, Warwickshire, which, as a common wheel plough, did excellent work; but its peculiarity consists in the addition of pulverizing knives attached to moveable bars or rods, extending beyond the end of the mouldboard. These knives are used in suitable soils for cutting off the angular summit of the furrow-slice just raised, and dividing it into two, or if requisite, into three portions. Having ascertained the draught of this plough in its ordinary state (see woodcut, fig. 1), one of the knives, *a*, was put in work to about the depth of two inches below the surface of the slice; and then a second knife, acting at a somewhat greater depth below the upper one. Under these conditions the dynamometer exhibited an increase of draught of four stones, or a little more than fifteen per cent. The skim-coulter, *b*, was then set down to the depth of about an inch ; this did not appear to cause any increase of resistance.

The woodcut shows the plough in perspective, with sufficient accuracy to illustrate the position of the knives, when out of work, and the simple arrangements for holding them and adjusting their depth of cut. Their shape is as drawn, but it will be understood that, when at work, their curved cutting edge is presented, at an angle more or less acute, to the furrow-slice, which is divided horizontally, in the plane of the plough's path.

FIG. 1.

The character of the soil upon which the trials were made was that of a sandy loam in a good mellow state, a crop of strong clover having been cut from it on the preceding day. The appearance given to the surface of the ploughed land by the action of the knives was that of a well-harrowed field, the soil being left loose and pulverized nearly to the depth turned up. The action of the plough was in no respect deranged by that of the slicers; it "swam fair" on the furrow bottom, leaving it clean and flat, and required so little skill in guidance, that Mr. John Stokes, of Pauntley Court, the exhibitor, who held the plough, frequently left it free for a long space to follow the horses. It possessed, therefore, like other well constructed wheel-ploughs, those properties approaching to self-action and government, which must be acknowledged to be no less essential to the perfection of an agricultural implement than to the steam-engine, the lathe, and machinery of all descriptions. It has been noticed that the great amount of pulverization effected by this simple combination of two knives with the common plough was obtained at the comparatively slight additional cost of fifteen per cent. of animal force; the whole draught of the plough, in this state, not exceeding that of several other good ploughs in the same soil, and being within the compass of the power of two horses. The judges were of opinion that the soil operated upon was as well pulverized by this single process, and to as great a depth, as if first ploughed and then harrowed; and they trust that subsequent experience may justify the expectations formed on the ground, that, by means of this remarkably simple combination, no unimportant economy and advantage may accrue to the farmer in pulverizing turnip and other soils preparatory to drilling the seed.

Fig. 2, drawn to a scale of one inch to the foot, represents the tail-part of the plough, and shows the knives a a in their working position. A furrow-slice, six inches deep by ten inches wide, would, if composed of perfectly coherent and elastic materials, assume the shape shown in section at c. Such, however, never is nor can be the case in practice with soil of any description. The slice of earth operated upon by a plough, whilst being raised from its horizontal bed, and forced into its new and oblique position by the torsion of the mouldboard, is irregularly extended, and much loosened or broken, owing to the imperfect cohesion of its particles, and to the absence of elasticity. It would, therefore, appear that the instant seized, and the place chosen, for assisting in the further disintegration of the slice by the action of the knives, are precisely those when its existing condition permits the greatest amount of pulverization to be effected, and with the least expenditure of power. The crumbling effect produced by severing each slice in detail, before it is pressed by the succeeding slices into a compact mass, and left to dry and harden, is analogous to the manipulations of the gardener, who bruises and pulverizes each spadeful of earth as he throws it up from the trench, and thus spares himself much subsequent toil, and his work much injury, by diminishing the after labouring and trampling on its surface to fit it for seed. The state in which the soil is left by this plough is attempted to be delineated at d; but it is evident that the degree of pulverization obtained will necessarily vary according to the greater or less friability of the particular soil acted upon, and according to its condition at the time of ploughing. Upon these circumstances depend both the figure of the furrow-slice c, and the extent of its dismemberment effected by the knives.

FIG. 2.

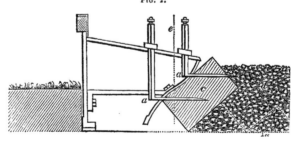

Mr. Stokes, who has continually used this plough since 1839, in soils varying as to tenacity, from light sand to stubborn clay, describes the appearance produced by the action of the knives on *stiff adhesive soils* to be that of a well spade-dug field, only that the work is more evenly and better performed, and that a sufficiently fine tilth is obtained, even on such soils, for the reception of seed to be drilled, without the use of the harrow, and with the further advantage of avoiding the poaching and trampling incident to it. The harrow is, unquestionably, the rudest and least efficient of all agricultural implements, and a promise seems at length to be held out that, in the preparation of land for subsequent drill husbandry, its use may be occasionally dispensed with ; nor does it seem unreasonable to expect that a single ploughing, with the knives, may, on some soils, save the time and cost of a second ploughing.*

Double-furrow and turnwrest ploughs.—The two double-furrow ploughs, the draught of which is recorded in the foregoing table were not in perfect trim for work. It is much to be desired that on future occasions the exhibitors of these implements, which are so much approved in certain districts, and on particular soils, would take the precaution to have them sent to the ground previously well set, and be provided with holders accustomed to their management. Others were also tried, but their draught was not taken, owing to the want of these precautions. The Society's prize was not awarded for these, or for the turnwrest ploughs. Two of the latter kind were tried —the one made by Mr. Huckvale, the other by Mr. Wilkie—but neither of them were in a condition to satisfy the judges that a correct decision on their merits or draught could be arrived at. Mr. Wilkie was not present, on account of illness. Ploughs of other kinds were also submitted to trial, but nothing worthy of note was elicited.

Draining and paring ploughs.—The premium offered for an open-furrow draining-plough was not adjudged. The show-yard contained one implement only of this kind, by Mr. James Comins, of South Molton, which was not tried. Mr. Johnson, of Leicester, exhibited Mr. Glover's excellent turf and stubble paring-plough, rewarded at Liverpool, which the judges were pleased to learn has met with the encouragement it merits.

In concluding these comments, the judges must express their consciousness that, owing to the insufficient time allotted for examining minutely so extensive an assortment of implements, they may have overlooked, or omitted the mention of, meritorous productions. Some implements, not rewarded, may also have been esteemed by visitors equal or superior in excellence to those which carried prizes ; and it is requisite to state that, for reasons unexplained and undiscovered, the show-yard contained numerous implements which were not entered for competition : of these, therefore no note was taken, as they did not pass under the observation of the judges.

Observations on ploughs.—Much useful instruction may be drawn from the experiments on the draught of ploughs, and on the quality of the work performed, now annually made at the instance of the society. The mean resistance of the five wheel-

ploughs registered in the foregoing list was 386 pounds, whilst that of the six swing-ploughs was 420 pounds, being a difference of nearly 9 per cent. in favour of the wheel-ploughs ; and the difference in the resistance of the best implement of the two kinds was 18 per cent. in favour of the wheel-plough.* It may also be safely affirmed that the quality of the performance in the same soil, by the respective ploughs, and under like circumstances of depth, width of slice cut, &c., is as the lightness of draught, *i.e.* in favour of the plough of least resistance.

On this occasion the judges took the precaution, after the trials, to suspend weights to the dynamometer, in order to verify the accuracy of its graduation, and to ascertain if any change had taken place in its indications during the experiments. The instrument was found to have given strictly correct results throughout the range of the draughts noted. It is also proper to state that the ploughs, after being got into trim, were successively brought to the same part of the field, and the indication of the force was recorded at the time of each plough's passage through similar soil, the pace being as nearly as possible alike in every case. The nature and form of the field selected for the purpose compelled the judges—at a considerable loss of time—to adopt this plan, as the quality of the soil varied materially in different parts, and the sharp slope of the ground in some parts of it would have rendered the experiments nugatory if the force of draught had not been taken pretty nearly in one locality.

An analysis and comparison of the results obtained at Liverpool, and Bristol, discloses facts of no slight importance to the agriculturist and ploughwright. The difference between the mean draught of the wheel and swing ploughs at the former trial was 17 per cent. in favour of the wheel plough, and there was an equality in this respect between the best implements of each kind. At Bristol one maker, Mr. Howard, of Bedford, produced a wheel-plough which beat his own swing by 18 per cent., the latter being equal to the best on the ground. At Liverpool, the difference between the maximum and minimum resistance of the plough was nearly 43 per cent., whilst at Bristol it amounted to 63½ per cent.; in both cases in favour of the wheel-ploughs. Whatever may be the cause of this enormous irregularity and disparity in the force required to perform work identically similar, it is apparent that the expenditure of animal power, and its cost to the farmer, are altogether dependant on the implement he employs, and proportional to the force used ; also, that in the single operation of ploughing, he is frequently consuming at least one-half more power than is necessary to perform his work. The elementary resistance of any given sort of soil is a constant quantity, and the skill of the ploughwright should be exercised in the endeavour to diminish, to its minimum amount, the excess of force employed to move the implement over and above that which is absolutely requisite to divide, under-cut, raise, and lay the furrow-slice ; all which operations are implied under the technical phrase ploughing. It is evident that, at Bristol, the difference between the extremes of draught required in the same soil by wheel-ploughs, and by those of the swing

---

* For additional information respecting this invention, see the end of this Report, p. 40.

* The draught of the double-furrow and turnwrest ploughs is not included in this estimate.

kind, was equivalent to a loss of power by the former of 36 per cent., and by the latter of 38 per cent.; and it resulted that a force not greater than 22 stones really sufficed to perform the same amount of work, or to produce the same useful effect, as a force of 32 and even of 36 stones, exerted by the same horses on other ploughs! The problem remains to be solved—by how much the least force used exceeds the resistance naturally and necessarily opposed to it? Its solution rests with the machine maker, and it will be found in the application of sound mechanical principles to the structure of the implement, when combined with a true knowledge of the nature and amount of the several resistances to be overcome.

The following particulars of the weight and dimensions of some of the principal parts of the wheel and swing ploughs submitted to trial have been obligingly furnished by the makers, at the request of the judges, who think that a record of them may, at least, present useful matter of study to the enlightened mechanic, and possibly induce him to experiment, extensively and carefully, on the effects arising from any change of these proportions as regards resistance and quality of work. He will, at the same time, be naturally led to investigate the influence produced by the line and angle of draught, as well as by the length and twist of the mould-board, and other properties which cannot be conveniently given in a table. The philosopher may meditate on these matters, as questions of interesting research; but the mechanician alone can arrive, though observation, experiment, and practical skill, at the construction of a perfect plough. A rich harvest of fame and profit awaits his labours; he may now work in confident security that the productions of his genius and industry will no longer—like the pulverizing plough—risk interment and oblivion in some corner of a secluded parish: the society offers him a fair and honourable field for the display of his labours, and its hand is open to encourage, reward, and proclaim them:—

Maker's Names.	Number of Wheels	Length from point to heel.	Width at the heel	Greatest width of Share.	Length of Share on the land side.	Weight.
		Inches.	Inches.	Inches.	Inches.	Lbs.
Howard	2	35	8½	8	9	220
Mason	2	34	10	6½	10	252
Brayton	1	32½	7½	6	10	196
Sanders and Williams..	2	36	6½	9	9	245
Carson...............	1	38½	6½ 10½ *	8½	12	193
Huckvale	—	29	9¼	9	12½	150
Earl of Ducie...............	Swing	27	8	6	9¼	161
Howard	do.	33	9	8	9	137
Brayton	do.	30	6	5	9	142
Carson...............	do.	38½	6½ 10 *	8½	12	174
Merrett	do.	38	9½	6¾	9	148
Law...............	do.	32½	8	6½	12	170
Wilkie...............	do.	36	7½	7½	12	230
				†	†	

* Moveable.

†† The cutting angle of the share is given by these two columns.

The judges trust that the importance of this subject will be a sufficient excuse for the space devoted to it; they feel it to be their province and duty to elicit, for the information of the society, all such truths as the experiments committed to their management may develope; and they do not hesitate to express their conviction that, if arrangements could be made at future meetings for a still greater extension of the time and means allotted to the trial of field implements, previous to the declaration of prizes, the zeal of constructors would be greatly encouraged, and the objects of the society more rapidly and surely promoted. The experience acquired by their having acted on several similar occasions induces them also to recommend that exhibitors be invited, as a condition of trial, to send their ploughs and machines in the best state for work, so as on future occasions to save the time of the judges, and to evolve more correct and useful results. It is evident that the acting parts of an implement put into the ground for the first time, or recently painted, are in a most unfavourable condition to fulfil one at least of the purposes of a trial, viz. the determination of its draught; and it is possible that the best implement may be in the worst trim for work. It is requisite too that the maker, or some authorised and sufficient representative should be present to manage his own implement. Several implements, the ocular inspection of which gave promise of novel merit, remained untried, or very imperfectly tried, at Bristol; whereas others, equally novel, had their principal qualifications and advantages sufficiently ascertained for the judges to report upon with satisfaction to themselves and to the inventors.

The justice of these remarks will be appreciated by all who witnessed the skilful management of Mason's plough by Mr. John Stokes, and the perseverance of the Hon. Mr. Nugent in bringing his untried subsoil-pulverizer into such working condition as to enable the judges to prognosticate favourably of its future efficiency. If the trials had produced no other result than that of directing the attention of the Society to these two implements in particular—of the merits of which no sound opinion could have been formed had they not been *practically ascertained in the field*—no inconsiderable advantage will have been derived; but it is a matter of regret to the judges that they

were unable to carry out to a much greater extent, and with greater precision, the objects of the Society in instituting these annual tests of the advance made in the science of agricultural mechanism. JOSIAH PARKER.
GEORGE LEGARD.
R. S. GRABURN.

NOTE ON THE PULVERIZING PLOUGH.

The following particulars of the history, use, and experience of these slicing-knives have been obligingly communicated to the judges by Mr. John Stokes of Pauntley Court, near Newent, farmer; by Mr. Allen Stokes, civil engineer, of Harvington, near Evesham; and by Thomas Brown, Esq., a magistrate of the county of Warwich, residing upon and farming his own estate at Kinwarton, near Alcester. The statement of these gentlemen is corroborated by Mr. William Mason, the maker of the plough exhibited at Bristol.

The knives were invented by Mr. Brown, who employed the father of Mason, a blacksmith, to fit them to a plough about twenty years ago. Mr. Brown originally placed one knife vertically, and another horizontally; but, finding the latter position to be most effective, he has continued to apply them in that form only; in which practice he has been followed by all who have since adopted them. Mr. William Mason at that time lived with his father, but afterwards engaged with a farmer as an agricultural labourer; and in his service acquired much skill as a ploughman, before settling himself at Grafton as a blacksmith and ploughwright.

In 1839 Mr. Allen Stokes altered the general form of the plough, which Mason was then in the habit of constructing; and, particularly, for the purpose of providing for the proper adaptation and adjustment of Mr. Brown's knives. The first of these improved pulverizing ploughs was sent by Mr Allen Stokes, in 1839, to his kinsman Mr. John Stokes, of Pauntley Court, whose farm contains between 300 and 400 acres of arable land (rented of Osmon Ricardo, Esq.), and consists of turnip and barley soil, with a portion of wheat and bean land.

Mr. Brown states, from his long experience of the knives, that they are particularly useful in pulverizing his adhesive and very difficult soil, as they save the harrowing, and thereby avoid the poaching of the horses' feet; that he last year ploughed with them a two years' old turf, and drilled wheat upon it without previous harrowing, using only a one-horse harrow to cover the seed. Mr. John Stokes also observes that stiff clay land is not left cloddy by the action of the knives, but will be found, in many cases, fit for receiving the seed as they leave it. He agrees with Mr. Brown that when the land is ploughed in an unkind state, perhaps one of the knives only may be found to work well; and, when the soil has been much trampled upon in wet weather, as on headlands, they will not work at all. In a mellow, friable soil, it is the practice to place the knives near to the extremity of the mouldboard, so as to catch and divide the slice as it falls over; but in a stiff soil it is found more advantageous to set them father off so as to make their cut just after the slice has taken its bed; also, that the most perfect pulverization is obtained by turning over the slice much more obliquely than is customary,

and even to reverse it as nearly as possible. Mr. Brown says, " I generally plough 8 inches deep and 10 inches wide with the knives. I now invariably use the horses in line in my stiff soil; nothing is so prejudicial as their treading out of the furrow. I have fully and fairly tried the horses abreast, but could not plough so well; the horses were worked too hard, and their trampling was very injurious." Mr. John Stokes uses the horses in both ways, according to the quality of soil, and the strength required. Both the Messrs. Stokes and Mr. Brown state their opinion that the advantage of the two-wheel plough, when using the knives, is so self evident, that there can be no question as to its superiority over the swingplough, for that purpose. Mr. John Stokes has applied them to a one-wheel plough, and it worked pretty well, but required holding : whereas, he observes, " the two-wheel ploughs, furnished with the knives and well set, require no guidance, and will go without a holder." When it is thought desirable to reverse the furrow-slice completely, Mr. Brown is in the habit of using only the upper knife horizontally, and he applies a lower one in a vertical position (as shown by the dotted line e. in fig. 2) so as to cut off about an inch or more of the inner or lower edge of the furrow slice just turned, to allow room for the succeeding slice to fall flat over, or nearly so; and, under these circumstances, the ploughs shallower and wider.

With respect to the economy per acre arising from this process, Mr. Brown observes, that he has no account of the cost of the old system of ploughing and harrowing on his estate, having abandoned it for so long a period. He expresses himself as so convinced of the important saving and superior work effected by the use of the knives, that he employs them throughout his farms, and for every kind of crop. Several farmers in the neighbourhood of Grafton, who had been in the habit of using Mason's ploughs, have sent them to him to be altered to this new patern.

TILE DRAINING AND TURNIP HUSBANDRY.

On Wednesday, the 16th November last, a dinner was given by Lady Bassett, at Bennetts, to those of her tenantry in the parish of Whitstone, who acting upon her advice had extended their cultivation of turnips. What adds much to the interest of this meeting is, that it also celebrates the commencement of a new era in the agriculture of the district, as on that day, previous to the dinner, furrow draining with tile was fully commenced under the superintendence of Mr. Peters, her ladyship's agriculturist.

EDWARD SHEARM, Esq., Stratton, Lady Basset's agent in this district, was in the chair. After the usual loyal toasts the chairman on proposing the health of Lady Bassett, said, it was under circumstances of no ordinary character, that they had met together. While this meeting was meant as a mark of approbation of the conduct of the tenantry who had so readily seconded Lady Basset's views of introducing improvement, they must also feel that there was something higher than mere personal interest attached to it. They might fairly say they were met to celebrate the first introduction of furrow and tile draining in the hundred of Stratton, and a new system founded upon that first foundation stone of all permanent improvement, in a district where draining was wanted as much, if not more, than in any district of the kingdom. The result he would not venture to predict; but that must be best known to those who had seen it carried into effect elsewhere; but if he were to judge from what he had seen of it on his own land, he had no doubt it would be most astonishing. He last year furrow-drained a field, and had it now in a state of preparation for a crop of Swedish turnips. If two years ago he had proposed putting that field into turnips, it would have been reckoned madness; but from its altered appearance since it was drained, he had no doubt of success; indeed it was now evident, that with proper management, this district was as capable of growing turnips as any other. He would ask Mr. Colville whether he would have believed five years ago that such crops of turnips could have been grown on Foxhall. Mr. Colville said, that twelve months ago he would not have believed any man who said that it was possible, as he now had the finest turnips he ever saw; many of them were very large. One he had seen that day was 2 feet 7½ inches round, and weighed about 12 pounds without the stems. Mr. Coles, of Bennetts, confessed that he had been afraid to venture with the tillage of so many turnips, as he did not consider his land was adapted for them, and even if they should succeed, he did not see how he could get them used, but Lady Bassett and Mr. Peters had got him prevailed upon to give it a trial, and he did not repent it. He found so much advantage from the turnips for his bullocks, that instead of not getting them used, his six acres would be little enough. Mr. Veal, of Oke, stated that although the field in which he had his turnips was as stubborn land as any in the neighbourhood, yet the turnips were a good crop, and from his success in that field, he would not be afraid of growing them on any of his land.

Mr. PETERS complimented the tenants present on the manner in which they had managed their turnip crop. If it was considered that they had five times as many turnips this year as ever they previously had, and that they had put them in upon a plan to them entirely new, was it to be wondered at if in some instances the management was not perfect; but really the cultivation of some of them was excellent. Mr. Colville's at Foxhall would do no discredit to any district; and as for Mr. Coles, of Bennetts, he (Mr. Peters) was proud of the manner in which he had acted, after hesitating so much at first. When once Mr. Coles had put his hand to the plough, he did not look back. He was glad to hear from every one of them that they were gratified with the trial they had made, and had all expressed a determination to extend their operations next year. He could assure them of a continuance of that encouragement from Lady Bassett which they had this year experienced. After a good deal of consideration, Lady Basset had set on a draining tile manufactory, and they had this day seen a sample of the mode of draining it was proposed to adopt. Her ladyship had in this not only conferred a boon on them, her own tenants, but had set an example in the district, which he was glad to learn from their friend, Mr. Shearm, was likely to be extensively followed by other great landed proprietors. It was hoped that the tile manufactory would be so extended next season, as not only to supply the demand on these estates, but also to allow others to test on their own properties

the utility of thorough draining, which he had no doubt would soon entirely alter the features of the country.

Mr. SHEARM begged to assure the tenantry of the great interest Lady Basset took in their welfare. Her ladyship was fully alive to the difficulties under which the farmers now laboured, but she also entertained the opinion, that there was still to be found in improved management what was calculated to turn the scale in their favour. With a determination therefore to assist in bringing about such improvements, she now comes forward to go hand in hand with them in the expence of setting about it. The farm buildings, and the mode of making and managing manure in this district, are found much fault with, and no doubt justly; but Mr. Shearm said, that he had authority from Lady Basset to tell them, that so soon as they showed themselves ready and willing to adopt improved management, she would erect the necessary buildings and farm yards for them. Mr. Shearm also stated that he was so well pleased with the result of what Lady Basset had done for her tenants, that he was resolved to carry out the system to the fullest extent wherever he could have the opportunity of doing so. He begged of the tenants to pay every attention, and learn of their friend Mr. Peters what they could, and he hoped that by doing so, although they were far behind their northern neighbours in the morning, they might overtake them before the noon of agriculture can be said to have arrived. It was rather unfortunate for them that Mr. Peters resided at such a distance, which made his visits far between, but he trusted that on the completion of arrangements now in contemplation this would be remedied.—*Cornwall Royal Gazette.*

APPLICATION OF SCIENCE TO AGRICULTURE.

EXPERIMENTS.

The impression has been gaining ground for some time, and has now become pretty generally prevalent, that considerable advantage will result from the application of chemical science to agriculture. The science of agriculture is indeed closely allied to that of chemistry; every plant is a laboratory, and a single leaf, by decomposing carbonic acid, proves itself to be a more powerful chemical agent than a galvanic battery. By the aid of chemistry we are enabled to learn the composition both of the soil and of the plants which it produces; and from the composition of the latter, we can see what are the substances necessary for their nourishment, and from that of the former, wherever it has been accurately ascertained, it has always been found that the abundance or deficiency of these substances assimilated by plants, is an exact indication of its natural productiveness or sterility. A soil, however, containing many of the elements necessary for the production of vegetables may be barren, on account of the absence or deficiency of one or more of the elements, the presence of which is indispensably necessary for the production of luxuriant vegetation. And it is on such a soil that opportunity is afforded to the agriculturist to display his skill. On examining, again, the common manures, we find the same agreement subsisting between their composition also, and that of the plants for the production of which they are known to be efficient; or, in other words, the elements contained in the manure supplied to the soil, are found in the plants which that manure aids in producing. For example, it is known that phosphate of magnesia is contained in large quantity in potatoes, and accordingly it has been found that phosphoric acid (supplied by means of bones or bran), and sulphate of magnesia (Epsom salts) are most valuable manures for increasing the produce of this root. The manures hitherto most generally used in agriculture have been putrescent animal excrements, and vegetable matter; and the composition of these substances demonstrates how admirably they are suited for the purpose. But, as they cannot always be obtained in sufficient abundance for the purposes of the agriculturist, it is evident that he may supplement the deficiency by the use of other substances containing the same elements. It may be possible too, to procure in this manner the elements of manure in so concentrated and portable a form, and at so cheap a rate, as to enable the cultivator of the soil to obtain a much greater value of produce, in proportion to the sum of money expended for manure, than he has hitherto realized. And that this *is* possible will not be doubted by any one who has studied the chemistry of nature. It is a point of great importance in the application of manure, that it be put into the soil in the state most suitable for being assimilated by the roots of plants. This remark is peculiarly applicable to the use of bones as a manure. Bones, if put into the soil without being properly reduced, may remain in it for a long period without being decomposed. The bones of antediluvian animals have remained in some soils for thousands of years almost unchanged. The exclusion of air and moisture tends to prevent their decay. They may be preserved for a long period even in a moist soil, provided they are surrounded by a tenacious substance preventing the access of rain and air; and in all cases when they are not reduced the exterior surface protects the interior (which is more gelatinous) from decay. Hence, perhaps, we may see a reason why bones have generally been found comparatively inefficient as a manure on stiff clay soils. It may be inferred, then, that a given quantity of bones will be much more serviceable as a manure when they are put into the soil in a state suitable for assimilation, than when they are returned to it in a very rough and imperfectly reduced state; and experience has shown that such is the case. It was stated in a report for the North East of Scotland, which appeared in the *Mark Lane Express* in the month of December last, that a solution of bones in sulphuric acid (the manner of preparing which the writer there explained, and for which see also Liebig's *Organic Chemistry*, p. 173, 2nd ed.) had been tried on a small scale, as a more economical and effective mode of supplying phosphate of lime to plants, than the common way of using crushed bones. This solution of bones has been used this season—and by some individuals in this district pretty extensively—as a manure for turnips. It was generally been used along with one-half the usual quantity of dung; and this is undoubtedly the way in which it is applied with most advantage. From its application in this manner, at the rate of 80 or 90 lbs. (of bones) per Scotch acre (1·261 ac. imp), very good crops of turnips have been obtained—crops fully equal to those raised by an application of the same quantity of dung along with 10 or 12 bushels of bones put into the soil in the common way. The advantages, therefore, that have thus been obtained are certainly,

in a pecuniary point of view, of great importance; a saving in the expense of manure of at least 1*l.* 5s. per acre having been effected. The amount saved on a field of 35 acres would thus be 43*l.* 15s. And this, be it observed, is not calculation founded on mere theory: a saving of greater amount than the above sum has actually been effected by some individuals this season. The bone solution has also been applied *alone*; but only on a small scale by way of experiment. The results thus obtained appear to be somewhat contradictory. In *all cases*, however, and even by an application of so small a quantity as from 60 to 80 lbs. of bones per Scotch acre, the most luxuriant growth was produced during the earlier part of the season; the turnips came up beautifully, were sooner ready for the hoe than those manured with dung and "drill" bones, and advanced rapidly for a considerable time; but in some cases in which the manure was applied in small quantity, and perhaps also not very well prepared, its effects failed during the latter part of the season. A good crop has, in some cases, been produced by an application of 160 lbs. of bones (digested in the requisite quantity of acid), per Scotch acre; but, from some other experiments, it does not appear that this quantity can be implicitly relied on for the production of a crop on poor soils. From the quantity of phosphoric acid found in the grain and straw usually produced on an acre, it has been calculated that 85lbs. of bones, properly prepared for assimilation, would be a sufficient quantity to apply to a Scotch acre, for supplying phosphates to three successive crops of oats, turnips, clover, &c.; but it does not appear that this holds good in practice. The bone solution, when used alone, ought, we think, to be applied at the rate of 300 or 350lbs. per acre. It has never failed—so far as the writer of this is aware—when applied in such a quantity, properly prepared, to produce a most abundant crop.

We repeat, however, that we prefer applying it along with a certain quantity of dung, because some ammonia, which, as well as phosphate of lime, is necessary to plants, is thereby afforded. It is is certain that bones, in whatever way they are applied, owe their beneficial effects chiefly to the phosphate of lime, which they contain to the amount of 51 per cent. (Berzelius); but at the same time it cannot be doubted but that, when bones are applied in the usual way, at the rate of 20 or 25 bushels per acre, the nitrogen of the gelatine which they contain must exert a very beneficial effect on plants. Bones, in a dry state, contain 33 per cent. of gelatine, and if we allow that gelatine contains (according to the analysis of Gay, Lussac, and Thenard) 16.9 per cent. of nitrogen, then 20 bushels or 1,000 of bones will give 55lbs. of nitrogen, or about 64lbs. of ammonia. And though this quantity cannot be *all* evolved for a considerable time, yet, as the decomposition of the bones proceeds, *part* of it will be gradually eliminated and become available for the promotion of vegetation. By the action of sulphuric acid on bones a *superphosphate* of lime is produced, and this salt being soluble—as all the *superphosphates* are—is in the state most suitable for assimilation. Phosphate of lime and nitrogen in the form of ammonia, seem to be the chief requisites in manure for almost every species of plants (phosphoric acid has been found in every plant hitherto examined); and the question therefore occurs—how can these substances be procured in the greatest abundance, and at the cheapest rate? Bones are the only source, at present known, from which we can obtain phosphate of lime in any considerable quantity. It is indeed reported—and Dr. Daubeny is at present, or was lately engaged in investigating the truth of the report—that *native* phosphate of lime (*phosphorite* or *apatite*) is to be found in Estremadura in Spain ; and, if such shall be found to be the case, this substance, so valuable as a manure, may yet come to be procured at a much cheaper rate than it has hitherto been. Ammonia, however, can be procured much nearer home, though indeed *it* seems to be much more highly valued by some, when brought in the shape of *guano* from the farthest coasts of America. Agriculturists have the means of procuring ammonia within their own reach, if they could be persuaded more generally to avail themselves of it. But though it certainly might be thought that advantage would be taken of our own in the first place, there is no reason why we should not purchase as much more as we can. Nor do we mean to say that *guano* is not a most valuable manure, containing as it does—besides 30 per cent. of salts of ammonia (which would give about 7 or 8 per cent. of the free alkali)—14 per cent. of phosphate of lime (Volckel's analysis). Its composition, therefore, and its beneficial effects as a manure, afford a proof of what we have stated above in reference to the value of phosphate of lime and ammonia. But to return. The chief sources from which ammonia may be obtained are animal and vegetable substances in a state of decay, and the urine of animals; and it is from the latter source more especially, that farmers have an opportunity of procuring it in great abundance. Human urine, after the conversion of all the urea, by putrefaction, into carbonate of ammonia, contains at the lowest estimate, 20lbs. of ammonia in 100 gallons of urine ; or nearly as much as is contained in 300lbs. of guano. "When it is considered," to use the words of Dr. Liebig, " that with every pound of ammonia which evaporates a loss of 60lbs. of corn is sustained, and that with every pound of urine a pound of wheat might be produced, the indifference with which these liquid excrements are regarded is quite incomprehensible." Besides ammonia urine contains phosphates and potash. The urine of other animals contains about one-fourth of the quantity of ammonia found in human urine. It is evident therefore, that, if the urine from cowhouses, &c., instead of being allowed to run to waste and its ammonia to evaporate, were collected in a tank or reservoir, constructed for the purpose, and properly managed by fixing its ammonia, which might be very conveniently done by mixing it, after being sufficiently putrefied, with a compost to which a considerable quantity of the solution of bones in sulphuric acid had been previously added, it would form a most valuable manure obtained at a very cheap rate. Such a compost would besides be a very convenient mode of applying the bone solution ; and it would be rendered still more valuable—more especially if it were to be applied as a manure for potatoes or grain—by the addition of a small quantity of sulphate of magnesia, which may be had at 13s. or 14s. per cwt. Sulphuric acid (oil of vitriol), gypsum or chloride of calcium may also be used for fixing the volatile carbonate of ammonia obtained from urine. H.

Ythanside, Aberdeenshire, Dec. 1.

GENERAL DRAINAGE AND DISTRIBUTION OF WATER.

Sir,—In your editorial remarks of the 24th ult. you pass some just encomiums upon the proposition of Mr. Blacker for draining the wet lands of the United Kingdom by means of assistance in funds from Government. Having given much attention to the matter of general drainage, I trust you will allow me to draw your attention to a proposition I have taken some pains to place before the agricultural public, and which it is my intention to explain fully before the committee of the approaching session, should the opportunity be afforded me. It appears to me to be much more feasible than the project of Mr. Blacker, and should it so appear to you, I hope to gain your advocacy to promote discussion on the subject. It is certain that the next session will see the passing of a *Sewerage* Act for *towns* (upon the sanatory reports), and will be also the advent of some general *Drainage* Bill for the *lands* of England. Although we cannot hope to see a compulsory measure for draining the whole of the clay lands, it is perfectly feasible for the Legislature to *unite the two objects of drainage of lands with sewerage of towns* by the making of *main drains* along the valleys where waters congregate *on* the surface, so as to put it in the power of landowners and occupiers to drain their lands *when they have the means and by degrees,* at the same time that these main drains or receivers may be made the vehicle (as conduits), of transporting the refuse of towns into the country for manure.

The passing of the act for the drainage of lands in Ireland, and improving the navigation and waterpower in connexion with such drainage, is evidence that the prejudice which has so long delayed the success of that measure has at length given way, and the principle *that the wishes of the majority should be binding on the minority* is now admitted in the matter of drainage, as well as in local improvements, such as inclosures, tithe commutation, and parochial management.

A general drainage act for Great Britain would effect improvements even more beneficial than those which will result to Ireland from the measure relating to that country ; for the necessary works being less expensive, they would receive the ready concurrence of landowners. Although we have not in Britain, in proportion to extent of surface, so much waste land to reclaim as they have in Ireland, we have many millions of acres of wet lands under the plough, as well as a considerable portion of bog and marsh lands. These, by the clearing of outfalls, would directly become capable of subordinate drainage, and be rendered, by means of recent chemical discoveries, which are inapplicable to them in their present state, susceptible of increased culture.

Professor Johnston, in his "Elements of Agricultural Chemistry and Geology," and other writers, have declared that we must look to our clay lands for the most profitable increase of our corn produce ; and since our clay lands are also our best wheat lands, the inclination of the whole agricultural community must coincide with that opinion, especially as the deficiency in wheat is greater than in other corn (the produce of the lighter lands), and we must necessarily be desirous, in a national point of view, of making that deficiency good.

Our annual produce is less than the demand by 1½ million of quarters, and we require for seed nearly as much more, making about three millions, which, at the average of the last 14 years (viz., 58s. per qr.), gives between eight and nine millions of pounds sterling paid for foreign corn. Apart from the benefit to be derived from the increase of produce, which would not be less, on an average, than one quarter of an acre to the land cropped with wheat, we must consider the effect of general drainage on the health of the population and cattle of the country. (See Mr. Chadwick's report for the Sanatory Condition of the Labouring Population.)

Upon the practicability of reducing the sewerage of towns, and the drainage of lands, to one system of arrangement, there may be a difference of opinion, if, in combination with that system, a care is to be taken of the refuse of the towns, for application as manure to land; still I hope you will consider the proposition with attention and inquiry. I have entered somewhat at length into this subject in the pamphlet published a few months back, and now enclosed, and I find that in *Mr. Chadwick's Report* (already alluded to), pages 302, *et seq.*, 392 and 393, he brings corroborative testimony in support of the proposition. Although of opinion that land and town drainage, with the preservation of the refuse of the latter is a feasible project, I look more to the *profitable use of the drainage, and surface waters, than I do to the improvement of the lands drained.* I feel assured, from observation, that by a judicious arrangement of a network of mains along the valleys of the country, not only might the pernicious waters which now stagnate on the surface, but the waters emitted from hill-side springs, which escape unheeded into the lower water-courses, be caught and concentrated, but might be advantageously applied and re-applied in irrigation and augmentation of inferior mill-streams, and in originating a motive-power for the establishing new mills, working of mines, &c. There are many instances on record where on private estates, this use of drainage waters has been carried out, but that case which approaches nearest to the object of the present proposition is the case of Lord Hatherton's improvement on his Teddesley Hay estate. There, drainage of a large tract of land, irrigation of a considerable portion of meadow, and the use of the drain water as a motive power, are all effected in one scheme. It is described by Mr. Burke, in his pamphlet, " On Draining, Irrigating, and Subsoil Ploughing," and has been corroborated by his lordship in a letter addressed to me.

The different mining districts of Wales, Cornwall, and Scotland, afford abundant proofs of the economy of water power over steam, where the water is immediately attainable—and the increasing consumption of coal supplies a reason for attention to any power which may be used as a substitute.

I have seen, within the last few months at the old Lanercost mines, near Lostwitiel, in Cornwall, rather an uncommon instance of the economy of water power. A small stream, into which the waters of a few springs have been collected from the adjoining hill, conveys to this mine a sufficiency of water to work 13 wheels of different diameters and for different uses. The water brought home and delivered to the highest wheel is equal to 60 horse power; but, by being re-applied, over and over again, to wheels lower down the hill, it produces in all a force of 578 horse power.

Another singular fact will serve to elucidate the feasibility of connecting drainage with the application of surface waters.

Mr. Dickenson, an extensive paper-maker, living near Watford, and having paper-mills on the river Colne, resorts to the following expedient to ascertain with what quantity of paper he may contract to supply his customers. On the hills in the neighbourhood of his mills, he has fixed a gauge buried in the ground a little depth below the surface. By consulting this gauge he is enabled to compute the amount of rain *which finds its way into the earth during the winter season, and which must be again emitted before it can be decreased by evaporation.* Experience has proved to him that, with this index, he can precisely ascertain the influx of tributary water which the river Colne, whereby his mills are worked, will receive. This statement was made at the Institution of Civil Engineers by Mr. Clutterbuck, and substantiated by Mr. Dickenson himself.

The above remarks I have had copied, so that I may place before you a few points which, I hope, will induce you to peruse the pamphlet enclosed, and to give the proposition your best consideration.

I am obliged by your notice of it in the Journal, and should not intrude it again on your attention were I not convinced that if the country was traversed with a series of " *mains,*" so as to concentrate the waters *which are now injurious,* all the expence of constructing those mains would be repaid by the profit to be derived from the use of the waters, *as a vehicle for the transit of town refuse— as a motive-force for machinery—as a supply for irrigating* —and as a partial remedy for present stagnation of flood-water.

Would not any funds from Government be better expended in the promotion of these combined objects than in any works of drainage of *detached* parts of the country ? It should be remembered, that by draining in unconnected districts the country will become a type of the confused state of the metropolitan sewerage. It can only be by uniformity *that the evil may be turned into good.*

I have presumed to score a few passages in the pamphlet (*which was published before Mr. Chadwick's Report*), to which I beg your attention ; and if you can oblige me by prominent mention of the foregoing views, I shall be proud and happy to communicate at any future period.

I have not written this letter with a view to publication, but you are welcome to use it in any way you please.

I am, Sir, &c. &c.,
J. BAILEY DENTON.
9, Gray's Inn square, Nov. 8, 1842.

P.S. I write from the Isle of Wight, and no one can travel from London hence, *but be struck with the want of* OUTFALLS.
—*Mark Lane Express.*

LIQUID MANURES.—Writers and lecturers on agricultural chemistry have long pointed out the importance of liquid manures, and enforced the benefits which would result to farmers by having a tank in their fold-yards for the preservation of this valuable liquid, but they have hitherto seemed loath to move out of the old beaten track of their ancestors, and heeded not the advice. Mr. John Milner, of Mindledale, near Kilham, has, however, been the first to set the example to the Yorkshire Wold farmers, by having a large tank made in his fold-yard, with underground channels from every available source, from whence any impregnated liquid can be obtained. The sink of the kitchen, the stables, and every other place where ammoniacal and other fluids are deposited, are made to contribute to this reservoir of liquid manure, so essential to luxuriant vegetable production. This liquid is said to be an excellent manure for grass; and cattle seem to eat the crops which have been thus saturated, with the greatest relish, and will even lick the manure from the grass.—*Hull Packet*.

ENGLISH AGRICULTURE.

BY MR. MAIN, CHELSEA.

(From the Quarterly Journal of Agriculture.)

In giving a sketch of the agriculture of England, I can only notice the general principles, and a few of the more prominent systems in actual operation. On such an extent of country many different kinds of soil occur, and we invariably find that, whatever the nature of the soil may be, whether clay or sand, or any intermediate quality, that character fixes the mode or system of farming which is followed thereon.

The soils which are most commonly met with and forming the agricultural face of the kingdom, are alluvial, diluvial, or other formation, all deposited from or by the action of water. The alluvial occurs in valleys through which rivers flow; the diluvial forms the level and slopes of the more elevated ground.

The alluvial soils are the richest portions of the country, and whether as meadow, pasture, or arable, yield the largest profits to the cultivator if dry, for some such soils are subject to occasional floods. Still this kind of land is the highest rented, pays the highest tithe (except hop and other gardens), poor, and all other county and parochial rates.

The diluvial deposites occupy by far the greatest portion of the cultivated surface, and are very variable in character. In some places, an obdurate unmanageable clay, in others, a light sandy gravel, and these often occurring on the same farm.

English farms vary in size from fifty to five hundred, or even to one thousand acres. They are mostly divided into separate fields by thorn-hedge and ditch-fences, the fields being larger or smaller according to the size of the farm. Some farmers keep the hedges low, and the ditches well scoured out especially where they act as drains; others scour the ditches and remake, that is, plash down the hedge every seventh or eighth year. There are usually hedge-row timber trees or pollards in the hedges, and which, though not necessary for the healthy growth of corn, give a dressy appearance to the country; and as shelter are certainly beneficial to live stock. In some parts, wood is the only fuel made use of, and there the topping of pollard trees, and fagots from the newly made hedges, are indispensible to the tenant. But the use of coal even for culinary purposes in farm-houses is rapidly gaining ground.

The occupiers of the smallest farms are only a superior class of labourers; and those of the large holdings are an opulent and highly respectable body of men. Among these the great graziers are preeminent, being located on rich tracts of land the most suitable for breeding and fattening all kinds of cattle, and manufacturing vast quantities of butter, cheese, bacon, and pork. Such farms require a great capital to stock them at first; and great vigilance and judgment to keep up a full and profitable store of both flocks and herds.

A few farms are entirely arable, except perhaps an orchard at the back of the homestead. But the greater number are of a mixed character, partly grass and partly arable, the most desirable proportions being one-third grass and the other two-thirds arable. Such farms are mostly on the diluvial deposite, and as already mentioned consist of various descriptions of soil, and of course require every expedient of agriculture to be practised upon them. I shall endeavour to give a detail of the business of a farm of this mixed character, and which will include most of the processes carried on by a great majority of English farmers.

The rents vary from twelve shillings and sixpence to forty shillings per acre; the medium from twenty-five to thirty shillings. To the rent must be added about a fourth for tithes, whether taken in kind, or paid by a composition in money; and a similar addition to the rent may be calculated on to pay poor and church and county rates.

Some landlords grant no leases; but in case of any expensive permanent improvement being executed by the tenant, the landlord generally pays one-half the expense, or finds materials, the tenant doing the labour. When leases are granted, they are what are called *running* leases of five, ten, or fifteen years, or what is more common, seven, fourteen, or twenty-one years, terminable at the end of any of those periods at the option of the tenant. Sometimes the landlord reserves to himself a similar option, or if not, by certain restrictive clauses in the lease protective of his own interests, the infringement of which annuls all the conditions. The great fluctuations to which the business of farming has been subject of late years has rendered the desire for leases less strenuous than formerly; and there seems to be a mutual feeling between the contracting parties to substitute equitable agreements instead of expensive leases.

In whichever way a farmer holds his farm, whether by lease or by agreement, one of the most common conditions is, that *he shall farm or cultivate the land according to the custom of the country*; that he shall sell no straw nor hay off the farm without bringing on an equivalent in dung; that he shall make no waste; plough up no meadow without being liable to pay a penalty of ten or twenty pounds per acre; and that he shall leave the farm in as good condition as it was when he entered upon it.

About fifty years ago, and after the custom of sowing turnips on the fallows, and grass seeds with barley or oats, was introduced, the general custom of the country was the *five-shift* course, namely, a fallow dunged for turnips to be fed off by sheep; next, barley with clover and rye-grass, or clover alone. Next year the clover is mowed once or twice, or mowed once in summer, and afterwards depastured with store-sheep until about the first of October, when it is ploughed up and sown with wheat, which is the crop of the fourth year; a part of the wheat-stubble is as early as possible dunged and sown with winter tares to be cut green for the stable in may and June, and the rest of the wheat stubble is sowed with oats in the following spring, and is the crop of the fifth and last year of the course.

This was the custom of the country at the time above stated, and was invariably adhered to, any deviation being considered ruinous. But it was a system in some measure imposed on the farmers not only by the mandates of their landlords, but from their inability to keep a sufficiently numerous herd of live stock, owing to their want of pasturage and other green or dry forage. Thus limited in live stock, they could not muster up in their yards, folds, and hovels, more dress or manure than was barely sufficient for *one-fifth* of their land annually. Notwithstanding the staid and grave character of the old farmers, they were not insensible to the loss they sustained by being obliged to sow two white crops consecutively, and those of them who could afford to do so, lamented that they could not depart from the old system, and banish oats entirely from the course; and by having turnips and other green crops every fourth year, enable them to keep more stock, and consequently get their land into better heart by dressing it every fourth, instead of every fifth year.

This improvement in the system of farming was soon proved to be absolutely necessary; and at the instance of several of the most influential landlords, many of the old trammels have been struck off, and the four-shift course has been adopted by every one who had the will and the means of doing so.

As already noticed, these farms are of various size; but whether large or small require a capital of not less than *fifteen pounds* per acre to stock them. The establishment of a farm of *one hundred acres* requires a team of four horses, a plough-man and plough-boy, a cow-man or shepherd, and a tasker or barn-man. The hedging, turnip-bowing, mowing hay, mowing and reaping corn, thatching ricks, and binding hay, is usually done by free labourers in the neighbourhood. This is the usual establishment on a farm of one hundred acres; but it is found that the larger the farm, the more economically is it managed. For instance a farm of four-hundred acres may be carried on with three teams; and on all farms the teams are reduced from four to three horses each, whether at plough or at cart, or waggon on the road. Ploughing with a pair of horses abreast is only introduced on light loamy or sandy soils, where only a light kind of plough can be employed. But on clayey gravels, and all heavy soils, the old Hertfordshire wheel-plough with an iron skeleton share, weighing half a hundred weight, is still used. One acre per day is the usual task of a plough team, whether done at one or two yokings. Ploughing with oxen, or with oxen and one horse as a leader is still the custom on the hilly parts of the west of England; and has been tried by many amateur farmers in other parts; but it is a decreasing rather than an increasing custom. On stony or flinty soils, oxen are unprofitable beasts of draught.

There are a few general principles by which all farmers are guided, wherever they may be placed, or whatever the kind of soil they may occupy. First, The land must be dry naturally, or rendered so by artificial drainage. Second, That aration, whenever performed, should be complete as to depth, perfect disintegration by the plough, harrows, and roller, and all this done only when the soil is sufficiently dry. Thirdly that no root-weeds be allowed to usurp and exhaust the land. Fourthly, That the various crops should succeed each other in the most judicious rotation; and, fifthly, That the soil be liberally supplied with the most suitable kinds of manure to keep it constantly in heart.

I shall now detail the proceedings of an English farmer as a tenant of a farm of a mixed character, and following the five-shift rotation. He commences fallowing his oat-stubble as soon in the autumn as he can; ploughing deeply, and striking up the

water furrows in order that the ground may lie as dry as possible throughout the winter. In the spring the first opportunity is taken to fill in the furrows by going *about* in each. The field is then ploughed athwart; and harrowed, especially if the original autumn furrows be still left in entire pieces, by the cross ploughing, and bound together by couch or other weeds. If many of these be barrowed out on the surface they are collected by women rakers, burnt or carried off. Some farmers never trouble themselves to burn or carry off weeds; but trust entirely to the plough and the sun to kill them; and this, I have seen completely accomplished in dry seasons on light soils. Another ploughing athwart is given before the end of May, which brings the surface to the same state it lay before the first cross ploughing was given. The ground by this time being perfectly loose and friable, the barrows are again put on, and which generally bring any root-weeds to the surface to be got rid of.

The next operation is drawing out the field into lands or ridges, and which are usually of eight steps unless the soil is liable to hold moisture, when the ridges are only four steps or less if very wet in winter. Ploughmen pride themselves much in drawing out a field accurately; and there are sometimes very amusing contests among the neighbouring ploughmen who shall most excel in this manœuvre; because on the regular breadths of the lands subsequent operations are more regularly performed.

The dung is next carted on, and laid in heaps along the middle of each land. Four horses, two in shafts and two in traces, are employed: the latter are shifted from the empty to the full cart alternately. The carts are large, the wheels having six or nine inch tires. From seven to twelve loads are laid on each acre, immediately spread and ploughed under the seed furrow.

The turnip seed (three lbs. to the acre) is sown broadcast and harrowed in; and if cloddy, rolled. The plants appear on or about the fourth day after sowing, and if the weather be favourable, and the fly keep off, they soon get into rough leaf; when they are considered safe. But if the fly alight upon the plants while in the seed-leaf they are soon destroyed, and then the field must be reploughed and sown again. This loss and extra labour often happens more than once, sometimes thrice, before a sufficient plant can be depended upon.

Soon as the turnip plants are sufficiently grown, the hand-hoes are set on, and paid by the acre, at the rate of six shillings for first going over, and two shillings per acre for the second setting out; and which finishes the culture of the crop. The varieties usually sown are Swedes, Norfolk-whites, and sometimes an acre or two of tankards. The last are eaten off first, as they are impatient of frost; and the first are reserved till late in the spring. An acre of good turnips maintains five score of sheep for one week, and on this as a rule, the flock are put on turnips sooner or later according to their number compared with that of the acres of turnips, so that they may last as long as they are wanted for the flock.

Folding with common hurdles is generally begun at the highest side of the field, not only that the sheep may have, when not feeding, the dryest lair, but also because the top of the field being generally of inferior quality to the soil at the bottom, is more benefited by the more frequent reposing of the sheep upon it. There should be a sufficient number of hurdles not only for penning the flock on the spot to be eaten, but enough to be set round against the hedges to keep off the sheep from leaving their droppings in the ditch, or on the bank.

The flocks usually consist of couples, that is, ewes and lambs, and four or six toothed wethers. The former have a fresh pen every day; and the wethers follow after to eat the principal part of the bulbs, which are picked out of the ground, and chopped in pieces for them. The whole have occasionally both hay and trough-ment either in the field or in the sheep-house, on wet or stormy nights. The entire flock, ewes, lambs, and wethers, are all intended for the butcher, and even if possible sold before the turnips are ended. There is a great demand for fat lamb about the festival of Easter; and every means are employed to pamper and push them forward for that season. The ewes and wethers are gradually draughted off to market, either before or after they are shorn; and if there be any "odds and ends" left, they are added to the store flock.

In the autumn, and as soon as the farmer can judge of the amount of his green and dry food for sheep, he buys in his forward ewes and wethers for fattening. The ewes are commonly those of the Dorset or Wiltshire breeds, which begin lambing about the end of November; and the wethers are mostly Southdowns, if the land be of middling quality; or Lincolns or new Leicesters, if the pasturage be plentiful and rich.

Sheep have a good deal of attention bestowed upon them at all seasons. The shepherd is generally a steady and trusty servant, and well acquainted with his business and charge. He acts as physician, surgeon, and butcher to the flock, shears and winds the wool, all which he attends to with the assistance of a boy and a dog. Sheep-shearing generally takes place about the beginning of June. In most parishes there is a gang of men called shearers, who on appointed days go from farm to farm, washing and shearing the flocks. They are paid at the rate of about three shillings and sixpence per score, with victuals and drink, ending with an abundant supper, of which the other men on the farm, together with their wives and families, are invited to partake. It is a rural festival, and looked forward to and partaken of with high glee.

On some large farms the business of suckling house lambs is a laborious and important part of the shepherd's duty. For this purpose a large commodious lamb-house is erected, and near it an enclosed yard surrounded by low sheds containing racks for hay and green meat, and troughs for brewer's grains for the ewes when their pastures are short. The floor of the lamb-house is divided into several compartments for the convenience of keeping the different classes of lambs apart, and also for keeping the unsucked ewes from among those which have been already sucked. The most forward part of the ewes begin dropping their lambs at Michaelmas, and are kept in a pasture during the day, until half a score or a score are dropped, when they are housed on nights, and from which the lambs are never allowed to come out till they are fit for market. At six o'clock in the morning of the day after the lambs are confined, their mothers are let out into the pastures; and at eight o'clock, if there be any ewes which have lost their lambs, these are brought into the lamb-house, and held by the head till the lambs by turns suck them dry. At twelve the mothers are brought in to their own lambs, and remain with them for an hour, when they are again let out to graze in the pasture. At four afternoon the ewes

having no lambs are again brought in to be held and sucked dry, and at eight the mothers are let in and pass the night with their lambs.

This mode of suckling is continued from year to year, the fat lambs being sent off as soon as ready, say in about two months, and other ewes and lambs taken in, so that the lambs are always proportioned to the quantity of milk. The price of house lamb varies from two to four guineas each, and in the early spring, with good luck, it is a very profitable business. Much depends on the conveniences of buildings, pastures, &c., and on the skill and assiduity of the shepherd in fattening house lamb, in keeping the lambs healthy, and the ewes unexhausted by their wasting exercise.

While the lambs are confined, they are allowed chalk to lick, both solid and in powder, in order to prevent looseness and fever, and their house must be always well littered with wheat-straw. They are fond of having little bundles of the same to nibble, some little of which they eat; this, however, is more to amuse them than for anything else. House lambs are neither castrated nor docked.

The business of fattening house lambs can only be profitably carried on within a moderate distance of London, or of fashionable watering-places. Cheltenham is famous for house lamb, and the London market is mostly supplied from Middlesex and the adjoining counties of Essex, Hertford, Buckingham and Berks.

Proceeding with the routine of the five-shift course, and keeping to the same field, the turnip ground is begun to be prepared for barley and seeds as soon as a sufficient portion is cleared. This is executed as follows:—The furrows (into which an undue portion of the tail dress has collected during the folding) are first opened out to scatter the droppings more equally, and that they should not be too deeply covered by the plough. The ploughing is then begun, but with a very shallow furrow. Four inches is considered quite deep enough, and for this reason the tail dress is all on the surface; and were this buried too deep, neither the barley nor seeds would receive that excitement in the first stage of their life which this dress is so well calculated to give, and, therefore, shallow ploughing is preferred. If the soil by this first ploughing turns up sufficiently dry and pulverized, the barley, two-and-a-half or three bushels to the acre, is sown broadcast, one cast before the first tine of the harrows, and one cast after or behind the harrows. A tine of the harrows, is going once in a place, a bout is twice in a place, reversing the movement. If the soil turns up cloddy, and cannot be reduced by harrows and roller to a perfectly fine state, it is ploughed again and again till the necessary fineness is obtained, for neither barley nor seeds prosper unless both rise simultaneously.

The barley being sown and rolled down, the grass-seeds are sown also broadcast as equally as possible. This is done either by what is called pinching, or by griping. The first is by taking up as much seed as can be held between the thumb and two fore-fingers of the right hand united, and jerking it forcibly here and there at every fall of the left foot, and not thrown downwards, but obliquely up in the air, that it may be better scattered. By griping, the hand is filled with all the fingers close, the thumb used as a lid is raised at every fall of the left foot, and here and there as before. Each land or half-land is sown twice over, once down and once up; and if two sowers be employed, they shift places at every turn. The seeds are next tined-in, and the whole is again rolled smooth.

The proportions of seeds for an acre, are 6lbs. broad clover, 2lbs. Dutch clover, 2lbs. yellow clover, and 3 half-pecks of rye-grass, all intimately mixed together. Sometimes 10lbs. of broad clover only are sown to the acre, and the next time the same field is similarly cultivated, the broad clover is entirely omitted, the yellow and Dutch in greater quantities being substituted. Sometimes the common rye-grass is only sown when it is intended to be thrashed for seed, or made into hay, it being for either rack or manger meat the heartiest of all other hay, if well and quickly got up, and not put into large ricks, for it heats violently.

Broad clover hay well got up is highly valued, either for the rack, or cut into chaff for the manger. Brewers use it chiefly for their highly pampered horses, but prefer that which has been sown very thickly, because it being of weaker growth, is easier drawn through the rounds of the rack by the horses, than that which is grown thinly ; the stems in the latter case being so very substantial and rigid, though when cut into chaff, is little inferior to corn for working-horse keep.

During the growth of the barley, it requires but little attention, no weeding being requisite; when fully ripe, which happens between nine to twelve weeks from the time of sowing, and when the ears are bent down, it is ready for the scythe, though no corn can stand longer without damage than barley. The earliest sown always turns out the heaviest in hand, consequently, fetches the highest price if not discoloured.

Barley is generally ripe in the month of August. It is mown with scythe and bow (a slender tough rod having one end fixed to the heel of the scythe, and the other end brought up in a bow and tied to the middle) across the lands if the wind permits, or as nearly so as possible. Laying the swathes across, renders raking-in easy and regular, two lands being raked towards the central furrow, which is left clear and open for the carriage and horses to pass along in loading. As the barley-land is perfectly smooth, the scythe clears off every particle of the straw, as well as the clover which has sprung up along with it. This sometimes forms a considerable portion of the swathe, and if showery weather sets in, retards the drying of the barley, and often renders the grain dark in colour, which is a certain loss, for it cannot be too bright in colour for malting. To gain this property it should be bleached in the field after it is cut, by turning it to the light of the sun, two or three times before it is ricked, or carried to the barn.

Carrying barley in good condition is a desirable affair, and many farmers run the swathes into wads to be immediately taken up, leaving the rakings to be got together afterwards by the horse or heel rake. Barley straw, especially when mixed with clover, is excellent fodder for store beasts in the yards in winter.

Almost every farm has a barley-barn, into which no other kind of corn is ever admitted, for no kind of grain is so seriously deteriorated by admixture with other kinds as is that of barley intended for the maltster ; a single oat in a sack will frighten away the most eager purchaser. Cockles, so often seen in barley, are not half so much dreaded in the sample as any kind of corn ; besides the seeds of this weed are easily riddled out by a properly constructed brass wire sieve. Bar-

ley is thrashed either by the machine or flail, and is cleaned up for market with very great care. A good sample should be bright in colour, round in shape, with a wrinkled skin, and in weight, per bushel, nearly approaching that of wheat. From four to five quarters to the acre is called a good crop. Mowing costs about three shillings and sixpence per acre, more or less, according to the thickness or quantity of clover on the crop. The barley stubble is lightly depastured with sheep during the autumn and winter, but withdrawn early in spring.

Some farmers who wish for a heavy growth of clover, and a moderate growth of the succeeding crop of wheat, give their young clover a dressing of dung, if to spare, if not, a dressing of coalashes, carted on and spread during the frost of winter. This certainly brings a heavy swathe, both at the first and second cuttings of clover, and being partly exhausted is not so apt to cause a too rank crop of wheat, which circumstances requires to be guarded against on land in high condition.

The young clover is cleared of stones or other matters in the spring, rolled down, and shut up for good about the 20th March. It is usually ready for the scythe about the 20th June, sooner to later according to the warmth of the season. The rule is to cut when the clover is in fullest bloom, and if rye-grass be among it, when this last is in flower. Clover-hay is soon made if the weather be favourable ; shaking up the butts of the swathe in the second day, and turning them on the third, in such way as that the whole leaves and stalks are partly withered, it will be fit to carry on the fifth day, if the swathes have been carefully opened to admit sun and wind. When properly made, it should remain of a pale green colour, and secured in small rather than in large ricks, lest it should heat too much, and so injure both colour and quality. But a moderate degree of heating in the rick is absolutely necessary, for unless this takes place, the hay is little better than straw. This circumstance is not attended to so much as it should be. Timid or indolent farmers often allow their clover as well as meadow-hay to lie too long in the field, both in swathes or in cocks, before it is ricked, and though hay may be carried too soon from not being withered enough, or carried too soon after rain, yet in either case, there is more hay spoiled by being taken up too late than too soon. A fermentation from the saccharine quality of the hay, renders it particularly palatable, as well as nourishing to cattle, and is a very different thing from a heating occasioned by too much moisture. When the first crop is carried, and which usually amounts to a ton or a ton and a half to the acre, it is determined whether the field shall be shut up for a second crop, or whether it shall be depastured. Some people, and especially amateur farmers and landlords, imagine it a downright robbery of the riches of the land to remove two crops of clover in the same summer. But this, like all other theoretical ideas, is a silly mistake. All land in this country is much impoverished by exposure to the summer sun ; but if constantly shaded, even by the heaviest green crop, it is but little deteriorated, as the succeeding crop of wheat fully and visibly proves. It is thought that, if the second crop be depastured, although by browsing off the herbage the surface becomes exposed, yet, the tail-dress left by the sheep makes up for the humid riches exhaled by the sun. But this is never seen unless it happens to be a dripping summer, when very little difference can be observed in the wheat, whether grown on the once or twice mown lea. The second crop turns out about one ton to the acre, is inferior to the first crop in quality, and is generally cut into chaff for the stable.

(*To be continued.*)

SIX LETTERS on the CURRENCY.

No. IV.

BY A COUNTRYMAN.

"Hic vivimus ambitiosa,
Paupertate omnes."—Juv. Sat. iii., 182.

"The face of wealth in poverty we wear."

TO THE EDITOR OF THE MARK LANE EXPRESS.

Sir,—I have previously alluded to a letter written by the late Sir Robert Peel, in 1826, to the two Houses of Parliament, and I will now make a further quotation from it. He says—" Having been long and extensively engaged in commercial dealings, I often witnessed a national embarrassment arising from a defective and impure currency, which resembled the present stagnation in trade; and I lament to observe that suffering and experience have failed in this instance of producing their usual good effects. In the enlarged scale of business carried on by this country, embracing a great variety of pursuits, a reliance on a metallic circulation alone *ever did*, and *ever will*, fail us. Gold, though in itself massy, often disappears in consequence of war or speculation; nay, the breath of rumour itself is sufficient to disperse it. Our domestic concerns are interrupted, and confidence lost, for want of an ample and approved medium of traffic." In confirmation of the latter part of the above extract, I may observe that, in consequence of the agitation at the time the Reform Bill was carried, in 1832, there was a slight run upon the bank for gold, who paid away on the 14th of May, in that year, 300,000 sovereigns. In addition to the foregoing, I will here introduce another high authority on this question, whose opinions are well entitled to attention—I allude to the late Mr. Huskisson, who, in a discussion on the corn laws, in 1826, says—" In considering the object now before the House, it would be impossible to legislate wisely, unless the currency, *in which are the soul and elements of prices*, should have been first disposed of; and this reason, not less forcibly than others, convinces me that the present period is wholly unfitted for the discussion." After making the above quotation in his late pamphlet, Mr. Enderby says—" From these remarks, we have a right to assume that, notwithstanding the passing of the Currency Bill of 1819, Mr. Huskisson was far from being satisfied that Parliament had arrived at a right conclusion." Some persons have endeavoured to throw much stigma upon the private country bankers, with respect to their issues not being regulated by the state of the foreign exchanges (with which, by the bye, they have about as much connection as with the twelve signs of the Zodiac); but this subject has been so ably handled, and Mr. Samuel Jones Loyd's notions so completely controverted by W. B. Brodie, Esq., M.P. for Salisbury (and a banker in that city), in a pamphlet published in 1840, in the shape of a letter to Sir Robert Peel, that I cannot do better than refer the reader to that document. He

estimates the issues of the country bankers at 11,250,000*l.*; and Mr. Leatham reckons the number of bankers in 1840 to be 1179, as under:—

English Bankers.......... 697
Scotch ,, ... 262
Welch ,, ... 66
Irish ,, ... 154

In order to shew the great regularity of the country circulation, I will give the amount for the whole county of Oxford, in December of each year from 1833 to 1840 (both inclusive), with the exception of 1840, in which the return is made in September, and also the same particulars for the county of Essex, both purely agricultural counties (*nine-tenths* of the country circulation being confined to the several agricultural counties of England and Wales):—

OXFORDSHIRE.

1833.	1834.	1835.	1836.	1837.	1838.	1839.	1840.
204000	204000	212000	214000	203000	237000	227000	210000

ESSEX.

200000	208000	199000	219000	224000	265000	200000	239000

It may be as well to remark, that the above returns are made at a period of the year when they are usually at the highest point; the same returns for July or August would probably shew a diminution from the above amounts of several *thousands*. It is a well-known fact to persons at all acquainted with country banking, that there can be no *over-issues*, as any attempt to do so would be *fruitless*, as the notes, if attempted to be put into circulation beyond the immediate locality of the bank from whence they are issued, would be returned directly, either through the London banks (where payable), or through some neighbouring bank. The amount of a banker's circulation is regulated principally by the prices of corn and cattle; if *they* rise in price, so does the banker's circulation; and if *they* fall, so does the circulation. It seems almost incredible that so much ignorance should exist as to the nature of country banking amongst men of the highest standing, and engaged in the most extensive mercantile concerns in London; in confirmation of which, I will refer to an extraordinary fact stated by Mr. Leatham, in his pamphlet, which was, "that a bank director of high standing, who was also an eminent Russian merchant in London, actually wrote down to him at Wakefield, to enquire if country bankers' notes circulated by endorsement from hand to hand, similar to a bill of exchange!" In my last letter I alluded to the panic of 1825-6, which produced such disasters through the whole extent of the country; and in connection with it I will mention "one fact" which has recently come to my knowledge, and which is said to be "worth a thousand arguments," as shewing the dreadfully ruinous effects of these periodical convulsions. An honest, industrious man (well known to my informant) had accumulated a sum of 2000*l.*, and a little before the occurrence above alluded to, he purchased a small estate for 4000*l.*, took up 2000*l.* on mortgage, and with his own 2000*l.* completed the purchase. The panic came on: the mortgagee required his money, which the poor man was unable to pay; neither could he, *at such a time*, borrow it elsewhere, nor sell the estate for more than half he had given for it; the consequence was, the mortgagee took it for his debt; the poor man was ruined, and obliged

E

to become a *day labourer*, in which state he now continues, and thus reduced from a state of comfort to
one of beggary, from circumstances over which he
had *no control*. This is only one amongst thousands
of instances which might doubtless be brought forward of a similar character.

I am, sir, yours respectfully,

Nov. 26th, 1842.   A COUNTRYMAN.

No. V.

SIR,—Notwithstanding the " glorious news "
from the East, of the cessation of hostilities with
China and Affghanistan, and the wide field for
commercial enterprise opened with the former
country, with its *immense population* of nearly
four hundred millions, rest assured we shall not
reap a *tithe* of the great benefit and advantages
we otherwise should do, by the treaty with the
" Celestial Emperor," unless our *money laws* are
at the same time altered, and the springs of industry once more loosened ; but if her Majesty's
minister *can be prevailed upon to do this*, then we
may *reasonably* look forward once more to that
state of prosperity and comfort to which we have
so long been strangers. I have been much interested in perusing a small pamphlet, published in
1840, by Joah Mallinson, a manufacturer at Leeds,
entitled " A Letter to Merchants, Manufacturers,
and Operatives, suggested by the enquiries more
frequently made than answered — ' What is the
Cause of our Present Distress?' and ' What will
become of our Commerce, our Manufactures, and
our Work-people?' " The following are some of
the *facts*, or *fundamental principles*, as recognised
by the author :—

1st.—That *wealth* is composed of industry, im-
pressible on all property, as lands, houses,
fisheries, cattle, hemp, wool, cloth, corn, shipping, &c., &c.

2nd.—That the *power of creating* wealth (commodities) infinitely exceeds the power of creating gold and silver, of *fixed* denominations, to
represent and diffuse such commodities.

3rd.—That a gold and silver (metallic) standard
is with ourselves purely arbitrary and conventional — as beads, tobacco, bits of cloth, or
shells, are so with others.

4th.—That *industry* and *capital* are both legally
and justly entitled to fair remuneration, in
order that taxes may be paid, as they ought to
be, out of *profit*, and not out of *capital*.

5th.—That money (purely considered as such) is
a bare conventional representation, or sign of
wealth—the oil of the machine, the channel of
comfort, &c.

6th.—That money is *necessarily and usefully* depreciated by taxation.

7th.—That a highly-taxed community requires,
and can neither prosper nor pay taxes without,
a *depreciated* or *expanded* currency ; more
money *being always required* to represent
commodities which *are* taxed than if *not* taxed
at all.

8th.—That " *price* " ever depends very greatly
upon the quantity of circulating medium that
can be encouraged to exist, by means of a
healthful state of *credit*.

He goes on to say—in reply to his own question
as to the *cause* of the distress, whether it is attributable to the corn laws or not—" The great question by which the country is at present agitated, is

the repeal of our corn laws, the advocates for
which are both numerous and respectable ; and it
is due to many of them to add, perfectly *honest in
their intentions*, desiring thereby to promote trade,
and alleviate the existing distress. Who can, for a
moment, doubt the sincerity of Earl Fitzwilliam,
himself an extensive land proprietor, in advocating
their repeal? His motive can be none otherwise
than pure ; and one might be led to presume also,
that a person of his lordship's intelligent mind had
carefully studied the question in all its bearings.
Other persons, however, equally honest, and as
sincerely desirous of obtaining relief as his lordship, and who look upon the corn laws *abstractedly*
as a great evil, entertain very strong grounds of objection to their *unconditional* repeal—*i. e.*, unless
other essentially necessary measures (viz., *an expansion of the currency, by a renewal of the Bank
Restriction Act of* 1797, *a regraduation of our
metallic standard, and a reduction of all existing
burthens*) be carried at one and the same time ;
hence the importance, and even complexity, of this
great question—which ought to be judged of not
separately from, but in conjunction with, those of
the currency and taxation.

Let us go back to first principles (for it is well
sometimes to begin at the beginning), and ask if
those who pay taxes ought not to be protected in
such interests as will enable them to pay those
taxes. The answer must necessarily be in the affirmative. Well, then, the true basis of the corn laws
is to enable the agriculturists to pay their portion
(say one-half) of the national burthens. Hence
their *protective principle* ; for it were worse than
Egyptian cruelty to place them (the agriculturists)
on a par, as to price, with *untaxed* foreigners, without
granting them at the same time a corresponding reduction in their burthens. Would these foreigners
accept of honourable terms of national co-partner-
ship, and take their share of our taxes and other
burthens, incurred to a great extent by subsidies to
them to fight their own battles ? I think not; and
therefore they are not entitled to send their produce
to us *unconditionally*. Moreover, if it be a fact—
and it is usually stated as such—that above *four-
fifths* of our manufactures are consumed by our
home trade, is it not a legitimate argument, in behalf of the agricultural interests, that a measure
tending to their injury (and as a necessary consequence to the injury of that important portion of
our trade, inasmuch as it would recoil back, and
that *speedily*, with a multiplied force, upon the
manufacturing interests), would be impolitic and
dangerous ? And it were mere infatuation to believe that such injury would be compensated by a
great additional foreign trade : it is, in my humble
opinion, contrary to both reason and the nature of
things. That foreign states would supply us plentifully with their corn, there can be no doubt, so
long as they got paid for it; but, with the exception
of America, little reliance could be placed on them
to take our goods in return.

That the total repeal of the corn laws would yield
to the exporting manufacturers temporary relief,
and enable America to pay off part of the debt
which she owes to them, may be admitted ; but the
result of such repeal, unaccompanied by the adoption of those other measures before alluded to,
would be inevitable ruin to thousands and tens of
thousands of all classes connected with the land,
and be followed by aggravated sufferings of all
other classes, beyond the present moment, in a ten-

fold degree. But, again, in order that we may decide this point correctly, let us look at America: there they have no corn protective laws—there they had, in 1830, as abundant a harvest as they were ever blest with—there they had commerce, and found the means to rebuild their fire-destroyed city (New York) only a few years since, and to project railroads and other improvements to an almost unlimited extent. But what is their present condition? Just the reverse of what it was only a very short time ago—without credit, their commerce languid, their improvements suspended, their stores "to let," and all but in absolute ruin; and perhaps that also awaiting them. Their corn laws—for they have none—cannot be the cause of their distress; but their circumstances press heavily, and with increasing weight, upon the country, especially upon the exporting manufacturers: there will be little or no trade with them this year, and less than heretofore for some years to come: confidence is fled, and it is only by a course of the most prudent proceeding, both on their part and ours, that we can be extricated from our perilous condition. In the meantime our commerce is suffering, and we repeat our enquiries—" What is the grand cause of our distress?" and "What will become of our commerce, our manufactures, and our workpeople?"

The foregoing remarks are so judiciously made, so temperately written, and so much in accordance with my own views on the subject, that at the risk of tiring the patience of my readers, and trespassing upon the columns of your valuable paper, I have made much longer extracts than I at first intended; but I cannot well conclude my letter without answering the above query in the words of the author: "*A crippled and inadequate legal currency, taken in conjunction with enormous taxation.*" He further remarks—" The currency laws of America have laid her energies prostrate; turned 'one of the finest and most rapidly-thriving countries on the face of the earth' suddenly from a state of high prosperity, comfort, and contentment, into that of ruin, of misery, and universal distrust;" affected the general commerce between the two countries, England and America, whose interests are bound up together; and with ourselves also the main evil will be found in our present currency laws, professing (and, as far as they are carried out, compelling us) to pay money of sterling gold value, which is an absolute impossibility, the relative amount of the precious metals to the entire property of the kingdom being only in the ratio of about 1 per cent., and hence these absurd laws expose the whole community to the most terrific risks. What is it, permit me to ask, which shackles the operation of our banking system? Is it not these very currency laws? And if so, it is perfectly useless, therefore, to accuse either the Bank of England or other banks, as some people do, of want of liberality, and disregarding sound principle; for the principle of *self-preservation compels* them to act with the greatest precaution, inasmuch as, in the event of a panic, they are the first to feel its effects—and the greater the amount of their issues, the greater the danger. Business and bankers, however, are so blended up together, that in times of prosperity, either real or apparent, the latter are induced to afford to their customers all the assistance they prudently can; and in too many instances, no doubt, joint-stock banks, in order to procure a business, have encouraged speculation,

and so far exceeded the rule of prudence as to injure or ruin themselves. What, I ask again, is the result (and I put the question pointedly to our merchants and manufacturers, who will very well understand it) of our banking system being thus shackled? Periodical panics—loss of credit and confidence—annihilation of hard-earned property—bankruptcies—and starvation of our poor. And what will be the sad sequel of these distressing circumstances? I answer, the first act of the tragedy is before our eyes daily—a sight too painful to witness: our operatives and aged men either sweeping our streets in droves, *as paupers* (I both *pity* and *respect* them), or begging their pittance of bread from door to door—starving, as some of them feelingly remark, in the midst of plenty. But this is nothing, compared to the distress and sorrow and suffering which are behind the scene, accumulating every day and every hour (brooding discontent and rebellion), and presenting to our imaginations such a dark picture of the last acts of the tragedy (unless a kind and gracious Providence interfere in our behalf), as to appal the stoutest hearts, and drive them from the shores of England, that they may not behold the sad spectacle." Earnestly recommending the little work from which I have made such copious extracts, to the attentive perusal of the members of the Anti-Corn Law League; and, hoping it may have the effect of inducing them to *agitate* for a repeal of the currency instead of, or in conjuction with, the corn laws, I remain, sir, yours respectfully,

Dec. 3. A COUNTRYMAN.

No. VI.

SIR,—In my preceding letters I have endeavoured to prove that much of the distress and commercial embarrassment which have at various times afflicted this nation during the last twenty years, have arisen from our present system of currency, by having a gold standard at a *fixed* instead of a *fluctuating* price; and I find the following remarks on this subject in a pamphlet, written by Mr. Enderby in 1837, entitled " Metallic Currency the cause of the Money Crises in England and America." " It is evident that the bank of England approve of the foundation on which our monetary system is based, viz., that gold should be the standard of value at 3*l.* 17s. 10½d. per oz., and that all paper money should be payable in that metal when demanded. I grant they are by no means singular in this opinion, for they have the majority of the nation with them; but it should not be forgotten that the arguments adduced in its favour have not been such as to convince foreigners of the correctness of the measure, for with the exception of the United States of America (where it has been made a joint standard with silver), *no country save our own has fixed gold as its standard.*"

I am glad to find by a " *feeler*" put forth in the city article of the *Times* a few days ago, in the following terms—that Sir Robert Peel and his colleagues have it in contemplation to introduce some important measure for the settlement of the " currency question;" and I earnestly hope they may have the *good sense* to take the *right course*, or I greatly fear " *perilous times*" are at hand, as there is a *point* when the *pressure* upon the *productive* and *industrious* classes will become *past endurance*, and which from *present* appearances cannot be far distant; then woe be to our national debt of eight hundred millions! for it is *utterly impossible* the *enormous amount* of our taxes can be paid, unless the currency is expanded sufficiently to enable the country to bear such *heavy burdens.* " An opinion prevails pretty extensively among the monied interest in the city that the approaching session of Parliament will bring forth some sweeping measure for the final settlement of the currency question, and for giving the best protection to the public that the case will admit, in regard to banking affairs generally. This opinion is founded on a variety of causes, but more especially these—*that the present system works as badly as possible*; that an abundance of materials for a reform have been provided by the enquiries of various committees of Parliament; that the Bank charter is at the disposal of the government for an early termination, if it is thought prudent to exercise that right; and finally, that Sir Robert Peel and his Ministry, being relieved from all foreign embarrassments, will possess the leisure and the ability to settle these perplexing questions. The present charter of the Bank of England dates from the 1st of August, 1834, and is for twenty-one years, but gives, by the 5th clause, an option to the Government of putting an end to the charter upon giving one year's notice within six months after the expiration of ten years from the above date; and the charter might, consequently, be reclaimed early in the year 1846; if that period is passed over, the charter will go on to the full term, expiring in 1855; after which, if no new charter is entered into, the exclusive privileges may be terminated at any time by giving a year's notice. The concurrence of the Bank itself in any new measure to be introduced is not impossible, as means might be found to make it acceptable to that corporation; but the more probable issue is, that the Government would have opposition to encounter from that quarter, and therefore it will be wise to be prepared for the worst that may happen, by as early a commencement of operations as possible. It will be at once courteous to the Bank and beneficial to the public to disclose, as soon as possible, any policy that may be adopted towards that institution. The great objects which men of business would desire to see attained are—such a regulation of the currency as will prevent it ever being greatly in excess or deficient in amount, and to *make it uniform in its character all over the United Kingdom.*" The following is an extract from a private letter, written by an extensive iron master in Staffordshire, a short time ago, in allusion to this important question :—" I believe that all the attempts now making to save the nation will be fruitless, unless the currency is put right at the same time. I mean that the taxes cannot be paid, and the poor man have employment with a gold standard as it is at present." It may not be amiss here to correct an erroneous impression that seems very generally to prevail, that because money has been, and still continues so abundant, in London, that the curreney is expanded *too much ;* but the fact is, although so plentiful in London, it is quite the reverse in the country, and almost universal complaints prevail of its scarcity in the various channels of trade and commerce : as is a plethoric subject with a flow of blood to the head (which ought to be circulating through the body) so it is with money. The periodical panics and convulsions to which we have been so frequently subjected since 1819, have spread such ruin and dismay amongst capitalists, that they prefer employing their money in London at 2 or 2½ per cent., to embarking it in any commercial transactions; *dear-bought experience* having taught many of them that under *our present* system of currency, we are constantly subjected to a *drain* for the precious metals, whenever the exchanges become *adverse* to us, and to correct which the Bank is compelled (in *self defence*) to *contract* its circulation, and thus *lower* the *prices* of *all kinds* of *merchandize.*

The remedies I have to propose for the removal of the evils which have so long afflicted us are the following :—In the first place I would withdraw all the gold now in circulation in sovereigns and half sovereigns (and which, by the bye, would be gladly dispensed with from the harassment, loss, and annoyance to which the holders have been for some months subjected in consequence of the proclamation issued as to their light weight); and I would also call in all the 1*l.* notes in circulation in Ireland and Scotland (which should be done gradually, by issuing no more stamps), and in future have an uniform circulation throughout the three kingdoms instead of (as of late years has been the case) gold in England, and 1*l.* notes in Scotland and Ireland. I would recommend the vacancy to be supplied by an issue of 1*l.* notes by the government (or by the Bank of England on its behalf), and which should be payable equally with Bank of England notes for all government taxes, excise, &c., &c. ; and in London they should be payable either in gold or silver, at the option of the holders ; the gold to be taken at the market price of the day, which should be fixed by a committee of bullion merchants, and published periodically in the *London Gazette.* I find the price of gold from 1801 to 1819, generally varied from 4*l.* to 5*l.* per oz. (never *under* 4*l.*), and in 1813 and 1814 was as high as 5*l.* 1s. and 5*l.* 4s. per oz. This would *effectually* put a stop to the *panics* and *commercial convulsions* caused by a drain for gold, in case of an *adverse* state of the exchanges, whenever extensive importations of foreign corn take place ; the price *rising at home,* as well as at *Paris* and *Hamburg,* and consequently making it *more profitable* to export our manufactured goods instead of gold. But even were it required, the bank would always have an abundant supply, if the amount now in circulation, in addition to its present stock, were deposited in its coffers. I would next prevent the great fluctuations in the value of money at the bank, by restricting them for ever charging *more* than 5 per cent., or *less* than 4 for discounts and loans.

It is a well known fact that in 1839, whilst they were charging six per cent. in London, they were at the very same time discounting at three per cent. for certain Joint Stock Banks who issued their notes. As a precedent for this I may observe that the Bank of France is compelled by a clause in her charter *not* to discount at a *higher* rate than four per cent., and has made a law for her own government not to *discount* or make quarterly advances *below* four per cent. The additional increase to our paper circulation in the shape of one pound notes would be but as "a drop in the bucket" when we consider that the total *annual produce* of the *soil alone* in this country is estimated at *two hundred millions pound* (wheat constituting *eighty-five million pounds* of it) estimating the quantity at *twenty-five millions* of quarters, and the price to average 68s. the quarter. In addition to the foregoing alterations I would suggest that something like the following plan should be adopted, which was proposed to the select committee of the House of Commons in 1822, viz., " The application of one million of Exchequer Bills to be employed through the agency of government in buying up a certain quantity of British wheat to be placed in store." I would recommend that in years when we have an abundant harvest, and wheat is reduced as low as 40s. or 45s. per quarter, that government should advance loans (through the Exchequer Loan Commissioners) as was the case to the different poor law unions for building their poor houses ; such advances to be made to the guardians of each union for the time being (the union being responsible) in the purchase of wheat to be placed in store, and whenever the price rose to a certain sum, to be agreed upon, the wheat to be brought out and sold, and the money borrowed be repaid to the Exchequer Loan Commissioners with interest at four per cent. By these means the farmer would be protected in years of great abundance by finding a ready purchaser, and in time of scarcity the poor would be benefited by having the price kept down at a moderate amount by the wheat in store being thrown upon the market; it would also prevent our depending so much upon foreign countries for a supply of the first necessary of life, and the parishes would also be relieved from their poor-rates (to a certain extent) by the *profit* on the wheat brought to market, and just at a time too when they would otherwise (from the high price of provisions) press heavily upon them. In addition to all these advantages the money would be advanced by government under the most favourable circumstances as regards the foreign exchanges, and would be repaid to them at the very time they were adverse, and a contraction of the circulation might be thought desirable. I also think considerable advantage would arise by converting some portion of our public debt into bonds, with coupons attached, for the dividends, and payable at the various continental cities, and to be used as a medium for regulating the exchanges instead of gold, but my limits will not allow of my enlarging upon this subject at the present time.

After maturely considering these various suggestions, I am decidedly of opinion that if carried out, we shall hear no more of Chartism, of Socialism, of Whiggism, of Radicalism, nor any other *ism*. We should neither have occasion to send out our population to New Zealand, to South Australia, to Van Diemen's Land, to Canada, or elsewhere, but they would find plenty of employment and good wages in their native land, and instead of ministers devising all kinds of schemes to raise the taxes of the country sufficient to meet its expenditure, the amount might be readily raised, and cheerfully paid, and the *obnoxious* income-tax repealed, and we should have the happiness of seeing our distressed country again restored to prosperity and comfort, and answering the vivid description of the poet, who designates it as

"A lovely spot
For all that life can ask,
Salubrious, mild ; its hills are green,
Its meadows fertile, and to crown the whole
In one delightful word, it is our home,
Our native isle."

I beg, in conclusion, to return you my best thanks, Mr. Editor, for allowing me to trespass so largely on your columns, and remain, yours respectfully, A COUNTRYMAN.

TESTIMONIAL TO W. SHAW, Esq.,

A MEMBER OF THE COUNCIL OF THE " ROYAL AGRICULTURAL SOCIETY," AND MANAGING DIRECTOR OF THE " FARMERS' FIRE AND LIFE INSURANCE INSTITUTION."

On Thursday, Dec. 8, a dinner of the subscribers took place at the London Coffee-house, Ludgate-hill, for the purpose of presenting to WILLIAM SHAW, Esq. (late Secretary to, and one of the original promoters of, the Royal Agricultural Society of England, Editor of the " Farmer's Magazine," &c.), " a public acknowledgment from the Agriculturists of the United Kingdom to that gentleman, for the zeal, the energy, the talent, and the success, with which he has long laboured in the behalf of the science of agriculture, and in support of every effort for the diffusion of knowledge amongst the cultivators of the soil." The number of subscribers was upwards of 500, and amongst them were the names of the Dukes of Richmond, Rutland, and Bedford; Earls Spencer, Brownlow, Ducie, Gainsborough, St. Germains, and Talbot ; Marquis of Downshire ; Viscount Campden ; Lords Leigh, Portman, Rayleigh, Ongley, Huntingfield, Worsley, Torrington, Rodney, &c., &c. The testimonial consisted of a splendid silver tea-service, a rich tureen, a beautiful cup, with a salver bearing the following inscription :—

" PRESENTED WITH OTHER PLATE
TO
WILLIAM SHAW, Esq.,
BY SEVERAL HUNDRED NOBLEMEN AND GENTLEMEN,
AS A TESTIMONY OF THE HIGH SENSE
THEY ENTERTAIN OF THE TALENTS, ZEAL, SUCCESS,
AND UNCOMPROMISING INTEGRITY
WITH WHICH HE HAS LONG LABOURED FOR THE
ADVANCEMENT OF THE BEST INTERESTS OF
AGRICULTURE, DEC. 8TH, 1842.

There were several other articles, the whole weighing about 650 ounces. The plate was executed by Messrs. Widdowson and Veale, of the Strand. The chair was taken precisely at six o'clock by FRANCIS PYM, Esq., of the Hazells, Biggleswade, Beds. There were in all about seventy gentlemen, who sat down to a dinner which was served up in a manner which did great credit to Mr. Lovegrove. The cloth having been removed—

The CHAIRMAN proposed successively, " The Queen," " Prince Albert and his Royal Highness the Prince of Wales," and " The Queen Dowager and the rest of the Royal Family," which were drunk with all the honours.

The CHAIRMAN then rose and said—It now becomes my duty, gentlemen, in reference to the next toast I have the pleasure to propose to you, to attempt a few words at the commencement of my undertaking, on the boldness with which I have taken upon myself the duty I shall endeavour to discharge on this occasion. I have undertaken it with some misgivings as to my ability to express the feelings I entertain towards the gentleman whose health I have to propose to you (*cheers*). Gentlemen, it is in order to show in some measure, however feeble, what a debt of gratitude the agriculturists of Great Britain are under to the gentleman who sits on my right hand (*cheers*). It is necessary for me to take a short review of the state of agriculture of this country, not only in the present time, but with respect to the advances that have been made in the last half century, not only in agriculture itself, but the reform of the other great branches of the industry and prosperity of.this great country (cheers). It is true that during a long period of war—it is not for me to say how long a portion of the land in general of Great Britain was under the influence of this circumstance, which is felt to this day (cheers)—during that period there were the most tempting and high prices, called "war prices," but more properly *paper* prices (cheers), that for a long time governed the sale of corn in this country. It is quite unnecessary for me to point out to you what has been the effect of those prices, and what would be the effect if they still obtained, in the peace, plenty, and happiness of this country (cheers). Still a return to prices more like what they have been in times of peace would be far preferable to those which, while they were productive of prosperity for a time, did not enable us to indulge in that long (hear). But, gentlemen, whatever may be the effect of war, or paper prices, whatever amount of temporary prosperity they produced, there is in the future a brighter and better state of things, which we all hail with unmingled satisfaction, and that is the power and capability of the soil of Great Britain (loud cheers). You will recollect, gentlemen, under the state of things I have alluded to, what was the position of the agriculture of this country with this gentleman in the front as its champion (cheers). Agriculture may be considered a science, a science worthy of the highest class of intellect which this our favoured country has produced (hear). That is the proud position agriculture should now take (cheers), not to be cried down as it has been, by other men, as if agriculturists could neither read nor write, and that all they could do was to dig the soil, as their forefathers before them, content with what Providence provided from day to day and year to year (cheers). But agriculture is a science, and should call to its aid all those elements in science and art which have raised commerce and manufactures to such a height as almost to throw agriculture into the shade (cheers). It is only by maintaining this most useful, most ancient, and honourable science (which I may with propriety I think call it), that this country can continue as great and as flourishing as it is at the present time (cheers). It was said, and well said, in the hall of Trinity College, Cambridge, at a meeting of the Royal Agricultural Society, that "Rome was destroyed by the decline of her agriculture." (Cheers). That is a fact you will do well to attend to, and there would be little advantage in reading the history of those nations who have gone before us if we did not benefit by their experience. (Hear, hear.) The Royal Agricultural Society of England is competent to do much to raise agriculture to the position it ought and will attain; and I know that it will not only relieve those who are in necessity of advice, but it will attempt to do what I trust it is perfectly able to do—to allow nothing to supersede it, or prevent its being established on a firm basis. (Cheers.) But there are other instruments at work, and we are indebted to the gentleman on my right hand, who, being the most uncompromising friend of agriculture, makes so honourable, so able, and so valuable an use of the instrument in his hands. (Loud cheers.) It is to the press of this country we are indebted. It is one of our greatest blessings (Cheers). It is only through the application of science and intelligence, and its general distribution, that we can avoid falling into degradation, and through which we may hope to hold up our heads, and by the blessing of Providence, who has blessed us with many advantages, become the greatest nation on the

face of the earth. (Cheers). It is by taking agriculture as the basis of national prosperity, and by the application of science and skill and intellect, that we can alone keep pace with other countries, or maintain the power and the position we now enjoy in the world, and continue a flourishing and prosperous country. (Cheers.) 1 have lately seen a pamphlet which tells us that all we have to do is to take a lesson from the agriculture of Scotland, who holds a more exalted position with regard to her agriculture than we do. But these are points not necessary for me to discuss at the present moment: it will be for my friend here to my right to use the instruments in his power to bring forward questions of that sort affecting agriculture before the public. (Hear.) It is through the discussion of important questions of this sort that agriculture can be fairly brought forward, and I am quite sure that while the subject is in his hands, and under his able guidance, its full importance will be maintained (Cheers). It was therefore under this conviction that I readily undertook to be a co-operator, in the position I have undertaken, in presenting to Mr. Shaw this handsome but ineffectual testimony of our gratitude which I see before me. I hope that he will long live in the enjoyment of the good opinion of all friends of agriculture, and that he long may live an useful and active member of society, acting upon the principles which he has so ably maintained. (Loud cheers.) I now, in your names, beg that he will receive this humble tribute of gratitude which I with the most thankful and grateful feelings present to him. I propose his health with three times three. (The toast was drunk amid loud applause.)

Mr. SHAW rose to return thanks, and was received with applause. He said: Mr. Chairman and Gentlemen—In your cause, or in any good cause, I trust that neither exertion nor readiness to act, nor perseverance will be wanting in me. But when I feel myself in the extremely awkward position of having to treat on such a subject as that upon which I have been called upon to rise, the difficulty of my position is not a little increased on account of the marked kindness with which you individually have been pleased to favour me. I feel most sensibly my utter incapacity to respond to your kindness, and the kindness of those other gentlemen who have been pleased to pay me this mark of respect. I say I feel utterly incompetent to at all express the grateful feelings I entertain towards you all (Cheers). If from any circumstances I have chanced to be so placed, that by means in my hand, or through any previous information I may have obtained, I have been at all instrumental in promoting that interest, which has been so well and so properly described by your chairman as the foundation of our national prosperity, it is to me an ample return (Cheers). But when I perceive that you have evinced such a kindly feeling, expressed in the warmest manner, and when I find names in the list of gentlemen who have thus complimented me extending from Dumfries in the North to the Land's End, I scarcely know how to believe that I am placed in such a proud position. I feel, as every man must feel, that the proudest moment of his life is this, when such a mark of respect is paid to him by his fellow citizens, and by those with whom he stands on an equal footing in the intercourse of life (Cheers). To return my thanks to you in the way I could wish, is wholly out of the question. I have indeed, I must admit, done something towards creating attention, or causing additional attention, to be directed to agriculture (*Cheers*). I would not for one instant assume to myself anything which I did not think right; but so far as regards that great Society to which your chairman has alluded, I take credit to myself in this, that in the year 1834, having the means in my hands, I first began to agitate the question of its establishment, and I never ceased when the opportunity offered to bring it before the public notice, pressing it repeatedly on those who had it in their power to bring it forward, and ceasing not until I had effectually prevailed on them to do that which I never had the vanity to suppose I could ever have effected singly. (*Cheers*). There is another institution, to which I am particularly attached, and so long as I shall have the power, I shall never lose sight upon fitting occasions to press upon the farmers of this country, that however great may be the advantage agriculture will derive from the "union of science with practice," in the existence of the "Royal Agricultural Society" (*cheers*), that there is no machinery that can be put in motion which will be so effective in working out the improvement of the mind, and in advancing the practical knowledge of agriculture as Farmers' Clubs (*Cheers*). I believe their real merits are as yet but little understood; and I trust that no opportunity will be suffered to pass, by those who have the means of aiding the formation of Farmers' Clubs, of doing all in their power, of using their utmost exertions to induce each to meet the other, to commune with each other, and to confer together in the discussion of those subjects which bear upon the practice of their occupation; being convinced, as I am, that immense, that great benefit to the whole country may be achieved by means of these institutions (*Cheers*). It would ill become me to occupy your time, but I cannot sit down without repeating that it is not in my power adequately to return my thanks for this proud public mark of your approbation. I can only say that I hope hereafter to be grateful; and that so long as my eyes shall, from time to time, meet any one of those articles you have so kindly presented to me, it will create a fresh stimulus in me to go on still forward; knowing that in receiving that handsome present I have incurred a debt (*no, no*), which it will never be in my power to repay (*no, and cheers*); but by perseverance in endeavouring to promote your interest, which I hope I shall never lose sight of so long as it shall please God to give me strength of mind and body (*Cheers.*) That is the only return I can hope to make to you for your kindness —kindness which has made such an impression on me as will never be eradicated while I live. May happiness and prosperity attend you and yours; and may the cloud, which seems to hang over us just now, pass speedily away; and by your exertion, your ingenuity, your talent, your industry, and your perseverance in sound English principles, may not only agriculture prosper, but this our dear native land be placed in that high position which your chairman has so eloquently described. (*Loud cheering*).

The CHAIRMAN next proposed "The Royal Agricultural Society of England," coupling with it the health of one of its distinguished members, Colonel Le Conteur (*Cheers*).

Col. LE COUTEUR, in returning thanks for the unexpected honour thus conferred upon him, and the great society with which he was connected, stated that his only object in being present on this occasion was to join his voice in giving praise to that gentleman ;who so well deserved praise, Mr. Shaw (*Cheers*). Living at a distance from the

Metropolis, he ever looked with interest for the journal with which that gentleman is connected, and turned over its pages with pleasure, because he saw that every interest of this great society was advocated. (*Hear*). He had watched that paper —the *Mark Lane Express*—and had seen on every occasion that Mr. Shaw had not used his power as some portions of the press had done, for particular purposes, but invariably for the best interests of the country, taking all sides of a question, and fairly placing it before the public.—(*cheers*)—leaving the public to form their own judgment thereon (*Cheers*). It was therefore to him (Col. le Couteur) most gratifying to see that the farmers throughout the country, from the north and the south, had come forward to present to that gentleman the truly elegant testimonial now before him, and he was truly happy to have been one to join in that presentation (*Cheers*). In acknowledging the toast on behalf of the Royal Agricultural Society, it would be fulsome to speak in its praise, because they were all before him members of that Society, as well as himself. He rejoiced to see this great country at peace. He confessed that he was one of those who looked with extraordinary alarm a-very short time ago, to the great measures passed; lately, for equalizing the burthens on the different classes of the country, but he knew that he was addressing those who would rejoice to bear, in common with the rest of their fellow citizens, the burthens of the state (*Cheers*). He rejoiced, as every one must rejoice, that peace with the great empire of China had been perfected, and that the portals of the greatest nation in the world had been thrown open to our manufactures. It was impossible to conceive adequately, the immense, the amazing benefits which would flow into this country from its amicable communion in commercial intercourse with so great a nation as that. Could any one conceive the effect of the intercourse of 300,000,000 Chinese with the 25,000,000 of beings in this country ? It was as if every *one* of us was required to supply the wants of *twelve* Chinese. He felt convinced that we should no longer feel the burthens under which this country had so long laboured. He would ask, what had been the cause of the great wealth and happiness of China but agriculture? (*Cheers.*) China was a nation of farmers, who were literally occupied in nothing but the cultivation of the soil. They were beyond a doubt a free, a great, and an independent people, although we called them barbarians, and they returned us the compliment (*Cheers and Laughter*). He was exceedingly proud to belong to the society which had been just honoured in so marked a manner, and he felt exceedingly obliged at having had the opportunity of expressing his gratitude to a gentleman who had done so much to promote the interests of that society (*Cheers*).

The CHAIRMAN then proposed "Success to the Smithfield Club," coupling with it the name of its indefatigable honorary secretary, Mr. Humphrey Gibbs (*Cheers*).

Mr. GIBBS, in returning thanks for the toast, stated that the present state of the institution with which his name had been connected was one of increasing excellence. The present exhibition, he thought, would speak for itself (*Cheers*).

Mr. SHAW then rose and said, he was truly happy in being permitted to propose the toast he was now about to introduce; first, because it afforded him an opportunity of expressing his gratitude to the chairman for his kindness in taking the chair on this occasion (*cheers*); and, secondly, because he knew there was not an individual who could be selected, who was more worthy of every mark of respect than his friend in the chair (*Cheers*). He could assure all present, that as regarded himself individually, nothing afforded him greater and higher satisfaction than when he learned that Mr. Pym had consented to take the chair on this occasion (*Cheers*). He would say unhesitatingly that, having mixed with many in the divers ranks in which he chanced to move, and knowing what he did of Mr. Pym—knowing his circumstances and his position, there was no one more deservedly respected than that gentleman, (*Cheers*). All knew the kindness of his manner and the urbanity of his general demeanour in every position in which he was placed—whether as a neighbour, a landlord, a magistrate, or as a private individual (*Cheers*). Knowing this, he would repeat that there was not an individual whom he could have wished to preside on this occasion in preference to the gentleman who now graced it (*Cheers*). In order to learn that gentleman's character or reputation it was only necessary to go into his own neighbourhood, and he (Mr. Shaw) would challenge any man to select another who stood higher in his own neighbourhood and in his own county than did Mr. Pym (*Cheers*). Without offering any further observations, he would call upon all assembled to drink long life, health, happiness, and prosperity to him. (*Applause*).

The CHAIRMAN briefly returned thanks, and then proposed "The healths of the Vice-chairmen and R. Westbrook Baker, Esq."

Mr. BAKER, in returning thanks, expressed the gratification he felt at being present on an occasion like this—to do honour to their friend, Mr. Shaw—for their friend they must all call him—a real working good friend to agriculture (*Cheers*). During the few years he had had the honour of knowing Mr. Shaw, he would say, that he never met with a man more determined to do that which he was able to do, combining with that determination great zeal, great energy, and a most powerful mind, and also good bodily strength (*Cheers*). He begged to bear his testimony to what Mr. Shaw had said with respect to farmers' clubs, and he was sure that if they were established in the various parts of England, Ireland, Scotland, and Wales, they would be generally taken up, and carried into the most distant parts, and would ultimately bring about truly practical good (*Cheers*).

Toast—"The Landlords of England, and the health of Henry John Adeane, Esq."

Mr. ADEANE, in responding to this toast, wished more of the landlords of England had been present on this occasion (*cheers*), in order to testify to Mr. Shaw the sense of their gratitude, which must be deep in the extreme. He trusted the time was not far distant, when the tenantry of this country would receive what they expected, and what their circumstances called for—sympathy from their landlords (*Cheers*). He considered that a liberal landlord made liberal tenants, and that on the other hand, liberality on the part of the tenantry begat a like liberality in the landlord (*Cheers*). There was a connection between landlord and tenant which, for the interest of both, should be indissoluble, and whatever injured the one, the other must suffer (*Hear*). It was true, as had been said, they were both in one boat. Their interests were united, and it was a merciful Providence that had knitted them together so closely, that if one suffered, that suffering must be extended to the other (*Cheers*.)

Toast—"The Provincial Agricultural Societies of England, and the health of R. M. Jaques, Esq."

Mr. JAQUES returned thanks, and expressed the gratification he felt at being indebted to Mr. Shaw for the honour of responding to this toast, as it was through that gentleman that he first became connected with any provincial agricultural society in this country. He only wished the testimonial to Mr. Shaw had been a thousand times more valuable, because he was satisfied that Mr. Shaw had rendered great benefit to the whole community. (*Cheers*). With respect to the agricultural societies, and the principles upon which they were conducted, he thought they were rather too much confined to exhibitions of stock. He thought that one of the important objects of such societies was that of bringing farmers more together, and more into communion. Last year the Richmond society expended in the purchase of agricultural implements one hundred guineas, and the amount of implements sold at the show was one thousand pounds (*Cheers*). The same society intended during the coming year to have a trial of implements that would extend from ten to fourteen days, and he hoped that experience would enable them to discover something that may be of benefit to all agriculturists.

Toast—"Farmers' clubs, and the health of J. Beadel, Esq."

Mr. BEADEL returned thanks in the name of the farmers' clubs and for himself, and with reference to the important object of showing the practical utility of farmers' clubs, he adverted to what might be done by improving the modes of cultivation, and of increasing the productiveness of the soil, and also the importance of diminishing the expence of production by obtaining larger crops from the land. The question was how to do that? and this question he thought might be answered by the adoption of a plan practised by himself, namely, spade husbandry, by which a labourer could earn 12s. 6d. per week. This plan he particularly recommended at the present time, when there are so many out of employ. It was true that the support of the surplus population fell very heavy upon the tenant farmer, but nothing could be worse than that they should be driven for relief to the unions (*Cheers*). Nothing, he was persuaded, could keep them out of the unions but providing them with labour, and that might be accomplished by adopting the mode pointed out by him—spade husbandry. Something must be done to give the honest, steady, and industrious labourers a fair amount of labour, and a fair remuneration for that labour. This might be accomplished without any additional expence to the farmer, if instead of keeping eight horses he kept only two (*Cheers*).

Toast—"The Tenantry of Great Britain, and the health of Mr. S. Jonas."

Mr. JONAS, in responding to the toast, hoped it would never be necessary for the British farmers to adopt the plan just alluded to. He hoped that the manufacturing interest of this country would ever be allied to the agricultural interest, and that the farmers of this country would never be called upon to relieve the poor labourers on their estates by cultivating the land by spade husbandry. It was only by confidence being restored to the farmers of England that they could be induced to exert their energies (*cheers*), and nothing would induce them to do that but an anxious and confident hope, and a firm reliance that their application would be answered by an adequate return for their capital and labour (*Cheers*).

Toast—"The Highland and Agricultural Society of Scotland, and the health of Mr. Wetherall."

Mr. WETHERALL returned thanks.

Toast—"The Royal Agricultural Improvement Society of Ireland, and the health of W. F. Hobbs, Esq. (*Three times three*).

Mr. HOBBS returned thanks. The Royal Agricultural Society of Ireland had done much to improve the cultivation of the soil of that country, and he felt persuaded that with the assistance and co-operation of different societies, the cultivation of that country would be greatly improved. He believed that Ireland was capable of increasing its productions to a very great extent, and that the spirit of the landed proprietors was tantamount to the capabilities of the soil, from the universal desire manifested in all parts of that county for improvement. The next meeting of the Irish Society was fixed to take place at Belfast, and he felt persuaded that if the English farmers would go over to attend that meeting, they would be highly gratified, and not only confer a benefit upon Ireland, but also upon themselves. He fully concurred in the observations made by the chairman respecting the presentation of the plate to Mr. Shaw, and he was glad to see among the list of subscribers to that testimonial some of the first agriculturists in the kingdom—among the leading nobility and landed proprietors, and also practical farmers. He was quite sure the testimonial was not equivalent to the services Mr. Shaw had rendered to the science of agriculture (cheers), and he was highly deserving of all that could be given to him. He (Mr. Hobbs) had watched him narrowly for a number of years past, he had worked with him, and he had always found him the staunch, the unflinching, and the zealous advocate of the interests of the farmers of this country (cheers); and he was sure that the farmers of England would ever respect him for the exertions he had made (Cheers).

Toast—"The British Agricultural Labourers, and the health of Mr. Hutley, of Essex."

Mr. HUTLEY (of Witham) returned thanks.

Toast—"The Treasurers of the Fund, and Cuthbert W. Johnson, Esq."

Mr. JOHNSON returned thanks.

Toast—"The Committee, and the health of James Dean, Esq."

Mr. DEAN returned thanks for the honour done to the committee and to himself, and expressed the gratification he had experienced at being placed in a position to assist in doing honour to Mr. Shaw, who had done so much to advance British agriculture.

Toast—"Agriculture, Manufactures, and Commerce, and the health of James Allen Ransome, Esq."

Mr. RANSOME returned thanks in a long and very eloquent speech, which was received with loud and well-merited applause.

[We regret extremely that our reporter should have neglected to take notes of Mr. Ransome's address, and in which regret we shall be joined by all who heard it. A more truly eloquent speech, fraught with sound principles, in reference to the great interests of " Agriculture, Manufactures, and Commerce," was never delivered.—ED. M. L. E.]

"The health and happiness of Mrs. Shaw."

Mr. SHAW returned thanks, and the chairman having vacated the chair, the party broke up.

During the evening the following song, entitled "The Altar, the Cottage, and the Throne," written by Mr. Thomas Hudson, and composed by Mr. N. J. Spoill, was sung with great effect :—

Let other countries boast of skies
Of azure bright and clear,
To England's praise I raise my lays,
My country ever dear.

England ! beauty's birth place,
Land of freedom stands alone,
Her strength is in the Altar,
The Cottage, and the Throne.

The altar—fraught with blessed words—
Our solace and our stay
In infancy, through childhood,
Up to manhood's latest day.

The altar, where man plights his vows,
Calls woman first his own ;
So blessed be the Altar,
The Cottage, and the Throne.

England ! beauty's birth place,
Land of freedom stands alone ;
Her strength is in the Altar,
The Cottage, and the Throne.

The Cottage, where pure rustic love
And labour are combined,
Maids with health—the finest wealth,
Their innocence of mind.

Where sons of toil, they till the soil,
And when to manhood grown,
Stand up ! defend the Altar,
The Cottage, and the Throne.

The Throne ! and where in all the world
Can such a sight be seen,
As reigning in her people's hearts,
Our young and lovely Queen ?

Old England still will favoured be,
With blessings stand alone,
Whilst all revere the Altar,
The Cottage, and the Throne.

England ! beauty's birth place,
Land of Freedom stands alone ;
Her strength is in the Altar,
The Cottage, and the Throne.

THE SMITHFIELD CLUB SHOW.

The past week has, as usual, been full of interest to those farmers who have visited the metropolis—the exhibition of the Smithfield Club, and the annual meeting of the Royal Agricultural Society, being the objects commanding attention, and of the proceedings at both of which we give full reports. The stock exhibited in competition for the prizes of the Smithfield Club was good, but in our opinion not so good as we have seen. Of the nineteen oxen and cows to which prizes were awarded eight were Short-horns, eight Herefords, one Long-horn, and two Cross-bred. As regards the number of prizes, the Short-horns and Herefords stand even ; but the Herefords carried off the first prizes in classes 1, 2, 3, and 4, and the Short-horns in 9 and 10 only. The gold medal, it will be seen, was awarded to a Short-horn exhibited by Mr. Maxwell. This animal was bred by Sir Charles Tempest, of Broughton Hall, Yorkshire, who is considered to have the best breed of short-horns in the kingdom. It was purchased of that gentleman in 1836, by Mr. Maxwell, of Everingham Park, near Pocklington, in the same county, and only stalled for feeding in February last. It gained the first prize at the York agricultural meeting, in August last, and its sister beast was recently sold to Sir Anthony Buller, for 150 guineas. Mr. Thomas Umbers, of Wappenbury, maintained his position as a Leicester breeder of sheep, carrying off the gold medal. Mr. Grantham and Mr. Samuel Webb were successful competitors for Southdowns. The general arrangements were excellent, and do much credit to Mr. Gibbs, the honorary secretary, and to the stewards. The Times newspaper, not usually wont to exhibit much interest in agricultural matters, thus speaks of the show-yard and the arrangements :—

" The removal of the Smithfield Show from the dirty yard in Goswell-street—in which for so many years it was a nuisance, to the space beneath the Baker-street Bazaar, where there is ample accommodation and every facility for the numerous classes of oxen, sheep, and pigs, has been a great step towards an improvement in the public knowledge of all that relates to the breeding and fattening of the animals on which the public subsist. There is now a better understanding on these subjects than there was a few years ago, and people do not go so much to stare at a fat bullock or a plethoric pig as a wonder, as to form a correct notion of the value of the system by which oxen, pigs, and sheep are brought to the state of perfection—to use the term by courtesy, which they exhibit. There is every facility afforded at the Baker street Bazaar for the public to see and judge for themselves ; and as everything is conducted in the best manner at this exhibition, and the place is as clean as the most fastidious can desire, every body will do well to go and see the Smithfield Show. Indeed it is almost a duty for all to go and see the result of the industry of British farmers, breeders, and agriculturists, now that so much has been said about tariffs, corn-laws, and so forth."

The exhibition of implements, of various kinds of seeds, roots, &c., was very large; of the former Messrs. Garrett and Son, of Leiston Works, Suffolk, exhibited a great variety. They have devoted much time and attention to the improvement of agricultural machinery, and their efforts have been productive of great good. Their "Drill for General Purposes" performs in one process the manuring and seeding the land ; the manure and corn may be deposited together down the same conductors, or through separate coulters, rakes being provided to cover the manure with a small portion of mould upon which the seed is deposited : the seed-box accompanying this drill is adapted to sow at the same time with spring corn and manure, or may be used as a separate implement for grass seeds, broadcast, or turnips and mangold wurtzel in rows, either with or without manure. By a patented improvement they have made a very desirable alteration in depositing coarse and damp manures. Their "Turnip and Manure Drill" has each lever made to swing independently of the other, so that the man following the drill is always able to keep the depositing coulters on the tops of the ridges : these are also affixed to this drill cast iron rolls for properly forming irregularly ploughed ridges.

The Iron Patent Horse Hoe is an implement of the greatest importance, combining simplicity with effectiveness, and we hope to see the ideas of the patentees fully carried out in establishing this as a principal implement in agriculture. One of their Thrashing Machines is so made as to thrash Wheat without injuring the straw in the slightest degree. We cannot give a full description of each particular implement. Their exhibition was one which does infinite credit to the manufacturers, comprising many other varieties of drills besides those described, Lever Drag Rakes, Clod Crushers, Iron Field Rolls, Chaff-cutting Engines, Dressing and Winnowing Machines, Hay-making Machines, Turnip-cutters, Cake-crushers for cattle and manure, Subsoil, Swing, Wheel and Ridge Ploughs, and many other implements of minor importance.

In viewing the agricultural implements His Royal Highness Prince Albert particularly noticed a very neat model of a Patent Clod-crushing Roller, and also the model of a newly invented Steamer, for the general purpose of steaming food for cattle, invented by Mr. Crosskill, who explained the simplicity and efficiency of their construction to his Royal Highness. This new invention obtained a prize at the Bristol Meeting of the Royal Agricultural Society.

Mr. Grant, of Stamford, exhibited his Patent Steerage Lever Horse Hoe, which obtained a prize at Peterborough, in October last.

Messrs. Barrett, Exall, and Andrews, of Reading, exhibited their improved Gorse-cutting Machine and several of their Ploughs, which are already well known in the agricultural world.

Messrs. Cottam exhibited an improved One Row Drill for manure and seed.

Mr. Hornsby exhibited his Drill for General Purposes, for drilling corn, seeds, and manure, for which the prize of £25 was awarded to him at the meeting of the Royal Agricultural Society at Liverpool, July 1841, and £30 at Bristol, July, 1842.

Mr. Cooch, an improved Winnowing machine.

Mr. Edmunds, Banbury, an Improved Turnip-cutting Machine, for beasts and sheep, and also his patent Land-presser.

The Uley Cultivator, or Ducie's Drag, which gained the first prize of the Royal Agricultural Society, held at Liverpool, in 1841; and also of the Yorkshire Society, held at Hull, in 1841, was also shewn.

The Tweeddale Drain Tile Machine was exhibited at work.

Messrs. Howard, of Bedford, exhibited their Patent Improved Plough and Harrows.

Messrs. Wedlake, of Hornchurch, Essex, had an excellent assortment of agricultural implements. Among which we noticed a newly invented Turnip-cutter, which answers a twofold purpose; it cuts the turnips in regular strips for sheep, and by reversing the handle cuts thin slices for beasts. An iron Cane Top or Chaff-cutting Machine on a very improved plan, made so that the frames can be easily taken to pieces, and put in the box, which forms a packing case. A wrought iron Plough, made for exportation, very light, and so constructed that the draught is very easy, and can be packed in a small compass. A Subsoil Plough, which by means of a screw can be elevated or lowered as required. Also a variety of Ploughs, Chaff-cutters, Oil and Rape-cake Cutters, and other improved agricultural implements.

Amongst the various implements exhibited was a Sheep Dipping Apparatus, invented by Mr. Thomas Bigg, of No. 15, Crawford-street, Portman-square, London, the well known proprietor of the "Composition" for the destruction of all vermin obnoxious to that valuable animal, the sheep. The above apparatus obtained Prizes both at the Highland and Agricultural Society of Scotland, and at the Yorkshire Agricultural Society's meetings, 1841.

Messrs. Thomas Gibbs and Co., the seedsmen to the Honourable Boards of Agriculture of England and Sweden, had the most splendid show of roots,

&c., that we ever recollect to have seen, and notwithstanding the superiority of their stand on former years, we consider this display one of the finest we ever witnessed. It would be useless for us to endeavour to enumerate the various articles of importance to agriculturists which we saw, but our attention was attracted by their turnips. The Swedes, in particular, grown by his Grace the Duke of Bedford, &c., from seed sent to his grace by these gentlemen, were remarkable for their beautiful form, and small top, and at the same time possessing the quality of size in its highest perfection. We think that no person interested in farming pursuits could fail to admire the fineness of top in Gibbs's Swedish turnips.

The large white Belgian carrots, some of which were ticketed as being grown by Jonas Webb, Esq., of Babraham, from Messrs. Gibbs's seed, were very fine; and one, as grown by Mr. Kendall, at Windsor, weighed 14lbs. We understood from the attendants at the stand that carrot seed is extremely scarce this year.

The enormous size of their mangold wurzel appeared to attract much attention; some weighed upwards of 35lbs., and the Globe mangel wurzel 30lbs.

Thomas Gibbs and Co. also exhibited specimens of the various natural grass from which they select in forming their mixtures, in which department the gentlemen have been so celebrated for many years.

Mr. Skirving, of Liverpool, exhibited a splendid show of his well known Swedes, stated to have been raised with the Guano manure alone.

Messrs. George Gibbs and Co., had an interesting exhibition of Roots and other agricultural produce, especially a Turnip they call "the Ashcroft Swede," particularly large, and appeared of excellent quality. The variety called "Payne's Kentish Green Crown Swede," were very handsome. Their Mangel Wurzel, Kohl Rabi, and Cattle Cabbage, grown by Samuel Crawley, Esq., of Stockwood Park, were beautiful specimens. They also showed samples in grain and ear of a new French Seedling Wheat, selected by that eminent agricultural experimentalist, M. Vilmorain, of Paris, now growing by Henry Cox, Esq. The Belgian White Carrot Roots, grown by Benjamin Curry, Esq., of Eltham Park, were of wonderful size.

Mr. Matson, of Wingham, exhibited specimens of long red Mangel, yellow and red Globe, not of large size, but of excellent symmetry. Also his Matsonian purple top Swede, green top Swede, white and green Globe. We noticed a green Globe Turnip, weighing about four pounds only, that seemed to be a very beautifully formed root.

Mr. Benjamin Edgington, of 2, Duke-street, Southwark, exhibited Models and Drawings of his temporary Pavilions and Marquees. We noticed a beautiful one which represented the saloon where the Queen partook of a dejeuné, as the guest of Lord Glenlyon, at Dunkeld. He also exhibited Rick-Cloths, Tents, Sacks, Horse-Cloths, Sheep-Nets, Royal Standard, Union Jack, and red Ensign in silk and bunting, improved waterproof dressed Cloths, &c., &c.—*Mark Lane Express.*

ANNIVERSARY DINNER OF THE SMITHFIELD CLUB.

The forty-second annual dinner of this society was held, on Friday, Dec. 9, at the Freemason's Tavern, Great Queen Street. The chair was as on former occasions occupied by the noble president of the club, the Earl Spencer. Among the distinguished patrons of the agricultural and farming interest present, we noticed his grace the Duke of Richmond, Earl Ducie, Baron Monteagle, the Hon. Col. Spencer, the Hon. Mr. Littleton, the Hon. Mr. Wilson, the Hon. Mr. Nugent, Mr. Pusey, M.P., Mr. Bennett, M.P., Mr. F. Pym, &c.

The company although not quite so numerous as we have witnessed in previous years, yet included several of the most eminent graziers and successful breeders of cattle in the country.

The health of the Queen, the Queen Dowager, Prince Albert, the Prince of Wales, and the rest of the Royal Family, having been successively drunk,

The CHAIRMAN rose to propose "success to the Smithfield Club." The noble lord stated that he had always been in the habit of prefacing the toast he was about to propose with a few observations, and, with their permission, he would do so on this occasion. The present was not quite so full a meeting as he had had the pleasure of witnessing on previous occasions, although he must say the cattle show of the day had been better than any he had ever seen before. The number of animals exhibited had been much greater than usual, and although certainly there had been, as there always would be, some rubbish among them, yet upon the whole he had never seen better animals in the yard. He had no hesitation in saying that he recollected shows in Smithfield in which first prizes would have been gained by seven or eight of the animals now in the second and third classes; and if that was not evidence of a good exhibition in the present year, he really did not know what was. The show was, some few years ago, held in a miserable, uncomfortable yard; but now, after three or four years' experience, not only had the breed of cattle been greatly improved, but the convenience and comfort of those who attended the show had been most extensively studied (*Hear, hear.*) There certainly were at this year's exhibition some animals not quite so good as he could have wished to see; the fault could not be stated to be want of size, although perhaps in some quarters there might have been a little more attention to the improvement of the quality. He thought that gentlemen ought to attend a little more to this matter, and not merely endeavour to produce animals of great weight and size. Mere size was an improper and unfair test in such a society as the present; a certain degree of size undoubtedly was requisite, but bulk alone was not what they ought to look to. Many of the company, he had no doubt, had heard some lectures lately upon this subject; at present those lectures were merely theoretical, but he hoped they would soon lead to practical results. The farmers must look to the most economical mode of feeding, as by that means alone they would be enabled to supply the markets with the cheapest food. Many of the animals in the show-yard were rather too fat for persons of ordinary taste. It was, however, quite a mistake for per-

sons to say, "Oh! what is the use of bringing such
fat animals to the market?" Why, undoubtedly
these beasts were not brought to the show as specimens of what might be done with the individual
animals at considerable expense of feeding, but as a
test of what might be done with that description of
animals by ordinary feeding. There were animals
which he would defy any grazier in England to
bring into such a condition as would render it
worth their while to bring them to market. Such
animals were utterly unprofitable to the grazier to
breed; but the animals which they required were
those which if they were well fed would yield an
adequate return to the farmer, and not those which
if the utmost trouble and expense were bestowed in
the improvement of the breed, would nevertheless
remain unprofitable both to grazier and butcher.
Having made these remarks, he would beg leave to
propose, "Success to the Smithfield Club."
The toast was drunk with loud applause.

The noble Chairman then proceeded to the more
immediate business of the evening—the distribution of the prizes which were awarded to the successful candidates. They were as follows:—

OXEN.

CLASS I.—Oxen or Steers, of any breed, under five
years of age, without restriction as to feeding, yet the
kind or kinds of food must be certified.

No. 11.—Mr. William Woodward, of Breedens Norton, near Tewkesbury, a 4 years and 6 months old improved shorthorned Ox, bred by himself, and fed on
hay, cabbage, Swedish turnips, barley meal, pea meal,
grass, green clover, and linseed cake. Travelled to
the show by van 5 miles, and by railway 143 miles.
Third prize 10l.

No. 18.—Mr. R. W. Baker, of Cottesmore, near
Stamford, a 3 year and 9 months old shorthorned
Steer, bred by himself, and fed on mangle flour,
oatmeal, and vegetables. Travelled to the show by van
30 miles, and by railway 105 miles. The second prize
of 15l.

No. 20.—Mr. Thomas L. Meire, of Cound Arbor,
near Shrewsbury, a 3 years and 11½ months old Hereford Ox, bred by himself, and fed on grass, hay, turnips,
carrots, grains, barley and pea meal, and oilcake. Travelled to the show on foot 3 miles, by cart 7 miles, by
boat 50 miles, and by railway 100 miles. The first
prize of 20l.

CLASS II.—Oxen or Steers, of any breed, under 6
years of age, weight 90 stone and upwards, that shall
not have had cake, corn, meal, seeds, grains, or distillers' wash, during twelve months previous to the
1st of August, 1842.

No. 32.—Mr. Samuel Bennett, of Bickering's Park,
near Woburn, a 4 years and 9 months old shorthorned
Ox, bred by himself, and fed on 16 bushels
of bean meal, 650lbs. of cake, turnips, carrots, and mangold-wurtzel. Travelled to the show on foot 1 mile,
and by waggon and railway 45 miles. The second prize
of 20l.

No. 35.—Sir William Wake, Bart., of Courteen Hall,
near Northampton, a 4 years and 10 months old Hereford Ox, bred by Mr. Perry, of Monkland, near Leo-
minster, and fed on 1,200lbs. of cake, 2 bushels of
bean meal, grass, hay, turnips, and mangold-wurtzel.
Travelled to the show by railway 60 miles. The first
prize of 30l.

No. 41.—Mr. John Slingsby, of Morton Hall, near
Manchester, a 4 years and 9 months old cross Ayrshire
Ox, bred by Mr. Stirling, of Keir, near Dunblane, and
fed on 441lbs. of cake, 253lbs. of corn, and grass. Travelled to the show on foot 3½ miles, and by railway 210
miles. The third prize of 10l.

CLASS III.—Oxen or Steers, of any breed, under 5
years of age, under 100 stone and above 70 stone

weight, that shall not have had cake, corn, meal,
seeds, grains, or distillers' wash, during 12 months
previous to the 1st of August, 1842.

No. 47.—Mr. Chamberlain, of Desford, near Leicester, a 4 years and 8 months old Hereford Ox, bred by
himself, and fed on 696lbs. of cake, 330lbs. of pea meal,
grass, hay, and green vegetables. Travelled to the show
on foot 10 miles, and by railway 102 miles. The second
prize of 10l.

No. 50.—Mr. John Manning, of Harpole, near
Northampton, a 4 years and 6 months old Hereford
Steer, bred by Mr. Josiah Dean, of Abbey Dare, Herefordshire, and fed on 800lbs. of cake, 4 bushels of bean
meal, grass, hay, and turnips. Travelled to the show
on foot 7 miles, and by railway 70 miles. The first
prize of 15l.

CLASS IV.—Oxen or Steers, of any breed, not exceeding 4½ years of age, under 85 stone weight, that shall
not have had cake, corn, meal, seeds, grains, or distillers' wash during 12 months previous to the 1st of
August, 1842.

No. 56.—Mr. George Payne, of Milton Keynes, near
Newport Pagnell, a 3 years and 6 months old Hereford
Steer, bred by Mr. Downes, of Medley Park, near Lud-
low, Shropshire, and fed on 250lbs. of cake, hay, and
Swedes. Travelled to the show on foot 6 miles, and by
railway 48 miles. The second prize of 5l.

No. 61.—Mr. E. Bouverie, of Dalapre Abbey, near
Northampton, a 3 years and 7 months old Hereford
Steer, bred Mr. John Meire, of Uchington, and fed on
742lbs. of cake, 2 bushels of oats in meal, grass, hay,
mangold-wurtzel, and Swedes. Travelled to the show
by van 4 miles, and by railway 60 miles. The first prize
of 10l.

CLASS V.—Oxen or Steers, of any breed, under 4½
years of age, under 80 stone weight, without restrictions as to feeding, yet the kind or kinds of food
must be specified.

No. 67.—Mr. Thomas Bridge, of Buttsbury, near
Ingatestone, a 3 years and 7 months old Hereford Steer,
bred by Mr. Hall, and fed on grass, lucerne, Swedes,
oilcake, and a little bean and barley meal. Travelled
to the show by van 26 miles. The first prize.

CLASS VI.—Oxen or Steers, of the Scotch or Welsh
breed, of any age, above 70 stone weight, that shall
not have had cake, corn, meal, seeds, grains, or distillers' wash, during 12 months previous to the 1st of
August, 1842.

No. 71.—Mr. John Manning, of Harpole, near Northampton, an upwards of 5 years old Scotch Ox, fed on
grass, turnips, 800lbs. of cake, and 3 bushels of bean-
meal. Travelled to the show on foot 7 miles, and by
railway 70 miles. The first prize of 10l.

CLASS VII.—Oxen or Steers, of the Scotch or Welsh
breed, of any age, under 70 stone weight, that shall
not have had cake, corn, meal, seeds, grains, or distillers' wash, during 12 months previous to the 1st of
August, 1842.
Withheld for want of merit.

COWS.

CLASS VIII.—Fattened Cows or Heifers, under 5
years of age. Freemartins and Spayed Heifers are
not qualified.

No. 74.—Mr. George Ellis, of Hatfield Peverell,
near Witham, a 3 years and 6 months old Hereford
Heifer, bred by himself, and fed on mangold-wurtzel,
Swedes, tare-meal, and hay. Travelled to the show by
van 40 miles. The second prize of 10l.

No. 76.—Mr. Robert Burgess, of Cotgrove Place,
near Nottingham, a 4 years and 3 months old Durham
Heifer, bred by himself, and fed on grass, oilcake, turnips, cabbages, and bean flour. Travelled to the show
on foot 6 miles, and by railway 126 miles. The third
prize of 5l.

No. 77.—Sir George Phillips, Bart., of Weston House,

Chipping-Norton, a 4 years and 2 months old cross-bred Heifer (Scotch and Durham), bred by himself, and fed on Swedes, common turnips, cake, linseed, bean and barley flour. Travelled to the show by van 40 miles, and by railway 56 miles. The first prize of 20*l.*

CLASS IX.—Fattened Cows, of 5 years old and upwards. Freemartins and Spayed Heifers are not qualified.

No. 9.—The Right Hon. Earl Spencer, of Wiseton, near Bawtry, a 7 years and 7 months old Durham Cow, bred by his lordship, and fed on hay, Swedes, barley and bean meal, and oilcake. Travelled to the show by van 22 miles, and by railway 180 miles. The second prize of 5*l.*

No. 82.—Mr. William C. Maxwell, of Everingham Park, near Pocklington, a 6 years and 8 months old shorthorned Cow, bred by Sir Chas. R. Tempest, Bart., of Broughton Hall, Skipton, and fed on grass, hay, bean and barley meal, cake, Swedes, and mangold-wurtzel. Travelled to the show by van 16 miles, and by railway 219 miles. The first prize of 20*l.*, and gold medal to the breeder.

CLASS X.—Fattened Cows, of 5 years old and upwards, that shall have had at least two live calves, at separate births.

No. 86.—Mr. W. Harbridge, of Brookend House, near Morton in Marsh, a 12 years and 8 months old longhorned Cow, bred by himself, and fed on hay, barley and bean meal, and oilcake. Travelled to the show by van 35 miles, and by railway 50 miles. The second prize of 5*l.*

No. 88.—The Right Honourable the Earl of Hardwicke, of Wimpole, a 10 years and 11 months old Durham Cow, bred by his lordship, and fed on oilcake, bean meal, mangold-wurtzel and hay. Travelled to the show by van 46 miles. The first prize of 15*l.*

No. 97.—Mr. James Watson, of Waldby, near South Cave, a 3 years and 9 months old shorthorned Ox, bred by himself, and fed on linseed cake and bean meal. Travelled to the show by railway 241 miles. Silver medal.

SHEEP

CLASS XI.—Longwoolled fat Wether Sheep, 1 year old, that have never had cake, corn, meal, seeds, or pulse.

No. 101.—Mr. T. Twitchell, of Willington, near Bedford, a pen of Leicester wethers, 20 months old, bred by himself. Second prize of 5*l.*

No. 107.—Mr. Thomas Umbers, of Wappenbury, near Leamington, a pen of longwoolled weth rs, 21 months old, bred by himself. The first prize of 20*l.*

CLASS XII.—Longwoolled fat wether Sheep, 1 year old, under 8 stone weight, that have never had cake, corn, meal, seeds, or pulse.

No. 114.—Mr. Thomas Umbers, of Wappenbury, near Leamington Spa, a pen of longwoolled wethers, 21 months old, bred by himself. The prize of 10*l.*

CLASS XIII.—Longwoolled fat wether Sheep, 1 year old, without restrictions as to feeding.

No. 115.—Mr. William Sandy, of Holme Pierrepont, near Nottingham, a pen of Leicester wethers, 20 months old, bred by himself. The first prize of 20*l.* and the gold medal.

No. 126.—His Grace the Duke of Bedford, of Woburn Abbey, a pen of Leicester wethers, 20 months old, bred by his grace. The second prize of 5*l.*

EXTRA STOCK—LONG WOOLLED SHEEP.

No. 134.—Mr. J. S. Burgess, of Holme Pierrepont, a long-woolled wether, about 32 months old, bred by himself. The silver medal.

CLASS XIV.—Shortwoolled fat wether Sheep, 1 year old, without restrictions as to feeding.

No. 146.—Mr. Grantham, of Stoneham, near Lewes, a pen of Southdown wethers, 20 months old, bred by himself. The first prize of 20*l.*

No. 147.—Mr. Samuel Webb, of Babraham, near Cambridge, a pen of Southdown wethers, 20 months old, bred by himself. The second prize of 5*l.*

CLASS XV.—Shortwoolled fat wether Sheep, 1 year old, under 8 stone weight, without restrictions as to feeding.

No. 152.—Mr. Samuel Webb, of Babraham, near Cambridge, a pen of Southdown wethers, 20 months old, bred by himself. The prize of 10*l.*

CLASS XVI.—Shortwoolled fat wether Sheep, 2 years old, without restrictions as to feeding.

No. 159.—Mr. Grantham, of Stoneham, near Lewes, a pen of Southdown wethers, 32 months old, bred by himself. The first prize of 20*l.*

No. 160.—Mr. Samuel Webb, of Babraham, near Cambridge, a pen of Southdown wethers, 32 months old, bred by himself. The second prize of 5*l.*

EXTRA STOCK—SHORT-WOOLLED SHEEP.

No. 171.—Mr. E. G. Barnard, M.P., of Gosfield Hall, near Halstead, a Southdown wether, 32 months old, bred by himself. The silver medal.

PIGS.

CLASS XVII.—Pigs of any breed.

No. 173.—Mr. W. Hobman, of Ewell, near Epsom, a pen of Neapolitan Pigs, 26 weeks old, bred by himself, and fed on peas and fine middlings (no milk). The second prize of 5*l.*

No. 179.—Mr. John Buckley, of Normanton Hill, a pen of cross Warwickshire and Neapolitan Pigs, 31 weeks and 3 days old, bred by himself, and fed on barley meal and a little bean meal. The first prize of 10*l.*

EXTRA STOCK—PIGS.

No. 183.—Mr. William Jarrett, of 77, Ratcliffe-highway, an Essex Pig, 33 weeks old, bred by himself, and fed on fine middlings, barley meal, and peas—brought up by hand. The silver medal.

The total amount of money expended in prizes exceeds 400 guineas.

The show is considered to be the best since 1839, in which year some very remarkable animals were exhibited. In the two classes which include Scotch and Irish oxen, there appears to have been less competition than usual, and in one of them both prizes are withheld through want of merit.

The exhibition, which was strictly private on Tuesday, was open to the public on Wednesday morning; and his Royal Highness the Duke of Cambridge visited it at an early hour, when Earl Spencer, the president, and several of the vice-presidents, were in attendance.

The following gentlemen undertook the office for cattle and long-woolled sheep :—Mr. Hewett, of Dodiorn, near Weedon, Oxon ; Mr. Druce, of Ensham, near Oxford ; and Mr. Buckley, sen., of Normanton-hill, Notts. For short-woolled sheep and pigs :—Mr. Arckoll, of Langley, near Eastbourne, Sussex ; Mr. R. Emery, of Hurston-place, Brighton ; and Mr. John King, Devonshire-place, Brighton.

The judges were selected by the stewards from the members of the club at an early hour in the morning, each steward appointing one.

The judges have hitherto been selected from among the most celebrated breeders of stock; but at the annual meeting held on Wednesday, Mr. Giblett, of Bond-street, proposed that in future one of the three for each class shall be a butcher.

SMITHFIELD CHRISTMAS CATTLE MARKET.

MONDAY, December 12th.

This being the day appointed for the holding of the Great Christmas Market, we had at a very early hour a large attendance of butchers and graziers from almost all parts of England, with an extensive number of the former residing in the metropolis; hence, as might be conceived, the greatest animation and bustle was apparent. Contrary to general expectation, the supply of Beasts derived from our grazing districts was much more superior than that brought forward for a series of years past; indeed, we may venture to observe that there were not 50 forming it in any way beneath the middle quality; hence it elicited the surprise and approbation of all present, and reflected great credit upon the skill and enterprise of the agricultural community. The competition between the Hereford, Devon, Durham, and Short-horned breeders was so extremely keen, that we scarcely know how, in the spirit of strict fairness, to award the palm to either in particular. However, for weight, size, and symmetry—including of course actual value—we might, we consider, state that the Herefords (except in the instance of the Scots which we shall have occasion to particularize below) were, as a whole, triumphant—embracing, as they did, some of the most wonderful animals we ever saw exhibited for sale in this market. Decidedly the best of this truly excellent breed were brought forward by Mr. Rowland, of Creslow, who had on offer about 40, estimated to weigh nearly 200 st., and for which 40l. each was asked, for the average of the drove. We next come to the Devons, which, though not quite so extensive in numerical strength, as at the corresponding market day last year, well sustained their long-established fame; yet, generally speaking, their weight was not quite so great as on that occasion. There were about 400 splendid pure Durhams, consigned to various salesmen, and which were fully as good as in many preceding seasons. As to the Shorthorns, these were more than usually prime, and those offering by Mr. Robert Morgan, the property of Mr. Goodall, of Deeping Fen, and Messrs. Thomas and Wiseman, of Holbeach, Lincolnshire—which gentlemen sent, also, some very prime Herefords—were certainly the best, and produced high figures: while they were surrounded by crowds of people during the day. The Scots next command attention, and notwithstanding we received very few really good ones from Scotland, those exhibited by Mr. Vorley, and owned by Messrs. J. and H. Rayner, of the Isle of Ely, Cambridgeshire, (10 in number) were scarcely ever equalled, much less excelled. These surprising creatures, which were estimated to weigh nearly 120 stones, were considered to be worth quite 32l. per head, which will at once show that we have not overrated them. Messrs. Gurrier and Maidwell, as also several others, had excellent shows of Beasts; in fact, to do justice to this admirable collection of stock, brought together, as will be conceded, under disadvantageous circumstances, would be impossible. As to the numbers, these were considerably less than last season, yet fully adequate to meet the wants of the buyers. At the commencement of the market, they purchased slowly; but, as the day advanced, the biddings became more spirited, and we are happy in being enabled to intimate that an advance in the quotations of beef, of from 2d. to 4d. per 8lbs., was firmly established, and a good clearance was effected, previously to the conclusion of the market. To prevent any misunderstanding, at a time so important as this is, we beg to state that the highest general quotations for beef were from 4s. 4d. to 4s. 8d. per 8lbs., though of course some cases could be named in which from 4s. to 5s. per 8lbs. were obtained; but as these figures were not those ruling, as an average, we deem it proper to omit them from our tabular statement. This we deem a matter of positive necessity to mention, as we find some statements giving higher rates for the general transactions in the market than are warranted by the actual trade.

The numbers of sheep were rather more than those last year, and quite an unusual improvement was observed in their quality and condition. Downs, though rather scarce, were very good, and we must say that that description of sheep, together with the Lincolns, Leicesters, Kents, and Somersets, excited our admiration; and we cannot pass unnoticed about 40 Downs and polled sheep in Mr. John Weall's pens, sent to that gentleman by E. F. Whittingstall, Esq., of Langley-Berry, Hertfordshire. For weight, size and shape, we should say the polled descriptions certainly exceeded those ever shown in this market; and we have no hesitation whatever in stating that, had they been shown in the yard of the Smithfield Club, they would have carried off the prizes offered by that society. Some of these extraordinary sheep weighed upwards of *thirty stones*, and for which 5l.5s. each were demanded. The mutton trade was somewhat renovated, and the currency had an upward tendency, say of from 2d. to 4d. per 8lbs.; the Downs reaching, without much apparent difficulty, 4s. 6d. per 8lbs. Calves came freely to hand, and were disposed of at last Friday's rise of 2d. per 8lbs. The Pork trade was tolerably steady, at fully, but at nothing quotable beyond, late rates.

From Lincolnshire, Leicestershire, Northamptonshire, and Warwickshire, we received 2,800 short horns, runts, and Herefords; from Norfolk, Suffolk, Essex, and Cambridgeshire, 320 Scots, homebreds, runts, &c.; from our Western and Midland districts, 700 Devons, Durhams, runts, Herefords, and Irish beasts: from other parts of England, 250 Herefords, runts, &c.: from Scotland, by steamers, 170 horned and polled Scots; from Ireland, 80 beasts; the remainder of the supply being made up by the stall feeders, &c., in the neighbourhood of London.

Not a single fresh head of stock was on offer from abroad, there being only a very rough Hamburgh beast received via Hull. The imports, as will be seen by the annexed returns, have been small indeed.

FROM GERMANY.				
	Beasts.	Cows.	Sheep.	Pigs.
London	5	2	—	—
Hull	30	8	—	—
Total for the week.	35	10	—	—
Previously this year.	1121	331	284	52
Grand Total.	1156	341	284	52

FROM HOLLAND.				
	Beasts.	Cows.	Sheep.	Pigs.
London	7	3	—	—
Hull	—	—	—	—
Total for the week.	7	3	—	—
Previously this year.	584	197	—	20
Grand Total	591	200	—	20

FROM SPAIN.			
	Beasts.	Cows.	Sheep.
London	12	—	—
Southampton	20	—	—
Week's arrival	32	—	—
Previously this year	726	85	230
Grand total	758	85	230

FROM FRANCE.			
	Beasts.	Cows.	Sheep.
Southampton	10	2	—
Hull	8	1	—
Week's arrival	18	3	—
Previously this year	350	32	140
Grand Total	368	35	140

It has been intimated that importations have taken place for our market from Calcutta and the Canadas; but we beg most distinctly to intimate to our readers that no receipts whatever have come to hand here from those distant parts; the cows named in some of the reports having merely belonged to the owners of vessels for the better accommodation of their passengers.

	Per 8lbs. to sink the offals.					
	s.	d.	s. d.			s. d. s. d.

	s.	d.	s.	d.			s.	d.	s.	d.
Coarse and Inferior Beasts	3	2	3	4	Prime coarse woolled Sheep	4	0	4	4
Second quality do.	3	6	3	10	Prime South Down	4	4	4	0
Prime large Oxen	4	0	4	2	Large coarse Calves	3	10	4	2
Prime Scots, &c.	4	4	4	8	Prime small do	4	4	4	0
Coarse and Inferior Sheep	3	4	3	6	Large Hogs	3	10	4	4
					Neat small Porkers	4	6	4	8
Second quality do.	3	8	3	10	Lambs	0	0	0	0

Suckling Calves, 16s. to 31s., and quarter old Store Pigs, 16s. to 20s. each. — Beasts, 4,541; Sheep, 25,380; Calves,160; Pigs, 408.

FRIDAY, Dec. 9. — Beasts, 722; Cows, 133; Sheep, 3,670; Calves, 183; Pigs, 345.

A STATEMENT and COMPARISON of the SUPPLIES and PRICES of FAT STOCK, exhibited and sold in SMITHFIELD CATTLE MARKET, on Monday, Dec. 13, 1841, and this day, Monday, Dec. 12, 1842.

At per 8lbs. to sink the offals.

	Dec. 13, 1841.				Dec. 12, 1842.		
	s.	d.			s.	d.	
Coarse & inferior Beasts	3	4 to 3	8	.	3	2	3 4
Second quality do.	3	10	4	0	.	3	6 3 10
Prime large Oxen	4	2	4	8	.	4	0 4 2
Prime Scots, &c.	4	10	5	0	.	4	4 4 8
Coarse & inferior Sheep	3	4	3	6	.	3	4 3 6
Second quality do.	3	8	3	10	.	3	8 3 10
Prime coarse woolled do.	4	0	4	4	.	4	0 4 4
Prime Southdown do.	4	6	5	0	.	4	4 4 6
Large coarse Calves	4	6	5	0	.	3	10 4 2
Prime small ditto	5	2	5	6	.	4	4 4 6
Large Hogs	4	6	5	0	.	3	10 4 4
Neat small Porkers	5	2	5	4	.	4	6 4 8

SUPPLIES.

	Dec. 13, 1841.	Dec. 12, 1842.
Beasts	6,334	4,541
Sheep	20,020	25,380
Calves	89	160
Pigs	419	408

GENERAL MEETING OF THE ROYAL AGRICULTURAL SOCIETY OF ENGLAND.

On Saturday, Dec. 10, the General Meeting of this Society was held at the rooms, 12, Hanover-square, and it is highly gratifying to us to state that the attendance of members was numerous, and that the whole proceedings passed off with great satisfaction to all present; amongst whom were—His Grace the Duke of Richmond, W. F. Hobbs, T. R. Barker, W. Smart, C. J. Smart, P. Pusey, M.P., S. Druce, Earl Spencer, H. Boys, R. Hodgkinson, sen., J. Gandern, W. Adcock, M. H. Shuttleworth, R. Boys, J. Clover, J. Dean, H. Manning, C. Hillyard, F. Pym, W. B. Wingate, J. Beck, W. W. Page, C. Alderman, J. Hind, C. Tawney, J. A. Ransome, W. M. Norris, W. Torr, jun., W. Richardson, H. Paget, B. Almack, G. Fownes, Col. Challoner, J. Gedney, R. Arkwright, Sir R. P. Jodrell, Bart., T. B. Saunders, R. Bromley, J. Bromley, C. W. Hoskyns, H. Fowler, R. Beman, Rev. C.

T. James, W. Lyne, H. Handley, J. Slack, H. Blanchard, J. Somerset, M.D., Rev. D. Gwilt, K. Hoskyn, M.P., J. Burgess, W. Pickering, F. Neame, H. Brookman, W. Astbury, H. Sadler, J. Walter, J. Beasley, R. Groom, T. Umbers, J. Kinder, W. R. Lawford, Professor Sewell, W. P. Gaskell, T. Mount, T. W. Granger, J. Gamble, J. H. W. Jones, J. Round, M.P., E. Divett, M.P., T. Knight, R. W. Baker, J. W. Bury, J. Dadds, sen., W. R. Browne, J. Browne, J. C. Clark, T. Beale, J. Gould, R. F. Shawe, W. Hall, J. Hedding, W. Beckford, E. Beck, E. K. Jarvis, R. Rigg, E. Matson, jun., W. Walter, C. Murton, H. Cobb, R. Cobb, G. Kilby, H. Dickinson, W. Beck, J. Houghton, Dr. L. Playfair, J. H. Turner, S. Grantham, E. E. Dawson, F. Tull, T. Bennett, T. Wells, P. Barnes, J. Mee, R. Herbert, G. V. Harcourt, M.P., &c.

His Grace the Duke of RICHMOND having taken the Chair, said, I have been requested by Lord Hardwicke to make an excuse for his non-attendance here to-day, his Lordship being engaged elsewhere upon important business; hence I take the chair for him on the present occasion.

The noble Duke then called upon the Secretary (Mr. Hudson) to read the report of the Society's proceedings for the past year, which was as follows :—

REPORT OF THE COUNCIL.

The society having now obtained an amount of nearly 6,500 members, and excited throughout the kingdom, and even in distant colonies of the empire, a lively interest in the prosecution and success of agricultural improvement, it has become a suitable subject of inquiry at the present moment, to ascertain in what manner and to what extent its labours have tended effectively to disseminate a knowledge of improved systems and carefully tested practices of modern husbandry, and to advance in their turn, by experiment, observation, and sound deduction, the standard of correctness in our general principles of agricultural reasoning.

This important task has been undertaken and accomplished by Mr. Pusey; and in the portion of the journal distributed within these few weeks among the members, your former president has given to the agricultural world a distinct and most interesting survey of the successful mode in which the objects of the society have slowly, but steadily and effectively, developed themselves during that brief period of its history. That contribution to your journal will be regarded as a most important document by the numerous members into whose hands it has, in the ordinary course of circulation, already found its way; and while it supplies to the council a ready exposition of the steady progress of the society in its career of usefulness, it affords to the members at large a satisfactory assurance of the important results which must ultimately be obtained in the prosecution of its national objects.

The council have to record with great satisfaction the successful issue of the annual country meeting of the society at Bristol. The distinguished reception given to the deputation by Mr. Phippen, at the termination of his mayoralty, and his subsequent co-operation, as a member of the local committee, during the preparations for the meeting, at once established that perfect cordiality between the citizens of Bristol and the members of the society, which the no less liberal, zealous, and hospitable co-operation of his successor, Mr. Franklyn, contributed to maintain. To Mr. Franklyn, as chief magistrate of the City of Bristol, the society were indebted for every attention, and especially for the excellent arrangements, made under his authority and that of the high sheriff, magistrates, and corporation, in maintaining the public order of the place, and in consulting the convenience and safety of the members who attended the meeting. The best thanks of the society have already been given to both of these gentlemen.

Mr. Handley, as your president, conveyed also at the time the thanks of the society to Mr. M'Adam, the chairman, and to the members of the Victoria committee, for the gratuitous use of the spacious and commodious rooms in which the official business of the meeting was transacted, and the council dinner took place ; to Mr. Adams, the owner of the site of the show-yard ; to the Bristol Institution, for the use of their theatre, in which Mr. Smith, of Deanston, delivered his valuable lecture on draining, to the members of the society ; and to the Commercial-rooms' committee, the Steam-ship Company, the directors of the Clifton suspension bridge, the vestry of St. Mary, Redcliff, and the other public bodies who gratuitously threw open to the free access and inspection of the members whatever they respectively possessed of general interest. The council felt equally under obligation, at the same time, to the Society of Merchant Venturers, Mr. Ireland Clayfield, Mrs. Worsley, and other individuals, who had liberally offered to the society the free occupation and disposal of their land. To Mr. Miles as the chairman, and to the local committee, the society were indebted for the excellent local arrangements of the period. The registrations of lodgings by Mr. Webb Hall, contributed essentially to the convenience of the members who attended the meeting ; and the devotion of time and energies so cheerfully given by Mr. Marmont, the secretary of the local committee, to the cause of the society, and the numerous surveys and plans of proposed and adopted sites for the purposes of the meeting, including a detailed plan of the Victoria Grounds, drawn to a large scale, constituted an amount of invaluable service, which the council most thankfully acknowledge.

In addition to the splendid exhibition of Devon cattle and other stock at the meeting, and an exhibition of the greatest variety of new agricultural implements hitherto made on any similar occasion, of which an elaborate report has been drawn up by the judges and printed in the journal, the numerous assemblage of persons interested in agriculture from every part of the kingdom, contributed to render the meeting of a highly interesting character. The presence of his Royal Highness the Duke of Cambridge as a governor, and of the Hon. Henry Everett, as an honorary member, and their lively participation in the proceedings of the meeting, were circumstances which, in many national points of view, added a peculiar interest to the occasion.

The council have received from the deputation to the town of Derby a favourable report of the various sites inspected as suitable for the purposes of the show-yard, pavilion, official-rooms, and lecture, to which they were conducted by the mayor, Mr. Colville, the chairman, and the members of the local committee ; and they have announced in the prize sheet, which has been extensively advertised in the public papers in that neighbourhood, as well as in the London agricultural papers, that the principal day of the show is fixed for Thursday, the 13th of July, and that all certificates will be required to be lodged with the Secretary by the 1st of June preceding. The council beg to call the attention of the members of the Society to this rule, they having decided that in no case whatever shall any certificate be received after that date.

The council have, since their last report, passed a resolution affecting the order of their meetings, and defining the character of the business to be transacted at them ; limiting to the first Wednesday in every month, at which any governors can be present, the deliberations and resolutions on the strict official details of the Society's business, and throwing open to the meetings held on the three other Wednesdays of the month the presentation and discussion of communications on subjects of agricultural interest, all members of the society being allowed the privilege of attending these last-mentioned weekly meetings of the council.

At the close of the session in August last, the council confided to Mr. Dean, as honorary director of the works, the arrangements required for adapting the various parts of the society's house to the several objects and purposes decided upon by them at their former meetings. To this important task, Mr. Dean, forming a quorum of the house committee, with the friendly co-operation of Mr. Burke and Mr. Gibbs, has devoted himself during the late autumnal vacation ; and with a success and amount of time and exertion which fully entitle him to the best acknowledgments of the society. Mr. Dean has presented to the council his detailed reports of the progress of the works, and has explained at length the various objects to which each department of his plan is adapted.

Mr. Dean has arranged the basement of the house as a depository for the display of such implements and other objects as the council may think fit to exhibit. On the first floor, in addition to the council and committee rooms, a library and reading room, open to members, has been provided, in which it is intended to form a standard collection of the best works on agricultural science and practice, and to take in, as they appear, the various English and foreign periodicals of an agricultural character, and where cases have already been fitted up for the exhibition of the collections of wheat, grasses, wool, and other objects of permanent interest. The remainder of the house comprises the secretary's apartments, the porter's hall, and dwelling room, the secretary's and clerks' rooms, and the various offices connected with the establishment ; all of which have been fitted up with the greatest attention to the comfort and convenience of the several parties to whom they apply, and, at the same time, with a due regard to judicious economy in the outlay.

The council have resolved not to give the prize to any of the samples of seed wheat selected at the Liverpool Meeting, and tried during the past season, with other varieties commonly grown in the respective neighbourhoods where the trials have been made, and of which the results are given in the last part of the Journal.

The council have to report to the general meeting the following adjudication of the prizes for the essays and reports of experiments in the present year:—

To Barugh Almack, late of Bishop Burton, in the East Riding of the county of York, and now of No. 11, Great George-street, Westminster, and 23, Alexandersquare, Brompton—the prize of 20 sovereigns, for the best report of experiments on the drill husbandry of turnips.

To Andrew Leighton, of Chelveston, near Higham Ferrers, Northamptonshire—the prize of 20 sovereigns, for the best account of the natural history, anatomy, habits, and economy of the wire-room, and the best means of protection against its ravages.

To the Rev. William Lewis Rham, M.A., Vicar of Winkfield, near Bracknell, Berkshire—the prize of 20 sovereigns, for the best essay on the mechanical properties of the plough.

To John Barton, of East Leigh, near Emsworth, Hampshire—the prize of 20 sovereigns, for the best account of the rotations of crops suited for light lands.

To George Fownes, doctor of philosophy in the university of Giessen, and chemical lecturer in the Medical School of the Charing-cross Hospital—the prize of 20 sovereigns for the best essay on the food of plants.

The Council have further to report that no essays were sent in to compete for the prize of 15 sovereigns, offered by the Society for the best account of the varieties of wheat suited to different soils, nor any essay of sufficient merit on the making of cheese. They have received from the judges appointed to consider the merits of the essays competing for the gold medal offered by the Society for the best account on record of the prognosties of natural signs of changes in the weather, their report on the relative merit of the essays on this subject, and, in accordance with the conditions of that prize, the Council have placed copies of the selected essays in the hands of Mr. Morton, jun., of the Whitfield Example Farm, for the purpose of a twelvemonth's accurate and extensive trial of the practical value and general correctness of the rules laid down by the respective writers of these essays, as indicating the signs of such changes of weather.

The council, in pursuance of the conditions of the prize of 10 sovereigns for an account of the best mode of curing butter for future consumption, and for preservation in foreign countries, have had the various samples sent in by the competitors, submitted to the examination and judgment of two eminent dairymen of the metropolis, who have decided, after a very careful examination, that the whole of the samples of butter competing for the society's prize are of very inferior quality, and utterly worthless as proofs of any efficient modes having been employed of curing the butter for future consumption.

The essays for the prize of 20 sovereigns, for the best account of the rotations of crops suited for heavy lands, have received the most careful examination and scrutiny of the judges in that department, without however agreeing in their decision on the particular essay most worthy of the prize. The council have accordingly appointed another member of the society to act as umpire on the comparative merits of the two contending essays, each of which has on this occasion been selected by the judges respectively as the best.

The council have placed the names of the Hon. Henry Everett, the American minister, of Dr. Playfair, the translator of Dr. Liebig's Organic Chemistry applied to Agriculture, and of Mr. Edward Solly, jun., Lecturer on Agricultural Chemistry to the Horticultural Society of London, on the list of the honorary members of the society; and they acknowledged with their best thanks the valuable service Dr. Playfair has rendered to the society in delivering before the members, at their present December meeting, two lectures on the important subject of the application of the principles of physiology to the fattening of cattle.—By order of the council,
London, Dec. 10, 1842. JAMES HUDSON, Sec.

The noble CHAIRMAN, after the Report had been gone through, read the following statement of the Society's funds for the period therein named :—

STATEMENT OF ACCOUNTS FROM JANUARY 1ST TO JUNE 30TH, INCLUSIVE, 1842.

RECEIPTS.	£	s.	d.
Balance in the hands of the bankers, Jan. 1st, 1842	1028	12	2
Balance in the hands of the Secretary, Jan. 1st, 1842	23	13	10
Half-year's dividend on £4,700, new 3½ per cents.	82	5	0
Half-year's dividend on £1,000, 3½ per cent. Reduced Annuities	17	10	0
Amount of subscriptions and compositions	3277	5	0
Sale of Journals	110	18	6
	£4540	4	6

PAYMENTS.	£	s.	d.
Permanent charges	399	10	0
Establishment	384	6	2
Expenses of Journal	790	1	1
Postage and carriage	28	14	6
Advertisements and miscellaneous payments	256	3	0
Country meetings' accounts	65	18	6
Cambridge prize to executor of the late Mr. Putland	15	0	0
Purchase of Stock	1000	0	0
Balance in the hands of the bankers, June 30th, 1842	1587	12	1
Balance in the hands of the Secretary, June 30th, 1842	12	19	2
	£4540	4	6

The above was signed by the auditors, and the Duke of Richmond intimated if any gentleman then present had any question to put, he should be glad to answer it, and that the ledgers would be open to the inspection of all parties after the meeting was over.

Earl SPENCER said, in offering myself to the notice of the meeting, I have to propose a vote of thanks to the gentlemen who formed the Judges at the meeting at Bristol. (*Cheers.*) Theirs was an onerous duty, and our thanks should, I think, be specially offered to them for the skill they exhibited, and the satisfaction they afforded in discharge of the task which devolved upon them. (*Cheers.*) I wish now to say something of the prospects of this society, which are, I am truly glad to say, favourable in every respect but one. This institution has extended itself over the country, and is exciting a great interest amongst all those engaged in agriculture. (*Cheers.*) We have men of great science connected with us, and who have done their utmost in support of that admirable science. (*Loud cheers.*) But there is one drawback to all; I mean the amount of arrears in subscriptions, which, it will be perceived, is not diminishing. This may be attributed to a great number of causes, but not to any disinclination of members to pay the amounts due to the society; neither am I apprehensive that any serious deficit will be apparent in the end. There are, it strikes me, many parties who are not aware of the facilities afforded them, by which money may be transmitted to us; yet I should say that it does require the exertions of every member to amend this state of things. And, I am quite of opinion, there are individuals in various counties who could greatly assist us in this matter. There is one remedy I would propose, that is, the necessity of members being made acquainted with the most simple way in which they could pay their subscriptions. I had not before heard the detailed statement of this report of the arrears, but it strikes me that, as we have nearly 6,500 members, only 3,000 of whom have paid, the readiest mode that could be suggested is, to pay by post-office order. If any, now present, should meet with those who have not paid, they might make this suggestion to them. This is the only objection I see, which, if allowed to go on, will be fatal. I have so often expressed my opinions upon the advantages of this society, that it would be unnecessary for me to dwell upon them now at any length; I shall merely conclude by proposing a vote of thanks to the judges.

F. PYM, Esq., seconded the motion of the noble Earl. He considered there were two ways of getting over the difficulties mentioned by Earl Spencer. One of them, it was true, involved expense—that of having collectors in different counties, who, for 6d. in the pound, would be glad to collect the subscriptions; the other was for members themselves to collect. Mr. Pym concluded by observing that, were the latter plan adopted, he would undertake to collect, with very little trouble to himself, nearly the whole amounts due in the county of Bedford. (*Cheers.*)

Colonel CHALLONER next rose and said :—From what Lord Spencer has said, I feel myself bound, after having been in the finance chair, to give as clear a statement as possible of the matter touching the arrears of subscriptions. Up to the 1st of January, 1842, there were 3,277 remaining unpaid. The proportion to arrears and composition, we have pretty accurately discovered; but how far we shall have to put the full determination of the Council into effect is rather difficult to determine. I should propose, then, that a much further investment should take place. We have now 102 Life Governors, which, at 50l. each, produces 5,100l.; we have, also, 376 Life Members, yielding, at 10l., 3,760l.—making a total of 8,860l., which sum, I think, ought to be invested. Last year, we purchased 1,000l. stock, and we have now in the funds 6,700l. It is, therefore, very evident that we ought to have laid out more money at interest; but the reason is the amount of arrear, which appears on the sheet I now hold in my hand. Your arrears at the same time in 1838, were 30l., but which have since been reduced to 7l., which amount was, it is conceived, owing by persons who are dead, consequently, not likely to be recovered. At the same period in 1839, they were 106l.; in 1840, 264l.; in 1841, 1,108l.; then, if you take the arrears with this and the preceding years, they will be found 2,315l.—altogether in three

F

years 1,714*l.*—making a total of 5,151*l.* A gentleman had said that a Committee should have been formed to collect the arrears, by which they would have been secured. A collector would, in my judgment, have great difficulties to surmount, and no satisfactory result could be looked forward to. I agree with Lord Spencer, that individual members as collectors would be useful; so would also be a county-list. In taking leave of the financial chair, I have to return thanks to the Committee; while I shall be most happy at all times to give this society every assistance in my power (*cheers*).

Mr. PUSEY said he had great pleasure in offering his best thanks to Dr. Playfair, who had given them two able lectures relative to agriculture (*cheers*). He (Mr. Pusey) did not think that hardly any person was in a position to offer any new feature in agriculture ; yet he had much gratification in offering his tribute of praise to one whom he hoped had opened a road which might prove valuable to him at no distant day (*cheers*). He therefore proposed that the thanks of the meeting be given to Dr. Playfair for his talented exertions.

The motion having been put from the chair, and carried unanimously,

The Duke of RICHMOND, addressing Dr. Playfair, said—I have great pleasure in conveying to you the thanks of this meeting. I join with it in the hope that future events may tend to your advantage (*applause*).

Mr. HANDLEY having proposed a vote of thanks to the Duke of Richmond for his able conduct in the chair, his grace replied by stating that he did not think any merit was due to him, as he there enjoyed a complete sinecure. But he agreed that this Society must prove of great benefit to agriculture, and consequently to the country at large (*cheers*).

The meeting was then declared dissolved.

At a Monthly Council held on Wednesday, the 7th of December—present, his Grace the Duke of Richmond, K.G., in the chair, Earl of Hardwicke, Earl of Ducie, Hon. Captain Spencer, Sir Hungerford Hoskyns, Bart., Colonel Austen, Thomas Raymond Barker, Esq., Colonel Challoner, C. R. Colville, Esq., M.P., James Dean, Esq., Henry Handley, Esq., W. G. Hayter, Esq., M.P., C. Hillyard, Esq., W. Fisher Hobbs, Esq., Samuel Jonas, Esq., George Kimberley, Esq., John Kinder, Esq., Philip Pusey, Esq., M.P., W. Woods Page, Esq., Dr. Lyon Playfair, William Shaw, Esq., John Villiers Shelley, Esq., Rev. J. R. Smythies, Professor Sewell, Professor Solly, Charles Stokes, Esq., and H. S. Thompson, Esq.—

Colonel John Le Couteur, Viscount of the Island of Jersey, and B. T. Brandreth Gibbs, Esq., of Half-moon-street, Piccadilly, and the Lodge, Old Brompton, were elected Governors, and the following gentlemen Members of the Society :—Thomas Holme Maude, Blawith Cottage, Cartmell, Lancashire ; James Harrison, Crimble, Rochdale, Lancashire ; Samuel Holker Haslam, Greenside Cottage, Milnthorpe, Westmoreland ; Daniel Robert Scration, Mitton Hall, Southend, Essex ; A. Thomas Edwards, Colchester, Essex ; Captain William Jones, Glanbrane, Neath, Glamorganshire ; Alfred Henry Cherry, Clapham, Surrey ; Edwin East, Streatham, Surrey ; William Beattie Booth, Carclew, Penryn, Cornwall.

Colonel Challoner presented the Report of the Finance Committee, and Mr. Dean that of the House Committee, which were respectively confirmed. On the motion of Mr. Hayter, M.P., it was resolved, that it be referred to the Finance Committee to suggest the mode which, in their opinion, is most advisable for the purpose of collecting the subscriptions in arrear ; and to report to the Monthly Council in February next.

On the motion of Mr. Handley, it was resolved, that the replies received to the letter addressed by him, at the request of the Council, to the members in arrear of their subscription, be referred to a committee, consisting of Mr. Shaw, Mr. Hayter, and Mr. Dean, with a re-

quest that they would report the result of their examination to the Monthly Council in February.

It was resolved that all Books, &c., borrowed from the Society by any of the Members, should be returned, for the purpose of completing the Catalogue of the Library.

The Draught of the Report to the General Meeting was laid before the Council, and referred to the Journal Committee.

Mr. Handley laid before the Council a report of his communication with the Chairman of the Great Western Railway, when he was requested to form, with Earl Spencer and Mr. Pusey, M.P., a deputation to confer with the Chairman and Directors of that Company on the subject of the complaints made in reference to the Railway charges at the period of the Bristol Meeting.

Mr. Handley also laid before the Council his report on the schedule of Prizes to be offered for Agricultural Implements at the Meeting at Derby ; when the Council having proceeded through the list of the various prizes proposed in that department, appointed a committee, consisting of Mr. Handley, Mr. Barker, Lord Ducie, and Mr. Shaw, to arrange and direct the publication of the General Prize Sheet and forms of Certificate for the ensuing Country Meeting.

Colonel Challoner presented the Report of the Members of the General Derby Committee, who had visited that town as a deputation on the 15th of November last, by direction of the Council, for the purpose of inspecting and reporting on the most suitable sites for the various objects of the meeting. This report was adopted by the Council, and referred to the General Derby Committee for the discussion of its details, and such communication as they may require with the Local Committee in reference to them.

On the motion of Mr. Handley, Mr. Parkes, C. E., was authorised to purchase for the Society, before the meeting at Derby, two standard dynamometers, each of different range of draught respectively, for greater and less resistance, to be reserved for the purpose of the trial of implements.

Mr. Gibbs gave notices of motion for the Monthl Council in February on points connected with the announcement (by means of a printed card) of the dates of meeting to the members of the Council, the rate of advertizing in the Journal, and the mode of its being printed.

The list of new committees to come into operation on the 1st of January, under the new bye-law, was discussed and settled.

The following communications and presents were received :—

Sir Francis Mackenzie, Bart., a letter to the Earl of Hardwicke, on a fair trial of the comparative merits of the various ploughs now in use throughout Great Britain.

Miss Molesworth: An ear and sample of barley raised from corns found amongst Turkish Wheat. It had ripened nearly a fortnight before the Chevalier in the same field. It was grown on loam : subsoil, yellowish, sandy clay, under-drained. Miss Molesworth expressed her willingness to place at the disposal of the Society a portion of the seed, should it be thought worth growing where its ripening a fortnight earlier than the Chevalier would be an advantage.

Miss Smedley : Specimens of wheat.

Sir Harry Verney, Bart. : A specimen of the Hope-toun oat.

Mr. Henry Price : Specimen of a prolific wheat found growing in a garden in Kent.

Mr. Hollist : Specimen of Talavera wheat grown in Sussex.

Sir Charles Morgan, Bart. : Samples of cloth made from the wool of the black mountain sheep of South Wales, made up without any process of dyeing.

Professor Lindley : Roots of the Bassano Beet, a sort of mangel-wurzel with turnip-like roots, from the north of Italy, probably a trial on land that will not carry mangel-wurzel.

Mr. Ormsby Gore, M.P., and Mr. Fisher Hobbs: Specimens of turnips.

Mr. J. F. Peacey: Regulations and premiums of the Winchcomb Farmers' Club.

The Duke of Richmond: Two impressions of a lithographic view of the Pavilion and Great Dinner of the Highland and Agricultural Society at Edinburgh.

Mr. Edward Dixon: An impression of the portrait of Mr. John Price, by F. Tatham, of Winchester.

Mr. Davis: A framed and coloured print of the Duke of Bedford's Prize Herefordshire Bull at the Cambridge Meeting.

Mr. Thompson: Specimen of a draining tile.

Highland and Agricultural Society of Scotland—the Quarterly Journal; Mr. Shaw—the Farmer's Magazine; Mr. Youatt—the Veterinarian; Martin Doyle—Cyclopædia of Husbandry; Mr. Stephen—Book of the Farm.

The Council then adjourned to Saturday the 10th of December; when there were present the Duke of Richmond, in the chair, Earl Spencer, Thomas Raymond Barker, Esq., James Dean, Esq., C. Hillyard, Esq., W. Fisher Hobbs, Esq., Philip Pusey, Esq., M.P., Francis Pym, Esq., and H. S. Thompson, Esq.

John Bell Crompton, Esq., Mayor of Derby, was elected a member of the Derby Local Committee.

Mr. Pusey laid before the Council the schedule of Implement Prizes, which was adopted and ordered to be advertised in the usual agricultural papers.

The report of the Council to the general meeting was received from the Journal Committee, and adopted.

The Judges of the samples competing for the prize offered by the Society for cured butter, transmitted the report of their examination of the several jars, when the Council decided that no prize should be awarded to any of the samples, but that a compensation of 9d. per lh., as the estimated original market price of the butter when made, should be allowed to each of the parties who had competed.

The Council then adjourned over the Christmas recess to the first Wednesday in February.

AN EXAMPLE TO LANDLORDS.—At a rent-day of G. C. Courthope, Esq., of Willegh, near Ticehurst, that liberal gentleman made a deduction of 20 per cent. from the rents of his tenants, who had complained of the great depression which existed, and observed that should the times not be more promising on the next occasion he would be willing to act accordingly. The farmer's labourers in the vicinity are raising a labour rate amongst themselves to keep them from going into the union.—*Morning Herald.*

REDUCTION OF RENTS.—Lady De Mauley, at the audit held at Paulett on Tuesday se'nnight, kindly authorized her steward to return to her tenants 20l. per cent. out of their respective rents. This considerate lady is the owner of very extensive property in and around Pawlett, including the fertile district of the Pawlett Hams; and has also very large possessions in Dorset and Gloucestershire, throughout which, the same generous manifestation will no doubt be extended.—*Taunton Courier.*

RENTS.—Francis Phillips, Esq., the proprietor of the Abbey Cwmhyr Estates, in consideration of the reduced prices of landed stocks and distressing pressure under which the farmers at present are labouring, has proposed, as an encouragement to his tenants, to reduce, at his next Christmas rent meeting, the rents due at Michaelmas next, ten per cent. This privilege his tenants who quit at Lady-day next will enjoy, as well as those that continue for the future.—*Hereford Times.*

We are happy to find that several of the landlords in Norfolk have postponed their audits, in consequence of the distressed state of agriculture, and wishing to give their suffering tenantry a chance of obtaining a better price for their corn, rather than compel them to sell out at the present ruinous prices. We trust and hope the Suffolk gentry will be actuated by the same good feeling, which we are sure will be highly appreciated by the occupiers.—*Ipswich Journal.*

DRAINAGE OF LAND AND TOWNS.

TO THE EDITOR OF THE FARMER'S MAGAZINE.

(See Advertisement.)

SIR,—The object of the advertisement, is to call attention to a publication now in progress—on the drainage of lands and towns—upon which I am desirous of laying an outline before your readers, and will, therefore, refer to the several articles in the order in which they appear in the advertisement.

Stratford Marshes.—These marshes were inundated to a serious extent in January in the last year, occasioned by a sudden thaw after a long frost and heavy snow, and a very high tide; and again in October, occasioned principally by an extraordinary high tide; also in November, from long continued rains and a high tide. So injurious were these floods to the occupiers of land in the marshes, and of houses in the village of Stratford, that several of the inhabitants really imagined that, from some neglect or something worse on the part of the marsh jury and bailiff, these unusually severe visitations had alone arisen; and, acting upon that belief, early in the last year got up a memorial assuming as facts things quite impossible, never once glancing at the true cause of the evils; and so satisfied were the memorialists that they would be able to prove every word in their memorial to be true, that they printed and circulated it, employed counsel to support the allegations contained in it, and during two long days, of nine hours each, battled their case before J. B. Bosanquet, Esq., (in the chair) Sir J. Henry Pelley, Bart., and eight other commissioners, with an ardour and an earnestness quite extraordinary. Mr. Turner (a very rising solicitor) and myself, on the behalf of the marsh jury and bailiff, printed and circulated a reply to the allegations contained in the memorial, together with a report which I had drawn up, from my professional as from my local knowledge of the circumstances which had mainly contributed to, if they had not wholly produced, the floods in question. In that report I have said—"I am convinced that the evils complained of in the memorial had their origin in causes far different from those stated; which causes neither the marsh jury, the bailiff, nor the commissioners themselves could have averted, nor can in future avert without more extensive powers than it appears they now possess; these causes being the insufficiency of the present rivers to convey away the flood waters arising from the drainage of the land on each side of the valley of the Lea for agricultural purposes; from the interruption of the free flow of the waters by the embankments of the Eastern Counties and Northern and Eastern railways, and from the deep cuttings in the marshes on each side of the railways for the purpose of raising the roadway, those cuttings conveying the flood waters with greater rapidity to the Thames than heretofore; hence the necessity for widening and deepening the ancient brooks and rivers where practicable, and where not practicable by the formation of new channels of outlet, and by those means only can serious inundations ever be prevented."

In the Stratford case almost every allegation of the memorialists was disproved to the satisfaction of the commissioners, and to a large assemblage of persons, brought together from very distant places, so important was the enquiry considered. One very important fact was mentioned by the chairman towards the close of the first day's enquiry, well deserving the serious consideration of philosophers and men of science. "He would," he said, "just mention that, from some reason or other, the tides have been higher of late years than formerly. In 1810 the greatest flood was 2 feet 5 inches above the Trinity standard; between that time and 1814, 2 feet 7 inches; in 1815, 2 feet; in 1824, 3 feet; and on this occasion, in 1841, the tide rose no less than 3 feet 4 inches above the Trinity standard: from which the memorialists would see that there were other causes for the evil beyond those alleged by them."

I refer in the advertisement to a report on the drainage of South Holland, undertaken by me at the instance of a noble duke, the late Right Honourable Sir Joseph Banks, Bart., and several other noblemen and gentlemen, to show that my attention has been called to the draining of land from a very distant period. The last considerable drainage carried into effect by me was in a parish in Huntingdonshire, partly fen and partly high land. As a land-agent I have ever considered draining to be the first step towards improvement, and to the landowner and tenant farmer, paramount, in point of advantage, over all other agricultural improvements, and as regards the health of the neighbourhood, of the very highest importance.

Why Mr. Handley's bill did not pass I cannot quite understand; its objects were such as every landowner must acknowledge to be just and necessary. Perhaps it would have better suited the taste of the aristocracy had it been an enabling and not a directing bill; with that change in its construction I have no doubt it would pass if again brought forward; and if, after some experience, it should be found to require enlarged and stronger powers, an amended bill might supply the defect.

Mr. Pusey's bill shared a better fate, although, practically, little advantage has yet arisen from it. Still it is a good point to start anew from, and I will hope that in another session of Parliament an amended bill will be introduced, taking away or modifying the power of the Court of Chancery to interfere, giving the jurisdiction to the Judges of Assize when on the circuit in the several counties; or, what probably would be better, converting the present Tithe Commissioners, whose labours are drawing towards a close, into a permanent Drainage Commission, with the requisite powers to enable them to deal with the whole subject. I hope also, that the provisions of the bill will be extended to the estates of corporations, ecclesiastical as well as civil, since no property is so badly managed as to drainage as are corporation lands generally.

The next matter in the advertisement relates to a subject of great and serious moment to the country at large, that of giving power to the surveyors of the highways to cleanse and deepen water-courses from their head or source to some main brook or river, the first great step to thorough-draining; nor does there appear to be any solid objection to that power being given to surveyors of highways which might not be urged with equal reason against allowing those officers to scour, cleanse, and deepen not only the ditches and drains which are on the sides of the public highways, but those also which are within the adjoining fields, if the ditches happen to be on the field side of the fences.

Those powers, it will be remembered, were first given to surveyors by the present General Highway Act, and have, as I know from experience, been attended with very beneficial results. But that would not be the only advantage of such an extended provision. Hundreds of labourers would get employment from the landowners or their tenants in these cleansings and deepenings during the winter season, upon finding that the surveyors had the power of ordering the work to be performed, and of charging the landowner or occupier of the land with a portion of the expense. Many a good labourer would then get work who now, alas! seeks relief at the union workhouse. As a guardian in a union of parishes, partly town, but chiefly agricultural, having a population little short of sixty thousand souls, it distresses me to witness week by week the claims of honest industrious men and their families famishing from the want of food, the guardians having no power to assist them further than offering relief to them in the house—to them a prison; because, when there, shut out from the world, who enquires for the poor man? who thinks of fetching him back to his home—once a home—some ten or twelve miles off, to do a day's work? It is not practicable to do so; there he pines away his strength. And when he quits the house, as the spring returns, broken-hearted and bowed down to the earth, his cottage and his furniture gone, he becomes good for but little, and his children—if he has children—from being made paupers in their younger days, remain paupers all their lives! His wife too, from mixing with the other inmates, many of them of the most vicious description, soon loses all self-respect, becomes idle, slothful, and careless, regardless of what may happen next—a burthen to herself, to the parish, and all about her.

Still, I am bound to say, I cannot blame the law, or the commissioners, or the guardians—at least not the guardians of the Edmonton Union. They would gladly adopt any means which the law will allow, of giving beneficial employment to all able-bodied labourers who apply for relief, if it were in their power to do so, and would hail any measure to which the legislature might give effect, that should have for its object the providing of beneficial employment for them.

That beneficial employment for a large number of agricultural labourers would result from rendering those provisions of the General Highway Act which relate to the appointing of district surveyors compulsory, it is impossible to doubt, particularly if the districts should be made co-extensive with the several Unions appointed for the relief of the poor; the guardians being authorized to make such appointments, and the district surveyors having such powers given to them as would enable them to scour, cleanse, deepen, widen, and extend all sewers, drains, and watercourses from their head or source to the nearest brook or other outlet within their respective districts.

When the Right Hon. the Speaker of the House of Commons, and a noble Duke, distinguished as the friends of agriculture and of the industrious labouring classes, were engaged in carrying the General Highway Bill through parliament, I had the honour of attending them upon several occasions, in reference to that Bill; when it was distinctly understood, that if the clauses which enabled the rate-payers to form parishes into districts for the purpose of appointing efficient paid surveyors should not be taken advantage of by parishes, it would be for parliament to amend the Act, by introducing clauses of a compulsory character, and such other amendments as experience might suggest. The experience of five years has shown that few, if any, parishes have formed such districts, and therefore it is that I venture to hope that the noble Duke will think the time has arrived when a compulsory measure may be introduced into parliament with the greatest advantage to the country.

The drainage of towns is the last item in the advertisement.

For illustration I have selected a densely populated neighbourhood, probably the worst drained town district in the kingdom, viz., the parishes of Whitechapel, Spitalfields, and Bethnal-green, situated north-eastward of, and adjoining to, the city of London, between Whitechapel road on the south-east, Bishopsgate-street and the High-street, Shoreditch, on the west, Hackney-road on the north, and Victoria-park, now in the course of formation, on the east. Between Whitechapel and low-water mark in the old river Lea, at Old Ford, the fall in the ground is very considerable, quite sufficient to effectually drain the district in question, and terminating in a situation most favourable for receiving, filtering, and preserving of the soil, issuing from the proposed great sewer for agricultural purposes.

In the advertisement I have given a general outline of the direction in which I would recommend the sewer to be carried, viz., through a line of streets to commence at the termination of the street now in progress at Spitalfields church, and proceeding thence to the new Victoria-park, also in progress, thence through the park and across the highroad leading from Mile-end and Bow, through Old Ford to Hackney, thence across the marshes below Old Ford; there to terminate in a series of ponds, the foul water to be filtered by means of sluices easy of construction, leaving the soil in a solid state, for removal by barge or otherwise, in the direction of demand for agricultural purposes, producing, beyond all doubt, thousands of tons of the finest manure yearly, and the filtered water, full of ammonia, might be conveyed into the marshes below Stratford, to irrigate the land to a large extent. Nor can it be doubted that a continuation of the road, after passing through the Victoria-park, across the marshes (about half a mile in extent) in the direction of the village of Stratford, terminating near to the new church, and to the stations of the Eastern Counties and Northern and Eastern Railways, would have a most beneficial tendency, not only in promoting a direct communication between the eastern and northern counties with the Victoria park, the City, the Regent's-park, and the west end of the town generally, but would increase the value of property in those directions to an extent of which but a very faint idea can at this time be formed. Nor would the continuation of the new street, now in progress, to Spitalfields-church, in the direction of Shoreditch-church, and following the present line of street by Hoxton-square to the City-road, be less beneficial than the one last described, because avoiding a narrow and most inconvenient portion of street, which is between the terminus of the Eastern Counties and Northern and Eastern Railways and Shoreditch church; besides which, it is more than probable that at no very distant period a market for butcher's meat, poultry, fish, roots, vegetables and fruits, upon an extensive scale, will be formed at or near to the terminus of

the railways in Shoreditch, in the stead of the present Spitalfields market; which is much too small and inconvenient for the amount of the traffic carrying on, and would also be a means of getting rid of a great nuisance in the narrow part of the street between the said terminus and Shoreditch-church. Such a market as that proposed would greatly increase the traffic on the railways, and would be beneficial to the farmers of Essex, Suffolk, Norfolk, Lincolnshire, and to the inhabitants of the neighbourhood of the market generally.

Since I first published an outline of the plan herein described, a commission has been appointed by Her Majesty the Queen, to inquire into the drainage and other considerable improvements of which London and its neighbourhood is susceptible; to those commissioners my labours will be submitted, in full confidence that they will have that attention which may be due to their merits, if any— and I require no more. J. DEAN.
Tottenham, Dec. 21.

FARMER'S CLUB HOUSE.

A meeting of the provisional committee, formed for the purpose of considering the propriety of establishing a Farmer's Club House in London, was held pursuant to notice, on Thursday, Dec. 1. About sixteen members of the Committee attended. There were also several gentlemen present who took an interest in the subject, but who were not members of the Committee. The chair was taken by John Hudson, Esq., of Castleacre, Norfolk. The object of the meeting having been stated, a lengthened discussion took place in reference to the amount of entrance fee and annual subscription, and also as to the locality in which a club house should be situated, so as to meet the convenience of farmers visiting the metropolis, and much useful information upon the subject was elicited. There was not the slightest difference of opinion on the advantage of establishing a Farmer's Club House. Some of the members were desirous of having a high entrance fee, with a view to form a fund for erecting a building at some future period; but the more general feeling appeared to be that both the entrance fee and the subscription should be kept as low as possible. Resolutions were agreed upon, and the Committee broke up. On Friday morning another meeting was held, and two resolutions were passed, first— "That it was highly desirable that a club house should be established, the members to pay an entrance fee, and an annual subscription." And, secondly—"That the Provisional Committee be requested to give their best attention to the subject, to prepare a prospectus, and adopt such means as they may deem best calculated to ensure the success of the object." We are given to understand that the Committee will go actively to work without delay, and that it will not be long before we shall be enabled to announce the prospectus. In the mean time any suggestions upon the subject will be acceptable to the Committee.— *Mark Lane Express.*

THE PROPOSED FARMERS' CLUB IN LONDON.

"Union is strength."

TO THE EDITOR OF THE MARK LANE EXPRESS.

SIR,—The above proverb I wish to see the agriculturists more generally adopt ; for, though few or none will deny its truth, yet our acts do not seem to imply that we wished to be strong, or believed in its efficacy. Doubtless some may say we have made great progress of late towards union, in assembling at county agricultural meetings, and at the great Royal Agricultural Society; and that our being scattered over the whole face of the country prevents our uniting, as townsmen may do who are all huddled together, and may be assembled at any time by the ring of a bell, or such like. But if we cannot be so easily called together, we can unite in petitioning, when our common interest is assailed ; could all subscribe something to promote our general interest, if needed ; could all patronise the Farmers' Club-houses in London.

It cannot be denied that we should be a powerful body if united, and should then be able to stand against our common enemy, the Anti-corn Law League, who were met together the other week, and giving from fifty to three hundred pounds each towards demolishing the little protection we now have on corn. It is owing entirely to union that they are become such a powerful body : by union they can make what laws they like, and take from us whatever protection best pleases them ; and by disunion we are unable to stand against them, for the good of ourselves and the agricultural population. I know not how it can be said of the manufacturers that they are a more distressed people than the agriculturists, when they subscribe their hundreds of pounds—which I know would be quite out of the power of the farmers to do—thereby shewing that they have more money to proclaim their poverty than we have to maintain our present situation.

All should now unite in patronising the Farmers' Club-house in London, for the many social and other advantages it possesses. There we could easily meet, since railroads are so common, for adopting measures to relieve our distress, or petition for the removal of grievances: it would be the agricultural focus. I fear many farmers will plead that they are very seldom in London ; but if they were never there, they had better subscribe the trifle it would require—for since we have such energetic neighbours in the north striving hard for repeal of import duties, we must stir too, and make small sacrifices to preserve the little we have, and prevent our whole stock in trade from being seized for debt and taxes.   A FARMER.
Dec. 20.

AGRICULTURAL QUERIES.

SIR,—Would you be kind enough to ask some of your scientific correspondents to answer you the following questions. I farm a magnesian limestone farm in the following course :—turnips manured with twelve 3 horse cart loads of rotten manure per acre ; barley, seeds pastured ; wheat drilled with 5 cwt. of rape dust per acre. The turnips are always eaten on the ground with sheep where grown. What is the quantity of organic and inorganic matter taken off by each crop ? and what is the quantity of those matters returned by the manure and rape dust, as well as by the droppings of the sheep whilst eating the turnips and seeds, and by the rotting of the roots of the clover and seeds ploughed in for wheat ?

Say my crops are—turnips, 20 tons ; barley, 38 hush. ; wheat, 27 bush. per acre.

The answering of the above queries will greatly oblige, yours,   C. C.

SIR,—I should feel much obliged to any one of your readers that could inform me what is the prevailing colour of the Ayrshire breed of cattle, and their peculiar qualities ? and at what price some of the best breeds could be procured for, say, two years old in calf ? An early reply in your paper will oblige, sir, your obedient servant,
Dec. 14.   A CONSTANT READER.

SIR,—I would feel under an obligation if any of your correspondents would favour me with the most expeditious and effective, and at the same time, economical method of reducing couch to manure ; and if they can give me the analysis of the manure so made, it would be an additional obligation.

I have an opportunity of obtaining a considerable quantity of the top and branches of the fir tree, principally larch, the ashes of which I wish to put upon my land ; perhaps some of your chemico-agricultural friends will oblige me by stating their composition, and the most rational mode of applying them as a fertilizer.

I am, your obedient servant,
Teeswater-side, Dec. 12.   A GOTH.

ANSWER TO QUERIES.

TO THE EDITOR OF THE MARK LANE EXPRESS.

SIR,—Your journal of the 7th November came to hand this evening. In it I observe a letter subscribed " A North Country Farmer," containing several queries in regard to the experiment in turnip husbandry inserted in your number for the 24th October last.

As this experiment was merely a repetition of a former one reported and minutely described in your journal for the 30th December 1839, I might simply refer " A North Country Farmer" to it, only assuring him that in the late instance there was no variation from the practice previously reported. By perusing that former communication he will also find that a heavier crop is not the only, or even the most important, advantage resulting from complete autumn tillage ; that it renders the farmer almost independent as regards the state of the weather at the period of sowing, while the land will be in a higher state of preparation than he can bring it to by any possible spring tillage.

That " A North Country Farmer" may have no room to complain that I evade his questions, I shall give answers to them all, though perhaps not in the order in which he puts them ; only premising that if he would be kind enough to reconsider the paper on which his queries are founded, and reflect that it is simply to report the comparative advantage as to quantity of crop, he may be led to perceive that the only question applicable to the case is the quantity and quality of the manure applied to both portions of the field.

The field on which the late experiment was made had lain at least fifty years in grass and pastured. For the purpose of draining and other improvements it was broke up in the autumn of 1838. In 1839 a crop of oats was taken; in 1840 a crop, partly turnips, beans, and potatoes—both the last without applying any manure; in 1841 the whole was cropped with wheat; and in 1842 turnips. Farmyard manure was used on both portions of the field, carted direct from the close, and immediately applied to the drills. No means were employed to ascertain the exact quantity; for having always a good supply, a liberal allowance is generally given.

Both portions of the field were equally treated as to quantity and quality. Before sowing the autumn prepared portion, a brush harrow, as in 1839, was passed along the drills to destroy any annuals that had vegetated, and a double-moulded plough was employed to lay up any portion of the soil that had fallen down. The spring prepared portion was ploughed from stubble the previous November, and the drills made up immediately before sowing. The practice on this farm was formerly to have the width of drills 28 inches; but farther experience seems to shew that 30 inches is preferable, and from 12 to 15 inches betwixt plant and plant. The weight reported included both bulbs and stems.

I am, Sir, yours most respectfully,
JAMES SCOUGALL.

Balgone, East Lothian, Nov. 30.

AGRICULTURAL REPORT.

GENERAL AGRICULTURAL REPORT FOR DECEMBER.

In laying before our readers a general review of agricultural affairs of the month, we will, in the first place, direct their attention to the atmospheric influences. That they have been, on the whole, favourable to vegetation no doubt can be entertained, yet the young wheat plants have stood in need of a few sharp frosts to check premature exuberance. It is, however, gratifying to learn that they are exhibiting, in almost all parts of England, a very flourishing and vigorous appearance, and bid fair for good forthcoming crops. From the month's commencement until its close scarcely a day elapsed without rain having fallen, yet the actual amount, in the aggregate, has not exceeded that at the corresponding period of some past years. On the 22nd and 25th the weather became seasonably cold, and thin ice was produced; but with these exceptions it has proved extremely mild, the barometer having stood unusually high.

The exertions of the agricultural body have, we have great pleasure in stating, been crowned with complete success in the process of committing the seed to the soil, and it is admitted by all that a finer period for that purpose has not been recollected since 1836. Thus far matters are cheering, but when we compare the value of the produce on hand with that of last year, we perceive much cause for despondency; and, notwithstanding some persons engaged in farming appear to be looking forward to an improved state of things bearing immediately upon their interests, we regret that we cannot lead ourselves to the same conclusion. Now it will be conceded that supply has much influence upon the ruling prices. Although partial failures of the wheat crop in this country have been apparent, we are firmly convinced that the actual yield was nearly adequate to meet every want until the conclusion of next harvest, unless, indeed, it should prove a late one. Add to this the immense imports of foreign corn, and we shall find a surplus on hand. We have all along contended, and still contend, that the quotations of corn must rule low, especially as relates to wheat, and the correctness of our assertions has been fully borne out by passing events. It is true, large quantities of wheat of foreign produce have gone into consumption during the last two months, yet the quantities in warehouse are still large, they amounting to nearly a million and a half of quarters, and both holders and speculators appear to be impressed with the belief that the spring markets will be anything but brisk; however, the transactions at the various shipping ports up the Baltic, Black Sea, and Mediterranean, for forward delivery, have been limited in the extreme.

A fewer number of really inferior samples of wheat offering at Mark Lane and elsewhere has been scarcely ever noticed; and the same observation may be applied to most other kinds of grain. The averages have again ruled extremely low, and any alteration in the duties for some time hence is wholly out of the question.

The potato crop has been more than usually large, with quality seldom surpassed, much less equalled. The process of raising it has occupied much of the time of the farm labourers, and the receipts at the various markets have been very large. This, together with the abundance of green vegetables, has caused the demand for all descriptions to rule heavy at very low rates of currency—the very best York reds have sold with difficulty at 60s. per ton. Only one or two small cargoes have arrived in London from Ireland, and from Holland and France about 70 tons have been received. The latter being of a very inferior description, have produced only from 20s. to 30s. per ton.

Owing to the absence of moisture in August, the growth of turnips has proved small. On some of the light soils, scarcely half a crop has been procured, with a considerable deficiency on the heavy ones; the graziers have, therefore, found it necessary to use more cake, carrots, hay, &c., for their stock, which has fared tolerably well. As to the epidemic, this has again made its appearance, though not with its accustomed virulence, in some of our northern and midland grazing districts, and great losses have been sustained in the transmission of the beasts and sheep to the different markets. We much hope that the Council of the Royal Agricultural Society will continue their spirited exertions to discover a remedy for this scourge, for such we may with justice term it.

Throughout our provinces, the supplies of Wheat offering direct from the farmers, have been but moderate, yet the demand has ruled dull. The finest descriptions of both red and white have mostly sold at previous rates, but the middling and inferior kinds have suffered a further decline. For free foreign wheat, there appears to have been a fair retail enquiry, and some few thousand quarters of bonded have changed hands at Liverpool, Hull, and Bristol, on speculation, at full quotations. Barley has been plentiful, and must be noted a shade lower in price. In malt, very little has been passing: nevertheless, its value has been supported. The oat trade has ruled dull in the face of small receipts. Beans, peas, and flour heavy.

As regards the importation of stock under the new tariff, it has been of a very meagre character during the whole of the month; the principal arrivals have been from Hamburgh and Spain. From the former, we have received about 100; and from the latter, 220 oxen and cows; about one-third has been in good condition; the remainder being much beneath the middle quality. Very few more supplies of stock can now be received from Germany or Holland until the spring, as most of the ports and rivers are becoming frozen up. From what we have been able to learn, some very extensive receipts of good stock may be then expected—many of the Dutch, German, and Spanish graziers having procured the aid of English feeders. Since the present measure has passed the legislature, the following arrivals have been reported, and which may serve as a good guide to those interested.

	Beasts.	Cows.	Sheep.	Pigs.
From Germany..	1191	356	284	52
Spain	878	114	230	—
Holland ..	594	204	—	20
France	401	38	140	—
Totals..	2064	712	654	72

Forming a grand total of 3502 head of different kinds of stock. Very few of the beasts from either Germany or Spain have realized a profit to their owners; while, in numerous instances, losses of from 2l. to 3l. per head have been experienced.

According to our Scotch advices, the corn trade has ruled heavy, yet no variation of moment has taken place in the quotations, but they have certainly had a downward tendency. It is admitted on all hands that the available supplies of grain are extremely good. The potato crop is represented as very abundant. Very dull accounts have reached us from Ireland, whence the shipments of produce to England, caused by the miserably low figures ruling in our markets, have been small. The deliveries of corn at the different markets have been good, with prices on the decline.

The following is a monthly statement of the supplies and prices of fat stock, exhibited and sold in Smithfield Cattle Market, since the date of our last report.

The supplies of beasts have amounted to 14,320; of sheep, 129,400; of calves, 1,132; and of pigs, 2,412. Those quarters from which the arrivals of beasts came to hand were as follow :—Lincolnshire, Leicestershire, Northamptonshire, &c., 7,100 shortborns ; Norfolk, Suffolk, Essex, and Cambridgeshire, 600 Scots and homebreds ; from our western and midland districts, 3,000 Herefords, runts, Durhams, Devons, and Irish beasts : other parts of England, 2,500 of various breeds; Scotland, by sea, 212 horned and polled Scots ; and from Ireland, via Liverpool, 300 Irish beasts.

The quotations have ranged as follow :—beef, from 3s. 2d. to 4s. 6d.; mutton, 3s. 4d. to 4s. 6d.; veal, 3s. 8d. to 4s. 8d.; and pork, 3s. 8d. to 4s. 8d., per 8lbs. to sink the offals.

The general quality of the stock brought forward has been more than usually good, indeed the collection has exhibited some of the most extraordinary animals both for shape and size we ever saw. For the primest qualities the demand has ruled firm, at full rates of currency ; and the value of the middling and inferior kinds has been freely supported, with a fair attendance of buyers.

A STATEMENT and COMPARISON of the SUPPLIES and PRICES of FAT STOCK, exhibited and sold in SMITHFIELD CATTLE MARKET, on Monday, Dec. 27, 1841, and Monday, Dec. 26, 1842.

At per 8lbs. to sink the offals.

	Dec. 27, 1841.		Dec. 26, 1842.	
	s. d.	s. d.	s. d.	s. d.
Coarse & inferior Beasts	3 4 to 3	6 ..	3 2	3 4
Second quality do.	3 8	3 10 ..	3 6	3 10
Prime large Oxen......	4 0	4 2 ..	4 0	4 2
Prime Scots, &c.......	4 4	4 6 ..	4 4	4 6
Coarse & inferior Sheep	3 6	3 8 ..	3 4	3 6
Second quality do.	3 10	4 0 ..	3 8	3 10
Prime coarse woolled do.	4 4	4 8 .	3 10	4 2
Prime Southdown do..	4 10	5 0 ..	4 4	4 6
Large coarse Calves ..	5 2	5 6 ..	3 10	4 2
Prime small ditto	5 8	6 0 ..	4 4	4 6
Large Hogs...........	4 6	5 0 ..	3 10	4 4
Neat small Porkers ..	5 2	5 4 ..	4 6	4 8

SUPPLIES.

	Dec. 27, 1841.	Dec. 26, 1842.
Beasts........	1.809	1,522
Sheep	16,910	13,180
Calves....	49	30
Pigs................	219	149

Up to Newgate and Leadenhall markets the receipts of slaughtered meat, since the commencement of the month, have proved great, viz. :—about 470 carcases of beef, 2,400 ditto of mutton, 1,200 ditto of veal, and 2,500 ditto of pork. The general inquiry has continued steady, at the following prices : —beef, from 3s. 2d. to 4s.; mutton, 3s. 4d. to 4s. 2d.; veal, 3s. 8d. to 4s. 6d.; and pork, 3s. 8d. to 4s. 6d., per 8lbs. by the carcase.

CALENDAR OF HORTICULTURE FOR JANUARY.

At the commencement of a new year it will be interesting to devote a few lines to the meteorology of the one just concluded. The first circumstance worthy of notice is the state of the land in 1841, at a period corresponding with the present. Then the floods were abroad, and field and garden were swamped with water. Now, though an ample supply of rain has fallen since the end of November, there is no superfluity—every concomitant is equally propitious to the gardener and farmer. The year 1842 has indeed, upon the whole, been beautiful, marked with singular coincidences, productive of great fertility in some degree, however affected by opposing phenomena. Every month of the year has witnessed two distinct periods of great elevation and considerable depression of the barometer (unless we except March, which in every respect was of an irregular and fluctuating character). The mercury was generally high in the early days of the month, and again about the 15th ; the second and fourth weeks were the periods of depression ; but the existing weather did not correspond with the indications, though it alternated very seasonably. December has been peculiarly fine and temperate to the present time, and so warm and sunny were the 13th, 14th, and 15th days, that the season resembled that of a genial April. No frosts, and few fogs have occurred, and vegetation is beautiful. The north-east winds have produced little cold, and many geraniums remain unaffected. Thus the anticipations of *early* severity have been negatived, and winter is at least curtailed.

The great height of the mercury, coincident with the turn of days, in a degree presages keen weather, and warns the gardener to be prepared with every appliance of protection. The best covering for ornamental shrubs—fuchsia, deutzia, azalia, kalmia, China rose, &c., &c.—is a deep layer of half decayed leaves, laid over the surface of the ground: this material protects and enriches; it also is congenial to all plants, and when mixed with white sand, produces an excellent substitute for bog-earth. The leaves of the shrubberies left on the ground, are too useful to be removed; and though deemed unsightly by many, are extremely protective.

The Operations of the Vegetable Garden

Must depend on the weather; if the land be open, and the weather mild, weedy ground can be improved by pushing the spade so as to cut up thin slices, and reversing the surface: thus the earth between rows of plants will be made neat, without disturbing any roots; and the weeds being turned, will be exposed to the frost. Vacant plots can be rough digged, and set up in ridges, and others deeply trenched.

If the ground be locked-up, dung and litter should be wheeled to places which require enrichment and protection.

The preparation of hot-beds and compost heaps ought to be undertaken. The common hot-bed for cucumbers is made by collecting the required quantity of the best and freshest stable dung of highly fed horses, heaping the whole, long and short, together. To this, one-third part of wet fresh leaves is added, forking and turning the two, parcel by parcel, till the whole be intimately mixed. Heat will be generated in the heap just in proportion to the existing quantity of urine and ammoniacal vapours will be liberated. In a few days then the heap should be turned and mixed with the fork a second time, and so soon as it shall again acquire strength, the hot-bed may be formed and moulded over within the frames. Danger of burning always exists in beds so constructed; therefore, numerous substitutes for the common bed and box-lights have been devised. None, however, equal the pits of Mr. Patrick, gardener to Colonel Vyse, of Stoke-green, Bucks, which we shall take the liberty to describe, by referring to a paper written by that excellent gardener himself.

An excavation is first made in the ground, three feet deep, ten feet wide, and of any length to admit of the extent of pits required. A 9-inch brick wall, a little-sloping outwards, is then built all round this space to support the earth, above which it rises a few inches. Mr. Patrick's range consists of 19 lights; but he observes that 6 lights of such pits will be sufficient for the supply of any moderate family, from the beginning of January to the middle of summer. The range of 19 lights begins with a pit of two lights, and ends with the same; but the intervening length is divided into pits of 3 lights each, and between each set is an open space of 12 inches wide, so that three, six, or more lights can be worked as required, in succession. The whole space within the 9-inch wall, and the

12-inch spaces between the ends of the pits, is at first filled with hot dung, but the dung between the ends when once put in, is not to be turned like the lining at front and back, because, as the pits are pigeon-holed, and without flues *at the ends*, the roots of cucumber or melon plants will work through, and receive nourishment from the decayed dung in the end openings. These end spaces are also exceedingly serviceable in cold and damp weather, as they afford means to top all round with fresh dung. The individual pits are narrow compared with their length; for, deducting two clear feet at the back and front of the whole range, between the 9-inch wall and the exterior of the pits, their breadth does not exceed 4 feet 6 inches outside measure. The outside wall of the pit is of 4-inch brick-work, pigeon-holed all round. Within this is a brick-on-edge wall worked up solid, excepting one row of pigeon-holes at the bottom, left for drainage. This inner wall is brought up one course higher than the pigeon-holes in the 4-inch work, or outer wall; and by covering the cavity between this and the outer wall with a double layer of plane, thin, 6-inch tiles, a flue is formed at the back and front of each pit. The tiles must be double, because the centre of each tile which finishes the flue must be firmly bedded over the joints of those first laid to make the flue steam-tight. By this means a mild and genial warmth (not a violent bottom heat) is circulated among the plants and the soil they grow in.

For cucumber and melon-growing, the pits are filled entirely with mould to the height of the fines, excepting about 6-inches of fresh turf, chopped to pieces, and placed at the bottom as drainage.

The cavity between the pits and 9-inch wall is filled, and renewed as required with hot-dung.

Our own observation at various periods has proved the correctness of the foregoing remarks; but it remains to say that, since Mr. Patrick has applied the same erections to pine-growing, a course of hot-water pipes has been added, which, in seasons of great severity, renders the pits perfectly secure and effective. In the frost of 1838, 2° below zero, succession pines were kept growing at 70°, being placed low in the pits, and the glasses closely covered by straw and mats.

It must be observed that wherever cucumbers and melons are grown, the pits are filled with mould; and no material is more appropriate than the earth of *decayed couch-grass.* But for pine-apple plants neither tanner's bark nor mould was introduced; but in lieu of either, a foot or eighteen inches of litter manure was placed at bottom, merely to support and embed the sides of the pots. The pine flourishes in the vapours emitted by this material; but Mr. Patrick disclaims fermenting bottom-heat, relying for equability of temperature upon the action of the flues, aided, if required, by that of the hot-water pipe.

The structure above described comprises every appliance of successful forcing in pits; but this is not all, for by it the farmer might avail himself of those masses of fermenting manure which he has ever at command, and effect the double object of husbanding that heat which is now expended in air, and converting it to the useful purposes of forcing the choicest fruits of the garden. It is surprising that persons who enjoy every possible advantage, should so neglect their opportunities.

Sea-kail is now coming in. We have on several occasions alluded to the superiority of boarded troughs over pots. Every facility is thus provided for ample growth, cleanness, and protection. A row of plants, raised from seed sown in April 1841, may now be bearing bleached kail, six or eight inches high, and proportionably strong : we have known several hundreds cut from a row 20 feet long. *Rhubarb* can also be blanched very early by similar means, and thus be had in perfection till the fine gigantic varieties come in, naturally early, in April.

Sow more peas and beans ; scatter saw-dust over the earlier rows that are up ; this material protects from frost and slugs.

FRUIT DEPARTMENT.

Do nothing in the way of planting, pruning, or training, unless press of time requires such operations, because the season is dormant, and nothing is gained ; February being in every respect favourable. But as currant and gooseberry bushes are often infested with moss, which disfigure the stems, they should be dusted or dredged all over when the dew or hoar frost is on them, with powdery lime, or a mixture of wood-ashes, lime, and a little soot. The ground between the trees may then be turned over, inch deep, to give the surface a neat appearance. This work ought, however, to have been done in November. Protect fig-trees with mats ; peach, nectarine, and apricot trees, with old flags or bunting.

Fruit-room.—Apples and pears keep wretchedly ; so it is reported, and so we find it. A wet autumn could not have been the actuating cause, for the autumn of 1842 was arid compared with that of the preceding year ; yet the fruits perish at the core with great rapidity. Attention then must be paid to the stores, for a decayed fruit is one in which not

only chemical decomposition is active, but whereon parasite fungi soon fix themselves, and taint all in contact with them.

Sow, under frames, radishes, small salad, lettuce ; also peas for transplanting. The latter are easily raised in reversed strips of turf, or in narrow boxes, laid on the floor of a warm vinery. Kidney beans in pots, and strawberry-plants for early fruit, should be introduced at successive periods. .

Early Vinery.—Keep the heat regularly active ; 70° is not too much by day, and 65° by night. Two opinions prevail as to moisture and air ; the latter cannot be excluded if the glass laps be at all open ; but vapour may be increased and diminished. If long open cluster be required, much moisture and strong heat at the time they show themselves will induce rapid extension. If flavour of fruit be the chief object, a dry house will promote it.

As the days increase, stimulate more and more the plants in the hot-house, and top dress many of those that begin to grow.

In the open Flower-garden little can be done. Every attention to the neatness of walks and lawns is proper, but it is futile to dig or plant. February is more favourable, and even that is too soon for most operations.

Small paddocks and orchard grass are much improved by admitting sheep to eat the herbage close. The manure should be raked or bush-harrowed to disperse it, and next month, or early in March, nitrate of soda, mixed with ashes and fresh loam, should be scattered over the grass. 28lbs. of the first are sufficient for half an acre.

REVIEW OF THE CORN TRADE

DURING THE MONTH OF DECEMBER.

Another year has closed around us, and to the agricultural interest throughout the United Kingdom, circumstances have occurred during its progress of more than ordinary importance. That degree of legislative protection to the property of the farmer which heretofore had been uniformly considered necessary to his prosperity, has now been to a certain extent withdrawn ; the Minister yielding to the principles of a false philosophy, and substituting the dreams of theory for the long and well established truths of practice. The alteration in the value of the produce of the fields which this most unnecessary, and in every respect unfortunate, event has occasioned, is certainly without parallel since the circulating medium was altered from paper money to a metallic currency ; and we much fear that the one will speedily be found as truly inimical to the farmer's capital and property as the other was about fifteen years ago. The new corn law has this season reduced the value of grain of every description from ten to fifteen per cent. under the cost of its production ; and in the value of live stock the farmer's property has already been deteriorated by little less than one-quarter of its value previous to the new Custom House tariff of import duties becoming the law of the land. We have yet to learn in what way any interest within the British empire is to be promoted by thus grossly injuring the proprietors and the cultivators of the British soil ; nor can we

conceive how any class, within our society, can flourish on the ruins of agricultural pursuits at home. That the wages of the productive labourers are regulated, and must continue to be regulated, by the amount of money in general circulation, is a self-evident truth, and that a free corn trade with foreign nations can under no circumstances increase, but must decrease the amount of money actually in circulation, is another axiom. When our population is supplied with food of home growth, it matters little what its nominal value may be ; the money paid for it not being for one moment abstracted from the amount of the currency actually in circulation, but continuing to give, in proportion to its abundance, adequate wages to all the productive classes. The real happiness and prosperity of the British and Irish people are therefore linked, we may truly say, with the soil on which they exist, and to improve the fields is to improve their condition in life. Foreign connections must be, and are always uncertain, and for the people of the United Kingdom to place their trust in foreigners for proper supplies of the necessaries and luxuries of life is neither more nor less than an act of political suicide. That, in the present state of civilized society, a barter trade is impossible, the experience of all ages now perfectly establishes ; and in our country the experience of the last five years should have taught this truth to all, excepting to those

who have some selfish pecuniary views in promulgating free trade doctrines, or are driven into
their adoption by blindfolded prejudices. Were
the doctrines of the modern political economists
founded on anything resembling truth and solidity, the virtually free foreign corn trade which
we have enjoyed now for five years, according to
their verbiage, should have long since produced,
at all events, a certain description of reciprocity in
trade amongst nations. During the last five years,
however, we have paid away, in cash alone, more
than thirty millions sterling to foreign land proprietors in exchange for foreign agricultural produce
imported into the United Kingdom for home consumption. That not one sovereign of the money
thus remitted to foreigners for food has been sent
back here for the purchase of British goods, the
daily complaints made respecting the rapidly declining state of our export trade to those foreign
communities from whom we have received these
large supplies of foreign produced food, affords but
too ample proof. This money is not at present giving,
and never will again give, productive employment
to any one class within the British Empire. It is
far more patriotically employed at home by its present proprietors. It is there partly embarked in the
improvement of German, Spanish, Russian, and
American agriculture, and partly in increasing and
in improving manufactures amongst those nations.
This is rather a strange mode, but certainly not
more strange than true, of increasing and improving
our manufactures at home by freedom in the corn
trade. It is the real cause, however, of one-half
the commercial and manufacturing distress which
has latterly prevailed throughout the United Kingdom, and which can alone be removed by the revival
of agricultural prosperity. We have extended to
poor and to serf-labouring nations the right hand of
fellowship, and we are now giving them the means
to cut that right hand off. Already, through the
agency of that money which we have latterly remitted to them in exchange for their agricultural
products, have we enabled them to increase so materially their manufacturing establishments, that it
has become an absolute necessity, on the part of
these foreign states, to establish such tariffs of import duties as to nearly prohibit British manufactures from competing, on anything like reciprocal
terms, with their goods in their own markets of
consumption. In thus giving legal protection to
home industry, the different foreign governments
are showing the most profound wisdom, and are at
the same time also perfectly contradicting the policy
and theories of our modern political economists.
The serfs of Poland and the boors of Germany do
not in general consume wheat, nor animal food of
any description, nor does their very paltry reward
for labour enable them to clothe themselves and their
families in British manufactured goods of even the
worst description; and the slaves in Russia are not
placed in any better position, in as far as the use of
British manufactures is concerned. The agricultural labourers in Poland are slaves in the true meaning of the word. In that the largest wheat-produ-
cing kingdom on the continent of Europe, no middle
men exist betwixt the land proprietor and his serfs.
Tenantry are nearly unknown, we may say, almost
in all those great wheat districts in America and Europe, from which we have, for several years past,
imported grain so very largely. The expence of its
production abroad is therefore not augmented by
rent, tithes, and public taxes; as is the case in the
United Kingdom, and a free corn trade, therefore,

betwixt us and them can only be attended by throwing many of our fields out of cultivation altogether.
With our heavy national debt, and with public rates
of every denomination to pay, we cannot compete
in price with foreign provision growers, even in our
own markets, and the consequences to us hereafter
it is easy enough to predict. For example, some
twenty years ago the manufacturers complained of the
heavy duty charged on foreign rape-seed, when imported into this country; the ministry then hearkened
to these complaints, and reduced the rape-seed duty
to a nominal charge. Without effective legal protection, however, rape-seed cannot be grown in this
country, and in consequence of the reduction in
duty to which we now allude, many farmers, engaged previously in rape-seed cultivation, were totally ruined. To the manufacturers themselves,
however, this alteration in the rape-seed duties has
been even more prejudicial than it was at the time
to the British agriculturist, who ceased to grow this
article when he could not profitably cultivate it.
The trade, therefore, has, for years now, been compelled to depend principally on foreign supplies;
and they being not equal to the necessary consumption, prices have been, and now are, much dearer
than they ever were previous to the reduction of
that duty, which was then so absolutely necessary to
the successful cultivation of rape seed within the
United Kingdom. Similar causes universally produce similar consequences, and to withhold from
wheat producers that degree of legislative protection which is absolutely necessary to the successful prosecution of their most national pursuits, must
eventually be followed by some great national calamity. The tillage of our fields will in many cases
be abandoned, and farther agricultural improvements
must also cease to be attempted. Thus, before we
experience, even for a dozen of years, the blessings
of cheap bread of foreign production, and the benefits
so much desired by all the cotton lords—of the wages
of labour being reduced even more in proportion
than the common necessaries of life may be, by the
existing corn law, and by the further proposed free
trade alterations in other laws—a deficiency in the
quantity of the common necessaries of life may begin
to be felt at home, and then, as rapeseed now
is, the value of all descriptions of grain and food
will be raised, and that too in a few years afterwards, very far indeed beyond the then limited means
of the consumers to pay. Indeed, then distress
may arise, and the means of applying a remedy to it
may be withdrawn even from the legislature itself.
The Minister, therefore, we trust, will maturely
weigh the consequences before he yields to these
dogmas; for the only object which the master manufacturers have at present in view is, that reduction
in the weekly wages paid to their workmen which
cheap bread must eventually occasion, though this
selfish purpose cannot long serve them; for, even
should they reduce their workmen to the condition
of Russian slaves and Polish serfs, they will still
find the coasts of America and of Europe bound
round with iron chains against the admission of their
goods to any extent into the great European and
American markets of consumption, for the larger
our imports of food may be from Europe and from
America, the greater will be the quantity of goods
manufactured in those portions of the earth, for the
consumption of the inhabitants at home. Their
agricultural produce consumed here must, however,
soon transfer our capital to them, and when we have
no longer money to give, then indeed, and not till
then, they will cease to send us food. The opera-

tives and artisans, however, know the intentions of their masters too well, to place any confidence in the purity of their motives. They are perfectly aware that dearness and cheapness are entirely relative terms, and are governed by the means to pay; a pound weight of bread at one penny would be dear enough to one man, and cheap enough to another, even if residing in the same neighbourhood. The value of wages alone can regulate this circumstance, and the people now are by far too much enlightened not to comprehend this fact: they know the value of money to them when it is abundantly in circulation; they know that then the wages paid for their labour are fully equal to their expenditure, when dear apparently provisions may be; they also are perfectly aware that abundance of money in circulation and abundance of foreign food in the market cannot exist at the same time in this country, and that labour is scarce, and wages uniformly are low, when the seasons prevent a plentiful growth of provisions at home. No schoolmaster is necessary to impress on them these self-evident truths, for a free corn trade with foreign nations, or a fixed duty on its importation, never can increase the foreign demand here for their labour, but must materially decrease the consumption of manufactured goods in all the home markets, which are by far the most valuable to them, both as to quantity and quality. It is not necessary to point out to them that there must be something wrong in the dogmas of the Anti-corn law advocates, when, almost with the same breath, they assert that, in the United Kingdom at present, there exist more men than can be employed at home, and, at the same time, recommend that the cultivation of our fields should be transferred from our own super-abundant population, as they denominate it, to the tillage of foreign fields, by foreign labourers. Here is a contradiction which none but those possessed, not of common but of uncommon sense, can reconcile; for we presume that these gentlemen cannot well deny that in the United Kingdom upwards of fifteen millions of acres of land are at present in a state of perfect unproductiveness; a great part of which may, by labour, science, and capital, be rendered eminently useful to the British community, and that, so long as a field so extensive exists for employment, the population cannot be considered redundant. The wealth of the nation may be considerably increased by the employment of thousands of families in the conversion of these waste lands into cultivated fields, for by labour of this description the public will be benefited for ages to come; but when the unemployed people are turned over to factories, their works endure only so long as they are patronised by the fancies of the day, and not one hour longer. They then become almost valueless, and afford a strong contrast to the labours of the agriculturist when directed to land improvements. Legal protection is alone necessary, we repeat, to render this empire perfectly independent of all foreign nations for food. We possess in the greatest abundance amongst ourselves means to support, in the best manner too, more than double our present population; but agricultural improvement is a plant of slow growth. In its infancy it requires protection, and time, talent, and capital, are all necessary to aid it in its growth to maturity. When the Anti-corn law lecturers began their orations, they asserted that cropping lands should be converted into pasturage; but our late tariff having destroyed this their former

favourite argument, they now consider agricultural improvement alone to be necessary to the restoration of agricultural prosperity, by enabling our farmers to undersell, in our markets, grain of all descriptions of foreign production. Under the beneficent protection of the late corn laws the improvement in agriculture during the last twenty-five years has, undoubtedly, been immense; and it is impossible to calculate the increased produce of grain fields during the last quarter of a century, at less than one quarter above its previous amount. Under corn laws equally protective, the progress in agricultural improvement, we doubt not, may be much more extensive during the ensuing quarter of a century than it was during the last, because both science and capital are now much increased; but it is idle to fancy that improvements can advance without legal protection to money embarked in them, and without time to bring them to perfection.

The present corn law, and the altered tariff on the importation of foreign provisions, therefore, we strongly suspect will place a bar to further agricultural improvement; for in the article of wheat, for instance, it is impossible that our farmers can, under the existing corn law, compete in our markets with foreign wheat. On the subject of the new corn law, we are surprised to find the London journal, the *Standard*, asserting that neither our farmers nor our land proprietors have as yet been injured, nor probably ever will be injured, by the alteration made last year in the scale of import duty; and this eminent journal founds its belief on the fact, that during the last three months in 1835 wheat was many shillings per qr. cheaper than it has been during the same period in 1842, and that no complaint of losses were made on the part of the farmers during the former period. The circumstances were, however, widely different in 1835 to what they now are. In the former year the value of wheat was reduced by the abundance of British-grown wheat sent into the market for sale, and quantity then made good to the farmer the loss he sustained in prices. Far different indeed, however, is the cause of the present depression in wheat prices. It most certainly has not been occasioned by the weight of the farmer's supplies at market, for during the last twenty years they never were so trifling in their amount as they have been since last harvest time, and therefore our farmers have not been paid this season in the same proportion as they were in that of 1835. The depression in prices has been solely occasioned, during the last six months, by an immense supply of foreign wheat having been pressed on the market for sale. In 1835 no foreign free wheat was in this country, and the law then protected the British farmer from foreign wheat in bond. Under the new corn law, however, we must have an annual renewal of the influence of foreign wheat in all our markets, and time will then show whether rent and taxes can be paid, and the farmer can be remunerated for his capital, science, and time embarked in agricultural pursuits and improvements, under the existing system. In the meantime, if he be by law duly protected, he has better prospects before him.

The young wheat plants are in a healthy state, though perhaps they are too luxuriant for the season of the year. He has also a prospect of obtaining for his wheat, during the next six months, prices nearer the cost of production than those heretofore offered to him; for an immense quantity of foreign free wheat has latterly gone into consumption, and the stocks remaining in granary are becoming weekly more moderate in their quantity. Still, however, we fear much that last year's crop cannot remunerate him for the expences of production, and that, therefore, either the landholder or the tenant must be injured by the late alterations in the corn laws. The landlord, however, may afford to subsist on a reduced rental, and the tenant may also maintain himself and his family, even amidst the ruin of his property embarked in agricultural pursuits ; but there is still a moral consideration on which the Anti-Corn Law Leaguers maintain the most profound silence. They never allude to the future condition of the great mass of the agricultural population, one half of whom, by these free corn trade measures, must inevitably be driven into the Union Houses, at the expense of the landed interest chiefly ; and the diminished wages paid to the other half for their labour, must eventually place them almost in the position of the half-starved portion of the community. The influence which these changes in our Custom-house duties may have on the public debt is of inferior consequence, although eventually they may lead to the adoption of Mr. Cobbett's favourite principle of an equitable adjustment being made in the half-yearly dividends now paid on that debt.

The commercial information received from North America since our last publication is dated on the 15th ult. in Boston, and on the 17th of the same month in Halifax. The contents of the letters are not of much importance. The severity of the weather had interrupted the communication with the Canadas, and inland navigation had in many places been obstructed by the same cause. Under these circumstances the Wheat and Flour markets were then dull, no business being practicable, excepting for immediate consumption at home; but in the United States the prospect of obtaining possession of the British corn markets, through the medium of our North American possessions, induced the merchants and millers to hold their property at prices too dear for our consumption, even after the payment of only colonial duties. It is thus annually that the importers of foreign grain into the United Kingdom for consumption, will be made the scape-goats of foreign agricultural speculation, so long as the present corn-bill is permitted to remain in our statute book. The American consignees will in future draw as largely as possible against their Wheat and Flour consignments, and should our markets not answer their sanguine expectations, the British consignees will be saddled with the loss. This is the new American method of transacting business, and no opportunity will be lost to take advantage of the privileges conferred on her merchants by the virtually free corn trade now established betwixt us and them. This will be, however, a very minor evil, which we must submit to in our future corn trade with the United States. It is by quantity, much more than by price, that the United Kingdom will be seriously injured by the changes which we have made in our importation duties. The growth of Wheat throughout the Union was much larger last season than it had ever been before, and the market which we have now opened for the consumption of American agricultural produce must annually lead to increased improvement in American agricultural operations. During the cold season, curing provisions of all descriptions suitable to our consumption was also at these dates prosecuted to a considerable extent; and in a few months hereafter we may, therefore, expect large supplies of American bacon, ham,

beef, and cheese, to the great *benefit* and *comfort* of the Irish and British producers of similar articles. The growth of live stock has heretofore been a most important consideration, and the curing of provisions has uniformly been a most profitable department of industry to the Irish nation. The American tariff of import duties on British manufactures, sufficiently proves that by smuggling alone can they be introduced to any extent into American consumption ; and, therefore, it is utterly impossible to conceive any benefit which the sacrifice of our agricultural interest to that of foreign nations, can confer on any class within her Majesty's dominions. Our eastern dominions, and the friendly nations throughout the Southern Ocean, are places much better fitted for our manufacturing commerce than North America now is, or ever can be. To this quarter our manufacturers should direct their undivided attention in future.

From the corn markets in the Black Sea, in the Adriatic, and in the Mediterranean, the intelligence received respecting the state of the corn trade since our last publication, is entirely devoid of interest. The weather had put a stop to business in the ports throughout the Black Sea, and the absence of demand had produced the same effect in those places where trade was not interrupted by the elements. During the season, very large shipments of Wheat and of Beans had been made to the British islands, and the stocks, consequently, of old grain were by no means abundant anywhere within those seas. The loss on Wheat received here from the South of Europe has been larger considerably than it would have been had more attention been paid to quality. The grain merchants in the lower ports are evidently but little acquainted with the condition requisite to render Wheat shipments safe for prolonged voyages, and several cargoes consequently arrived here heated, and in the worst state possible. Should a grain trade with the ports within these seas be persevered in by our merchants, the condition of the cargoes should be inspected previous to the commencement of the voyage, and a remedy may thus be applied to evils of a similar description in future. But for the sake of British agriculture, we sincerely trust that years may elapse before we have again any necessity to look to this quarter for supplies of food. The voyage is far too difficult to be safe for perishable articles, and seldom indeed has any profit been derived by the merchants engaged in these operations.

The letters from the North of Europe are dated in due course of post, but the information which they communicate is not of much consequence to those engaged in the corn trade in this country. The season for activity throughout all the markets in the Baltic has closed ; and as no speculation existed then in the corn trade, very little business was transacted ; the value of Wheat remaining much the same as we noted it in our last publication. The inland navigation having continued open much longer than usual, the stocks on hand had been considerably increased, particularly at Stettin ; and early in next season, when the rivers become again navigable, the quantity of Wheat on sale was expected to be large. Prices, of course, will then be regulated by the quotations from Mark-lane, and during the summer months we shall again be inundated with foreign Wheat, whether our wants require it or not.

Should financial matters permit the Chancellor of the Exchequer to draw the attention of the legislature to the excise laws during the ensuing session of Parliament, very important benefits may be the consequence to the public in general, and more particularly to the producers and to the consumers of manufactured barley. Last season our Custom-house duties were examined, and were very materially reduced in their amount. It is at present, however, a matter of uncertainty whether these reductions will be generally beneficial to the community; but no doubt can be entertained that those portions of the new Tariff which apply to agricultural products are in the highest degree unjust towards the agricultural interest at home. The farmer's property, invested in live stock, has been deteriorated already very considerably by the alterations which were made in our Custom-house duties last year, and should some modifications not be made in the public charge now imposed on the importation from foreign states of live stock and of cured provisions, the fall in the value of home-grown articles of similar descriptions must still more seriously affect the capital embarked by our farmer in the cultivation and future improvement of the fields. It may, however, at all events, be hoped that the Ministers will now turn their attention seriously to the duties now collected on malt and on spirits manufactured in England; for they, in a very material degree, affect the growth of barley throughout the United Kingdom, and likewise are injurious to the finances of the empire, in as far as, by their outrageous extravagance, they confine consumption to the lowest point possible. Although, during the month of December, the supplies of barley in all the great markets of consumption were certainly, for the season of the year, not unusually large, still they were considerably larger than the maltsters and the distillers required, and consequently sales of it were difficult at gradually declining prices. The maltsters naturally confine their malting operations to the probable consumption of malt during the year, and the English distillers regulate their purchases of barley by similar rules. The quantity of barley therefore annually converted into malt is certainly not one-half of the quantity which the consumption of beer would require, if the malt duty was reduced to moderation—for the present rate is much too high to permit the use of beer amongst the people beyond a most miserable pittance to each individual within the United Kingdom. At the existing malt duty, four and a half millions sterling are not at present paid into the Treasury from this source of annual revenue; but were the duty only 1s. per bushel, at least ten millions of quarters of barley would be converted into malt annually, and even this quantity would furnish a very short allowance of beer when divided amongst thirty millions of human beings. By this modification of the malt duty, as we have repeatedly shown, two millions of acres of land, at present unproductive, may be brought forward into barley tillage; may add three millions sterling annually to the rents of land; may give agricultural employment to thousands of families now in a state of want, and the profits which would flow from this new channel of improvement would be much greater than the expence attending the additional consumption of beer amongst the industrious classes of society. The revenue likewise would be materially increased by the introduction of moderation into the malt duty, and not one class in society could receive even the slightest injury from this alteration. But even should this proposed change in the malt duty eventually be attended by a loss to the revenue, the Chancellor of the Exchequer has a most legitimate

quarter at present, wherein any deficiency may be made good. We now allude to the duties already collected, and which, we fear much, will continue to be collected, on foreign grain, cattle, and cured provisions, when imported here for home consumption. By this great alteration in our custom-house duties the agricultural interest is the primary sufferer, and it is therefore only fair and reasonable that that portion of those duties which is raised on the importation of foreign grain and foreign provisions, should be applied to remedy the injuries which land proprietors and their tenantry suffer from this violent change in our long established institutions. These duties will amount annually to from one to two millions sterling, and annually now must they be on the increase. The application of them therefore to the reduction of the malt and the home-made spirit duties, is not only an act of common justice to our landed interest, but it must also materially benefit the great mass of the working classes throughout the United Kingdom; and on this account we most seriously direct the attention of our readers to the numerous advantages which must result from our proposed alterations in the malt duty particularly, and likewise in that at present levied on spirits manufactured in England. In this part of the United Kingdom the spirit duty is upwards of three hundred and fifty per cent. on the intrinsic value of home-made spirits, and this high charge opens a door to smuggling of that description which human nature cannot resist. It opens a door to vice, which can only be closed by its very material reduction. It is the real origin of idleness and drunkenness, and any sacrifice on the part of the public revenue itself, should be made to the removal of the evil we now complain of. It is perfectly well ascertained that more than one half of the spirits now used in England, is the produce of the smugglers' illegal trade; and that these spirits are of the worst description. The importation of them is ruinous in the extreme to the public morality, and the consumption of them is destructive to the public health. The character of British spirits, legally manufactured, is the reverse of this. Like every thing else, however, moderation in their use is the true way to arrive at the virtue of temperance; and to reduce the heavy duty now levied on them to 5s. on each proof gallon would, in a great measure, alter the habits of those who at present are the great consumers of foreign smuggled spirits. This alteration would at least double the quantity of wholesome British spirits at present used in England, for it would entirely suppress the use of foreign deleterious spirits, by rendering their illegal importation no longer profitable to the smuggler. To raise the duties now levied on spirits manufactured in Scotland and in Ireland to 5s. on each proof gallon, and to reduce the duty in England to the same figure, would also materially improve the revenue; at the same time that it would decrease the quantity of ardent spirits now annually consumed here, under the existing most vicious system; and eventually it would lead the people into the peaceful habits of moderation in their spirit consumption. The alteration in the duties to which we now allude, would likewise lead to a reduction of little under half a million sterling annually in the sum now expended for the prevention of spirit smuggling into England alone; and to supply the markets throughout England with British-made spirits instead of foreign smuggled spirits, as is the case at present, would open a market for the consumption of nearly half a million quarters of British grown barley, in addition to the quantity now used by the British and Irish distillers annually. On every principle therefore, either of morality or of national interests, the duties now charged on home-made spirits should be modified to meet the times, now so pregnant with alterations in our internal institutions. A great deal is now said and written on the spirit smuggling trade. The advocates of the free trade principles attribute this nefarious custom to the high duties levied on foreign spirits in this country, and they urge their reduction as the means of putting an end to illicit spirit importation into our markets of consumption. With these doctrines, however, the experience of facts prevents us from coinciding, for, in wholesomeness, no spirits can be distilled from any article equal in quality to the genuine extract of Sir John Barleycorn, who, from his connection with our landed interest, as well as from his own intrinsic value, should certainly, in this country, be preferred to any *spirit* of the age. To gain a high character in this respect, is the highest ambition of the worthy knight, but his good intentions are thwarted by the laws of the excise.

Since our last publication the supplies of oats in all our great markets of consumption have been larger than the demand required, and, notwithstanding the great superiority of the quality of last year's growth over that of the preceding one, still prices have been weekly on the decline. The average now is only a shade above 17s. per quarter, a price which must eventually put an end to the profitable cultivation of this article throughout the United Kingdom. To the landed interest in Ireland this depressed state of the oat trade is in every way detrimental, and should some steps not be soon adopted to remedy the evil, a stop must in a very few years indeed be put to agricultural improvement throughout the sister island. To sell Irish oats in London, Glasgow, and Liverpool, at an average price of 17s. per quarter, and to deduct the expences of drying, shipping freight from the west coast of Ireland to the British market, expences there of commission, del credere, metage, insurance, and numerous et ceteras, we fancy that even an Anti-corn-law leaguer himself must admit that little can remain to the farmer, for the payment of his rent and the charges of production. In Great Britain, to suppose that the farmers can continue oat cultivation under such prospects, would be indeed an act nearly resembling absurdity ; and, as we have asserted in a previous part of this article, the certain consequence must end eventually in higher prices being paid to foreign nations for oats than has been the case during the last twenty years. The production of them probably will within a few years, under the present system of the corn-laws, become extremely limited indeed ; and then, as in the case of the consumers of rapeseed, the great body of the community will have severe cause to regret that the ministers—yielding to a false feeling of humanity—altered those laws which protected internal industry of every description from the interference of foreign with British agricultural produce in all our markets of consumption. The corn-law offers at present no impediment whatever to the importation of foreign oats into our markets, even for immediate consumption. From the opposite coast on the continent, to all our markets betwixt Cornwall and the north of Scotland, the oat freight is only 1s. to 1s. 3d. per qr., and as the best qualities are always from 4s. to 6s.

per qr. superior in value to our average prices, this difference in value will pay the import duty. In the ensuing spring months very large supplies, therefore, may be expected to arrive from the continent, for prices can be there so regulated as to render the trade profitable enough even at a farther reduction of prices in our markets. These oats will be imported by vessels under foreign flags, and navigated by foreign seamen. This alteration will transfer a part of our valuable coasting trade to foreign shipping—in as far as the Irish, Scotch, and north of England oat carrying trade is concerned—and the advantages promised to the agricultural interest, to the British ship-owner, and to the British sailor for such great sacrifices, are the chances of seeing the oat growers in the north of Europe dressed in Manchester cotton, in Leeds wool, and in other descriptions of British manufactures. For the chance of a little additional employment to the labourers in the manufacturing districts, the property of the national debt itself is to be hazarded, and the whole system of our internal polity is to be convulsed. That the evils must come is a moral certainty, and that the good can never come, may with equal confidence be depended on. So long as we have silver and gold these foreign oats will be paid for in the precious metals ; and this money, when once remitted to the continent, will never return here. It will thereafter be employed in foreign agricultural improvements, and in extended commercial and manufacturing operations amongst those states from whom we receive supplies of foreign produce and provisions. It is undoubtedly the duty of our Government to attend to the wants of the people, and to enable them to support themselves on the cheapest terms possible. This good, however, can never be obtained by transferring from our own field labourers to those of foreign states the cultivation of agricultural produce necessary to the general support of our inhabitants ; and we strongly fear, therefore, that the truth may be discovered after the time for applying a remedy to the evil has passed away.

CURRENCY PER IMP. MEASURE.

DEC. 26.

	Per Qr.			Per Qr.
WHEAT, Essex and Kent, red	4C 52 54	White	50 54 58	
Irish	46 48	Do.	48 50	
Old, red	— —	Do.	— —	
RYE, old	32 —	New...	32 —	
BARLEY, Grinding 24 27 Malting	30 32	Chevalier	32 34	
Irish	21 23	Bere .19	20 22	
MALT, Suffolk and Norfolk	56 58	Brown..	50 54	
Kingston and Ware	56 60	Chevalier	60 —	
OATS, Yorksh. & Lincolnsh., feed	20 23	Potato..	23 25	
Youghall and Cork black	16 17	Cork, white	18 19	
Dublin	17 18	Westport	18 19	
Waterford, white	17 18 19	Black ..	16 17	
Newry	20 21			
Galway	12 15			
Scotch feed	22 —	Potato..	21 24	
Clonmel	18 19 20	Limerick	18 19 21	
Londonderry	18 19	Sligo ..	18 19	
BEANS, Tick, new	30 32	Old	32 34	
PEAS, Grey	31 33	Maple..	31 33	
White	32 33	Boilers .	35 38	
SEED, Rape...... —l. —l.	Irish..—l. —l. per last.			
Linseed, Baltic....40 46	Odessa	48		
English Red Clover....	— — per cwt.			
White	—			
Mustard, White —	9	brown 11 12 per bush.		
Tares, old 28 30	new	36 40 per qr.		
FLOUR, Town-made 43 45	Suffolk 34	— pr sk. of 280 lbs		
Stockton and Norfolk, 35	—			

FOREIGN GRAIN AND FLOUR IN BOND.

OATS, Brew	15 17	Feed...	12 14	
BEANS	18 24			

IMPERIAL AVERAGES.

Week ending	Wheat.	Barley.	Oats.	Rye.	Beans.	Peas.
Nov. 12th	48 8	27 11	17 9	32 2	31 8	33 2
19th	49 8	28 1	17 10	31 8	31 6	34 2
26th	49 6	28 1	17 0	32 2	31 4	33 7
Dec. 3rd	48 6	27 9	17 9	28 1	30 11	33 5
10th	47 3	27 1	17 3	29 5	30 8	32 3
17th	46 10	26 5	17 2	28 11	29 10	32 2
Aggregate average of the six weeks which regulates the duty	48 5	27 7	17 7	30 5	30 11	33 3
Duties payable in London till Wednesday next inclusive, and at the Outports till the arrival of the mail of that day from London ..	20 0	0 0	8 0	10 6	10 6	9 6
Do. on grain from British possessions out of Europe	5 0	2 0	2 0	1 6	1 0	1 0

COMPARATIVE PRICES OF GRAIN.

WEEKLY AVERAGES by the Imp. Quarter, from the Gazette, of Friday last, Dec. 23rd, 1842.		AVERAGES from the corresponding Gazette in the last year, Friday, Dec. 24th, 1841.	
	s. d.		s. d.
WHEAT	46 10	WHEAT	52 10
BARLEY	26 5	BARLEY	30 2
OATS	17 2	OATS	21 1
RYE	28 11	RYE	44 8
BEANS	29 10	BEANS	37 0
PEAS	32 2	PEAS	36 6

Account shewing the Quantities of Corn, Grain, Meal, and Flour, imported into the United Kingdom, in the month ended the 5th Dec., 1842; the Quantities upon which Duties have been paid for Home Consumption during the same month, and the Quantities remaining in Warehouse at the close thereof.

Foreign Grain and Flour.	Quantity impo'ted.	Quantity entered for consumption.	Quantity remaining in warehouse.
	qrs. bush.	qrs. bush.	qrs. bush.
Wheat, from British Possessions	415 6	574 6	866 3
Peas, from do.	308 0	249 4	446 5
Indian Corn, do.	83 6	—	1277 1
Wheat, foreign	53801 3	643 3	185563 0
Barley, do.	531 2	3849 6	60308 5
Oats, do.	2719 7	1308 1	61042 4
Rye, do.	—	—	1366 6
Peas, do.	1226 3	2538 6	33457 0
Beans, do.	8897 0	1735 1	82770 2
Indian Corn, do.	2965 6	286 5	14311 1
Buck Wheat, do. ..			....
	cwts. qrs.lbs.	cwts. qrs.lbs.	cwts. qrs.lbs.
Flour and Meal from British Possessions	20355 2 23	12922 1 13	21041 2 10
Flour & Meal, foreign	11432 3 9	38 0 8	42265 1 21

STOCK OF GRAIN, &c., IN BOND, IN THE PORT OF LONDON, ON THE 5th DEC.

Wheat.	Barley.	Oats.	Beans.	Peas.	Rye.	Flour.
qrs.	qrs.	qrs.	qrs.	qrs.	qrs.	cwts.
85,037	12,330	35,134	26,652	9,424	—	31,505

Cloverseed, 19,025 cwts.

PRICES OF SEEDS.

DEC. 26.

Linseed, English, sowing 48   56
Baltic .... —   —   crushing 42   45 per qr.
Mediter. & Odessa 45   46
Coriander.............. 10   16   old.... 16   20 per cw'.
Mustard, brown, new .. 10   11   white.. 10   10s.6d p.bush.
Trefoil, new............ 18   22   old.... 12   16
Rapeseed, English new.. 31l. 33l. per ton.
Linseed Cakes, English.. 10l. to 10l. 10s.
Do.   Foreign.. 7l. to 7l. 10s.
Rapeseed Cakes........ 5l. 5s. to 6l. 0s.

POTATO MARKET.

SOUTHWARK WATERSIDE, Dec. 26.

Per ton.		Per ton.	
	s. s.		s. s.
York Reds .... 50 to 60		Wisbeach Kidneys.. 40 to 45	
Scotch do. (from vessels) .... 45 to 00		Jersey Whites (from store)... .... 00 to 30	
Do. do. (from store) 30 to 35		Jersey and Guernsey	
Devons............. 45 to 50		Blues............ 40 to 45	
Kent, Essex, and Suffolk Whites .. 40 to 45		Yorkshire Prince Regents .... 45 to 50	

WOOL MARKETS.

LIVERPOOL, Dec. 24.

	s. d.	s. d.	s, d.
Laid Highland Wool, per 24 lbs..	6 9	to 7 3	
White do. do............	9 3	10 0	
Laid Crossed do..unwashed..	8 0	9 6	
Do. washed do.............	8 6	11 0	
Do. Cheviot unwashed do.	8 6	10 0	
Do. washed	12 0	15 6	
White do. do.............	19 0	22 0	

FOREIGN.

LEEDS, Dec. 23.—Although this is the season of the year when business generally is done on a more limited scale, the transactions of the past week, though not perhaps equal to the average of the fortnight or three weeks previous, have nevertheless been fully as extensive as might reasonably have been expected, and prices continue very steady.

PRICES OF MANURES.

Subjoined are the present prices of several sorts of manure:—

Bone dust, 22s. to 23s. per qr.
Half-inch Bone, 21s. 6d. to 22s. per qr.
Rape Dust 7l. 7s. per ton.
Rape Cake, 6l. 10s. to 7l per ton.
Rags, 4l. to 4l. 10s. per ton.
Graves, 5l. to 5l. 10s. per ton.
Gypsum, at the waterside, 35s. per ton; landed and housed, 38s. to 42s. per ton, according to quantity.
Agricultural Salt, 34s. per ton.
Lance's Carbon, 12s. per qr.
Ditto Humus, 14s. per qr.
Soap Ashes, 10s. per ton.
Poittevin's Patent Disinfected Manure, 13s. 6d. per qr.
Poittevin's Highly Concentrated Manure, 30s. per qr.
Nitrate of Soda, 22s. 9d (duty paid) per cwt.
Nitrate Potash (saltpetre) 30s. per cwt.
Petre Salt, 4s. per cwt.
Willey Dust, 4l. 4s. per ton.
Urate, 5l. per ton.
Chie-fou, 21s. per cwt.
Daniell's new Bristol Manure, 13s. 4d. per qr.
Hunt's new Fertilizer, 13s. 4d. per qr.
Grimwade's Preparation for Turnip Fly, 10s. 6d. per packet, sufficient for three acres.
Wolverhampton Compost (Alexander's), 12s. per qr., subject to carriage to London, or forwarded from Wolverhampton.
Guano, 10s. to 14s. per cwt, according to quantity.
Potter's Artificial Guano, 15s. per cwt.
Dr. Daubeney's Sulphate of Ammonia, 12s. per cwt.
Muriate of Ammonia, 24s. per cwt.
Muriate of Lime, 12s. per cwt.
Clarke's Compost, 3l. 12s. 6d. per hhd., sufficient for three acres.
Wright's Alkalies, 28s. and 42s. per cwt.
Soda Ash, 20s.
Chloride Lime, 28s per cwt.
Sulphuric Acid, 2½d. per lb.
Sulphur for Destroying Worm on Turnips, 16s. per cwt.
Hunt's Artificial Guano, 12l. per ton.

Printed by Joseph Rogerson, 24, Norfolk-street, Strand, London.

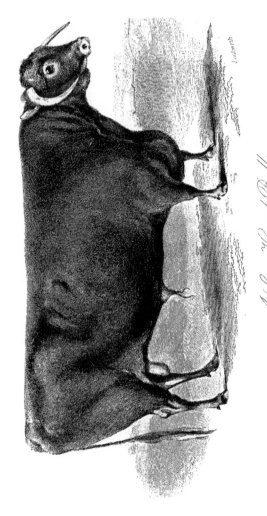

A Long Horned Bull.

Getting into a Difficulty.

London, Published by Smith Fllcr & Co. 65 Cornhill & 18 Waterloo Place Pall Mall. Feb.y 1. 1843.

THE FARMER'S MAGAZINE.

FEBRUARY, 1843.

No. 2.—Vol. VII.]   [Second Series.

PLATE I.

Our first plate represents a long-horned Bull, which was exhibited at the Meeting of the Royal Agricultural Society, held at Bristol, in July last, and gained a prize of Twenty Sovereigns, awarded to the Hon. M. W. B. Nugent, of Higham Grange, Hinchley, Leicester. The animal was bred by Mr. Horton, of Sherborne, Warwick.

PLATE II.

GETTING INTO A DIFFICULTY.

TO THE EDITOR OF THE FARMER'S MAGAZINE.

Sir,—The Essay on Ploughs, which I herewith send you, though unsuccessful in obtaining a Prize from the Royal Agricultural Society of England, has been thought to contain some hints to plough-makers, which may be useful. If you will therefore give it insertion in your next Magazine, you will sincerely oblige

THE AUTHOR.

Rainham, Kent, Jan. 17, 1843.

AN ESSAY on the MECHANICAL PROPERTIES of the PLOUGH.

BY WILLIAM SMART, OF RAINHAM, IN KENT.

In an attempt to investigate the merits of the plough and its mechanical properties, it will not be irrelevant, by way of preliminary, to enquire what that implement is intended to perform.

And, as it will be readily allowed that the preparation of land to receive seed, corn, &c., is the main point, so it will as necessarily follow, that to have the land properly and effectually ploughed is a matter that ought to be fully understood.

Few things connected with the almost daily occupation of agriculturists can vary more than their notions of good ploughing. In some counties, ploughing the land three or four inches deep, and flapping it over nearly as flat as the unploughed land, is considered well done ; in others, turning the furrow three-fourths over, so that it may form an angle with the field of about forty-five degrees, is much admired ; while, in other instances, ploughing from six to eight inches deep, and turning the furrow completely over, so that the share-mark is exposed quite at the top, and the old

OLD SERIES.]

surface turned into the bottom, thus effecting an entire change, is the only way to obtain the approbation of ploughmen and farmers. The general habits of ploughing in various counties may probably have great influence in forming these various opinions ; the instruments employed being such as have been handed down from former times, without questioning their perfection, may also add to these predilections. The ploughs in general use in Essex, Suffolk, and most of the midland, western, and northern counties, and the work they perform, may be instanced as furnishing a practical comment upon the two first cases ; and that of the Kent or turnwrist or the latter, by which to estimate the value of each. The swing and wheel ploughs having fixed breasts— the cutting and moving parts of which generally measure about three feet in length, and in breadth at the bottom about nine inches, increasing to about twelve at the upper part—may be classed among those whose work satisfies the farmers in the two first cases, because the ploughs are incapable, from their construction, of performing the work required by the last—the power to effect which will greatly exceed that of the other two, and will account for the difference of strength applied.

It cannot be denied, for instance, that two furrows of equal breadth, one six inches deep and the other three, must vary in weight as two to one— of course, a power varying in the same ratio will be required to move it.

It is equally undeniable that, to turn a furrow completely over requires a greater degree of force than to leave it half or three-quarters turned. For example, a furrow nine inches wide, *six* deep, and moved fifteen, may be calculated thus : $9 \times 6 = 54 \times 15 = 810$; whereas, a furrow nine inches wide, three deep, and moved twelve, will appear thus : $9 \times 3 = 27 \times 12 = 324$. The compa-

G   *[No. 2.—VOL. XVIII.*

rative power required will be as 810 to 324, or 5 to 2. The importance of deciding what is efficient ploughing will thus appear no very trifling matter. This difference may appear to many greater than they expected; but every practical ploughman will understand that a furrow *cannot* be turned properly over, if the opening in which it is to turn be less in extent than the depth and breadth of the said furrow added together.

It would be superfluous to show that a furrow, ploughed six inches deep and turned quite over, is preferable to one of half the depth and half the turning; or that the more completely the stale or surface earth is buried, and the greater portion of fresh earth is brought to the surface (supposing it to be of similar quality to that on the surface), in a proportionate degree will the fertility of the soil be increased, and the seed-furrow improved.

If, therefore, three or four inches in depth, and turning the furrow partly over, can be called effectual ploughing, the foregoing calculation will shew that if a power equal to *two* horses be sufficient, those persons who require their land to be moved to a depth of from six to eight inches, and their furrow turned completely over, have to perform a task which will require a comparative power equal to that of *five* horses, and an instrument so constructed as to accomplish the work.

Much has been said, and much written, upon lightness of draught as applied to ploughs, but efficiency of work is the first consideration; and, if this efficiency be either unattainable or incompatible with lightness of draught, can it be desirable to sacrifice the greater to the smaller advantage?

The construction of ploughs, and their mechanical properties, have not been hitherto much considered, neither have the capabilities of the various sorts in use been shewn. It may be doubted if the fixed breasts before referred to are *capable* of executing work in the most effectual way? They have not the power, for instance, of turning the land bottom upwards; because, to effect this, the plough must have a double action; and they have but a single one, of which more hereafter. Having thus endeavoured to shew that efficiency is the grand essential, I come now to consider the mechanical properties of the plough, under the several heads proposed by the Royal Agricultural Society of England.

First—The form of the cutting and moving parts of the plough as affecting the work to be performed on various soils.

Second—The form of the same as affecting the draught.

Third—The true line of draught as derived from the shape of the plough, and the structure of the animals employed in drawing.

First—The form of the cutting and moving parts of the plough should be that of the *wedge*; and, as the power of the wedge is allowed to be according to the angle which the inclination of its sides presents, and equality of that angle throughout its whole length : so of the plough. Should the fore part of the wedge incline in a more acute angle than the after part, though the friction may be diminished in the first instance, it must be proportionately increased at the latter; the pressure should be equal throughout the whole length. A specific opening is required with ploughs, because the opening or excavation which the plough makes *must* be sufficiently wide to receive the succeeding furrow; and therefore what is gained by the small

angle at one point is counteracted by the required greater angle at the other; the land also having by this inequality to pass a curved instead of a straight line, will be more broken, and the friction consequently much increased.

It has already been stated that a furrow six inches deep and nine inches wide must be moved fifteen, in order to obtain sufficient room to turn; should this be attempted with a plough whose cutting and moving parts are only three feet in length, the angle required to effect this will be twenty-four degrees; but should it be done by one of five feet in length, the angle will be reduced to fourteen and a-half degrees. The length of the cutting and moving parts of a plough are of great importance, inasmuch as the angle is dependent upon it, as well as the convenience of using it. Let the opening or excavation of the furrow be fifteen inches ; the longer the cutting of the plough, the smaller the angle required, and vice versâ. Again, allowing the axiom "the smaller the angle the greater the power," as well as the greater facility of passing through the land, yet a medium length is most desirable ; for, by carrying out the length to an extreme, in order to obtain a small angle, the plough may be rendered useless. A plough fifty feet long, for instance, could not be conveniently employed. Extreme shortness should likewise be avoided, as the obtuseness of the angle will thereby be increased, so as to render the difficulty of its passing through the land very great.

Five feet in length, therefore, is proposed as the most eligible, which will require an angle of fourteen and a-half degrees without being inconvenient in length. Should four feet be thought of, the angle will be increased to eighteen and a-half degrees ; if three feet, twenty-four degrees, if two feet, thirty-six degrees; if of one foot, seventy-five degrees; and if a right angle, then it could not possibly pass at all. See the annexed scale.

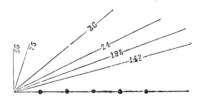

The various powers of these angles cannot be so well ascertained by calculation in reference to ploughs as by the dynamometer, but they are certainly considerable. If the plough is formed with a single action—such as those with fixed breasts before referred to, having simply a lateral wedge—it will not have sufficient power to turn the land, but will merely push it aside. If it possess a double wedge, or rather two wedges acting together, one vertically the other laterally, then an effectual turn can be given to the land which no other can accomplish.

These observations will apply to all soils ; of course the advantage will be more felt in adhesive than in those of a more free character. Sandy soils will pass any line which the breast or wrest of a plough may bring in contact with it ; but those which stick (or load, as the ploughmen term it) will slip past a straight line with greater facility than a curved one.

Second :—The form of the same as effecting the draught.

The draught is effected in four ways; first, by the weight of the instrument; secondly, by that of the body to be removed; thirdly, by the distance to which that body has to be removed; and, fourthly, by the facility with which an instrument to effect these objects can be made to pass through the land.

First—The weight of the various instruments differ too little to make a discussion upon them necessary, further than to say there must be suffi- cient substance in each to bear occasional high pressure, unless it be thought necessary to keep a greater number than is usually done, as light ploughs for light work, and heavier for heavy work. But even in such a case, the difference of draught is not so much affected by the weight of the instrument as by the pressure to be over- come.

Secondly.—The weight of the body to be re- moved. The furrow can only vary in weight by the varying depth, supposing it to be always nine inches wide. A furrow six inches deep must always, in the same soil, be twice as heavy as one of three only. In the report of several trials with ploughs given by Philip Pusey, Esq , and published in the Jour- nal of the Royal Agricultural Society, vol. i. part iii. page 229, the trial shows the varying weight of the draught as the depth increased from five to twelve inches, which strongly corroborates this hy- pothesis ; for though the weights therein set forth do not increase in a regular and equal ratio with the depth, yet the difference may be accounted for in several ways without affecting the principle. The following are copied from the report :—

Furrow nine inches wide.

Depth.	Draught stones.
5	23
6	22
7	25
8	30
9	31
10	40
11	50
21	50

It may be supposed that the two first results have changed places ; for it cannot be easily ac- counted for in any other way that six inches in depth should be of less draught than five, or that the va- riation of weight in the three last should. have been exactly according to the report. Some ex- traneous cause may possibly have intervened to produce such an inequality as ten stone between ten and eleven inches, and perfect equality be- tween eleven and twelve inches ; upon the whole, however, seeing, that ten, eleven, and twelve éx- actly double those of five, six, and seven, the exam- ple given is a very strong one.

Thirdly—The distance to which that body of earth has to be removed has before been shown. It must be equal to its breadth and thickness, and the draught will consequently be very materially affected thereby ; it will also be increased by the increase of depth, as the distance of removal must go on increasing with the increase of depth.

Fourthly—The facility with which an instrument can pass may be partly determined by the obstruc- tions a furrow has to encounter while in the act of passing, as may be exemplified by two angles, thus—

The angle with straight sides will surely pass with greater facility than the one presenting several projections ; so a plough with straight sides will, by the same rule, pass more freely than one whose sides are curved.

Thirdly—The true line of draught, as derived from the shape of the plough, and from the struc- ture of the animals employed in drawing.

The true line of draught to propel an instrument possessing and displaying the properties of a wedge with the least expense of labour, may be proved by the operation of the wedge itself, and the applica- tion of the power that propels it ; if a wedge is most effectually propelled when the power is ap- plied in a perpendicular line with the intended pas- sage of the wedge, so must it operate on the plough possessing the same property ; for instance, apply the propelling power to a wedge in any other line, and it is immediately forced into a new direction, and that in proportion to the angle of the line in which the propelling power approaches it. If a beetle is made to descend perpendicularly upon a wedge which is placed at right angles with a log of wood, and the log is placed in a true horizontal po- sition, it is forced forward into the timber without altering its direction ; but should the said beetle fall thereon in any other line, the wedge will imme- diately swerve from its first position, and its power to open a passage will be deteriorated to an amount equal in degree to the angle of incidence : so with the plough. The line of draught which requires the least labour, is that which approaches nearest to the parallel direction of the plough's passage. Could the application of power be placed in the same line as the cutting and moving parts of the plough, or parallel thereto, it would require less la- bour than when applied in an angular direction ; but as that cannot be obtained by horse power, and as no other is in general use, so the nearer the true line can be approached or obtained, the lighter the draught.

The propelling power being derived from the shoulders of horses, and the line of draught extend- ing from thence through the axle to the heel of the plough, will form an angle with the horizon according to the height of the horses, and the dis- tance at which their shoulders are placed from the point of contact ; this ought to be preserved a right line as much as may be (indeed all curved lines should be avoided), which can be always regulated by the height of the wheels. If they should be too high, the line of draught will be elevated in the centre, and the tendency will then be to lift the heel of the plough, already under that lifting in- fluence from the angular line of draught; if they should be too low, the tendency will be to lift them from the ground, but as this tendency is rather de-

G 2

sirable in a small degree, because it assists the ploughmen in canting them into the furrow, when turning at the end, so it is a deviation less to be avoided than the other. Supposing the length of the plough from the heel to the axle to be seven feet, the line of draught attached to the heel of the plough to be six inches from the sole, and the axle of the wheels to be eighteen inches high, the angle formed by the horizontal and true draught lines would be one of about nine degrees : but as the height of the horse's shoulders, from whence the power is derived, is about forty-eight inches, and at a distance from the heel of the plough of about fourteen feet, the angle of the actual draught and horizontal lines will be found to be one of fifteen degrees ; this will depress the draught line at the axle about eight inches, which will serve to show that wheels of less than three feet in height are not desirable.

Should it be necessary to use more than two horses, the line of draught, by which the leading horse or horses is attached to the plough, will (from the distant place they occupy) bring their draught into a right line from the heel of the plough through the axle to their own shoulders. This tendency in the plough to delve—occasioned partly by the angular line of draught which gives the heel of it a continual inclination to rise, and partly by the inclination of the buck and share—may be in a great measure counteracted by placing the fore end of the plough-beam on a rest or bolster, as much above the line of draught as the horizontal line is below it, so that the draught line will be about midway di-

Beam line.
Draught line.
Horizontal line.

viding the angle formed by the inclination of the beam and the horizon in its centre, and thus neutralizing the tendency of the heel to rise, by the depressing tendency of the draught upon the beam.

In swing ploughs this counteraction is left in the hands of the ploughman, and is regulated either by his discretion or caprice ; in order to effect which the cutting and moving parts of the plough are made very short, and the handles very long, that the lever (upon which principle they act) may give him sufficient control, which could not be obtained if the handles were short, and the cutting and moving parts of a more appropriate length.

Figure 1 in the annexed sketch represents a turn-wrest plough with the double wedge complete.

The buck E G has a vertical action, whereby the furrow is raised on the edge, after being separated from the main land by the coulter M, and from the subsoil by the share E ; this process occupies the first part of the plough ; the second or after part is the lateral wedge, which is formed by the wrest C D, which then comes into operation, and completes the turn of the furrow, laying it bottom upwards.

The shelve-wrests G K are intended to continue the line of the buck as far as useful, but chiefly to prevent the loose earth from falling over the fore part of the wrest before it has acquired its perpendicular position, and has no other use, so that its line being exact with the buck is not important ; because the furrow has ceased to pass up the first wedge shortly after it has arrived where they join to it, rolling away over its side.

The rod bat N is intended to act as a lever in removing the coulter from one side to the other ; from the left side of the share, which is its proper place when the right wrest is extended, and which maintains it in that position, by being hooked into a catch, till the plough turns at the end of the furrow, when it is shifted to the right side of the share, when the wrest on the left side B D, (figure 4), is pushed out, by that on the right side being pushed in, and so on alternately till the field is finished ; having, by means of this turn-wrest plough, every inch of land turned over, and not one open furrow left in the whole field, instead of leaving a twelfth part of the said field unmoved, as is the case with ploughs with fixed breasts, and another twelfth left in open furrows.

The chain O O, called the tow, is the draught chain or line before described.

Figure 2.—The angle, which may be termed the governing principle of the plough, every angle of which, vertical or lateral, is upon the same scale. It is five feet in length and fifteen inches at the base, making an angle of fourteen and a half to fifteen degrees. These dimensions have been fixed on as the just medium between too great length of plough and too great obtuseness of angle, as well as from several trials, which have approved themselves to the judgment of practical men.

The apex of the lateral wedge is the edge of the coulter, and in the vertical the edge or plate of the share. It will be easily seen in the lateral in figure 5, where the black mark (|), representing a section of the coulter, completes the angle A B C upon the scale of figure 2, the dotted lines converging to that point from the ends of the wrests, B D and C D, completing it.

Figure 3.—Section of a turn-wrest plough, cut horizontally about nine inches from the bottom, with two wrests, B D and C D, placed close to the chep or sole. The fore part, E, is the chisel-point or share, six inches wide and three long. It lies quite plane at the bottom of the furrow, which it cuts at the depth required, six or eight inches ; and which furrow, as the plough proceeds, passes up the buck E G, or vertical wedge, till it is placed on its edge, when the work of the first wedge is done. The furrow being thus placed, figure 4, representing the wrest, B D, extended, and forming the lateral wedge, begins to operate ; and as the plough passes on pushes the furrow over, and completes the work. The spindle, B C, is that which being connected by a pin with the ends of each wrest, is made to slide through the plough ; the holes in it are used as stops, which by means of a small pin prevent the extended wrest from receding by the pressure of the furrow. The foremost ends of the wrests are fastened to the sides of the chep or sole by moveable joints, so that they can be raised or lowered at pleasure, extended more or less as occasion may require, according to the depth of the furrow, which is managed by using a longer or shorter spindle, by which means the opening of the furrow is extended or contracted at the pleasure of the ploughman.

Figure 5, which has been already noticed, is the counterpart of figure 4, having the extended wrest C D on the opposite side, and its companion B D close to the plough.

Figures 6 and 7.—The two wrests separated from the plough and viewed edgways, one for the right, and the other for the left, side of the plough ; they can, however, be placed on either side.

Figure 8.—A wrest four inches wide viewed flat-

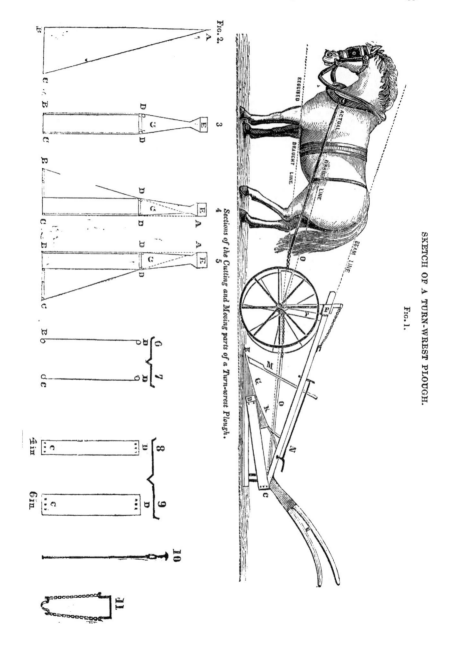

SKETCH OF A TURN-WREST PLOUGH.

Fig. 1.

Fig. 2.

Sections of the Cutting and Moving parts of a Turn-wrest Plough.

ways; this is intended to be used where the land is unbroken, as figure 9, six inches wide, is, where the land is loose, such as stirring fallows, &c.

Figure 10.—The rod bat, an iron lever with a hole for the coulter, which places the coulter on the side of the share required; this is effected by having the coulter hole in the beam sufficiently large to allow the coulter to swing; and which is fixed to the side required by the rod bat, being held in its place by an iron catch.

Figure 11.—Collar and collar chains, P P. These are used for the purpose of keeping the plough steady. The chain is passed through a ring in the tow, and hooked on the collar, which is made to fit the plough beam, so that the inclination to land in ploughing one furrow is made to coincide with that on the other or return furrow. It has the further effect of making the plough compact, by rendering it more like a single piece, by tying it together in a firm manner; this tying also gives the ploughman complete command of the wheels when turning at the end of each furrow, so that he can cant them into their place with ease and at his pleasure.

It may here be observed, that the two wedges have their lines cross each other without interfering; the lateral wedge, for instance, does not begin to act till the furrow has passed the vertical one; but immediately after it is raised on the edge by the latter, the former begins to take effect, and thus continues the motion in a rolling manner, instead of pushing it away; thus effecting the work at the least expense of labour, in the same manner as a piece of timber can be removed with greater ease by rolling than by pushing.

The three sections of a field partly ploughed are given to show the process of cutting and turning, by which the peculiarities of the turn-wrest plough are developed.

Sections of a field partly ploughed by a turn-wrest plough, showing the various positions which the furrow obtains while in the act of turning.

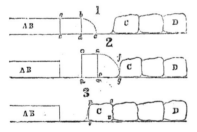

Section 1.—The part of the field A B is the whole or unploughed land, six inches deep; the part C D, the furrows as they lie after the process of ploughing is completed, being each turned completely over. The roundness of their appearance is chiefly caused by the corner of the furrow at *d* being rubbed off in passing the wrest, unless the land be very strong or clayey, in which case they retain their square or angular shape. The side of the furrow, *f g*, is as it remains after the plough has passed, leaving the opening, *b d f g*, fifteen inches wide, which is equal to the depth and breadth of a furrow, the space required for the succeeding furrow to turn in.

a b c d.—The furrow last noticed is now to be turned. The chisel-point E, figure 5, enters the line *c d*, cutting two-thirds of it next to *c*, called the land side, and leaving one-third uncut next to *d*; it is not desirable to cut the line *c d* in its whole extent, because if entirely separated it would be liable to slide away by the lateral pressure in some degree, and so far diminish the opening too much to allow the entire turn to be effected: the chisel point must also be equal on each side, in consequence of its having to cut another furrow on its return, and turn it on the reverse side.

The coulter M begins to cut the line a c, when the chisel-point has entered two or three inches, and before the furrow begins to rise up the buck. If it should be placed further back, it would allow the buck to break up the furrow while attached to the whole land, and not only cause the furrow to be broken to pieces, but would increase the draught greatly; if put more forward, it would be placed in the solid land, and could not be restrained from grasping the land too freely; if allowed to fly too wide, it would also cut into the solid earth, so that the share could not so easily raise the furrow, and would moreover cause the plough to *land* too freely —that is, the bevelled edge of the coulter would draw away the plough, causing it to press too eagerly after a larger furrow. If not sufficiently wide, the plough would not land freely enough, and would turn up some earth on the land side; its proper place is to make it meet exactly the two lines of the wrests forming the apex of the angle. Having the coulter thus in the right position, which is very material, the separated furrow on the side *a c* begins to rise up the inclined line of the buck E G, as the plough proceeds, bringing down *b* to *c*, when, having passed the vertical wedge, and being thereby set on its edge, as may be seen in section 2, where *a b c d* will be observed in that position.

The wrest C D, which forms the lateral wedge, then begins to act, and rolls the furrow over, bringing down *a* to *g*, and *c* over to *f*; the position of the furrow *a b c d* is now completely reversed, *a b* being at the bottom, and *c d* on the surface. See section 5.

Sections of a field partly ploughed with a fixed breast, nine inches wide at bottom and twelve at the upper part, of the depths of three, six, and nine inches, showing the different degrees of turning obtained at each depth.

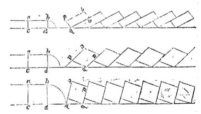

The rolling manner in which the furrows are removed, when in mellow land, has the effect of rubbing off the square corner *d*, so that the furrows acquire a roundness in appearance, the matter rubbed off falling under it, and thus prevents the fitting in of the squares so as to make a seam between.

It will now be necessary to show—as was intimated in the first part of this essay—the impossibility of such work as is described above being effected by the ploughs with fixed breasts, such as are in general use in the western, midland, and northern counties, their dimensions being, as before stated, about three feet in length in the cutting and moving part, and their breadth at the bottom nine inches, increasing to twelve in the upper part; of course the opening between the ploughed and unploughed land cannot exceed that extent.

Let a furrow nine inches wide and three deep be attempted with such an instrument, and the following consequences must ensue:—the first motion of the furrow, in order to turn, must be to raise it on the edge, which will occupy three of the nine inches of width (the extent of the opening), leaving six only to receive the breadth of the furrow, which is nine. See section 1, of a field ploughed. Again:—Let the depth be increased to six inches, and the first motion occupies six, leaving three only to receive nine. See section 2. But should the depth be increased to nine inches, then the furrow on the first motion will occupy the entire space; and the furrow must remain on its edge, or half turned, there being no space left to receive a second movement. See section 3.

The foregoing sketches of ploughing with a turn-wrest and other ploughs, are supposed to be done on clover leys, where the roots hold, or upon lands which from other causes are held together, so as to constitute a whole furrow. In loose lands, such as fallows, pea and bean stubbles, which have been cultivated during the growing of the crops, and undergone spuddling or scarifying since their removal, so as to break to pieces the surface, and which are perfectly clean, the difference of ploughing is less apparent, and also less material. Lands in this state, upon which full crops are grown, are often drilled, or sown upon after being creased; and numerous instances can be shown, where ploughing under such circumstances is altogether omitted.

It may be answered that a fixed breast is not necessarily limited to nine inches in width at the bottom, but can be set as wide as any other. Should this be the case, the angle must be more obtuse, which will give greater draught. Should the length be increased, so as to allow the angle to remain the same, yet the fixed breasts necessarily impose round ploughing, and the open furrows thus left will be of very great extent, and the field exceedingly uneven.

Doubtless the wish to mitigate this undesirable appearance has induced farmers to use instruments such as have been described (though but little advanced in science), chiefly from local habits, and an indisposition to enter upon any new thing. An unprejudiced trial will in all probability be made, and the merits of each duly set forth, which may be already anticipated. The "turn-wrest plough" will then be properly appreciated.

A very full meeting of the subscribers so the Leicester Monument was held at Norwich, on Saturday, January 21, when it was determined, by a large majority, that the Monument should be erected at Holkham. The sum now subscribed is 4,600*l*.

CHEMISTRY APPLIED TO AGRICULTURE.

(*From the Annals of Chymistry.*)

The analysis of soils is often of great importance to the agriculturist, and in this particular he has frequently to address himself to the chymist. The instructions for undertaking such analyses differ materially from each other. Of themselves they are very simple and easily executed, if a certain plan has been previously laid down for attaining the object in view. This object is twofold—viz. firstly, to know how much and what substances of organic origin, (that is to say, how much humus) is contained in the soil; and, secondly, with what disintegrated minerals the inorganic part of the soil is mixed.

The answer to the first question falls entirely within the compass of organic analysis. The soil is dried in an oil-bath at 266° F.; then treated—in the apparatus figured p. 281 of the *Annals*—first with ether, then with alcohol, water, and so on consecutively. By this process several different matters are extracted from the soil; but it is very uncertain if any of them will be distinguished as previously already known. We have not yet sufficiently examined the products of the decomposition of organic bodies to be able to execute this kind of analysis in such a manner that we can finally decide what products of decomposition the soil contains. This examination, therefore, becomes difficult; and yields, even if executed with precision, not very valuable results, until we shall have previously made ourselves acquainted with these products of decomposition by a close examination of them.

Two circumstances respecting humus may be positively ascertained, viz., 1st—its quantity; which is found out by burning a weighed quantity of soil, after being dried at 266° F., in an open crucible, until all the combustible parts are destroyed, when the loss shows the contents of organic matter; and, 2ndly, the azote therein contained, which is ascertained by combustion, according to the method of Varrentrapp and Will. The results of these experiments are seldom of much value; since the quality of humus in soils varies according to the manure added, and as the succeeding crops may absorb the several components of each manure.

The inorganic components of the soil, again, are easily ascertained. An air-dried sample of the soil being disintegrated as much as possible between the hands, is weighed, and sifted through a tin-plate sieve, consisting of several plates succeeding each other, with less and lesser holes. The sieve is then shaken, with the cover on, until the mass is divided according to the different size of the holes in the different compartments of the sieve, and each of these quantities is then weighed, in order to give an idea of the different sizes of the various ingredients.

Another air-dried sample is likewise weighed, and then dried in the water-bath, until it ceases to lose weight. A smaller portion of it is then weighed, placed in a glass tube, which has been closed at one extremity by fusion, and heated in the oil-bath to 266° F., until it ceases to lose weight, after which the contents of water are found by calculation. This sample is heated to redness in an open crucible until the whole of the carbon is consumed, and the organic matter of the whole is found by a calculation based thereon.

The greater portion of the sample is likewise exactly weighed, put into a glass vessel, infused with water, and then stirred with a quill. After being left undisturbed for a few moments, all the lighter parts are skimmed off, and the turbid water poured through a muslin sieve into another vessel, where it is allowed to stand for the purpose of depositing. There remain on the sieve fibres of roots, undecomposed portions of straw, stalks, &c. This operation is repeated until the freshly added water no longer becomes turbid by stirring. The finally remaining residue is dried and weighed, but not exposed to a red heat.

This residue is spread on paper, and, if required, examined with the aid of a compound microscope, in case of the parts being very small. The practiced eye then detects the grains of those minerals, the *debris* of which form the soil. Grains of transparent quartz, milk-quartz, red and white field-spar, scales of mica, lime, clay-slate, &c., are thus detected, and have been obtained from such minerals as are met with in the neighbourhood; and this easy examination is sufficient to elucidate of what minerals the soil is composed—on which point chymical analysis would not be able to give positive information. In proportion to the more finely pulverised portions contained in soil from the recent formations of mountains, the greater is its fertility, if mixed with the requisite manure. The *debris* of limestones, and different tertiary kinds of aluminous slate, mixed to a certain extent with quartzoze or granite sand, form the best mixtures.

From this residue the corbonate of lime (in case of the same being contained therein) is extracted by a mixture of one part of nitric acid and 100 parts of water, which are allowed to act on it without heat. When the effervescence has ceased, although the liquor still reddens litmus paper, the liquor is decanted, and the calcareous earth, after being neutralised with caustic ammonia, is precipitated therefrom by oxalate of ammonia. The magnesian earth is then ascertained (if present) by mixing the liquor in excess with carbonate of potassa, and boiling it therewith.

The residue left undissolved by nitric acid is washed, dried, weighed, and treated with concentrated muriatic acid. This solution is then further treated in the way directed for analysing silicates, which are soluble in muriatic acid. The muriatic acid frequently disengages siliceous acid without dissolving it. These are then extracted by boiling the undissolved parts with a ley of carbonate of soda. The undissolved residue is then weighed. It is in general nothing but sand composed of quartz or granite.

We now return to the parts left after being skimmed. That portion which passed through the muslin sieve is a mixture of decomposed organic substances (humus), clay (alumina), and extremely fine sand, which frequently contains siliceous shells from infusoria. After being left undisturbed for an hour, the sand and humus have settled; the clay, however, still remains suspended. The water is then decanted from the thick pap of clay, and gradually evaporated to dryness in a weighed bason or a crucible, after which the remaining clay is dried by the application of a rather higher degree of heat *e. g.*, in the oil-bath at 302° F., and weighed.

The deposited mass beneath the pap of clay is placed on a filter previously weighed. The turbid water which passed during the washing of the mass through the filter, together with the clay solution, is exposed to evaporation. The filter, together with all therein contained, is dried at 212° F., weighed, and burnt to ashes; after which the residue is examined under the microscope. It is then further treated in the same way as above stated for the coarser powder.—*Berz. Lehr. d. Chimie*, vol. x. § 123.

FOURTH REPORT OF THE WRENTHAM FARMERS' CLUB.

The committee of the Wrentham Farmers' Club, in presenting this, their fourth annual report, beg to observe they have examined the minutes recorded of the proceedings which have taken place at the different meetings held during the past year; and although they have to regret, that on some questions, the amount of information obtained has not been so extensive as could have been desired (occasioned in some measure by the imperfeet attendance given), still they consider it a duty they owe to the members generally, to lay before them, in as condensed a form as possible, the result of the discussions on those subjects which have been brought under the notice of the club accordingly.

At the first meeting of the present year, the members present, proceeded to the consideration of a rather important question, at that period, "The best method of filling up the plant of wheat, where a deficiency exists, and of which there appeared great probability, in consequence of the extreme wetness of the season." It was observed, that where the deficiency did not amount to the loss of more than one-half of the plant, no material benefit would result by sowing any additional seed, but that care should be taken in keeping that which remained free from weeds through the summer. Harrowing and rolling in the spring were recommended in such a case; and raking by hand, was also stated to have been found very efficacious in destroying much of the red-weed and other annuals, and causing the plants to tiller more rapidly.

Where, however, the plant was so far deficient, that re-sowing would appear indispensable, in order to obtain a crop, the best system was considered to be that of planting Talavera wheat, or, (in some cases) the same as sown in the autumn, provided it be some time in February, or early in March; but at a later period than that, either barley or oats was preferable: barley was allowed to be the most advantageous, particularly on light lands, as generally producing a heavier crop. Dibbling, and afterwards hand-raking in the seed, was to be preferred to drilling, as by the latter system, many of the plants would be destroyed, and the seed would frequently be deposited where not required. A resolution was afterwards adopted, in accordance with the above observations.

At the following meeting, a discussion took place on "The best method of feeding and keeping hoggets in the turnip season so as to prevent loss from dropping." The member introducing the question, who had, in former years, been a sufferer to a great extent from the above cause, had recently adopted the plan of drawing his turnips two or three days previously to being used; and he was induced to believe the system had proved effectual, as, since having pursued it, he had lost none, on lands where in past seasons his loss had been very great. It was however objected, that this system was not decidedly practicable, as it could not be. generally adopted, particularly in frosty weather; and it was thought that as much soil would be eaten with the food when the turnips were drawn previously, as there would be, if allowed to remain in the ground. Another instance was stated in which no losses had occurred for several years; here the plan adopted was, that of allowing the sheep to range ou stubbles or pastures for a few hours during the day. Several statements were afterwards made, in which the evidence was so conflicting that no satisfactory conclusion could be arrived at, as the same method of keeping had frequently in different cases produced entirely different results; high keeping had invariably been productive of the greatest losses. The system of feeding in troughs had also failed as a preventive, as one member who had recently adopted it had lost a great number of his hoggets. The prevailing opinion appeared to be, that the principal cause of dropping proceeded from an excess of fluid in the gall (commonly called overflowing of the gall) producing scouring, and causing the death of the animal in a very short time. Not having the advantage of professioual assistance, and in the absence of sufficient information on the subject, it was ultimately agreed that the purport of the foregoing observations be forwarded to the secretary of the Royal Agricultural Society, in order to be laid before the council, hoping, that through their veterinarian professor, some specific remedy may be pointed out as a preventive.

Your committee here beg to acknowledge the receipt of a communication afterwards received from the secretary, stating that the subject had been laid before the council, and referred by them to the veterinary committee.

The next meeting was occupied in a discussion with regard to "The merits of boiled barley for the purpose of feeding cattle, as compared with other kinds of artificial feeding." The member who introduced this subject, stated he had been induced to make use of boiled barley in consequence of the inferiority of his root crop, and the low price which that grain then realised in the market. In an experiment he had been making with two yards of bullocks, on linseed cake, pea-meal, and pollard, he found that by substituting boiled barley for the oil cake (still giving the same proportion of pea-meal and pollard), that they grazed equally as well, with this great advantage, that they did not consume so many roots by a bushel per day (for cach beast), as when feeding on oil cake. He had also been feeding pigs with barley, and considered it equally fattening.

Another member who had been giving it to milch cows, was perfectly satisfied with its results, as it affected a decided saving of his roots; he considered it a very healthy food for young stock of every description, but thought it rather slow fattening. Others spoke in favour of its use as far as their observations had extended; but the meeting not being in possession of sufficient practical experience on the subject, adopted the following report in lieu of a resolution :—

Report—" From the observations which have been elicited with regard to the use of boiled barley, it appears that where the system has

been practised, it has been attended with success, but having only been pursued by a few members, it is not considered expedient to adopt a specific resolution, but to urge the propriety of individually proving its fattening properties, even on a small scale, in order that satisfactory conclusions may be arrived at. One important feature deserving of notice, connected with its use, appeared in the saving of roots, as where boiled barley had been given a less quantity was consumed. With regard to the merits of boiled barley, as a substitute for linseed cake, it is inferred that the use of either the one or the other, must be regulated by the comparative price of each ; the low price of barley at the present time operating in favour of its consumption in lieu of oil cake or any other artificial."

The subject at the next meeting was on "The management of wool." This question did not elicit much discussion ; it was observed, that in order to obtain a good fleece, it is necessary sheep should be kept in good condition, as by such means, more wool is produced, and that of a better staple. Much attention was considered requisite to be paid to washing, so as to eradicate all sand, and that from ten days to a fortnight, (according to the condition of the animal) should intervene between washing and shearing, during which time the sheep should be kept as much as possible from pits and sandy banks. It was remarked that but little difference was seldom made by buyers in the value of wool of good quality, and that of any inferior description.

In a subsequent discussion on "The cultivation of white carrots," the opinion of the meeting was as follows : —

Resolved—" The land having been previously well cleaned, should be ploughed up a good depth, but it is not considered desirable to manure for them at the time of sowing, as by such a system the carrots generally become fangy. The second or third week in April is the best time for sowing; and about four pounds of seed per acre are required, mixed with a portion of sand or saw-dust, at the rate of two bushels to five pounds of seed. Either drilling or sowing can be pursued as circumstances may render desirable ;—if the land be subject to annual weeds, drilling is to be preferred from the opportunity afforded of horse hoeing, in which case, the rows should be about twelve inches asunder."

At the following meeting, the subject before the club, was "The best method of rearing and improving the breed of cattle." From what was advanced on this question, it appeared desirable (in order to check the system which had lately prevailed, of buying in at a high price and selling out at a low one) that more cattle should be reared in the neighbourhood. An objection was urged by some, that in following out this system, too much stock of a particular description, would have to be kept on a farm for a long period before making any return, and that the manure made from such stock would not be so valuable, neither would so much be produced. There was nothing to recommend the Suffolk breed of cattle but their milking properties. As regarded the more preferable breeds, the Ayrshire was considered the most profitable for the purposes of a dairy, and the short-horn for grazing. It was however, thought very desirable that greater attention should be given to improving the present breed, and the following resolution was therefore adopted :—

Resolved—"That in endeavouring to improve the present breed of cattle, the most important step appears in the selection of a male animal of the best description, and that a cross from the Durham or Ayrshire breed would tend most to effect that object."

At the next meeting, a discussion took place, with regard to "The best method of working or making summer-lands," in which the general opinion appeared to be, that where the land is intended for early roots, ploughing immediately after harvest is almost indispensable to the making a good [fallow, as one earth at that season of the year would be found more effectual in extirpating grass and other weeds than two or three at any subsequent period. If the land be foul, or much grass exist, scaling or ploughing without the breast, was recommended in preference to clean ploughing the first time; in either case it is very desirable the previous crop of wheatstubble be mown, that the stubble be no impediment in the way of cleaning.

The number of ploughings requisite would depend much on the state of the land. One member of much experience had observed that his turnips where the best where only three earths were given. This would apply principally when a fallow is made in the previous autumn, but even at any time, if the land be clean and in good tilth, frequent ploughings are not considered beneficial, from having the effect of causing the moisture necessary for vegetation to be absorbed, and thus often proving detrimental to the root crop. It was thought that the system of early ploughing would be attended with some inconvenience on light lands, as in many instances the stubbles were required for sheep to range upon, but as far as regards a preparation for roots, it was generally allowed to be decidedly the best plan.

The meetings in harvest and the succeeding month were but thinly attended, consequently no discussion ensued; but at the latter meeting, a question of much usefulness, (at that particular period) arose, as to the "Best method of mending maiden layers deficient in plant." It was observed, that where the deficiency in a layer is confined to spots, or is what is termed gappy, sowing red suckling on such parts was the most advisable plan; but if the failure be the same in all parts of the field, the best method appeared to be that of drilling a portion of tares among what is still remaining, in ridges at nine inches apart, and at the rate of one bushel per acre. This latter system was recommended by several experienced members, who had invariably derived more benefit from pursuing it, than from any other.

At the last monthly meeting of the Club, after the inspection of an excellent exhibition of roots, a discussion was entered into on the "Most approved treatment of Cattle for grazing purposes." The introducer of the subject, stated, that his system was to commence feeding with common turnips, afterwards proceeding with Swedes, and beet, or carrots, in the season to which each was more particularly adapted for consumption, together with a small quantity of corn or cake, which he increased as the

beasts improved in condition. This latter system of giving artificial food from the commencement he considered of much importance in grazing, as upon a favourable beginning often depended a successful issue; and it was much more advantageous to give a small quantity for a lengthened period, than a large quantity for a short time, or beginning when the animal is in part fattened. He preferred giving artificial food the last thing at night, when, if loose in a yard, they would feed more evenly; others considered it more desirable to be given at intervals of two or three times a day, as well as a portion of hay or chaff. An occasional change of food was stated to be beneficial to beasts in a forward state, as an inducement to feed, and with regard to which, much regularity and attention was necessary. The system of giving an excess of food was particularly reprobated, as no more than a satisfying quantity should be allowed at any one time. The meeting adopted the following resolution:—

Resolved—"That the most approved system of grazing appears to be that of commencing with common turnips, and about four pounds of cake, or a equivalent in corn, per day, for each beast, and increasing the quantity and quality of the food, as the animals improved in condition."

In summing up this brief Report, your committee would observe, that as the success of any society will at all times depend on the support it receives from the members of which it is composed, they feel, therefore, that the thanks of the Club are justly due to those gentlemen who have given regular attendance, and by their observations tended to elucidate such questions as have been brought before them; but at the same time, they would urge the desirableness of prosecuting still further enquiries on all agricultural subjects, instead of being contented at remaining stationary, or as indeed doing so would almost imply retrograding. They are aware that success does not at all times crown the efforts of the cultivator of the soil, as many unforeseen events, over which he has no control, such as unfavourable seasons, and sudden transition of prices, often tend to paralize his energies, and which would appear to be particularly the case at the present period; but it is not, however, on that account, that there should be a relaxation in attempts at improvements; on the contrary, such circumstances call for increased exertions, and should rather act as a stimulant in the pursuit of a more extensive knowledge of agricultural affairs; and they will only observe, in conclusion, that it is a duty incumbent on all, as responsible and useful members of the community, to use those means, which an enlightened judgment, and greater facilities of cultivation offer, in endeavouring to increase the produce of the soil, combined with a due regard to practicability and individual circumstances; and having done so, trust the issue to the unerring dispensations of Providence.

JAMES HINGESTON, Chairman.

AGRICULTURAL CHEMISTRY.

A PRELIMINARY TO THE PUBLIC APPOINT-
MENT OF ANY AGRICULTURAL CHEMIST.

TO THE EDITOR OF THE MARK LANE EXPRESS.

SIR,—It is a circumstance of much promise to agriculture, that there seems to be growing up, among practical agriculturists, a disposition to make the resources of science available to their art, and more especially the resources of chemistry. This is a disposition that ought to be encouraged. Incalculable advantages, there is not the sightest doubt, might be expected to arise to agriculture from a prudent and well-advised application of chemical principles; but what I much fear is, that if at the outset a wrong direction shall be taken by agriculturists, not only must reasonable expectations of advantage be disappointed, but a discouragement to perseverance may be the result, and thus, in the end, as much harm be done by unadvised zeal, as must be endured under the downright indifference of ignorance, indolence, and prejudice.

This apprehension has arisen from the consideration of a very well-intentioned proposal that has been made by some agriculturists in Scotland, to appoint, by subscription, a competent chemist to be employed by them in making such analysis, and in giving such professional advice as the subscribers throughout Scotland may require. It is because I can hardly but think that the enlightened projectors and subscribers to this project have not rightly apprehended the direction that should be given to efforts, in order to make the science of chemistry available to improvements in agriculture, that I take the liberty of addressing you on the present occasion.

A few observations may suffice to give an idea of one important unsettled point in agricultural science that chemistry alone can determine.

All the matter in any plant may be divided into two kinds—the organic and the inorganic. The organical parts of a plant may be partly dried away, and the remainder may be entirely burnt off. When the plant is thoroughly burnt, only a white ash remains. This white ash is the inorganical part.

The organic parts of a plant appear, from the chemical investigations that have been made, to be derived either from the atmosphere itself, or from the organical matter in the soil acted upon by the atmosphere. The inorganical parts of a plant are admitted on all hands to be derived, not from the atmosphere, but from the soil. Indeed, the organical parts of a plant may be regarded as essentially vegetable, the inorganical parts as essentially mineral.

The mineral ingredients of a plant vary in kind and in proportion, according to the nature of the plant; but as to the kind and proportion of the mineral elements, chemists have as yet ascertained, with accuracy, next to nothing. Yet, without such information, of what use can chemical analysis be? Different plants no doubt require not only different proportions of mineral matter, but mineral matter in part of a different kind. This is indeed apparent from the circumstance that certain wild plants abound in one description of geological districts, and are totally wanting in others. I will take upon me to affirm that until the mineral ingredients of a plant be ascertained with all the accuracy that befits the agricultural importance of the subject, even the chemist is not prepared to

do justice to the analysis of a soil. This will not be easily comprehensible, except by persons experienced in the business of chemical analysis; but this much must be obvious to every body, that so long as the chemist does not know what mineral parts must pass from the soil into the plant, so long he is ignorant of the most essential mineral parts to seek for and determine with accuracy; and neither the chemist nor any other man, supposing him to have before him a much more unexceptionable analysis of a soil than is yet known by chemists ever to have been performed, can be prepared to pronounce whether the soil abounds or is deficient in those particular mineral elements that are essential to the plants that are intended to be cultivated in the soil. Ignorant as we are on a point so fundamental and so essential, we may increase the number of chemical analyses of soils as we please, and we may even with truth account them of high value; but they can be valuable only as those things were that sunk off Spithead, in the Royal George, and had to remain at the bottom of the sea for two or three generations before they could be recovered for the use of mankind.

So long as the kind and proportion of the mineral ingredients of plants remain thus undetermined, of what use, allow me to ask, would the projected appointment of a chemist be for the analysis of soils? and permit me to suggest for consideration, whether the determination of the kind and proportion of mineral elements be not an essential preliminary step in order, not only to make such an appointment as the projected one useful, but even to make any single chemical analysis of a soil, whensoever or wheresoever performed, of any avail in the practice of agriculture.

I own I think the money subscribed would be thrown away.

Should then nothing be done? Should the praise-worthy ardour of the projectors and subscribers be repressed? Should the stillness and stagnation of ignorance and indolence remain undisturbed? By no means: but, as surely as that without ploughing and sowing there can be no reaping of corn, so surely the mere indolent admission, or the loudly pronounced conviction of the necessity of scientific enquiry for the service of agriculture, will not alone enable agriculturists to reap the advantage that would be secured by the institution and completion of the contemplated investigation.

By whom can such an enquiry be conducted? Certainly by no person but a scientific chemist, and he would require to be one of no mean attainment, industry, and conscientiousness. It is proper to mention, because possibly such an idea might not occur to agriculturists, that the enquiry suggested, although conducted by a competent chemist, devoting to it the whole of his time, is of such extent that it could not be accomplished in so short a period as two years. Can the patrons and friends of agricultural improvement expect that any competent chemist will, of his own accord, undertake and satisfactorily perform an enquiry of such extent, although of such undoubted importance to agriculture, merely as a labour of love? Surely such an expectation cannot be reasonably entertained. Few scientific chemists of attainments adequate to such an undertaking can command the time that would be necessary, and assuredly the research, of incalculable importance to agriculture although it be, holds out no promise of chemical discovery, or of reputation such as could induce a competent chemist to enter on the investigation. I apprehend, accordingly, that no full and satisfactory investigation of the mineral ingredients of plants can be looked for from the spontaneous labours of the only persons competent to make the investigation.

Permit me then to submit for consideration, whether the offer of a becoming remuneration for a man of science, qualified for such an investigation, would not be an object worthy of some of the great agricultural associations?

Under this plan, one of two courses might be adopted : either a special chemist, British or foreign, of such scientific reputation as to afford adequate security for the fidelity and the value of his experiments, might be employed ; or an adequate reward might be offered for the competition of all chemists. The subject of the mineral components of plants is so very wide, that it would appear expedient to limit the enquiry at the outset to the mineral elements of certain specified plants. The selection of the particular plants would have to be made with the assistance of competent scientific advice, and of course by such advice also would the merits of the prize essays, in case of a competition, come to be determined.

It is not with the most distant view of taking any part in such an investigation, or of offering myself among the competitors, that I have been induced to address you ; but solely from a desire that no misdirection be given to efforts, such as I cannot but approve of, and to intentions such as I cannot but wish to promote.

Various other serious practical mistakes appear to me to have been made in the formation of the project that has given occasion to these remarks ; but, having already occupied so much space, I must, for the present, delay further observations on the project.

I am, Sir,

Your obedient servant,

A Professor of Chemistry.

January 18*th*, 1843.

TO THE FARMERS OF SUFFOLK.

[This letter is equally valuable to, and demands the attention of, the farmers of any other county as well as of Suffolk.—Ed. F.M.]

LETTER I.

(FROM THE BURY POST.)

Gentlemen.—As our county press has wished me to believe that my late address to the Hadleigh Farmer's Club, on the theory of manuring, contained matter of interest to the agricultural portion of their readers, I venture to address myself to you in general. You may remember that I did not profess to point out anything *new;* and that I merely attempted to draw a few inferences from recorded facts and the opinions of others. My object was to diffuse information for the sake of some who might not be aware of the importance of a correct theory of manuring, or might be unwilling to believe that science can ever be expected to do much for the improvement of practice. Two or three of my practical friends have since then communicated with me on the subject ; and certain inquiries and expressions in their letters have inclined me to think

that if I were to put on paper a few remarks upon some points more or less connected with your important pursuit, I might probably stimulate some among you to make further inquiry, by showing you what it is that science wants you to attempt, in order that she may be put into possession of a sufficient number of positive facts for improving and perfecting her theories. I am told that very few practical farmers are sufficiently instructed to comprehend, or to profit by, the information which science puts before them ; and in the excellent publication called the *Gardener's Chronicle* of this week, (published Dec. 31,) I find a confirmation of this statement. " It is certain," says the editor, " that among the aids which cultivators must now look to with most anxiety is that of chemistry. It is evident to all who understand the principles of tillage, whether in gardens or fields, that the dear old empirical rules of action are inadequate to the wants of the world ; that if we are not to starve, or be otherwise ruined, we must have more out of the land than our fathers had ; and that the common modes of cultivation will not give us more. This is as plain as the sun at noon-day. Under such circumstances, what is it that we English do ? Why, our agricultural associations talk of chemistry as a fine thing—listen to lectures on chemistry, often, we fear, without understanding them, and are contented to rest there, &c. The truth is, that English education—including that of Cambridge and Oxford, does not enable men to appreciate the value of such inquiries."

This misfortune of that incompetency of which the editor here speaks is, that it not only disqualifies persons for availing themselves of every important discovery in science which may bear upon their practice, but frequently most fatally misleads them in their very desire to do so. In an account which I published twenty years ago, of the geology of Anglesea, I traced on the map a particular district under the name of the " Coal-measures," applying this term, in its strict geological meaning, to a particular series of our strata, in which the principal coal fields of England are situate. But some zealous speculators choose to fancy that coal must necessarily be hid somewhere in a district with so inviting a title ; and, consequently, very foolishly to throw away their money in searching for it in places where any geologist would have told them they might have spared themselves the cost. I was informed that if I had visited the island shortly afterwards I should have run some risk of being ducked in the Menai. Now, I have no desire to have my nose rubbed in a dunghill, if any one of you should so far either chance to misinterpret me or to trust me so as to be induced to put yourselves to fruitless expense. I had rather find you all sceptical and over-scrupulous than hasty and over-confident in adopting any suggestion of mine. *You must experiment for yourselves!* If you do not, you may be fifty years in determining some point of importance to you, which might be settled in fifty months or in fifty days.

I will tell an old college acquaintance and worthy friend of mine that he must *disprove*, and not dispute with me, Liebig's suggestion to add gypsum to your dunghills, if you wish to retain that important but invisible ingredient, ammonia—which is continually escaping from them, and upon which plants mainly rely for one of those elements absolutely essential to their growth. My friend chooses to quiz me for having drawn attention to Liebig's suggestion, as though he did not value that tact which a knowledge of natural science confers upon her votaries for making suggestions of this kind. Talk of our making comparative experiments (he thus writes to me), and then tells us to mix gypsum in the manure heap! In 1860 some such paragraph as this will appear :— "So, the absurd practice of mixing gypsum in our manure heaps, for which no assignable reason can be given, took its rise from an incidental hint given by a learned professor now no more."

My friend well understands how a mathematical education confers a power of comprehending a variety of natural phenomena, in a way which no popular view or exposition of them can possibly supply; and why should he refuse to an eminent chemist the right of expecting that the suggestions of his science should be fairly and fully tested? But I know my friend's energy too well not to believe that he intends trying the necessary experiments for testing Liebig's conjectures. In fact, he has just bought some gypsum! Only I don't mean that he shall have all the credit to himself; and, therefore, I shall challenge every farmer in Suffolk to compete with him. If only fifty among you can be found willing to accept the challenge, I shall hope to see the scepticism of my friend set at rest, by proof or disproof, I care not which, within as many months as he has suggested years for the possible duration of my mortal career. My challenge is this—

The best comparative experiment for testing the value of Liebig's suggestion that Gypsum should be added to manure heaps to fix the Ammonia. This experiment to be tried by every farmer in Suffolk who feels any interest in the progress of Agriculture.

The mode of trying the experiment should be as follows:—Two dunghills are to be prepared, as nearly alike in all respects as it is possible to make them; one with, and the other without, the addition of gypsum. Two separate and equal portions of the same field are to be manured with these. I shall say nothing about the respective quantities of the materials, or the time they are allowed to rot. A little variety, among the numerous trials which I expect to hear of, will be useful, and indeed necessary, to the speedy determination of the important problem to be solved. Let the gypsum be sifted over the several layers as they are deposited in one of the heaps. I would suggest there should be about enough to just cover the surface, without placing it on very thick. The returns should give precise information of the following particulars, and any others that may suggest themselves. I shall be happy to report on them before this day twelvemonth; and I will plead for the thanks of all the agricultural societies in Suffolk being given to every contributor :—

1. The quantity of straw used in each heap.
2. The quantity of animal excrement.
3. On what day each was begun.
4. On what day each was completed.
5. On what day they were carried and deposited in the soil.
6. The number of loads, and weight of each.
7. The extent of land manured by each.
8. The quantity of gypsum used to one of the dunghills.

N.B.—A comparatively small quantity is all that can be required.

9. Any difference in the coming up and appearance of the crops, on each piece of land.
10. When each arrived at maturity.
11. The *precise* amount of produce.

N.B, It is needless to reply to this ques-

tion by guess or estimate. It must be swered by the *scales.*

12. Any peculiarity in the qualities of each produce.

Although these particulars may require nothing more than an ordinary degree of intelligence, and a little industry to note them, yet, if they are correctly stated by about 50 experimenters, without any attempt to coax the results into accordance with previous notions and prejudices, they may determine a very important problem in the present state of agricultural science.

Your obedient servant,
J. S. HENSLOW.

P.S. If the farmers of Suffolk consider an occasional letter from me likely to be of service to them, perhaps they will endeavour to prevail upon the editors of the several journals they may happen to take in to copy from that one which I take in myself. The editors will not expect that I should furnish more than one copy of MS.; and having ascertained from the editor of my own paper that he is willing to insert any communications of the sort, I shall send them to him.

Hitcham Rectory, Jan. 7.

EXPERIMENTS IN TURNIP GROWING.— At the annual exhibition of the Sussex Express Root Show which took place at Lewes, two samples of Swede turnips among the extra productions were the subject of considerable inquiry—one was grown by R. Gray, Esq., at Barcombe, with bran as a manure, the other by T. Richardson, Esq., in the same parish, with oil as a manure. Both these experiments seemed to have answered their purpose. Bran was equal to yard manure, and oil had an evident effect in keeping off the fly and nourishing the root. We may here remark that no manure can be applied advantageously for turnips, unless there be present phosphorus in some shape or other, for the turnip contains in itself the chemical properties of carbon, oxygen, and hydrogen as water, nitrogen, silicon, potassium, phosphorus in a large degree, and a slight shade of sodium. In all cultivated soils carbon is present in the shape of decayed vegetation. Rain-water contains oxygen and hydrogen. Nitrogen is invariably present. Silicon, in the shape of gravel or sand. Potassium is found in all clays, but phosphorus has generally to be brought to the land incorporated with the manures applied. Fish oil contains a large portion of phosporus, as does also brans and hence may be traced the value of these two manure, for turnips. It should be borne in mind that fish oil, until it has undergone a chemical change, is injurious to both seed and plant; it is consequently applied after having been incorporated with wood ashes, in which there is a quantity of potass; this immediately changes the oil into soap, and the manure, therefore, actually is soap, and not oil, when thrown upon the land. Where wood ashes are not readily to be obtained, the oil mixed with soda, dissolved in water, will produce the change necessary for its becoming a useful and active manure, and may then be incorporated with road scrapings, or other materials, to fit it for drilling. To destroy the rapacity of the grubs, no plan seems so effectual as turning up the ground rough late in autumn, so that it may be exposed well to the frost. Salt thrown sparingly over also additionally cleanses the soil. Upon stiff lands a winter fallow is a great sweetener, and those who have tried it for roots have ever been well compensated for their labour. To prevent the depredations of the fly several plans have been adopted,—dry lime after a shower has been of great service, but nothing has as yet been presented to public attention more effectual than spreading coal tar or gas ashes over the land after sowing. The smell of the bitumen is so offensive to the fly as to ward off their attacks. An easy method for applying this preventive is to obtain coal tar, and mix it with a solution of sub carbonate of soda (the common soda used in houshold affairs). A chemical combination takes place, and the tenacity of the tar is in a great measure destroyed. Mix the tar so prepared with road scrapings, ashes, or mould : let the compost be turned over several times, and when well incorporated it is ready to be used, and may be spread broadcast after the sowing is completed. We may mention that coal tar forms a leading ingredient of one of the patent manures, but as it does not contain phosphorus in any shape, it possesses scarcely any other value to the crop except protecting it from the ravages of the fly. As a manure for wheat or any other straw crop its application has been very advantageous. As much public benefit is expected from the growth of carrots, we may be excused for offering some observations upon its culture upon stiff clays. The land should be ridged up in the latter end of October or November, and being exposed to the winter's frost, will be ready early in the following year for the reception of the seed, which should be sown as early as possible after February. As there is at the present time a great deficiency of agricultural work for the labourer we can confidently recommend the farmer to employ spade husbandry in preparing the ground for the crop. It will amply repay the extra expense.—*Sussex Express.*

QUERIES ANSWERED—OTHERS PROPOSED.

BY CINCINNATUS.

Your correspondent "Economist," of York, inquires in p. 445 for December, "whether in sandy or gravelly soils through which water percolates freely, a portion of the subsoil may not be brought into activity without the expense of draining?" &c., &c.

Having been in the regular habit of using a subsoil-plough, many years before it came into fashion, I can, from experience, answer decidedly in the affirmative. I have in several instances removed rushes and other water-plants, without any drain being within 200 yards, by the following easy and inexpensive mode of operation.

First, I plough up the pasture for oats; on mowing the oats they are immediately carted away,* the land ploughed on the same or the following day, and by attentively observing the proper state of the soil, for a powerful drag and a heavy iron roller, the soil is reduced into a proper state for drills. After setting potatoes, or sowing Swedes, or mangel-wurzel, I introduce the subsoil plough between each *alternate* drill. The effect is beautiful; as the plough advances the rising and sinking of the summit of the drill on each side is very perceptible; three horses in a line draw the plough about 11 inches below the bottom of the previous furrow, which I feel effectually disturbs the crust of moor pan, marl, &c., that obstructed the uniform descent of rain to the roots of the crops, compelling our best agricultural assistant (or enemy, if we by neglect abuse the bounty of Providence), *water,* to pass away through cracks, fissures, worm-holes, &c., into an abyss of sand, where it wends its way until it breaks out in some lower level.

I have several fields in the farm on which I reside that a superficial observer would have con-

* As described in the *Farmers' Progress, No.* 1, for November, 1839, p. 316.

sidered it necessary to drain at a great expense; they are now as dry as I would wish them, and with less than one mile of drains where ten are now almost universally recommended. I never go to the expense of draining a field without digging a number of small pits ; if no water lodges in those pits I make no drain in that part of the field ; where water lodges I make several of those pits, until I have ascertained the *cause* of the lodgment of water. If the water proceed either from a spring, or because it is confined by a stratum of clay, I make one deep drain, or rather culvert of *large* tile, stone, or brick, whichever costs the least, to the nearest outlet : this done, I wait *with patience* to see the effect of this deep drain. Not unfrequently, the little pits previously full of water become perfectly dry—so far as they become dry I save the expense of additional drains. Not unfrequently, pits within a few yards, or even feet of the deep drain, retain water, whilst others 10, or even 100 yards distant, are drained, probably by some connecting gravel bed, or fissure, acting as a syphon : no matter what the cause, here again I save the expense of draining. Where water lodges in the shallow pits near the deep drain, I know that moor-pan, or clay, or other substance impervious to water intervenes, requiring only a little common sense and observation to remove it—a very small drain, or the removal by spade husbandry of a knoll to some hollow place near at hand, I have generally found a perfect cure. About half a score years ago my attention was drawn to the low part of a valuable meadow, so wet that we could only turn cattle upon it in very dry weather. I soon ascertained that there was no spring — it was merely a basin receiving more than its own share of rain; it was, however, an evil which must be obviated. It would have cost me 10*l.* or 12*l.* to have conveyed the stagnant water to the nearest outlet. After a little consideration I ordered my labourers to dig a drain *up the hill* to carry off the water from the lowest part of the meadow—they looked aghast, but my orders must be obeyed. I had some difficulty to preserve my gravity when I gave those orders. The fact was that I had long noticed a part of the field, 30 or 40 yards higher up, much burnt in dry summers ; by pitting the place I found a bed of gravel—it was to this point I directed my new drain, of course deepening it as I proceeded. I began with tiles about 20 inches below the surface ; when I got to the gravel the drain was about 8 feet deep ; I there dug a deep hole, filled it with clean riddled gravel, and thus at an expense of less than 30s. I effected a perfect cure.

As I shall, ere long, fulfil my promise given in the *Farmers' Mag.* for September, p. 181, of narrating the "Farmers' Progress," No. 9, on a more extended scale of public utility, and on the important subject of draining a large extent of moss land, I shall confine my present observations to the recommendation of caution as respects the great expense of draining. If I am not much deceived, enormous sums are now employed *injudiciously* in draining. Mistake me not—until superfluous water be removed farming cannot answer, but if twenty pounds be expended where five pounds or a smaller sum will have equal effect, I call it extravagance. If I am not mistaken, millions of the tiny tiles to be seen in various parts of the kingdom will, before 20 years are past, be found to be useless, or worse than useless, for drains, when they cease to carry away superfluous water, add to the evil, increasing the growth of water-plants, and destroying those which supply food to man and beast.*

I beg leave to add, that my observations apply principally to hilly land where porous soils prevail. Flat clay land I have only occasionally had to deal with, but even on this description of land I have found that a smaller number of *deep* drains left open during dry weather, until the sides are parched and cracked, with a *well levelled* culvert at the bottom, and filled with stone, covered with a reversed sod a foot from the surface, with short minor spit drains, about 2 feet deep on the square, and a narrow spit of about 8 inches at the bottom, covered with turf or flat stone, emptying into the culverts, equally effectual and less expensive than more numerous parallel drains, laid with tile or stone.

TANKS.

Several of your correspondents have enquired as to the construction of tanks, and the application of liquid manure. If the situation be low or flat, I have nothing to say; but if the situation be so elevated that the surface of the tank can be below the drains from the farm buildings, and the bottom of the tank be above the land to be irrigated, I beg leave to refer them to the *Farmers' Magazine* for March, 1840, p. 174, for a description of the simplest and best tank I ever saw, and to p. 331 for November, 1840, for the place, where it is to be seen by any agriculturists who like to look before they leap.

GUANO.

I shall look anxiously to the *Farmers' Magazine* for the next four months for information as to the application of Guano; not from parties interested in the sale, or the result of small experiments, but from practical farmers who will correctly and impartially state what they have witnessed, be it favourable or otherwise.

Though I allow no farm-yard manure to escape or evaporate, some years must elapse before enough can be provided to restore a large extent of land in a distant estate, exhausted by repeated cropping and great neglect; therefore I resort to guano, and I am desirous to know, not merely how to apply it alone, but in connexion with alluvial soil, soil from decomposed clay slate, bog soil, clay, wood-ashes, either with or without the ashes of bog and clay, charcoal from the croppings of oak and other timber. Of each of these I have an inexhaustible supply; how to combine them, or any of them with guano most advantageously for newly seeded grass-land, old meadow land recently well drained, lucerne, Italian rye-grass, barley, oats, Swedes, turnips, mangel-wurzel, and carrots. Authentic information on any one of these numerous queries I shall be grateful for, and consider a point gained.

My present idea, if not better instructed, for grass land is to mix guano with alluvial soil next February, having at least six inches of soil outside, to turn it over in March, adding about 3 bushels of wood-ashes to 1 of guano; the first damp weather without wind after 15th of April, to spread the compost, aiming at 1½ cwt. of guano per acre, and hush-harrow to follow the first dry day; a roller when very dry.

* In improving two small farms that I purchased several years ago, it cost me more money to search out and take up numerous old drains, nearly all choked up, than to drain the land effectually.

For Swedes, mangel, &c.—Having previously got the land into fine condition, and having everything ready, I think of sowing broadcast about 3 cwt. to the acre of guano; immediately plough into 27-inch drills, spread 8 or 10 tons to the acre (all I can afford) of farm-yard dung in the drills; upon the dung in the drills spread 3 or 4 tons to the acre of wood-ashes, mixed with burnt clay and bog that covered the wood when burning, to exclude the air; stroke up with the double-breasted plough, roll the top of the drills that the seed may be near the manure; sow turnips with the drill, mangel with the dibble, and finish by flattening the outsides of the drills with the spade to prevent evaporation.

Though experienced in the improvement of land in its various branches, and in the production of hay and milk, I consider myself a novice in farming generally; therefore I am sincerely desirous of receiving instruction in the interesting science of agriculture, particularly as respects the application and combination of manures with any one of the soils above mentioned—viz., alluvial, bog, clay, and decomposed clay-slate.

CHARCOAL.

I read in a hundred places of the excellence of charcoal as a manure, of its affinity and retention of ammonia, but scarcely a word of the mode of applying it. A description, concise, intelligible, of the quantity, the size to which it should be ground, in short of anything practical as respects charcoal, would, I think, be acceptable to many of your readers; it would be attentively and gratefully perused by

Your obliged humble servant,
Dec. 19, 1842.   CINCINNATUS.

Since writing the above, I have perused in page 6 to 10 of your last number, with pleasure and instruction, Agricultor's perspicuous remarks on the "Principles of Draining, &c." His lucid explanation of a neglected, but *most* important principle of agriculture, *capillary attraction*, is, in my humble opinion invaluable, and well worthy the best attention of every gentleman desirous of improving his landed property. And, I also gratefully acknowledge the practical information emanating from the Preston Agricultural Meeting, in pages 18 and 19 of the same number; the clear, concise, and well considered Reports of that Society, unmixed with trifles of mere local interest, are doubly valuable for the information they contain, and as an example to other agricultural societies.   C.
Jan. 12, 1843.

FARMERS' CLUBS.

TO THE EDITOR OF THE FARMERS' MAGAZINE.

SIR,—I concur with you that the advancement of agriculture is greatly aided by the formation of Farmers' Clubs throughout the length and breadth of the land, as by their means any improvement in the management of stock or the growing of crops, made by a member of such club, is no longer kept a profound secret, but is discussed in public, and if approved of, immediately adopted by the whole neighbourhood; thereby benefitting not only the farmers themselves, but every class in the community. I regret such societies are as yet rarely to be met with in many parts of England (I know of only one within

the limits of the great agricultural county of Somerset, that of Bradford, near Taunton); and I would call upon the farmers of the whole kingdom to come forward and establish clubs in every locality, reminding them that, since'the protection we so much needed is now unhappily (in a great measure) withheld from us by the alteration in the duties on the importation of corn, cattle, and provisions, it requires strenuous and increased individual and united exertion for the British farmer to maintain that elevated position he has hitherto held. I hail with pleasure the time when every knot of villages shall possess its farmers' club, calculated, as I am convinced they are, to enlighten the understanding of the agriculturist, and in so doing to disperse the mist of prejudice now unfortunately obscuring the path of too many amongst us; and certain am I that it is not only the agriculturist who will benefit through the dissemination of knowledge by these clubs, for if the farmer can only increase his crop of wheat two bushels per acre, price being regulated by the supply and demand, will not every class of the community, more especially the half-starved operative, reap an advantage in the reduction of the price of bread— the first necessary of life? Seeing then that so many and great benefits will arise from the formation and support of such institutions, why should the farmers of England display such great apathy and listlessness in not coming forward at once in support of so good a cause? Many, I am aware, who would gladly lend their aid, when once set on foot, are from a want of education and general knowledge of public business unfit to take an active part in the formation of such societies; then why do not the clergy, the landlords, and the independent gentlemen, who possess every requisite for such an undertaking, nobly step forward, and by their example stimulate others to exertion? I trust it is evident that the cause of humanity calls upon them to assist in the great undertaking, not only from the reduced price of bread to the manufacturing operative, but, from the increase of employment arising from an improved system of farming, to the agricultural labourer, whereby the poor-rates would be reduced, crime would be lessened, and the morals of the lower classes greatly improved; and all this affected at the expense of no individual interest whatever. Trusting the subject will receive the consideration it deserves,   I remain, sir, yours respectfully,
          ·   A TENANT FARMER.
East Somerset, Dec. 24, 1842.

ON BURNED CLAY AS A MANURE.

TO THE EDITOR OF THE FARMER'S GAZETTE.

SIR,—I shall feel obliged by your informing me, through the medium of your truly useful paper, how kilns should be constructed for burning clay? and will peat suit as fuel?

Is common yellow clay suitable for burning, or would a mixture of loam or calcareous earth be an improvement?

Would the ashes produced be a good manure for green crops?

Would it be advisable to use it mixed with any other ingredient?

Any other information on the subject you will be kind enough to impart, will be thankfully received by   Yours,   A FARMER.

[To CONSTRUCT THE KILN,—Let sods be cut, of a convenient size to handle, say a foot wide and 18 inches in length; with these form a parallelogram or "long square," let the walls be a couple of feet thick, and tramped or beaten firmly together, and raised at least three feet high; the kiln should be so situated that the wind may blow against one of its sides; the kiln may be from four to six yards long, by three yards wide, and an aperture within one yard of each end, and others at a distance of about five feet from these, should be left in the side walls when building them for the purpose of forming drain-like openings across the kiln; should there be a likelihood of the wind changing so as to blow against the end of the kiln, it is advisable to make one of these drain-like openings from end to end in the length of the kiln; these funnels are to be built also with sods. Some dry turf, such as is used for fuel, is to be put into these funnels, and over it and between the funnels well dried sods, or any other combustible materials, are to be laid on to the depth of a couple of feet over these sods, partially dried, to the level of the walls of the kiln. These materials being set on fire, a powerful heat will be produced, quite capable of burning clay without previously drying it; care, however, will be necessary to avoid throwing it on in too great a quantity at once until the mass appears red, when a large quantity may be thrown on. The sod walls are to be raised as the heap rises, and as soon as it is perceived by the strength of the smoke and the glow of heat that the mass is ignited in all its parts, the apertures may be closed up, and the kiln left to become charred. Should appearances indicate a likelihood of the fire being smothered, it will only be necessary to open one or more of the funnels to secure its acting. It is customary, as soon as a sufficient quantity, say twenty cubic yards, has been heaped on the fire, to cover it up closely with sods, but this, although a good practice, we have found not to be necessary. Clay only, and not loam or earth of any kind, is suitable for burning. If the land on which the burned or charred clay is to be applied be deficient in calcareous matter, earth containing it, being burned with the clay, would improve it much. We have seen layers of finely broken limestone completely burned in clay kilns. We have seen excellent crops of turnips produced on indifferent land by the use of the ashes of clay-kilns, and there can scarcely be a better preparation for rape. Farmers with whom we have conversed, in the county Monaghan, where the burning of clay is general, have assured us that, but for the manure so produced, they could not raise crops of either potatoes or corn, nor pay their rents, and they assert that the land so treated, time out of mind, is better now than formerly. As a considerable quantity of the surface sods and earth are burned every time potatoes are planted, we cannot but doubt this latter part of the assertion, and these lands being peculiarly suited to the turnip husbandry, were that crop once introduced, and its value fully tested, burning would, we have no doubt, notwithstanding the present notions of those who adopt it, soon be given up. No doubt the action of the fire causes combinations capable of affording food to plants, still we look upon burned clay rather in the light of an alterative, as improving the texture of the soil by rendering it more friable and permeable to moisture, than as a manure. We have seen composts formed of burned clay, bog-stuff, and lime, and consider such mixtures valuable.]

ON THE PROGRESS OF AGRICULTURAL KNOWLEDGE DURING THE LAST FOUR YEARS.

BY PH. PUSEY, M.P., F.R. AND G.S.

(From the Journal of the Royal Agricultural Society.)

As four years have passed since our Society was founded for extending the knowledge and improving the practice of husbandry, it may not be useless now to enquire how far, if at all, its working has hitherto carried out the views of our founders. Though we could not be fairly required to have done much in so short a time, we certainly ought to have done something, strengthened as we have been by the hearty aid of the English farmers. We should be encouraged, I think, by knowing what we have done, if indeed we have succeeded in anything; we shall be more likely to advance farther, if we look at the difficulties we still have to deal with; and the best encouragement, perhaps for active men, is the knowledge that they have yet a great deal to do. The extension of science may, however, mean two different things, either the spread of existing knowledge among a wider number of persons—and this is a most important object in our department; for if the best practice of each different district would become general in the country, a very great improvement in farming would at once be effected—or it may mean the discovery of principles hitherto entirely unknown. In examining how far we have advanced in either way the knowledge of farming, it may be convenient to begin with the soil itself, proceeding afterwards from tillage and seed-time to harvest; and as no soil, however good, can yield what it ought while it is drenched with water, we must first consider drainage.

It is only seven years since we heard in England, chiefly through the present Speaker of the House of Commons, that a manufacturer in Scotland, now well known as Mr. Smith of Deanston, had found the means of making all land, however wet and poor it might be, warm, sound, and fertile, and that this change was brought about by two processes, thorough-draining and subsoil-ploughing. His rule of draining was this : that we are not to endeavour merely to find out hidden springs, and to cut them through by a single drain, which in some of our books appeared to be regarded as all that was necessary; but that, as the whole surface of retentive soils is rendered wet, not by accidental springs, but by the rain, the whole surface of the field must be made thoroughly dry by under-drains, running throughout at equal distances; any field, he said, however wet, might be so dried, provided these under-drains were cut sufficiently near to each other. This was the principle of thorough or frequent draining asserted by Mr. Smith of Deanston, in 1835; and this principle, which was then new and startling, may now be regarded as firmly established. But though it was then so novel, I have discovered accidentally that it has been long practised to its fullest extent in one part of England. I do not speak of furrow-draining, which was well known in many districts, for the drains were not generally so deep nor so numerous as they are on the Deanston system. But an old drill-man from Suffolk having observed to me, that if he were the tenant of a strong clay farm in this neighbourhood, he should drain the whole of it with drains cut 12 feet apart and 3 feet in depth ; I was struck with this remark of an old man who had never read the new system of drainage, yet described it as carried to its utmost extent, for drains could scarcely be cut nearer or deeper. He told me, on being further questioned, that it was the method which he had seen as a boy at his native place. Mr. Allan Ransome, at my request, inquired into the matter, and informs me that forty years ago three properties, one of them Lord Huntingfield's, near Yoxford, in Suffolk, were drained in this manner. I have reason to believe that the same effectual mode of draining has long been practised in Essex, so much so as to he called the Essex system even in Scotland. Now, in proving that Mr. Smith's system is not new, I do not lower his claims to our thanks, for he probably invented it also, and at all events carried it out with an energy which made it new in his hands ; but I think the fact of its previous practice in Suffolk and Essex worth notice for two reasons : one, that any new method, however highly recommended, must be received with doubt as long as it continues new, and that consequently the best praise by which any method can be recommended to practical farmers is, not that it is new, but on the contrary that it is old and tried ; the other reason is this, that here was a plan of drainage which was regarded as novel, yet had been employed and established for half a century at no great distance from London ; and this is by no means a singular proof how little the farmers in one part of England knew, until lately, what the others were doing.

All, however, who are at all acquainted with improved husbandry, are now agreed that on wet land thorough-draining is to a farm what a foundation is to a house. There is no doubt now what ought to be done ; the difficulty is to find means for doing it, since one third of England, I believe, requires to be drained. It would be easy to bring forward instances of great profit resulting from drainage ; and I may refer to the accounts of Sir James Graham's operations at Netherby,[*] and of Lord Hatherton's[†] at Teddesley, where the water which gushes out of the underground drains is thrown over a water-wheel, thrashes the corn, and does the other work of the barn; still great returns cannot be held out in all cases, yet every wet farm ought to be drained. But the advantage of draining is not to be measured merely by the additional bushels of corn that may be grown on an acre ; though I believe five or six bushels of wheat per acre would be a fair estimate of the increase ; for such land is usually thrown up into very narrow ridges, perhaps 10 feet wide, and no corn grows in the bare furrow, so that one-tenth of the land is lost altogether ; the lower half of the ridge, too, on each side of the furrow bears often only straggling ears. Long tracts of such fields must have been seen between Birmingham and Liverpool last year by many of our members ; and it may be useful for landowners to know that every arable field which is laid up in ridges probably requires more or less to be drained ; in fact these deep furrows were devised by our ancestors for drying the ridges piled up between them. An intrinsic advantage, however of draining is this, that the character of the farm is changed. It is difficult to obtain a good tenant for a cold clay farm ; and I am inclined to think that some of these farms have

---

[*] Journal, vol. i. p. 32.

[†] Ibid., vol. ii. p. 273, on the drainage of land: by J. F. Burke.

II

gone backwards in the last fifty years. On two such farms, now in wretched condition, I found it was in the memory of living persons that they had once borne far better crops. No long time ago it was the clay lands that fed the country; but since the great change effected in light-land farming by turnip husbandry, every farmer wishes to occupy what is called a stock-farm—a farm where he can fold his sheep on the land at all seasons—consequently the clay-farms have become less and less popular; and, in some cases, have fallen into inferior hands.* Nor can we be surprised at the unpopularity of a wet farm, for its discomforts are endless, as well as its losses. The acts of husbandry are at all times liable to interruption by excess of rain. The farmer does not know when he can plough or sow; often his teams cannot go on the land, so that the work to be done accumulates; yet when the favourable moment arrives, in which all the work must be done at once, he requires more horses for each plough than the light-land farmer, while he has less time for doing that work. In a wet autumn he must sow his wheat too late; perhaps not sow it at all. If he does sow wheat, and the rain continues, the seed sometimes rots in the ground; or if it has come up well, winter soaks the hollows thoroughly, if it does not fill them, with standing water; and in spring, on each side of the furrow, large blanks are seen in the crop.†

---

* A main reason why clay-farms have, to a considerable extent, fallen into "inferior hands" is the circumstance that they are the only farms which, from the moderate outlay required to enter, come within the reach of a certain class. If, for instance, a farming servant or cottager, either by marriage, bequest, or a long course of industry, shall have become possessed of a few hundred pounds, and desire to be himself an occupier, he is debarred from entering upon a grazing, a mixed, or a convertible farm, by the capital necessary to purchase stock or artificial manures; but for a small clay-farm a team of horses and a few implements are alone essential. He ploughs, sows, and reaps, and converts his straw into what he calls manure, by the mouths and feet of a few starved calves or yearlings, mainly aided by the winter rains, and then carts it on his land, little better than rotted straw. No wonder the condition of small clay-farms should be low. Yet, however disagreeable the enumerated drawbacks to a clay-farm, and I admit they are many, there is none more grateful for capital expended, either in draining or manure. Once drained, the art of clay-farming consists in the art of ploughing, and the art of making manure. If, on the one hand, the clays could advantageously spare their superfluous moisture to the thirsty, gravelly, or sandy soils; on the other hand, they do not burn like these under a summer sun, and, at all events, carefully retain, until required by the crop, whatever manure is put into them.—H. HANDLEY.

* I have also heard from a farmer on a very stiff clay, that the wetter the winter the more rain is required on such land by the wheat in the following summer; the more consequently it suffers in a season of drought. The reason, I think, must be this, that the water lodged in winter condenses the soil, destroying the looseness which the plough had produced in it, and thus rendering it when dry once more a close clay, through which the roots of the plant cannot make their way, and which moderate summer rains cannot penetrate; but this is not generally applicable to clay lands.

In fact, a perpetual struggle is going on between the ploughman with his horses on one side, who endeavours to reduce this stubborn clay into mould, and the rains which render it solid again. There are some such farms, so hard in dry weather, so tough in their best state of moderate moisture, so deep and impassable in wet winters, so cold and backward in spring—I have one such farm myself—that farmers who are accustomed to warm, sound land, fit at all times for stock and for labour, say they would not occupy such ground free of rent. No one who knows the effect of thorough-draining can see without regret such farms, and the starveling crops which they bear. If the occupier be a bad farmer, his own circumstances are probably in proportion to the poverty of his land; if a good one, half his exertions are lost, and he does not obtain the fair reward of his industry and enterprise. If I were a working farmer, nothing would induce me to enter on a cold wet farm, unless there were a fair prospect of its being drained, either with my own money under a long lease, or with the aid of my landlord. Our Society has wisely abstained from entering into questions between landlords and tenants; and I will therefore merely mention that sometimes in Scotland, on a lease for nineteen years, the tenant pays for the draining himself; sometimes the landlord finds materials, and the tenant the labour, or the landlord pays for the whole, receiving interest for his outlay. The landlord, however, may not find it convenient to make heavy advances over a large property; but, as Lord Stanley recommended, he may borrow the money for such a purpose. In districts, indeed, where under-draining is still unknown, the tenant may not be aware of its advantage, and therefore may not meet his views. In that case a few fields may be drained at first, in order to prove the advantage; or if a poor wet farm should fall in, it may be taken in hand and reclaimed, which is more useful and more interesting for a country gentleman than to occupy a farm ready made to his hands because it is the one nearest his dwelling. I am sure a strenuous effort ought to be made for attaining this object. All cannot be done at once; but in justice to our tenants, we ought to begin in earnest, not regarding with indifference farms poached with water, but considering the want of drainage on any part of our property as a defect, and in some degree a discredit. Every land-steward should survey his employer's estate with this special view, lay the result before his employer, and suggest matured plans for drying the soil.

The best materials for draining are tiles: indeed, where the fall is slight, the water does not flow through broken stones; and if the stones must be brought from a distance, the labour of drawing them is too heavy. Hitherto, however, the cost of tiles has been a great check to their employment; but two years ago we discovered that while 40s., 50s., and even 60s. per thousand were paid for tiles in the south of England, Mr. Beart, of God-manchester, five years before, had invented a simple machine by which he had reduced the price of tiles from 40s. to 22s. throughout Huntingdonshire. His statement was as follows:—

"The price of furrow-draining tiles has fluctuated here from 20s. to 22s. per 1000; at these reduced prices the consumption of tiles has increased greatly. As a proof of that increased consumption, and of the great quantity manufactured, it was publicly stated at a late meeting of agriculturists at Huntingdon, that one tenant-farmer last year consumed 520,000 draining-tiles. I wish to point out to tile-makers, that whether the making of draining-tiles be performed by machinery or by hand-labour only, they may be made at prices much below what they now cost in many parts of the country, and thus enable the makers so to reduce the price of tiles that the consumption will augment as it has in this county. Though the profit on a single thousand of tiles will be less, still the quantity they would sell would be so increased that the profits of their works would be larger. By the introduction of machinery, which led to the change of system in this county, a reduction of 15s. per 1000 was effected in one season, and *during the last five years the number of tile-works has been doubled.*"*

The price of tiles depends partly on that of the coals used in burning them. Mr. Beart states that in Huntingdonshire, where coals cost 23s. per ton, tiles are sold for 22s.; and that with one ton of coals he burns 3500 tiles. Where coals then cost 16s., tiles would cost 20s.; and where 37s., 26s. per thousand. At our Bristol meeting a new tile-machine was shown by Mr. Irving; it is praised by our judges, and described in this journal by Mr. Ford, whose estimate of the cost of labour in tile-making agrees closely with Mr. Beart's. Lord Tweeddale's most ingenious machine is also now reduced in size, so as to be worked by hand-labour. Those who wish to make tiles will determine for themselves which is the best. Mr. Burke entertains, and has expressed in a note,† a decided

---

* See account of Mr. Beart's machine, Journal, vol. ii. p. 93.

† The owners of all tile-machines severally profess theirs to be the best. I am not personally interested in any of them; but having written on the subject, and not only made anxious inquiries regarding it, but also practically examined several of the tiles in different parts of the kingdom, I unequivocally state that those made under the Tweeddale patent are superior to all others; for they are made at one operation, by the uniform power of machinery, the compression of which renders them more solid, and consequently more durable, than those made by hand. In saying this, I have no wish to detract from the merit of Beart's invention; but the so-called "*machine*," though useful in the preparation of the clay, is, in fact, a mere *tool*, and goes no farther; the tile being actually made, as in every other case (except the Tweeddale), entirely by hand. In comparing the price of tiles and soles, the *length* is seldom named, and they are usually not longer than 12 inches: now the Tweeddale tiles are *fifteen inches*, wherefore, the number required by Beart's tiles, at the closest distance of drainage, is 2440, whilst those of the Tweeddale patent would only be 1952. The price of the latter, as I learn from the patentees, varies, according to the price of coals, from 25s. to 45s. per thousand. The cost of draining an acre could, therefore, never be much more than that of Beart's, while the difference, both in quality, labour in laying down, and real usefulness, would be still greater than in quantity.

It is false economy to drain land with inferior tiles. They may suit the object of a tenant who looks only to the duration of his lease; but the owner of the soil, who has at heart his own interest and that of his heirs, should see that the work is done in the most substantial and imperishable manner. The saving of a few shillings in the price of the tiles is

opinion; but I need not enter into that question. Whichever of the three be the best machine now, there is no doubt that, seven years ago, Mr. Beart greatly reduced the price of tiles in Huntingdonshire. Here we then paid 50s., and even 60s. for tiles; there Mr. Beart sold tiles of the same length

---

to him, therefore, not worth consideration; and I should imagine that landlords and trustees, when raising money for that purpose under the Drainage Act, will be compelled by the Court of Chancery to use the most efficient means in their power. The subjoined letter from the agent to the Tweeddale patentees will afford all the necessary information regarding the price and formation of their tiles.—J. FRENCH BURKE.

"I understand that you want some information in regard to the improvements recently patented in the Tweeddale drain-tile and brick machinery, and as those additions are of very great importance to agriculturists, as well as to the trade, I have much pleasure in complying with your wish.

"The Tweeddale machinery, in its original state, was intended to perform several functions in the manufacture of bricks and tiles beyond what were absolutely necessary in most cases. In consideration of those objects it was indispensable to employ great *power* to work the machines, and the expense was consequently, perhaps, too heavy for general adoption. On this account the company instituted a series of experiments, and at much outlay have effected the important result of—1st, a considerable reduction in the price of the machinery; 2nd, a vast abatement in the patent dues on seignorage; and, 3rd, a diminution of power from that of horses down to the labour of one man, or even a boy. Hence I can confidently assure you that, in the essential points of *quantity*, *quality*, and *cheapness* (length for length), it is utterly impossible for any other existing machine to compete fairly and successfully with those of this company. Among other advantages, I would beg leave to mention that our machinery, as now arranged, may be profitably adapted to the very smallest establishment; that it may be worked by one person as easily as a grindstone; that it is portable; and that bricks and tiles, of the best kind, can be produced by ordinary labourers and boys. You are probably aware that tiles and soles, of 10 and 12 inches in length, are often named in comparison of price with ours, which are not only 15 inches long, but also of very superior quality. It may indeed be some evidence of their estimation in the agricultural world to state that this year we have made *upwards of twenty millions of draining-tiles and soles.*

"I beg to enclose for your attention a short account of our machines, and the rates of seignorage for their use. I shall have much pleasure in showing the hand-machines at work to you or your friends at any time, and to give any information as to the cost of working them. I wish it to be understood that we find no fault with any other tile-machine, but claim only for our own that superiority which we are certain it deserves. The very great durability of our tiles, arising from the compression employed in their manufacture, may be the more readily understood by comparing the weight of the common tile with those made with the aid of the pressure we employ. It will be found that common tiles weigh about 35 cwt. per 1000; while those made by us will weigh about 45 cwt. per 1000. The price of a hand tile-machine is 45*l.*; and with it two

H 2

(1 foot) and the same quality for 22s. : here soles, one of which is required with every tile, cost 30s. ; there, from 8s. to 10s. So that, in fact, for the same sum which the soles alone cost us here, the Huntingdonshire farmer *obtained the tiles into the bargain.* Yet the price of coals would justify a difference of 1s. only. If the Huntingdonshire scale could be made universal, the highest price of one-foot tiles would be not 60s., but 27s. per thousand: and what has been done in that county for seven years, being now known, ought to be imitated. Indeed, if a landowner have a kiln of his own, he may make tiles, as Mr. Beart does, for 15s. per thousand : the machine costs only 12*l.*, and can be used by a common labourer ; as doubtless can Lord Tweeddale's and Mr. Irving's. I will only add a short estimate of the expense of tile-draining on the

Huntingdonshire scale of prices—in a district where coals cost 16s., and tiles would sell, consequently, at 20s., soles at 10s. Those who know the necessity for draining wet land, the difficulty of defraying the expense where hundreds or thousands of acres require to be drained, and consequently the importance of saving 4*l.* or 5*l.* per acre in making land dry, will agree, I think, that if the manufacturers remember the names of men who have improved their machinery, Hargreaves or Arkwright—even though their inventions may have been long superseded—we must not forget what we owe Mr. Beart for his, which is still producing tiles at half cost. The fourth column shows the outlay required for tiles at the high standard—50s. for tiles, and 30s. for soles.

COST OF THOROUGH-DRAINING ONE ACRE AT HUNTINGDONSHIRE PRICES.

*Distance between Drains.	Length of Drains in 1 Acre.	Number of Tiles.	Cost of Tiles and Soles at high prices.	Reduced Cost of Tiles and Soles.	Cost of making Drains at 3½d. per Pole.		Total Reduced Cost per Acre.		
Feet.	Furlongs.		s.	s.	s.	d.	£	s.	d.
66	1	660	53·	20	11	8	1	11	4
44	1½	990	80	30	17	6	2	7	6
33	2	1320	106	40	23	4	3	3	4
22	3	1980	160	60	35	0	4	15	0
16½	4	2640	213	80	46	8	6	6	8

At this reduced price of tiles the cost of thorough-drainage certainly no longer appears formidable, for the greater portion of our land which requires to be drained would be laid sufficiently dry by drains cut at intervals of 44, 33, and 22 feet. I know many farms, the whole character

men and one boy can easily make 500 perfectly-formed draining-tiles, 15 inches long, per hour.

" The following are the rates of seignorage charged to licencees :

	Per 1000.
	s. d.
On any number up to 100,000, made in any one season	1 0
On all beyond the first 100,000 up to 150,000, made in the same season	0 11
On all beyond the first 150,000 up to 200,000, made in the same season	0 10
On all beyond 200,000, made in the same season	0 9
On soles for draining-tiles, one half the above rates."	

* This calculation has been made by ascertaining the expense of cutting one drain of 40 poles in length ; the price of labour being usually calculated per pole : and 40 poles or 1 furlong, are the length of an acre when the breadth is 66 feet. If the price of labour or the cost of tiles be higher than is rated in the table, an addition must of course be made to the estimate for the single furlong ; but when the cost of one furlong is ascertained, the expense of draining at the different distances is easily seen. For more detailed calculations see Mr. Stephens's " Book of the Farm," chap. 28. Some addition may be required for breakage and for main drains. The carriage of the tiles is not included because it is not considerable, and would therefore be done by the ordinary horses of the farm.

and management of which would be permanently changed by drains cut at 33 feet apart ; this could be done for the very moderate cost of 3*l.* 3s. per acre. The greatest number of drains that can usually occur (16½ feet interval, or 4 furlongs per acre, cost only 6*l.* 6s. I must admit, however, that on very strong land it may be necessary to fill in with stones over the tiles, which raises the cost of workmanship from 3½d. to 6d. per pole, that is, from 11s. 8d. to 1*l.* per furlong. But, if the ground be sloping, broken stones may be used alone, where they are to be found near at hand. In many districts flat stones are common, which may be set upright in the drain, so as to give the same free current as tiles, without their expense. Mr. Holcomb states that he has used mere wedges of peat,* which cost only 6s. per thousand, as substitutes for tiles. The Duke of Richmond has also applied peat, cut into the circular shape of tiles, for the same purpose. There is a method of draining grass-land called wedge or sod draining, fully described by Mr. Handley Brown in our last number ; in which the roof of the drain is supported by a mere wedge of the natural turf. It is exceedingly cheap, costing in Lincolnshire only 18s. 6d. per acre, at an interval of about 30 feet. I think it must require a strong clay subsoil, as a weak clay would hardly maintain an open passage, but would probably silt in. It is, I believe, an old practice in North Wiltshire, where such drains are executed at a depth of 20 inches for 9s. or 10s. the furlong, so that grass-land is there drained at the very narrow interval of 16½ feet for the trifling ex-

* Mr. Pym, however, has found that some peat drains he has made in Bedfordshire have fallen in. The field is subject to floods, which had backed up in the drains.

pence of 2l. per acre. Mr. Brown advocates the use of these thorn-drains on arable land also, and states that he has known them draw well where the water has lain over tile-drains. But in thorn-draining, sooner or later, the whole work must be done again. Tile-drains are made once for ever, since any occasional repairs would fall into the common management of the farm. His statement, however, that tile-drains will not draw on his land, deserves great attention. I have seen the same failure here in drains only 20 inches deep, on some very strong land; but that the clay from the sub-soil had been thrown back on the tiles in these drains. In the next field, though the drains were 30 inches deep, yet being covered slightly with stones, and filled in with surface mould, they ran well even after one strong summer rain. Some high authorities tell us that the clay should be pressed down on the tile, and that no water should penetrate the drain from above; but I must say on this much-argued question, that practice, I think, is against them. Still Mr. Brown is no doubt right in saying that there is some land in England so extremely retentive of water, that there may be a doubt whether it can be drained with tiles; and as it is on such land that the expence of tiles is heavy, from the necessary nearness of the drains, it may be well to use the old system of filling with thorns as has been long practised in Suffolk. There the drains are cut to the full depth of 30 inches, a narrow open channel being left at the bottom in the solid clay, a twisted rope of straw forming the roof with thorns or heath over it. This system has been found to answer; and indeed on the strongest clays appears to afford more certainty that the drains will run than the new plan of tile-draining. They last sixteen years, and may be completed for 10s. a furlong, so that 6 furlongs of drains may be allowed to the acre—that is, the drains may be placed so near as even 11 feet to each other, for the trifling expence of 3l. It appears to me a fortunate circumstance that on those very heavy soils where on the one hand the great num-ber of drains which is necessary might raise the expence of even cheap tiles beyond ordinary means, and on the other hand there is some doubt whether tiles will draw off the water, we should find an old established method of draining, which certainly does draw off the water, which is suited particularly to stiff clays, because the stiffer the clay the longer will an open channel underground remain open, and which is so cheap as to bring our estimates once more within a moderate com-pass. On such land, therefore, I should recom-mend thorn or wedge draining, because I think many more farms will be drained at 3l. than at 10l. per acre. The drain, I am told, is placed by the side of the furrow, not under it, and is not trodden in, as we might fear, on arable land. Not only, however, do tiles and stones fail to act on some very heavy land, but on such land, if under grass, I have been told that drainage when it has acted has even been found injurious; and I mention this because we ought not to shut our eyes to ob-jections, and because nothing I believe has more checked the advance of farming than the unwil-lingness of eager improvers to admit that their remedies can in any single instance be found to fail. Still, with regard to draining, the exceptions, if any, can be but few. Those large tracts of the country which require drainage can generally be drained easily, and our Society has done a great service to the country by making known the means

of draining them with the best and most lasting materials, according to the Huntingdonshire me-thod, cheaply. Further reductions of price I know are in progress. If Lord J. Hay should perfect his invention of concrete draining-tiles, another large saving may be effected. But I trust that the coming winter will not pass by without a vigo-rous commencement of under-draining throughout the country; for besides the benefit to the farm, draining in its execution of course gives great employment to the labourers, who may this year be in much want of employment; and even beyond this temporary relief, every landowner who drains and then breaks up with the plough 25 or 30 acres of indifferent pasture, provides employment throughout future years for an additional family. Notwithstanding the covenants in old leases, I believe that on many farms weak pastures not worth more than 20s. an acre might be so broken up after drainage, with advantage to both owner and occupier, and that many village families might be so founded.* At all events, the necessity of draining is so certain, that within the next ten years a large part of England will probably be thorough-drained, and at no dis-tant day a soaked field will be as little tolerated as ruined barns or foul crops; but I am anxious to see a great exertion made at once for this na-tional object, and, if I have dwelt too long on the matter, my excuse must be this—that it is vain to speak of good farming until we have land which deserves to be farmed well. There can be no profit in farming highly land on which stock does not thrive, and on which half the crop may be drowned by one rainy week; wet land is well adapted for slovenly husbandry.

Before we leave wet land I ought to say one word on subsoil ploughing, but the accounts of its effects are as yet contradictory. It does not ap-pear to suit very light soils, as it makes them too loose, unless indeed there be a retentive subsoil under them, near the surface; nor very strong clays,† since these run together again. As it should only be done after draining, we can scarcely ascertain which of the two operations has produced any improvement that may have arisen. It seems, however, to do most good where the subsoil is a mixture of rubble and clay; and I have heard of one farm of that nature, near Taunton,

* There are also thousands of acres, perhaps mil-ions, that are at present worse than lying waste, causing whole districts to be unhealthy to man and beast—acres that will not support a goose, or at best a sheep, per acre; some let to farmers at from 2s. 6d. to 5s. per acre, all of which with little excep-tion, if properly drained and well cultivated in a regular course of alternate husbandry, would in-crease in value from 150 to 300 per cent., forward the harvest from 14 to 20 days, improve the cli-mate of the country, and add to the produce in a direct ratio to the higher value of the land.—Geo. Kimberley.

† There is great ambiguity in the term clay, as used in different districts; sometimes, when a clay is said to have been reduced to mould by subsoil ploughing, it turns out to be what those who live upon a strong clay would not consider a clay. A really strong clay when dry has no roughness or grittiness which show the presence of sand, but is smooth like soap, though extremely hard and diffi-cult to break with the hand. If it contain lime it is marl.

which had been thorough-drained without benefit, but on which the subsoil plough produced a large immediate increase of crop. This was a red clay, and it was on a red clay also that Mr. Thompson* found subsoiling to have answered in Yorkshire. It appears to answer best on those parts of the country, the northern and western, where most rain usually falls. I would try it, however, after draining, on any strong land ; but the original plough seems to me too bulky in its underground parts, as the thick iron sole on which it rests can only be forced through the land by great exertion of the cattle.† The implement shown by Mr. Nugent at Bristol must stir the land as thoroughly with its thin deep tines or teeth fixed in a framework above ground. Where the subsoil is very stony, a single tine will move it thoroughly. Subsoil ploughing, however, should be tried cautiously, as in two instances—one a farm near Exmoor, in Somersetshire, where the subsoil is a wet blue slate ; the other a farm also with a stony subsoil—it did permanent mischief. The trial, however, can be easily made, as many common ploughs, if the mouldboard be removed, will serve as well as one made for the purpose. Altogether, though we must not speak too confidently of subsoil ploughing, I cannot but hope that we shall probably have to thank Mr. Smith of Deanston for this invention, as well as for the zeal and ability by which he has succeeded in restoring the ancient English practice of thorough-draining.

Hitherto we have considered only one defect of land—too great cohesiveness, and consequent retention of too much moisture. There is an opposite fault, however, well known to farmers—too great looseness. This fault may be seen on tracts absolutely barren, as on Bagshot Heath, or on fields under culture, which are termed blowing sands, because the surface-sand drifts in high winds. In different degrees it is a common fault in land, and shows itself by thinness of the corn-crop, shortness of the straw and of the ear. Formerly, indeed, rye was grown on such land instead of wheat. Folding with sheep, pressing and shallow ploughing, diminish the evil, but do not remedy it. The practice of our ancestors was to cover such land with marl, which is usually a strong clay, containing a great deal of lime. Marl was said indeed to benefit the land at first, but to injure it afterwards—to be " good for the father, but bad for the son." This injury, however, arose, I believe, from improvidence ; marl was found to act without dung at first, and the fields which had been marled were consequently tilled without dung until their soil was completely exhausted. It fell into disrepute, and many farmers are perhaps not aware that it is still largely used in England. I have been surprised to find, in the successive numbers of our Journal, how often it is mentioned casually by members of our Society. To take first the most striking example: the improvement of the late Lord Leicester's property, as described by Lord Spencer.‡ I doubt if that la-

mented nobleman, with all his enterprise, could have fed oxen where rabbits had previously browsed, as was his just boast, unless those sandy commons had first been made solid with marl. It is used also largely in Bedfordshire on a yellow sand about Woburn* The practice is general, I believe, in Norfolk, and also in Suffolk, where, at some recent agricultural meeting, a prize was given to the farmer who had drawn the largest quantity in one year—and that quantity, if I am not mistaken, was 10,000 cart-loads. It is mentioned by Mr. Dugdale† as existing in Warwickshire ; and we have a very good account of an entire farm which had been marled, at Sheriff Hutton,‡ in Yorkshire. Marl is commonly applied in Cheshire to light soils at the rate of 128 cart-loads to the acre.§ I have had also specimens of marl so used sent from the New Forest in Hampshire. The greatest improvement of recent times, the application of clay to peat and peaty sand in Lincolnshire and the wide district of the fens, by which in one instance, as we learn from Mr. Wingate,‖ on land which had been almost worthless, two white crops had been grown every three years, one of them wheat, yielding 40 bushels per acre—an unexampled rotation, not used, however, only when the land was fresh, but continued for eighteen years—this improvement, which equals anything that has been done in Flanders, is another instance of the same principle. It is, therefore, important, to examine the facts accurately : as yet, however, we have not the means.

The substance applied is sometimes called marl, sometimes clay. Of the specimens I have received, even those which were called clay, have generally turned out to be marl, for they contained lime, which constitutes the distinction. The difference, however, is important, because marl is a much rarer substance than clay ; and if lime be an indispensable ingredient of clay fit for manure, many districts of England must be cut off from this source of improvement. I am inclined, however, to hope that it is not indispensable. One specimen of the Lincolnshire clay which I have examined certainly was not a marl. Again, the Flemings, as Mr. Rham¶ informs us, have converted their sandy desert into one of the most fertile districts of Europe by bringing up year after year 2 inches of subsoil from trenches shifted each year, until they reached a depth of 2 feet. Their sands, I believe, rest often upon yellow clay, and their fields have in some places the singular appearance of light sand on the surface, while water is standing in the ditches 2 feet below. I do not think that the clay of the Netherlands contains much lime. I have met with an instance of a strong clay without lime in Suffolk, which has been applied to a poor light calcareous soil, and paid itself the first year, in the clover-crop.** Near Reading, too, the same effect has been produced by the clay dug out from the railway on a thin burning gravel. That clay is certainly not a marl. We have also a striking account†† in our last No. of the application of blue shale to a field of gravel and sand, on which dung

* Journal, vol. ii., p. 30.
† See the Report of the Judges of Implements. The mechanical construction of this ingenious invention will be improved, I believe, at Lord Ducie's Iron-works. Mr. Gabell, of Crickhowell, works his single-tine subsoil plough 18 inches deep with two horses.—Journal, vol. ii., p. 421. I have also found my own answer the purpose.—Ibid, i., 433.
‡ Journal, vol. i., p. 1.

* Journal, vol. iii., p. 233.
† Ibid, vol. ii., p. 259.
‡ Ibid, vol. ii., p. 67.
§ Mr. Cuthbert Johnson on Fertilizers, p. 271.
‖ Journal, vol. ii. p. 408.
¶ Outlines of Flemish Husbandry.
** Prize Essay of East Suffolk Agricultural Association, by Captain Alexander.
†† Journal, vol. iii. p. 161.

and bones had equally failed to produce either turnips or barley, yet 50 cart-loads of this shale brought on each acre 40 bushels of barley. Now shale is clay half hardened into blue slate. I do not know whether there was lime in the shale, probably not; but here is an answer to a question sometimes asked when the admixture of soils is proposed—Is clay better than dung? The answer is, Yes. For on very light land even dung will not produce wheat, but clay will; and I may now give a case in point, which happened this year on my own land, a piece of barley, containing 12 acres, the soil a poor, loose, peaty sand. When the blade appeared, one-half of the piece looked green and healthy, the other half yellow and sickly. On inquiry I found that to the thriving portion there had been applied two slight dressings of strong clay (not marl, for it had been examined), amounting only to 50 loads on the acre. The boundary was distinct. But in the middle of the sickly portion was also a square patch of vigorous growth. Here there had been a dunghill one year before. The result at harvest was this, that on the clayed portion there was a thick crop of good colour up to the boundary, and even where a detached heap of clay had been laid; on the unclayed portion the crop was thin, many of the plants having perished. An acre of each was fairly selected and thrashed separately. The unclayed acre yielded 34½ bushels of barley, the clayed acre 46 bushels; so that this lasting improvement of the soil was paid in the first year. Where the dunghill had been, the barley ripened prematurely, was of a dark brown colour, and the seed was shrivelled. It is commonly said by farmers on our burning land that the better a field has been dressed in the previous winter, the worse will the barley be in a hot summer; and I see that they are right. This amounts to the remark of Mr. Handley, that dung will not benefit land beyond a certain point—will produce not wheat, but straw. It is, I believe, a fundamental principle of agriculture, that each soil has a limit beyond which manure cannot force it, and the principle should never be lost sight of. I would add another rule. Strengthen the soil itself where you are able, and you raise that limit permanently. Corn, especially wheat, requires solidity in the soil. A principal cause of barrenness,* as Mr. Rham has shown us, is the coarseness of its particles—I suppose because the rootlets are not in contact with such soil. Marl, I believe, does not act merely by its lime, but corrects this defect by interposing finer particles in the soil. Clay certainly acts in this way. But on this important subject I hope that our practical members will send statements of their experience, and specimens for examination. It is remarkable that, among the many analyses of soils reported by Dr. Liebig, all the fine close sands are fertile, and the coarse loose sands, with one exception only, are barren.

But though clay may act which is not marl, and does not contain lime, there is no doubt that the lime contained in marl is also beneficial. In Mecklenburg sandy marl† is used as well as clay marl. In the county of Suffolk there is a loose rubble called craig now largely used by farmers as a dressing for land. The account of its discovery, given in a prize-essay of the East Suf-

folk Agricultural Society, by Captain Alexander, is so remarkable, that I will quote it at length:—

"I now come to the shelly deposit denominated red craig: it consists of shell mixed with sand and gravel. It is barren in its own nature, and is therefore used, instead of gravel, to form garden-walks; it contains much oxide of iron, and was first discovered to be useful as a stimulus to soils overcharged with sour, black, vegetable deposits, from the following accident. A person was carting some of this craig for a garden-walk, and, in conveying it over a black barren soil, the cart broke down and scattered the contents; the driver, instead of collecting the craig, spread it over the surface where it lay. The field was after this prepared for turnips in the usual way, and, much to the surprise of the occupier, there was a good crop of full-sized turnips where the craig had been cast, while the rest of the field afforded only a miserable crop of stunted turnips. By this accident was the application of craig first made efficient; and *it is almost impossible to calculate the increase added to our agricultural produce by this discovery in the craig districts.*"

Such is the origin of a widely-spread provincial practice. On the same loose earth my own neighbours have observed that, where limestone-rubble has lain, or a road has passed, the turnips are better, and they spread rubble upon such land. Mr. Charnock* not only applies clay to sand, but he adds, "I have attempted to improve my farm by an admixture of soils, and have found it by far the most certain way of making permanent improvements. The calcareous (limestone) sand here mentioned, which in the neighbourhood has been considered perfectly poisonous to plants, I have found, by mixing liberally with the soil, to contribute to a considerable increase of my crop."

There is another ancient practice of the kind, which I mentioned in a former number†—the application of chalk brought up from pits dug 20 feet deep, on the chalk hills of Hampshire, and wheeled over the land in barrows to the extent of 2000 bushels per acre; but I was mistaken in calling it an expensive operation, for the usual price is wonderfully low, only 45s. per acre, and I believe I was also misinformed in stating that it is useful where the soil contains chalk already. It is remarkable that the red clay of these hills, though very thin, and resting upon chalk which is pure lime, contains, so far as I can ascertain, no lime at all. Hence the chalk acts probably in two ways—chemically by supplying the lime which was wanting; mechanically by loosening the clay, for its application renders these hills more mellow to work with the plough.‡ Chalk, I find, is also used largely on the wolds or chalk-hills of Yorkshire, and there it is found to render loose soils more firm.§ This is a very cheap mode of transposing

* Journal, vol. iii. p. 162.
† Ibid., vol. i. p. 1.
‡ Mr. Thorpe's paper in the present number.
§ This opposite effect of chalk, in loosening Hampshire soils and binding those of Yorkshire, may be explained, I think, as follows:—The chalk, which is lime, mixes with the Hampshire clay, and, expanding in a different proportion during frost, shakes the texture of the soil. On the Yorkshire soil it falls also to powder, and this powder interposed between the coarse particles of soil gives compactness. Mr. Schweizer, of Brighton, has also discovered phosphate of lime in chalk.

* Mr. Rham on the Analysis of Soils.—Journal, vol. i, p. 47.
† See Mr. Handley's paper in this number.

soils; but on the coast of Essex, where chalking, as Mr. C. Johnson* tells us, is largely practised, it is brought by sea from Kent, and is applied at a rate of from 10 to 30 tons per acre, the poor lands requiring more than the rich ; and in the clay districts of Windsor Forest the farmers sometimes bring chalk a distance of 10 miles for the same purpose, at an expense, as Mr. Rham has told me in his own case, of 8*l.* per acre. If it be carted 10 miles, where it cost 8*l.*, certainly not an acre of the hills themselves on which the chalk will act should remain without it, where it can be spread from wheel-barrows for little more than 2*l.* The chalk-hills occupy a large tract in England, but whether the soil be generally so strong or so light as to be benefitted by chalking I do not venture to say ; we want information on this point also. I have brought forward these cases of admixture of soil, not imagining that a sudden transformation of English soils can be effected at once, but in the hope that, in districts where any such practice is known to be beneficial, as on the fens of Lincolnshire or the hills of Hampshire, it may be applied with increased spirit; that some of these practices, as that of claying or marling, may turn out to be useful in districts where they are not hitherto know ; that men of science may explain the action of these materials, and so some light be thrown on the laws of vegetation ; and that possibly, as in the case of the overturned load of craig, practical farmers, by observing any casual difference in the verdure or growth of their crops—for nature or chance are constantly making such experiments, if our eyes were open to mark the effect, or our minds to inquire for the causes—may be so fortunate as to find some new application of the same principle. There are many other cases in point, such as the use of the honeycomb-stone† (the lava of ancient volcanoes) as a manure in Devonshire and Scotland, or of peat upon clay-lands‡ in Germany and Sweden : those which have been mentioned are enough to show that in this, as in many other matters of farming, our practice is in advance of our science.

(To be continued.)

ON THE CULTIVATION OF LIGHT LANDS.

TO THE EDITOR OF THE FARMER'S MAGAZINE.

I observe that the Royal Agricultural Society have offered a prize for the best essay on the cultivation of light land, and also on the management of farm yard manure ; and I dare say there will be many deep and scientific papers sent in to compete for them. But if you think this worth a place in your magazine it is much at your service. It is an account of the management of a light land farm that has been in my occupation for between thirty and forty years, and I believe the mode of management may fairly be said to be according to the best management of the present day, that is, in England. In Scotland and the north of England, some variations from the difference of climate, &c. may be perhaps made, with advantage ; and if so, our northern neighbours know

well how to make that variation. The farm consists of 190 acres of light arable land, of about the value of 20s. to 25s. an acre, tithe free, and about 100 acres of pasture and meadow. I began with the four-course system, and an excellent one it is ; but latterly I have varied from it a little, the land being in a high state of cultivation, and instead of the four-course, I farm it on a four and a half course. It was 45 acres of turnips, 45 of barley, 22½ red and 22½ white clover, timothy, cock's foot and trefoil, 45 acres of wheat, sowing a few acres of tares on the turnip land—a bad plan, as the fallow is almost always imperfect after the tares, at least on moderate land, and the crop of turnips very inferior—and 10 acres of sainfoin. My present plan is 40 acres of turnips, 40 of barley, 40 of seeds, 40 of wheat ; 6 acres of tares, 2 acres of peas, and 12 acres of oats—total, 20 acres after the wheat ; after the red clover, 10 acres of sainfoin and 3 acres of lucerne in one of the fields most adapted to its growth. By this means there are 6 acres of tares, 4 sown in the autumn, 2 in the spring ; 2 acres of peas to start the pig feeding, and 12 acres of oats to cut up for the farm horses, which saves the farmer putting his hand into his pocket and going to market to buy oats. The turnips and seeds come twice in 9 years, instead of 8 ; and wheat is of most importance, the red clover once in 9 instead of 8 years, by which and good management it will generally stand.

FIRST, TURNIPS.

The land for fallows is of course ploughed before Christmas—the first time over, as deep as possible, endeavouring every course to increase the depth of soil ; cross ploughed, &c., &c., as all good farmers know perfectly how it should be done. One acre of potatoes planted the first week in May, and a certain portion of mangold wurzel as the farmer pleases, and as many Swedes as can be well got in by the 10th of June. All after that time the best common white top to be sow the 20th of June and finishing by the 20th of July ; to be all well manured in ridges with the best manure from cake-fed beasts, horses, and pigs. If the manure will not hold out, the remaining white top to be drilled in with bones or rape cake, and plenty of ashes on the flat, at 18 inches apart. The ridges 27 inches apart (all the turnips drilled with ashes); this distance, 27 inches, fits the cart wheels. Some persons sow their turnips 20 inches apart, which equally suits the wheels ; but I have never tried it, and I should think the drills too narrow to be well horse-hoed. The turnips, &c., to be well horse and hand-hoed. The potatoes to be taken up at the usual time. The mangold wurzel as soon as the wheat sowing is finished and safely stowed away ; the Swedes to follow, and all finished before the severe frosts are expected ; a portion of the Swedes to be cut up for the farm horses and beasts in the yards, and the remainder cut up for the sheep in the field ; and after trying many ways of storing, I know no better way than that mentioned in the "Farmer's Magazine" for July, 1842, p 42, by Col. Wood. There cannot be too many ashes drilled in with the turnips, and on sand land I have twice used salt, and with great advantage ; 10 bushels an acre, at about 10d. a bushel, harrowed in a day or a few days before sowing the turnips. I have this year a field of 9 acres, 5 well manured in ridges and 4 drilled with bones and ashes; a part of the manure was omitted, and 2 acres of boned ; it shows

---

* Mr. C. Johnson on Fertilizers, p. 262.
† Journal, vol. iii. p. 27.
‡ The present number, Mr. Handley's paper.

on the manured, but on the boned most particularly the turnips are of a different colour and twice as good. The benefit to the crop I should conceive arises from the salt retaining the moisture in the land, and also acting in some measure as a stimulant or as a manure. One great advantage of thus taking up the Swedes is, that the land is not injured by the drawing or exhausting the land by a growth in the spring, but is left in quite as good a state for the following crops as after common turnips. All the turnips to be cut with Gardener's cutter, as by so doing three advantages are gained—the turnips go much farther, the sheep do much better, and it gives much employment to the labourers and their children. All the sheep have chaff, cut hay, or sainfoin, with a little barley straw ; the fatting sheep and the male, provincially the Heder lambs, oil-cake with their chaff. By this means the fatting sheep are soon ready for market, and the Heder lambs are in such forward condition that they sell at the highest price at the spring fairs, or are carried forward with cake on the seeds or feeding pastures, clipped and sold fat in June ; by which another advantage is gained, that the pastures are eased early in the summer. The sheep should be on turnips in good time, that they may get well established before the wet weather sets in ; and giving the oil-cake, I need scarcely say, leaves the land in the best state for the barley crop.

BARLEY.

Barley should be got in by the end of March, if possible ; and to accomplish that, I last year, on eight acres of Swedes (the turnips having been previously drawn and heaped), whilst the sheep were eating one four acres, I ploughed and sowed the other four acres, and as soon as the first four were finished, shifted the troughs on to the sown land, and sowed the first fed off ; by which time was gained in getting the field sown, and I think the treading of the sown land did rather good than harm both to the barley and seeds. I sow the Chevalier, as I find it equals any sort in quantity. I do not find it more likely to be laid, and the price averages considerably higher than any other. If the ground is hard, as it often is in spring, I use the presser, ploughing across the ridges, which I find answers exceedingly well ; so much so, that I am inclined to think I shall sow most of my barley with the presser, as last year I pressed part of a field, and that part came up two or three days first, and kept its superiority quite to harvest ; and there is very little more labour, as it does not require so much harrowing ; and after the presser the land is left just as you could wish it.

SEEDS.

20 acres of red clover and 20 acres of white ; viz., 1 stone of white clover, 7lbs. of trefoil, 3lbs. of timothy or cocksfoot, 3lbs. of rib grass, and some parsley. The red to be mown for soiling and for hay. The second crop, what is not wanted for soiling, to be fed off by the fatting sheep and Heder lambs when in flower. The white to be fed by the ewes with twins, provincially double couples and Heder lambs—giving them chaff and linseed cake ; by which means the land is in the best state for a crop of wheat ; the increased quantity of herbage, and the superior doing of the sheep, about paying for the cake. A better plan than putting on rape-cake at seed time, as the cost then falls entirely on the wheat crop ; and I think

the linseed plan will produce a better crop than the rape cake. I have always until lately, following Arthur Young's advice, kept my seeds unstocked until the spring, as they are injured and are later in the spring if hard stocked in the autumn, but have now tried another plan to a certain extent. I have stocked them with lambs at the rate of one or one-and-a-half an acre for three weeks or a month, before going to turnips, giving them linseed cake and chaff. I find the seeds little injured, perhaps as much benefited by the manure from the oilcake as injured by the feeding. The lambs have done excellently, and I have not lost one since going on turnips to this date (Nov. 20).

WHEAT.

The red clover to be manured with farm-yard manure, and if you have not enough with rape cake, soot, or pigeon manure, as the wheat on the red clover is to be followed by oats, &c., the white clover will require no manure. The land to be ploughed, pressed, and the wheat sown between the 1st and the 20th of October as nearly as possible. 3 bushels an acre (hand-hoed in spring if necessary), well harrowed in the spring, 7lbs. of trefoil an acre, being first sown according to the plan mentioned by Sir J. Sinclair, as pursued in the Netherlands ; the expense of the trefoil is little, and if it hits, which it generally does, the keeping is very useful for the flock in the autumn. The wheat to be mown at harvest—a mode superior to reaping, particularly on light lands, but also in almost every case, as being cheaper, the straw better, and in a wet time infinitely superior, as I myself experienced a few years ago. I had a ten acre field half reaped, half mown, the weather showery ; the mown was carried uninjured three days before the reaped ; the reaped three days later, and considerably grown.

OATS, PEAS, AND TARES.

4 acres of tares ploughed, pressed, and sown immediately after harvest ; 12 acres of oats the end of February or beginning of March ; and 2 acres of tares after barley sowing is finished.

SAINFOIN.

Having natural meadow I have only 10 acres of sainfoin, otherwise I should increase the quantity, as I am clear that it is one of the most profitable crops on the farm. For on land of 20s. value you have a crop equal to the best meadow, and this lasts for six or seven years. I am only surprised that much more is not grown in the midland counties on light land, as is the case in Kent and in the southern counties. I can only account for it from supposing that it has been tried, and perhaps failed from improper *management, which is*, however, very simple. Sow the land in high order after turnips with 3 bushels an acre of barley, 5 bushels of sainfoin seed, and 7lbs. of trefoil. The trefoil is only for the first year, to fill up the crop before the sainfoin gets strong, and then dies away. The sainfoin seed should be clean as possible from grass seeds, and weeded from grass, particularly oat grass, as much as it can the first year ; after that, if there is any oat grass, send the labourers over it with sharp scythes when it is in flower, which will be before the sainfoin is in flower, and let them mow off the heads of the oat grass to prevent it from seeding, and by degrees smothering the sainfoin.

The eddish should not be stocked with sheep (it

is better with lambs only) later than the first of November, as sheep later than that eat the heart out, which shows itself early, and which eating destroys the plant. When it is going off the last year, or last year but one, sow gypsum over it at the rate of 6 bushels an acre, as is the custom in East Kent; the only thing is to get the right sort of gypsum; I have tried two sorts myself that were absolute failures. But I believe the Burnham gypsum, near Bawtry, is the right sort for agricultural purposes, having formerly tried it with success, and mean to try it again.

LUCERNE.

I have about three acres. It comes in before the tares and red clover, and is always very useful. I sow 20lbs. an acre broadcast, manure it every year with farm-yard manure, or half the land farm-yard manure and half gypsum alternate years, and get three good cuttings.

MANURE.

My practice has been a very simple one, with little trouble or expense—and that with a farmer goes a great way; for we know very well that very few like or will follow any new plan if attended with either much trouble or expense, and turn away at once if you begin to talk about tanks, hydrogen, oxygen, &c., &c. I claim no credit for the plan, for many farmers may, I dare say, follow the same plan; but many certainly do not. The yards are moderately hollowed when empty; they are then covered with about six inches of earth, and when that is covered with about a foot of manure, which, when the yards are full in the winter, will be in about a week or ten days, cover it again lightly with earth from banks, roadsides, or wherever it can be got, and so on alternately until the yard is full, or it is led away. By this management the earth is as it were lost in the manure, but really comes out as so much manure, and the manure is improved—in fact, the manure is increased in quantity and improved in quality. At the proper time let it be carted to the turnip fallows, thrown in a heap, well covered down to keep the steam in it, and banked up at the sides. It will want no turning, but will come out forty-nine times in fifty in the best state for turnips. This manure is made from the farm-horses—which are never turned out winter or summer, except on Sundays in summer, to please the waggoner—pigs, and beasts fatting on oilcake. All the straw is trod into manure, except a small part cut into chaff with the sainfoin and clover, and a small quantity given to beasts for about a month in the spring, with about six pounds of oilcake each, before they go into the feeding pastures. And here I will take the liberty of giving this advice to the young farmer—never to be afraid to lay out his money in oilcake (linseed). I pledge myself it will return with interest; his farm will be in high heart, and his crops will never disappoint him. As to any new manures that are found out, let him feel his way.

Nitrate of soda I have tried for three years. On sand I have found it answer perfectly; on other land it has perhaps just about paid its way for wheat and oats; and so well on meadow, that I shall go on with it.

Guano I tried this year on turnips. I drilled in two cwt. an acre, with plenty of ashes, for Swedes—not one came up. I then sowed the land with common turnips, and there is a moderate crop. So it

has been with me; but a neighbour tried one cwt. (and ashes) only for Swedes, and the crop is as good as a well manured crop on each side of them. I have now tried an acre of wheat with two cwt., and one with one cwt. an acre—what will be the result, we must wait until next harvest to see.

GYPSUM.

If I find the Burnham gypsum the right sort, and that it answers on my land, I shall sow six bushels an acre over all my red clover annually. April and the beginning of May is the usual time for applying it, but I am inclined to try as an experiment sowing some in autumn. The red clover often looks beautiful all through the winter, but dies away in the spring; in that case sowing in May would be useless. Perhaps applying it in the autumn might prevent this; and if so it would be invaluable, as securing a red clover crop.

In this statement I have but little entered into detail, as it would have made the paper too long, and would have been unnecessary, as it is addressed to farmers. It is simply an outline which any practical man can fill up. I believe the above to be a good and profitable system, but I am not bigotted, and shall look out for any improvements that may be suggested in your Magazine, and also to the prize essay on the management of light land, that we shall soon expect to see in the Royal Agricultural Society's Journal.

Nov. 20th, 1842.   X.

ON THE ADVANTAGES OF A SPECIFIC EDUCATION FOR AGRICULTURAL PURSUITS.

SUBSTANCE OF AN ADDRESS TO THE FAIRFORD AND CIRENCESTER FARMER'S CLUB, DELIVERED THE 14TH OF NOVEMBER 1842, BY MR. R. J. BROWN.

I have undertaken to make a few remarks on the subject of education: a subject, the importance of which it is impossible to over-rate, and for this reason—all other animals come into the world with faculties that expand with their growth to individual perfection; man alone arrives, and continues (if left to himself), a perfectly helpless and ignorant being. He could neither feed nor dress himself without the benefit of instruction and example; his mind would be a blank, his voice would be inarticulate, indeed (if he survived) he would be very inferior to the lower animals. This is a fact that should be kept always in view; and is the real foundation on which the necessity of education is established. It would appear, at first sight, a great neglect on the part of a benevolent Creator, that man should be so circumstanced; deeper consideration will convince us, that it is the greatest proof of His wisdom and love; for we shall discover that it arises from His gracious design of advancing man step by step, to a far higher destiny than the lower animals; even to almost indefinite perfection, and endless life. For this purpose education begins with the cradle, and only terminates (if it does terminate) with the grave.

Education, though long neglected in this country, appears now to obtain the attention it deserves; but there are facts which show, that it is still far from being fully appreciated; one is, the common remark, that it may be carried too far. It may be inappropriate, or bad, we allow; but that a man can know too much of what relates to the things around him, or to his particular employment in life, it is not easy to understand. Another proof of neglect is the way it has been treated by government; some small amount is now doled out, but if appreciated as it ought to be, the subject of the education of the mass of the people, and the arrangement of plans for its success, would be considered by far the most important business of each session of parliament; reports from every district would be received and considered, and ample funds devoted to its support; it will be a happy day for England when the cost of her school-masters exceeds that of her army. As the public have shown neglect of the subject, so have societies and individuals. Happily the cause of education has not been quite so treated abroad. In Austria universal education is prescribed by authority; every village has a school. It is said that a man who cannot read and write may not even marry or obtain employ. Prussia and Saxony have systems of public instruction; every parish has a school for elementary knowledge, connected with schools for the higher branches; and these are specimens of most of the continental nations. In nearly all the states of America large funds are devoted to this object; affording the most favourable augury of her future advancement. The state of New York, with a population of about two millions, in addition to six colleges for the higher branches of learning, expends one million of dollars annually on the support of common schools; and of this sum 400,000 dollars are raised by taxation. Massachusetts, with a population of 700,000, raises by taxes 120,000l. per annum for the purpose of education; these are samples of the rest. In China universal education has existed for centuries; it has been the moving principle of her system. Every Chinese is educated; and, as there is no order of nobility by birth, the most intelligent and best educated are drawn from the lower schools, and, step by step, are qualified for the highest posts of government.

Some of the objections to education that we find existing, may be traced to errors in the mode of effecting it; too much importance having been given to it merely as a means of intellectual advancement; but even to this extent, the argument that it tends to diminish crime, is proved by the statistical returns of our prisons. But education to produce perfectly satisfactory results, must not be so confined. In carrying it out there are three principles in man never to be lost sight of or neglected, commonly called the heart, the head, and the hands; in other words, the affections, the understanding, and the practice. Good affections are to be fostered, by instruction in what is right, both by precept and example, and by the practice of it; and these principles should be kept in view in every pursuit. How difficult to succeed in anything without the love of it; how imperfect our endeavours without a knowledge of the best mode of effecting it; and how impossible to succeed without patient application of that knowledge!

Having dwelt on the importance and nature of education, we naturally come to the consideration of the best mode of effecting it; this has been proved to be by classes. Class education has the advantage of greater cheapness, and of being more complete (who present would not prefer a veterinary surgeon to a common farrier?). More means can be collected and adapted to a distinct class of pupils than to a general school; the comparative cost of expensive aids is in its favour, and there are stimulants to the acquirement of knowledge that other bodies want. Class education in Great Britain has been almost entirely confined to divinity, physic, and surgery; even the Duke of Wellington was obliged to obtain his military education in France. Of late the army and navy, engineering, designing, teaching, and singing, have their schools. *Agriculture is still without a public institution where it is taught.* That such an institution is wanting there are many proofs, chiefly the slowness with which improvements have been adopted by the mass of agriculturists, and that they have been chiefly made, and first practised, by men of liberal education. As proof of the former I may mention, that Jethro Tull showed the advantage of drill and horse-hoe culture at the beginning of the last century, whereas in China and Japan, it had been practiced from the earliest times; and yet it is only now becoming general. The history is the same of the introduction of the artificial grasses and roots, whilst the proper husbanding of them by stall feeding, &c., is, in these parts, very little attended to, although practised for ages in some countries. Frequent underground draining, introduced afresh by Mr. Smith, of Deanstone, was practised with success in Essex and elsewhere fifty years ago. The names of Bedford, Coke, Spencer, Ducie, Richmond, Sinclair, Morton, Ellman, Davy, Liebig, Young, and Marshall, will prove the advantage of a liberal education, even when not so specific as it might be. If a higher order of education had been awarded to the practical farmer, would the advance of agriculture have depended so much on the more theoretical classes?

There is no class of society to whom a good education is so important as the agricultural, not with a view to the wealth and resources of the country alone, but also on account of its position. The larger part of the population must be very much dependent on it for their character and advancement; its influence is almost omnipotent in the country districts. How important, then, that it should receive every possible advantage that a complete education can give! It is worthy of all the pains and expense that are necessary to effect this object. There are circumstances in the position of the farmers of England that remarkably adapt them for a superior class education—their numbers, wealth, and frequent occasions of meeting. Once establish a higher order of education amongst them, and it must of necessity be sustained. They would not acquire knowledge merely as an accomplishment; they have daily use for all the practical knowledge they can acquire; there is scarcely a science that they have not need of, which we shall see if we take only a rapid glance at them. The knowledge of all that relates to animals, both the useful and noxious—the cattle and flocks that give nourishment to man; the birds, insects, &c., that are injurious; their history, or all that relates to their different species; their physiology, or what relates to their internal structure and functions; their economy, or all that relates to their increase, food, health, &c. The same of vegetables—the plants productive of food, the weeds that impede the labours of husbandry, their history or botany, their physiology, their economy; the sciences that relate to all inorganic substances; geology, or the knowledge of the strata of the earth as they affect the surface soil, and have an influence on cultivation; chemistry, or the component parts of the things around us—what causes their combination, or promotes their dissolution; a knowledge of soils; of minerals; of the nature of heat and light; without which no product of the field comes to perfection; what lessens or increases their action; of the subtle yet immense powers that act upon and control matter, generally so unobtrusive, yet always in operative energy around us; of electricity, and the other attractive and repulsive forces; of physics, in relation to extension, weight, solidity, mensuration, drawing; of book-keeping; all of constant use on a farm in calculating and registering the results of experiment and culture; of mechanics, and their practical application to machinery; of the moving powers applied to implements of husbandry, a subject of daily increasing importance; of hydraulics, in reference to draining and lifting of water and liquid manures; of hydrostatics, as manifested in the solid, fluid, and gaseous states of water, and their effect on soil, vegetation, health, and climate; of all that relates to the atmosphere, of such importance to the farmer, that after all means have been used, his success depends on weather; the finest crop may be destroyed by a single storm of hail (an effect, in Italy, said to be avoided by the use of electric conductors); the formation and character of clouds, and their effects; of seasons; of temperature; of wet and dry air, and their effect on vegetation and animal life. The science of the atmosphere is only just receiving attention, observations are only now commencing; it is not at all improbable, at future periods, our knowledge will have so increased from accurate and extended observations, that we shall be able to predict the nature of coming seasons; but this probably will require observations to be taken, not only in our own country and Europe, but concurrently in the extreme parts of the earth, and this will be done when men become convinced of the folly and wickedness of national jealousies, and all combine in furthering general science and in advancing whatever will increase the happiness and welfare of their fellow creatures.

Enough has been enumerated to show that a farmer had need know almost everything; and yet no public institution can be pointed out where in early life (the time for acquiring these sciences), he may be instructed in them at a moderate cost; not that education will make every man a genius, or even a discoverer of new facts; but we know not who has the necessary qualifications until all are well educated—and by such an education as we have glanced at, minds will be expanded, and ready to receive and apply facts, by whomsoever discovered. We know not what new grasses and vegetables are in store for the use of man. The Falkland islands have been known for ages, but it was only the other day, when they became the temporary residence of well-instructed men belonging to Captain Ross's expedition, that a grass was noticed that bids fair to be a most useful addition to our present stock, as it is said to flourish in marshy soils subject to the access of sea water, and to be exceedingly palatable and nourishing to horses and cattle; moreover, what a blank and mystery must the world around him be to the man who only knows things by the obvious characters that address the sight and touch—to get rid of such mental darkness would be alone a sufficient reason for advancing our object.

Institutions for teaching agriculture theoretically, and in some cases practically, exist in most of the continental states of Europe; in Prussia, Bavaria, Wirtemburg, Austria, Hungary, Switzerland, and Italy, they have long existed; in France, at Grignon, in the department of Seine and Oise, youths are educated on a farm of 500 or more acres of various soils, stocked with sheep and cattle of different breeds; it contains a botanical garden, nursery, orchard, &c. The instruction requires two years; in the first are taught the elements of mathematics applied to mensuration, plans and levels, topography and drawing; the principles of electricity, physics, and chemistry; botany and vegetable physiology applied to cultivation and planting; the first principles of the veterinary art; rational principles of cultivating and farming; of rural economy; of the employment of capital, and management of farms. The second year : the principles of husbandry applied to production and employment; mathematics applied to mechanics; hydraulics; and the elements of astronomy; physics and chemistry applied to the analysis of earths, waters, manures, &c.; distillation and economy of keat; mineralogy, and geology; the culture of the kitchen garden, orchard, woods, &c.; the knowledge of useful and destructive insects; architecture applied to rural buildings, including drains, making mortar, lime, cement; the laws of property in land; the principles of health as respects man and animals; practical experiments, and the use of implements. Here we have a sufficiently expansive course of study. Another large establishment exists at Gran Jouen, in the department of Loire Infereure, for practical and theoretical agriculture.

In our own kingdom a successful example has been set in a quarter where we should have least expected it—in Ireland. At Temple Moyle, near Londonderry, a college has been established on a farm of about 300 acres, which I will describe from personal observation. That this experiment has been made under the most unfavourable circumstances you will allow, when I state that the land is on the slope of a hill with a north east exposure, and that the soil is a clay of so tenacious a nature that the farmer of the establishment stated, it would be improved by deep under-ground drains of only one yard apart. The farm is sheltered by a belt of trees, but there are no inclosures; a single road runs up the centre; at the lower part stand the buildings, presenting a neat front, and wings that enclose behind a spacious court; then succeed stalls, &c.; in front of the house the ground is laid out in a kitchen and botanic garden, where the various grasses, &c., are kept distinct. In 1840 there were 70 pupils of from fifteen to twenty years of age, paying 10l. per annum, being chiefly the sons of the neighbouring farmers; half the number are in class under a master and tutors, and half on the farm under an intelligent Scotch farmer; and a more active, vigorous, yet intelligent body of young persons I never saw. The farm with all its disadvantages was making a profitable return, and though of such natural sterility, the drained part was covered with excellent crops of wheat, &c. This institution has been in operation a dozen or more years, and has turned out some hundreds of well informed young men; some of whom have taken the situation of bailiffs with great credit to themselves and the institution; and the testimoney of the supporters and officers of the establishment was, that in scarcely a single instance had they been disappointed in the character of the young men who had been instructed there. Here we have almost an exact model of what is wanted in England; a little expansion to meet the larger scale of farms in this country would make it complete. In China agriculture is considered of so much importance, that the emperor himself holds the plough on one day in the year to insure its being considered an honourable employment; and the consequence is that the

Chinese have advanced beyond others in this noble art, so much so, that it is said, you may go miles without meeting with a single weed. After this enumeration of what has been done elsewhere, it does appear extraordinary that there should be a total absence of any public school of agriculture in England. Let us do our part in endeavouring to do away with this deficiency, and agreeing that such an institution is desirable, I will just sketch out a plan of one that will be adapted to our own district. We must endeavour to commence well and take advantage of the experience of existing institutions ; and by so doing, we shall probably find that our object would be effected by a college established on an example farm of from 300 to 500 acres, situated on a central part of the Cotswold Hills : the district for its support to be defined, not by any artificial boundary, but by its geological formation ; that is to say, the soils resting on the volitic series of rocks, including the forest marble. These would embrace a district of nearly 50 miles in length, from Bath to Camden, and a breadth defined by the vales of Severn and the Warwickshire Avon on the one side, and of the Thames and Wiltshire Avon on the other—leaving out the vale lands of each river respectively. This would give scope for an establishment for 200 pupils of 15 to 20 years of age ; and it is probable that £20 per annum from each—in addition to the produce of the farm—would defray the expenditure. The estate might be obtained on a long lease ; the buildings to consist of proper class and sleeping rooms, sufficient stallage, and other farm buildings ; to be supplied with a library, philosophical apparatus, &c. ; the farm with the best description of stock of various breeds, the best implements, &c. ; each pupil to be half the day in class, learning the sciences applied to agriculture—both theoretically and experimentally, as have already been adverted to—and half the day on the farm ; where, under a good farmer, and with the example of a few picked labourers, he will acquire such dexterity in the various operations of husbandry, as will enable him in after life, not merely to tell a labourer how he ought to work, but to take a tool and shew him. He will thus obtain the respect of his men, and be able to appreciate their work.

Another important advantage of part of the day being spent in manual labour, is the assistance it will afford to moral training. I have no doubt you will agree with me that moral training is of the greatest importance ; all present can judge of the consequences of bringing a number of young persons of this age together in one establishment without a strict system of discipline. We do not wish to see our sons intelligent only ; but, from their morals and character, a credit to their class, and a blessing to their country. This object will be very much forwarded by such a portion of labour as shall still leave sufficient time for mental culture ; thus bringing into action two of our principles—the hand and the head—and making both operate (as we hope) on the heart.

Such a college would also be a fit place for the annual exhibition of stock, for the trial of new implements, of new manures, seeds, and systems of husbandry on portions of the farm, and all without extra expense.

We now come to an important question. How is our object to be effected, and at what cost ? We may safely reckon that the sum requisite for the buildings, stock, &c., will be from ten to twenty thousand pounds ; and the best mode of raising this sum would be by shares—say of £20. If each land-owner in this extensive district would subscribe one share to every five hundred acres of his estate, and each tenant one to every three hundred to five hundred acres he occupies, we should have ample funds ; each share might recommend a pupil. It has been suggested that such an institution should originate with the Agricultural Society, or with Government. We shall find that the practical way is to do our own business ourselves. We shall thus have an institution adapted to our wants. No one situation will do for all England. We hope that every district, the vales, the chalk, the red sand, &c.—that each will have its college. If one large establishment was reared, we may fear that it would be a failure ; anything rather than the substantial practical institution that will turn out—not the finical gentleman, afraid of soiling his hands—but intelligent, active, hardy young men—who will maintain the substantial honest character of the English yeoman, combined with all that modern science and advancement, and careful training and moral and religious culture can do, to elevate them to the station in the country that they ought to fill. We are each of us the centre of some little circle. Let us advance the cause by advocating it amongst those we know ; and, with God's blessing, we may hope that, ere long, the cry for the efficient practical education of the rising generation of farmers will be so loud and general, that all difficulties will disappear, and we shall have the happiness of seeing an agricultural college on the Cotswold Hills—a model, we trust, for many others in the land.

ON THE SUBSIDENCE OF THE SAP IN TREES IN CONSEQUENCE OF THE PRESENCE OF SHEEP.

(FROM THE ANNALS OF CHYMISTRY.)

" L'Echo du Monde Savant" contains, in the number for the 30th of October, the following article :—

" M. Bouteille has written to us, in reference to an article having for its title as above, and which appeared in our journal of the 23rd instant, by M. Poiteau,—' The inhabitants of the country,' says M. Bouteille, ' particularly the wood-cutters who remove the bark from oak trees in forests, all know that the neighbourhood of a flock of sheep will hinder them from pursuing their work, by preventing the circulation of the sap, which renders it almost impossible to decorticate the trees. This fact, so worthy of exciting the attention of physiologists, has never been studied. Many instances of this singular phenomenon have been noticed by different journals, but they have never given the least explanation thereof.' M. Bouteille complains, and with some reason, that they never sought to render an account of it.

" M. Raspail inserted, in the Réformateur of November 25th, 1834, the following article :—

" ' Fascination de la sève des arbres ;
Riez en, mais ensuite vérifiez.'

" ' We find, in a number of the Annals of the Society of Agriculture of Charente, an opinion that we scarcely dared to announce, until it had gone the round of all the country papers.

" ' The author asserts, that the presence of a flock of sheep suffices to arrest the course of the sap of trees, which causes, according to the author, the bark so to adhere to the wood, that the barking is thereby rendered most difficult. What should be the cause of this fascination? We are ignorant.'

" M. Raspail afterwards published his Vegetable Physiology, and the second edition of his Organic Chemistry, but these works contain nothing on the subject.

" M. Bouteille demands that the Academy should institute a commission to study the subject. He thinks that if the air be analysed, so as to ascertain the principles it contains, particularly at that period of the year when the sheep are still covered with their thick fleece, impregnated with a large quantity of greasy matter, this latter will be found to give out much ammonia to the atmosphere, which may be perceived at some distance from the flock. M. Bouteille attributes to this odour the cause of the phenomenon in question, but he does not account for the manner in which it acts. It is more than probable that M. Bouteille is in error; the ammoniacal exhalations would only assist vegetation.

" M. Maleysie goes much farther than M. Bouteille; for he believes that the neighbourhood of a flock is opposed to the growth of young trees,—an opinion which is partaken by most cultivators. The only harm that sheep can commit is to rub the bark from the young plant, which thereby perishes. We must, then, seek elsewhere for the cause of this singular phenomenon."

[We would suggest, for the consideration of our contemporary, that if the air adjoining the forest be analysed at the time when the neighbourhood of sheep is simultaneous with the arrest of the sap, such air will be found to be very deficient in *caloric*, which not only prevents the flow of sap, but excites the instinct of the flock to seek the shelter of neighbouring trees.—ED.]

CULTIVATION OF TURNIPS.

SIR,—In my last letter I pointed out some of the advantages experienced by me in working heavy land intended for turnips in the autumn, instead of doing so in the spring, as we have been accustomed doing, not only in very much lessening the labour of pulverisation, but doing so far more effectively than it is possible to do in the old way of working.

But there are other advantages than these, which I shall state as shortly as possible, and which will appear very obvious to most agriculturists not wedded to the practice of their grandfathers—for this is the great obstacle to all improvements, not only in agriculture, but in every other science—they *canna be fashed*, as we say in Scotland. Sir H. Davy has long ago laid it down as a maxim, to be as seldom departed from as possible, never to allow manure to lay in farm-yards and dunghills until it becomes decomposed and almost useless from the evolution of the various gases, that a large portion of the most valuable properties of the manure is thereby lost, not only to the farmer but to the country—so much so, that he states it as his opinion that one-third and sometimes a half of the manure is lost by allowing it to be too much decomposed. It is true that a very serious objection has again and again been started, by stating the impossibility of using rough dung, particularly for turnip husbandry,

which most unquestionably works very foul; but here you will observe the objections are obviated by working the land, and putting in the dung in the fall instead of in the months of May and June, when the weather is generally so warm and dry—indeed the rougher the dung is, the better when thus applied. By so doing a great deal of manure which would otherwise lie in the courts and farm-yards all winter going to waste, would be applied to the land with the greatest possible advantage, not only in a pecuniary point of view (i.e., less dung will serve), but the land by its numerous absorbing vessels will imbibe the ammonia, &c., from the dung in the process of decomposition, and is then in a better state of preparation for the deposition of the seed than when sown immediately above smoking hot dung and litter moisture; thereby generating in many seasons the fly fingers-and-toes, mildew, &c., with a number of other evils which turnip husbandry has to contend with.

There is still another advantage to be derived from autumn dunged land, intended for turnips the following year, which is well adapted for all farmers, but more especially to those who are far from dung, or have to depend altogether upon what they make themselves, which is to give them land, say from 15 to 20 tons of farm yard or other dung per acre in the drills, in the fall of the year, as described in my former letter, and from four to six bushels of prepared bones along with the seed at sowing, and, if partly eat on the land with sheep, particularly if the land is light, will put it in first rate order for any ordinary rotation of crops. The best way to use the bones, or whatever stimulant is used, is to dibble them in with the hand, at nine or ten inches apart on the top of the drill after being rolled, which can be done by a man and two girls, for about 2s. 6d. per Scotch acre, (a machine has been made by a person, in the neighbourhood of Stirling, for doing this work, and for which a premium was awarded to him by the Highland Agricultural Society) and will be found a far more effective mode of using any of our new manures, than by scattering them on the surface or on the top of the drill, as is the practice in many parts of the country. The seed is thus placed in immediate contact, not with hot dung, but with one or other of the stimulants used; the young plants, so soon as there is a braird, reaping the whole advantage (i e., the stimulating qualities of the manure) whatever may be used—whether it be bones, guano, rape-dust, or nitrate—while, if run into the whole length of the drill, there is a positive loss of manure being pushed away from the plant when it most needs nourishment by the hoe in singling, and is thereby of comparatively little use to the turnips, but rather has a tendency to encourage the growth of weeds between the drills, which, in wet seasons, are sufficiently troublesome without receiving a premium to grow.

There is another advantage—and though last not least—and it is this: that by this means a great deal of turnips, which are now a very important crop to the country, might be grown to the great advantage of the farmer instead of bare fallow, and would enable many, not only to increase the quantity of manure, by enabling them to fatten more stock, but put those into far better condition for the butcher than they are able otherwise to do when their land is not naturally adapted for turnip husbandry.

I am, sir, your most obedient servant,

Piffer Mill, Nov. 26.   PETER THOMSON.

ENGLISH AGRICULTURE.

BY MR. MAIN, CHELSEA.

(From the Quarterly Journal of Agriculture.)

(Concluded)

If the second crop of clover is off in good time, the lea is hard stocked to eat up every green leaf before the ploughs are introduced. The ploughing is done with much care to lay the ridges in the best form for throwing off surface-water. Between the end of September and the 12th of October is said to be the best season for sowing wheat. The seed is prepared for sowing by being steeped in brine from eight o'clock in the evening till five o'clock next morning. While in the steep it is frequently stirred, and every thing that floats is carefully skimmed off. The brine is made strong enough to float an egg. At every farm-house there are a couple of tubs kept for this purpose ; a large one to hold a sack of wheat, and as much brine as will serve to cover it. This large tub has a tap at bottom at which the brine is let off—the wheat being kept back by a tap-wisp. When the wheat is sufficiently drained, it is turned out on a paved floor ; and quicklime is sifted over it and turned backwards and forwards until every grain is coated with lime ; it is then formed into a heap and covered with sacks till it is wanted on the field. There are many different ways of preparing seed-wheat, all of which are practised for the purpose of freeing the seed from the sporules of the fungi, called smut, and mildew, rust, or blight. The spori or seeds of those diseases are supposed to be killed by the brine and caustic quality of the quicklime. It cannot be doubted that such preparation is partly, though not entirely, effectual ; and certainly a dressing of lime to wheat-land is a preventive of smut.

If the summer has been showery, slugs most likely will be prevalent, and to prevent their motions in the soil, a pressure follows the plough, and closes the creases between the furrows, and presses closely down the furrows themselves before the seed (two and a-half bushels to the acre) is sown ; and then harrowing twice or thrice in a place finishes the work. If no pressure be used—and especially if the ground works light and dry—the land is, in such circumstances, well trodden down with a flock of sheep driven repeatedly over till the surface remains smooth and firm ; and this not only to obstruct the motions of the slugs, but to prevent an uncommon birth of seed-weeds, charlock, and poppy, in the spring.

The field, if inclined to wetness, has every furrow struck up, and every water-furrow scoured out, and the whole smoothed and levelled with the spade. Thus the wheat field is left to nature until the spring, when sometimes the harrows are usefully employed to roughen a compacted surface, and afterwards rolled to produce a concussion of the bed in which the *coronal* roots are spreading themselves. And if any top-dressing has been provided it is now thrown over, especially on such spots where the wheat is thin or weakest.

Soon after this the weeders with their paddles go over the field, cutting or pulling up every dock, thistle, or other noxious weed they can eradicate by such means ; and which weeding is, if necessary, continued till the wheat is two feet high.

Wheat harvest usually begins in the last week in July, and is often finished in a fortnight. It is mostly reaped by some few of the constant men, aided by a few others called *month's men ;* these are extra hands taken on to assist getting in the harvest, whether it continues three or six weeks. A fixed price for the harvest is previously agreed upon, varying from three pounds ten shillings to five pounds, besides beer, four or five pints (English) of which are allowed per day, but no food. Some farmers allow food also, in which case the harvest wages are much less. Sometimes reaping is wholly done by extra hands, who are paid by the acre, charging from ten to twenty shillings, but without either beer or food. I have had a fair standing crop reaped for eight shillings per acre ; and after a wet and windy time had paid twenty-four shillings for a like bulk of crop ; the reapers earning less money at the latter than at the former rate.

The wheat is bound either by single or double bands—that is, by one length of the straw instead of two lengths united below the ears. The first are necessarily small sheaves, which are soon ready for housing ; the second are often too large, and require more field room ; though the latter is mostly practised. Scotch *shearers* penetrate as far as Lincolnshire occasionally, and from thence work their way homewards. Irish reapers are plentiful in the west and southern counties, and are mostly employed by the largest farmers.

Wheat is generally housed, but it is no misfortune if a rick or two be required to be set in the rickyard. They are mostly set on stone or metal staddles, with either octagonal or square frames.

The yield of wheat in this country varies from sixteen to forty bushels per acre, with from one and a half to two loads of trussed straw. The grain is gradually threshed with the flail ; and to thrash and clean a sack, and bind the straw in trusses of 40lbs. each with two bands, is the daily task of one man ; which, besides laying a fresh flooring for the next morning, he finishes about three o'clock in the afternoon, after which hour he is not called on to do any work, except in hay-time and harvest.

About an acre, more or less, of the wheat-stubble is, as soon after the wheat is carried as possible, dunged, ploughed, and sown with winter tares ; and the rest of the stubble is fallowed up preparatory to being sown with oats in the spring.

As soon in that season as the ground is sufficiently dry the field is again ploughed, sown, and harrowed. The quantity of seed—from four to six bushels per acre ; the kinds, either common white, black Poland, black or white Tartarian, or small black. In March or April the oat field is rolled, in which state it remains till harvest.

Oats are mown with scythe and cradle, or with a bow only. The crops are seldom heavy, unless on very rich ground, or when the ground has been liberally dressed for the crop, in which case it must be reaped and bound in sheaves. But ordinary crops are sometimes so short and light, that a good cradle-mower will cut down four or more acres per day, for which he is paid at least half a crown per acre. After lying in swathe for a few days, they are raked in, carted to the barn or rick, like barley ; and, when flail-thrashed, the tasker must clean two sacks per day, tie up the straw in bundles, and remove it to the cribs or straw-house.

The oat crop thus cleared off, and which usually yields from four to ten quarters per acre, is the last of the five-shift rotation, when the same proceedings and course of cropping is recommenced, as has been already detailed.

The defects of this system of cultivation are, as

already said, having two white crops together, too many raised for sale, and too few green crops for home consumption. Consequently, a sufficient number of live stock cannot be kept to make dress enough to keep the land in heart, and thereby increase the general fertility of the farm; and yet, notwithstanding the defects and positive loss sustained by an adherence to this system, many extensive farms on the diluvial formation are still conducted according to this irrational custom : nay more, many tenants are compelled by the terms of their leases, or agreements, to follow this system, and no other !

But within the last twenty years, a change has been gradually taking place, by introducing what is called the Norfolk or *four-shift* rotation ; and which is merely by throwing oats out of the rotation, which allows fallowing for turnips and other green crops every fourth instead of every fifth year. This prevents the accumulation of weeds, which always appear among the oats—renders fallowing an easier process, and the succeeding crops more abundant, in consequence of a more numerous head of live stock being kept and fed for sale. More pastures have been laid down ; drilling the crops instead of broadcasting has been adopted ; and improved implements of several kinds, and for various purposes, have been invented and introduced into the business of farming.

These improvements were partially begun fifty years ago, and fully carried out at Holkham, Woburn Abbey, and at many other places ; so that both the practice and knowledge of agriculture have been widely diffused by imitating the examples set by the noble owners of the above-named places, under the superintendence of Mr. Blaikie, at Holkham, and of the late Messrs. Wilson and Sinclair at Woburn. To these eminent practical and botanical agriculturists have succeeded a numerous class of their pupils and followers, who are disseminating their opinions and practices far and wide. So that it may be truly said that agriculture is making rapid strides towards all practical perfection in the central counties of England, where it has hitherto been behind both the northern and eastern counties. In furtherance of this progressive improvement, the Royal English Agricultural Society, with the extensive influence of its members, will greatly contribute to reform what is still amiss or inexpedient in the leasing of farms, as well as in recommending the best practices.

The soil of the Duke of Bedford's farms in the vicinity of Woburn is a fine sandy loam, chiefly arable ; it was, and I believe still is, managed under the following course of cropping ; namely, 1. Turnips, on a dunged fallow, sown in drills twenty-seven inches apart; 2. Barley, with broad clover ; 3. Clover, either soiled with sheep or made into hay; 4. Wheat, sown on a stale furrow, well harrowed down, and in drills nine inches apart ; 5. Turnips, as before ; 6. Barley, with clover and trefoil ; 7. Clover, &c., depastured with sheep ; 8. Pease, drilled ; and 9. Wheat, which ends the course.

The turnip ground is prepared with much labour, thoroughly and repeatedly ploughed until it is quite pulverized, as well as cleared of root-weeds. The drills are first opened by a double-breasted plough ; the dung is then carted on, and spread along the bottom of the drills, and the ridges between are split right and left to cover the dung, and over which the seed is drilled. The intervals are stirred by horse-hoe, and the plants are set out with the hand-hoe.

The crop is partly drawn for feeding cattle, and partly eaten with sheep ; each intermediate row being drawn for the former purpose. Along with the turnip crop, No. 5, as much ground is sown with winter tares as will suffice for cutting green in May ; and which ground in afterwards sown with turnips.

In the execution of this course of cropping there. is one particular which may be noticed ; it is, in ploughing the leys a skim-coulter is always used. This addition to the plough lays the clover, stubble, and weeds in the bottom of the open furrow, to be completely buried by the next slice. The same is done for the pea crop, which gets the roots of the clover out of the way of the drill-shares. From two to three bushels are sown, are kept clean by horse and hand hoes, and are fit to reap or pick in July, with a hook in each hand of the reaper, one to hold up the straw, and the other wielded horizontally to separate it from the ground. The crop is then rolled into small wads or bundles, and require turning once or twice before being ricked.

In this country peas are a precarious crop, being subject to be attacked by the *aphides* in dry summers, and often exposed to frequent showers in July, either of which casualties are fatal to the crop. On heavy clayey soils peas do better ; their rank growth on such land, offends the aphides, and ripening later in August escape the July rains.

In the above course peas occur only once in nine years, and wheat only twice, which, from the high condition of the land, is not considered too often ; and as broad clover is only sown and mown once, there is no fear of sickening the soil with it.

As there is always an opportunity of having a two-year old ley, or a portion of worn-out pasture to break up, such portions of the farm are invariably appropriated to the production of oats. When old pastures are broken up in order to be laid down again with the best grasses, the ground undergoes the following course of culture and cropping. The sward is ploughed in December, and when mellowed by the frost, is well harrowed and sown with five bushels of the Polish variety to the acre. The crop is heavy, and though cut with the scythe is afterwards bound in sheaves—the yield eight or nine quarters per acre. The oat stubble is ploughed soon after harvest, and immediately harrowed, in which state it remains till the beginning of November, when it is ploughed a second time, laying the lands as high in the middle as can be done. Soon as spring weather invites, the field is again harrowed and sown with beans in drills twenty-seven inches apart, requiring three bushels to the acre. The growing crop is kept clean by the horse and hand hoes ; the crop is reaped, and bound in sheaves, yielding about 40 bushels to the acre. Soon as the beans are off, the ground is scarified by a powerful implement going as deep as the plough. If the scarifier brings any weeds to the surface, they are picked off, and then the land is in order to be ploughed and sown with wheat in October. The seed is drilled at twelve inch intervals ; this distance being found best for autumn sowing.

The wheat stubble is immediately begun to be prepared for turnips cultivated as before detailed ; and these, when consumed, are followed by barley, and sown with permanent grasses to form the new meadow.

If a field, intended to receive a similar process of conversion to arable, and reconversion into meadow, be inferior in quality, the succession of crops is somewhat different—as follows :—1st, oats; 2nd, turnips; 3rd, Barley ; 4th, clover for soiling or hay ; 5th, wheat; 6th, turnips; 7th, barley and seeds, for permanent pasture.

Grass-land, if sufficiently extensive, is divided into any number of equal portions, and mowed in rotation ; that portion to be mowed always receiving a dressing of good rotten dung in the winter previous. By this management no part is impoverished by cutting too frequently ; and when cut for hay, the crop is always abundant, usually yielding from one and a-half to two and a-half tons to the acre.

Hay-making is well understood, and well performed in England. It is indeed reduced to a regular system, when weather allows, and which is as follows, viz. :—

When the day is fixed for the mowers to begin, they are at their work as early as four o'clock in the morning ; the makers, mostly women and boys, turn to alter breakfast, and with small forks ted out all the grass mown before breakfast. This tedding is done very carefully and equally over all the surface, and in the course of the forenoon it is turned once or twice. In the afternoon it is raked into single wind-rows, each raker taking about three feet in width of the tedded grass, and thereby leaving clear spaces between. When the wind-rowing is finished, the rows may be turned once, if there is time ; but every row must be run into grass-cocks before sunset.

On the second day, the first work is tedding out all that was mown after breakfast on the first, and up to the same time on the second day. Next the grass-cocks are shaken out into staddles, or long-beds, four or five yards wide, leaving a clear space between the staddles raked clean. These are turned once or twice during the forenoon ;· and that which was tedded in the morning is turned once or twice, wind-rowed, and at last made into grass-cocks for the night. After dinner the staddles are raked into double wind-rows, and before sunset are made into cocks twice or thrice the size of grass-cocks.

On the third day, the work of tedding out, wind-rowing, shaking out into staddles, shaking out the large cocks, and turning these last from time to time to the sun and air, the hay will be in good order to be carried to the rick about four o'clock afternoon. This is the usual process, every day's mowing becoming fit, with the necessary attendance, to be carried on the third or fourth day after mowing. This, it may be thought, is an expeditious way of getting up hay ; but if the weather be fine, it is the usual course in the south of England. I have often made scores of acres in a season, without making a single cock ; but in uncertain weather it is impossible to go on safely without cocking-up every night.

Hay-ricks are generally built rectangular, about six yards wide, and of any convenient length, say seven, eight, or nine yards, according to the quantity wished to be put together. Square ricks are most suitable for binding into trusses three feet long and two feet over ; the thickness varies according to the closeness or hollowness of the hay. Each truss weighs 56lbs., thirty-six of which make what is called a load in the markets. (For the method of binding, see a paper of mine in vol. iii., p. 850, of this Journal.)

In some of the eastern counties, the hay is put up in large cocks in the rick-yard, or in a corner of the field in which it is made. These being well pulled, very little straw is required for thatching, and that only on the crown of the cock. Whereas square ricks have the whole roof thatched, consuming much straw, and causing expensive labour.

As grass-land is invaluable to the arable farmer, as enabling him to keep more live stock, so has it been particularly guarded by restrictive clauses in leases. But sometimes old grass becomes mossy and unprofitable. In this case, a renewal of the sward is necessary ; and in order that this may be effectually performed, the land undergoes a preparation and course of cropping, as has been already detailed.

The system which has now gained the title of "convertible husbandry," that is, the conversion of grass-land into arable, and its reconversion into grass, is no doubt an improvement of the old system ; because there is certainly much heavier crops of corn produced on the newly broken-up land during the transition, and when again laid down, larger crops of grass of the most approved species. Great advances have been made in the choice and collection of the seeds of the best grasses since the publication of our friend the late Mr. G. Sinclair's *Hortus Gramineous Woburnensis*. Farmers are now well aware how much it is to their advantage to deal with a respectable seedsman, who can serve them with pure samples of the sorts they want, and which are most suitable for the land they cultivate.

Permanent pasture is advised to be sown with the following kinds and quantities of seeds per acre, viz. 10lbs. white clover, 3lbs. trefoil, 2lbs. rib-grass, and 3 pecks cock's-foot ; or instead of the latter, 1 peck perennial rye-grass, or 3 pecks meadow-fox-tail, and 1 peck rough-stalked meadow-grass. These together are a very liberal quantity for an acre ; but as seedling grasses are subject to many casualties, erring on the safe side is commendable.

Besides the above species, there are a few others which are found in the best pastures, and recommended to be sown, namely, smooth-stalked meadow, sweet-scented vernal, meadow fescue, and golden oat-grass.

Italian and several other superior varieties of rye-grass have lately been introduced into cultivation for ordinary purposes, and are by many farmers highly approved. The flesh-coloured clover introduced about the same time has been fairly tried, but has not realised the expectations entertained of it as a green forage plant.

The rough cow-parsnip, and Bokhara and flesh-coloured clover, as forage plants, have all been tried, and all have had or still have their admirers ; but as yet there are no signs of either being admitted into the regular routine of farming.

Having given an outline of the usual proceedings of English farmers on the almost obsolete five-course system, and the gradual change to the Norfolk or four-course shift, I may add, concerning the latter, that this also begins to be less popular than it was at first. It is objected that, in this rotation, clover occurs too frequently, and the consequence is, that the land is everywhere getting *sick* of it, so that a really good crop of clover is rarely to be seen. Changing the kinds of clover, that is, substituting the white and yellow species instead of the red every alternate fourth year, is found not to be so effectual as it was once presumed to be ; and other rotations have been devised, one of which is that suggested by the experienced Mr. Morton for light turnip soils.

1. Turnips and Swedes on a manured fallow.
2. Barley and seeds.
3. The seeds pastured with sheep or other live stock.
4. Second year seed, also pastured by sheep or other ditto.
5. Oats.
6. Potatoes, mangel-wurzel, beans, or winter tares, dunged.
7. Wheat.

The superiority of this round of cropping consists in there being only three crops of corn taken in the course of seven years, and which, from their so seldom occurring, are likely to be extraordinarily abundant; nor will the land be exhausted of the nourishment corn particularly requires, when so seldom called upon. The intervening crops are either resting, cleansing, or otherwise ameliorating products, and, when disposed of to live stock at home, return as great a profit in the shape of wool, mutton, and beef, as the corn grown on the same land would have done if carried to market. And, moreover, the land would be kept in constant better heart and higher state of cultivation.

Very little rye is sown, an acre or two of the wheat land only being devoted to it, but never admitted as an object in the rotation. It is an exhausting crop, though profitable, as far as it goes, when the straw can be sold to the *plaiters* or the mattress makers. Rye, as well as bere, is sometimes sown for sheep keep, but tares or coleseed are mostly preferred for such purposes.

The cultivation of hemp and flax are quite given up in the south of England; but there are various districts in which saffron is grown for the druggists, as well as liquorice; and for clothiers, the teazle; and poppies for the apothecary; all of which are as profitable as common farming, otherwise they would not be cultivated. In some places, as in the neighbourhood of Colchester, in the county of Essex, many farmers turn their attention to growing garden and agricultural seeds for the London seedsmen, which is said to be a profitable pursuit. Rape and mustard are cultivated in various places in the northern counties, and brank on the light lands of the south.

Hops are extensively cultivated on the rich lands of Kent, Sussex, and Surrey in the south, and Worcester and Gloucestershires in the west. In the same counties the production of fruit, from the filbert nut up to the luscious fig, are important items in the profits of farms, and, though all of a precarious character, are still trusted to as sources of income.

The circumstances of English farmers are as various as are their persons. When untiring industry and steadiness of conduct are united with a competent capital, all may go on well, but capital without practical knowledge is very rarely successful. We have witnessed many attempts of amateur farmers to introduce what they call the Scotch system of farming into England. Not only the modes of ploughing and sowing, reaping and mowing, thatching and stacking, &c., but every other adjunct of men, implements, cattle, with all the paraphernalia of the *bothie* system, even to an old Ellen to sweep the house. The low nominal rents of many parts of England were seductive to many half-informed Scotch farmers, who too eagerly engaged English farms; but when called upon for their quotas of tithe, poor-rates, church and county rates, together with the higher prices of necessaries and of labour, they found themselves deceived; and when they thought of shielding themselves from the two latter items of cost by the introduction of their own countrymen and customs, in this they were also defeated by the desertion of their men for better engagements in the neighbourhood, and fresh importations only served to linger out an attempt which was so different from the customs of the country where tried, and where it could not be pleasantly carried out. But still Scotch farming and Scotch farmers are much respected; the first, for the economy with which it is conducted, and the second, for their intelligence and steady character. But in countries which differ so much in manners and customs, and particularly in the modes of paying farm servants, the one entirely in money, and the other partly in money, but chiefly in provisions, must make uniformity in the success of the masters, as well as in the views, habits, and moral conduct of the labourers impossible. It often happens, from the improvident mismanagement of the English labourer, that towards the end of the week, his cottage, if he has a family, contains none of the comforts of a home to him; no resources of either "meal or malt" to lean upon, and only looking forward for Saturday night, to receive his ten or twelve shillings, which are mostly dissipated before he receives them. This improvidence has been chiefly brought about by the leniency of their old poor laws, and though these laws are now more stringent, dependence upon the overseer will never be obliterated until the present generation has passed away.

English labourers are, however, a most useful and hard-working class of men, and, when working by the piece, indefatigable; they excel in all the various labours of the husbandman, and many of them fare hard as well as work hard, merely because they must have the most costly food. Very few of them have any education; but the rising generation will be greatly improved in this respect, from the more general diffusion of elementary knowledge.

TO THE EDITOR OF THE NORTHAMPTON MERCURY.

Sir,—The old-fashioned method of holding for a series of years the precious products of the earth is quite exploded as a theory, but there are many who practically adopt it, as the following facts will prove. A friend of mine has five years' wool on hand, for which he was offered each year the prices at foot. Having often argued with him upon the impolicy of this practice with little effect, I put into his hand the following calculation, which has induced a change in his opinion, and may cause others to think upon the subject.

Yours, &c., R. B.

				£	s.	d.
1838—50	Tods at	43s.	....	107	10	0
1839—50	..	35s.	....	87	10	0
1840—50	..	28s.	....	70	0	0
1841—50	..	28s.	....	70	0	0
1842—50	..	28s.	....	70	3	0
				405	0	0
Present value—250 tods at 25s....				312	10	0
Loss		....		92	10	0
Interest and Compound Interest to next show day				74	13	6
Total loss		....................£167			3	

DEAD WEIGHT OF SOME OF THE PRIZE CATTLE EXHIBITED AT THE SMITHFIELD CLUB CATTLE SHOW FOR 1842.

OXEN—Class I.

No. 1. The right hon. Earl Spencer's four years and nine months old short-horned ox, 124st. 13lb.

No. 5. Sir T. B. Lennard's four years and nine months old Durham ox, 109 st. 10 lb.; loose fat 13 st. 2 lb.

No. 7. Mr. William Richardson's four years and eleven months old Durham ox, 115 st. 6 lb.

No. 8. Mr. Thomas Crisp's three years and four-and-a-half months old short-horned ox, 125 st. 10 lb.; loose fat, 15 st. 6 lb.

No. 9. Mr. William Loft's four years and eight months old Durham ox, 128 st. 12 lb.; loose fat, 13 st. 2lb.

No. 14. Mr. Benjamin Wilson's four years and nine months old short-horned ox, 125st. 10lb.; loose fat, 11st. 6lb.

No. 17. Mr. William Mason's four years and ten months old short-horned ox, 151st. 3lb.

No. 18. Mr. R. W. Baker's three years and nine months old short horned steer, 116st.; loose fat, 13st. 11lb.

No. 20. Mr. Thomas L. Meire's three years and eleven and a-half months old Hereford ox, 113st. 2lb.

No. 21. Mr. J. T. Senior, four years and six months old Hereford ox, 102st. 12lb.

No. 22. Mr. T. J. Mack's four years and ten months old Durham ox, 114st.; loose fat, 12st.

No. 28. Mr. John Millar's three years and nine months old Durham ox, 106st. 4lb.; loose fat, 14st. 4lb.

No. 30. Mr. Dudgeon's three years and eight months old short-horned ox, 120st.; loose fat, 14st. 6lb.

Class II.

No. 31. Mr. Charles Gibbs's five years and eleven months old Devon ox, 113st. 11lb.

No. 33. Mr. William Loft's four years and ten months old Durham ox, 119st. 8lb.; loose fat, 15st. 10lb.

No. 35. Sir William Wake, Bart., four years and ten months old Hereford ox, 124st. 8lb.; loose fat, 14st. 4lb.

No. 36. The Hon. Charles Arbuthnot's four years and six months old short-horned ox, 131st. 6lb.

No. 37. Mr. Henry Towndsend's four years and six months old Durham steer, 119st. 4lb.; loose fat, 10st. 5lb.

No. 38. The Right Hon. Earl Spencer's four years and six months old short-horned ox, 108st. 7lb.

No. 39. Mr. Abraham Perkins's three years and eleven months old Hereford steer, 77st. 2lb.

Class III.

No. 42. Mr. Robert Smith's three years and three and a half months old improved short-horned steer, 91 st. 6lb.

No. 43. Mr. G. F. Wills's three years and six months old short-horned ox, 93st. 10lb.

No. 47. Mr. Chamberlain's four years and eight months old Hereford ox, 96st. 6lb.

No. 48. Mr. Christopher Smith's under three years and eight months old short-horned ox, 95st. 6lb.

No. 49. Mr. Abraham Perkins's three years and eight months old Hereford steer, 83st. 2lb.

No. 50. Mr. John Manning's four years and six months old Hereford steer, 97st. 2lb.

No. 51. Mr. William Hay's four years and nine months old short-horned and Aberdeenshire ox, 103st. 5lb.

Class IV.

No. 52. Mr. J. W. Bailey's three years and seven months old Devon ox, 94st.; loose fat, 11st. 6lb.

No. 57. Mr. J. T. Senior's three years and one month old Hereford steer, 80st.

No. 62. Mr. Dudgeon's two years and five months old Highland and short-horned cross ox, 70st. 12lb.; loose fat, 9st. 13lb.

Class V.

No. 65. Mr. W. F. Hobbs's three years and seven months old Hereford and Durham steer, 80st. 2lb.

No. 66. Mr. W. J. Bailey's three years and ten months old Devon ox, 64st. 8lb.; loose fat, 9st. 2lb.

No. 68. Mr. John Tucker's under two years and five months old Durham steer, 80st.; loose fat, 10st. 10lb.

Class VI.

No. 71. Mr. John Manning's five years old Scotch ox, 89st. 2lb.

Class VII.

No. 73. Mr. John Manning's upwards of five years old Scotch ox, 81st. 2lb.

COWS—Class VIII.

No. 76. Mr. Robert Burgess's four years and three months old Durham heifer, 75st. 10lb.; loose fat, 8st. 13lb.

No. 77. Sir George Phillips's, Bart., four years and two months old cross-bred heifer (Scotch and Durham), 76st. 6lb.

No. 78. Mr. Robert Ayres's four years and four months old Durham heifer, 86st. 12lb.

Class IX.

No. 79. The Right Hon. Earl Spencer's seven years and seven months old Durham cow, 84st. 8lb.

No. 80. Mr. William Harbridge's five years and six months old long-horned cow, 82st. 4lb.; loose fat, 9st. 2lb.

No. 82. Mr. William C. Maxwell's six years and eight months old short-horned cow, 101st. 12lb.; loose fat, 14st. 4lb.

Class X.

No. 86. Mr. W. Harbridge's twelve years and eight months old long-horned cow, 105st. 2lb.

No. 88. The Right Hon. the Earl of Hardwick's ten years and eleven months old Durham cow, 98st. 4lb.

EXTRA STOCK—Cattle.

No. 90. Mr. John Millar's three years and eight months old Durham ox, 102st. 12lb.; loose fat, 14st. 4lb.

No. 91. Mr. Abraham Perkins's three years and ten months old Hereford steer, 86st. 10lb.

No. 92. Mr. Thomas Bridge's three years and eight months old Hereford steer, 89st. 10lb.

No. 97. Mr. James Watson's three years and nine months old short-horned ox, 117st. 10lb.; loose fat, 14st. 12lb.

No. 99. Mr. John Manning's upwards of five years old Scotch ox, 81st. 2lb.

No. 100. Mr. Dudgeon's three years and eight months old short-horned ox, 131st. 6lb.

SHEEP—Class XI.

No. 101. Mr. Thomas Twitchell's pen of Leicester wethers, twenty months old, 9st. 4lb., 8st. 13lb., 8st.

No. 102. Mr. Chamberlain's pen of new Leicester wethers, twenty months old, 9st., 9st. 7lb., 9st. 11lb.

No. 104. Mr. Joseph Perkins's pen of new Leicester wethers, twenty months old, 7st. 8lb., 7st. 6lb., 7st. 3lb.

No. 107. Mr. Thomas Umbers's pen of long-woolled wethers, twenty-one months old, 9st. 10lb., 9st. 12lb., 9st. 8lb.

Class XII.

No. 109. Mr. Chamberlain's pen of new Leicester wethers, twenty months old, 8st. 6lb., 7st. 2lb., 7st.

No. 112. Mr. J. S. Burgess's pen of long-woolled wethers, twenty months old, 7st. 12lb., 6st. 12lb., 7st.

Class XIII.

No. 115. Mr. William Sandy's pen of Leicester wethers, twenty-one months old, 10st 6lb, 10st 10lb, 11s. 9lb.

No. 116. Sir E. C. East's, Bart., pen of cross long-woolled wethers, twenty-two months old, 10st, 10st 8lb, 9st 13lb.

No. 119. The Right Hon. the Earl of Radnor's pen of Leicester wethers, twenty months old, 8st 9lb, 10st 4lb, 9st 2lb.

No. 121. Mr. Charles Large's pen of long-woolled wethers, twenty months old, 12st, 13st 2lb, 13st 2lb.

No. 122. Mr. Edward Chapman's pen of Leicester wethers, twenty months old, 10st, 9st 10lb, 10st 2lb.

No. 124. The Hon. Charles Arbuthnot's pen of Leicester wethers, twenty months old, 9st 6lb, 10st, 10st 4lb.

No. 125. Mr. J. S. Burgess's pen of long-woolled wethers, about twenty months old, 7st 6lb, 7st 8lb, 7st 9lb.

No. 126. His Grace the Duke of Bedford's pen of Leicester wethers, twenty months old, 10st 1lb, 11st 2lb, 11st 6lb.

EXTRA STOCK—LONG-WOOLLED SHEEP.

No. 130. Sir E. C. East's, Bart., cross long-woolled wether, twenty-two months old, 11st 6lb.

No. 133. Mr. Edward Chapman's Leicester wether, twenty months old, 14st 8lb.

No. 134. Mr. J. S. Burgess's long-woolled wether, about thirty-two months old, 14st 4lb.

No. 135. Mr. Thomas Carpenter's long-woolled Oxfordshire ewe, four years and nine months old, 14st 6lb.

No. 193. Mr. R. Beman's Cotswold wether, thirty-three months old, 13st 12lb.

CLASS XIV.

No. 145. Mr. Jonas Webb's pen of South-down wethers, twenty months old, 9st 7lb, 9st 5lb, 9st 2lb.

CLASS XV.

No. 150. His Grace the Duke of Richmond's pen of South Down wethers, twenty months old, 8st 4lb, 8st, 7st 12lb.

No. 151. Mr. Grantham's pen of South Down we-thers, twenty months old, 8st 4lb, 8st 11lb.

No. 152. Mr. Samuel Webb's pen of South Down wethers, twenty months old, 8st 5lb, 7st 13lb, 8st 4lb.

CLASS XVI.

No. 153. His Grace the Duke of Norfolk's pen of South Down wethers, thirty-two months old, 10st 11lb, 11st 11lb, 10st 8lb.

No. 154. Mr. W. Bennett's pen of short-woolled cross wethers, thirty-two months old, 10st 2lb, 10st 10lb, 13st 10lb.

No. 155. Mr. John Harris's pen of South Down wethers, thirty-two months old, 10st 6lb, 10st 10lb.

No. 156. His Grace the Duke of Bedford's pen of South Down wethers, thirty-two months old, 10st 10lb, 9st 3lb, 10st 5lb.

No. 157. His Grace the Duke of Richmond's pen of South Down wethers, thirty-two months old, 10st 12lb, 11st 4lb, 10st 7lb.

No. 158. The Right Hon. the Earl of Lovelace's pen of South Down wethers, thirty-two months old, 9st, 8st 11lb, 8st 13lb.

No. 159. Mr. Grantham's pen of South Down we-thers, thirty-two months old, 9st 13lb, 9st 11lb, 10st 10lb.

No. 161. The Right Hon. Lord Western's pen of short-woolled wethers, thirty months old, 8st 13lb, 8st 1lb, 10st 8lb.

EXTRA STOCK—SHORT-WOOLLED SHEEP.

No. 163. Mr. William Bennett's short woolled sheep (Down and Leicester cross), thirty-two months old, 13st 6lb.

No. 167. The Right Hon. the Earl of Lovelace's South Down wether, forty-four months old, 11st 3lb; loose fat, 1st 3lb.

No. 170. Mr. Samuel Webb's South Down wether, twenty months old, 10st 6lb; loose fat, 1st 4lb.

PIGS—CLASS XVII.

No. 173. Mr. W. Hobman's pen of Neapolitan pigs, twenty-six weeks old, 16st 4lb each.

No. 174. Mr. J. Crawther's pen of improved Middle-sex pigs, twenty-eight weeks old, 11st 9lb, 11st 12lb, 13st 2lb.

No. 175. Mr. W. F. Hobbs's pen of improved Essex pigs, twenty-three weeks and two days old, 9st 6lb each.

No. 176. Mr. T. M. Goodlake's pen of Wadley pigs, thirty-two weeks and three days old, 15st 6lb each.

No. 177, Mr. William Bryant's pen of improved Essex pigs, twenty-nine weeks and three days old, 10st 4lb each.

No. 178. Mr. G. Carrington's, jun., pen of mixed breed pigs, thirty-seven weeks old, 16st 12lb each.

No. 179. Mr. John Buckley's pen of cross Warwick-shire and Neapolitan pigs, thirty-one weeks and three days old, 18st 4lb each.

EXTRA STOCK—PIGS.

No. 181. Mr. Jacob Crawther's improved Middlesex pig, twenty-eight weeks old, 14st 12lb.

No. 184. Mr. William Bryant's improved Essex pig, twenty-nine weeks and three days old, 12st 2lb.

No. 189. Mr. William Hobman's Neapolitan pig, twenty-six weeks old, 16st.

ON THE SELECTION OF SEED GRAIN AND VEGETABLES.

TO THE EDITOR OF THE FARMER'S MAGAZINE.

SIR,—Public men and public writers are open to public criticism; and well it is for the good of society that this axiom is generally received, or, in many instances, an incalculable amount of injury would be sustained by the world, owing to the many ill-digested and often groundless theories that are propounded by men of literary eminence.

On perusing your December number of the "Farmers' Magazine," I have observed what I conceive to be a lamentable instance of the above, bearing the name of an agricultural writer of un-doubted talent—to wit, "Peter Cowan," and I humbly solicit the favour of a short space in your columns to refute, from practical knowledge, his groundless theory; and in order that I might not fall into the same error myself, I have consulted several practical farmers and market gardeners in this neighbourhood on the subject. The result of my enquiry is, that I have obtained the most deci-sive evidence of the instability of Mr. Cowan's statement, that a "watery, unripened, bad-to-eat potato is the best for seed;" on the contrary, I have found that the best seed invariably brings the best crop, if planted under the same circum-stances. My authority for this information I con-ceive to be indubitable, from this circumstance,—that one of the individuals I have consulted (an in-telligent market gardener) has been induced to make the experiment with various species of plants, and he therefore spoke from facts, and "facts are stubborn things."

Mr. C. also states, "all cultivated vegetables have a tendency to degenerate, but this tendency is more than counteracted by the cultivation be-stowed, until they arrive at a degree of perfection beyond which it does not appear possible by any cultivation to push them; and if this is attempted a recoil is induced, and a degree of degeneracy and inferiority in the produce appears to be inevitable." Again, " if fine grain is used as seed, what will be the result? Of what quality will be the produce? Will it not be found to have degenerated—to be much inferior to the seed used? Improve it cannot," &c. Monstrous doctrine, truly! Enough to dishearten the host of individuals who have turned their attention to the improvement of seeds generally. It is true that all cultivated vegetables have a tendency to degenerate, but it is not true that when they reach a certain degree of perfection, they inevitably recoil; the fact is, that the tendency in vegetables to degenerate seems to be one of the innumerable and all-wise regulations of Divine Providence, intended as a suitable punishment to those who neglect to employ the powers he has given them, in improving, as far as nature will allow, the several creatures intended for the use of man. With respect to the assertion that a recoil inevitably ensues, on any attempt being instituted to push a vegetable beyond a certain degree of perfection, I am content to refer the reader to the great and wondrous improvements that have been, and are still making in the quality and size of vegetable productions—satisfied that they afford positive proof that whatever exertion may be made, if made with reason, will be rewarded by an improvement. I therefore am bold to make this proposition, in direct opposition to Mr. Cowan's theory—that although, for the punishment of the indolent, vegetables, if neglected, will degenerate, yet, for the reward of the industrious, if cultivated, they will improve. It is observed in the second quotation, that the finest grain must degenerate. "It cannot improve," says Mr. C.; if such is the case, and if Mr. C. is justified in advancing this opinion, he must be prepared to state to what degree of perfection grain may be brought, beyond which it is impossible to improve it. When he has furnished this information without doubting—not on supposition, as in the paper referred to—then I shall be prepared to contest this portion of his theory.

One other quotation only: "Those who have been attentive observers will be led to conclude that when vegetables, animals, or even the mental powers of man, attain an extraordinary degree of perfection, degeneracy in those particulars in which they have been superior seems invariably to await their offspring." It is an extraordinary fact, that the offspring of men gifted with great mental powers are generally deficient in that respect; but what has this to do with vegetables or animals? What comparison can possibly be drawn between the mind of man and a plant? None whatever; and it ought not, therefore, to be cited as an example. But how ignorant must Mr. C. be of practical agriculture, to state that animals degenerate when they have attained a great degree of perfection, if the slightest attention is paid to them. We have certainly had no instance yet of superior animals begetting bad stock. If Mr. C. is aware of any such, perhaps he will communicate it in his next letter.

In fact, I have perused Mr. Cowan's letter very attentively, and I am firmly persuaded that it contains theories calculated to have an injurious tendency, inasmuch as they are directly opposed to the results of experience; but, however closely and severely I may have criticised his letter, I trust a right interpretation will be put upon the motives which have actuated me in so doing,

since my only object is to elicit the truth; and seeing statements made which I knew were in opposition to all the information I had previously obtained on the subject, I could not forbear giving the results of my short observation.

I am, Sir, yours obediently,
PRACTICE WITH SCIENCE.
Lion-street, Kidderminster, Dec. 23, 1842.

CULTIVATION OF TURNIPS.

TO THE EDITOR OF THE MARK LANE EXPRESS.

SIR,—In this day of enterprise I always feel great pleasure in reading the practice and experiments of my brother-farmers in the cultivation of that noble root the turnip, especially the Swede. It having been my lot for some years to have only stiff heavy land to cultivate, I have adopted every method I could think of to cultivate the Swedish turnip on this kind of land to advantage; but I confess it never occurred to me to adopt the method so highly recommended by Mr. Thomson, of Piffer Mill, in your paper of the 21st of November, and repeated again last week. It is indeed a new method, but to me it appears a very costly one. If I rightly understand Mr. Thomson, his land is one year devoted to the growth of tares, the second to turnips. Now here are two green crops succeeding; I must contend here is a positive loss of a crop of barley, which ought to have succeeded the tares, which is one of the best preparative crops for barley on heavy land. Turnips ought at all times to be sown upon land that would otherwise have been a summer's fallow.

If Mr. Thomson will adopt my method, which is the following, all the difficulties he so much complains of in working the land in the spring will be obviated. The land I intend sowing with turnips, mangold wurzel, and potatoes, was ploughed up last August, as soon as the wheat was carted, and well scarified and harrowed; it was next cross ploughed during the harvest, and again scarified; after the harvest it was all picked over by women, the weeds burnt; the land was then put upon the ridge to remain until March, when it will be again ploughed. About the third week in April I put the dung on, plough and drill the mangold wurzel; the second week in May I put the dung on for Swedes, plough it in, and drill in the seed as quick as possible. I drill in with the seed as many coal and wood ashes, mixed, as my drill will deposit; and I find them a great stimulant to the young plant, and the ashes adhering to the bulb as it increases in size, preserves them from the grub. It is an error of Mr. Thomson's to suppose that when manure is drilled in, that much of its virtue is lost. Turnips are seldom left in the row more than eighteen inches apart, consequently the plants have only nine inches each way to seek for the manure.

I quite agree with Mr. Thomson that too many farmers are prone to be wedded to the systems of their fathers, and condemn new methods without giving them a trial; at the same time I think it quite necessary to be cautious in adopting new methods we so often see recommended. My maxim is to try all new things upon a small scale, and I generally find some of them good.—I am, Sir, yours most respectfully, H. C. WENTWORTH.
Harlow, Dec. 30.

THE LAST CENSUS.

STATEMENT OF THE POPULATION, IN COUNTIES OF GREAT BRITAIN, AND THE ISLANDS IN THE BRITISH SEAS, ACCORDING TO THE CENSUS OF JUNE, 1841; AND THE COMPARATIVE POPULATION OF 1821 AND 1831, TOGETHER WITH THE HOUSES INHABITED AND UNINHABITED AT THE LATE CENSUS.

ENGLAND.

Counties.	1821.	1831.	1841.	Houses inhabited.	Houses uninhabited.
Bedford	83,716	95,483	107,937	21,235	521
Berks	131,977	145,389	160,226	31,472	1,566
Buckingham	134,068	146,529	155,989	31,071	1,157
Cambridge	121,909	143,935	164,509	33,112	1,218
Chester	270,098	334,391	395,306	73,390	5,845
Cornwall	257,447	300,938	341,269	65,641	4,956
Cumberland	156,124	169,681	177,912	34,444	2,369
Derby	213,333	237,170	272,202	52,910	2,484
Devon	439,040	494,478	533,731	94,637	6,117
Dorset	144,499	159,252	174,743	34,559	2,012
Durham	207,673	253,910	324,277	57,450	3,272
Essex	289,424	317,507	344,995	67,602	2,482
Gloucester	335,843	387,019	431,307	80,856	5,790
Hereford	103,243	111,211	114,438	23,461	1,428
Hertford	129,714	143,341	137,937	30,155	1,305
Huntingdon	48,771	53,192	58,699	11,897	373
Kent	426,016	479,155	548,161	95,547	5,013
Lancaster	1,052,859	1,336,854	1,667,064	289,166	23,604
Leicester	174,571	197,003	215,855	44,649	3,260
Lincoln	283,058	317,465	362,717	73,038	2,250
Middlesex	1,144,531	1,358,330	1,575,895	207,814	9,854
Monmouth	71,833	98,130	134,349	24,880	1,417
Norfolk	344,368	390,054	412,621	85,922	3,711
Northampton	162,483	179,336	199,061	40,903	1,674
Northumberland	198,965	222,912	250,268	48,704	3,031
Nottingham	186,873	225,327	249,773	50,541	2,749
Oxford	136,971	152,156	161,573	32,141	1,440
Rutland	18,487	19,385	21,440	4,297	120
Salop	206,153	222,938	239,014	47,203	2,093
Somerset	355,314	404,200	436,002	81,632	4,702
Southampton	283,298	314,280	35,940	66,589	3,274
Stafford	345,895	410,512	510,206	97,676	5,455
Suffolk	270,542	296,317	315,129	64,081	2,317
Surrey	308,658	486,334	582,613	95,375	3,948
Sussex	233,019	272,340	299,770	54,066	3,647
Warwick	274,392	336,610	402,121	81,445	6,899
Westmorland	51,359	55,041	56,469	10,848	870
Wilts	222,157	240,156	260,007	50,986	2,149
Worcester	184,424	211,365	233,484	46,962	2,922
York (East Riding)	154,010	168,891	186,813	37,098	1,647
City of York and Ainstey	30,451	35,362	38,322	7,710	269
York (North Riding)	187,452	190,756	211,496	43,801	2,680
York (West Riding)	801,274	976,350	1,154,924	226,473	18,870
England	11,261,437	13,091,005	14,995,508	2,753,295	162,756

WALES.

Anglesey	45,063	48,325	50,890	11,488	746
Brecon	43,603	47,763	53,295	10,634	833
Cardigan	57,784	64,780	68,380	15,102	811
Carmarthen	90,239	100,740	106,482	23,485	1,383
Carnarvon	57,958	66,488	81,068	16,869	771
Denbigh	76,511	83,629	89,291	18,485	991
Flint	50,784	60,012	66,547	13,320	446
Glamorgan	101,737	126,612	173,462	33,205	1,466
Merioneth	34,382	35,315	39,238	8,467	547
Montgomery	59,899	66,482	62,220	13,650	884
Pembroke	74,009	81,425	88,262	18,804	1,021
Radnor	22,459	24,651	25,186	4,687	234
Wales	717,438	806,192	911,321	181,166	10,133

SCOTLAND.

Counties.	1821.	1831.	1841.	Houses inhabited.	Houses uninhabited.
Aberdeen	155,387	177,657	192,283	32,193	1,095
Argyll	97,316	100,973	97,140	18,514	917
Ayr	127,299	145,055	161,528	30,247	1,297
Banff	43,561	48,604	50,076	11,228	478
Berwick	33,385	34,048	34,427	7,405	382
Bute	13,797	14,151	15,695	3,067	93
Caithness	30,238	34,529	36,197	6,962	214
Clackmannan	13,263	14,729	19,116	3,593	110
Dumbarton	27,317	33,211	44,295	7,986	372
Dumfries	70,878	73,770	72,825	14,375	724
Edinburgh	191,514	219,345	225,623	38,903	2,861
Elgin	31,162	34,231	34,994	8,133	370
Fife	114,556	128,839	140,310	28,965	1,502
Forfar	113,430	139,606	170,380	36,153	2,036
Haddington	35,127	36,145	35,781	8,009	739
Inverness	90,157	94,797	97,615	19,182	578
Kincardine	29,118	31,431	33,052	7,274	314
Kinross	7,762	9,072	8,763	1,806	114
Kirkcudbright	38,903	40,590	41,099	8,159	316
Lanark	244,387	316,819	427,113	80,531	3,964
Linlithgow	22,685	23,291	26,848	5,309	327
Nairn	9,006	9,354	9,923	2,396	109
Orkney and Shetland	53,124	58,239	60,007	11,426	267
Peebles	10,046	10,578	10,520	2,119	154
Perth	139,050	142,894	138,151	29,172	1,798
Renfrew	112,175	133,443	154,755	24,626	1,092
Ross and Cromarty	68,828	74,820	78,058	16,166	385
Roxburgh	40,892	43,663	46,062	8,674	365
Selkirk	6,637	6,833	7,989	1,446	76
Stirling	65,376	72,621	82,179	15,837	795
Sutherland	23,840	25,518	24,666	4,972	167
Wigtown	33,240	36,258	44,068	8,512	296
Barracks	..	..	4,425	17	..
Scotland	2,093,456	2,365,114	2,628,957	503,357	24,307

SUMMARY OF THE POPULATION.

	1821.	1831.	1841.	Males.	Females.
England	11,261,437	13,091,005	14,995,508	7,321,875	7,673,633
Wales	717,438	806,182	911,321	447,533	463,788
England and Wales	11,978,875	13,897,117	15,906,829	7,769,408	8,137,421
Scotland	2,093,456	2,365,114	2,628,957	1,246,427	1,382,530
GREAT BRITAIN	14,072,331	16,262,301	18,535,786	9,015,835	9,519,951
Islands in the British Seas	89,508	103,710	124,079	57,598	66,481
Total	14,161,839	16,366,011	18,659,865	9,073,433	9,586,432

It will be thus seen, that the total population, according to the census just completed, is as follows:—

	Males.	Females.	Total.
England	7,321,875	7,673,633	14,995,508
Wales	447,533	463,788	911,321
Scotland	1,246,427	1,382,530	2,628,957
Jersey, Guernsey, &c.	57,598	66,481	124,079
	9,073,433	9,586,432	18,659,865

These numbers, including 4,003 males and 893 females ascertained to have been travelling by railways and canals on the night of June 6, make the grand totals 9,077,436 males, and 9,587,825 females. The population, therefore, of Great Britain amounts to 18,664,761 persons.

The returns include only such part of the army, navy, and merchant seamen as were at the time of the census within the kingdom on shore.

The increase of the population, as compared with the returns of 1831, is at the rate of 14.5 per cent. for England; 13 per cent. for Wales; for Scotland, 11.1; for the islands in the British seas,19.6; making the increase for the whole of Great Britain 14 per cent., being less than that of the 10 years ending 1831, which was 15 per cent.

The returns of the census for Ireland have not yet been published, but it is understood that the entire population numbers, as near as possible, a total of 8,200,000 persons.

The following table shows the comparative difference as to the number of houses in Great Britain in the years 1831 and 1841 ;—

	In 1831.	In 1841.	Increase in 1841.
Inhabited	2,886,595	3,464,007	597,412
Uninhabited	133,331	198,061	64,730
Building	27,553	30,631	3,078
	3,027,479	3,692,699	665,220

THIRD REPORT OF THE FRAMLINGHAM FARMERS' CLUB.

PRESENTED AT THE GENERAL MEETING, NOVEMBER THE 15TH, 1842.

December 28th, 1841. *Subject—"Sheep Stock on heavy land Farms."*

There were nearly 50 members present this evening, and a very lively and spirited discussion ensued; but as the prescribed limits of a Farmers' Club Report, will not permit us to touch upon all the points arising out of the several subjects appointed for investigation during the year, it is thought that the better plan will be to record only the resolutions past, afterwards noticing such arguments as were strongly supported in opposition, and such observations either for or against, as seemed to be received with marked attention. Proceeding upon this plan, our notes supply the following report.

Resolved—" That Sheep stock to a fair extent are very desirable even to the heavy land farmer."

" That half-bred Down and Leicester *lambs* purchased as early as convenient, say June, (with a slight cross of Norfolk if more size be desired) are most suitable for this district."

" That yarding sheep during winter is the better practice, provided they are allowed to run out upon a pasture for an hour each day, and have sufficient troughs in the yard for all to feed at once."

" That when the common turnips are finished, Swedes are best for fattening, but that mangel wurzel are preferable for breeding ewes, causing more milk and finer lambs."

" That oil cake at the rate of ⅓ lb. per head per day, is better for fattening than corn."

" That cutting hay, clover, and turnips (parti-

cularly Swedes) and feeding in troughs, amply repays the additional outlay for labour by the saving from waste, and that cutting is more especially necessary for lambs, as they frequently suffer from shedding their teeth."

" That sheep should have frequent changes of food; and free access to either rock, or common salt."

" That netting is preferable to common hurdles, for dividing fields, &c."

The propriety of the heavy land farmers keeping sheep, seemed to be fully justified by the excellent effects said to be produced by their manure upon the soil; by the destruction which ensues to the wire-worm and very many slugs by feeding old clover layers with them, and by the great benefit which often results from turning sheep upon young wheat in the spring.

A good deal of opposition was shewn in favour of hoggets purchased early in the spring, and there were members present who contended for breeding sheep. One gentleman spoke of a heavy land farmer who keeps twelve score breeding ewes, yarding them continually all winter upon one bushel of beet per day to every ten sheep, with fresh pea straw, &c.; and no one, he added, has better success either in the number or quality of his lambs.

Netting was advocated by some of the members for folding on account of its comparative cheapness. There appeared to be only one member present who used wheeled hurdles, and his decided opinion was that their durability and the ease with which they may be removed and fixed, gave them many advantages, particularly in the summer season; he generally folded his long fallows with them—six hurdles (of iron he recommended) each twenty-one feet long on four wheels, afforded room for 100 sheep.

January 25th, 1842.—*" The best management of Fences and planting of Quick."*

Upon this subject it was resolved " that a new ditch should be four and a half feet wide, well sloped to about six inches at the bottom, the upper spade being added to the bank, the facing set back six inches, and raised sixteen or eighteen inches for the spring, something like eight inches more earth being placed above the spring." " That the bank should be four feet in width, and have the dead fence pushed into it by hand without making a trench for it with the spade." " That white-thorn spring should be good, and that it should be planted with intervals of five inches, first slightly cutting the roots, leaving the operation of topping until the second year." " That quick, or spring, should be planted as early as possible, before Christmas better than after, and not later than February." " That on account of the great demand for faggots in this neighbourhood for cattle yards, and firing, the meeting expressed a decided opinion that cutting down to the bottom is the best plan; the fence grows faster, and as it was said, fully bears out the truth of the old adage, " cut bushes, and have bushes."

There were but two points presenting any notable difference of opinion—the one relating to the distance which the young plants should be placed from each other (four, five, and six inches being respectively contended for) and the other referring to the cutting of fences; some members asserting that in cutting a fence the first time, it should be buck-headed.

February 22nd.—" Top-dressings."

The employment of artificial manures for this purpose was brought before the club on its first establishment now two years ago, and it would seem from the resolution which follows, little additional light has been thrown upon the subject since that period. It appears however that one proposition at least is brought to a tolerable degree of certainty—we mean the inutility of the nitrated alkalies on soils of good staple quality in high condition ; and so far as our experience and observation has gone, little doubt remains of their being well worth the attention of cultivators of light soils, or strong clays. The resolution adopted by the club on this occasion was to this effect, viz.: " That the results from similar experiments as tested by different individuals are so various, that the club cannot yet arrive at any determinate opinion as to the particular . cases in which the several artificial manures ought to be applied ; and when they find that their farmyard manure seldom if ever fails, and that their trials with chemical manures are often unsuccessful, they cannot come to any other conclusion than that the knowledge which they greatly require is, how to detect the particular ingredients deficient in their soils, or how to make such a compound top-dressing as shall combine the greater portion of the fertilizing principles of farm-yard manure ; notwithstanding this, when they take into account those cases in which some of the artificial manures have produced really good effect, they still feel convinced that it is desirable members should individually continue to test experiments on a small scale until satisfied as to their applicability."

March 29th.—" Deficient Layers."

Upon this subject the following opinions were expressed by the Club—" That clover should not be repeated more than once in eight years ; that from ¾ of a peck to a peck per acre of good new seed is the proper quantity ; that it should be sown broadcast or with the barrow, at the same time the barley is put in ; that the land should be rolled before the plant comes up ; that rye-grass is best for filling up ; and should it be thought expedient to plough up the layer and plant beans, the ploughing is best done in November, and ought in no case to be delayed beyond February.

There was much diversity of opinion in regard to filling up a deficient layers. Cow-grass found many opponents on account of its generally coming to the scythe but once ; tares had some advocates, but the majority are favourable to ryegrass sown soon after harvest.

Drilling clover was said not to do well ; the rows make bad ploughing. Some members held that clover should not be sown at the same time the barley is, if the latter is put in very early, lest the young plant should suffer by frost ; whilst others asserted that they had never known clovers to take harm from such cause. Much stress was likewise laid upon the injury which rolling is supposed to occasion, if done when the plant is very young.

Insufficiency of seed, old or bad seed, too early or too late sowing, bad tillage, dryness of the season, the length of time which the land has been under the plough, were each and all of them assigned as sufficient to cause deficiency or failure of the clover crop ; but instances were adduced of the one-third of a peck per acre producing a good crop. Claying was also allowed to be of great service ; at the same time, it seemed that every one finds it necessary to allow some years to elapse between clover crops. It appeared obvious, therefore, that previous and too frequent cropping with it, or with plants analogous in character, is the main cause of deficient layers ; hence the disputed questions arise, viz., whether the injurious consequences of growing plants of the same class in too quick succession result from a deposition by the plant of matter unfavourable to the growth of that class ? or whether failure arises from the exhaustion of any peculiar matter of the soil which may be essential to the well-doing of such plants ? This forms a subject of great national importance, and well worthy of philosophical research, inasmuch as it involves the questions whether certain *determinate intervals of time must of necessity* be allowed between the cultivation of any given crop, thus restricting the aggregate amount of such crop throughout the kingdom, or whether any certain means exist of making land capable of growing the same kind of crop in closer succession.

April 26th.—" Rearing and Weaning Neat Stock."

From the observations addressed to the meeting, the following are selected as being approved by the majority of those present. " That calves, whether intended for grazing or for the dairy, should be kept better than they commonly are in this district through the first year ; to this end it was recommended (supposing the calves to fall in February, which was considered the best time), that they should remain upon the cow three weeks, or, if a young cow, a month ; when taken off, they should have about a gallon of skimmed milk twice a day for the first week ; this may then be diluted with water more and more daily for three weeks longer, or until the animal is put to grass, when it may be entirely discontinued. In the interim, the calf should be induced to pick at hay, roots, pollard, or cake. A constant supply of water should be kept by them, and during the hot summer months, when flies are troublesome, it is advisable to provide a shed with green clover, tares, or cut grass ; and when taken up in November, hay and turnips, with liberty to shelter themselves in a warm covered place as they choose ; warmth, dryness, and cleanliness being deemed very important requisites. If possible, nothing but wheat straw should be used.

Some casual remarks were made during the evening, which went to show that calves when taken from the cow do better upon oatmeal gruel made with water, than upon skimmed milk.

A gentleman had so constantly escaped the disease known under the name of garget (which is believed to be incurable), that he attributed his success to his keeping his young stock warmer and drier than his less fortunate neighbours are in the habit of doing. Another stated that he always dressed his calves in November, with a view of preventing the disease.

May 24th.—" The best mode of making Hay and Clover."

It will occur to the readers of our last annual report, that this subject had already undergone consideration by the Club ; its importance, however, is such, that some members expressed a desire to bring it again under notice. The re-discussion of it was chiefly a repetition of that which we heard last year, and concluded by an unanimous confirmation of the resolutions then adopted ; therefore, beyond the additional weight which may thence attach to those resolutions, we have gained little by the past year's experience.

A curious article upon hay-making, written by a German some forty years ago, was read to the meeting, the most striking portion of which was a recommendation to gather clover in a green state into immense large cocks containing three or four loads each, with the view of bringing on a state of fermentation; a similar practice, it appears, is prevalent in Ireland in the present day. Be the weather wet or dry, of course it must be spread out after a few hours; the labour of cocking, or rather of stacking and unstacking, must consequently be very great, and excited surprise in those who heard it, that such a curious system should be persisted in; the fact, nevertheless, was listened to with attention, because it recognises the principle of fermentation upon the cock.

A gentleman complaining that his stacks always moulded beneath the thatch, was advised to leave the thatch open at the top until the heat of the stack has entirely subsided. It was likewise confidently stated that a layer of faggots placed just where the roof commences, is of much use as a preventive of mould in the body of the stack. The bad state in which hay was harvested last year has, we believe, made many converts to the practice of salting; many members assenting that hay which seemed entirely spoiled appeared to become by its use both palatable and wholesome.

June 27th.—" The best management of Cows."

Resolved,—"That in feeding cows great regularity is required; that from February to May they ought to be kept well with roots, hay, and perhaps cake, that they may go out to grass in good condition; that mown grass or clover, if the meadows are bare, should be supplied to them under cover during the extreme heat of the summer; that their keep in the winter months should consist of roots and hay, or if short of these, straw and one cake per day, diminishing the quantity of cake towards the time of calving; that great care should be taken that cows are well milked, and also that they are kept moderately warm, dry, and clean; that common turnips should be given first, then Swedes or beet—if beet, cautiously, particularly towards the time of calving; that selling new milk or butter at per pound or pint, answers best where there is a convenient market for them, and that where this is the case, stall feeding with tares, &c., may be practised, but that butter from such feed will not stand in firkin."

So far as the subject was discussed, the manage-ment of cows appears to be dependant in a great measure on soil and locality. Some pastures are remarkable for their yield of butter, others for curd or cheese, and some for quantity more than quality of milk; after-grass, bran, pollard, and grains, were each said to be favourable to the flow of milk, but not of butter. Several members thought that some artificial keep ought to be re-sorted to when the meadows are bare in the latter part of the summer as well as in the spring, in order to keep the animals in milk, if possible, un-til they calve; this, it was said, may be generally done, and it was deemed bad management to suffer cows to fail in their milk at any period of the year. A general objection, however, was raised to artificial keep by those who firkined, because the butter will not keep; but during the winter months, when the demand for it pinted or pounded is generally equal to the supply, cake at the rate

of two per day with straw only, is thought to be a good substitute for a scarcity of turnips, and it seems doubtful, from a calculation that was made (taking into account also the superior value of the manure), whether there is not an actual saving: at all events, the carting of turnips at an unfavourable time may be avoided by their use. Beet, it was asserted, will not do to take the place entirely of turnips, because the produce has an unpleasant flavour, and young stock are paralysed by them; their ill effects were stated to arise from their being used too plentifully.

Barley-meal was also recommended in lieu of cake. Alderney cows were highly extolled by two or three members for the richness of their milk; and it was mentioned as a fact worthy of note, that be their food what it may, the milk never tastes of it. Frequent change of pasture in small enclosures was considered highly desirable.

In country districts, selling milk cannot be carried to a great extent, dairying (which needs great attention from the mistress), is consequently the only alternative, but whether one-meal cheese or butter best answers the purpose was not decisively determined. One shilling per pound for butter was thought by many to pay better than the usual price obtained for one-meal cheese. Our flet cheese, *as such*, was declared to possess superior qualities if made properly; the current jest applied to Suffolk cheese was therefore resented.

July 19th.—" On Agriculture as a Science."

On this occasion a resolution was passed, "That the members present, recognising the benefits already derived from science as applied to agriculture, are strongly of opinion that still further improvements will be attained by its aid."

From a body of men whose experience has taught them that it is generally safer to adhere to what may be termed hereditary notions, than to trust to scientific theories which they do not fully understand; a learned disputation on a subject embracing such a boundless field for philosophic speculation was not expected. The only useful objects which could be gained by discussing such a question consisted in ascertaining the value attached by the practical farmer to the labours undertaken by scientific professors on his behalf; and in giving those who are able to appreciate the influence of the sciences an opportunity of explaining, for the benefit of their less reflective neighbours, how and to what extent the improvements in modern husbandry have depended upon those influences, and how other improvements may still be expected to result from them.

Not many years ago, the farmer who presumed to consult his understanding, and to depart from certain universal rules, incurred the ridicule of his neighbours; he was pointed at as a man seeking his own ruin by reckless adventure. The art of farming, it was supposed, had reached the point of perfection—the right way of doing everything was known; hence, he who questioned its truth must be wrong.

We take no credit to ourselves for having effected the change; it is, nevertheless, satisfactory to observe that progress has somehow been made towards more enlightened views. We hail it as one step towards improvement to hear a community of farmers acknowledge that science has been of beneficial service to their art; and the terms with which they appeal to men of science to continue their efforts in furtherance of agriculture, give still further reason to hope that they are ready to avail themselves of such assistance, and to profit by it.

The mere question whether or not agriculture is receiving advantages through the sciences, hardly existed as a question with the members of the club; the proceedings of the meeting were consequently directed to some of the more conspicuous features of modern farming; and praise is due to some of the members for their attempts to point out the connection of agriculture with the sciences, and how some recent improvements have sprung from them. The observations of one gentleman were peculiarly pleasing and instructive; he alluded to numerous instances in which farming has been promoted, as he believed, by the direct application of scientific principles, and called the attention of the club to many others wherein hints have been borrowed from the sciences and turned to useful account. He concluded by a recommendation that the study of the sciences should form a prominent part of the education of the young farmer. He thought also that advantage might be gained even from the study of the languages—it makes the technicalities of science intelligible, and enables persons to read and to understand valuable works which might otherwise remain closed to them. The education of farmers, said he, is too limited, and in no respect such as it ought to be. Agriculture, it is admitted on all hands, is or ought to be governed by principles admitting of the exercise of talents of the highest order; the reasoning powers of the young farmer ought, therefore, to be suited by proper education to the noble and scientific pursuit for which he is intended. Any fool will do for a farmer, is a common expression, but it is a mistaken one; the want of education not only prevents the advancement of agriculture through the farmer himself, but he is thereby incapacitated for carrying into effect the recommendations of those who are better instructed. In the above views the meeting seemed entirely to acquiesce. Perhaps we may be permitted to ask if any adequate means exist through which such a desirable object can be obtained? Surely, whilst every endeavour is making to provide suitable instruction for the poor labourer, some arrangement should likewise be made to place within the reach of the farmer more appropriate means of educating his sons. Located in districts remote from capable and experienced teachers, the farmer is denied the advantages enjoyed by the citizen; he is compelled to go to the expense of placing his children at some distant boarding-school, where the kind of instruction is but little adapted to their future station in life, or to be content with the meagre knowledge to be obtained from a village schoolmaster.

September 20th.—" The Rotation of Crops."

At this meeting the club passed a resolution approving of the four-course shift usually practised in the neighbourhood, and recommended that long fallows should occur at least once in eight years.

The general character of the soil may be supposed to have originally determined the kind of rotation best calculated for different districts; but we know that the constitution of it becomes in some degree altered by cultivation; a different system of cropping may, therefore, be rendered necessary both from this circumstance, as well as from the fact of a greater variety of field vegetables having been introduced from other countries. The necessity of taxing the powers of the soil to the fullest extent is likewise so continually pressed upon the mind of the farmer of the present day, that the possibility of dispensing with long fallows or of lessening their frequency have become questions which naturally force themselves upon his attention. We find accordingly that longer shifts and even perpetual cropping have been successfully adopted by agriculturists of great repute; a knowledge of this circumstance makes the rotation of crops a subject well worthy of investigation. Rotations of four, five, and six courses were severally canvassed by the club, and led to the conclusion above stated. The member who introduced the subject enquired which of the three systems, without exhausting the land, and fouling it with weeds, would ultimately prove the most advantageous after taking into account the additional expense of cultivation? Suffolk and Norfolk, he observed, stand high as agricultural counties, and this he thought might be partly attributed to our adherence to a rotation suited to the character of the soil. He thought the farmer should be cautious how he departed from long-established local customs in these matters: a crop in lieu of fallow is not always a crop into pocket. He believed that the attempts to substitute improved rotations in this district had uniformly failed, except where the individual has had access to an unusual quantity of manure. Another gentleman said that no advantage could result from an extended rotation, unless it includes two crops of wheat; and these would necessarily succeed too quickly each other; such a system also requires so much extra manure to compensate for exhaustion and fruitless labour in weeding, &c., that a doubt remains after all, whether the additional crop counterbalances the expense and injury to the succeeding crops. A third member stated that he had repeatedly endeavoured to introduce a different system, but his deviations from the usual custom, notwithstanding that they have been tried upon choice land at the expense of the remaining portion of the farm, have always left his fields so foul that he has been ashamed of them, and he found the second crop of wheat very deficient. Upon the whole, he was inclined to think he gained nothing by it; how, then, it was asked, can any such practice be expected to answer when applied to an entire occupation?

There are few farms, it was observed, which will permit the cultivator to choose which portion shall be under certain crops. An opinion was expressed that too many tares are grown upon our heavy lands; it would answer better to let a larger portion be in fallow; the failure of the clover crop was thought to be sometimes owing to this practice. Again it was considered that a few acres well prepared for a root crop was preferable to a larger breadth badly manured. Much stress was laid upon the advantages of getting tares off early; to this it was answered that the land which would most benefit by so doing will not grow them early; ploughing the wheat stubbles in was spoken of as a means of obviating this difficulty, but it appeared that such backward land will not readily decompose stubble. From some other observations which followed, it seemed to be the conviction of the members present, that whilst there are tracts of soil which will produce an average under whatever crop the farmer may choose to plant, and consequently permit him to make choice of such a rotation as may be considered most convenient ; there are others which will admit of the cultivation of a limited class of plants only, and which therefore require frequent fallows to prevent the too close succession of them, and to compensate for the absence of those manure crops which they are not calculated to grow. Such land, it was remarked, would not even withstand the four-course shift, were it not supported by other land of better quality.

October 18th.—" On the necessity of keeping Farming Accounts, and the best method of doing so."

In regard to the first part of this subject, hardly two opinions can exist; it was therefore resolved by the club, "that to conduct farming business properly, the keeping of correct accounts is not only necessary, but highly advantageous and useful; and that it becomes still more important in a business point of view, if carried to the extent of keeping a regular register of every operation carried on upon the farm."

Several books published by different authors, and which facilitate this desirable object, were laid before the meeting ; as, however, the majority of those present had never had an opportunity of comparing their several merits, it was deemed advisable to purchase a copy of each for circulation amongst the members. The complicated nature of farming accounts, it was said, had deterred many persons from keeping them, although aware of the importance of doing so ; great merit was consequently conceded to those gentlemen who have undertaken the task of simplifying them. Other persons have neglected to keep accounts because they were not aware of the ease with which, through the assistance of such helps, it can be done. Three or four members bore testimony to the great aid which they received from these works, and stated that with a little trouble, attention, and regularity, a farmer is enabled to take an account of all his business transactions with great accuracy and satisfaction to himself. Although, as might have been expected, none of the published systems appeared to accord entirely with their ideas, alterations were suggested which a better acquaintance with the works in question may enable the club to recommend to the notice of the publishers. It was observed during the discussion, that nothing so greatly contributed to the formation of business habits, [and to bind the attention to its proper occupation, as the regular keeping of accounts. Nothing forms so sure a guide for future proceedings as it does, by affording the means of detecting the cause of failure in past practice. It has a value beyond this—its infallible property of teaching all men how to adjust their outgoings to their incomes.

November 15th.—General Meeting.

The Prizes for Roots, &c., were adjudged as follows :—For

Red mangel wurzel ...... Mr. JOHN EDWARDS,
Yellow ditto .... Mr. JAMES READ.
3 best Swede turnips...... Mr. JAMES READ.
3 best round white turnips Mr. PEIRSON.
Best white wheat .... Mr. JAMES READ.
Best red wheat .... Mr. JOHN EDWARDS.
Best Barley.............. Mr. G. GOODWYN.
Best Tick beans.......... Mr. G. GOODWYN.
Mazagan beans .... (none offered)
Maple peas .... Mr. PEIRSON.

About twenty-five prizes were likewise awarded to the labourers of members for garden produce.

JOHN PEIRSON, Chairman.   HENRY CLUTTEN, Sec.

SECOND REPORT OF THE GREAT OAKLEY FARMERS' CLUB.

PRESENTED AT THE ANNUAL MEETING, HELD AT GREAT OAKLEY, NOV. 14, 1842.

Your committee, in presenting you with their second annual Report, beg to congratulate you on the increased number of your members, and on the countenance which farmers' clubs receive from all parties. They believe that, in the absence of a more scientific knowledge of the properties of soils and plants, these clubs are, from the practical knowledge they bring together, of the greatest possible benefit ; and that, when such knowledge shall be acquired, they will prove the best medium of bringing it into general use.

Your committee desire particularly to allude to the minutes of the July meeting. They are induced to do so, that similar societies, which may see our report, may, if they have not done so, be led to give that part of it, alluding to education, their best consideration.

It is there stated that the present improvement, both in habits and farming, has arisen from the improved education of the cultivators of the soil ; that their further advancement depends upon it ; and that the still further knowledge required, is to be obtained without materially increasing the present time or expense allotted to young men of this class.

Your committee have reason to believe, that this all important subject of agricultural education is occupying the attention of its ablest and best friends ; and that the day is not far distant, when we shall have a class of schools calculated to impart knowledge on all subjects that will promote the objects of agriculture ; and it must ever be borne in mind, that it is only by our superior skill and knowledge, that we can, under a rewarding Providence, maintain the position we enjoy ; for our competitors abroad, with whom we have to contend, in the production of corn and cattle, have every other advantage over us.

FIRST MEETING, 27TH DECEMBER, 1841.

Subject—" On Grazing Cattle."

That it is the opinion of this meeting, that bullocks cannot be grazed advantageously without the aid of artificial food ; but are not unanimous which is the best, cake and roots, or corn, cake and roots.

But it is the opinion of the meeting, that when the price of corn was such as to render it equally advantageous as cake, that the corn ought to be resorted to, being the produce of our soil, and that a warm and equal temperature is of great importance.

Moved, that bullocks should have food allowed to remain by them only 12 hours ; in which the meeting fully concurred.

The interest of the discussion was much increased by the remarks of two medical gentlemen present, showing the necessity of giving chaff, or dry food, to assist the digestive powers of the animal, to obtain all the nutritious part of the food, and especially if consuming a large proportion of oil cake.

SECOND MEETING, 24TH JANUARY, 1842.

Subject—" On cultivating Beans and Peas."

A member introduced the subject by stating, that he considered it of considerable importance to the bean crop, to have the land manured and ploughed up before Christmas ; the land by the means of an early ploughing acquired solidity, and was in a better state to receive the seed; six rows on an eight-furrow stetch he considered better than more, affording a better opportunity of keeping them clean. He thought beans, generally speaking, were not dropped thick enough, that two or three beans in a hole were required, or not less than three bushels per acre.

Another member concurred in the plan of ploughing strong lands up before Christmas; but considered mild land was best ploughed just before setting the beans; he also preferred seven rows on a stetch, and one bean in a hole; or one bushel and a half per acre. After some discussion on these various points, it appeared that the meeting were not unanimous as to the best time of ploughing mild land for beans; but it was the general opinion of the meeting, that beans should be planted with two beans in a hole, and with six rows on an eight-furrow stetch.

It is the general and approved plan, in the neighbourhood, to put peas in in the autumn, directly after wheat sowing.

THIRD MEETING, 21ST FEB.

Subject—"On cultivation of Barley."

A member considered, when turnips were fed on the land, it should be ploughed twice before sowing, as by this plan the large proportion of manure deposited in the furrows in feeding, would be left on the two outside furrows; he strongly recommended waiting until the lands were perfectly dry before the seed was deposited, and the earliest time in the year the land was in this state, ought to be taken advantage of. He also considered less seed per acre than was generally used, might be adopted with advantage; he thought more than eight pecks per acre was not only a waste of seed, but injurious to the crop.

Several members who last year, upon a small scale, adopted the plan of putting only eight pecks per acre for seed, spoke highly of the plan, and strongly recommended further trials to be made. After considerable discussion on this point, the meeting resolved, it being the almost uniform practice, that from ten pecks to three bushels per acre of seed was required. The land in this neighbourhood being generally too wet to admit of feeding, it was also resolved, that one good ploughing, after the turnips were removed, was sufficient.

Considerable discussion took place upon the benefit of scarifying. A member moved that the scarifier should be used, as it enabled you to leave the stetch in a better form to lay down with seed; and gave a greater depth of mould for depositing the seed.

Another member stated that land, in consequence of being laid up very round for turnips, after the first ploughing, might be laid with good ploughing, sufficiently flat to be laid down with seeds; and for any other purpose he considered scarifying worse than useless.

He moved, that heavy harrows should be used instead, as he did not consider the great depth of mould acquired by the scarifier, beneficial to the barley crop.

The meeting did not come to a division; for, although the scarifier was evidently getting out of repute as to its general use, there were cases, it was considered, when it might be used to advantage.

FOURTH MEETING, 21ST MARCH.

Subject—"On Under-draining."

A member stated, that on hilly land the drain he thought required to be of sufficient depth on the hill, so that the bottom of the drain formed an inclined plane; but on flat land, the distance and depth must be regulated by the nature of the subsoil; and, where that was uniformly sound, he thought sufficient water furrowing answered every purpose.

A second member stated, that on hilly land, where the land was springy, and the subsoil sandy, he had known several acres drained by sinking a small well, and leading a drain from it.

A third member stated, that from his experience, he had found 30 inches in depth to answer every purpose; and he thought, all things considered, that tiles were not only the most effectual, but in the end the cheapest to fill up with. Stone was admitted to answer well; but except in a few localities it was too difficult to obtain.

A fourth member had found great benefit from the use of the mole plough. Several members spoke of it as being highly useful on some soils, but did not consider it generally applicable to this neighbourhood. The fourth member stated, that he used the mole about three yards apart.

After some discussion on the best mode of filling up drains, and the comparative expenses of the different plans, it was resolved :—

It is the first and most essential improvement that can be made on wet lands; it is an improvement on which all others must be based; but this meeting can lay down no plan, either as to depth or distance of the drains, the soil in this neighbourhood varying so much; but were unanimous in agreeing that tiles were best, and in the end the cheapest to fill up with; but tile draining was so expensive, and the improvement of such a permanent character, that it could not be incurred by a tenant, without the aid of his landlord, to any extent.

After the discussion some interesting facts were stated, upon the cause of drains being stopped or blown. The roots of trees had been known to pass a long distance, and especially the willow, and to block the drain up, by entirely filling it up with its fibrous roots.

A member stated, a few years since he discovered a drain blown, on a piece of land on which a piece of white turnips were standing late in the spring, and on digging down several feet, he found the drain was entirely filled by the roots of the white turnips.

Another instance was named, where the same effect had been produced by the roots of mangel wurzel.

FIFTH MEETING, 18TH APRIL.

Subject—"On the Preparation of Manure for Turnips."

A member introduced this subject by stating, that his conviction from several years' experience was, that manure was applied with most advantage in a raw state; this conviction was forced upon him, as he had been much prejudiced against the system, until he saw the benefit of it on an adjoining farm.

There were other members, who had been applying their manure in a raw state, avoiding fermentation as much as possible, and spoke very highly of the result of such a practice. Sir Humphrey Davey was quoted, as high authority in favour of the application of raw manure. They also contended that by allowing the manure to undergo great fermentation—no unusual thing, even twice before it was applied to the land—a great portion of the volatile salts was allowed to escape, and the strength of the manure was much lessened, if not injured ; but by allowing decomposition to take place under the soil, every property of the manure was secured to it.

On the other hand, it was contended by another member, that fermentation was not so injurious, but was necessary to destroy seeds. After considerable discussion on the best mode of mixing, and the fermentation of hills, it was resolved, that the majority of this meeting are decidedly in favour of mixed manures; but admitted that the practice of applying manure as soon as it was mixed was daily gaining ground; and the spirit of enquiry being generally agitated on this most important subject, the management of manures, aided as practical men now were by men of science, it was much to be hoped that some generally acknowledged correct principles, for every variety of soil, would be ascertained.

SIXTH MEETING, 23RD MAY.

Subject—"On the best mode of keeping Farming Horses during the summer."

A member stated that he believed red clover, mown and used in the yard, was the best food and plan of feeding horses during the summer months ; that clover on land in a good state would admit of being mown several times; but he considered, in addition to green food, where horses were kept fully employed, they required an addition of a bushel of corn per week; he preferred the plan of keeping rather under the usually admitted required horse strength of 1 to 20 acres and keeping them high. It was calculated that where 12 horses were required, if allowed corn all the time they ate green food, thirteen might be kept at the same expense by restricting them from corn during three months out of the four that green food was generally consumed. Tares were generally admitted to be a most valuable green food for horses, and particularly at the time they were in bloom.

A second member stated his practice was to allow his horses no corn or dry food for the first week he gave them tares ; he considered the purgative effect they had on the horses, in the spring of the year, for a few days highly beneficial to their health. He had lost but one horse during the last 16 years ; after a week he gave them a little corn and chaff, until the tares or green food approached their full growth, when he considered corn was not required.

A third member stated that he had mown the Italian rye grass into his yard for his horses, and he found they would do better on it without corn, than they would with other green food with the addition of corn.

It was resolved as the opinion of the meeting, that horses are kept with most advantage in the yard, upon green clover, tares, or Italian rye grass ; and the majority of the meeting concurred in the opinion of the second member, that corn was not required during two or three months of the time the horses were eating green food, except under peculiar circumstances.

SEVENTH MEETING, 20TH JUNE.

Subject—"On the Management of Swine."

A member said he considered the first litter of pigs ought to fall sometime in January, and with great care and good feeding they ought to arrive at the weight of three score pounds in six months.

He considered the diseases, to which pigs were

so liable, were to be attributed in general to the want of cleanliness, or to the confined size of the piggeries.

Another member said, he believed from his own, and from the experience of a neighbour, whose success in the management of pigs was well known, that pigs were much injured by being turned out too early in the morning ; their natural habits were opposed to this, except compelled to it by hunger or force, and green food, with either white frost or dew on, he considered very liable to engender disease. Beet root to any extent, was stated to be unfavourable food, either for sows or pigs.

The members were not agreed as to which would make the most pork—barley or peas, of equal weight ; but it was considered, that pigs would fatten best with barley and peas ground together,

EIGHTH MEETING, 18TH JULY.

Subject—"On the best mode of keeping Farming Accounts."

A member introduced the subject by commenting on the importance, and pointing out the many advantages of farmers keeping correct accounts. He stated that " Swinborne's Account Book" was one of the earliest that appeared before the public, and the trouble and expense taken by Mr. Swinborne to make it generally known, gave it an extensive circulation ; and the attention of farmers being drawn to it, many works emanated from the press, and the meeting fully appreciated the exertions made by Mr. Swinborne, on a subject but too little attended too, although of so much importance.

Several members congratulated the meeting on the improved habits of farmers; instead of meeting, as was too generally the case some few years since, to indulge in the pleasures of the table to excess, meetings were now becoming general throughout the country for the enjoyment of social and intellectual intercourse, and for the promotion of objects in which all classes were interested.

And the meeting could not but feel that this great and improved change had mainly arisen from the improved education of the cultivators of the soil ; but great as had been the good effected, the meeting still felt that the education of young men, intended for agricultural pursuits, was still very defective, and that a knowledge of every branch of science bearing on agriculture, ought to form a part of their education ; and the meeting believed, that these desirable objects might be accomplished, without materially increasing the present expense and time allotted for the education of young men of this class.

NINTH MEETING, 19TH SEPTEMBER.

Subject—"On the best mode of keeping Farming Horses during the Winter."

A member stated he believed, all things considered that oats, beans, and clover stover, were the best food for the use of the cart horse, and on the whole as cheap. His own plan was to allow each horse two bushels of oats, one and a half cwt. of stover, during the busy time of wheat and spring sowing, and in the winter months one cwt. of stover. About ten pecks of beans were considered equivalent to a sack of oats, but it was not thought desirable to use them alone. He also stated, that so much depends on the feeder and the driver as to horses being kept in condition, that if we failed in having a steady intelligent man, a master cannot expect his horse to look well with all his care in providing for them He believed it was a good plan to allow them to go into a yard at night, if the yard was provided with good shelter and sheds.

The meeting, after discussing the various plans of keeping horses, on part vegetables and part corn, all concurred in adopting the plan first suggested, as most adapted to this neighbourhood.

It was stated by a member, that much injury was sustained, where carrots were used, by washing them previously to giving them to horses.

An unlimited use of clover stover was stated by a member to be injurious to the wind of many horses.

TENTH MEETING, 17TH OCTOBER.

Subject—" On the advantages of Top Dressing."

A member introduced the subject by stating he had applied manure as a top dressing to wheat during the winter; but as far as could be judged by comparison, with but little advantage. Several members spoke to the same effect; but it was stated by another member, that manure applied last season, either as a top dressing, or ploughed in from the wetness of the season, was unusually ineffective. Several members highly approved of manuring young clovers in the autumn. It was also stated that as good wheat was grown after clovers manured in a young state, as when manure was applied immediately before the wheat sowing.

An artificial top dressing, that could be applied with advantage to clover, was much wanted. As regarded artificial manures they had been so little used in the neighbourhood generally at present, that the meeting could come to no correct conclusion as to their particular merits; but those members who had tried them, gave the preference to nitrate of soda.

All who had tried them acknowledged there was a benefit to the crop from the use of the nitrate of soda, and other artificial manures; but at present the price of them was too great to admit of their being used to advantage.

The Prizes were adjudged as follow, for—

White Wheat	Mr. W. Thompson.
Red Wheat	Mr. M. Cooper.
Barley	Mr. J. Barker.
Oats	Mr. J. Hempson, jun.
Peas	Mr. W. Thompson.
Beans	Mr. E. Cooper.
Swede Turnips	Mr. Stanford.
Common Turnips	Mr. W. Keer.
Beet Root	
For the best of two acres ⎰ Beet Root in one field.. ⎱	Mr. W. Mason.

BARN FLOORS. — (To the Editor of the Salisbury and Winchester Journal.)—SIR,—Observing in your widely circulated paper of the 19th ult., an inquiry as to the best material to be substituted for oak in barn floors, I beg to name what I conceive to be a very superior substitute, both as to quality and price—I allude to the wooden pavement now so generally used in the streets of London. The blocks are all pinned together; they require no sleepers; but are laid on a firm concrete foundation, thus affording an elastic and improved floor for thrashing; and, being one solid mass, is impervious to rats. The cost is from 7s. to 10s. per square yard, and I can speak from experience as to the floor being equal, if not superior, to oak.—Your obedient servant, A CONSTANT READER. —Romsey, Dec. 1, 1842.

FERMENTATION OF HAY AND MANURE.

SIR,—Feeling the deep necessity for a chemical investigation of the subjects herein to be mentioned, and not being a chemist myself, I beg leave to bring them, through the medium of your paper, to the attention of those qualified for their consideration. I mean the loss sustained by hay and by manure in different stages of fermentation—as fermentation I believe I must call it.

Every one knows the sweet smell of new-mown hay; it has not this smell while standing in the growing state, but immediately on being cut down, the grass dies, and begins to give off a quantity of, I presume, gaseous matter, which produces this peculiar odour; this is followed by a great loss in weight and a great loss of nutrition. One perch of grass will certainly feed more than two perches of hay. Would it be possible in any degree to fix this volatile matter, which seems by the effect of its loss to be the chief nutritive ingredient?

When hay is put into a rick, it sometimes heats, which some people insist improves it—an assumption which seems at variance with common sense, as while the process of heating is going on, a strong saccharine smell is perceived; by which it is evident that a quantity of saccharine matter is being evolved in the shape of gas, and is dissipated in the atmosphere. Is this beneficial or not? and would it be useful or not to take measures to prevent it? I know it will be asserted by some that horses prefer heated hay; but is there not a loss sustained?

I make a heap of compost manure every year; the substratum is composed of bog stuff or peat earth, a substance probably unknown to most of your English readers; it serves to absorb some of the liquid matter which would otherwise be carried off, and it suffers itself at least a partial decomposition, and adds to the heap. Some of our Irish theorists say a useless addition, but notwithstanding, practically, most extensively used in Ireland. Over this is placed the farm-yard dung, according as it is produced, and any other gatherings which can be had. I used to turn this heap in spring, whereby all the ingredients became intimately mixed. Immediately after this operation, the mass seemed to ferment, and a great quantity of gas was given off. I know not of what description, whether ammoniacal or what else, it may be, only that, as usual in such cases, there was a shocking bad smell, which after a few days went off by degrees, and the mass now was sensibly diminished in bulk, and that to a very considerable extent, and the substance was reduced to a more homogenous form, and more near than formerly in appearance to the condition of rich black mould. It had evidently suffered decomposition in a great degree, the putrefactive process had had its effect, and there was a loss of substance, which had evidently gone off in the atmosphere. Query, therefore, what was the matter which was lost? Was it a loss to lose it? Had it been retained, would it have been of use to future vegetation, and if so, how could its loss be prevented?

This latter is a question in which every farmer is deeply interested, and I should hope be deemed worthy of an answer by some competent authorities; many of whom, I presume, look over your pages. I have felt its importance so much, that these last two years I have desisted from turning manure, and I would like to know whether I am right or wrong. I think it goes further, but it has a crude appearance when going out, and the bog earth particularly seems to be in a great measure unchanged.

Further, as a question interesting to your Irish, and probably some of your Scotch readers, bog or peat earth is certainly composed of half-decayed vegetable matter. Aquatic vegetables grow on the surface of the bog, and die in succession, and so form yearly accessions to the substance of the bog, which is in a state apparently of semi-decomposition, its structure being preserved from total putrefaction by (I believe) a principle called tannin—a principle which is well known operates in a great degree to the preservation of matters which have often been found in bogs. I conceive it would be important if, in order effectually to decompose this bog earth, we could get rid of or neutralize this tannin. Query, how is this to be done? I do not think lime does it; at least my experience does not tell me so. I have made some experiments with bog earth. I have put it on a meadow just as it came off the bog, and also when mixed with quicklime, and left for a year in the heap twice turned, and found no benefit in either case; and though I always use it, and that at considerable expense for the drawing home in compost manure, I am yet undecided whether it confers any benefit on the land of itself, or whether it only acts by its mixture in more equally distributing the really essential matters, and as an absorbent of some which would otherwise go waste.

If I do not convey information by this letter, I hope to elicit it, and am,   Sir, yours, &c.,
Dec. 3, 1842.   CULTORIUS.

REMARKS

RELATIVE TO A PAPER BY P. PUSEY, ESQ., M.P., ON THE PROGRESS OF AGRICULTURAL KNOWLEDGE DURING THE LAST FOUR YEARS. BY GEORGE THOMPSON, JUN.

The writer of the following lines has had frequent opportunities of ascertaining the views of practical agriculturists with respect to the formation and encouragement of societies having for their express object the advancement of agriculture; and he has thereby become convinced that many members of those societies are undecided as to the tendency of such institutions; indeed, that some unhesitatingly declare it to be their conviction, that they are, and have been, productive of no possible advantage. Now, by what mysterious influence such individuals are induced to remain members of societies which they think can be of no possible benefit, remains to be explained; it is only necessary for the writer to state that he is acquainted with such individuals. But, independent of this class of persons, there is another which includes within its pale by far the greater portion of the agricultural world, and it is that class who professedly and practically oppose the present progress of agricultural knowledge. Much it is to be regretted by every philanthropist, that men should be so blind to their own interest; and it is still more to be regretted that this is the case, when it is known that this blindness does not arise so much from wilful prejudice as from mistaken impressions. Every friend to agriculture (and who ought not to be so?) must inevitably desire to remove such an unfortunate impression from the minds of all interested parties. Such is the desire of the writer, and with this view he calls particular attention to Mr. Pusey's paper, published in the third volume of the "Journal of the Royal Agricultural Society;" a paper containing the clearest synopsis of the advantages of agricultural societies, that has ever yet been submitted to the public. Being founded on

fact the arguments are conclusive. Nothing is inserted but what bears the stamp of experience; in fact the paper is, as its title implies, " a retrospect of the state of agriculture during the last four years.' During which four years, greater advances have been made in agricultural knowledge than were ever before made in an equal period. Mr. Pusey proves those advantages to have been made chiefly from the institution of the Royal Agricultural Society.

But, however excellent the paper may be, and however conclusive its arguments may prove, it is a source of considerable regret, that in its present shape the circulation must be limited to that body of individuals who least require it—the members of the society, in justification of which it has been written; therefore, the writer of these remarks ventures to hope that the author of that paper, or the directors of the Royal Agricultural Society, will republish it, in a cheap form for general circulation; inasmuch as such a composition, founded on indisputable and well authenticated facts, is calculated to remove many dangerous prejudices still existing in the minds of a great portion of the agricultural community.

Nevertheless, there are some few conclusions relative to manures which are incorrect, or insufficient; and which arise from the circumstance that Mr. Pusey has not instituted inquiry sufficiently far in that department of agricultural science; but still are no argument against the utility of agricultural societies, rather one in their favour.

The first instance is the exception of tanner's bark from being available as a manure, since it is generally known that this article forms a very useful material to incorporate with other and stronger fertilizers; not only this, but the writer has seen it applied on a small scale, for onions and turnips, with the most beneficial result; indeed, a chemical analysis of its composition must at once pronounce it to be a valuable manure.

Again, with respect to nitrate of soda, Mr. P. observes, "There are the most undoubted proofs from numerous quarters of an enormous increase in the produce after its use; there are as undoubted instances of its utter failure, nor have we any clue to the mystery." An instance is then quoted, where in one year nitrate of soda produced eight bushels of wheat; in the next it gave but three, and in consequence it was abandoned as a manure. Yet the cause was obvious: the land did not require anymore of that particular manure, therefore the mystery was elucidated. Indeed, Mr. Pusey afterwards quotes Liebig's theory, which at once accounts for this hitherto mysterious effect, and therefore it is somewhat strange that he could not solve the mystery.

But the fact is, that Liebig himself, although he has produced the ablest work on agricultural chemistry which was ever written, yet has not given " a clue to the mystery." The clue will never be found until agriculturists become chemists. They must adopt the motto of the Royal Agricultural Society, namely, " Practice with Science;" and they must apply it as well to manuring as to every other branch of agricultural science. Then they will " have a clue to the mystery," not before.

With the exception of some few erroneous conclusions, as to the causes of failure in some particular manures, Mr. Pusey's paper cannot be regarded in any other light than as a valuable addition to the library of the agriculturist; and it is hoped that so great a desideratum will not be exclusively reserved for the members of the Royal Agricultural Society.

Lion-street, Kidderminster, Nov. 28th, 1842.

A LECTURE ON AGRICULTURE,

DELIVERED AT THE WADEBRIDGE INSTITU-
TION ON FRIDAY, 10TH DECEMBER, 1842,
BY MR. JOHN WILLS, OF SOUTHPETHERWYN,
NEAR LAUNCESTON, CORNWALL.

MR. PRESIDENT,—It is with no small degree of pleasure that I receive permission to address such a distinguished and enlightened an audience on the important and daily interesting subject of agriculture as I have now the honour of seeing before me.

That anything I am able to bring forward should be thought worthy the attention of this institution I consider a high compliment, and I shall endeavour to prove how deeply I feel the honour, by laying before you whatever knowledge I have gathered in this most useful art.

I would commence by requesting you to keep your attention on the subject; and, notwithstanding my incapability to do justice to this important matter, still I trust I shall show you that each of us, and the community at large, are vitally concerned in its prosperity, and that " there is nothing better than agriculture."

Of all the arts and sciences that can engage the attention or excite the industry of mankind, agriculture, or the cultivation of the earth, must stand pre-eminent, for on its being properly understood depends the comfort, happiness, and welfare of the millions that inhabit the earth. On opening the gate of this wide field what an extensive view presents itself !

Man in all ages have found it necessary to cultivate the soil to procure the necessaries and comforts of life. Thus holy writ tells us that David, both before and after he was anointed king, employed himself in husbandry, and made a feast at the sheep-shearing. Rachel kept her father's flock. Ruth got into the good graces of Boaz, by gleaning at his harvest. Elisha was called to be a prophet as he drove one of his father's twelve ploughs ; but it is useless to particularize all those luminaries of ancient days who have encouraged agriculture : still, if it was worthy the attention of kings in the olden times, surely it cannot be less so now, when our great and rapidly increasing population demands all the energy, skill, and industry of the sons of agriculture to grow, if possible, two ears of corn and two blades of grass where only one grew before. I have been engaged in this pursuit from my infancy, and if there is any advantage to be derived from farming lands of various descriptions, in different climates, and fairly testing their productive qualities, paying due regard to the expense of cultivation of each particular soil, thereby clearly ascertaining their respective value ; I repeat, if there is any advantage to be derived from these things, I do without ostentation, and can with great propriety, lay claim to it. It is always pleasing to me to see any well cultivated district, and whenever my eye alights on this favoured and really beautiful country—when I call to mind that I have toiled many a day, and watched my fleecy care by night in some of your most fertile fields, and remember too, that they are the same " that my grandfather tilled," I do feel, and that most strongly, for this delightful neighbourhood, and am anxious to see the proprietors and cultivators of this favoured land take the full advantage of your fertile soil, your beautiful climate, and your invaluable river ; and as that river, with its hundreds of tributary branches, drains many a lofty hill and waters many a thirsty plain in its numerous windings, yet pours its waters at last through one channel into the bosom of the wide ocean ; so may you, my brother farmers, by study and application bring all the resources that are within your reach into one bold stream, and pour it on the bosom of agriculture, and make you stand as examples to the agriculturists of England. It is with this feeling, sir, I venture to read a paper to you this evening ; not that I can advance anything to win your admiration, but I stand here to say to my brother farmers that they hold responsible situations, for they are the producers of food for the people ; but they must not allow their time to be misspent, but they must read, " learn, and inwardly digest," and put in practice what is deemed improvement, and come here, and at other such valuable institutions, and occupy the place I so unprofitably fill, and tell their hearers the result of their observations and experiments.

Let the farmers of England do this, and the tree of prejudice that has taken such deep root amongst us will be destroyed. It will silence the complaint by removing the cause ; and the way to do this is expressed in two words, " Improve Agriculture."

It is a truth well known, that our minds, like our bodies, are naturally much affected by the character of the food they receive. I wish, sir, to impress this observation most fully on all, but with redoubled force on the minds of young men, who, as plants in a nursery, are very soon to fill situations where the food on which they have feasted their minds will be put to the test. And here I cannot but lament the very imperfect education that class of young men receive, who in time are to be the producers of the food on which our very existence depends. I know I am addressing many a wealthy and a generous yeoman, and I rejoice in the opportunity. I trust it will be the means of awakening a feeling that has unconsciously been slumbering too long. I do not hold it necessary for a farmer to be a chemist and an engineer ; still I contend it is highly desirable he should understand so much of the facts connected with these subjects as to enable him to know his business as a farmer on the most correct principle.

I beg to offer my best congratulations to you, sir, and the highly respectable audience I have the honour to address, on the formation of many valuable agricultural societies and farmers' clubs lately established in different parts of the kingdom, the good results of which are becoming visible every day—the meeting at Truro for roots, seeds, &c., so lately as the 1st instant to wit. It fully bears out an old observation, that agriculture must and surely will command attention ; the longer we live the more clearly we shall see its importance, and the more highly will it be praised by England's best sons ; for depend on it, " nothing is better than agriculture."

The Royal Agricultural Society of England will in this case, and very properly too, be the leading star. This society is formed of noblemen and gentlemen of station and character—men of sterling worth, who will, and who can well afford to spend time and money in advancing the prosperity of agriculture, and they are stoutly supported in this great cause by the most intelligent farmers of England. Without detracting from the merits of the prizes offered for live stock, their prizes for essays on different subjects must be attended with the greatest advantage. It must be equally gratifying to you as it is to me, to know that the prize for the best essay for storing turnips was awarded to Mr. Geach, a Cornish farmer. You have now your farmers' club ;

K

and I am delighted to find the noble house of Pen-carrow has mingled its influence with others of minor degree fully to carry out the benefits intended for the landowner, occupier, labourer, and consumer. This is as it ought to be; for until we feel the interest of the one to be the interest of the whole, we shall be grasping at the shadow and losing the substance. These things may probably tend to the revival of the agricultural meeting that for many years was held in your neighbouring town.* With this view I am induced to speak more fully on the subject. It is as important to the country that agriculture should be scientifically understood and studied as that manufacturing science should progress. The mere culture of the land is nothing except it be conducted on the best possible principle. To do only as those who have been in the field before us did (but are now passed away), is no great merit. The resources of the mind ought to be brought to labour, and profiting not only by experience, but in learning by experiment, we may hope to see improve-ment progress in an equal ratio in agriculture as in mechanics; and the knowledge of the stores of ex-perimental philosophy affords to be applied to this most useful of all the arts, because it produces the raw material on which the human race is fed and clothed. When the merely operative farmer knows the value of science he will then see that it is the stepping-stone to agricultural wealth, and learn the secret why his better informed neighbour, who has devoted some little attention to such pursuits, has beat him in the career of enterprize. Agricultural societies are particularly beneficial in communi-cating this knowledge. They bring the results of all systems into competition, and must set those who are behind in the contest thinking why they are so. Whatever experiments have been tried, whatever improvements made, whatever failures ex-perienced, are brought under the views of all: the first as lessons to instruct, the last as rocks to avoid. The real value in crosses in breeding, of intermixing soils, of the action of peculiar manures, of the intro-duction of seeds, and of the utility of implements, are tested. The landlord and the tenant, whose interests are identical, are brought together, and may profit by the intercourse.

These are some, but not all the advantages de-rived from societies of this kind. I have been in the habit of attending various agricultural meetings in the west of England for many years, and can, and do with much satisfaction, bear testimony to the benefits resulting from them. To say I never heard any objections to meetings of this kind is not what I am prepared to do; but the strongest I have ever heard advanced is this—that it is opening the eyes of landlords, or in other words, giving them too great an insight into the returns made from land. Now, sir, I, as a tenant farmer, from my experience am ready to confess that this is a strong reason for promoting these societies, and establish-ing them on a firm and solid basis. For I contend, and I appeal to every man of experience, if it is not better to rent a farm under a nobleman or gentle-man who, or whose agent, understands the art of farming, and knows the value of an enlightened, enterprising, and good farmer, than it is of a man who knows little or nothing about it; whose only guide in choosing a tenant is the man that pro-mises to pay the most rent. Can it in this our day be supposed for one moment that the proprietors of the soil of England, old England, would say to Λ,

" You are farming an estate of mine not better than B's, but you show prize cattle, produce more corn, and make a far better return than him; and, not-withstanding your rent is quite as high as his, still from these circumstances it will bear, and therefore must be increased?" That such landlord is not to be found is more than I am warranted in saying; but, thank God, public opinion has such weight with mankind, that such a man would be placed by the world below, far below his industrious and praiseworthy tenant, the value of whom his sordid views would not allow him to estimate. But, sir, it is to be hoped where we shall see one instance of this kind a hundred, ay, a thousand, will occur where merit will meet its due reward. And here I will give you an instance. At an agricultural meeting very recently in our neighbouring county,* a tenant farmer received the prize for the best cultivated farm. At the next court day his landlord highly and deservedly complimented him for his good management, and presented him with a handsome present, assuring him that tenants of his descrip-tion were fully entitled to every encouragement from their landlords, and the best thanks of the public.

Having, sir, said thus much on agricultural so-cieties, I beg to observe that, as he who would grow good fruit must graft from a good stock, and he who would have clear water must go to the head of the fountain, so agricultural societies to be made useful to farmers, and beneficial to mankind, must be cherished and fostered by the kind and generous hand of the proprietors of the soil; unless this is done, and the estate agents in England are capable of acting as tutors to the tenantry, and able coun-cillors to the landlords, we never can progress ra-pidly in agricultural improvements.

The tenant must feel an interest in the soil, and no-thing that I know of would tend to give more confi-dence than to fall back on the good old custom of granting terms of twenty-one years, which are as necessary for the prosperity of the landed proprie-tors as their tenantry. The grand and great object of every farmer should be to raise the greatest quan-tity of produce on a given quantity of land.

Many a farmer who now grows 20 acres of corn, if he were to put the same manure and labour to 15, would in all probability grow quite as many bushels, and instead of increasing his acres was to properly cultivate those he occupies, would find his profits greater. This observation would also apply to some landlords. Landlords who are very reluctant in laying out money in draining, and otherwise improving their lands, even when the tenant ensures them 5 per cent. for the outlay, do not hesitate to purchase land, well knowing at the time it will not pay them more than 3 or 3½ per cent. This, sir, I am sure you will per-ceive is not turning capital to the best account, neither is it improving agriculture. It is highly de-sirable the productive qualities of the land should all be brought into action; but how to accom-plish this much-wished-for object is a matter that re-quires sound judgment, as no one rule can be laid down for the cultivation of all soils. It must be admitted that many valuable and useful works have been written on the subject, but a man can never learn the art of farming from reading alone. Agri-culture is a science of no ordinary kind, and cannot be properly understood and comprehended except from practice. In trade and manufactures certain rules are laid down by which all are instructed during their apprenticeship, but husbandry is an

---

occupation of boundless variety, extending to more objects, and fettered by fewer positive regulations, than any other. The time and conditions on entering a farm are of great importance, but a tenant can rarely choose his time of entry; but to cultivate a farm on the right principle he must be fully aware of the properties of the lands he occupies, and his judgment and skill will be called into action to classify them. To class a farm judiciously is what I call laying the foundation of agricultural prosperity: it is not the work of a moment, neither can it be effected by the stroke of the pen. I never yet saw a farm but some portion of it was better calculated for tillage than others, and certain fields, from having water, shade, and situation, better adapted to pasture. Now this is a matter in many countries so nicely distinguished, and so highly prized, that tenants are prohibited from ploughing certain lands, which is as much for the benefit of the occupier as the owner.

After the pasture lands are deducted a certain number of acres remain for tillage. Now the question arises—What system or rotation of crops shall be adopted so as to keep the land in good heart, and yet draw from it the greatest possible profit? It has been well observed, that no branch of husbandry requires more sagacity and skill than a proper rotation of crops. Here I have often seen the folly of leases laying down the same rule for all lands—lands that require direct opposite treatment. It is a well known fact that different systems prevail in the same district; and it is also well known that on a vast number of farms there is no system at all. Fields are taken from grass and laid down again quite at random. The numerous systems that prevail have arisen out of local habit, or they arise from improvements that have not been generally made known. Now, sir, from my experience, which has been upwards of thirty years standing, I give it as my decided (but not hasty) opinion, that the system to be adopted, or the rotation of crops to be grown on a farm, must depend on the soil, climate, situation for manure, and markets. The great secret for both landlord and tenant is to lay down such course for cropping the land as will enable the tenant to improve it; at the same time to pay a fair and reasonable rent, which the landlord has an undoubted right to receive. We will now suppose the best system for all parties being ascertained, the intelligence of the farmer is called into action to rightly determine what number of people and working cattle are requisite to cultivate his estate, so as to bring all the productive qualities of his land into operation. Here it is that agricultural economy is called into play. If a farmer employs one more man than can be profitably employed, it detracts from his profits. On the other hand, if he suffers his land to be unproductive for want of labour, he is injured in a tenfold degree. This is a matter worthy every farmer's best attention. As it is highly desirable to have a system for the management of the estate, it is no less so for the establishment. Reasonable and proper rules should be laid down and observed; due regard should also be paid to moral and religious character. The heads of families will do well to remember the responsible situation they hold, and that they are accountable for their treatment to those under their care and in their employ, as well as they are in discharging their duty to them. By putting these hints into practice it would facilitate labour, promote industry, encourage good behaviour, and relieve the mind of both those whose duty it is to command, and those who are also to obey, from much confusion that must prevail where neither rule nor order is observed. I am now, sir, arrived at a very important consideration for the farmer—the number and description of animals to be kept on his estate, and the quantity and quality of food to be provided for their sustenance. In the early ages, and we may even come down to the time previous to the introduction of the field culture of green crops, the cattle were, comparatively speaking, few, and those miserably provided for. In the summer months they got into tolerably good condition, and a sufficient number was then slaughtered while they were so to provide animal food for the thin population, until nature again clothed the pastures with the natural grasses. As time advanced the attention of man was called to the providing of food for cattle during the winter and spring months—hence the introduction of green crops and stall-feeding. The number of cattle to be kept on a farm must be entirely guided by the quantity of food there is for their consumption; and every owner of stock will do well to remember that if his cattle are not improving, the food they consume is wasted. How frequently are bullocks seen during the winter months losing in condition; and how common is it to see sheep, more especially young sheep, not so heavy in March as they were the November previous! How is this to be accounted for? Why, sir, for want of three things; namely, attention, shelter, and a sufficient quantity of food, and that too of the right quality for carrying the stock properly through the winter. Notwithstanding this, improper management is to be found. Still I am proud to say, there are farmers in Cornwall, as well as in other counties, where you may find all the cattle during the winter and spring months in nicely built houses or yards, well fed and comfortably littered: there they not only retain their condition, but are actually growing more, and fattening faster than when in the pastures. Nor is this all the advantage; the quantity of rich manure produced is the farmer's treasure. I cannot refrain from again repeating the very great and serious loss that is occasioned in this county for want of better farm buildings—a subject I have often pressed on the attention of landlords, agents, and tenants—and a better plan of preserving farmyard manure. When I have been speaking of the propriety of confining cattle in the house or yards during the winter and spring months, I have by more than one been asked—how is it possible to provide food for them during so long a period?

I admit this is a question of vast importance, and the man that cannot answer it has much to learn to make him a good farmer. I have said to such persons, and I would now say, if there be any one present that wished to be informed on this valuable head, visit some of those farms that are regularly and properly cultivated, and go and do likewise; and he will soon find it to prove to his comfort and advantage. From this improved mode of treatment we find our best and fattest stock come to market in abundance in those very months that, under the old system, a fat animal was rarely to be seen; so we have now a constant daily supply of roast beef for the good people of England. It is also a fact deserving notice, that the food on which cattle are supported, and their state of condition, make an essential difference in the quantity and quality of manure. Let a man that has not given this matter proper attention manure any given quantity of land from that which is made from cattle kept on straw alone by night, and allowed to wander the lanes or neighbouring common by day, and select another piece of land of the same quantity and quality, and use the same quantity of manure made from cattle in high condition that are richly fed in the stall; and the contrast will be so great that it will teach him such a profitable lesson as he will never forget. That nothing is better than agriculture, as I at first asserted, and consequently nothing is of greater importance than its improvement, will not, I think, in this our day be questioned. If any friend to this great cause, who has hitherto been slumbering at his post, will ask or think, "What shall I do to promote it?" the answer is, join your fellow labourers with heart and hand, and support everything that will tend to improve the practice or diffuse the science of agriculture. This spirit of improvement—this thirst for knowledge that is beginning to manifest itself, and is spreading widely through the country—give it your best support; for if we look to the history of manufactures for the last century, if we see what it has done for them, we shall not doubt its capability of benefitting every practice to which it is applied. If we look at what it has done for agriculture itself within the last twenty years we may hope—and I would say reasonably hope—great things for the future.

Perhaps, sir, few things within our recollection have so vitally touched the landed interest as the two great questions that have recently come under the consideration of the legislature—questions that all must acknowledge to be of such magnitude and importance as to require the best energy, skill, and talent of the ablest statesman to encounter. I allude to the Poor Law and the Tithe Commutation Acts. The old Poor Law, or I would rather say, the administration of that law, was arrived at such a frightful pitch, that there was neither safety for person or property. If we were wanting proof for this we have only to turn to the extracts from the information received by his Majesty's Commissioners as to the administration and operation of the Poor Laws, published by authority in 1833, and we shall be abundantly supplied. To those who have not read this work I strongly recommend them to do so, because in this peaceful part of the country you can form no conception of the trickery, imposition, and wretchedness there stated. It will afford a useful lesson to the young, and will stagger those of more mature age, at the depravity of human nature. If I shall not be too tedious I will give you a case or two (*go on, go on*). You will find in Mr. Chadwick's Report, page 278, the following statement:—"Mr. Brushfield, a tradesman residing in Spitalfields, and one of the parish officers of Christchurch, Spitalfields, states:—The first day I was in active office (25th March, 1831), a woman, named Kitty Daley, came to me for relief on account of the illness of her child—she came without her child. I knew this case, as the doctor had said something ought to be given to her, on account of the child being ill of the small-pox. I gave her sixpence to serve until I had the opportunity of visiting her. In the course of the day, between the hours of ten and two o'clock, about forty or fifty applications were made to me for relief. Usually it is the practice of the parish officers to give away money on the representation and the appearance of the parties; indeed, it is scarcely possible for a tradesman who has a retail shop to avoid giving away considerable sums of money, as the applicants excite the sympathy of his customers, and if he does

not comply with their demands they (the paupers) may and do raise mischievous tumults, and injure his business by their clamours and obstructions. They did injure my business in this way, and must injure the business of any man who does his duty. However, I determined to give no relief on the mere representation of the parties. I therefore took down the names and address of the applicants for the purpose of visiting their residences. In the course of the forenoon three women came to request relief, and each brought in her arms a child, which she said had the small-pox. The child was muffled up very carefully; one woman showed me the arm of the child, the other showed me the face of the child which she had, the third gave me a glance at the face of the child she had. It appeared to me strange that there was so much small-pox about, but when I saw the face of this third child it immediately struck me as being the same child that had been shown to me before, though it was now in a different dress. On visiting the places where the parties said they resided, it was found that about one-third of their statements of residences were falsehoods; no such persons were to be found. The names of some on the list were immediately recognised by the beadle as overseer-hunters—persons who make it their business to seek out and impose upon new overseers. Ultimately relief was not given to more than about twenty, the remainder, after much exertion (which had never been undertaken before), having been ascertained to be cases of imposition. Few tradesmen who had the inclination would have had time to go through the same investigation, which I dare say was even then very imperfect. I found no where the three mothers who had each come with the infant afflicted with the small-pox; but on visiting the residence of Kitty Daley, there I found the very same infant I had last seen, and it was dressed in the same dress. She did not deny the fact that it was the same child that had been brought that morning in three different dresses by three different women. I accordingly gave her no relief. Subsequently I pursued my investigations into the cases of other applicants for relief, and struck off many cases of fraud. My general mode of investigation was not to make enquiries elsewhere, but to visit the residences of those persons I suspected (which, by the way, was most of the paupers) first on the Saturday, and next on the Sunday. On Saturday they expect us, and I had generally some cause to doubt the appearance of their dwellings on that day. In general those who wished to impose upon us over-coloured the picture, and certainly the pictures they drew were often very appalling. One Saturday one of the churchwardens accompanied me, and we visited ten places—the scenes of distress were quite frightful; there were two cases which appeared to be cases of extreme misery. In one house, that of a man named Bag—a man with a wooden leg, residing in Pelham-street, we found there sitting as if sunk in despair. He said he had no work, and had had no food for that day or since the evening before. His wife was afflicted with a bad leg; she was in bed, and stated that she had not been able to get out of bed for six weeks. The room was in a miserable plight—dirty and wretched. I looked into the cupboard and found no provisions there; the appearance of the place was such that the churchwarden could not forbear giving the man some pecuniary relief at once. The other case was one of a man named Ansler, of Red Lion-street, who had for some time before been chargeable to the parish as an out-pauper; we found the appearance of the place most deplorable. There was no appearance of food or comfort, and the children were ragged, dirty, squalid, and wretched. I told the wife to tell the husband to apply to me for relief in the evening, when I would give him relief, as I intended to do, being fully convinced of the necessity by the extreme misery which I had witnessed. The husband and wife came together to my house in the evening. I expressed my regret that they should be obliged to come to the parish, and asked if the husband had no prospect of getting work. He declared he had neither work nor any prospect of getting any at present. I judged by his appearance that he had been drinking, and said,—' Well, call upon me in the morning, and I will see what I can do for you.' They said they were very much obliged to me, and went away, apparently quite pleased, although, according to their representations, they were absolutely in a state of starvation.

"On Sunday morning I renewed my visits to most of those whose residences I had visited on the afternoon previous. The first case I visited was that of the man Ansler; I went at about nine o'clock in the morning. I opened the door, and then knocked, when I found they were in bed. I saw the wife jump out of bed, and in great haste she ran to a table which was standing in the middle of the room, and covered it over with a cloth, but in her haste to get away, and in her confusion she pulled the covering off, and exposed to my view a large piece of beef, a piece of mutton, and parcels of tea, sugar, bread, &c., &c. The man called from the bed, 'B——t 'em! never mind them; you know they belong to your father.' I told them that was enough, and immediately left the place. They have never applied for relief since. When I visited the house of Bag, I found Mrs. Bag out of bed, at her breakfast; she had her tea, and he had his coffee. I saw a neck of mutton on one shelf and two loaves on another shelf of the cupboard which was empty the day before. I went into his workshop (he was a silk dresser) which I found full of work. The man swore horribly, and I left the place. I do not know that he ever again applied to the parish. My impression now is that nearly the whole of the cases which we had visited on the Saturday were found to be each partially or entirely similar cases of imposition." I will give you another case, which will be found in Mr. Cowell's Report, page 393.

"*Swaffham, Norfolk.*"

"A woman in a neighbouring parish had five illegitimate children, for which she was allowed 10s. per week, and 6s. for herself. Finding herself pregnant for the sixth time, she employed a man to go round to various persons with whom she might or might not have had connection to acquaint each of them separately with the fact of her pregnancy, and of her intention of swearing the child to him unless he consented to send her a sum of money, when she would engage to swear it on some one else. Her demands for this hush money ranged as high as 10*l.* in some instances. The first man to whom her ambassador applied gave him 10*l.* The ambassador returned, and represented to his employer that the man had laughed at her threat, but had sent her half-a-crown, out of which he thought she ought to give him 1s. 6d. for his trouble. To this she consented, so he benefited 9*l.* 19s., and she 1s. by this first negotiation. She carried on this course with several persons with various success, and at last swore the child to a man who resisted, and on

his appeal succeeded in getting the order quashed. This case was tried at Swaffham, where the above circumstance came to light in court. This woman was never punished. She gave birth to her child, was allowed 2s. for it by the parish, and is now in the receipt of 18s. per week, the produce of successful bastardy adventures."

So much, sir, for the Poor-law.

The old Tithe-law, we all too well know, was in many instances oppressive—a bar to the improvement of agriculture, and in numbers of cases put the pastor and his flock at variance. These matters duly considered will form objections so strong, and of such weighty nature, that posterity will look into the history of tithes with amazement at the manner in which they were so long paid. When we look at the tenths on the titheable produce of land, calculating on the improved principle of cultivation, the vast outlay made in implements, buildings, manure, labour, &c., and all to increase the produce of the land, and view the prominent place it takes in the returns of a farm, we need not wonder at the increase made in most cases of commutation. The agreements are now generally finished, and the apportionments are rapidly progressing. The spirit and letter of the Tithe Act puts the principle and the detail of the apportionment entirely into the hands of the landowners. They may select what valuers they please, and what number they please; they may give these valuers specific instructions, or leave them to apportion by their own discretion, guided only by the general rules of the act. They may by means of these specific instructions apportion the rent-charge field by field, or on their gross estates, or with the assent of the tithe-owners they may charge it on certain portions of their estates, leaving the other portions tithe free. Thus, sir, you see the vast power placed in the hands of the valuer. Landlords are beginning to see the propriety of selecting men for this important part of the bill of practical knowledge—men that know how to estimate the titheable produce and the productive quality of land. The apportionment being confirmed the rent-charge will be paid accordingly; and here many a tithe-payer will be at a loss to know why he should pay more in 42 than he did in 41, and perhaps less in 43 than in 42; but a very few years will unriddle this mystery, and I trust we shall "one and all" find it an improvement; for while it gives the tithe-owner a better security, it holds out to the cultivator of the soil a great inducement to increase its produce, the good effects of which must be felt by the community at large. Improvements of various kinds will be made through the country, and amongst others draining will form a striking picture. It cannot be too strongly recommended to those whose lands are about to be, or have lately been drained, to have the plan of the drain marked on the plan of the field (for I take it for granted every man has, or shortly will have, the map of his estate), that the mouth of the drains may be found. Many a drain has been ruined for want of being kept open, consequently a vast deal of money has been wasted; when the present occupier makes his exit, all knowledge of this matter too often ceases.

I am now, sir, drawing to a conclusion of my paper. Could I hope that some of my observations may tend to the improvement of my favourite pursuit, agriculture, I shall be amply repaid for any little time they have cost me. This I confidently anticipate, that the enquiry and study of agriculture will be pursued, and the results will afford new aids to this most useful and interesting science.

The soil offers inexhaustible resources, which, when properly appreciated and employed, must increase our wealth, our population, and our physical strength. We possess advantages in the use of machinery and the division of labour belonging to no other nation ; and the same energy of character, and the same extent of resources which have always distinguished the people of the British islands, and made them excel in arms, commerce, letters, and philosophy, apply with the happiest effects to the improvement of the cultivation of the earth. Nothing is impossible to labour aided by ingenuity. The true objects of the agriculturist are likewise those of the patriot. Men value most what they have gained with effort—a just confidence in their own powers result from success. They love their country better because they have seen it improve by their own talents and industry, and they identify with these interests the existence of those institutions which have afforded them security, independence, and the multiplied enjoyments of civilised life.

HADLEIGH FARMERS' CLUB.

IMPORTANT LECTURE BY PROFESSOR HENSLOW ON THE THEORY OF MANURING.

The anniversary meeting of the Hadleigh Farmers' Club was held at Hadleigh, on Friday, the 16th December.

As is usual at these meetings, there was a good shew of neat stock and sheep in the market-place, and there was also an excellent show of beet root and turnips in the Corn Exchange.

Soon after four o'clock upwards of 90 gentlemen partook of a most excellent dinner provided by Mr. Stephens of the White Lion, in the assembly room. Robert Kersey, Esq., the president of the club, took the chair, supported on the right by the Rev. H. B. Knox, and J. Grouse, Esq., and on the left by the Rev. the Professor Henslow, and Richard Newman, Esq. There were also present J. Last, Esq., Messrs. R. Partridge, sen., Partridge, jun., H. Partridge, R. Rand, J. Rand, Ansell, Matthews, C. Brown, H. Hardacre, R. Hawkins, W. Hawkins, J. Hudson, H. Sallows, W. Strutt, jun., J. Everett, W. Lott, R. Postans, W. Green, R. Sallows, A. Syer, J. Norman, Makin, C. Kersey, C. Fenn, W. Grimwade, H. Clayden, J. Cook, &c. Mr. J. Rands officiated as Vice President.

After the usual loyal and patriotic toasts had been drank

The SECRETARY read the report of the Society's proceedings for the past year.

The report commenced by alluding to the valuable information given to the club at several of its meetings by the Reverend the Professor Henslow, and then went on to recommend that a separate fund be raised for the purpose of giving premiums to deserving labourers and their families.

February 5th.—The members took into consideration the internal diseases of sheep and neat cattle. This discussion rested principally on what is commonly called drop sheep, and blown and hoven, or blown animals. Several members having expressed their opinions, the following recipe was recommended for a beast when it has become

blown or hoven : 1 lb. glauber salts, ¼ lb. of treacle, and 1 oz. of ginger, mixed with one pint and a half of warm water. The following resolution was also adopted :—

" That before any direction can be given with regard to the drop in sheep, the disease upon which most difference of opinion existed, a minute inspection of the internal parts was required to ascertain the seat or cause of it, in order to offer a remedy ; but with respect to hoven or blown animals, powerful stimulants should be administered, and Mr. Grouse recommended the different preparations of ammonia as likely to be the most efficient.

" In cases of scour in sheep, a small dose of castor-oil to be given to remove any offending matter from the bowels, after which about four grains of opium and one ounce of chalk, and then put upon dry food,"

April 22nd.—The preparation of the land for vegetable crops, especially turnips and beet root, was the subject which engaged the attention of the club.

The following resolution was passed :—

" That breaking up the land as deep as the soil will permit immediately after harvest is highly advantageous, it being thereby more easily cleaned and pulverized, and rendered in a better state for the root crop. The seed to be planted upon the ridge or Northumberland system : 27 inches apart for mangel, and from 18 to 27 inches for turnips, was also strongly recommended."

May 20th—The subject which stood for discussion was—on paring and burning earth—when the following resolution was adopted :—

" That the application of burnt earth to heavy and strong lands is highly beneficial, but injurious to such soils as are principally composed of silicious earth."

June 24th—The fermentation of manures came under consideration.

The member who commenced the subject, recommended that the manure should never be carted from the yard except when in a moist state, and if not wanted for immediate application to the soil, to put it into a heap and compress it, by carting over it with the tumbril and horses, to prevent rapid fermentation.

Another member recommended laying down a quantity of earth, then carting the manure from the yard upon it, and when the hill was completed, to cover it with earth upon the top to prevent evaporation, and a short time before it was required for use to stub it over and mix it together.

It was also thought the quality of the manure would be much improved by allowing it to remain in the yard a longer time than was generally the practice, the urine and the other droppings from the stock being absorbed, and retained by the increased depth of straw and fodder.

Another member put the query, whether manure is improved in quality by being subject to any fermentation.

There being a very short attendance of members, and the subject being considered important, and the want of chemical knowledge severely felt, it was unanimously agreed to adjourn the consideration of it to some future meetings, and that Professor Henslow be respectfully invited to give a lecture upon it.

At the next meeting the most advantageous mode of consuming the root-crop came under discussion. The member who brought it forward considered the manner of its disposal depended to a certain extent on the nature of the soil upon which the roots were grown, and he thought the most advantageous manner of consuming the turnip crop was feeding sheep upon the land.

After an interesting discussion, the following resolution was agreed to :—Upon soils of a light and mixed description the turnip crop is most advantageously and economically consumed by sheep where they are grown ; the Scotch and Swede varieties to be cut and put into troughs; carrots to be consumed by horses and colts ; potatoes, where grown in large quantities, to be steamed or boiled, and given to fatten bullocks and pigs : mangel to be stored from the frost, and adapted for all descriptions of neat and sheep stock in the spring, although if required, a small quantity may be given to cows and pigs during the winter.

At the last meeting in November, the subject of liquid manures was brought forward by a member who had tried its effects upon land intended for barley and wheat, by applying about 16 hogsheads per acre to the soil about a month before the seed was sown ; that for wheat was applied to the old clover-lay a short time before it was ploughed and no apparent increase visible in their production ; but where he had applied the same quantity to his pasture land, a great benefit resulted from it. The application of it he also recommended to dung-hills, especially if required for immediate use, as it caused a very quick decomposition, and added materially to the quality of the manure.

Another member supported the opinion very strongly of its beneficial application to pasture lands, as tending materially to increase the produce, and that it should be carted on in moist weather or in the evening.

Other members were of opinion, if proper management was exercised in keeping the fatting stock under sheds or in houses, and a sufficient quantity of straw allowed them for fodder, no liquid of any value would escape, and it might be entirely prevented by putting a layer of earth at the bottom of the yards where the manure was made.

After some desultory discussion, the following resolution was agreed to :—

" That it is highly necessary to prevent, by every possible means, the escape of the liquid manure, although from the situation of different premises, it is rather difficult to give any definite directions. The general opinion was in favour of retaining it in the straw, recommending all the buildings to be troughed, and allowing no extra or surplus water to run through the manure-yard ; but where the situations of the buildings renders this method impracticable, that tanks be provided for its reception and applied to the pasture land."

The report concluded as follows :—

Your committee beg to remark, as we appear to be arrived at a time when it will be necessary for the British farmer to exert every energy in his power and to cultivate the strictest economy in his management, it becomes his duty by every means to promote the success of societies like the present, whose established object is the dissemination of every improved system ; and as the benefits of association can only arrise from individual support, they earnestly call upon *one* and *all* to join heart and hand in promoting as far as possible the noble cause in which we are engaged, and upon the prosperity of which so many materially depend

for support ; and adopting the language of the poet, would say—

" Success to the Hoof and the Horn,
Success to the Flock and the Fleece,
Success to the Growers of Corn,
With the blessings of Plenty and Peace."

The Rev. the PROFESSOR HENSLOW :—I have permission to propose to you a toast, which I am sure will meet with a hearty welcome. We all know that societies of this description are chiefly promoted—at least, the success of them is chiefly promoted—by the officers who superintend their proceedings. I need not say anything with respect to the merits of the gentleman who presides over this club. You have all experienced for three years that no person could possibly have presided in a better manner than he, or have kept you together in better style. In his presence it would ill become me to say much more on the subject ; I shall therefore propose the health of Mr. Kersey. (*Applause.*)

The CHAIRMAN :—I rise from a sense of duty to acknowledge the toast which has been so very kindly proposed by the gentleman on my left, and which has been so cordially responded to by this large and respectable assembly. The only answer I can possibly make is, I feel deeply convinced that nothing I have done—that in fact my poor services do not in any way merit the compliment you have paid me. I can, therefore, only echo back the sentiment, that success may continue to attend the Hadleigh Farmer's Club. But, as we are assembled to commemorate our third anniversary, you will perhaps allow me the liberty of taking a short review of our past proceedings ; and in doing this, I may say that when I consider the benefits which have already arisen from the establishment of this and similar societies—when I reflect upon the important and interesting topics connected with agriculture which have been brought under discussion —when I remember the harmony of feeling that has always prevailed at our meetings upon mutual interchange of sentiment—when I reflect, as I do with pleasure, upon the lectures delivered by the learned Professor upon my left, directly and indirectly connected with agriculture—when I recollect and reflect upon all these things, I have only to say, that the reminiscences of the Hadleigh Farmer's Club will always give me interesting and profitable to my mind. (*Applause.*) But having taken this short review of the past, you will allow me to direct your attention to the future. I do not pretend to be gifted with prophetic vision—I would not cast a shade over the pleasing scene which now presents itself before us ; neither would I check for a moment the spirit of hilarity which now pervades this meeting ; but you will allow me to urge upon you the great importance of acquiring all the practical knowledge of agriculture which may come within your reach. Remember that you are entering upon the field of competition—I do not say who your competitors are, and I will not say who they may be ; but should they arise from every quarter of the globe, I believe the determined and the never-failing spirit of the agriculturist, aided, as I trust he is, and as he ever will be, by men of science, by men of genius, and by men of talent— by men whose names stand high in the page of literature—and by men whose, I may say, university honours adorn and dignify their brows— with such assistance I believe we shall surmount every difficulty : I believe we shall carry the palm in competition, and I trust the British farmer will continue to see his fields clothed with flocks, and his fields covered over with corn. (*Applause.*) Thus as English agriculture has flourished through uncounted years, I trust it will continue, and that Britain, the land of our fathers and the land of our birth, will remain, as she ever has done,

" First flower of the earth ;
First gem of the sea."

(*Applause.*) I now beg again to return my sincere and grateful thanks for the honour I have received ; and I can only regret that you have not appointed for the ensuing year a chairman who would more efficiently than myself discharge the important and interesting duties of the office. I have now the pleasure and also the honour of introducing to your notice the Reverend the Professor Henslow. (*Loud applause.*)

The Rev. Professor HENSLOW, after the cheering had subsided, said.—You requested me to prepare for the present meeting some sort of statement or report on the theory of manuring. I have, in consequence, occupied all the leisure I could command since I met the club in October last, in studying the opinions of various authors, who have treated the subject scientifically or practically. The opportunity which I possess of consulting publications more immediately devoted to the practice of husbandry is very limited, and there are several authors, whose opinions I wish I could have seen, but which I have had no means of examining. Among those whom I have been able to consult, I may mention Davy, Liebig, De Candolle, Sprengel, Payne, Daubeny, Johnston, the author of British Husbandry in the Farmer's Series of the Library of Useful Knowledge, and the Edinburgh Encyclopædia. I have also read all the papers relating to this subject in the Journal of the Royal Agricultural Society, in the Gardener's Chronicle, and in some of the later numbers of the Gardener's Magazine. These are the chief materials from which I have endeavoured to form my judgment. You all know that I am entirely unacquainted with the practical details of husbandry, and I have no further acquaintance with a dunghill than what I may have been able to cultivate by the sense of smelling. When I tell you that the most experienced chemical philosophers have pronounced the subject of manuring to be one of the most intricate, as it is one of the most important applications of their science, you must not expect that the exposition I am about to give you can be otherwise than imperfect. I do not pretend that it will contain a thoroughly digested view of the great variety of opinion which I have met with, but I offer it to your notice merely as the impression left upon my own mind of the present most plausible view of the subject. I bring to this inquiry no greater knowledge of chemistry than what any man of liberal education may be supposed to possess that has attended two or three courses of chemical lectures in a university, and has occasionally burnt his fingers in attempting to repeat a few of the simpler experiments which he may have seen his instructor perform. I have, certainly, no greater knowledge of chemistry than what I conceive every one engaged in so important a pursuit as agriculture ought to have acquired, as a matter of course, and as part of his professional education, if he would hope to profit by those researches of professed chemical philosophers, which are calculated to throw light upon the

science of husbandry, and enable him to turn to the best advantage the means which he has at his command. For myself, I must confess that I have felt somewhat in the position of the cock in the old fable, who, whilst scratching on a dunghill, stumbled upon a precious stone of which he could make no use, and professed that he would rather have found a single grain of barley than every such precious stone in the world. I do not mean that I have discovered any new fact of great value whilst I was fulfilling the task you set me : new facts are not to be discovered without experiment, or personal observation. But I must declare that I have satisfied myself there are a vast number of precious facts recorded in books, which are not sufficiently known to the generality of practical men. It is for you, gentlemen, to play the part of agricultural lapidaries, and work up these precious jewels into more marketable shapes, and contrive to turn them into profitable commodities. I am sure that you are not likely to play the part of dunghill cocks, and to despise such jewels when you learn the real value of them. The general impression left upon my mind by these inquiries has been of a mixed character. I have felt cheered at finding the decided progress which has been made, and the good promise held out of further rapid advances ; and I have been impressed by a feeling of regret that the want of chemical knowledge prevents so many practical men from either availing themselves of the knowledge already acquired, or of adding anything of real value to the common stock. I do not say of my countrymen what the celebrated German chemist (Liebig) has declared of his, that they have no desire to avail themselves of the information which science proposes. I think I know the spirit of the English nation much better than to say this of any class of my countrymen. I will quote to you the opinion he expresses of the present race of German agriculturists :—" Agriculture has hitherto never sought aid from chemical principles, based on the knowledge of those substances which plants extract from the soil on which they grow, and of those restored to the soil by means of manure. The discovery of such principles will be the task of a future generation ; for what can be expected from the present, which recoils with seeming distrust and aversion from all the means of assistance offered it by chemistry, and which does not understand the art of making a rational application of chemical discoveries? A future generation, however, will derive incalculable advantage from these means of help." Whatever may be the case in Germany, I much prefer the view which Sir Humphrey Davy took of the prospects of British agriculture in his day, and which appears to be now verifying to a very great extent.—" Science cannot long be despised by any persons, as the mere speculation of theorists ; but must soon be considered by all ranks of men in its true point of view—as the refinement of common sense guided by experience, gradually substituting sound and rational principles for vague popular prejudices. The soil offers inexhaustible resources, which when properly appreciated and employed, must increase our wealth, our population, and our physical strength. We possess advantages in the use of machinery, and the division of labour, belonging to no other nation—and the same energy of character, the same extent of resources, which have always distinguished the people of the British Islands, and made them excel in arms, commerce, letters, and philosophy, apply with happiest effect to the improvement of the cultivation of the earth. Nothing is impossible to labour aided by ingenuity."

Before I proceed to offer you my remarks, I must express a hope that no one will be induced to adopt any suggestions which I may happen to make, without first experimenting for himself on a limited scale, before he ventures to operate upon a large one. My wish is to stimulate to enquiry, not to dictate to practical men what it may be most expedient for them to adopt—I have no desire to direct, but to suggest. I fear that after-dinner speeches are not very well calculated for conveying that description of information that is likely to be of real profit to the listener ; but, as I see some gentlemen of the press present, who are prepared to book my observations, I shall take the liberty of offering them my services in securing a correct report of what I may say. With all due deference to their ability to report me correctly, I know from experience that where persons are not perfectly familiar with the use of technical terms, important mistakes will sometimes creep in ; and, if my observations are to go abroad, I should wish to avoid any such inaccuracy, lest it might tend to mislead. With this preamble, then, I proceed to my task. But I must first beg you to have a little patience with me, and allow me to proceed in my own way. I find, when an old woman with a long tongue has to give evidence before me as a justice, that it is always best to let her tell her story in her own way, without interrupting her, or attempting to arrive at the conclusion by some short cut. And so, if you shall think what I am about to state in the first part of this address, to be somewhat irrelevant, I trust you will bear with me, and perhaps you may find the second part of it a little more to the purpose, for I propose to divide this address into two parts ; in the first of which I shall allude to a few of the general principles of nutrition, and in the second I shall endeavour to show how it is that manures are rendered serviceable according to those principles. There exists so intimate a connection between the different branches of natural science, that it is impossible to treat of any one of them without alluding to some other. I find that I cannot well explain to you what are the chemical principles involved in the theory of manuring, without referring to the botanical principles upon which the nutrition of vegetables is supposed to depend. I need not, however, on the present occasion, refer you to more than two of these principles, and they are of so simple a character that every one may easily comprehend the facts which they illustrate. All those plants which are the objects of attention to agriculturists are possessed of roots and leaves. The roots are the parts, or " organs," of the plants by which matter in a liquid state is absorbed into the system ; and the leaves are the organs by which matter in the gaseous state is exhaled, or discharged from the system. A portion of the crude matter absorbed by the roots is modified in the leaves by a peculiar process depending upon the action of light, and is thereby fitted for affording nourishment to all parts of the plant. It is nearly all the rest which is exhaled in the form of gas, especially water, under the form of steam and oxygen. There are many striking analogies between the functions performed by plants and animals ; only plants are more simply organised than animals, and their functions are fewer and not so complicated. Plants are without that internal sack which

in animals we call the stomach, and with the practical use of which we have just been giving distinct evidence that we are well acquainted. Now when animals have received food into this stomach of theirs, it is immediately acted upon by certain juices, secreted for the purpose, by which it soon becomes converted into a semi-fluid mass, called " chyme." Whilst this chyme is gradually passing through the intestines, it is, in its turn, acted upon by certain absorbing vessels, called " lacteals," which take up from it a peculiar milky fluid, which is named " chyle." This chyle is carried along the lacteals into the veins, where it is mixed with the blood ; and after passing through the lungs, where certain changes are effected, it is itself converted into blood. The blood which has thus been derived from the food of the animal contains the materials necessary for the nourishment of all parts of the system, and circulates, as we all know, through the whole body. In different parts of the animal frame there are certain glands, as the liver and the kidneys, &c., which are destined to prepare peculiar secretions from the blood, and to carry off such matters as are not required, or are no longer serviceable to the purposes of nutrition. These are discharged, as well as those superfluous portions of the food which are not essential to the formation of the chyle. In comparing the nutrition of plants with that of animals, we perceive some marked differences, as well as some general resemblances in the two processes. Plants have no stomach, and there appears to be no very direct analogy between the first process in their nutrition, and in that of animals. Plants absorb, indeed, through the extremities of their roots, water holding many substances in solution ; but it is hardly correct to consider the extremities of the roots as so many distinct mouths. There are no openings at those points, neither does anything in a solid state pass into them. They cannot imbibe even the most impalpable powders—they can absorb fluids only. This action then seems to be more analogous to that of the lacteals in animals, which absorb the chyle from the matters of the intestines. There is also this great distinction to be noted in the materials which afford food to plants and food to animals, that whilst animals are fed only from matter which has been previously organised (that is to say, which has formed part of a living being, either animal or vegetable), plants are nourished by materials which they prepare out of inorganic matter. The water that enters their system at the extremities of their roots contains a small per centage of various earths, salts, and grass, of which I shall say a few more words presently. Having been subjected to a process analogous to the respiration of animals, the result is the formation of that " proper juice " of plants, which may be considered as their blood. So that what entered in the form of inorganic matter has become changed into organic. Though chemists are able to imitate nature in compounding various inorganic substances out of the simple elements, they cannot so prepare any portion of organised matter. It requires the agency of life, of vegetable life, to effect this in the first instance. Vegetable life is the power, if I may be allowed the expression, which the Creator applies to that engine or laboratory which we call a plant, for the purpose of combining a few elements in those particular proportions in which they constitute " organic matter." It is upon the continued production of organic matter out of inorganic, that the very existence of all animals depends. No animal can feed directly upon inorganic matter, upon earths, salts, or grasses, &c. When beasts and birds of prey devour the flesh of other animals, they still feed on matter which was originally derived from the vegetable kingdom. So true to the very letter is the general declaration announced in the first chapter of Genesis :—"And to every beast of the earth, and to every fowl of the air, and to everything that creepeth upon the earth, wherein there is life, I have given every green herb for meat." A great variety of matters are to be found in different parts of organised beings, whether animal or vegetable ; but several of these substances do not appear to be absolutely essential to their constitution. Several have been accidentally introduced with the ordinary food, and do not occur at all times in the system. Others, again, form only a very small per centage of organised matters, although their more constant presence seems to show us that they are absolutely necessary to its formation—or at least to the healthy condition of the individual. Setting aside for the present all considerations of such substances as these, we find the main bulk of that organised matter of which animals and vegetables are composed, is formed out of only three or four elements, united in a considerable diversity of proportions. In the three lectures which I have had the pleasure of delivering to the Club during the past year, I endeavoured to make you acquainted, by experiments and illustrations, with the nature of those four elements which enter most largely, though we cannot say exclusively, into the compositions of organised matter. Those elements are carbon, oxygen, hydrogen, and nitrogen. The three first are the principal components of plants, though nitrogen is also essentially present in small proportion ; not as it should seem in their very tissues, but in some of the organic products formed within them. Nitrogen enters more largely with the general composition of animal matter. I can imagine that there are persons who, not being familiar with chemical terms and ideas, may have seen no use in my attempts to explain them. Certainly, to those who have no desire to become acquainted with the first principles of chemistry, such explanations can be of very little service ; but to those who consent to turn their attention to the acquisition of such knowledge, those technical terms which it is necessary to employ will soon become as familiar as household words ; and you will find the words carbon, and oxygen, and hydrogen, and nitrogen, to bring to your recollection as distinct ideas as the words furrow and stetch. When I came to reside in Suffolk, little more than three years ago, I recollect that at our first village ploughing match, I was obliged to inquire the difference between a furrow and a stetch ; but I have not forgotten what I was then told. Such information, however, is not very likely to be of much use to me in my pursuits, whilst a correct apprehension of such terms as those to which I have alluded may certainly become of real service to you, provided you wish to advance a few steps towards the acquirement of chemical knowledge. Since I have said that animals are wholly dependent upon the vegetable kingdom for their nourishment, and since plants contain less nitrogen than animals, we may perceive one reason why animals discharge so large a portion of their food in the form of excrement, without its having ever entered into the composition of the chyle. I have stated that whilst all animals require previously organized matters for their food, plants are nourished by forming their nutritious juices out of unorganized matter. This assertion may seem to be contradicted by the fact, that the manures which are most frequently applied in culture, are organic. It is also certain, that if plants are watered with weak solutions of certain organic products, as gum and sugar, they will thrive upon such nourishment. With respect to organic manures, I have undertaken to show you presently how it is supposed that they served to nourish plants ; but I am not prepared to say how such soluble substances as gum and sugar, when introduced by absorption at the roots, are acted upon by the system. I do not think it has been clearly ascertained whether they are directly assimilated or not. In the case of parasitic plants which absorb a nutritious juice directly from those plants to which they are attached, we see an example where it is not necessary that plants should prepare such juices for themselves. So in the case of the foetus, which we find to depend for nourishment upon the blood prepared by the mother ; but, even if it be possible to nourish plants by certain soluble organic matters, without these undergoing any previous decomposition in the way, we shall presently show to be necessary in all ordinary cases ; still we must see that wild plants are never dependent upon their nourishment upon the juices of others. They must cater for themselves out of the abundant natural supply of inorganic materials prepared for them. Some plant or other may grow on any spot of the earth's surface below the limits of perpetual snow, and not absolutely in the burning crater of a volcano, provided it can obtain a sufficiency of moisture. It is moisture that plants require in the first instance. Water of itself can supply them with two out of the four elements essential to the formation of organized matter. Water is a compound of oxygen and hydrogen ; but all water on the earth's surface naturally contains also carbonic acid, which is a compound of carbon and oxygen. This substance is every where present in small proportion in the atmosphere, and is readily dissolved in all waters, so that the rains and dews cannot descend upon the earth without bearing with them some portion of it into the soil, from whence it may be absorbed by the roots together with the water in which it is dissolved. Plants, it has been clearly established, derive their carbon by decomposing carbonic acid. The carbon is fixed, and the oxygen discharged so long as their leaves are exposed to the influence of light. Although nitrogen forms the greatest portion of our atmosphere, plants do not obtain it directly from this supply. It should be remembered, as a fact of importance to the theory of manuring, that no element in its free state is directly assimilated by plants. Those elements out of which they prepare organic matters, are obtained by the decomposition of compound substances. The material which is now considered to furnish nitrogen to plants is ammonia. This is a compound of nitrogen and hydrogen, and is found dispersed through the atmosphere, though in very minute proportion, and in combination with carbonic acid. So that we ought rather to say, that it is the carbonate of ammonia, that substance commonly called "smelling salts," and not ammonia itself, which is the source from whence plants obtain their nitrogen. There may possibly be other substances besides water, carbonic acid, and carbonate of ammonia, from which plants may derive one or other of the four elements of which they are mainly composed; but this has not been thoroughly and so satisfactorily shown to be the case as with regard to the three above mentioned. It will be observed that whilst water may supply two, and carbonic acid two of these elements, the carbonate of ammonia contains all the four.

Having now given you this rapid and imperfect sketch of the mode in which vegetables are nourished out of certain inorganic compounds, whose elements they re-arrange into the form of organic matter, I shall pause a little, before I enter upon the second part of my address, that we may be able to proceed with the more regular business of an anniversary dinner.

The CHAIRMAN : I have now the pleasing duty of proposing the health of a gentleman, whose very valuable services have placed the Hadleigh Farmer's Club under great obligations. It is very evident we have arrived at a period of time when science and practice must be combined, and when we see gentlemen of acknowledged talent and patriotic mind willing to come forward to our assistance, I have only to add that they place us under very deep and lasting obligations (*Applause*). I am happy to congratulate the meeting upon the fact, that the Reverend the Professor on my left, distinguished as he is by literary fame, by the rank he enjoys, and by the honour he receives from the University of Cambridge, has condescended upon this occasion to give us a lecture upon a subject deeply and intimately connected with agriculture. I have only to repeat that I have great pleasure in proposing the health of Professor Henslow (*Applause.*)

The Rev. the Professor HENSLOW : I feel exceedingly obliged by the kind expressions that have fallen from the Chairman, and my thanks are equally due for the kind manner in which you have received the toast. I have now been connected with the Hadleigh Farmer's Club sufficiently long to convey to you the assurance that it affords me the greatest pleasure if I can at any time afford either instruction or amusement; and I trust that as long as it pleases God to continue me in health and strength, I shall always have inclination and opportunity to co-operate with you in your investigations (*Loud applause.*)

Song—Mr. Hardacre, "England, the land of my soul."

Mr. LAST proposed the health of the Vice-President.

Mr. RAND returned thanks, expressing the pleasure he felt in being connected with a society so exceedingly respectable and liberal.

The Secretary then read the awards to the successful competitors.

Mr. RAND proposed the health of the judges of cattle, Mr. Turner, of Woodbridge; Mr. Hudson, of Romford; and Mr. Holton, of Wiston; as well as the healths of the judges of roots, Mr. Sallows, Mr. Hawkins, Mr. Norman, and Mr. Matthews, with the thanks of the club for their exertions (*Applause*).

Mr. TURNER returned thanks in behalf of himself and the judges, expressing the pleasure he felt individually in being present to witness their interesting proceedings.

The Reverend the PROFESSOR then resumed :—
I am now arrived at that part of my enquiry which must be considered of main importance to the agriculturist—the manner in which manures may be supposed to supply plants with materials for supporting the functions of nutrition. I propose first to say a few words on the theory in general, and then I shall notice the composition and effects produced by certain specific manures. By so doing I hope to be able to confirm and support the theory in a way which may make it more thoroughly intelligible. If we regard manures as the actual food of plants, we must look upon the soil as the stomach of the vegetable kingdom. For it is necessary that certain changes should take place in all organic manures which are placed in the soil before they can benefit the plants they are intended to nourish. The farmer, therefore, should as carefully watch the condition of this capacious plant-stomach, as a skilful physician would be attentive to the digestion of a dyspeptic patient. He must remember that his crops are not under the sole care of nature ; who never would have placed them in the soil or situation where he chooses they shall live. When left to nature, plants, like animals, will range themselves spontaneously over the surface of the earth in those regions and localities where each, after its kind, may have its peculiar wants supplied by the climate, soil, or other circumstances best adapted to its constitution. Whatever each receives from the soil, that it restores again in the natural progress of decay. But still, whatever a plant derives immediately from the soil, forms, as we have said, a very small proportion of its entire bulk; being only that small per centage of ashes which remains fixed, after all the rest which can be dissipated by burning. The main bulk of every plant being derived from water, carbonic acid, and carbonate of ammonia (matters which are primarily derived from the atmosphere) cannot be considered as any part of the soil, though plants absorb them from the soil after they have found their way into it. When a plant dies and is decomposed, these three ingredients are again formed during its decay, and are restored to the atmosphere. And yet no practical man considers that his crops can feed on air alone; but he is careful to supply them with manures of various kind, solid or liquid, organic or inorganic: and experience teaches him that his crops have relished such food. But for all that, plants do not attack such food directly. Such food is often useless, even poisonous, to them in its raw and unaltered state. It must be first digested, (as it were) either before it is put into the soil, or whilst it is beneath the soil, in order that those particular inorganic compounds may be formed out of it, which plants absorb in the way I have described, and from which they form organic matter. We may then, I think, consider the fermentation, putrefaction, and decomposition of organic manures, as a substitute for digestion in the feeding of plants, when we compare their functions with those of animals. By this process the elements composing an organic manure are restored to the condition of inorganic matter, and then they combine afresh to form those inorganic compounds from which plants prepare their proper juices. As for the few inorganic matters found in the ashes of plants, the presence of some of them is no doubt essential to the healthy condition and even to the existence of particular species ; and therefore it is quite necessary that they should be restored to the soil. In many cases it is probably even more necessary that these inorganic matters should be replaced, than

those organic parts of certain manures which serve to keep up a supply of the four most abundant elements of vegetation. For nature cannot readily restore to the soil the various inorganic matters which may be gradually abstracted by continued cropping; but she can always do so with respect to water, carbonic acid, and carbonate of ammonia; as for instance, during a fallow. When we supply organic manures capable of restoring the three last named substances to the soil, we are hastening the operations of nature in this respect. Now, with regard to one of these three substances, water, the aid we thus afford to nature must be very trifling, compared with the supply which she herself so bountifully furnishes. With respect to another of them, carbonic acid, her supply is at all times generous, since every drop of water that penetrates the soil carries with it a certain amount of this ingredient, in solution. Still it is very possible that the decomposition of organic manures, under particular circumstances, and indeed, in ordinary cases, do render very effectual aid, in directly affording a large additional supply of carbonic acid for the nourishment of plants. It was considered by Sir H. Davy that this supply of carbonic acid was the principal benefit derived from the decomposition of organic manures; but more recent experiments appear to have placed it beyond doubt, that the regular supply of the carbonate of ammonia is of far greater importance. Although plants require little of this material for furnishing the small quantity of nitrogen necessary to their growth, yet it must always be present to a certain amount, or they cannot live. Little as they require, and ample as the supply may be for plants growing spontaneously, it appears that in removing crops from the soil, we abstract the carbonate of ammonia which is retained there, more rapidly than nature can readily restore it. Hence the necessity of furnishing the soil with organic manure, or at least with some material which may afford nitrogen to the ensuing crop. Such being the general theory on which chemists explain the manner how it is that organic manures are considered to act, I shall now proceed to an examination of some of those specific manures which farmers are in the habit of providing for their crops.

That which is generally admitted to be the most important of all manures to the British farmer, and of which he is most careful to obtain a supply, is the common farm-yard manure from which dunghills are prepared. This is composed partly of vegetable matter, and partly of the dung and urine of animals. On putting such manure into the soil, we are evidently restoring the inorganic matters which were taken directly from it, and in addition we are supplying it with a quantity of organic matter. When this organic matter is decomposed (but not until then) it affords the three inorganic compounds, water, carbonic-acid, and carbonate of ammonia, essential to the nutrition of plants. It is a subject of anxiety to agriculturists, to ascertain the extent to which they should allow the process of decomposition to be carried in the dunghill; or, whether they need allow the materials to ferment at all, before they are applied to the land. The question is not yet considered to be completely decided. Whatever I have to say on this subject must therefore be viewed as suggestions for further enquiry. I shall here set aside all considerations of the extent of those be-

nefits which may be afforded by the vast variety of matters to be found in a dunghill after it has been thoroughly rotted; and I shall confine my attention to the consideration of the single ingredient, the carbonate of ammonia. Ammonia itself is said to exist frequently in small quantity in the excrements of animals, more especially in their urine. We must, however, look for our main supply to the decomposition of a variety of organic products, which are either dissolved in the urine, or more sparingly intermixed with the solid excrement. The whole of such materials, however, form a very small per centage in the entire mass. In urine, for instance, water alone forms above 90 per cent., and of the materials which make up the remainder, some of them contain no nitrogen at all. In the progress of the decomposition of those products which contain nitrogen, this element is set free, and immediately unites with hydrogen, also set free, and the result is ammonia. But ammonia cannot exist long in a free state in the atmosphere. It enters into ready combination with any acid it may meet with. Now carbonic acid is another of the inorganic compounds which is formed in abundance during the progress of the decomposition; and some portions of it enter into immediate combination with the ammonia, and the result is a new substance, the carbonate of ammonia. Ammonia itself is highly volatile; it rises readily into the air and is dispersed. Carbonate of ammonia is also volatile, and escapes in a similar manner, though not with equal rapidity. In its solid state it is a white substance, looking something like a piece of marble; and I will hand round the table a lump of it for your inspection. You will find that it emits a highly pungent odour, and if any gentleman present is unacquainted with the smell of a dunghill, he may obtain a notion of what it is like by smelling at this lump of carbonate of ammonia. Though this substance is so volatile, it is readily dissolved in water, and will then be retained for a considerable time, the evaporation going on very slowly, except the temperature be somewhat elevated. It has been stated that gypsum may be advantageously employed in effecting the decomposition of the carbonate of ammonia, as fast as it is formed in the dunghill. The consequence would be, that we should have the sulphate of ammonia, instead of the carbonate; and that salt is not volatile. But though plants may be able to obtain their nitrogen from ammonia, or the carbonate of ammonia, it does not follow that they may therefore do so from the sulphate, or any other of the salts of ammonia. This is a subject which chemists have not yet fully elucidated. It seems, however, to be quite certain, that all the salts of ammonia do produce a beneficial effect on vegetation; and therefore it is highly important to secure as many of them as possible, whether by retaining the liquid in which some may be dissolved, or by preventing the escape of such of them as can assume the gaseous state. Perhaps I may be permitted to allude to a trifling experiment which any of you can easily repeat, and which may serve to show how the ammonia may be fixed in the state of the sulphate of ammonia upon decomposing the carbonate with gypsum. If you place in a wine-glass a little powdered carbonate of ammonia, with a little more than an equal quantity of powdered gypsum, or of plaster of Paris, which is burnt gypsum, you will still perceive the strong odour of the carbonate of ammonia. But if you now add a little water to the mixture, and stir it well, the odour immediately ceases, and a slight effervescence in the glass shows us that a chemical action is taking place; and if we were to examine the result at the end of a little time, we should find it consist of carbonate of lime and sulphate of ammonia. The affinities of lime and ammonia for the sulphuric and carbonic acids are so nearly balanced, that a mere difference in temperature will determine which of the two shall combine with each; and it is a singular fact, that if carbonate of lime (*chalk*) be mixed with sulphate of ammonia, and then moistened, a reaction takes place; and whilst the sulphate of lime (*gypsum*) is forming, the carbonate of ammonia (which is also formed) gradually escapes, till the water becomes pure, with nothing but the nearly insoluble sulphate of lime left in the glass. Without detaining you further with any disquisition on these effects, I recommend you to try such simple experiments as may seem to make the matter clearer to yourselves. Since the whole amount of the salts of ammonia which may be procured during the decomposition of the organic matters in a dunghill, depends upon the quantity of nitrogen which these may contain; it is evident that under ordinary circumstances, a portion only of that amount has been preserved at the end of the process: since there has been a constant escape of some part of the carbonate of ammonia, in an invisible form, whilst the process of decomposition was going on. It should seem, therefore, that a prudent step to get the manure into the ground as speedily as possible; and perhaps even before the decomposition of the materials has commenced; or at least before it is much advanced. But let us look a little more attentively at this important question before we come to any definite conclusions. Suppose I represent the quantity of nitrogen contained in the organic matter of a certain portion of unrotted manure, by 100. Suppose that this gradually combines with hydrogen, and forms 100 parts of ammonia, and this again combines with carbonic acid, and forms 100 parts of carbonate of ammonia. In such an estimate of the amount of these several materials, I make no allusion to their respective weights; I am merely looking to the relative proportion between the atoms of each substance, and this will be the same in the compounds as in the simple element nitrogen. Whilst this formation of 100 parts of carbonate of ammonia was proceeding, let us suppose that half of this substance escaped into the atmosphere, and the other half was retained, some how or other, in the manure. We may suppose the moisture retains it; or that it has been decomposed by some acid, as the humic acid, or the sulphuric acid, and that the salts thus formed are dissolved in the liquid parts of the manure. At the end of the process, then, we shall find fifty parts of ammonia, in some form or other in our rotted manure; the other fifty parts having been lost. Compared with unrotted manure, then, it is enriched by these fifty parts of serviceable material, whilst there is not an atom of any such in the other. Suppose we now put a certain quantity of unrotted manure into a patch of ground, and leave a like quantity till it has become thoroughly rotted, and put it also into another patch of ground of the same dimensions. In the latter case we apply, suppose, fifty parts of the fixed ammonia directly to the soil, ready for the crop; but in the former case we have not any. Still in the unrotted dung we have the 100 parts of nitrogen, capable of forming 100 parts of am-

monia. Provided, then, we can secure the conditions necessary for effecting the decomposition of the manure after it has been placed in the earth, we shall now have command over 100, and not 50 parts only of ammonia, in some form or other. But possibly the decomposition may not commence, or not proceed with sufficient rapidity to benefit the crop to the same extent as the already rotted manure. Let us suppose, however, that it does begin immediately, and that whilst the crop is growing, 50 parts of the nitrogen have been usefully employed in keeping up a regular supply of ammonia. The unrotted manure will then have done its duty as efficiently, and perhaps more so, than the rotted; and when the crop is removed there will . still remain 50 parts of the nitrogen which has not yet been abstracted. It does not follow that the whole of this can be rendered available for the succeeding crop; for the decomposition will proceed, possibly with an increasing rapidity, so that before another crop can be benefitted by the nitrogen that was left, this may be greatly diminished. I don't mean to say that this can be considered a precise representation of what can really happen in any case; but it may serve to show you the complexity of the subject, and why it is that we cannot always expect so great an advantage from the use of unrotted manure as we might have fancied we should have done. The process of putrefaction requires a certain degree of heat, of moisture, and the access of air, or it cannot take place. This process may, therefore, be very much advanced or retarded by the particular circumstances. Thus, for instance, in a very dry sandy soil the vegetable matter of the manure may be preserved for some time, as effectually as the dried plants in my herbarium; here moisture was required. Or, in a stiff clay, the ready access of air may be cut off, and the decomposition, in consequence, proceed very slowly. Lastly, the weather may be too cold, and thus decomposition may be entirely arrested. We all know that in Russia the markets are supplied during the winter, with frozen provisions, and that these will keep perfectly fresh as long as the frost lasts. Indeed, there seems to be no limit to the length of time which organized matter may be preserved in ice; and I dare say that most persons here present have heard of the entire mammoth which had been embedded in the ice of Siberia, in all probability, for thousands of years, until it was thawed out one hot summer, when the dogs and bears devoured the flesh. The skeleton and parts of the skin are still preserved in the museum at St. Petersburgh. I have, perhaps, been unnecessarily tedious in these remarks, but I wish to impress upon you how requisite it is that every farmer, or at least every superintendent of agricultural proceedings, should be able to determine, upon correct principles, to what extent he should allow his manure to decompose before he makes use of it, in order that he may apply it to the very best advantage. He must distinctly understand that the longer he suffers any organized matter to continue rotting, the less nitrogen he can command for the formation of ammonia and the salts of ammonia. In cases where the greatest good may be expected from using the manure in its unfermented or very slightly decomposed state, there is an objection, of a mechanical nature, to its application, on account of the difficulty of getting the long straw into the ground. But surely any mechanical difficulty may easily be overcome in an age of mechanical contrivances. I have no doubt that our Ipswich friends, Messrs. Ransome and May, would readily invent, if such an instrument should ever be required, some smasher or crusher of long muck, which would masticate this plant-food as effectually as our own jaws have chopped up the excellent dinner we had lately on the table. Science certainly advises against any long continuance of the process of decomposition, and her suggestions in this respect are backed by a recorded practice of the late Lord Leicester, to whose opinions all practical men will be willing to lend most serious attention. He is stated to have said that by allowing farm yard manure to be only half rotted, he found it went twice as far as when entirely rotted. I think I do not misstate him ; and that he also had adopted the practice at the suggestion of Sir H. Davy. I am careful not to give any very positive advice on practical matters, but I shall venture to forego a little of my caution in what I have to say further on the subject of dunghills. Much is yet to be learnt as to the best mode of preparing and employing farm yard manure ; but I think, that as a general rule of management, farmers should be more anxious about retarding than accelerating its decomposition. Whenever they perceive a great heat arising, and a strong smell escaping, they may know that the chemical action is violent, by which the re-arrangement of the elementary substances it contains is taking place ; and the carbonate of ammonia will be rapidly forming and escaping. They should take precautions to prevent this. Just attention should be paid to mixing the materials as equally as possible, and I will even venture to recommend, till good reason shall be shown against such practice, that a little powdered gypsum be scattered from time to time over the materials as they accumulate. It can do no harm, and I believe may do much good. Let a sufficient quantity of water be sprinkled over it, to wet the gypsum thoroughly. If the manure is to be kept for any time, it may be covered over with the richest mould, which will retain some portion of the escaping carbonate of ammonia ; and if peat can be procured conveniently, it may be serviceable for the same purpose. But I must not trespass upon you by entering into details of this sort, which you will find better explained by practical writers. I should certainly avoid using lime on the dunghill ; and I do not understand the use of covering a dunghill with chalk, which I see is sometimes the practice of this neighbourhood. Those who adopt it no doubt find it beneficial ; but I question whether they would not be equally benefitted by carting the chalk directly on to the land. If some parts of our enquiry are encumbered with difficulties and uncertainty, there are some points upon which I find both scientific and practical writers appear most cordially to agree, and upon which indeed I should have thought very little judgment was required. It should be no question with a farmer that he cannot be too careful in the preparation and preservation of his manure. It should at all times be under his immediate inspection and control. The too common practice of leaving it exposed by the roadside is as impolitic as it is illegal. A proper place should be provided, where it may be protected from undue influences of the weather, and where the farmer may secure from waste every drop of that rich brown liquid which I so often see oozing out and running away, but which may be considered as the very life blood

of his crops. There are sundry suggestions to be met with in professed treatises on the subject, and I shall not presume to decide which is the best mode of preparing a site for the dunghill. Perhaps a flooring of asphalte might be useful in some cases instead of stone or brick. If the practice of leaving dunghills by the roadsides is objectionable, on a variety of accounts, so I consider there can be no doubt it is wrong to carry such manure on the land in the manner generally adopted in this neighbourhood. I see it for a fortnight together scattered over the field in little hillocks. If there are any matters capable of rising in a gaseous state, their escape must be facilitated by such a process; and if there be any liquid matters oozing from the manure, they will penetrate the soil immediately under each hillock in undue proportion. I must incline to the practice of those districts where, I have been informed, whilst the manure is carted on the land in rapid succession of load after load by one set of men, another set of men attends to put it under ground as soon as possible.

Having spoken so fully on the subject of farmyard manure, I shall not attempt to discuss very minutely the differences between this and other organic manures. The chief objection to farmyard manure is its bulk, and perhaps the day is arriving when means will be contrived for extracting from it all that is really essential to vegetation in some very small compass. I shall now pass on to what must be considered a still more important description of manure than that which I have just mentioned, although in this country we are far behind other nations in understanding its proper management. I shall quote to you a passage from Sprengel on the subject :—" Although there can be no doubt that night-soil is one of the strongest manures, it is still in most places managed with less care than any, and in many altogether neglected ; yet the greater or less value attached to it in any country is certainly a proof of the degree in which the agriculture of that country is advanced. Where pains are taken with it, husbandry will be found in other respects excellent ; where it is little thought of, the art in general will usually be less perfect." In these observations I perfectly coincide. Both theory and an intelligent practice unite in declaring that the mixture of fæces and urine, termed night-soil, is among the forms of animal excrement which abound the most in nitrogen. Besides this, such a material must contain all those inorganic substances, to be found in the food of man, some of which may not be restored to the earth with the excrement of other animals, because they may not have formed an essential part of those plants upon which they fed. In the case of wheat, for instance, though we restore the straw to the earth, still the seeds may have required that something should be extracted from the soil, essential to their development, and which may not be retained in the straw itself; this, in fact, is known to be the case. Such a substance would not necessarily be returned to the soil, in restoring the straw alone, or even the dung of other animals, which may never be fed on corn. But such a substance would be restored by the use of night-soil. The rapidity with which this manure enters into decomposition renders its management more intricate, and fully justifies Sprengel's remark. If, then, the farmers of England are prepared to avail themselves of what he tells them, I have no doubt they will soon find it to be well worth their while to establish some general system of saving every particle of night-soil they can command in the towns and villages. I would go further in my recommendation, and, though my advice may seem ironical, I believe it to be sound and wholesome advice. I would say to them, to care less about the number of cattle you may require for securing an abundance of manure, and feed your labourers well and better than they are now fed, and you will find it more to your interests to do so. I shall not dilate upon the manner in which night-soil should be prepared, but content myself with the statement that there are means for entirely depriving it of unpleasant odour. It can be no small convenience to be able to concentrate the useful part of twenty-five tons of farm-yard manure into thirteen bushels; and this is about the proportion in which a given quantity of night-soil is said to excel the more bulky material. The liquid portions of animal excrement contain the greatest quantity of nitrogen; but the effects they produce are more transient from the rapidity with which they decompose; so that great waste must occur unless they are applied in a very diluted state, and from time to time whilst the crop is growing. If it were expedient to apply such manure, little at a time and frequently, the effects would probably exceed those of all other kinds. But the management of liquid manure requires tact and experience. Perhaps in places where it is secured from waste by being collected in tanks, the constant presence of gypsum would be found very serviceable. With respect to other organic manures of animal origin, I need say scarcely anything—they are all serviceable—not a particle of them should ever be wasted—every farm-yard might have some pit or general receptacle for all kinds of offal, blood, feathers, dead rats, mice, or whatever else is of animal origin — by covering such matters with earth (and again I would add a little gypsum), and mixing with them some vegetable refuse, a rich compost might be prepared of great use in the good cause. There is one description of animal manure upon which I wish to make a few remarks. Every one is aware of the value of bone manure, of which such immense importations have taken place of late years. The effects produced by fresh bones must be considered of a two-fold character; one depending upon the decomposition of the organic matters in the bone, and the other on that produced by the action of the earthy or inorganic matter, which is chiefly phosphate of lime. Those who have never seen the experiment tried, will be surprised to find how large a portion of every bone, and even of the teeth, is composed of animal matter. I have here prepared two bones from a leg of mutton which I will send to the right and left round the table. They have been steeped for a few hours in dilute muriatic acid, which has extracted every particle of earthy matter without very materially altering their general appearance. But if you take them in your hand, you will find they are as flexible as if they were made of leather. This explains the use of bones in the manufacture of glue, or in making soup, so large a quantity of animal matter must be serviceable in its decomposition in supplying ammonia. Intermixed as it is with the earthy parts of the bone, it decomposes very slowly; and traces of it may be found in the fossil bones which have been buried in caves and dens of extinct animals which perished thousands of years ago. But when all this animal matter has been extracted from

bones, whether by boiling, burning, or by long decay, the earthy matter that remains is also a most valuable manure. It is chiefly composed of phosphate of lime, a substance of at least one of the materials of which, seems to be very generally if not universally essential to the structure of plants, or the perfecting of their seed. Very little of it, however, is taken up by each individual plant. The same substance forms the greater part of that particular form of dog's excrement, called " album græcum," of the shells of crabs and lobsters, &c. It is highly advisable that all such matters should be added to the compost pit. Some simple contrivance may be employed for breaking them into small pieces, or for reducing them to powder. Perhaps something on the principal of a stamper; a vertically-placed beam of timber with an iron shoe, which may be raised and then allowed to fall on the materials to be crushed. It should be remembered that different animal matures enter into decomposition with very different degrees of rapidity. Those which are soft and juicy readily decompose, whilst such substances as horn, hair, feathers and woollen rags are sometimes not thoroughly decomposed till after the lapse of several years. These latter are generally much the richest in nitrogen.

With respect to organic manures of vegetable origin, I shall say but very little. They contain little nitrogen compared with animal manures. They ought all to be carefully collected, and added to the compost heap. Even the docks which are now pulled up in full seed, and placed in the middle of the road, I presume for the purpose of disseminating them in all directions, might be collected before they went to seed, and added to the general stock. The more juicy the vegetable matter the more readily it decomposes; but even the decomposition of the more fibrous kinds may be secured by mixing them with other matters. In foreign countries, farmers seem to make much greater use of manuring with green crops, by ploughing them in before they have gone to seed, than is considered to be expedient among ourselves. Perhaps there may be cases in which attention to this practice would not be misplaced. If a fallow be required for improving the condition of the soil, and not merely for destroying weeds, then I can conceive that a green crop, which may be suffered to grow for the sole purpose of being ploughed in, might be of real benefit. At first sight, it might seem that such a crop could add no more to the soil than it had taken from it. But this is not strictly true. Some portion at least of its carbon has been derived from other sources, and thus an alteration must be effected both in the chemical composition and mechanical condition of the soil when the crop is ploughed in. The roots of the green crop are also employed in bringing up towards the surface certain saline and earthy matters which lie at some depth, and are thus placed in a more convenient position for the crop which is to succeed.

I shall pass on to the subject of inorganic manures, though I cannot say much on them, after the length of time I have already occupied your attention. These substances are calculated to supply plants with some of those materials which enter into their composition to a much smaller extent than the four elements supplied by organic matter. Some of them, as the salts of ammonia, and the nitrates, may possibly be sources from whence plants are able to derive a portion of their nitrogen; but this is an undetermined question. Some of them seem to be serviceable to one kind of plant, and some to another. In general, I should consider that they ought to be applied in comparatively small quantities; and frequently, rather than much at once. I may remark upon a few of them, which seem to produce a specific effect upon particular plants. This appears to be owing to different plants having the power of selecting, to a certain extent, particular substances from the soil, which other plants growing in the same soil either do not require at all, or only in much smaller quantity. For instance, all the grass tribe take up a large quantity of siliceous matter, the substance of which flints are composed. This it is which gives the polished surface to the straw of corn and grass. So much of this material is taken up by the gigantic grass called bamboo, that lumps of it ooze out of the stem like masses of gum, and are contained in the hollow parts between the joints. 1 will send round for your inspection some fragments of this curious substance. Gypsum, again, is found abundantly in the plants of clover, and others of the same natural family. It is stated that as much as three or four bushels may be obtained from the plants which have grown on one acre. Where a soil does not contain gypsum, we may reasonably suppose that clover will not prosper; but the manner in which gypsum should be applied to the soil admits of further enquiry. It is stated to produce most remarkable effects in some places by being merely scattered on the soil itself; whilst in other instances it produces no effect unless it is scattered over the leaves of the plant in the form of plaster of Paris, or burnt gypsum. The nitrate of soda seems to be decidedly useful in invigorating the grass tribe (among others), and in all probability will generally be found to increase the produce of a hay-field, provided it be applied with other manures. For with all these inorganic manures, it is hardly judicious, in the present state of our knowledge, to think of dispensing entirely with such as are of organic origin. That nitrate of soda accelerates the germination of seeds, I had an opportunity of witnessing in the effect it produced upon some wheat which I had steeped in it, and which came up more readily, and, for a time, grew more rapidly than other seed sown with it. Salt again, is another inorganic manure, about which there is great difference of opinion. If I should be asked, as a botanist, to what plants I should consider its application likely to be beneficial, I should say at once, try it upon all those which, in their native state, are found only growing near the sea side, or upon the very shore. I name asparagus, seakale, cabbage, all the forms of beet and mangel wurzel, perhaps celery also, as plants which nature shows us need salt for their healthy development, and consequently which might most probably be assisted in those more monstrous states under which culture has brought them. I dare say that most of you are well aware how grateful salt is to all cattle. It seems to be as essential to their perfect health as it is to our own, that they should obtain it with their food, as in fact they generally do to a greater or less extent. If a lump of rock-salt be fastened at one end of the manger, a horse will be found to lick it daily, and we may fairly conclude that it is wholesome to him. If salt then is used as a manure on grass lands, and it should be found to produce no very decided benefit, yet it is not unlikely that the grass will have become more grateful and serviceable to cattle, simply by its having absorbed some portion of it. A mixture

of lime and salt has been recommended as a manure. Perhaps chalk and salt would produce the desired effect still better. I know that one valuable member of this club once tried it, and succeeded in giving his field a coat of hard mortar, which he was afterwards obliged to scrape off again. But possibly he was in too great a hurry. For when lime and salt are left to the long continued action of the atmosphere, I can easily suppose that a carbonate of soda, and a muriate of lime will be the result, two salts which are said to have been found beneficial, and both of which are soluble in water. But I must really desist from further comment. What I have been saying will I hope assist in convincing the members of the club, or any others who may have patience to read this long-winded address, that practical men ought to be better acquainted with some of the leading principles of chemistry, than they generally are. Such knowledge is not merely required of them for the purpose of directing their own concerns; but without it they cannot hope to make chemists acquainted with the results of their practice in a form and shape which may be available for scientific purposes. A celebrated French botanist has pointed out the manner in which persons engaged in different departments of science may co-operate in elucidating the general theory of vegetable physiology. On referring to agriculturists, he is very particular in pointing out the necessity of their being far more accurate than they generally are in their details. I shall quote to you his remarks:—
" The radical fault which so much detracts from the use that might otherwise be made of the experience of practical men, consists in the too frequent absence of all comparative experiment. I mean of such as are rigorously comparative. We read daily in works of husbandry, and we hear repeated in conversation, accounts of some particular process, which is pronounced to be good or bad without any reference to an exact comparative result. What a multitude of boasted processes we meet with in agricultural journals, which in reality can neither prove beneficial to practice, nor serve to throw any light upon theory. The first step towards curing this evil, is to bring practical men to understand that a single trial never proves any thing. It is much to be wished that the host of agricultural and horticultural societies which now cover the face of Europe, would determine never to pay attention to the results of any but comparative experiments, detailed under a precise form of numerical expression." Provided agriculturists will turn over a new leaf in these respects, it is from them that science might expect to derive the most considerable mass of facts upon which she may hope to improve our knowledge of the laws of vegetation, and bring the art of agriculture to the dignity of a science. Sir John Herschel, in his " Discourse on Natural Philosophy "—a book which every one should read who wishes to know what science means—has some excellent remarks upon the possibility of almost every one who chooses it, co-operating in some way or other for the advance of knowledge. " It is an object of great importance to avail ourselves as far as possible of the advantages which a division of labour may afford for the collection of facts, by the industry and activity which the general diffusion of information, in the present age, brings into exercise. There is scarcely any well informed person, who, if he has but the will, has not also the power to add something essential to the general stock of knowledge, if he will only observe regularly and methodically some particular class of facts which may

most excite his attention, or which his situation may best enable him to study with effect." May I then advise you to omit no opportunity of keeping an exact register of all the positive facts you can obtain in the cultivation of your crops. I would say register, register, register these facts, and in the end you will find that such a proceeding will be ser-. viceable to yourselves in particular, and to science in general. I shall here close my remarks on the subject you have requested me to look into; but before I sit down, I shall venture to say a few words upon another subject, on which I feel myself much more qualified to give an opinion, than upon how your crops should be manured. There is a description of culture which requires its special manure, and in which I conceive you are as deeply interested as in any which you carry on in the fields. You have the proper cultivation of your labourers to look to. This is not the place, nor is this a befitting occasion for me to appeal to you on any higher grounds than mere worldly policy, for recommending attention to their moral, intellectual, and social condition. One of the best manures which you can provide for the description of culture I now allude to, is to secure your labourers constant employment. I shall not enter upon the wide field which this question embraces ; but I put it simply to you as a matter of worldly policy to do so. I am no prophet : but it needs no prophet to foreshow you what will certainly come to pass, if your labourers are thrown out of employ. If profits are to depend in future upon increased produce, and not upon high prices, then must there be an increase of general intelligence among your labourers, to enable you to take advantage of improved methods of culture ; and there must be increased labour also to carry them out. I recommend to your serious attention that glorious maxim of the wisest of earthly monarchs—"There is that scattereth and yet increaseth; and there is that withholdeth more than is meet, but it tendeth to poverty."—Prov. xi. 24.

"The health of the Secretary." (Applause.) Mr. GRIMWADE returned thanks.

AGRICULTURAL QUERY.

TO THE EDITOR OF THE MARK LANE EXPRESS.

SIR,—In your paper of December 19th, Mr. James Beadel, of Witham, stated that he was digging a field with a peculiarly constructed fork, which enabled him to keep the present top soil on the surface. I shall feel much obliged by Mr. Beadel giving a description of the fork, and how used, in your paper. By so doing you will confer a benefit on manual labour.—I remain, Mr. Editor, yours respectfully, A YORKSHIREMAN. Jan. 18.

ANSWERS TO QUERIES.

In answer to " A Young Farmer," I would burn the heath preparatory to bringing in moor-land, because the heath would tend to keep the furrows too open in the first process of cultivation ; but, unless prompted by necessity, I on no account countenance the burning of vegetable matter on a farmer's field, such as scutch, &c., for it is like a man lighting his own lamp, that the character " Bad farmer" may be more legible to all around. But to the point in question. After the heath is burned, go along with a plough, taking a furrow of 2 or 3 inches deep ; then follow with another plough

in the bottom of the first furrow, throwing up 3 or 4 inches more on the top of the first; and so on until the whole is completed. This done in Autumn, and exposed to Winter's frost, will make it ready for sowing a crop of Hopetown oats along with 2 cwt. of Guano in the Spring. This crop may not make the farmer rich, but it will bring the land into a proper state of cultivation for next year's turnips or potatoes.

In the Spring preparations for the above green crops, a moderate liming would be necessary. I have found it answer very well to throw the lime upon the drills after the potatoes were planted, and then hoe or harrow it in.

Having had much experience in Scottish agriculture, I shall be most happy at all times to give information regarding any of the late improvements.

A CHESHIRE STEWARD.

SIR,—In answer to the " Goth" of Teeswater, the most rapid way of reducing the couch grass collected from his land into the state of decomposing manure, is to mix it with either common salt or lime (say half a bushel of salt, or one bushel of lime, to a ton of the couch grass).—See Johnson and Shaw's Farmer's Almanac, for 1843.

As to the analysis of the ashes of the larch tree, the composition of these vary with the soil on which they are raised. 100 parts of some from a limestone hill were found to contain—

Soluble salts 15
Phosphates of Lime and Magnesia.... 12.25
Carbonates of Lime and Magnesia 44
Silica 2
Metallic oxide 2
Loss 22.75

The most rational way of applying these as a fertiliser is as a top dressing to the grasses.

PETER VANDEL PRIGGENS.
Newcastle, December 16th, 1842.

AYRSHIRE CATTLE.

SIR,—In answer to the queries of a " Constant Reader," in the Mark Lane Express of this week, as to Ayrshire cattle, the prevailing colour is red and white, occasionally roan ; their milk is superior in quality and quantity. In the autumn of 1841, I tried the milk of four against that of four well-bred short-horned cows ; the milk of the Ayrshire outweighed that of the short-horned. The Ayrshire eat little, and from their lighter weights do not poach the land in wet weather, and they are hardy ; my county is Lancashire, and the land rich dairy land. A commission agent purchases them for me at Falkirk in general. This autumn he has sent me a considerable number of calving cows and heifers, high-bred and handsome. Average price, 8l.6s.6d. ; some yearling heifers, 5l. 5s. ; a two-year old bull, 15l. 15s.; and a one-year old bull, 8l. 8s. ; also a full-bred and perfect beauty in-calf heifer, 10l. 10s. These prices are exclusive of commission and travelling expenses.

If the " Constant Reader " wishes for further information, and will address to H. P., post office, Blackburn, he shall with pleasure have all particulars.

THE EPIDEMIC.—We beg the most particular attention of our readers to a cure for the epidemic, announced in our advertising columns; upon the efficacy of which we place implicit reliance, provided care is taken in the application.

ON MANURES.

By MM. Boussingault and Payen.

(*From the Annals of Chemistry.*)

In a former memoir we sought to establish the comparative value of manures by the results of analysis. The practical observations which have since come under our notice seem to justify the principle on which we had based our calculations; at least, no serious objections have been raised against it ; and the kindness with which enlightened practical men received our first attempts decided us on completing the task of examining all the manures that it has been possible for us to obtain.

For the better comprehension of the remarks contained in this second paper, it will be necessary to repeat the definition which we gave of powerful manures. At the present day, this definition is equally applicable as it was formerly, and appears to be the exact expression of well-ascertained facts.

Manure is the more valuable in proportion as the quantity of organic azotized matter is stronger, or predominates over the non-azotized organic matter ; and in proportion as the decomposition of quaternary substances acts gradually, and agrees with the progress of vegetation.*

We intend to define here the value of manures applicable to such cultivated lands as receive the benefit of preceding crops, containing residuary vegetable matters poor in azote, but rich in ternary organic substances. It may be admitted that the intelligent farmer can obtain, at a low cost, the mineral matters which enter into the composition of the soil, and thereby assure himself of the influence of manures. In order that manure spread over the ground may *alone* serve for vegetable nourishment, it would be requisite that it should contain all those elements, organic and inorganic, which, without being borrowed from the atmosphere, should be in reality assimilated during the life of the plant, and contained in the crop. In this case the manure must necessarily vary according to the nature of the ground, the climate, the season, the species of vegetable cultivated, the laying down and slope of the land, and lastly, according to the influence of the subsoil and the residue of preceding crops. If we admitted this hypothesis, the composition of manures would become so variable and complex, that any general rule would be impossible. Scientific data would be useless, for it would be utterly impossible to re-unite economically the required conditions : it is convenient, therefore, as formerly practised, to divide the substances which increase the fertility of the soil into two great classes—the inorganic compounds, which independent of the chemical properties they procure to soils, by furnishing such mineral substances as are indispensable to the complete development of vegetables, evidently contribute to the physical qualities of the land under cultivation. Such are the salts particularly suitable for certain plants, as gypsum (*platre*) for leguminous plants, and those which have an alkaline reaction, and are found in the greater number of vegetables, as lime, solutions of soda or potassa, wood ashes, &c., which generally assist vegetation on all soils. These matters, so useful to the agriculturist, are comprised under the denomination of *amendments* and *stimulants.*

We may consider either as stimulants or as manure, substances by whose assistance plants are furnished with the water necessary for their most productive development : organic remains macerated in ponds, irrigation even (too often neglected where it might be managed), serve to attain this desirable end.

Manures, correctly speaking, are of organic origin ; they ought to supply to land the want of *gaseous or soluble aliments,* such as vegetables can assimilate.

But among these aliments, we should do wrong if we considered those as most desirable which give rise to the production of the greatest quantity of carbonic acid. It were wrong, we repeat ; for these almost always abound in lands continually cultivated, whilst decomposable azotised matters, experiencing the most rapid losses, ought consequently to be more frequently rendered to the soil : it should always be our care to renew the supply of these latter, which are unceasingly being exhausted. We may, then, with propriety point out these to cultivators as most worthy of their attention ; and if we determine accurately their proportion in the commonly-used manures, we shall have given useful information, and furnished the best means of detecting the frauds so prejudicial to the agriculturist, which occur in commercial manures.*

Besides, it is now a question that has been decided by numerous concordant facts, generally admitted by the most distinguished agriculturists. They know also that certain manures furnish at one and the same time amendments—stimulants, water and organic aliments, more or less azotised ; such are the majority of manures, which ought, from the many functions which they serve to fufil, to be very appropriate to the soil, and especially for cultivation : *fresh* for dry or sandy lands : *warm* for wet and cold *argillaceous* soils.

As to rich manures, capable of being transported to long distances, they may be fruitfully applied on all lands, for all kinds of cultivation, provided that their action be assisted, and the power of the soil developed by amendments, and by irrigation, contrived on the spot, or not far removed from the farm.

To fix our ideas clearly on this subject, we cite the following example :—On a dry and sandy land, where manure, strongly impregnated with moisture agreed very well, it was attempted to replace this manure by dry blood, of equal value. It was easy to foresee the result : the crop failed.

Ought we, from this, to conclude that a manure, rich in strongly-azotised matter, was useless or injurious on a light soil? Undoubtedly not : mixed with a small portion of fresh manure, so as to contain altogether the same quantity of azote, it rendered the vegetation far more luxurious and abundant than by the customary method of cultivation, where fresh dung alone had been employed.

---

* Thus it is the azote in combination, contained in a manure which is especially useful, and the proportion of this, when ascertained, indicates the richness of the manure.

* The numerous disputes between agriculturists and merchants, relative to disinfectant manures, and to the black residua of refineries, have shown how illusory were the old tests for manure. The proportion of azote replaces these very advantageously : it has been adopted by M. Malagutti, one of the learned Professors of the Faculty of Rennes, not far from localities where agriculture has derived much profit from the vast applications of these manures.

TABLE OF ANALYSES AND COMPARATIVE VALUE OF MANURES.

NAME.	Normal Water.	Weight of dry matter employed. (Gr.)	Nitrogen in cubic centimetres of 1 cent. cubic = 13·434 grs. of water at 39·5 F.	Temperature. F.	Barometric pressure.	Nitrogen per cent. in the dried matter.	Nitrogen in per cent. in the Normal matter.	TITLE. Dry substance. A.	Substance in the Normal state. B.	REMARKS.
Farm dung	79·5	4·0755	661	49°	0·743	1·95	0·4	100	100	Roots, stalks, leaves, and flowers
Autumnal leaves, oak	24·99	0·333	475	58	0·751	1·565	1·175	80	293	
" beech	39·3	0·492	8	50	0·761	1·906	1·177	77·7	294	Previously dried
" poplar	31·1	0·553	5·5	59	0·761	1·166	0·538	66	134	Hops, 1st quality
" acacia	53·6	0·372	5	59	0·7516	1·557	0·721	79·8	134	Vinous, process of M. Dombasle
" peartree	14·5	0·593	8·2	66	0·743	1·53	1·36	813	340	Ditto
Madia sativa t manure	70·55	0·31	14	67	0·761	1·534	0·45	78·6	112·5	Ditto
Branches and leaves of box	59·26	0·488	19·25	63	0·756	2·89	1·17	147	292·5	
Residue from cyder apples	6·4	0·716	3·7	43	0·747	0·63	0·59	32·3	147	
" hops	73·05	0·439	8·50	60	0·749	2·28	0·60	114	150	
Beetroot lees and scum	67·0	0·488	6·5	59	0·769	1·579	0·535	80·9	134	
Exhausted slices of beet	94·50	0·691	10·25	59	0·7695	1·758	0·009	90·1	22	
Cakes of cotton-grains	11·02	0·333	13·25	72	0·7607	4·584	4·02	232	1000	Ditto
" camelina	6·5	0·668	32·3	45	0·754	5·93	5·515	304	1573	
" hempseed	5·0	0·364	24·7	45	0·753	4·78	4·21	245	1032	
" poppies	5·0	0·714	33·2	44	0·733	5·70	5·36	292	1340	
" beech-nuts	6·2	0·718	20·7	44	0·732	3·53	3·31	181	838	
" walnuts	6·0	0·719	34·0	45	0·752	5·59	5·24	286·6	1310	Very woody, employed as fuel
Dung from inns (du midi)	60·58	0·493	9	62	0·745	2·683	0·79	107	197	Communicated by M. Gasparin
Guaino into England	19·56	0·766	40	58	0·766	6·201	0·59	323	1247	Normal state [ed by sifting
" cleaned by sifting	23·40	0·480	60	60	0·744	7·047	5·398	361	1349	Globiliferous concretion, remov-
" imported into France	11·28	0·266	37	65	0·746	15·732	13·950	806·7	3487	Distinct putrid odour
Litter of silkworms (5. age)	14·29	0·498	15	61	0·754	3·483	3·285	178·7	827	From Neuilly
" (6· age)	11·39	0·361	11·25	59	0·773	3·709	3·290	190	822	From Senart
Chrysalides	78·30	0·318	25	64	0·750	8·987	1·942	461	485	Dirt
Urine from the public urinals	9·57	0·563	25	59	0·751	17·556	16·853	900·2	4213	Ded in a stove
Ditto	96·889	0·150	35	58	0·752	23·108	0·715	1153	179	1543 grs. of liquid gave 3·617 grs. of residue; the volatile ing-
Animal charcoal from the refineries (Mayenne)	27·65	1·038	16·5	53	0·774	1·901	1·375	97·4	343·7	dients have been remov
Dutch manure	54·12	0·382	8	57	0·764	2·478	1·36	127	340	
English black	13·45	0·260	18	59	0·751	3·022	6·952	411·4	1738	Blood + lime + coal soot
Residue from Pruss. blue + blood	53·40	0·466	11	59	0·7704	2·8031	1·306	143·7	326	
Marine plants mineralised	19·54	0·645	15·5	66	0·757	2·8051	2·408	141	602	Dried in the store
Ditto	11·72	1·008	24·5	58	0·760	2·756	2·408	602	598	Ditto
Rotten man	—	1	9·7	46	0·759	1·03	2·395	52·8	—	Horsedung in a dry state, & previ- ously sifted to remove the straw
Sea-shells	—	2·130	1·00	76	0·7655	0·652	0·052	2·67	13	Previously dried.

Note.—In the column A, the title of each manure, supposed dry, is compared to that of dry dung, represented by 100. In the column B, the title of each manure, in its usual moist state, is compared with the title of moist dung, represented

L 2

SYNOPTICAL TABLE OF EQUIVALENTS OF MANURES.

SUBSTANCES.	Equivalent of the substance dry.	Equivalent of the substance in its Normal state.	OBSERVATIONS.
Farm dung	100	100	Taken as a term of comparison
Autumnal leaves, oak............	125	34	
" beech..........	102·3	33 98	
" poplar	167·2	74·34	
" acacia	125·2	55·47	
" peartree....	127	29·40	
Madia sativa, recent manure........	126	88·88	Roots, stalks, leaves, and flowers
Box	67·5	34·18	Branches and leaves
Residue of apples used for cyder..	309	67·79	Residue dried in the air, taken as the Normal state
Ditto hops for brewing	87·6	66·65	Residue containing 0·73 of water
Scum and lees	127·1	47·65	From a beetroot sugar factory
Exhausted slices of beetroot.......	110·7	4136·50	From beetroot macerated
Cake of cotton-grains	32	9·99	
" camelina	32·8	7·25	
" hempseed	40·8	9·50	
" poppies	34·2	7·46	
" beech-nuts............	55	12·08	Very woody, used for burning
" walnuts	34·8	7·63	
Inn dung........................	93·7	50·63	Inland
Guano	31·4	80·40	Imported into England
Ditto	27·7	74·10	Ditto sifted
Ditto	12·4	28 60	Imported into France
Litter of silkworms	56	12·17	5 ᵉ age
Ditto	52·5	12·15	6 ᵉ age
Chrysalides of silkworms..........	21·6	20·61	
Urine	11·1	2·37	From public urinals (dried)
Ditto	8·4	55·95	Liquid (ammonia included)
Refineries' black.................	102·5	27·91	From Mayenne, obtained at Paris
Compost (termed) Dutch	78 6	29·40	At Lyons, animalised black
English black....................	24·3	5·75	Blood + lime + coal soot
Residue of Prussian blue	6·9	30·62	Animalised with blood
Marine plants..	7·0	16·61	Ditto with fæcal matter
Ditto	7·1	16·70	Ditto
Decomposed manure..............	189	33·33	Horsedung, dried and sifted
Sea-shells	3750	769·23	From the shores of Dunkirk.

Note.——The figures in the first column indicate the quantity of each manure which would be required to replace 100 of dry dung. The figures in the second column indicate the quantity of manure which would be required to replace 100 of fresh dung (moist).

Comptes Rendus, Oct., 1842.

by 100.—It will be perceived, that farm dung differs chiefly from inn dung in its proportion of dry matter: the first contains 0·2 and the second 0·4 of solid matter. These data may serve to calculate the amount of profit that might be realised by drying manures, in order to reduce the cost of carriage.

CALENDAR OF HORTICULTURE
FOR FEBRUARY.

The season and weather, so far as the year 1843 has advanced, have been extraordinary. Every prognostic of the autumnal equinox is verified; the winter is mild, open, rather damp, and of late somewhat boisterous. Still high winds have not been frequent, and very few fogs have occurred. The phenomena peculiar to the entire season are those singular and remarkable fluctuations of the barometer fortnightly, the mercury attaining great altitude, and gradually becoming depressed to a still greater extent. In 1822, at Christmas, and but for one day, it approached to 28 inches in the Isle of Thanet; and then a little rain followed, but

no marked commotion. In the present year, it fell progressively, continuing nearly a week below 29 inches, till the 13th of January, when our instruments showed 28 inches 20 cents. Subsequently they have risen; and now we have very nearly 30 inches 40 cents (19th). It will soon be known whether any violent meteorological commotion has occurred abroad, independent of the eruption of Etna.

Of the crops and plants—one and all—in the open air and under glass, the report is singularly propitious. Garden vegetables are prime: and a nurseryman aptly observed, that he has been put to little comparative trouble this winter, as his delicate plants had very few dead leaves, the foliage being healthy and active; hence, there is little danger of mouldiness. Every person who values his gerania, calceolarias, and such species, ought to be on the alert to remove decayed leaves before and during winter, because they foster those parasites which constitute what is called " mould," and also communicate a taint to the healthy adjoining foliage.

Every green-house plant now requires abundance of air when the atmosphere is clear and drying; foggy weather induces damp. Fire has been little used at present, but some should be applied in very cold evenings, because the buds are advancing, and many juicy plants suffer much in February.

Camellias that have passed blooming may now be excited in a moist heat to accelerate the spring growth. When growing they require abundance of water, a frequent gentle syringing, and a somewhat shady situation.

Indian and Chinese azalias are coming into bloom. Some gardeners force these sweet plants in a moist heat of 60°, others never remove them from the greenhouse; by adopting both plans a longer succession may be kept up. One precaution must be observed. If the azalias are potted in heath-soil only, that earth must never be suffered to become quite dry, else it will be difficult to re-moisten it, and the tender fibres of the roots must perish. This remark applies extensively.

Sow the seeds of gloxinia, streptocarpos, and gesneræ, on the surface of a shallow pot, or pan of fine heath-mould; sprinkle, and cover the pot with a piece of glass. Sow also, early, seeds of the several varieties of thumbelgia half-an-inch deep, and many choice annuals. A small propagation-house, with a pit of damp sand in the middle, kept gently warm by a branch of the flue, or hot-water pipe passing through it, will facilitate every operation of sowing, and of striking cuttings, graftings, and of inarching the camellias and other choice shrubs. The propagator should however bear in mind that cuttings ought to receive their moisture from the bottom; therefore, a pot of them, properly prepared with drainage-soil and upper layer of sand, should be placed in another large pot, its bottom covered an inch or more with small pot-sherds; on these the small pot may rest, sand being interposed between the sides of both to a level with the two rims, and a bell-glass pressed therein. The sand should be thoroughly moistened by the syringe, when the outer pot may be kept in a trough standing upon a temperate part of the flue, in this an inch of water should constantly be kept; and thus a gentle bottom heat and due moisture will be maintained, as the water will be drawn up by the sand as required. The glass need never be moved; and thus that loss of foliage which always results from top waterings, may generally be obviated.

The early vinery should be kept moist and pretty close, with a temperature of 70° by day and 65° at night. Considerable precaution is required just at the drawing-out of the clusters and when the flowers open; the water should fall upon them at that time.

The pine-stove must be maintained at 70° to 75° for fruiters; and the succession-pits moist, at 70°.

Cucumbers succeed well if forced now, and the pits or beds should be well attended to, that the heat decline not.

Small salads and kidney-beans may be sown; strawberry plants, and dwarf rhubarb in pots, covered with others, may now be introduced into a warm forcing house. Asparagus may again be forced for a late crop prior to that of the open beds, also potatoes and sea-kale.

VEGETABLE OPEN DEPARTMENT.

Earth up, and stick peas. Sow another crop of Charlton's or Cormack's early May-pea. Several new sorts are announced, of which we know not the merits. Repeat the sowings of beans and peas, twice in the month. The following may be sown in the last week, if soil and climate are known to favour early sowings; but in general March will be soon enough: early York, and red cabbage, savoy, Brussel's sprouts, horn carrots, onions, and leeks.

Give air abundantly to cauliflowers under frames and glasses. Move the earth, if the ground be dry enough for the hoe, about the rows of winter spinach, cabbage sprouts, and all other vegetables in rows; or pass the spade horizontally along the surface, so as to cut up an inch of earth, and reverse it; thus thousands of rising weeds will be obliterated, and a neat appearance given to the beds.

Sweet herbs can be propagated by rooted off-sets or suckers. Choose a fresh site, and make the soil rather rich.

HARDY FRUIT TREES.

Gooseberry and currant bushes should be pruned without loss of time, for the buds will soon expand unless very severe weather occur. Ample directions have been repeatedly given for the selection and amputation of shoots in the former, and the close spurring-in and shortening the latter; therefore, we may refer to former calendars: yet it will be right to observe that a shoot of a currant-shrub, if cut back, rarely fails to die down, or become feeble, two joints below. Therefore, while the gardener should resolutely cut out crowding branches, and spur close the laterals, it would be as well to forego shortening the reserved leaders till several green shoots have become an inch long; then, the sap being active, and the foliage sufficiently expanded to absorb and transpire, the leaders can be cut back to the lowest growing shoot but two, and thus a clear healthy lead will in general be secured.

Raspberry rods may be pruned back to a swelling bud or at the point where the shoot takes a curve. They then can be staked, and the ground cleared of wandering suckers.

When the berry-bearing shrubs are regulated, every one which is infested with moss or lichens ought to be well dredged with a mixture, of wood-ashes two parts, powdered lime the same, and coal-soot half a part, all by weight or measure. This done, while dew or hoar-frost is on the twigs, the ground should be forked, or turned over to make the plots and borders neat.

Apricot, peach, nectarine, plum and cherry trees on walls, ought to be pruned, the time being determined by the condition of the buds. It is never unseasonable to cut quite close all the projecting breast wood, and to disbud those at the back; but the well placed bearers that can be led in close to the wall ought to remain till some young shoots break, and begin to expand their leaves, for the reason just assigned under the direction for pruning the currant. After the walls are put in order, it will not be amiss to turn the soil, and sow a few light crops, such as lettuce, salad, and radish, but never within a yard of the trees.

Espalier apple and pear-trees are not shortened, unless the remote branches interfere with other trees: but all the small laterals and spurs ought to be pruned back to a fertile bud; and the boughs should then be secured close and in regular order to the stakes or trellis.

FLOWER GARDEN.

Sweep and roll lawns and gravel walks, trim away dead shoots of herbaceous plants, but still leave the ground undisturbed till March. It is better far to sow annual plants in pots, protecting them in frames, or over the gentle hot-beds ; time and security are thus gained. But beds of tulips ought to be cleared of weeds ; and ranunculus roots planted in beds, deeply prepared and enriched, about the end of the month.

Look over the auriculas, remove dead leaves, and top-dress the soil.

Polyanthuses in pots are also to be dressed with maiden turf loam mixed with a little old manure.

If there be dead wood in the evergreens it ought to be sawed or cut out—nothing more disfigures a laurel than such branches, which soon cause hollow places.

Scatter heath soil mixed with a little sandy loam over the American borders ; this dress will particularly assist the hardy azalias, by promoting the growth of young roots near the surface.

Prune hardy roses to low, well situated buds, whether they be bushes or standards—to confer vigorous growth and compact figure.

AGRICULTURAL   REPORTS.

GENERAL AGRICULTURAL REPORT FOR JANUARY.

At most previous corresponding periods of the year, we have had occasion to notice what is usually termed " seasonable" weather, but that of the past month has been the mildest, as a whole, almost ever recollected. For the first ten days, however, and about the 15th and 16th, the temperature was low, and which was productive of some rather sharp frosts, so as to produce ice, in exposed situations, of about an inch in thickness. Since the date last mentioned the atmosphere has continued unusually fine and open, but without being creative of much rain. Of snow, we have had very little, in any part of England. Notwithstanding that prevailing circumstances have been anything but favourable to the young wheats, it is gratifying to observe that they have not exhibited that rapidity of growth as might have been anticipated. True it is, that in some instances the plants have become proud and spindly, especially in bottoms ; but, generally speaking, we think there is no great reason to complain. All out-door farm labours are well in their place—the land has received frequent stirrings and workings, uninterrupted by superabundant moisture—while the fallows are much more free from weeds than could reasonably be expected.

The fine seed-time, in the autumn of last year, was a great boon to the agricultural body; since not only did it allow them to finish the sowing of the usual breadths of land with wheat, but many of them determined, when it was practicable—and particularly as that description of grain was yielding a fair return—to bring an increased number into cultivation. The ravages of the slug and other insects, have been only to a moderate—perhaps we might say limited—extent, compared with former years ; hence, should the months of February and March prove equally fine, the prospects for the next harvest are undoubtedly good. It has been argued that the present depressed prices of wheat will, doubtless, cause many large farms to grow less of that article this year; consequently, that a large crop cannot be fairly calculated upon. We take our stand upon a very different footing to this. That quotations are ruinously low, we admit ; but then a question arises in our minds, what other produce can, in the ordinary course of things, be made to give a greater return than wheat? If attention be the more directed to barley, oats, beans, or other grain, it is reasonable to suppose, that from their superabundance, even greater losses would be the result. It is not to be imagined that, because the value of the staple commodity is *now* beneath that which it ought to produce, that it is always to continue so. Our candid opinion is, that if the growth of wheat be once neglected in this country, distress and ruin would be speedily felt. There is one thing very evident : we must have it for our subsistence, and if not produced here, we shall be compelled to import more largely. Here, then, a question of the most vital importance to all classes of the community arises, which is—are we to make use of the appliances within ourselves (and which, by the way, are of no ordinary character), or are we, by our own neglect, to be dependant upon the foreigner? The former can be brought into action without difficulty ; the latter would inevitably produce a great national loss, never to be repaired. Take, for instance, a deficient harvest in this kingdom : say the yield of wheat has fallen two millions of quarters under an average of years, and then we shall soon find where " the shoe pinches." To purchase this immense supply, we should have to export not less than *four millions of sovereigns*, hard cash, which ought to be in free circulation amongst the home growers. It is a folly—as is here demonstrated—to wish for what are called " high" prices ; these neither benefit consumer or producer—indeed they are injurious, in the long run, to both—for the withdrawal of so much money from the country—and that too for ever—is an event, at any time, to be regretted ; the more so, as very little reciprocity of feeling is scarcely, if ever, evinced by the recipients abroad. But some have argued that the more corn we take the greater will be the demand for our manufactured goods. A greater fallacy than this never entered into the mind of man, as we shall presently show. Now, if we could find that the principles of reciprocity *were* recognised and adhered to, we could offer no opposition to an easy importation of grain ; but it certainly does occur to us that it would be as difficult to prove that it does exist, on anything like a liberal scale, as to solve the whole of the problems of Euclid, or give an example of the theorem of a " body *irresistible* meeting a body *immoveable !*" Although we may be considered as travelling somewhat out of the path usually allotted to us in an Agricultural Report, we beg to lay a few facts before our readers, in order to work out the position we have here assumed. If we take last year, we shall find that the exports, from this country to Russia, with a population of no less than sixty millions, was not 2,000,000*l.* ; to France, with thirty-two millions of inhabitants, 1,700,000*l.* ; to Prussia, having *fourteen millions,* not 200,000*l.*; to Spain, with the same amount of population, 500,000*l.* To Portugal, Sweden and Denmark, we send about one million seven-hundred and fifty thousand pounds worth of goods, while the number of inhabitants of those countries is about eight millions : hence, it will be observed that our exports to those parts—with a united population of about one hundred and twenty-eight millions, and from which we have derived,in the same period,an immense supply of wheat—exceeded little more than 5,000,000*l.* Why, our shipments to the West-India Islands, and to the North American and Australian Colonies, with a population of only two millions and a half, exceeded 7,500,000*l.*; or about one half more than those to the countries above named, with their hundred and twenty-eight millions! To particularize further, we might add that, if anything were requisite to show the necessity of giving ample protection to the capital and labour employed in the cultivation of the land in the United Kingdom, and to prove more forcibly that we should endeavour, as the foreigners are, to have the means of subsistence within ourselves, we might adduce the following curious and important statement of the proportion per head which the population of several foreign countries and British Colonies received of British exports last year : Prussia consumed, per head, 3½d. worth; Russia, 5d.; Portugal, 8d.; Spain, 8d.; Sweden, 9d.; Denmark, 11d.; France, 11d.; the United States of America, 17s.; Australian Colonies, 11*l.* 15s.; West-Indies, 3*l.* 12s.; and our North American Provinces, 1*l.* 11s. 6d.! It is also a singular and instructive fact, that, while Russia receives from us articles of the value of only 2,000,000*l.*, Great Britain annually pays to that nation a balance, over and above the value of the goods she sends her, ranging from 5,000,000*l.* to 6,000,000*l.*! This does not look *much* like reciprocity, at least not to our way of thinking; but "facts are stubborn things," and so, we think, they will ever continue.

The extremely dull state of the Corn trade, and the miserably low prices consequent thereon, have been productive of great injury to the interests of the Agriculturists. The operative class has likewise suffered to an extent hitherto almost unknown; and this leads us to the consideration of the future prospect of the trade. To arrive at anything like an accurate conclusion on this head would, in the absence of any official details, by which we could form a pretty correct opinion as to the actual supply of English wheat on hand, be a matter of no little difficulty. It seems to be generally understood that the aggregate produce in this country last year was rather over-rated by some of the dealers. In the county of Essex, in particular, the yield has exhibited a considerable falling off; and we cannot conceal the fact from our readers that we have nearly or quite a sufficiency on hand, including, of course, the foreign supplies, to meet every demand until next harvest. There is one thing very much opposed to any national advance in the currencies for some time to come, viz., the excellent quality of the grain now in the hands of the growers. We could sincerely wish the farmers to receive fair returns for their skill and industry, but it would ill become us to give publicity to any opinion or advice by which they might be misled. Prices may rise somewhat above their present level ; but we much question whether they will this season come up to that obtained during any period of 1841.

The early lambing season has gone on remarkably well, and been productive of a fine fall of strong and healthy lambs; but, as respects the epidemic, we regret to observe that very numerous instances have occurred of a fatal character. Depastured stock has fared unusually well, in consequence of the plenteous supply of herbage and succulent roots.

The working of the tariff has been closely watched by those most immediately interested. On this occasion, we have to notice very scanty imports of stock from any quarter into England, while their quality has certainly been beneath an average. Some of the supporters of the present measure refer, with some apparent degree of satisfaction, to what they consider the limited arrivals, but it should be borne in mind that there is every prospect of a very great and decided increase in the numbers, as well as a great improvement in the condition, of the importations which will take place in the spring. Sir Robert Peel told us that we had nothing whatever to fear from Spain, from the impossibility of bringing beasts across the Bay of Biscay, but what will be said when we intimate that the "Lady Mary Wood" steamer brought in safety through the tremendous gale that occurred on the 13th, eighteen oxen across that dangerous portion of our navigation ? As yet, nothing has arrived at Liverpool; but preparations are in progress to bring large quantities to that port from Spain. The following statement will show the total numbers which have arrived under the new act :—

	Beasts.	Cows.	Sheep.	Pigs.
From Germany..	1228	361	290	101
Spain	992	134	230	—
Holland ..	672	220	--	40
France....	401	38	140	—
Total..	3273	753	660	181

Forming no less than 4,867 head, or an increase over our last month's statement of 655—the latter being the importations from the 1st till the 26th.

The general state of the demand for live stock in Smithfield—if we except that for veal having ruled firm—since our last, has been inanimate, and the quotations have suffered some abatement, owing, in a great measure, to the immense arrivals of country slaughtered meat up to Newgate and Leadenhall markets. We are glad to state that comparatively few of the beasts have been affected with the disease; but the sheep have come to hand in very bad condition, and great losses have in consequence occurred on the roads. The supplies have comprised about 13,500 beasts, 124,000 sheep, 1,100 calves, and 2,600 pigs ; the former of which have been derived as follows :—About 2,000 Scots and homebreds, from Norfolk, Suffolk, Essex, and Cambridgeshire; 3,000 short horns and runts, from Lincolnshire, Leicestershire, and Northamptonshire; 2,000 short horns, runts, Devons, and Irish beasts, from our western and midland districts ; 3,400 of various breeds, from other parts of England ; 230 horned and polled Scots, by sea from Scotland ; 200, *via* Liverpool, from Ireland ; the remainder being chiefly brought in from the neighbourhood of the metropolis. The prices have ranged thus :— Beef, from 3s. 2d. to 4s. 6d.; mutton, 3s. 4d. to 4s. 6d.; veal, 4s. 10d. to 5s. 8d.; and pork, 3s. 6d. to 4s. 0d. per 8lbs. to sink the offals.

A STATEMENT and COMPARISON of the SUP-
PLIES and PRICES of FAT STOCK, exhibited
and sold in SMITHFIELD CATTLE MARKET, on
Monday, Jan. 24, 1842, and Monday, Jan. 23, 1843.

At per 8lbs. to sink the offals.

	Jan. 24, 1842.		Jan. 23, 1843.	
	s. d.	s. d.	s. d.	s. d.
Coarse & inferior Beasts	3 2 to	3 6 ..	3 0	3 4
Second quality do.	3 8	3 10 ..	3 6	3 8
Prime large Oxen......	4 0·	4 4 ..	3 10	4 0
Prime Scots, &c......	4 6	4 8 ..	4 2	4 4
Coarse & inferior Sheep	3 4	3 8 ..	3 0	3 2
Second quality do.	3 10	4 2 .	3 4	3 6
Prime coarse woolled do.	4 4	4 6 .	3 8	3 10
Prime Southdown do..	4 8	4 10 ..	4 0	4 4
Large coarse Calves ..	4 10	5 2 ..	4 2	4 10
Prime small ditto	5 4	5 6 ..	5 0	5 4
Large Hogs............	4 6	5 0 ..	3 10	4 4
Neat small Porkers ..	5 2	5 4 ..	4 6	4 8

SUPPLIES.

	Jan. 24, 1842.	Jan. 23, 1843.
Beasts................	2,741	2,698
Sheep	24,020	26,720
Calves...............	130	76
Pigs.................	412	381

The demand at Newgate and Leadenhall markets has been very dull, at low quotations. There
have been received about 3,000 carcasses weekly
from Scotland and various parts of England. Beef
has sold at from 3s. to 3s. 8d.; mutton, 3s. to 4s.;
veal, 4s. 2d. to 5s. 6d.; and pork, 3s. 10d. to 4s. 6d.
per 8lbs. by the carcass.

AGRICULTURAL REPORT FOR JANUARY.

We continue to witness the regular progress of
the growing crops. Large breadths of wheat of a
beautiful verdure, but by no means luxuriant,
that is, unduly gay; this we can testify, as refers
to the condition of wheat in the east of Berkshire. We, therefore, can by no means justify the
assertions of some who tell us of an untimely advance. However, it is proper to observe, that
from a Northamptonshire correspondent there is
advice of an unprecedented healthy verdure, and
that many have fed off the wheats with sheep; but
no mention whatever is made of any injury, either
incurred or to be apprehended—on the contrary,
the writer asserts the confident hopes of the
growers.

Some frosts have occurred, and January is much
colder than was December. The unusual depression of the barometer (as it prognosticated) was
followed by a fierce tempest, which broke or tore
up some trees, destroyed chimney-pots, and dis-
placed much thatch; but the rain was wholly dis-
proportionate to the fall of the mercury, and that
was soon contrasted by a rise almost equal to the
previous depression.

The meteorology of the first month warrants
the hopes of a fine season; and if February be of
its accustomed character, and the rains be succeeded by a drying but not rigorous March, the
prospects will be cheering indeed.

Of crops, besides the growing wheat, we can
form but little judgment. Clover is good—so are
the vetches, but no conclusion can be yet arrived
at; the land, however, turns up most capitally,
and a famous bed is thus preparing for all the
spring corn. What a contrast with the condition
of the ground in 1842!

The flocks of sheep appear to be very fine, and
the lambing season has hitherto been propitious.

There are increasing evidences of the stimulus
which has been applied to chemical research. New
manures multiply, but we question whether there
be not much of empiricism abroad. Were our
own rich materials economised, we should find
occasion to congratulate ourselves. The Chinese
are patterns; not a grain of ordure is wasted by
them; all is applied with industry, and the land
becomes the grand laboratory of animal excretions.

If we are likely to hold intercourse with this
strange and exclusive people, it will be wise to
observe and copy them in all things which are
found to produce great results.

But though many things which are offered to
the farmer be useless, it is proper to say that
some we are acquainted with flatter themselves
as possessing manures of recent discovery which
will extensively fertilize, at a very trifling cost of
money or labour. We propose to keep in view
one or more trials that are likely to be made close
at hand. Whoever can cause the land which now
yields three and a half quarters to produce five
per acre, will be a benefactor to the state, and
hereupon it is rational to entertain hopes. Something indeed must be done to increase produce, in
lieu of indulging in the vain expectation of lower
rents and higher prices.

Supply and the demand. These are the governing principles which render nugatory all the enactments of law; and were the agriculturists
really scientific, and acquainted with the components of land and crops, they would not seek for
or depend upon scales or restrictions, which, in
solemn fact, tend to little else than to produce dangerous speculations and fictitious reports.—Jan. 25.

SOMERSETSHIRE.

I now commence my report after the completion of
another year, but from which in its events must the
matter it contains be chosen, grounding the prospects
before us on the facts of the past. 1842 will for many
reasons be a marked one to the agriculturist, a year of
changes, of perplexity, and loss; and yet as far as refers
to the seasons we shall seldom witness more favourable
ones, and should the next be similar, we may look for
great abundance, but on this it would be unwise to
speculate. If we compare the appearance of the wheat
in ground with last year, it will be generally acknowledged there is scarcely any comparison; the danger
and the eventual deficiency in the crop last year, arose
from seed and plant being destroyed by the wet, and
the state of the land when put in; but this year no seed
could have come up better, or thicker, and the only
fear is its expending itself; it certainly looks strong and
healthy, but much more forward than is thought desirable; that an unusual breadth is put in, I think admits
of no doubt, and should the crop be no better than the
last year the quantity will far exceed it, but with such
a season there is a greater prospect of ·abundance.
Vetches are also very forward, and we have not for
years saved so much hay from the growth of grass; our
fields have scarce the least appearance of winter, and
there is a freshness in the green that reminds one of the
spring rather. Complaints are made of the winter roots
growing out, and spoiling from the mildness of the
season; cowslips were gathered in the field not long
before the shortest day. Although it has been so unusually unfavourable to the butcher, and they have in
many instances suffered by having more meat killed
than demand for it, there is from the scarcity of stock
a tendency already to advance; but it is expected later
in the spring there will not be the usual scarcity of the
season, many of the dairy farmers having to winter-

graze their dairy cows, in consequence of so many of them proving barren, so much so, that we may expect a good sale for cows and calves to supply their places. Mutton is much scarcer, the low price has caused a good consumption. The lambing season has commenced favourably, the ewes being in good condition. The price of pork has gone down to 6s. 6d. per 20 lbs., but it has now rallied to 6s. 9d. to 7s.; and bacon 4½d. to 5½d. per lb. by the side. Cheese has also shared the depression, although the make is decidedly less than last year, 42s. to 50s. having been about the best prices; and last week there was a very poor sale, but it is expected the demand will improve should we have a dryer atmosphere. Good, or rather extra beef, has not been under 10s., with a good demand; but that which was only half fat was a drug on the market, as yet at the low price, 6s. 6d. to 7s. per score, such were purchased, it occasioned considerable slaughter, and has made a proportionate clearance of live stock. The sale of beef and pork, *sold for foreign*, has been much lessened, and unless our fresh meats are much higher than they have been since the alteration of the tariff, there is nothing to be feared from salt meat; and if parties have sent out orders, grounded on the demand a few months back, they will be deceived, novelty had more to do with that demand; and with it, I am persuaded, in these parts the sale will cease also. If the grazier can begin by purchasing his stock in place, so as to sell at from 7s. to 9s., according to quality, at a profit, he will not be affected much by foreign competition. As regards the alteration in the corn laws, no doubt the consumer is benefited, but it makes the corn trade one of the worst capital can be engaged safely in, and inflicts an injury on those growers who stand in need of the greatest protection; for, in consequence of the quantity poured in to meet the lowest duty, and with the panic which ensued rents were to be made up *at very low prices* by large quantities *from a deficient* produce per acre, forced into the market just at the worst time for sale, the consequence is, that when the deficiency begins to be apparent from the supplies falling off, the price

rises too late to benefit the parties who are least able to bear the low prices; at the present time there, is apparently, in *this country much less of wheat in the growers' hands than for years*, and that in comparatively few hands. Of barley, beans, oats, and cloverseed, there is more than an average stock; but of oats and barley, I should consider there was about the usual consumption, and will not accumulate in stock, as there is no disposition to buy these articles beyond the usual wants of the trade. But the consumption of beans has from some cause much fallen off, and a good many that have appeared have gone into store. Peas have also with difficulty found buyers. The price of cloverseed is not fixed, the quality is good, and the quantity saved exceeds greatly what it has been for years: I have heard of prices from 36s. to 50s. per cwt., very little yet sold. I should quote the price of grain as follows:—wheat, 62 to 65 lbs. per bushel, 6s. 3d. to 6s. 9d., red, 5s. 4d. to 6s. 3d.; flour, per 280 lbs., 34s. to 37s.; barley, 3s. to 3s. 3d., grinding and malting, 3s. 3d. to 3s. 8d.; beans, 3s. 8d. to 4s., old, 4s. 3d. to 4s. 6d. Since the above was written, the effect of the rise in London has become more apparent, and at Bridgwater, yesterday, 6s. 9d. was refused for very prime white, 64 lbs. per bushel; flour, 37s. to 38s. was the price some millers stood for; foreign wheat would fetch full 4s. per qr. more than three weeks since, but to have a good sale English must sell higher; to show how low we have been, flour has been down to 34s.; the Union contract has been taken as low as 4½d., but generally at 5d. to 5½d. best 4lb. loaves. Neither millers or bakers have an average stock, and there is an increasing conviction that the crop was much overrated. Beans are still a drug. We have had this week several hail storms, and Mendip has been covered with snow; last evening it froze, but about the middle of the night the wind got round to the south-west, and it was rough, accompanied with rain; it is now west, and has blown all the day a *hurricane*, with occasional showers, and trees falling, &c., &c., and we shall hear, I expect, of much damage.—Jan. 13.

AGRICULTURAL INTELLIGENCE, FAIRS, &c.

OSWESTRY FAIR.—The supply of sheep was small; good mutton averaged fully 5½d. per lb., inferior 5d., bacon pigs and porkers 3½d. An improvement of 3s. to 4s. per head took place in the price of small stores, for which there was a considerable demand. The cattle market was a bad one, good beef not exceeding 5d., and lean stock almost unsaleable. Good cows and calves were enquired after, and sold tolerably well, there being few in market.

NEWARK FAT STOCK MARKET, on Tuesday last, was well supplied with beasts and sheep of a very good quality, which realised pretty good prices.

HIGHLAND AND AGRICULTURAL SOCIETY.—At the late general meeting of this Society, it was stated that a gold medal had been awarded by the Committee to James Stuart Menteath, Esq., yr. of Closeburn, for a paper on the Geology of Dumfries-shire, accompanied by a map and an extensive collection of specimens: a premium of twenty sovereigns was voted to George Bell, Esq., Woodhouselees, for a distinct report, with plans and specifications, of a tile-work suited for proprietors or tenants who may wish to manufacture drain tiles for their own use. Mr. Scott, of Craigmuie, made a report of the progress which had been made in obtaining subscribers for the society's journal and transactions, at a reduced price. He need not remind the meeting that the desirable object could only be attained by guaranteeing to the publishers a certain number of subscribers. The privilege of obtaining the work on the terms proposed was open to the members of this society, and to the members of

local associations in communication with the society, to whom it had also been extended. If there were 1,500 subscribers, the publishers had agreed to make the price two shillings to these classes. Every exertion had been made by the committee, by sending circulars and otherwise, to induce the members to come forward; and he was happy to report, that 880 members of the society had subscribed, and 131 members out of seventy local societies, making a total of 1,011. Though this fell short of the number required, yet he had no doubt it would soon be made up, as the proposition had been favourably received by every one; and he had no doubt the delay that had taken place, on the part of many members, was to be imputed entirely to oversight. He begged that the members present would urge upon their friends to delay no longer; as the last number of the old series of the Journal would be published in March, and the first number of the new series would be issued in June. He was gratified to state that this matter had attracted the attention of members of local societies in the north of England; and the publishers had handsomely agreed to extend to them the same privileges with the members of this society and of the local agricultural societies of Scotland. He might take this opportunity of stating, also, that measures were in process by the Directors for making up a complete list of all the local societies in Scotland; and he would be glad if gentlemen would assist the committee by giving information respecting the associations in their respective neighbourhoods. Mr. Norman Lockhart reported the preliminary arrangements in progress for the Glasgow Cattle Show in 1844. Sir William Jardine, in the absence of Lord Greenock, gave in a report on the state of the museum. In every respect that institution kept up its interest; and, as the Society were aware, it was the best arranged and the most capable of being rendered useful of any similar Museum in the country. In the year 1841, 3,700 individuals visited the Museum; last year no fewer than 10,286 had inscribed their names in the visitors' book. These consisted of persons of all ranks and classes, and presented a gratifying instance of the interest which the museum had excited. The donations of models, implements, roots, seeds, &c., continued to flow in as before; and he might particularly notice a splendid collection of geological specimens of Dumfries-shire, from Mr. Menteath, younger, of Closeburn. The monthly meetings of the Society, held in the museum, continued to be as attractive as hitherto. The Directors had resolved to change the hour of meeting to three in the afternoon, that the farmers might attend immediately after the market. It was intended that papers of practical interest should be read at these meetings, as well as papers of a more scientific character; and it would be well if those who had influence would urge them to attend and take part in the discussions that took place, as their practical experience would be of much value to those who were more intimately engaged with scientific pursuits. In the establishment for 1843 we find (connected with this district); *Vice-Presidents*—the Right Hon. William, Earl of Mansfield, K.T.; *Extraordinary Directors*—the Right Hon. Lord Wm. Douglas; *Ordinary Directors,* —Sir William Jardine of Applegarth, Bart.; Norman Lockhart, Esq., Tarbrax; William Scott, Esq., of Craigmuie; James Allan Dalzell, Esq., Whitehouse Villa; *Chairman of Standing Committees, Cottages*— William Grierson Yorstoun of Garroch; *Deputy Chairman of Monthly Meetings*—Sir William Jardine, Bart.

ROSS FARMERS' CLUB.—The members of this club held their annual meeting at the New Inn, on

Thursday last, when the accounts were audited, leaving a considerable balance in the treasurer's hands. H. Chellingworth, Esq. was unanimously elected president for the ensuing year, and F. Woodall, Esq. vice-president; and a vote of thanks was passed to the secretary (Mr. Price, of Bechell), for the assiduity and attention he had paid to the society hitherto; after which the members sat down to a most excellent dinner, and the whole passed off with much spirit.

FRAMLINGHAM FARMERS' CLUB.— SUBJECTS FOR THE YEAR.—Feb. 14, The propriety of paying more attention to preserving the drainage from our farm yards—Mr. Jeaffreson. March 14, The best description of Vegetables, to cultivate for stock feeding—Mr. G. Goodwyn. April 11, Merits of rye grass, and other artificial grasses'—Mr. Chapman. May 16, On the payment of labourers' wages, partly in kind—Mr. Peirson. June 13, The management of swine—Mr. E. Gooch. July 11, The dairy *versus* grazing—Mr. James Read. August, no meeting. September 5, The best mode of breaking up pasture; also the best way of laying down old ploughed land to permanent pasture—Mr. J. Laws. October 10, The desirability of changing occupations at New, instead of Old Michaelmas—Mr. James Barker, Jun. November 7, Annual meeting.

LOUGHBOROUGH AGRICULTURAL ASSOCIATION.—The Members of this Association held their fourth quarterly meeting for the discussion of subjects connected with the welfare of agriculture, on Thursday last (the 19th inst.), at the Plough Inn, Loughborough; S. B. Wild, Esq., of Ibstock, in the chair. The subject for discussion was ably introduced by Mr. Walker, of Bradmore, "On the best method of depositing grain and small seeds;" and some valuable practical knowledge on this important branch of agriculture was displayed by several members. At the close of the discussion, the following resolution was agreed to:—" That this meeting recommends the drill system as the best method of depositing grain and seeds, and that grain be placed not more than two inches deep, and small seeds one inch."

REVIEW OF THE CORN TRADE

DURING THE MONTH OF JANUARY.

The new year has not commenced under favourable circumstances to the cultivators of British and Irish fields. For that portion of the crop of 1842, which they have forwarded heretofore to market for sale, they have obtained prices much under the expenses of its production, and strong doubts and much anxiety have been created in their minds respecting the future; for the alteration in the corn laws, and the reduction in the duties charged on the importation of various articles of foreign agricultural produce, continue to be universally considered as by no means favourable to the agricultural interest of the United Kingdom. Experience has taught the farmers the expenses of grain production at home, but they know not the lowest price at which foreign agricultural produce can be profitably sold in this country. After payment of rent, local and public taxes, tithes, fair wages to their labourers, and numerous other expences attending tillage in this country, they are practically convinced that, when the average price of British grown wheat is under 58s. per qr., the farmer suffers in his capital; and in the existing state of the corn trade, therefore, they feel little confidence in their ability successfully and profitably to cultivate the fields of their forefathers hereafter. Within the last quarter of a year, the average price of wheat has been under 47s. per

quarter, and, during the same period in the current year, similar causes may produce a similar effect on the value of their property. Now, in the minds of our farmers, an impression has been created that even this low average cannot prevent the importation of foreign wheat of fine quality into this country for consumption. Polish wheats are generally worth from 7s. to 10s. per qr. more in Mark-lane than the average price of English wheat; and as in Poland rents and tithes are unknown, and as the field-labour is performed by half-starved and unpaid serfs and slaves, the great land-proprietors generally on the continent of Europe can afford to pay, we may say, under all circumstances, our maximum duty, and have sufficient profit to themselves also, after payment of freight and all the other expences of importation into this country. The prospects, therefore, of the agricultural interest are at the present time any thing but cheering, for only by short crops in future have they any great chance of reaping remunerating prices for their wheat produce. For the remainder of their wheat, however, of 1842, some prospect exists at present that remunerating prices may soon be obtained. The consumption of wheat during the last four months has been chiefly supplied by the importers of foreign wheat, and the quantity of this description in granary has consequently been very materially reduced since that period. . Of duty-paid wheat not much above half a million of quarters now remains in the granaries, and under the Queen's lock the quantity is somewhere about two hundred thousand quarters, the cost price of which has been so high, that to pay our present duty would subject its proprietors to a considerable pecuniary loss. It is, therefore, not probable that this bonded wheat will be entered for home use, until a considerable improvement in its present value occur; and the farmers, therefore, may naturally conclude that in the wheat markets, until the end of June at all events, their property cannot be interfered with, except by the small quantity of foreign duty-paid wheats at present in the United Kingdom. There, therefore, as we have said above, may exist fair grounds for expectations and hopes that the remainder of last year's crop may still be disposed of at prices which may in some measure remunerate the British growers for its cultivation. During last month, indeed, some improvement, but to no great extent, in the value of various descriptions of grain actually occurred; and so long as the farmer's deliveries are confined within the bounds of prudence and moderation, this advance will be maintained, and may even be increased, until the arrival of the time when our supplies may be again rendered redundant by foreign importations. This, however, cannot be the case to any extent before the month of July, or the beginning of next harvest season; and then prices, as they usually are at that season of the year, will be chiefly regulated by the appearance of the crops in the fields, and by the state of the weather. Our farmers have, therefore, before them the prospect of nearly exclusively supplying the markets with wheat during the next four or five months—a privilege which it would be well for the best interests of the United Kingdom if the law gave to them in all times, and under all circumstances, excepting when actual want may be the consequence of unfavourable seasons; and there is, therefore, as we have already said, a chance at all events that, by prudential management, a partial degree of prosperity may be restored to them, although we much fear that it cannot be lasting in the present state of the agricultural laws of the British Empire. A moderate advance in the value of grain during the next six months must be attended by an universal good; indeed the benefit will be much more extensively felt by our artizans and commercial and manufacturing labourers, than by the landholders, the farmers, and the field labourers themselves; the agricultural interest having always within itself abundance of provision for immediate support, even under the most adverse circumstances, but with the other classes in our society circumstances are widely different indeed. Bad seasons and damaged crops, no doubt, may render occasional supplies of foreign food absolutely necessary; but when this misfortune occurs, distress amongst the manufacturing and trading interests is the inevitable consequence. During the last four or five years we have had but too much expetience of the evil consequences to commerce of large supplies of foreign grain, even before the late alteration of the corn law gave encouragement to this description of trade. This most extensive importation of foreign grain has not been attended during these years by any corresponding increase in the quantity or in the value of British goods exported to those empires, kingdoms, and states, from which such immense supplies of grain and provi-

sions have been received by us. On the contrary, the custom-house returns but too clearly establish the melancholy fact that annually have our exports of manufactures to these foreign grain-exporting states been on the decline. In our trade with any of them, reciprocity exists not. We are compelled to pay for their agricultural produce in the precious metals, and this money never is again remitted to this country in exchange for any article produced by British or by Irish industry. It is now embarked in the improvement of the fields in those states to which it has been remitted, and in extending their manufactures, thereby rendering them annually more and more independent of British manufactures, in proportion to the value of the grain and provisions which we receive from them. This is not the way to extend the foreign consumption of British manufactures, for a barter trade in clothing and provisions has never yet been established betwixt any two foreign communities, and the whole history of civilized society most abundantly has established the painful fact that it never can. The unfortunate state of our grain crops latterly, joined to the reduction made in the import duties on various articles of foreign produce and manufactures, and to the alteration effected in the corn laws during the last session of Parliament, is now visibly making a deep inroad on our finances themselves; to which, unless some bar be immediately raised, it is impossible to predict the fatal consequences which may ensue to the people in general. In the year 1842, we paid to foreign agriculturists upwards of six millions sterling in money for wheat alone, which is a dead loss now to the British nation. So far from having increased the foreign demand for manufactured goods, the effect has been decidedly the reverse; and it has also most materially decreased the home consumption of goods amongst the landholders, farmers, and the agricultural labourers; and we cannot be surprised that manufacturing distress has been the natural effect of this most unfortunate state of our affairs. Had these six millions sterling been paid to British farmers for provisions, instead of having been remitted to foreign nations in payment for foreign wheat, that sum would never have been withdrawn from circulation in this country; but it would have been employed now at home in increasing the wages of the industrious classes of society generally. This, however, is only a small part of the money remitted during 1842 to foreigners in exchange for their manufactures, and for many articles of their agricultural produce, which, under protective laws, we could grow or manufacture in far greater perfection at home. To this false system of free trade are we now indebted for even a deficient revenue. The money which we pay to foreigners for various articles of their production would be far more profitably employed now had it been paid away to our workmen at home for similar articles. For instance, in minor matters even, we cannot at the same moment pay for and wear French boots and English ones; and if we prefer the foreign ones, we throw the English makers out of employment. Now, so long as this most impolitic trade exists—by which our money is sent to foreigners in exchange for grain, provisions, or for any description of foreign manufacture, which we can manufacture at home—so long must distress continue to exist amongst all the productive classes in British society. Poverty must continue to be their chief companion, and low wages must deprive them of those means of living which they enjoyed under laws patriotic and protective to home agriculture and to internal industry. The deficiency now existing in our public revenue has its origin, we repeat, solely in the reduction—or, we may more truly say, in the want of living wages amongst many of the industrious classes. The money which would have been employed by them in the consumption of duty-paid articles has been paid away for foreign grain and for foreign labour, and thus is the revenue injured by encouraging foreign instead of English labourers. A few, and only a very few, of the Cotton Lords may make princely fortunes on the ruins of British agriculture, and on the reduction of the wages latterly paid to the manufacturing labourers ; but this selfish principle will not be long permitted to exist within the United Kingdom ; for if it be tolerated only for a few years, the public creditor may begin to whistle for his dividend, which assuredly cannot be paid so long as the wages of the industrious afford them not the means of paying for and consuming duty-paying articles. Income-taxes and property-taxes may be doubled and tripled on the community, but without the aid of powerful indirect taxation, they can, under no circumstances, be of any avail in restoring the national finances. Under the influence and protection of laws now either repealed entirely—or, at all events, modified—large crops formerly rendered our agricultural interest flourishing. No money was then paid away for foreign agricultural produce, unless when the crops at home were bad. It remained in active circulation at home. It rendered labour abundant, increased the wages of industry, and reduced the expenses of living. It rendered the revenue more than equal to the public expenditure, and it filled the people with gladness. A material improvement in the value of agricultural produce may, however, take place within the next six months ; and even this alteration will do good to the community, short though the period may be in which it may be enjoyed. But, after all, the only true plan for the restoration of general prosperity is to enact laws by which our internal industry may be sufficiently protected. With our immense capital, energy, and science, applied to agricultural, commercial, and manufacturing improvements at home, double our present population may be well fed and productively employed. The wages of labour may then be always placed above the expenses of living, whatever may be their amount, and no complaints will be made afterwards of any deficiency existing in that part, at all events, of our revenue which is collected by the officers of the excise.

But now circumstances have put it beyond the power even of the Anti-Corn Law Leaguers themselves, any longer to attribute the partial distress to which a portion of the manufacturer's operatives have latterly been subjected, to the high price of provisions ; for, during the last half year at any rate, wheat has certainly been far under the price at which it can be, with profit to the grower, produced in this country ; and had the doctrines inculcated by these our modern political economists, *of the possibility of a purely barter trade existing amongst nations in the present artificial state of civilised society,* any foundation whatever, the vast quantities of grain which we have imported during the last five years from foreign nations, should long before this time have illustrated the soundness of these principles, and enabled them to point to a happy, well paid, and well

employed manufacturing population for a confirmation of the good conferred by their acts on the inhabitants generally of the United Kingdom. The commercial operatives, however, now know by experience, that when the value of provisions is reduced by foreign supplies, their wages are much more in proportion reduced by the same cause. The home market they know to be the most valuable, because the most extensive, for the consumption of British manufactured goods, and this channel for consumption mainly depends on agricultural prosperity. Our colonies and India possessions are the next best consumers, for throughout Europe and the United States of North America, our free trade laws have been met by the imposition of nearly prohibitory duties on the importation of British goods into any one of them, and yearly now does our export commerce with them decline. The Anti-Corn Law Leaguers now finding little or rather no favour in the eyes of the manufacturing labourers, are turning their attention to our agricultural labourers, and are extending to them their philanthropy. Here, however, their labour is equally unfortunate and unproductive, for the agriculturists, consisting of at least two millions and a half of males, cannot understand how their condition in life can be improved by our purchasing the produce of foreign fields, and giving employment to foreign labourers in producing grain and many other descriptions of provisions, which can be most abundantly grown at home by themselves. When a real equality in circumstances is established amongst nations, when British labourers come on an equality in mind, in intelligence, and in living, with those of Russia or of Poland ; when the wealth of the United Kingdom, and that of the corn districts in Europe may be placed on a level, then indeed something like reciprocity in trading may be established. The equal circumstances may then teach the free trade doctrine of giving and receiving according to their wants amongst nations ; but so long as the immense riches of Great Britain render the customs and manners of the population so very different to those in any other country, a barter trade cannot exist. The time, however, must speedily arrive when an unanimous demand will be made on the British legislature by the British people, for protection to their industry in our markets of consumption against the industry of all foreign communities. Until this be done the state of the British empire must continue to be unsatisfactory in the extreme, and none will suffer more than those whose labour is their property, until some change in the present system be effected.

In the barley trade the month of January has effected very little alteration. The finest samples have advanced somewhere about 1s. per qr. ; but this, unfortunately, has been occasioned by small supplies of the finest qualities, and certainly not by any increased consumption. The consumption of malt has most materially fallen off during the year 1842, and we fear much that this decrease must annually occur in a greater degree until the cause in which it has its origin be removed. During the last session of Parliament the attention of the representatives of the British empire was mainly directed to our tariff of Custom-house duties, which were materially reduced, we presume chiefly for the encouragement of foreign labourers, and of foreign industry, by making the British markets more profitable to them, and by enabling them to possess themselves of a share of our surplus money, the employment of which at home is now felt to be so difficult and unprofitable. To the excise laws no attention was given, nor was any alteration in them attempted either by her Majesty's Ministers, or by the Opposition during the last year. The reduction of the duties levied on foreign wines and on foreign spirits was mentioned, but the reduction of the duty levied in England on British spirits did not enter, even for one day, into the contemplation of the British legislature. These duties are upwards of three hundred and fifty per cent. on the original value of spirits, and in this source alone originates the immoral practice of smuggling. In affording relief to the inhabitants of the United Kingdom generally all the duties levied by the excise should have been very materially reduced, for by these means alone can consumption be legitimately increased, and an addition be made to the productive employment of many of the industrious classes of society. By the reduction of the duty now charged on British spirits, consumed in England for instance, the labour and profit of producing an additional quantity of oats and barley, to the extent of not less than half a million of quarters, would be gained by the community, the revenue would be increased, and it is no paradox to assert that at the same time the consumption of ardent spirits by the British people would be most materially decreased. Moderate duties in England, such as they now are in Scotland and in Ireland, would destroy the trade of the smuggler by rendering it no longer profitable; and in this highly important alteration would the temptation to drunkenness be in a considerable degree suppressed. Somehow or other, spirits, which have paid no duty, possess, we may almost say, an exclusive charm for the consumption of the people; and the encouragement which the high spirit duties in England hold out to the illicit trader, both at home and abroad, renders the field for smuggling at present not to be resisted. The quantity now annually and illegally imported, and passed into use, cannot be less than ten millions of gallons; on which the British Government obtains no revenue, and in the production of which neither the British farmer, the British workmen, nor the British distiller receives either useful employment or profit. It must therefore be apparent that, for the interest of morality amongst the people, for the interest of the public revenue, for the interest of the improvements in agriculture, and for the extension of productive employment amongst the industrious classes of society generally, a material alteration in the duty now imposed on home-made spirits in England, should be effected immediately on the next meeting of parliament. The British distillers form a most important class in society. By them, even under the existing most impolitic system, the public revenue is benefited to the extent of at least six millions sterling annually, and to grant to them facilities for increasing their operations in England is certainly a much greater national advantage than to encourage the distillers of France or of Holland. Those who consume brandy and geneva can well afford to pay the present import duty, but it is widely different with the great mass of the community. Our rectifiers can give all the flavour to British brandy and gin which the foreign distillers can do, and in real wholesomeness no comparison can be made. For the sake of the public health, therefore, as well as for that of morality, smuggling of spirits should be suppressed, and fair encouragement should be

given to the manufacturers of good spirits at home. We have stated that high spirit duties in England prevent an additional consumption of British grain to a very considerable extent; and our high malt duty prevents the quantity of barley now used by the public brewers from being much more than doubled; for so far from the consumption of malt keeping pace with the increase of population, it has annually been falling away, until the quantity now used by the licensed brewers has declined to little above three millions and a half of quarters. Under a proper system of taxation, and under better regulations for the maltsters than the present excise laws permit, the consumption of barley by the brewers may, in a very few years, be more than tripled. A duty of 1s. per bushel imposed on barley intended to be converted into malt, and permission to the maltster to use his experience and his talents in producing the best article possible, would speedily be attended by this much desired effect. As matters now are regulated, in many instances, no science can enable the maltster to accomplish his own intentions. He is now compelled to apply the same rules to his trade, whether the barley be flinty or soft, whether it be grown in a warm or a cold climate, and whether the temperature at the time of malting be suitable or not for his operation. If the excise permitted him to convert his barley into malt, according to circumstances, a superior article would always be the result of his labour, and to charge the duty on the raw barley itself would remove every objection which can now be made to our proposed alteration. It would save the exciseman a great deal of very useless trouble, and it would also save the public the still more useless expense of maintaining many officers, who would be much better employed in following up pursuits far more useful to the public, though certainly less profitable to themselves. It only requires a small portion of nerve to be exerted by the Chancellor of the Exchequer to enable him to remove, at all events, a considerable part of the depression under which the community is now labouring. The cultivation of at least two millions of acres of land, now entirely unproductive, will be one effect necessarily arising from the reduction in the present rate of the malt duty. When accomplished, this improvement will add to the value of land rents at least two millions sterling annually, and thus increase the nation's wealth; it will likewise give a great deal of productive employment annually to many thousands of families now unemployed, and the profits arising from this source alone would go far in paying for any expence which the increased consumption of beer would occasion. Another powerful reason for the reduction of the malt duty to some point within moderation, may be found in the solid benefit which the community would derive from the enjoyment of cheap and unadulterated beer. At present more than one half of the population have not the means to pay for even the smallest pittance of this article, not more to them a luxury than a necessary of life; whilst the other half, whose incomes permit the use of it, consume it in a highly adulterated state, and they are in fact defrauded by by many of the vendors, who cannot afford to sell it at any thing like moderate prices, unless after a mixture with it of the most deleterious ingredients. A reduction in the malt duty and an alteration in the regulations, by which the maltsters are at present restricted in their operations, is a duty, therefore, which the legislature imperatively owes to the best interests of the inhabitants of the United Kingdom. No doubt can be entertained of the revenue drawn from this source eventually being improved by a financial measure of this description, for the increased consumption would render an increased revenue a necessary consequence. But even should the reduction of the malt duty create a contrary effect, no deficiency in this respect should be permitted to stand in the way of a great public benefit, for there are other channels from which any deficiency in the malt tax may be easily supplied. In our late publications we have pointed to the duties now levied on the importation for home consumption of foreign grain, pulse, and various other descriptions of agricultural products. As the alteration in the corn laws, and the late reduction in the duties chargeable on cured provisions of all descriptions, press heavily on the agricultural interest, it is but common justice that the revenue arising from the introduction into consumption of those articles, by which farmers are so severely injured in their property, should in future be applied to the reduction of those taxes which restriet, in a great manner, the progress of agricultural improvements. Sir John Barleycorn—and from his long and varied experience, his authority ought at all events to be attended to, even by the Chancellor of the Exchequer himself, on a subject of this vast importance—asserts, that he can afford to pay more than one quarter of the public expenditure; indeed, that he has nearly done so, till he was overtaxed within the last five or six years, and that he would contribute in a far greater degree still to the same object, if the law only gave him a fair opportunity to do his best for the public service. The worthy knight also is under some fear that the national creditors will not long receive their dividends, unless his valuable representations be immediately attended to, and the malt and spirit duties be materially reduced.

The oat trade during the whole of last month has continued in a most deplorable state of depression, but prices had previously been so low, that it would require talent of a peculiar description to make them less valuable than they latterly have been. As it is, however, a fall of 1s. per qr. on the finest qualities has occurred since our last number went to press. Improved quality on the contrary has raised the price of the lowest descriptions about 1s. per qr. during the same period. The average price is somewhere about 17s. per qr. The greater portion of the Irish supplies in London is sold at present even under that low price, and it must be perfectly obvious, we may almost say to the Anti-corn Leaguers themselves, that this article cannot be grown in Ireland at anything like that price, if rents, taxes, and even the lowest wages to agricultural labourers, are to be in future paid. To the north of Europe, therefore, should the existing system be persevered in, must the Oat consumers in Great Britain ultimately look for suitable supplies, and the labour of production will be then transferred from British and Irish workmen to those of foreign states. This is one way certainly to improve our excise duties, which requires more than common sense to comprehend. But, even in this loss of field employment at home, the evil does not end. We have been accustomed to admire, and foreign maritime states to fear the British navy heretofore, and it would appear that the modern plan for strengthening our commercial navy, is to transfer a large portion of our oat carrying trade from the British flag to those of foreign communities; for most undoubtedly the greater

part by far of foreign oats consumed in this country always has been, and ever will be, imported in foreign ships, navigated by foreign seamen. As soon as the season opens, the freight of oats to Scotland and to all the ports in England, betwixt Berwick and the Land's-end, will be from 1s. to 1s. 3d. per qr. at most, and these freights will be carried out of the British empire in hard money, as will be also the cost price of the oats themselves. In manufactured goods not one cargo of them will be paid. On the contrary, this money will be invested in foreign improvements of various descriptions, and must hereafter increase the difficulties which our manufacturers now experience in competing with those of foreign states even in our home market. Oats for some years past have been profitably cultivated in Ireland, chiefly because in the British markets they received prices generally more than equal to the expenses of their cultivation ; but now this advantage has been to a certain extent withdrawn, for the sole purpose apparently of enriching foreign agriculturists, and from the vain expectation that a part of this money may be returned by them afterwards, and expended amongst the Manchester manufacturers. For a theory, therefore, the future improvement of the Irish soil, and the productive employment of the Irish people in their native country, are to be put in jeopardy ; but the truth may be discovered when a remedy cannot be applied to the evils which generally arise from experiments so truly absurd as those are, to which the public attention has been so frequently directed of late. From the United States, and from our American colonies, the letters received since our last publication, are dated in the first week of January ; but they communicate no commercial information in any degree interesting to corn traders in this country. Throughout the American Union flour and wheat for home consumption had not declined, at these dates, materially in value ; but when the season allows the prosecution of that trade, we are informed that prices in a great measure will be regulated by those in Mark Lane, for the last crop was uncommonly productive, and the quality also was fine. It was not supposed, therefore, that our West India colonies, and the different states in South America, would be able to take off the surplus of the American growth, and therefore it was then generally concluded that much must depend on appearances in Great Britain for a favorable vent, for at all events a portion of the last American wheat crop. In the meantime the shipments of dairy products were weekly on the increase. The quantity of American cheese now in this country is exceedingly large, and it is therefore obvious that any farther increase in the supplies of it must hereafter materially interfere with the value of this article in this country, to the great detriment of our dairy farmer's property embarked in it. Jonathan's reciprocity in this article is not unlike his reciprocity in all other commercial matters. We charge less than $1\frac{1}{2}$d. of duty on each pound of his cheese entered here for home consumption, whilst the American duty on English cheese, when imported into that republic, is upwards of $6\frac{1}{4}$d. per pound. This is another valuable sample of freedom in trade amongst friendly nations ; one by which Great Britain will not considerably add to the quantity of Manchester goods now consumed in that republic ; but to hurt the capital of our dairy farmers is only another small sacrifice made to the illustration of, we do not call it political economy, but of a false philosophy now daily propagated amongst the British people. The information respecting the corn trade, which we have received from various parts of Europe, is not of any interest whatever to those concerned in the corn trade here. The elements have closed all the corn shipping ports within the Baltic sea, and the doubtful prospects of the trade in the United Kingdom have prevented speculative bargains from being entered into for shipment when the seasons permit. At Dantzig, Stettin, Rostock, and all the large wheat markets within that sea, prices of wheat were nearly nominal, the best high mixed Polish samples being quoted at 33s. to 35s. per quarter; but, as no purchasers for exportation were then in any of these markets, sales of only small quantities could be then effected. When the inland navigation, however, became again free, large supplies were expected in all of them from the interior, and then the value would be regulated by the future appearances in Mark-lane. If no improvement occur here, the best Dantzig wheat, it was generally expected, would fall under 30s. per quarter on board, and at Stettin and Rostock Silesian wheat of the best qualities will probably decline some shillings below Polish, under similar circumstances; for the last crop was abundant, and of superior quality almost everywhere throughout the Northern corn districts. In the ports in the Mediterranean and Black seas, the corn trade is still in a very depressed state, and the value of all descriptions of grain is purely nominal at the latest advices. Unless a demand should arise from England, little improvement in this state of affairs was expected in those parts, for the supplies, during the spring, will naturally exceed the home consumption. On the whole, we regret that our January prospects are so gloomy, and so little qualified to remove the fears of our Agriculturists, who have a chance certainly of obtaining during a few months remunerating prices, for last year's wheat crop; but, we repeat, that this is only a prospect which depends on the future supply of British wheats, and which may be removed within a few months by the favourable appearance of the coming wheat crop, when harvest approaches towards its completion.

CURRENCY PER IMP. MEASURE.

JAN. 23.

WHEAT, Essex and Kent, red	4C 52	White 50 54 58
Irish	46 48	Do. 48 50
Old, red	— —	Do. .... — —
RYE, old	32 —	New.... 32 —
BARLEY, Grinding 24 27 Malting	30 32	Chevalier 31 33
Irish	21 23	Bere .19 20 22
MALT, Suffolk and Norfolk	56 58	Brown.. 50 54
Kingston and Ware	56 60	Chevalier 60 —
OATS, Yorksh. & Lincolnsh., feed	20 23	Potato.. 23 25
Youghall and Cork black	16 17	Cork, white 18 19
Dublin	17 18	Westport 18 19
Waterford, white	17 18	Black .. 16 17
Newry	20 21	
Galway	12 15	
Scotch feed	22 —	Potato.. 21 24
Clonmel	17 18 19	Limerick18 19 21
Londonderry	18 19	Sligo .. 18 19
BEANS, Tick, new	30 32	Old 32 34
PEAS, Grey	31 33	Maple .. 31 33
White	32 33	Boilers . 35 38
SEED, Rape...... —l. — l.	Irish..—l. —l. per last.	
Linseed, Baltic....40 46	Odessa 48	
English Red Clover..	— — per cwt.	
White		
Mustard, White 7 10	brown 8 11 per bush	
Tares, old 28 30	new 36 40 per qr.	
FLOUR, Town-made 43 45 Suffolk 36	— pr sk. of 280 lbs	
Stockton and Norfolk, 36 —		

FOREIGN GRAIN AND FLOUR IN BOND.

OATS, Brew	15 17	Feed... 12 14
BEANS	18 24	
PEAS	20 24	
FLOUR, American, per brl	22 24	Baltic .. — 22

IMPERIAL AVERAGES.

Week ending	Wheat.	Barley.	Oats.	Rye.	Beans.	Peas.
Dec. 10th	47 3	27 1	17 3	29 5	30 3	32 3
17th	46 10	26 5	17 2	28 11	29 10	32 2
24th	47 2	26 5	17 4	28 5	28 11	31 2
31st	47 1	26 3	17 2	28 1	28 3	31 0
Jan. 7th	47 1	26 5	17 2	31 7	28 0	29 11
14th	47 10	26 5	16 11	29 4	27 5	29 7
Aggregate average of the six weeks which regulates the duty	47 2	26 6	17 2	29 4	28 9	31 0
Duties payable in London till Wednesday next inclusive, and at the Outports till the arrival of the mail of that day from London ..	20 0	10 0	8 0	11 0	11 6	10 6
Do. on grain from British possessions out of Europe	5 0	2 0	2 0	1 6	1 0	1 0

PRICES OF SEEDS.

JAN. 23.

The demand for Cloverseed does not augment much and having a fair quantity offering this morning sales proceeded slowly at about our quotations. In the value of other descriptions of Seeds little change has occurred during the past week, and the only article which was actually cheaper this morning was Canary.

Linseed, English, sowing 48	56		
Baltic	— —	crushing 42	45 per qr.
Mediter. & Odessa 45	46		
Large, foreign....	— —		
Clover , English, red 40	56	white 42	58 per cwt.
Flemish .. 42	46	do..	none
New Hamburgh .. none		do.. 40 60	
Old do. 40	43	do.. none	nominal
French 40	48	do.. none	
Coriander............ 10	16	old.... 16 20 per cwt.	
Mustard, brown, new .. 9	11	white.. 9 10s.6d p.bush.	
Trefoil, new............ 18	22	old.... 12 16	
Rapeseed, English new.. 31l. 33l. per ton.			
Linseed Cakes, English.. 10l. to 10l. 10s.			
Do. Foreign.. 7l. to 7l. 10s.			
Rapeseed Cakes .... 5l. 5s. to 6l. 0s.			
Hempseed, small........ 35 38	large.. 46 48 per qr.		
Rye Grass, English...... 30 42	Scotch 18 40		
Tares, winter .... — —	New 4s 0d 5s 0d p.bush.		
Canary, new............ 64 65	fine 65 66 per qr.		
Carraway, old .... — —	new 42 44		

PRICES OF HOPS.

BOROUGH, MONDAY, Jan. 23.

Prices for Hops of this year's growth are rather better since our last, and the quotations are as follows for pockets, bags being very scarce :—Wealds, 79s. to 87s. ; East Kent, 101s. to 114s. ; and Sussex 77s. to 83s. per cwt. Farnham, 140s. to 160s. ; Pockets of 1841, 60s. to 70s ; choice ditto, 70s. to 84s. ; and bags, 60s. to 80s. ; old olds, 35s. to 42s. per cwt.

Accounts from the German breweries state that owing to the deficient crops, cargoes had been received from the United States, some of them being, however, of very unequal quality. There had been a good deal of speculation in Bavaria, &c. The duty on Foreign Hops brought to England is £4 14s. 6d. per cwt.

WORCESTER, Jan. 21.—Until within the last week or two our Hop market has worn a very gloomy appearance ever since November last, some weeks passing without a single lot going through the scales, and the few parcels disposed of were generally at very reduced rates ; now, however, things are changed, the demand for all descriptions being general, and prices have again rallied to nearly the highest quotation since the season commenced. To day some considerable sales were made at the quotations given below. There is not so much enquiry for old liops, though good yearlings are very saleable.

1842's 78s. to 86s. choice, 90s. per cwt.
1841's 65s. to 72s. .. 78s. ..
1839's 48s. to 56s. .. 60s. ..
Old odds 25s. to 40s. .. 45s. ..

POTATO MARKET.

SOUTHWARK, WATERSIDE, Jan. 23.

The supply of Potatoes to the London market during the past week is not so large as have been lately received. The receipts for the week are as follows, viz., from Yorkshire, 975 tons; Scotland, 440; Devonshire, 225; Jersey, 110; Wisbeach, 90. Total, 1840 tons.

The demand is much firmer for good samples of the best sorts, and the supply being limited, sales have been readily effected, and our last quotations freely obtained ; and if the supply continues short, with a prospect of improvement.

PRESENT PRICES AS ANNEXED.

	Per ton.		Per ton.
	s. s.		s. s.
Scotch Reds	50 to 55	Jersey and Guernsey	
York do.	— to 60	Blues	— to 50
Devous,	— to 55	Yorkshire Prince	
Kent & Essex Whites	— to 45	Regents	— to 45
Wisbeach	40 to 45		

WOOL MARKETS.

BRITISH.

LEEDS, January 20th.—There has been rather more doing in sales of combing wool this week ; and prices are firmer at last week's quotations. In clothing wools we have not any alteration to notice either in demand or prices.

WAKEFIELD, January 20th.—We have little variation to notice in our report of the wool trade this week ; a few sales have been made in light haired combing wools at former limits—and as stocks are very bad, the market is firm. We have scarcely any inquiry for clothing or blanket wools, and prices are nominal.

LIVERPOOL, JAN. 21.

SCOTCH.—We have nothing new to report in laid Highland Wool ; the trade only continue to take for their immediate wants at late rates. White Highland has been in fair request, and is now scarce in the market. Good crossed Wool is still in demand at late rates, but inferior is quite neglected. There is no demand for Cheviots of any class, but as a few government orders are being given out, it is expected there will be a little more demand soon.

	s. d.	s. d.
Laid Highland Wool, per 24 lbs..	6 9 to	7 3
White do. do.	9 3	10 0
Laid Crossed do..unwashed..	8 0	9 6
Do. washed do.	8 6	11 0
Do. Cheviot unwashed do.	8 6	10 0
Do. washed	12 0	15 0
White do. do.	19 0	22 0

FOREIGN.

JAN. 23.

The wool market keeps firm, although some of our manufacturers feel disappointed that there has not been a more animated demand for the China trade. The secret is, however, that our merchants have already suffered too severely from the experience of late years to run headlong into extensive and uncertain speculations, though there is no question but that both from the English and Scotch ports there are shipments making. The statement copied from a German correspondent's report of the Leipsic fair, wherein are noticed ar purchases by English houses, of cloth intended forexportation to China, because cheaper than our own fabrics, seems to be partially incorrect, since it is now admitted by other commercial writers that the Germans themselves have begun to move in the shipment of articles to China, and intend freighting several vessels. Might not these said English purchases be therefore a mere weak invention of our rivals to alarm the British manufacturers, and encourage their own ?

Upon the 7th inst., the cloth market of Leipsic had not been brought to a close. Ord. descriptions were at first neglected, but afterwards there arose some demand for exportation to Sweden and Norway, at the rather lower rates that were current. Not so much was done in middling cloths. Fine qualities at about 40 guter groschens were most sought after. Of English woollens the supply was very limited, but still quite adequate to the demand. There was a larger stock of German fabrics, but no extensive buyers. Most of the raw wool at market found buyers. Combed was in principal demand, and a shade dearer.

Accounts of Sept. 3, from Sydney, give the exports of Wool to England during the first six months of 1842, at 25,130 bales. The market for English manufactures continued to improve.

At Paris some woollen fabrics appear to have rather advanced in price, or at least the holders are firmer.

From the Cape-of Good Hope, accounts of Nov. 26 notice an increase in the exports of Wool during the preceding quarter ; the shipments to October 10 having amounted to 4997l. from Table Bay ; and to 3732l. from Port Elizabeth.

PRICES OF MANURES.

Subjoined are the present prices of several sorts of manure :—

Bone dust, 22s. to 23s. per qr.
Half-inch Bone, 21s. 6d. to 22s. per qr.
Rape Dust 7l. 7s. per ton.
Rape Cake, 6l. 10s. to 7l per ton.
Rags, 4l. to 4l. 10s. per ton.
Graves, 6l. 10s. per ton.
Gypsum, at the waterside, 35s. per ton ; landed and housed, 38s. to 42s. per ton, according to quantity.
Agricultural Salt, 34s. per ton.
Lance's Carbon, 12s. per qr.
Ditto Humus, 14s. per qr.
Soap Ashes, 10s. per ton.
Poittevin's Patent Disinfected Manure, 13s. 6d. per qr.
Poittevin's Highly Concentrated Manure, 30s. per qr.
Nitrate of Soda, 22s. 9d (duty paid) per cwt.
Nitrate Potash (saltpetre) 30s. per cwt.
Petre Salt, 4s. per cwt.
Willey Dust, 4l. 4s. per ton.
Urate, 5l. per ton.
Chie-fou, 21s. per cwt.
Daniell's new Bristol Manure, 13s. 4d. per qr.
Hunt's new Fertilizer, 13s. 4d. per qr.
Grimwade's Preparation for Turnip Fly, 10s. 6d. per packet, sufficient for three acres.
Wolverhampton Compost (Alexander's), 12s. per qr., subject to carriage to London, or forwarded from Wolverhampton.
Guano, 10s. to 14s. per cwt., according to quantity.
Potter's Artificial Guano, 15s. per cwt.
Dr. Daubeney's Sulphate of Ammonia, 12s. per cwt.
Muriate of Ammonia, 24s. per cwt.
Muriate of Lime, 12s. per cwt.
Clarke's Compost, 3l. 12s. 6d. per hhd., sufficient for three acres.
Wright's Alkalies, 28s. and 42s. per cwt.
Soda Ash, 20s.
Chloride Lime, 28s per cwt.
Sulphuric Acid, 2½d. per lb.
Sulphur for Destroying Worm on Turnips, 16s. per cwt.
Hunt's Artificial Guano, 12l. per ton.

Printed by Joseph Rogerson, 24, Norfolk-street, Strand, London.

A Short Horned Cow.

Drawn by I. Cooper. Engraved by J. Scott on Copper. Published as the Act directs, by J. Harding, St. James's Str. London.

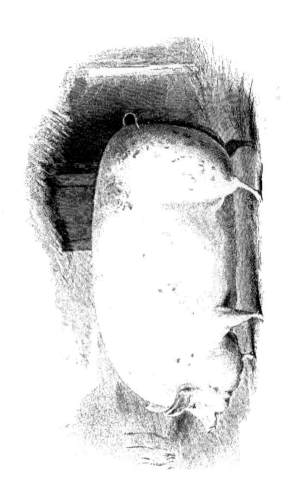

THE FARMER'S MAGAZINE.

MARCH, 1843.

No. 3.—Vol. VII.]   [Second Series.

PLATE I.

The subject of our first plate is a six years and eight months old short-horned Cow, for which a prize of Twenty Sovereigns was awarded to W. C. Maxwell, Esq., of Everingham Park, near Pocklington, Yorkshire, at the Smithfield Club Show in December last. The Gold Medal was also awarded to Sir Charles Tempest, Bart., of Broughton Hall, Skipton, as the breeder of the animal. She was likewise exhibited at the Meeting of the Yorkshire Agricultural Society, and obtained a prize of Ten Sovereigns.

PEDIGREE.

She was calved 7th of March, 1836, got by Scrip (2604), dam Modesty by Magnet (2241), grandam Prudence by Don Juan (1923), g. g. dam Modesty by Sir Anthony (1435), g. g. g. dam by Romulus (564), g. g. g. g. dam by Snowball, g. g. g. g. g. dam by Wellington (684), g. g. g. g. g. g. dam by Young Wynyard, g. g. g. g. g. g. g. dam by Simon (590), g. g. g. g. g. g. g. g. dam by Simon.

ON THE PLANTING, MANAGEMENT, VALUE, GROWTH, AND HARVESTING OF FOREST TREES CULTIVATED FOR PROFIT.

By John Morton.

Observation of nature is a source whence much valuable knowledge may be obtained on almost any branch of rural economy, and particularly in the management of forest-trees; but of all the sources from which assistance may be obtained on this subject, none has been more generally neglected. Yet when we seek for knowledge of any kind, it is surely best to apply to that authority which appeals for the superiority of its principles to the success of its practice. Now, if we test this matter so, where shall we find a name connected with the production of timber of higher authority than that of nature? Where are there finer trees than those cut in her forests? Should we not then apply to her for information? The present mode of managing timber shows that no such application has as yet been made. The practice of an age which could not call science to its assistance seems still to be preferred to that which might be founded on an examination of any of the great natural forests. The axe and the saw, in conformity with the maxims of a long-past age, are still used to destroy plantations in their youth. Did we consult nature she would tell us that no pruning-hook ever entered the precincts of her domain—that she pays no forester to superintend the growth of her timber —and that it is by neglecting the use of those means alone which are now considered essential that she succeeds in raising those trees, without which our ship-builders might shut up their yards, and our navies would be mastless. It is very evident that a great deal of error lies at the foundation of the general practice of our foresters. In order, then, that we may be better able to state with clearness our views on this subject, it will be well to arrange them under different heads.

There are many things—such, for instance, as the influence of light on vegetation—which, while they are very important as regards the assistance they afford us in our inquiries into the best mode of managing plantations, are yet so purely scientific in their nature, that it may be well, in the first place, to give a short statement of that science which connects them together, and draws from them results regarding the mode in which the bulk of trees is annually increased, and regarding the circumstances favourable to the amount of that increase.

The two great organs in the plant, the one for administering and the other for qualifying and modifying the food supplied to it by the soil, are the roots and the leaves. The body or trunk of a tree is that which connects these two parts together, and it is that part of the tree the growth and increase of which is the object of the forester in adopting all the different modes of managing plantations. In a transverse section of this part of the tree a number of circular rings of various breadths are observed. These circular rings are larger and more distinctly marked in some kinds of trees than in others. There is a remarkable difference in the texture of the inner and outer side of the circular ring in some kinds of timber. In the pine tribe particularly the outer side is much more dense and compact than the inner; it is by this difference indeed that these rings are so easily distinguished in some trees, and with such difficulty in others. Each of these circles is the growth of one year, and thus the age of the tree is known by their number—its diameter depends on their number and breadth. These circular rings are so many integuments, each of them encircling the older portion of the tree. The growth of the tree every year is owing to the annual addition of a new integument. The newest of them, or so many of the newest as are distinguishable from the others by greater softness, and generally also by a whiter colour, gets the name of the alburnum; it is through this alburnum alone that the sap ascends from the root to the leaf. There are many theories to account for the way in which the food of plants, after having been prepared in the soil, is taken up by the roots. The roots terminate in fibres, whose extremities consist of small tubes which are closed by a porous, membranous substance. This, from its nature, gets the name of a spongiole. The commonly-received opinion is, that the ascent of the sap is owing to capillary attraction, which, as the tubes through which the ascent takes place are very fine, would be sufficient to raise it to a very considerable height. Others have supposed it to be owing to a process they have termed endosmose; they suppose that the substance of which sap is composed has a strong affinity to water, and that, while the pores of the spongiole are sufficiently open to allow water to pass through them inwards, they are fine enough to hinder the passage of sap outwards. The consequence must be, that water will be constantly passing through; it is evident there is a limit to this process where irritated artificially, for the syrup generally employed instead of the sap will, by the constant influx of water, eventually become so diluted as to lose its attraction for the water without the membrane; but this limit can never occur in nature, for, while the moisture absorbed below tends to dilute, the evaporation going on

from the leaves has the effect of concentration, so that its consistence remains unaltered. A third party, but with probably less reason than the others, attribute the whole of the phenomenon to muscular action. Perhaps each of these causes is partially effective in producing the result. Whatever be the nature of the propelling force, it is a well-established fact that sap does ascend. It proceeds upwards through the alburnum, or newly-formed part of the stem, to the leaves, and is there acted upon by the air of the atmosphere. A great portion of it is there evaporated, and when it has at length assumed a proper consistence it descends by the inner coating of the bark, supplying, as it passes downwards, the wants of the various growing parts of the tree. In the course of one season a new coat or integument is laid on over the last year's growth, between the bark and the old part of the tree, and at the same time a new bark is produced within the last year's bark; between this new wood and new bark another layer of wood and another layer of bark will next year be made. The first year's growth, the oldest part of the wood, is thus always in the centre of the tree, where it remains in its original size, neither growing in length nor circumference; and the oldest part of the bark is always on the exterior of the tree, where it remains till the annual increase of the bulk of the tree bursts and splits it, and at length, in some cases, causes it to fall off. It is very evident that the annual addition of a layer of wood around the older part of the tree gives to trees a tendency to grow in a conical form, because the number of these annual layers must diminish of course from the root to the top.

The use of the leaves of plants is most important; a leaf is merely a curious development of the stem, all the different parts of which may be distinguished in it; it is formed of a thin portion of a succulent, cellular substance, covered by a skin or cuticle on each side. The upper surface of it is not nearly so porous as the lower, at which accordingly all the changes effected by heat, air, and light are supposed to take place. Water is here evaporated, and the amount so lost is astonishing; it is so great, that it has been proposed, and in some cases, I believe, carried into effect with considerable success, to drain marshes in the first place by planting trees in them, which by the copious evaporation from the leaves would at length remove the stagnant water. The concentration of the sap by evaporation is, however, not the only effect produced by the leaves; oxygen gas is given out by the green parts of plants while the sun shines, and during night is absorbed in smaller quantity. This is supposed to take place by the absorption of the carbonic acid gas contained in the air and its decomposition in the plant under the influence of light, the carbon being taken and appropriated as food, while the oxygen is set at liberty. During the absence of light this process is exactly reversed; but the amount of oxygen then absorbed is not so great as that given out during the day. The foliage thus appears not only to be a most beautiful, but a most useful part of the tree. The sap, thus prepared by the leaves of each branch, gives increase of bulk first to the branch as it descends towards its junction with the stem, and then to the trunk and roots. The trees, consequently, that have branches from the the ground to the top naturally take a conical form, tapering from the bottom upwards. This is particularly the case in trees of the pine tribe. Their limbs are distributed with regularity, growing in whorls from the ground to the top of the tree, at almost equal distances, and there is always one circular ring less above each tier of branches.

In almost all that has been here said a strong resemblance may be observed between the plant and the animal. The root may be compared to the mouth, the leaves to the lungs; and the analogy between these two last sets of organs is very striking. The sap, like the blood, circulates; each is at length divided and subdivided, and spread over an immense surface, by which it is brought into contact with the air; and though, on the whole in the one case the fluid is oxidised, carbon being given off, and in the other carbon is absorbed, yet, under certain circumstances, the operation is precisely the same. Neither the plant nor the animal will benefit by the nourishment they receive, unless they also receive the aid of the atmosphere. The air must lend its vivifying and enriching properties, or they cannot live. The power of converting food into material fit for nourishment is said to be in proportion to the size of the lungs in animals; so it is with trees; for as it is the leaves of plants which convert sap into a substance capable of nourishing them, we must conclude that, the greater the extent of its foliage, the greater will be the growth of the tree. It by no means follows from this, however, that of two trees that which is placed in the situation most unfavourable for the production of leaves will not eventually produce the most valuable timber.

Each kind of tree, however, has a character and external appearance peculiar to itself. The oak is a noble and majestic tree. It stretches abroad its sinewy arms, and conveys to the mind the idea of strength. The beech too throws out its wide-spreading branches, but it wants the rugged outline and abrupt roughness characteristic of the oak. The Spanish chesnut may be said to hold a place between these, and accordingly partakes in part of the character of each. The ash again is known by the scantiness of its foliage, and the size and peculiar arrangement of its limbs. The elm rises to a height superior to the oak or the beech, extending its arms aloft. All the pine tribe take the form of cones, their limbs being arranged in whorls stretching out horizontally, and decreasing in length towards the top. These descriptions, however, apply to the trees when growing solitarily under favourable circumstances. Trees, as well as plants of every kind, accommodate themselves to circumstances, adapting their growth to their situation. Thus the roots of a solitary tree, growing in an exposed situation, are large and numerous, having a deep and firm hold of the ground, to enable it to withstand the force of the storms to which it is exposed; the trunk too is short, and it sends out a great number of limbs abounding in small twigs and foliage, and the whole tree appears stunted and dwarfish compared with one of the same species growing in a low and sheltered situation. A similar contrast also is observable between trees growing on the sea-shore and those situate in deep valleys, sheltered either by surrounding hills or by trees growing around them. Near the coast the limbs are observed to grow almost exclusively on one side; they shrink, as it were, from the apparently withering effect of the sea-breeze, and those which front it have degenerated to mere bushy twigs, and are covered with a thick but stunted foliage. In the sheltered valley the trunk is straight

and tall, and the limbs are vigorous. It is curious to observe the near connection which exists between the roots and the limbs of a tree. A single tree, having a large head spreading over a considerable extent of ground, is always possessed of very large roots, extending deep into the earth, and spreading in every direction from its centre to a much greater distance than the extremities of its limbs; a complete net-work is thus formed under the surface, the roots interlacing each other in every possible direction. But a tree of the same kind growing in a thick plantation, having a tall trunk and few straight branches, has also very few roots, and those are long and slender, taking but a slight hold of the ground; yet the strength of each tree is similarly proportioned to the resistance which each requires to make for its support during stormy weather. Thick plantations are much less agitated by wind and storm than when they are thinly planted, for the tops only of the plantations in that case present a resisting surface of leaves and branches; hence trees in sheltered situations are easily blown down when that shelter has been taken away by improper thinning.

It is this tendency in trees to accommodate their growth to their situation that puts it in our power to give them almost any character which we choose; for, in whatever way we wish them to grow, we have only to place them in circumstances fitted to produce that effect, and nature will perform the rest for us. If, then, we plant for profit, the first thing to be done is to inquire into the mode of growth which is most profitable, producing the finest and most valuable timber—then to ascertain under what circumstances that growth will take place—and lastly to act upon the information so obtained.

Forest trees may be classed, according to their external characters, induced by the circumstances under which their growth has taken place, into two great divisions.

The natural propensity of a tree is to spread its foliage to the light; when, therefore, it is solitary, or on the outskirts of a forest, there being no obstruction to this propensity, a large head is formed, abounding in limbs, with numerous small branches and thick foliage. This then may be taken as a specimen of our first class—the solitary tree, abounding in branches and limbs of various sizes.

When, however, trees are situated close together, each, that it may surmount the obstacles which oppose its lateral growth, increases in height, and expends but little of its sap in the formation of limbs. Here then is an individual of our second class—the tree of the thickly-wooded forest, having a long trunk and few limbs.

These then are the two classes between which we have to judge.

The answer to the question as to which is most valuable might doubtless be easily guessed, for it is well known that the value of timber depends not so much on the solid contents of trunk, limbs, &c., as on the length of scantling; so that, although it may be perfectly true, as was before stated, that, other things being equal, of two trees, that which was single and therefore fully exposed to the action of heat and light will in the course of a given number of years increase in solid contents, altogether more than the one which is situated in a closely-wooded plantation, yet the difference in the amount of growth does not compensate for the difference in the value of the growth per cubic foot. Trees that grow close together soon lose their branches; the trunk, though it does not increase so much in diameter, increases greatly in length, and the timber is much finer than that of single trees.

The limbs and heads of trees, where they have been allowed to grow solitarily, may be considered as about three-fourths of the weight of the whole; while in trees raised together in a plantation they not unfrequently bear so small a proportion to the whole as one-fourth only. In order, however, that we may not seem to make assertions without proof, we shall refer to a table at the end of this paper, in which, by not only giving the measurements, but the value also, of the limbs, trunk, and branches of three oaks which grew single, and of three cut down in a plantation—also of the same number of beech similarly circumstanced—the statements here made are fully borne out. These trees were not selected for the purpose of illustrating the argument; but having been cut down for sale they were measured; and the results will be found fully to corroborate all that is here stated.

Having thus shown what kind of growth produces the most valuable timber, and the mode in which that growth may be obtained, the next point is to ascertain the best way of adopting the principles here laid down: and for this purpose we shall go into the details—first, of planting, then of management of young plantations, and, finally, of harvesting the timber when fully matured.

The second branch of our subject, therefore, is planting. In planting, as in almost every branch of rural economy, we should study to adopt all the operations of nature. Nature seldom or never plants more than one kind of tree in the same district; each tract is generally well stocked with only one kind of timber. In England nature has her forests or plantations of oak and beech, and we believe that, before the lowlands of the middle and southern counties were brought into cultivation, the greatest part of them was covered with elm. Because, however, the elm takes possession of good deep land, it was rooted up to make room for the production of food, and is now found only in hedge-rows—while some forests of oak and beech, because those trees prefer poor clay or thin calcareous soils, have been allowed to remain.

In Scotland the natural forests are of Scottish fir (*pinus sylvestris*), and here there is no mixture of any other sort of tree. In Norway, Sweden, Poland, Russia, and America, there are numerous forests of various species of pine; also without mixture. Each species of pine occupies the district allotted to it without the interference of any other variety.

There are two reasons for planting individuals of only one sort of tree together. The first is, because, as the different forest-trees differ in their choice of soils, that which is adapted for any one of them might not be suitable for a variety. The other is this:—some trees are more hardy and have a greater tendency to throw out lateral shoots than others; this, when the wind rises, causes them to lash and irritate the stems of their more delicate neighbours, the sap-vessels of which are thus bruised, their growth retarded, and the trees themselves ultimately destroyed.

If we mix hardwood trees and evergreen together, the latter very soon get the mastery over the others; thus, when either spruce, Scotch, or silver fir is one of the sorts of trees growing in a plantation where there is a variety, their lateral limbs growing very strong, they will not only occupy the ground allotted to them by the planter, but will also extend their limbs in every direction,

assuming a right to the allotments of their more tardy neighbours. When, however, a plantation is composed solely of any one of these firs, each individual tree being placed under similar circumstances with its neighbours, they will grow up side by side as if they had come to a mutual understanding that each should only occupy its own portion of ground; and if this allotment be very limited, tall straight trunks will be produced without any lateral branches. What is true in respect of the Scotch fir is true of any other kind of tree. If, however, in planting we select those trees which resemble each other in their tendency to throw out lateral branches, there cannot be the same objection as there is to the mixture of trees varying in the amount of this tendency. Thus the growth of the oak and the Spanish chesnut—the elm and the ash—the beech and the sycamore—the larch and the poplar—and of the Scotch firs, the spruce and the silver fir, is similar as regards both rapidity of growth and character, and their propensity to throw out lateral limbs is equal: these, therefore, may with propriety be planted together. If, however, all are mixed up in one plantation, we shall find that the Scotch and spruce firs, &c., will occupy most room, and have the superiority over the others, forming trees with large heads and a great quantity of limbs; next to these in the vigour of their growth will be the larch, then the beech and the sycamore, then the oak and the Spanish chesnut—lastly, the ash, the elm, and the poplar.

Nature may be supposed to begin her operations in the formation of forests by sowing clumps and patches over the surface of the ground hereafter to be covered with wood, the size and form of the plots being regulated by circumstances. A seed is carried by a bird or by some of the many other means adopted by nature for transporting it, and is dropped in the midst of a barren waste. It grows up and becomes a tree; after the lapse of years the seed which it has scattered around it also springs up, and a clump or plantation is thus formed: if seeds of any other kind should have been dropped in the midst of them, one of the kinds will eventually obtain the mastery of the other. The seeds thus scattered grow up around the parent plant—the plantation will increase annually in extent until it meet the progeny of trees of the same or of another species whose ancestors have been transported in a similar way. In this way natural forests are raised, and they may be of the same kind of tree for a great extent, if the soil and subsoil be uniform, or they may grow in different masses of trees, varying with the nature of the soil and of the climate. The tediousness of this process evidently precludes the possibility of our imitating nature here; but although we cannot adopt all the details of her practice, we can, and we should, admit the correctness of the principle upon which she acts, and take it as the rule of our conduct. We should with her plant thickly together, although we may not take the same method of putting our seed into the ground; and the only variety we should admit into our woods ought to be, as with her, that which depends on variety of soil and of situation.

Having thus laid down the principles on which we are to act, we shall now consider the details to be founded upon it. The plan to be adopted should have a reference to the natural habits of the trees to be grown. If the ground proposed to be planted be of a uniform nature, then, as we have said, only one kind of tree should be planted. If, however, the soil vary considerably, then we should plant in masses of different trees, each kind being planted on that soil which it prefers.

By thus planting in soils and situations natural to the tree to be grown, we may calculate on success in all our plantations.

There are several points which should be taken into consideration before proceeding to plant at all.

We must in the first place inquire if the value of the timber grown after a certain number of years would be greater than that which might be produced from the same land if under agricultural management. The value of the produce in the one case must be compared with that in the other before we can determine on which side the profit would be greater. Thus, if a field be worth so much per acre per annum for the purposes of agriculture, it ought when planted not only to pay the same yearly rent with compound interest thereon, but also the expence of planting, with the interest on such expense, and that for as long a time as the ground is wholly occupied by it; and if the sale of timber after a certain period amounts to more than this accumulated sum at the time it is harvested, then, and then only, is it more profitable to plant than to farm the land.

There are, however, besides the mere return of cash, other advantages to be taken into consideration as due to the growth of timber. Thus trees and plantations in many cases increase the value of surrounding land. The profits accordingly of plantations formed for the purpose of shelter must be sought for in the improvement which the adjoining land has received from them, and in cold bleak situations this advantage has been very great. In this way the beauty of an estate is often greatly improved by the very means taken to increase its value; and ornamental plantations, if laid out with judgment in the form of belts, screens, and clumps, so as to take up the poorest land and occupy the bleakest situations, are frequently the means of adding greatly to its market value.

Some soils, with a view to their improvement, might be planted with the intention of clearing them again after not many years, and restoring them to the common purposes of agriculture. If this be our object, viz. the preparation of land for future cropping, the larch is the best of all trees for the purpose—the quantity of its leaves is greater, and they decay much sooner, than those of any other tree. The fertility frequently given to poor soils by the decayed vegetable matter thus left on the ground is astonishing. One great advantage which larch possesses over most other trees for this purpose is that twelve or fifteen years' growth is in general sufficient to kill all the natural plants on the ground, and if the wood be intended for an open grove, it will, when thinned out, soon get covered with a sward of fine rich grass. The change of the value of poor mountainous districts thus effected would amply repay the expense of planting at the end of twenty or twenty-five years, independently of the value of the poles and bark.

The planter should consider all the expense he has incurred in the formation of woods as so much capital sunk for the purpose of creating a provident fund for a future generation, to enable it to meet extraordinary demands on the estate, such as planting waste land, repairing and erecting buildings, and other permanent improvements. As soon, accordingly, as the timber is harvested, the proceeds should be laid out in this way, or in the purchase of an additional extent of property. The timber of an estate should never be sold to meet the annual expense of an establishment.

Before the planting is entered upon, the soil should be prepared for it. Wet soils should be drained, and soil of every kind should be fenced and cultivated to a certain extent to protect and prepare it for the reception of the seed or plants. In some wet and thin soils the surface should be laid out into one-bout ridges with the plough, after having been pared and burned, drained with open ditches—for close drains would soon be choked by the roots of the plants—and subsoil-ploughed: the trees should be planted on the tops of these ridges in rows, the earth being drawn up about their roots. In most soils the previous preparation should be that of double-digging, if the subsoil will admit of it, and a crop of potatoes or turnips should be taken off it the year before the planting is to be commenced. The ground is thus left in a clean state, fit for the reception of the seed or young plants—sometimes great advantage results from bringing up the subsoil and mixing it with the soil. There are instances in which the soil does not suit a particular tree, while the subsoil is such as that tree would grow in to perfection. It is in cases such as this that this operation is attended with such beneficial effects. If, for instance, we attempt to grow larch on black moor or peat earth lying on a gravelly subsoil, we shall certainly fail; while, had we previously turned the land so deep as to mix with it some of the subsoil, our operations would have been attended with success.

This shows us the necessity of not only examining the soil before determining on the kind of tree to be grown, but the subsoil also, as we may by this examination be enabled to grow a more valuable tree than we should otherwise have been justified in attempting.

When the climate will allow, it is always better to sow trees than to plant them. Sowing the ground we intend for a plantation of hard wood with acorns, beech-masts, or ask-keys, according to the tree we have determined on, is the best and most profitable way of raising timber. The plantations raised in this way will grow quicker, and produce straighter and more uniform shoots, and are found in eight or ten years to outstrip those of the same age raised from seedlings transplanted from a nursery. Oaks grown from acorns sown in the field in which they are allowed to come to maturity grow taller and are more kind in their growth than those which have first been sown in a nursery, transplanted, and then put out into the field where they are destined to stand. The reason seems to be that no check is put to the growth of their tap-roots, and they are therefore not only enabled to take a firm hold of the ground at an early period of their growth, but also go deeper into the earth in search of their food. Those which have been transplanted grow stunted and dwarfish, throwing out lateral shoots for many years after they are planted.

We have already stated that trees, in order to produce valuable timber, should be sown thick. Oaks, ash, and beech should be sown in rows about two feet apart, and about two or three inches from seed to seed in the rows, and they should be kept clean for four or five years; good seed should be selected, not the heaviest and largest, but that gathered from the finest, fastest growing, and largest trees of the kind. On examining the various experiments that have been made at Welbeck, the property of the Duke of Portland, the plan that seems to succeed best in raising the oak is that where the acorns had been sown in rows varying from eighteen inches to two feet apart, and having a furrow every five or six rows to take off the surface water. The acorns in many places came up as thick as beans in a garden, and they have thus been allowed to grow for sixteen or twenty years, till they were eighteen or twenty feet high, at which time nine-tenths of them had been thinned out by the natural death of the most backward of the lot, the remainder being the finest and most vigorous plants. The dead plants soon rot, and thus not only prevent weeds and rubbish from accumulating, but furnish by their decomposition manure for those that remain. These are at that age about three feet apart, all the dead and imperfect ones being cut down.

Although, however, almost every fact bearing the least on the subject shows the propriety of thick planting, we should not on that account forget to vary this thickness according to circumstances ; and if we use nursery plants of perhaps from two to three years old, though it is certainly more profitable to sow, it is a good rule to plant thinnest, and the largest plants, in the most sheltered situation and the richest soil, and *vice versa.* The thickness of our planting may then vary from two to three feet between the plants, which is from 11,000 to 5,000 plants per acre.

I have already stated my opinion, and the reason for it, that individuals of only one sort of tree should be planted together. This is contrary to the prevailing fashion on this subject, for we are constantly told that there are certain kinds of trees, as larch, spruce, and Scotch fir, which are good nurse-plants, and are accordingly recommended to be mingled with the hardwood intended to be grown as a protection to it. They are good nurse-plants, it is said, because they grow fast ; now this is a very excellent property, if they unite strength and durability, which the trees mentioned do to a very considerable extent ; then these of all others are those which a view to profit would recommend us to grow. That, however, is not the mode generally adopted, and the larch, the spruce, and Scotch fir are cut down to make way for the tender and less profitable growth of a hardwood plantation.

I do not here advocate the growth of these trees to the exclusion of the oak, the beech, and other hardwood trees. All that I here mean is, that it is unprofitable to attempt the growth of hardwood in situations where these nurse-trees are required, and it is highly so to use these nurse-plants in situations where the hardwoods flourish without them.

We now come to the consideration of the proper mode of managing plantations, from the time they are planted till the time they are harvested.

Numberless are the plans, of various degrees of complexity and expense, by which man's ingenuity attempts to perform that which nature does with simplicity, regularity, and no expense. In the case before us, the object is the growth of the greatest number of cubic feet per acre of the most valuable timber ; the production of trees that have the least offals, that will cut up for every use with the least waste, and whose length fits them for every purpose. It should here, therefore, be the aim to throw the greater portion of the weight of wood, which would otherwise form the head of

the tree, and then be fit merely for fire-wood, into the trunk, where it will become valuable timber. This being the object, what are the means in general taken to obtain it ? The young trees, oaks for example, are transplanted from a nursery, where for four or five years they have grown on a rich soil, to a situation where the land is probably too poor for profitable cultivation ; they are planted here and there among a plantation of young firs, larches, &c., the intention of which is to give them shelter, but the effect of which is in most instances to choke their growth and destroy them ; they are then gradually allowed to see the light by the cutting down and removal of the nurse-plants ; and, whereas it was formerly almost entirely excluded, they have now a superabundance of light, and room is given for the lateral shoots to grow and increase in size, which they will not fail to do. These, as the forester knows, not being calculated to improve either the form or the quality of timber, are cut off ; they grow again, and are again pruned, and so on till the upper branches of the young trees, having at length met one another, exclude the light and stop any further tendency to growth in that quarter. The plantation, after a lapse of years, is ready for market, and the forester wonders that, after having followed the usual practice of pruning and thinning, and thinning and pruning, in order that it may not be said, as we have heard it remarked of plantations, "These trees could not grow for want of air," the timber is of bad quality, full of knots, and still, after all his precautions, with a large proportion of offal.

How does nature act ? We have already described the mode of growth in natural forests. The trees are there so close together that light is excluded from their trunks, and their growth is therefore entirely upwards ; there are no lateral shoots, and that which would otherwise have formed a head produces a trunk. Thus it is that the spars used in our navies are of such perfect straightness, so very long, and so perfectly free from knots. In the forest thus coming to perfection, a great many trees are choked by the superior growth of others, and, as the food supplied to those which remain decreases every year, owing to the gradual exclusion of light, there is annually a smaller quantity of sap-wood formed, and a greater quantity of that which remains is hardened, till at length the whole becomes of equal excellence with the heartwood. The growth of the tree is thus entirely stopped, and if it is not felled by the axe of the woodman, who knows the value which the timber-merchant sets on it in that state, it stands a few years till, the process of decay having been carried sufficiently far, it at length falls, and furnishes nourishment for the growth of those that remain.

The work thus gradually and spontaneously proceeds, and the results of it are far superior to anything that can be referred to by the advocates of the system of spoliation, which is generally considered as necessary to perfect timber in artificial plantations.

Here, as in other cases already mentioned, though it would be far from profitable to follow nature through all the details of her management, it would be highly so to adopt the principle upon which she acts. We should with her avail ourselves of the effects of light in accomplishing our purpose. After planting or sowing thickly, the natural influence of light will have the effect of raising trees perfect in form and quality. Light has everything to do in directing the growth of trees, and it will be a powerful engine in the hand of the manager of woods if he make use of its influence in attaining his object, but it will be too powerful for him if he work in opposition to it. If it be let in upon the trunk of the tree in excess, then lateral shoots and branches will make their appearance, and lopping them will only increase the injury, for it is useless to attempt to work with the knife against the influence of light. No art can set aside the laws of nature.

I should much rather leave nature alone to adopt her method of thinning, than let a forester enter a plantation and thin it out in the way it is always executed; although I should rather it were thinned, if it were done in a proper time and manner.

The question, to what extent will it eventually be profitable to thin out a plantation, hinges upon two important facts: first, that too small a quantity of limbs and leaves will check the growth of the tree, a certain quantity being required to maintain the growth in undiminished vigour; and secondly, that too large a quantity will injure the value of the timber. Now, extensive thinning, by admitting the light, will not only produce limbs and lateral branches, but also greatly diminish the number of trees per acre; and too slight a thinning may, by excluding the light, give a check to the growth of the tree. There will therefore be a medium, by adopting which we shall raise valuable timber, and at the same time run no risk of checking the growth of our plantation. I would commence, when the trees are from 10 to 15 feet high, according to their thickness on the ground, by cutting down all those that are choked and dying or dead, and I would let these lie and rot on the ground, rather than run the risk of bruising the sap-vessels and injuring the bark of those that remain by taking them out of the field. Their value will, at any rate, be scarcely beyond the expense of cutting them up and fagoting them, and they will by their decay give food for the young plants that are left.

In no instance should a plant be cut down because by the vigour of its growth it is likely to overtop and choke those around it; nor should any be felled because the operator thinks they are too thick—the only rule to guide him should be this: cut down the dead and those that are dying. He may err in cutting down a growing tree; he cannot do so in letting it stand. Time will decide if the plantation is too thick; and when we require to go over it a second time, we shall then be no longer in doubt whether this tree or that of those which remained after our first thinning shall survive, for all that we have to do is to abide by our old rule. We should not be scrupulous to thin them out to a certain distance, those merely should be felled upon which nature has set her mark. Our anxiety should be to take out the worst, and leave the best and most thriving, for it is these which occupy the land with their roots, and fill up the space above them with their foliage.

By proceeding thus, we shall keep the trees just so thick as to let them have just the room and the light that is necessary for the healthy production of the quantity of branches and leaves required for the preparation of the sap that will profitably augment their trunks. The knowledge of the quantity of branches that is necessary for the vigorous growth of trees of various kinds and size can be obtained only by long experience.

Practice also will teach how to vary the details of management according to the habits of the trees grown. With respect, for instance, to a general rule, which we have found useful, to double the distance between the trees as they triple their height, it may be sufficiently correct, and yet it may be improper to follow literally the table of distances which may be deduced from it; thus, if the trees be 3 feet high, three years after planting, and 2 feet apart, the following table will show how to proceed:—

	Feet.	Feet.	Feet.	Feet.
Length of tree	3	9	27	81
Distance between them produced by death or thinning	2	4	8	16

This table should vary according to the kind of tree grown. Thus, while larch, and Scotch fir, and others of the pine tribe may be benefited by the thinning being commenced at an early stage of their growth, which indeed will spontaneously take place, oak, ash, and other hardwood trees, for the first fifteen or twenty years of their growth, will grow faster and to greater perfection by being thick together. They may then be thinned out, if about 15 feet high, to the distance of 3 feet apart, all the dead wood being cut down. When about 25 feet high, the removal of all the dead trees will increase the average distance between them to four or five feet. The thinnings may this time be taken away, as the operation of removal will not be likely to injure the trees, the room being greater; they are also now of more value. When from 30 to 40 feet high, they may be thinned out to 6 feet apart, about 1200 trees being left to the acre. The operation of thinning, that is, of removing those trees whose growth is checked, may be continned till ultimately, when the trees are ready for harvesting, they will be found to be from 12 to 18 or 20 feet apart, or about 120 in number per acre.

The details of management should, however, not only vary with the habits of the tree, but also with the nature of the ground planted. Thus on poor land the same kind of tree should be thinned less, and should be brought to maturity closer together, than when grown on rich land, well calculated for the production of timber of the first magnitude. On soil of this character trees will grow longer, and occupy the ground profitably for a greater number of years, and the thinning process may therefore be carried on a longer time, than when the land is thin and the situation bleak.

It is evident that trees which will grow to two tons of timber will require more nourishment and greater room than those which will grow to half a ton only.

(To be concluded in our next.)

THE VALUE OF A SHILLING.—For one shilling per week, paid yearly, half-yearly, or quarterly, a person thirty-six years of age may secure 100l. to his widow, children, or representatives at his decease.— For one shilling per week, a man aged 30 may secure for his wife, not exceeding his own age, an annuity of 10l. per annum at his death, whenever it may happen.—For one shilling per week a person twenty-one years of age may secure an annuity of 10l. on attaining the age of 50; a person twenty-eight years of age on attaining 55; a person aged 36 on attaining 60; and a person aged 44 on attaining 65. Either of these benefits may be secured in the Farmer's Fire and Life Insurance Office.

FARMERS' CLUB HOUSE.

PROPOSED TO BE ESTABLISHED IN LONDON FOR THE USE
OF FARMERS AND OTHER PERSONS INTERESTED IN THE
CULTIVATION OF THE SOIL, OPEN TO PRACTICAL
FARMERS AND SCIENTIFIC MEN OF ALL COUNTRIES.

Since the formation of the Royal Agricultural
Society of England, the want of a Club House in
London, at which members of that Society, of the
Smithfield Club, and agriculturists from different
parts of the country when visiting the metropolis,
might meet each other, and where those who may
have long known each other by name, and perhaps
have been in correspondence with each other, might
become personally acquainted, has long been felt.
The subject was brought under the notice of the
Committee of the British Farmers' Club in December, 1840, and was highly approved. Several attempts have been made to effect the object, but a
serious difficulty always interposed in the outlay of
capital requisite for the formation of such an establishment. A plan has, however, been devised by
which that difficulty is completely overcome.

Each succeeding year furnishes fresh proofs of
the necessity of union among Farmers, and that it
now more than ever behoves them to adopt in earnest
the means pursued by the other classes of society,
viz., that of associating with each other, as well for
the purpose of mutual information as for the general
good of the body.

It is proposed that this Club shall be established
as a point of union for agriculturists, and with a
view of affording to its Members accommodation
similar to that of the London Club Houses already
existing, but more comprehensive in its objects, and
much less expensive. That arrangements be made
with the proprietor of an hotel to let to the Club a
suite of rooms to be devoted *exclusively* to the use of
its Members, and to supply viands, wines, &c,. of
the best quality, at a fixed rate of charge to be agreed
upon.

It is proposed at first to have a reading-room, a
dining-room, both of large dimensions, and one or
more sitting-rooms for the use of Members who have
private business to transact.

The reading-room will be supplied with the leading daily papers, and all newspapers and magazines,
British, colonial, and foreign, connected with agriculture and horticulture. An agricultural library
will be formed, to contain all works upon agriculture, horticulture, and the sciences bearing upon
them, such as geology, botany, chemistry, &c.; also
Parliamentary reports and returns, bills and acts of
Parliament having reference to the same subjects.
A register will be kept of estates to be sold or let,
and similar information of any description will be
entered, so that persons requiring it may obtain the
best and readiest information upon all matters bearing upon agriculture. It is intended also, through
the medium of this establishment, to form a central
point of communication between all the Farmers'
Clubs in the kingdom, so that the information to be
supplied from each may be collected and communicated to the others. A book will be kept for entering
the addresses of Members while staying in London,
so that persons desirous of communicating with
them may be enabled so to do. This slight outline
will serve as a specimen of the objects contemplated
in the establishment of a Farmers' Club House; once

established, it will afford the means of carrying out
many others which time and circumstances will develope. In order to render the use and benefits of
the Club House extensively available to Farmers,
the entrance-fee and annual subscription has been
fixed as low as possible.

All persons sending in their names to the Secretary before the 25th March will be admitted Members, subject to the rules as to admission and general
government of the Club, upon payment of an entrance-fee of one guinea, and an annual subscription
of one guinea; and after that period upon payment
of an entrance-fee of two guineas, and an annual
subscription of one guinea.

The Provisional Committee have had communication with a person occupying premises in a central
situation between the Cattle Market of Smithfield
and the Corn Market in Mark Lane, for suitable
apartments for the Club, until the number of Subscribers shall have so increased as to warrant their
taking to rent or purchasing a house, and providing
the requisite establishment. From the extent of the
premises in question further temporary accommodation can always be had if needed, and should the
number of Members so increase as to require further
permanent accommodation, it can be afforded; and
the Provisional Committee have received an offer
from the party to the effect, that he will furnish
good viands, wines, spirits, beds, &c., &c., at a
moderate scale of charges, to be hereafter agreed
upon by the Committee.

The following Gentlemen compose the Provisional
Committee:—

ANDERSON, W., Oakley, Bedford
BAKER, ROBERT, Writtle, Chelmsford, Essex
BEADEL, J., Witham, Essex
BEMAN, R., Donnington, Stow-on-the-Wold, Glouc.
BRAGINTON, G., Torrington, Devon.
COOPER, J. R., Red House, Westleton, Suffolk
DEAN, J., The Yews, Tottenham, Middlesex; a Mem-
   ber of the Council of the Royal Agricultural Society
EMERY, G., The Grange, Banwell, Somerset.
GATES, R., Marshall Vale, Bramley, Guildford
GIBBS, HUMPHREY, Half-Moon Street, Piccadilly,
   and Amphill, Beds.; a Governor and a Member of
   the Council of the Royal Agricultural Society
GRANTHAM, STEPHEN, Stoneham, Lewes, Sussex
HOBBS, W. F., Mark's Hall, Coggeshall, Essex; a
   Member of the Council of the Royal Agric. Society
HUDSON, JOHN, Castle Acre Lodge, Swaffham,
   Norfolk
HUTLEY, W., Pown's Hall, Witham, Essex
JACOBS, W. H., Chale Abbey, Isle of Wight
JAQUES, R. M., Easby, Richmond, Yorkshire
JOHNSON, CUTHBERT WILLIAM, 14, Gray's
   Inn Square, London
KING, FIELDER, Buriton, Petersfield, Hants.
LOFT, W., Trusthorpe, Alford, Lincoln
OAKLEY, J., Frindsbury, near Rochester
PRICE, H., Hartlip, Sittingbourne, Kent
PURSER, W., Copie, near Bedford
DAVID, E., Radyr Court, Cardiff, South Wales
RUSBRIDGER, JOHN, Goodwood, Sussex
SHARPE, W., Scarthing Moor, Tuxford
SHAW, WM., 346, Strand, London; a Governor and
   Member of the Council of the Royal Agricultural
   Society
STEVENS, T., Atherston, Ilminster, Somerset
TORR, W., jun., Riby, near Caistor, Lincoln
WEST, J., Collingham, Newark, Notts.
WESTBURY, GILES, Andover, Hants.
WETHERELL, WM., Durham.

WM. SHAW, 346, Strand,
Honorary Secretary.

CULTIVATION OF TURNIPS.

TO THE EDITOR OF THE MARK LANE EXPRESS.

SIR, — In 1840 it was proposed by the Royal Agricultural Society to try certain experiments on the growing of Swedish turnips, upon the following conditions. See the *Journal*, 1840, Part IV.

Model Experiment on the growing of Swedish Turnips.

CONDITIONS.

Seed—" Purple-top," to be procured of Mr. Thomas
    Gibbs, Half Moon Street, Piccadilly.
Manure—Dung, 20 tons.
    Bones, 20 bushels.
    Poittevin's Manure, 26 bushels.
Distance—18 inches and 27.

In the following year (1841) I was induced to make my humble attempt, not only from a desire to aid in an experiment emanating from this much valued Society, but in consequence of a prize being offered in this county (Rutland), upon the following conditions :—

" For Swedish Turnips, cultivated on any system, in quantities not less than five acres, and situated within the county of Rutland, first prize, 7l. The entries made previous to sowing, &c."

The particulars of the trial, for which I received the first prize, were handed to the Royal Agricultural Society, but were not selected and set forth in the *Journal*. See vol. iii. p. 423-4-5-6. I trust that should you feel disposed to give the particulars herewith sent publicity in your excellent publication, the *Mark Lane Express*, you will not only oblige my inquiring neighbours, but many other experimental agriculturists.

I remain, Sir, your obedient servant,
RICHARD WESTBROOK BAKER.
Cottesmore, Feb. 14th, 1843.

(COPY.)

The seed from Mr. Thomas Gibbs, Half Moon Street, Piccadilly.

The five acres were cultivated alike, with the exception of bones to one acre, and had been so cultivated for some years, viz., upon the four course system of turnips, oats or barley, seeds, wheat. The field is situate upon a high tabling, say two hundred feet above the valley. The soil is red, and the subsoil red kale with iron stone, and valued in 1814, with the average of wheat at 72s. 1d., at 30s. per acre, tithe free, and is by no means naturally a powerful soil. Gorse grew abundantly thereon but a few years back. The whole was ploughed in December, 1840, after wheat, ten inches deep, being three inches deeper than any former ploughing ; and was covered with lime fresh from the kiln in March, 1841, at the rate of twenty qrs. per acre ; was harrowed a few days afterwards, and ploughed a second and third time, and harrowed to admit the weather and incorporate the lime with the soil—between the 20th of March and the 10th of May. On the following days the land was ridged twenty-eight inches wide, and twenty tons of farm-yard manure per acre moderately rotten was deposited, and immediately covered by the double mould-board plough. A single horse drill which will deposit bones and seed, or the latter without the former, followed, and two lbs. of seed per acre were sown ; and on the first acre twenty bushels of bones were used. Poittevin's manure could not be procured. The turnips were

horse-hoed in the usual mode, and set out with the hand hoe at nine inches from plant to plant.

The summer was unfavourable — first, from drought, with severe frost, east winds, fly, and wire-worm ; and, afterwards, from excessive rains and cold weather.

Having a great objection to depend upon weighing a portion of an acre, I determined to have (as I had in former years) the whole acre, No. 1, that had the bones applied, drawn on the 1st of December, carefully cleaned from top, bottom, and soil, and weighed, the land being correctly measured : also the acre, No. 2, that was not boned. The result was as follows :—

	tons.	cwt.
No. 1, with bones	23	1
2, without bones	21	0
In favour of bones ..	2	1

Cost of bones 3l. It is further stated that in former experiments similar to this, the *exact* acre measured, and the crop cleaned as in this case, the weight in no one instance exceeded twenty-six tons.

Application of lime and winter ploughing did not appear as a preventive to wire-worm.

(Signed) RICHARD WESTBROOK BAKER.
Cottesmore, Dec. 24th, 1842.

TURNIPS.

At the recent meeting of the West Suffolk Agricultural Association, Mr. R. B. Harvey (Harleston), being loudly called for, said he had been peculiarly gratified that day by the observations of a gentleman opposite upon the show of roots, which he considered a point of the greatest importance. However good the cattle might be, it was necessary that there should be good food to give to them. He had had in the present week, an opportunity of seeing the vast difference between a good and a bad crop of roots, grown on the same land and at the same expence. On the same field were grown Skirving's turnips (of which doubtless most present had heard) and two other varieties, and the difference was as much as 30s. per acre in favour of Skirving's over one variety, and not quite so much over the other. Looking at the matter in this light it must be of the greatest importance to obtain a good stock of seed, and he for one was obliged to the gentleman who had offered an increased premium with this view.

Mr. GAYFORD felt rather called to make a few observations after what Mr. Harvey had stated, and would observe that if the agriculturists wished to make the association as beneficial as he wished it to be, they would communicate what they could, throw aside prejudice, and receive information. It happened that it was his field to which Mr. Harvey had alluded—this field and his books were open to any one who might choose to go over them. He had a quantity of Skirving's seed, and some from Mr. Raynbird's, and some from Mr. Grayson's. His drill deposited four drills at a time ; Skirving's seed was put into two of them, and the other descriptions into the other two ; and Mr. Harvey had not exaggerated when he said that the difference in favour of Skirving's was 30s. per acre. He pledged himself that there was no difference in the manure, they were all drilled at the same moment, and there could not be an advantage to one and disadvantage to the other.

Mr. GEDNEY said that he should not have risen

but for the turnip question being brought upon the carpet. He thought the subject was a most important one, for they could not have good meat unless they had good roots. They all saw that they were to have very cheap meat; however, that was not a matter to disturb themselves about at present, though it might very soon be. His friends Messrs. Harvey and Gayford had told them that one sort of turnips (Skirving's) were worth more by 30s. an acre or upwards than another description; but the question was whether they did not grow water instead of sugar. He himself was no novice in growing turnips; he had been endeavouring to instil a few of his notions into the mind of the Rev. Mr. Gwilt, who was sitting by his side, but that gentleman told him that they were things of bygone times, and his notions about the turnip crop he supposed were the same. He had ceased to grow Skirving's turnips, for he entertained an opinion that it was not a turnip to grow upon a light or mixed soil—his belief was that it might be grown safely on a heavy soil. It had been said that Skirving's turnips were the best because game would eat them in preference to any others, but he thought the reason for this was that they stood high out of the ground, and the game would not eat dirt. He had put some turnips of two different sorts, and grown on different kinds of land, into a chemist's hands to be analyzed; he asked him if he could take a square inch or a grain weight out of each turnip, but he preferred analyzing the whole turnips. He had done so, and he would now state to the members of this Association the result arrived at, giving the weight and specific gravity of the various turnips (six in number) taking water as a standard at 60 degrees of temperature, reckoning in grains troy.

No.	Description of Turnip and of Land.	Weight of whole Turnip.	Specific gravity of Turnip.	Weight of fibre per 1000.	Sugar, Gum, &c.	Water.
1	Skirving, on stiff clay soil	31270	1015.4	36	108	856
2	Ditto, ditto	24560	1005	28	90	882
3	Ditto, very light land.....	25813	1003	34	96	870
4	Ditto, ditto	25812	1009.3	37	120	843
5	Short top purple, mix'd soil	17718	1017.3	46	120	834
6	Ditto, ditto...............	19875	1012.7	36	90	874

What was considered fibre was wood, and nothing more nor less. No. 4 was small and very deficient in weight as compared with No. 1, yet it produced 120 grains of sugar, or nourishment. No. 5 was a very small turnip, yet yielding 120 grains of sugar, whilst No. 1, almost twice its size, yeilded but 108. On this ground he should build his argument that in a small turnip there might be a great deal more nourishment than in a large one. He hoped some of the members of the Association would take courage and go to a chemist's, and find out what they really did grow. It was desirable at this time of day that they should begin to understand what they were doing: the gentleman by his side might say that these things were understood years ago, but he could tell them that there was a necessity that they should now open the door, and it would not want oiling, for it would be forced open. (*Hear, hear.*)

The Rev. D. Gwilt explained that when he talked to Mr. Gedney of bygone things, he meant to say that these matters had been laid before the public in the *Quarterly Journal of Agriculture* and in the *British Farmers' Magazine*. He agreed in Mr. Gedney's remarks about turnips. He recollected that when Skirving's turnips were first introduced at Smithfield,

Mr. Gurney bought some of them, as well as the seed, but he (Mr. Gwilt) could get no seed. Two years after he saw Mr. Gurney and he said they would not do—they were coarse and bad. He thought Matson's a superior turnip, and that that small sort against Skirving's would be found to produce more saccharine matter. That time three years Mr. Gataker gave him a challenge against his Swede turnips; they were thrown down in the committee-room, and folks said he was fairly beaten, but they were afterwards cut up and he believed his own were allowed to be the best. But he was of opinion, in looking over the field with farmers, that they would not stand with Matson's, which were longer necked and better turnips. He would have an opportunity of testing some varieties, and would communicate the result.

ON GUANO.

BY CUTHBERT W. JOHNSON, ESQ., F.R.S.

The exertions now making in every direction to increase the supply of all kinds of manure, is perhaps one of the best proofs of the great modern increase of agricultural enterprize. The farmers of a former generation would have been little prepared for the information, that the town-made dung of London was capable of being profitably conveyed, by sailing vessels, to all the southern and eastern counties—that it was even carried to Northumberland, as ballast for the coal vessels; they would have been still more surprised to learn that distant countries were exhausted of their refuse bones to manure the turnip lands of England—that they were brought for this purpose from the Baltic, and even from the Atlantic Ocean. And if they deemed these facts matter for astonishment, how much more would they consider marvellous the very recent importation of the excrements of sea birds, brought from the Pacific Ocean — the guano of the Peruvian farmers? And yet it appears to be a fact, that within the last two years from twenty to thirty thousand tons of guano have been brought into this country from those islands on the western side of South America, which are only situated within the latitude of perpetual dryness.

Guano is, it seems, the European mode of pronouncing the Peruvian word "huano," or manure.

This substance exists in large quantities in some of the rocky islands off the coast of Peru, where, in the course of ages, it has been formed by the deposit of the excrements of innumerable multitudes of sea fowl, who haunt these localities, especially during the breeding season.* It exists, according to M. Humboldt (*Davy's Elem. Ag. Chem. 296.*) in the greatest abundance in some of the small rocky islands of the Pacific Ocean, as at Chincha, Ilo, Iza, and Arica. Even when Humboldt wrote, some twenty years since, fifty vessels were annually loaded with the guano at Chincha alone, each trader carrying from 1,500 to 2,000 cubic feet.

* " It forms irregular and limited deposits, which at times attain a depth of 50 or 60 feet, and are excavated like mines of red ochre. Its real origin was well known to the Government of the Incas, and its national importance fully understood. It was made a capital offence to kill the young birds on the Guano Islands."—*Professor Johnston, Jour. Roy. Ag. Soc. v.* 2, p. 103.

In a communication (January 29, 1843) from a gentleman who has visited these islands, he observes:—" The Chincha Islands (three in number) are in a line with each other, north and south, and about half a mile distant from each other. Their greatest extent is north and south, and each island is from five to six miles in circumference. Their base is *granite*, and the covering *huano*, in some places 200 feet thick, stratified horizontally ; the strata varying from 3 to 10 inches in thickness ; in colour from light to dark brown, and unmixed, (to all appearance), with the slightest particle of sand or earth of any description. When I was last at the Chincha Islands, in April, 1842, I saw a perpendicular surface of huano *exposed*, of upwards of a hundred feet, and no difference whatever in its appearance from the surface to the bottom. The underneath part was probably somewhat heavier than the upper. The different shades of strata seemed to be mixed indiscriminately. The depth of the huano formation, however, is by no means the same all over the islands. In some parts it does not exceed three or four feet. Supposing the huano to be really the dung of birds, there was one fact which we who visited the islands found difficulty in accounting for ; pieces of granite in considerable quantity, some of them weighing twenty pounds, are found strewed over the surface of the island, in parts where the huano is from fifty to a hundred feet thick. I enquired particularly of the labourers if any of these pieces of granite had been dug out of the huano, and they answered they had not. They were found only on the surface. The only substances occasionally found in the huano (at all depths) are skeletons of birds and eggs, or rather lumps of ammonia, with the form and colour of an egg, which when exposed to the air are dissipated in three or four days."

The guano is the putrefying excrements of innumerable sea-fowl that remain on the islands during the breeding season. It is used by the farmers of Peru chiefly as a manure for the maize or Indian corn, and it is said sometimes in the small proportion of about one cwt. per acre. "The date of the discovery of the guano and of its introduction as a manure," says Mr. Winderfeldt (*Brit. Farm. Mag.* vol vi. p. 411), " is unknown, although no doubt exists of its great antiquity. In many parts of America, where the soil is volcanic or sandy, no produce would be obtained without the guano. It has been calculated that from 12,000 to 14,000 cwt. are annually sold in the port of Mollendo for the use of the country round the city of Arequipa. In the province of Taracapa and in the valleys of Tambo and Victor the consumption should be something more, as where all kinds of fruit, trees, and plants, with the single exception of the sugar cane, are manured with the guano ; which is not the case with the district of Arequipa, where maize and the potato alone require it. In the district of Arequipa 3 cwts. of guano are spread over an extent of 5000 square yards (about an English acre) ; but in Taracapa and the valleys of Tambo and Victor, 5 cwt. are required. The land thus manured in Arequipa produces 45 for 1 of potatoes, and 35 for 1 of maize, where wheat manured with horse-dung produces only 18." There are, it appears, three varieties of guano, which bear on the coast of Peru different prices. "The white guano is considered the most valuable, as being fresher and purer. It is found on nearly all the islands along the coast. The red and dark grey are worth 2s.

3d. the cwt. ; a higher price is given for the white on account of its greater scarcity ; it is sold at the port of Mollendo at 3s. 6d. per cwt., and at times, as during the war, it has obtained as high a price as 12s."

In a recent obliging communication (Dec. 29, 1842), from a gentleman who has resided many years on the coast of Peru (Henry Bland, Esq., of Liverpool), he observes, in answer to some questions which I had addressed to him, with regard to the uses of the guano, the soils, and the climate of Peru : " The valleys on the coast of Peru consist chiefly of a light sandy soil. No rain falls upon that part of the coast where I have seen guano used. Neither are the dews so copious as to be considered by the Peruvian farmer to be of any importance in promoting vegetation in the valleys. On the tops of the coast hills, a slight verdure is produced by the dews in the winter season, but it does not remain for more than from one to two months. The land of the valleys is irrigated, but without the the limits of irrigation all is a desert, with the exception of the slight vegetation I have alluded to. This is the state of the coast, from about 5 degrees to 22 degrees south latitude. I do not believe that so small a quantity as one cwt. of guano per acre is found sufficient for the soil upon any part of the coast of Peru. In the neighbourhood of Arequipa, the first crop is maize (Indian corn). The seed is sown in drills or trenches, and the bunches (three or four plants I call a bunch) come up about two feet apart. When the plants are six or eight inches above ground, a pinch of guano (as much as can be easily held between the thumb and two fingers) is placed around each bunch, and the whole is usually irrigated immediately afterwards. Guano is again applied when the plant is about throwing out its fruits ; a handful is then applied to each bunch, and irrigation immediately follows. The next succeeding crops, potatoes and wheat, are produced without any further application of manure. In the valley of Chaucay, distant from Lima about 40 miles, a soil, which without guano is capable of producing only fifteen for one of Indian corn, with guano is made to produce 300 for one. In speaking of guano, the Peruvians say, ' Aunque no sea santo hace milagros'—Guano, though no saint, works miracles. Guano to be good, being in some measure soluble in water, can never be found in its most powerful state in any climate where rain falls ; and consequently any that may be brought from the coast of Peru, taken from without the limits of dryness, must be of inferior value compared with that which comes from the Chincha Islands, situated in about 14 degrees south latitude, and about ten miles distant from the main, and from Paquica on the coast of Bolivia, in latitude 21 south. Upon these islands and at Paquica, is the principal deposit of guano. Two or three cargoes of guano from the coast of Chili (where rain is frequent) have found their way into this country, and have, I believe, been sold for Chincha guano ; thus injuring both the character of the best guano as a manure, and the importer of the genuine article.* I may men-

---

* " It is the dryness of the climate," observes Professor Johnston, " which has permitted the guano to accumulate on these coasts. When we reach a region in which from local causes the dews are heavier, and the rains more frequent, the accumulation ceases ; cold water dissolves at least three-fifths of the guano in the state in which it reaches

tion a circumstance to show the little estimation in which nitrate of soda, compared with guano, is held by the Peruvian farmer. "On the coast of Peru nitrate of soda is produced at a distance of about 45 miles from Iquique, the port at which the principal part of the nitrate is shipped. For mules to transport the nitrate from the place where it is made to the port of shipment, the nitrate merchant, who sells for export, depends chiefly upon the farmers who reside in the immediate neighbourhood where the nitrate is produced, and he can only secure their services by having always ready for them in the port of Iquique, a return load of guano, which they carry back to manure their farms, after having carried a load of nitrate, almost from their own doors, to the port of Iquique."

Guano appears in the state in which it has been lately introduced into this country, to be a fine brown or fawn-coloured powder, emitting a strong marine smell : it blackens when heated, and gives off strong ammoniacal fumes. When nitric acid is mixed with it, uric or lithic acid is produced. The composition of guano varies, however, considerably. According to the analyses of MM. Voelckel and Klaproth, the varieties which they examined contained—

	Voelckel. Parts.	Klaproth. Parts.
Urate of ammonia	9	16
Oxalate of ammonia	10·6	0·0
Oxalate of lime	7	12·75
Phosphate of ammonia	6	0·0
Phosphate of ammonia & magnesia	2·6	0·0
Sulphate of potass	5·5	0·0
Sulphate of soda	3·3	0·0
Chloride of sodium (common salt)	0·0	0·5
Chloride of ammonia	4·2	0·0
Phosphate of lime	14·3	10
Clay and sand	4·7	32
Undetermined organic substances, of which about 12 per cent. is soluble in water, a small quantity of soluble salt of iron, water	32·53	28·75

In a few words it may be regarded as an impure compound of phosphate of lime, of urate of ammonia, and other salts. There is no doubt but that it is a very powerful manure; the very composition of its salts would indicate this fact. Thus, uric or lithic acid, which is a fine white powder, nearly insoluble in water (1720 parts of water only dissolving 1 part of uric acid), is composed, according to Dr. Prout (*Thomson's Chem.* vol. ii. p. 187), of—

Hydrogen	0·125
Carbon	2·250
Nitrogen, or Azote	1·750
Oxygen	1·500
	5·625

us. A single day of English rain would dissolve and carry into the sea a considerable portion of one of the largest accumulations; a single year of English weather would cause many of them entirely to disappear."—(*Jour. Roy. Ag. Soc. v. 2 p.* 315.) As the guano is, we have seen, of different qualities, and is easily adulterated, the farmer should be careful to procure it of the large dealers, such as Messrs. W. J. Myers, and Co., or Edwards, Danson, and Co., Liverpool, the London Manure Company, or Mr. Mark Fothergill, Lower Thames-street.

The fresh guano, says Professor J. F. Johnston (*Jour. Roy. Ag. Soc.*, v. ii. p. 311), is more valuable, because it contains more of the uric acid. We have no analysis of the recent droppings of any of the birds which frequent the shores of Peru; they would probably be found to differ in some degree, not only with the species of bird, but also with the kind of fishes on which at different seasons of the year they were found to prey. We possess analyses, however, of the excretions of other birds which live chiefly upon fish, from which we are enabled to form an opinion as to what the recent guano is likely to be. Thus Dr. Wollaston found those of the gannet (*Pelicanus bassanus*), when dry, to contain little else but uric acid, while in those of the sea eagle Coindet found—

SOLID EXCRETIONS.		LIQUID EXCRETIONS, DRIED.	
Ammonia	9·2	Uric acid	59
Uric acid	84·65	Earthy and alkaline phosphate, sulphates, and chlorides	41
Phosphate of lime	6·15		
	100·0		100

The most elaborate set of experiments with the guano, with which I am acquainted, were made in 1810, upon potatoes and mangel-wurzel, in the Island of St. Helena, by the late General Beatson; and they are the more valuable from being comparative. The soil on which these experiments were made was rather stiff, being composed of blackish mould, intermixed with friable fat clay. The following table gives the results of every experiment : 35 loads of horse-dung litter per acre were used, 35 of hogs' dung litter, and 35 bushels per acre of the guano. With potato seed the size of walnuts, planted whole :—

Six inches deep. Bushels.		Three inches deep. Bushels.	
Guano	554	Guano	531
Horse-dung	583	Horse-dung	479
Pigs' dung	447	Pigs' dung	414
Soil simple	395	Soil simple	311

The total comparative produce in lbs. of potatoes, from a series of experiments on these manures, was therefore—

	lbs.
Guano, or sea-fowl dung, at 35 bushels per acre	639
Horse-dung, 35 cart loads per acre	626
Hogs' dung, 35 cart loads per acre	534
Soil simple	446

With mangel-wurzel the produce per acre on a similar soil was as follows :—

	Leaves. tons.	Roots. tons.
Soil simple	38	19¼
Hogs' dung and ashes, 360 bushels per acre	131	66¼
Guano, 35 bushels per acre	153¾	77¾

In an experiment of Mr. Henry Barton, of Caldy (*Brit. Farm. Mag.* v. vi. p. 555), with Swedish turnips, the following were the results :—

	tons.	cwt.	lbs.
Two rows manured with 6 cwts. per acre of guano produced	19	3	3
Two rows manured with 16 cart loads per acre of compost produced	16	0	6

In those of Mr. Pusey with Swedish turnips, upon a strong but shallow loam upon limestone, the following were the products (*Jour. Roy. Ag. Soc.*, v. iii. p. 425) :—

	At 18 inches.			At 27 inches		
	tons.	cwt.	lb.	tons.	cwt.	lb'
With 20 tons of dung per acre.........	13	13	40	13	1	36
With 20 bush. of bone	14	0	36	9	18	40
,, 26 bush. of Poittevin ....:	12	5	80	12	5	80
With 3 cwt. of urate.	13	1	48	12	1	48
,, 3 ,, of guano	13	10	16	12	3	16
,, 20 bush. of pearl ashes............	8	16	0	10	16	60

At the meeting of the Isle of Man Agricultural Society, in August, 1842, Mr. Lyle gave the results of some experiments with this manure on a light, poor, hungry soil, on which grew two patterns of grass—one of Stickney's rye-grass, mixed with small quantities of holcus lanatus (woolly soft grass), and poa trivialis ; the other of Italian rye-grass. Both were top-dressed on the 12th of May with guano, at the rate of 3 cwt. per acre. On the 20th June following, one square yard of the dressed and undressed spaces, taken as fairly as possible, was cut and carefully weighed; the following were the results:—

Stickney's rye-grass, and small quantities of Holcus lanatus and Poa trivialis.

Of one square yard, dressed with guano at the above rate, the produce weighed .... 7½lbs.
Of ditto, not so dressed 2¾

Italian rye-grass.

Of one square yard, dressed with guano as above, the produce weighed............ 10½lbs.
Of ditto, not dressed 4¼

The guano was also applied at the same time (12th of May,) and at the same rate, to rows of young elms, larches, and strawberries, and on the 20th of June these rows could be distinguished, even at a considerable distance, from the others, by their deep and healthy green, and more vigorous growth. — (*Johnson and Shaw's Farmer's Almanac, v. 1. p. 290.*)

The experiments hitherto reported, made in Ireland with guano, appear to have been on a small scale, and attended with all the disadvantages arising from a first attempt with a new manure. The results of several of these were communicated to Lord Gosford's annual meeting at Market Hill, in December, 1842, from which I find that the Rev. R. Archer, of Hilltown, obtained the following results from the admeasurement of a square perch of each.

Kind of Manure, and Quantity per acre.	Sort of Turnips.	Crop, per acre.			
		Ton.	cwt.	qr.	lb.
Carb. of ammonia, 50lbs........	Skirving's Swede,	16	14	0	22
	without tops	13	16	1	20
Guano, 3¾ cwts. .	Ditto	25	14	1	4
	without tops	19	18	2	8
Guano, do.	Yellow Aberdeen,	38	17	0	8
	without tops	31	10	0	0
Carb. of ammonia, 100lbs.	Dale's Hybrid,	31	10	0	0
	without tops	18	12	3	2
Guano, 3½ cwts..	Ditto,	39	10	2	24
	without tops	27	16	1	20
Farm-yard manure perhaps 30 tons	White Norfolk,	33	7	2	20
..	without tops	23	15	2	24

The results of the experiments of Mr. Alexander Kinmouth, of Deer Park, were as follows : —

MANURE, Per English Acre.	PRODUCE, PER ACRE.				
		Tons.	cwts.	qrs.	lbs.
Farm-yard manure, 36 carts	Turnips	30	8	3	0
.. ..	Tops ..	8	15	3	0
Guano, 4 cwt.	Turnips	28	17	0	16
.. ..	Tops ..	4	4	1	4
Bones, 25 bushels	Turnips	20	17	0	16
.. ..	Tops ..	4	17	0	16
Compost of clay and lime — 30 barrels of lime mixed with the scourings and deepenings of flax-holes, which, when dry, lay 4 months before using	Turnips	28	1	1	20
	Tops ..	7	10	0	0

These experiments upon guano I have selected from the most recent with which I am acquainted (and others will be found in the subsequent pages of this Magazine) ; from these we may arrive at the conclusion that the effects which it has been noticed to produce when used in sufficient proportions, are exactly those which might be calculated upon, from a knowledge of its chemical composition. The salts of ammonia, with which it abounds, of necessity produce that early vegetation, and those dark green coloured leaves in the after stages of the growth of the plant, that the salts of ammonia, in other forms, are pretty certain to induce. Rapid, however, in their action, they of necessity speedily lose their fertilizing powers, since decomposed by the growing plant, the nitrogen and the hydrogen of which the ammonia is composed, are assimilated by the plant. The salts of ammonia being decomposed, nothing of any material consequence remains for the service of the growing crop but the phosphate of lime. This salt, it is well known, forms the chief fertilizing ingredient in bones ; if this was removed from them the bones would become of little value. Now, this mode of comparison may be some guide in directing us to the true proportion in which the guano should be applied to the soil. Guano there contains phosphate of lime in varying proportions, but always in quantities very considerably inferior to bones ; sometimes 10 or 15, at others 22, and in one specimen 30 per cent. of this salt was detected. Now this is not half the amount of the same salt that bones contain. M. Berzelia found 55 per cent. in those of the ox. 67 per cent. has been detected in those of the horse, and 70 in those of the sheep. How then is it probable if the farmers of the turnip soils of England find it necessary to use from twelve to sixteen bushels per acre of crushed bones, how is it likely that a much less quantity of guano can be needed? It is true that in the watered lands of South America, only three or four cwts. per acre are applied ; but then these soils are *irrigated* immediately after the guano is applied, so that its salts of ammonia are dissolved and form a liquid manure ; and every farmer is well aware that the very object and effect of all liquid manures is to reduce the amount of the organic matters, which is, in other forms, necessary to apply to the soil. And as I have elsewhere remarked, I have every reason to believe that for grass lands, especially those in moist situations, guano, in liberal proportions, will be found to be an excellent top-dressing. To assert, however, as some persons have, that guano may be successfully used in the proportion of about one cwt. per acre, is to injure the cause of the guano ; it is an error which could only arise from an ignorance of its mode of action and chemical composition, and can only be compared to the absurd story once so gravely detailed, that a single bushel of common salt would permanently fertilize an acre of grass.

ROYAL AGRICULTURAL SOCIETY OF ENGLAND.

The Council held their first monthly meeting at the Society's House, in Hanover Square, on Wednesday, the 1st of February; present—His Grace the Duke of Richmond in the Chair, Earl of Euston, Colonel Austen, Thomas Raymond Barker, Esq., French Burke, Esq., Colonel Challoner, F. Clifford Cherry, Esq., Charles Robert Colvile, Esq., M.P., James Dean, Esq., Humphrey Gibbs, Esq., B. Brandreth Gibbs, Esq., Henry Handley, Esq., W. Goodenough Hayter, Esq., M.P., C. Hillyard, Esq., W. Fisher Hobbs, Esq., John Houghton, Esq., John Kinder, Esq , Francis Pym, Esq., Rev. W. L. Rham, Professor Sewell, William Shaw, Esq., and John Worsop.

Mr. Raymond Barker, Chairman of the Finance Committee, presented to the Council the Committee's Monthly Report, on the state of the funds of the Society, the current cash balance in the hands of the bankers on that day being 1,772l., and the amount of invested capital 6,700l. stock. The Report announced the decision of the Committee on the two resolutions referred to them by the Council, the committee recommending two additional clerks for the execution and despatch of the increasing business of the Society, and the continued adoption of post-office orders for the transmission of subscriptions to the Society's office.

These recommendations were unanimously adopted by the Council.

Mr. Pym reported to the Council the steps he had taken for getting in the arrears of subscriptions in Bedfordshire, and the success which had attended his applications to the Members in that county, the subscriptions received by him on the part of the Society having amounted to the sum of £54.

Mr. Wyon, her Majesty's Chief Medallist at the Royal Mint, having transmitted to the Council the great seal confided to his execution, it was declared by the Council to be unanimously adopted as the common seal of the Society ; and Mr. Dean having laid before the Council, on the part of Mr. Bicknell, the Society's solicitor, and of Messrs. Lowe, the solicitors of Sir George Talbot, the approved lease of the Society's house in Hanover-square, for a term of 99 years, at an annual rent of £300 for the house and £30 for the fixtures, the seal of the Society was affixed to the lease in the presence of the Council, and the contract signed by the Secretary, in the name and on behalf of the Society, agreeably with the terms and condition of the Royal Charter, the Duke of Richmond as the Chairman, and Mr. Handley as a Trustee, attesting, by their signatures to the document, the validity of the contract.

On the motion of Mr. Gibbs, seconded by the Earl of Euston, the following resolutions, of which due notice had been given, were carried unanimously :—

1. That a card be printed for the use of the Members of the Council, showing the dates at which the stated meetings of the Council will take place throughout the Session.

2. That the Duke of Richmond, Earl Spencer, the Chairman of the Journal Committee, the Chairman of the Finance Committee, and Mr. Gibbs, be appointed a Committee to inquire into, and report upon, a more economical mode of printing and getting up the Journal; and that they be requested to report the result of their inquiries as early as convenient.

3. That the Finance and Journal Committees be requested to settle a scale of charges for the insertion of advertisements in the advertising sheet of the Journal; and that the publisher be instructed to receive advertisements accordingly on the account of the Society.

Notices of Motion.—The Rev. W. L. Rham gave notice that he should move, at the next Monthly Council, for the appointment of a Sub-Committee of the Journal Committee, to whom all papers and agricultural correspondence should be referred, and who should meet monthly to examine and classify the papers, and make their reports to the Council; and Mr. Raymond Barker, for the appointment of a permanent House Committee, entrusted with given powers; and Mr. Gibbs, that an annual list of the Members be printed showing the state of arrears (if any) due from each Member, no Member being allowed to have his copy of the Journal delivered or sent to him for any year until the subscription for that year shall have been paid.

The Duke of Rutland placed at the disposal of the Society a cow on the Belvoir Castle Farm, whose extraordinary case of preternatural enlargement of one side of the body without any apparent cause, and under the condition of perfect health and uninterrupted functions, had already been brought under the notice of the Council by the Duke of Richmond. The best thanks of the Council were voted to the Duke of Rutland for this instance of his Grace's interest and liberality ; and Professor Sewell undertook, at the request of the Council, to communicate with the Duke of Rutland on this subject.

The Marquis of Downshire, and Mr. Blacker, of Armagh, transmitted communications to the Council, having reference to the recent agricultural meeting at Markethill, in Ireland.

The Baron de Cetto, the Bavarian minister, communicated to the Council a request on the part of the Bavarian Agricultural Society on the subject of the Alpaca.

Mr. Richard W. Nash, Secretary of the Western Australian Society, transmitted to the Council an acknowledgment on the part of that Society, of its having been placed on the list of the corresponding Societies of the Royal Agricultural Society of England ; and a statement of the intention of its members to communicate every information in their power upon any subject regarded as of sufficient importance.

Mr. Ridgway, of Piccadilly, sent in a proposal to undertake the printing of the Society's list in a compendious and economical manner.

The thanks of the Council were ordered for these communications, and for those of Sir Francis Mackenzie and Mr. Houghton, laid at the same time before them.

Numerous donations were received of books for the Society's library, and for the museum the model of a new roller, invented by Mr. Clifford Cherry, for pressing and equalising the surface of land.

The Council adjourned to Wednesday next, the 8th of February.

A Council was held at the Society's House in Hanover-square, on Wednesday, the 8th of February; present, Philip Pusey, Esq., M.P., in the chair; Thos. Raymond Barker, Esq.; James Dean, Esq. ; Humphrey Gibbs, Esq. ; Brandreth Gibbs, Esq. ; William Goodenough Hayter, Esq., M.P.; W. Woods Page, Esq.; Wm. Shaw, Esq.; and W. R. Crompton Stansfield, Esq., M.P.

The various communications presented to the Society

since the former meeting were received with the best thanks of the Council.

The Council then adjourned to Wednesday next, the 15th inst.

At a Council, held on Wednesday, the 15th of February — present, William Miles, Esq., M.P., in the chair; Colonel Austen; David Barclay, Esq., M.P.; Thomas Raymond Barker, Esq.; French Burke, Esq.; Colonel Challoner; F. C. Cherry, Esq.; Brandreth Gibbs, Esq.; Humphrey Gibbs, Esq.; William Goodenough Hayter, Esq., M.P.; Philip Pusey, Esq., M.P.; Rev. W. L. Rham, and William Shaw, Esq.

Communications were received from His Grace the Duke of Portland, on the application of bones as a manure; from Sir John W. Lubbock, Bart., on the agricultural instruction of cottage tenantry; and from Mr. J. H. Charnock, of Wakefield, on the subject of drainage.

The Council adjourned to Wednesday next, the 22nd instant.

NEW MEMBERS.

The following gentlemen have been elected members of the Society during the month.

Thomas John Moysey Bartlett, Esq., solicitor, of 5, Beak Street, Regent Street, London, was elected a Governor.

Adams, Edward, Bassford Hall, Newcastle, Staffs.
Alsop, John, Darley Dale, Bakewell, Derbyshire
Ames, John, 33, Green Street, Grosvenor Square, London
Ansdell, John, Glàsllyn, near Abergavenny, S.W.
Argile, George, Heage Hall, Belper, Derbyshire
Baker, Benjamin, Acle, near Yarmouth, Norfolk
Balmer, Thomas, Fochabers, N. B.
Barber, John, Derby
Barker, James, The Hall, Bakewell, Derbyshire
Barrow, G. H., Ringwood House, near Chesterfield, Derbysh.
Baring, John, Oakwood, Chichester, Sussex
Bate, Samuel, Beech, Swinnerton, Stone, Staffordshire
Beeley, Samuel, Palterton, near Chesterfield, Derbysh.
Belcher, the Rev. George Paul, Butterton, Ashbourne, Derbyshire
Bentall, Edward Hammond, Heybridge, near Maldon, Essex
Biddulph, Robert, Charing Cross, London, and Ledbury, Hertfordshire
Bilbie, Thomas, Nettleworth, Notts.
Bird, John, Westerfield, Ipswich, Suffolk
Bloodworth, Thomas, Kimbolton, Huntingdonshire
Boden, Henry, The Field, Derby
Braddock, Henry, Bury St. Edmunds, Suffolk
Brittlebank, William, Winster, Bakewell, Derbyshire
Brightmore, John, Highlow, near Bakewell
Brooke, Thomas, Pencraig Court, near Ross, Herefordshire
Brown, Thomas, Kinwarton, Stratford-on-Avon, Warwickshire
Buckley, the Rev. Henry W., Hartshorne, Burton-on-Trent, Staffordshire
Buckley, John, jun., Normanton Hill, Loughborough, Leicestershire
Bulpet, W. W., Winchester
Burgess, Joseph Stubbins, Holme Pierrepoint, Nottingham
Burgess, William, Wiggenhall, Saint-Mary-Magdalen, near Lynn, Norfolk
Burnell, Edward Pegge, Wimburne Hall, near Southwell, Notts.
Butler, Sir Thomas, Bart., Ballin Temple, County Carlow, Ireland

Calvert, Edward, Derby
Campion, William, jun., Heben-Abbot, Winchester
Campion, Rev. H., Danny House, Brighton
Cantrell, Rev. William, Alvaston Field, Derby
Cantrill, Joseph Thomas, 21, Old-square, Lincoln's Inn, London
Carpenter, Thomas, Hull Farm, Chipping Norton, Oxon.
Carr, Walter Edmund, Milfield House, Wooler, Northumberland.
Capel, Arthur, Bulland Lodge, Wiveliscombe, Somersetshire
Capron, George, Stoke, Northamptonshire
Carson, Rev. Thomas, Vicar of Crich, near Alfreton, Derbyshire
Cathcart, Sir John Andrew, Adlestress House, near Chipping Norton, Oxon.
Chambers, John, the Hurst, Alfreton, Derbyshire
Charles, Charles, Wollaton, Nottingham
Charlton, Thomas Broughton, Chilwell Hall, Nottingham
Clarence, John, 21, Cullum Street, Fenchurch Street, London
Clarke, Charles, Matlock Bath, Derbyshire
Clavering, William, University Club, Suffolk Street, London
Cleave, John, Hereford
Cleave, Benjamin, Newcombe, Crediton, Devon
Crundwell, George, Castle Hill, Tunbridge, Kent
Cocker, Henry, Hathersage, near Bakewell
Coke, Major, Vice-President of the North Derbyshire Agr. Soc., Woodhouse, Mansfield, Notts.
Conyton, George, Pentillie Castle, Plymouth
Copeman, W. W., North Wilts Bank, Devizes, Wilts.
Corney, Thomas, 65, Old Broad Street, London
Cotterell, Jacob Henry, land-agent, Bath
Cox, L., Ardington Mill, Wantage, Berkshire
Crompton, Gilbert, Chesterfield, Derbyshire
Curtis, Samuel, Justice of the Peace, Wellington Valley, New South Wales
Davis, John, Mapperton, Wincanton, Somersetshire
Day, Thomas, Spaldwick, near Kimbolton, Huntingdonshire
Deane, Thomas, Hambleden, near Henley, Oxon.
Dean, Alexander, Pershore Road, Smithfield, Birmingham
Deans, Rev. Joseph, Vicar of Melbourne and Chellaston, Derbyshire
Dyott, Captain, Frenford, Lichfield, Staffordshire
Ella, William, Wimeswold, Loughborough, Leicestershire
Elliot, William, Grislow Field, near Bakewell
Fawcett, Rev. Christopher, Boscombe Rectory, near Amesbury, Wilts.
Fairman, William Creed, Gore House, Sittingbourne, Kent
Featherstonhaugh, Timothy, the College, Kirkoswald, Cumberland
Forrester, George, Bryanston, Blandford, Dorset
Fremantle, Rev. Wm. Robt., Rector of Middle Claydon, Winslow, Bucks.
Frost, Jonathan, Baslow, near Bakewell
Frost, Matthew, Buxton, near Bakewell
Fuller, Augustus Elliot, M.P., Rose Hill, Roberts'-bridge, Sussex, and 26, Clifford Street, London
Gamble, Joss Christopher, Sutton House, St. Helen's, Lancashire
Garlick, John, Gosberton, near Spalding, Lincolnsh.
Gibbons, Edward, Minster, Isle of Thanet, Kent
Godfrey, Thomas Spragging, Balderton, near Newark, Notts.
Goodwin, George, Langar, near Bingham, Notts.
Goodwin, William, Birchwood, near Alfreton, Derbysh.
Gorham, John, Wittering, Chichester, Sussex
Griffith, Edward Humphrey, Ty-newydd, near Denbigh
Hall, Joseph, Castleton, near Bakewell, Derbyshire
Hall, Jas. Wallace Richard, Springfield, near Ross, Herefordshire
Hallowes, Thomas, Glapwell Hall, Chesterfield, Derbyshire

Halton, Rev. Immanuel, Winfield Manor, Alfreton, Derbyshire
Harris, James, Long Sutton, near Odiham, Hants
Harrison, Thomas, Risley, Derby
Haworth, S. R., 21, High-street, Hull
Hawkins, John, Heage, Belper, Derbyshire
Heathcote, Arthur H., Blackwell, near Bakewell
Heathcote, Cockshutt, Teignmouth, Devonshire
Heath, John, Amersham, Bucks
Henson, John, Walton, Loughborough, Leicestershire
Heywood, John Thomas, Brimington, near Chesterfield, Derbyshire
Heyworth, Ormerod, Everton, Liverpool
Hill, Edward, Brierly Hill, near Dudley, Wore.
Holmes, John, Alfreton, Derbyshire
Howard, John, Bedford
Hoy, Barlow, Thornhill Park, near Southampton
Hubbersty, Rev. Nathan, Wirksworth, Derbyshire
Hubbersty, Philip, Solicitor, Wirksworth, Derbyshire
Hughes, William, Framfield, Sussex
Humbert, Charles F., Stanmore, Middlesex
Hunt, Charles Brook, Bowden Hall, Gloucester
Hunter, Charles Vickers, Kilbourne, near Derby
Hurley, Richard, Gaddon House, Collumpton, Devonshire
Ingle, Thomas, Solicitor, Belper, Derbyshire
Keppell, Hon. Colonel, Ashley Lodge, near Lymington, Hants.
Jepson, William, Edensor Inn, near Bakewell
Jones, Thomas, Kensworth, Market Street, Herts.
Keary, H. W., Holkham, Norfolk
Lacey, William, Adbolton, Nottingham
Leech, John, Fox and Owl Inn, Derby
Lees, Benjamin, Eastling, Feversham, Kent
Llewellyn, Pearce, Merrion Court, near Pembroke, S.W.
Lingen, Henry, 4, Essex Court, Temple
Longcroft, Chas. Richard, Llanina, Cardiganshire
Longsdon, William, Longstone, near Bakewell
Luckham, Levi, Broadway, near Weymouth
Mac Cound, Henry, Cressbrook, Bakewell, Derbyshire
Martin, Wm. Bennett, Westborough, Barnsley, Yorkshire
Martin, Charles Wykeham, M.P., Leeds Castle, Maidstone, Kent
Mead, Rev. David, Brewham, Bruton, Somerset
Miller, Giles, Goudhurst, Kent
Mills, Samuel, 20, Russell Square, London
Mills, John, Bisterne, Ringwood, Hampshire
Milnes, William, Stubbing Edge, Alfreton, Derbyshire
Milnes, James, Wood End, near Matlock, Derbyshire
Mold, John, Alderwasley, Belper, Derbyshire
Morris, Thomas, Woolpack Lane, Nottingham
Mosley, Ashley Nicholas Avery, Burneston House, near Derby
Mundy, William, Markeaton, near Derby
Murdock, James Gordon, 11, Haymarket, London
Nash, Daniel, 60, Strand, London
Newdigate, F., Blackheath, Kent
North, Nicholas, Wiggenhall, Saint-Mary-Magdalen, near Lynn, Norfolk
Oakes, Thomas, Riddings House, near Alfreton, Derbyshire
Ord, Capt. Harry Gough, Manor House, Bexley, Kent
Ormerod, George, Fern Hill, near Rochdale, Lanc.
Parkinson, John, Kepnersley, Herefordshire
Paxton, Joseph, Chatsworth, near Bakewell
Peach, Robert, Fansley, near Derby
Pearson, John, South Winefield, Alfreton, Derbyshire
Pell, Albert, Penner Hill, Watford, Hertfordshire
Penton, Thomas, Middleton-street Farm, Longparish, Whitchurch, Hampshire
Phillips, John Friend Pering, Gitcumbe, near Totness, Devon
Philips, Fred. Charles, Rhual, near Mold, Flintshire

Portman, Wyndham B., R.N., Hare Park, Newmarket
Potter, Joseph, Horsley Woodhouse, Derby
Poyser, Thomas, Solicitor, Wirksworth, Derbyshire
Price, Joseph, Monmouth
Radford, Edward, Tansley Wood, Matlock, Derbyshire
Rea, George, North Middleton, near Wooler, Northumberland
Read, John, Derwent Hall, Sheffield
Rees, John, Flimston, near Pembroke, S.W.
Reed, John, Hopton, Suffolk
Redfern, William, Middleton, Bakewell, Derbyshire
Rendlesham, Lord, Rendlesham, Woodbridge, Suffolk
Riches, John, Uxbridge, Middlesex
Roberts, Charles, Tedmore, near Stourbridge, Worcestershire
Rogers, Captain William Henry, Newland, near Coleford, Gloucestershire
Rothwell, Richard Rainshaw, Preston, Lancashire, and 6, Alfred Place, Bedford Square, London
Round, George, Colchester, Essex
Sadler, William Ford, Nurseryman, Derby
Scarsdale, Lord, Kedleston Hall, near Derby
Scriven, George, Castle-Ashby, Northampton
Sergeant, John, Stratford-on-Avon, Warwickshire
Sharman, Alexander, Bedford
Sheppard, Sir Thos. Cotton, Bart., Thornton Hall, Stoney Stratford, Bucks
Simpson, James Blyth, Derby
Sitwell, Edward Degge, Stainsby, near Derby
Slater, John, Shottle, Belper, Derbyshire.
Smith, Alfred, Banker, Derby
Smith, Thomas, Cotton Court, Manchester
Smith, John George, Crediton, Devon
Spencer, Griffin, Alfreton, Derbyshire
Stedman, Robert, Great Bookham, Leatherhead, Surrey
Stedman, Robert, Pakenham, Ixworth, Suffolk
Stevens, John, Breaston, Derby
Stirrup, Samuel, Mansfield, Notts.
Stokes, Thomas, Wilford Place, Leicester
Stone, Thos., Barrow, Loughborough, Leicestershire
Story, Nathaniel, Derby
Strutt, Jedediah, Belper, Derbyshire.
Symonds, Thomas Powell, Pengethly, Ross, Herefordshire
Swinborne, Robert, Great Oakley, Colchester, Essex
Taylor, Robert, Treeton Mills, Rotherham
Taylor, John, jun., Coed-Du, Mold, Flintshire
Taylor, Henry, Pilsley, near Bakewell
Taylor, John, Mereworth, Wrotham, Kent
Tebbs, John, Walcot, near Lutterworth, Leicestershire
Thomas, Le Marchant, Billingbear Park, Wokingham, Berks.
Thomas, Ilted, Hill House, Swansea, S.W.
Tooke, Rev. Alfred, East Mordon, Blandford, Dorset
Turbutt, Gladwin, Ogston Hall, near Alfreton, Derbysh.
Tuck, Henry, Avon, Ringwood, Hampshire
Turner, the Rev. Arthur, Ladbroke Rectory, Southam, Warwickshire
Vandeleur, George, King's Newton Hall, Derby
Vickers, Abraham, Manchester
Wakely, Thomas, Rainham, Rochester, Kent
Watkins, Samuel, Worksop, Notts.
Webster, Frederick, Marley Farm, Battle, Sussex
White, T. H., Chevening, Kent
Wheatcroft, Abraham, Cromford, Derbyshire
Willis, Charles, Cranbrook, Kent
Worsley, Charles Carill, Winster, Bakewell, Derbysh.
Wright, Henry, Kelvedon Hall, Chipping Ongar, Essex
Wright, Charles, Wirksworth, Derbyshire
Wyley, James, High Onn, Stafford
Wyatt, Harvey, Acton Hill, near Stafford
Wyatt, William, Eyam, near Bakewell
Wyatt, Robert, Foolow, near Bakewell

THE CORN LAWS.

SIR,—You are at liberty, if you think proper, to publish the following observations and remarks on the all-absorbing question of the corn laws. They are the conclusions arrived at after closely watching the working of those laws for more than thirty years. About 1810, I first began to consider the subject, and was then a decided advocate for those laws, and continued so for ten years. Since then my opinions have taken a retrograde bias, and at this time am in favour of an entire repeal. From 1813 to 1837 I was a *rent-paying farmer*, and I am still so connected with land in various ways, that if the corn laws are any benefit to those interested in land, they will be to me. But, however connected I was with land, I should be very sorry to advocate any law which might benefit one part of the community at the expense of the other.

My intention is to prove the following points :— 1st, That the corn laws were no benefit to the landowners from the year 1800 to 1815. That they were of considerable benefit to them from the latter period to 1830, and that from 1830 to the present time it is extremely doubtful whether they have not been injurious to them. 2nd, That the corn laws, instead of being any service to the tenant farmers, from 1800 to the present time, they have been extremely injurious to them, and of course to the rural population. In short, that they have produced a worse effect upon these two classes than upon any other class, or upon all the other classes. 3rd, That although I consider these laws have not had a good effect on the interest of the trading and manufacturing classes, yet I am far from thinking they have done the mischief which those classes imagine. It is my intention in this paper to steer clear of all party or interested views, and to fearlessly state what I consider to be the truth, whoever I may offend or whoever I may please.

There is little doubt but the real intention of the landowners in carrying the corn laws always has been to keep up the rent roll, but, at the same time, I feel persuaded that one part of the benefit, in their ideas, fell to the lot of the tenants and their labourers. They are charged with selfishness. I believe they have just as much of this vicious ingredient in their composition as the other classes of the community have, and no more. We have all too much of it, from the highest to the lowest ; the only difference is, that the wealthy, in every class, have the most power to injure his neighbour when he allows it to get the upper hand of his better feelings. England will never be a happy country till there is less of it. The aristocracy have a great number of faults, and some of them great ones. But, notwithstanding these faults, and notwithstanding the injury they have unintentionally done to their tenants and to their labourers, in the passing of the corn laws, they generally make the best landlords. Where it is otherwise, it is as often the fault of the agent as the principal.

I shall now proceed to prove my first proposition. From 1805 to 1815 the law allowed free importation of wheat at 6d. per quarter, when the price was above 66s. Now, during the whole of those ten years, with the exception of 1814, the price never averaged so low as 66s.; consequently,

there was a constant free importation previous to 1814 from this time, and, notwithstanding it being then stopped, corn still continued to fall in price till 1816, when we had a very bad harvest. In several of these ten years prices averaged 120s. or 130s. per quarter, although there was free importation at 66s. It is therefore clear that the corn laws were not the cause of these high prices, and of the high rents put upon the land, during those ten years, or I will say fifteen years—namely, from 1800 to 1815. The causes evidently were, the paper money and the war. During the whole of those fourteen years, when the ports were always open to foreign corn, and of course a free trade in it, the importation of wheat never amounted in any one year to one million quarters, except in 1810, when it amounted to near one and a half millions. My object in stating this is to prove that we should never be able to import even one-sixth of our consumption, and that we should always be dependent on the British farmer for a supply under any circumstance.

I know it will be said that in those fifteen years we were at war with France, and that the seat of war was generally in the corn-growing countries of Europe, and from which the armies would have to be supplied. But we were at peace with America most of the time, and the war was never carried into Poland or Russia till 1813 ; and, as we were master of the sea, those countries were open to us, and where it is said we can get the cheapest grain.

In 1815 wheat got down to the average of 63s. 8d. per quarter, and the landowners considering that with the rents and burdens upon land, at that time, it could not be grown for less than 80s., they passed a law prohibiting importation when the price was below that sum. And, under the idea that the general average would be near 80s., landowners, valuers, and farmers, made their valuations and estimates accordingly, and, of course, rents remained at the point which they had gained before the conclusion of the war. Then it was that the ruin of the tenant and the labourer commenced. Then it was that the landowners were receiving thirty per cent. more rent than they ought to have done ; for, notwithstanding the prohibition when the price was under 80s., and notwithstanding, of course, that there was none imported, except in 1817 and 1818, the prices kept averaging lower and lower (except in these two years), till 1822, when the average was 43s. 3d., only 3s. 3d. above one-half of the prices contemplated by the landowners, farmers, &c., at the passing of the Act of 1815. The average in these seven years never reached 80s., except in 1817 and 1818, which was caused by the two extremely bad seasons of 1816 and 1817 ; and, excluding these two years, the average price of wheat of the other five years was 62s. 5d. It is clear the corn laws in these seven years could not keep the prices up anything near 80s.

The landowners, seeing that in 1822 wheat only averaged 43s. 3d., and seeing the ruin which was taking place amongst farmers and all the rural population, concluded there must be something wrong in the law as it then stood, and, of course, in 1823 passed a new law. Now this law was a proof that all who voted for it were either extremely deficient in common sense, or in firm upright integrity ; because if they had marked the working of the preceding law, they would have seen that it had been ineffectual. They would

N

have seen that it had not prevented wheat coming down to an average of 43s. 3d., without any importation, except after an extremely bad harvest; therefore, it was very clear that the new law could not have that effect. Those who had not marked this were unfit for law makers, and those who had, and still voted for it, were not honest men, as it is evident they intended to do an injustice to the farmers by keeping their rents up a little longer.

The law of 1823 prohibited importation of wheat when the price was below 70s., with a duty of 17s. per quarter when above. It was again supposed by the farmers and land valuers that the price would average near the above price; of course, rents were still fixed higher than they ought to have been. Landowners and all the other classes also supposed, or pretended to suppose, that wheat would never be much below 70s., while the law of 1823 remained in force.

This law continued in force till 1828; and how does the fact stand? Why, that the average never reached 70s., and only reached 60s. in two out of the five years. The lowest average of a whole year was 51s. 9d., and the average of the whole five years was 58s. 5d., or 11s. 7d. below the price prohibiting importation; of course, it could not be foreign corn which reduced the price in England, and it follows that the law was worse than useless to the farmers, as without it they would have expected low prices. The consequence was, they were still sinking deeper in poverty, and of course the landowners still getting more rent than their due—that is, where the tenants could stand the screw, and the landowners were true "Shylocks."

In 1828 the late law was passed, and has been one of the greatest humbugs that has been enacted of late years. However, the injury it has done the farmers has not been so great as was the case with the two former bills. 1st, They had had two excellent lessons taught them by the preceding laws, and had not much confidence in any corn laws. 2nd, What little confidence they had was shaken by the sliding scale, as the price of corn abroad was represented to be so low as to afford the foreign corn merchant to pay almost any amount of duty fixed by the law. They were therefore extremely cautious in their offer of rent, and there had also been a general reduction, to a considerable amount, all over the kingdom, but particularly in the agricultural districts.

Having shown that the corn laws of 1815 and 1823 had entirely failed in their object of keeping prices and rents up, and of course had brought ruin on the great body of *farmers* and their *labourers*, I shall next show what the *sliding scale* humbug has done for these classes. In 1828, the miseries of the rural population were such as to make property completely unsafe in the agricultural counties. Seeing this state of things, and still clinging to the corn laws, like a drowning man to a straw, and being urged by the trading interest to make some alteration in those laws, and wishing to appear liberal in making the change, our law-makers enacted the sliding scale.

For nine years (ending 1837) after the passing of this act, the price of wheat averaged 56s.; and if 1838 had not been an *extremely deficient harvest*, and the three following ones below an average, the price would still not have averaged more than 56s. In 1835, the average was 39s. 1d., and in one week in January, 1836, as low as 36s. Therefore in these nine years there was little or

no foreign corn in the market; of course importation was not the cause of those low prices, and it follows that the *corn laws* could not keep prices up. And, if they fail in the object intended, why keep such laws in force—or, at all events, why not have a low fixed duty, which would assist the revenue?

Previous to the passing of the late act in 1828, I have said that rents and other expenses of farming were very considerably reduced throughout the country; of course the prices under the last law, previous to 1838, did not produce the same ruinous results to the farmer as the preceding I aw had done; but their capital had been so much reduced, that the wages of their labourers could not be advanced, on account of the farmers being unable to employ the number of hands they otherwise would have done. But it is very clear that the sliding scale would still have slided money out of their pockets, if new bargains had not been entered into as regards rent, &c.

Since 1838, we have had several general gaol deliveries of foreign corn, which, with a great quantity on which duty has been paid, above the nominal duty of 1s. per quarter; so that we may say that we have had open ports for corn since 1838, so far as competing with the British farmer; and I feel convinced that little more foreign corn would have entered our ports for the last three years, if they had been entirely open the whole time. It is therefore very clear that the *sliding scale* could not prevent wheat coming *down* to 36s. per quarter, or advancing *up* to 80s. From what I have stated above, and from what I have felt in practice, I am quite satisfied that the corn laws, previous to 1828, were the cause of the ruin of hundreds of farmers, and of the starvation of thousands of their labourers; and that since 1828, the late law has been no manner of use to them, or to the landowners. It is evident that the amount of *paper money*, combined with the *productive* or *unproductive seasons*, have more to do with the prices of grain than the corn laws have.

The landowners on one side, and the trading interest on the other, may say that, if there had been no corn laws, prices might have been considerably lower than they have been. I do not believe it, neither can they prove it; and by-and-by I shall prove that it would not have been the case; it is therefore idle talk to say, as the trading interest do say, that these laws double the price of bread.

Previous to 1842, we had four deficient harvests, two of them very much so. The crop of 1838 was not more than two-thirds of an average one in this parish, and was little more in any part of England or Scotland.

I will now endeavour to prove that, had the ports always been open, the prices of grain would not have averaged much, if any, less than they have done.

I have already shown that, with *open ports*, from 1800 to 1815 wheat scarce ever averaged below 80s., and several years above 100s. per quarter. In 1817 and 1818 *open ports* could not keep it below the average of 80s.

With all the foreign corn which has come into the English market the last four years previous to 1842, a great part at a nominal duty, the average price has not been much below 70s. (68s.), even with the great quantity of inferior grain which has been brought into the market. Without this it would have been nearer 80s. than 70s. I repeat that it is quite clear that, when we have either an *excess* of *paper money* or a *deficient harvest*, prices cannot. be kept down with *open ports or free importations* at a nominal duty; of course, at *such times*, corn laws do nothing *for* the *interest* of the landowner, and not half the injury to the consumer as is represented by that class. To the farmer they never did anything but injury.

It is quite clear that the average price of wheat for nine years after the passing of the late act could not have been so low as 56s., if we had not grown sufficient for home consumption; and, as the farmers were at the end of those nine years in far better circumstances than at present, it proves that 56s. is a remunerative price to the British farmers, when we have *average crops*, and, supposing rents and other burdens the same as in those nine years. Now, supposing that we had had open ports those nine years, would the prices have been much lower upon an average than 56s.? or would they have fluctuated more? I feel convinced they would not. It would not do for England to purchase foreign corn to any extent with *hard cash*. If we must import extensively, so as to injure the British farmer in his own market, wheat must be laid down in the manufacturing districts at a less price than 56s.; and the foreign corn merchant must take goods in exchange, not cash. Now our manufacturers say this will be the case; but stop, my friends, do not be sure of this. What advantages have the farmers in *Russia, Prussia, Poland, &c.*, over the English farmers? It is said, *little or no rent, few if any taxes, very low wages*, or no wages *at all* in some parts. This is a very pretty picture till examined very closely, when it will be seen that there are a few blemishes in it. But I will let these alone till I have examined the other side of this pretty *gilded* picture. Well, then, what are the *disadvantages?* Well, there is the English corn merchants' profit; carriage from the English port to the interior; the English port dues; the freight, insurance, and risk from damage while on board ship; the foreign port dues; the foreign corn merchants' profit; carriage by water from the interior, with damage and waste; carriage by land from the farm to the river—from one mile to perhaps fifty, sixty, or a hundred miles, over *bad roads.* There are neither *canals* or *railroads* in those countries, where there are no *rents* or *wages* paid. The farmers are deficient in capital, and both them and their labourers are deficient in skill, in comparison with the British farmers and their labourers — although these have plenty of room for improvement. Grain is continually wasting and taking damage, from its being first cut from the land till it gets to the consumer: in the stack, in the barn, in the granary, on board ship or boat, in the warehouse, at the mill, it it is continually *wasting*, or taking damage from *insects, vermin*, or *moisture.* When all these advantages and disadvantages are balanced on both sides, I say, I do *not fear the foreign farmer a fig, with open ports and without duty.* It is the increased skill and industry of the British farmers and their labourers which has enabled them to produce wheat at 56s., with the present rent and taxes; and there is little doubt in my mind, that, by applying more capital and skill to the British soil, it will be raised at considerably less price than that.

There has been no more grain raised in foreign countries than what has been consumed there or exported; and, from accounts from all travellers, all the land near *good roads* or *rivers* is occupied in the cultivation of grain. Of course, if their exports must be extensively increased, the cultivation of grain must be greatly extended; and this cannot be done without a greater outlay of capital in the cultivation of the land at present in tillage, or by extending the cultivation of grain at a *greater distance from good roads or water carriage.* To intersect the country with common roads, railroads, or canals, will also require capital. The Russians, Poles, and Germans are poor, and while they continue to export corn at a very *low price*, they will *continue so*, whether they take our manufactured goods or not. If they were to sell grain at a higher price, it would require considerable time to acquire this necessary capital; and at present they seem inclined to expend what they can spare on manufacturing for themselves, and by-and-by I will show that they will continue to do so, however free and open the British ports are for their corn.

If foreign landowners get *little or no rent*, and if the foreign *labourers* and *farmers* get *little or no wages or remuneration*, how will it be possible for them to take our manufactured goods to any extent for their corn? The labouring classes must be content with the plainest and coarsest of clothing, and not sufficient of that; neither can the higher classes (there is seldom any middle class in such countries) afford any luxury either of dress, equipage, or furniture. Where there is little coming in, there will be little going out. It will just amount to this: while they remain in such circumstances as to afford grain *lower than the British farmer*, with their advantages, they will not be in circumstances to take our goods at a price to pay the manufacturers; and, if their circumstances improve by *higher rents* and *higher wages*, then they cannot afford grain at the same low price. It is the low wages which are now given in England to all classes of labourers which prevent them from purchasing clothes and other articles of comfort; and very low wages will produce the same effect everywhere. I maintain that *high wages* and *low-priced provisions* can never go together; the nature of the thing will not allow it. Labour constitutes a great portion of the expense of raising grain; I therefore repeat that; if wages rise abroad so as to afford the labourers good cloth, furniture, and houses, the expense of raising grain will be increased in the same proportion. At present the Germans, Russians, &c., want only *cash;* and while they do this, it will be ruin to us to take much of their grain.

For ten years ending 1840, the average price of wheat at Danzig was 37s. 7d.; at Petersburgh, 36s.; at Odessa, 27s. 9d. With respect to expenses, it is difficult to get a correct statement, as they are generally made out for party purposes; and I never saw one yet but I could find several holes in it. According to a writer in favour of corn laws, the average expense, interest, and profit, from the above ports, is 13s. per quarter; but the writer has made no allowance for damage by moisture, heating, English port dues, porterage, and warehouse rent at the British port; or carriage inland, British corn merchants' profits and interest; no allowance for feeding rats, mice, insects, sailors, porters, carters, and millers—for no man will starve who works in grain. It is therefore clear that 13s. will not cover all expenses, risk, and waste. Again, the grain from the above ports is not equal in *quality* to the British in fair average seasons, and of course would not sell in the same market at the same price by several shillings per quarter.

It will be seen from the above, that wheat from the above foreign ports could not have been sold in the English market on an average of ten years, for less than 50s. or 51s.; and, taking the quality into account, could only meet the British wheat at about 55s. or 56s. The average of England for those ten years was 57s.—only a difference of 1s., or 2s. at the most. There needs little more said to prove that, taking *quality into account*, wheat is at an average from 16s. to 20s. per quarter less at the above ports than the average price of English wheat. For six years ending 1837, the ports were entirely closed to foreign corn, and of course, in consequence of no demand for it, the price at the above ports would be at its *lowest point* for remunerating the foreign grower, and perhaps even lower than that. Well, the average of these six years in England was 50s.; the average at the above three foreign ports was 32s.; difference, 18s. We will take the lowest average in England for one year out of the above six years—namely, 1835—which was 39s. 1d.; average of the same year at the above ports, 28s. 4d.; difference, only 10s. 9d., which would not pay expenses, saying nothing of risk, &c. And yet the farmers in England were in better circumstances in 1835 than at present. It must be remarked here, that in England the average of these six years was 50s., and for 1835 only 39s. 1d.; difference, 10s. 11d.; while the difference at the above foreign ports was only 4s. 8d. between the average of the six years and 1835.

It is seen that with closed ports for six years the average price in England was 50s., and at the three foreign ports 32s., a difference just sufficient to cover all expenses, profits, waste, damage, &c., and difference of quality. Well, we will suppose the *ports had been open* those six years: what would have been the result? There *would have been* foreign corn imported, or there *would not*. *If not*, then prices would have remained at home and abroad as they were; but, if importation had taken place to that extent as to *reduce the average below* 50s. in England, it would also have raised *the average abroad*, in consequence of the greater demand, and would have acted upon the foreign corn merchant like burning a candle at both ends. It is to be seen from facts, that, as the foreign exports of corn *increase*, so the price there *advances*; for it is there, as it is here—*supply and demand* affect the prices.

Let us peep at the good old times of England, before the *French war*, when the "old English gentlemen" were so very generous and hospitable. The average of wheat in England for twenty years ending 1790 was 45s. 4d., ; the average at Danzig for the same time was 28s. 8d.; difference, 16s. 8d. The difference in England between the average of those twenty years and the last ten years is only 11s. 8d.; and the difference at Danzig is 8s. 11d. At that time the "fine old English gentleman" frequently gave the corn merchant 5s. per quarter for exporting wheat, so that prices could be kept up to 45s. He was then *frightened* of his *rent-roll* just as the "young English gentleman" is at present. At that time the rent of land was less than half the present rent—wages about one-half—lays at land taxes nothing in comparison to what they are at present; *no rural police;* yet the average price

of wheat was only 11s. 8d. below the average of the last ten years, in which we had several bad seasons. At that time (from 1770 to 1790) ports were generally open to foreign corn, and yet there is a difference of 16s. 8d. between the English price and the price at Danzig, which clearly proves that it required *that sum at that time* to cover expenses, profits, damage, and waste; and taking the difference of the value of money at the two periods into account, the cost of importing at this time should not be less than 30s.

I contend that, at the very lowest estimate, the *English landowners* enjoy an advantage of not less than from 16s. to 20s. per quarter over the *landowners of Poland and Russia*. This, I contend, is quite sufficient to cover the difference of the burdens upon the land, and, of course, that we may safely repeal the corn laws. As to the *tenants and their labourers*, they have *lost millions* by the corn laws.

I think I have shown that we cannot exchange goods for corn to any extent on the European continent, so as to pay the British manufacturers, on account of the poverty of the people; but it may be said, and is said, this may be done with America, as there the people get good wages, and spend very considerably on the various necessaries, comforts, and luxuries in and on their bodies, dwellings, &c. There, it is said, "they have corn enough, and to spare." We will soon see whether this is, or will be, the case to any extent or not.

Brother Jonathan talks loudly *at this time*, how he could befriend his old hard-worked brother John, by taking his manufactured goods, if Johnny will but take his corn in return for payment. But this is only because he finds that his brother, *at this time*, is selling his goods at *less than prime cost*, and has been giving *more than the average prime cost* for his corn. Now what Jonathan says is very well, and would without any doubt be the case, and would have been of late years of considerable benefit to England; and, of course, is one reason why the ports should have been open, and the corn laws repealed. But let wheat keep at its present price, and let manufactured goods *get up in price*, so as to pay the workmen *fair wages*, and masters and merchants a *fair remuneration*; I say, let these state of things come round again, and brother Jonathan will call out, "Oh, brother Johnny, brother Johnny! I cannot afford Wheat at that price and pay all expences; and I also begin to think of manufacturing for myself. However, if you will take my cotton, tobacco, and other produce of that nature, which you do not produce, and give me a good price for it, I will exchange with you; but I cannot stand your prices of corn, as my labourers are determined to have good wages. I have to give a dollar for wages where you give 1s. 6d."

I have said before that *cheap corn* and *high wages* cannot stand together. In an entirely new settled country, where there is little to do but plough, sow and reap, this may be the case; but in all that part of America east of the mountains, except the barren or unimprovable land, has now been in cultivation some time, and to raise good crops will require cultivating in the English or Scotch style; and of course with high priced labour, will make the expence of raising corn as great as in England. If the prices of grain in all the seaports be examined, it will be seen that little will come to England when the price is down here at 56s. Besides, in America there is a rapid increase of inhabitants, from births and *emigration*, so that the cultivation of grain has to be rapidly extended to supply their own wants, and brother Jonathan will not be content with the same quantity and quality of food as the Russian and Poland *serfs*, or even the *English labourer*. It is quite clear to me, that very cheap corn cannot be produced in America east of the Alleghany mountains, for reasons above stated ; and it can only be raised at *little cost* on the *fresh land* in the valleys of Ohio, Mississippi, and Missouri. An American writer says, wheat can be laid down at Liverpool, from these valleys, at 47s. the quarter. But in making out his bill of charges, profits, &c., he has left several items out, so that I feel convinced it cannot be brought from thence for that money.

If grain can be raised so very cheaply in the United States, why not in Canada ? There the rents and taxes are no higher than in the United States, and the land is superior to that in the eastern division of the United States. Canada is under the British government, and of course our markets are open to their produce, and every facility is afforded them for taking our articles of merchandise in return. There is sufficient of territory to raise grain for nearly all England, and the Canadians have their eyes open to profit where there is any to be had. Yet, with all these facilities for a traffic in food, there is never any extensive importations of corn from thence. The reason is obvious : corn cannot be raised without hands, and those hands *want wages and food*, and the Canadian farmers and labourers are both *better fed and paid* than the English. It is clear, from facts, that they have not sent, or will send, much corn when wheat is below 56s. here. Therefore, I for my part do not fear the American farmer with a free trade in corn. And I feel convinced, that whenever the corn laws are repealed—and most assuredly they will be repealed before many years are rolled over—the English landowners will find that their property will be depreciated very little if any in value. If I should recommend any duty at all upon foreign corn it should be a *low one, and fixed*, for the sole purpose of *raising revenue*.

I shall here say a few words on the objections of a fixed duty when prices are high. We will suppose it 10s., and the average prices in England 80s. If the duty was then taken off, the only difference it would make would be advancing the price at the foreign ports 10s., the price in England would remain the same. I will prove this from facts : on June 5th, 1841., wheat free on board at Danzig was 40s. Supposing wheat shipped on that day, by the time it arrived in England (five weeks) the duty was 24s. On August 17th it was seen that the duty would soon be down to 1s., and wheat was then 60s. at Danzig. That is, as the *duty fell* from 24s. to 1s. in England, *prices rose at Danzig* from 40s. to 60s. When prices are high here, the duty can be no object abroad, and prices will be high here, whether we have corn laws or not, when we have *more than one bad season in succession*, or when we have an excess of paper money. I am an advocate for a repeal of the corn laws, because I feel they are no benefit to the farmers or their labourers, or labourers of any class, and at this time, or for the future, no great benefit to the landowners. But at the same time, I am of opinion they have not done that injury to the manufacturer as is represented by

that class, although I admit they may have done some harm. It may perhaps then be asked, is there no remedy for the present depression ? I will give my opinion as to the causes, and leave it with the manufacturers to judge for themselves as to a remedy or remedies.

There were always ebbs and flows in trade, and ever will be. But notwithstanding this, ever since the conclusion of the war the profits on trade and commerce have regularly been getting less. Before I go into the causes of this, I will state what I conceive to be the cause of the *present deep and long continued depression*.

One cause, no doubt, is the four deficient harvests we have had, in consequence of which provisions have been so high that the labouring classes could only purchase food. Another cause in my opinion is, that there has been too much money spent in too little time in making railways ; particularly upon those which will never pay anything like fair interest. This, therefore, has been mis-spent capital. If one half the money which has been spent on railways had been spent upon the cultivation of waste lands, or in the better cultivation of the land at present in cultivation, it would have produced a *greater amount of manual labour*, and would have produced *double* the quantity of provisions we have imported. This would have assisted trade by *lowering* the price of provisions, and giving *more wages* to the labourers.

It appears to me very strange that almost any upstart, if he can raise a fine coat, sport a gold or silver watch-guard, smoke a cigar, and tell a plausible story on some speculative concern, can easily raise the means for carrying his project out ; while a drab coated farmer would be kicked out of doors for even having the presumption to ask for assistance in the improvement of his farm.

I will now give my opinion as to the causes of the falling off in the profits on trade, and which I say commenced at the conclusion of the war.

One cause, and the *principal* one, is *excessive taxation*, caused by that war. This cuts like a two edged sword. First, it has enabled foreigners to compete with us ; secondly, a great portion of the earnings of the people is taken to pay taxes, and of course cannot purchase sufficient of the comforts and necessaries of life, in clothing, furniture, &c.

Another cause is, *excessive extravagance* in the higher and the middle classes, and also *at times* in the labouring classes when they had the means to be so ; for there has been times when even this class could have saved money. The estates of the nobility are nearly all in mortgage. They cannot support the younger branches of their families out of their estates, and they are thrown upon the country ; that is, kept out of the taxes in some shape or other, and in which they are of no manner of use, but generally do harm. They are thus fed by the people, and fed extravagantly. It is an axiom which cannot be denied, that the more extravagantly one portion of the people are kept, the poorer the remaining portion will be. Extravagance in the merchant, tradesman, manufacturer, or farmer, has equally as bad effect. When these live up to their incomes in prosperous times, they cannot keep their merchandise, goods, or produce, when demand for a season declines. All must go to market, and prices sink so as to produce ruin, and injure their neighbours, and their workmen. Too great a desire for luxury, pomp, and power, leads to immorality, and these combined will lead either a man or a nation to ruin. These were the ruin of the Grecian and Persian empires. They caused the downfall of the Roman empire. They were the ruin of the French monarchy, and it is very doubtful if they will not be the downfall of England.

Another cause of the gradually declining profits in trade is, that foreigners are begun to manufacture for themselves. And why should they not do so? why should we have the presumption, or the selfishness, as to expect that we should manufacture for the whole world? When the war was over, the world was open for every nation to do the best it could, by every fair means in its power. When foreigners saw the wealth we had acquired by commerce and manufactures, it was natural they would attempt to follow our example. They have done so, and they will do so. At the first they only required *capital* and *skill.* The latter is easily got, as it can be imported, so far as management goes, and they are acquiring it rapidly. The former is not so easily got, but they are acquiring it, and it will be like a snowball—it gathers slowly at first, but increases more rapidly in proportion as it augments. They will find that, for a long time yet to come, capital will pay a greater per centage expended in manufactures than if expended on land. If low priced food and low wages are a benefit to the English manufacturer, those on the Continent of Europe have both these benefits in perfection, and are also exempt from excessive taxation. The masters themselves are more simple in their manners, and of course live at less expense than the same class here.

Having now given my opinions and ideas upon the various subjects connected with the corn laws, I will sum up the conclusions at which my arguments point.

First, that we have grown, and shall continue to grow, sufficient for home consumption *in fair average seasons,* and that we can afford wheat in such seasons at from 50s. to 56s., and other grain in proportion.

Secondly, that the foreign corn grower cannot produce corn *lower* than this laid down in the manufacturing districts of England, on account of their great distance from this market, the ineffectiveness of their implements of husbandry, their deficiency in skill and that of their labourers, their want of capital, and want of good internal communication in the country.

Thirdly, that these *disadvantages* are sufficient to counterbalance their *advantages* of lower rents, wages, and taxes.

Fourthly, that as the principles of the late corn law and the present one are grounded on the idea that the only danger to the British landowners will arise from fair average crops at home, of course, if my conclusions rest on good grounds, the corn laws may safely be repealed.

Fifthly, that corn laws were never anything but an *injury* to the *tenant farmers and their labourers.*

Sixthly, that all sliding scales are grounded in error; as, however low the duty, when the prices are *high here,* this will not affect the prices; for as the duty is reduced in England in seasons of scarcity, so the prices will rise in foreign markets, and of course all the advantage will go to the foreign farmer or corn merchant. Common sense will tell any one this, audrit only requires facts to be examined to prove its correctness. Sliding scales, however easy and graceful, will lead to un-

certainty in the business of corn merchants, but particularly to importers.

Seventhly, that there are other causes than the corn laws for the present depression in trade; for, according to their own statements, when food is *lowest trade is best,* and of course *trade is best* when there is the *least foreign corn imported;* therefore, corn could not have been taken in exchange for goods.

I ground my objections to any corn laws, principally, that they lead to everlasting uncertainty in the affairs of almost every class, by *raising* or *depressing* their expectations *above* or *below* par, and leads to everlasting agitation and ill feeling between the different classes which ought to go hand in hand together. Through them men's minds are always in an unsettled state. Repeal them and we shall soon know what we are all about. We could not be worse than we are. If we have a fixed duty, let it be a low one, of about 4s. per quarter for the purpose of revenue.

I am yours respectfully,

Winwich, Jan. 20th.   W. ROTHWELL.

A WORD TO THE BRITISH AGRICULTURIST.

If there is one department of agricultural science more neglected by the practical farmer than another, it is that of manuring. Chemists have made calculation after calculation, experiment after experiment, but all to little or no purpose. The farmer, I mean the working farmer—him who is a farmer from necessity—has derived little or no benefit from the host of eminent individuals who have concentrated their whole attention on agricultural chemistry. Why is this? Why is it that the great and all-important discoveries of Davy are still laughed at by many—paid but slight attention to by all; at least by all those who would reap the greatest profit from them? 'Tis true that a wonderful progress has been made in agriculture within the last few years;[*] and much has been done in the improvement of stock, perfection of machinery, &c., but very little in the science of manuring. And the circumstance appears to be still more unaccountable when we call to mind the fact that there are greater means of improvement in this particular branch of husbandry than any other; in no other department are the rudiments so well understood and so generally circulated as in this. We know the constitution of every agricultural plant, we have analyses of all descriptions of soils, we are well versed in the respective compositions of air and water, we have abundant means of ascertaining the constitution of all manures; indeed, we know and perceive all but the peculiar operation of the vital principle, and yet we are daily applying matter to soils in which a sufficiency already exists. Why is all this? Why is it that in some departments agriculture is rapidly advancing—in others making no perceptible progress? It is unpleasant and by no means the choice of the writer to give the cause of this anomaly; but "facts are stubborn things," and it becomes no one to conceal the truth.

[*] See Paper by P. Pusey, Esq., Jour. Royal Agric. Society, Vol. III., Parts 2, 3.

It is well known that the improvements which have been made in stock, are owing to the exertions of *experimental farmers* and those who farm for example ; independent of which it requires little or no calculation to improve stock—there are no scientific rules to be perused and committed to memory —it can be accomplished as well by a man of mediocre ability, as by one of a high order of intellectual capacity, provided he has perseverance. It must not be supposed, therefore, that no credit is due to those who have by their exertions improved the breed of any kind of stock. Immortal credit is due to any one who confers the smallest benefit upon his fellow creatures ; but the purpose is to shew why our breeds of animals have been so much improved, and another department of husbandry almost totally neglected. The cause, then, is that much in this respect has been done *for* the agriculturist, and there being little difficulty in what has been accomplished.

With respect to machinery, in which, perhaps, the most extensive as well as the most beneficial results have taken place, it need only be asked, who take the majority of prizes for machinery at agricultural prize meetings ? Not farmers, but machinists. This then speaks for itself: the improvements, the wonderful improvements made in machines have been brought about by the machine vendors, and not by farmers. It is readily admitted that it would be of no avail for Messrs. Ransome, Garrett, Crosskill, &c., &c. to construct new implements if the farmer had no disposition to encourage their laudable exertions ; still, it must be confessed, that the advance of agriculture in this department is not owing to agriculturists themselves.

All this puts a different feature upon the question, since it is obvious that the rapid strides which have been made, and are now making, in agriculture, are not to be attributed to the exertions of the working farmer. Now, it is no longer unaccountable that manuring should remain stationary, since it is a pitiable but undeniable circumstance that three-fourths of the working agriculturists are men who rest satisfied with pursuing the customs of their ancestors, and who invincibly resist the introduction of science. Science is a bane to them—the very word is a nuisance to John Bull.

Then what is this word science, that practical men seem to be so averse to ? If we refer to Johnson, we find that *science is art*—a most ridiculous signification, truly. In the mind of the practical farmer it is too frequently interpreted to be a system of human invention, cunningly devised for the base purpose of rendering a subject incomprehensible to any but the most learned ; and, truly, when we see the pains which some *professors* take to clothe their thoughts in pedantic phraseology, it is not surprising that some individuals should arrive at this conclusion. But the *true* signification of the word *science* is, a knowledge of all that *exists*, and of the laws that govern the operations of nature—a knowledge of matter, things, and systems. Whatever is done by a system is done scientifically : nature does nothing, except by the interposition of nature's God, without a system. A knowledge of these systems is science, *generally* ; a knowledge of any one system is *a* science. The numerous terms, the difficult rules, the complicated calculations, the mysterious analyses, are not *the science ;* they are the handles, the guides, the agents which render the science comprehensible by the human mind, invented by human beings for that purpose. They are

the channels through which the Newtons, the Lockes, the Davys, the Liebigs convey the researches of their expansive minds to unborn generations. If science, then, is a knowledge of the operations of nature, it must be from some unwholesome influence that so many individuals neglect to profit by it. That influence in the present instance is *prejudice*—yes, prejudice—however disagreeable it may sound to those interested, it is too true ; for what can it be but prejudice that prompts men to say— " Our forefathers prospered without science, and why should'nt we ?" What can it be but prejudice which induces men to believe that the system they adopt admits of no improvement ?

In order to render the question more intelligible, it may be asked for what purpose do men apply manure to soils ? Most assuredly to supply a something which is requisite to the growth of a plant, and which does not exist in the soil. Then, as we have the means of ascertaining what portion of a plant is supplied from the atmosphere, what from the rain which falls, and what from the soil, is it not evident to the most prejudiced that the slightest exercise of our reasoning faculties must enable us to judge with some degree of accuracy what particular bodies or compounds should be added to the soil, in order that it may furnish the plant with due proportions of each of its component materials? If we once admit the possibility of the above statements—and who can deny that they are rational ? —we become advocates of science.

But, in order to explain the subject more clearly, and that there may be no doubt as to the advantage of calling in the help of science, in the application of manures—in making manuring a science instead of an art, we will imagine an instance which has frequently occurred :—two neighbouring farmers enter upon the occupation of adjoining farms at the same time, and it so happens that they have adjoining fields of three-year-old turf; the soil in each field being composed, as far as ocular examination can detect, of the same materials. Being old friends they make no secret to each other of the system of cultivation they intend to pursue ; consequently, being convinced that some application is necessary to the turf, and having heard that nitrate of soda has had a beneficial effect upon such crops in many instances, they each decide on applying this manure at the same rate per acre, and as nearly as possible at the same time. The result is, that a great increase in the crop is produced in one instance—in the other, no benefit whatever can be discovered. The consequence is, that the one individual denounces the use of nitrate of soda, the other applies it indiscriminately in almost all cases. Meanwhile, this trifling circumstance probably engenders ill feeling between the two old friends, and all because they cannot discover (to use the words of an existing agricultural writer) " a clue to the mystery." The foregoing is by no means an exaggerated picture of everyday occurences. This is the consequence of making manuring an *art*.

We will now suppose the same case treated scientifically—the parties being fully aware that a plant cannot abstract that from the soil which does not pre-exist in it. Their first impulse is either to submit a portion of the soil to the analytical examination of an operative chemist, or, being chemists themselves, to ascertain of what the soil is composed—the one individual finds it will be improved by the materials contained in the nitrate of soda ; the other, not only that this manure will be useless, but what composition is required ; now this is manuring *scientifically*—this is making manuring a *science*. The advantage of the latter system is obvious.

A little consideration will, nevertheless, render it by no means remarkable that, notwithstanding the means of making the application of manures a *science* have been long placed within reach of agriculturists, yet that they have been utterly neglected ; since it is generally known that the application of *artificial* fertilizers is comparatively of a recent date, prior to which period the evacuations of animals, combined with decayed vegetable matter, formed the staple manure of the country. Now, *farm-yard manure*, which was the chief application, contains every material that a plant requires ; hence, if applied in sufficient quantities, it can never fail. But within a few years soils have been brought into cultivation, and those systems of farming have been adopted which have compelled the agriculturist to introduce artificial manures, in order to supply the deficiency of natural. And, from the circumstance that no artificial manures have been found (with one or two exceptions) to contain *every* material abstracted from the soil by plants generally, it is apparent that any one artificial manure is insufficient to maintain fertility in the soil. This renders it imperative upon the agriculturist to call in the assistance of chemistry, in order that he may be enabled to compete with agriculturists in this country and all others ; for, if the soil requires phosphate of lime to produce a wheat crop, of what possible utility will it be to apply a manure which does not directly or indirectly afford that particular matter ? And who can ascertain by mere ocular observation whether the manure or the soil contains phosphate of lime ?

If this problem cannot be solved by looking at the soil and the manure, what is the course to be pursued ? We must endeavour to ascertain the composition of each, which cannot be done without the help of science. It is very well to say, " science was not necessary when my grandfather or great-grandfather was a farmer." It is very well to say at the market dinner-table, " farmers have done well without science, and therefore it is unnecessary." But we must remember that our forefathers tilled the *richest* soil, at a time when there was no foreign competition, when farming produce realised almost double its present value, when receipts were larger and disbursements smaller, and when they had abundance of farm-yard manure to preserve the fertility of soil, without resorting to the application of rape-cake, nitrate of soda, *cum multis aliis*. Still it is by no means extraordinary that farmers of the present day should be opposed to the application of scientific rules ; or, if not opposed to their application, at least careless in applying them ; for, as they justly observe, farming has been conducted without science, and they cannot yet perceive the very different position in which they are placed, compared with farmers even of the last generation. The human mind is so subject to the unhealthy influence of prejudice, that it is no wonder farmers of the present day should be disposed to follow with almost invincible determination the customs of past ages ; yet, however natural it may be that they should thus act, it must be a source of sincere regret to the enlightened, unprejudiced mind,

that they should thus be heaping up trouble for a future day. If English farmers would but avail themselves of English discoveries ; if they would but instantly adopt the sure path of *science*, in preference to the uncertain one of *art* ; if they would but avail themselves of all the important inventions which are open to them, they would once more be enabled to compete with those who till the soil in any country on the face of the earth.

May they adopt those rules which will make agriculture a *science*, before they have cause to regret their culpable neglect in not doing so, by the overwhelming and ruinous consequences attendant upon the introduction of the untaxed produce of more fertile countries.

GEORGE THOMPSON, JUN.

Lion Street, Kidderminster,
Feb. 4th, 1843.

GUANO.

EXTRACTS FROM AN ESSAY, BY MR. J. NAPIER, JUN., WHICH OBTAINED A PRIZE AT THE LATE MEETING OF THE NORTH DERBYSHIRE AGRICULTURAL SOCIETY.

From MR. JOHN HORNCASTLE, Agent to H. G. KNIGHT, Esq., M. P.

The Yews, near Tickhill, Aug. 8, 1842.

To MR. JAMES NAPIER,

DEAR SIR,—I fear you will think me negligent for not replying sooner to your queries respecting the Guano, but I have been from home, and otherwise much engaged, owing to the return of Mr. Gally Knight into the country.

I will answer your questions as correctly as I can, in the order they are put.

The quantity of Guano we applied, was 4 cwt. per acre, and it was mixed with about an equal quantity (in measure) of wood ashes. It was drilled in with the turnip seed, the manure of course being let in a little deeper than the seed. The nature of the soil is limestone, averaging 5 or 6 inches deep. It is on a hill, and consequently dry. The turnips were drilled on ridges 21 inches apart. They were drilled on the 11th of June last, when the weather was very dry. There has not been the slightest appearance of fly or wire worm, but this observation will equally apply to the remainder of the field, which has been differently treated. The present appearance of the crop (Swedes) where the Guano has been applied, is highly pleasing, the plants being strong, and of a dark healthy green colour.

The adjoining portion of the field is of the same nature and quality. The same description of turnip seed was drilled, and part of it the same day, but instead of Guano and wood ashes, we put on good farm yard manure and rape dust.

The ridges were first opened, and about nine one-horse loads of good rotten manure (per acre) were spread. The ridges were then closed, and 4½ cwt. (per acre) of rape dust was drilled in with the seed. The Guano-tilled turnips came up three or four days before the others, *grew much faster*, and are now *most decidedly superior ; so much so as to be easily distinguishable by a stranger in walking past.* They have all been cleaned and hoed alike, and when arrived at maturity, I shall have equal quantities of land measured, and the bulbs weighed.

I will not speculate upon the effects to be derived by the succeeding crops, but at present, *the Guano is certainly deserving of the preference.*

I estimate the cost of one acre, tilled with 4½ cwt. of Guano and wood ashes, at 4*l*. 10*s*., and I consider the quantity and value of the manure and rape dust to be the same; in both instances of course including an allowance for labour and expences.

I am, dear sir, yours very faithfully,
JOHN HORNCASTLE, JUN.

From THOS. DUNN, Esq.' (Sheffield Coal Company), *Richmond Hill, near Sheffield, July 30, 1842.*

To MR. JAMES NAPIER,

SIR,—I beg to acknowledge the receipt of your note of 26th inst., relative to the trial of Guano, which I have made on the Colliery Farm, at Birley. I had 3¾ cwt. of Guano, which I applied on one acre of land. The Guano was mixed with about six bushels of wood-ashes, and then drilled along with the seed. The land is dry, of moderate quality; the subsoil stony, resting on porous rock. The depth of the soil about 15 inches. The fallow was clean, and the whole field in what we call "good heart," previous to the application of the manure for the turnip crop.

The ridges are 22 inches apart. The Guano was drilled with Skirving's seed, which I had direct from him. The sowing took place on 12th May, the land being in beautiful order for the reception of the seed. The plants came up well, have not been troubled with the fly, nor yet with the grub, and at present look as well as possible. The remainder of the same field was sown with the same seed on 14th of May, having 16 tons of good farm yard manure per acre. The plants came up equally well, and for the first six weeks or two months, took the lead of the plants where the Guano was drilled. *Now, they are more on an equality;* indeed a stranger would have difficulty in deciding on which part of the field the Guano had been used. My own opinion is, however, that the plants on that part of the field where farm yard manure was used, will produce the greatest crop. They look, I think, more vigorous, and form the bulbs better. It is however, but fair to say, that the *cost of dressing the field* where the farm yard manure was used, was *much more than where the Guano was used.* I intend to weigh a fair sample of the produce, say in December, and shall be glad to give you the result.

I am, sir, your obedient servant,
THOMAS DUNN.

From BENJAMIN SWAFFIELD, Esq., Bailiff to His Grace The Duke of Devonshire.

Chatsworth Farm, Aug. 16, 1842.

To MR. J. NAPIER,

SIR,—Enclosed is the best answer I can give to the questions touching the Guano, which I hope will be satisfactory to you, and you have my best wishes for your success at the approaching meeting.

On the 20th June last, I drilled 3½ cwt. of Guano mixed with wood ashes, along with the turnip seed on 2½ acres of land, in ridges 2 feet 6 inches apart. The weather was then showery. The nature of the land is a poor peaty soil; the subsoil, a yellow clay. On the other part of the field, I used bones and rape dust, mixed in the following proportions:—

Bones, 1¼ qr. per acre, at 22*s*. per qr.
Rape dust, 1½ cwt. per acre, at 7*s*. 0*d*. per cwt.

and I also applied a small dressing of yard manure equally over the whole field.

The present appearance of the crop is very equal. It is an excellent crop, and looking remarkably healthy. I consider it *the best crop I ever saw on land of the same quality,* the land being very poor.

I am, sir, yours respectfully,
BENJAMIN SWAFFIELD.

P. S.—I applied 1½ cwt. of the Guano on an acre of eddish as soon as the hay was got, and the *improvement in the eddish is wonderful.*

From THOS. STANIFORTH, Esq., Hackenthorpe.

Hackenthorpe, near Sheffield, Aug. 3, 1842.

To Mr. JAMES NAPIER,

DEAR SIR,—I beg to hand you the following statement of my trial of the Guano manure, in reply to your application of yesterday.

I drilled the Guano at the rate of 2½ cwt. per acre, (mixed with ashes) with my turnip seed on 1st June last. The field, which is a two acre one, is of a strong soil on a stiff clay bottom, and was in good condition prior to the application of the manure. On the other half of the field, I drilled bones at the rate of half a ton per acre, the cost of which was 6*l*. per ton. I also applied good fold manure upon the whole field at the rate of 12 loads or tons per acre, which I value at full 11*s*. per ton. The plants where the Guano was applied, are looking *better than those dressed with bones,* and judging from present appearances, will, I think, produce a greater weight of turnips.

I am, dear sir, yours truly,
THOMAS STANIFORTH.

From Mr. SAMUEL LINLEY, Hackenthorpe.

Hackenthorpe, Aug. 2, 1842.

To Mr. NAPIER,

SIR,—I mixed 12 cwt. of Guano with about four cart loads of sod ashes, and drilled it in with the common white and Dale's hybrid turnip on the 24th June last, at which time the weather was rather showery. The size of the field is 8 acres, and it is situate on Birley Common. The land is of a very thin, poor, and gravelly nature. I drilled the Guano on about five acres, the drills being 18 inches apart; and on the remainder of the field, I used bones (also mixed with ashes), at the rate of half a ton per acre. The cost of these was 7*l*. per ton, at Woodhouse Mills. The plants where the Guano was used, are looking *much better and healthier than those manured with bones,* and will, I doubt not, produce a much more abundant crop.

I should also add, that *they have scarcely been troubled in the least by the wire-worm,* (with which the land is greatly infested), whilst the others have been *very much injured* thereby.

I am, sir, yours respectfully,
SAMUEL LINLEY.

From Mr. EDWARD HOBSON, Rirley, near Sheffield.

Birley, 8th mo. (Aug.) 12, 1842.

Respected Friend, JAMES NAPIER,—On 23rd of 6th mo. (June), we mixed 2 cwt. 2 qrs. 17 lbs. Guano, with a sufficient quantity of sod ashes to make it spread well out of a hopper, and applied it broadcast on an acre of land. I then sowed the turnip seed, (Dale's Hybrid), also broad-cast, and ploughed the Guano and seed into ridges with a double mould-board plough, rolling them afterwards with a light roller.

The cost for the acre, was 2l. 7s. 5d.

On three acres adjoining, we applied about 17 cwt. per acre of pulverized bones, and ploughed them into ridges in the same manner, but sowed the seed with a drill attached to the plough, and rolled them also with a light roller.

The cost per acre, was about 2l. 15s. 5d.

The turnips on the Guano are rather thinner, but in colour, exceed those on the bones. The soil is of a light nature, on a gravelly subsoil; and the weather was rather showery before and after sowing. 　　　I am, respectfully, thy friend,
EDWARD HOBSON.

From Mr. GEORGE WOODHEAD, Birley.

Birley Common Side, Aug. 12, 1842.

To Mr. J. NAPIER,

SIR,—The following is an account of my trial of Guano manure on turnips:—On 20th May, I drilled it in with Swede turnip seed (*unmixed* with ashes), at the rate of 4 cwt. per acre. The weather was then dry. Rain fell a few days afterwards. The quantity of land whereon it was applied, is exactly half an acre. The soil is a gravelly loam, on a subsoil of shaly gritstone. The ridges are 24 inches apart. On the other part of the field I applied good rotten fold manure, (mixed with a few ashes), at the rate of 14 loads per acre. I consider the value of this, to be at the least, 10s. per load or ton. The turnips dressed with Guano, *came up a full week before the others.* They have kept the lead, and at the present time are *almost as good again as the others, both in size and colour.* They have not been *in the least affected by grub or wire-worm,* neither did we meet with any in hoeing them, whereas on those dressed with yard manure I often destroyed as many as *eight or nine wire-worms at one root.*

On a rood of the same field, I also drilled (a fortnight later than the Swedes) the seed of the Scotch yellow turnip, with Guano, in the same proportion as before. They are *greatly superior* to the remainder of the crop, which was dressed with yard manure of the same quality, and in like quantity as the Swedes.

They have never been injured by vermin of any kind, and are easily to be distinguished by their size and healthy colour. I have this day, (merely for the sake of curiosity), weighed a fair average sized turnip, including bulb and top, from the different parts of the field. The weight is as under:—

	lbs.	oz.
Swede turnip, dressed with Guano	3	8
Do., do., Yard Manure	2	2
Present balance in favour of Guano	1	6

	lbs.	oz.
Scotch yellow, dressed with Guano	3	5
Do., do, Yard Manure	1	9
Present balance in favour of Guano	1	12

I shall be glad to show the crop to any one who may wish to see the great benefit derived from the use of the Guano manure, and am, sir,
Yours respectfully,
GEORGE WOODHEAD.

The result of my own experiment with Guano is as follows:—

On the 10th of June last, I mixed a hundred weight of Guano with two bushels of wood ashes, and drilled it with Swede turnip seed on half an acre of land. The weather at the time of sowing, was fair, but cool. The land is of a strong nature, resting upon a subsoil of stiff yellow clay, and is by no means good turnip land.

The depth of soil is about ten inches, and the ridges are 24 inches apart.

On the remainder of the field, I used good well-rotten yard manure, at the rate of 12 tons per acre, the worth of which I estimate to be about 10s. per ton. The plants on that part of the field where the Guano was used, came up sooner than those whereon yard manure only was applied, but at first did not look so vigorous.

Now, however, (Aug. 4th) they are far superior to the others, and the difference both in size and colour is very apparent. I must likewise mention, that when we hoed the Guano'd turnips, we did not find either wire-worm or slug; but in other parts of the field, and even in the next row to them, we were much infested by them, and the crop has suffered accordingly.

I also observed during the *hot weather* we have lately had, that the *ridges containing the Guano were invariably moist, whilst the remainder of the field was quite parched by the heat.* This, I think, proves its utility in retaining moisture in the soil, and also its power of absorption thereof from the atmosphere. I likewise sowed broad-cast, and mixed in like manner with ashes, a hundred weight of Guano, on about the same quantity of land, in a field of barley, which was so much injured by the slug, as to convey the idea, that in some parts it had been left unsown.

In a very few days after this dressing, the effect was surprisingly visible. The barley is now so much improved, as to give every promise of an abundant crop. The ears are well filled, and the straw is both stronger and taller than that on the remainder of the field. 　　JAMES NAPIER, JUN.

Hackenthorpe, Aug. 4, 1842.

Guano has also been applied with very great success to wheat, clover, grasses, potatoes and other vegetables, as well as to exotic and other plants.

The following statement from a correspondent of the "Gardener's Chronicle," establishes it as a valuable manure for all purposes of horticulture.

"As I see many questions in the "Chronicle" concerning Guano, I send you, for the benefit of your readers, the following observations which I have made during a period of sixteen or seventeen months, having used it both in its natural and in a liquid state. I find the following method of applying it to succeed best on soil which is of a light sandy nature, on a red sandstone formation. For peas, beans, onions, &c., and all other crops for which the ground is prepared in the autumn, it should be used at the rate of one pound to four square yards, (mixed with half its own quantity of wood ashes, where they can be procured.) When used in spring, or any other season, it should be well dug into the ground before planting or sowing, for if seeds come into contact with it during germination, the stimulus is too strong for them. The cabbage tribe seems particularly benefited, as it not only *promotes their luxuriance,* but prevents *them* from *clubbing.* Our cauliflowers have this year been *very fine,* and *free from that pest;* whereas last year they were *literally devoured;* and I attribute it *entirely to Guano having been used this year instead of other manure.* I may also mention, for the information of those who are *now troubled with slugs,* that if they will *dust the ground now and then with it, those enemies will very soon disappear.* Potatoes, turnips, lettuce, &c., and every thing for which it has been used as a manure, show its beneficial effects. When the crops are gathered, I will send the comparative weights of the produce of it and other manures. When used in a liquid state, four pounds will be sufficient for ten gallons of water; and in this way I prefer it for all plants in pots, having used it for camellias, pelargoniums, and many other things, with the most gratifying results. I water with it twice a week. The leaves of the camellias are dark green, and from their shining appearance, seem as if they had been washed : they have made good wood, and show abundance of flower-beds for the next season. Cucumbers also, watered twice a week with the liquid, assume a healthy green peculiar to Guano. We have cut many this season, 22 inches and 2 feet long, (a cross between Kenyon's and Walker's) grown at the back of a pipe stove, and watered as before stated. The pine apple luxuriates under similar treatment, and I have now about forty black Jamaicas, swelling fine fruit, which I think would not have been half the size, if they had not been watered with the liquid twice a week. I may state, that I allow it to stand twelve hours after mixing, and I prefer using it before it has stood too long, as it *then* gives off its ammonia.''

The following statement of " the effects of Guano as a manure," has lately appeared in a number of " The Cumberland Pacquet." A correspondent of that journal writes as follows :—

" Having paid considerable attention to the effects produced by this manure in the different kinds of crops to which it has been applied in this district, I am able to furnish your correspondent with the information he desires, and also to give him such respectable references in the names of those whom I shall mention, as having tested the productive powers of this manure, as will leave no doubt upon his mind [with respect to the efficacy of Guano in the production of grain crops, turnips, &c.'

".This year, Guano has been used by the Earl of Lonsdale, on Monkwray farm, where it has been applied both to turnips and hay-grass with surprising efficacy. The turnips are a *splendid crop,* and the hay-grass was *one third more in quantity than was produced by the same extent of land to which the Guano had not been applied.*"

" Mr. Todd, of Tarnflat, made an experiment with this manure, which he applied to *barley, oats,* and *turnips,* and the result has been *most 'successful,* as his crops, thus favoured with the application of this manure, will testify.''

" Mr. Carter, of St. Bees; Mr. James Fox, of High Street; Mr. Mossop, of Rottington; Mr. Hodgson, of Low Walton; and a great number of other spirited cultivators, have also made trial of Guano this season, and are prepared to prove its efficacy by a reference to the splendid and luxuriant crops now growing upon the lands to which it has been applied. With respect to the *qualities of the soils* on which Guano has been tried in this district, I may at once state that they consist of *every variety,* in consequence of the application having been so extensive, and I have not heard of *one single failure on any kind of soil.* A correspondent of

last week is anxious to know, if Guano would answer upon *cold land in summer fallow for wheat.* My answer is that *it would,* and I ground it upon the following reasons :—First, it has been found to answer upon every variety of soil to which it has been applied in this district; and in the second place, Guano *is so tenacious of its fertilizing powers,* that it does not, like some other manures, *lose them in one season at least;* for I know a gentleman in this neighbourhood, who tried the effect of Guano in 1841 with success, and *this year its productive qualities have exhibited themselves on the same soil without any fresh application, and with undiminished effect.* How long this manure will retain its virtues in the soil after its application, is a question which time alone can solve; but it is no mean circumstance in the way of its recommendation, to be enabled to state, that for two seasons its productive qualities have undergone no diminution.''

The following has recently appeared in a number of the " Liverpool Albion," published in October last.

" GUANO.—We are happy to hear from our agricultural and horticultural friends, that this manure, which was tried in this neighbourhood last year, for the first time, with such favourable results, has again proved itself to be one of the most valuable manures ever introduced either for field or garden crops. It has been used to a considerable extent in this county, both in a dry and in a liquid state; and in every instance when properly applied, it has answered well for crops of every kind. *It has also been proved to be a lasting manure ; for very good crops have this year been obtained, without any manure whatever, from the land where Guano was applied, and had given large crops last year.* Our farmers and gardeners have, no doubt, much to learn with regard to the proper quantity to be used of this new manure; but, as a great many experiments have this season been made with it, we may expect this point will soon be settled. In this neighbourhood, Guano has been applied on wheat and other grain crops, and on grass lands, as a top dressing, at the rate of two hundred weight per statute acre, with most excellent effect. For turnips, four hundred weight has been used to she acre, and given very good crops; and four and six hundred weight used for potatoes with the same success. In the gardens and nursery grounds, Guano has been applied principally in a liquid state, and in that manner has surpassed every manure yet discovered. Its effects on young fruit and forest trees are wonderful; also upon greenhouse and hothouse plants of every description ; even the exotic heaths, to which manure of any kind has been considered injurious, seem to flourish beyond all precedent when watered with it. About four pounds to twelve gallons of water are enough for the liquid. The water should stand twenty-four hours before use ; and when drawn off, twelve gallons more may be put to the same Guano.''

AGRICULTURAL STATISTICS. — The total number of horned cattle in the United Kingdom is estimated at 7,000,000, and the total number of sheep at 32,000,000. Valuing the first over-head at 10*l.,* and the last at 25*s.,* both together will give a total value of 110,000,000.—*Manchester Guardian.*

LANDLORD AND TENANT.

PRESENT STATE AND FUTURE PROSPECTS OF AGRICUL-
TURE, AS RELATES TO LANDLORD AND TENANT, AND
AS AFFECTING THE COMMUNITY AT LARGE. AD-
DRESSED TO THE LAND-OWNERS OF ENGLAND—BY
" A TENANT FARMER."

MY LORDS AND GENTLEMEN—For a long series of
years, whether in peace or war, the loyalty and devotion of the tenantry of England to the interests of
their country, have never been called in question,
and scarcely less proverbial has been their fidelity
to you, whose lands they have so greatly improved.
Hitherto in times of civil commotion, whether from
Ludditeism, Chartism, incendiarism, or whatever else
may have threatened the peace of the country, your
tenants have come at your bidding, and enrolled
themselves as peace-officers for the protection of
your persons and property. In more modern times,
a strong current has also set in in the populous districts against your interests; by the aid of your tenantry, you have successfully repelled those attacks,
and that aid has been rendered not more, we think,
from interest than principle. The more intelligent
of your tenantry looking at the peculiar circumstances of the country, since the commencement of
the French war, the manner in which the debt and
consequent taxation has influenced the price of land-
mortgages, and all other contracts relating to the
soil of the country have, (in their opinion) rendered
security to the domestic markets necessary, by the
wise policy of protecting laws; and this they have
thought not merely beneficial to agriculture, but
also conformable, permanently, to the best interests
of the country. So far, then, you have doubtless
taken with you a large portion of the more enlightened of the tenantry of the country; besides which
they have been wont to regard their interests as mainly
identified with your own. It would be idle, however, now to deny that recent events have produced
a most fearful reaction in the minds of the tenantry
at large, without any reference to party politics; the
identity of interests is doubted, and that of sympathy
for your tenants in many instances denied.

Facts are stubborn things, and it cannot be disputed that within two short years one-fourth at least
of the entire property of the tenantry of the country,
as far as it was invested, in the live and dead farming stock, and cropping of the farm, has been completely swept away, and that not from disastrous
seasons or providential visitations.

I do not say that Sir Robert Peel and his coad-
jutors have been the wholesale plunderers! I leave
that point for others to settle; all I know is, that
the very men who could never assemble in the company of agriculturists two years ago, without anathe-
matising the Whig Radical Government (as it was
called), and calling upon the farmers to Petition—
Petition—Petition! at the late autumnal meetings,
have been horror-stricken at the very name of politics. " For *God's sake, don't introduce politics!"*
and the old cry of Petition—Petition—Petition!
has been superceded by " *Cultivate—Cultivate—
Cultivate!"* There can be no mistake as to what
this means—" The profits of you tenants are gone,
that is quite certain; and, by Jove! if you abate
one iota of cultivation our rents must go too."

My Lords and Gentlemen—I appeal to you, Is
this the treatment that the tenantry of England deserve at your hands? That there are, however,
among you many noble minded and generous men
who will honourably meet any emergency I do not

for a moment question, but it is useless to deny
that the representatives of the farming districts
stand convicted before the tenantry of the country,
and you must not imagine that this great political
dishonesty can go unpunished.

Henceforth you may retain the homage of a vassal,
but not that of a bold, honest-hearted yeoman!

These observations, I am aware, more or less
partake of party: but it is not on that account I
introduce them; the main object of this letter is to
bring before the public a subject too big for party,
and one in which the very best interests of the country are involved—it is *the Law of Landlord and
Tenant, as affecting the community at large.*

My Lords and Gentlemen—You are accused by
large bodies of people in the more populous districts
of holding exclusive privileges. This angry feeling, I believe, is not at all confined to the question
of Corn-laws; that question settled, the rancour
would remain. You have made a large number of
electors by the 50*l.* clause of the Reform Bill, who
cannot independently exercise their elective franchise; besides which it is a fact, which cannot be
controverted, that while large portions of the community have been suffering great privations, your
property has been ascendant. This is easily accounted for, and it is time now that the truth
should come out. The despotic (not to say dis-
honest) principle, on which much of the land has
been let in England for a series of years by the
wretched tenant-at-will system, enables the landlord to put in his pocket by far the greater part
of all the tenant's improvements. By the statute
law of the land the tenant is punished for dilapidations; but it affords him no protection as to his
improvements. Let the tenant only farm high, by
the purchase of manures, by draining and marling
his land, or by any other ameliorations, however expensive, and in six short months a needy, avaricious landlord may pounce upon those improvements, and make them his own.

Nor am I writing at random. I can name farms
(if called upon) in the county of Bedford—and
there are doubtless thousands elsewhere—where
the tenants thirty or about thirty-one years ago,
sold a waggon load of wheat for upwards of 70*l.*
On the same farms they have been compelled
during the present winter to sell the like quantity
and quality for about 30*l.*, while the rent of the
farms are from ten to fifteen per cent. higher now
than at the former period, *and this when no part of
the improvements have been made* by the landlord.
No wonder then that such landlords should call
out, " *Cultivate! cultivate! cultivate!"* This state
of things, followed as it has been by the recent
loss of property among the tenantry, added to their
total inability to employ our redundant population,
cannot but have produced the most serious heart-
burnings in the country. The labourers will not,
nor ought they to be allowed to, starve or to be
penned up in district workhouses. The great increase of incendiary fires is seriously ominous!
Landlords of England, look on these things! I do
not wish to alarm your fears so much as to awaken
you to a sense of justice and sympathy. The
competition for farms deceives you. The truth is,
farmers increase, while the average of the country
remains stationary; and, for the most part, they
have no alternative but to hire on your own terms,
or (regardless of friends and kindred) leave the
country, and try their fortunes in foreign lands.
You have, however, the remedies for your country's

ills very largely within your own reach; and if you have not honesty and patriotism enough to adopt them, *you must know where the responsibility rests.* Let the first acts of the sessions of 1843 be such as shall enable you *to stand erect before the country.*

First, regardless of all party considerations, repeal so much of the 50*l.* clause of the Reform Bill as relates to *tenants-at-will.* It imposes a responsibility on the tenant, and gives a despotic power to the landlord, both totally at variance with the spirit of the British constitution. It is not in this point, however, that I have to deal with it; in its operation upon the condition of the tenantry and upon cultivation, it is infinitely worse. It imposes a great barrier to the granting of leases, reduces the tenant to a mere state of vassalage; giving him comparatively but little interest in the future, it dams up the sources of employment, and consequently greatly retards improvements.*

The second point—and that which I regard as fraught with the greatest benefits to the country— is some amelioration of the law of landlord and tenant. In a short but comprehensive act comprising few words, all that is wanted might be accomplished. Take the following as a rough draft, and improve it all you like, but do not damage it.

Whereas the population of the United Kingdom seems to be rapidly outgrowing the ordinary capabilities of the soil for its maintenance; and, moreover, it being vastly important for the better employment of her Majesty's dutiful and loyal subjects in the rural districts, as well for the happiness, wealth, and independence of the United Kingdom, that all obstructions should be forthwith removed, and full scope given to the employment of the capital, skill, and enterprise of the agriculturists. Be it therefore enacted by her Majesty's special command, with the consent of the Lords Spiritual and Temporal, and the Commoners of the United Kingdom in Parliament assembled, that from and after the passing of this act, any farmer being a tenant-at-will, or under a lease for a less term than twelve years, It shall and may be lawful on such tenant receiving a notice to quit from his landlord, to call in a valuer, and to give notice to the landlord to appoint a person on his part to meet such valuer, to assess the amount of compensation that shall be due to the tenant for any improvements he shall have made during his occupancy, the full benefit of which he shall not have received—any lawful claim of the landlord for dilapidations and mismanagement to be deducted: the decision of such valuers or their umpire to be final.

And when the act is passed, you may call it, if you please, the Farmers' " Magna Charta."

It is quite clear that the landlord who wishes to hold his tenant in a state of vassalage, and immediately grasp his improvements, will demur to such a piece of even-handed justice. There are those however in the country who would doubtless spurn to avail themselves intentionally of what in common justice must belong to the tenant. The late Duke of Bedford, to wit, once said to a tenant of

* I am frank to admit however that this clause of the Reform Bill, seemed but a fair balance of power against the 10*l.* borough voters, but descending down to tenants-at-will in its operation it is most mischievous; such a person under a lease may exercise his elective franchise with some degree of independence—a tenant-at-will cannot.

his—"That the law of landlord and tenant doubtless required revision, and he hoped to live to see the day when it should be accomplished." That generous and truly patriotic nobleman, however, did not live to see it accomplished.

The importance of some such measure is not fully seen at the first glance. Among some of the benefits which would accrue the following may be enumerated.

It would greatly conduce to the granting of long leases, giving the tenant a sort of co-proprietorship in the lands; raise him in the scale of society; inspire confidence in the outlay of capital; secure the employment of an otherwise redundant population; and provide food in our own country for almost an indefinite increase of mankind.

Apologising for the length of this letter,
I remain, your very obedient servant,
THE BEDFORDSHIRE REPORTER.

P.S. I know it may be objected that in these changing times no one knows how to hire land on a lease. A lease for land ought however, at any time, to contain a clause enabling a tenant to vacate, providing any great depreciation of farm produce should be effected by legislative enactments. It is time, however, *this system of plunder was put an end to.* If further concessions are to be made, it would be infinitely better to do it once for all, at whatever cost. The writer however has no hesitation in saying, let whoever may live to see it, extreme low prices for any lengthened period, in the circumstances of this country, cannot fail to produce the most serious convulsions. Had Sir Robert Peel stopped in his alteration of duties on wheat, it might have been well; to blast everything the farmer grows was entirely uncalled for.

AGRICULTURE AND COMMERCE.

TO THE EDITOR OF THE MARK LANE EXPRESS.

SIR,—A subscriber, I send for your consideration a letter, which I trust you will insert in your paper and magazine, believing it to contain views of the utmost importance, in themselves essentially correct, and, at the present juncture, peculiarly appropriate.

We see agitation on every side, the consequence of embarrassment and conflicting interests; we hear discussion, and yet the questions in dispute seem at best but imperfectly understood. The rival claims of the two great classes of agriculture and trade furnish the matter of debate; and although the interests of any two classes in a community should, in a well-regulated state of things, not be directly at variance with each other, these evidently are so, and reconciliation is apparently almost impracticable. With much declamation on the subject, however, the case is yet never fairly stated between them—the real difficulty never fairly met.

Now, what is the actual position, what the supposed interests of the respective parties? A question this, whose answer fairly stated, would obviously indicate as well the true state of the case, as the course to be followed in our present emergency.

"Repeal of the Corn Laws," on the one hand,

"No Repeal," on the other; such at the present moment are the respective party claims.

The English manufacturer demands "Repeal," in other words, he demands cheap provisions, and he thus argues: 1. Wages will inevitably fall to the price of the necessaries of life. 2. A low priced manufactured article will give a profit at low wages, which same article would be ruinous at high ones. 3. England is heavily taxed directly and indirectly. The English manufacturer, therefore, demands "Repeal," because he has to compete in the market with a foreign merchant, who enjoys the advantages of cheap provisions and light taxes. He complains, and justly, of the corn laws being injurious to trade; but when he assumes them to be a monopoly existing for the benefit of the land, at the expense of the rest of the community, he is manifestly wrong, inasmuch as the farmer does in no degree pocket the proceeds.

He demands corn laws, i.e., protection, not for his own private interest, but because heavily taxed he has to compete, at great odds against himself, with the foreign agriculturist. In a word, he requires protection against foreign competition. But to put his case in the clearest possible light: suppose a farm, subject to certain money payments, rent, &c., convert the several sums into their equivalent bushels of wheat, at the respective rates of 8s. or protection, and 6s. or no protection—the figures 8 and 6 being assumed for illustration sake —free trade would not give him 5s. per bushel. Precision of figure is here, however, of less consequence than the presenting a comparative result in bushels of wheat, instead of pounds of money.

Farm .. 200 acres.

	£	Bush. of Wheat at 8s. per bush.	Bush of Wheat at 6s. per bush.	Difference.
Rent ..	300	 750	 1000	 250
Taxes ..	30	 75	 100	 25
Rates ..	36	 90	 120	 30
	366	915	1220	305

Tithes 60l. with the standard of wheat fixed by law at 7s. per bushel, also a 20 per cent. depreciation of stock.

Omitting the depreciation of his stock, what, in the case of repeal, shall give the English farmer the extra 305 bushels of wheat necessary to make up the same sum total in money? Improved system or science? Can the farmer with diminished receipts afford expensive artificial manures, or costly machinery, or superior stock? No; the very means of improvement are taken from him. But, says the free trader, all things are reduced alike; the farmer on the whole will be no loser. Evidently the receiver of a fixed income will be no loser; on the contrary, he will be a gainer to the amount of the reduction, as prices will have fallen 25 per cent. while his money income will remain the same. With the farmer, however, it is not so; his main outgoings are his fixed payments—rent, tithe, taxes, rates. In wages really he can save next to nothing, though nominally he reduces them; he pays them in bushels of wheat, and his labourers already are reduced to the barest necessaries of life. His expenditure in his other matters is but small, at least the savings on these can be but trifling. If his great money payments remain nearly the same, even the present modified duty will, with every economy on his part, scarcely support him; but total repeal would annihilate rent.

The interests, then, of the two classes are rival, and in existing circumstances irreconcileable.

Why is repeal essential to the existence of our foreign trade; why destructive to English agriculture?

The whole resolves itself into a question of taxation.

Supposed all nations taxed alike, there would be comparatively but little need for prohibition or protection; but in our artificial state, heavily taxed as we are, protection against the lightly taxed foreigner is absolutely necessary; or our home interests are ruined. To enable us to bear the immense taxes imposed on us, prosperity, in other words highprice, is necessary; and then here is our dilemma, with high prices at home, our foreign demand gradually ceases, and of course distress of trade ensues; with low price at home, the pressure of our fixed burdens is at once acutely felt, and we have immediately the cry of distress; and if to relieve trade we lower the farmer, we do but involve him in the difficulty, and also to the same extent injure our home market. And extension of trade is not the panacea the free trader would have us believe. We want remunerating prices as well as extension. Now, the official returns of our exports and their value, prove beyond doubt, that depreciation has at length taken place to the extent of nearly one half; in other words, our trade has been forced at any sacrifice. Hitherto improved machinery, together with gradual reduction of wages, has supported the profit of the employer— until at length machinery has gone abroad, giving the foreigner in that respect an equality with ourselves—and the English price of the necessaries of life will admit of no further reduction of the miserable artizan. Hence the cry for cheap corn; hence the Anti-Corn Law League. With what justice to the farmer, however, the demand for repeal can be made, is, I trust, made evident; certainly justice to the artizan can form no part of the argument in its favour.

The only just course would be for the English farmer to pay his landlord, the state, and his local taxes in bushels of wheat, instead of pounds of money. As he receives so let him pay, and then he would not object to repeal; price to him in such case being of no consequence. But to compel him to pay the same sum of money with depreciated produce, is at least as much a breach of national faith as Sir J. G.'s proposed 30 per cent. reduction of the interest of the debt. Such proposition is obviously equivalent to a reduction of taxes, which, so says the deficient revenue, cannot be collected with the great interests of the country steadily declining.

Is such reduction unjust? Where is the injustice of cutting down our expenditure to our means; of leaving in the hands of the toiling labourer enough of his hard earnings to furnish him with daily bread? Is reduction necessary? The state of the country affords a sufficient answer. Of that state the falling revenue is a marked index, pointing as it does for its cause, to the dreadful privation, the horrid suffering which must, which does exist; confirming too, as that deficiency does, the statements of the "Sanitary Report;" a confirmation shocking to Christian, to common humanity, subversive of our claim to superior civilization, and yet desirable (if the reality be, as it is, true) as furnishing the most imperative call for earnest and honest consideration for prompt remedy.

And the suffering, the difficulty, is now not confined to the lowest, it pervades to a great extent the middle classes also; meanwhile the shocks to credit are becoming more dangerous, the condition of our labouring class more brutalized, all together threatening to involve the general interests of the country in one common ruin. Once again, what is the remedy? Temporizing, inasmuch as it deals only with detail, leaving the cause untouched, must ultimately fail. Sir R. Peel nevertheless hopes, by the revision of old and the imposition of new taxes, to make up the deficiency, and so meet the difficulty of his position. His hope has proved, will prove, to be fallacious; he can but shift the burden from one shoulder to the other, if the burden itself remain the same. What is that burden? Fifty millions of state taxes, more than twenty more of local taxes for the church, the poor, &c. Seventy millions! can there be no saving in any of the various items of this monstrous total? Are there no unnecessary offices, no overpaid services? Can we much longer afford such expences?

With retrenchment the corn laws, any monopoly, may be repealed, and yet all classes flourish, and then England would take equal, if not vantage ground. Without retrenchment, skill and force may do much to delay, but they cannot prevent national bankruptcy.

Jan., 1843.   J. B. I. N.

Amongst the most useful of modern inventions, the doctrine of chances, as applied to assurances on lives and survivorships, stands undoubtedly pre-eminent. The certainty with which the duration of human life is now ascertained, renders this mode of providing for a family the most eligible of any, to individuals whose incomes are dependant on their personal exertions; and whose families, deprived by sudden death of their natural protector, would be often plunged into misery, did not the salutary provisions of life assurance furnish a means by which, on the investment of small annual contributions, the future comfort of those most dearly loved and fondly cherished is rendered certain, safe, and permanent. Yet, little more than two generations have passed away, since, instead of a graduated scale of premium, so arranged that each age shall pay its own risk, every age was insured at the common premium of five per cent.; and the establishments trading on life risks were tenacious of speculating even at that exorbitant rate of premium. Dr. Halley and M. de Moivre were the first on the continent who attempted to apply a graduated scale, fixing the ratio of decline in human life; which attempts stimulated the ingenuity of our own countrymen to apply the new theory to the actual decrement of life, as furnished by the London Bills of Mortality; and Mr. Simpson gave rules for constructing tables of expectation, which were improved on by the celebrated Dr. Price, and afterwards perfected by the talented secretary of the Equitable Society, Mr. Morgan, who has since applied the doctrine of chance to almost every variety of contingency incidental to man in a state of society. Still with the fear which naturally governed these speculations, before experience had convinced the framers of schemes of life assurance that their principles

and doctrines were perfectly sound, the conductors of the Equitable Insurance Society set apart a reserve fund to provide against the period when, according to Dr. Price's suggestion, a maximum of decrement would bring on a maximum of claims, and the immense profits attendant on their speculation may be fairly inferred from the fact of this reserve fund having accumulated to nearly 20 millions of pounds sterling. Added to this, almost all the old companies admit the fact of their scale of premiums being too high, by allowing their insurers a share of profits, not exceeding two-thirds; and even with this allowance thrown back, the various offices continue to realize capital, though it must be confessed at the expense very often of many praiseworthy insurers struggling through difficulties to make a provision for the future well-being of their families; who, by being called on to pay more than the risk actually demands, are frequently deprived of present comforts while they are not able to realize commensurate benefits in the future. Many of the premiums in the older establishments are notoriously 20 per cent. in excess. Thus the insurer who wishes to invest savings out of his present income sufficient to secure a thousand pounds on his death, is obliged to pay one-fifth more than the office has a right to demand. Now, though this does not appear to make any difference in the end, in cases wherein the insurers are entitled to share profits, it will be found to operate most grievously when the policy of insurance is held as a security. For here the insurer is taxed far beyond his just proportion, while another takes the profits to which the excess of premium he has paid fairly entitles him. Besides, the office taking one-third of the accumulated premium as its own share of the profit, the debtor who has given a policy of insurance, by way of collateral security, is thus deprived of the whole 20 per cent. for the benefit of parties who can have no just claim to the sacrifice. Prudence, therefore, should dictate to individuals who may have occasion to ensure their lives, whether for investment, security, or otherwise, to seek out establishments whose scale of premium is as low as is consistent with the guarantee of the sum assured, both as furnishing the most certain, because the least onerous mode of paying the premium, and preventing the accumulation of undue profit in the hands of the company. We repeat that companies, trading on calculated results, from the experience of the Equitable Society, might even reduce the premiums of the older offices, in some cases 25 per cent., and yet retain in their hands a sufficient remunerating profit. Life assurance will be found highly beneficial to persons having offices, employments, estates, or incomes which cease and determine with their lives; more especially to clergymen, physicians, lawyers, and persons holding pensions for life, as it enables them to secure a sum to be paid at their decease to their families or representatives; it is also useful to persons holding offices, leases, &c. during the lives of others, as by the same means they may secure themselves from the loss which they would otherwise sustain by the death of such persons. But while prudence dictates the necessity of life assurance to individuals so situated, it imperatively calls on them to seek out such offices as will at the least possible diminution of their present income guarantee them the exact sum required, instead of continuing to pay an excessive premium for a share in profits, the principal part of which must find way into the pockets of the company, and not into those of the insurer.

FOUR LETTERS ON THE PLANTING OF FOREST TREES.

TO THE EDITOR OF THE MARK-LANE EXPRESS.

LETTER I.

ON THE PREPARATION OF THE SOIL.

SIR,—Conflicting opinions having recently appeared, and those too of distinguished writers,* as to the necessity and advantage of previous preparation of the soil for planting, it seems requisite to say a few words with the preliminary object of clearing away the doubt that such a discussion must raise, upon the very threshold of the subject, in the minds of those who have not proved the fact for themselves. Indeed it would be practically absurd to enter upon the directions and details of a step, the total necessity of which was disputed. But we hope this question may be easily set at rest.

The writer who maintains (upon experience) that a young plantation will thrive as well as it is possible for it to do, without the previous double digging or trenching of the soil, is either speaking of land too good to plant (except as may be required for ornament, or particular purposes unconnected with profit), or else he asserts what common experience contradicts. In fact the question as to the amount of preparation required, is a mere question of difference of soils. If the soil be deep, rich, and loamy, giving free percolation to the surface-water, the expense of double digging, trenching, or subsoil ploughing, is obviously unnecessary, though the additional oxygenation of the soil occasioned by them cannot but do good. But where, as in the great majority of land *to be planted*, we have to deal with a thin-skinned piece of ground either too light or too heavy for profitable cultivation ; or a piece of recently inclosed common land ; or the side of a hill ; or any rough nook or corner of land, over-grown with furze, ling, heather, fern, thistles, nettles, or any such gipsey-like occupants of neglected territory—there can be no more doubt of the extreme advantage, if I may not say *necessity*, of previous preparation of the kind above-mentioned for profitable planting, than there is of the use and value of man's labour upon any other of the various forms of matter which nature has thrown 'in the rough' before his industry and skill. In a word, common sense bids us so to prepare a middling or bad soil as to approximate as nearly as art can do to the character and qualities of a good one ; and, of

course, in proportion as the soil already possesses by nature the qualities desired, so will it demand less from human labour. If, however, it may be assumed that really good soils are not those usually or properly devoted to forest planting, I do not hesitate to lay it down as an unassailable general principle, that *deep cultivation*, either by the spade or the plough, is an absolute essential to the best, and I mean by that *the most profitable*, planting.

But then the *expense!* Here is the stone against which several reasonable and practical-seeming writers have stumbled. And men who would think nothing of a year's naked fallow, with Heaven knows how many ploughings and harrowings, with liming, manuring, and the loss of a year's rent, as the preparation for a crop of wheat—put their hands into their pockets, and look wise and prudent about the expense of a double digging or double ploughing for a crop, *not of one year, but of centuries*.

A piece of ground is about to be made woodland. The question is, shall it be made good woodland once and for ever, by an outlay of 4*l*. or 5*l*. an acre ? or shall it be made a waste of stunted stag-headed oak—mossy, coarse, unhealthy-looking ash—thin, straggling, feathery larch—getting worse and worse every year as their roots get deeper into the hard, weeping subsoil of a wet clay, or the dry and hungry substratum of an uncultivated sand ? Which shall it be ? The future produce of the latter may be worth from half-a-crown to five shillings an acre per annum, the former from fifteen shillings to a guinea. When you have taken your choice, *you have taken it for ever*; because *you cannot recultivate the soil in which your trees are growing*. If you make an error, it is the error of a hundred years. And do not imagine, as one writer has done,* that two feet depth of double-dug soil is only an improvement *pro tanto*, i. e., until the roots of the trees get deeper. For it is a most important truth in arboriculture, that the vigour and health imparted to the tree by free growth when young, will give it root-strength to overcome almost every difficulty of soil and situation afterwards : besides, that ash, the most profitable perhaps of all, seldom penetrates deeply into the soil ; and the deeper the soil is loosened, the sooner the roots of the oak and other deep growing trees get out of its way, and both species are enabled to grow healthily *nearer to each other*, causing thereby a greater crop on the given space. In fact, whatever may be asserted oe denied as to the importance and value of deep cultivation for annual crops, it is impossible to say too much in its favour as a necessary preparation for trees, whether for grove plantations or coppice, a description of crop which when *once sown* will show, *and that irrevocably and irremediably*, during the life of the planter, and for generations afterwards, results corresponding with the due preparation of the soil to which it was committed.

Now the roots of the sapling of any forest tree have this advantage over the annual crops of the farmer and the gardener, viz., that from their hardier and more permanent nature they will more readily betake themselves to active growth, in soil or subsoil well broken up, which (to use a farmer's phrase) " never saw daylight before." Double digging, therefore, by which the upper layer of soil, with all the coarse vegetable matter in and upon it, is effectually buried, and the subsoil exposed at the top, is

---

* Mr. Selby on the one side ; Mr. Withers of Norfolk, Mr. Shaw, Mr. Johnson, and the *Editor* of the *Mark Lane Express*, on the other.

* Sir Walter Scott—a great novelist and a great planter, but whose fame survives better in his novels than his plantations.

not only a safe but perhaps the best method of preparation. If any thing be added to stimulate early growth, lime is preferable to other manures, because its effect upon the coarse and raw soil thus superimposed, is both more *specific*, and more lasting. Every subsoil contains more or less of metallic salts and of crude unoxydised earths, both of which are chemically acted on, and corrected by lime, which in this case cannot be applied too hot. Its operation upon inert vegetable matter is still more familiar to all : and lime having a tendency to *descend*, and be carried into the subsoil by rain, operates upon the buried vegetable soil, at the very time when the hidden treasures of this layer are required for the extending roots of the young trees. If mixed in the course of the work, with the subsoil thrown to the top in double-digging, it will be found the best and most permanent, as well as generally the cheapest application that the planter can use. It particularly favours the growth of the beech and the Spanish chesnut. It would be well, if convenient, that this operation should be performed about six months before the setting of the plants : early in spring, for instance, with the view of October planting.

But in stiff or wet land, or ground that lies low, a thing, if possible, still more important than double-digging, is the cutting of *deep, open drains*. This is an advantage peculiar to plantations and coppice : because not an inch of ground is lost, and the drainage far more perfect than even the best tile-draining will afford. They should be cut at least three feet deep, and this may be done between rows of trees not more than five feet apart.

It is difficult to overstate the advantages of these drains : for, besides the principal object of them, viz. the getting rid of stagnant surface water, the soil thrown out adds considerably to the depth of the adjoining land : and they contribute to loosen the whole of the ground, by allowing of greater *lateral expansion*, which even in the stiffest soils, the planter will soon observe to be taken advantage of. By means of them more air is admitted to the soil, and stagnant gases and moisture released. The freedom thus afforded to the spread of the minute fibres of the roots, is of incalculable benefit, years and years after the most deeply broken soil would have set to almost its original hardness.

These open drains, or " grips," may be made from 20 to 30 feet apart, according to the wetness and tenacity of the soil : and as this work can be better judged of when finished than double-digging, it may safely be set by the perch or rood for job-work. I have found, and consider it of such importance, that in soils of the above description, I should never think of planting without it. To prove its importance, let the planter only try the experiment of making some deep open cuttings, so directed as to carry off the water, wherever bad patches are observable in wood and coppice : the good effect will be remarked, even after one summer's growth. I have recovered a great deal in this manner : indeed it is the only remedy that may be said to be applicable to plantations already growing. And in large tracts, where, perhaps, double-digging might be out of the question, one deep ploughing, followed by deep open drains, at about 30 feet apart, and the soil out of them spread and broken over the adjoining " lands," is as good and effectual a preparation as circumstances will sometimes admit of. But let the planter ever bear in mind that the preparation of ground for trees is a thing which when done is done once for all. When the roots have once begun to travel in a network

through the ground, it is too late to regret the mischief which original neglect of cultivation soon begins to shew. Truly is the motto in this case applicable,

" *Dimidium facit qui bene capit, habet.*"

I remain, Sir, your very obedient servant,
　　　　　　　　　　　　　MISLETOE.

LETTER II.

THE CHOICE OF PLANTS.

SIR,—The preparation of the ground being completed, our next consideration will be, what description of trees to plant.

The number of those which are found in practice most profitable is not great. The ash, larch, Spanish chestnut, oak, elm, and birch, with the hazel, alder, and withy, seem to comprise all which, for the purpose of mere profit and a ready sale, would occur to the planter in ordinary situations and cases. Second to these in point of value, but not therefore to be excluded, even where ornament and diversity of effect may be disregarded, I would name the beech, lime, abele-poplar, wych-elm, maple, locust (*robinia pseud-acacia*), and walnut, with the spruce and silver firs. And thirdly, as chiefly for ornament and variety, the plane-sycamore and tulip, hornbeam, mountain-ash, horsechestnut, copper-beech, black-walnut, holly, and box, with the cedar, Scotch fir, and yew-tree.

The order in which I have named them will seem arbitrary ; but botanical arrangement being out of the present question, I have endeavoured to do so as nearly as possible in reference (taking one district with another) to facility of sale and private use.

To the *ash* I have given the very first place ; and few I believe will now dispute its precedency. The rapidity of its growth, its specific utility for a variety of purposes answered by no other wood, and the consequent steadiness of demand and high price, give it an importance less affected by season, situation, or circumstance, than any other tree. As coppice it will flourish even in soils where it would never become fine timber ; which I have never seen it do in a subsoil of coarse, hard, or wet clay. Wherever this is the case, it is useless to plant it for timber without double digging. Indeed it is only in the best soils that this tree will come to perfection without it. So much does it shun all contact with a hard unbroken subsoil, that its roots will travel far and wide, scarcely a couple of inches below the surface, in search of vegetable mould. Well, therefore, may the farmer regard it with dislike when planted for hedge-row timber ; though *a clean barked and healthy appearance of it*, in that character, is perhaps one of the best letters of credit that the land can offer to a new comer. A foe to the plough while living, it is however its best friend afterwards. Mr. Selby speaks in the highest terms of its beauty ; but I confess that even during its brief term of foliage, and without considering its late bloom and early unpicturesque decay, it seems to me far behind the Spanish chestnut, oak, elm, or beech, in this point.

The value of the *larch*, after the struggle of more than half a century, is at last understood. From a peculiarity in the deposition of its woody fibre at each year's growth, it is almost unique in its combination of lightness with strength, durability, and longitudinal bearing. On this account it is peculiarly suitable for roofing, and for building purposes generally; and makes excellent gates, preventing by its lightness both the slamming and the drooping at the nose, which so often destroy oak gates prematurely. When planted originally very close, the first thinnings are admirable as hop-poles; and at the next thinning it is superior to everything else for scaffolding. In consequence of the complexity of its grain above alluded to, and to which it mainly owes its strength, it will not cleave, but must be sawed into scantling. Mr. Selby calls it "the rival of the oak"—a name which I would rather make it share with

The *Spanish chestnut*, a tree whose virtues are not yet so generally known or appreciated as it well deserves. For coppice it is surpassed by nothing but the ash, and its growth is very nearly as rapid. Allowance being made for any peculiarities of situation and demand, a coppice of ash and Spanish chestnut is fit to cut from two to three years earlier than one of oak and hazel; and being certainly more valuable would afford on calculation an advantage of from twenty-five to thirty per cent. in profit. As timber, the Spanish chestnut comes to maturity in less than half the time of the oak, and is at its prime from forty to sixty years old. Some of the finest and soundest beams in old houses that have been pulled down, have been found to be of this tree.* The bark contains the *tannin* principle in the degree of about two-thirds to that of the oak; and it generally sells for half price, but at the present value of bark this would hardly compensate the disadvantage of summer felling. After the age of sixty, it is apt (except in the finest specimens) to bleed from small fissures near the neck of the root, caused probably by wind-shakes, in consequence of its excessive weight of foliage. *There is no tree which seems to me to combine profit with ornament in so great a degree as this.*

The *oak* and the *elm* require but little remark. In a light, dry, and deep soil, the latter is certainly the best of all hedge-row timber. Its shade is both less, and less injurious to growing crops or grass, than that of the oak; and, in suitable soil, its roots will descend below the reach of the plough. It bears the removal of its lower branches more kindly than the oak (an amiability that is sadly abused), and heals the wound very rapidly. And as it bears transplanting, and *standing alone transplanted*, better perhaps than any other tree, it is convenient, if not one of the most beautiful, for ornamental purposes. Here again the foe most to be dreaded is a wet clay subsoil, in which the elm soon takes the character of a slow-growing, mossy tree, often found heart rotten when felled. On such a soil the oak will generally grow the quicker of the two. Unrivalled, however, and well known as are the qualities of this truly British tree—the *oak*, the slowness of its growth is so great a drawback, that

as hedge-row timber, especially, I much doubt whether, at the present and probable future prices, it ever pays for the land it spoils. Our dockyards are full of foreign oak, in consequence of the immense expense of its conveyance by land: so that, except in the somewhat problematical emergency of universal war, its value, even for naval purposes, will ever be little better than a mere speculation. If war were, according to the views of some, a sort of essential and perpetual condition of mankind, then I would still place this emphatically "war tree" in the foremost position: but if we may hope that that best of national civilization, which is founded on the increase of education and corrected views amongst all classes of the great families of the human race, will gradually convince mankind of the mutual inutility and disastrous consequences, not to speak of the wholesale crime, of trying to settle differences by mutual butchery; I see no good reason why our friend the planter should attach more than that due share of importance which the ordinary purposes of trade and commerce, and private utility give, to a tree which is hardly arrived at maturity when his grandson, if he ever have one, is near his grave. The practice of summer felling deducts from the real value, even of the heart wood; and must, upon every principle of vegetable physiology and the chemical history of decay, constitute the main predisposing cause of dry-rot. The sap wood of the oak is far less valuable than that of the larch, or Spanish chestnut.

I have mentioned the hazel, alder, and withy, of course as underwood only; but I doubt whether the latter should ever be grown except in a bed by itself, in which condition it is a most profitable way of employing wet land. But in mixed coppices it is like the poplar, a bad neighbour, whipping the leaders of the nearest trees, in consequence of its rapid growth and pliancy to the wind; and in oak coppices, becoming rotten at the stool and mouldy in the bark before the time of cutting arrives. In some localities, the alder, which also delights in wet and even marshy ground, is very profitable; but it may otherwise be well substituted by the hazel and Spanish chestnut.

Of the trees in the second class I may speak more briefly, though of course there are districts where, in consequence of peculiarities of soil or of local demand, many of them assume a more primary importance. The partiality of the *beech* for a calcareous, or indeed a pure chalk, soil, is well known. In a damp climate, like that of England, timber which will not bear exposure to wet is apt to fall even below a fair discount. Such is the case with the beech, whose firmness of grain, and consequent adaptation for the turner's lathe, prove how much higher its character would stand in a steady atmosphere. As a park tree it is beautiful, and autumn owes it some of her richest tints. In several places I have observed that rooks show a great partiality to this tree for the establishment of their clamorous but respectable communities. To accomplish which end (for those who may desire it), the trees should be planted pretty thickly, that they may draw each other up to that particular height which the crafty rook seems to measure with the gun-accomplished eye of a Manton, Egg, or Purday. In coppice, however, this tree should be planted very sparingly, being almost the only one which, however close pressed on every side, will not abandon its tendency to spread. Even the ash and the larch—the former the most baleful, and the latter the most intolerant, neighbour of the forest—cannot

---

* During the recent alterations at Hampton Court, in Herefordshire, the ancient and truly baronial seat of the Lords Coningsby, some beams of very great antiquity, and in a high state of soundness and preservation, were found on being cut to be of Spanish chestnut. Mr. Selby, alluding to some other instances, suggests that oak beams might possibly, through the similarity of the grain, have been mistaken for chestnut; but there is abundant reason to doubt the suggestion more than the reality of the instances he alludes to.

keep within bounds the overbearing and interfering shoots of the well-named *" patulæ fagi."*

But the detail, however brief and sketchy, of the respective merits of our " forest friends " have led me into trespass ; and I must beg the reader's indulgence for the postponement of the conclusion of this letter to a future number of a journal whose every page is too well filled, and at this busy time too preoccupied with parliamentary information, for the insertion of country communications, which savour in every sense of the " Long Recess."

And I beg to subscribe myself, Sir,
Your very obedient servant,
MISLETOE.

ON THE PROGRESS OF AGRICULTURAL KNOWLEDGE DURING THE LAST FOUR YEARS.

BY PH. PUSEY, M.P., F.R. AND G.S.

(From the Journal of the Royal Agricultural Society.)

[Continued.]

There is still a practical point of view, however, which strikes me so forcibly, with regard to these common admixtures of soil, that I cannot but shortly advert to it. They are all permanent in their effect, and nevertheless all exceedingly cheap. Chalking land on the hills costs little more than 2l. per acre ; pays itself often in the second year ; and its effect lasts for twenty years. Marling cannot cost more ; repays itself as soon ; and lasts even longer. Claying the fen-land costs 36s. an acre ; converts very bad into very productive land ; and lasts twenty years. Yet there is a great deal of land in each district to which these improvements are applicable on which they are not practised, although they are permanent, while farmers elsewhere lay out 3l. an acre for bones which hardly last above two or three years. It is not that the farmers of these districts have any doubt of the efficacy of each process. Why, then, is not each universally carried out upon every acre of land within its own limits? This is a difficult question to answer. In some degree none of us carry out all that is in our power ; but want of capital, or want of confidence in the tenure of farms, are, I suppose, the two principal causes of this omission. Without entering minutely into the remedy, I think the more landowners acquaint themselves with the real merits and real difficulties of farming, the more these two obstacles will be smoothed ; and I must say that land-agents might promote such improvements more than they do, if they would make themselves acquainted, not with the theory, which is difficult, and may be mischievous, but, as they easily might, with the common practice of their own neighbourhoods. We have many intelligent agents ; but it is an evil that any land-agents should be utterly unacquainted with land. Besides these three cheap and lasting improvements of the soil itself, we have found a still more necessary and almost equally cheap improvement, draining, which, it now appears, can be accomplished by some well-known method or other on all laud, at little more than

3l. per acre, the cost, as I before said, of a good dressing of bones. Now, as the varied surface of England passes through my mind, I do not see that in any large portion of it one or other of these acknowledged improvements might not be at once put largely in practice, with an absolute certainty of success. The chalk hills span the whole south of the country in four branches. We hear of marling in Norfolk, Suffolk, Warwickshire, Bedfordshire, Cheshire, Yorkshire, and Hampshire. I do not know the extent of the fens ; but I have seen the extent of land which empties its waters into Boston Wash and at a million of acres. As for draining, there is not a county, nor any large proportion of parishes, or even of farms, in which it ought not to be done. These improvements must cost, no doubt, many millions ; but there is no want of idle capital. The misfortune is, that, according to an old remark, I forget by whom made, the capital and the soil of the country are not acquainted with each other. I wish it were a standing rule on every estate, and, if possible, on each individual farm, that some employment should be given every winter to the labourer, by doing some lasting good to the soil.

We may proceed, however, from the soil to its tillage, and first the plough. As more as been done by our society in the last four years for its improvement than might have been expected with regard to so ancient an implement, I will endeavour to trace the progress of our inquiries. At the time of our foundation, four years back, the Scotch iron swing-plough was stated to be the most perfect form of plough. Lord Spencer having remarked that, from his observation of ploughing-matches, he doubted whether swing-ploughs had any advantage over those with wheels, a prize was proposed by our council for the best essay upon the subject, which was won by Mr. Handley, who applied the draught-gauge for measuring the strain arising to the horses from different ploughs, and found that those wheel-ploughs he tried inflicted the least labour upon the cattle. Following his example, I tried several ploughs in the same manner, and with the same result. It further appeared that there was a much wider difference in the draught of ploughs than had been suspected, and even that, of two ploughs used by two farmers in the same parish and on the same soil, one was heavier for three horses than the other for two ; the old Berkshire plough costing the cattle a muscular strain of twenty-three stones, while Hart's improved one-wheeled plough was drawn by them with an exertion of fourteen stones only. One of Messrs. Ransome's was hardly surpassed by Hart's in lightness, and it certainly made better work. The Scotch were the heaviest of the swing-ploughs. The next trial was by Mr. Freeman* at Haverfordwest, in South Wales, who set an old Welsh plough of the country against Hart's. Here again the old plough was more severe for three horses than Hart's was for two. The old plough stood at twenty stones ; Hart's at thirteen. The next experiments were made by Lord Tweeddale, and in these the Yester plough equalled Hart's plough in lightness. The next trial was before our judges at Liverpool, whose words I will quote from their report :—†

" It appears that in almost every case the draught of the wheel-ploughs was less than that of the

* Journal, ii. p. 105.

† Ibid., p. cxiv., Judges' Report.

o 2

swing kind : and it must not be concealed that the wheel-ploughs in every case actually turned over more soil than the swing, for the share and sole of the former maintained a flat, horizontal position, whereas all the swing-ploughs leant more or less to the land-side, cutting to a less depth on the right than on the left hand side. Consequently, the furrow-bottoms left by the wheel-ploughs were more even than those excavated by the swing-ploughs."

On this occasion, a wheel-plough by Messrs. Barrett, of Reading, was the lightest, marking 22 stones ; Hart's the next, 24 stones ; a Scotch and a Northampton swing-plough the heaviest, standing each at 40 stones. I cannot but remark how little our mechanists yet know of the draught of their ploughs, when implements could be brought forward to compete for a prize at a great public meeting, some of which gave as much work nearly for four horses as others for two.

The latest published record of trials* is a very careful set of experiments by Mr. Hannam, of Dorchester, in Oxfordshire. Here again, as in Wales and in Berkshire, the lightest plough stood at 13 stones, the old Oxfordshire plough at 22 stones, the Scotch swing-plough at 20 stones. The lightest plough in this instance was Messrs. Barrett's.

There only remains the interesting report of our judges on the ploughs which competed at our Bristol meeting. There, again, it will be seen that the lightest plough was a wheeled one, Mr. Howard's of Bedford, which stood at 22 ; the heaviest, a Scotch swing-plough, which marked 44 ; the next heaviest, another Scotch swing-plough, which marked 36 ; and, in the words of our judges, " it is worthy of note that the resistance of Mr. Howard's two-wheel was less by four stones than that of his swing-plough."

From these repeated trials, which have arisen out of Lord Spencer's remark, we may now come to the conclusion that wheel-ploughs, as he suspected, are superior to swing-ploughs, in ease for the cattle, and are also superior in the work they perform ; that the Scotch swing-plough in particular is very severe for the cattle ; that, since in three country trials the draught of the ploughs was found to differ as two to three—that is, as two horses to three—more attention is required on the part of our ploughwrights to the easiness of their draught ; and lastly, that, since in our two public competitions at Liverpool, and again at Bristol, the draught of some competing ploughs doubled that of the winning plough, as if at Epsom one horse had only run half the course when another was winning the Derby, it appears very clearly that our plough-makers, as a body, are not thoroughly acquainted with the qualities of their own implements, otherwise the race could not be so unequal. It may not be useless to them, therefore that we should inquire what it is in ploughing which constitutes the work of the horses? Some makers appear to think that if their plough is light in weight it will be light in draught; but this supposition is a mistake, as the report of our judges at Bristol will show. The lightest weight of a wheel-plough there stated is that of the plough which was heaviest but one in draught ; and the swing-plough worst in draught was the lightest in weight of its class.

* Journal, iii. p. 9.

	Draught.	Weight.
Howard's wheel-plough, lightest in draught............	22 stones.	220 lbs.
Carson's wheel-plough, heaviest but one in draught....	32	193
Earl of Ducie's swing-plough, lightest in draught........	26	161
Wilkie's swing-plough, heaviest in draught............	44	125

This distinction between lightness of weigh and of draught should be observed by the makers of ploughs who intend to compete at future trials ; and it is satisfactory to the employers of ploughs, since it shows that solid construction of the implement is by no means inconsistent with ease to their horses. Again, if the weight of the plough has little effect on its draught, I believe that the weight of the earth to be raised has not much more—for the furrow-slice, when the plough has severed it, can be turned over by the hand without much exertion ; neither can the perpendicular cutting of the earth by the coulter occasion much of the draught in ordinary land, because implements with numerous teeth, each performing a similar cut, can be drawn by four horses. But a plough, when merely drawn along the surface of a furrow, requires considerable force to move it. This arises of course from friction—the resistance of the rough particles of the soil to its progress. If the furrow were coated with ice, a finger would draw the plough. Locking the wheel of a waggon at a descent shows the power of this kind of friction. Before the iron shoe is placed under the wheel the horses may scarcely be able to hold back the waggon ; afterwards they may be obliged to pull it : but when the plough is at work, every part of it below ground grates downwards, sideways, or upwards, against the earth, as the shoe of the wheel grinds the road. You must therefore add to the labour of a plough-team when you increase the rubbing surface of the sole or of the mouldboard. Our manufacturers of impleme n y should, I think, therefore inquire whether they may not improve the draught of their ploughs bc diminishing the surface of the parts which are below ground. Captain Carr pointed out to m that the draught of a plough is diminished if the coulter be set towards the land-side. The reason must be this,—that the coulter so set prevents a side of the plough from rubbing against the land.

There is another cause of draught, which, though similar, is not precisely the same with friction. In my first trials I found that a plough drawn along a furrow on clay land in a very wet state occasioned nearly as much labour to the horses as when actually doing its work. The friction on so smooth a surface as wet clay cannot be much ; the strain must be occasioned, I believe, by its adhesion. The strength of this adhesion is shown by the difficulty which a labourer finds in digging strong clay, from its adhering when wet to the back of his spade. On such lands in this neighbourhood a wooden mouldboard is used, the clay being found to adhere less strongly to wood than to iron.* The length of a mouldboard must

* The same soil which when wet adheres to the plough becomes exceedingly hard when dry, because its particles cohere together, and then the splitting action becomes a source of draught; hence, of course, the difficulty of ploughing most soils when

increase adhesion as well as friction, but practically on clay land it is impossible to use a short mouldboard, because, if we endeavour to throw such land too suddenly over, it will roll before the plough when it is very wet. This happens sometimes indeed even with the long mouldboards now used on such ground; and consequently it is very difficult to make an improved plough for such clays. But for other soils I think plough-makers will do well to regard diminution of friction as a leading principle of their attempts at improvement, varying its application according to the land which their ploughs are intended to work; for we never can have a standard plough suited to all descriptions of land. If land be light and free, the plough should be short above ground, that the horses may be nearer their work, and short below, that there may be less friction. Hart's is such a plough; and is now generally used on such land in this neighbourhood; but if you put this plough on strong or stony land, it will rise out of the ground when at work. On strong or stony land a wheel-plough must be long in the beam, that the horses may hold it down when they pull it; and taper in the breast, that it may undermine the obstacles which it meets. Different depths of ploughing, again, require a different shape of the mouldboard. These, however, are matters for the makers of ploughs; the question for farmers is, the advantage to be derived from the use of light ploughs. Where the difference is between the draught of two horses and of three, that advantage is of course very clear; even where it is less, the improvement may bring the plough within the command of two horses, upon land which before was too strong for a pair. Where four horses are the usual team, pair-horse ploughing may be impossible, and its advocates were wrong when they asserted that there is no land which two horses are unable to master. But in many districts, where three horses were the usual number, country ploughing matches have tended to introduce the two-horse system. On the first occasion the curtailed team is viewed with some incredulity, but does its work. The next year more pairs come forward. At last the triple team becomes singular in its turn, and ultimately disappears.

Even if the number of horses be not reduced, it is of course right for their sakes and our own to lighten their labour; but there is another point in which lightness of ploughs may be useful. I mean increase of pace, and this is a matter deserving more attention than it has received. It is remarkable that more work is done in a day at plough in the north of England than in many parts of the south. Here three-quarters of an acre, I believe, is the daily task in winter, whereas an acre is the Scotch amount at that season, and a quarter more as the days lengthen. It is stated, however, by London,[*] that in Suffolk farmers plough, with two horses, 1 acre a-day on stiff soils, and 1¼ to 1½ acre on sands. In Northumberland even 2 acres are sometimes accomplished, I am informed, during the hurry of turnip-sowing. I think our farmer's clubs in the slow-ploughing districts ought to inquire whether this practice of the northern and Suffolk farmers does not deserve imitation; and I may repeat one circumstance which struck me much in my former experiments,

as it appears to bear out quickness of pace. It might be supposed that the more rapidly the plough works the greater would be the exertion of the horses, so that, although more work might be done in a day, the ultimate wear of the cattle would be the same. But I found by the draught-gauge that, when a plough was made to move quicker, though more earth was of course moved, there was no increase in the draught, at least as between the pace of 1½ and of 2¾ miles in an hour. Strange as this fact appears, it agrees with what is known by mechanicians, that in many cases the resistance arising from friction does not augment with increase of speed, and it tends to confirm my belief that friction is a principal cause of the labour of ploughing teams. An example of increase of pace without addition of draught may be found, I believe, in the descent of a carriage with a drag on the wheel. The horses, indeed, who have to cover more ground at plough, have of course to carry their own weight a greater distance each day. But, if they be in good condition and nimble, I doubt if they feel it; and the northern horses appear to me to be naturally quick stoppers. The best Clydesdale horses, such as the pair of greys which Lord Derby sent to our trial-ground at Liverpool, or Lord Ducie's browns, which were seen by many of our members at Bristol, appear to unite the merits of our three English breeds—the compactness of the Suffolks, the power of the old Lincolns, and the courage and quickness of the Cleveland race.

I have dwelt at great length on the construction of the plough, because each successive trial has shown that it is a subject which rewards our inquiries in practice. Mathematical calculations have been framed for it, but the mouldboard of Lord Ducie's plough, so highly praised by our judges at Bristol, had been cast on the day before the trial from a mould shaped to the actual curve of the furrow-slice: and it may be best thus to fit on the plough to different kinds of soil. There is evidently much to be gained, and a great reduction of horse-labour to be effected. Only we must not go too far by asserting that all land can be worked at all times by two horses only.[*] Soils differ much too widely in their resistance, as appears from the following numbers, which have been already published,[†] shawing the average draught of numerous ploughs tried by me on three neighbouring farms:—

	Draught.
Sandy loam	17 stone.
Clay loam..........	30 "
Strong clay	47 "

Mr. Hannam too, in his interesting trials, has shown that the same field, in different stages of

---

they are dry, which becomes impossibility on a strong clay.

* Loudon's Encyclopædia of Agriculture, p. 1136.

* Even if two horses could draw the plough in winter on our heavy clay-lands, the surface is so soft that the horse which must necessarily walk upon the unploughed land does great harm by trampling it together. I believe that the best plan upon such farms would be this: to have a plough with two shifting mouldboards, a short iron one for summer use, with two horses abreast, and a long wooden one for wet weather, to be used with three horses walking in line. Both Mr. Bennett of Tempsford, near Bedford, and Mr. Moore of Coleshill, have adopted this plan of a changeable mouldboard. The plough should have one wheel in summer, and in winter a *foot* which clogs less than a wheel.

† Journal, vol. i. p. 219, Inquiry on Draught in Ploughing.

cultivation, varies widely in its resistance ; for he measured the draught of some ploughs during the process of barley-sowing, and the difference with Hart's plough was as follows :—

	Draught.	Furrow.
April 2. Seed-furrow with single horse	9 stones 2½	× 8
April 3. Breaking up turnip-ground trodden in rain 21	5	× 9
" Ditto less trodden.... 18	5	× 9
April 20. Ditto drier and harder, with the same plough...... 25	5½	× 9

The difference of draught between three farms worked with the same ploughs as one to three, and here on the same field the difference within one month is again one to three. Such variations must encourage active inquiry, but should check hasty conclusions.

There is no doubt, however, that in many parts of the country the third horse might be discarded, and that two horses would be ample for each plough. But it may be said that ploughing is not the only employment of farm-horses, and that if the same number of horses be required as at present for other farming operations, each in their due season, the farmer cannot reduce his horses, since for these operations he will require his present establishment ; that his stables must be as full as they are now ; and consequently the only advantage of putting two horses instead of three to his plough will be that one-third of his cattle may remain idle at home during the season of ploughing. Now it happens, singularly, that another saving of horse-labour has been proposed, which would precisely meet this emergency. In southern England the harvest is brought home on heavy waggons drawn by three horses ; and the dung is carried out on equally heavy carts, to which three horses are also attached : but in Cumberland and the north all this is done with light carts drawn by one horse only. Here we have practice on each side, and certainly there appears no particular reason why three horses drawing three carts should be able to convey more than three horses drawing one large cart only : but the contrary would seem more likely. Still there is a strong opinion on the part of those farmers who use the one-horse cart that their system is best. This is a difficult matter to test ; but we have had a paper from a south country agriculturist, Mr. Hannam, who has used one-horse carts for ten years, at Burcott, near Dorchester, in Oxfordshire, and who thus states his own experience :—

" My farm, of 370 acres, was some years ago under very able management, with a strength of twelve horses and six oxen. Just previous to my taking it into my own occupation *sixteen* horses had been employed by another spirited cultivator. I have gradually, by the joint operation of two-horse ploughs and single-horse carts, reduced my number to *eight* horses....Let farmers take the two-horse plough as a first, and the single-horse cart as a second step, and I have no hesitation in asserting that they will find themselves gradually, as they are able to master the working of the system, able to perform their labour, as I have experienced, with something approaching to half the number of horses that they now use, and with at least equal facility and comfort."

This is a strong statement from ten years' experience, supported by calculations for which I

must refer to Mr. Hannam's own paper;* and founded on the practice of the north of England —that one half of the purchase-money of horses, their wear and tear, their food, the bills for shoeing them, forming together a large part of the outgoings upon a farm, may be saved by the use of two-horse ploughs and one-horse carts. Now I would not advise a farmer even on these grounds, to part with his waggons, because further inquiry is needed ; but I do think this question of one-horse carts well deserves that further inquiry, and ought not to be put aside ; and I will avow, though living in a country of waggons, that, from what I have seen of one-horse carts, I believe these heavy waggons are doomed. One merit of the carts is their readiness in service. On a large farm near Wantage, Mr. W. Edmunds has adopted them ; and last year I witnessed them accidentally carrying barley : it was done most briskly by a man loading on each side, and one on the cart. The time occupied to load a cart high, and tie it by two ropes thrown over from each hind corner (which was done instantaneously), was five minutes by the watch, and the succeeding driver standing in his cart trotted up in his turn, keeping his time regularly, though the field was a hilly one. Carts certainly offer an important saving to a young man entering upon business. For Mr. Hannam says that, where waggons are used, there " would be required, on a farm of 400 acres, six dung-carts, at 16*l*. ; two Dutch (mould) carts, at 10*l*. ; one marketing-cart, at 16*l*. ; and five waggons, at 35*l*.: total, 295*l*." On the other hand, Mr. Hannam uses skeleton harvest-carts ; but, elegant as they are, they are not necessary. His own or any other light cart, fitted with rails and ladders, answers, I find, the same purpose ; and eight of these carts, at 16*l*. each, would amount to 128*l*. only ; so that here would be a saving of capital to the amount of one half. Leaving this subject, however, to the consideration of farmers, I must return for a moment to ploughing.

As to the modes of ploughing, it is not to be expected that much should have been brought to light in four years : but I may mention one point for which northern farmers have sometimes blamed those of the south—I mean shallow ploughing. On our trial-ground at Liverpool a southern farmer observed to me that the furrow prescribed (six inches) was too deep, and immediately afterwards a northern farmer found fault with it as being too shallow. I have already detailed the practice of my own neighbours in ploughing light barren soils very shallow indeed.† Where they have ploughed sands deep even for turnips, in trying the Scotch practice, it has decidedly failed. Firmness is, I believe, quite as important for loose land as looseness for land which is over close. On some very loose land of my own I have seen the most remarkable improvement produced on a turnip-crop, for which tightness of soil is least requisite, by the passage of waggons in a previous year, and by the trampling of horses where a rick had been built. For a wheat-crop firmness, as all farmers know, is indispensable. Firmness, however, is not a positive but a relative term—relative to the soil, to the crop, and also to the climate.

* Journal, vol. ii. p. 73. On the Reduction of Horse Labour by Single Horse Carts ; by H. Hannam.

† Journal, vol. ii. p. 400. On the Practice of Farmers in cultivating Peaty Land.

In part of Norfolk, according to Loudon, "they plough with two or four horses very shallow, carefully preserving the hard basis formed by the sole of the plough, which is called the pan of the land; breaking this up is said to let down the riches into the hungry subsoil. One of our members, Mr. A. Edmunds, who has long farmed 200 acres of peaty land in Gloucestershire, tells me that he always ploughed it shallow, and that for wheat he did not stir it at all, but skimmed it only with a breast-plough. The summers there are probably hotter than in Lincolnshire, where peat is ploughed deeper. Near Coblentz, on the Rhine, where the summers are very burning, it is stated that the farmers only scratch the ground with a one-horse plough, because they find deeper ploughing injurious. I dwell on this point the more because high authorities in Scotland in recommending not only deep ploughing but trench-ploughing, that is with one plough following another in the same furrow, and throwing up the subsoil on the surface from the depth of a foot. This may be useful where the surface is light and the subsoil is a good clay, and it may be less dangerous to make the ground so hollow where rain falls constantly, and the land is seldom very dry; but, apart from the looseness produced, I should think that, as Mr. Denison observes, "in very few cases is the soil underneath more fitted for vegetation than that of the surface;"* and I believe such an operation would be destructive on many of our southern farms.

The use of the plough may be sometimes even dispensed with altogether, by means of a class of implements on wheels, with teeth or tines that tear up the land. One of them is Biddell's scarifier, which I believe to be a good working tool, because I see many farmers purchase it, and because one of my own I constantly find has been borrowed by my neighbours. A Suffolk farmer states† that " by the use of this implement he can equally well cultivate his farm with 12 per cent. less of horses." Lord Ducie's cultivator is also well spoken of, and our Bristol judges commend another by Messrs. Cottam. They likewise speak highly of a Warwickshire plough with slices behind, which pulverise the soil like a harrow. If this simple contrivance of Mr. Mason's should answer, it will be a remarkable discovery; but time and use must show its merits or its defects, and the soils to which it can be applied.

The land being worked, we may proceed to the crop. The sower, with his accurate hand and eye, is now seldom seen; but I am unable to detail the various modes of spreading the seed which have taken his place. The large drill is generally used for corn in the south, and the intervals between the rows of young corn enable the hoer to keep the land clean. As every seed, too, is covered with earth, less corn is required for the purpose. In Suffolk wheat is dibbled in by the hand, and a still further saving of seed is effected, one bushel being sufficient, instead of two or of three. This seems a strangely tedious process; but some of us, who may look on it as unworthy of a large farm, probably set out beans by hand, and should blame the Scotch farmer,‡ who sows broadcast four bushels per acre, while we find one bushel enough

for that crop. Even corn, I believe, is but little drilled in Scotland. Should Mr. Rham be able to bring his dibbling-machine to perfection, he will have the satisfaction of saving the country one bushel per acre of wheat. I should mention that there is a question on the advantages of thick and thin sowing. Lord Western strongly advocates liberal use of seed, but I am unable to bring forward any facts on this point.

Great hopes have been entertained that by attention to the selection of seed, we might be able to increase the yield of our wheat, and many new varieties have been from time to time advertised, with favourable testimony as to their produce. Farmers, however, rightly view with mistrust very long, loose heads of corn and a great bulk of straw, having found such wheat liable to be laid, and subject to mildew, a disease which appears to arise whenever the vegetation of the plant, either from its own habit or from the manure applied to it, surpasses the strength of the soil. This I believe to be an important law of agriculture. Such long, loose heads of corn are often found to contain very little and very thin grain; or where the grain is large, the millers will not purchase it, because the bran is too thick. Our Society has offered prizes for the best specimens of seed-wheat, to be adjudged after trial by appointed judges; but as yet we have had no award, because the wheats selected at Oxford were mixed in the sack, and the Cambridge prize-wheats were not found to excel those against which they were tried. There is a doubt even about the principle of our selection, because though the prize is for seed-wheat, our judges can only tell us which are the best samples of corn; but many farmers say that the plumpest sample is not the best seed;* that plump corn is most liable to rot in the ground in wet weather: they certainly do not use inferior wheat as seed from mere economy; for sometimes lean wheat is sold as seed at a higher price than other corn which is better for grinding. Still I believe that we have done good already by directing attention to old as well as new sorts of prolific wheat. It is impossible that so great a difference of yield should be found as four bushels an acre in many trials, and that some wheats should not give more than others, were it only half a bushel, in a regular course of farming; and though half a bushel be little, I need scarcely remind our members that in all calculations for general improvement of farming our multiplier for these small numbers is millions. I believe, however, that a greater increase than this may be hoped for, especially upon good land, for it is on good land, as far as I can ascertain, that the different qualities of wheat show themselves most; which might be expected, and is another instance of the principle, that soil will not bear to be forced beyond given limits. A familiar instance of this principle is the growth of white wheat, which, although more valuable than the red, has been abandoned excepting upon superior soils. It has been often tried in the parish where I am writing, but the ear produced is of a dingy colour externally, the grain poor, and, what is remarkable, of a red colour. Amongst the good wheats which have come to my knowledge, I may mention the Red Marigold, shown by Mr. Fisher Hobbs, at

---

* Journal, ii. p. 32.
† Journal, vol. i. p. 348. Account of the use of Biddell's Scarifier.
‡ Professor Lowe's Practical Agriculture, p. 274.

* Sprengel I find also states that the best wheat contains too much gluten for seed—the gluten converting the starch into vinegar instead of sugar which is the food of the young sprout.

our Oxford meeting, the Burwell, the Chidham, the Golden Drop, the Silver Drop, the Golden Swan, the Bellevue Talavera (but upon good land, for on a moderate soil I have seen this last wheat fail in several cases), Hunter's White, the Hopetoun, an excellent Scotch wheat, propagated by Mr. Shirreff (to whom we are also indebted for the Hopetoun oat), and a wheat not yet known, a seedling raised by Mr. Jonas, of Ickleton, in the county of Cambridge : but for more accurate information we must await the result of future trials.

No improvement has been made during the last four years in barley ; but a new kind had been already widely adopted, and is regularly quoted in market reports, which proceeds from a single ear picked by the Rev. Mr. Chevalier, at Debenham, in 1819, and is now well known by his name. A new kind of oat, however, is mentioned in our present Journal, which is remarkable not for larger produce but for early maturity. This property is hardly important in ordinary English farming, but those who have seen the oat-harvest tardily ended, as I did last year on the elevated moors of West Somerset in mid-November, will be aware of its value for such mountainous districts where the chill summers seldom ripen the crop, and a doubt is entertained whether it be worth while to raise corn at all. There are such tracts in Derbyshire, and must be many such, I imagine, in Wales. Cumberland and Westmoreland, with a considerable portion of Scotland, have the same bleak and rainy atmosphere. The farmers of those districts, and it is to them I address myself, will value the account which Mr. Fisher* gives of the oat raised from a single ear by Mr. Dyock, near Aberdeen, in 1830. It ripens a fortnight or even three weeks earlier than other kinds, and is equally productive with potato-oats in the elevated situations to which it is fitted. Its use appears to have spread gradually in Scotland. Mr. Fisher tried this oat for the first time last year in Westmoreland. He sowed it side by side with the potato-oat, reaped the Dyock oat on the last day of August, the potato-oat on the 20th of September, and obtained the largest return from the Dyock oat, as well as the heaviest sample. If this oat should maintain its character, a greater boon could not be given to the mountainous parts of Great Britain, since it would remedy at once for their staple crop the main difficulty of their farms.

But if we have not learned much that is new as yet respecting white crops, the information we have received upon green crops has made amends to us ; nor is there any more interesting branch of farming. It is well known that the stock which furnished our forefathers with meat were fattened on the rich grass lands, but that, by a great revolution in farming, the light arable soils now chiefly supply the country with animal food. In the four-course rotation, consisting of barley, clover, wheat, and turnips, successively, while the wheat gives us bread, and the barley beer, a great part of the clover and all the turnips are converted into mutton, or sometimes into beef. But there is another ground for inquiry into green crops. It is commonly said that the farmers of the south of England are greatly inferior to those of the north, and the charge is hardly denied ; yet I do not think that in the south we are at all backward in

the management of our corn ; on the contrary, I am told that our corn-fields are more free from weeds : our grass lands have also a decided superiority. It is our turnip-fields, with poor roots and large patches of bare ground, that offend the sight of those who are accustomed to the neat, and vigorous aspect of ridges crowned with close-set heavy bulbs, in northern husbandry. A keen controversy has been carried on for some time, chiefly in the *Farmers' Magazine* by practical farmers on this very subject, and has been called "The Turnip Question." The chief point on which it turned was, the weight of turnips that could be grown on an acre of land—the northern farmers asserting high weights, the southern denying them. Having attentively read the arguments, I will state what appears to me to be the result.* It is clear, I think, that the northern crops do greatly exceed those of the south. Five-and-twenty tons to the acre of Swedish turnips are not an unusual yield in Scotland with ordinary good farming. Here the best crop I have grown with a heavy dressing did not exceed sixteen tons ; one neighbour I believe has reached twenty. But in Lancashire prizes have been given during the last ten years by two district societies. The average weight of the prize crops of Swedes has been thirty tons : such a crop has never been seen in the part of the country where I am writing. To what, then, is their superiority owing ? Undoubtedly to the ridge system, which has been so admirably described by Mr. Grey,† of Dilston, in his account of Northumberland farming. In the first place, the dung being in the centre of the ridge immediately under the seed, the young plant is forced up more rapidly, and is sooner safe from the fly, which so often destroys the whole crop at its birth. In the next place, it is a great advantage that the horse-hoe can be used instead of the tedious hand-hoe. Lastly, there is no doubt that the plant placed immediately over the dung attains a much greater bulk. Hence arise the fine turnip-crops of the north ; and southern farmers are often blamed for not following this example ; but wrongly, as I now see, for having endeavoured, during many years, to introduce the ridge system into my own neighbourhood, I must admit that on some soils so far south it does not answer. Nor ought we to be surprised that it does not ; for one object doubtless of the ridge-system is, by raising the turnip above the level of the soil, to free it from excessive wet ; and this is a great gain in those northern and western parts of the country, Scotland, and even Lancashire, where the summers are constantly wet. But in many parts of the south we have to fear not wet, but dry springs and summers, at least upon turnip lands ; and it is not unusual that six weeks together should pass without rain. What is advantageous, therefore, in Scotland, may

---

* Journal, present number, Mr. Fisher on the Dyock Oat.

* The relative expense of raising Swedes in the north and south has never been fairly compared. In the north it is not uncommon to manure very heavily for Swedes, and plough it in the ridges, and also to drill bones or other expensive artificial manures with the seed on the top of the ridge, the whole amounting to from 12l. to 15l. per acre ; in the south a fair coat of dung, at less than half that cost, is the usual practice, while in many cases great crops of Swedes are raised at a less charge than 2l. per acre for manure.—GEO. KIMBERLEY.

† See Mr. Grey on Northumberland Farming, Journal, vol. ii. p. 151.

be hurtful here; and on this point I cannot do better than state the opinion of one of our members, Mr. Brooks, of Hatford, near Faringdon, a practical farmer, which ought to have the more weight, because, having tried the ridge system for many years, he has retained it upon one part of his farm, and abandoned it upon the other. It is upon adhesive land that he has found it fail, and, in his opinion, from two reasons :—When the ground is thrown over the dung by the plough, the small clods which such land almost always contains fall exactly into the centre; that is, in the line where the seed is to be sown, and form a bad seed-bed. Again, if dry weather follow, moderate showers do not penetrate the hardened surface of the ridges upon cohesive land. Upon a light sandy soil, on the other hand, Mr. Brooks finds ridging answer, and perseveres in it with success. There is indeed an advantage in ridging, where it is practicable, which I have not seen adverted to, but which I believe to be real. It is common to see on a field of green corn that the blade grows stronger in a line along the crown of each land, in consequence of the double portion of surface mould collected by the plough, where the two slices of earth are lapped over each other in ploughing; now a turnip set on a ridge has this very advantage of a double foundation of the best mould. Still in the south of England, on some soils, we must give up the hope ef establishing the ridge system; but it does not follow that we are to renounce all endeavour at improving our turnip crop. Even flat-drilling, I am told, has great advantages over broadcast sowing of turnips; for although dung cannot be placed immediately under the rows, bones and other artificial manures can. On one farm in Oxfordshire, 1,600 bushels of bones are drilled every year in this way. There is, besides, a much greater certainty of a crop, because the drill deposits all the seed at the proper depth, and thus the unseemly blanks in our turnip fields may be prevented. Another great disadvantage in the broadcast system is the expense of hoeing them twice, or even three times, by the hand, which costs 10s., or even 14s., per acre. I do not know any good horse-hoe for flat-drilled turnips; but at Holkham, where mangold-wurzel is sown in this manner, an implement is used which hoes three rows at once, being drawn by two horses abreast. A good horse-hoe for flat-drilled turnips is, I believe, one of the most useful machines that could be invented; or if there be a good one already in use, though confined to its own district, that could be made known.

But when we have done all, applying to our turnips or Swedes as much manure as the northern farmers, I doubt if it be possible for us to obtain in the south crops generally equal to theirs, for a reason to which I must now advert. In the north the Swede and white turnip are each sown nearly a month earlier than in the south. Hence they have a longer time for their growth. For many years I have seen repeated attempts made here to follow this Scotch practice, and they have all signally failed; for as soon as warm weather comes, white filmy spots appear on the leaves of the turnip, which soon creep over its whole surface. This is mildew, and at once arrests the growth of the plant, rendering the root hard and stringy. In a bad case of mildew I have seen a large field of these early Swedes struck in July, and filling the air with a most offensive odour. Last year, if ever, early sowing of Swedes might have answered

in the south of England. At the time of our meeting in 1841, there were beautiful crops of Swedes near Liverpool, of which the leaves already met, and in that rainy region were, no doubt, perfectly safe. Here I found a last attempt which had been made at early sowing of Swedes by Mr. Brooks, and I watched them with much anxiety. During the six chilly wet weeks which followed, they went on perfectly well. But no sooner did the sun shine forth in September, than after four drys the white tint appeared, and the plants grew no more. I do not mean that nowhere in the south turnips can be planted early; for on the top of the chalk hills I know that they can; and it is well worth observing how very slight an elevation affects the climate, and consequently the growth of crops. On the Cotswold hills, which are of no great height, Lord Ducie, who has occupied a farm there, doubts if it be worth while to grow wheat. But generally in the south, I do not believe we can sow Swedes or turnips as early as in the north; nor have we moisture enough for carrying them forward; consequently, though we ought to manure them more highly than we do, we cannot fairly be blamed, as we are sometimes blamed, for not raising crops equal to those of the north. Still many of us might grow much better turnips than we now do; and it is one of the points to which we ought in the south to give our most earnest attention.

But if our southern climate be against us in the growth of turnips as well as of oats, there is a root which our warm summers favour as they do wheat—that root is mangold-wurzel, or beet. I state this on the high authority of Mr. Lowe, Professor of Agriculture at Edinburgh, who says—

" Beet, however, requires a somewhat favourable climate. It is accordingly more cultivated in the southern than in the northern parts of this island. Although in Scotland very good crops are occasionally produced, the plant is not so well suited to cultivation there as the Swedish and yellow turnips; while in the southern counties the beet is probably a more productive crop than the turnip. Thus also in France and the warm countries of Europe the turnips are not to be compared with the crops which are produced of beet."[*]

Professor Lowe's opinion, that a heavier bulk of beet can be grown than of Swedes, is confirmed by Mr. Hillyard, who has raised both for many years, and informs me that where he gets twenty-five tons to the acre of Swedes he would expect thirty tons of beet. The question then arises, can the farmer apply the mangold as profitably as the Swede ? It is well known that the Swede is not very good for ewes suckling in February; the turnip is better, but does not keep well until that time, unless it be small; so that many farmers sow very late turnips for their ewes, which stand the frost indeed, but give a very small bulk. The mangold is known to be good for all animals giving milk. But it also appears, from a remarkable experiment of Lord Spencer's,[†] that this root is good for fatting also. The two beasts put up by him made even more progress when fed alternately upon mangold than upon turnips, and he considers the result to have been decisive. Mr. Hillyard, however, has undertaken to renew the experiment with regard to horned cattle; and it might be desirable to try it respecting the fattening of sheep. Still enough

---

* Lowe's Practical Agriculture, p. 334.
† Journal, vol. ii. p. 200.

is known to encourage the growth of mangold ; and Mr. Miles has given* us some good rules for its cultivation. The only difficulty is in the sowing ; because, unless the seeds are put in very shallow, they will not grow. But the dibbling wheel† removes this objection. After the young shoot is come up, all anxiety is at an end. It is attacked neither by fly, slug, nor wireworm. Unlike the Swede, it can be sown early in April. It can be grown, too, on heavier lands than even the Swede. The common long red beet exhausts the land rather more, in Mr. Miles's opinion, and requires rather a better soil ; but the orange globe will flourish wherever the Swede will succeed. I find in Count de Gourcy's Travels‡ that Mr. Fisher Hobbs, who has grown beet for many years, and has tried twenty-eight kinds, regards the red and the yellow globes as the most productive varieties. It appears also certain that in our four-course system the turnip crop returns too often. All the manure we bestow on the turnip does not produce such fine roots as were seen forty years since, when it was new to the land, and the site of a freshly-grubbed hedge puts our best cultivation to shame.§ For these reasons, and because the beets keep longer in spring than any turnip, I think they should be allowed a share of the root-fields on every farm to which they are suited. The merits of the four-course system are great, but a great defect too is its monotonous circle of wheat, turnips, barley, and clover.

(To be continued.)

TO THE FARMERS OF SUFFOLK.

LETTER II.

GENTLEMEN,—I stumbled yesterday upon the following notice in a newspaper, by whom sent I know not. Whether the suggestion it contains, of using common salt for fixing ammonia, may be of equal value with that of Liebig, which I laid before you in my first letter, it *is for you to determine.*

"MANURE.—It is well known that in a close stable, where there are a good many horses, there is a very pungent smell affecting the nose and eyes, more particularly when the stable is being cleaned out. This smell is occasioned by the flying off of ammonia, which is the very essence and value of manure, and which volatilizes or flies off at a very

---

* Journal, vol. ii. p. 298.'

† It is stated that a double wheel answers still better. Journal, vol. iii. p. 164. A small frame with a short row of dibbles, held in the hand, may also be used.

‡ A translation of this very interesting agricultural tour is now appearing in the " Farmer's Magazine."

§ It is well known that all varieties of beet require to be stored before the setting in of severe frost. This is now frequently done with Swedes also. They are either earthed up in the field, or carried home to the yard, where care should be taken that they have a free circulation of air. It is one of the advantages of this extending practice, that it affords a busy month of employment for women at a time when other labour is scarce.

low temperature—even the warmth of the dung in a stable will send it off, and it goes off in great quantities by the common heat of the dung in a farm-yard, whether thrown up in heaps or not. There is however a very cheap and simple remedy for this. Before you begin to farm out your stable, dissolve some common salt in water ; if a four-horse stable, say 4lbs. of salt, dissolved in two buckets of water, and poured through the nose of a watering-pan over the stable floor an hour or so before you begin to move the manure ; and the volatile salts of ammonia will become fixed salts from their having united with the muriatic acid of the common salt, and the soda thus liberated from the salt will quickly absorb carbonic acid, forming carbonate of soda ; thus you will retain with your manure the ammonia which would otherwise have flown away, and you have also a new and most important agent thus introduced, viz., the carbonate of soda. As this is the most powerful solvent of all vegetable fibre, and seeing that all manures have to be rendered soluble before they can act upon vegetation, it will be at once apparent that the carbonate of soda so introduced must be a most powerful and valuable agent. If 1 cwt. of salt were used for these purposes every week for each one hundred acres of land under cultivation, it would be quite ample to sprinkle frequently all the feeding places and the farm-yard, for the latter the salt may be sown by the hand in rainy weather. The weekly cost would be, say 1s. 6d. to 2s. 6d. The advantage to be derived from this simple measure is very great indeed, and can only be known by actual trial. Suppose the cost to be 2s. per week, the advantage may be safely estimated at ten times that amount."

In this account I observe, what appear to me, some inaccuracies. It may be true that a little free ammonia does escape in a stable ; but I believe that chemists teach us it is rather the carbonate of ammonia which we smell there than ammonia itself. Ammonia cannot long exist in a free state wherever carbonic acid is present; and this acid is everywhere present in the atmosphere. Moreover, whilst ammonia is forming from the decemposition of certain organic compounds in the dung and urine of animals, carbonic acid is also forming abundantly, and will instantly unite with the ammonia. The abuse or misuse of terms is too common, even among some of your best agricultural writers. This is very unwise. Precision in the application of technical terms is the very soul of science. But I find chapters on the use of lime in agriculture, where lime is treated as existing under a variety of forms ; when all the while the author is speaking of so many perfectly distinct mineral substances, of which lime happens to be one of the constituents. Nothing, again, is more common than to hear mention of a soil containing lime, or mild lime, when it is the carbonate of lime which is intended. Some will think me trifling in this matter ; but really it is of great importance. The action of a particular substance may be very different in an uncombined state, from the action of another substance of which it may form a constituent part. For instance, both sodium and chlorine act intensely upon the human frame, and rapidly destroy life if received into our stomachs ; but when chemically combined, these substances, united with water, form common salt, one of the most harmless and most necessary articles of life. We might just as well call salt a form of sodium or of chlorine, as carbonate of lime a form of lime. We might as well call our flesh a form of carbon. Unless attention be paid to the application of terms, according to their strict meaning, a confusion of ideas is always to be dreaded. Thus, in the extract I am noticing, I presume we ought rather to consider that the carbonate of ammonia and the muriate of soda have mutually decomposed each other, than that the latter was decomposed by ammonia, and the soda afterwards united with carbonic acid. The result of such mutual decomposition would at once lead to the formation of muriate of ammonia (sal ammoniac) and carbonate of soda (commonly called soda). Now muriate of ammonia is described as being beneficial to vegetation, but what relation it may bear in this respect to the sulphate of ammonia, that form in which Liebig directs you to fix the ammonia, I am not prepared to say ; *this must be left for yourselves to determine.* The author of the above communication directs attention more particularly to the carbonate of soda, which has, I believe, been found very serviceable on some lands ; and I remember that I alluded to it in my Address to the Hadleigh Club. But I must beg leave to doubt the explanation which he gives us of its mode of acting. It is stated to be " a most powerful solvent for all vegetable fibre ;" whereas I have experimentally ascertained that we may preserve both animal and vegetable substances in solutions of carbonate of soda, much better than in most other chemical salts. The precise manner in which the alkaline salts—of potash, soda, and ammonia—act on the vegetable system is at present an undetermined point ; but that their action is more or less beneficial appears to have been fully proved. Provided, therefore, our informant is correct in saying that salt fixes the ammonia, his *advice* may be considered valuable, though his *theory* should turn out somewhat premature. I shall here mention a little experiment I have lately tried, as it bears upon the subject I am discussing, though it absolutely proves nothing that was not previously known ; because I was not careful about making the necessary *comparative* experiments essential for enabling me to draw positive conclusions. Two quarts of urine were saturated with salt, and allowed to stand for a fortnight, when two quarts of water were added to them. A strip of grass in a grass plot which is kept constantly mown, in front of my house, was now watered with the mixture, on the 13th of December last. In about eight or ten days a visible effect had been produced, the strip became greener than the rest, and at this moment is very distinctly marked by its darker colour. I have another strip, which was watered with a weak solution of nitrate of soda in July or August last, which is also of a darker green than the rest of the grass. No effect has been produced upon a strip that was watered with a solution of common salt at the same time. In these experiments I merely wished to see whether those solutions would produce *any* effect ; and not to estimate the precise effect. But I am so satisfied with the effect produced by the urine, that I am intending to have an underground tank for the reception of all liquid " *rejectamenta,*" such as soap suds, scullery water, and urine. I think of dividing my tank into two compartments, and allowing the liquid to collect alternately in one or the other ; and then, in the first week of every month, to clear out the compartment which has been filling, and carrying the contents over a grass field, or applying them to the garden. Whether I shall place gypsum or salt in the tank will be for future

consideration. I have been informed by practical men in this county, that the use of liquid manure has been tried and abandoned in several cases. Why it was not considered expedient to persevere I know not. The effects which it produces must be expected to be more transient than those of solid manure, and especially so on stiff soils, which may not readily imbibe it ; but perhaps it may still be worthy your consideration, whether it would not be expedient to apply it, in certain cases, *very much diluted,* and with frequency. But, however unadvisable such a practice may be thought for arable land, perhaps it may be recommended for pasture. It is the liquid parts of manure which are richest in materials suited for generating ammonia. It is to me a continued cause of surprise to witness the supineness of some of my neighbours, who persist in adhering to the bad and proscribed practice of preparing their dunghills by the roadside—a practice which not only scientific enquirers, but all intelligent *practical* writers, have denounced.

The preparation of manures should be watched and attended to at home, as carefully as the food you prepare for your cattle. My friends of the vegetable kingdom like good food as well as your stalled oxen ; and they will not be put off with half allowance, and yet yield you double measure, you may depend upon it. Your obedient servant,

J. HENSLOW.

Hitcham Rectory, Jan. 14, 1843.

TO THE EDITOR OF THE BURY POST.

SIR,—Permit me to make one or two observations upon the letter of Professor Henslow, on the subject of Manures, which appeared in your last number. In that gentleman's excellent remarks upon the necessity of making experiments with the sulphate of lime (gypsum), he has, inadvertently I have no doubt, omitted the consideration of one fact, which is, that gypsum itself acts as a powerful manure—and consequently that the experiments suggested with *two* heaps of manure must be inconclusive as to the power of gypsum in fixing ammonia, inasmuch as the experimenter will be at a loss to know whether his increase of produce (if such is the effect), is owing to the gypsum, *per se,* or to the sulphate of ammonia formed by the decomposition of the sulphate of lime. The action of gypsum on grass land and clover layers is different from the effect which it is intended to have in the heap of manure. In the former instance, it acts as Liebig points out, by decomposing carbonate of ammonia absorbed from the rain and moisture of the atmosphere : in the latter, it is intended to *fix* a *volatile* body. Now the decomposition of the sulphate of lime by ammonia is a *very gradual process,* and will not, according to Liebig, take place at all, unless in a state of solution, for which it requires 400 times its weight of water.

The question of the degree of affinity between lime and ammonia for sulphuric acid is, however, by no means clearly decided. In " Turner's Chemistry" it is stated that lime has a greater affinity for sulphuric acid than ammonia, but at the same time the writer admits that causes may so modify the action of affinity, " that it is conceivable that ammonia may in reality have a stronger attraction for sulphuric acid than lime, and yet the latter, from the great influence of disturbing causes, may succeed in decomposing the sulphate of ammonia."

I think, then, it is quite clear that the experiments with the gypsum alone must be unsatisfactory.

I would therefore take the liberty of suggesting that a third heap of manure be added to those recommended by the Professor, and that this be watered with *dilute sulphuric acid*, or oil of vitriol. One ounce of the concentrated acid to a gallon of water will make a solution sufficiently strong for the desired purpose. Let this be used in the same way as the Professor instructs the use of gypsum, each layer of manure being watered by the dilute acid. *The ammonia will be thus fixed at once.* Care must however be taken, in this experiment, not to supply too much acid, or the result will not be correct, because sulphuric acid in excess acts as a manure itself by uniting with lime in the earth and thus forming gypsum. The test of the whole of the ammonia being fixed is the following :—Take a piece of rag, and dip it into muriatic acid ; hold this immediately over the dunghill, and if ammonia is escaping, there will be a white layer of muriate of ammonia on the rag.

In conclusion, let me express how deeply I consider the agriculturists of Suffolk are indebted to Professor Henslow for the exertions which he is making in their behalf, in bringing his well known talents to bear upon one of the most important subjects that can possibly affect the interest of the British farmer.

I am, sir, your obedient servant,
Stowmarket, Jan. 14.   C. R. BREE.

LETTER III.

GENTLEMEN,—Mr. Bree has correctly asserted that two comparative experiments *alone*, such as those I have suggested to you, cannot afford *conclusive* evidence of the utility of gypsum in decomposing the carbonate of ammonia, formed during the decomposition of certain organic matters in a dunghill. It was not from inadvertency, as he supposes, that I proposed to restrict you to the consideration of those two comparative experiments. By referring to that address to the Hadleigh Club, which has been the occasion of my commencing these letters, you will see that I have noticed the direct action of gypsum upon plants ; and also, that I have briefly alluded to the anomalous relations under which lime and ammonia appear to stand with regard to each other, in their affinities for carbonic and sulphuric acid, to which Mr. Bree has likewise referred. But for the present I had rather not enter into these considerations. Let us only get the two experiments I have proposed to you, repeated by not less than fifty experimenters, in different parts of the county, and I think it very possible that we may need no further trials. Should any ambiguity remain, it may easily be cleared up by a few very simple experiments afterwards. I am very anxious, in a first effort, not to involve the question in greater complexity than may be absolutely necessary ; and I am afraid that a third heap watered with sulphuric acid would not much assist us. If you are desirous of ascertaining whether free gypsum is capable of producing any effect in the particular soil in which the experiments are being tried, it may be applied at once to that soil without the manure. If I had supposed that only one or two of yourselves were likely to attempt the solution of the problem I have set you, I should have asked for a dozen different modes of preparing the dungheaps ; and I had thought of proposing that five, and not two pieces only, of ground should be set apart ; but afterwards, I considered the plan I have suggested would, upon the whole, prove to be the best. Only we are dependent upon *numbers* making the trial, if we are to hope for anything like success. Although I am still of opinion that the challenge may rest as it is framed, for the general sweepstakes ; yet, as Mr. Bree has suggested an improvement (for no doubt it would be one), for you to determine whether some free gypsum in the dunghill may not be producing a specific effect, I will suggest to the *doubly energetic* among you a second brace of experiments, viz. : To set apart two pieces of land of the same size as those you propose to manure with our two dunghills, and let one of these be prepared with gypsum and the other left untouched. If the results should not be needed otherwise, it may be of importance to you to ascertain whether the particular field in which the experiment is made require gypsum or not.

From a private communication which I have received, I fear I have been imperfectly understood as to the scale upon which it may be considered necessary to carry on these experiments. My correspondent expresses his fears that the necessary care, time, and expense required will prevent many of you from attempting them—" To comply with your terms (he writes), it would be requisite to put two equal bullocks into two equal yards, equally exposed to the weather, equally drained, equally littered, equally fed ; and this carried on for three months at least ; and the result carried out into a heap and turned, and left for three months more, and then applied to equally good land : the coming up and growth of the crop watched for nine months ; thrashed and marketed in three months more ; in all eighteen or twenty months. The patience of no farmer would hold out so long." Now, I certainly had no idea of taxing a farmer's patience with all these minutiæ. In leaving it open to the zeal or judgment of every one to proceed as far as he might choose, I have perhaps said too much about noting the time it may take in preparing the dunghills, though I did not suppose this would at most include more than a few days. I will state, therefore, what may be considered as sufficient for those who have no inclination to go further.

1. Mark out two pieces of land, each about one-eighth of an acre, in the same field ; and settle before-hand how much manure you consider they may require.

2. Weigh out as much straw as may be required for preparing the requisite quantity of manure.

3. Measure out and mix well together as much fresh dung, of any or of all sorts, as may be required.

4. Place the straw and dung in alternate layers, sifting the gypsum over the dung in one heap as already directed, &c., &c.

All this need not occupy more than a good morning's work ; though if larger dunghills are to be prepared, the time of preparation should be noticed, on account of the possible escape of the carbonate of ammonia. In those preliminary experiments which chemists or botanists may attempt for the purpose of interrogating nature, there cannot be too minute or laborious attention paid to all the details ; but when the results of such experiments appear to have ascertained some natural law of vegetation, which may be considered as bearing directly on the pursuits of agriculture, then the further experiments which the agriculturist himself is called upon to make, are of a much coarser and less elaborate character ; and none of them need be made a tax upon his time, patience, or pocket, to any very formidable extent. An ordinary degree of attention to weights and measures is generally all that will be called for—little more, in fact, than the practice of the market itself requires. But success is mainly to be looked for *in the multitude of co-operators* accumulating a sufficient number of positive facts. All England might be converted into one great experimental farm, if our different agricultural societies would prepare accounts of the exact mode in which some hundred farmers might perform a set of easy comparative experiments at the same time, and send in the results of them. This is what is most needed for accelerating the present jog-trot progress of agriculture into something like a railroad pace of advancing. A multiplicity of most important questions might then as speedily be settled as you, gentlemen, farmers of Suffolk, mean to decide whether Liebig is right or wrong in recommending gypsum to you for fixing ammonia in your dunghills.

In concluding this letter, allow me, once for all, to thank the few gentlemen who have already, and those many gentlemen who intend hereafter, to assist in these discussions. The greater the number who enlist under the banners of free discussion the better. I, for one, shall be quite ready to acknowledge any error that may be detected in my statements, or to attend to any suggestions which I may feel convinced are improvements upon them ; for you must understand that I am not an accomplished chemist, and that I have no experience as a practical agriculturist, and am therefore very likely to be caught tripping. But let us all agree to dispense with mutual compliments, and to preserve our tempers, and truth in the end will not be far from us.

Your obedient servant,
Hitcham Rectory, Jan. 21.   J. S. HENSLOW.

PROBUS FARMERS' CLUB.

BONE DUST AND TURNIPS.

In consequence of the severe weather which occurred at the late anniversary of the Probus Farmers' Club, the members were prevented from visiting the farm of Carnwinick, and examining the improvements made thereon as intended ; and, accordingly, Thursday, the 26th of January, was appointed for this purpose.

This farm is the property of C. H. T. Hawkins, Esq., and is under the management of Mr. Trethewy, of Trewithen. Previous to the year 1835, it was a barren waste,—heath and fuize being the only covering of the soil ; and it had been let for *two shillings per acre*. Some attempts had been made to cultivate small portions of this waste, about twenty-one years since, using lime as a manure, but without success. In the spring of that year, Mr. Trethewy resolved on trying the effect of bone dust, which had just been introduced into the county, by Mr. Strong, of Exeter ; and, accordingly, some few acres were broken and sown with turnips, one portion of which was manured with bones, at the rate of three quarters to the acre, the price then being 17s. per quarter. In the years 1836 and 1837, it was cropped with oats, and then laid down to pasture up to the present time.

The attention of the members of the club was particularly drawn to this field. The portion where the bone dust had been used, had a most luxuriant appearance, whilst the other part exhibited a state of the greatest sterility. It was as if a line of distinction had been drawn between rich and scanty herbage—between a green meadow and a barren soil ; and we understand that the effect of the bone dust was as perceptible in both crops of oats, as it is in the pasture at the present time.

In the year 1836, Mr. Trethewy broke up another piece of the waste, which was sown with oats ; and on the following year a similar crop was taken, using as a manure for about one half only, two quarters of bone dust to the acre, sown broad cast, after which the whole was laid down to pasture. We understand that where the bone had been used, the crop of oats was particularly good ; and at the present period, the line of distinction on the pasture is so perceptible, that the effect of the bones might be seen at almost any distance where the eye could reach, and from all appearances will remain so for years to come.

This was a convincing proof to the members that bone dust was not only valuable for a present crop, but that it was a manure that left its durable effects on the soil beyond every other kind.

Other similar cases were shewn us, where the same beneficial effects had been experienced, in two patches particularly, one being broken in 1837, and the other in 1838. They had been sown with turnips, and manured with bone dust, which produced most excellent crops ; after which a crop of oats was taken, and then pastured, up to the present period. And in another piece of about six acres, which was broken in 1839, and sown with Swede turnips, an excellent crop was produced ; since which, other crops have been taken, and the clover at the present time is very luxuriant, and equal to land let at 40s. per acre.

In 1840, another piece was broken and sown with turnips, with bone as before, and oats in the following year ; both crops were excellent. In November, 1841, it was ploughed *once* only, and without any other cultivation sown to turnips in June, 1842. This crop was also good, and plainly proved that turnips after grain may be produced without either spring or summer ploughing. In 1841, another large portion was broken, sown with Swedes and afterwards cropped with oats, using the bone manure only, which answered as well as before ; and last year, another piece of six acres was broken, four of which were sown with Swedes, and manured with bone dust. The members of the club acknowledged that this was decidedly the best crop of turnips which they had seen for the season.

The general plan adopted by Mr. Trethewy through the whole period had been to consume about one-half of the turnips on the land, by folding sheep thereon, whilst the remaining half was carted to the farm yard for the cattle. In a few instances, in order to test the value of some other manures against the bone, he has instituted experiments on small portions of the different fields, with Lance's, Poittevin's, and Clarke's manures, the urate of the London Manure Company, and Guano, all of which he found to be extremely useful, though failing evidently in their durability on the land.

The estate of Carnwinick is about 100 acres, 50 of which Mr. Trethewy has thus brought into good cultivation, in the manner we have described, since 1835. Its general appearance is that of patches of verdure and sterility—the cultivated portions strongly contrasting with the uncultivated ones, and the naked and barren waste of Trelyon common adjoining.

In the farm yard, there were twenty head of cattle feeding on turnips, among which were a few tolerable specimens of the Devon breed, some good specimens of a cross between the Devon and the Short-horn, and four of the West Highland breed—a hardy race, possessing great aptitude to fatten, and well adapted to some of our mountanous districts. In addition to the members belonging to Probus, there were several practical agriculturists from the adjoining parishes also present, who expressed themselves not only pleased at what they saw, but surprised at the improvements which had been effected in so short a period, and at so trifling an expence—an expense evidently within the reach of every farmer, since there was a decided profit produced en the outlay even on the first crop, whilst the land in appearance was equal to the same let at from 20s. to 30s. per acre. The soil lies on the clay slate rock, and may be considered as a fair average of the commons and downs lying on the same stratum, in the parish of St. Stephens, which might all be brought into a similar state of cultivation by using the same means.

CORN AVERAGE PRICES.

Opinions differ much on the effect produced by the addition of the 138 towns by the Corn Law Act passed last session. The subjoined table shews that the effect has been to raise the averages in every case except one.

		Averages published weekly in the London Gazette.	Averages taken from the 150 Towns only, named in 9 Geo. IV. c. 60.	Averages taken from the 138 additional Towns only, named in 5 Vic. I. c. 14.
		s. d.	s. d.	s. d.
Week ending }	1842. July 9	64 10.321	64 7.838	65 10.463
	16	65 8.006	65 8.612	65 5.726
	23	65 4.251	65 3.006	65 8.563
	30	63 9 357	63 8.907	63 10.692
	Aug. 6	61 2.999	60 10.739	62 1.024
	13	58 11.035	58 3.182	60 5.878
	20	56 5.149	55 11.019	57 8.521
	27	55 0.928	54 6.866	56 4.737
	Sept. 3	53 3.010	52 10.738	54 3.318
	10	51 6 744	51 2 071	52 9.079
	17	52 8.992	52 7.801	53 0.627
	24	54 0.564	53 9.384	54 9.845
	Oct. 1	53 2.200	52 3 206	55 11.601
	8	51 6.765	51 3.286	52 5.273
	15	51 1.216	50 11.043	51 7.620
	22	50 9.465	50 5.281	51 10.237
	29	49 5 492	49 1 431	50 6.349
	Nov. 5	48 7.668	48 3 227	49 9.007
	12	48 8.671	48 3.816	49 10.336
	19	49 8.340	49 7.033	49 11.967
	26	49 6 570	49 3.645	50 3.265
	Dec. 3	48 6.007	47 6.722	49 3.362
	10	47 3.904	47 1.695	47 10.534
	17	46 10.546	46 9.104	47 2.871
	24	47 2.276	47 1.387	47 1 897
	31	47 1 280	46 10.979	47 7.903
	1843. Jan. 7	47 1.211	46 9.093	47 9.096
	14	47 10.107	48 8.592	48 2.753
	21	49 1.692	48 9.117	50 2.616
	28	49 3.082	48 11 703	50 0.603
Aggregate weekly average........		52 10.394	52 6.949	53 8.188

CHELMSFORD FARMERS' CLUB.

REPORT OF THE COMMITTEE OF THE CHELMSFORD FARMERS' CLUB FOR THE YEAR 1842.

The committee have much satisfaction in communicating to the members of the Chelmsford Farmers' Club a summary of its proceedings during the last year, and they look with confidence for its continuing prosperity and usefulness. Since the formation of the club, external circumstances, in some little degree unfavourable, have occurred ; but on the whole the results have been both gratifying and valuable. The discussions at the monthly meetings have been productive of considerable information on some of the most important questions of agricultural practice ; and the absence of the restraint which practical men sometimes feel in large public assemblies, has, in these monthly meetings, elicited many most useful remarks and opinions, which, there is reason to believe, would not have been delivered in meetings of a more mixed and public character.

The experience of every day affords abundant proof of the value of farmers' clubs in diffusing a knowledge of the principles on which the cultivators of the soil may or may not be successful in the various operations of their practice.

Abstract science alone cannot make a good farmer ; and but a few years ago practical men were too apt to treat all theory as worthless—if not mischievous—speculation ; but a new light has now broken in upon those who are engaged in agricultural pursuits, and the elucidations of some of the most scientific men of the age have clarly shown, that with a view to improvement, it is necessary to look to the nature of the root and trunk of the tree, and not to remain satisfied with the fruit its branches may spontaneously yield. The committee, therefore, earnestly recommend to their brother agriculturists the study of principles as an important guide in practice, at the same time rejecting idle projects, which, though specious in appearance, are, on examination, found to be inconsistent with long and successful experience. The value of scientific principles can only be tested by experiments—the best of all possible instructors for intelligent men, having general practical knowledge of the matter to which the experiment is applied.

With these few preliminary observations, your committee deem it proper to lay before you the following sketch of the proceedings of the club during the year 1842.

The club was formed at a public meeting, held on the 17th December, 1841, Mr. Robt. Baker, of Writtle, in the chair ; and after several meetings of a provisional committee, rules for the governance of the club were drawn up, and a committee, a chairman, and a secretary for the ensuing year were appointed.

The first monthly meeting was held on Friday, the 28th of January, 1842, at the Chelmsford Institute, and the subsequent meetings have been held at the same place.

At the first monthly meeting, on the 28th of Jan., the chairman favoured the club with a valuable dissertation on draining, illustrating it by drawings. Mr. O. Copland also made some useful observations on the same subject, accompanied with drawings. After a very interesting discussion as to the best methods of draining (in which several other members joined), the meeting separated without agreeing to any resolution ; and the subject will be renewed at an early period.

The other subjects of discussion, and the resolutions of the meetings thereon, have been as follows :—

The causes, prevention, and remedying of defective plants of wheat, and preventives of the devastation committed by slugs and insects.

Resolved—That the slug and wire worm are most destructive to the wheat plant.

That the application of lime and salt to the seed previous to sowing the wheat is destructive to the slug and wire worm, and that lime is beneficial both before and after sowing the wheat.

That dibbling or drilling in wheat is the best mode of remedying a defective plant.

The making, managing, and applying, of farm-yard manure.

Resolved—That the best method of making manure is to do so under cover, with as little water as possible; and in the absence of sheds, to do so as far as the available means will admit.

The soiling of horses and cattle upon green crops in yards, as a means of economizing the food, and increasing the quantity and quality of the manure.

Resolved—That as a general principle for economizing food, and producing the best manure, green crops should be mown and fed in the yards.

That horses should not be permitted to feed out of the yards during the summer.

That cattle upon farms with little pasture should be kept in the same way.

That sheep should be folded on the clovers, having the fold changed frequently.

That rye, Italian rye grass, lucerne, tares, and red clover, are best adapted to keep up the proper succession of green crops, for soiling, so as to ensure a constant supply.

The best method of producing and securing a good crop of turnips.

Resolved—That in fallowing land for turnips the land should be ploughed early in autumn, and immediately after the removal of the grain crops.

That manure put on at this season and ploughed repeatedly with the land will produce better turnips than if put on immediately preceding the sowing.

That the land should be allowed to remain as long as possible between the two last ploughings.

That immediately the land has been ploughed, it should be sown, rolled, and harrowed, without allowing opportunity for the moisture to escape.

That the ridge system of 18 or 27 inches is best adapted to produce Swede turnips. The ridge should be formed, the dung deposited, ploughed in, drilled and rolled without any delay, which can be easily effected upon large occupations.

That turnips should be hoed as early as possible, to prevent their being drawn up weakly and to facilitate their growth.

That a plant is better secured from the fly, by manuring well and drilling a large quantity of seed.

That in pulling turnips for storing, the tops should be wrung and not cut off; the roots should be left on with the earth attached, and the turnips should not be pulled with a hook.

That in storing, the turnips should either be collected in heaps of about ten bushels each, covered with straw and then with earth, or be carted home, placed between hurdles of the width of six or eight feet, and slightly thatched, and further protected by placing mulch or straw round the sides during severe frost. They should on no account be carted before they are perfectly dry.

That if turnips be put in clamps, great care be taken not to cover them too closely, nor to put them in clamps of more than six feet in width.

That Swede turnips should not be stored in enclosed buildings, as so doing would render them liable to get into fermentation and rot. Swede turnips may also be stored by ploughing into furrows, and covering them with earth from the next furrows, and so on in succession.

The best method of cutting and harvesting grain crops.

Resolved—That it is the opinion of this meeting that the system of bagging; or, as it is otherwise termed, fagging, is the best mode of cutting wheat.

First—Because it occasions less loss of grain, the labourer, if expert at the work, being able to secure nearly every ear.

Secondly—Because all the straw is obtained, and the expense of haulming dispensed with; the value of the straw so obtained being equivalent to 20s. per acre.

Thirdly—Because the sheaves of wheat by standing further above the stubble, are more exposed to the air, and admit it more freely.

Fourthly—Because no earth is taken up in the process, as is frequently the case with mowing wheat; and the wheat is not tied so closely as in reaping.

Fifthly—Because the land is at once cleared for the next crop, without the process of haulming, which is a saving of at least from three to four shillings per acre.

That the proper time for cutting wheat is when the straw has become yellow for three or four inches below the ear; but if mildew be apprehended, and the wheat has not changed to a yellow colour so soon as might have been expected, then it cannot be cut too early, and it is advisable at all times to commence cutting a little too early rather than too late, both as regards the improvement of quality and the quantity of grain.

That as regards oats it is advisable to cut them before they become quite ripe, as the straw is thereby greatly improved for the purpose of food, and the oats are preserved from shelling in the field, and if a few not quite ripe should adhere after thrashing be kept on the straw, they are not lost, as the cattle will find them.

That it is advisable to bind oats, especially if the crop is a heavy one; but they should not be bound immediately after cutting, but merely be laid in the band two days previous to binding.

That beans should have the latter green beans cut out and laid in the furrows a few days previous to cutting the general crop. The beans should be placed in the form of a cone, and bound round securely with those which have been previously cut, and if they are well managed they may be pitched on the waggon and transferred to the stack with almost the same facility as those bound with spun yarn; the beans also will resist rain much longer by this mode than if they were bound in the ordinary way.

The resolution respecting the bagging of wheat is strongly recommended to the attention of the members of the club; and it is hoped that the utmost exertion will be used to adopt it immediately in this district, as from the forwardness of the present harvest there is almost a certainty of its succeeding. It is also recommended to use the bagging hook with the improved bent shank.

The best method of preparing land for wheat—the varieties best adapted for light or for heavy soils—the best method of steeping or wetting—and the best method of sowing.

Resolved—That a good clover ley is best calculated to produce a full crop of wheat—that it should only be ploughed once previous to sowing—that if there is a misplant of clover, the land should be ploughed fleet or struck at Midsummer.

That a bean or pea etch kept clean is the next best preparation for wheat—that on tender or light soils cultivated on the four-course system (when the beans or peas take the place of clover) the etch does not (if clean) require to be ploughed more than once for the seed, but that on heavy soils farmed on the six-course system of husbandry—when the beans are grown in the fifth year and far from the fallow, it is best to gain tilth for the wheat, by ploughing the land about immediately after harvest.

That on most soils it is not advisable to manure a good clover ley for the wheat crop, as the manure may be more profitably applied to other crops.

For heavy land in a good state of cultivation rough chaff white wheat is best adapted; for mixed soils, the hedge-row or Taunton Dean, Syer, and Smoothey's red are best.

That the best method of wetting wheat is in a solution of sulphate of copper (blue vitriol). The quantity recommended generally for a sack of wheat is one pound of the sulphate to two gallons of boiling water; the solution to be applied while warm.

That as soils and circumstances are so various, the club can come to no determination as to the best method of seeding. They consider that it must be left to the judgment of the practical farmer to make use of the drill, the dibble, or the broad-cast system of sowing wheat, according to circumstances.

The best and most economical method of keeping farm horses.

Resolved—That one bushel of oats weekly is sufficient for a farm horse during the summer and winter months, between the seed times.

That it is injudicious to take horses entirely from corn during the winter.

That Swede turnips, carrots, and mangel wurzel, may be economically used in feeding horses, but as it is considered that the greatest consumption of food upon the farm most benefits the land, it is most advisable under all circumstances to feed the horses on grain, and to use the green food for neat cattle and sheep.

That salt is beneficial to horses, and ought to be used at all times—in moderate quantity.

That beans are beneficial when used in small quantities, as a substitute for oats, in the autumnal months, but it is best to use them with bran or pollard, which may be effected with less expense than with oats.

That it is advisable, both with regard to economy and benefit to the horses, to cut hay and straw together for them in preference to feeding them with hay alone; the proportion to be 56lbs. of hay to two trusses of straw : wheat or oat straw to be preferred. From 24 to 30lbs. of the chaff daily is sufficient for an ordinary sized horse. During the seed-time, or in any period of hard work, from 10 to 15lbs. of oats daily are required in addition ; but the quantity of chaff should be diminished in proportion as the quantity of corn is increased.

That it is advisable at all times to bruise the oats before using them.

That the principal point with regard to economy in feeding horses is the assiduity of the horseman, and his giving the food in small quantities at each time, feeding them regularly, and for a long time together.

What varieties of stock pay best ; the causes and best method of treating the disease that has for some time past been so injuriously prevalent among stock.

That Kent sheep are decidedly best for marsh land, as being hardy and producing an excellent carcase ; but they are not so well adapted for arable land.

That Southdowns are best adapted for dry pasture or dry arable land, and the Hampshire downs for general purposes, especially upon the heavier descriptions of land.

That half-breds, between the Leicester and Southdown are most disposed to fatten, and they come to maturity earlier than any other description of sheep, and are well adapted, when the food is of good quality, but the mutton is not so valuable as either the Southdown or Hampshire down.

That pure Leicesters are disposed to fatten beyond any pure breed of sheep, but as they are not grazed to any extent in the county, their qualities have not been fully discussed.

That Hereford oxen are best adapted for stall feeding and dry and warm pasturage.

That Durham and Devons stand next in position, Galloway Scots the next, and all the short-horns and Scots before the Welch varieties, of which the best are the South Wales oxen.

That the Highland Scots, the North Wales, and the Durham are best adapted for summer grazing, with Herefords, &c. ; but in every point the West Highlands are best adapted for the marshes.

The discussion on the question of disease was principally relative to its affecting sheep, and it was resolved,

That the disease was originally entirely infectious, but is now more frequently epidemic, or both.

That the disease is inflammatory. The system is first affected, subsequently the feet. The inflammatory action goes on until matter is found between the sensible part of the foot and the hoof, and continues until it finds vent at the top of the hoof, which ultimately comes off, and foot-rot frequently succeeds.

That the principle of cure is obvious, and the experience of persons in the meeting confirms the utility of first giving the animal one ounce of salt, and the dose repeated in twenty-four hours. The hoof should be cut away between the claws, until bleeding ensues, or the matter escapes. The sheep should be kept on dry pasturage until the cure is effected.

Your committee next beg to call your attention to another subject, viz., the formation of a permanent library for circulation and reference. This has been attended to so far as the funds of the club would allow, and a nucleus has been formed, around which it is hoped a large accumulation of books will, ere long, take place. Several periodical agricultural publications are regularly added to the library, and a few members have kindly lent some books for the general use of the club. The committee beg to remind the members of the utility of such a library, and hope that in the present year it will receive a large increase either by gift or loan.

The next point to which it is the duty of the committee to advert, is the present state of the club with respect to the number of its members, and to its funds. The present number of members is 73. The receipts have been the annual subscriptions of members (10s. each), and the items of expenditure, the rent of Institute, purchase of books, advertising, printing, stationery, and postage—leaving a balance in hand of about 8l.

As several gentlemen who are not members have on this occasion honoured the club by their presence, the committee beg to introduce the following brief sketch of the objects and rules of the institution :—

The objects of the club are the advancement and diffusion of agricultural knowledge.

The officers are a chairman, treasurer, and secretary, and a committee of management, elected annually.

The members of the club meet monthly, on the Friday on or next succeeding the full moon, for the discussion of subjects connected with agriculture.

The chair is taken at half-past four o'clock, and the meeting terminates at half-past seven.

Any member may propose for discussion a subject connected with agriculture, on giving notice to the secretary.

A candidate for admission as a member must be proposed and seconded by members at a monthly meeting, and balloted for at the next meeting.

No person can be admitted as a visitor more than once, without the consent of the committee.

An annual meeting of the members is held in January.

The annual subscription is ten shillings per annum, to be paid to the secretary in advance.

Having noticed all that occurs to your committee, of information and explanation, they conclude by expressing a confident hope that the members of the club will continue to attend the monthly meetings as often as may be in their power, and use their utmost endeavours to enlarge the sphere of its utility. The agriculturists have too long been passive and disorganised. While every other class of the producing part of the community have been uniting and labouring together for the benefit of their general interests, the cultivator of the soil has been isolated from his brother cultivators, and without the means of advancing the general interest of the body to which he belonged. Each agriculturist laboured and improved but for himself, and had not the opportunity of offering to others the expensive and laborious advantages of his own experience, with a certainty or even a probability of an equivalent return. But the time has arrived when he finds that he must be up and doing. The spirit of enquiry—the desire for improvement, and the acquisition of knowledge, are no longer confined to the factory or to the general hive of manufacturing industry. The why and the wherefore are now asked on the broad acres of Britain as well as in the laboratory or the workship; and the aid of science is now called in to ascertain the qualities and capabilities of soils—the principles of vegetable and animal organization and growth—the best applications of manure, and to promote the improvement of agricultural implements. Agriculturists now meet to give and to receive information, and there is diffused into their body at large a spirit of enquiry and a unity of feeling which must produce the happiest results, not only to the cultivator of the soil, but to every inhabitant of Great Britain. These ends and these results cannot be better promoted than by a zealous, and, above all, by an active personal support of institutions formed on the principles of the Chelmsford Farmers' Club.

THE PLOUGH.

TO THE EDITOR OF THE FARMER'S MAGAZINE.

SIR,—In your last month's magazine your readers are favoured with what purports to be an "Essay on the mechanical properties of Ploughs." Had the author contented himself with treating generally of the principle upon which all ploughs ought to be constructed, and their various properties, I should not have thought it necessary to say anything on the subject; but, conceiving the purport of the "essay" to be rather to puff a particular implement—its object an attempt to convert a fancied superiority into reality—I am induced to forward a few remarks in reply, by way of protest against so unwarrantable an inference being drawn from your correspondent's positive affirmations.

Mr. Smart's sole end and aim appears to be to show that the turn-wrest plough possesses properties of which the fixed-wrest plough cannot boast, and which, indeed, may in some degree account for his "essay" being unsuccessful in obtaining a prize from the Royal Agricultural Society.

The chief advantage Mr. Smart contends for, is the power the turn-wrest plough has of turning the furrow slice completely over. Now, what more effectual plan could be adopted to leave the land flat (which Mr. Smart so properly deprecates) than just to invert its original flat position, and which the figure in the "essay" shows that the turn-wrest plough accomplishes?

The two figures that Mr. Smart introduces to elucidate his position, are quite sufficient, in my opinion, to disprove what he wishes to establish.

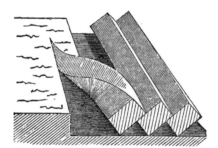

Work performed by "Turn-wrest Plough," as described by Mr. Smart.

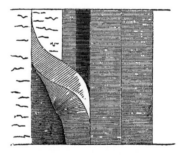

Work as performed by "Fixed-wrest" Plough.

The practical man, at a glance, will not hesitate to give his preference to the lie of the furrow-slices —as shewn by the section of the work performed by the fixed-wrest plough over that performed by the turn-wrest; first, because parts of two sides of the slice are exposed, which will the better enable the weather to penetrate, if that is the object wished; and, secondly, the angles will afford greater facilities for obtaining a mould, by means of the harrow, than a flat surface can furnish.

I fully agree with your correspondent, that ploughing is one of the most important operations in husbandry; but, at the same time, I must beg to retain my opinion that if the work can be performed efficiently with two horses, it is nothing but sheer waste to use four.

In the concluding paragraph in the "essay" Mr. Smart expresses a hope that an unprejudiced trial will be made of the various ploughs. He appears to forget that many such trials have been made, and that the result has ever been to prove the "turn-wrest plough" to be the most burdensome implement (nearly one-third more than any other plough). With regard to efficiency of work, I conceive there is just as much corn grown on land ploughed by two horses as there would be though four were employed.

Should Mr. S. wish to see his gigantic implement tried once more, an opportunity will be afforded him at the next annual meeting of the East Suffolk Agricultural Association, when I understand it is intended to have a general trial of implements, but more especially ploughs.

I have the honour to remain,

Sir, your most obedient servant,

Suffolk, Feb. 21.   HARRY FLOWERDEW.

P

AGRICULTURAL ECONOMY.

Every thing on a farm ought to be turned to account. The farmer must have horses to labour his fields, and cart his produce. He must feed these horses at considerable expence ; and shall he not turn their dung, urine, and litter, to the best account? He must have cattle also to consume his straw, to breed, and yield milk, and thus enable him to pay a part of his accounts. Shall he not turn the excrement of these cattle to the best account? He requires an establishment of servants and labourers ; if these have not employ· ment, they will steal from him, or leave him. His wisdom then is to consider how he can employ them with economy and advantage.

We hear much of foreigners taking our manufactures for their produce. Will foreigners take our farm dung for their guano and bones? I trow not. What then? The farmer has an article which he can neither sell nor barter ;.and this article, when properly prepared, is the *very best* manure for raising his crops. Is he to throw it down the water, or allow it to go to waste, that he may give a large sum to foreigners for an uncertain substitute ?

If, as on entering a new farm, he needs to purchase part of the manure for the first crop, it may be important to know at what market he can obtain the cheapest and best supply; or, if part of his farm is too hilly to admit cartage of dung, he may find it cheaper to use bones or guano ; but in all ordinary cases he may, with skill and attention, supply his wants from his own resources. It is, therefore, unfair to charge the price of farm dung in opposition to that of *purchased* articles, because it has cost the farmer almost no expence but what he would have incurred, even if he had neglected it. The charge of dung is putting money out of the farmer's right hand into his left; while the charge of other manures is sending his money abroad.

I have said that farm dung is the *very best* the farmer can have. In mine of 29th Nov. last, I showed that its chief function is to supply carbon to plants in the form of carbonic acid, and that by the combined aid of warmth, air, moisture, and slight alkaline reaction, it gives off carbonic acid, to be taken up by the roots as they need it. When soils are rich in *decaying* vegetable matter, a slight dressing of alkaline or saline manure will assist the evolution of carbonic acid, and bring forward a good crop. But it is the tendency of all other manures except dung or decaying vegetable matter, to exhaust and impoverish the soil. It is true that plants take up between one and two per cent. of inorganic matter from the soil ; but it is also true that they contain about *fifty* per cent. of carbon. Every farmer knows four facts which bear on this subject. (1.) He knows that if he go on liming and cropping without dung, he will gradually render his fields barren. Thus lime enables him to exhaust the soil by removing its carbon. (2.) He knows that the period in which his fields are chiefly exhausted is the *ripening* season, a period when plants are giving alkalies back to the soil, and largely accumulating carbon. (3.) He knows that wheat requires a warmer and richer soil, and is more exhausting than oats. Wheat, in ripening, takes up carbon much more rapidly than oats ; but wheat does not contain half the weight of inorganic matter which oats contain. *Ergo,* wheat robs the soil chiefly by abstracting carbon

or decaying vegetable matter. (4.) He knows that a crop of turnips, though it takes up more than *ten times* the weight of inorganic matter which a crop of wheat takes up, enriches rather than impoverishes the soil ; and why? because the turnips are not allowed to ripen their seed, and perhaps draw more of their carbon from the atmosphere. Corn plants ripen chiefly after their leaves have become hard and begun to fade. Hence it is absurd to suppose that these dying leaves can absorb from the air the carbon which fills the husk.

The inference from these facts plainly is, that no manure can permanently support fertility, except what contains carbon in a state capable of giving off carbonic acid ; and as no manure equals good farm dung in this quality, it is obviously the best (as it is the cheapest) which the farmer can have. But it not only contains carbon in this state ; it also contains all the inorganic matter required by agricultural crops. The farther discussion of questions connected with this important point must be deferred.

By the kindness of Professor Johnston, of Durham University, I am favoured with a very interesting detail of experiments performed on different crops in 1842, with a view of answering several important questions connected with manures. The sheet will probably be published in the next number of his Lectures on Agricultural Chemistry. I can at present refer only to the first set of experiments, performed on the estate of Lord Blantyre, near Haddington, on a field which had been furrow-drained and subsoil-ploughed. The object of these experiments was to ascertain—(1.) "What are the relative effects of different saline substances upon the turnip crop under the same circumstances ? And (2.) How far may these substances be employed *alone* to supersede farm-yard manure in the culture of turnips?"

The part grown with "farm-yard manure was a fair average crop," and this shows the field to have been in fair condition for culture. Not one of the ten lots treated with other manures (as salt, rape-dust, nitrate of soda, sulphate of soda, guano, soot, and mixtures of these,) yielded one-fourth of a good crop. "They show (says Professor Johnston)—(1.) That saline manures in that locality cannot economically take the place of farmyard manure, even for a single season. (2.) That saline manures are even *hurtful* in the present condition of the land, when employed alone—producing a smaller crop than if no manure had been applied at all, and some of them in a remarkable degree. This appears to be especially the case with common salt, which, at the rate of one cwt. an acre, reduced the crop of bulbs nearly to one half of what was yielded by the *unmanured* portion of the field. It is still more striking that nitrate of soda, applied at the same rate, should diminish the crop, though in a less degree than common salt, and that soot should almost kill it entirely, and that fifteen cwt. of rape-dust per acre should produce scarcely any effect. In regard to guano, it was applied in too small a quantity to do all the good of which it was capable had it been laid on more largely. If six or eight cwt., instead of one and a half cwt., per acre had been used, the crop would probably have *equalled* that obtained by the use of *farm-yard* manure."

I may remark that both soot and guano have been found valuable in gardens, and wherever there is an excess of decaying organic matter along with a deficiency of alkaline matter.

In answer to the request of "An Agriculturist," I beg to refer him to Professor Johnston's Lecture "On Liming." His last number on the theory of the action of lime, just published, contains substantially the same view which I stated in the *Herald* of 1st December last, and treats the subject with much perspicuity. Liebig's "inorganic" theory will soon be a matter of history.

Feb. 13, 1843.   G.

GYPSUM AS MANURE.

TO THE EDITOR OF THE MARK LANE EXPRESS.

SIR,—An interesting letter appears in your last number, written by the Rev. Professor Henslow to the *Bury Post*, in which experiments on the application of gypsum to manure heaps, for the purpose of fixing the ammonia, are suggested to the Suffolk farmers.

Gypsum in many parts of England is difficult to procure, and in such places would be expensive; in addition to which, it is almost invariably sold in the state of rock, and requires grinding or pounding before it is applied, which, with most farmers, would be found a troublesome operation; and every little difficulty of this sort would operate against its use.

Again, gypsum is so sparingly soluble, that under the average circumstances of the farm-yard dung, the moisture would be insufficient to its solution; and consequently a large portion of the gypsum would remain undissolved, and of course could not act.

Now, common salt is almost everywhere to be had cheaper than gypsum, is very soluble, requires no pulverising, and will act equally beneficially in fixing the ammonia.

If gypsum is used, the carbonate of ammonia becomes sulphate, and the sulphate of lime becomes carbonate of lime, which is comparatively useless.

If common salt be employed, the carbonate of ammonia becomes muriate, and the common salt is converted into carbonate of soda.

The muriate of ammonia is as fixed a salt as the sulphate of ammonia, and thus the important end in view is equally answered at less cost and less trouble. The generality of farmers having no chemical knowledge, and perhaps little faith in the results of these plans, it is desirable to render the operation as simple as possible.

We have, however, another most important advantage in using common salt as compared w gypsum, as the double decomposition in this case leaves us in the manure carbonate of soda instead of carbonate of lime, as in the case of gypsum.

Now, carbonate of soda is a most powerful solvent of vegetable fibre, and consequently a most valuable agent in preparing the manure to act on plants.

The description of salt to be used should be the common rough salt of commerce, which is to be had in Liverpool at from 10s. to 15s. per ton; and I should suppose that a peck measure full applied to the farm-yard manure once a week, by sowing it all over the surface with the hand, would be sufficient for a farm of 100 or 150 acres; and I believe the result would be highly beneficial to the farmer.

Salt would appear to have been anciently used on the dunghill, from the expression in scripture—that if the salt has lost its savour, it is neither fit for the land or the dunghill.

I am, sir, yours, respectfully,
AMMONIA.

BURTON-UPON-TRENT FARMERS' CLUB.

We hope to be able to present our readers with a monthly report of the proceedings of the Farmer's Club of this town, which cannot fail to interest many and to advance in some degree the object of that society in spreading useful information on agricultural subjects.

At the last meeting, held on the 13th January, the discussion turned on one of the most important branches in the art of agriculture—"the best method of draining land." Mr. Bass had engaged to introduce the subject, and as he was unable to attend, a short essay, which by the assistance of an intelligent friend he was enabled to lay before the meeting, by way of directing the discussion to the points he thought most worthy of examination, was read for him. He chiefly wished to seek the advice of the club, on the plan of "draining strong lands," now known as "thorough draining." Where the land is wet from springs, the under-water must be removed, or the draining could not be called thorough. Where the land was wet through the retention of the water which fell on the surface, the difference between a thorough and an imperfect drainage, chiefly consisted in the depth and distance of the drains. He thought the right principles were those advanced by Mr. Smith, of Deanston, and his followers. The land which lies on a retentive bed should be brought as much as possible to resemble that which rests on a porous bottom. To do this, the drains must be as deep as plants penetrate. Two feet was the least depth. They should be as near together as was necessary to lay the ground dry, not only effectually, but quickly; sometimes as near as ten, and in lighter loams forty feet asunder. The depth should be greater if the soil were porous at two feet deep, because if as much water passed through the side of the drains in the third, as the second foot downwards, the distance apart need not be so great. The proper distance apart and the depth of the drains, were the first requisites of their efficiency. If the trenches could be left open the draining would be perfect. The construction of the closed drain should be with a view to preserve the same advantages as the open trench. In such soils the water is removed by percolation, through its substance and the side of the drain, was the filter. It must therefore be preserved, and there must be a free channel below to give vent to the water. In proportion as a drain fulfilled these purposes it approached to efficiency, and its importance next to its efficiency was its permanence. If the trench were filled with thorns in the lower parts, and covered well, to prevent direct openings through the top, an efficient drain would be made, but not lasting. Nevertheless in heavy clays they would remain a long time. In lighter soils the sides of the drain would fall in and choke the passage. A rubble drain of stones made a better drain, and if well made might continue an indefinite time. It would answer best in heavy soils. In light soils the side and bottom of the drain would fall and the mud could not be removed, but would rest in the crevices of the stones. This was its inferiority to the tile. Besides it was not cheaper except where stones could be gathered on the ground. Conduit drains of stones were as good as tiles, but usually more expensive. Tiles were the best drain, if well made and properly filled up. He thought that a perfect drain was a tile with a sale, covered with stones, and a turf over the stones to prevent the soil from falling in above. But stones could not often be had without too much expense. A turf over the tile and upper soil over it was the usual way of filling. It was very well at first, but the turf would decay, and there would be soil washed into the channel. There ought to be a layer of stones, or of screened gravel immediately above the tile and around it, or the soil would gain access. A quick fall in the drains was good to remove collections of mud, and was open to no objection where a sole was used to the tile. He thought a sole needful in every case of either clay or more open soil to prevent the sinking of the tile. The filling up with a porous material was the first essential, without it the water could not flow into the drain. To prevent the wear of the bottom of the drain, and the falling of soil into the channel, were the secondary, but not less important things to be attended to; they were all too often neglected.

Thorough draining was opposed to surface draining; but pure clays could not be thoroughly drained, and poor soils would not pay for a thorough drainage. They must be thrown in a good form by ridge and furrow. Every soil of good texture would pay for thorough, better than for imperfect drainage. In conclusion he thought such improvements as draining ought always to be effected by the landlord, who might charge interest to the tenant on the outlay, or increase the rent according to the increased fertility of the soil. In the first case the tenant took the risk, and in the second the landlord; but he thought there were few cases in which it would not be the landlord's interest to take the whole risk and chance of profit on himself. It was seldom the interest of the tenant to invest money in draining, because he required a return of ten to fifteen per cent. on his capital, and the tenancy from year to year, which is the common custom of letting lands, made the case in which it was his interest still more rare.

Mr. Pratt, of Cauldwell, in consequence of the unavoidable absence of Mr. Matthew Gisborne, was called to the chair, and gave great satisfaction by his adroit manner of eliciting the opinions of each gentleman supposed to be most conversant with the subject for discussion.

The experience of the club had been mostly in deep draining for springs. Mr. Roper of Blakeley Lodge, gave many instances of the good effects upon the land effected by drainage. He agreed with the opinions of the proposer as to the efficiency, and the practicability of the system on strong lands on an impervious subsoil, but he doubted whether it could be applied in any case where water could find its way from below (Mr. Bass had in his paper expressed his opinion that there might be such cases). Mr. W. Higgott, of Branston, also explained the methods he had pursued and had found a thorough draining profitable. Mr. W. Hollier, of Walton, and several other gentlemen, also took part in the discussion. Mr. George Greaves, Mr. Joseph Nadin, and Mr. Robert Chapman, of Gresley, put the meeting in possession of some valuable geological information respecting the rise and progress of springs; and the best methods of obviating their injurious effects upon the land. The club expressed their concurrence in the views of the proposer, though there was much difference of opinion as to the necessity of soles to the tile in strong soils. Mr. George Greaves doubted whether the system of thorough draining laid down by Mr. Smith, of Deanston, and

adopted in the essay just read, were applicable to the generality of the land in England, believing as he did, that the land in Scotland on which Mr. Smith's experiments had been chiefly tried, differed widely in its geology from the generality of land in this country. We believe the meeting did not coincide with the opinions of Mr. G. Greaves.

Mr. Bass was requested by the club to permit the paper to be published, as they thought it would do good to direct the minds of the farmers of the neighbourhood to an examination of the subject. We have reason to believe it will be circulated in the shape of a pamphlet.

At the meeting, February 9th, M. Gisborne, Esq., president, in the chair, the club took into consideration "the advantages to be derived from a more general adoption of the drill system both on light and heavy soils." There was scarcely the slightest difference of opinion as to the superiority of the drill over the broadcast method of sowing for every description of crop. The increase of crop caused by the destruction of the weeds, and the diminution of the labour of cleaning the land in the intervals of the crops, were thought to afford an ample return for the extra expense of drilling and hoeing. There arose a good deal of discussion on the question how far it was practicable to extend the practice to the heavy soils, as well as on some other imputed advantages of the drill. Mr. Roper, the proposer of the subject, thought drilling both pulse and white crops might be applied to the very heaviest soils, if they were on a dry bottom, and said that during an extensive experience on the estates of Mr. Pole, of Radbourn, he had never been prevented from drilling on strong land, except during the wet winter of 1841. As soon as the crop was gathered in the autumn, he ploughed the land, and, if possible, got out the weeds, and laid it up in ridges till the spring, when he scarified the land, and drilled upon a stale furrow. He preferred three yard lands, so that the horses might never step from the furrow and poach the ground; but this could not always be done on lands which had long been used in another form, for the form could not be changed without much damage. If the land were ploughed early enough, he thought there would seldom be any difficulty in getting the strongest soils fine enough for the drill, and whether we sowed drill or broadcast the same fine tilth would repay the labour. Some of the members thought that in many soils, and in wet seasons, it was impossible to use the drill for spring sowing, but the majority agreed that it might be much more used than it is in heavy lands, and the club came to this resolution on the point:—"That the practice of drilling was beneficial wherever it could be followed, and that its use might be greatly extended to the heavy soils." The next question was the saving of seed. Mr. Roper thought seed was saved in two ways by the drill. All the seed sown by drill was sown at the depth required, while of that sown by broadcast some was much too deep, and some much too shallow. A given quantity of seed would produce a greater quantity of plants. The saving of seed in white crops from this cause would average one-sixth. The stirring of the soil around the young plants, and the destruction of the weeds, caused each individual plant to extend its roots further, and to thrive more vigorously, and, consequently, fewer plants were needed; and he is of opinion that one bushel of seed by the drill would yield as much as two sown broadcast. There was a vigorous opposition to the latter opinion. Mr. Daniel advocated the doctrine laid down in Lord Western's letter, which is a liberal allowance of seed at a rather wide distance. He was followed by the majority of the members present, and the club came to this resolution :— "That no saving of seed was effected by the drill farther than by its producing more plants from a given quantity of seed." Then as to the saving of manure. Mr. Roper contended that not only was the application of manure rendered more efficient by being put in the immediate neighbourhood of the plants, but that a less quantity of manure was re-quired in a course of husbandry to produce a given quantity of produce. He had found two quarters of bone dust go as far when drilled with the seed as three quarters sown broadcast, and when the turnips were eaten on the ground the subsequent crops were quite as large from the smaller quantity of duet. He had seen the same thing with rape cake. He was joined in opinion by Mr. Wm. Greaves, who said that part of the manure scattered broadcast must be necessarily consumed by the weeds, which was consumed by the additional crop when the weeds were hoed up, and that the weeds did not return the manure back again. He thought also that in light soils it was not good to give more manure than the immediate crop required, as it would evaporate into the air, or be washed through by water, instead of remaining for the subsequent crop. The majority of the members argued, on the other side, that crops consumed manure in proportion to their bulk, and that if the immediate crop consumed more the sub-sequent ones would fall off; but it was admitted freely that by placing the manure in the vicinity of the plants, their vigorous growth was ensured with more certainty, and the club came to the resolution —"That there was no saving of manure by the drills, but a more efficient and beneficial application of it." As to admission of light and air, and heat, between the rows, there were various opinions. Some members thought the drills should run north and south, in strong lands, to catch the sun, and east and west in light lands, to escape his rays. Mr. Roper did not attribute much of the good effect of drilling to this cause. Mr. Joseph Dickin was of opinion that it was of little importance in white crops, which carried their leaves and flowers at the top to admit the current of air and the light between the rows, but of great advantage in bean and pulse crops, which podded low. The podding at bottom was always the mark of a good crop of beans, and he had found this greater in the drill than by broad-cast. Mr. G. Greaves also thought that mildew was favoured by damp, and that the intervals of the drill rendered the wheat less liable to it. As to the de-struction of weeds, all agreed that this was the main object of the drill, and the chief source of the in-crease of the crop. Mr. Roper thought that to drill and not to hoe was to favour the growth of weeds, and diminish instead of increasing the crop. There were no advantages which could be put in com-parison with those springing from the hoes. Some members thought that the use of the hand hoe in white and pulse crops was not effectual in quelling the root weed as well as annuals, and many that the horse-hoe was much more efficient. Others, on the contrary, said they had experienced a great falling off of the root-weed, and thought the hand-hoe as efficacious as the horse-hoe in this respect. In crops at wide intervals, the horse-hoe stirred the ground deeper and admitted air, and was less expensive; but in white crops the hand-hoe was thought safer

and better. No horse-hoeing, it was thought, could kill weed as a fallow kills it by exposing it to the sun, and it only checked weed as the hand-hoe does, by cutting off the early shoots, and keeping it down till the roots of the crop have obtained possession of the soil. It was resolved on this point—"That the hand-hoeing of crops has great effect in diminishing the quantity of root-weed." After these main ad-vantages of an increased produce, a destruction of weeds, and consequent lessening of labour in the tillage, others of lesser weight were insisted on. The clover and grass seeds were put on a clean bed, and on unoccupied spaces, and they throve better. One member remarked, that the red clover often ex-hansted itself in the first year, if sown early, and with the drill it was hoed in late. Drilled crops, by being free from weeds, stood up better, and rose more quickly after being beaten down; for the same reason they required less field room. One member said it was customary with him to mow his barley in the morning and carry it in the evening.

The subject proposed for debate at the next meet-ing, is the " growth of turnips on strong lands," by Mr. Daniel.

PLOUGHING MATCH.

On Tuesday, February 14, a ploughing match of a first-rate character took place at Baumber, on a piece of land (kindly lent for the occasion) in the occupation of Joseph Hunter, Esq., between seven farmers' sons—most of them having gained cups at other meetings. The following are the names of the young men for a sweepstakes of 20s. each :— John Richardson, Sturton ; Edward P——, Stur-ton ; Joseph Hance, Borwell ; — Nicholson, Tel-ford; John Gilbert, Sturton ; — Evison, Wes-pington ; — Strawson, Hemingby. They ploughed half an acre with two horses abreast in four hours. It was a slight frost in the morning ; towards noon a great many gentlemen and farmers in the neighbourhood were present, and were highly gratified at the superior manner in which the work was done by all. Mr. Thomas Hodgson, of Market Stainton, and Mr. Thomas Westoby, of Belshford, were the judges. The first prize was awarded to young Strawson, of Hemingby ; the second to John Gilbert, of Sturton ; and the third to young Nicholson, of Belshford ; and the judges expressed great pleasure in find-ing the work done in so masterly a manner. A dinner was provided by Mr. Addison, at the Ram Inn, where nothing but good feeling pre-vailed.

TO THE EDITOR OF THE FAR-MER'S MAGAZINE.

Sir,—A writer in your magazine for the present month, who subscribes himself "Practice with Science," must be told that he, as well as Peter Cowan, is deficient in an acquaintance with, at least, one science—I mean that of phrenology ; otherwise he would not have so dogmatically as-serted that the same law which influenced the pro-gress to perfection in animals and in plants, did not hold good when applied to the improvement of the mental faculties in man. I admit that numerous instances may be cited where " the offspring of men gifted with great mental powers are deficient in that respect," but the cause of that deficiency can generally be traced by the phrenologist.

When "Practice with Science" shall have devoted the same attention to the consideration of the moral improvement of the human race as he has evidently done to that of the improvement of agricultural animals and plants, probably he may see reason to admit that the operation of the laws of nature are in both cases the same.   N.

AGRICULTURE.

TO THE EDITOR OF THE REPORTER AND CHRONICLE.

SIR,—If you can afford space for such quiet subjects as those which concern agriculture, when the proceedings of Parliament fill your columns with more interesting matter, I should be glad to be allowed to offer two or three observations on the agricultural report in your last, from a North Derbyshire Farmer. From the spirit of his own remarks I feel sure that he will be pleased to have an opportunity of answering the objections I think may be made to some of his opinions.

I agree with him that the farmer is now-a-days placed in circumstances which require all his skill and energy to meet the difficulties of his condition. I do not quite agree with him that these difficulties have been brought on by the alteration in the Corn Law and Tariff, though certainly the sliding-scale has not been much of a protection during the last half year. I can remember, too, many times in which agriculture was depressed while the so-called protection of the corn-law was greater than now to attribute the present low markets to a remission of the protective system. But without disputing about the source of the altered state of things, it is certain that we must now-a-days bestir ourselves and seize every improvement which can lessen our expence or increase our produce.

Your reporter has, I think, somewhat indiscriminately disparaged three of the most useful innovations in the practice of farming; and without attempting to go at length into their merits, I will endeavour to remove the objections he makes to new manures, the subsoil plough, and thorough drainage. He classes them all among those things advised by politicians, which, if followed, would increase the payments of the farmer without a corresponding increase of his produce.

"If, for instance," he says, "new manures be injudiciously applied in forcing and stimulating white crops continuously, the land will be exhausted, and the condition of the farmer made worse." Here, I think, he overleaps the true point of danger as to new manures, and places it where there is none which does not equally belong to our staple farm-yard manure. The danger is lest farmers should rashly waste the new manures on land which is not fitted for them. But if it be admitted that the new manures will increase the white crop to a profitable degree, they will also increase the green crops, and I see no reason on earth why farmers should be more injudicious in over-cropping their land with old than with new manures. I have been accustomed to regard the new manures, and to see them used to increase the quantity of farm-yard manure, and to add to instead of diminishing the fertility of the land.

Agreeing with Mr. Smith, of Deanston, that a thorough drainage is the first step to good farming, and agreeing with him further as to the distance and parallelism of the drains, the reporter goes on to say that he thinks a deeper drain than twenty inches superfluous—the subsoil-plough useless, and that the drains should be in the furrows. It must be confessed that the plan of draining tenacious clays, described by him, is an excellent system of surface draining, but still it is not a thorough drainage, nor according to the Deanston principles. That there are soils so tenacious and impervious as not to admit of the method of Mr. Smith, I can well conceive. The principles of thorough drainage I take to be, that the water should all pass through the soil and subsoil into the side of the drains. In a pure clay this is not possible, and the water must be removed by suffering it to fall down steep ridges into the furrows, either over the surface or by percolation through the upper soil, and fall into the drains through the top. By this plan the drainage cannot be called thorough, for the subsoil is not drained, and the roots of the deep seeking plants are still in the wet. But in any subsoil which does admit of percolation through its substance by placing the drains near enough and deep enough, the whole body of the soil and subsoil is laid dry to the depth of the drains. The use of the subsoil plough, considered merely as an agent in draining, is to improve the texture of the subsoil, and to convert an impervious into a permeable substance. It is recommended by Mr. Smith to wait two or more years after draining tenacious clay lands before the subsoil plough is used, in order that the soil may become more friable, and the numerous crevices it makes may be more permanent. By means of it the whole subsoil is made capable of admitting the flow of water from side to side, and I cannot suppose the channels by the mole-plough, at distances of eight or ten feet, can drain the subsoil in an equally efficient manner. I do not doubt, therefore, that the plan of Mr. Smith would more effectually drain such a soil as the reporter describes, though, perhaps, the less perfect plan may be most expedient on clay pastures. As to the depth of the drains, when the subsoil is impervious at the depth of twenty inches, so that no water will flow into the drain lower, it is of course useless to go deeper than is necessary to make a secure drain; neither, I believe, would Mr. Smith recommend it except the subsoil plough be used, in which case the drain needs to be deeper to allow the plough to pass safely over it. But in all soils which are permeable at the depth of two feet or more, I believe the land is greatly improved by being drained to that depth, and in most cases by making the drains deeper we are enabled to widen the distance and effect a much greater saving of materials than the cost of the extra cutting. As to the question whether the drains should be in the furrows, I admit that in the plan of drainage described by the reporter that it is necessary to place them there, as he says, to "facilitate the discharge of water into the drained furrows." But I believe he would find it difficult to prove that "more sun and warmth" are given to the land by laying it ridge and furrow. Mr. Smith, in his lecture, told us why the land should be laid flat, and if a thorough drained field be in the same condition as a field naturally well drained, I see no reason why one should be laid in a different manner to the other.

I agree with the reporter that tile drains, well

made, are better than stone. It is only when stone is at hand, and tiles not to be come at, that I would use rubble drains. I do not believe it possible for any sediment to be removed from a rubble drain, and they therefore require extreme care in making them, and are very liable to get out of order. I wish our farmers in this district would imitate the excellent method of using the tile practised by the reporter. We too frequently see the tile laid without a sole at the bottom, and no care bestowed in filling up the drain with porous material—two things which I consider essential to a good and lasting drain.

The reporter seems to me to do great wrong to the subsoil plough in considering it merely as an assistant in thorough drainage. He says "the truth resolves itself into this, that the whole credit claimed by the subsoil plough is due to the efficient drainage previously applied;" thus he not only denies it any efficiency in draining, but also any merit in improving the soil or favouring vegetation after it. Now, I believe, if he will consult the reports of those who have used the subsoil plough, he will find that its efficacy in draining tenacious soils is admitted by all, but that its effect in this way is infinitely less than its value in improving soils which are already drained. The soils which do not require drainage have, in fact, been those which have been most benefited by its use. It would take up more space than you could afford me, if I were to adduce any proof of what I have advanced, and I fear I have written at too great a length already. In conclusion, I beg to assure your reporter that my wish is like his —the improvement of agriculture and the benefit of the farmer; and I shall be glad to meet him again in a friendly spirit if he thinks what I say worthy of comment.

I am, Sir, your obedient servant,
Feb. 8.   A SOUTH DERBYSHIRE FARMER.

NEW AGRICULTURAL IMPLEMENT.—There was exhibited in the Market-place on Monday, a patent "convertible cultivator," the invention of Mr. J. Hall, of this town. The peculiar properties of this machine are, that it is made with parallel and tilting motion frames, now for the first time, it is stated, brought into operation, and that in the machine may be fixed *any* instrument for the general purpose of tilling the soil, the frame being alike suited to *all*. Previously to setting this machine to work, the delvers and crushers can be fixed, so as to penetrate to any required depth into the soil, and the arrangements for this purpose can be easily and quickly varied when necessary. Motion is given to the delving and crushing wheels, by the delvers and crushers acting against the ground in a contrary direction to the line of draught of the horses or other animals employed to draw the machine. From the bind wheels revolving in the spaces between the front wheels, they not only serve to break up any clods or lumps which may have been imperfectly acted on by the front wheels, but are also of great use in clearing away any earth or rubbish which may adhere to the delvers and crushers of the front wheels. For a full description of this instrument, which has been pronounced "one of the most cleverly contrived and efficient of the kind" ever invented, we refer to the *Mechanics' Magazine*, of January 21st, to which we are partly indebted for the terms of the above notice.—*Cambridge Advertiser.*

ON THE FERTILIZING PROPERTIES OF BONE MANURES.

SIR,—In Professor Liebig's "Agricultural Chemistry," page 184, Playfair's translation, is an important practical receipt. He is treating upon the fertilizing properties of bone manures; and, after stating that 40lbs. of bone-dust per acre is sufficient to supply three crops of wheat, clover, potatoes, turnips, &c., with the requisite quantities of phosphates, he goes on to say—"But the form in which they (the phosphates) are restored to a soil does not appear to be a matter of indifference; for the more finely the bones are reduced to powder, and the more intimately they are mixed with the soil, the more easily are they assimilated. The most easy and practical mode of effecting their division is to pour over the bones, in a state of fine powder, half of their weight of sulphuric acid diluted with three or four parts of water; and after they have been digested for some time to add 100 parts of water, and sprinkle this mixture over the fields before the plough; in a few seconds the free acids unite with the bases contained in the earth, and a neutral salt is formed in a very fine state of division." He afterwards proceeds to shew the beneficial effect of it thus applied, and states that neither corn nor kitchen-garden plants suffer in consequence.

The practical value of this suggestion is well known, and has been adverted to in the public journals, and particularly, I believe, in the *Mark Lane Express,* by a very intelligent correspondent from Scotland: it has become the property of chemistry; but, if it belongs to any individual, it certainly is the property of the learned and illustrious Professor of Giessen, to whom the scientific world is under manifold obligations; and doubtless numbers of the readers of your valuable journal are at present engaged in putting this ingenious suggestion to the test of experiment. Of that number I am one, and being so, permit me to draw the attention of yourself and readers, as it is a subject of some interest to the British farmer, to the specification of a patent lately published in the *London Journal and Repository of Arts and Science and Manufactures,* an extract from which is published in the *Chemist* of the present month, page 72. After stating that the improvements consist in decomposing bones, bone-ash, &c., &c., previous to using them as a manure, by mixing them with a quantity of sulphuric acid, sufficient to set free as much phosphoric acid as will hold in solution the undecomposed phosphate of lime, the notable discoverer, John Bennet Lawes, Esq., of Rothampstead, Berks, goes on to claim, amongst other things, firstly, "The combination, for the purposes of manure, of bones or any other substances containing phosphoric acid with sulphuric acid, as aforesaid;" secondly, "The combination, for the purposes of manure, of phosphoric acid with any of the alkalies, potash, soda or ammonia, or any of the alkaline earths, lime, or magnesia or alumina, as aforesaid:" thus, in the first place, claiming the whole of Liebig's process; in the second, the practical application of its resulting compounds to agricultural purposes.

Having made these remarks, I leave the public to draw their own conclusions, and will merely remark that scientific discoveries ought ever to minister to the arts of life, and to individual interests only when a fair and *legitimate* claim can be made to them or their practical application.   CHEMICUS.
Feb. 6.

THEORY OF MANURES.

TO THE EDITOR OF THE MARK LANE EXPRESS.

Sir,—In the last number of your valuable and improving paper, a Dumfriesshire correspondent makes some remarks on the theory of manures.

He admits that soils are exhausted by crops, but denies that " by applying to soil those matters which one crop has taken up, we restore it to its original condition, and render it capable of yielding another crop equal to the first." He was sure that Mr. Hannam would find this verified by making the experiment on an exhausted wheat field, and that, even if he applied, proportionally to the crop of wheat he expected to reap, the nicely estimated quantities detailed in Sprengel's analysis of this grain, allowing, as he prudently proposes, "a little for rain," and adds " the field will be barren indeed if it does not contain a little of each to help his crop."

Your correspondent must surely be aware that no soil, capable of supporting vegetation, is utterly destitute of organic salts and acids and the mineral alkalies or alkaline earths in some measure, and he may easily satisfy himself of this by a glance at the mineral composition of rocky masses in general ; but he is mistaken in supposing that on this account most or all soils contain " a little of each of them." A soil may even produce tolerable crops of various kinds, and still be destitute of one or other of these desirable elements. Of this he can easily satisfy himself also, by again consulting the celebrated German chemist whose high authority he has cited.

No scientific agriculturist for a moment supposes that he is justified in expecting a crop of wheat, merely if to a soil almost destitute of the necessary elementary bases and acids, &c. a proportion of all these he applied equivalent to what a crop of wheat should remove from it. But he holds that if a crop of wheat is reaped from the soil, and the straw returned to it, and the grain sold, and that he returns also a proportion of fertilizing matter proportionate in chemical value to the grain he has sold and so removed, he will be preserving his land in a state of uniform fertility. That in every rotation he is bound, as nearly as his circumstances will admit, to restore to the soil in one shape or another a quantity of fertilizing matter as nearly as possible proportionate to what has been removed from the soil during the course of that rotation.

Who could reasonably suppose that the roots of a single crop could extract from a barren soil every particle, minus " a little for rain," of a measured estimated quantity added to it, with the vain hope of securing by this measured quantity a crop of a certain bulk and value? It is not possible that any one could imagine that the roots of a single crop could so effectually and unsparingly permeate and exhaust every interstice and particle of soil of its accidentally appropriated portion as to recover and embody in its own organization the whole of the limited quantity so added. But if a crop of wheat is reaped and a fertilizing equivalent added, the fertility of the soil may be indefinitely preserved.

Another consideration too is worthy of attention, viz., that the various fertilizing substances in the soil are constantly preserved in a ceaseless and unvarying state of progressive decomposition and recomposition—that they must undergo many such changes before they are capable of entering by the root pores or spongioles, so as to be afterwards deposited as a portion of the substance of the plant, and that very few substances indeed can be applied to the soil as manures in a form calculated for their immediate absorption by vegetables; and that usually a much longer time must elapse before the entire produce of the substances are in a fit state to be appropriated by plants, than that which passes from the period of sowing to the reaping of a grain crop. But if a crop of wheat be reaped from a fertile soil, it only exhausts a portion of its fertility, that portion which has undergone the changes necessary to fit it for the wheat plant ; and by restoring this portion in chemical value the fertility of the soil may be rendered permanent. But the roots of the plants would only remove such congenial particles as came within their reach, and could by no means exhaust the soil of its fertilizing principles. It is wrong to suppose that if a soil be effectually exhausted, and even a very large portion of raw restoratives added with a view to its recovery, that it is immediately placed in the same situation as a soil that has never been so exhausted, but has had its energies carefully nursed by a uniform interchange of enriching manures for equivalent produce reaped in every rotation. The last contains fertilizing compounds in every varying stage of progress—the first, though the chemical elements have been copiously superadded, still requires a certain time to prepare and mature these compounds.

Your correspondent also says that " if the rhemical action of the roots is of the healthy character, a slight excess there, in part, compensates deficiency of solar action at the leaves ; but if the solar and terrestrial actions do not nearly balance each other, little value will be reaped." Most certainly if the " terrestrial action," as I understand his meaning, is in excess, the plant is likely to increase too much in length without perfecting its seeds in time. It must however be borne in mind that lime in the soil tends to encourage early maturity in the crops. And your correspondent would also do well to remember that the " solar action" always increases the " terrestrial action" in a great degree, particularly in a rich soil, and with abundant moisture also encouraging ligneous development. When the soil is poor or infertile, of course the ligneous growth is diminutive and soon checked and over. The " solar action" has therefore quite as great an influence as the " terrestrial action" has " on the leaves."

He is quite correct in saying that " the effect of the disposing influence is extensively manifest in all natural agencies." For instance, the formation of acid compounds in the soil is much promoted by the presence of lime. Lime promotes the decomposition of the organic substances it accidentally meets with in the soil, by pre-disposing them to the formation of such acids. Therefore raw elements added to a fertile soil, always, in this latitude, containing lime, &c., pass rapidly through the various successive preparatory stages, and are much sooner converted to fructifying usefulness than they would be in a soil either barren or containing noxious principles, which they would require to combine with previously perhaps and neutralize.

He is wrong in talking of an excess of manure being necessary to produce permanent fertility; only so much is required as just to render the soil sufficiently rich, and afford, by a gradual and sustained decay, a moderate but uniform supply of wholesome vegetable food. To effect this it is not necessary to lay on manure in excess. This would be waste.

He is perhaps right in remarking generally that too little attention is paid to climate.

Nevertheless it is unquestionable that draining, liming, and sufficient manuring, particularly bone manure, have enabled the Highland farmer to creep up eminences with a stealthy but steady step; and, if not retarded by the late deterioration in value of agricultural produce and stock, there can be little doubt that these encroachments on the domain of the heath and the dingle for turnip ground, so indispensable to ensure winter food and numerical increase for the neighbouring flocks, will go on rapidly increasing in extent and value.

I have the honour to be, Sir,
Your very obedient servant,
Hampstead, 18th Jan.   J. A.

STEEP LIQUORS, DISINFECTING NIGHT SOIL, BONE DUST, & GYPSUM.

TO THE EDITOR OF THE MARK LANE EXPRESS.

Sir,—Having as little inclination as leisure for additional correspondence, yet desirous to have the proposed steep liquors, referred to in your last, discussed by intelligent practical men, I hand you a copy of the original letter, in which the inquirer will find the information he desires. It is a practical, not a chemical question, that it requires to be examined, and your correspondents must not expect me to take any part in the discussion.

There is another question in your last, which may as well be answered whilst the pen is in my hand—" How much gypsum will fix the nitrogen in night-soil, and how long will it be in disinfecting it?" The proportion required depends chiefly on that of urine present; but as gypsum is a useful manure and cheap, it is as well be sure to put enough—say 1½ cwt. per ton; even 2 cwt. would do no harm. But gypsum does not "disinfect;" that is, destroy the offensive smell: it only fixes the ammonia, which contains the nitrogen. Burnt bones will do both; and best when burnt in covered vessels, so as to be only charred, not calcined. But, whilst their " disinfecting" power is great, they are not so good fixers of ammonia as gypsum; and as, in calcining, they lose almost half their weight of animal matter of the most fertilizing quality, more will be lost in this process than will be gained by their action on the night-soil. Gypsum is perhaps the best fixer of ammonia; and dry coal ashes in towns, or *charred* hedge-sods in the country, the best destroyer of the bad smell, they both do almost instantly. Sods do not act so well when the black is burnt off them; the carbonaceous matter being the chief disinfector. Turf ashes answer almost as well. Any of these ashes will fix the ammonia also if pretty freely used, and so will tanners' refuse bark, or acid matter of any kind. Peat or bog-turf is an excellent fixer of the ammonia; adding, at the same time, much to the quantity and value of the manure. But for destroying the odour, ashes and charred substances are best: soot mixed with saw-dust answers both purposes.

This is a hasty and abrupt account of what might be much better explained in fuller detail; but I have only leisure to add that, is it pity ever to burn bones for manure. They may be broken and fermented with wet sheep's-dung, well bedded and covered with moist earth, peat, or sods, to absorb all gases, when they become much more active

and friable. Stable-dung may do where sheep's dung is not at hand; but they must not be allowed to get dry and fire-fanged.

To a former letter from a " Lancashire Agriculturist" I may take this opportunity to observe, that it was not for my own " pleasure," but for the benefit of the farmer the letter he referred to was written; that, whether the " farmer will believe it" or not, seems rather his business than mine; but that if he will turn back to your paper of the 19th December, he will see an account of good crops of turnips from 160lbs. bone-dust per acre, instead of the 1,000lbs. allowed by, Sir, yours, &c.,

J. PRIDEAUX.

SEED PICKLES, OR STEEP LIQUORS.

TO THE EDITOR OF THE PLYMOUTH HERALD.

" Let us bear always in mind, that while the country grants protection to agriculture, it will expect, in return, that the land shall be cultivated in the best and most productive manner."—DAUBENY.

Sir,—The practice of steeping seeds may have a two-fold object—the cure or prevention of disease; or quick germination and early growth of the young plant. The first is the purpose for which seed-wheat is generally pickled; the latter being more applicable to spring sowing. Of all the plants that would profit by quick germination and early growth, none would gain more than *turnips*, by getting out of reach of the fly. An objection here meets us at the outset; experience has abundantly proved the advantage of sowing turnips with the drill; in which damp seeds would hang, and soft ones might be crushed. The dampness may, however, be cured by shaking with fine sifted and dried bone dust; and there are some drills in which soft seeds may pass without crushing. At any rate, if great advantage can be gained by steeping, we may safely leave this mechanical objection to the ingenuity of the machine maker.

I throw out the suggestion for the consideration of practical men; and *now*, out of the season, to allow time for its consideration and discussion. The liquors are borrowed from Sprengel, whose works not existing in English, are accessible to few British farmers: but he must be exonerated from whatever impropriety there may be in their application to turnips, as he does not mention that seed in the case; only saying, generally, that seeds thrive best, after steeps of the same nature as the manures which best agree with them when growing.

" Phosphoric acid," he says, " properly diluted with water, effects such extraordinary quick germination and early growth of the young plant, as to have often struck me with surprise. This acid does not corrode the seeds, even in a strong solution; thus quite unlike the other mineral acids. I have employed it for steeping a great variety of seeds, and found it useful to *all*. The strength was one acid to 400 water, and the seeds remained in 15 to 20 hours; but even 48 hours does not hurt them. Since this is so prompt a promoter of germination and early growth, I should recommend its employment on the large scale; first ascertaining by experiment, the smallest proportion that will answer; not from fear of hurting the seed, but on account of the expense, phosphoric acid being a costly article."

Thus far Sprengel. The only objection he finds is its dearness, which is so easily obviated, that the method could only have escaped him in the multifariousness of his subject. Bone-dust, decomposed by sulphuric acid, forms sulphate of lime (gypsum), and super-phosphate of lime, which is very soluble in water. It may be thus prepared :—1 lb. sulphuric acid, mixed with 5 lb. of water, will become very hot. When half cold stir in 2 lb. fine bone dust, and let digest 48 hours, stirring occasionally to prevent clotting. It may then be diluted with 10 or twelve gallons water, adding it gradually at first, and stirring it quite smooth. When the water is all in, let it settle, and pour off clear.

Gypsum will fall to the bottom, and the clear solution will contain the super-phosphate of lime, with about one-fourth per cent. of gypsum, and a very little free sulphuric acid. These are no way injurious ; the solution of gypsum being itself an excellent steep liquor, strongly recommended by Sprengel for peas, beans, and vetches : and sulphuric acid found by him not injurious even in much larger proportion.

Steep liquor thus prepared will, therefore, be not only cheap, but probably better than mere phosphoric acid, as containing also phosphate of lime and gypsum, both considerable ingredients of turnips, as well as other crops.

Phosphoric acid, and this preparation of it, may be regarded as mere accelerators, not likely to destroy infection, unless so far as the strengthening of the young plant may help to do it. But the other material which strikes me as deserving the consideration of your practical readers, is already partially known as a disinfecter ; though its employment has been restricted by the prudent caution it unquestionably requires.

Arsenic was found by Sprengel to produce such extraordinary effects on the germination and early growth of wheat and rye, that the rye showed the effects of it even in May : an object where the rye is wanted for green food. He used one part white arsenic to 50 water, and steeped the seeds ten hours.

Now arsenic is a terrible poison. If we allow weight for weight of steep liquor, to seed, 50 lb. seed will contain 1lb. of arsenic, a quantity not likely to carry any injurious proportion into the crop even of corn ; and in the turnip seed quite insignificant. Nor seems there much ground of apprehension from mismanagement of this dangerous material by unpractised hands, farmers being already in the habit of using it in sheep liquor.

It must be observed that arsenic is *not an ingredient* of plants, but it possesses many chemical properties in common with phosphorus, and may therefore have some analogous effect in germination. Even its objectionable poisonous quality seems to offer some important advantages over phosphoric acid.

If the diseases of wheat and rye are due, as is now pretty generally understood, to fungi and animalcules, there seems nothing more likely to destroy them than arsenic: and in the case of turnips it might not only force the young germs generally out of reach of the fly, but perhaps kills the flies and grubs which were forward enough to attack them. It is used on the continent, in little balls, with flour, &c., to kill vermin in the soil.

It has been long since recommended for experiment in the second volume of " British Husbandry." I should like to see its applicability fully and searchingly discussed by practical men.

ON GYPSUM.

TO THE EDITOR OF THE MARK LANE EXPRESS.

SIR,—In your paper of the 30th ult. a reference is made to the fixing of ammonia by the application of gypsum, and during the last year many suggestions have appeared in your paper of the advantage of using it for that purpose, and that by persons who appeared to be conversant with its chemical properties, which in substance were to the following effect, viz. :—" That by mixing or sprinkling ground gypsum with carbonate of ammonia they would each become decomposed, and form new compounds ; the sulphuric acid would leave the lime and unite with the ammonia, and the carbonic acid would leave the ammonia and unite with the lime, thus forming sulphate of ammonia and carbonate of lime." Conceiving that these suggestions were founded on correct principles, I was induced to incur some expense in procuring gypsum for the purpose, but after having tried it, the gypsum did not appear to fix the ammonia, which led me to ascertain the affinity that these respective substances have for each other, and found that the sulphuric acid has a greater affinity for lime than it has for ammonia, or than carbonic acid has for lime. It is a well known fact that heat will separate or dispel carbonic acid from lime, which takes place in the conversion of limestone into pure lime, but heat will not dispel or separate sulphuric acid from lime. Should the gypsum contain an excess of sulphuric acid, which is sometimes the case, then the acid to that extent would combine with the ammonia ; but is it economical to purchase gypsum to be thus applied ? It has also been recommended to mix peat-ashes with manure, or substances containing ammonia for the same purpose ; but upon ascertaining what peat ashes are composed of, we find that their most powerful constituent is carbonate of potash , a substance the most efficient in volatilising ammonia.

Should these hasty and crude remarks upon a subject that is attracting considerable atttention among agriculturists be deemed interesting to your numerous readers, they may induce similar communications on *practical* subjects, which are the only test of correct theory.   I. J. M.
Balgian, Feb. 3, 1843.

NITRATE OF SODA AND GUANO.

SIR,—It my be acceptable to some of your readers to have a ready mode of detecting adulterations in nitrate of soda and Guano; and if you think the following information worth a corner in your paper, you are welcome to make use of it.

A ready test for nitrate of soda is to throw a little on a clear fire. If the nitrate burns freely with a yellow light and hissing noise, it is pure ; but if there is any tinge of blue in the flame, accompanied with a slight cracking noise, it is adulterated with common salt.

The pure nitrate burns very much like saltpetre, and may be substituted for it in making a weaker gunpowder.

Guano possesses a peculiar fishy smell, not easily mistaken ; but some kinds now offering are totally devoid of even this peculiarity. A very easy mode of detecting the best sample is to moisten a small portion of each with water, and place them whilst wet on a line of fresh lime. A strong smell of ammonia will instantly be perceptible, and that which yields the strongest smell will be the best Guano.

I am, sir, your obedient servant,

CHARLES SQUABBY.

Salisbury, Feb. 8, 1843.

ON GUANO.

SIR,—If you think the following observations on guano, crops, &c., worthy of a place in your invaluable journal, you at pleasure may insert them. The first thing I shall notice is a part of my experiments this year, on an eight acre field, sown with 3 cwt. of guano and 3 bushels of Italian rye grass per acre on the 29th of April, cut on the 3td of August, weighing when green eighteen tons, and when dry and ready for stack four tons per acre. Much of this crop was upwards of five feet long ; so rapid was the growth that fifty hours after cutting, it had again sprung up to the height of 3½ inches. With the above in view I see no reason to doubt that the cottager, with his five roods of land, could supply his house with vegetables, and cow with winter and summer food, thereby providing for his family an almost entire subsistence. Who with a Scotch eye in his head can view without regret the richest plains of England lying in a state of nature, in what are called "meadow-lands," on which are laid a large portion of the best dung from the farm-yard (not from the liquid tanks, which would be infinitely better), there to be exposed to and carried off by the action of the atmosphere ?

Surely in this day of intelligence these lands might be turned to a better account.

Second, an acre of oats sown with two cwt. of guano, mixed with an equal quantity of gypsum, had a powerful effect in producing a growth ; but in this case it did harm in laying the crop flat to the ground, thereby deteriorating the quality of straw and grain, nevertheless proving itself to be most valuable when the land is too poor for a crop. Thirdly, on potatoes six cwt. of guano mixed with one cwt. of gypsum produced a crop equal to twenty tons of good farm-yard dung. Fourth, on turnips, one acre of yellow bullock manured with four cwt. of guano, mixed with equal quantity of gypsum, produced a crop of thirty tons. One acre done with two cwt. of guano, mixed, produced twenty-seven tons. The portion done with four cwt. pushed at first a rapid growth into the tops, so that for long, that done with the two cwt. bade fair to be the best crop, but when then the tops began to fail of the first portion, they shot past the other and took their place in degree of crop, as will be seen by the above weights.

Along with all my turnips I sowed one cwt. of gypsum per acre, mixed with a like quantity of fine wood or other ashes, so wet, as to pass through the machine freely, which greatly assists in the first stage of vegetation.

On no account would I sow such manures as guano, bone-dust, rape-dust, &c., upon the surface for a turnip crop, which is too commonly done by machines for the purpose, although those machines have coulters making ruts of two or three inches deep for receiving the seed and manure ; yet the depositing of that manure so near the surface induces the plant in seeking food to push its roots along the top of the drill, thereby exposing them to all the changes of our variable climate, and materially checking the growth of the plant. Another evil attends sowing manure so near the surface, which is in the first hoeing or thinning of the turnips, a large portion of it is drawn away from the plant altogether.

The manure, be what it may, for a turnip crop ought to be deposited in the bottom of the drills, and then with the plough covered in about six inches deep ; the seed then sown on the top of the drill along with the before mentioned mixture ; the plants will push their roots in the natural direction, where they will find their food in a comparatively uniform temperature.

Were it not for the uninteresting nature of the foregoing remarks I might with less hesitation trouble you with the following observations on the practical system of farming of an east Lothian friend of mine, which may be summed up in these words — Drain well, clean well, and manure well. In following out these valuable and comprehensive sentences, in the first place leases must be granted of from fifteen to twenty-one years, according to the state the farm is in when agreed for, which alone will give that security absolutely necessary to the improver. This done, drain effectually, the landlord giving the tile, and the tenant putting them in under the direction and inspection of the proprietor's agent (not at a per-centage, that appearing as an addition to rent, and rather objectionable to the tenant at a collecting day), parallel to ridges of from sixteen to thirty feet apart, and from two to three deep, according to nature of subsoil.

Of all the materials with which drains are filled I should prefer tile, because, by giving ready facility to the farmer, the tide of profit is so much sooner turned into the pocket. After the above drainage, subsoil plough (there are now two-horse subsoil ploughs very answerable for small farmers) ; then plough, cultivate, and harrow, as occasion requires, not with a team of from three to eight horses one before another, necessarily involving the labour of two men, but by two horses abreast, which can be managed perfectly in every respect by one man. All scutch and other weeds being now brought to the surface, so many little boys and girls must be in readiness to gather them into heaps, to be carted off to some convenient place (not to be burned), where they should be mixed with dung for a future crop.

The ground being now drained and cleaned ready for receiving, say a turnip crop, I would only add that turnip manure ought to be of a mixed description, on purpose to obtain both an early and late growth. My last year's general crop was raised from a mixture of farm-yard, bones, and guano, at an expense of four guineas an acre, some of the yellow bullock measuring thirty-eight inches in circumference.

Agricultural associations established in every district, sending one member to the annual meeting of the great parent society, bearing to and from every useful information would, tend much to the advancement of agriculture.

In removing that vassalage and moral restraint under which the tenant-at-will lies, by granting leases, would do more, in the way of food and labour to the poor, and general advantage to all classes, than any other act of emancipation that could be granted to the people of England.

A CHESHIRE STEWARD.

DRAINING BY THE PLOUGH.

Considering the rapidity and cheapness with which this fundamental improvement can be executed by the drain plough, we think the following experiment, reported in the *Stirlingshire Observer*, well worthy attention:—

"We have much pleasure in drawing attention to the subjoined statement of the performance of Mr. Alexander's drain ploughs, on Tuesday week, on the farm of Forthbank, lately entered to by Mr. Robert Forrester. Mr. Forrester is going over the farm with a regular system of draining, and his friends and neighbours, along with Mr. Alexander, turned out to give him a day's darg, and we must say, that we never witnessed work performed in so masterly a style. Mr. Alexander's two ploughs opened the drain, the tiles being put down and laid in at the same time, and so rapid was the performance, that a field of 10½ acres was opened in every furrow, the greater part of the tiles put down and laid in, in the short space of seven hours.

"The ploughs were drawn by a team of twelve horses each, the first or top plough taking out from fourteen to fifteen inches, the second or bottom plough followed, taking out from ten to twelve inches, and in less than seven hours from starting (including twenty minutes for feeding), opened 10,080 yards of drains ready for the tiles, excepting the removing of the small earth from the bottom with the cleaner, that had fallen in from the sides, and opening the parallel drains into the main drains with the spades (the main drains having been previously put in). The levels were taken with the greatest accuracy, and we have conversed with several gentlemen experienced in draining who were on the spot, and who gave it as their opinion, that they had never seen drains opened with spade or plough so neatly, or the levels taken so correctly.

"The following is an estimate of the expence of opening drains both with the spade and plough in the same field :

Cost of opening 10,080 yards of
　drains with the Spade, and lay-
　ing in the tiles at 11d. per 36
　yards of drain,..................... £12 16 8
Cost of opening 10,080 yards with
　the Plough,
12 pairs of horses at 3s. per pair,
　including drivers,...........£4 16 0
2 conductors to each Plough, at
　2s. each..................... 0 8 0
2½ days of a man cleaning drains
　and laying in tiles at 2s,....... 2 15 0
　　　　　　　　　　　　　　　　 ————
　　　　　　　　　　　　　　　　 £7 19 0
　　　　　　　　　　　　　　　　　　　 £7 19 0

Balance in favour of Plough draining £4 17 8

" Besides, in estimating the expence of drains opened by the plough, the expence is less real than apparent, because at this season of the year the horses are not required for farm purposes, and would, in all probability, be standing idle in the stables. The objection, too, which is sometimes urged to the number of horses required for plough draining, is at once removed by the facility of two or more farmers clubbing together, as was done in the present case, and which is now getting general over the district.

" We were glad to observe a number of gentlemen connected with the agriculture of the district, and others present during the performance of the ploughs, who all seemed particularly pleased with the result."

———

AUSTRALIAN AGRICULTURAL COMPANY.— The nineteenth annual general meeting of the shareholders in the above association was held last week at their offices, 12, King's Arms-yard, Moorgate-street. Mr. Broderick, chairman of the board of directors, having been called upon to preside, the report for the year 1841, the latest period to which the accounts were made up, was read. It stated that the whole of the shepherds, labourers, &c., sent out to Australia in 1840 had arrived in safety, and very favourable accounts regarding their conduct had been received. The great depression of employment in the colony rendered it unadvisable to send any more labourers from this country, and, in consequence of the substitution of free for convict labour, the expenses of the association had increased, and the wages of the workmen been reduced. In the year 1841, 2,033 acres of land had been cleared for cultivation, being an increase of 101 acres above that in the previous year. The harvest had, however, been very unfavourable, 80 acres of wheat having been destroyed by the excessive drought and the southerly winds ; but in other respects the crops, up to August, 1842, were in a promising condition. The live stock up to December, 1841, were—sheep 79,961, lambs yearned during the year 16,994, which with the purchase of five Leicester sheep, was 96,960. There had been sold from December, 1840, to December, 1841, 2,279 ; slaughtered for the use of the establishment, 5,782 ; and 9,836 had died from age and disease. The horses and ponies numbered 566, and the horned cattle 5,251. In consequence of the great drought an unusual number of sheep had died ; and the sale of live stock in 1841 only realised 5,985*l.* 6s. 1d., while in the preceding year it amounted to 21,498*l.* 1s. 10d. In the agricultural department, 143 free labourers were employed, 118 ticket-of-leave men, and 269 convicts. In the collieries, 63 free men and 120 convicts, showing an increase during the year in the former of 26, and a decrease in the latter of 73. The produce of the sale of coals, live stock, and wool, was 37,574*l.* 12s. 5d. The entire expenditure left a balance in favour of the association of 3,173*l.* 11s. 1d. The surplus in hand in 1840 was 19,145*l*, and it was then annouced that a call of 1*l.* 18s. per share must be made, or the dividend suspended. The call was made, and paid in July last ; but the directors regretted to state that in consequence of the great depression in colonial affairs they were unable to announce a dividend this year. The balance-sheet, exhibiting the receipts from all sources, proved a balance in hand of 8,074*l.* 1s. 1d. The debtor account was 362,460*l.*, and the creditor, 354,386*l.* 1s. 6d. The value of the property of the association was 798,926*l.*16s. 6d. The report having been adopted, the meeting broke up.

———

A GRAZIER'S PROFITS. — A grazier brought to Wakefield Fortnightly Cattle Fair, on Wednesday se'nnight, twenty fat sheep for sale ; he asked 37s. each for them, but was bid only 30s., which price he ultimately took. Three months ago, the same sheep were bought by the grazier at York at 2*l.* 2s. 6d. per head, and he had fed them upon turnips, which cost him 2*l.* 12s. 6d. per acre. The amount of his *profits* will be easily ascertained.

THE WEATHER OF 1842.

My report of the weather for 1841 (published in the *Carlisle* Patriot of the 22nd January, 1842) began, as well it might, with remarks on the great quantity of rain which had fallen in that year, and particularly during the last six months of the year. Very different must be the beginning and end of this report of the weather in 1842; for the words "drought" and "continued drought" need only be used, and they will almost express the weather for the whole twelve months, as will be seen by reference to the following table of

RAIN.

	QUANTITY FALLEN.		AVERAGE OF LAST 7 YEARS.	DAYS RAIN.	
	1841.	1842.		1841	1842
January ..	2.364	2.331	2.516	23	16
February ..	1.249	1.315	2.106	19	15
March	2.407	2.962	2.580	22	23
April	2.429	0.418	1.255	26	7
May......	2.172	1.671	1.475	18	17
June......	3.243	1.849	3.052	18	13
July	3.166	2.529	4.458	25	16
August....	6.210	1.675	3.568	23	14
September .	3.863	1.812	3.681	18	20
October ..	5.360	1.795	3.266	25	9
November .	3.231	1.925	2.838	17	18
December .	3.388	1.543	2.280	23	18
	39.082	21.825	33.056	257	186

By examining this table in detail we find that March is the only month in which the quantity is above the average, and that only rather more than a quarter of an inch; also that February and March are the only months in which 1842 exceed 1841; all the other months being so much deficient that in the first six months the quantity of 1841 exceeds the quantity of the same months in 1842 by three inches and a quarter (3.318); and the last six months of 1841 in like manner exceed by nearly fourteen inches (13.939), while the total quantity for 1841 exceeds the quantity for 1842 by seventeen inches and a quarter.

The total quantity for 1842 is less than the average by 11.231 inches; or nearly eleven inches and a quarter. There is no other year on record in which so small a quantity of rain has fallen here.

There have been also 71 fewer days on which rain fell in 1842 than in 1841, March being the only month in which 1842 exceeds 1841, and the most remarkable difference being in the months of April and October. The number of days on which snow fell in 1842 was 15; while in 1841 there were 21, and in 1840, 22 such days. The following table will shew in what months this difference occurred.

SNOW.

NUMBER OF DAYS.

	1842.	1841.	1840.
January......	8	14	5
February	3	6	10
March	1	—	3
April	1	—	—
October	2	—	—
December	—	1	4
	15	21	22

If we follow the plan of 1841, we come next to the consideration of the winds; and here we find from the following table that the number of days on which the wind was westerly in 1842 is less by four than in 1841. The most remarkable feature has been in the force of the wind during the past year; for we had the strong winds in June and July which we usually have in September.

WINDS.

NUMBER OF DAYS.

	EASTERLY.		WESTERLY.	
	1841.	1842.	1841.	1842.
January............	15¼	17	15¾	14
February	22	8¾	6	19¼
March	10¼	4¼	20¾	26¾
April	10¼	19	19¾	11
May	8½	13	22½	18
June	14½	12½	15½	17½
July	6¾	13½	24¼	17½
August	5¼	11½	25¾	19½
September..........	16½	15	13½	15
October............	15¾	5¼	15¼	25¾
November..........	14½	21¾	15½	8¼
December	7½	9	23½	22
	147	150½	218	214½

The following table exhibits the indications of the thermometer during the past year as respects the mean of each month, as also the maximum and minimum; and we find that the mean temperature of the year has been the same as the average mean temperature, namely, 48 degrees. The mean temperature of the first six months of the past year was 45 degrees, and of the last six months 51 degrees. The lowest degree of temperature (14 degrees) was registered on the night between the 20th and 21st of October; the highest (81 degrees) was registered on the 18th of August. In 1841, the highest degree of temperature was 77 degrees (on the 27th May), the lowest was 2 degrees (on the 7th January); the mean of the whole year being 49 degrees. If we look only at the *mean* temperature of the year, we find that the difference between one year and another is seldom more than two degrees, generally only one, however much the two extremes (the maximum and minimum) may have varied :—

THERMOMETER.

	MEAN.	HIGHEST.	LOWEST.
January............	33.2	45.5	21.5
February	40.1	53.4	24.0
March	44.0	56.6	33.3
April	47.6	67.0	31.0
May..............	54.3	67.3	38.8
June..............	58.5	77.0	41.8
July..............	57.0	72.6	33.8
August	61.5	81.3	42.8
September	57.5	67.5	39.8
October	44.5	60.0	14.8
November..........	39.6	53.8	24.8
December	44.6	55.0	29.5

The remarks which have just been made on the the uniformity of the mean temperature apply still more strongly to the mean pressure of the atmosphere. The average mean pressure at Carlisle is 29,800; the mean pressure of 1842 was 29,826; of 1841, 29,724; and of 1840, 29,868. These differences, considering the range of the mercury in the barometer in this latitude, may be set down as nought; for a very small error in taking one observation might cause them all easily enough. The greatest height to which the mercury in the barometer attained in 1842 was 30,563 (on the 9th of April). The lowest point to which it fell was 28,465, on the 23rd October, during the great storm at Madeira. The difference between the two points was, therefore, 2,098, or rather more than two inches.

BAROMETER.

	MEAN.	HIGHEST.	LOWEST.
January	29.916	30.511	28.804
February	29.789	30.412	28.918
March	29.608	30.290	29.062
April	30.145	30.563	29.199
May................	29.838	30.485	28.820
June................	29.972	30.387	29.214
July	29.245	30.393	29.272
August	29.989	30.393	29.623
September..........	29.847	30.412	29.284
October	29.913	30.514	28.465
November..........	29.665	30.443	28.659
December	29.991	30.453	29.016

The following table of the weather presents very few new features, when looked at in conjunction with the table given last year. We find, however, that the frosty days of 1842 were fewer in number than those of 1841, by 12; that the clear days of 1842 were more than those of 1841 by 16, and that there were 46 days in the past year on which the sun did not shine. The days on which hail fell, in 1842, were 16; in 1841, there were 8 such days; and in 1840, only 3. The days on which we had thunder, in 1842, were 8; in 1841, we had 12 such days, and in 1840, 9.

WEATHER.

NUMBER OF DAYS.

	Clear through out.	Cloudy without rain.	Rain.	Frost.	Sun Shone out.
January	3	12	16	24	21
February	4	9	15	5	26
March	0	8	23	0	29
April	15	8	7	1	29
May........	4	10	17	0	27
June........	9	8	13	0	30
July	5	10	16	0	30
August......	2	15	14	0	28
September ...	0	10	20	0	28
October	4	18	9	7	28
November ...	1	11	18	15	20
December ...	0	13	18	6	23
	47	132	186	58	319

Upon a review of the weather for the whole year, we find that it has been an extraordinarily favourable year for the farmer and the gardener. The winter month of January was not inordinately severe, the temperature having never been lower than 21 degrees, and the succeeding spring months were so dry that the farmer had every opportunity of cleaning his land; indeed, such opportunity as seldom occurs; and we know that it was not lost in this part of the country at least. As soon, however, as this cleaning had been got over, the farmer began to express fears for the grass and the

subsequent hay harvest; and, as it proved, such fears were not groundless; for we had so many days of dry easterly winds in April, and so little rain, that it soon became too evident that the grass and the hay would be failing crops. So turned it out; but this was fortunately the only failure of the year; unless we reckon the failure of the after grass as another and separate blemish in the weather of this remarkable year; for, though after each successive dry month we persuaded ourselves that the next *must* be a wet month, and though our hopes of rain were put off from quarter to quarter, no rain came in such quantities as to make up for the dryness of the preceding months. The grain, however, flourished amidst all the dryness; and such a produce has not been known for many years; the quantity per acre, in many places, being nearly double the produce of the few last years. The harvest began ten days sooner this year than last, and, on account of the grain being all ready for the sickle, it was housed fifteen days sooner than in the last year. Of course, in this respect, reference is only made to the harvest of this immediate neighbourhood. With respect to the potato crop, the farmers actually complained that they were taken up too dry, and have subsequently attributed to that fact the rot which in some parts of the country—more particularly on the borders of Scotland—has considerably reduced the quantity available for human food. If we judge by the price, however, there seems to be no fear of there not being sufficient to feed us all till next crop. The mildewed tops of the turnips seemed to alarm the farmer, and not without reason; for hay being scarce and straw short, if the turnip crop failed too, the natural question arose, what was to be done with the live stock during the approaching winter, which winter (during the severe frost in October, when the thermometer was seven degrees lower than it had been in January), every one prophesied would set in soon and be remarkably severe; a prophecy, by the bye, not hitherto fulfilled; for cows might be seen enjoying their mid-day grassing on the 27th of December. On the strength of all these fears and prophecies, however, hay rose from sixpence a stone to ninepence before the close of the year; but the openness of the winter will prevent such a price being sustained, it is hoped.

When the wheat seed-time arrived the farmer had still to contend with the drought, which in some places prevented his getting into the land. Such an obstruction as that he seldom has to complain of. Since then we have had such remarkable open weather, that the wheat has got too high to be able to bear the frosts of January—at least so say the farmers. Certainly a more open December has seldom been known; for we had the violet, hepatica, primula, polyanthus, leopard's bane, gentianella, and other spring flowers, in full bloom, as if it were March instead of December; and tulips, which were planted in the middle of November, were appearing above the soil in the middle of December —the usual time for their appearance being the beginning of February. Before leaving the garden it may be as well to state that the past year has been remarkably favourable for flowers and fruit; the summer flowers having come to such perfection in bloom and in seed as we seldom witness here; and the fruit having been so plentiful that apples might truly be called a drug in the market. We had not even the usual strong winds in September to blow them off the trees. We were obliged to bestir ourselves, and undergo the hardship of *pulling* them all off. With respect to the frost in October, which killed the dahlias and other half-hardy plants, it may be a useful hint to the gardener, in the way of *protection*, to inform him that for the last four years his dahlias have been injured almost exactly on the same day: thus it happened in 1839, in October, on the 6th; in 1840, on the 3rd; in 1841, on the 4th; and in 1842, on the 4th. From this it will be seen that protection during the first week in October will most likely preserve the enjoyment of those beautiful flowers for many weeks after.

It remains only now to say that we were not much better off for moisture in December than we were in June. Complaints of wells and water-holes being without water were then still rife, and if you had occasion to transplant a tree or a shrub, you still, even then, found the soil about its roots as dry as dust; and yet we are given to understand that 1842 is only the beginning of a series of fine years, and we are implored by meteorologists to live till 1844, when, say they, those that live so long *shall* see a fine year. JOSEPH ATKINSON.
Harraby, near Carlisle, 7th Jan., 1843.

AGRICULTURAL QUERIES.

SIR,—I should be much indebted to any of your correspondents who would furnish in your next number, a plan, or description of a cow house, which would be suitable for stall-feeding seven or eight cows.

I should be glad to be informed as to the dimensions of the stalls, arrangement of the racks and mangers—whether the cattle are to be tied up or left at liberty; and any other particulars useful to a novice in the plan, in a part of the kingdom where nothing of the kind is to be met with.

I should be also thankful for any hints on the cultivation of lucerne—whether it will bear transplanting, and if it is capable of enduring an exposed northern (sea) aspect. The soil is light, rich, and dry, with a granite bottom.

Your insertion of the above queries will be appreciated by A RECENT SUBSCRIBER.
Near the Land's End, Feb. 4th, 1843.

SIR,—Your last number contains a letter from Mr. J. Scougall, on the important question of autumn cultivation for turnips, to which Mr. S. replies, and refers to a communication to the Mark Lane Express. As I take your magazine only, I should be glad to know if Mr. S.'s practice is to prepare and manure the land fully in autumn, as appears to be the practice of Mr. P. Thompson.

Mr. Matson's "autumn cultivation" has also been referred to, but, as his statements appeared in your journal before I became a subscriber, I should feel obliged by your republishing his system and its results. Several queries in late numbers remain unanswered: in September on "winter vetches," in November on "carrots."

We have alabaster in plenty in this neighbourhood, which I understand is your gypsum. Will you inform me if it is absolutely necessary that it should be burned before use; also if two cwt. of the calcined alabaster is the proper quantity for an acre of clover or grass. Is the advantage great if it is mixed in the manure heap? How long should urine remain in the tank before using?

I should feel greatly obliged by answers to the above, and if you are thus indulgent I may venture to trouble you with further queries, as I believe the time is fast approaching when all owners of small properties in land must exert themselves to the utmost to exist. The general impression here is, that there must either be a low fixed duty on corn, or none at all, and we must alter our system of husbandry altogether. At present we grow corn in a grass country. Now, sir, it appears to me we ought immediately to commence a change by increasing our number of cattle, &c.; this involves the important question of house-feeding, on which I may address you hereafter, if you treat my present attempt with indulgence.

I am, sir, yours very respectfully,
A CUMBERLAND YEOMAN.
Egremont, near Whitehaven, January 21, 1843.

TO THE EDITOR OF THE MARK LANE EXPRESS.

SIR,—As a constant reader of your Journal, I take the liberty of submitting the following questions, replies to which, either from yourself or readers, will be valuable.

Would spade husbandry be advantageous on a light gravelly soil?

Could the four course system be pursued on such, viz., clover or seeds every four years, by the application of gypsum; also when should the gypsum be applied, at the time of sowing the seed, or as a top-dressing in the spring following?

Would not the cleansing of a spring water pond succeed as a substitute for gypsum?

How would lucerne succeed on such a soil, and how is it cultivated—is it fit for cutting the same season as sown, or not till the following—is it a productive plant, and would it be suitable for milking cows on the soiling system?

Your insertion of the above will much oblige,
A YOUNG FARMER.
Alderton, near Tewkesbury, Feb. 10.

ON SUBSOILING.

SIR,—As some gentlemen favour the idea that subsoiling *light* lands (viz., those which have their subsoils of gravel, sand, and chalk) is beneficial, but which I consider quite contrary to my ideas upon the subject, I have here proposed a few remarks, which I will thank you to insert in your next number.

It is of consequence to know how this species of tillage benefits the lands, as it is very expensive. I, not having had any experience upon this subject, shall only argue upon the supposition of the case.

We must first know, then, in what way subsoiling benefits lands which have a subsoil of clay. In two ways it effects this—by allowing the superfluous water to soak lower into the soil, which the drains carry off much sooner; and in a deeper soil, which is also very beneficial. But when we come to talk of *light* lands being subsoiled, it is to be considered *how* it benefits *them*, for they are already too dry, and by subsoiling them they will be made much drier.

By ploughing at a certain depth, I consider a *pan* is formed, which much prevents the water from soaking lower; but subsoiling would destroy this pan; and some will perhaps say that subsoiling these lands will make a deeper soil; but to accomplish this, these lands may be *ploughed* much deeper.

If this should happen to meet the eyes of any of your readers who differ with me upon this subject, and still consider subsoiling *light* lands beneficial, I shall feel obliged to them if they will state their reasons for so thinking. Your obedient servant,

Sandon.   A YOUNG FARMER.

GUANO.

SIR,—The present fine open weather encourages farmers to begin sowing beans, peas, oats, spring wheat, &c., and many of us are desirous of using guano, now that the price has fallen to 10*l*. or 12*l*. per ton; but we are at a loss to know in what manner to apply this great fertiliser in the most advantageous manner. We are told that two or two and a half cwt. is amply sufficient for an acre of land; the cost per acre would not, therefore, exceed 24s. to 30s. per acre, and the smallness of the bulk will render the expense of its application very small. A great service would be rendered to the farming interest if some one or more of your intelligent correspondents, who have tried guano, would give the result of their experiments, and communicate to their brother farmers the best modes of applying this manure—to what soils it is especially applicable—in what manner it is best applied—at what seasons—to what crops—and in what quantities. Plain instructions on these heads, which the least scientific of us could readily comprehend and carry into practice, would confer no small benefit on the farmer and the public; and, if my letter should elicit such information, I shall rejoice at having addressed you on the subject.   A. B. C.

SIR,—The pastures in the counties of Monmouth and Hereford are much infested by a strong growing weed, commonly called "hard heads," or "hard tops;" it is found both in dry and wet fields, and I have observed it grow particularly strong on the tops of the drains, in ground drained within the last two or three years. The blossom of it is purple, much the shape of a thistle; but it does not turn to down, like the latter, and blow away by the wind, but dries on the stem, and continues until the plant dies down in autumn, as the cattle never meddle with it. It grows from one to two feet high. If any of your correspondents can suggest a means of extirpating it without ploughing up, it will much oblige your obedient servant,

Dec. 30.   ENQUIRER.

SIR,—May I trouble you to call the attention of your readers, more particularly the professional ones, to the disease now prevailing amongst cattle? It is not the same, I understand, as that with which the whole country was visited a year ago, and for which various remedies were speedily announced, but of a far more fatal character. In some districts in this county, Derbyshire, it appears most destructive; most of those, on some farms, very shortly dying after they are attacked. The veterinary surgeon seems quite lost. If any remedy is at present known it is highly desirable that the county should be made acquainted with it. If not, that the attention of scientific men should be called more particularly to it, as also that of the Royal Agricultural Society, that by it a suitable and sufficient remuneration may be afforded to those that may give up their time to the discovery of a remedy for so fatal a malady. The small farmer must inevitably be ruined if nothing can be done to save his stock. Already

I have heard of more than once instance where such is the case; and the loss to the county must be immense.   Your reader, and admirer,

Feb. 10, 1843.   AGRICOLA.

SIR,—Observing in your excellent Journal that one of your correspondents highly extols the Ayrshire breed of cows, I shall feel obliged to that gentleman if he would inform me, if he does not find that they go a much longer period dry before calving than any other breed. I have changed my breed of short-horns to the Ayrshire, because I thought they would suit my pastures better; but from some cause, or from their nature, I find it to be the case, as at this time I have three cows which have been dry ever since the end of November, and I do not expect them to calve before next month and the month after. If there is any reason from neglect of the dairy-woman, or other cause, I shall thank the correspondent to inform me.

Your obedient servant,

Saltwood, Hythe, Feb. 4, 1843.   SUBSCRIBER.

MR. EDITOR,—Allow me to express my obligations to the "Cheshire Farmer" for his kind reply to my former enquiry respecting the best method of bringing heath land into cultivation. For want of being more explicit in describing the nature of the land, I did not give him the opportunity of giving me the information I wanted. The heath, or grig, grows to the height of eighteen inches or so, quite covering the surface, and by its shade has destroyed all herbage underneath. The soil is loose and friable, but the *roots* of the heath, after the bushes are burnt off, remain and make it very difficult to plough, and so matted together that it cannot be crop cut by the plough, nor raked out by the harrows. One part I wish to convert into pasture: can it be done without ploughing?

Is there any instrument by which the roots can be torn out or cut? or, if there is not, is there an implement by which it can be pared off by horse-power?—Any information will greatly oblige,

A YOUNG FARMER.

On reading the report of your Nottinghamshire correspondent in your last week's journal, I see that the murrain has made its appearance amongst the sheep and cattle in that county; and that from their method of treating the disease very few of either die from its effects. The same disease being prevalent some seasons in this part of the country, a great favour would be conferred on myself and neighbours by being informed of the manner in which the disease is there treated, as with us it generally proves fatal.

A CONSTANT READER.

Near Highworth, Wilts., Feb. 19.

"A Constant Reader" says—you, or any of your correspondents, will oblige by answering the following query:—

I am going to leave land next Michaelmas, hired on lease; this lease restricts me from having more than a certain quantity in cropping; this quantity I have already sown with wheat, but I want to set a field with potatoes. My landlord says that potatoes are considered as cropping, as is everything that comes to maturity and ripens. Shall I be departing from the terms of my lease if I set potatoes in addition to the quantity already sown with corn?

SHORT HORNS.

TO THE EDITOR OF THE MARK LANE EXPRESS.

SIR,—Allow me through the medium of your valuable and widely-circulated paper, to make a few enquiries relative to the improved breed of short horns. I wish to establish a small but choice herd, and should be glad to obtain information as to the requisite outlay per head, the best mode of management, and whose blood is considered the choicest? Should this meet the eye of any old breeder willing to lend a helping hand to an ardent admirer of short horns, he will by so doing confer a favour on yours, truly,

Feb. 16.   GRAZIER.

"A Correspondent" wishes to know which is considered the best mode of feeding horses with Swedish turnips—steamed, or in their natural state —and what quantity per day should be given?

Perhaps some of your correspondents could inform me what is the best means of rotting a large heap of grass sods and twitch roots. Would it hasten the decomposition by mixing farm-yard manure, &c.? Would lime, or *salt* be useful?

Your obedient servant,   ENQUIRER.

ANSWERS TO AGRICULTURAL QUERIES.

AYRSHIRE COWS.

In answer to "Subscriber," H. P. has to inform him that his cowman states his Ayrshire cows generally go dry from six to ten weeks previous to their time of calving; last year one of his Ayrshire cows, a superior milker, went dry only a month before she calved, and this year she has gone dry full three months before her period of calving. In this respect his cowman finds no marked difference between Ayrshire and other cattle. H. P. cannot see that any blame can be attached to a dairy-woman on this account. H. P., Post-office, Blackburn, will be happy to give "Subscriber," if he will favour him with his address, his opinion, or rather that of an experienced agricultural friend, on the breed of Ayrshire and short horns.—Feb. 16.

SIR,—I have only just time to say to a "Young Farmer" that there is no doubt heath land can be turned to pasture, by first mowing or burning the heath, then giving it a good dose of quick-lime, and in the next spring after that is done, give bones small ground at the rate of one ton per acre; but I am quite satisfied that by breaking such land up, and giving it a thorough working and filling its heart full of proper manure, then sowing it down with a proper quantity of mixed seeds suited to the soil, would be much more profitable and pleasing to the eye. I cannot fancy there can be any insurmountable difficulty in ploughing heath lands a first time. If the roots be so closely entwined as to preclude a thin ploughing, give it a good furrow below all roots, with a plough which have irons file-sharped and coulter well bent forward; if two horses be not sufficient for the task, four will, two and two abreast.   A CHESHIRE FARMER.

"Enquirer" asks what are the best means of rotting grass-sods and twitch-roots? "A Tenant" informs the writer that, a few years ago, he mixed up a quantity of twitch-roots with horse-dung, in the month of July; he turned over the heap in November, when the roots were partly decomposed, and early after Christmas he carted the compost upon his meadowing land, and the roots were then completely decomposed; the grass-sods would undoubtedly decompose sooner than the twitch-roots. —Feb. 16.

SIR,—In answer to the letter of "A Northumbrian," in the *Express* of the 16th January, the following is submitted by the writer of the paper to which he refers:—

The bone solution is prepared as follows:—Procure the bones in a state of fine powder, the finer the better, and pour over them half their weight of sulphuric acid (oil of vitriol), previously diluted with three or four times its weight of water; stir the mixture, and allow it to stand for three or four days, or for a longer period if convenient, repeating the stirring occasionally. A soluble *super*-phosphate of lime is thus formed, along with the sparingly soluble sulphate of lime. The way in which the solution has hitherto been *most generally* used, is to dilute it, when thus prepared, with from thirty to fifty times the weight of the bones used of water, and to spread it into the drills by a machine for the purpose. The solution *has*, however, been applied in a dry state, but not hitherto to any great extent. I last season mixed up a small quantity of it with peat-ashes, in sufficient quantity to take up the free acid (the additional quantity of water, of course, not having been added), and then expose the mixture to dry. This was applied at the rate of about 340lbs. (of bones) per imperial acre, and, without any dung, produced, on a very poor and light soil, a very fair crop of turnips. This may be repeated by way of experiment, but on an extensive scale it would be advisable to use along with it a certain quantity of dung, in order to *ensure* a good crop. From this, however, and some other similar experiments, it appears that the efficacy of the manure is not lessened—or, at least, not materially so—by being mixed up with ashes and applied in a dry state. And, if "A Northumbrian" can command a supply of wood-ashes, they will certainly form a most excellent mixture for the solution. Wood-ashes themselves—especially if not lixiviated—form a valuable manure, containing as they do a large quantity of potash and some phosphates. "A Northumbrian" will see in the paper in the *Express* of the 26th of December, to which he refers, that it was recommended to mix the bone solution with compost, and then to saturate this compost with urine, by which the important object would be gained of fixing the volatile carbonate of ammonia of the urine; and the mixture thus formed would be a most valuable manure, as it would contain phosphate of lime and nitrogen (in the form of fixed salts of ammonia), two grand requisites for almost every kind of crop. With regard to the influence of the bone solution on the after corn crop, experience does not warrant the expression of any decided opinion. The experiments made in 1841 were on a small scale—a few drills of turnips in different fields—and from such narrow stripes it is impossible to speak with any confidence; and we do not wish to make any statement without seeing clearly the ground on which it rests.

Q

Sir,—A "Yorkshireman," in your last number, requests a description of the fork which I use for digging, and a statement of the method I adopt so as to keep the top soil on the surface.

The fork has three prongs ; it is fourteen inches long, seven and a half wide; each prong is three quarters of an inch wide, and half an inch thick, made rather tapering, and the ends are chisel-pointed ; the weight, including the handle, is 8lbs. It is difficult to give an intelligible description of an implement; and if "Yorkshireman" will favour me with his address, I will procure one and forward it to him—the cost is only 4s. 9d.

The plan I pursued, so as to keep the top soil on the surface, in the field which is now finished, was as follows:—The men were required to dig up the old furrows fourteen inches deep ; the plough then took a slice of four inches deep on each side, and turned them on the part dug. The furrows so left were then dug, and an adjoining slice turned on to them. The process was repeated till the whole was dug, and the land left in the same sized stitches as before.

The digging costs 2½d. per rod, or 33s. 4d. per acre, to which is to be added the expense of one ploughing. The advantages are—additional depth of soil, the capability of growing green or root crops without the usual manuring, and a diminution in horse and a corresponding increase in manual labour. Spade husbandry may not be adapted for every soil ; but, as a means of improving the land, increasing the produce, and affording profitable labour, it is entitled to more attention than has been hitherto bestowed upon it.

I remain, Mr. Editor, your obedient servant,
Witham, Jan. 28.　　　　　　　　James Beadel.

TO THE EDITOR OF THE FAR-MERS' MAGAZINE.

Sir,—It would afford me the greatest pleasure to see in the pages of your widely circulated magazine, a paper by some of your scientific contributors on the best means of steaming fodder, together with an account of the best apparatus for that purpose, and an exposition of the mode in which the constituents of fodder are affected by steaming so as to render it more nutritious to cattle.

I am the more desirous to see this subject treated of in consequence of the nature of the soil where I am located being unfavourable to the growth of turnips, and as large numbers of cattle are kept a great interest would be excited and much benefit conferred on many of your readers in this quarter by an article on the subject referred to.

I am, sir, yours very respectfully,
A Constant Reader.
Little-Hallam, Derbyshire, February 22, 1843.

BARN FLOORS.

TO THE EDITOR OF THE FARMERS' MAGAZINE.

Sir,—In your magazine of this month there is a letter copied from the *Salisbury and Winchester Journal*, and signed a "Constant Reader," respecting barn floors. His suggestions are very good as to upright blocks being used for that purpose, except that rats are as likely to burrow under wooden blocks as under planking, the superiority of the

one floor over the other would consist in the longer time it would take the rat to get to the surface of the one to that of the other. I would therefore call the attention of the writer of the letter to a barn floor superior to any other, viz., asphalte, through which no rat will burrow, no damp raise through it, even if laid on a springy clay and as no dust would rise as from a clay floor, or damp as from a stone one, a better sample would be delivered. The value of liquid manure being now fully appreciated, asphalte is one of the best floorings for stables, bullock and cow sheds, and pig-styes, and is a most excellent coating for tanks to receive the liquid manure in.

I am, Sir, yours &c.
Norwich, Feb. 23, 1843.　　　　　A Subscriber.

CALENDAR OF HORTICULTURE FOR MARCH.

The sudden attack of winter, which commenced in the evening of 13th ult., was very decisive in its character : fierce easterly wind, a copious but drifting fall of snow, and a frost progressing from 7° to 9°, 10°, 11°, to the 17th, produced their full effects; we use the terms of horticulture, and imply degrees of actual depression below the freezing point (32°). The lowest grade observed on our instruments was 21° of Farenheit, on the third morning; but we have heard of 18°—that is to say, 14° of frost. After the snow commenced, the temperature rose five degrees, and a gradual thaw succeeded, with some rain on the 19th.

We suspect that many geraniums, calceolarias, and such-like semi-succulent plants, have suffered, because the long continuance of open weather naturally tended to induce security. But, though the attack was sudden and waspish, we had the satisfaction to observe that in dry houses, coverings and moderate fires operated very effectually. So much depends upon habits, and what we call the education of a set of plants, that, unless they be exposed to a degree of rigour which actually decomposes the tissue, a very low comparative temperature will be beneficial rather than hurtful.

From the character of February—cold, fluctuating, and moderately wet—(circumstances which remind one of the sayings of old)—we anticipate a true March, and if that be the case, the employment for the gardener will be ample. In the

Vegetable Department

Sow, at intervals, all the summer crops, excepting the kidney bean, and where any vegetable is required in succession, it may be a good rule to sow so soon as the plants of the previous sowing appear above the surface. It will be advisable to dig before sowing, and it should appear that much may be done towards cleaning and enriching the ground by attending to the following simple processes :—

First of all, lay the spit-dung, leaf-mould, decayed vegetables, or whatever manure be employed, over the plot ; then scatter over this dress, a mixture composed of dusty ashes one peck, powdered air-slaked lime half the quantity, and common salt about a quart—the whole sifted together ; being dusted over a pole of land, every slug upon the manure touched by the dust would be killed or debilitated. This mixture ought to be applied at night, and again in the early morning, prior to digging.

The sowing may then be made as the work proceeds, but after its completion a second two-fold dusting will be proper.

The spade and rake will carry some portion of the first caustic materials into contact with vermin below the surface, the turning-up of the ground will raise more of them, and the last dressing made immediately after every portion is sowed and raked, will do execution upon the slugs so exposed. Fortunately the ground is pretty free already, the dry weather of August having thus proved the gardener's friend; and now, by a little attention at every favourable opportunity, we believe that nine-tenths of the moluscous pests may be destroyed, and that without any risk to a crop.

Here it will be relevant to advance a hint upon the fuel which a forcing gardener might adopt with advantage. We find no kind of coal so cheap or effectual as that called *Moira*—it does not produce binding clinkers, but consumes to a grey ash, fine as hair-powder. This ash contains saline matter, and hence resembles wood-ash, and acts as a manure. When the fire is banked up at night, we have known a lump of 7lbs., covered with screenings of coal and small cinders, to retain strong heat for ten hours, insomuch that, for many weeks, we have no occasion to rekindle the fire. The ashes are capital, used with lime and salt.

Having thus premised, taking advantage of the state of the soil and weather, sow—broad beans, i. e. long-pod, toker Sandwich, Windsor, and the green-seeded.

Peas—the new early sorts, also Prussian, scimitar, and imperials.

Cabbage—including brocoli, Brussell's sprouts, borecole—all these towards the end of the month.

Lettuce, radish, small salad, spinach, parsley.

Beet-root in drills. Carrot, parsnip—some prefer broad-casting, but, however sown, the loam cannot be too fresh and pure, nor too fine and free from stones.

Sow early turnips.

Onions require deep tillage and sound manure; afterwards the surface may be beaten hard, sowing the seed upon it as broad-cast, or in mere scratches or shallow drills, covering the seed by a slight screening of sand and light manure mixed, which may be patted to a level flat surface. Sow also leeks.

Plant out cabbage from the beds—a few red ones for pickling; cauliflower, from glasses and frames; lettuces, of the autumn sowings.

The sweet and pot-herbs—as purslane, chervil, coriander, basil, dill, fennel—are sown about the last week.

Dress the artichoke plants, removing litter and dead leaves, and prepare land for fresh plantations, and for new rows of asparagus and sea-kale, in the following manner—rhubarb can be included. Our plan was suggested by observing the work performed in one of the finest old gardens of Berkshire (of conventual origin we believe)— that of Shottesbrook, whose old church and appendages are the admiration of the antiquary.

Dig out two feet wide trenches, screen the earth, if the good soil will admit it, thirty inches deep; if not, add to the depth, but by no means raise bad subsoil. Throw cabbage-stalks, strawberry-refuse, or any vegetable offal into the trenches; tread them level, and fill up with the screened earth or old turf loam, blended with an equal quantity of the best manure that can be obtained. During the mixing and turning, scatter salt or nitrate of soda, to the extent of two pounds to every trench of twenty feet length; these saline inorganic manures will furnish a supply for years, but their immediate effect will be the destruction of soft insects. Leave the land so prepared till April.

Earth up peas, beans, &c.; hoe all intervening spaces; fork asparagus beds and rows, and remove every kind of litter.

FRUIT DEPARTMENT.

Gooseberry, currant, and raspberry bushes, if not already regulated, should be pruned forthwith, according to the directions given in former articles. Scatter wood-ashes, lime, and soot, over the branches, or dredge them over with a tin box, containing powdered lime, sulphur, and a little coal-soot. This application will at least clear the bark from parasite vegetation, and, moreover, may check the progress of some insects lodged therein. After the regulation, the ground should be turned, and sprinkled with a very small quantity of dry and finely powdered salt. A pound will go far, and a particle the size of a grain of celery-seed, will annoy a small slug—it is more effectual than lime.

Prune and nail all the wall-trees, study the habits and process of bearing of each, then apply the knife accordingly. The leading maxim is to furnish every half foot of the space occupied by a tree, with fertile wood.

Spur-prune apple and pear espalier trees, tie the branches to form a well-trained figure, and, if mossy, wash the limbs, or syringe them with lime water.

Trench and prepare ground for new strawberry rows; 18 inches to two feet is not too deep; apply manure as dress and nitrate of soda before digging and turning, and select three aspects to prolong the season. If the beds be ready by the 15th plant before the end; Keen's, the Hudson's Bay, and Knight's Elton, will not be surpassed.

Give air, proper supplies of water, and increased heat, as the season advances, to the pine-stoves and vineries. Keep a steady growing heat with the cucumbers, and begin to sow melons.

FLOWER GARDEN.

In the first favourable weather dig in all the leaves that have lain on the ground of parterre or shrubberies; add leaf-mould and old cow manure; and, in digging, separate and replant herbaceous plants in new earth. It is a great advantage to remove the old earth from all the fancy beds upon lawns, and to replace it, according to the habits of any choice plants, either with the best maiden turfy-loam or leaf-mould and heath-soil: the effect produced is most striking.

Sow at the end of the month, the seeds of approved annuals, and carefully thin out and give much air to the pots of annuals sown under glass. Propagate freely, by cuttings, calceolarias, cinerarias, and some geraniums. A ready method to obtain the former is to look over some strong plants of last year, and to select some of those low shoots which begin to protrude root processes. These emerge near the point of junction of the older with the last made young wood; taken off just below the embryo root, and planted in light soil, aided by a very gentle heat in a closed frame, plants will be secured in a very short time.

Auriculas require attention; prepare a soil of equal parts—reduced turfy loam, heath-mould, leaf-mould, or three year old cow-dung and sand ; mix, and sift them twice, remove all the best offsets, and plant three in a forty-two pot.   Scrape away the old top soil from the parent plants, and top-dress them ; expose to air and morning sun.

Look over all the green-house plants, remove dead leaves ; dress the surface ; repot growing pelargonia ; cut back to well placed buds all that have a bad unbalanced figure.   Water timely given, and the regular use of the syringe are essentials.   The Indian azalia, if suffered to become heart-dry, seldom revives ; its hair-like roots perish in a dry ball, and it is notorious that heath mould should always be gently moist.

Heaths require abundance of air, free watering,

and a shifting, if the roots fill the pot, before growth takes place.

Camellias out of bloom, may be safely excited in a shady warm house ; they like water while growing.

Whether a plant be in stove, conservatory, greenhouse, or pit, as the solar power increases, so ought our application of stimuli to be called in aid.   More heat, more water, more air ; these form our principles—but we say by day—for night is not the season for excitation, but for repose.   Early closing all the houses with sun on them, is a conservative precept ; and where fire or hot water is applied, let the heat fall 10 or 12 degrees during the night.   No injury will result even with plants which revel by day in 90°, by a decline to 60° in the hours of darkness.

AGRICULTURAL   REPORTS.

GENERAL AGRICULTURAL REPORT FOR FEBRUARY.

Notwithstanding there have been several extraordinary changes in the temperature of the past month, the weather has proved, as a whole, seasonably fine.   From the 1st until about the 10th, the atmosphere was very damp and humid ; after that period, a cold north-easterly wind was experienced for several days, which had the effect of causing the young wheat plants, though they thus received a wholesome check, to assume rather a withered appearance.   Fortunately, however, at this crisis a fine and deep fall of snow took place, which, while it sheltered the wheats from atmospheric inclemency, tended to produce a favourable influence upon the soil ; such, indeed, as the farmer is always desirous of beholding.   On the 19th the wind worked round to the south-west ; hence the snow speedily disappeared, and we have since been favoured with several genial rains.   This, then, is a brief history of the month's weather.

In reference to vegetation in general, we may state that it was never remembered to be in a more healthy and flourishing state than at the present moment.   As to the wheat, in particular, it is true several instances have come under our notice in which premature growth has been exhibited ; but, comparatively speaking, there is cause for congratulation on this head, and we think the prospects of the forthcoming harvest are certainly good.   There is one thing certain, that our agriculturists are in a much better position, as regards their heavy wheats, than they were at the corresponding period last year.   Then scarcely a moiety had been sown ; but now we find that every patch of land destined to be sown with that description of winter grain has growing upon it most luxuriant crops.   Preparations are in active progress for sowing the Lent corn, which, we trust, will be satisfactorily accomplished.

A question of the highest importance to the agricultural community now arises ; and which, by the way, has been productive of some very erroneous details, offered in a variety of forms, regarding the stocks of wheat of home produce now in this country.   That these are the great governing principle of future prices, none will be found to deny, though the supplies of foreign may be large.   With much care have we collected every fact bearing upon this topic of consideration, in

order to arrive at the truth of the position we are about to assume.   Now, it will be remembered that, for several months past, we have stated it to be our honest conviction that, from the circumstance of the supply of wheat being *about an average*, we were fully convinced that no permanent rise could, in the ordinary course of things, take place.   That we were correct in our views, is evidenced from the fact of the trade and ruling prices corresponding exactly with them.   If reference be made to the stocks now on hand for the whole country, it will be found that, though deficiencies are observed in many districts—such, for instance, as Essex, Suffolk, and parts of Norfolk—they are quite equal to those at the corresponding period of last year.   Whilst holding in view that present rates are extremely low, and perhaps unprofitable, we cannot conceal the fact that the future prospects are far from flattering ; yet we entertain this conviction, that prices have seen their minimum range.   It is far, very far, from our wish to represent matters or circumstances worse than they really are ; but it would, in our opinion, be a dereliction of duty did we withhold any statement which would be a guide to the agricultural body of the kingdom.   At Mark Lane, as well as in nearly the whole of our provincial markets, the supplies of wheat offering, direct from the growers, have been very scanty, and of middling and inferior quality.   With some difficulty previous rates have been obtained for the finest parcels, but the middling and out-of-condition sorts may be called 1s. per qr. lower.   Foreign wheat—both free and in bond—has ruled very heavy, and prices, in many instances, have remained almost nominal.   Good sound barley and the best malt have maintained their value, but other kinds have commanded little attention.   Oats, beans, peas, and flour, have ruled about stationary.

The early lambing season has gone on favourably, and been productive—especially in the southern districts, including the Isle of Wight—of a good fall of strong and healthy lambs.   The epidemic, however, has been again very prevalent, and some rather severe losses have been sustained by the graziers, both as respects their beasts and sheep.

The turnip crop is well represented, while the depastured stock, from the supply of grass being more than usually abundant, have fared extremely well.

In Ireland and Scotland the wheats are looking remarkably well, with every prospect of an abundant harvest. The corn trade, however, as with us, has ruled dull, and rather lower rates have been accepted for low parcels of grain.

With respect to the tariff, we have but few observations to offer this month; so scanty have been the importations, that they are quite unworthy of notice. At Smithfield, no fresh foreign beasts or sheep have been on sale, yet we have good authority for stating that large importations will take place in the spring from Germany and Spain.

The following is our usual monthly statement of the supplies and prices of fat stock exhibited and sold in Smithfield cattle market. The former have amounted to 12,020 beasts; 105,233 sheep; 992 calves; and 2,312 pigs : the latter have ruled as follows :—Beef, from 2s. 10d. to 4s. 4d.; Mutton, 3s. to 4s. 6d.; Veal, 4s. to 5s. 6d. ; and Pork, 3s. 4d. to 4s. 4d. per 8lbs., to sink the offals.

On each market day there has been a fair attendance of buyers, but, owing to the large arrivals of slaughtered meat up to Newgate and Leadenhall markets, from Scotland and various parts of England—they having exceeded 20,000 carcasses—the demand has ruled inactive, and lower prices has been the result. As to the quality of the stock, this has been pretty good, and we are glad to be enabled to state that the Norfolk droves, as well as the receipts from Scotland, have more than equalled our expectations.

A STATEMENT and COMPARISON of the SUPPLIES and PRICES of FAT STOCK, exhibited and sold in SMITHFIELD CATTLE MARKET, on Monday, Feb. 21, 1842, and Monday, Feb. 20, 1843.
At per 8lbs. to sink the offals.

	Feb. 21, 1842.		Feb. 20, 1843.	
	s. d.	s. d.	s. d.	s. d.
Coarse & inferior Beasts	3 6 to	3 8 ..	2 10	3 0
Second quality do.	3 10	4 0 ..	3 2	3 4
Prime large Oxen	4 2	4 4 ..	3 6	3 8
Prime Scots, &c.	4 4	4 6 ..	3 10	4 2
Coarse & inferior Sheep	3 8	3 10 ..	3 0	3 2
Second quality do.	3 10	4 2 .	3 4	3 6
Prime coarse woolled do.	4 4	4 6 .	3 8	3 10
Prime Southdown do.	4 8	5 0 ..	4 0	4 4
Large coarse Calves	5 0	5 6 ..	3 10	4 6
Prime small ditto	5 0	6 0 ..	4 8	4 10
Large Hogs	4 6	4 10 ..	3 4	4 0
Neat small Porkers	5 0	5 2 ..	4 2	4 4

SUPPLIES.

	Feb. 21, 1842.	Feb. 20, 1843.
Beasts	2,602	3,113
Sheep	19,650	26,220
Calves	61	94
Pigs	419	392

In Newgate and Leadenhall markets the trade has again ruled very dull, and low prices have been with difficulty realized for all descriptions of meat.

AGRICULTURAL REPORT FOR FEBRUARY.

On the 15th a keen frosty air from a north-eastern quarter, which in the earlier days of the month had brought merely a bracing temperature, ushered in a degree of severity perfectly Siberian when compared with the general mildness of the three preceding months. The frost increased daily till the 18th, when the mercury rose 6 degrees, i. e., from 21 of Fahrenheit—its lowest—to 27°. A fierce wind then accompanied, as it had preceded, a considerable fall of snow, which, had there been a calm, would have covered the surface to the depth of four

inches. As it was, we have obtained only drifts and snow-water to fill the ditches ; for a thaw took place in twelve hours, and by the 20th hardly a patch of snow remained. The thermometer has now attained 40°, and rain falls.

The consequences of these mutations must be, first, a complete check, at this late period, of winter vegetable growth, and an end to all anticipations of premature luxuriance.

February puts on its old-fashioned garb : the land will be replenished with water at a period when the drying winds of March are likely to carry off every particle from the surface. In 1841 the floods of December had poached, nay, drowned the lands ; and then, as early March proved again rainy, the drains and water-courses were replete with water in April.

Crops of all kinds *now* occupy a genial, mellow bed ; every thing is secure and unscathed. Enough of winter has occurred to retard, but nothing to injure ; and if we be blessed with those genuine influences which bring plenty of March dust, we may safely congratulate the agriculturist upon the progress of one of the finest of seasons. We use the term *genuine*, because, of late years, the dust of March has been raised by parching, rigorous, east winds, accompanied by five or seven degrees of unseasonable frost : a dry atmosphere, a keenish air, and plenty of sun, are the legitimate concomitants of a health-confining March.

What will the landlords and farmers think, say, or do now ? The quotations cited in the leading article of last Monday's "Express" are quite decisive—they appeal to the understanding ! The progress of events, and the spirit of the times are therein laid down as in a well-drawn map.

"God helps those who help themselves"—says the proverb ! Which, being applied, will instruct, that they to whom the wisdom is granted to strike at the nail which will drive ; and, taking advantage of every available method of improvement, employ the means placed within their command, will, by the exercise of a liberal economy, be rendered prosperous.

We know not that sudden alterations, or abolitions of restrictive measures, would be wise ; but certain we are that, whatever is the relics of a warlike, contentious spirit, ought not to be upheld by men who profess a love of peace ! Let all men love as brethren, generally and individually—in states and in families, and it will be as plain as the sun at noonday, that it is their interest to cultivate an interchange of *all comforts* ; and that the opposite system must be purely evil in its origin and results.

Every prospect is cheering, if we could but lay aside anticipations of what may never occur. The land is in the most excellent condition, the plough (prior to the frost) discovered *that*; in every situation the grass lands are covered with healthy verdure ; the turnips hold out sound and abundant, and the flocks are thriving. We ought to be grateful and wise ! Legislator, landlord, and occupier, ought to pull together, and feel but one common interest ; whereas, we stand still, revile, and abuse ; then cry out " Wolf !"—and despair of a remedy !

Assuredly rents, in hundreds of instances, are too high, and tenancies far too limited ; but the farmer is also too profuse and lavish : horses are superabundant, machinery is too expensive, force is not economised ; and in addition, every market day shows us equipages and general appliances of wealth ! Is complaint legitimate with the maintenance of three hunters? It is not that we would argue for old, bygone customs, and the self-denial of even delicacies: none better merit the enjoyments of the earth's bounty than they who labour on the soil; but then, why should we enjoy and complain,—why prognosticate ruin, while we revel in superfluity?

The arts and sciences are open to this favoured generation; and our Scots brethren have well, diligently, and economically availed themselves of their aid—and become rich.

Difference of clime, of seasons, and habits, certainly claim allowances; but still, we of the south may learn. Our advantages are pre-eminent also; and herein, perhaps, we may trace a primary cause; for experience has ever shown, that a land rich by nature, that produces almost spontaneously, is comparatively neglected, while another, which would be barren were it not courted and tasked to the uttermost, repays the labourer with double interest. Thus is verified the text that says—

"The band of the diligent shall bear rule."

ESSEX.

The appearance of our county bears full promise, as far as wheat is concerned. of very great abundance. Genial weather cheq ered with but little frost has been the pred minant feature of the season, and though many farmers are in favour of rather more severity on the young wheat plants, yet we are inc ined to the contrary opinion, and prefer a mild winter as being far more beneficial than a severe one to the productiveness of the crop. For the last three or four seasons frost has prevailed to a greater extent than in the preceding ones, and short roduce has generally been complained of. So far as appearance of other vegetation goes, tares and young clovers are generally promising. Grass has continued growing all through the winter, and has carried stock to an unusually late period. The time for spring sowing has arrived, but little appears yet to be done with the exception of a few beans. The land is still in a very rotten state, but should the weather improve it may probab'y work well, as the fine dry tilth in which it was laid up last autumn must have tended much to have that effect. The utmost gloom broods over the markets for all descriptions of agricultural produce. Good red wheat is selling in our markets, at 47s.; barley, 28s.; beans, 24s.; and oats, 18s. per qr Clover-seed may be bought from 20s. up to 34s. Live stock of all descriptions begaring the sellers, and proving the fact to be indisputable that the late and threatened measures of our Conservative government are rapidly producing a state of things decaying comparison with anything that has occurred during the last twenty years. In the year 1835, one of the most productive as well as the lowest priced year of any during that period. wheat averaged 39s. 4d., with an abundant crop, what is it now with but an exceedingly limited one in our county, 47s. 5d.! Barley, 29s. 11d.; what is it now with a bad crop, 27s. 1d.! Oats, 22s.; what are they now, equally unprolific, 16s. 11d.! Beans, 30s.; what are they now, with a wretched crop, 27s. 5d.! Peas, 30s. 3d., now 30s, 1d. Clover-seed in a far worse plight, and the meal markets more wretched than all; and yet the Agricultural Interest still slumbers, and patiently waits its downfal. No threat seems now to alarm it. Without a leader to protect it, its energies seem all

at once prostrated, and sullen inactivity has succeeded the glorious struggle of the last election. The events of the last session are perhaps without a parallel in the history of legislation. An open attack is made by a previous Government on the Agricultural Interest—that attack is resented—an appeal is made to the country—a vast majority of representatives are returned to repel encroachments—and the chosen leader, "The Farmer's Friend," demands an immediate recantation of their allegiance to the soil; away go the hopes of the constituency, and still paralyzed, they heed not the Government announcement but lately made, that the whole continent of North and South America is to have free access to our markets by the payment of 3s. per qr. duty to the Canadian treasury. This proposal ought to be sufficient to strike terror into the hearts of every man who has aught invested in British land. Farmers of England! we urge you to your duty—we appeal to you. Rouse from your fatal apathy, and demand justice, aye, and good faith from your representatives ere your all is gone. The tenant class is first to fall; the landowner may live without the tenant. Do what you can to disperse the fatal mesmerism that broods over the once independent spirit of the Legislature. Mark ye! Twelve more months will not have passed before the farmers of England shall demand, as they have hitherto done, measures for immediate justice. If native industry is to have no claim upon the legislature, the legislature must reduce its claims on it. Native industry must then determine whether it is just that the hierarchy should have their increased demands met without abatement. Native industry must, then, with rigid scrutiny analyse the various imposts to which she is now subjected. If nothing but noise and agitation is to be successful, we must try that too. We want but a rallying point. That gained, the Agricultural Interest may yet be saved. Its strength is not yet gone. Like the lion, it may sleep till shorn of its last hair, but its sleep is only adding to its strength; for encountering the hostile ranks which have gathered round it while in its state of lethargy.

YORKSHIRE.

The extreme open weather, which resembled April more than January, continued until the latter end of that month, and vegetation was stimulated to a degree of forwardness rarely witnessed. The wheats were shooting upwards, the hedges budding, and the woodbines in full leaf; the turnips very nearly in flower, and the birds singing, quite to remind us of the Spring in the very middle of the season called Winter. A change, however, took place towards the close; a little snow, and some frosts occured in the beginning of February; and on the 4th a storm of wind, little inferior to the hurricane of January 1839 passed over the county, and upturned hundreds of stacks, unroofed and blew down several buildings, and uprooted many beautiful trees. No damage beyond a considerable waste, has been done to the corn, as the weather was happily fine for a time, sufficient to enable the farmers to get the scattered sheaves together again. Vegetation is, however, severely checked. The wheats are shrivelled, and the recent spring the plants have made are again levelled with the ground; indeed the shrivelled blueness of the wheat plants gives a degree of extreme baldness to many a field, which a month ago was more like a fog-layer than any thing else. The turnips are also checked, but not so far as to affect their juicyness, nor cut down their large foliage. Fodder, though certainly spared a good deal by the open winter, is by no means abundant, and beasts and sheep are beginning to come out of the graziers' hands pretty rapidly—sufficiently so, or more so, than the wants of the markets require. Prices are very low. Spring wheat is being sown, but not by any means to the extent of last Spring; indeed, the price of wheat is by no means such as to tempt the farmer to extend his breadth of that grain beyond its wonted limits; five and sixpence per bushel is the prevailing price for that article. Sir Robert Peel's declaration has given universal satisfaction amongst the farmers here. The league is powerless so long as he holds his present position.— *Feb.* 14.

AGRICULTURAL INTELLIGENCE, FAIRS, &c.

NORTHALLERTON FAIR.—This celebrated fair commenced on Monday, the 6th, and terminated on the 14th. There was a large attendance of respectable dealers from London, Edinburgh, Manchester, Liverpool, and other places, and also several foreigners. During the early part of the fair the show of first-rate coaching horses, hunters, and nags, was good, most of which met with ready sale at fair average prices, particularly the first sort, which appeared to be most in request. One dealer, Mr. Burford, of London, purchased upwards of 150 of that description, and gave great prices. As the fair progressed, the middling and inferior description of horses became plentiful, and although the prices obtained for such were low, yet there was a better demand for them than for several years pas .

GODALMING WINTER CATTLE FAIR, held on Monday last, brought together an unusually large show of animals, of which the working horses were the best. On this occasion the usual collection was reinforced by the addition of some pens of sheep, which were a novelty in the show. Nothing could exceed the beauty of the day and fineness of the weather, for the season, and the attendance was both numerous and respectable. Buyers sharing in the influence of the depressed state of markets, were few, and much of the stock remained unsold.

ASHBOURN FAIR, Feb. 13th, was well supplied with all kinds of cattle. Fresh barren beasts were better sold than any other stock, and those at indifferent prices; all other stock were scarcely saleable at all; in fact we never witnessed so dull a fair as this in cattle. But few sheep were penned, and in them sales were dull. The horse fair commenced at the latter end of last week, was but thinly supplied, and little business was done in them.

BIDEFORD SPRING FAIR.—The show of cattle was larger than we ever witnessed at any spring fair previously held in Bideford. Fat bullocks were sold at 9s. 6d. to 10s.; store cattle, from 7s. to 7s. 6d. per score; cows and calves, from 9l. 9s. to 13l. 13s. each. Sheep—the number of sheep penned was not so large as last year. Prime fat wethers fetched 5¾d.; ewes, 5¼d. per lb.; couples sold for 26s. to 36s. Horses—there were but few good horses in the fair, with the exception of those in the hands of dealers, and high prices were demanded. There were a good many rough colts, which sold at from 3l. 10s. to 7l. each. The fair generally was tolerably brisk—the cattle and sheep being in excellent condition for the season; and we are glad to state that this fair is greatly improving every year. The attendance of graziers, dealers, and men of business was very numerous indeed.

DEVIZES CANDLEMAS FAIR was largely supplied with all descriptions of cattle; but owing to the low prices offered, little business was transacted throughout the day. Towards the close, however, some few sales were effected; beef selling at from 9s. to 10s. per score; but on the whole the trade was exceedingly dull.

BATH FAIR was well supplied with fat cattle, and of an excellent description. Sales were effected at better prices than have ruled at late fairs. Beef fetched from 9s. 6d. to 10s. 6d. per score, and mutton sold as high as 5¾d. to 6¾d. per lb. There was a fair supply of lean stock, but sales were rather dull.

At DORCHESTER CANDLEMAS FAIR there was a very numerous attendance of farmers and graziers, and much business was done. The supply of fat beasts was limited, prices being from 8s. to 10s. per score. There was a large supply of Cows and Calves, among which were many of prime quality; ready sales were effected at from 10l. to 15l.

FARINGDON CATTLE FAIR, although larger than the corresponding one of last year, was by no means a large one. A few excellent horses sold well, as also a few fat Oxen. There was a full attendance of dealers, but trade on the whole was considered dull.

INFLUENZA AMONGST CATTLE AND SHEEP.—The contagious disorder which has now for nearly four years more or less attacked the cattle and sheep brought to the London markets has this year returned with unabated violence. On every market-day both Smithfield market and all the leading lines of intercourse from it exhibit this from the number of sheep which are seen lying in a condition incapacitated for walking. The principal effects on the sheep are shown upon the hoof, as inflammation, and subsequently suppuration takes place round the coronet of the hoof, which from that cause is thrown off, thus differing from the common foot rot, the seat of which is between the claws. The extent of this disease is so great, that numbers of the sheep are obliged to be brought to market in carts, and in cases where the pens are not crowded, the poor animals lie down, and are incapable of again rising. There is no doubt, however, that the complaint is considerably increased by the crowded state of the pens, which are quite inadequate for their accommodation, whilst this circumstance defies the judgment of the butcher, who is thus prevented examining them. The disease is also extremely prevalent amongst cows and other cattle, and since Christmas Mr. Rhodes, the extensive cowkeeper at Kingsland, has lost 170 of the former. Another cowkeeper in the neighbourhood of Gray's Inn-lane also has lost 42 within the last four weeks. In these the chief seat of attack is the lungs, and if not rallied within 48 hours after the attack, their loss is certain. Their hoofs, as well as those of the sheep, are also thrown off, and the tracks from the bleeding limbs of the animals in Smithfield market present a pitiable picture of the sufferings which they must undergo. The epidemic, if such it may be termed, is not so prevalent on the Surrey as the Middlesex side of the river, although the cows at many sheds in Bermondsey, and particularly in the Grange-road, have recently suffered much. Although there is no doubt the quality of the meat must be very much impaired by the prevailing disease, there is no criterion by which such may be distinguished after death from the meat of the healthy animal. The sufferings of the sheep in Smithfield-market, and the impossibility of butchers distinguishing the diseased from the healthy animal, is a very strong plea for the enlargement of the market for their accommodation, particularly as the means for doing it are now offered at a reasonable expense to the corporation.

DISEASE IN CATTLE.—A destructive disease has recently broken out amongst the cattle in certain districts of this county, which has hitherto defied the power of medicine or treatment to overcome. It chiefly affects the lungs, and comes on so imperceptibly, that it has generally advanced to its last stage before the state of the animal is discovered; and by that time the lungs are found to be greatly wasted, and incapable of performing their functions. It does not appear to be contagious; as the cattle on farms situated on each side of those in which it rages, are exempt from the disease; whilst on the farms where it has broken out, cattle at the stall, in the yard, and in the pastures are all alike liable to it. On some farms in the neighbourhood of one town in this county, as many as from 23 to 32 head of cattle have died from its effects, and a number are yet suffering.—*Shrewsbury Chronicle.*

GUANO.—The Liverpool United Brokers' Circular states that 2000 tons of the new manure, called guano, have been recently sold in this town at from 10*l.* to 12*l.* per ton. This quantity will raise ten thousand acres of turnips, as four cwt. per acre has been found sufficient for that purpose. With that quantity, which at the present price will only cost two pounds, we ourselves raised larger crops of turnips last year than we were able to raise with eight pounds' worth of common manure. If the original importers of this valuable manure had been satisfied to offer it to the public at the present price, the consumption would have been ten times as great as it is now; for having tried guano with every description of crop, we do not hesitate to pronounce it the cheapest and most valuable manure ever introduced into this country. As we are buyers, not sellers of the article, our praise of it is at least disinterested.—*Liv. Times.*

GUANO.—The superintendent of the hardy department reported that he had tried several experiments with guano upon plants in pots. In loam, containing one-fiftieth part of this substance, Verbenas and Salvias became luxuriant in about the same degree as if potted in rotten dung. The same plants also flourished exceedingly in sand containing a similar proportion of guano. The same effect, or even a more beneficial action, was produced upon them when peat was substituted for sand. But when rich garden soil was employed with the same proportion of guano, the plants became languid and died. It was therefore inferred that the value of guano as a manure, will depend upon the soil with which it is employed, and that a quantity which would be highly beneficial in poor soil will become deleterious upon land previously rich and well manured.—*Proceedings of the Hort. Soc. No.* 17.

APRIL WHEAT.

TO THE EDITOR OF THE FARMERS' MAGAZINE.

Mr. EDITOR,—As you did me the favour to insert, in your December number, my former communication on the "April Wheat," I must now beg your permission to occupy a small space in the forthcoming number of your valuable journal to state the result of my last year's growth.

I find the portion of my field sown last year with the April wheat measures 8 logs less than 3 acres, and my crop is exactly 26 sacks 2½ bushels, including tail—making on the [average full 9 sacks per acre.

The sample is very good—weighs 12 score 16lbs. per sack—and is put by the millers who have seen it, at the highest market price.

It will be in the recollection of your readers that this wheat was sown on the 19th April, and was reaped on the 12th August—before it had been four months on the ground—and that a small quantity sown on the 20th of May, not only ripened well but produced more than an average crop.

The advantages of such a wheat for late spring-sowing are so self-evident that it would be a waste of time to dwell on them. I shall therefore only call the attention of those farmers who may be disposed this year to give it a trial, to the circumstance, that whenever it has not succeeded well, I have had reason to know or to suspect, that the land had been left too rough. It cannot be made too fine, and should in fact be prepared as if for barley; and the wheat should be sown at the rate of 2 bushels, or 2½ bushels per acre.

I am, Sir, with thanks for your kindness, yours faithfully, A CONSTANT READER.

Wilts, Feb. 20th, 1843.

REVIEW OF THE CORN TRADE
DURING THE MONTH OF FEBRUARY.

The meeting of Parliament has not in any manner dispelled the gloom which for many months now has been suspended over the heads of our agricultural interest. On the contrary, this gloom is rapidly on the increase, the Minister having plainly intimated that, should it be necessary to make any alteration in the corn laws hereafter, the change will render them, if possible, even less protective to the cultivators of the fields at home than they are at the present moment. It is therefore now the general fear and expectation that the system of fixed duties being levied on foreign grain of all descriptions, when entered for home consumption throughout the United Kingdom, will eventually be adopted by the British legislature, and thus will an effectual bar be placed to the progress of agricultural improvements throughout the three kingdoms. These unfavourable prospects very naturally are daily increasing those doubts previously entertained by the entire body of British farmers respecting the result of their future agricultural operations. Even on the best soils, at the present prices of agricultural produce, they are perfectly persuaded that to pursue the present system without better protection, can only end in the loss of the large capital embarked by them in the cultivation of their farms, and afterwards in placing one-half of their field labourers in Union-houses, and reducing the other half to that condition in life which is closely allied to starvation. It is utterly impossible to conceive in what manner the general interests of the British Empire can be promoted by transferring the productive labours of the fields from our own population to the inhabitants of foreign empires, kingdoms, and states; or what advantages can be gained by placing our agricultural labourers on a level with the serfs of Poland and the slaves of Russia. This is, to be sure, a system of liberty and equality which may be suitable to the inhabitants of a kingdom like Utopia, but can never be palatable to the enlightened and comfortably supported subjects of the Queen of the British Isles. It is surely a novel and most extraordinary plan for providing for what the Anti-Corn-Law Leaguers denominate a surplus population, to transfer from them the productive and healthy labours of the fields to" German boors,

Polish serfs, and Russian slaves. It is likewise a still more extraordinary plan for increasing the wealth and adding to the strength and power of the British empire, to cease agricultural improvements at home, to throw millions of acres of land, now eminently productive, out of cultivation, and to cultivate foreign fields instead of our own with British money, which under the existing corn law has already been, and must continue to be, remitted abroad to an immense extent, in exchange for numerous articles of foreign produce and manufactures. These sums of money sent abroad by us, in exchange for foreign grain and for the products of foreign industry, must for the future be employed in foreign agricultural improvements, or embarked in foreign manufacturing establishments. It is inconsistent with experience and common sense for one moment, to suppose that our parting with money can give the slightest encouragement to reciprocity in trade. So far from being hereafter exchanged by its now foreign proprietors for British manufactured goods, its influence will for the future produce widely opposite effects. It is already limiting the quantity and value of our export trade to those countries from which we import provisions, and it must continue to diminish it annually until it arrive at *nil*. We are giving to foreign corn-producing communities the means of speedily competing with us, not only in their own but also in our markets, in the sale of manufactured goods. We are enabling them, by our false liberal principles of trade, to build up manufacturing establishments in all directions, rivalling our own in extent, entirely at the expense of the British Empire. By our corn laws we are extending productive employment annually amongst foreigners, and we are at the same time reducing our own labourers to idleness and to poverty. We are also yearly adding to the strength of what may soon be hostile nations, by actions which are gradually undermining the power and greatness of the British Empire. And for what are these sacrifices made? Certainly for no other national, or rather rational, object than to increase the riches of a few of the cotton lords. These traders want to manufacture cheaper than they do at present, but this benefit to themselves they cannot obtain unless by the reduction of the wages now paid to their artisans and workmen, the preliminary step to which is the reduction of the prices of the necessaries of life. To obtain this their end, they care not for the safety of the national creditors, nor have they any objection to place the foreign slave and the British labourer on a perfect equality in mental intelligence and in worldly circumstances. Under an entirely free trade in grain with foreign states, or under any fixed duty on the importation of grain into this country, it is vain to expect that fifty millions sterling of taxes and upwards can be annually collected in the British Empire, and the receivers of the public dividends must be the first sufferers from any deficiency occurring hereafter in the revenue. Without a perfect system of protection to industry at home, the general annual expenditure of the inhabitants of the United Kingdom cannot be, for any length of time, maintained at its present amount, and the consumption of all tax-paying articles must be also eventually very materially reduced by this cause. The certain consequences of an actual freedom in the foreign corn trade, or the imposition of fixed rates of duty on foreign grain

when entered here for home use, must be, we repeat, ruinous to the industry of all classes in the British Empire, and must place in great danger that sacred property which is embarked by the fundholders on the faith and honour of the English nation. But even this interest, however important it undoubtedly is, is still vastly inferior in its intrinsic value to the one which the industrious classes at present possess in productive employment. This is the real property of the great majority of the British community, and out of it springs the real wealth of the nation. To transfer even a portion of this property to foreigners is to defraud British labourers, and, as soon as the mist of prejudice is removed from their eyes, an universal demand will be made by them, whether they be employed in agricultural or in commercial pursuits, on the legislature for protection to their labour, which now affords them the means of comfortable living, against the interference of foreign labour in the British market. To employ Poles in the production of wheat, is to defraud the Essex farm labourer of a part of his property; and to employ foreign bootmakers, hatters, or any other foreign handicraft, for British consumers, is to deprive British labourers of their legitimate property in the production of similar articles at home. During the whole of last month, the fishmongers, for instance, have been most abundantly supplying the people of England with Dutch fresh salmon and with foreign caught fresh fish of every description, which is an extraordinary plan for increasing the means of our fishing interest for the payment of tax-paying articles of consumption. There must therefore, we repeat, soon arise loud and universal complaints amongst workmen of every denomination, against tampering with the corn laws in the British legislature, and petition on petition will be then presented to Parliament for the re-enactment of many laws, latterly either repealed or greatly modified, by which our internal industry—which had for many years been properly protected, and under which the people generally existed in a flourishing condition, and the British Empire rose to the greatest eminence amongst the nations of the earth—may be again restored to its pristine state of real prosperity. Within the United Kingdom we at present possess, and the people universally are acquainted with the fact, in the greatest abundance, the means of supporting triple our present population in that independent state in which the British people have for generations now been accustomed to live; and until these means be exhausted it is in the extreme improper to attempt to reduce them to a level with the working classes in any part of Europe, Asia, or America. The waste lands alone in Great Britain and Ireland, which at present are entirely useless to the people, but at the same time are perfectly capable of being brought into the highest state of cultivation, render the idea of a surplus population truly ridiculous and contemptible. We have immense resources for converting these wastes into grain and grass fields, and certainly we have abundance of money at present unemployed, which, under wise regulations, may be most productively employed in these important undertakings. Lands may be reclaimed from the banks of rivers, from arms of the sea, and from morasses themselves, by the labour of man, and the capital embarked eventually must be doubled and tripled by operations of this description. Nothing which manufacturers can produce, can be placed in the scale against the advantages which may easily be obtained from further agricultural improvements. The products of manufacturers speedily perish, but agricultural improvement is, not like them, the plant of a kindly sun. It does not, like them, rise quickly to its height, nor does it soon decay. As it approaches to perfection it benefits mankind, and it blesses the human race for many centuries afterwards. The labours of the manufacturer are widely different from those of the farmer also, in the health and real happiness of the workmen. The labourers of the manufacturer breathe a heated atmosphere, and are subjected to numerous complaints; whilst the agricultural labourer does his quiet duty in the fields, where he inhales only the pure air of heaven, and consequently he lives in comparative contentment with his condition in life. To compare the state of the agricultural labourer with that of the manufacturing workman, is only necessary to establish the great truth, that the former is infinitely superior in his habits to the latter, and, therefore, that to sacrifice the one to the other would be an act of the greatest injustice to the working classes generally in this country, in as far as the one enjoys sturdy health, whilst the squalid appearance of the other universally denotes a broken up constitution; and therefore, we repeat, it is the duty of the legislature to give the greatest encouragement to agricultural pursuits, in as far as to do so best serves the real interests of the commonwealth. The wages of labour cannot be maintained, we again assert, at their present rates, in any department of industry, unless the cultivators of the soil be fairly protected in all our markets of consumption against agricultural produce of foreign growth; and the same justice should be extended to manufacturing labourers, to artisans, and in fact to every interest in the state. The admission of foreign goods into consumption should be prohibited altogether unless on the payment of duties sufficiently protective to industry at home, and, at the same time, adding to the national revenue. By these means alone can the capital of the British Empire be retained at home for the public use, and profitably applied to the productive employment of the British people. The experience of farming during the last year is as little satisfactory to the cultivator of the British soil as are his future prospects. For that portion of the last wheat crop which he has already sent into consumption, the prices received by him have not remunerated him for the expenses of its production; and the millers' demand generally has been during that period supplied by wheats of foreign growth, on which the British importers have sustained a heavy loss of money. Under the new corn law, good and sound wheaten bread is now selling in the metropolis at one penny halfpenny a pound; but the wages of labour render this price far dearer to the consumer than it was when he paid 10d. for the four-pound loaf; and this reduction in his pay is mainly, if not entirely, occasioned by the transfer of a portion of our productive labour from our own to the workmen of foreign communities. Thus both manufacturers and agriculturists are now paying heavy penalties for the illustration of the principles of free trade with foreign nations; and some speedy alteration must be made in the present system, if our legislators be inclined to avert from the British nation still greater calamities. The manufacturers complain of want of markets everywhere for their goods; and the farmers know not whether their prosperity for the future depends on good or on damaged crops. In all departments of industry, in fact, confusion of the worst description prevails. The manufacturer can find no remunerating market for his finer descriptions of goods; because the agriculturist obtains not for his produce prices nearly equal to the expenses of growing it. Money is collected into large masses by the capitalist, who can find no channel at home in which he can productively to himself send it again into circulation. Legal protection to agricultural and to manufacturing pursuits can alone alter this unwholesome condition of British society. With protection against foreign agricultural produce in all our markets of consumption, abundance of money will be speedily invested in agricultural improvements; and soon afterwards must prosperity again attend the labours of the industrious. It will then soon become sufficiently apparent, that in the United Kingdom means exist for supporting triple her present population, and for productively employing our commercial, fishing, and manufacturing labourers, if the number of them should hereafter be doubled. As matters are at present, the farmers find themselves in the distressing position of not knowing whether abundant or damaged crops will in future be most advantageous to themselves, and therefore they have paid little attention to the seasonable check which the winter wheat plants received during the progress of the last month. That this occurrence must tend to increase the chances of an abundant wheat crop next harvest, cannot be disputed; but it may also tend still to reduce farther the capital now embarked in agricultural pursuits. Indeed, the markets seem already to be labouring under its influence; for the supplies of wheat, and particularly of north-country flour, have since our last publication considerably exceeded the demand, and to effect sales declining prices must be submitted to. It was, some time ago, generally supposed that, after the turn of the year, the wheat trade would have assumed a more cheering aspect; but in this hope the cultivators of the soil have been as much deceived as they have been since the meeting of parliament, by the conduct of the farmers' friends, placed by their exertions in the House of Commons. At the one event they are much disappointed, whilst the latter circumstance fills the great majority of them with amazement.

The information received from North America, since our last publication, is neither of recent date nor is it interesting either to traders or to agriculturists in this country. In all the corn export markets throughout the United States, the supplies of wheat and flour were much larger than the demand required; prices had consequently given way considerably, and a still further depreciation in the value of agricultural produce was confidently looked for by the exporters. The low prices in England did not encourage speculation at these dates, for a confident opinion was entertained that the sellers must eventually submit to those prices which would render shipments both of wheat and flour to this country practicable. In the meantime, shipments to a considerable extent continued to be made of dairy farming produce, and of cured provisions of various descriptions. Even the advantages to be obtained in this country from ship-biscuit baking had not escaped the attention of Jonathan, and considerable shipments of this manufactured article continued to be made to this country, and goes into consumption here, we presume, for the benefit of our bakers at home. In return for agricultural products, Jonathan at present receives not one article on which British industry has been employed, unless on the payment of heavy duties, partly for the protection of American industry at home, and partly for financial purposes. In this way, certainly, the American system of reciprocity in trade is gradually becoming wonderfully successful. Manufactures of all descriptions are rapidly increasing amongst them, because they are perfectly protected against foreign competition, and large sums of specie are weekly arriving in their various ports, to pay for the balance of their export commerce. Money consequently had become so abundant throughout the American Union, that a considerable portion of the loan which the American government had latterly but vainly endeavoured to raise in Europe, had been advanced by a few merchants in New York, paying par for a six per cent stock. We dare say that these bonds will find their way speedily into this country; be purchased by our capitalists, and the annual interest on them eventually be repudiated by our transatlantic brethren. Thus do our corn laws encourage the shipment of specie to foreign states, in exchange for foreign agricultural produce. Thus does our system of free trade give most productive employment to foreign workmen, and drive our own labourers into Union-houses, or into destitution even of a worse description. During the month preceding the latest dates, upwards of half a million sterling, in specie, had been received from this country by the American Union, whilst scarcely any goods of British manufacture had arrived in that period. Still larger sums of cash have been since then forwarded to America, and the shipments made of goods are still less. Thus progresses reciprocity in commerce with that country.

The season of the year having suspended the corn trade between the ports in the Mediterranean and Black seas, and those in the United Kingdom, the reports from these markets during the last month have not been interesting. The depressed state of the corn trade in England had, for a time, rendered sales of wheat for exportation impossible, and had reduced the quotations to rates nearly nominal, more particularly in the Adriatic. In all those markets the stock of wheat was gradually accumulating, and its value decreasing. Prices at Trieste were quoted at 26s. to 28s. per quarter, but no business had been latterly transacted there, and it was the general opinion that actual buyers would have been supplied even at lower rates; the crops in that country being large, and immediate sales being preferred by the proprietors, to holding for still higher rates. The stock of beans had then been considerably reduced, and an improvement in their value had occurred, which rendered them too dear for shipment to our markets. In the lower ports of Italy the trade was in an equal degree depressed, no animation whatever being exhibited in any article of agricultural produce. When the season, however, removes the danger of heating created by the length of the voyage to Great Britain, it is not improbable that exceedingly low prices may encourage speculative shipments being made during the next summer and harvest months.

The internal navigation betwixt the wheat districts in the interior and the shipping ports in the Baltic and the German ocean, being at present interrupted by the elements, the information received, since our last publication, from Dantzig, Rostock, Hamburg, and the other foreign corn markets in the north of Europe, is not of any interest, for scarcely any business was doing in any description of grain. The prices of wheat at Dantzig were nominally quoted at the latest dates, at somewhere about 35s. per quarter, free on board; but the future value of this article depended much on the advices which may hereafter be transmitted to the foreign corn merchants from Mark-lane. Lower down in the Baltic and without that sea, wheat prices were proportionately lower, and the future depended on similar circumstances. One lesson, however, may be drawn from the state of the corn trade in America and in Europe at the present moment. It may shew clearly to the advocates of a free corn trade, or of fixed rates of import duties, how injurious these changes would be to the best interests of the British people. Dantzig wheat, without duty, could at the present prices in the ports of shipment, be sold here, to a good profit, at 42s. per quarter. In quality it is certainly equal to any grown in the United Kingdom, and here it cannot be produced at any such rates, if the interest on our national debt is to be paid in future, and if our labourers are to be permitted to live in the comfortable manner to which they have heretofore been accustomed. But even under the existing corn law, it is generally expected that when the season permits, we shall be inundated with grain from the Baltic, for its value will conform with the prices to be obtained in Mark-lane.

In the barley trade no improvement whatever has occurred during the last month. On the contrary, the supply has regularly exceeded the demand, and sales have been consequently forced at declining prices. This circumstance, so exceedingly injurious to the barley farmer, has its origin in various causes, the principal one of which most unfortunately is to be found in the reduced consumption of pure and unadulterated beer by the great mass of the people. Herein too are the evils of reduced rates of wages operating most disadvantageously, not only on the interests of agriculture, but most particularly so on the comforts of the entire population itself. When our internal industry was duly protected by law, more particularly the profitable cultivation of the soil, the home market universally consumed such quantities of manufactures and of various other articles of necessaries and luxuries, as gave much productive labour to various descriptions of industry, and remunerated the workmen with excellent wages. The new theory, however, of political economy, and the almost fatal practice which we have now for sometime had of the principles of a false system of free trade, have, even already, reduced the wages of labour throughout Great Britain so very materially, that although the people have the inclination, still they have not the means to consume their wonted regular quantity of beer. From this cause have arisen the late falling away in quantity in the manufacture of barley into malt, the at present great heaviness in the sale of, and continued depression in the value of barley, and, what the Chancellor of the Exchequer considers to be the greatest evil of all, the immense falling away which occurred during the last financial quarter, in the excise department of the public revenue. The present state of the corn trade generally, and that depression in prices which is gradually depriving the farmers of the capital which they have em-

barked in the cultivation of their fields, must hereafter, however, add more and more to the present
depression, in proportion to that diminution which
is now annually occurring in the means of the great
body of consumers in the home market to pay for
their usual quantity of goods for the use of their
families and of themselves. Already has the rapid
decline in the home market, in the consumption of
manufactured goods, thrown hundreds of thousands
of human beings out of their daily bread, and the
future prospect of receiving remunerating wages for
their labour hereafter is gloomy in the extreme.
The barley grower is severely feeling the decreased
value of his produce, nor has he any more cheering
prospects before him than the great body of consumers of beer. In one way most certainly
have the ministers of the crown means to diminish,
if not entirely to remove, the complaints at present
made by the barley farmers of the want of remunerating prices for their crops, and by the great
body of consumers, that beer is too dear when
compared with the wages now paid to them for
their labour. To this channel of national relief we
have often directed the attention of our readers,
and we shall continue to call the public attention
to this deplorable state of affairs until the legislature be pleased to apply a real remedy to this evil.
It originates, in a certain degree, in the weight of
the malt duty, and also in the manner in which the
maltster's operations are interfered with by the
absurd malting regulations of the excise office.
The high duty now charged on malt not only restricts the quantity of barley manufactured into
malt, but it is likewise the cause of that adulteration in the quality of beer which is so extremely
pernicious to the health of the lower orders of consumers, and also detrimental to the revenue itself.
A moderate rate of duty on all taxed articles
universally places much more money in the
treasury than is done by oppressive duties, and the
whole history of the malt-tax perfectly establishes
this fact. Its present high rate is gradually decreasing the quantity of barley converted into malt.
Indeed, at present the quantity of malt now consumed by the common brewers is reduced considerably under four millions of quarters; but to
remit in some degree a portion of the malt tax,
would certainly very materially increase the quantity of malt at present manufactured in Great
Britain. On properly dried malt the duty now
is somewhere about 25s. per quarter, which in
metallic money is fully as high as the former
charge of 34s. 9d. was in a paper circulating medium. It is nearly one hundred per cent. on the
value of the raw material, and the natural consequence of this oppressive charge is an annual decline in the quantity of barley now manufactured
into malt. The malt duty of 34s. 9d. never paid
more into the treasury in one year than three millions sterling. In the second year, however, after
its reduction to 20s. per quarter, upwards of six
millions of quarters of barley were converted into
malt. Even this quantity, however, when used by
the brewer, served out beer in very limited quantities to the entire population. Not much above
one-half of that quantity of malt is now used in
the brewer's trade, and the consequence is, that
adulteration of beer has latterly become so prevalent amongst the minor retailers. A large loss
of revenue is likewise a result of the same cause.
To reduce the malt duty to 1s. per bushel, will in
a great measure remedy these evils, and that, too,
within a very short period after its reduction. The

increased consumption of malt will add to the present sum paid into the treasury from this source
of revenue very considerably; and eventually it
will more than triple the quantity of barley converted into malt under the existing system of restriction. At a time when it is proposed to reduce
the duty now charged on foreign wines, which even
now is upwards of thirty per cent. lower than the
duty charged on British made spirits, surely some
attention should be paid by the ministers of the
crown to the malt duty, which is chiefly paid by the
productive classes of society. On the mass of the
English people a material reduction in the malt
duty would confer a great benefit, and in doing so
the legislature would be only doing to them an act
of common justice. The benefit, however, would
not be confined to the lower grades of British society, for the alteration would be fully as advantageous to the proprietors themselves of barley
lands. The increased consumption of beer would
render necessary the cultivation of at least two
millions of acres of land, at present entirely unproductive, in addition to the lands at present in
barley cultivation. This conversion of waste
lands into barley fields, would add upwards of one
million sterling annually to the income of land
proprietors; and the after-profits arising from
their cultivation would much more than pay for
the additional expense which the additional consumption of beer would occasion amongst the
people. Instead of transporting many thousands
of our agricultural labourers for the purpose of
cultivating the wilds of the Canadas, surely common sense and the common feelings of humanity
should dictate their employment within the British
islands, so long as one acre of land remains
in a state of perfect nature, and so long as
even the best cultivated lands at home are still
capable of much more important improvement by
the application to them of capital, of labour, and of
legal protection to the produce of that labour. If
the malt duty, however, be unnaturally high, the
duty at present charged in England on the manufacture of spirits is extravagantly high, being nearly
three hundred and fifty per cwt. on the value of
British spirits themselves. This excessive duty
renders the profits and the pleasures of the smuggling trade irresistible to the people, and is a great
corrupter of public morality; it encourages the consumption of illicit spirits, defrauds the public
revenue, and destroys the health and the characters
of all employed in this nefarious system of trade.
In Ireland and in Scotland smuggled spirits do
not at present exist, because low duties have rendered their importation not sufficiently profitable.
In England, however, high duties render the system
widely different, for at least one-half of the spirits
now consumed in this portion of the United Kingdom is of the worst description, and pays not one
farthing of duty to the public revenue. There is no
cause whatever for the duty on home-made spirits
in Scotland and in Ireland being lower than it is
in England, for we do not find that the ladies of
Lambeth, and of the Seven Dials, are more prone to
the consumption of spirits than are those of Scotland and of Ireland. At all events, if we may be
allowed to judge from appearances, we are persuaded that excessive duties do not cure the evil;
for the smuggler renders the supply at all times
fully as large as the demand requires. To equalize
the duties on home-made and on colonial spirits
would speedily remedy the evils of the present
system. To fix the duty throughout the United

Kingdom at 5s. per proof gallon would improve the revenue, because it would destroy the temptation to the illicit importation of spirits, and the morals and health of the people would likewise be improved by consuming pure and wholesome home-made spirits, instead of the deleterious and pernicious trash with which they are at present supplied by the smuggler. The reduction of the duty on home-made spirits in England, and the suppression of the smuggler's trade, would open a channel for the consumption of at least half a million of quarters of British-grown grain, in addition to the quantity consumed under the present system by the distillers of the United Kingdom. The excise taxes require revision in a far greater degree than those of the customs did last year. By the reductions made in the latter, a vast deal of productive employment has been transferred by the legislature from British labourers to those of foreign nations, without in any manner whatever serving one interest within the British empire. Manufactured barley latterly paid one quarter of the public expenditure, and if the excise laws were modified, as they certainly should be, this article would contribute still more largely towards the national income.

In our last review of the state of the corn trade, we reported the trade in oats to labour under much depression, and prices to have nearly reached the lowest rates possible. During the last month we are unable to quote the slightest amendment, and to say that this article is not now of less value than it was in January last, would be but little cheering to the producers. To the farmers in Great Britain, oat prices now are not nearly so interesting as they were twenty or thirty years ago, because they are not now so generally cultivated either in England or in Scotland as they formerly were; but to the agricultural interest in Ireland, the state of the oat markets in Great Britain is in the highest degree important. In that island agricultural improvements have been slowly but surely progressing during the last quarter of a century; and the ready sale which Irish agricultural produce of all descriptions has met with in all the British markets, has been the chief spur to enterprise in the sister country. The attention of the farmers there has heretofore been chiefly directed to oats, and they cultivated them not only to their own advantage, but likewise to that of the British consumers. Moderate prices were sufficient for the farmers' profit, and were, of course, of much consequence to the great body of the general buyers in this country of this article. At the present value, however, it is almost impossible that they can be produced in Ireland, and still more impossible to grow them with any chance of profit in Great Britain. The existing depressed value is not occasioned by unusually large supplies, nor is there any visible falling away in the quantity required for general consumption. The uncertainty which the alteration in the corn laws has created in the United Kingdom, respecting the future value of agricultural produce, is the chief, if not the sole, cause of that dulness in the corn trade which at present exists so extensively, and which is doing so much injury to the best interests of the British community. In London a great part of the Irish supply of oats has for several months been selling at about 16s. per quarter; and when the expenses of preparing them for the voyage by kiln-drying and of shipping them, the after charges of freight, sea insurance, and London expenses of sale, are deducted from that price, we strongly suspect that little

remains to pay the farmer for their production, and still less is left to pay the land proprietor for the rents of the fields on which these oats have been produced, The great fear at present entertained by our growers is, that the highest duty now charged on foreign oats cannot prohibit the importation of the finest qualities of them at any time into this country ; the maximum duty not being more than the difference in price is betwixt the best descriptions of foreign oats and the average price of those grown at home. The current year, therefore, in every probability, will shew whether foreigners can, under the present law, undersell Irish oat growers in the British markets. That a contest of this description should have been sanctioned by the British legislature is certainly not one of the smallest wonders of these times of liberty, for in it is distinctly included the future continuation of those principles on which our empire has been mainly raised. The trial hereafter must be whether Great Britain is for the future to employ Irish or foreign labourers in the production of oats, consumed by her population ; whether these oats are to be carried under the British or under foreign flags, and whether the money to be paid for these oats is to continue in circulation amongst the productive classes in the British Empire, or to be remitted to foreign nations, for the improvement of foreign fields, and for the encouragement of foreign manufactures. The experiment is certainly a dangerous one, for on its issue depends also, in a material degree, the future progress of agricultural improvements in Ireland, and the future productive employment of the agricultural portion of her population. In Ireland upwards of eight millions of the human race are at present supported chiefly by agricultural pursuits ; and it appears to us hazardous in the extreme to place in jeopardy the very means, limited though they be, by which they are now maintained, even should the wages of the manufacturing labourers in Great Britain (amounting, as they do, to something considerably less than half a million of males) be doubled by the depression of the wages of the Irish population. Great Britain is, however, considered by foreign agricultural and manufacturing workmen to be extremely wealthy, and they accordingly are hovering around her, like hungry vultures, to have their share of the prey. At this certainly, on their part, no wonder need be entertained, for they are only acting on the great laws of nature ; but the wonder is how any person calling himself a British statesman, can encourage and promote these most extraordinary and violent attacks on the sacred property of the industrious labourers in the United Kingdom, by transferring even the smallest portion of it to foreign workmen ; for it must be eventually a fatal policy to pay foreigners for labour which can be well performed at home—particularly when multitudes of our own workmen cannot procure any labour, and are consequently reduced to a state of perfect destitution. The certain consequences of persevering in the present falsely-called system of reciprocity in trade, must be the transportation to the colonies of multitudes of valuable labourers annually, and the reduction of still greater numbers of them to the union-houses. It is not by means such as these that the public revenue can be rendered equal to the public expenditure ; nor indeed can it be maintained at anything like its present amount by reducing to pauperism a vast portion of the productive classes within the United Kingdom.

CURRENCY PER IMP. MEASURE.

FEB. 20.

WHEAT, Essex and Kent, red	46	52	White 50 54 58	
Irish	46	48	Do. 48	50
Old, red	—	—	Do. .. —	—
RYE, old	32	—	New... 32	—
BARLEY, Grinding 24 27 Malting	30	32	Chevalier 31	33
Irish..................	21	23	Bere .19 20	22
MALT, Suffolk and Norfolk	56	58	Brown.. 50	54
Kingston and Ware	56	60	Chevalier 60	—
OATS, Yorksh. & Lincolnsh., feed	20	23	Potato.. 23	25
Youghall and Cork black	17	18	Cork, white 18	19
Dublin	17	18	Westport 18	19
Waterford, white 17	18	19	Black .. 17	18
Newry	20	21		
Galway	15	17		
Scotch feed	22	—	Potato.. 21	24
Clonmel 17	18	19	Limerick18 19 21	
Londonderry...........	18	19	Sligo .. 18	19
BEANS, Tick, new.............	30	32	Old.... 32	34
PEAS, Grey...................	31	33	Maple.. 31	33
White	32	33	Boilers . 35	38
SEED, Rape......—l. —l.	Irish..—l. —l. per last.			
Linseed, Baltic....40	46	Odessa 48		
English Red Clover....	—	— per cwt.		
White	-			
Mustard, White 7	10	brown 8 11 per bush		
Tares, old 28	30	new 36 40 per qr.		
FLOUR, Town-made 42	45	Suffolk — 36 pr sk. of 280 lbs		
Stockton and Norfolk, —	36			

FOREIGN GRAIN AND FLOUR IN BOND.

WHEAT, Dantzic	—	—
Hamburg	—	—
Rostock	—	—
BARLEY	20	—
OATS, Brew....................	15	17 Feed... 12 14
BEANS	18	24
PEAS.........................	20	24
FLOUR, American, per brl......	22	24 Baltic .. — 22

IMPERIAL AVERAGES.

Week ending	Wheat.	Barley.	Oats.	Rye.	Beans.	Peas.
Jan. 7th	47 1	26 5	17 2	31 7	28 0	29 11
14th	47 10	26 5	16 11	29 4	27 5	29 7
21st	49 1	27 2	17 0	28 2	27 7	29 5
28th	49 3	27 8	17 0	30 4	27 10	30 4
Feb. 4th	48 1	27 5	16 9	28 2	27 3	29 11
11th	47 5	27 1	16 11	30 1	27 5	30 1
Aggregate average of the six weeks which regulates the duty	48 1	27 0	16 11	29 7	27 7	29 11
Duties payable in London till Wednesday next inclusive, and at the Outports till the arrival of the mail of that day from London ..	20 0	9 0	8 0	11 6	11 6	11 6
Do. on grain from British possessions out of Europe........	5 0	2 0	2 0	1 6	1 0	1 0

COMPARATIVE PRICES OF GRAIN.

WEEKLY AVERAGES by the Imp. Quarter, from the Gazette, of Friday last, Feb. 17th, 1843.		AVERAGES from the corresponding Gazette in the last year, Friday, Feb. 18th, 1842.	
	s. d.		s. d.
WHEAT	47 5	WHEAT	60 0
BARLEY	27 1	BARLEY	28 5
OATS	16 11	OATS	19 8
RYE	30 1	RYE................	37 1
BEANS..............	27 5	BEANS..............	32 5
PEAS	30 1	PEAS	33 11

PRICES OF SEEDS.

FEB. 20.

The demand for Cloverseed was excessively slow this morning, and considerable difficulty was experienced in making sales at last week's quotations. In other descriptions of seeds there was scarcely anything passing, and prices remained nominally unvaried. The enquiry for both Linseed and Rapeseed Cakes was slow and the latter was somewhat easier to buy.

Linseed, English, sowing 48	56			
Baltic	—	— crushing 42	45 per qr.	
Mediter. & Odessa 45	46			
Large, foreign....	—	—		
Clover, English, red	40	58	white 42	60 per cwt.
Flemish, pale'....	42	46	fine.. 50	53
New Hamburgh ..	none		do.. 40	60
Old do...........	40	43	do..	none
French	40	48	do..	none
Coriander..............	10	16	old.... 16	20 per cwt.
Mustard, brown, new ..	9	11	white.. 12	16 p.bush.
Trefoil, new............	18	22	old.... 12	16
Rapeseed, English new..	32l.	35l. per ton.		
Linseed Cakes, English..	9l.	10s. to 10l.		
Do. Foreign..	5l.	15s. to 6l.		
Rapeseed Cakes........	5l.	10s. to 5l. 15s.		
Hempseed, small........	35	38	large .. 46	48 per qr.
Rye Grass, English......	30	42	Scotch 18	40
Tares, winter	—	—	New 4s 0d 5s 0d p.bush.	
Canary, new...........	62	63	fine 64	65 per qr.
Carraway, old	—	—	new 42	44

PRICES OF HOPS.

BOROUGH, MONDAY, Feb. 20.

The quantity of business doing is rather limited, the buyers appearing to think that the quotations are run up somewhat beyond the sum they ought to pay; there is notwithstanding a short supply, and much firmness in the rates, which we quote as under :—

Pockets 1841 : 60s. to 70s. ; choice do., 70s. to 84s. Bags 1841 : 60s. to 80s. per cwt. Pockets, old olds, 35s. to 42s. per cwt.

Pockets 1842: East Kent, 101s. to 141s. ; Weald of Kent, 80s. to 89s. ; Sussex, 77s. to 83s. ; and Farnham, 140s. to 160s. per cwt.

POTATO MARKET.

SOUTHWARK, WATERSIDE, Feb. 20.

Owing to the weather during the past week being colder, and more seasonable, the demand has consequently been brisker, and our market has had a much firmer appearance than of late, but without any material variation on our former quotations. Present prices as annexed :—

	Per ton.		Per ton.
	s. s.		s. s.
York Reds	— to 60	Wisbeach .... 40 to 45	
Scotch do.	50 to 55	Jersey and Guernsey	
Devons............	— to 55	Blues.......... 50 to 55	
Kent, Essex & Suffolk		Yorkshire Prince	
Whites..............	— to 45	Regents ...... 45 to 50	
	Yorkshire Shaws, for planting, 50s.		

WOOL MARKETS.

BRITISH.

LEEDS, Feb. 17.—We have not any material alteration to report in the markets during the present week, either as to demand or prices.

WAKEFIELD, Feb. 17.—We cannot report any improvement in any branch of the Wool trade ; on the contrary less is doing, and in order to effect sales a shade lower prices have been submitted to.

LIVERPOOL, Feb. 18.

SCOTCH.—The same inactivity pervades our market for all kinds of Scotch Wool. Laid Highland is light in stock, and prices are maintained ; white Highland is scarce, and enquired for at our quotations. There is very little good cross in our market to offer, and inferior is quite neglected. There is rather more doing in Cheviot this week, but at lower prices.

	s.	d.	s.	d.
Laid Highland Wool, per 24 lbs..	6	6 to	7	0
White do. do...........	9	0	9	0
Laid Crossed do..unwashed..	8	0	9	3
Do. washed do.............	8	6	10	6
Do. Cheviot unwashed do.	8	3	10	6
Do. washed	12	0	15	0
White do. do.	18	0	21	6

Import and export of Foreign and Colonial Sheeps' Wool and Goat's Wool, into and from the ports of Great Britain, for the years 1840, 1841, 1842, with a statement of the quantity of lbs. of Foreign Wool upon which duty has been paid for home consumption, compiled principally from official returns.

FOREIGN IMPORTS.

1842.	London.	Liverpool.	Hull.	Total.
	bales.	bales.	bales.	bales.
German	11,133	22,581	37,904	49,100
Spanish	2,834	2,074	4,658	4,958
Russian	11,606	858	1,303	13,916
Bristol.........				19
South America...	2,097	18,712		20,809
Africa..........	230	5		235
Turkey and Goats	6,867	714		7,581
Sundry	69	210		279

QUANTITY OF FOREIGN WOOL CLEARED FOR HOME CONSUMPTION.

	London.	Liverpool.	Hull.	Total.
	lbs.	lbs.	lbs.	lbs.
1842	9,388,274	9,427,033	17,313,069	30,981,376
1841	10,283,517	6,083,870	17,246,011	33,553,398
1840	12,873,228	9,190,397	16,251,517	38,304,142

COLONIAL IMPORTS.

1842.	LONDON.		LIVERPOOL.		TOTAL.	
	bales.	Weighing about lbs.	bales.	Weighing about lbs.	bales.	Weighing about lbs.
New South Wales....	32,005	8,248,415	5,531	1,421,407	37,536	9,669,893
Leith............	473	192,561			473	192,561
Van Dieman's Land.	14,071	3,978,543			14,071	3,978,543
Cape of Good Hope.	6,431	1,382,665			6,431	1,382,665
East Indies......	5,123	1,770,549	6,733	2,222,586	11,865	4,003,435
Sundry	24	6,108	9	2,313	33	8,481

	LONDON.		LIVERPOOL.		TOTAL.	
	bales.	lbs.	bales.	lbs.	bales.	lbs.
1842	57,795	14,086,881	12,973	3,746,605	70,409	18,854,557
1841	54,764	13,845,555	13,172	4,021,845	67,936	17,867,400
1840	41,573	10,911,037	11,179	2,947,437	52,752	13,955,074

TOTAL IMPORT, FOREIGN AND COLONIAL.

	Foreign.	Colonial.	Total.
	bales.	bales.	bales.
1842	96,897	70,409	167,306
1841	148,080	67,936	216,016
1840	137,198	52,752	189,950

EXPORTS, INCLUDING ENGLISH.

	London.	Liverpool.	Total.
	lbs.	lbs.	lbs.
1842	1,836,851	1,693,285	3,530,136
1841	1,779,896	845,149	2,625,045
1840	717,405	188,363	905,768

Bales.

From the foregoing statement it will be seen that the decrease in the import of Foreign Wool as compared with the year 1841 amounts to the large quantity of.......... 52,083

This decrease, however, consists principally in the quantity of small bales imported from the West Coast of South America, the import of which into London and Liverpool was

  in 1841 54,883
            1842 20,809
    Decrease .... —34,026

In German and Danish, the quantity imported into London, Liverpool, Hull, and Goole was, in 1841 63,092
                1842 49,048
    Decrease .... , —14,008
In Spanish there is also a decrease of 2,383
            —————50,416
            1,667

To which, adding the increase in Imports from Russia, viz........ 1842 13,916
                1841 10,634
            —————3,282

    Leaves 4,949

For decrease in the imports of other descriptions of foreign Wool, not enumerated above, and which will be found to consist principally in Turkey, Italian, &c.

The quantity of foreign Wool which has actually paid duty in the past year for home consumption has not decreased in anything like the same proportion as the imports; the amount on which duty was paid in
    1841 being 33,553,398 lbs.
    1842 „ 30,981,376 „

Showing a decrease of .... 2,572,022 „

Or rather more than two and a-half millions of pounds, whereas the weight of the bales above named as short imported would, at the lowest calculation, be upwards of nine millions of pounds. It is also worthy of remark that the decrease in the amount on which duty was paid in 1841 as compared with 1840, showed a much greater decrease of consumption of foreign Wool than the past year, being very little short of five millions of pounds, which decrease however was nearly balanced by an increased import of Colonial, which latter we assume to be entirely used for our home manufactures; and from this it would appear that in the year 1841 there was no decrease in the total quantity of Wool consumed for manufacturing purposes.

In Colonial Wool there has been an increase upon the total import in 1842, viz.,

	1841.		1842.
New South Wales	39,372	..	38,099
Van Diemen's Land ..	12,988	..	14,071
Cape of Good Hope ..	4,951	..	6,431
East India...........	10,579	..	11,865
	67,890		70,466
			67,890
			2,576

Bales, which would average, one description with another, about 780,000lbs. against the decrease above alluded to in foreign Wool of two and a-half millions of pounds, thus showing a decrease in the actual consumption of Wool of about 1,700,000 lbs. in the year 1842.

FOREIGN.

CITY, Feb. 20.—The imports of wool into London last week were 500 bales, of which 365 bales were from Turkey, 122 from Rio de Janiero, and 13 from Germany.

The public sales of Colonial wool commenced on Thursday, the quantity advertised for the whole series being about 9000 bales, and which it will take till the close of next week to offer. At first the attendance was barely so good as at the last auctions, but since it has improved, and may now be called fair; the wool which was partly withdrawn on the opening, and which has gone lower, having since shewn a tendency to rally a little. Perhaps as the better flocks come forward prices may rise a little.

PRICES OF MANURES.

Subjoined are the present prices of several sorts of manure:—

Hunt's Bone dust, 18s. per qr.
Hunt's Half-inch Bone, 16s. per qr.
Hunt's Artificial Guano, 8*l*. per ton.
Rape Dust, 7*l*. to 8*l*. per ton.
Rape Cake, 6*l*. 10s. to 7*l*. per ton.
Rags, 4*l*. to 4*l*. 10s. per ton.
Graves, 6*l*. 10s. per ton.
Gypsum, at the waterside, 32s. 6d. per ton; landed and housed, 38s. to 42s. per ton, according to quantity.
Agricultural Salt, 34s. per ton.
Lance's Carbon, 12s. per qr.
Ditto Humus, 14s. per qr.
Soap Ashes, 10s. per ton.
Poittevin's Patent Disinfected Manure, 13s. 6d. per qr.
Poittevin's Highly Concentrated Manure, 30s. per qr.
Nitrate of Soda, 18s. to 18s. 6d. (duty paid) per cwt.
Nitrate Potash (saltpetre) 26s. 6d. per cwt.
Petre Salt, 4s. per cwt.
Willey Dust, 4*l*. 4s. per ton.
The Urate of the London Manure Company, 5*l*. per ton.
Chie-fou, 21s. per cwt.
Daniell's new Bristol Manure, 8s. per qr.
Huut's new Fertilizer, 13s. 4d. per qr.
Grimwade's Preparation for Turnip Fly, 10s. 6d. per packet, sufficient for three acres.
Wolverhampton Compost (Alexander's), 12s. per qr., subject to carriage to London, or forwarded from Wolverhampton.
Guano, 10s. to 14s. per cwt, according to quantity.
Potter's Artificial Guano, 15s. per cwt.
Muriate of Ammonia, 24s. per cwt.
Muriate of Lime, 12s. per cwt.
Clarke's Compost, 3*l*. 12s. 6d. per hhd., sufficient for three acres.
Wright's Alkalies, 28s. and 42s. per cwt.
Soda Ash, 14s. to 16s.
Chloride Lime, 28s. per cwt.
Sulphuric Acid, 2½d. per lb.
Sulphur for Destroying Worm on Turnips, 16s. per cwt.
Sulphate Soda, 7s. 6d. per cwt.

PRICES OF SHARES.

No. of Shares.	Div. per Ann.	IRON RAILWAYS.	Price per Share.
6,300	1*l* 4s p.c.	Birmingham & Derby ..100*l* sh pd	42
6,300	8s	Do. Thirds, iss. 8⅛ dis. 33⅓*l* sh 25*l* pd	
		Do. Eights................1½*l* pd	2⅜
9,500		Do. and Gloucester ...100*l* sh pd	
10,000		Do. New, iss. 7½ dis. 25*l* sh 17½*l* pd	
15,000	4*l* per ct	Bristol and Exeter..100*l* sh 70*l* pd	57 a 6½
7,500	2*l* 10s	Cheltenham & Great Western 100*l* sh 80*l* pd	31½
3,000		Clarence..............100*l* sh pd	
64,000	18s p sh.	Eastern Counties ....25*l* sh 23*l* pd	9 a ⅛
		Ditto New............8*l* 6s 8d pd	11⅛ a ¼
64,000		Ditto Debentures .. 8*l* 6s 8d sh pd	11⅛ a 11
12,500	3½*l* per ct	Glasgow, Paisley, and Ayrshire 50*l* sh pd	
18,000	5*l* per ct	Edinburgh & Glasgow .. 50*l* sh pd	45½ex-d.
18,000		Ditto New..........12½*l* sh 7½*l* pd	6¾
16,000	7s 6d p.sh	Glasgow, Paisley, and Greenock, 27*l* sh 25*l* pd	
10,918	10*l* per ct	Grand Junction........100*l* sh pd	198
11,000	5*l* per ct	Ditto Half Shares ......50*l* sh pd	
10,000	2½*l* per ct	Great North of England. 100*l* sh pd	
25,000	4*l* per sh	Great Western .... 100*l* sh 65*l* pd	94 a
25,000	3*l* per sh	Ditto New..............50*l* sh pd	69¾ a
37,500	5s per sh	Ditto Fifths........ 20*l* sh 12*l* pd	17⅝ a
		Ditto Bonds....1849	
		Ditto Bonds 1850, Letter C	
2,000		Hartlepool............ 100*l* sh pd	
8,000	1*l* per sh	Hull and Selby .... 50*l* sh pd	
2,100		Leeds and Selby........100*l* sh pd	
5,100		Liverpool & Manchester. 100*l* sh pd	
7,968		Ditto Half Shares......50*l* sh pd	
11,475		Ditto Quarter Shares ..25*l* sh pd	
36,000	4*l* per ct	London and Brighton....50*l* sh pd	36 a 5⅞
		Ditto Loan Notes....... 10*l* sh pd	
48,000		London & Blackwall Av. 16*l* 13s 4d	5⅛ a 5
43,077	3s	London & Greenwich Av. 12*l* 15s 4d	4¾ a ⅞
11,136	5*l* per ct	Preference or Privilege Av. 18*l* 17s 2d	
	5*l* per ct	Ditto Bonds (183,300)............	
25,000	10*l* p sh	London & Birmingham 100*l* sh pd	211 ex-d.
25,000	2*l* 10s	Ditto Quarter Shares....25*l* sh pd	52¼ex-d.
31,250	3*l* 4s	Ditto Thirds............ 32*l* sh pd	
	2*l* 14s	Ditto New.......... 32*l* sh 2*l* pd	36½ex-d.
		Ditto Bonds 1843	
46,200	3*l* per sh	London & South West. Av. 41*l* 6s 10d	64¾ a 5
		Ditto Bonds 1842	
33,000	13s 4d p s	London & Croydon..Av. 18*l* 15s 9d	10
13,000	3*l* 17s p sh	Manchester & Leeds 100*l* sh 70*l* pd	
13,000	1*l* 13s p sh	Ditto New Shares ....50*l* sh 30*l* pd	
	4s	Ditto Quarter Shares........2*l* pd	4¾
30,000		Manchester & Birming. 70*l* sh 40*l* pd	23 a ½
		Ditto Extension......70*l* sh 7*l* pd	
10,000	3*l*	Midland Counties......100*l* sh pd	62
10,000	15s	Do. ¼ Shares, iss. 10 dis. 25*l* sh 15*l* pd	15½
		Newcastle & Darlington Junction 25*l* sh 6*l* pd	
15,000	2*l*	North Midland........ 100*l* sh pd	65
15,000	1*l* 0s	Do. ½ Shares, iss. 10 dis. 50*l* sh 40*l* pd	32½
22,500	13s 4d	Ditto Thirds, iss. at 11*l* 13s 4d dis. 21*l* 13s 4d sh pd	21⅜
10,256	2*l*	Northern & Eastern 50*l* sh 45*l* pd	34 ex-d.
3,136		Do. Scrip...iss. 5 dis. 50*l* sh 5*l* pd	10⅞ a ¾
12,208		Do. ¼ Shares...12*l* 10s sh 1*l* 5s pd	2½ a ⅜
72,000		Paris and Rouen ....20*l* sh 20*l* pd	20⅛ a ¼
40,000		Rouen and Havre....20*l* sh 2*l* pd	2½
7,000	5 per ct	Sheffield, Ashton-under-Lyne, and Manchester .... 100*l* sh 82½*l* pd	
1,000	1*l* 15s	Sheffield and Rotherham 25*l* sh pd	
1,500	15*l* per ct	Stockton and Darlington 100*l* sh pd	
28,000	4*l* per ct	South Eastern and Dover 50*l* sh pd	22½ a ¼
28,000		Ditto New, iss. 25 dis. 25*l* sh 25*l* pd	22½ a ¾
6,700	10*l* per ct	York & North Midland..50*l* sh pd	93 a ½
6,700	10*l* per ct	Ditto New Shares.... 25*l* sh 20*l* pd	30

Printed by Joseph Rogerson, 24, Norfolk-street, Strand, London.

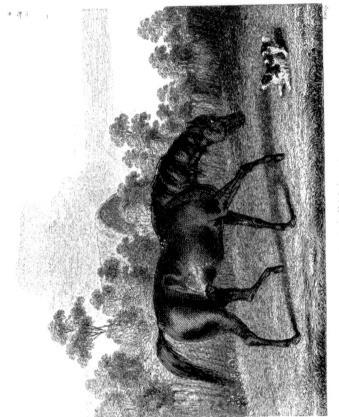

Sir Hercules

The Fox and Badger.

THE FARMER'S MAGAZINE.

APRIL, 1843.

No. 4.—Vol. VII.]   [Second Series.

PLATE I.

SIR HERCULES.

THE PROPERTY OF MR. WEATHERLEY, OF EAST ACTON.

In presenting our readers with a portrait of this celebrated stallion, it is not too much to say that in popularity on the turf or in the stud, he ranks as high as any of his contemporaries. He was bred by Lord Langford, in 1826; got by Whalebone, out of Peri, by Wanderer—Thalestris, by Alexander—Rival, by Sir Peter—Hornet, by Drone—Manilla, by Goldfincher—Mr. Goodricke's old English mare—Cullen, Arabian, Cad*,

PERFORMANCES.

In 1828, at the Curragh September Meeting, won a match, carrying 7st. 10lb., agst. Mount Eagle, 8st. 2lb.; New T. Y. C.; 100 sovs.; and won a Two-years-old-Stakes, New T. Y. C. At the Curragh October Meeting won a Two-years-old Stakes, T. Y. C., beating three others; and walked over for a Two-years-old Stakes.

In 1829 won a Three-years-old Stakes at York Spring Meeting; last mile and three quarters (8 subs.); beating Netherby, Flambeau, Flacrow, c. by Viscount, out of Nell, Maldon, and Brielle. At Doncaster ran third for the St. Leger; beaten by Rowton and Voltaire, and beating 16 others; and won a Three-years-old Stakes; one mile (23 subs.) beating Fortitude and Zodiac.

In 1830, at Newmarket Craven Meeting, won the Claret Stakes (5 subs.), beating Morris Dancer, c. by Gustavus, out of Canvass, and Spaniard.

Sir Hercules is the sire of Mulgrave, Maria, The Gipsey, Water Witch, Birdcatcher, Arthur, Langford, Cruiskeen, Honest Ned, Honesty, The Hydra, The Corsair, Jenny Jones, Coronation, Hereford, Iole, Robert de Gorham, and several other winners.

PLATE II.

THE FOX AND BADGER.

ON THE PLANTING, MANAGEMENT, VALUE, GROWTH, AND HARVESTING OF FOREST TREES CULTIVATED FOR PROFIT.

BY JOHN MORTON.

(*Concluded.*)

The evils attendant on improper thinning are without remedy, and tend sometimes to the destruction of entire plantations. At Wilbeck, the seat of the Duke of Portland, where the management of the oak is carried on in a scientific manner, there is an instance of injury done by over thinning. The lawn, I think, was planted in 1743, and was in 1825 eighty-two years old. The oaks here were then about 30 feet high, and the average quarter girth was about 7 inches; while the oaks in Lord Harley's wood, close by, that were planted in 1725, and were consequently 100 years old, were about 60 feet long, and the average quarter girth was 9½ inches. The trees on the lawn were thinned too early and too much. This is the cause of the stunted growth of its timber. There is another evil attendant upon reckless thinning besides that which tells upon the quality and quantity of the growth of the plantation—one that is often most destructive in its consequences. It has been shown that in thick plantations the whole of the trees unite in the resistance they make to a storm, and that the wind glides over the smooth surface presented to it by their tops, without being able to make any impression on the body of any individual of their number. It has been also shown that trees grow tall in proportion to the shelter they receive, and that they are provided with roots according to the resistance they are required to make in the particular situation in which they grow. If, then, this smooth surface be broken in upon by imprudent thinning, gaps being made, and each tree being more exposed, then, as they are not prepared for the resistance they are now required to make, it must be evident that, if a storm attack them before the roots have acquired sufficient strength, they will not be able to withstand its violence. There are many instances of this. The following is one. A field of larch in Renfrewshire was thinned out by a gardener ignorant of the business: the trees were at once thinned out to the distance of 20 feet apart: soon after the operation was finished, the first storm of wind that occurred threw down nearly all those that remained.

In summing up all that has been said on this subject, we must protest against the method in which it is handled by most foresters. Their object seems to be—and indeed the object has been commended by many authors on the subject—not to raise a valuable crop of timber, but to make the ground pay a certain annual return after the first six or eight years, by the sale of thinnings and prunings. This mode of arrangement renders useless any attempt that may be afterwards made to produce timber; for the wood has become so knotty as to be worth very little per foot; and there is so great a proportion of offal, that there are but few trees in the plantation which exceed in solid contents a very small number of cubic feet. However various the details of management may require to be in different cases dependent on the habits of the tree and the nature of the soil, yet

the principle here laid down should be adopted as the foundation of them all.

The following remarks on circumstances affecting the value of timber will be placed here in their most natural position, between what has been said on the management of plantations and that which remains to say on the harvesting of timber.

For general purposes timber requires to be hard, tough, and clean; and if with these properties it unite great length and considerable diameter, it is then the most valuable of its kind. If timber be short, although it may be of great diameter, the short scantlings into which alone it can be cut will require no considerable thickness : a thin tree, therefore, will serve as well as a thick one for these purposes. If, however, it be of great length, the long scantlings will require proportionate thickness. Such trees, however, are rare : consequently the value per foot increases more rapidly with the length of the tree than with the diameter.

There are many circumstances which must influence us in the price of timber besides the variations in the demand. Thus its value is dependent on soil and situation. If it has grown on a poor soil, the timber is harder and more durable; it is of finer grain, and has a finer texture; and consequently, though the trees of a sheltered situation have grown in the same time to a much greater height and bulk, they are worth less per foot than those of a bleak and poor district. The strongest and best timber is grown on the north side of the hill. Timber grown in hedge-rows is much heavier and harder than that grown in a plantation, its bark is also thicker, and contains more tannin; yet this has not much influence on its value per foot, as, although superior in these respects, it is not only greatly inferior in the length and bulk of its growth, but, in consequence of its limbs and branches being coarse and full of knots, it can be used only in short and bulky masses. It does not answer well to be cut out in small scantling, as it warps at every knot.

The quality of timber, again, is better, and its value per foot is therefore greater, when grown on soil suited than when raised on soil not natural to it. Thus oak that has grown on clay is much more valuable to the consumer than that grown on sand or any other soil. The wood is tougher, harder, and more durable, and the bark is thicker and has more tannin in it. On sand, the wood of the oak is brittle and soft, and, like the Dutch oak, spoils the carpenter's tools, probably owing to its containing a portion of silex. The value of timber will depend also on a variety of local circumstances. It will vary with its distance from the market, and also with the nature of the demand. If near a manufacturing or a seaport town, the demand will raise its price. In valuing trees for sale, besides all these circumstances, we must also take into account the proportion which the head of the tree bears to the trunk; for not only is the wood of the limbs of less value than the trunk, but it injures that part which is valuable by forming knots at its junction with the trunk. Generally speaking, the timber of the trunk of the tree, however large the limbs may be, is double the value per foot of the wood of the branches.

We now come to the last branch of our subject—the harvesting of timber. A great deal has been said and written on the planting and management of plantations, but very little has been said on the proper time and mode of harvesting them.

Notwithstanding, however, the neglect which this branch of the subject has hitherto sustained, it is one of the greatest importance, as I shall show, that heavy losses are frequently due merely to improper management as to the period of bringing the timber of a plantation to the market. Trees should be felled as soon as their growth becomes unprofitable; and this is the case whenever their annual increase of growth is of less value than the interest upon the sum for which they could be sold. It must be evident that, though the value of a plantation may increase 10l. annually, owing to a yearly increase of bulk, yet it must be advantageous to cut it down, if by bringing it to market we could obtain 15l. interest per annum for its value. We by so doing not only gain 5l. a-year, but the ground occupied by the wood becomes available for other purposes. It should therefore be the object of the forester to ascertain the period when the growth of the plantation become unprofitable. This knowledge can only be obtained by repeated measurements and comparisons of the growth of one year with another. Signs of decay are very easily distinguished; but they should never be allowed to make their appearance in the trees of a well-managed plantation. We often hear it observed of a tree, "It should be cut down, for it has done growing; it is beginning to decay;" whereas it is more than probable that the trees should have been cut down many years, perhaps generations, before, and the proprietor has all this time been sustaining a great annual loss. There are instances in which the loss sustained in this way may be proved to be immense.

There are very few individuals who hear of the progress and growth of their timber, and yet there is no other way of securing ourselves against this loss; for, although there are many signs which indicate decay in a tree, there are none which point out the period when it has reached its greatest yearly growth. This period will vary with many local circumstances. It will be dependent on the kind of tree grown, and on the nature of the soil and situation, being later in those trees which are raised on a soil and in a situation most fitted for it. Thus oak will grow profitably longer on a clay soil than on any other; elm on a deep loam; and beech on a calcareous soil; and the pine tribe in bleak situations, those being natural to them. The only accurate way, however, of determining this period is by the measurement of the annual growth of the tree; and every proprietor of a timbered estate should have his plantation looked over by a person qualified to report on the state of their growth; all those trees whose growth is unprofitable should at once be brought to the market. If possible, they should be cut down in the month of October, in a year when there has been a good crop of seeds, so that their places may next year be supplied by young plants at no expense.

I shall now give some instances which I have collected of trees of great bulk growing solitarily, giving in some of them data by which the growth at various intervals may be ascertained. These instances are brought forward with the view of showing the wondrous growth which sometimes takes place in solitary trees, and of proving the impropriety of drawing general conclusions from the results of individual trees, not for the purpose of encouraging the growth of isolated trees with a view to profit, of which I have already shown the impropriety, involving as it does wrong formation of wood as well as a great waste of ground. They are worthy of being put upon record, although they do not bear upon the point immediately to be established. Having mentioned a few of them, I shall return to the course of my argument and endeavour to prove the result of the foregoing statements:—

1. "The Golenos oak grew about four miles from Newport, in Monmouthshire. It was cut down and converted by Thomas Harrison, his Majesty's purveyor for Plymouth dock-yards, in 1810. The trunk was nine feet in diameter and ten feet in length, containing 450 cubic feet; but there were twelve limbs—

The 1st of which contained 472 cubic feet.

2nd	"	355	"
3rd	"	235	"
4th	"	156	"
5th	"	113	"
6th	"	106	"
And six others, in all		540	"

2427 cubic feet

of sound convertible timber. The bark was estimated at six tons; five men were twenty days in cutting it down and stripping the bark, and a pair of sawyers were five months in converting it, without missing a single day. This tree had only 400 rings in its trunk, and (a convincing proof that it was in an improving state all that time) it had increased 8-10ths of an inch in circumference annually, and produced six cubic feet of excellent timber per annum during the whole time of its growth. It was sold by Mr. Harrison to government after it was converted, and delivered at Plymouth dock for 600l."

The two following instances are given in a letter from R. Mansham, Esq., to J. Reeves, Esq., of Hithel, in Norwich, dated 1st October, 1799, 1st vol. Bath Papers:—

2. "I have a memorandum of a former rector of Honingham, wherein it is written that in 1610 be planted two chestnut-trees by his church-porch. "The largest of these was, in 1778, seventeen feet eight and a half inches in circumference, showing an increase of 176½ inches in 168 years."

3. "Near Honingham, on the road to Norwich, were planted oaks in 1580, the largest of which, in 1778, was sixteen feet three and a half inches in circumference, an increase of 195½ inches in 198 years."

4. The Bowles oak in Nymphsfield parish, Gloucestershire, was cut down in 1826: the trunk was fourteen feet long, and 164 inches in circumference under the bark at the girting place. It contained 163 cubic feet of timber; one limb was twenty-one feet long and nineteen inches round it, making fifty-five feet; there were twenty-five other limbs, containing in all ninety-eight feet, making in all 310 cubic feet; besides smaller limbs, from which were made 145 posts six feet long and twenty-four inches in circumference; this is equivalent to 200 feet more. This tree had only 150 circular rings in its trunk, and its age was therefore only 150 years: so that it had increased in circumference one inch and one-tenth, and produced two cubic feet of timber per annum, exclusive of small limbs.

5. In the parish of Standish, Gloucestershire, on Butts farm, an oak was cut down in 1825, the trunk of which was 176 inches in circumference, and only nine feet long. It contained 121 cubic feet of timber, two limbs containing in all 180 feet; and seven other limbs containing 122 feet; making in all 423 cubic feet of convertible timber,

besides fifty-six posts containing eighty-four cubic feet. This tree was only 140 years old; it had therefore grown one inch and a quarter per annum in circumference, and had increased in bulk three cubic feet annually, exclusive of small branches.

6. In 1816 a beech was cut down in Woodchester Park, the seat of Earl Ducie. It was ninety-two feet long, and at five feet from the ground it was seventy-two inches in circumference; it contained 177½ cubic feet of timber; it was 147 years old, that being the number of its circular rings; it had consequently increased in circumference half an inch per annum, and had produced one cubic foot and two-sevenths of timber annually.

7. Not far from the same place was cut down another beech; it was 115 feet long, and its circumference at five feet from the ground was seventy-four inches: it had only 119 circular rings, and had therefore increased in circumference six-tenths of an inch per annum, and produced one cubic foot and seven-tenths of timber annually. These two last instances seem to give a slower growth to the beech than to the oak; they however grew in a thick wood, and their head was so small that a couple of men might have carried that of either of them down the hill on which they grew.

8. A solitary elm which grew on Mr. Barber's farm, Tortworth, Gloucestershire, was cut down in 1825; its circumference at five feet from the ground was eighteen feet and a quarter, the trunk was only nine feet long, and there divided into three limbs. The total solid contents was 685 cubic feet; it had grown 188 years. This gives one inch and two-tenths as the annual increase of its circumference, and three cubic feet and six-tenths as the annual increase of its bulk.

9. In 1816, 400 larch were cut down at Dunkeld. The following table shows their growth at ages varying from forty-seven to seventy-two years:

No. of Trees.	Age.	Average contents in feet.	Growth per annum.	
60	72	65	⅞ of a foot.	78
70	68	56	¾ do.	78·20
120	57	40	⅗ do.	96
100	..	36	.. do.	72
50	47	30	⅔ do.	30
				354·20

10. Thirty-six years ago a number of larch were planted in a clump in the midst of Colliers Wood, in the parish of Avening, in the county of Gloucester; thirty of them only remain, the others having been cut down. The length of the tallest is eighty feet, and at five feet from the ground the circumference is forty-two inches; at fifty feet high it contains twenty-six cubic feet. The average contents of the thirty were about ten cubic feet, and they occupy ten square yards each, which gives 4860 cubic feet per acre.

11. The oaks sown at Welbeck, the seat of the Duke of Portland, in 1803, at twenty-two years old (1825) were about twenty feet high, and about six inches in circumference breast high: they were thinned out to three feet apart. Cowclose was partly sown and partly planted in 1785 with oak; when forty years old they were from thirty-five to forty feet high, and from sixteen to twenty inches in circumference at five feet from the ground; then standing from two to three yards apart: this was the finest growing oak-plantation at Welbeck. The Lawn plantation was eighty-two years old in 1825; the average length of trunk was here only about thirty feet, and the circumference about twenty-eight inches. The trees stood at an average distance of twenty-four feet from one another. The dwarfish state of this plantation has been already pointed out as the effects of over-thinning: their growth had not been four-tenths of an inch in circumference annually. The average length of trunk in Lord Harley's wood, planted in 1725, and therefore a hundred years old in 1825, when I took all these particulars, was about sixty feet, and the average circumference at the girting-place was thirty eight inches: they were thinned out to twenty-five feet apart. The annual growth for 100 years was here about one-third of a foot.

12. The following table marks the progress of the growth of twenty-six oaks raised in Woodchester Park, Gloucestershire, felled in 1825. The circular rings at the root, indicating their age, were 146 in number. The largest tree contained 134 feet of timber, and was forty feet long; the smallest contained only twenty-seven feet, and was twenty feet long: they averaged sixty-four feet apiece, and their average length to the limbs was thirty-six feet. A section was taken from three trees nearest the medium size, and their average at five feet from the root, was twenty-five inches and three-tenths in diameter. At eighteen feet from the ground it was twenty-one inches and three-tenths; and at both these places the increase in diameter was ascertained at intervals of ten years by a careful examination of the rings, and a calculation of the increase in the contents founded on them:—

Periods of 10 Years each	Increase of Diameter at 5 feet from the Ground for each Period, in Inches and Tenths.	Increase of Diameter at 18 feet from the Ground for each Period, in Inches and Tenths.	Amount of Quarter Girth for each Period, at Girting-place.	Amount of Cubic feet at the end of each Period, the length being 36 feet.	Increase of Cubic feet for every 10 years.
	25·3	21·3			
10	1·5		·9		
20	3·0	2·9	3·9	2·5	4·75
30	2·5	2·4	5·6	7·25	5·
40	2·4	2·0	7·1	12·25	5·75
50	2·0	2·0	8·5	18	5·75
60	1·9	1·9	9·9	23·75	6·25
70	1·8	1·8	11·1	30	6
80	1·6	1·7	12·3	36	6
90	1·4	1·5	13·3	42	7
100	1·2	1·4	14·2	49	7
110	1·0	1·2	15·	56	4
120	·8	1·0	15·	60	4
130	·5	·8	16·	60	4
140		·5	16·	64	4

This table is instructive, as the last column proves the annual growth of the tree to have increased up to the age of 130 years, at which it began to decrease. Such an increased growth of timber as this is not, however, to be expected on any entire plantation.

Having given these instances of remarkable growth, from which no decided inference can be drawn, but which I thought might not be without interest for the society, I shall now proceed, lastly, to that point which is the most important of all, and shall bring forward in detail the result in value of timber which arises from thin and from thick growth of timber.

The following is a measurement and valuation of six oaks cut down in 1825, in the parish of Woodchester, in the county of Gloucester, by the particulars of which I intend to shew the superiority of the plan of growing trees with few limbs over that of growing trees with many limbs. The three first oaks which I shall mention grew in a thick plantation surrounded by other trees of equal height. The three last were each solitary:—

No. 1.

Measurement of an oak at the Farm Hill, Woodchester:—

	£	s.	d.
52 feet long by 19 inches quarter-girth, 130 cubic feet, at 4s. 6d. per foot	29	15	0
1½ cord of wood, which is equal, at 10s. per cord, as it requires 40 cubic feet of solid wood to make a cord of wood, so that 1½ cord is equal to 60 cubic feet, at say 3d. per cubic foot	0	15	0
20 faggots, worth 8s. 4d. per 100, or 1d. each, say 30lbs. each	0	1	8
16 cwt. of bark, at 8*l*. per ton	6	8	0
	£36	19	8

N.B.—There is a cwt. of bark for every 12 cubic feet of timber.

The trunk of this tree is rather more than two-thirds of the whole tree, taking all the cord-wood into the account.

No. 2.

Measurement of an oak by the mill-pond, Woodchester Park:—

	£	s.	d.
56 feet long by 18 inches quarter-girth, 126 cubic feet, at 4s. 6d. per foot......	28	10	0
1 cord of wood, equal to 40 cubic feet, at 3d. per foot........................	0	10	0
20 faggots, at 1d. each................	0	1	8
15 cwt. of bark, at 8*l*. per ton..........	6	0	0
	£35	1	8

N.B.—There is 1 cwt. of bark for 11 cubic feet of timber.

The trunk of this tree is just three-fourths of the whole tree, taking all the cord-wood into account.

No. 3.

Measurement of an oak at the top of Shade Hollow, Woodchester Park:—

			£	s.	d.
The trunk is 41 ft. long and 22 in. ¼-girth,	137	cub. ft. at 4s. 6d. per ft.	30	16	6
One limb is 18 ft. long and 10 in. ¼ girth, 12½....... Another is 14 ft. long and 10 in. ¼ girth, 9½........	22	do. at 2s. 6d. do.	2	15	0
	159				
1 cord of wood, equal to....	40	do. at 3d. per foot	0	10	0
20 faggots, at 1d. each................			0	1	8
1 ton of bark, at 8*l*.................			8	0	0
			£42	3	2

N.B.—There is 1 cwt. of bark for 10 cubic feet of timber.

The trunk of this tree is rather more than two-thirds of the whole tree, taking into account the limbs and cord-wood.

The following is a recapitulation of the above three oaks, which grew in a thick plantation, surrounded by other trees of equal height:—

No.	Trunk.	Limbs.	Cord-wood.	Cubic ft. of Cord-wood.	Fagots.	Bark.	Value.		
							£	s.	d.
1	130	..	1½	60	20	16	36	19	2
2	126	..	1	40	20	15	35	1	8
3	137	22	1	40	20	20	42	3	2
	393	22	3½	140	60	51	114	4	6

From the average of these three oaks the following facts are shown. The trunks are about three-fourths of the whole trees, including limbs and cord-wood; there is only one faggot for every six cubic feet and a half of the trunk, being fifteen faggots per hundred cubic feet; one cord of wood for every 112 cubic feet of trunk; one cubic foot of limbs for every eighteen feet of trunk, being less than six per hundred feet; and for every eight cubic feet of the trunk and measurable limbs there is one cwt. of bark. These trees were above 150 years old, and their timber was of the most valuable quality. The whole were sold at an average of 4s. 1½d. per cubic foot.

No. 4.

Measurement of a solitary oak then standing in Milbarn Ground:—

	No.	Length. Feet.	Quarter-girth. Inches.	Contents.		At per ft.	Value.		
							£	s.	d.
Trunk.		18	26½		88	5s.	22	0	0
Limbs,	1	18	12	18					
	2	12	12	12					
					30	3s.	4	10	0
	3	18	9	10					
	4	20	9	11					
	5	6	9	3					
	6	18	8½	9					
	7	18	8½	9					
	8	24	7	8					
	9	26	7	9					
	10	16	6	4					
	11	16	6	4					
					67	2s.	6	14	0
50 posts, worth 1s. each, containing each about 1½ foot of timber; in all				75		1s. 6d.	2	10	0
3 cord of wood, 10s. per cord of timber, say....				120		3d.	1	10	0
					195				
60 faggots, at 1d. each							0	5	0
24 cwt. of bark, at 8*l*. per ton							9	12	0
					380		£47	1	0

There is 1 cwt. of bark for 11 cubic feet of timber, including the measurable limbs; and the trunk of this tree is not quite one-fourth of the whole tree, taking all the limbs, posts, and all the cord-wood in account.

No. 5.

Measurement of a solitary oak by the Shade, near Mr. Almond's:—

No.	Length. Feet	Quarter-girth Inches.	Contents.	At per ft.	Value. £ s. d.
Trunk.	19	24½	76	5s.	19 0 0
Limbs, 1	9	13	10¾		
2	8	12½	8½		
			—19	3s.	2 17 0
3	20	10	14		
4	12	10½	9		
5	14	8½	7		
6	14	8½	7		
7	20	9	11		
			—48	2s.	4 16 0
30 posts, worth 1s. each, at 1½ foot of timber in each			45	8d.	1 10 0
2 cord of wood, 10s. per cord, equal to			80	3d.	1 0 0
			—125		
40 faggots, 1d. each			. . .		. 0 3 4
1 ton of bark, at 8l.			. . .		. 8 0 0
			268		£37 6 4

There is 1 cwt. of bark for 9½ cubic feet of timber, including the top; and the trunk is about one-fourth of the whole tree, including the limbs, posts, and cord-wood.

No. 6.

Measurement of a solitary oak in the long ground, near Mr. Almond's:—

No.	Length. Feet	Quarter-girth Inches.	Contents.	At per ft.	value. £ s. d.
Trunk.	15	27	76	5s.	19 0 0
Limbs, 1	6	22	20		
2	14	12	14		
			—34	3s.	5 2 0
3	14	9	8		
4	12	8½	6		
5	10	8½	5		
6	10	8½	5		
7	18	7	6		
8	18	7	6		
			—36	2s.	3 12 0
50 posts, worth 1s. each, say 1½ foot of timber in each			75	8d.	2 10 0
3 cord of wood, 10s. per cord equal to..			120	3d.	1 10 0
			—195		
60 faggots, at 1d. each	.	. .	.		. 0 5 0
25 cwt. of bark, at 8l. per ton		.			. 10 0 0
			341		£41 19 0

There is 1 cwt. of bark for 9 cubic feet of the whole tree; and the trunk is nearly one-fourth of the whole tree, including the limbs, posts, and cord-wood.

Recapitulation of the above three solitary oaks now growing in Woodchester Park:—

No.	Trunks in Cub. Ft.	Limbs in Cub. Ft.	Cord-wood only.	Cord-wood and Posts in Cub. Ft.	Posts. No.	Faggots.	Bark.	Value. £ s. d.
4	88	97	3	195	50	60	24	47 1 0
5	76	67	2	125	30	40	20	37 6 4
6	76	70	3	195	50	60	25	41 19 0
	240	234	8	515	130	160	69	126 6 4

From the average of the above three solitary trees the following facts are shown:—the trunk is not quite one-fourth of the whole of the tree, including trunk, limbs, posts, and cord-wood; there is also 1 faggot for 1½ cubic foot of trunk, being 75 per 100; there is a cord of wood for every 30 cubic feet of trunk, being 3½ per 100 feet; there is 1 foot of limbs for every foot of trunk; and it takes 10 cubic feet of trunk and measurable limbs to produce 1 cwt. of bark.

Statement of the particulars of the value of the above three solitary trees:—

	£ s. d.
240 cubic feet of trunk, at 5s. per foot	60 0 0
83 do. of limbs, at 3s. do...	12 9 0
151 do. do. at 2s. do..........	15 2 0
474	
130 posts, at 1s. each	6 10 0
8 cord of wood, at 10s. per cord	4 0 0
160 faggots, at 1d. each.....	0 13 4
69 cwt. of bark, at 8l. per ton	27 12 0
	£126 6 4

If the growth of these three trees had been according to that of those three growing in the thick wood, then the following would have been a statement of their value:—

We find that the contents of measurable timber, trunk and limbs, are .... 474 feet
130 posts, at 1½ foot each.............. 195 „
8 cord of wood at 40 feet .... 320 „

989 „

Now three-fourths of this wood, if the trees had not grown single, would have been in the trunk. Therefore, ¾ of 989 cubic feet is—

	£ s. d.
740 feet, at 4s. 6d. per foot	166 10 0
The limbs would amount to the remainder, 249 feet, of which 29 feet might have been measurable at 2s...	2 18 0
And 220 may have been cord-wood, which, at 40 feet per cord, is 5½ cord, at 10s.	2 15 0
There would have been about 120 faggots, at 1d. each	0 10 0
And 98 cwt. of bark, which, at 8l. per ton, is	39 4 0
Their value, thus calculated, would have been	£211 17 0

This shows a loss of upwards of 80*l.* on the three trees; and we may accordingly safely infer that there is a loss on an average of 50*l.* per cent. by growing trees solitarily instead of in a thickly-wooded plantation. This loss would of course be greatly increased if we were to calculate that due to the immense waste of land involved in that mode of growing trees. A similar loss is of course sustained where the trees, by over thinning, are allowed to assume the character of those growing solitarily, by throwing out lateral branches, and forming large heads.   JOHN MORTON.
Chester Hill, August 4, 1840.

ON STRICTURE IN THE ŒSOPHAGUS OF THE COW.

BY MR. W. HAYCOCK, V.S. (MEMBER OF THE ROYAL VETERINARY COLLEGE, EDINBURGH), HUDDERS-FIELD.

TO THE EDITOR OF THE FARMER'S MAGAZINE.

SIR,—As the magazine which you edit is one devoted to the best interests of farmers, cattle keepers, and I may add to society in general, I beg leave to offer you the present paper upon a case of disease which has occurred in a cow, and which very lately I had the management of. The disease to which I allude was stricture of the æsophagus; an affection rarely, I believe, observed in the lower animals, which perhaps in a great measure may account for the silence of writers upon cattle pathology respecting it. Mr. Blaine, in his work, the first edition of which appeared at least eighteen years ago, just devoted seven lines and a half to the description of its symptoms, situation, part affected, and mode of treatment; so that I leave every inquiring reader to judge for himself as to the amount of information he would be likely to derive from the perusal of so short an article. Mr. Percival, however, does not pass it over quite so lightly; he devotes about three pages to it, but his observations have reference only to its existence in the horse. Professor Dick, in the article "Veterinary Science," written by him in the 7th edition of the "Encyclopædia Britannica," does not even allude to its existence; while Mr. Youatt again, in his work published by the "Society for the Diffusion of Useful Knowledge," applies about half a page, or scarcely that, to the elucidation of the disease in question; and he informs us that during the whole of his practical career up to that period (the period at which he wrote)—which practice must have been very extensive—he never met with more than one case of this affection in the cow. Seeing, then, that so little is said respecting the existence of such a disease in the above-named animal, I may deem it a sufficient apology in thus venturing to address the agricultural portion of your numerous readers with the history of a case, together with a few observations upon the subject—a subject so palpably overlooked, and at the same time I may say so intimately connected with their interests, that it cannot fail of proving of some little utility.

The cow affected as I have intimated, was the property of Wm. Brook, Esq., one of the magistrates for this borough. The history of the case is as follows. The animal was in the daily habit of receiving an allotted portion of cut turnips in a raw state, and one evening, about two or three weeks after Christmas last, the usual quantity was placed before her, and after she had eaten about one-third of the whole she suddenly exhibited symptoms of choking. The abdomen became greatly distended, while every four or five minutes the hind extremities were brought forwards, the back thrown into an arch, and the nose protruded as though endeavouring to vomit. These very violent symptoms in part subsided, but for some weeks after, whenever she took food, they returned with more or less violence; sometimes, in consequence of eating, the animal would be thrown into such agony, that she would leap or place her fore feet upon the rack from whence she fed, and after violently straining for a considerable time, vomit everything back again; then again resume her natural position as though nothing was the matter. A cow-leech residing somewhere in the country, was at this time entrusted with the management of her, but all the medicine he administered was a pint of castor oil: he saw the case was a perplexing one, so he altogether abandoned it. For a time, however, the animal appeared to have recovered; her food was masticated and properly swallowed, and for two or three weeks all was going on well, when a relapse took place, and most of what she eat was vomited back. Such was the account I received from the man who desired my attendance, and accordingly I lost no time in proceeding to make an examination, and ascertain if possible the disease under which the animal laboured. I found her pulse beat with moderate regularity, but feeble; she was in very fair condition, and lively in appearance; in short, after the most rigid examination, I was unable to detect the least constitutional derangement, save the existence of a slight degree of debility. She appeared desirous of food, and I requested some to be given, in order that I might perceive its effects upon her, or if vomiting would be produced; a small portion of hay was placed before her, which she eagerly seized, masticated, and swallowed. I then stood watching her every motion for a considerable time, but could not perceive any improper movement, or anything like a desire to vomit; more hay was given, which was also swallowed, but I did not wait long before I saw a mass of something move very gently backwards and forwards in the œsophagus—it moved for about half a minute, when she jerked forth the point of her nose, relaxed the lower jaw, and a portion of the hay she had just masticated was vomited forth, seemingly with the greatest ease. These movements were continued until the whole had returned, after which the cow appeared as desirous as ever for a fresh supply. I was much puzzled, as any one may be certain I should, for I had never seen vomiting induced in the cow before; I had heard of one or two solitary cases, but doubted their truth. Here, however, to all appearance, was positive evidence; and the next step in the matter was to know the cause. After weighing the matter over in my mind, I thought perhaps the whole phenomena, strange as it was, might possibly be induced by the lodgment of some foreign substance, or by the growth of a tumour at the back part of the mouth, or at the entrance of the pharynx, and that such substances giving rise to irritation in these parts, vomiting was produced, or was the consequence of a kind of reflex action. It is well known that irritation, however slight, in these parts in the human being, will produce vomiting; and, judging from the similarity of the parts in both, I concluded if the effect is produced by such a cause in the one, possibly it may in the other. I accordingly procured a ball iron, and minutely examined the structures, but found everything in a normal condition. I was therefore necessitated, as it were, to suppose that the cause lay in the paunch or the first stomach—that, in short, a morbid excitement existed within this organ, whatever might be urged with respect to its want of sensibility. Medicine was given to act upon the bowels in the first place and afterwards produce a sedative effect; and upon visiting the beast a second time, the cowman informed me that the vomiting was less frequent, and that the gruel which he gave her was retained altogether. I considered this a sign of amendment, but it proved of very short duration; for upon visiting her a third time, I found her worse than ever—gruel and everything she partook of was returned immediately, and she evidently laboured under great depression and feverish excitement. It now for the first time occurred to my mind that *a stricture must exist in some distant part of the œsophagus.* I lost no time, therefore, in procuring one of Monro's flexible probangs, which I passed with every necessary caution down the œsophagus; it proceeded for a considerable distance without any interruption, when it suddenly stopped, and force was required to again send it onwards, and at the moment it proceeded a quantity of thick and very fetid pus rushed from the upper extremity of the probang, which proved satisfactorily that my conjectures respecting the existence of a stricture were well founded. In a little time the instrument was withdrawn, and about two quarts of thick gruel administered to the cow, which did not return. I visited my patient again the day following, and found her worse—the pulse almost imperceptible, the extremities cold, the eyes sunk in their orbits, and a discharge of thick yellow mucus came from their inner conthus, the abdomen distended with gas, pus discharged from the vagina, and when food was given to her the greater portion of it was, as usual, vomited back. I saw that the vital energies were rapidly on the decline—that the undigested substances within her, in consequence of the decline of such energies, were beginning to decompose, and that unless a speedy alteration for the better took place, the termination would shortly prove unfavourable. Recourse was a second time had to the probang, which was again obstructed in the same part as on the day previous, but vomiting was never afterwards observed. The cow, however, in spite of every effort and every assistance, medical or otherwise, continued to sink, until at last she died on the 6th of March.

Examination eight hours after death.—I dissected out very carefully the whole of the œsophagus from one extremity to the other, and upon cutting it open and exposing its internal surface, *I found at the commencement of the œsophagean canal the situation of the stricture. The cuticular membrane of the canal at this part was gone for more than an inch, which of course exposed the muscular fibres entering into the formation of the organ; for five or six inches below the seat of injury, and for two inches above it, the whole was in a state of gangrene.*

The abdominal and thoracic viscera were healthy throughout; the paunch contained a moderate

quantity of food, but the third and fourth stomachs were empty. In conclusion, then, I would remark that from the time which intervened from the first appearance of choking, which I mentioned as occurring soon after Christmas, and from the healthy condition of the abdominal and thoracic organs, that if measures of an efficient kind had been put into force at the first, when the constitutional energies were vigorous, that the animal would undoubtedly have recovered. The injury in the first instance I cannot suppose was either very severe or very extensive, but the food which the cow constantly received, being of a rough or coarse nature, would necessarily keep up the irritation in the part, where probably a sharp piece of turnip fixed itself when the symptoms of choking manifested themselves, and which exhibited such extensive disease when exposed after death. Cattle always, at least generally, when in health devour their food very greedily, and the sharp angles of turnips when cut into slices are extremely liable, from the hasty manner they gulp them, to lacerate or otherwise injure the interior of the æsophagus. I would therefore recommend every owner of cattle (as I invariably do when called to a choking cow from eating raw turnips), who partly feeds his milch cows upon turnips, never to give them in a raw state, *unless they be* CRUSHED, but to either steam or boil them—modes of preparation which will altogether prevent choking, and perhaps be the means also of preventing the loss of many a valuable animal.

ON MAKING BUTTER.

TO THE EDITOR OF THE FARMER'S MAGAZINE.

SIR,—I wish to make a few observations on a paper read by Professor Traill (who is the author) at the last monthly meeting of the committee of the Highland Agricultural Society. The paper is entitled "Experiments and Observations on the production of Butter."

Having myself that is, with my own hand—previous to being thirty-five years of age, when I gave up that labour—churned considerably more than 50,000 lbs. of butter; and having watched the process in the dairy, first under my mother, who was noted for producing a good article, and then under my wife, who followed in the same track, I consider that my experience may be of some service. My "experiments and observations" differ, in some respects, materially from those of the Professor.

I shall only make remarks on those parts of his paper wherein we differ.

1st. He says, "The quantity of butter was smallest (I suppose from a given quantity of milk) just after calving."

I have found the quantity greatest at that time, from the same quantity of milk, from the same animal. The butter is also far more easily separated from the milk at that time. The more distant after calving, the more tardily the separation was, under the same circumstances of temperature, &c.

2nd. He says, "That the addition of some cold water during churning facilitates the process, or the separation of the butter; especially when the cream is thick and the weather hot."

Cream should always be thick before the churning commences; but when it requires cold water to make the butter separate, it is a proof of the cream being at too high a temperature; and, in this case, both the quantity and quality will be much deteriorated. If the weather be hot, and the cream churned at its proper temperature, to add a little cold water, after the separation has taken place, will make the butter collect easier into larger lumps. The churning should continue a little while with a slower motion, after the water is added.

3rd. He says, "That cream alone is more easily churned than a mixture of cream and milk."

The separation will take place sooner, at the same temperature, but the butter will be of no better quality, while the buttermilk will be worse.

4th. "That butter produced from sweet cream has the finest flavour when fresh, and appears to keep longest without becoming rancid ; but that the buttermilk so obtained is poor, and small in quantity."

No butter can be got from sweet cream while it remains so. Cream may be sweet when the process of churning commences but it will, become acid before the separation takes place. To commence churning sweet cream is labour lost. It is because it has taken a long time to churn it makes the buttermilk bad. The quantity will be the same. Common sense will tell any one this. Whatever weight goes into the churn the same weight will come out in the shape of butter or buttermilk. There will be no more butter, of course; the quantity of buttermilk cannot be less.

If the butter becomes rancid it is from bad management in the dairy. If the wife and daughters ride in their pheatons every day, the butter is almost sure to be spoiled. There are a few dairy-women who are proud of doing their duty without being looked after. Rancid butter is caused by the cream being kept in too high a temperature, and has become acid too long before churning. It has "heaved" in the vessel. There is also what we call, "binged" butter, which is as bad, or worse, than the rancid. This is caused by the cream being kept in too low a temperature, and, of course, has been too long in turning acid, or too long before the churning has commenced.

5th. "That churning the milk and cream together, after they have become slightly acid, seems to be the most economical process on the whole ; because it yields a large quantity of excellent butter, and the buttermilk is of good quality."

Quite right, if the temperature of the mixture be right when the churning commences, and the churner does his duty; but a deal depends upon these two things. If the temperature be too high, or too low, or if the churner be a lazy fellow, (it is no woman's work) or if he dine out, or receives company three days a week, the butter is sure to be less in quantity, and both it and the buttermilk worse in quality than it otherwise would be.

6th. "That the keeping of the butter in a sound state appears to depend on its being obtained as free from uncombined albumen, or caseine, and water, as it can be by means of washing and working when taken from the churn."

To speak in language which every farmer and dairy-woman can understand, the butter, to make it excellent, and to keep it so, requires to be made free of buttermilk or water. Now, how can

washing it in water make it free of water ? Nothing can make butter firm, sound, and sweet, but well working, and never to let water to come near it after it is taken out of the churn. To wash butter is a wrong notion altogether.

7th. The author states "the interesting fact that, in the course of his experiments, he found when sweet milk and cream were churned together, and though cold water was added after an hour and a half, and then after three hours churning, not a particle of butter was obtained."

There is nothing curious in this "interesting fact." The mixture either had too little cream in it, or was at too cold a temperature, and made colder by the addition of cold water, or that the churner was exceedingly lazy.

According to my experience and observations by the following rules, if strictly followed, prime butter and butter milk will be produced ; the former to keep sweet and solid for twelve months.

1st. Let the dairy and everything about it be kept perfectly clean, and be well ventilated and shaded from the sun. If the floor be two feet below the surface of the ground the better; but I do not like a cellar, except to keep the butter in after being made up for use or keeping.

2nd. Let the cream be taken from, say, three fourths of the milk (that which is first taken from each of the cows), after this milk has stood in proper vessels in the dairy twenty-four hours. Mix this cream with the remaining fourth of the milk, or "afterings," in proper earthen vessels, and let them stand in a temperature of about 50°, so that it will turn acid in about three days. It should not exceed four days.

3rd. As soon as it has turned acid, or before twenty-four hours after, it should be churned.

4th. If the temperature of the room where the churning is performed in, be below 60°, let the cream and milk be about 65°, when the churning commences ; but if the temperature of the room be above, or at 65°, let the mixture be about 60°.

5th. Whether the churning be performed by steam power, horse power, or by manual labour, the motion must be quick at first. If by man there must be a regular supply of what we, in Lancashire, call "elbow grease." The separation should take place within the hour, or there is something wrong either in the temperature or in the churner. I frequently see men or women dabbling in the churn for half a day, or more, when there is nothing more required but "elbow grease" to make the separation take place in proper time.

6th. As soon as the separation takes place, churn slow till the butter collects into lumps. If the weather be hot, adding a little cold water will effect this sooner.

7th. Immediately after the churning is finished, let the butter be taken out of the buttermilk and worked a little, to get a great portion of the milk from it. Then add a little fine salt and work it again, still taking the milk from it as it springs. Then add what salt is intended to be put in, more or less, according to the time it is intended to be kept, but never make butter without salt if it be only intended to be kept one week. Make the salt fine. The dairy-woman must then use some "elbow grease" in working the salt in ; and, in doing this, all the milk will come out. The butter will then be sweet and solid, and will remain so for twelve months if it be put into proper vessels, and has had a proper quantity of salt put in it. Butter washed in water will never keep so well as that managed in the above way.

I shall conclude with two remarks. 1st. The very best dairy-women, who make their fingers into thermometers, will sometimes spoil a churning of butter. 2nd. Cream which has been once frozen, will be difficult to make butter of afterwards, even if raised to a proper temperature.　　　　I remain, Sir, yours, &c.,

Winwick, March 20th.　　　　W. ROTHWELL.

ON THE MANURES WHICH ARE GENERALLY FOUND ON THE FARM.

BY CUTHBERT W. JOHNSON, ESQ., F.R.S.

Although there are few farms in our islands whose profitable culture cannot be assisted by additional artificial manures, yet it is equally certain that it is rarely found that the fertilizers which the land itself produces are used to the extent to which they are profitably capable. These means of agricultural improvement, therefore, will be the subject of this paper. Of the many neglected sources of fertility commonly met with in most districts, is the mixture of soils—the rendering the sands and gravels more tenacious, and more fertile, since more retentive of moisture, by the addition of clay, marl, or chalk, and the addition of sand or ashes, or lime to the clays to render them more friable. This source of improvement, and of *permanent* improvement too, is one that hardly any farm of any tolerable extent is entirely without; or if the desired earthy manure is not to be found on the surface of the farm, or at only a tolerable depth, yet still within an easy distance, some earth or other is usually found which is capable when spread over the fields of more than repaying the cultivator for the expense of its transport. It is in this way that the farmers of some of the clay soils of north Hants bring to the surface, by sinking deep pits, considerable quantities of chalk, many cubic yards of which they with great profit spread over their lands. It is thus, too, that the farmers of Norfolk have imparted a sufficient degree of solidity to their blowing sands, by bringing to the surface the clay and the marl, which so often forms the substrata of these now celebrated barley districts. The deep calcareous sand pits, which the Suffolk farmers have formed in the craig formation of that county, betray by their very extent that even the most ferruginous sand is not without its agricultural value when carefully spread over certain soils. In all parts of the island, in fact, this judicious admixture of earths is to a certain extent carrying on; it is only the extension of the system that I am advocating. The farmers of the northern counties have long burnt their limestones and spread the lime thus produced over their cold, wet soils. The peaty lands of Lincolnshire have been long since, to a large extent, clayed and marled, and thousands of cubic yards of the calcareous sands of the shores of Cornwall are annually spread over its heavier soils.

All these efforts, let the young farmer remember, have for their object, not only to bring the three earths—silica (flint), alumina (clay), and lime—which constitute all cultivated soils, into a more fertile proportion to each other; but it is a very common result, when the soil is chemically examined, that a deficiency of some essential earthy constituent of plants is found in it (of carbonate of lime for instance), which deficiency the earthy manure is found to contain. To determine this, careful practical observations can alone supply the absence of chemical analysis. Of the invariable presence of the earths—silica, alumina, and lime—as constituents of his ordinary crops, although in varying proportions every intelligent farmer is aware; thus as I have in another place had occasion to remark (and the chemistry of the operation cannot be too generally understood) M. Schræder obtained from thirty-two ounces of the seeds of wheat *(Triticum hybernum)*, of rye *(Secale cereale)*, barley *(Hordeum vulgare)*, oats *(Avena sativa)*, and of rye straw, the following substances, the weight being given in grains—*(Gehlen Journ.* vol. iii. p. 525):—

	Wheat.	Rye.	Barley.	Oats.	Rye Straw.
Silica	13·2	15·6	66 7	144·02	152 0
Carbonate of Lime...	12·6	13·4	24 8	33·75	46 2
Carbonate of Magnesia............	13·4	14·2	25·3	33·09	28·2
Alumina	0 6	1·4	4·2	4 05	3·2
Oxide of Manganese	5·0	3·2	6·7	6 95	6·8
Oxide of Iron	2·5	0·9	3.8	4 05	2·4
	47·3	48·7	131·5	227·8	238·8

The earth, silica, or flint, abounds in almost every description of vegetable matter, especially in the grasses, and Equisetum (horse-tail). In the Dutch rush it is so plentiful that that plant is used by the turner to polish wood, bone, and even brass. It forms so considerable a portion of the ashes of wheat straw, that when these are exposed to the action of the blow-pipe, it unites with the potash found also in the straw, and forms an opaque glass. Davy found it most copiously in the epidermis or outer bark of the plants he examined.　　　　Parts.

100 parts of the epidermis of bonnet cane
　contain of silica .... 90·0
100 parts of the epidermis of bamboo cane.. 74·5
100 parts of the epidermis of common reed.. 48·1
100 parts of the epidermis of stalks of wheat 6·5

In the joints of the bamboo a concrete substance is found, which Fourcroy and Vauquelin examined, and ascertained that it consists of 70 parts of silica, and 30 parts of potassa. This substance, which is named *tabasher,* can only be furnished by the soil.—*(Gehlen,* vol. ii. p. 112).

Silica, according to M. Saussure, constitutes 3 per cent. of the ashes of the leaves of oak gathered in May, 14·5 per cent. of those gathered in September, and 2 per cent. of the wood. In the ashes obtained by burning the wood of the poplar, it exists in the proportion of 3·3 per cent.; of the hazel, 20·5 per cent.; of the mulberry 0·12 per cent.; of the hornbeam 0·12 per cent.; 0·5 per cent. in peas *(Pisum sativum)*; 61·5 in the straw of wheat; 0·25 in the seeds; 57·0 per cent. in the chaff of barley; 35·5 in its seeds; and in the oat plant 60 per cent.

Lime is, if possible, still more generally present in all plants than silica. "The salsola soda," says Dr. Thomson, "is the only plant in which we know for certain it does not exist." *(Syst. of Chem,* vol.

iv. p. 190). It is, however, united with carbonic acid as carbonate of lime; or it exists as the base of some other salt, such as in oxalate of lime, or in sulphate of lime (gypsum). It was found in the ashes remaining after the combustion of oak wood, at the rate of 32 per cent., by M. Saussure. In that of the poplar at the rate of 27 per cent. He discovered also 8 per cent. in those from the wood of the hazel; 56 in those of the mulberry wood; 26 in the hornbeam; 14 in the ripe plant of peas; 1 per cent. in the straw of the wheat, but not any in its seeds; 12 in the chaff of barley, but none in either its flour or its bran; neither did he find any in the oak plant; but then, in the ashes of the leaves of the fir (*Pinus abies*), raised on a limestone hill, he found 43·5 per cent.

Alumina is found in most vegetables, but in much smaller proportion than either silica or carbonate of lime, and the same remark applies to magnesia. M. Schræder found, as we have before seen, in two pounds weight of the seeds of wheat only $\frac{6}{10}$ths of a grain of alumina, in rye $1\frac{7}{10}$ grains, in barley $4\frac{3}{10}$ grains, in oats $4\frac{1}{2}$ grains, and in rye straw $3\frac{7}{10}$ grains. In 12 ounces of wormwood there are about 5 grains of alumina. This earth, however, necessarily exists in all fertile soils as the food of plants; for although the proportions in which it is found are rather small, yet still there is no reason to believe that its presence is not essential to the healthy growth of the plant. M. Saussure found the ashes of the *Pinus abies*, growing on a granitic and on a calcareous soil, to contain nearly the same quantity of alumina (15 per cent. on the calcareous and 16 per cent. on the granitic), although these soils differed widely in the proportion of the alumina they contained; for 100 parts of each were composed of—(*Thomson's Chem.* vol. iv. p. 317):—

The Granitic soil.	Parts.	The Calcareous soil.	Parts.
Silica	75·25	Carbonate of Lime	98·000
Alumina	13·25	Alumina	0·625
Lime	1·74	Oxide of Iron	0·625
Iron & Manganes	9·00	Petroleum	0·025
	99·24		99.275

Such are the earths that constitute all cultivated soils, and such is the proportion in which they form the elements of some of the plants which they support. In the soils of the cultivator, however, they exist in an endless variety of proportions; it is by rendering these proportions more fertile that earthy manures are so permanently valuable to the soil: thus, I found 68·5 per cent. of silica in the gravelly soils of Great Totham, in Essex, and 62 in those of Kintbury, in Berkshire. Davy discovered about 50 per cent. in the soil of the Eudsleigh Pastures, in Devonshire; 54 in that near Sheffield Place in Sussex; 15 in the turnip soils of Holkham, in Norfolk; 32 in the finely divided matters of the wheat soils of West Drayton; and about 97 per cent. the soil of Bagshot Heath. Mr. George Sinclair found about 66 per cent. in the grass garden of Woburn Abbey.

Of alumina, or pure earth of clay, the proportions are equally varying. I ascertained the presence of 4·5 per cent. of this earth in a gravelly soil of Thurstable in Essex, and 8·5 in one at Kintbury in Berkshire. Mr. G. Sinclair found 14 per cent. in the soil of the grass garden at Woburn Abbey. Davy detected 8·5 per cent. in that at Endsleigh, 6·25 in one at Croft Church in Lincolnshire, 7 in that in Sheffield Place, 11 in that of Holkham, 29 in a field at West Drayton, and about 1 per cent. in the soil of Bagshot Heath.

Of carbonate of lime, the presence is just as varying in amount as that of the other earths. I found 18 per cent. in a soil at Totham, and 19 per cent. in a soil at Kintbury; Sinclair 2 per cent. in the soil of the Woburn Abbey grass garden. Davy discovered 8 per cent. in that from Croft Church, 3 per cent. in that of Sheffield Place, 63 per cent. in the finely divided matters of the soil from Holkham, and about 1 per cent. only in the soil from Bagshot.

The expense of carrying clay or marl from the pit, and spreading it over the field, is not so expensive an operation as is sometimes supposed. In some extensive trials of Mr. Linton (*Jour. Roy. Ag. Soc. v. ii. p.* 67), where marl was added to the soil at the rate of 150 cubic yards per acre, the expense was 5*l*. 9s. 8d. Mr. Rodwell carried many thousand cubic yards at 8d. per cubic yard (*Farmers' Encyclopædia*, p. 862); and in Bedfordshire Mr. Overman, who applies about forty loads (of forty bushels) per acre, pays his men 3d. per load to fill and spread. And in estimating the expense, the farmer must not forget that this mode of fertilising the soil is not like the application of decomposing manures, beneficial only for a brief period, but that the very staple of the soil is improved.

When, however, we have accomplished all that can be effected in adding the simple earths or mixtures of earths to the soil, there is yet much to be effected by the use of earth mixed with organic matters—such as commonly occurs in headlands, old hedge-rows, pond-mud, ditch scrapings, &c.—to which, in order to promote the dissolution of their decomposing matters, it is a common and excellent practice to add to each cubic yard a bushel of lime, or half a bushel of refuse common salt (the marine variety of the bacon merchants is excellent); or even to saturate the mass with urine or other concentrated liquid manure. This compost is generally found to be an excellent top-dressing for grass lands or for potatoes (especially with salt), wheat, or spring corn.

The wasteful drainage from the farm-yard, and the readiness with which liquid manure may be prepared on all farms, to increase the cultivator's stock of organic fertilizers, will be perhaps the subject of another paper; for much yet remains to be accomplished in its extended use; for, as Mr. M. Milburn very truly remarks (*Trans. High. Soc., v. viii. p.* 275), "The generality of farmers are too apt to allow the whole of the urine made by their stock, the drainage of the fold-yards, and the liquid from the mixens, to run down some sewer, and enrich the rank grass and weeds which it approaches, or run into some distant river.'

To the collection and preparation of weeds, turf, roadside parings, &c., the same remarks in general apply as to the use of pond-mud, &c.; and let it be remembered that this kind of labour has moreover this superadded advantage, that while manure is collected weeds are destroyed; the land is enriched while the tillage is improved.

And then, again, with regard to the preparation of "home-made" manures applicable by the drill— a mode of fertilising the land now advancing with rapid strides, and which I venture to predict is an excellent practice, that will annually continue to extend — much may be done by the farmer from his own resources; by a little care in collecting and storing under cover valuable mixtures of night-soil, ashes, &c., a dry, sufficiently friable, and valuable drill manure may be readily prepared, sufficient for a considerable extent of turnip land. And if to the ashes procured from burnt earths, &c., only a limited proportion of rich animal matter is added, the supply may be extended to almost any extent. Mr. Marshall, of Riseholme, has given (*Jour. Roy. Ag. Soc., v.* iii. *p.* 164) the composition of several preparations of this kind which he has successfully used for turnips, of which the best varieties seem to consist of, per acre :—1. A mixture of twenty bushels of night-soil and cinder ashes, worked together, with forty bushels of clay ashes. 2. Of twelve bushels of crushed oyster shells, six gallons of whale-oil, with forty bushels of ashes. 3. Six bushels of crushed bones, four gallons of whale-oil, and forty bushels of ashes.

In some trials by Mr. George Sherborne, in Middlesex, about forty bushels per acre of common cinder ashes, mixed with three or four gallons per acre of train oil, was found an excellent drill manure for Swedish turnips.

And then, with regard to the formation of compost with the farm-yard dung, much more may be effected in extending its bulk without materially diminishing its power than is commonly believed; f. r instance, it may be mixed before it is fermented with peat with tanners' refuse, bark, or sawdust, with considerable advantage. The compost may In this way be easily increased in bulk, from one-third to double its former size.

It is by such economical additions to his stock of fertilizers that the cultivator will readily be enabled to diminish the necessity for purchasing the powerful drill manures now importing from abroad or prepared in this country ; and the intelligent farmer will remember that, when he is thus availing himself of the resources of the land he possesses, that he is not only saving his money, but he is giving extended employment to the labouring population around him; so that while he is increasing the internal resources of his farm, he is adding to the comforts of his poorer neighbours.

ILLOGAN PLOUGHING MATCH.

(FROM THE CORNWALL GAZETTE.)

On Monday, February 12th, a most interesting display of agricultural skill took place in Tehidy Park, where there was a large attendance to witness the competition, and to promote by their presence and encouragement the truly English object of " Speed the Plough." Nineteen ploughs competed, of which no less than twelve were without drivers. All were drawn by horses except one, which had two yoke of oxen. The quantity of ground marked out for each was 12 yards wide, and 160 yards long, being one-third of a customary acre. Printed rules for their guidance were delivered to all the ploughmen before starting. The arrangements were made under the direction of Lady Basset's agriculturist, Mr. Peter. The Judges were Mr. Gill, of St. Clements, Mr. Rosewarne of Gwinear, and Mr. Davis of Probus. The merits of the competitors were judged of simply by the appearance of the work when finished, without regard to time, the judges not attending on the field until after the ground was ploughed. The following were the awards.

Ploughmen.	Owner.	Time.
1st. 2l. Benj. Rowe.	.Mr. Williams, Bosproul	4h. 40m.
2nd. 1l. And. Lumsden.	Lady Basset, Park farm	3 85
3rd. 10s. W. Thomas.	.J. S. Enys, Esq.	Enys 4 10

WITH DRIVER.

1st. 1l. 10s. Rowland White, Mr.Martin, Carnhill		5 10
2nd. 15s. T. Chenowth (oxen) Lady Basset, Tehidy		4 35
3rd. 7s. 6d. S. Parkville, Mr.Carthew, Tregogiran		4 8

HIGHLY COMMENDED.

John Skewis, Lady Basset, Park farm ; Thomas Chenowth, Lady Basset, Tehidy ; Andrew Stephens, St. Erth, who would have obtained a prize if the second half of his work had been equal to the first. Both the first prizes were won by Ransome's Rutland plough.

Towards the close of the match, Mr. W. Short, sen., exhibited a plough manufactured by himself, which is new to this part of the country, and indeed has been brought very little into notice, though it was invented about twenty years ago by Thomas Brown, Esq., of Kinwarton, Warwickshire. One of these ploughs was exhibited at the Bristol Meeting last year, and is very highly commended in the report on the exhibition of implements, which is published in the Journal of the Royal Agricultural Society. A full description with plates, will be found in the Farmer's Magazine for January 1843. The chief peculiarity consists in the addition of two pulverizing knives attached to moveable bars extending beyond the end of the mould board. The effect of these knives is to cut off the angular summit of the furrow slice just raised, and to divide it into two or three portions, thus almost combining harrowing with ploughing. The additional work is done with a very small increase of power. The action of the plough, which is called the surface pulverizing plough, afforded much satisfaction to the practical farmers present, and the invention appears very valuable. The action of the subsoil plough was also shewn, working at a depth of eighteen inches. Its power and effect in heaving and breaking the subsoil without bringing any to the surface afforded much surprise to those who had not before seen it in action, and many a stick was thrust down into the furrow to mark the depth to which the ground was broken.

At four o'clock 34 gentlemen, farmers, and others, sat down to an excellent dinner at the Basset Arms, Pool. The Rev. G. Treweeke, rector of Illogan, presided, supported by W. Reynolds, Esq., of Trevenson, the Rev.—Wulff, rector of Gwinear, the Rev. E. Pridmore, &c. Mr. Hichens of Fairfield acted as vice-chairman. The usual loyal toasts were drunk, after which the award of the judges was read. The Chairman then proposed the health of Lady Basset, prefacing it with commendations whose justice was fully acknowledged by all present, and particularly noticing, what was so remarkable in a lady, her zeal in promoting agriculture, and teaching the best methods of cultivation.

The Vice-chairman then gave the health of a friend who had given the Illogan Farmer's Club important assistance by a valuable present of books, and who felt much interest in their proceedings, and who regretted that he was unable to attend—John Basset, Esq.

The chairman next gave the health of the umpires, whose great credit as agriculturists, and their impartial and honourable characters, could leave no doubt of the justice and truth of their award.

Mr. GILL acknowledged the compliment for himself and his colleagues. They had performed their duty to the best of their ability. The ploughing was very good. He had never seen better. He feared their award might not give satisfaction to every one, for the fact was, that three or four of the numbers came so near together, that the judges were nearly an hour before they could decide.

The successful competitors were then called in, and the chairman addressed to each some appropriate remarks in delivering to him his prize. This gratifying part of the business of the day being concluded, the health of Mr. Peters was drunk, and the chairman called upon him to deliver his Lecture on Ploughing.

"Before commencing the operation of ploughing, the first requisite is to have a plough, the next a sufficient power to draw it along.

"There are many sorts of ploughs now in use, each having its advocates; and possibly different descriptions might answer in different localities. In some places wheel ploughs are approved of; in others, swing ploughs. The old Cornish plough is a swing plough, and a very simple implement, which, with some improvements, might be rendered useful, as it is at any rate very inexpensive.

"There is a description of ploughs which in my opinion deserves to be more noticed—that is, 'Turnwrest ploughs', or those which plough the land all one way, with the mould plate first working on the right, and then on the left. There was an iron plough here to-day belonging to Mr. Grey of Endellion, and exhibited by the maker, Mr. William Short, of Camelford, which seemed to have some useful improvements; the small skim coulter, for paring off the surface, from that part of the furrow which, when turned, came near the surface, and more especially two furrow slicers, working on the furrow after it was turned over, and placed horizontally behind the mould plate, were calculated to pulverise the ground, and save a good deal of labour. Such a plough, I think, might be most usefully employed in ploughing turnip land on which sheep had been folded.

' Amongst all the different sorts of ploughs, my own opinion is, that a plain iron swing plough has a decided preference, when competently managed, being so readily adapted to the various operations on a farm; but this opinion on my part may be strengthened by the circumstance of my having been most accustomed to such ploughs.

"There is now I believe little difference of opinion as to what is the most convenient power for drawing along the plough—a pair of horses yoked abreast, the ploughman driving with reins, being preferable to most others;—although we have seen very good work to-day by Lady Basset's four oxen, and even in less time than some of the ploughs with horses.

"The first thing in commencing to plough a grass field is to mark off with a slight furrow the intended breadth for end ridges for turning the plough and the teams upon; and the next, is marking out, or opening the ridge. There are different modes of doing this; but what I approve of is, first to plough a small shallow furrow, laying the next or "backing" furrow over the first, so as to set its angle upright; the third and fourth furrows should be rather narrower and shallower than the ploughing intended, and should meet the other in such a manner as to leave their angles on the same level. If properly managed, the second furrow should present the same angle and appearance as the rest of the furrows, leaving the place of opening almost imperceptible. The breadth of ploughing should be regulated by the depth. There is a difference in this proportion in different ploughs; but a depth being given, the ploughman can at once proportion the breadth, by seeing that one furrow is laid upon the other, so that the angle may stand upright, and that measuring from the top each way the distance may appear alike on both sides after the work is finished. The finishing of the ridge is of much importance, and the necessity for more attention to this must have been apparent to-day. Another thing is the ploughing of any corners or angular pieces. This is best done as for example in a piece shaped like the letter V, by beginning your work in the middle of the wide end first making a very narrow opeaing directed towards the narrow point, and gradually extending every furrow, keeping as nearly parallel to the outer boundaries as possible. Thus not a single hoof need to trample on the ploughed land. No field that is correctly ploughed should have any part trampled by the horses in turning after it is ploughed. Short angles may be laid to the rest with a single furrow, that is, by returning empty, if with a common plough.

"The next thing I shall consider is the ploughing of stubble, or arish. This is done in different ways. By reversing the order in which it was ploughed from grass—by ploughing across—by trench ploughing—by ribbing (or coombing)—by double ribbing, that is, by first ribbing in the ordinary way, and then to turn over in the same direction the ground left unturned before, along with the coomb previously turned. This is reckoned to give great facility to the cleaning out of couch, or "stroil," by laying it open to the operation of the harrow, &c. My worst objection to it is, that the land is not turned to the proper depth before winter—a point I consider most essential.

"In cross-ploughing, or otherwise ploughing the land for fallow in spring, the openings should be made by throwing out two furrows—one in going, and the other in returning to the right of the former, leaving as little in the middle as possible; part of these furrows being returned in ploughing in the fast ground under them, so as to form something like a ridge drill in the middle. Thus every part of the ground is broken without being but slightly elevated above the rest of the field.

"It is of much importance that attention be paid to having such openings quite straight, and at regular intervals, much time being often occupied needlessly in ploughing such land, from the supposed indifference as to whether it is done straight or not. This is the best field for young beginners, or others learning to plough straight, as corrections can be made without much injury. The operation of the subsoil plough, which was exhibited at work to-day, is simple. The upper furrow being first turned by the common plough, the other follows, loosening the subsoil under, without bringing any of it to the surface.

"The next thing I shall advert to is drilling for green crops of mangel wurtzel, potatoes, turnips, &c. This is done in different ways—with the common plough, making a drill by going and returning; this has one advantage. Although requiring more time, as by taking on a greater width with the " taking in" furrow than required for the drill and cutting off this part with our next furrow, the land is most effectually loosened. With the common plough, making the drill with a single furrow; this is a most expeditious and in my opinion the best way of drilling for turnips, especially when dung is to be applied.

" The ploughman begins at a short distance from one side of the field and makes a number of drills, into which is placed the manure. He then, after making a drill on the right side of his work, returns to the drill first made and splits it with the plough, covering in the manure. He thus proceeds, alternately making a drill to the right and splitting a furrow in returning, always leaving a sufficient number of drills in the interval for the operation of manuring.

" Any number of ploughs can follow each other in this operation, the drill being made always to the right of the last. By some, a simple contrivance is used to regulate the width, a rod being placed over the mould plate, with a fastening forward, to which a small "marker" is suspended. The required distance being marked off, the plough is carried along the mark, by which the greatest regularity in width is secured. The advantage of this plan is apparent in dry weather, as the drills being newly opened are moist, and the manure being applied and covered in almost immediately insures a regular braird.

" Another mode is by drilling with a double or banking plough, as it is termed, with a mould plate on each side, but I have seen but few who could make very efficient work with this, it being difficult to manage; and it does not so well loosen the ground, as it works much by pressure. Following out the working of these crops, there is the use of the horse hoe and small plough, and the banking up, which does not require much tact. There is one thing I may mention, that when the ground is hard and requires loosening between the rows, when about to be banked up, both are most effectually done by using the small plough, giving three furrows to each drill, taking away the furrow, first from the left hand drill, and in returning taking it from the other; but this to be a larger furrow and thrown over to bank up that from which the first was taken; the third furrow taking away part of the last and deepening the middle distance, breaking up the other drill at the same time.

" To finish a course, the next thing I shall advert to is the ploughing of land after green crops, preparatory to its being laid down with a corn crop to grass. Great caution ought here to be used to render the ground as level as possible. When not to be ploughed in ridges the turnwrest plough does this to most advantage; but where ridges are adopted, the marking off should be most correct, for which purpose a small cross staff should be used to mark off parallel lines for measuring, and two or more poles should be set up in opening the ground so as to insure correctness. A ploughman having two objects to bring in a line before him can direct his course and open his furrow straight. Whatever difference of opinion may exist in regard to the depth or breadth of ploughing, no doubt in the world can be entertained of the advantage of straight and correct ploughing, both as regards economy of time, and efficiency of work. Such land is generally ploughed rather narrow and not so deep as in other cases,

especially in ploughing where sheep have been folded.

" There is one other thing to be mentioned—drilling for wheat on barley with the small plough, which is done in the same way as the single drilling of turnips, by always going to the right of the last furrow, leaving the drills at any required distance, say nine, ten, twelve, or fifteen inches, as may be required. The corn sown in this after being properly harrowed appears in drills. Beans and peas are sometimes put in on the same principle.

" As I expected my friends the ploughmen here I could not let the opportunity pass of stating the advantage of, and strongly recommending, the better education of ploughmen. The necessity of a certain degree of arithmetical knowledge must be apparent; a knowledge of some of the first principles of geometry will enable them to lay out their work, and also give them a correct taste for the execution of it.

" The questions likely to arise to them in those branches are pretty numerous. I may instance, quantities of seed to be sown in a certain space of ground—quantity of bone dust or other manure per acre; how far should a bushel or a cwt. extend either in drill or otherwise at given widths? A certain number of loads of dung per acre, how far should a cart load go? So many tons of lime per acre, how many heaps (if put into heaps) form the cart load of a given weight? These with many other questions will often occur; how convenient for a master, and how pleasant for the farm labourer or ploughman, if he is capable of executing an order from his master exactly under any of the above circumstances. So in geometry, a knowledge of the rules by which he could most readily take the lines for determining the contents of irregular piece of ground by simple calculations.

" There is another thing, calculating the weight of cattle, hay, &c. by measurement: this enables a man in some degree to correct his ideas as to their value.

" Most of the above, nay, all these questions are learned by simple rules; and a small work on the subject, with familiar terms and explanations, would be very useful. The time and opportunities of ploughmen would allow them to reap great benefit as self teachers, or by teaching one another. Adult teaching in the practical rules necessary for particular trades or occupations is the best revival of the rudiments of education taught in youth.

" There were several other things which I intended to recommend to ploughmen and others. The use of the line for correct work, clearing out water courses, sides of hedges, &c.; how neat such jobs look if correctly executed, compared to what we too often see of work executed at random. The keeping of ploughs, carts, harness, &c. clean; a tidy disposal of all implements about the farm yard, so that when any article is wanted they can place their hands on it at once; no better general rule for which could be given than the old one of " having a place for every thing, and every thing in its place."

The Rev. E. PRIDMORE rose to propose the thanks of the company to the lecturer, and took occasion to notice the great improvement which had lately taken place in ploughing in their neighbourhood. At their ploughing match only two years ago, prizes were refused to those who ploughed deep, for it was supposed that our soil would only admit of shallow ploughing, and only one of the competitors then ploughed without a driver. To-day the furrows were six inches deep, and prizes were refused to shallow ploughing ; while of nineteen ploughs in the field no less than twelve were guided by the ploughman himself without a driver.

The proposal was responded to by acclamation, and the chairman with many around him left; but there were many who remained discussing the peaceful contests and triumphs of the day to a late hour.

WARWICK CORN AVERAGES.

We beg the attention of our readers to the following communication from Mr. Umbers, of Wappenbury, on the subject of the returns for Warwick. Should many such *mistakes* occur a serious effect must be produced on the averages. The subject is of a nature so serious and important as to demand the attention of the Government, and should be noticed in parliament. We have no doubt that in this case it was entirely a mistake ; it shows the necessity of a check ; but for Mr. Umbers the mistake would not have been discovered; and if any number of persons in any other places were to make false returns, unless there be some authorised check, or a Mr. Umbers in each place, the law may be evaded, and injustice inflicted on the whole agricultural class. The thanks of his brother farmers are due to Mr. Umbers for his vigilance, and we trust that his example will be imitated, and a watchful eye kept on the returns generally. Farmers are too apt *to leave the care of their interests to others.*

(COPY).

TO GEORGE JOYCE, ESQ., COMPTROLLER OF CORN RETURNS, BOARD OF TRADE, LONDON.

First.

SIR,—At Warwick market, on Saturday last, the 28th inst., I was surprised to see the Inspector of Corn Returns list exhibited upon a board in the corn market, for the week ending the 21st of January, 1843—a copy of which I send you herewith, viz. :—

			Average.	
qrs.	bush.		s.	d.
851	0	Wheat	51	6
460	0	Barley	31	10
163	0	Oats	20	4
62	0	Beans	41	6
6	5	Peas	33	4

Being a regular attendant at this market, and generally a seller of grain as a grower, my attention was called to the above return. I called upon the inspector in order to ascertain how the mistake originated. I was informed that the returns were correct, as received from parties making them. I requested to inspect the book or the returns (but was informed that was not allowed) in the hope of detecting the error. It is a most egregious return, and calculated to prejudice the interests of the growers of grain of this country, if allowed to continue.

I will engage to say that not 50 qrs. of barley was sold in Warwick market, on the day to which this return refers, at so high a price as 31s. per qr. ;

and as to beans, the finest quality of old ones in the market, during the last four months, would not command 34s. per qr.

I trust that you will institute an immediate enquiry into the matter, in order to discover and expose the parties in whom the error originated, to prevent a recurrence in future. In haste,

I am, sir, your very humble servant,
THOMAS UMBERS.

Wappenbury, Jan. 31st.

Second.

SIR,—I addressed a letter to you on the 31st ult., and feel very much surprised that I have not received an acknowledgment of the receipt from you. I shall be glad to be informed, per return of post, if my letter came to hand. In haste,

I am, sir, your humble servant,
THOMAS UMBERS.

Wappenbury, Feb. 12.

COPY OF LETTER FROM GEO. JOYCE, ESQ., AFTER RECEIVING MY SECOND.

TO THOMAS UMBERS, ESQ., WAPPENBURY, NEAR LEAMINGTON SPA.

First.

SIR,—I beg at the same time that I acknowledge the receipt of your two letters of the 31st ult., and the 12th inst., to apologize for any apparent neglect on my part in not having replied to your former communication before this. The fact is, that *immediately* on its receipt, I addressed a letter on the subject, to the corn inspector, at Warwick, and from whom I have not yet received any answer.

As, however, this gentleman is appointed by the Excise, and, consequently, is under their instructions, it is possible that he will not move in the matter without their direction. I would, therefore, suggest (in case such be his feeling) that you should address the Commissioners of the Excise on the point, or ascertain from him if such be the fact. I will, however, write to him again by this post.

I am, sir, yours, very obediently,
GEO. JOYCE.

Corn Department, Board of Trade, Feb. 14:

Second.

SIR,—I have just received a letter from Mr. Hopps, Inspector of Corn Returns for Warwick, in answer to the one I addressed to him on the 1st inst., relative to the high averages of barley and beans, which you were so kind as to call my attention to ; he informs me that the error arose from the imperfect manner of the dealers' sale ticket, from which he copied bags as bushels, which caused the difference of price in his calculations. I have desired him to give the necessary explanation and take this opportunity of thanking you for the trouble you have taken on the subject.

I am, sir, your obedient servant,
GEO. JOYCE.

Corn Department, Board of Trade, Feb. 17.

COPY OF LETTER FROM INSPECTOR OF CORN RETURNS, WARWICK.

SIR,—On this morning, I received a communication from the Board of Trade, respecting the averages of barley and beans reported on the 21st ult., and directing me to investigate the matter.

Upon examination it appears that from the very confused manner in which some of the corn factors had made out their returns, and sending them to me without remarking whether the quantity purchased by them were qrs., bush., or bags; I, consequently, mistook bags for bush. and *vice versa* on two occasions, which was the cause of the errors alluded to. Herewith I have sent you the true averages for that week.

I am, sir, yours, very obediently,
HUGH JAMES HOPPS,
Inspector of Corn Returns.
Excise Office, Warwick, Feb. 15.

COPY OF TRUE AVERAGES FROM INSPECTOR.

COUNTY OF WARWICK—TOWN OF WARWICK—DATE, JAN. 21, 1843.

An account of the quantities and prices of the several sorts of British corn sold in this market, or the said town, during the week ending Saturday last, according to the returns made to the inspector by the corn-factors, &c.; computed by the standard imperial measure :—

		Total amount.	Price per qr.
qrs.	bush.	£. s. d.	£. s. d.
Barley 480	0	643 14 9	1 6 9
Beans 88	2	128 13 0	1 9 1

The quantity and amount of each article have been carefully examined and compared with the entries of all the purchases stated in the returns delivered to me by the corn-factors, &c., for the week above mentioned, and the average price of each article has been duly calculated.

HUGH JAMES HOPPS, Inspector.

THE CELEBRATED RED STEER. — An excellent lithograph of this ox, the property of R. W. Baker, Esq., of Cottesmore, and which has attracted so much attention in the agricultural world, has just been published by Mr. W. H. Davis, of Chelsea, animal painter to her Majesty the Queen Dowager. It is said to be an excellent likeness of the animal. According to the description on the print this animal has won eleven prizes. In 1839, the second prize in the 7th class at the meeting of the Rutland Agricultural Society. In 1840, the first prize in the 12th class at the Bourne Agricultural Society. In 1841, the first prize in the 7th class at the Bourne Agricultural Society, the first prize in the 7th class at the Stamford Agricultural Society, and the first prize in the 6th class at the Waltham Agricultural Society. At the Waltham meeting the age of the steer was disputed, since which attention having been called to the question of age, no successful opposition has been made, and the following ing prizes have been awarded to him. In 1841, the 1st prize, 3rd class, at the Rutlandshire Agricultural Society, and the 1st prize, 3rd class, in the Leicester Agricultural Society. In 1842, the 1st prize, in the 1st class at the Stamford Agricultural Society, the 1st prize, in the 1st class at the Rutland Agricultural Society ; and the 2nd prize, in the 1st class at the Smithfield Club Show in December last, there being 23 competitors.

AGRICULTURAL DEPRESSION.

TO THE EDITOR OF THE FARMER'S MAGAZINE.

SIR,—Although I may only be repeating arguments that have already been much better explained in your magazine, still, with your permission, I shall beg leave to recal the attention of your readers to the following facts.

One apology that is often urged for the income-tax is, that the reduction in the price of provisions caused by the alteration in the duties on corn, live stock, &c., will enable each head of a family to save the amount of his income-tax in his household expenditure. Now, let us observe how this applies to the farmers. The reduction in the price of wheat is at least 2s. a bushel since last year, and live stock has diminished one-quarter—some say one-third—in value ; so the farmer has not only his income materially reduced, but an extra tax on his industry to pay into the bargain. If this be not "helping a lame dog over a stile," I do not know what is. It is said that should prices continue so low rents must be reduced ; and this is my opinion. But no reduction in rents can meet the loss sustained by the present value of corn. Land in this neighbourhood, which produces twenty bushels of wheat per acre, is let at 20s.; thus the loss of 2s. a bushel amounts to double the entire rent.

I am not sufficiently conversant with the subject to say how the corn law question ought to be eventually settled ; but this I can positively state, from sad experience, that the present alteration has already proved of serious injury to the agriculturists ; and I will add one or two observations on what appear to me evident facts. Of late years most of the European countries, as well as the United States, have been forbidding the importation of our principal manufactures for the purpose of encouraging their own. This has been done by means of prohibitory duties, to enable the natives to compete in price with our artizans. The late alterations that I have had the opportunity of seeing in the tariffs of foreign nations seem to me delusory, and only intended to amuse this country, without being of any material benefit to our manufacturers. I think when the duty on corn was reduced last year, it should only have related to those countries that were willing to receive our principal manufactures on the payment of duties equally moderate. I know it is said that, in that case, corn would be sent from one country to another that had made a more advantageous treaty with England, and the introduction of corn from the United States into the Canadas urged as a precedent ; but, with proper care and attention in the arrangement of treaties, surely our experienced statesmen would be able to conquer this difficulty.

To conclude, as I have already stated the reduced value of agricultural produce, I will only add the increase in the farmer's expenses taken for the parish in which I reside. The poor's rate has increased 95 per cent. since the establishment of the new poor law. The tithes are augmented about ten per cent. by the Commutation Act ; and a new impost is added in the form of an income-tax. I have made these few observations quite independent of any party feeling, intending them for the consideration of persons of all political opinions, and only affirm that they contain a concise statement of the real state of things in our neighbourhood.

With many thanks for the information I have derived from the perusal of your magazine,

I am, Sir, your obedient servant,
Chepstow, Feb. 27. VERITAS.

ON THE PROGRESS OF AGRICULTURAL KNOWLEDGE DURING THE LAST FOUR YEARS.

BY PH. PUSEY, M.P., F.R., AND G.S.

(*From the Journal of the Royal Agricultural Society of England.*)

[*Concluded.*]

There is another root, however, which promises also to break through that monotony, and has been made known in England since the foundation of our society, though it has been common for two centuries in Flanders and Germany. I mean the white carrot, of whose produce such surprising accounts have been published. It has been stated to give thirty tons to the acre, each ton selling in some neighbourhoods at £2, or double the value of Swedes. Lord Ducie grows it regularly on Whitfield-farm, and obtains twenty-four tons to the acre: the green tops alone, which may be given to sheep when the root is taken up, are said by Mr. Harris to be equal to a second crop of clover. The only difficulty in its cultivation is the slow growth of the young plant, which can scarcely be distinguished from weeds, unless by women cleaning them on their knees; but this may be obviated by drilling the carrot; and I am told it may be grown on ridges, and therefore horse-hoed. They will thrive on rather strong land, though light warm land is most natural to them. Sub-soiling is almost indispensable, which may be done, however, with a common plough. As this root seems likely at last to take a permanent place in English farming, and as it may be interesting to know in future times how it was introduced, which has been often questioned with regard to the turnip, I may put on the records of our society, that it was brought over in 1835 by Mr. Rham, of Winkfield. There is another carrot, the early horn, of which Lord Ducie obtained sixteen tons to the acre—no trifling yield—and which, by its almost globular shape, appears suited to very shallow soils.

With regard to the use of the carrot, it is known to be good for horses, though too much of it should not be given them before spring, as it is supposed to weaken their eyes in winter. It is also excellent for milch cows. All stock, indeed, is so fond of the carrot as to produce a difficulty in its use, for it makes them refuse other roots; but it may be mixed with them after steaming. It appeared from the account which Colonel Le Couteur has given us of the great bulk of parsnips raised in Jersey, that we might have had to add this root also to our field-crops; but he has since found the white carrot yet more productive, and the tapering growth of the parsnip makes it very difficult to draw from the ground.* I have therefore only to add the mangold-wurtzel potato, which is very coarse but extremely bulky, and is said to be the only potato that should be given to pigs without previously boiling. Of its merits, however, I know nothing positive.

Such is the information we have received on those roots by which our stock are sustained in winter; and I cannot but look back to the former

---

* Parsnips have one advantage over carrots, that hares and rabbits seem not to touch them.—BRAY, ROOKE.

history of farming on this point. The castles of the old barons were victualled at Michaelmas with salt beeves and sheep, because there was little hay for their winter keep. Afterwards more hay was made, and fresh meat was obtained through the year. When our population exceeded the extent of our meadows, the common turnip was introduced: but as this does not well resist frost, it would last only till February. Then came the Swede, which carries us on till the end of March. Another class of summer food, clover, had been also introduced, but would not be ready so soon: vetches therefore were sown in autumn, to be fed off in spring. But there is still an interval to be filled—for vetches do not come in as soon as Swedes are ended. Mangold-wurtzel indeed will carry us through this space of time; but it appears also that, while winter-feed may be prolonged, spring-feed may be hastened by growing an early variety of vetches; and Mr. Williams, a farmer of Ilsley, informs us that last year he had vetches three feet high in the beginning of May, on a backward soil in a high situation. An account is given of this vetch in another part of the present number. Its importance will be seen at once by all flockmasters; if it should stand the trial, the circle of artificial food will be completed throughout the year, and a wonderful triumph, I must say, be secured by the farmer's skill over the seasons. Early rye, indeed, has long been used for the same purpose though some farmers do not approve of it; for while young it gives little food, and it shoots up rapidly to a harsh stalk, which stock do not relish. Clover of course is the mainstay during summer; but it is acknowledged that generally land will not bear its recurrence well every four years, though we have not yet found a substitute. The Italian rye-grass is evidently an acquisition, as it gives not only a greater bulk than the common rye-grass, but is also preferred by sheep. This is a new plant; but in the present Journal we have a strong recommendation of an old one, lucerne, which is the more interesting because Mr. Rodwell brought it before the Board of Agriculture in 1811, and speaks of it with unabated confidence now in 1842. It requires, however, I believe, some depth of soil, and perhaps a favourable climate. Rape, the green crop of the fens, is evidently at home upon poor peaty land, pared and burnt, or dressed with peat-ashes; for such land has a tendency to produce leaves rather than roots; and ashes throw up the rape so strongly, that a flock of sheep is hidden among the stems when at feed in the pen. Sanfoin, on the other hand, is known to prefer a soil full of natural lime. There are many new plants recommended for summer soiling —the Bokhara clover, the Siberian vetch, the Siberian bear's-claw—all three of gigantic growth; but of their merits we know nothing as yet, nor of spurry or of maize (Indian corn), which was recommended at the Doberan meeting of German farmers to be fed off green.

From green crops we are naturally led to the stock which is fed on them; but so much has been done during forty years by the Smithfield Club for our cattle, that little can be expected in four years from our society beyond a wider exhibition of the superiority of English breeds. As those, however, who have not studied the subject undervalue sometimes the show of fat cattle, because the individual animals are too fat for consumption, I think it may be useful to prove what the Smithfield Club has really done. Grazing animals in a wild state, according to Dr. Liebig, will hardly become fat at all. Deer in a park, for the same reason, are not killed before they are six or seven years old; and many may even now remember that mutton was once eaten when five years old. But by selection of individuals in breeding it was found that this time might be shortened. First, the Leicesters—then our larger long-wooled sheep, the Cotswolds—and last, the short-wools, or Southdowns—have been cultivated on this great principle of early maturity; and the Southdowns, as well as the others, have been brought to market as mutton in four, three, two, and lately on some farms at one year of age: so that, to say nothing of root crops having been multiplied four times in weight, the same amount of green food which formerly gave us a sheep only every fifth year is able to produce us now a sheep every year—that is, five sheep for one. A deduction must of course be made for the breeding ewes. It is but common justice to the Smithfield Club to show this vast good which they have done to the country. There is also a Scotch breed of improved sheep, the Cheviot, which I believe would be better suited than our Southdowns for the mountainous parts of Southern England. The same principle has been applied to horned cattle, of which we have also three established breeds—the Short-horns, the Herefords, and the beautiful Devons. Though early maturity has not been carried so far with them, no breed out of Great Britain can compare with them in aptitude to fatten. It is said, indeed, that better milkers may be found than even the shorthorns; and this may be the case; but milk alone cannot be made the test of cattle even for a dairy farm, because the cows which are necessarily discarded each year, for age or barrenness, ought to be suited for fatting. In cattle, too, a Scotch breed, the Ayrshire, may stand by the side of our own, as it appears to unite in a high degree the two requisites of milking and grazing, both upon moderate land; but whether it be suited to our rich southern meadows must be very doubtful.

All these breeds are now fatted chiefly, not on grazing pastures, but on arable ground. The origin of this practice was no doubt the production of meat for an increased population; it is continued and extended, not from a view to profit in the sale of the meat, but for the production of dung, and the consequent increase of the corn crop. It is well known to farmers, though not to others, that the dung of an ox fattened with corn or oil-cake is far more valuable than that of a cow kept in merely ordinary condition—perhaps worth twice as much. This principle is the great distinction of English agriculture, and constitutes what is called high farming. It is worked out in different ways.

Every autumn horned cattle move across England, from Devonshire, Herefordshire, parts of Yorkshire, and Scotland, to the eastern coast, where they are fattened. I do not know why this practice should be confined to that side of the country; but though it may be known elsewhere to individual farmers, all the counties in which stall-feeding seems to be established lie to the east—Essex, Suffolk, Norfolk, Cambridgeshire, Lincolnshire, Yorkshire, Northumberland, and in Scotland the Lothians. There is some variety, however, in the mode. The more common method, I believe, is to tie up the beasts in stalls in close houses. In Northumberland, Mr. Grey, of Dilston, informs me that this plan is given up, and that the cattle are

kept loose (eight or nine together) in small yards, with an open shed on one side; he gives as the reason of this change, that they appear to be more healthy when so treated; that they turn the litter more regularly into manure, do not lose their hair, and, their joints not being stiffened, are better able to travel to market. In Lincolnshire, again, many good farmers find it answer not to fatten beasts at all, but to keep young stock in straw-yards; not, however, upon straw only, as in the old system of low farming, but pushing them forward with oil-cake: for this is one great merit of improved farming, that whereas, by the old practice, the animals which serve for our food were kept often on the brink of starvation for several years—by the new one they are maintained in an improving state from their birth; and so their comfort, as long as they live, coincides with our profit. Such is the high farming of the eastern side of England—there so well known that it may appear superfluous to have described it at all; but in the counties with which I am more conversant—Oxfordshire, Wiltshire, Hampshire, and Berkshire—a feeding-house full of oxen on an arable farm is almost, if not quite, unknown; yet here, too, we have high feeding, which is high farming, but it is the high feeding of sheep penned on the turnip-field, receiving hay, peas, barley, oats, or oil-cake, with their turnips sliced for them in troughs (nor is there a better mark of good farming for the traveller than a turnip-slicer in the fold), and brought to market sometimes at the age of one year. This is excellent farming: and I have been repeatedly told by farmers, that where two flocks have been kept in one field—one fed with corn, the other not—the difference may be distinctly seen along the line where the hurdles had stood in the following crop of barley, marking the efficacy of high feeding.[*] Still, good as the system is, it has this disadvantage in comparison with the feeding of beasts, that the straw grown on the farm is not made into strong dung, but is merely trampled in large yards, from which it comes out very little changed even in its appearance.

But Mr. Childers has brought forward interesting experiments, which show that sheep, as well as oxen, thrive much better for warmth and shelter. He states that "eighty Leicester sheep, on the bare field, consumed about fifty basketfuls of cut turnips per day, besides oil-cake." "On being brought into the shed," he proceeds, "to my surprise, they were immediately only able to consume thirty baskets, and before a month had elapsed the quantity had decreased to twenty-five baskets; thus economising one-half the turnips: they also ate less oil-cake. I found, nevertheless, that their increase was as rapid this year as it was the year before."[†] In the year before, the sheep in the shed had gained one-third more than those in the field: so that here was a saving of one-half of the turnips, with a gain of one-third of meat. Now this result agrees precisely with the most recent discoveries of Dr. Liebig, who has shown that the natural heat of the body is kept up by the use of food, and that the greater the cold the larger must be the consumption

---

[*] In one instance, where a very dry summer followed, the advantage was in favour of the less highly dressed land; a strong instance of the power of dung to injure barley in a dry summer upon burning land.

[†] On Shed-feeding, by Mr. Childers—Journal, i., pp. 169 and 407.

of food; and he instances the Samoyedes, who eat ten pounds of meat daily. "Warm clothing," he adds, "is a substitute for excess of food." Now, I do not say that we are at once to house all our sheep —because, apart from the labour of carting home the turnips and carrying out the dung, the treading of the sheep is almost indispensable on light soils for rendering them firm. But I do think Mr. Childers's discovery most important, and well worth the serious consideration of sheep farmers; and that, in time, it may become the foundation of a change of practice—that the fatting sheep, for instance, may be housed, and the breeding ewes be left on the land, or the fatting sheep be housed by night in winter, or as Mr. Childers suggests, during the heat of the sun in September. It may be said, indeed, why house sheep in heat, if cold is to be guarded against? Partly because heat disagrees with them, as is shown by their panting beneath the sun and seeking the shade, and partly because one advantage of housing them is the saving of dung; for many farmers suspect that there is sometimes a great loss of manure when made by sheep on the land. In dry weather, when the ground is hard, either from heat or frost, a portion of it evaporates rapidly; in wet weather, on light lands, I doubt if it be not sometimes washed downwards below the reach of the following crop. The change, however, would be so great that it would be unwise to make it at once; and, indeed, we require some further experience of its effects on the health of the sheep.*

There is another principle in Mr. Childers's concise paper, scarcely, if at all, less important than that of shed-feeding, which I confess had escaped me altogether, until it was ably pointed out by the Rev. Mr. Thorp, in a paper † read by him before "The Yorkshire Society." That principle is rapid feeding. The usual course, I believe, in feeding sheep, is to keep them about four months upon turnips, increasing the additional food, such as corn and cake, towards the end of the period; but Mr. Childers proposes to feed them to the utmost from the very first. "I think," he says, "the greatest profit would be made by shedding them for about ten weeks. By giving them cake and a little crushed barley I think you may gain from 33 to 40 lbs. per head in that time; their increase in value during that time cannot be less than 15s. to 20s. per head; and in this way you may feed off two or three lots during the winter. In ten weeks they consume half a ton of turnips each. Thus, with artificial food, an acre of 30 tons will feed no less than 60 sheep. The artificial food will cost from 6d. to 1s. each per week."

This would not be exactly a saving of food, as in shed-feeding, but a substitution of other and expensive food for so many turnips, and the further question must be asked, whether this substitution will pay. Assuming Mr. Childers's figures to be correct, that 15s. are added to the value of the sheep, and that the additional food costs about 9d.

---

* Mr. Thompson, of Kirby, has just informed me that shearlings bear shedding better than lambs, and that one farmer who tried shedding last year had considerable loss by purging; he therefore recommends that the back of the shed should be made of open wattle, or that moveable sheds should be used in the field.

† On the Feeding of Sheep—Supplement of his Number.

a week for ten weeks, there would be left 7s. 6d. for the half ton of turnips, which would be enough. The outlay on extra food is large; but then the return would take place in a shorter period, namely, ten weeks, when the money would come back, and a fresh purchase be made. If the system would pay, it is self-evident that a vast increase of the best manure, the whole object of all feeding, would be obtained; and though it is somewhat startling to hear of 60 sheep being fattened on a single acre of turnips, still it would be worth doing, and ought to be done for the sake of the public, if it can be done without loss. This principle of rapid feeding which Mr. Childers has brought forward seems well deserving inquiry; since if it be practicable it must greatly increase our manure, and consequently our crops, according to the bountiful provision of nature, that the more meat we raise on our land, the more corn we are enabled to grow; and that thus, again, having obtained more corn, the more stock in return we are able to feed.

This brings me to the most difficult subject in agriculture, which I have therefore reserved for the last. I mean manure, on which it may be said that we have learnt a great deal in the last four years, but know nothing; for we have learnt many of the chemical principles on which manures act, but we do not yet know how to apply those principles to the daily work of the farm. It is now established that the most important ingredient of farmyard dung is ammonia—the same substance as common smelling-salts—known to escape very readily in the air; and there is a growing opinion that a great deal of it does so escape from our farmyards, which is doubtless the case; though I am not sure whether the alarm on the subject be not somewhat exaggerated. For ammonia arises chiefly from the urine of the cattle, but it does not form itself until after some days; and by that time in a well-littered yard it has sunk from the surface, and has been trampled down fast, so that it can less easily evaporate. Whilst it is forming itself, too, the straw begins to decay; and it is the opinion of Sprengel that an acid called the humic acid, formed from the decaying litter, has the property of combining with the ammonia, and removing its volatile property.* This must be doubtful, of course, and various means of fixing the ammonia have been proposed. Sulphuric acid is one, either in the shape of gypsum, which has been found not to answer, or in that of green vitriol, or as a pure acid; but these are at present only suggestions. We have been also strongly urged to imitate a foreign practice of using liquid manure, spread from a water-cart; but this I believe to be a very doubtful innovation. For if the urine be collected separately, it is the opinion of Sprengel † that a still

---

* Where peat can be obtained, it assists in fixing the ammonia when mixed with the dung, according to Lord Meadowbank's process—See Journal, i., p. 147.—Mr. Dixon on Compost Heaps.

† Dr. Sprengel, after describing the various methods of employing liquid manure, uses these strong words:—"Whoever is obliged for want of straw to collect the urine separately—whoever, if he be compelled to do this, mixes no water with it, or who fails also to employ some neutralising substance to combine with the ammonia which is produced in so great a degree during the summer—suffers a loss of manure which exceeds

greater escape of ammonia takes place, unless some substance, which is not yet ascertained, be added to fix it, or it be largely diluted with water, which occasions great labour in its application. This last objection lies also against the other form of liquid manure, the runnings from the yard collected in a tank; for after heavy rains they sometimes do not contain above two per cent. of salts, and are then not worth the labour of carriage. It appears that this foreign practice has arisen from two causes; one, the want of litter, and where the same cause exists, as on some of our dairy-farms, the method might be well introduced: the other motive is the desire in Flanders of applying a liquid top-dressing in May to the corn growing on sandy land, or else to a second crop, such as carrots sown amongst beans; but this last case does not arise in England. Some loss, however, must arise by the runnings from every farm-yard; for whether the ammonia be fixed or escape in the air, there is no doubt it is still soluble and runs away in the water. One remedy is, to prevent the rain from flowing down the surrounding roofs into the yard, by placing gutters under the eaves. Perhaps another would be what I have seen in an old-fashioned yard, a hollow space, like the basin of a dry pond, three or four feet deep, with a drain near the top that prevents it from overflowing. This hollow I was about to do away with as unsightly; but when filled as it now is with couch-grass—leaves or stubble would certainly have a better appearance —it seems likely to answer the purpose of detaining valuable salts that would otherwise run away. It is also supposed that great waste arises when dung is spread on a field; and this theory has been carried so far that a serious charge has been brought in a daily publication against the farmers of the Vale of Aylesbury, for dressing their meadows, not at a wrong season, but for dressing them with dung at all, as if the whole essence of the dung must be evaporated, though the farmers had not yet found out their mistake. Some waste, I suppose, takes place, for which on meadows there is of course no remedy, but perhaps not so great as is imagined. Mr. Handley informs me that he has observed for years a common field, on part of which, occupied by cottagers, the dung was sometimes allowed to lie spread for many weeks, while on the remainder it was ploughed in at once, but he never could detect any difference in the succeeding crop. Possibly after the dung has fermented, a great part of the ammonia is reduced, as Sprengel supposes, to a fixed state. If so, we must hesitate to adopt what many have recommended and practised, the ploughing in of dung in a fresh state. After all, if the yard be well littered and the dunghills be covered with earth, I doubt whether, excepting on grass farms where the tank may be necessary from the want of straw, the present management of dung can be greatly improved, though in many districts the quality certainly may be.

But besides farm-yard dung, we have an infinite variety of artificial manures or hand-tillages; indeed, it may be said that there is no refuse of any trade, provided it be animal or vegetable, except

tanner's bark, which is not or might not be used for this purpose. It would be useless to enumerate all, as they are well known, and the supply of many is very limited. The two principal articles are bones and rape-dust; the former suited for light land, and used chiefly for turnips. It is remarkable how very local is the use of both these manures; that of bones, indeed, is spreading, but rape-dust is not much known in the south; and certainly where artificial manures are new, there is some unwillingness to lay out money upon them, though dung perhaps is bought at 5s. the cart-load, and carted with great labour at a long distance. When bones were first used, it was thought that unboiled bones must be better than those from which the animal oil had been extracted; but the reverse appears now to be true— not that animal oil is useless, but that it sheathes probably the bone, and checks its action upon the plant. There remains, however, in the bone another animal compound—gelatine, or the matter of jelly; but Sprengel states he has repeatedly found that bones act as strongly after they have been burnt,* when the jelly of course is removed; and this is well worth remarking, because the body of the bone consists of phosphate of lime, evidently another powerful principle, which is found also abundantly in urine, and consequently in dung. But though the character of bones is established upon light land for turnips, even this manure fails on some soils of that quality. I have some light land where it acts very feebly, some where it does not act at all, and on which many hundred bushels of bones have been quite thrown away. There is also some light land near Baldock, on which bones have been proved to be useless. This shows that we cannot be too cautious in prescribing even the most approved remedies for the first time upon land.

Rape-dust appears to be established chiefly among the farmers of Nottinghamshire, Yorkshire, and Lincolnshire. As it is one of the few hand-tillages which can be applied to clay, and as some of our south-country clays are much in want of assistance, I may mention that, according to an excellent prize-essay† by Mr. John Hannam, the best mode of using it is drilling with autumn-sown wheat at the rate of four or five cwt. to the acre, the price being about 7s. per cwt.

As another instance of the local prevalence of manures, woollen rags may be cited, which are the only hand-tillage familiarly known to farmers in my own neighbourhood. Mr. Hannam states, " 20,000 tons of rags are said to be used annually by the farmers of Kent, Sussex, Oxford, and Berkshire. The price is about 5l. per ton. They

---

all belief. It is indeed only a gaseous substance and not a solid material visible to the eye, which thus escapes and is lost; but for all that, it is of greater importance to the plants than any other portion of the droppings."

* Since this was written I find that Mr. Hannam, of North Deighton, near Wetherby, has this year repeated the experiment with the same result. " In order to solve the question," he says, " we burnt in a pit a quarter of bones and drilled them with turnips (both Swedes and white ones); and on two other patches we applied a quarter of unburnt bones from the same stock as the burnt ones were taken. The turnips are now growing, and, as far as can be determined, seem to thrive with the burnt bones as well, if not better, than with the unburnt."

† Any member who is desirous of trying rape-dust will find full information upon it in this prize-essay of the Wetherby Agricultural Society upon Rape and other Hand-tillages, published last month at Leeds.

answer extremely well for hops and wheat. They are usually cut by a chopper into shreds, and applied by the hand at the rate of half a ton per acre." Six or seven cwt., I believe, is a fair dressing for wheat upon light land ; on heavy land rags are not used here at all.

With regard to nitrate of soda, from which so much was once expected, there are the most undoubted proofs from numerous quarters of an enormous increase in the produce after its use ; there are as undoubted instances of its utter failure ; nor have we any clue to the mystery.* On the same land where it gave me eight bushels of wheat one year, it gave barely three in the following ; and having tried it largely at that time on four different farms, nowhere with success, I have given it up. Still there is evidently a principle of fertility in it which will some day be found out, and some farmers continue to use it, but in several cases it has produced mildew in wheat and barley by forcing the crop beyond the strength of the land. By the side of the nitrate I tried on several fields the sulphate of ammonia, extracted from gas-water, for the first time. It acted precisely as the nitrate of soda, darkening the colour of the plant, and lengthening the straw and the ear even more than the nitrate, but it certainly did not pay. Again we have the principle, and we must learn to combine it.

I can speak with more confidence of the last new manure, guano, having used it on a small scale last year, and to the extent of five tons in the present season. There are two circumstances in its favour beforehand : one, that it is in fact dung, though of very ancient origin, still birds' dung, which is known to be the most powerful of all manures—the other, that it has experience in its favour, though a distant experience certainly, at the other side of the globe, in Peru—still an experience of 300 years. It appears to be best calculated for root-crops. On a light loam, where it has been used here this year for turnips at three cwt. per acre, costing 45s., it has nearly equalled twenty loads of very good dung, and has beaten twenty bushels of bones costing 65s., as well as several other artificial manures beyond any comparison. Where it has been broadcast and harrowed in with late turnips, it has pushed them on well, while on two patches left without guano there is no plant at all. Last year, when drilled with the seed, it killed half the seed. This year, though mixed with sand and drilled separately, with earth spread over it, some of the plants have perished ; and two farmers have told me that, with the same precaution, though the seed grew, the plant also died when the root reached the guano. It is a curious fact that the same thing once happened to one of our members, Mr. Graburn, when he placed the ordinary allowance of rape-cake immediately under the seed. Drilled in with barley on a very poor sand, it has acted very decidedly ; but I find it has only given me one quarter of barley, so that, unless it acts next year, it will not have paid back its cost.† It has failed as a top-dressing on corn and on clover. But hav-

ing stated these cases of failure, I must say that guano seems an excellent manure for root-crops, if rightly applied,* and, as it is now sold at 12s. per cwt., a very cheap one ; but I should be sorry if any of our members tried it largely in consequence on a different soil without success.

Quicklime, again, is so largely used on the west side of England, that it bears there the name of manure, to the exclusion sometimes, I am afraid, of dung ; while on the other side of the country it is almost unknown. Whether lime could be adopted elsewhere is a very interesting question, and what is its mode of operation ? Sir H. Davy's theory that it dissolves vegetable matter is given up ; in fact, it hardens vegetable fibre. Some persons think that it should be applied hot to the soil, founding their view upon chemical principles, but at present it seems better to follow practice ; and where it has been mixed heretofore with five times its bulk of earth, and left so in heaps for some weeks before it is applied to the surface, it would be well to do so still. Indeed, I am told farmers near Totnes, in Devonshire, have given a fair trial to fresh lime, and have found it act not at all better than when it is slacked.† Dr. Liebig has recently discovered that lime has the power of decomposing clay, and producing potash and soda, which are manuring principles ; now, if this be the mode in which lime acts, there could not be a better course than to mix lime with earth before it is thrown upon grass-land, and the old practice would agree with the true theory, as is often the case. Of all things we must guard against premature inferences from abstract science; but be the cause what it may, the effect of lime in sweetening sour pastures is wonderful throughout the districts where it is used, and it is well worth inquiry whether it could be applied in those districts where it is at present unknown.

We have then several substances more or less simple which produce the effect of dung. The mode of their action belongs not to the practice but to the theory of agriculture, into which I am not competent to enter ; but as important discoveries have lately been made in that department, I will endeavour to state the modern German theory, as founded by Sprengel, and lately established by Dr. Liebig.

Plants consist in the main of several vegetable substances, which are, however, all composed of *four* kinds of air variously combined ; these gases are named oxygen, hydrogen, carbon, and nitrogen. Dr. Liebig supposes that the two first are derived

---

* A full statement of all the recorded experiments on nitrate of soda is contained in Professor Johnston's " Chemistry and Geology applied to Agriculture," whose book is the most complete account of agricultural chemistry that we possess.

† Mr. Pryme has found guano fail when drilled in with barley.

* I think that guano should either be sown broad-cast (mixed with mould), and harrowed in rapidly before sowing the seed, if the crop is flat-drilled ; or when it is ridge-drilled, I have sown the guano broad-cast upon the first ridges. When these are split, the guano is brought home to the roots of the plant as it stands on the second drill.

† On the other hand, at Woburn, I have just met with a case in favour of recent lime. The soil was a light sand with a tendency to blackness at top ; half a turnip-field had been dressed with fresh, and half with slacked lime, and there was a marked difference in favour of the fresh lime. As far as our knowledge goes, which is not far, lime appears to me to act wherever there is a natural tendency in the soil to cover itself with heath on waste places, and also wherever the soil is of a deep red, which colour indicates a peculiar salt of iron.

by the plant from water; the third, which is charcoal, from the air; and the fourth, nitrogen, which constitutes the most nutritious part of our food, from ammonia; which substance he has found not merely in the dung of animals, but in the water of rain, a new and remarkable fact. But there exists also in crops a considerable quantity of earthy matter; in every ton of oat-straw, for instance, nearly one cwt. of flint, whence, if a hayrick be burnt, lumps of a substance like glass are often found in the ashes. These mineral substances vary in different plants as to quantity, but eight are generally to be found in their ashes, *four* of the eight being acids, namely, that of flint, which is silica; of bones, phosphorus; of brimstone, sulphuric acid; of common salt, muriatic acid; and also *four* alkalies, potash, soda, lime, and magnesia.* These, Dr. Liebig says, cannot of course be formed in the plant, but must be derived from the soil; and accordingly there they are generally to be found when the soil is examined by chemists, but in limited quantity, so that the soil may become exhausted of one or more of them. But further, all these eight mineral substances are to be found in farm-yard dung, besides ammonia, the source of nitrogen; hence the excellence of dung for all crops indifferently. Some crops, however, require more of one ingredient than of another; hence the good effect of bones upon turnips, which contain a great deal of phosphorus, and of gypsum or peat-ashes, which contain sulphate of lime, upon clover; of Epsom salts also, Dr. Liebig states, which contains magnesia, upon potatoes. Some soils, again, may contain so much of one of these eight minerals, that it may be useless to add any more. Thus gypsum is found to be useful in one part of a field and not in another, and bones are useless in Mecklenburgh, where the fields are dressed with a marl full of phosphorus; or, on the other hand, a tract of country may be deficient altogether in some one of the eight ingredients which is necessary for all crops, as in lime; in such a district lime will be a standing manure. This is a very superficial view of the new theory of agriculture, which, though but a theory at present, certainly promises important results. In order to test it first, and, if it hold good, to apply it afterwards, two courses of inquiry are requisite—one, as Dr. Liebig informs me, a more minute examination of the ashes of plants, in which these mineral substances are found, and further a more accurate analysis of our various soils, in which last particular English science is sadly defective; for Dr. Liebig observes, " Davy has made several analyses of various fertile soils, and since his time numerous other analyses have been published, but they are all so superficial, and in most cases so inaccurate, that we possess no means of ascertaining the composition or nature of English arable land." This reproach on our science ought certainly to be removed; and it is easy to see how varied a field of inquiry is opened by the new theory. At the same time, though it is a most promising theory, it would be premature to expect that for some years to come chemistry should be able to direct, or materially to benefit, actual husbandry. But though we have not yet seen the secret workings of nature, I believe that we are near the

* A very small quantity of alumine, or the earth of clay, is also usually detected in the ashes of plants.

door, and that the veil will soon be raised. Any young chemist, who will take up the late brilliant discoveries of general principles and devote his life to patient research into the means of applying them, may hope to acquire an imperishable reputation; and it is evident, from the ardour with which chemists now embark in agricultural research, that they feel they are making progress. But we certainly have to thank men of science generally for the readiness with which they have come forward; Dr. Buckland, Mr. Murchison, Sir H. Delabeche, have helped us in geology; Professor Henslow has given us a complete history of the diseases of wheat; Dr. Daubeny, as the Oxford professor of agriculture, might be said to belong to us. Mr. Johnston, of Durham, has contributed an excellent account of guano, in addition to his own valuable publications; and the Society has engaged Mr. Curtis to write for us a complete history of the insects which are injurious to crops.

Such are the principal facts which have come to our knowledge in the last four years. I ought to have spoken of machinery, but the shows in our implement-yards have spoken for themselves, and we have most able reports from our judges; yet I cannot but advert to two circumstances: one, that a manufacturer informs me his threshing-machines, which seven years ago only threshed 15 quarters of wheat in a day on an average, now thresh 25; the other, that, in accordance with a suggestion made in the first number of our Journal, travelling threshing-machines worked by steam were brought forward by two makers at Bristol, Messrs. Ransome, and Mr. Cambridge, of Market Lavington, in Wiltshire. I may add that Mr. Howden and the Messrs. Tuxford, of Boston, have each constructed for travelling men similar machines, which are now commonly let for hire in the fens of Lincolnshire. The most gratifying discoveries, however, have been the discoveries of old practices unknown beyond their own districts. I am certain that four years ago no one knew how much good farming there was in the country. Now that these things are come to light, we may hope that they will not only be spoken of, but be practised more generally: that draining-tiles will be greatly cheapened, more drains be cut, more chalk be laid on the downs, the wolds, and the clays, marl on the sands, clay on the fens and peats, lime on the moors, many of which should be broken up; that old ploughs will be cast away, the number of horses reduced, good breeds of cattle extended, stock fattened where it has been hitherto starved (though this is now rare), root crops drilled and better dunged, new kinds of those crops cultivated, and artificial manures of ascertained usefulness purchased. It is the knowledge of these weapons which we actually have in our hands that may make us look back with satisfaction to the efforts we have already made, and forward, with cheerful confidence to the improvement of husbandry through the collective experience of our farmers.

Pusey, Oct. 7, 1842.

ADDENDUM.

Having had the advantage of seeing in Bedfordshire, since these pages were written, practical examples of some of the points which I have ventured to bring before the society, I am desirous of shortly mentioning them. On the estate of my friend Mr. Pym, at the Hazells, may be seen the admirable effect of *marling*. His neat and productive farm is a light yellow sand, which naturally was covered with heath, as may be seen on a small portion reserved for the beauty of its scenery, which strongly resembles a Highland glen, being not only covered with heath, but also with grey lichen, like the grey moss of trees— a kind of vegetation which shows a great degree of sterility. The whole farm has been made fertile by means of a dark grey clay, which is full of lime, situated at the foot of the sandy hill, and the moderate dose of 60 cart-loads per acre is found to last at least 20 years. On this *sandy* farm both turnips and Swedes were *ridge*-drilled, and looked remarkably well. In going from the Hazells to the town of Bedford I travelled for 10 miles across the valley of the Ouse. Here may be seen on almost every farm admirable crops of Swedes, in fields of 40 or 50 acres, without a defective spot of bare earth. The soil is rather a *strong* loam, upon gravel not unlike the land near Salthill; and the Swedes were *flat*-drilled, not upon ridges. At Bedford I had the pleasure of seeing the county ploughing-match. There were forty ploughs, all upon *wheels*, and, though the land was rather strong, all *two-horse ploughs*. Next morning I was permitted to go over the home-farm of the Duke of Bedford at Woburn. Here are two or three fields of very strong land, which had been *thorough-drained* and also subsoil-ploughed; which latter operation was thought to have rendered them much lighter to plough. The land, however, is not clay, but marl, a more crumbling substance than clay. But the arable farm in general, which contains 500 acres (besides 700 of permanent grass), is a sandy hill, resembling Mr. Pym's—indeed a continuation of the same low range; and has been dressed with *marl* in the same manner. One of the fields had not only been covered with heath within a few years, but had been the common turbary of the neighbourhood, so that the surface-soil had been carried off by the poor for fuel. The whole appeared now highly productive. I went over 180 acres of root-crops, and I do not remember a single bare spot. The turnips and Swedes on this *sandy* land were grown upon *ridges*. There were also *white carrots*, a heavy crop; and I was particularly glad to see a 14-acre piece of *globe* mangold-wurzel of the most luxuriant growth, on some newly-broken land indeed, but land which had borne so rank a grass when in park that no animal would touch it; and it was said that even a Highland Scot, confined to this part of the park, had been starved. Mr. Burness, the Duke's bailiff, informed me that he intended to increase the growth of the globe mangold-wurzel; and that by his highest farming he could grow 22 tons of Swedes, 30 tons of turnips, 36 tons of long mangold, and no less than 40 tons of globe mangold—rating the superior yield of globe mangold over swedes still higher than Mr. Hillyard. Mr. Burness also told me that the *same experiment with Lord Spencer's on the comparative feeding properties of Swedes and of mangold*, had been *tried with bullocks at Woburn, and with precisely the same result*. He also told me that, whenever he wished to push a beast on in condition, he changed it from Swedes to mangold-wurzel. The farm-yard is a vast assemblage of buildings, with sixty bullocks, chiefly Herefords, fatting in the stalls—partly on linseed, which is ground on the premises by the same water-wheel which threshes

the corn. The flock is Sussex Down, but a part are crossed with the Leicesters, for one generation only of course, all the lambs being made up for the butcher. Mr. Burness stated that for this purpose he thought the half-cross was the best, as the meat fetched the same high price with the Downs (a halfpenny a pound more), while the Leicester blood gave a greater disposition to fatten. This noble farm is certainly a model of light-land husbandry; and I did not discover a fault in it. I should add that on these 1500 acres no waggon is used. The harvest is brought home and the dung carried out upon *single-horse carts*; nor in this respect is there any departure from the practice of the neighbourhood, for I find that in Bedfordshire and a part of Hertfordshire the farmers use nothing else—so that the advocates of single-horse carts need not go so far north as Cumberland in support of their innovation.

LEASES.

Speaking of leases and covenants, Von Thaër says—" The proprietor should always direct his attention to obtain from his land a gradual increase of produce, or to augment its value continually. The farmer only desires the greatest profit during the continuance of his lease, without caring for the value of the land afterwards. Whilst the proprietor can content himself with a trifling produce during a few years, in order to attain greater and more durable profit subsequently, the tenant must, on the contrary, endeavour to obtain the greatest produce, even though its amount should be diminished during the latter years of his lease ; because the proprietor who wishes to farm on the best system, finds at the same time both pleasure and profit in laying out on his property as much capital as he can spare, whilst the tenant, on the contrary, withdraws as much of his pecuniary resources as possible, to employ it in other ways, or to place it at interest. The improvement of the land constitutes the pleasure of the proprietor, while the mere occupying farmer only thinks of augmenting his income. Thus the longer the lease may be, the more do the interests of the landlord and tenant become identified ; the shorter the term, the more conflicting are those interests. With a lease of twenty-four years, a tenant ought, at least during the first two-thirds of its duration, to follow out the views of the proprietor. But the time will come when he will act on different principles, and endeavour to extract from the land a return in proportion to his outlay at the commencement. To this must be added, that a tenant cannot have the means of laying out so much on the land as the proprietor, even if he wished to do so. The latter must pay the rent, whilst a proprietor anxious to improve can economise something from the net produce to expend on his property. The first may be compared to a merchant who trades on borrowed money ; the second to one who speenlates with his own funds. The former must first provide for his rent, the latter need only think of extending his speculations."

WENLOCK FARMERS' CLUB.

The first anniversary meeting and dinner of the Wenlock Farmers' Club took place at the Raven Inn, on Monday, January 16th. The president, Thomas Mytton, Esq., took the chair at three o'clock. After dinner was over, and a few of the usual toasts given, the secretary was called on to read the following report.

Your committee, in presenting to you the first annual report of your club, beg to congratulate you on the proud position in which you stand, as being the first to introduce the principle of farmers' clubs into this great and flourishing agricultural county, which shows that although the farmers in this neighbourhood may be (as declared by some) the least conspicuous on all good farming, they are determined not to be the last in adopting any means that may have a tendency to improvement; and your committee think that nothing is so likely to attain that object as the formation and support of farmers' clubs, which have of late conferred so much benefit on those localities where they have been established. But whilst your committee are enabled to congratulate you on the steady attendance of the farmers of the surrounding neighbourhood, they observe with regret that the great majority of landowners and their agents have as yet kept aloof from our proceedings. This, if continued, will tend much to damp the energy of the farmer to persevere in the good cause; and whilst your committee witness with delight the steady attendance of the nobility and gentry at the meetings of the clubs established in other parts of the kingdom, they are at a loss to account for the apathy of the great landowners of Shropshire, but fondly hope that the establishment of this and similar meetings in different parts of the county will ere long arouse them into action. Your committee fear that they have perhaps exceeded their province in some of these remarks, and have extended this part of their report to an inconvenient length; but before proceeding to lay before you the substance of your past discussions, they think they cannot do better than close this portion of their address with the concluding paragraph of the Report of the St. Peter's Club, which says—"We are living at a time when it becomes every farmer throughout England to cultivate the most industrious and frugal habits, both in-doors and out. At your first meeting after the organisation of your club, you deprecated the conduct of her Majesty's late ministers in their attempt to remove the protecting duties on corn, and you may have little less to fear from the project of those at present in power. Your struggle, in consequence of the alterations now making, will be a hard one; but for our own sakes, for the sake of our families, and for the sake of our country, let us try, and try heartily, and try cheerfully, and may the sunshine and the showers, and the blessing of Heaven, sustain and succeed our efforts." To which, in behalf of the Wenlock Club, your committee sincerely say amen.

The first meeting, on the 23rd of May, was entirely occupied with the preliminary proceedings consequent on the formation of the club, which does not call for any remarks from us.

At the second meeting, the subjects were—"Is it advisable to shear lambs?" and, "On the best mode of harvesting hay and clover." But before they were brought forward, a good deal of time was taken up in a vain attempt to unite the club to the Wenlock Reading Society, which induced many of the members to leave, and the subjects for the evening were therefore but very indifferently discussed. The first, as to "the shearing of lambs," was confined to the observations of the member bringing it forward, who merely related an experiment he had tried with sixteen lambs—the eight shorn produced 32lbs. more mutton than those left unshorn, and at the two clippings 3lbs. more wool; but owing to the high price of hogget wool at that time (1839), the two lots produced pretty nearly equal profit, the eight shorn having made 18l. 17s. 11d., and the eight unshorn 18l. 17s. 6d. The next subject, "the harvesting of hay and clover," was more freely discussed. The member bringing it forward related his practice at some length, the substance of which will be embodied in the resolution. The chairman then took up the discussion, and commenced his address by stating, that if farmers would pay more attention to the condition of their meadow land they would greatly facilitate the harvesting of the crop, for by the plants of grass being kept in a healthy and vigorous state, they were enabled to throw out a larger quantity of flowering stems, which not only added very considerably to the bulk and nutritive quality of the hay, but by the stems keeping the bottom grass when cut in a less compact form, the crop was ready for carting much sooner than a thin, meagre crop would if cut on the same day. He also very justly observed, that sun and wind were very great auxiliaries in the harvesting of hay; and instanced the injury sustained from high hedges and overhanging trees. He also pointed out the necessity of farmers paying more attention to the formation of their ricks, exemplifying this by two very ingenious little drawings—the one showing a cross section of a rick, where the sides in making had been kept the highest, the layers sunk down in a concave form, proving admirable conductors of wet into the middle of the rick; the other showing that where the middle was always in advance of the sides, the layers sunk down in a convex form, that safely protected the rick from the ingress of rain: but strongly recommended his brother farmers to possess themselves of one or two rick cloths. The vice-chairman followed, and fully bore out the assertion of the chairman as to the harvesting of a heavy and light crop of hay from actual experience of several years on a meadow, part of which was under the influence of water and part not. After a few observations from two or three other members, it was resolved, "That whilst every hand should be got among the hay when fine, yet that in anything like uncertain weather it was better to let it remain in swath until the weather settled, only turning when the bottom became yellow, and that a liberal supply of salt should at all times be thrown into the rick at the time of making."

At the July meeting the time of the club was again a good deal occupied with an attempt to connect it with the Wenlock Library, the previous knowledge of which, and the hay harvest not being completed, there was but a very thin attendance of the members, consequently the subject put down for discussion ("The best mode of cutting and harvesting wheat") was but indifferently inquired into. It was brought forward by the secretary in a plain, straight-forward, matter-of-fact form, he giving it as his decided opinion that mowing wheat had the advantage over every other mode of cutting, in its being ready to cart home much sooner, securing the whole of the straw, and removing all annual weeds from the field to be separated from the grain by the machine, when they could be burnt or otherwise disposed of. Some of the members spoke strongly on the sickle and hackling system; but owing to the thin attendance of members the subject was postponed without coming to any resolution. The practice of the members present went to show that mowing wheat greatly facilitated the harvesting, but that by hackling you got a very superior sample.

August and September being harvest months, there were not any meetings of the society.

In October the subject for discussion was, "The best description of wheat, and the best modes of pickling and sowing it"—brought forward by the chairman. He stated that he had tried several of the new varieties of wheat, but had abandoned the whole of them, as being too delicate for our cold climate, in favour of a white wheat long and successfully grown in this neighbourhood, called Rennie's white wheat. He had also tried several modes of pickling, and found them all more or less defective, except a solution of sulphate of copper, known as blue stone, which if properly used never failed to prevent smut. He was not prepared to give a decided opinion as to the comparative merits of drilling or broadcast. The subject was taken up by the members generally, some advocating the drill system, others as strongly supporting the broadcast mode. The discussion was ultimately postponed without coming to any resolution, owing to the little experience the members have had as yet in drilling.

At this meeting G. Pritchard, Esq., placed at the disposal of the club two prizes for best and second best ploughmen, the match to take place before the next meeting, for which your committee think the thanks of the club are due to Mr. Pritchard.

The match ultimately came off in a field belonging to Mr. Pritchard, of Buildwas, when eight ploughs only started. Mr. Oakley, of Wroxeter, kindly consented to be judge, and expressed himself highly gratified with the way in which the work was generally performed. Mr. Pritchard's, of Buildwas, servant obtained the first prize, and Mr. Wood's the second, which were given to the men at the following meeting of the club, with some very seasonable remarks by the chairman.

The subject for discussion in November was, "The best mode of storing turnips." There was a very large and full attendance of members, and the question assumed a most interesting and animated form. There were a few roots shown, one immense large Swede by Mr. Wood, called Laing's improved. The member bringing the subject forward urged his brother farmers to adopt some mode of storing, a subject scarcely ever thought of in this neighbourhood; and afterwards related the several practices that had come under his observation, and expressed his determination to adopt Geache's plan (vide prize essay) for the great bulk of his turnips. Several very novel plans were related; but after a very lengthened discussion, it was finally resolved, "That where turnips were consumed in troughs in the field, the best plan was to throw a cart-load in a ruck and earth them up, leaving the top unclosed for

the circulation of air until frost sets in, then close over with the tops; and where the turnips were carted off, that Geache's plan appeared to the club to have many advantages."

December—"The best mode of keeping cart horses," occupied the attention of the club at this meeting. Abraham Darby, Esq., read a long and interesting statement of the weekly expenses incurred in keeping one hundred cart horses attached to his iron works. Mr. Darby divided his statement into three tables, the first showing the expense of keeping eighty-two horses for forty-eight weeks. Your committee find great difficulty in arranging this table so as to meet the views of the farmer, as the period extends over the winter and summer months, consequently the green food cut and the pasturage are included in the average cost per week, which amounts to 14s. per horse; Your committee have divided this into two tables; first, adding the hard grain and bran together, of which we find the average expense per week per horse to be 9s. 7d., and the cut stuff, pasturage, &c., to be 4s. 5d. And again, we have taken the bran (which forms a very considerable item in these accounts, and in some degree partakes of a substitute for cut chaff, &c.) from the hard grain, and then the expense will stand thus:—grain 4s. 6d. per week per horse, bran and chaff, &c., 9s. 6d. Or, it may be stated thus—hard grain 4s. 6d.; bran 5s. 1d.; cut stuff, pasturage, &c., 4s. 5d. Mr. Darby's other two tables go to show a saving which occurred in the keeping of the horses attached to the Bradley farm, by abandoning the use of the nose-bags. These horses are chiefly used in drawing limestone; and in the first instance were not allowed to bait in the stable until their day's work was finished, but were fed out of nose-bags. The expense per week per horse was 16s. 6d.; but Mr. Darby conceiving that a portion of their food was spilt, adopted the plan of baiting an hour in the stable, and doing away with the nose-bags, from which a saving of 3s. 5d. per week per horse was effected. The great thing to be observed in these accounts is that everything is cut and charged, which swells the expense to what would appear to the farmer a frightful amount. But it should be borne in mind that a considerable portion of this expense is charged to cut hay, bran, &c., for which the farmer uses chaff, &c., as in some measure a substitute. But Mr. Darby's paper is altogether so full of useful information, that your committee have requested the secretary to insert it in the minutes of your proceedings. Your committee conceive it to be a matter of high gratification to find a gentleman so extensively connected with manufactures and commerce, associating himself with the farmer; and your committee are satisfied they only anticipate the sentiments of every member of our club in saying that Mr. Darby is entitled to our best thanks.

The subject in discussion called forth a good deal of remarks from the members generally, one of whom strongly recommended boiled barley, having used it with every success for the last two years. The subject was eventually adjourned, the hour of separation having arrived; but it appeared to the majority of the members present, that a very considerable saving would be effected if horses were more generally fed with cut food.

Your committee cannot conclude this report without expressing the obligation which the members of the club are under to Richard Thursfield, Esq., surgeon, for the very great zeal he has shown in behalf of our club, having given us several very valuable recipes for horse and cattle medicine, which have been placed in the hands of Mr. Horton, druggist, to be made up for the use of our members at the lowest possible rate. Mr. Thursfield has also shown a most praiseworthy readiness to impart to the club some useful information on the probable cause of some of the diseases affecting horned cattle, particularly that frightful one abortion (a most laudable example, which we hope to see followed by others), and for which your committee need hardly say the very best thanks of the club are due.

Your committee have thus endeavoured, though in a humble manner, to lay before you the substance of your discussions for the year past ; and, in resigning into your hands the trust you have imposed upon them, they sincerely and heartily wish your society every success, and earnestly hope that each year may add to its efficiency and beneficial effects.

RICHMONDSHIRE FARMER'S CLUB.—This excellent provincial society is progressing rapidly in public favour, and numbers nearly 200 members ; a reading room and library have recently been formed.—The following have been the subjects discussed during the last three months and the decisions respectively recorded thereon :—In December, the subject was, " The best method of winter feeding cattle and sheep." The decision—" That cleanliness is of the greatest consequence ;—and that, in feeding cattle, loose sheds are best adapted for bullocks ; (two in each shed,) and that cows and heifers fatten best, when tied up. That turnips, and oilcake or meal with a sufficient quantity of hay or cut straw, answer well for feeding cattle." Cut turnips and hay were recommended to be given to sheep, experience having proved that they thrive much better when the turnips are cut and given to them in troughs.—Introduced by Mr. John Outhwaite. In January, the subject was " Agricultural Chemistry." On which no positive decision was come to, as on the whole there seemed to be much difference of opinion amongst the members present, as to the benefits received by agriculture from the agricultural chemist ; and the majority seemed to be of opinion that hitherto they had derived little advantage from the labours of the scientific man.—Introduced by Mr. Raw. In February, the subject was, " The best method of preventing the ravages of vermin in and about farm-steads." The decision—" That traps, ferrets, and terriers might all be used with good effect in destroying rats and mice. That it is advisable for the purpose of banishing these vermin, that corn should be stacked upon pillars, care being taken that nothing is placed against or under the stack :—and that all holes in buildings should be perseveringly stopped with glass and lime, or black slag from the lead smelt mills." The meeting also recommends that all drains connected with the house and farm-stead, should have grates properly walled into them.—Introduced by Capt. Harland. The following are the subjects appointed for discussion during the three ensuing months :—On Thursday, the 16th March, " The best method of managing ewes, especially during the lambing season," to be introduced by Mr. James Bell. On Thursday, the 13th April, " The properties and application of lime," to be introduced by Mr. T. Smurthwaite, Holme House. On Thursday, the 11th May, " The best method of paying the wages of agricultural labourers," to be introduced by Mr. Lister.

PARLIAMENTARY PAPER.
CORN.

Return to two several Orders of the Hon. the House of Commons, dated respectively 10th August, 1842, and 3rd February, 1843 ;—for,

RETURNS of the QUANTITIES and AVERAGE PRICE, for each six weeks of all Corn sold in places included in the Act 5 Vict., c. 14, from the commencement of the operation of that Act to the latest period :—Also, of the QUANTITIES and AVERAGE PRICE, for each six weeks, calculated according to the provisions of the Act 9 Geo. IV., c. 60, of all Corn sold in the Towns specified in Section 8 of the said Act, for the same period.

WHEAT.

WEEKS ENDED.	Total Quantities for each six weeks, sold in places included in the Act of 5 and 6 Vict., c. 14.	Weekly Aggregate Averages, by which the Duty on Wheat is regulated by the Act 5 and 6 Vict., c. 14.		Total Quantities for each six weeks, from the Returns of the cities and towns named in the Act of 9 Geo. 4, c. 60.	Weekly Aggregate Averages, calculated according to the provisions of the Act of 9 Geo. 4, c. 60.	
	Qrs.	s.	d.	Qrs.	s.	d.
1842—April 29	367,487	59	3	367,487	59	3
May 6	380,445	59	8	380,445	59	8
— 13	396,729	60	0	396,729	60	0
— 20	414,433	60	5	414,433	60	5
— 27	431,220	60	9	431,220	60	9
June 3	447,865	61	3	447,865	61	3
— 10	462,489	61	9	462,489	61	9
— 17	477,763	62	3	477,733	62	3
— 25	481,699	63	0	481,204	63	0
July 2	478,829	63	7	476,157	63	7
— 9	486,634	64	1	468,846	64	1
— 16	513,308	64	5	471,028	64	5
— 23	525,015	64	7	460,266	64	7
— 30	530,531	64	7	443,922	64	7
Aug. 6	543,017	64	2	432,557	64	1
— 13	539,591	63	3	410,132	63	1
— 20	509,200	61	10	377,893	61	7
— 27	454,787	60	1	331,357	59	9
Sept. 3	427,773	58	1	307,349	57	8
— 10	426,571	56	0	306,912	55	7
— 17	437,027	54	7	317,750	54	2
— 24	489,376	53	10	358,439	53	5
Oct. 1	557,194	53	3	410,432	52	11
— 8	609,937	52	8	451,155	52	5
— 15	641,795	52	4	474,431	52	1
— 22	651,406	52	2	481,139	51	11
— 29	637,256	51	8	471,344	51	4
Nov. 5	605,664	50	9	449,180	50	5
— 12	583,980	50	0	432,352	49	8
— 19	581,384	49	8	428,649	49	5
— 26	581,054	49	5	428,820	49	2
Dec. 3	584,677	49	1	431,060	48	9
— 10	603,429	48	8	444,419	48	5
— 17	607,293	48	5	447,244	48	2
— 24	599,918	48	2	442,595	48	0
— 31	588,551	47	9	435,671	47	6
1843—Jan. 7	572,993	47	4	425,128	47	1
— 14	572,494	47	2	425,822	47	0
— 21	580,298	47	6	430,280	47	4
— 28	587,852	47	11	434,592	47	8

GEORGE JOVEE,
Comptroller of Corn Returns.
Corn Department, Board of Trade, Feb. 10, 1843.

THE CULTIVATION of TURNIPS.

TO THE EDITOR OF THE MARK-LANE EXPRESS.

SIR,—In your paper of the 2nd inst., I observe that Mr. H. C. Wentworth, Harlow, makes a few remarks on my letters published in the *Mark Lane Express* of November 21st and December 19th, which, in my humble opinion, he has somehow or other in a great measure misunderstood—and in more than one instance makes me say what I did not even dream of saying.

In the first place, it is quite true that the field upon which I tried the experiment of drilling and dunging in autumn, was tares in 1841, and turnips in 1842 ; but I did not state that it was our common practice to take two green crops consecutively. And I do think that, if Mr. W. had read my letter of the 21st of November with a little more care, he would have seen what was the *cause* of my taking turnips instead of a white crop—viz., that the field was *somewhat foul*—as I have no idea of sowing either barley or any other grain on land where there is likely to be a *contention* for the *mastery* between the crops sown and the weeds. In one word, our practice is to take—after turnips—barley, grass, and oats : this is our common rotation.

In the second place, Mr. W. states that turnips ought always to be sown on land that would otherwise be summer fallow. Now, sir, this is one of the advantages which I have pointed out, and which I think is not a small one, when summer fallow would be the only alternative ; but I would whisper in Mr. W.'s ear, that if there were no more turnips grown in our neighbourhood than on such land, their *breadth* would indeed be *narrow*.

In the third place, Mr. W. states that, if I would adopt his method, all the difficulties complained of in working the land in spring would be obviated. Now, sir, I am old enough to be aware that not only in working turnip land, but in many other matters, the old proverb will hold good—that *" Every crow thinks his own birds whitest ; "* but I can assure him that I have tried the plan recommended by him more than once, and find the one adopted by me last year, and described in my letter of the 21st of November, infinitely the best I have yet tried ; and I am much mistaken that, if Mr. W. would be persuaded to try a few drills on my plan, *cheek* by *jowl*, with the same number on his own, I am confident he will approve of it as much as I do—or his land is not of that *stubborn* nature that mine is. At the same time, I feel obliged for Mr. W.'s kind intentions.

In the fourth place, Mr. W. says it is an error in me to suppose that, when manure is drilled in, much of its virtue is lost. Now, Mr. Editor, if I had said anything that could be construed into the above meaning, I most assuredly would have been in error ; but I have said nothing of the kind, but have given the opposite as my opinion, and would again repeat that if, instead of allowing our manure to lie and decompose in our dunghills and court-yards, it ought to be carted to the fields intended either for potatoes or turnips, and covered in by the plough as often as opportunity offers after the harvest is over. I yesterday finished dunging ten acres for turnips on the new plan.

In the fifth place, Mr. W. says, turnips are seldom left in the row more than eighteen inches apart—consequently the plants have only nine inches each way to seek for the manure. Now, I am not sure if I understand Mr. Wentworth in what he has stated above, because I stated in my first letter that we draw our drill or ridge with the plough at from twenty-eight inches apart—viz., from apex to apex—and when *singling* out the young plants, we leave them at from nine to eleven inches apart ; so that in the row they are, say ten inches from each other ; but the other way they are twenty-eight inches apart, and some of our East Lothian farmers think this too close—that when the land is in high condition, the drill or ridge should be thirty inches instead of twenty-eight, as it is perfectly obvious that plants require room to breathe as well as animals.

But if Mr. Wentworth means to say that in his part of the country they seldom make their drills or ridges wider than twenty-eight inches from apex to apex, I apprehend that this in a great measure will account for the difference of weight of crop with him and with us ; and, from what I have stated above, it would appear we manage things differently in Scotland.

In the last place, Mr. Editor, I would beg to state that I would not have troubled you either now or with my former lucubrations, but from a principle which ought to regulate our conduct in every instance where we either intuitively or by chance stumble upon what we conceive to be an improvement, of whatever nature it be, by which our crops are improved either in bulk or quality. This, and this alone, has been my motive in addressing you.

I am, sir, yours most obediently,
Peffer Mill, Jan. 7.   P. THOMSON.

OBSERVATIONS ON LIEBIG'S ORGANIC CHEMISTRY.

BY GEORGE THOMPSON, JUN.

This work appears to be a tissue of contradictions ; little is broached that was not long previously generally known and well established ; and that which forms the very foundation of the whole work is a series of ill-digested statements, so absurdly contradicting each other, as to render it a matter of the greatest astonishment that so much respect should be shown to the author's production. If there is one unfortunate circumstance more demanding our regret than another, it is to see men loaded with temporal honours, which command our respect, devoting their mental powers to the promulgation of absurdities, which wear an enticing garb, from being professedly the production of individuals whose high order of intellect has entitled them to be made members of various learned societies. That this is peculiarly the case with Professor Liebig needs but a small share of penetration to discover ; since, at page twenty-one of this despotic writer's composition, he states —" One hundred volumes of air have been found at every period and in every climate to contain twenty-one volumes of oxygen, with such small deviations that they must be ascribed to errors of observation." Now, this is not the discovery of the Professor, or there might be some grounds for questioning its accuracy ; but it is the result of numerous experiments, made by various chemists at several periods. Then is it not extraordinary, is it not preposterous, that after thus quoting and confirming the opinions of men far more eminent in chemical science than the Professor ever will be, that he should contradict, from the mere fungi of his own brain, the well established experience of ages? But he does so. For, at page twenty-eight, we have—"The various layers of wood and mineral coal, as well as peat, form the remains of a primæval vegetation. The carbon which they contain must have been originally in the atmosphere as carbonic acid, in which form it was assimilated by the plants which constitute these formations. It follows from this, that the atmosphere must be richer in oxygen at the present time than in former periods of the earth's history."

And by way of further proof of this most singular statement, it is advanced on the same page that—"In former ages, therefore, the atmosphere must have contained less oxygen, but a much larger proportion of carbonic acid, than it does at the present time—a circumstance which accounts for the richness and luxuriance of the earlier vegetation."

Here, then, we have *opinion* versus *fact*, and it might be a question with some individuals as to which authority was entitled to the greatest respect —the *dreams* of Professor Liebig, or the *demonstrations* of the host of eminent chemists who have gone before him—but that he contradicts his own opinion, for at page twenty-five he states—"Animals on the other hand expire carbon, which plants inspire ; and thus the composition of the medium in which both exist—namely, the atmosphere—is maintained constantly unchanged."

Compare this opinion with a former one, to the effect that the atmosphere contains much less carbonic acid at the present than at a former period.

All this may appear wonderful—it may seem to be the production of a great genius in the estimation of the learned—but it is contrary to common sense.

Another portion of this work cannot fail to excite some degree of astonishment ; for at page seventy it is observed—"We cannot suppose that a plant could attain maturity, even in the richest vegetable mould, without the presence of matter containing nitrogen ; since we know that nitrogen exists in every part of the vegetable structure." With all due deference to the opinion of *a Professor*, it is a well established fact that many plants exist, into the composition of which not a particle of nitrogen enters. But we have a still more startling statement with respect to this gas ; for, at page seventy, will be found—

"We have not the slightest reason for believing that the nitrogen of the atmosphere takes part in the processes of assimilation of plants and animals ; on the contrary, we know that many plants emit the nitrogen which is absorbed by their roots either in the gaseous form or in solution in water. But there are on the other hand numerous facts, showing that the formation in plants of substances containing nitrogen—such as gluten—takes place in proportion to the quantity of this element which is conveyed to their roots in the state of ammonia, derived from the putrefaction of animal matter."

Thus our author first denies the supposition that plants obtain their nitrogen from the atmosphere ; and, secondly, attempts to show that it is obtained by the roots from ammonia contained in the soil. Very good. But what have we at page seventy-two? Why—

"A certain proportion of nitrogen is exported with corn and cattle, and this exportation takes place every year without the smallest compensation ; yet, after a given number of years, the quantity of nitrogen will be found to have increased. Whence, we may ask, comes this increase of nitrogen? The nitrogen in the excrements cannot re-produce itself, and the earth cannot yield it. Plants, and consequently animals must, therefore, derive their nitrogen from the atmosphere."

It may be urged by some admirers of this *most extraordinary* man, that in denying that the nitrogen of the atmosphere contributes to the sustenance of plants, he does not intend to include that portion which exists in the ammonia that has been proved to fall with the rain, and that this is the nitrogen referred to in the last extract. But how will such individuals reconcile this idea to the statement of the Professor, already quoted, that those substances containing nitrogen exist in plants just in proportion to the quantity of ammonia contained in the soil which has been derived from putrefied animal matter? They must confess that there is a most absurd contradiction.

Again, at page fifty-eight — "Substances containing a large proportion of carbon are excreted by the roots and absorbed by the soil. Through the expulsion of these matters unfitted for nutrition, the soil receives again with usury the carbon which it had at first yielded to the young plants as food in the form of carbonic acid."

And page fifty-nine—"A soil receives more carbon in this form"—that is, in the form of excretory matter—"than its decaying humus had lost as carbonic acid." We must beg the reader to bear in mind the above, whilst we refer to the following extract from page sixty-one:—"Large forests are often found growing in soils absolutely destitute of carbonaceous matter ; and the extensive prairies of the western continent show that the carbon necessary for the sustenance of a plant may be entirely extracted from the atmosphere." Now, granting that the first theory—of plants excreting more carbon than they abstract—be correct, what becomes of the second theory—that extensive forests and prairies of *excretory plants* are found to be growing in soils absolutely destitute of carbonaceous matter ? It is manifest that the Professor must allude to the present constitution of the soils referred to, since there is no data to show the composition of them prior to the existence of the forests ; it is also quite clear that the plants or trees have been growing for ages in these soils ; and, as the Professor himself propounds the theory, that plants of this nature return more carbon to the soil than they extract from it, we may fairly ask what has become of the excreted carbon in the forests spoken of? And we must conclude, at all events, that the author has again contradicted his own statement.

These are not the only errors in the work, for several eminent chemists and physiologists have detected and exposed many contradictory statements in the more elaborate portions of the composition ; but those we have quoted are the most palpable. They are those which must convince the most ignorant of the absurdity of submitting a work so ill-digested to the perusal of a public not absolutely unacquainted with scientific truths, still less destitute of common sense. All previous critiques upon this work have been so replete with scientific terms and subtle arguments, that the *practical* man has not ventured to wade through the stream of technicalities which repel rather than invite the uninitiated ; but in the present article the object has been to select such passages as afford a striking proof of the author's inconsistencies, without diving into those portions which, although incomprehensible, or rather tiresome to the unlearned, yet contain even more serious errors than those exposed in this paper—more serious, because not so easily discovered.

If then the author has shown such marvellous ignorance of the contents of his own composition as to contradict on a following page what he has stated on a preceding one ; if he had but fallen into this dilemma in one instance only, what respect should be shown to his production ? Decidedly none! If he had so committed himself by a train of powerful reasoning, such as the able counsellor would employ in cross-examining a witness, until he compelled the man to contradict his own assertions ; if even this course had been adopted, the inconsistency would have been less glaring ; or if any doubt had been expressed as to the verity of one of the conflicting statements, little foundation would there have been for questioning the correctness of the work. But when one chapter contradicts itself—indeed when one page contradicts the following—and all without the slightest doubt being expressed as to the correctness of either statement, it must be the conclusion of every man possessing common sense, that such a work, instead of being taken as a text-book by the learned, should be treated with profound contempt.

It is not denied that the object of the work is good, that there are many valuable hints contained in it ; but those valuable parts are of no use, save to the individual who is already acquainted with them ; since the man who is ignorant of them, on discovering such a manifest contradiction in the early part of the composition, as that the quantity of oxygen contained in the atmosphere is always proportionately the same, and yet increasing proportionately the same, must instantly conclude that no future statement of the same writer is entitled to the slightest respect. Hence, that portion of mankind who are most in want of the work, will receive no advantage from it , and the author's contemporaries in the walks of science will either merely confirm those statements which are correct, or contemptuously reject the whole work as not being entitled to the slightest credit.

It is obvious that the professor has propounded theories from the fertile resources of his own imagination, to give stability to others equally destitute of any rational foundation. That many parts of the work are highly valuable is admitted, but what consistent man can possibly depend upon them ? The writer of this article did not peruse the work with a mind prejudiced against its contents ; on the contrary, he had heard and seen so much in its favour as almost compelled him to deny the evidence of an ocular examination ; but of all errors in composition contradictory arguments and conflicting statements are the most prominent. It is impossible that those who read for information, and think on what they read, can overlook or fail to observe such inconsistencies. It is indeed a matter of astonishment that this work should occupy such an enviable position in the libraries of the learned, and it cannot be fully accounted for, except by concluding that scientific men have devoted more attention to the numerous novel theories contained in its pages, than to the general connection and conformity of the argument. The object in exposing these manifest

discrepancies has been solely a desire to promote the progress of agricultural science ; for it is apparent that if the chief votaries of science are guilty of propounding adverse theories, that they must inevitably retard the advancement of the work they are engaged in. The foregoing remarks have not been penned from any conceited idea of superior, or even equal attainments, with Professor Liebig ; no vain opinion of self-sufficiency has actuated the writer in submitting them to the perusal of an enlightened public ; but simply a desire to oppose the circulation of those publications which irretrievably injure the cause they advocate. It is, therefore, much to be regretted that the work was ever published in its present ill-digested form, and it becomes a duty on the part of those who discover its imperfections to retrieve the cause of agricultural science from the degradation into which it may be plunged by its enlightened *professors*.

Lion Street, Kidderminster,
March 1st, 1843.

TO THE FARMERS OF SUFFOLK.

Letter IV.

Gentlemen,—Before I change the subject, I shall once more address you on the little experiment I have suggested to your notice. I was rather surprised, two or three days ago, to hear a practical agriculturist of this county declare that he was not acquainted with more than one farmer whom he considered *qualified* for undertaking the experiment I have proposed to you. I explained to him how very little was really required, and I hope I convinced him that even the tenant of any common cottager's allotment was quite as well *qualified* for conducting our experiment to a successful termination, as the first chemist in the land. A scientific friend, also, has written to me, and he says,—" As for hoping to get results *registered* by the farmers, if you succeed, you will either prove yourself a magician, or else that your Suffolk farmers are very different from the Shropshire ones whom I have been accustomed to." Now, I have certainly no desire to be considered any way implicated in the " black art," but I shall most heartily rejoice to find the farmers of Suffolk thus far in advance of the farmers of Shropshire, as to be willing to attend to the suggestions of those chemists who would have them try a few simple experiments for themselves. All the world knows that the husbandry of Norfolk and Suffolk is generally in advance of that of every other county in England ; I am afraid we may not say in Great Britain. But this will be very little to the purpose, if the Suffolk farmers have become unwilling to adopt the only sure steps which have *now* become necessary for their carrying to still greater perfection the craft they follow: and indeed, of converting the *art* of husbandry into the *science* of agriculture. In order that I may understand whether you are really inclined or not to co-operate in determining the question I have proposed to you, I shall take the liberty of requesting every one who is so disposed, to inform me of his determination. The penny postage, and the liberal conduct of our provincial journals, afford us such ready modes of communicating, that I do not hesitate to suggest the following arrangement:—Let every gentleman who may be willing to co-operate, furnish me with his address by post. I will prepare precise instructions for the conduct of our experiment, leaving blanks to be filled up by each experimenter. Provided I shall have received not fewer than fifty applications for these instructions before the end of February, I will then get them printed, and will forward them by post to all who shall have favoured me with their addresses. In the meantime I will endeavour to persuade some neighbour to allow me to superintend the preparation of two small manure heaps; and I shall thus be able to form a more accurate judgment of the number of pounds of straw, bushels of dung and urine, and pints or pecks of gypsum, which may be required for manuring a rood of land. I shall not think it worth while to proceed further in this question, unless fifty at least can be found to engage in it; but I shall hope to engage your attention by some other topic.

Although a knowledge of chemistry and botany is not necessary for any one who may be disposed to try the description of experiments which are called for from agriculturists; yet every farmer who will acquire a few precise ideas on such subjects will find himself in a better position for appreciating the value of these experiments, and will be able to reason for himself on the propriety of performing others. I shall, therefore, take the liberty of suggesting to those among you who may be utterly ignorant of chemistry, to make a beginning, by trying a little experiment illustrative of the subject before us. On the next market day enter any chemist's shop and ask for

One ounce of muriatic acid (spirits of salt) value 2d.

One ounce of sulphuric acid (oil of vitriol) 1d.

One ounce of carbonate of ammonia (smelling salts) 1d.

Procure also a small lump of pure chalk or marble, value nothing; and a tea cupful of powdered gypsum, value about one farthing.

Before I propose the experiment which will serve to illustrate what may *possibly* take place in our gypsumed dunghill, I shall advise two or three preliminary experiments, for the purpose of your acquiring a little insight into the nature of the ingredients I have mentioned above. Take four wine glasses, A B C D, and drop three or four drops of muriatic acid into A and B; and three or four drops of sulphuric acid into C and D. Add two or three times as much water as there may be acid in each glass. Scrape a little of the carbonate of ammonia, and drop it into the glasses A and C, you will perceive a strong effervescence take place. Continue adding more of the carbonate of ammonia till this effervescence ceases. The acids are then *neutralised*, as chemists say, by having combined with a sufficient quantity of ammonia contained in the carbonate of ammonia. The effervescence was occasioned by the escape of carbonic acid set free, and which appeared under the form of a gas. In glass A, we have now a muriate of ammonia (sal ammoniac), and in glass C, a sulphate of ammonia. We do not *see* these new compounds, because they are both dissolved in the water; but if the glasses were set aside for a time, until the water could evaporate, we should then find both these salts of ammonia in a solid form.

Next, into glasses B and D drop a little powdered chalk or marble, and a strong effervescence will take place, as before. These substances are composed of lime and carbonic acid united; and here also the carbonic acid has been set free, whilst the lime has

entered into union with the muriatic acid in glass B, and formed a muriate of lime a very soluble salt; and in glass D the lime has combined with the sulphuric acid, and formed the sulphate of lime which is the same thing as gypsum. As sulphate of lime is not soluble except in a very large proportion of water, it will appear in this glass as a dense white powder.

When you have actually *tried* these experiments, and have thought about the changes which have been effected, you will find yourselves in possession of more accurate ideas of what chemists mean by decomposition, affinity, and neutralization, than you would have obtained by merely reading about them.

Having thus made these preliminary experiments, let us next attempt one which may serve to illustrate the manner in which Liebig intimates that the escape of carbonate of the ammonia may be arrested, during the decomposition of manure. Whilst dung, but more especially urine, is decomposing, carbonate of ammonia is continually forming and gradually escaping into the atmosphere. But you cannot see this, because the carbonate of ammonia escapes in the form of invisible vapour. If you smell at the pennyworth of this substance you have obtained from the chemists in a solid form, you may be made conscious that it is gradually evaporating, just as a piece of camphor would do. This essence of your pocket dunghill must, therefore, be kept close shut up in a box or jar, if you wish to retain it for any length of time. Ocular proof, as well as nasal, may be obtained, that the carbonate of ammonia is escaping; for if you unstopper the phial in which the muriatic acid is contained, and bring the mouth of it near the lump of carbonate of ammonia, you will immediately perceive dense white fumes floating about. These fumes arise from the muriatic acid (which is escaping in the form of vapour from the bottle) uniting with the carbonate of ammonia (also escaping in vapour), and the result is the formation of this muriate of ammonia.

I shall now propose the little experiment I alluded to. Put about half a tea-spoonful of powdered carbonate of ammonia into a wine glass, and add about a tea-spoonful of gypsum to it; and stir them well together. Smell the mixture, and you will still perceive that the carbonate of ammonia is escaping. It is evident, therefore, that the gypsum has not yet acted in "fixing the ammonia." Next add water enough to cover the mixture; stir it up and smell again. You will no longer perceive the odour of carbonate of ammonia. Now, water *alone* will act in *retarding* the escape of the carbonate of ammonia, though it cannot prevent this gradually taking place; as you may easily prove by dissolving a little of the carbonate of ammonia in water, and smelling it. But where the gypsum is also present, chemists tell us that a mutual decomposition of this substance and the carbonate of ammonia will occur; and at the end of a certain time you will find in the glass two new substances, viz., carbonate of lime, and sulphate of ammonia, Here, then, you see in miniature what is supposed may *possibly* be effected on a large scale by adding gypsum to a dunghill, provided we keep it sufficiently moist. But this is the very point I wish to-be settled one way or the other. I have no decided opinion on the matter; and it is never safe to feel positive of success on a large scale, merely because an experiment succeeds on a small one. The same precautions are needed in agriculture as in mechanical arts. Many a working model has been contrived which will act to admiration; and yet when the principle it was intended to illustrate, has been applied to machinery, the engineer has been disappointed by something coming into play which he had not foreseen, and he has failed in producing the results upon which he had calculated.

I am afraid that some persons will consider that I am descending to matters which are far too elementary for the columns of a newspaper, and that I had better refer those who are ignorant of chemistry to some elementary work on that science. But my desire is to convince those who never opened a work on chemistry, how very little energy is required for attempting to gain some slight degree of information on the subject. I am an old hand at the art of teaching. For several years it was my lot to tutorize men at Cambridge in the rudiments of mathematics ; and I know by experience how very necessary it is to place the first, and most elementary propositions, in various lights, before some men can be brought to catch the idea of what is intended. The first few difficulties fairly mastered, an advance afterwards becomes comparatively easy. " Ce n'est que le premier pas qui coute," say the French—"The first step is everything." Let the first step be made to the chemist's shop for the four pennyworth of articles I have named above, and I suspect it will not be the last. But let not the first step be forgotten towards performing the experiment I have suggested, viz., that I be favoured with the addresses of those who are willing to try it.—Your obedient servant,

J. S. HENSLOW.

Hitcham Rectory, January 28, 1843.

THE GYPSUM EXPERIMENT.

TO THE EDITOR.

SIR,—The objections which I urged against the experiment proposed by Professor Henslow have not been removed by that gentleman's observations in his last letter. It is of the utmost importance, for the credit of that somewhat novel branch of science, agricultural chemistry, that all experiments should be conducted upon correct principles ; and, as Mr. Henslow has invited discussion with the sole object of arriving at truth, I again trouble you with some remarks upon the subject.

Professor Henslow proposes that dry powdered gypsum should be spread between the layers of a heap of manure, for the purpose of fixing the ammonia which escapes during fermentation in the form of the carbonate of that salt. I contend that gypsum in such a position *cannot* fix ammonia, because the salts of lime and ammonia are not brought together in a state necessary for the exercise of chemical affinity. This is the question I propose to discuss.

Mr. Henslow states that his experiment is the proposition of Liebig. On this point I think I can prove that Mr. Henslow has mistaken the meaning of Liebig. I am not sure that many of Liebig's *theories* are not open to grave objection ; but we will not open this subject. The present is a question of fact; and, as Liebig as a *chemist* is justly distinguished among the *highest* authorities, I will be content to abide by his chemical opinions alone.

But I have looked in vain through Liebig's "Organic Chemistry in its application to Agriculture and Physiology" for any recommendation like that of Professor Henslow ; on the contrary, I think I can prove from this work that such a proposition is *not* founded upon correct principles.

It will be allowed that the principal part of the ammonia generated in the dunghill is volatilized during the process of fermentation, or, as it is commonly called, " heating," and that this process is temporary and dependant upon the quantity of fermenting matter. In the small heap required in Professor Henslow's proposed experiment it would be over in a few days. If the ammonia is not fixed in this time it is irretrievably lost. Now Liebig states, at page 88 of his work, that—" Water is *absolutely necessary* to effect the decomposition of the gypsum on account of its difficult solubility (*one part of gypsum* requires 400 parts of water for solution), and also to assist in the absorption of the sulphate of ammonia by the plants : hence it happens that the *influence* of gypsum is *not* observable on *dry* fields and meadows."

" The decomposition of gypsum by carbonate of ammonia does not take place instantaneously ; on the contrary, it proceeds very gradually, and this explains why the action of gypsum *lasts for several years.*"

Now mark—it results from the above statement of Liebig that, for every pound of gypsum used, you must have also present 400 pounds or 50 gallons of water ! or else no decomposition takes place. If you are to rely upon rain to promote its gradual decomposition, you must wait " several years ;" and where in the meantime is the *volatile* carbonate of ammonia ?

But Liebig expressly states, at page 190, that it is the *liquid excrement* which gives to the solid " the property of emitting ammonia—a property which they (the solids) possess only in a very slight degree." Solid dung, where mixed with decayed vegetable matter in the form of stable manure, does not, as Liebig has pointed out, act as a manure through the agency of ammonia. " The peculiar action of solid excrement is limited to their inorganic constituents, which thus restore to a soil that which is removed in the form of corn, roots, or grain," which, he further states, are " the silicate of potash and the phosphates of lime and magnesia." p. 181. By solid manure we in fact " supply a soil with all that is requisite for the formation of the woody fibre, the grain, the roots, and the straw." p. 188. But if we wish to increase the nutritive produce of corn, we must supply it with more food in the form of nitrogen, which it obtains from the atmosphere, from rain, from salt in the earth ; and it is the *object of agricultural chemistry to increase the supply by fixing the ammonia, which would otherwise become volatilized in the process of fermentation—in the liquid excrement of animals.* Upon this principle Liebig recommends the *stables* to be spread with gypsum ; because here it obtains its water of solution, p. 194 ; or to strew the fields with gypsum and *then* apply the liquid excrement; or the drainage of dung-hills, p. 193. He sums up the matter thus :—

" From the preceding remarks it must be evident that the greatest value should be attached to all liquid excrement, when a manure is desired which shall supply nitrogen to the soil. The greatest part of a superabundant crop, or in other words the *greatest increase of growth which is in our power,* can be obtained exclusively by their means."

I think then I have fairly made out from Liebig's authority the following positions :—

First.—That gypsum will not decompose carbonate of ammonia, unless dissolved in 400 times its weight of water, or acted upon by the rain in the course of several years ; and therefore *that it will not* fix the ammonia of fermenting manure, if spread between the different layers in the form of powder.

Secondly.—That Professor Henslow's experiment must be unsatisfactory, even if the salts were brought

together in a state favourable for the action of chemical affinity; because the ammonia in all manure
heaps depends chiefly upon the fortuitous circumstance of the amount of *liquid* excrement they contain
and not upon the much smaller proportion in the
solids, or that which results, if any, from the process
of fermentation or heating.

Thirdly.—That as the solid manure supplies to
land the silicate of potash, and the phosphates of
lime and magnesia, which salts are not volatile—
which are essential to the growth of the plants, and
which *must* be supplied to replace that removed by
the previous crop—we must not look here for our
additional supply of nitrogen, unless we can fix the
volatile ammonia by a direct agent.

Fourthly.—That the principal benefit—if not at
present *the only* benefit which chemistry has been
able to confer upon agriculture—is that of fixing the
ammonia in *liquid* excrement, and in the drainage
from dunghills. This is, however, a most important
improvement; for Liebig states that for *every pound*
of liquid excrement with the ammonia fixed, there
will be a produce of a pound of wheat. The ammonia may be fixed either with gypsum dissolved in
400 times its weight of water, or by sulphuric or
muriatic acids diluted with water—100 parts of
sulphuric acid diluted with 1000 parts of water,
being equal to 175 parts of gypsum.

100 pounds of burnt gypsum will fix the ammonia
of 6250 pounds of horse's urine.—Liebig, p. 88.

I trust that Professor Henslow will find that, in
this my feeble attempt to elicit truth, I have attended
to the wise recommendations at the close of his last
letter.—I am, Sir, your obedient servant,

                                  C. R. BREE.

Stowmarket, January 25th, 1843.

LETTER V.

GENTLEMEN,—I had intended to have turned over
a new leaf, by discussing, in this letter, some of the
functions of the leaf; but I must trespass once more
upon you by a few remarks I wish to make upon
Mr. Bree's comments in yesterday's paper. He has
stated that Liebig has not recommended the addition
of gypsum to *manure heaps*; and also that he himself
considers the experiment I have proposed to you
would be *useless*, because the carbonate of ammonia
and gypsum would not mutually decompose each
other, under the circumstances of the case. I certainly did not turn to Liebig's work when I wrote
my letter, to ascertain the precise words under which
he had recommended the application of gypsum to
farm-yard manure, but the impression which his
statement had left upon my mind inclined me to
believe that his advice was *general*; and that where-
ever the carbonate of ammonia might be forming in
the materials of which dunghills are prepared, there
it might be useful to apply gypsum to decompose it.
I had sent to Dr. Daubeny, the Professor of Agriculture and Chemistry at Oxford, a copy of my Address to the Hadleigh Club, after it appeared in the
papers, with a request that he would point out to me
any errors into which I might very possibly have
fallen, owing to my partial acquaintance with chemistry. In his reply (Dec. 28) he assured me that
he saw none, but added this remark: "I may notice that Mr. Pusey, in the last number of the *Agricultural Journal*, states that the application of gypsum to stable-yard dung has proved a failure. I
know not why this should be so, and therefore think
it deserves to be enquired into further." I had pre-

viously written to Mr. Pusey to ask his reasons for
the assertion here referred to; and in his reply (Dec.
15) he had stated, "A farmer wrote to our Secretary desiring him to inform me that he had used a
considerable quantity of gypsum, and had found it
do no good—I did not mean that gypsum would not
decompose the carbonate of ammonia, but that it had
not done so in a farm-yard. Your experiment indicates the cause of failure to have been the absence
of sufficient moisture." The remarks of these gentlemen satisfied me that the question had not yet
received that degree of attention which the interests
of agriculture required; and this was the reason
which induced me to propose the experiment in the
form I did. (Jan 7)—not as one which had been
suggested in that form by Liebig, but as one which
I thought would test the *general tenor* of his suggestions. I shall quote to you a few passages from
Liebig, and Dr. Daubeny, which I consider fully
justify my inference. Liebig says, at p. 192. "In
dung-reservoirs, well constructed and protected from
evaporation, the carbonate of ammonia is retained in
solution." "When it (the carbonate of ammonia)
is lost by being volatilized in the air, which happens
in most cases, the loss suffered is nearly equal to
one half of the weight of the urine employed, so that
if we fix it—that is, deprive it of its volatility, we
increase its action twofold;" and p. 193, "The carbonate of ammonia formed by the putrefaction of
urine can be fixed or deprived of its volatility in
many ways. If a field be strewed with gypsum, and
then with putrified urine, or the drainings of dunghills, all the carbonate of ammonia will be converted
into the sulphate, which will remain in the soil.
But there are till *simpler* means of effecting this
purpose; gypsum, cloride of calcium, sulphuric, or
muriatic acid, and super-phosphate of lime, are all
substances of very low price, and completely neutralize
the urine, converting its ammonia into salts which
possess no volatility." And p. 194, "The ammonia
emitted from stables and necessaries is always in
combination with carbonic acid. Carbonate of ammonia, and sulphate of lime (gypsum) *cannot be
brought together, at common temperatures, without mutual decomposition.* The ammonia enters into combination with the sulphuric acid, and the carbonic
acid with the lime, forming compounds which are
not volatile, and, consequently, destitute of all smell.
Now, if we strew the floors of our stables, from
time to time, with common gypsum, they will lose
all their offensive smell, and none of the ammonia
which forms can be lost, but will be retained in a
condition serviceable as a manure." And Dr. Daubeny, in speaking of the composition of *dung-heaps*,
thus comments upon Liebig: p. 83. "Hence Liebig
advises the addition of sulphuric or muriatic acid,
both cheap substances, to the other materials of the
dung-heap, which, forming with the ammonia present
the sulphates and muriates of that alkali, would at
once prevent any loss of it by evaporation. If these
expedients be not adopted, it should at least be borne
in mind, that unless means are taken to prevent it,
the most valuable portion of the manure is constantly
escaping, during exposure to air and sun, by evaporation, and also by draining off into the ground;
whence, instead of a material calculated to afford a
ready supply of nitrogen to the plant, we obtain an
effete mass, in which that element is in a great measure wanting, and which, therefore, can only influence the growth of plants, by virtue of the phosphoric salts and other fixed ingredients still present
in it;" and p. 84, "The above theory of its use, (viz.
of gypsum as proposed by Liebig) being admitted,

we may be encouraged to extend its application to other crops besides the Leguminosæ, and also *to mix it with the dung of our stables*, so as to prevent the waste of this valuable material, which is constantly occurring." Now, whether I am justified or not in supposing that Liebig intended to recommend the application of gypsum, and the other materials no ticed by him, to your common manure heaps, I still retain my opinion that it will be highly expedient for you to try the little experiment I have suggested to your notice. All your manure heaps contain urine as well as dung; and surely they are as moist as the floor of the stable. No one can deny that a large quantity of carbonate of ammonia is driven off from them during the process of fermentation; and even the solid dung and the vegetable matter assist in supplying some of it. Whether gypsum will serve your purpose or not, is the question at issue. Mr. Bree is positive that it will not; because carbonate of ammonia and gypsum, *in a dry state*, do not mutually decompose each other. If you will refer to my address to the Hadleigh Club, you will see that I expressly stated that the gypsum should be *wetted*, "Let a sufficient quantity of water be sprinkled over it to wet the gypsum thoroughly." Upon referring, however, to my first letter, I see that I have inadvertently neglected to repeat this caution; and hence I have misled Mr. Bree to suppose that I did not consider the presence of any moisture necessary to secure the decomposition of the two salts. But still Mr. Bree has further argued, that as gypsum requires four hundred times its weight of water to dissolve it, we could never supply this menstruum in sufficient quantity to the dunghill, to enable the carbonate of ammonia and gypsum to act upon each other. But this, I think, is an incorrect inference. I conceive it cannot be necessary that all the gypsum should be in solution at the same time, and as fast as one portion is decomposed, the water would be able to take up another. If this be not admitted, I can still refer to the known principle, that the mutual decomposition of a soluble and insoluble salt may take place, provided the former be in a state of solution. Thus, the carbonates of potash and soda, in solution, are used to decompose the sulphate of barytes. I read in Ure's *Dictionary of Chemistry*, that in the manufacture of sal-ammoniac, an impure solution of the carbonate of ammonia (obtained from the destructive distillation of animal substances) is passed through a bed of pulverised gypsum, when mutual decomposition ensues, and the result is sulphate of ammonia in solution, and an insoluble carbonate of lime. In this case, the gypsum was not in solution; and why should we suppose it to be absolutely necessary that it should be so in the dunghill? Provided there is sufficient moisture to dissolve the carbonate of ammonia, it seems to me very likely that the mutual decomposition of the two salts will take place. Upon such points, however, I do not feel myself competent to speak positively. Where Liebig asserts that gypsum strewed over a field remains a long while before it is wholly decomposed, I had fancied that he meant to say, this was owing to the very gradual manner in which the carbonate of ammonia was supplied by the atmosphere; otherwise he appears to contradict himself. It was certainly an oversight on my part, in not alluding, in my first letter, to the necessity of moistening the gypsum in the experiment I have proposed; and I am under obligations to Mr. Bree for having noticed the omission. I shall not dwell upon the further remarks of Mr. Bree, which are sufficiently interesting to you, as tending to illustrate the use of li-

quid manure, but which do not apply so directly to the question at issue. Liebig's remark on this subject is worthy your most serious attention—p. 201. " When it is considered that with every pound of ammonia which evaporates, a loss of 60lbs. of corn is sustained, and that with every pound of urine a pound of wheat might be produced, the indifference with which these liquid excrements are regarded is *quite incomprehensible*. In most places, only the solid excrements, impregnated with the liquid, are used, and the dunghills containing them are protected neither from evaporation nor from rain!"

If Mr. Bree is still unwilling to believe that the experiment I have suggested can be of any service, perhaps he will be so good as to propose to you an experiment for testing some other method suggested by chemists for fixing the ammonia in dunghills. The objection which occured to me against the use of free sulphuric acid on a dungheap, was the probability of the acid entering into combination with other ingredients than the carbonate of ammonia, and thus not waiting till all of this salt was formed, which might be afforded by the thorough decomposition of the organic materials. However, I shall be delighted to see some of you attending to Mr. Bree's suggestion, as well as some of you to my own. In order that he and I may not be jealous of any preference you may be inclined to show to one or other of us, I propose that all who intend to co-operate should toss up, and let heads or tails decide for each of you, whose experiment he is to try.

I have received a communication from a gentleman, who informs me that he is a manufacturing chemist, and that he denies the fact asserted in the extract I quoted from a newspaper in my second letter, viz,. that common salt can fix the ammonia formed in stables. I am inclined to believe that he may be correct; for, on dissolving common salt and carbonate of ammonia together, I do not find the smell of the latter to be destroyed. If you refer to my letter, you will see that I was merely attempting to correct the informant's *theory*, and not to dispute his *facts*; and that I cautiously remarked, " *Provided*, therefore, our informant is correct in saying that salt fixes the ammonia, &c." I should be prepared to assent more freely to the contradiction I have alluded to, it I had not perceived that Dr. Daubeny, in his lectures, inclines to the same opinion as the anonymous author of the extract—p. 86 : " Chloride of calcium, *common salt*, sulphuric and muriatic acids, phosphate of lime, and other salts, may, it should seem, on the principles laid down, be substituted when gypsum cannot be obtained." Who shall decide when doctors disagree ? This is precisely the sort of question which a person like myself, who am not a professed chemist, is unqualified to decide for you. My object in addressing you is not to dispute with chemists the facts they assert ; but to endeavour to put before you the theory which explains their facts, in such a manner as may convince you how necessary it is *that you should experiment for yourselves, with some definite object in view*, and not in that hap-hazard sort of manner in which agricultural experiments are most frequently undertaken. My advice is, that you trust not implicitly to the suggestions of the most celebrated chemists; nor adopt their notions into your practice, without previously making *a set of comparative experiments* for yourselves, in order to test the value of their suggestions. I feel more and more convinced that some plan for securing co-operation, such as I have thrown out in these letters, might be made a most effectual means of greatly accelerating the progress of agriculture. If you could enlist

T

some first-rate chemist into your service, who should lay down for you precise rules for trying certain simple agricultural experiments, and you would then consent to act together *by hundreds and thousands* in attending to his directions, and in *registering* results, he would soon strike out for you such decided improvements in the art of culture, that your important interests would be able to maintain that state of prosperity in which it is so essential to the general wellbeing of the country they should exist. If the arrangements of your various agricultural societies were only as complete for securing abundant returns of *comparative experiments*, as they appear to be perfect for exhibiting fat cattle and fine roots, or even for discussing good dinners and promoting good fellowship, I should then hope to live long enough to see the farming produce of Great Britain double that which is now extracted from the soil. If you consider me too sanguine in this expectation, and that my assertions need some qualification, I will, for the present, fall back upon the declaration of the President of the Hadleigh Club, at their last anniversary,— "Though we have to compete with all the world, I firmly believe, with the aid of science, that the energy of the British farmers will carry them through every struggle and every difficulty." Your obedient servant,   J. S. HENSLOW.

Hitcham Rectory, February 2, 1843.

LETTER VI.

On Stripping off the Leaves of Plants.

GENTLEMEN,—More than one person has fancied that he could increase the produce of his potato crop by pulling off the leaves. I have been told by an experimenter that he once pulled all the leaves from his potato plants, under an idea that by so doing he could divert the sap into the tubers, and thus greatly increase their size, by not allowing any portion of the nutriment in the sap to be wasted in developing such comparatively useless appendages as the leaves. The result of this experiment was a crop of tubers so minute that it almost needed a microscope to enable the disappointed experimenter to see them. The result of this single experiment renders it highly *probable* that it is not advisable to pull off the leaves of potatoes. Possibly it may be expedient to adopt such a practice in certain other cases. For instance, it may serve some good purpose to pull off the leaves from mangel wurtzel ; or *possibly* it may be useful to strip a peach-tree or an apple-tree of its leaves, in order to divert the sap to the fruit, and thus increase its bulk or flavour. In the case of the mulberry-tree, indeed, it has been long ascertained by the experience of those who rear silkworms in the South of France, and elsewhere, that such a practice by no means improves the growth of that tree. On the contrary, such constant pulling off the leaves, which they are obliged to have recourse to, produces a decidedly bad effect upon the health and stature of the trees. They become miserably stunted objects, and would die outright if the leaf-pullers did not take the precaution of allowing a few leaves to remain on the ends of the boughs. It should seem, then, to be sufficiently proved that neither potatoes nor mulberries rejoice in being despoiled of their leaves. But may we safely generalize from no more than *two* facts of this description, and conclude that no plant can be benefitted by abstracting its leaves? There are some opposing facts to be taken into consideration. There are certain

plants, those for instance commonly called cactuses, which have no leaves; and there are, moreover, certain agriculturists (so I have been told) who strip the mangel wurtzel of its leaves; which we must presume they would not do unless they were well satisfied the practice was advisable. We have, then, potato and mulberry *versus* cactus and certain agriculturists. Ought we not to have recourse to further experiment in order to test the value of the practice to which I have referred, since it has not been universally adopted, and (as I have also been informed) it is even objected to by some agriculturists as useless or perhaps injurious?' Possibly I am under some error as to the extent and nature of this practice. I have been informed that in some places the leaves are pulled two or three times during the growth of the plant, whilst in other districts the practice is to pull them only a short time before the roots are dug up. I have, however, been asked my opinion, as a botanist, what result may be expected from pulling off the leaves of this plant. To which question I can only reply by alluding to those particular functions of the leaf which are connected with the nutrition of plants in general. What is your opinion, Mr. H., said a practical gentleman to me, about pulling off the leaves of mangel wurtzel? May I ask, was my reply, what may be your *motive* for doing so? I did it because my excellent neighbour, Mr. So-and-So, had adopted the practice ; and Mr. So-and-so, it appeared, had seen it recommended in some journal. I asked whether the object was to *diminish* the size of the root-stalks ; because I did not feel quite sure that this might not be advisable in some cases. But I was immediately informed that this was not to be *desired* in any case. There must, then, be some *expediency* in this practice which more than counterbalances whatever risk may be incurred of diminishing the size or weight of the root-stalks. I have no desire to interfere with any approved practice in agriculture ; but it would be exceedingly desirable that science and practice should not be at issue; and as this practice, however modified, must still bear some relation to the functions of the leaf, perhaps you will not object to hear what botanists suppose they have ascertained concerning those functions; and then, possibly, some of you may feel inclined to try a little *comparative experiment* for the purpose of determining for yourselves whether their theory is correct or not. I need hardly invite so many experimenters to step forward in this case as for our projected gypsum experiment. An ordinary petty jury of twelve may be considered quite sufficient for adjudicating on such a subject as this ; and I suspect they will find they run less risk of being puzzled in doing so, than they have sometimes been when sitting in a jury-box, mystified by the quirks and quibblings of opposing counsel. I shall not, in this letter, enter further upon the subject; but I will endeavour to prepare for you, in my next, some little account of the functions of the leaf, and perhaps I may then suggest an experiment by which you may test the utility of the practice of pulling off the leaves of mangel wurtzel. In the meantime I shall be very glad to know to what extent the different factions of anti-pull-mangel-leaf and pro-pull-mangel-leaf practitioners prevail. Even if you should consider this question of too trifling a character for discussion, it may not be wholly unadvisable for me to offer you a few remarks upon the general functions of the leaf, which is so far from ever being an appendage of little or no value, that it is absolutely essential (wherever it is provided) to the health of the individual, to the full development of the tuber or root-stalk, and to the perfecting of the seed. In leafless plants, a special provision is made for securing the purpose for which leaves serve in other cases: the resources of Infinite Wisdom being as multifarious in providing the conditions essential to the well-being of each particular species of plant, as we find them to be in adopting the numerous forms of ani-mated nature to the variety of circumstance under which they are destined to exist.

Your obedient servant,

J. S. HENSLOW.

Hitcham Rectory, 11th *Feb.*, 1843.

P.S.—A few more last words, if you please, about our Gypsum Experiment. I do not wish to add to the arguments I have already brought forward in urging you to co-operate in attempting this little ex-periment; but I may state that I have received a second communication from the gentleman to whom I alluded in my fourth letter, and that he has allowed me to use his name in support of his testimony. It is Mr. Burgess, a manufacturing chemist, of Up-well, near Wisbeach, who informs me that he has had great experience in preparing both the carbonate and muriate of ammonia; and he states positively that the carbonate of ammonia in solution will com-pletely decompose gypsum *without the necessity of this substance being first dissolved*. He has suggested the following experiment, which any one sceptical on this point may easily try for himself—

"Take an ounce of powdered carbonate of ammo-nia, and add to it half a pint of soft water : put this in a phial and shake it occasionally, till it is com-pletely dissolved. Take two ounces and a half of finely powdered gypsum and add to the above : shake the whole occasionally for two or three days, and the result will be a solution of sulphate of am-monia, and an insoluble precipitate of carbonate of lime."

I have been invited to extend the challenge I have offered you to the farmers of all England, under an idea that I shall not find fifty persons among your-selves who have *sufficient public spirit* to co-operate in the way I have suggested. I cannot believe this. But I can readily suppose that I may not be able to meet with fifty among you who feel sufficient con-fidence in myself to think it worth their while to attend to my advice : and if so, I must be content to withdraw my challenge altogether. I should not think myself justified in extending it to all England. Such a proceeding might come with a good grace from a body like the Council of the Royal Agricul-tural Society, acting under the directions of a Liebig or a Faraday : but I am taxing my own opportunities (to say nothing of my presumption) to the utmost, in attempting to persuade you to help yourselves in that way which seems to me the most likely to se-cure a rapid improvement in the practice of agricul-ture; I mean by your *co-operating in performing comparative experiments, with a definite object in view*. It is not I, or any mere follower of science, but it is many among the best-informed of your own body, who are daily assuring you of the absolute necessity that now exists for your attending to the suggestions of such chemists as the late Sir H. Davy, Liebig, and others, who have directed their attention to agricultural chemistry. All will be of no use, or rather worse than useless, if you do not take the *right method* of testing the value of their suggestions. That method I believe I have pointed out to you, in advising extensive *co-operation* for making *comparative experiments*. I am still far from

having received the addresses of fifty willing to try our gypsum experiment; but there is yet a fortnight to the end of February. Those gentlemen who have already favoured me with their addresses, must not take it amiss if they find that I decline accepting a less number than fifty. I am willing to devote time and attention to a useful purpose ; but as I consider fewer results would lead to no satisfactory conclu-sions, I must decline proceeding any further, if I find that my advice is not capable of influencing a suf-ficient number of you to make an attempt so simple and unexpensive as the one I have proposed.

THE GYPSUM EXPERIMENT.

SIR,—When Liebig stated that gypsum and car-bonate of ammonia cannot come together at common temperatures without decomposing each other, there can be no doubt he used the expression as a chemist, leaving it to be understood that they were brought into contact in a state favourable to decom-position. If he did not do this then he contradicts his own statement—that "water is essential to the decomposition of the gypsum," and that the process is "slow" and "very gradual," as there can be no doubt that, if the *cohesion* of the sulphate of lime is overcome—and if there is present "*quantity of matter*," which the celebrated Berthollet considered compensates for a weaker affinity—that decompo-sition of the two salts will occur. I do not think it necessary to discuss this part of the subject further, or to point out the difference between "chemical affinity" and "chemical decomposition," which are often opposed to each other, as in the instance of the carbonate of potash decomposing sulphate of baryta, the most insoluble salt in nature ; but I will merely remark that, in the exercise of chemical affinity the change takes place at once, as in those instances of elective affinity where muriatic acid is added to a carbonate, or sulphuric acid to a muriate; but when the exercise of affinity is produced in instances of double decomposition, where two salts are brought into contact, the decomposition which ensues is in-fluenced by "modifying circumstances." The prin-cipal of these is *cohesion*. It is a law in chemistry, that when two acids and two bases are brought to-gether, the salt which is most insoluble is invariably formed. Now sulphuric acid has a greater affinity for lime than ammonia. But carbonic acid has a great affinity for lime, and as the sulphate of lime and the carbonate of lime are about equally in-soluble, the tendency to insolubility cannot have much influence in the decomposition of the salts ; but upon the same principle that the carbonate of potash decomposes sulphate of baryta when they are brought together in water, so will the carbonate of am-monia decompose the sulphate of lime under the same circumstances, and the only rational explanation of the decomposition is that the water absorbs an ex-cess of carbonic acid, which thus produces quantity of matter, which, as we have seen, Berthollet consi-ders compensates for a weaker affinity. Leaving, however, this part of the subject, let us return to the question of the extent to which this decomposition takes place in the dunghill. In the preparation of sal ammoniac, a solution of the impure carbonate of ammonia is digested with gypsum, until decompo-sition takes place, when there is water, time, and quantity of matter all favouring the decomposition. In the dunghill water is required not only to cause the decomposition of the salts, but also to absorb the soluble sulphate of ammonia. When I stated that a pound of gypsum required 400 pounds of water I did not mean that it was necessary that the whole of the gypsum should be in solution before decompositiou ensued ; I made use of the expression in a relative sense, to show the great quantity of water necessary to ensure the mutual rapid decomposition of a volatile, and an almost insoluble, compound. If it is urged that it is not necessary to have the entire amount of water of solution to cause partial decomposition, then I contend, the less water, the longer is the time required ; and as, from the constant evaporation, you never can have sufficient water to ensure rapid decomposition, so will the ammonia be volatilized, and the experiment fail, as in the instance pointed out by Mr. Pusey.

To test the matter, however, fairly, to prove at once the power of gypsum in fixing ammonia, and the relative merit of that salt and sulphuric acid, I will take the liberty of suggesting to Professor Henslow's notice, and I hope, through his recommendation, to the farmers of Suffolk, the following simple comparative experiment.

Procure three vessels made of wood, with lids, (old beer barrels will do very well) each capable of holding 36 gallons, and numbered 1, 2, and 3. Into No. 1, put at different times, three pounds of concentrated sulphuric acid and one gallon of water ; into No. 2, five pounds of finely powdered gypsum and one gallon of water ; and one gallon of water into No. 3. Let these vessels be filled with urine as it can be collected either in houses or stables, the former to be preferred, as it contains four times more ammonia. The acid and gypsum had better be divided into three portions, one pound of acid with the gallon of water, and a third part of the gypsum, to be put into the barrels at once. When about a third full, add another pound of acid and no water, and another third of gypsum ; and the remaining portions when about two-thirds full. Then mark out, as directed by Professor Henslow, four patches of land, about the eighth of an acre each, and number them 1, 2, 3, and 4. As corn crops require the salt contained in stable manure, if it has not been done in the autumn, let each patch have an equal portion of manure taken from the same heap, and previously to its being ploughed in let the contents of each barrel be spread regularly over the portion of land corresponding to its number—weigh the seed required for each piece—register every step of the experiment—note the difference, if any, in the crops upon each—carefully weigh the straw and grain—and communicate the result to your respective agricultural associations. Of course No. 4 will have received no liquid, No. 3 will have had the liquid without any means taken to fix the ammonia, and Nos. 1 and 2 will have had that alkali fixed by the means recommended by chemists.

The trouble will be very little—the expense less. The price of sulphuric acid wholesale is fourpence a pound, of gypsum rather more than one farthing a pound.

I have made my calculations, as to the quantity of each required, from the statements of Liebig that 100 pounds of gypsum will fix the ammonia of 6250 pounds of horses' urine, and that 100 parts of concentrated sulphuric acid, diluted with 800 or 1,000 parts of water, are equal in effect to 175 parts of gypsum, and I have put the amount in round numbers for the sake of convenience. It is quite possible, as human urine contains so much more nitrogen than horses, that if the former is used, as

recommended, more acid and gypsum will be required. This will be known by the escape of ammonia, which is detected either by its pungent odour, or by the simple test which I mentioned in a former letter. If more of either be added, the amount should be noted and communicated with the result of the experiment. If Liebig's theory be found correct in practice, and the experiment be carefully performed, then we ought to have an increase of produce in No. 3 over No. 4 of 150 pounds of grain, and in Nos. 1 and 2 of 300 pounds, being at the rate in the former of 80 and in the latter of 160 stone of grain per acre. Corn is the best crop to give the experiment a trial, because grain or beans eliminate or take up more nitrogen than esculent roots, and an important fact to the practical farmer arises from this. It is well known that if land is too highly manured with stable manure the result is an increase in the bulk of straw, and, if anything, a decrease in the weight of grain. Chemistry easily explains this, because it proves that that manure supplies the material upon which the growth of the stalks, leaves, and roots depend. But the liquid manure is rich in ammonia, which gives nothing to the straw, but is entirely eliminated by the grain, and this circumstance not being visible in the growing crop may have led some to have prematurely laid aside the use of liquid manure.

I am, Sir, your obedient servant,
C. R. Bree.

Stowmarket, Feb. 18, 1843.

P.S.—I think there is very little doubt but that salt will to a certain extent fix ammonia. The law is, when two soluble salts, the decomposition of which does not form an insoluble salt, are mixed together, the two acids are divided between the two bases, and four salts are yielded, as in the present case—muriates of ammonia and soda, and the carbonates of soda and ammonia.

WIRRIL AGRICULTURAL CLUB.

The Ploughing Match of this club came off on Monday, the 13th Feb. The ground selected for this interesting trial of skill was a field of about eleven acres, in the township of Ness, adjoining the turnpike-road leading to Neston. The judges were Messrs. Longton, of Rainhill, Lancashire ; Simpson, of the Court House ; and Wm. Davies, of Mostyn, Flintshire.

Reaching the spot we found it laid out in half-acre allotments, that being the quantity of work to be performed by each plough, and the allotments numbered respectively, from one to twenty inclusive. The surface soil, being an old pasture ley, is loose loam, well supplied with boulder stones, and resting upon a subsoil of dry hungry, gravelly ramel. The time limited for the completion of the work was four hours and a half, the width of the furrow being nine inches, and the depth six inches. Only seventeen teams started, viz., fifteen for the first class prizes for men of all ages, and two for the second, for young men under twenty years of age, so that the allotments 10, 11, and 12, were unoccupied. Not knowing and purposely omitting to enquire to whom the ploughs belonged, we can only remark upon the work in reference to the number drawn by each ploughman, and which corresponded in every case with the numbers marked upon the ground.

The work was laid up into three-yard bouts or ridges, and each ploughman had to clear up five rains or water furrows—the great test of skill in the present case, for reasons which we will explain presently.

The ploughs were all of them swings, and for the most part iron; made either by Wilkie, or West of Lundie, though the one used by No. 4 was by Moreton, of Upton. The horses were double, and some really splended pairs there were. We particularly noticed No. 19, a pair of chesnuts, admirably adapted for the purpose, but rather slow; they were not larger than the Clydesdale horses, but heavier in the limbs. The iron ploughs were universally admitted to run "sweeter" than the wooden ones, though No. 13, which was of wood, made very good work. The following is, in our opinion, the order of merit in the several performances, without reference to time:—

FIRST CLASS.—First prize, No. 19; second ditto, No. 4; third ditto, No. 17.

The work of Nos. 13 and 18 was also very good, as well as No. 20; but that of No. 14 was equally bad. There were but two candidates for the second class prizes; the first of which was won by No. 7, and the second by No. 8.

The ploughman No. 19, a Scotchman, was decidedly the most business-like man of the kind we ever saw; he husbanded the strength of his horses so as to leave but two minutes to spare in time, and his execution was really beautiful. His plough (a Wilkie) was so set that his furrow-slice was turned completely, and the acute angle of it (and that too, with scarcely a deviation) was turned well upwards, so that the harrow in covering the seed would do it most effectually. To show that he was completely master of his implement and its capabilities, we were informed that he changed the sock of his plough, after finishing his ridges, and before he began to clean up his rains or water-furrows, for one with a narrower wing, which enabled him to finish his work better. The work of No. 4, too, was very excellent, and he had also this in his favour, that from the superior activity of his nags his work was done in much less time than that of No. 19. We observed the best hands invariably left all their water furrows to be cleared up after they had finished all their ridges; and this was quite the most difficult part of the work, because the surface soil, being only about the depth of the furrows, and the subsoil being as before remarked, dry, loose, and gravelly, the sod roved before the plough, and instead of being turned over, merely rose on its edge, and then fell back again, grass uppermost. "No handling" then became the cry, and the very best man amongst them was glad to catch the falling sod with his foot, and press it to its place; but notwithstanding the cry, every man in the field we believe used his hands for this purpose, more or less.

The beauty of the day attracted a large concourse of spectators; and we observed on the ground several implements from Messrs. Cartmell's manufactory, in Liverpool, consisting of chaff cutters, bean and grain crushers, horse hoe, &c. &c.

The dinner of the club took place at Neston, C. Stanley, Esq. of Denhall, in the chair; but as the dinners upon these occasions are, in our estimate, quite the least attractive part of the proceedings, we make no apology to our readers for omitting an account of it.

BRAINTREE FARMERS' CLUB.

The annual meeting of the members of this club took place on Wednesday, Feb. 15, and was respectably attended by the agriculturists of the district. The following report of the committee for the past year was read to them:—

REPORT.

The committee of the Braintree and Bocking Farmers' Club, in presenting to the members at their annual meeting a report of the proceedings for the past year, cannot but regret that it should be their painful duty to state that the meetings of the club for the past year have not been so well attended, the discussions consequently less spirited, and the information elicited not of that importance which the growing intelligence of members, and the continued influence of the club, would seem to warrant.

Your committee, anxious to ascertain the cause of the general non-attendance of members with a view to remove it, cannot be insensible to the altered position of the farmer, and without enquiry as to the circumstances which have led to the general depression, they are fearful such depression has at present, and will for a time, have the effect of retarding the progress of institutions calculated to improve and elevate the British farmer.

Your committee however desire to impress upon the minds of the members of the club the necessity of a more constant and uniform attendance at their monthly meetings, if the purposes for which the club was originally instituted are to be carried out, or the ends it proposes to attain are to be realized. The necessity for legitimate combination and mutual interchange of opinion amongst agriculturists afforded by the Farmers' Clubs, was never more urgent than at the present moment, and independently of the personal and individual advantages to be gained, they are calculated to be mainly instrumental in placing the agricultural interest in a situation which its importance demands, and will readily be yielded to it, if those who "till the land" are not hindered through prejudice, or enervated by continued prosperity. The manifest advantages resulting from Farmers' Clubs are so great that your committee feel it unnecessary to dwell upon that subject at any length; they afford the most simple, yet effective, means for discussing the various scientific discoveries and improvements which those who lack practical knowledge are daily making and suggesting, and although the purely practical farmer may view with apprehension the rapid strides which science is daily making in its favourite pursuit, he is as it were by mixing with his fellow cultivators almost insensibly led to adopt some of the many suggestions which from time to time are brought under his notice, and subjected to the severe, but proper, test of practical experience.

Your committee, with the hope that their endeavours to excite a greater interest in the club may be attended with success, are anxious to press upon the attention of the members the importance of combined effort to raise in the scale of society the cultivators of the soil. The times in which we live, the exertions which are made to educate the lower classes, the deference paid to real knowledge, the rapid strides which science is daily making, all tend to show that it can be only by steadily pursuing the path of inquiry, by diligent research, by patient investigation, and a careful observance of phenomena which are daily occurring, that we can hope to maintain our position or keep pace with the increased intelligence of the times in which we live.

The isolated position of farmers, the few opportunities they have of meeting, the limited means of improvement till lately within their reach, are all difficulties which can only be overcome by a deep conviction of the importance of the art they follow, and its pervading influence in all the other arts of life. We may not only anticipate but be positive that certain causes will produce certain effects, and although it may not be our privilege to witness the full perfection of the fruit, nor perhaps may the opening blossom be apparent, yet your committee desire to cheer you on in the useful path you are pursuing, and with a confidence not in the slightest degree abated, anticipate the realization of all and every the advantages which from time to time have been stated as certain to result from the increased knowledge and improvement to be derived from farmers' clubs.

It cannot but be profitable to every farmer to watch with interest the progress which agriculture has made, and is making; nor can any more satisfactory proof of such progress be adduced than the increase in the general average of the country, which is universally admitted; the causes which have produced this are doubtless various, as well as numerous; but surely no one will deny that the increased and increasing intelligence of the farmers as a body has had some influence in producing it. Let us then proceed in the firm conviction that as our knowledge increases we shall be able to penetrate deeper and deeper into the secrets of nature, and, as the fruits of our exertions, induce her to yield still more abundantly the fruits of the earth for the sustenance of her numerous and hardy sons.

Your committee cannot close their report without again alluding to the difficulties which seem to surround the farmers' interest; and although it is no part of their duty to enlarge upon the causes which may have produced them, still they would urge as a means best calculated to dispel the cloud, renewed and vigorous exertions. The farmers of the united kingdom are a numerous, influential, and important body; their occupation is the most ancient and the most honourable; their welfare necessarily influences every other class of the community, and in times like the present, assailed almost on every side, they must buckle on their armour, and prove that whatever may await them they at least deserve success.

Your committee are inclined to suggest as a means of improving the usefulness of the club, and making it more subservient to the purposes for which it was instituted, that arrangements should be made for the delivery of three or four lectures in the course of the year upon subjects connected with agriculture, and upon which a discussion could afterwards take place, but the committee will await the decision of the general meeting upon this subject. With the foregoing remarks your committee beg to submit the following brief summary of the proceedings of the club for the past year.

March 16, 1842.—Subject, "*The best method of preparing the land for sowing Mangold Wurtzel, Turnips, and other Root Crops.*"

The discussion was commenced by a member, who stated he had obtained several prizes for his roots at agricultural meetings. His plan was as follows:—

For mangold wurtzel he ploughed the land as early in the autumn as possible, and endeavoured to get it into good tilth, and immediately before the last ploughing in the spring he applied fermented ma-

nure; he drilled the seed and applied a very heavy roller, and afterwards during the growth of the plants used a horse hoe. He grew Swedes upon nearly the same plan. Common turnips for feeding he prefers sowing broadcast, and uses seed of several years' growth, by which he thinks he is more likely to secure a good plant. The seed should not be more than three years old, or the crop will run to rose crowns which crack, admit the water, and the turnips decay. Several other members addressed the meeting, and recommended that for mangold the land should be made as solid as possible. That for turnips the Northumberland balk of 27 inches was preferable.

The following resolution was proposed and agreed to:—

"That it is expedient in preparing land for mangold wurtzel to get the cultivation as forward as possible in the autumn, and to put on the manure in an unfermented state immediately before the last ploughing, and to scarify and roll in the spring, keeping the land in a solid state for the reception of the seed, and using a portion of some artificial manure for the purpose of forcing the growth of the young plant. And that the best method of sowing Swedes is upon the balk, varying the plan in some degree with regard to the quality of the soil, but never losing sight of the advantage of having the land in a good state of cultivation."

April 13, 1842.—Subject, "*The most judicious and efficient method of managing Agricultural Labour.*"

The importance of this subject was generally admitted, and a long discussion ensued. The system of letting work was strongly recommended, and that masters should endeavour by example and precept to create and maintain a good feeling between themselves and their men, encouraging and rewarding the industrious and steady workmen who were valuable to the farmer; to induce their men to join benefit clubs, as having a tendency to give them a feeling of proper and manly independence; to avoid the use of improper language, and adopt such means as are best calculated to improve the moral character of the labourer. A member recommended the master to be punctual to and regular in all his arrangements as it regarded his men. After an animated discussion, in which many of the members joined, the following resolution was carried:—

"It is the opinion of this meeting that in all cases when practicable it is desirable to let the labourers their work. That day work is not desirable either for master or man, inasmuch as it is productive of dissatisfaction to both. That it is also important to keep the men as regularly employed as possible, and not to turn them away without ample cause. To encourage them to join benefit clubs, and to promote steady, sober, and industrious habits, encouraging the honest and good in preference to the idle and dissolute."

May 18, 1842.—Subject, "*The best method of feeding Farm horses and other Cattle upon the green produce of the Farm.*"

A member stated that from experience he found no green food so good as grass, especially that which grew upon marsh land; that tares are too relaxing when young, and occasion much waste by decaying at the bottom when in more advanced growth. Mown clover was recommended in the absence of grass. It was considered advisable to mix hay with the green food, to cut the whole, and for a short time after commencing the green food to give the cattle a small portion of corn. The feeding in yards was strongly recommended, and as one of the effects besides the improvement in, and the increase of, manure, good beef might be produced on heavy land farms during the summer months. A difference of opinion arose as to the growth of lucerne. One of the members contended that considering the farmer lost his crop of wheat in the usual course, and the heavy manuring necessary for lucerne, it was not profitable to grow it. Several who had grown and used lucerne spoke of it most favourably, and contended that it increased the quantity of the manure to a much greater extent than it required it. The meeting was addressed by occupiers of soil of almost every description; and after a lengthened and spirited discussion, the following resolution was adopted :—

"That it is the opinion of this meeting that the best method of feeding farm horses and other cattle upon the green produce of the farm, is by mowing and feeding in the yards, commonly termed soiling, and at the commencement of the season to cut it with a portion of hay into chaff. And for horses, lucerne is strongly recommended for its substantial quality, and as yielding early and successive crops, and being exceedingly healthy and nutritious food."

JUNE 15, 1842.—Subject, "Hay-making."

Upon this subject a very interesting discussion arose, but as the resolution embodied most of the remarks made by the various members, it is subjoined without any further explanation.

"That it is the opinion of this meeting that the proper time for cutting grass for hay is when it is in full blossom; great care must then be taken that it be well strewed out either with the tedding machine or by hand, for on this in a great measure depends all the remaining stages of the operation. It must afterwards be rake-rowed and cocked according to the state of the weather, and the nature of the grasses. This meeting strongly recommends the use of the tedding machine, and the Leicestershire hay rake, which is considered decidedly superior to the common wooden rake in consequence of its size and convenience, and its great saving of time. With respect to clover-hay this meeting recommends making it principally on the swarth not turning it more than once, as much shaking it about has a tendency to break off the leaf, but if the weather be not favourable, it may be put upon the cock after being partly made. And as to tare hay, it recommends that it be made principally by cocking, beginning with small ones and enlarging them frequently. It is further the opinion of this meeting that care and vigilance are requisite during the hay season, and that the farmer ought ever to bear in mind the old adage, 'to make hay while the sun shines.'"

JULY 27, 1842.—This meeting was very thinly attended, and the subject proposed to be discussed was adjourned till the next meeting. A conversation took place amongst those present, upon the new mode of reaping practised by a member, that of cutting within two inches of the bottom. The extra cost was stated at 10s. per acre, the advantage in straw and corn 20s. per acre; that the extra quantity of manure would amply repay the increased cost of reaping low. No greater risk from the weather was incurred, nor if properly managed would the crop cost more to thrash. The sheaves were more compact and regular than when mowed, and no dirt was pulled up with the straw as in bagging. Mr. Lungley tried the following experiment, and presented it to the club; general publicity was given to it in the reports of the meeting of the Witham Ploughing

Match, but the committee beg to introduce it into their report.

[Here follow the tabular statements of the experiments by Mr. S. Lungley, which we published in our report of the Witham meeting.]

SEPTEMBER 14, 1842.—Subject, "The covenants in Leases of farms."

This subject was introduced by defining the objects of leases to be mutual protection, giving to the landlord every security, and affording every possible elasticity to the operations of the tenant. Increased reserved rents were thought very objectionable, the offence bearing no proportion to the punishment. The covenant of re-entry, except in very serious cases, led to the ejectment of tenants for very trifling breaches; that, unfortunately, the difficulty or loss in farming, according to the usual specified covenants in strict leases, led to a general disregard of them, and that the alteration in the system of farming rendered necessary different covenants to those usually adopted. Long leases were required to induce tenants to invest their capital in improving the soil, and render the land permanently more productive. It was stated by a member that in one lease which came under his notice, the tenant was bound to sow one-fourth of his land in clover every year; by another that there was nothing in a lease with which he was conversant to prevent the cropping the whole of the land with cole seed or wheat in the last year. A member stated he had let two farms recently, and allowed the occupiers the option of paying interest during the term upon the amount of the valuation, which they much preferred to paying the money. The meeting came to no resolution, as the subject will probably be discussed again ; but the following suggestions for farming-covenants were considered to be generally applicable:—

The tenant to farm the land in a good and husband-like manner, keeping the land clean and free from weeds ; not to take two white straw crops in succession without manuring for the second ; to have one-eighth of the arable land in clover every year ; to consume all the hay, straw, and green crops upon the premises, or bring an equivalent in value of manure ; to use all the manure where most needed upon the land.

OCTOBER 26, 1842.—Subject, "The weeds injurious to the farm."

The member introducing this subject gave a description of many of the common weeds injurious to crops, and stated that it was difficult, if not impossible, entirely to exterminate some weeds indigenous to certain soils, but by good farming and proper management their injurious effects would be scarcely perceptible. A member suggested a long fallow as the best means of eradicating weeds, but it was considered high farming would accomplish the object much better, and make the crops smother the weeds, instead of the weeds smothering the crop. The following resolution was carried :—

"It is the opinion of this meeting that the weeds growing upon the land are much more numerous and injurious than is generally supposed, and it recommends great care and vigilance in detecting and destroying them in their young state before they have seeded or become deep rooted in the soil ; the best remedies appearing to be draining, manuring, and general good farming."

NOVEMBER 16, 1842.—Subject, "When it is the best season of the year for carting manure from the farm yard, for beans, young clover, or clover layers. Is it desirable to make bottoms twelve inches thick, with earth from waste lands, parings of banks or chalky clay, a year *previously, to stir them over and eradicate the weeds in them?"*

It was recommended to make bottoms for muck heaps a year or two before they are wanted, in order that the seeds or roots of weeds may germinate and be eradicated by digging or ploughing the intended bottom; it was suggested as a good plan to cover the bottom of the farm yard with nine or twelve inches of earth, and about Lady-day to stir over and well mix the earth with the manure. The following resolution was carried:—

" In the opinion of this meeting it is a good plan, where practicable, to cart earth or clay as a bottom into the yards. But where manure is required for beans or young clovers, it is advisable to make bottoms a year before they are wanted, as near as possible to the field to which the manure is to be applied. The heap is to be stirred over once or twice, and carted on to the land as soon as convenient after harvest."

DECEMBER 14, 1842.—Subject, " *The best and most advantageous method of applying Farm-yard manure.*"

The discussion on this subject was limited, and the subjoined resolution embodies the opinions expressed upon the subject :—

" It is the opinion of this meeting that the best method of applying farm-yard manure is in a highly fermented state to the green and root crops. If turnip land to turnips and mangel wurzel ; if not, to the young clover, beans, and peas. "

JANUARY 11, 1843.—Subject, " *The best season of the year for ploughing up Land for long Fallows, with a view to the extermination of charlock and other weeds.*"

This meeting was very thinly attended, although the subject must be most interesting to the practical farmer ; a desultory conversation rather than a discussion took place, and the following resolution was proposed and carried :—

" It is the opinion of this meeting that the best time of the year for breaking up land for fallows is early in the autumn, which causes the seeds of charlock and other weeds to vegetate, many of which are destroyed by the frosts of winter. It is further recommended to drill the fallow crop, and hoe it constantly, and to spare no pains to keep the land clear of all weeds, more particularly of charlock."

The committee was then elected, Mr. Baines was chosen president for the ensuing year, and Mr. W. Fisher Hobbs, vice-chairman ; a vote of thanks was passed to Mr. Wm. Hutley, for his efficient conduct as chairman during the past year.

AGRICULTURAL EDUCATION.

TO THE EDITOR OF THE FARMERS' MAGAZINE.

SIR,—Much has been written for the benefit of farmers respecting the improvement of agriculture, and much censure has been passed on that class of men, because they are slow to adopt the improved systems that have been offered to them. The following observations have been occasioned by reading a paper in your March number, entitled " A Word to the British Agriculturist." Your correspondent there says, " It is a pitiable but undeniable circumstance, that three-fourths of the working agriculturists are men who rest satisfied with pursuing the customs of their ancestors, and who invincibly resist the introduction

of science. Science is a bane to them—the very word is a nuisance to John Bull." And again— " If science, then, is a knowledge of the operations of nature, it must be from some unwholesome influence that so many individuals neglect to profit by it. That influence in the present instance is prejudice—yes, prejudice—however disagreeable it may sound to those interested, it is too true ; for what can it be but prejudice that prompts men to say, ' Our forefathers prospered without science, and why should not we ?' What can it be but prejudice which induces men to believe that the system they adopt admits of no improvement ?"

My object is not to reflect on your correspondent for using such strong language, neither is it to attempt to justify " three-fourths of the working agriculturists" in their extreme cautiousness in adopting scientific methods to improve their culture ; but simply to endeavour to trace the evil to its proper source, and then to suggest a remedy.

1. The reason why " three-fourths of the working agriculturists rest satisfied with pursuing the customs of their ancestors, and invincibly resist the introduction of science.

Liebig has offered to the farmer a " Treatise on Chemistry in its Application to Agriculture and Physiology," or, in the words of the editor's preface to the second edition of that work, " A Treatise on the Chemistry of Agriculture." By a reference to the contents, the working agriculturist finds the *first part* treats on the " chemical processes in the nutrition of vegetables," and then referring to the contents of the several chapters, he comes to the " constituent elements of plants" —" the assimilation of carbon"—" origin and action of humus"—" the assimilation of hydrogen" —" origin and assimilation of nitrogen"—" the organic constituents of plants," &c., &c. ; which alone is sufficient to deter him, or any other man similarly circumstanced, from proceeding to the examination of the book. Professor Johnston's " Elements of Agricultural Chemistry and Geology " is a clear and simple introduction to the subject, but it must be observed, that even elementary knowledge cannot be acquired without study. Here, we perceive, is the source of the farmer's prejudice— science cannot be made familiar to him in the ordinary way by which he receives an increase of information. The terms used convey to him no ideas—he can attach no definite meaning to them, and consequently he is uninterested and unimproved. During the whole period of life allotted to education, he probably never heard the name of any of the constituents of plants, nor of the distinction of *organic* and *inorganic.* Is it marvellous, then, that the farmer is prejudiced, when he has had no opportunity of becoming acquainted with the first lines of science.

This view of the source of the farmer's prejudice will be confirmed if we take a glance at the education which he has received. In many instances it has been limited to what instruction could be had at the village school ; in this respect the children of farmers have been disadvantageously circumstanced ; and then, the utmost that was formerly attempted was a knowledge of reading, writing, arithmetic, and land-surveying. A tolerable knowledge of these was deemed *sufficient for a farmer.* All that was connected with farming was to be learned from the father, who had learned it from his father, and thus the whole art had been handed down from generation to generation. There is, therefore, nothing sur-prising in the fact, that at the market dinner, three-fourths of the working agriculturists should shelter themselves behind the plea that their an-cestors had done *without science.*

2. The remedy for this state of things.

If we have succeeded in showing that the source of the evil is a *defective* education, then the remedy is obvious—an *improved* or *extended* course of in-struction.

At this day we are ready to wonder how men could, by possibility, have thought that so limited an education was all that was required for a farmer. Such a conclusion could not have been arrived at, had there not been extreme igno-rance of the nature of his occupation. That knowledge which is merely recreation to the com-mercial classes, is absolutely *vital* to the agricul-turist. There is scarcely a science to which he ought to be a stranger. This was strikingly set forth in Mr. Brown's address to the Fairford and Cirencester Farmer's Club, on the advantages of a specific education for agricultural pursuits, in-serted in the February number of the " Farmer's Magazine," to which we beg to refer. There can be no doubt that farmers especially, in their ordinary education, ought to be made acquainted with the elements of physical science, particularly statics, pyronomics, dynamics, mechanics, hy-draulics, pneumatics, electricity, meteorology, chemistry, and geology. A question may arise whether such an extended education is practicable in ordinary schools. Our reply is, if parents and schoolmasters are both alive to the importance of a scientific education for young farmers, it is of easy accomplishment. Not by the antiquated method which teaches and learns everything by committing it to memory, and which is as speedily lost as it was gained. The intellect of the pupil must be engaged—with the text he must have illustration—experiment. Time, which is sadly squandered away upon useless subjects in many, if not in most schools, must be husbanded for the purpose of science. The course of instruction must be enlarged in ordinary day schools : in boarding schools the specious must give place to the solid. Let there be but a groundwork of scientific knowledge laid—the elements acquired in the term ordinarily devoted to education, and then the youths will be fitted either to enter upon the more specific studies of agricultural colleges that may hereafter be called into existence, or they will be prepared to embrace and act upon those scientific principles which professional men may propose to them. Liebig will, with farmers so educated, become a favourite author, and scien-tific treatises on agriculture will find readers and purchasers who are able to form some estimate of their merits.

Before I conclude this letter, I will just observe, that I have to a limited extent adopted the system of instruction above recommended in my own school. I have a class of youths studying the elements of agricultural chemistry. On the con-clusion of the first division of their subject, the class gave a coffee party to their fellow pupils and a few friends, after which a conversation was introduced by myself on the organization of vegetables, and the chemical conditions essential to their life and development, which was creditably sustained by the pupils, and afforded complete evidence of the practicability of a course of

scientific instruction answering the wants of the practical agriculturist.

I think I have succeeded in showing that *defective* education is the source of the farmer's prejudice, and that the remedy is an *improved* and *enlarged* course of instruction. If it meet your approval, I shall on a future occasion endeavour to point out the means by which this desideratum may be supplied.

I am, sir, yours obediently,
JOHN KAY.
Grafton House Academy, near Stratford-on-Avon, March 10th, 1843.

ON THE COLOUR OF THE ROOTS OF SWEDISH TURNIPS AND MANGOLD WURTZEL.

SIR,—Having been engaged in my early life in an extensive business of farming, I had not in con-sequence an opportunity of carrying out by experi-ment (which I then thought trifles), those observa-tions to which my attention had on various occasions been directed, until having retired to a much smaller business. I had often been struck by the preference given by live stock to one colour in pre-ference to another ; having a lot of wether hoggets in a pasture adjoining my house, over which I had a window, from which I had a view, they being fed twice per day on mangold, my attention in the first instance was excited by the sheep running over the whole quantity given them, merely tasting each root, after which returning and remaining until they quite finished each root that was of the white flesh kind in preference to those of purple or mottled. This having been the case for two or three successive seasons, induced me to cultivate the long orange with white flesh, which I had the satisfaction to find to be more nutritious, and not so purgative as the purple ; and still further to confirm my opi-nion of their superiority, in the winter of 1837 I had half a score spayed Hereford heifers on store feed of mangold and hay in a warm yard (for I find warmth to be essential to benefit in feeding with mangold), having them until the 25th of January on purple mangold. I then commenced the orange coloured ; after having been upon it about a fort-night, though the weather being not so favourable, I could perceive a manifest difference in their con-dition ; their coats had altered from a rough hungry look to a sleek and mellow appearance, with a decided better feel on the points. This I could not account for, as the hay was precisely the same quality, and the weather decidedly colder, with wet and storms, upon any other cause than the greater nutritious qualities possessed by the yellow in comparison to the purple. I in consequence directed my attention to the land whereon they grew, expecting to find the succeeding crop of wheat less whereon the yellow was ; but the contrary was the case, having, as near as I could judge, from three to four bushel of wheat per acre more on the land on which the yellow was, the quality of the land being the same, as was likewise the manuring the field, half of one kind and half the other. To confirm myself of the fact the succeeding year, I merely had an acre of the purple in the centre ridges of the field, and was careful that the manur-ing was equal. The same result followed on the barley crop; I found the acre of barley upon the land whereon the purple grew to be five bushels per acre less than the average of the remaining portion of the ten acres, and the same result as I had previously observed in the beasts doing better on them when stall fed with cake. I found upon weighing the crop that there were 36 tons per acre of the purple, and 32½ tons of the yellow; this was by no means in proportion to their respective qualities of feeding, and the superior increase of the succeeding crop. The success attending this proof directed my attention to the more important root, the Swedish turnip. In 1839 I sowed a field of Swedes, one half of the common purple, the other half the yellow skinned kind, with yellow flesh, which I had previously selected, and which had always been a favourite for hardness in withstanding the winter. Here again I had the satisfaction of experiencing the superiority of the after crop of barley on the land whereon the yellow grew, and the sheep appeared to do better from their greater brittleness; they do not appear to tire so soon as when on the purple kind; in their mouths, independently of the decided greater sweetness to the taste of the yellow, the purple is more of the flavourless taste of the cabbage stalk. This season has again given me an opportunity of ascertaining another quality which I was not aware they possessed, that is, their superiority in withstanding the mildew better than the purple. I divided a field into three divisions, one of the Liverpool, one of the Manchester, the remainder of the yellow skinned. The soil being of a light turnip loam, suffered from the drought in the month of August; the mildew followed as a consequence. The Liverpool being naturally inclined to run to neck, were in consequence of the mildew a mere mass of neck; the Manchester, a much more delicate sort, were killed in great quantities; but the yellow skinned kind, though considerably affected on the first attack of the mildew, quickly recovered themselves, and nearly doubled in produce the other two kinds. I find upon reference to Dr. Lindley's lectures upon mildew, he there states that dark or purple colours are much more liable to be attacked by mildew than light green or yellow colours of plants generally. This has so confirmed my opinion of the superiority of yellow in preference to the purple, that I shall in future grow no other than yellow-skin Swedes, and orange mangold wurtzel.

I am, Sir, your obedient servant,
A NORFOLK FARMER.

NORFOLK FLAX SOCIETY.

A meeting of the subscribers to this society was held at the Norfolk Hotel, on Feb. 25th. A committee, to have the entire management and control of the society's funds, was appointed. Nearly 80 noblemen, gentlemen and farmers have already joined the society, and upwards of 300l. has been subscribed.

The following letter, from the *Norfolk Chronicle,* will, we doubt not, be read with interest.

ON THE FATTENING OF CATTLE WITH NATIVE PRODUCE, AND ON THE CULTIVATION OF FLAX.

In the pamphlet that I lately published, three important projects were considered, viz.: the fattening of cattle upon native produce, the growth of flax

for the sake of the seed (linseed) as a substitute for foreign oil cake, and the cultivation of the prolific plant with reference principally to the value of the fibre.

With respect to the first.—Three years' experience has established the superiority of a compound made of linseed and grain over foreign oil cake. The instances of success are numerous, while no cases of failure have occurred. It is impossible to particularise them, but the inquirer may obtain abundant references, and correct information, on Thursday, at North Walsham.

An experiment is being tried with twelve bullocks by Mr. John Postle, of Smallburgh, under circumstances of peculiar interest, to which I desire to make an especial reference, and to attract particular attention; because I am confident that the most prejudiced must be convinced, unless he is under the influence of some enemy worse than prejudice.

The North Walsham Farmers' Club offered a challenge, through the county papers, to put the comparative merits of compound and oil cake to the test; which challenge not having been accepted, Mr. Postle determined to satisfy the public himself upon that point, under the following regulations viz.:—

That twelve bullocks should be equally divided by judges, selected for the occasion; six to be fed on Swedish turnips and compound, and six on Swedish turnips and oil cake. Both lots to have an unlimited quantity of turnips, but an account was to be kept on the weight that each lot consumed per day, and the cost for compound and cake to be equal; that is to say, if the cost for compound was only 6d. per day each for one lot, the other was to be allowed oil cake to the same amount. Accordingly, the bullocks were divided, weighed, and numbered, and placed in separate yards. I saw them myself last week for the first time, and so great is the advantage perceptible on the side of the bullocks fed with compound, that had I not been acquainted with the fact of their having been weighed, and the rectitude of all the parties concerned, I should have concluded them to have been unskilfully divided. Mr. Postle is a gentleman of great experience, has undertaken this experiment on public grounds, and has pledged himself to carry it through with the strictest impartiality. The bullocks are fed in a yard at Worstead, near the church, and are freely open to inspection.

With respect to the second project, the last year's crop of linseed, both as to quantity and quality per acre, must exceed, according to the best sources of information, those of any other part of the world, being in several instances worth from 8l. to 12l. per acre, independent of the flax.

The third project originated the Society for the Promotion of the Growth of Flax in Norfolk, which cannot fail to confer immeasurable benefits on every class of society, if conducted with spirit and energy, and in strict accordance with those patriotic principles which actuated its formation.

An agriculturist from Belgium is now actively engaged as the society's agent, in making preparations for the manufacture of the past year's crop of flax, examining the soil, and instructing in the management of their land those who intend to be growers of flax this year in Norfolk.

Thus far have these projects proved singularly successful. In adverting to them my only motive is to show, that the cultivation of flax primarily for the fibre, is no more a chimerical scheme than that of

fattening cattle upon native produce, or that of growing linseed as a substitute for oil-cake. I think I shall be excused for bringing them so promiuently forward, and for reminding the country that 100,000l. a-week are sent out of Great Britain for the purchase of flax, and about 400,000l. u-week besides, for oil-cake, linseed, hemp, oil, &c., &c., all of which can be produced from our own resources. I think I shall be excused for reminding agriculturists in particular, that their property continues to sink in value, and that the most fatal consequences are to be apprehended. Again, I think I shall be excused for calling upon landowners, occupiers, clergymen, and every one who is directly or indirectly concerned in the welfare of agriculture, not only to support the Flax Society of Norfolk, but to promote the formation of similar societies in every county in the kingdom, because I am persuaded that the cultivation of flax only requires to be nationally adopted, to obtain for the redundant population the employment, agriculture the support, and trade the encouragement, which each so greatly needs. Because the cultivation of linseed, the making of artificial food to fatten cattle, and the sale of flax, will be fresh sources of wealth to the British farmer: because hands must be drawn from the manufacturing towns to prepare the flax for market; and because an impetus would be given to home trade in general by the increased price of wages, and by the consequent increased consumption of all the common necessaries of life:—for these reasons, and not for the sake of courting popularity, which at best is an uncertain privilege, I offer to the public the information that I have been able to collect during the last three years, on the subject of flax, and also my personal assistance in the formation of flax societies in any part of the kingdom.—I remain, Sir, your obedient servant, JOHN WARNES, JUN.
Trimingham, March 1.

ON THE CONSTRUCTION OF AN ECONOMICAL TILE-WORK ADAPTED TO FARMS OF ORDINARY SIZE.

BY GEORGE BELL, ESQ., WOODHOUSELEES, DUMFRIES-SHIRE.

(From the Transactions of the Highland and Agricultural Society of Scotland.)

[Premium Twenty Sovereigns.]

When about to erect a tile-work on the farm of Woodhouselees, for the purpose of thoroughdraining about 500 acres of land with a very retentive subsoil, I found great difficulty in procuring plans or obtaining information to enable me to construct the work at a moderate expense; for the object in view being merely that of making tiles for the draining of the farm, it was inexpedient that any great outlay, such as might be necessary for a permanent work, should be incurred.

I derived much valuable information from the papers by Mr. Taylor, Mr. Bcart, and others, in the "Transactions of the Highland and Agricultural Society;" but none of the plans I at first obtained, for a work on such a scale as to admit of turning out 300,000 tiles in a season, could have been erected for less than about 300l.

Finding, in the course of my inquiries, that much greater economy in the outlay on tile-works had been practised in Cumberland than in those generally hitherto established in Scotland, I advertised amongst the tile-manufacturers employed in that district, for contractors willing to undertake the making of the tiles I might require for three years; and desiring that each party offering to contract should describe the size and construction of the kiln and drying shed he required to be erected.

From the information thus obtained, a modified plan, combining all due economy with efficiency, was adopted to suit the views of responsible and respectable contractors, who undertook the manufacturing of the tiles.

The result has been in every respect most satisfactory.

In the season of 1841, the number of tiles made was—

286,478 three-inch tiles,
and 29,671 four-inch do.

Total, 316,149

The kiln was drawn twenty times, giving an average of 15,807$\frac{9}{20}$ tiles for each kiln.

Dates of drawing the kiln each time.

April 29	June 14	Aug. 2	Sept. 14
May 10	.. 22	.. 10	.. 25
.. 18	.. 31	.. 19	Oct. 2
.. 31	July 10	.. 31	.. 16
June 7	.. 20	Sept. 7	.. 25

The quantity of coals used was 154 tons.

In 1842, the number of tiles made was—

221,796 three-inch tiles
and 21,204 four-inch do.

Total, 243,000

The kiln was drawn fourteen times up to the 18th September, when a sufficient number for the season was obtained, giving the average of 17,357½ tiles for each kiln.

Dates of drawing each kiln-full.

May 3	June 11	July 19	Sept.
.. 14	.. 18	.. 29	.. 18
.. 23	.. 27	Aug. 6	
.. 31	July 11	.. 19	

The quantity of coals used was 113 tons 15 cwt.

There were also burnt, in 1842, 1500 soles for the bottoms of drains. More have not been burned, as slates, suitable for soles, are obtained at a lower cost.

It will be seen from the detailed account, afterwards given, of the expenses of erecting the work, that the whole cost, exclusive of the carriage of materials, was 139l. 0s. 10½d.

The wood was got particularly cheap, having been purchased at a sale of trees that had been blown down in 1838, and was consequently well seasoned.

No repairs whatever have hitherto been required, and the only additional outlay has been the purchase of 500 fire bricks for the flues, which cost 1l. 16s. 3d.

Coals are delivered at the work at 7s. 4d. per ton of excellent quality.

The three-inch tiles, the size mostly used, are delivered to me at 18s., and the four-inch at 23s. per 1000 ; the contractor having a free house and horse's grass.

It is hoped that the details given may encourage the establishment of similar economical works, by proprietors or their tenants, where thorough-draining is required and clay can be met with ; for there is not only a great saving, from the comparatively small sum that requires to be added to the price of the tiles, to repay the cost of the works, but there is also a saving in carriage to the tenant, and an advantage afforded of making the time of leading the tiles subservient to the other operations of the farm, in place of interfering with them.

Copy of Specification of Shed for drying the Tiles.

The shed proposed to be erected to be 105 feet in length and 17 feet in width over all. To have 4 lines of shelving, and 11 shelves in each line. The shelves to be all prepared for putting up. The space between the lines of shelving to be left at such distances as the contractor for making the tiles shall please.

Wall-posts.—The posts which form the walls of the shed to be about 6 inches square, of larch trees, with the bark either left off, on, or peeled, as will be thought best ; to be each 9 feet long, and set at intervals of 7 feet between centres for the side-walls ; and those at the end 8 feet. The posts to be sunk in the ground to the depth of 2 feet below the level of the floor of the shed. Where the ground may be found soft, a flat stone of 15 or 16 inches square to be laid in the bottom of the pit and the post set upon it. The pit to be then filled with stones and earth well beaten down. The heads of the posts to be levelled off at 7 feet above the floor, and a tenon 1¼ inch long formed on the head of each of the four corner-posts.

Beams.—The wall-head beams to be 8 by 4 inches, in two or more lengths for the side-walls, scarfed over the head of a post—those for the end-walls to be in one length ; to be joined at the corners by half lapping, and mortised for the tenons of the corner-posts. The beams to be secured to the posts by an oaken treenail 12 inches in length, passing down through the beam into the head of each post.

Roofing.—The rafters of the roof to be 6 by 2½ inches. The tie-joist, at the foot, to be 6 by 2 inches ; and the balk, at half height, to be 5 by 2 inches. The couples to be set at 21 inches between centres, each couple having a tie-joist and a balk ; the former to be dovetailed at the ends, and let into the rafter one half inch, and securely nailed with a strong spikenail to the wall-plate. The couples to rest on the tie-joist and heel of the rafters—the latter being notched for that purpose. The roofs to be formed with pavilion ends, the hip-rafters being 7 by 2½ inches ; and these, together with the common rafters of the ends, to be all properly tied at the foot. The roofs to be covered with Welsh slate, of the cheapest quality that may be procured, consistent with a due regard to strength and durability ; to be laid on laths, and the ridges to be finished with two boards 7 inches broad, spliced together and nailed down firmly into the rafters.

Shelving.—To be of spruce-fir, all sawn and squared for putting up. The third of their number, or thereabouts, to be of the whole breadth required, viz., 13 inches ; and the remainder in halves, ¾, or 1 inch in thickness, to be supported in manner following :—For the single lines of shelving, a post, 3 by 2 inches, to be set up at intervals of 14 feet, answering to the alternate posts of the walls, and at 14 inches distant from the posts. In the double lines, a set of three posts of like dimensions to be set up at each of the same intervals—14 feet. The distance between the posts of each set to be 14

inches, so that, when the shelves are laid, there shall be a space of 2 inches clear between their back edges. The whole of the posts here described to be set on sleepers of wood laid in the floor, the feet of the posts being nailed to the sleepers. The latter to be 3 feet in length for the double lines, and 1½ foot for the single. The other dimensions may be 5 by 2 inches or thereby. The heads of the posts to be fastened to the tie-joists, care being taken in setting the roof, that a joist shall fall to answer each cross line of shelving posts. The beams of the shelving to be 2¼ by 1¾ inches ; to be checked into the posts not less than ¾ of an inch, and well nailed. The height, from the top of one beam to the top of the next, to be 6¾ inches, or equal to 6 inches clear between the shelves. The shelving to be farther supported by two upright lines of beams, placed intermediate between each cross line of posts ; the intermediate supports to be simply pieces of inch-board, 6 inches broad, placed on edge between the shelves, rising from the bottom upwards, directly over each other, thus reducing the distance between the points of support to 4 feet 8 inches. The shelves when fitted into their places, to be nailed to the bearers to prevent warping. A portion, say 1-sixteenth, of the shed may be shelved at 7 inches in the clear, to receive main drain tiles.

Sundries.—No. 1. In order to prevent any tendency to shifting of the roof, waling pieces of 3 by 1½ inches to be nailed to the lower side of the joists, and bear against the wall head beams. These walings to run the entire length of the shed on either side. No. 2. To give stability to the shed, shores or stays to be applied to each post.

Materials.—All posts, beams, roofing, and sleepers, may be made of larch or Scotch pine timber. That part of the wall-posts which goes into the ground to be slightly charred over a fire, and, while hot, coated with tar.

N. B.—The shed was made 113 feet long. See note at the end of joiner's contract.

Copy of Estimate for the Joiner Work of the Shed.

Woodhouselees, 18th March, 1840.

I hereby promise to put up the shed for the draining tiles according to the specification, completing the whole in a strong, workmanlike manner, to Mr. Bell's satisfaction, or of any one whom he may appoint to inspect the work ; also all tools made of wood, appertaining to the tile work—two bow barrows, and frame of clay pug-mill, and all boards requisite, for the sum of 19*l.* 15s. ; and to find nails of the best quality, which shall not be scantily used, for 4*l.* additional ; which is in the whole 23*l.* 15s. The whole work to be finished by the 1st day of May, under the penalty of 2*l.* sterling.

(Signed) ROBERT BELL, Joiner.

N.B.—Agreed, at the same time, to make the shed 8 feet longer for 12s. more.

Woodhouselees, 4th Feb., 1840.

Conditions to be observed in Making Draining Tiles for Mr. Bell.

The kiln, shed, tools, and every other article appertaining to the work, will be required to be kept up in the best order and condition, and left in the same.

The clay for the ensuing year's manufacture to be annually turned over in the months of November, December, and January ; and for this season, as soon as the contract for the work is made (not a day to be lost).

The tiles, bricks, or soles to be manufactured of

the very best quality, made in the most proper form, from moulds to be approved of; and none to be paid for that do not meet the entire approbation of Mr. Bell, or overseers whom he may appoint. The clay to be fairly and properly wrought; the whole surface to be cleared off before the clay is thrown out; no waste of clay to be allowed, but wrought to the bottom. No bricks to be burned twice over, but when properly made, and up to their full dimensions, shall be paid for by the Excise gross account, and no more. The tiles shall at all times be made to the full thickness and sizes, sufficiently dried, lapt, and kept in good order before being put into the kiln; and when taken out they shall be kinched up in a proper manner; and when laden, none to be taken but such as are sufficiently good. No carts to be loaded out of the kiln. The size or openings of the tile-moulds to stand as follows at the time of making:—

2 inch tiles, 13⅜ inches long by 7½ inches broad
3 " 13¼ " 9 "
And 4 " 13¼ " 10½ "
All others in proper proportion.

The contractors may engage for three years, with the power either to them or Mr. Bell, at the end of any one year, to put an end to the agreement, on giving one month's warning.

Copy of Contract for Making Draining Tiles, &c.

We, J. Irving and James Little, tile-burners, do hereby engage, in terms of the foregoing specification, to make draining tiles and building bricks, of a proper and sufficient quality, at the following prices, viz.:—

3 inch tiles, at 18s. per 1000.
4 " 23s. "
6 " 28s. "
And building bricks, 21s. "

The contractors to be allowed any materials that may be necessary for repairing the kiln. They shall also be allowed a dwelling house, a stable for their horse, and grass for the same during the season. Regular accounts to be kept and certified by Mr. Bell, his overseer, and the contractors. Subsisting money to be paid as the work advances, and the balance at the end of the season.

(Signed) J. Yule, witness. (Signed) J. Irving, And Jas. Little.

List of Tools to be kept up by the Contractors.

4 Moulding Tables	4 Long Furnace-irons for putting up Tiles
4 Sand-boxes	2 Iron Pokers for Kiln
4 Water-pails	1 Pair Iron Tongs
4 Benches for horses	1 Iron Scraper for clearing the eyes of the kiln
9 Horses for 3-inch Tiles	1 Coal Rake
3 " 4 "	2 Coal or Ash Buckets
3 Moulding-frames for 3-inch Tiles	Wheeling Planks
1 Do. for 4 do.	1 Large Pole
3 Barrows	Curtains for Shed.
4 Small Iron Scrapers for Tables	

The Kiln.

The construction of the kiln will be better understood from an inspection of the plan, than from any specification of it. It is seventeen feet long by ten feet wide, inside measure; and eleven feet in height: built of stone outside, and lined with brick. It is tied firmly together with large flat stones, and also above the eyes, of which there are five on each side. Great care should be taken to use clay instead of lime in building every part which the fire reaches. Fire-clay, if to be had, is of course best for this purpose.

A shed is placed against the west side of the kiln, to afford shelter to the fireman.

Detailed Expense of the Erection of the Tile-work.

	£	s.	d.	£	s.	d.
Stones for kiln, 6*l.* 0s. 6d., common bricks, 7*l.* 18s. 6d.	13	19	0			
3050 fire-bricks (which quantity left sufficient for setting the kiln)	11	3	9			
35 measures of lime (each containing 3 imp. bushels) at 10d., 1*l.* 9s. 2d., building kiln, 14*l.*	15	9	2			
100 long fire-bricks........	1	13	0			
				42	4	11
Sheds.—Wood got at a sale, part of which was left over for palings and farm purposes..................	22	0	0			
2290 feet of boarding, at 1½d. for shelves, ready to put up, and laths	16	3	1			
Sawing 3122 feet of boards for shelving, at 2s. 6d. per 100 feet	3	15	6			
Joiner work of shed, per contract, including nails	24	7	0			
Additional sawing of boards and planks required	1	10	0			
				67	15	7
10,000 Welsh slates, 13*l.* 6s., slate nails, 2*l.* 15s.......	16	1	0			
303 yards slating, at 2½d. per yard	3	3	1½			
				19	4	1½
Iron-work for clay-mill, and all other iron-work, or tools made of iron, necessary for the work	4	5	0			
Linen for curtains	2	18	9			
				7	3	9
Coopers' work on pug-mill..				0	7	6
Cost of shed against the kiln				2	5	0
				£139	0	10½

The carriage of the materials is not included in the above.

On the Manufacturing of the Tiles.

The best clay that could be procured on the farm was but of very coarse quality, being mixed with some portion of sand, and with a good many small sand-stones; it is such as most tile-makers would have been afraid to use if they had not had practical experience in it, or seen similar worked. To prove its fitness, I had some tiles made of it in a neighbouring tile-work; and it has been found, with judicious management, to make a strong and useful, though not a fine-looking, tile.

I mention this circumstance that landlords or tenants may be encouraged to have a trial made of their clay where they are desirous of erecting works, although it may not have a promising appearance.

1. *Raising and Turning the Clay.*

After the soil has been removed from above the clay, and the depth of the bed has been ascertained, a drain of sufficient depth should be cut to take off the surplus water.

The contractors by the stipulations, it will be seen, are bound to turn over what may be required for the following season early in the winter, when it is cut out in thin slices, and the stones, so far as practicable, carefully picked out. A little water requires occasionally to be thrown over it. Should the weather be frosty when this operation is going forward, it is beneficial for mellowing it.

2. Milling the Clay.

When the operations of the work are about to commence in spring, the period for which is regulated by the absence of all frost, the clay that has undergone the above process is wheeled in barrows along planks to the pug-mill, which is driven by a horse, and is of the ordinary simple construction. The clay is emptied into the mill from the barrows, and pressed out through a hole at the bottom, where it is again deposited in a barrow, and wheeled into the drying shed, where it is turned out in lumps convenient for the moulders.

3. Moulding.

In the open space in the drying shed, tables are placed for the moulders, each with a sand and water box. The milled clay being, as already stated, deposited conveniently for the work, the moulder having placed the mould (which is described in the specification) on the table, lifts with both hands a large piece of the clay, which he brings down with considerable force into the mould, so as to fill it; the clay above the mould is then cut off with a wire stretched on a bow. The small stones, if any, left with the clay in the mould are picked out, and any defects that may appear are filled up by beating small pieces of clay into them.

The surface is smoothed with a flat piece of wood, about 4 inches broad, and 10 inches long. The mould is then lifted, leaving a rectangular cake of clay on the table, a little sand having been previously used to prevent the clay adhering to the table, or to the tile-horse on which it is placed to receive the shape of a drain tile, and on which the tile also is smoothed by the hand and a little water. Some sand is also thrown on one of its sides, to prevent it adhering to the tile next it on the shelf, where it is now deposited by the boy attending the moulder. It is necessary for preserving the proper shape of the tiles that the attendant be furnished with two tile-horses, one always being left in the last made tile on the shelf till another is made and placed close by its side. This has the effect of preventing any derangement of shape that might occur by leaving the tile unsupported on one side. The time required for the tiles to stand on the drying shelves before being removed into the kiln, depends entirely on the state of the weather, but it is of great importance to have them thoroughly dry before being removed from the shelves.

If the kiln has been previously emptied, the tiles, when ready, are carried at once from the shelves, and placed in it for firing; but if the kiln is not ready, or if the weather be unfavourable for filling it when the tiles are fit to be moved from the shelves, they are deposited in the open space in the shed.

4. Method of Filling and of Firing the Kiln.

It may be mentioned, that when the distance from the shed to the kiln is short, which should always be the case where practicable, for the purpose of economizing labour, it is found speedier and better, as doing less injury to the tiles, to carry them, in place of using barrows, from the shed into the kiln, where the contractor places them carefully on end. The whole space between and above the flues is filled up in tiers, until it gets to within two tiers of the top, when a space about the width of a tile is left between the walls and the two upper tiers all round the kiln.

About 24 hours after the fires are lighted in the flues, this space is filled up with round pieces of coal; and the top of the kiln (on which bricks or other covering had been previously placed to assist in regulating the draught) is then thinly covered with small coal. When these are fired, the heat from the flues, by proper attention on the part of the burner, is equally diffused through the whole kiln, the door-ways having been previously bricked up and made air-tight.

The supply of coals and admission of air to the flues is the most difficult part of the process to describe; but a competent practical knowledge of it is soon acquired by any intelligent and steady workman.

During the season of 1841, the fires were kept lighted 3 to 3½ days for each kilnful; but this season, by allowing them to burn 4 days, and by some slight alteration in the method of filling the kiln with the tiles, the average turn out has been very considerably increased, whilst the consumption of coal has been slightly diminished; the coal required for each 1000 tiles made in 1841 having been about 9¾ cwt., and in 1842 about 9¼ cwt.

5. Cost of making Drain Tiles.

It would not, in my opinion, be profitable for either a proprietor or farmer to carry on the work in a satisfactory manner by day's wages.

The cost to the contractors for the different parts of the process is about as follows :—

	3-in. Tiles, per 1000.		4-in. Tiles, per 1000.	
	s.	d.	s.	d.
Removing the surface and casting of clay	0	10	1	0
Grinding and sand	2	6	3	6
Paid for moulding	3	9	5	0
(Out of which the moulder pays the boy attending him 10d. per day.)				
Filling into the kiln	1	2	1	3
Coals—9¼ cwt. 7s. 4d. per ton	3	6	4	0
Burning (the fireman attending day and night)	1	6	2	0
Taking out of kiln	1	0	1	2
Superintendence, incidents, and upholding the shed, kiln, and implements	0	9	1	1
	15s.		19s.	

The hands employed have generally been—three moulders, three boys, two men at the clay, and assisting at the kiln, and one of the contractors assisting at moulding and taking a general superintendence.

6. Size of the Tiles.

In burning, the length of the tile contracts to about 12½ in. The thickness of the 3-in. tiles is a little above ⅝ in.; the 4-in. ¾ in.

Fig. 1.

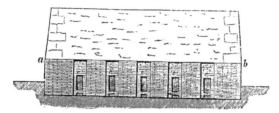

Fig. 2.

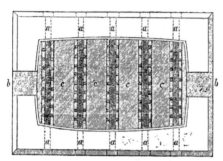

Fig. 3.

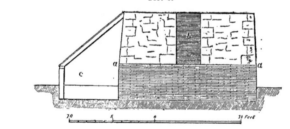

Fig. 4.   Fig. 5.

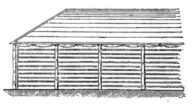

(*For Description see next page.*)

Description of Engravings.

Fig. 1 is an elevation of one side of the kiln, which is 23 feet in length at the height of the line *a b* ; the width over walls at the same height, *a a* of fig. 3, is 16 feet, and the height is 11 feet; *c c*, &c. are the five furnaces, 2 feet in height and 8 inches in width.

Fig. 2 is a plan of the kiln taken above the level of the furnaces and fines. The dotted lines *a a* &c. represent the position of the furnaces, and the continuation of these across the floor of the kiln are the main flues. These fines are formed by a wall of brick on bed, built up to a height of 2 feet on each side of each flue; they are built with openings or minor flues, as represented by the darker shaded spaces in these walls, which serve to admit the flame and hot air from the furnaces into the spaces *c c*, &c. The spaces *c* are each 2 feet wide, except the end spaces, which are only 9 inches, and in loading the kiln they are all filled with brick or tile requiring to be burnt. The two doors *b b* are required for loading and drawing the kiln, and while the firing process is going on, they are built up in the usual manner. The inside dimensions are 17 feet 1 inch in length, width at the ends 9 feet, and at the middle 10 feet ; the height, as already stated, being 11 feet.

Fig. 3 is an elevation of one end of the kiln, *a a* the extreme breadth being 16 feet ; *b* is the door, 4 feet in width, the sole of which is at the height of 4 feet above the sole of the furnaces ; and *c* is a section of the shed for the fireman.

Fig. 4 is an elevation of a part of the tile-shed, or drying shed. The entire length of it is 113 feet, and the height of the side-posts 7 feet. The protecting cloth screens are represented as brailed up to the eaves of the roof.

Fig. 5 is an end elevation of the shed, the width of which is 17 feet over all; *a* is one of the passages running between the lines of shelving, and *b* is the open space allotted for storing up dried tiles previous to their being placed in the kiln.

STATISTICAL SOCIETY, Feb. 20.—T. Tooke, Esq., V.P., in the chair. A paper was read, entitled "The Agricultural Statistics of Five Parishes in Middlesex—Norwood, Greenford, Perivale, Hanwell, and Ealing," by Mr. H. Tremenheere. Norwood contains 2259 acres ; it is divided by the Uxbridge road into two nearly equal portions ; that of the north is composed of a heavy clay soil ; that on the south of a light loam, and of gravel. The rent of land varies from 40s. to 50s. per acre, and the farms in the southern division let for 20s. per acre more than those in the northern. The surface of the soil in the northern part indicates that almost the whole of it was within no very remote period in a state of arable cultivation. It is now almost entirely pasture land. The soil is richly manured, abundance of dung being procured from London ; but there is a very general inattention to the preservation of manure made on the farms. The liquid produce of the stables and outhouses is permitted to run into the farmyards, and to stagnate in black ponds in the winter, and evaporate in the summer. There is a strong prejudice against all modern inventions for facilitating or abridg-

ing labour. The wages of labour vary from 12s. to 15s. per week. A farm of 250 acres gives permanent employment for 14 labourers. The produce of Wheat, in 1842, was 32 bushels per acre. Barley, 40 ; oats, 32 ; potatoes, 7 tons ; and hay, three-fourths of a ton. The number of live stock was 886. Greenford consists of 2,032 acres ; it contains about twelve farms, the largest 221 acres. The rent of land varies from 32s. to 3*l*. per acre. There are 1,605 acres of meadow-land, 371 of arable land, and 54 of woodland. The soil is a strong clay, well calculated for the growth of wheat, beans, and tares. Much of it is susceptible of improvement by a good system of draining. In some parts the land in winter becomes so saturated with water as to be unfit for the support of cattle. No modern machinery of any kind was observed. The agricultural produce, in 1842, was as follows :—wheat, 24 bushels per acre ; barley, 38 ; oats, 40 ; and potatoes, 74. The number of live stock was 673. Perivale consists of 626 acres. It belongs entirely to one proprietor, and is divided into five farms. The soil is a heavy clay, requiring four and occasionally six horses to plough it. The most profitable mode of managing the land is found to be the production of hay for the London market. The drainage is very defective, and the farmers are little disposed to attempt any mode of improvement. The wages of labourers vary from 12s. to 14s. per week. The agricultural produce per acre was, wheat 22 bushels, and hay three-fourths of a ton. The number of live stock was 599, of which 531 were sheep, these animals being taken in to feed at the rate of 2s. 6d. per score. Hanwell contains 1,363 acres. The rent of land is about 50s. per acre. Manure is supplied from London. The agricultural produce, in 1842, was, wheat, 48 bushels per acre ; rye, 24 ; oats, 48 ; potatoes, 6 tons ; and hay 1 ton. The live stock amounted to 186. Ealing consists of 3,807 acres. It is composed of two different descriptions of soil ; the heavy, or clay and light rich loam, the former constituting meadow or pasture land, the latter arable farms and market-gardens. The rent paid for arable and pasture land varies from 40s. to 60s. per acre. Farms are generally held on leases for 21 years. Little use is made of modern agricultural machinery. The implements of husbandry are of the same kind that were in use 30 years ago. A considerable portion of Ealing consists of market gardens, and forms a part of that large area in the vicinity of the metropolis, lying on both sides of the western road, which may be regarded as the great fruit and vegetable garden of London. The fruit gardeners have an upper and an under crop growing on the land at the same time. The soil is an excellent dry loam, and is abundantly manured. The number of labourers employed on these gardens is very great, and is estimated at 30 persons to each acre. The average rent paid is 10*l*. per acre. The wages of labour vary from 10s. to 15s. per week, and the proportion of women to men employed is as two to one. An important benefit was conferred on the labouring population, and on the poor of this parish in the year 1832, by the Bishop of London, as lord of the manor, who granted 20 acres of waste land for the purpose of enclosure and allotment. The proportion allowed to each person is 20 rods, at a yearly rent of 5s. The land is now divided into 146 allotments, and so great is the demand for those that are vacant, that there are, at the present time, 50 applicants. This system is found to be attended with most beneficial results. The occupier undertakes to live soberly, and to abstain from working on the Sabbath, on pain of forfeiting his allotment in case of non-compliance. The average assessment for the relief of the poor, from 1827 to 1833, was 4s. in the pound, and from 1835 to 1841 it has been reduced to 2s. 8½d. The wages of labour vary from 12s. to 15s. per week. The agricultural produce of 1842 was, wheat, 35 bushels per acre ; barley, 50 ; oats, 43 ; potatoes, 85 ; and hay, 1 ton per acre. The number of live stock was 1,430, of which 1200 were sheep.

BOKHARA CLOVER.

TO THE EDITOR OF THE MARK LANE EXPRESS.

SIR,—I observe in your report of the proceedings of the Council of the Royal Agricultural Society, that Joshua Rodwell, Esq., presented some dried specimens of the Bokhara clover, some of which were 13 feet in length, &c.

As this plant is little known, any information upon its feeding properties must be beneficial to agriculturists.

Some seed was presented me in the spring of last year, which I had sown upon a piece of rich garden ground; the progress it made was vigorous and rapid, and in the space of two months many of the plants reached a height of 4 feet, the leaves being of light pea green, more resembling lucerne than any other plant I have seen, and equally tempting in appearance for the purposes of food.

Upon examination I found if bruised it gave out an unpleasant odour, very much resembling the scent of mellilot, or heart liver, and to which it bears some resemblance in the leaf, but whether of the same class or not my investigation did not lead me to examine.

I had portions of the plants cut and offered to various kinds of stock, none of which, except horses, would partake of it, and even those that did refused to eat it in any quantity, rather tasting than eating it; and so convinced was I of its inutility as an article of food, that I took no further pains to preserve it.

I am ready to admit that the cattle to which it was offered had the usual access to other food; but tares, clover, grass, &c. were taken with avidity after the Bokhara clover had been refused by them.

The Alsike clover I have grown with considerable success upon a small scale; it has a property unusual with other varieties of clover, as it grows readily by transplanting; is eaten freely by cattle, and is very productive; a single plant has covered a space four feet in diameter, with a great number of closely set stems of a creeping character, and bearing a resemblance to the white or Dutch clover (upon a gigantic scale), and to appearance quite as productive as the red clover. It shoots again quickly after cutting, and formed the principal food through the summer of some tame rabbits, which however, entirely refused the Bokhara clover when presented to them.

As similar experiments have probably been carried out by others, they would oblige me, as well as your subscribers in general, by communications upon the subject, through the columns of your paper. I am, sir, your most obedient servant,

Writtle, March 17. ROBERT BAKER.

CALENDAR OF HORTICULTURE FOR APRIL.

A few retrospective remarks may lead to useful comparisons. The early days of March were bracing, sunny, and frosty; the ground not being penetrated by frost remained open, and free to the spade, and we receive evidence by distant reports that everywhere throughout the kingdom the condition was similar. The season, however, which promised to be precocious, had become late, and though localities, and differences of soil and exposure, must produce some effect, we believe, as a general fact, that few wall-trees had expanded their bloom in the middle of the month. Even the berry-bearing shrubs were backward; but such is the influence of a really genial spring, that an apparent retardation becomes not only a point of security, but is converted into early productiveness. In the

CULINARY DEPARTMENT

most of the operations of March will be still performed; but there are others which are more peculiar to the season, thus:—Asparagus plants can be put into the beds prepared in the way lately described (p. 227); many persons are of opinion that there is but one sort of this vegetable, and as a species this may be true—but of varieties, produced by culture and treatment, there are several. The large giant asparagus is unquestionably the most rapid in its growth: it was introduced by a person of the name of Grayson, about twelve years since, who also gave written directions for planting it in single-row beds. Much depends upon soil and situation; the rich alluvial beds of Fulham, and near the banks of the Thames, within a few miles of London, being most favourable to it. But in any garden, provided the plot have been properly prepared, it will thrive, and yield luxuriantly. Two years old plants are preferable, set in double rows, twelve inches apart, but the plants alternating in the rows, as in quincunx. If the season prove dry, copious watering should be given till the growth be assured.

Sea-kale is sown about the same time, namely, the first or second week in the month, the plot having been deeply prepared during the best weather of the winter. A very good (tried) method is that described by Maher:—" Divide," he says, " the ground into beds, four feet wide, with alleys of eighteen inches; after which, at the distance of two feet, sow five or six seeds two inches deep in a circle of about four inches diameter. If the seed be good the plants will rise regularly in about six weeks."

Sow cabbage, Brussel's sprouts, for the second crop; cauliflower in the first week, to come in use in August; brocoli for 1844, thrice, and purple Cape about the 12th, or thence to the 15th. Some do not transplant Cape brocoli; but in that case future directions must be given. Savoy (the small green globe is preferred) early and late in the month, to prolong the season for families, where this best of winter brassicas is much used.

Sow silver-skinned onions twice, for drawing young; and all the salad herbs; also radish, the taper and turnip-rooted.

Summer turnips, as the Dutch or early stone, make two small sowings.

At the third week, or even earlier, if the season be mild, sunny, and the ground merely moist, but quite warm, begin to sow the varieties of kidney-bean.

The artichoke is now, in some of our best gardens, treated as a biennial, or almost annual plant. Instead of the mouldings, coverings, and other laborious winter operations with old stock plants, the strongest rooted suckers are detached from the best stocks, and planted out, about two feet asunder, in rich deep beds of light loam.

Showery genial weather, like that of old fashioned April, is almost essential to success, for a dry spring is very inimical. Whenever the weather is favourable, early or late in the month, the transplanting should be made, and the variety called the globe ought to be preferred; these young plants will bear one or two fine heads, and that is suffici-

cut. Older plants are only retained to furnish suckers, and thus a constant succession is maintained. By combining the culture of new plants with some two or three years old, heads may be obtained from June to October.

Transplant cabbage, cauliflower, and lettuce, but in respect to the last, it is always preferable to sow the seeds after the middle of March, for these late transplantings generally fail, as the plants speedily run to flower.

Plant second crops of potatoes to succeed the early varieties; these come in after September, and are very desirable. After all that has been said or written, no kind of potato surpasses the early "Shaw" and true "Champion," unless it be that mealy delicate variety called, in west Wiltshire, the "early purple-eye."

FRUIT DEPARTMENT.

While we write (18th March) though the temperature has been nearly 60°, currant bushes have not started a leaf, raspberries are equally bare, and gooseberries are only so forward as we have many times seen them in February; thus a winter of the mildest character may be ultimately followed by a very late spring. The fruit, however, promises to be most abundant.

Wall-trees are also late, and we hope secure; the peaches and nectarines must be attentively watched after the fruit sets, to prevent, by fumigation, washing with tobacco-water, or frequent syringing, the ravages of the aphis.

The bladder-blight is, we fear, irremediable; it is a disease by which the leaves become bloated and horribly distorted; these subsequently may become the nidus of insects, but the cause is either in the sap, or perhaps may be traced to a chill, which destroys the pores, and thus produces a plethoric surcharge of the cells.

As peach borders are repeatedly trodden by the workmen, they should not have any crop near the trees, nor ever be deeply digged.

Apple and pear trees on walls or espaliers ought speedily to have the best regulation: and in this we include close spurring and cutting back all the long projecting spurs; thus those unsightly stag's-horn processes, which so disfigured the old trained trees, will be avoided. The same direction applies, in a degree, to dwarf standards, and finally a dusting with powdery lime, or copious syringing with fresh lime-water, will remove mosses and lichens, and keep the bark clear and bright.

The early vinery will in some instances be so forward as to have its clusters colouring; air is more required in this stage than at any other, and the heat must be strong by day—65° is ample during night; moisture is to be abated, and no water should fall on the fruit while colouring.

The pine stoves and pits must be kept active, and now succession plants must have their spring potting; the best soil for which is an unctuous friable loam, with one-third of decayed manure and some bone dust. If the roots be white and healthy, not one should be removed; if black and inert, that portion may be safely amputated. After these operations the plants cannot be kept too close in shaded pits at a heat of 80°. Here it is a duty to observe that a good hot-water apparatus is the safest and most effectual mode of heating, and it can be constructed at a most trifling expence.

Any common second-hand or old copper can be fitted with two tubes by a brazier, one above the other, about the middle, and flush with the metals;

these orifices should be three or four inches in diameter. These pipes should pass into a range of common tile drainage tubes, made to fit by joints, one within the other, each supported by a brick set off, let into the back, end, and front walls of the pit or house, and cemented, water-tight, by Parker's cement. The upper copper pipe should pass into the earthern pipes that run along the back wall, then across the further end, returning by the front wall, and by a bent copper pipe, terminating in the copper, which thus receives the water at the lower of the two orifices.

The entire descent need not exceed four inches in a range 30 feet long, and the merits of the apparatus will consist in its extreme simplicity, economy, and perfect applicability to all the processes of cucumber, melon, and pine growing, and the propagation of dahlias and other tender plants, by cuttings or shoots.

Hot water so employed, offers one great advantage; it will flow through a properly constructed range of pipes, so long as two different degrees of temperature are maintained, however high or low that temperature may be; thus a house can be kept at 45° or 50° throughout its length, or be raised to 75° or 80°; and, if Moira coal be used as fuel, a fire can be kept up for twelve hours, by the simple regulation of the ash-pit and chimney damper.

A smoke-flue varies in its heat throughout, and is far less under controul.

Stove plants can be propagated by cuttings, at the end of the month, and so may all the tribe of geraniums. Air, water, strong day temperature, with a vaporous condition of the house, raised by almost deluging the floor early, are essentials.

The greenhouse plants grow freely now, and will require great attention; some must be repotted, all will need due supplies of water, and free air in dry and sunny weather. Dead leaves should be removed, and if aphis appear, the house should be closed, fumigated by tobacco smoke twice while dry, after which the plants should be thoroughly cleaned by the dexterous use of the syringe.

Camellias like moist heat (60° or more), shade, and abundance of water, while growing, for thus they form their growth, and develop their flower-buds early in the summer.

In the open ground departments, the shrubberies and parterres should be kept quite clean; numbers of annual plants, raised in pots, may be planted out in appropriate situations, and, at the same time, herbaceous perennials may be divided and replanted.—March 21.

ROYAL AGRICULTURAL SOCIETY OF ENGLAND.

At a Council held on Wednesday, the 22nd of February, present—Philip Pusey, Esq., M.P., in the chair, Colonel Austen, T. Raymond Barker, Esq., T. M. Bartlett, Esq., T. W. Bramston, Esq., M.P., F. Burke, Esq., Colonel Challoner, F. C. Cherry, Esq., H. Gibbs, Esq., B. Gibbs, Esq., W. G. Hayter, Esq., M.P., Rev. C. Keene, W. Miles, Esq., M.P., W. W. Page, Esq., W. Shaw, Esq., and G. Wilbraham, Esq.

Mr. John Gillott, a farmer, residing at Bridge Norton, near Witney in Oxfordshire, communicated to the council the result of his trial of the Bokhara clover, and expressed his intention of transmitting to the society the result of his trial of the April wheat last year. This communication was received with thanks and referred to the general committee; the author being requested to state the nature of his soil and the result attending his trials during the ensuing summer. Mr.

Pusey and Mr. Miles expressed their intention of instituting trials of the Bokhara clover and Khelat lucerne on peat soils, and Mr. Gibbs undertook to obtain for the society further information on the subject.

Mr. Illingworth, of Bristol, submitted to the council his suggestion for a systematic establishment of farmer's clubs in connexion with the poor law unions and local associations throughout the country, for the purpose of collecting and transmitting to the Royal Agricultural Society of England the result of their practical inquiries. The Council returned their thanks to Mr. Illingworth for the favour of his communication, but did not feel justified in entering on so extensive an undertaking as as the one he proposed to them.

Mr. Pusey reported, as chairman of the Journal Committee, the result of a correspondence with the Duke of Portland and the Rev. W. Thorpe, and the reception of various other papers for the Journal.

Mr. Stratton, of Bristol, presented to the society a series of lithographic drawings, of his collection of waggons and implements exhibited last year at the meeting at Bristol.

The Council then adjourned to Wednesday, the 1st of March.

At a monthly Council held at the Society's house in Hanover Square, on the 1st of March, present—Philip Pusey, Esq., M.P., in the chair, Earl of Euston, David Barclay, Esq., M.P., Thomas Raymond Barker, Esq. John Benett, Esq., M.P., French Burke, Esq., Col. Challoner, F. C. Cherry, Esq., Humphrey Gibbs, Esq., Brandreth Gibbs, Esq., Stephen Grantham, Esq., H. Goodenough Hayter, Esq., M.P., C. Hillyard, Esq., W. Fisher Hobbs, Esq., Rev. C. E. Keene, John Kinder, Esq., Francis Pym, Esq., Professor Sewell, and W. R. Crompton Stansfield, Esq., M.P.

Mr. Raymond Barker, Chairman of the Finance Committee, presented to the Council the monthly report of the Committee's examination of the accounts, and the state of the funds of the Society; from which it appeared that in addition to the invested capital of the Society, the current cash balance in the hands of the bankers on that day was 1,593l. This Report, together with the recommendations of the Committee, in reference to the additional clerks and official arrangements, was adopted and confirmed.

On the motion of Mr. David Barclay, M.P., it was unanimously resolved, " That in future the carriage shall not be paid for the Journals of Members whose subscriptions have been in arrear; but that, on receipt of the said subscriptions, a letter shall be addressed to the parties by the Secretary, informing them that the Journals to which they may be entitled are ready for delivery at the Office of the Society, in Hanover-Square, on application, with an order in writing; and can either be forwarded immediately at their own expence, or with the next number of the Journal, at the expence of the Society."

Colonel Challoner, as the last year's Chairman of the Finance Committee, presented to the Council the general balance-sheet of the accounts connected with the Society's Meeting at Bristol, from which it appeared that, independently of the amount of 1,300l., given by the Society in prizes for stock, implements, &c., and the various sums offered for the Prize Essays of the year, the Society had contributed out of its own funds the sum of 573l., to promote the objects of the Meeting, and supply the deficiency arising from the excess of the expenditure over the receipts on that occasion: the total receipts being 4,202l., while the outlay required for various arrangements of the meeting had amounted to 4,775l. Colonel Challoner then proceeded, as Vice-Chairman of the General Derby Committee, to read to the Council the Report of the Committee in reference to the arrangements for the meeting. This report was unanimously adopted, and the contract with Mr. Manning for the execution of the whole of the works connected with the show-yard and Pavilion for the sum of 2,200l. confirmed.

Mr. Raymond Barker obtained leave to postpone his motion on the appointment of a permanent House Committee, until the Special Committee had made their final report to the Council.

Mr. Gibbs gave notice that he would move at the next Monthly Council, "That all annual Members shall be considered to be in arrear of subscription after the 1st of June in each year."

Mr. Pusey, M.P., gave notice that he should move at the next Monthly Council, "That in future the Journal should be issued in half-volumes twice in the a , containing the same amount of matter as heretofore."

Mr. Pusey, having then informed the Council that the Reports on the Model Experiment on the growth of Turnips, furnished by the Hon. R. H. Clive, M.P., and Mr. R. Westwood Baker, had not been made use of in the Journal, on account of the parties not having complied with the regulations of the experiment proposed; proceeded to inform the Council that agreeably with their request he had applied to the Earl of Aberdeen for letters of introduction and safeguard in favour of Dr. Daubeny, who in a few days would proceed on his tour of enquiry through Estremadura and other districts in Spain where the phosphorite mineral (containing so large a proportion of the earth of bones) was known to abound.

Mr. Pusey informed the Council that Dr. Playfair having declined to accept an appointment of the value of 500l. per annum, in order that he might remain in England to devote himself to the study and profession of Agricultural Chemistry, he should propose at the next Monthly Council that Dr. Playfair be appointed the " Consulting Chemist" of the Society, giving to the Society his gratuitous opinions on all questions of a chemical nature transmitted to him through the Secretary, making a charge, according to a given scale, only for such analyses as might be required. Mr. Pusey stated to the Council the important advantages that would accrue to the Society and its members at large in their thus securing the talents of so distinguished an individual as Dr. Playfair.

Professor Sewell reported to the Council that he had communicated, as requested by them at a former meeting, with the Duke of Rutland respecting the cow which he had offered to the Society, and whose case had attracted the notice of the Members; and that, with his Grace's permission, Mr. Batchelder, Veterinary Surgeon at Grantham, had examined the animal, and ascertained the case to be that of a ventral or abdominal hernia. Professor Sewell having informed the Duke of Rutland that such diseases not being common in the London dairies, the case in question would be instructive to a large class of pupils attending the Veterinary College. His Grace had expressed great satisfaction at the opportunity thus offered to him of contributing to the promotion of the objects of the Society and of the College, and sent the animal to the College infirmary, where she had safely arrived by railroad.

ALSIKE CLOVER.

Mr. Fisher Hobbs informed the Council that he had lately met with a kind of clover which he thought might prove useful to practical farmers, although, as he found Mr. H. Gibbs was well acquainted with it, he could not bring it before the Council as a new variety. His attention had been called to this plant by a gentleman of the name of Sewell, residing in the county of Essex, who had originally sown with great care in his garden a few of the seeds presented to him by a friend, the same plants being seeded two or three consecutive years with the slightest apparent exhaustion; a fact which Mr. Sewell assumed as proving the plant to be a perennial. He described the growth of this clover as being very strong, the plant throwing out in some instances as many as thirty stems from the same root, these stems resembling those of the common red clover, while the blossom had a pink hue, bearing, with the seed-pods and leaves, the greatest analogy to the white or Dutch clover: the roots throwing down tap-roots like the one variety, and shooting out numerous small lateral fibres like the other. From these striking similarities to the two common varieties, Mr. Sewell concluded that the clover he had thus cultivated must be a hybrid between them. Mr. Hobbs stated that Mr. Sewell strongly recommended this hybrid clover to be sown in conjunction with the red clover, on account of its great length of stem, especially when grown on rich land, and its inadequacy consequently to support itself erect; the plant becoming bent and trailing, and thus difficult to mow without loss, excepting by very careful and expert labourers; and that, on account of the smallness of the seed, he considered the common quantities per acre as quite unnecessary; from six to seven pounds per acre, carefully distributed, being quite sufficient, or half that quantity mixed with half a peck of red seed.

Mr. Humphrey Gibbs stated that the clover alluded to by Mr. Hobbs, was the Alsike Clover, or Trifolium hybridum. A foreign correspondent of Messrs. T. Gibbs and Co., had cultivated it for six successive years, and had found it an excellent article, as it withstood the greatest degree of frost, which the other clover would not do over there. On middling descriptions of soils it produced fair crops, on richer soils very heavy ones. The stalks are said not to harden like those of the red clover, but remain soft. After being cut it soon shoots again, and seed crops had been taken three successive years from the same plants—giving the plants a top dressing of stable manure in the winter. The habit of the plant is horizontal in its growth. Messrs. T. Gibbs had also received some of the seed and specimens from Mr. Sewell, the gentleman from whom Mr. Hobbs had the seed presented to the Council, and that Mr. Sewell had stated that, " It is, I have no doubt, likely to prove a very valuable acquisition to that class (clovers) of plants. It is a perennial and possesses all the good qualities of the common red and white (clover) as a sheep feed, &c., but its produce is very considerably more than the latter, I should say nearly or quite double." Mr. Sewell grew some acres of it last year, which were fed all summer with sheep, and he had reason to be highly satisfied with it, both for quantity and quality; he considered from 6lbs. to 7lbs. amply sufficient seed required for an acre.

Mr. Hobbs having stated that he intended to make trial of the Alsike clover, the Council requested him to furnish the Society with the results.

The Duke of Richmond transmitted to the Council a communication from the Moray Farmer's Club; Mr. Read, of Regent's Circus, various specimens of cylindriac tiles, with an account of the manufacture, price, and peculiar merits; Mr. Squarey, of Salisbury, a specimen of phosphate of lime; Mr. Francis Clowes, of Hemsby, a communication of experiments with various manures; and Mr. Danson, Dr. Ure's Report on Analysis of Guano: all of which were received with thanks, and referred to the Journal Committee.

Mr. Cherry submitted and explained to the Council the advantages of his equalizing roller for land, and his portable forge, which he had employed for twenty years.

The Council then adjourned to Wednesday, the 8th of March.

––––––––––

At a weekly Council, held at the Society's house in Hanover-square, Wednesday, March 8; present, Philip Pusey, Esq., M.P., in the chair; W. R. Browne, Esq., French Burke, Esq., John Walbanke Childers, Esq., M.P., Humphrey Gibbs, Esq., Brandreth Gibbs, Esq., Sir John V. B. Johnstone, Bart., M.P., Rev. Edmund C. Keene, W. Woods Page, Esq., William Shaw, Esq., John Spencer Stanhope, Esq., and Henry Wilson, Esq.

BOKHARA CLOVER.

A letter was read from Joshua Rodwell, Esq., of Alderton Hall, near Woodbridge, Suffolk, informing the Council that he had forwarded by the Waterloo, Captain Laws, from Woodbridge, a packet of dried specimens of the Bokhara Clover ("alba altissima"),

of his own growth in the years 1841 and 1842, which he hoped the Council would accept for the use of the Society, as an interesting exhibition to the members in the rooms of the Society, and at the Derby meeting.

The plants measured nearly thirteen feet in length; specimen No. 1 being of the growth of 1841, from seeds sown in April; No. 2, the growth of 1842, from the roots of plants sown in 1841, gathered and pressed when in bloom; and No. 3, the growth of 1842, from the roots of plants sown in 1841, gathered and pressed when in seed.

Mr. Rodwell expressed the satisfaction it would give him, if in any way he could furnish details as to the properties or growth of that gigantic plant.

This present was received with the thanks of the Council, and a request for all the information Mr. Rodwell could supply on this subject, especially in reference to the point whether the plant was liked or disliked by cattle.

VETERINARY PREPARATIONS.

J. Allen Stokes, Esq., of Harvington, near Evesham, Worcestershire, addressed to the Council a communication on the subject of the loss he had just sustained of a five years old thorough-bred mare, apparently from common inflammation and constipation of the bowels; but on a post mortem examination, as it was found, from an extraordinary strangulated hernia, the intestines having passed through the diaphragm, and thereby caused inflammation and death. Dr. Lloyd having thought the specimen a valuable one, had preserved it in spirits; and the case being the more curious from the hernia having evidently existed at least twelve-months. Mr. Stokes was desirous of presenting it, with Dr. Lloyd's particulars of the case, to the Veterinary Department of the Museum of the Society, should the Council think it desirable.

On the motion of Mr. Shaw, the Council accepted the present with the thanks of the Society, and directed that it should be deposited under the charge of Professor Sewell at the Veterinary College.

COTTAGE TRACTS.

The Secretary informed the Council that in addition to the 6,000 impressions of Mr. Main's paper on Cottage Gardening already reprinted from the Journal, for cheap distribution, at the prime cost of one penny each, among the labouring cottagers of the kingdom by members of the Society, the 3,000 impressions of Mr. Burke's compilation on Cottage Economy and Cookery, was nearly exhausted, and a new re-print of a further similar number of impressions required.

BAVARIAN AGRICULTURE.

The Baron de Cetto (the Bavarian Ambassador) having signified to the Society on a former occasion his willingness to promote the objects of the Society to the utmost extent of his opportunities, by effecting a communication between the Society of the Royal Academy of Sciences of Munich, the Council received at this meeting the valuable donation of the various Transactions of that distinguished and learned Academy; containing, in their several volumes, many papers of an agricultural character, along with a separate treatise (with coloured plates) on the potato-sickness, or injury from disease to the potato-crop of Germany.

The thanks of the Council were voted by the Council for these communications, which were specially referred to the notice of the next Monthly Council.

SPECIMENS OF WHEAT.

Professor Henslow transmitted to the Council 33 Specimens of Wheat for the Library of the Society, each specimen (with its root, plant, ear, and seed) being arranged with great care on a white papered ground, and the frame enclosed with glass; the particulars relating to the specimens being recorded on the back of the respective frames.

Mr. Pusey informed the Council of the great labour and devotion of time these specimens had cost Professor Henslow in their due arrangement, and that they formed a portion only of the series of specimens that gentleman had so kindly undertaken to arrange for the Society.

Mr. Pusey informed the Council that as their weekly meetings (namely, all meetings of the Council during the session, not held on the first Wednesday of the month, and which any member of the society was privileged to attend), were intended to be set apart for the reception and discussion of papers on topics of agricultural interest, he would on that occasion proceed to read to them an account of a series of experiments with various manures, presented at the last monthly Council, and made by Mr. Francis Clowes, of Hemsby, near Yarmouth, in Norfolk.

The reading of this paper excited much interest among the members present, who, in the course of their discussion on the various points to which Mr. Clowes called the attention of the Society, stated such facts within their own experience as had a bearing upon the subject.

The Council then adjourned to Wednesday, the 15th of March.

———

At a weekly Council, held at the Society's house, in Hanover Square, on Wednesday, the 15th of March, present, the Duke of Richmond in the chair, Earl of March, Earl of Essex, Lord Camoys, Thomas Alcock, Esq., Barugh Almack, Esq., Col. Austen, Thomas Raymond Barker, Esq., W. R. Browne, Esq., French Burke, Esq., Colonel Challoner, F. C. Cherry, Esq., Charles Robert Colvile, Esq., M.P., A. E. Fuller, Esq., M.P., Humphrey Gibbs, Esq., Brandreth Gibbs, Esq., W. Goodenough Hayter, Esq., M.P., Sir John V. B. Johnstone, Bart., M.P., W. Woods Page, Esq., Henry Wilson, Esq., and Colonel Wood, M.P.

The Duke of Richmond informed the Council that a successful operation had been performed at the Royal Veterinary College, by Mr. Simmonds, the Professor of the Cattle Pathology in that establishment, on the cow presented to the College by the Duke of Rutland, and whose remarkable case of hernia had already excited so much interest on account of the extent of the protrusion, the long standing of the case, and the healthy condition of the animal ; when it was decided that Professor Sewell should be requested to recommend to furnish a detailed account of the case to the Journal Committee.

Francis Hart, Esq., of Alderwasley, informed the Council of his intention to introduce the Dyock Oat on the Derbyshire-hills, in consequence of the favourable account Mr. Pusey had given of it in the Journal, as suitable for high and light lands ; and the rev. R. W. Fisher replied to the inquiries made of him as to the best mode of obtaining the seed for that purpose.

Richard Illingworth, Esq., of Bristol, suggested the publication, under the sanction of the Society, of concise practical tracts on particular topics of agricultural interest, as the best mode of applying Guano, &c.

Edward Oldfield, Esq., of Ashill, near Walton, Norfolk, communicated the case of one of his foals, which had died from the obstruction caused by the accumulation of a compact substance, 2¼lbs. in weight, 9 inches long and 13 inches in circumference. This communication, and the specimen enclosed, was referred to Professor Sewell.

Professor Johnston, of Durham, transmitted for the members of the Council, several copies of the third number of his printed " Suggestions and Experiments in Practical Agriculture," containing the results of experiments made in 1843. Professor Johnston considered these papers of great value, not merely for the actual information they contained, but on account of the new suggestions to which they gave rise, and the hopes they held out for the future.

Mr. T. E. Hardy, of Liverpool, transmitted a copy of his correspondence on the subject of Guano, and the results obtained from its application.

Mr. Macgregor Skinner, Secretary of the Flax Improvement Society of Ireland, presented several copies of the printed Reports of the proceedings of that Society ; informing the Council that through the agency of the Flax Society two similar institutions had been established in England in the counties of Norfolk and Essex.

Mr. Walrond, Secretary of the Gloucester Farmers' Club, presented the Third Annual Report of that Association, containing a detailed account of their proceedings during the year 1842.

Earl Fitzwilliam applied, through the Rev. J. W. Harman, for copies of the tracts on Cottage Gardening and Cookery—reprinted from the Journal—for the purpose of distributing them among his labourers, and leave was granted accordingly.

Mr. Fuller, M.P., Col. Challoner, Sir John Johnstone, and Mr. Browne, having reported to the Council their experience in the amount of the turnip crop grown on different soils, under different management, and with different manures, the Duke of Richmond explained to the meeting the success which, in Scotland, had attended the trials made with bones converted by chemical agency, and at a cheap rate, into a manure of a modified character, the details of which he had communicated to the Journal Committee.

The Council then adjourned to Wednesday, the 22d of March.

———

At a weekly Council, held at the Society's House, in Hanover Square, on Wednesday, the 22nd of March, present, Thomas Raymond Barker, Esq., in the Chair ; Hon. George Henry Cavendish, M.P. ; Thomas Alcock, Esq. ; W. R. Browne, Esq. ; French Burke, Esq. ; F. C. Cherry, Esq. ; E. D. Davenport, Esq. ; C. Hillyard, Esq. ; Robert Henry Hurst, Esq. ; Rev. C. Keene ; Sir Francis Mackenzie, Bart. ; W. Woods Page, Esq. ; William Shaw, Esq. ; T. Spencer Stanhope, Esq. ; and W. R. Crompton Stansfield, Esq., M.P.

MODEL AND EXPERIMENTAL FARMS.

Sir Francis Mackenzie presented to the Council a detailed statement of his plan for the establishment of a Model Farm in each county of England and Wales, by a public subscription, at an estimated sum of 117,297*l.*

Henry R. Sandbach, of Hafodunos, near Llanrwst, in North Wales, communicated to the Council his offer of any quantity of land in North Wales, on any reasonable terms, for the establishment of an experimental farm, provided it were managed under the immediate direction and responsibility of the Society.

RED WATER IN SHEEP.

C. Hillyard, Esq. informed the Council that he had received information of the great loss of turnip-feeding sheep which had recently occurred in the county of Northampton, in consequence of an accumulation of red-water in the abdomen ; at the same time stating that, from information he had received on the previous day, the following recipe, taken from an old author, had been employed with the greatest success :—

> Epsom salts, six ounces.
> Nitre, in powder, four ounces.
> Boiling water, three pints (poured upon the salts and nitre).

When new-milk warm, add

> Spirits of turpentine, four ounces.
> Bole Armenian, in powder, half-an-ounce.

Mix and shake the whole well together, when given. The dose is from three to four table-spoonfuls.

N.B. The sheep must be bled before administering the medicine.

" When this medicine is intended to be given to a considerable number of sheep, they must be taken from the turnips, or whatever they are feeding on, and put into a pen or fold-yard for two hours before it is given. Then, a small horn should be provided that will just hold the quantity proper for each sheep. Let the bottle be well shaken each time it is poured into the horn. This method of giving drinks will be found very advantageous when many require it at one time.

They must be kept from food two hours after the medicine is given, either in a fold-yard, or a pen; after which, they may be put in their pasture as usual. When this disease is so severe that several die every day, it will be necessary to repeat the medicine every third day, for three times or more, if thought proper, and to change their diet, and remove them into a more elevated situation. This medicine, together with bleeding, will be found a powerful preventive to most inflammatory complaints which sheep are liable to, while feeding on turnips, or in a luxuriant pasture."

EXPERIMENTS WITH GUANO.

William Gibbs, Esq., of 13, Hyde Park Street, London, communicated the following results of the trials of guano with Swedish turnips and wheat:—

ACCOUNT OF FOUR EXPERIMENTS ON THE GROWTH OF WHEAT, MADE IN THE PARISH OF WRAXALL, IN THE COUNTY OF SOMERSET, 1842.

Nature of Soil.	Preceding crop.	Character & quality of manures and quantity per acre.	Cost of Manures sowing.	Time of sowing.	PRODUCE. Ground sown. A. R. P.	Bushels Wheat per acre, weighing 84lbs.	Straw per acre, per doz. sheaves.	Remarks.
No 1. Poor land, light loam, stony, upon limestone rock. High & exposed situation.	Potatoes 12 tons.	Guano, cwt. qrs. lbs. 3 3 20	At 14s. per cwt. £1 17 6	February.	0 1 20	34½ bushels.	32 doz.	Guano sown after the seed was drilled in and harrowed at once.
No. 2, ditto.	Ditto.	At 5s. per ton. £3 0	At 5s. £3 0	Ditto.	0 2 0	34 do.	29 doz.	Nos. 1, 2 & 3. Well manured with dung for the potato crop. The land in good heart & tolerably clean, though naturally poor.
No. 3, ditto.	Stable dung 12 tons.	At 23s. per qr. £2 17 6		Ditto.	0 1 20	28½ do.	23 doz. and 3 sheaves.	
No. 4, ditto.	Bones, 20 bushels.			Ditto.	0 3 19	20½ do.	18 doz. and 4 sheaves.	No. 4, Very clean.
Summer Fallow.								

N.B. All the land was prepared for Wheat sowing in the Fall, but the season would not admit of the seed being put in till February.

ACCOUNT OF THREE EXPERIMENTS ON THE GROWTH OF SWEDES, MADE IN THE PARISH OF WRAXALL, IN THE COUNTY OF SOMERSET, 1842.

Nature of Soil.	Preceding crop.	Character and quality of Manures per Acre.	Cost of Manures per Acre.	Time of sowing.	How often sown, and what quantity.	How Hoed.	What disease, if any.	When pulled.	Weight per acre, after being topped and tailed.	Cost of Manure per ton of net produce.	Remarks.
Light loam on limestone. High and exposed situation.	Wheat.	Guano Monk! Charcoal. lbs. qrs. cwt. 2 0 0 1 2 3 0 1 11	Guano at 14s. per cwt. 1 10 10 Charcoal Pounding, &c. 5 0 £1 15 10	Drilled in, the 18th May.	Once 2½lbs. per acre.	Hoed three times & hand-weeded early in August.	Slight Mildew first observed 10th to 16th Nov.	From the Ground pulled.	tons. cwt. qrs. lbs. 0 3 20 16	s. d. 5 11	Guano compost laid in rows, covered with the plough, and seed drilled in upon it.
Ditto.	Ditto.	20 tons stable yard dung.	Dung at 5s. per ton. £5 0 0	Ditto 18th May.	Once 2½lbs. per acre.	Ditto.	Ditto.	Ditto.	13 1 1	5 11	
Ditto.	Oats.	32 bushels bones.	Bones at 23s. per Quarter, £4 12 0	Ditto 25th May.	Once 2½lbs. per acre.	Ditto.	Ditto.	Ditto.	9 3	5 9½	

Mr. T. E. Hardy, of Liverpool, transmitted the Reports of recent Experiments made with Guano in various parts of the country.

Captain Shedden of Bittern Manor House, near Southampton, presented a box containing a sample of very fine field-peas grown by him last year; and the Secretary was directed to request of Captain Shedden the favour of all the information he could supply connected with their character, history, and cultivation.

Mr. Benjamin Bond, of Draycot, Staffordshire, presented a copy of the list of premiums offered by the Draycot Parochial Agricultural Society for October in the present year; and an impression of the mezzotint engraving of two Durham Oxen, reared and fed by the late Mr. John Bond, of Brancott, near Stafford.

Professor Solly, of the Horticultural Society, presented a copy of his *Rural Chemistry*, and Mr. Cuthbert Johnson a copy of his *Agricultural Chemistry for Young Farmers*; Mr. Shaw, copies of the *Farmer's Magazine*; Sir James Murray, of his *Trials and Effects of Chemical Fertilizers*; Mr. A. Low, of Overgate, Dundee, copies of his treatises on the *Potato Crops*, and the Cultivation of *Flax*; and Messrs. Lawson, of Edinburgh, a copy of their treatise on the *Cultivated Grasses*, and other Herbage and Forage Plants.

The following papers were referred to the Journal Committee:—Sir Francis Mackenzie's Suggestions on the Establishment of Model Farms; Mr. Sandbach's offer of Land for an Experimental Farm; Mr. White's Reports on the operations of Thorough-Draining and Subsoil-Ploughing, together with a statement of the crops on the farm of the Hon. R. H. Clive, M.P., at Priors Halton, in 1841, and the result of experiments with different Manures in the growth of Turnips and Barley; and Mr. Rodwell's paper on the result of his cultivation of the Bokhara Clover.

The Council then adjourned to Wednesday, the 29th of March.

NEW MEMBERS.

The following gentlemen have been elected members of the Society during the month.

Aitchison, E., R.N., Groombridge, Sussex
Anderson, James, Gortleck, N. B., and Mount Ver. non, Hampstead
Alcock, Thomas, King's Wood Warren, Epsom, Surrey
Allsop, Joseph, Woodington Farm, East Wellar, near Romsey, Hants
Andrews, Charles James, Reading, Berks.
Bass, Abraham, Burton-upon-Trent, Staffordshire
Bass, Michael, Burton-on-Trent, Staffordshire
Bates, the Rev. C., Castleton, Derbyshire
Beardsley, Samuel, Callow, near Wirksworth, Derby- shire
Belcher, Robt. Shirlay, Burton-upon-Trent, Staffordsh.
Blane, Sir Seymour, Bart., the Pasture, Derby
Bond, Benjamin, Draycot, Stone, Staffordshire
Brodhurst, John, Crow Hill, near Mansfield, Notts.
Brown, John Lees, Farewell, near Lichfield, Staffs.
Burne, William, Alfreton, Derbyshire
Cantrell, William, surgeon, Wirksworth, Derbyshire
Champion, the Rev. I., Edale, Castleton, Derbyshire
Champion, Francis Beresford, Edale, near Castleton, Derbyshire
Charge, John, Chesterfield, Derbyshire
Charrington, Nicholas, Leytonstone, Essex
Clark, John, Kirby Hardwicke, near Mansfield, Notts.
Clement, Hampden, Snareston Lodge, Atherstone, Warwickshire
Clowes, William Legh, Spondon, near Derby
Cocking, Joseph, Tupton, near Chesterfield, Derbyshire
Coffin, Captain Henry Edward, R.N., Firtree Cottage, Bartley, near Southampton
Cox, Edward Soresby, Brailsford, Derbyshire
Cox, William, Brailsford, Derbyshire
Cox, Henry, Parkfield, near Derby
Cox, John Henry, Parkfield, near Derby
Cremorne, Lord, 3, Great Stanhope-street, and Dartry, Rockcorry, Ireland
Darwin, Sir Francis S., Sydnape, near Matlock, Derbyshire
Doncaster, George, Middlethorpe, near Newark, Notts.
Erne, The Earl of, Crumb Castle, Lisniskea, Fer- managh, Ireland
Evans, Rev. Charles, Blackwall, near Wirksworth, Derbyshire
Evans, Samuel, Darley Abbey, near Derby
Fielding, Rev. H., Langley Rectory, near Derby
Filder, James Moses, the Pages, Bexhill, Sussex
Forbes, Sir John Stuart, Leamington
Foster, John, Rumbridge, near Southampton
Fox, H. W., solicitor, Derby
Foxwell, Thomas, Shepton Mallet, Somersetshire
Garton, John, Lumsdale, Matlock, Derbyshire
Gill, George, jun., Daccombe Court, Coffinswell, near Newton Abbot, Devon.
Godwin, Richard Bennett, Long Eaton, Derbyshire
Grant, Henry John, Gnoll Castle, Neath, Glamorgan.
Hale, Gervoise Cressy, Alfreton, Derbyshire.
Herring, John Barnwell, Watering Farm, East Dere- ham, Norfolk
Rigg, Samuel, Abbey Holme, near Wigton, Cumber- land
Holden, Rev. James, Pleaseley Rectory, near Mans- field, Notts.
How, John, Beech Farm, St. Alban's, Herts.
Huddlestone, Peter, Little Haugh, Norton, near Ix- worth, Suffolk
Hughes, John, Donington Priory, Newbury, Berkshire

Hulme, James Hilton, Cliffe House, near Baslow, Derbyshire
Hunter, John, Stanton Hall, Derbyshire
James, Henry, M.D., Treton Wood, near Wirksworth, Derbyshire
Jessop, Michael, Alfreton, Derbyshire
Johnson, Rev. Nathaniel Palmer, Ashton-on-Trent, Derbyshire
Johnson, Samuel, Somersall Hall, Chesterfield, Derby- shire
Johnson, John Goodwin, Bentley, near Ashbourne, Derbyshire
Lambard, William, Beech Mount, Sevenoaks, Kent
Leach, Francis Edwardes, Kylybebil, Swansea, S. W.
Mason, William, Neeton Hall, Swaffham, Norfolk
Masters, Charles L. H., Barrow Green House, Oxted, Godstone, Surrey
Maynard, Edmund Gitting, Chesterfield, Derbyshire
Meynell, Godfrey, Langley, near Derby
Meynell, John, Langley, near Derby
Meynell, John, Tapton Grove, near Chesterfield, Der- byshire
Meyrick, Owen Fuller, Bodergam, Anglesey, N. W., and Clifford-street, London
Mills, John, Castlegate Nottingham
Moore, Thomas, Syston, Leicestershire
Moss, John, Derby
Mousley, John Hardcastle, Derby
Mousley, William Eaton, Derby
Murton, Frederick, Sturry, near Canterbury, Kent
Oxford, Earl of, Eywood, Kington, Herefordshire
Parkinson, William, Sawley, near Derby
Phillips, Rev. W. J. G., Eling Vicarage, near South- ampton
Pollard, George Augustus, Brockhurst, near Coven- try, Warwickshire
Rammell, Edward Wootton, Dent-de-Lion, Margate, Thanet, Kent
Read, John, Hopton, West Harling, Norfolk
Ricardo, David, Gatcombe Park, near Minchin Hamp- ton, Glouc.
Robinson, George, Winthorpe Hall, Newark, Notts.
Rushout, Captain, first Life Guards, Hyde Park Barracks
Sampson, William, Church Broughton, Derbyshire
Sampson, Benjamin, Tullimaar, near Truro, Cornwall
Shaw, Francis, surgeon, Wirksworth, Derbyshire
Simpson, Frederick, Spondon, near Derby
Sitwell, Robert Sacheverell, Merley, near Derby
Smeddle, William, Ordnance office, Tower of London
Smedley, John, Lea Bridge, Matlock, Derbyshire
Smith, Francis, Salthill, near Chichester, Sussex
Smith, The Right Hon. Robt. Vernon, M.P., 20, Saville Row, London, and Farming Woods, near Thrapstoue, Northamptonshire
Spence, Rev. Isaac, the Plantation, Acomb, near York
Spurr, Jeremiah, Wigthorpe, near Worksop, Notts.
Stedman, Dudney, Horsham, Sussex
Stevens, Henry Isaac, Derby
Stevenson, Richard, Barton, near Nottingham
Stokes, John Ruddington, near Nottingham
Strachan, J. M., Teddington Grove, Middlesex
Swan, James, High, near Stone, Staffs.
Sylverwood, William, Somercoates, Alfreton, Derby- shire
Thomas, Thomas Edward, Glennor, Swansea, S. W.
Thornhill, Thomas, jun., Pakenham Lodge, Ixworth, Suffolk
Timson, Rev. Edward, Woodlands House, near South- ampton
Tongue, Edward, Aldridge, Walsall, Staffordshire
Townsend, Henry, King's Newnham, Brinklow, War- wickshire
Tweed, Thomas, Bowater Crescent, Woolwich
Walkden, — Rushall, near Pewsey, Wilts
Walker, William, Compton, Abdale, Gloucestershire
Walker, George, Wootton Park, near Ashbourne, Derbyshire
West, William Henry, Cliffass, Crickhowell
Whetham, Colonel, Kirklington, Southwell, Notts.

Willer, George, Hungerford Park, Hungerford, Berks.
Wilson, Edward, jun., Lydstep House, Tenby, Pembrokeshire, S. W.
Withers, Henry, 10, above Bar, Southampton
Woodbourne, James, Kingsley, near Alson, Hampsh.
Woodhouse, John, Over Seale, Ashby-de-la-Zouch, Leicestershire
Woodhurst, Lieut.-Col. M. L., Oxted, near Godstone, Surrey
Wright, Charles, Bilham House, near Doncaster, Yorkshire
Yeates, James, Mint Cottage, near Kendal, Westmoreland

TO THE EDITOR OF THE FARMER'S MAGAZINE.

Sir,—I am accused (by a correspondent to your Magazine for March, who subscribes himself "N."), of having "dogmatically asserted that the same law which influenced the progress to perfection in animals and in plants, did not hold good when applied to the improvement of the mental faculties in man." Now, whether I so dogmatically asserted this theory or not will be better judged of by your readers, after a perusal of the passage in my communication, to which "N.' refers. It is as follows:—" One other quotation only :—' Those who have been attentive observers will be led to conclude that when vegetables, animals, or even the mental powers of man, attain an extraordinary degree of perfection, degeneracy in those particulars in which they have been superior seems invariably to await their offspring.' It is an extraordinary fact, that the offspring of men gifted with great mental powers are generally deficient in that respect; but what has this to do with vegetables or animals ? What comparison can possibly be drawn between the mind of man and a plant? None whatever; and it ought not, therefore, to be cited as an example." Should your readers decide that I have too authoritatively disputed the accuracy of the quotation, they can only do so under the impression that there is cause for doubt upon the subject, since error cannot be opposed with too much firmness; and no rational individual, I apprehend, will for one moment entertain the idea that, if my argument be substantial, I have maintained it immoderately.

Well then, in order to prop up my unstable theory, I am content to refer the reader to an admission of the very individual who attempts to disprove it :—" I admit," writes "N.," "that numerous instances may be cited where ' the offspring of men gifted with great mental powers are deficient in that respect,' but the cause of that deficiency can generally be traced by the phrenologist." Did I question the ability of the phrenologist to explain the cause ? "Dogmatically" not. I merely propounded the theory that animals and plants did not necessarily degenerate. "N." has admitted that there are numerous instances of mental degeneration ; yet he has not questioned the possibility of preventing the deterioration of plants and animals ; consequently it is a premature and exceedingly dogmatical deduction that I am either ignorant of the science of phrenology, or incorrect in my theory that " no comparison can possibly be drawn between the mind of man and a plant." The former argument is insupportable ; the latter is disproved by "N." himself.

But, probably, "N."intends it to be understood that, if by the general cultivation of the science of phrenology, as much attention was devoted to the object of maintaining incessant and constant improvement in the mind of man, as is paid to that of animals and plants, this extraordinary but too certain mental degeneration would not ensue. This is the only argument that can justify the statement that the law of nature is the same in both cases. If such should be the argument I would humbly beg to submit the question, whether "N." entertains a conviction, that by the cultivation and application of the science of phrenology, the mental powers of the son would be necessarily equal, or superior, to the mental powers of the parents ? If he does not entertain this conviction, his attempt to disprove my theory is manifestly nugatory. Whilst, if he does entertain it, I respectfully solicit his proofs of its correctness; and in the absence of such proofs I shall still retain my former opinion, that procreation has no influence on the mental faculties, and that no comparison can possibly be drawn between the mind of man and a plant.

I am, sir, your obedient servant,
GEORGE THOMPSON, JUN.,
Practice with Science.

Lion Street, Kidderminster,
March 13th, 1843.

TRIALS AND EFFECTS OF CHEMICAL FERTILIZERS, WITH VARIOUS EXPERIMENTS IN AGRICULTURE.

BY SIR J. MURRAY, M.D.

When we reflect upon the following alarming statistics (for England alone), published by the Commissioners in their Report on the Condition of the Labouring Population, we should try to augment land produce, and furnish food and employment in proportion to the increase of our people :—

" The extent of new territory required annually by the annual increase of the population, viz., 230,000, would form a county larger than Surrey, or Leicester, or Nottingham, or Hereford, or Cambridge, and nearly as large as Warwick. To feed the annually increasing population, supposing it to consume the same proportion of meat that is consumed by the population of Manchester and its vicinity (a consumption which appears to us to be below the average of the consumption in the metropolis), the influx of 230,000 of new population will require for their consumption an annual increase of 27,327 head of cattle, 70,319 sheep, 64,715 lambs, and 7,894 calves, to raise which an annual increase of upwards of 81,000 acres of good pasture land would be required. Taking the consumption of wheat or bread to be on the scale of a common dietary, i. e., 56 ounces daily for a family of a man, woman, and three children, then the annual addition of supply of wheat required will be about 105,000 quarters, requiring 28,058 acres of land, yielding 30 bushels of wheat to an acre; the total amount of good land requisite for raising the chief articles of food, will therefore be in all about 109,000 acres of good land annually.''

At a time when half our poor are unemployed—when we have scarcely any manufactories but land, and in a country where land was not hitherto considered a *manufactory* at all, it is our sacred duty to open up new resources of work for our people, and to make them *producers* rather than *consumers.*

Seed, taxes, and rent, cost nearly as much for half a crop as for a whole one. Our damp clay land is not half moulded, broken, or pulverised; we trust too much to horse labour, and too little to manual. Steady boys and girls, having each the care of a field of crop, *and encouraged by premiums*, could soon become as expert in the charge of a series of drills, as in the management of a number of spindles in a factory.

We hope that our chemical efforts will lead to this result, that thousands of children, now *blanching* in work-houses, will be engaged in drill-husbandry—become little farmers, and earn at least 6d. per day each for themselves, and as much more for their employers.

For this purpose it is necessary that *garden husbandry* should be established in our fields; let every farm be made a *garden*, and we shall have plenty of work for all our people, and plenty of bread for them to eat.

Manual labour can accomplish many objects which machines and horses cannot effect. As plants require weeding, hoeing, moulding, and sprinkling, the hand can effectually dress the earth round the stalks—put them into a condition of fertility, and feed, weed, and nourish every individual plant, as if it were a little tree.

The feeding of plants separately during their growth in small mounds of earth, and the deepening of the intervening space around them, would soon convert our fields into gardens—gardens of Eden to the health and morals of our people.

Children feed poultry in pens. Why are fowls *crammed*, and vegetables *starved?* Were the spirit of the above system carried out, farmers would become more reconciled to their present high rent, because they could soon well afford to pay it.

Although, for the sake of emulation, it is best to put an acre or field under the management of each particular boy or girl, yet when such field is being planted, or sown, four or five boys should be employed together, so that the seed may be all introduced in one day.

One lad spaces the lines, opens a thin groove, trench, or drill, and breaks and levels clods. A second follows, scooping out the seed-holes (as in the plan below at A). At any defined distance, marked upon the handle of his scoop, he rapidly turns out a pint, quart, or other quantity of mould, which he leaves in a little heap. The third youth blends this pile of earth with a small measure of the " *acidulous and alkaline fertilizers*; this *tiny compost, when well mingled*, is scooped again into the seed-hole, and covered with a thin sprinkling of earth, to separate the seed from the compost. A fourth lad follows, plants his seed, covers it over, presses it down, and advances to the next little hot-bed. In this manner an acre can be effectually planted in a day, for 2s. wages. The seed-bed is thus brought to a much *finer tilth* than by the common plans, and therefore less seed and manure will suffice in land *properly prepared.* The boy's feet press down the surface sufficiently to solidify the mould over the seeds, and prevent them from being lost by the depredation of birds, or dried up by the sun, when they have first begun to vegetate. All this accelerates and secures the certain and uniform germination of the plants.

" In our wet clay lands, the wells left by the feet of horses would then be avoided, and slugs, weeds, and stones picked up, whilst white carrots, chicory, and many valuable vegetables would be brought to perfection by hand, which are out of the way of horse-work.

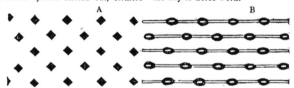

A shews the opens or seed-holes made in the small trenches when ready to receive the fertilizers and seed. B shews the banks or mounds raised around each plant during its growth. The intervening white spaces, or trenches, are to be turned up, *on the principle of subsoiling* in *diagonal* cuts or furrows, crossing each other, as represented in the above plan B.

Were all culinary and green crops dibbled, sown, or transplanted at a proper distance, and *earthed up* regularly, by young persons, the produce could be increased to almost any amount. A single potato plant thus reared and fed by hand, yields from seven to fourteen pounds of tubers.

THE EDEN HALL OX.—A striking likeness of the short-horn ox, the property of Sir P. Musgrave Bart., of Eden Hall, Cumberland; which obtained a prize from the East Cumberland Agricultural Society two years in succession, has just been published. It is a lithograph by I. W. Giles, from a painting by Mr. T. Bland, a young artist who displays much talent. The ox, 6 yrs. old, was killed at Eden Hall and weighed 160 stone. In accordance with his well-known kindness and beneficence Sir Phillip Musgrave distributed the greater part of the meat amongst the poor.

LIQUID MANURE.—We quote from the Boston Cultivator, (America,) of Dec. 17th, 1842, the following portion of an address delivered before the members of the Housatonic Agricultural Society:—
" By an accurate experiment, made by Mr. Young, with fourteen cattle, in one year he made two hundred and eighty-eight loads of compost of loam and muck simply from the *urine* of these cattle. During the same time, their solid excrements and litter amounted to two hundred and forty loads. With compost saturated with urine, he manured seven acres, and with the solid excrements, five acres. After ten years' accurate trial, he came to this result, that the liquid excrement of this stock would manure as many acres of land, last as long, and produce as large crops as their solid excrements. Let this experiment, of one whose good deeds in this great cause speak to us from the grave, teach all a lesson never to be forgotten in the *economy of the manure heap.*"

AGRICULTURAL QUERIES.

TO THE EDITOR OF THE FARMER'S MAGAZINE.

SIR,—In pursuing the enquiries I purposed on addressing you on the 21st of January, I am happy to find I am already joined by two of your subscribers—one requesting a plan of a cow-house on the most improved principle, and "whether the cattle are to be tied up or left at liberty", the other requesting to be instructed in the best mode of steaming fodder, the best apparatus for that purpose, and in what state the fodder is nutritious? In both these enquiries I cordially join, adding to the first a request that the plan may be extended to a greater number of cows, with liquid manure tanks of size sufficient to contain each cow's week's liquid. To the second, the queries —are not all descriptions of fodder rendered more nutritious by steaming; and should the different kinds, hay and turnips, or mangel wurzel, be given in each feed together? I would be inclined to follow up these queries by at once requesting your opinion on the important question of house feeding; but as I have already trespassed on your space, and am expecting answers to my former questions on the use of gypsum and urine, I defer this for a future communication. Your last number contains two valuable letters recommending the use of common salt in dung-heaps instead of gypsum; and two from Professor Henslow in favour of gypsum. Though late in adopting the use of liquid manures, I trust that from such discussions we may find out the most beneficial mode of fixing their volatile properties, and applying them. Allow me to suggest the propriety of your giving a leading article on house-feeding for milch cows. I am sure it would be approved of by all your northern subscribers, who would have the benefit of your knowledge to guide them as to the best practice in feeding and rotation of crops.

I am, Sir, yours very respectfully,
A CUMBERLAND YEOMAN.

TO THE EDITOR OF THE FARMER'S MAGAZINE.

SIR,—On looking over your magazine for the present month I perceive the attention of your readers particularly directed to the use of guano manure. From Mr. Johnson's article on the subject, I should imagine this description of manure particularly adapted to moist situations; I also perceive it is best applied with wood or sod ashes. Being the holder of a large tract of old bog, which I am now in the act of draining, and which I hope to have sufficiently drained to till with turnips and mangel wurzel this season, I would feel much obliged to you—or such of your friends or readers as may be able to give me any information on the subject—if you will let me know whether you would think guano calculated for such ground? The quantity of ashes which will be raised off the bog will be by no means sufficient to insure a fair crop. I will, therefore, be under the necessity of using other manure; and, from what I have just read of guano, I am induced to solicit your opinion on it. Say whether I am right in supposing that four cwt. of guano, mixed with the sod ashes, would be likely to procure a fair crop of Swedes or mangolds; and whether you would prefer laying both on the soil before drilling, or first drilling and putting in the manure with the seed.

I can scarcely conclude without expressing my sense of the many and great advantages I have derived from two years constant reading of your magazine. I have no doubt if many of my neighbours and countrymen would follow my example of subscribing to this publication, they would soon have reason to be glad of it. Quite sure that you would do everything in your power to circulate useful information, I beg leave to remain, sir,
Yours sincerely,
March 10.   AN IRISH SUBSCRIBER.

YARDING OF SHEEP.

SIR,—At a meeting of the Maidstone Farmer's Club it was stated that the custom of "winter yarding sheep" was much increasing; and that many flock-masters had abandoned the use of cattle in their straw-yards to make manure, and substituted sheep. That a portion of the turnip crop should be consumed in the yards is obvious, in order with the straw to make good manure for the ensuing turnip crop; but it is on this account only that many farmers keep cattle stock, who would much prefer giving the entire of their turnip crop to sheep, if they could substitute them for cattle in the yards during winter, but the fear of foot rot, &c., has prevented. If any of your correspondents accustomed to the yarding of sheep will state the particulars of the winter management of them in yards where it has answered, and whether best adapted to the breeding ewes, or feeding sheep, the information will be useful to many farmers, as well as to   Your obedient servant,
Feb. 20, 1843.   ENQUIRER.

MR. EDITOR,—For the last two seasons the gooseberry and currant trees in our garden have been completely stripped of their leaves, and the fruit in consequence entirely spoiled, by a common green and black caterpillar which have infested the trees and all the surrounding beds in myriads, destroying almost every thing before them—peas, beans, cabbages, &c., &c.

Can you, or any of your correspondents, inform me what would be likely to destroy them? Could the trees be fumigated, or washed with any preparation which would destroy the enemy before it be hatched, as my idea is, the larva lies concealed in the branches and stems of the trees?

These caterpillars do not range over the whole garden (which is one of considerable size), but confine themselves almost entirely to one-half of it, and this has been the habit of these voracious little creatures for the two last summers.

Any information on this subject, will oblige,
Mr. Editor, your obedient servant,
Wellingborough, Feb. 20, 1843.   G. G.

SIR,—By mixing common salt with lime it is said that an excellent fertilizer is produced, in the shape of carbonate of soda and muriate of lime. I would feel greatly obliged by an answer to the following queries:—

First—Is muriate of lime not of so extremely subtile a nature as to pass very rapidly through the soil to a considerable depth below the roots of vegetables? If so, how does it act as a manure? Is it by leaving some fertilizing property behind in filtering through the earth? or by entering into some new combination with some of the component parts of the soil? And in what way is it beneficial to vegetation?

Second—What would be the result of mixing

soot along with salt and lime ? Would the compound be a still more valuable manure ? And if so, would its increased value be in proportion to the additional expense ?

Feb. 22, 1843.　　　　An Old Farmer.

ON CHANGE OF SEED.

Sir,—I should be glad, through the medium of your journal, to learn something about the changes of wheat for different sorts of land. For example, supposing I have been in the habit for many years, of using my own seed wheat, on a gravelly soil, on which I am now recommended to try a differently cultivated seed ; I should like to know whether such fresh seed should be from a heavy or a lighter soil.　　　I am, sir, your much obliged,

York, Feb. 24, 1843.　　　　Economist.

TO THE EDITOR OF THE MARK-LANE EXPRESS.

Sir,—I have read with considerable interest in your paper, the letters of Professor Henslow to the farmers of Suffolk, and think he has clearly demonstrated the principle of gypsum being the best mode known at present of fixing the ammonia in manure heaps.

I believe I express the sentiments of all your readers, when I say the Rev. Professor merits the warmest thanks of every person interested in agriculture, for the indefatigable trouble he has taken in investigating experiments, as well as for the popular and lucid style in which he communicates the results to the public.

There are some men who, the moment they hear of a scientific subject, seem to think it a necessary qualification to make a grand parade of chemical terms and verbiage (as quacks formerly quoted Latin without much attention to its precise meaning) which sounds " prodigiously fine," as Dominie Sampson would say, in print, but is in my humble opinion much less effective in its practical application and its desired ends, than the Professor's simple and easy mode of teaching.

But the questions I wish most particularly to ask some of your readers are—would not the application of gypsum be equally effective to clover leys when that peculiarly volatile manure of the sheep-fold is exposed to the greatest heat of the sun's rays for perhaps four months? And would it not be equally useful as a food to the clover plant, by supplying to the soil what the growth of the plant exhausts? And also what quantity is it necessary to sow per acre ?

By inserting the above in your next number, you will oblige,

Your obedient servant,

Sandon, Hants, March 17.　　　R. D. W.

TO THE EDITOR OF THE MARK LANE EXPRESS.

Sir,—I have procured several hundred bushels of pure charcoal dust from the skreenings of wood charcoal used in a forge, but I am quite at a loss what ingredient to mix with the dust for turnips. I shall therefore be most thankful and deeply indebted to any of your readers for the necessary information, saying what to mix with (say one hundred bushels) of charcoal dust, and how many bushels per acre should be drilled with the seed to insure a good crop of Swedes. The soil is a light sandy loam ; the field was wheat last year, and was limed with one hundred and twenty bushels per acre in the autumn of 1841. The wheat was

top dressed last spring with one cwt. of nitrate per acre, but the crop was a poor one, and the nitrate was not of the least good.

I have a field of wheat growing upon the same description of land, and limed in the autumn. I shall feel greatly obliged by being informed what top dressing this should have.

I cannot suffer this opportunity to pass without returning Mr. Rogerson my humble but grateful thanks for his admirable letter in your valuable paper of the 13th instant, calling upon the Royal Agricultural Society to send us farmers " lecturers." I sincerely and anxiously hope Mr. R.'s plan will be carried out at once, with the addition that the professors give lectures wherever a farmer's club is established. Ardently wishing you every success in the great cause you have taken up,

I am, Sir, your's very truly,

March 23rd.　　　　　P.

" A Constant Reader " will be very much obliged if any of our readers will inform him how to apply the following manures for growing turnips :—

Guano, what quantity per acre, and how deep it should be covered in the drills.

Urate, quantity and depth.

Gypsum, quantity and depth.

Sulphate ammonia, quantity and depth.

Daniel's patent manure, quantity and depth.

Nitrate of soda, quantity and depth.

" A Correspondent " inquires if the water in which mangel and Swedes are boiled is injurious as food for pigs ; and if so, why and what is its deleterious property. Also, where he can get the best and the cheapest portable one-horse threshing machine. And also, a light implement to skim the surface after the corn has been removed, as well as the spine of grass ley.

ANSWERS TO AGRICULTURAL QUERIES.

TO THE EDITOR OF THE FARMER'S MAGAZINE.

Sir,—I observe in your last number a letter addressed to you, wishing some of your correspondents who have tried guano to send you the results of their experiments, and by so doing they would confer no small benefit on the farmer and the public. I communicate to you the result of my experiment with guano and other manures on various kinds of crops : if they are of any service to you they are quite at your disposal.

I tried last season four different kinds of manures on potatoes ; the produce of eight yards of a drill each, were as follows :—

Animalised Carbon................23½ lbs.
Farm-yard Dung.................21½　,,
Guano ....19¾　,,
Bone-dust......................15½　,,

Carbon, at the rate of one ton per imp. acre.

Dung ....15 tons.
Guano.........................2 cwt.
Bones ....50 bush.

I sowed six drills of the small tick bean—length of each drill 175 yards—two with guano, two with carbon, and two with farm-yard dung, all at the same rate per acre as with the potatoes ; the result was as follows :—

Guano produced ....244½ lbs. of beans.
Carbon ....224 ,,
Dung ....130 ,,

The bulk of straw on the drills manured with guano and carbon was much the same, but on the dung there was much less. The three samples looked beautiful, and to the eye there was no difference; but their weight after the guano was 70lbs. per bushel; the carbon and dung 67lbs.—3lbs. more per bushel in favour of guano.

I used guano pretty extensively last season for turnips along with farm-yard dung, and they have produced very good crops. Our land being a heavy clay soil, I was afraid to risk the guano alone ; I tried it on a small scale by itself on a few drills, and it raised a splendid crop. I intend to use it more freely this season on turnips, as I have seen its effects proved. The way that I deposit the guano is with Sydney's dibbling machine, (procured from Messrs. Drummond of Stirling) which deposited it in parcels at nine inches apart, and partially covered with earth a few seeds being then dropped directly over each parcel.

When I used dung along with guano (the drills being made), I put in about seven and a-half tons of dung per acre ; after the dung was covered in the drills by the plough, the machine followed with the guano and seed—the guano at the rate of two cwt. per acre.

I tried guano at the same rate per acre as before on two 18-feet ridges with oats, sown with the hand, and harrowed in with the seed, which produced an excellent crop. Another part of the field was manured with carbon, one ton an acre ; the crop was superior to the two ridges manured with guano. Two ridges of the same field got no manure, and were much deficient to either the guano or carbon. I tried guano on a ridge of barley. I could perceive no difference between that ridge and the other parts of the field ; but the weather was uncommonly dry at the time, which was against it.

I have this year a ridge of wheat manured with guano, harrowed in with the seed, which looks better than any part of the field, although manured with good farm-yard dung.

" A Correspondent" wishes to know which is considered the best mode of feeding horses with Swedish turnips—steamed, or in their natural state ; and what quantity per day should be given ?

After an experience of twelve years, I am convinced that steaming or boiling them with chaff is the best mode. I have always found horses very fond of them in that manner, and very healthy. A common stable pailful, or half an imperial bushel, mixed with chaff, should be given once a day ; oftener scours them too much. At night I prefer them to be given.

I am, Sir, your obedient servant,
Castle Malgwyn March 11. J. HENDERSON.
[Land steward to A. L. Gower, Esq.,
Castle Malgwyn, South Wales.]

TO THE EDITOR OF THE FARMER'S MAGAZINE.

SIR,—In reply to "Enquirer" respecting the plant he calls " hard-heads," I have little doubt it is what in the northern counties are sometimes called " hard-irons" by the peasantry. Some years ago, part of my fields—which had for many years been mown—produced this pest, which no stock

will touch whilst growing, and is a nuisance in the hay ; which I got rid of most completely by the following means :—During the winter months I pastured the fields with sheep, principally young ones, of about a year old. With their sharp cutting front teeth they scooped out the root, which destroy the plants ; and in two years not one was to be found, nor have they ever appeared since, though it is now many years since it occurred.

I shall be very glad if this information is of any service to your correspondent, and am, Sir,
Your obedient servant,
March 12. S. W.

TO THE EDITOR OF THE FARMER'S MAGAZINE.

SIR,—In your March number a " Young Farmer" wishes to know if subsoil ploughing gravelly or light soils is at all beneficial ? He also gives his opinion that it is not of any benefit to subsoil gravelly soils.

As I have had a four years' practice in subsoiling—having subsoiled above two hundred acres, both on gravelly soils and those of a very retentive clay, the clayey parts being previously well furrow-drained at a depth of thirty inches six yards apart, having done above 120 miles of such drains in the four years—I have found subsoil ploughing both descriptions of soils to answer most admirably, the crops on the subsoiled parts having far exceeded those on the same description of land not done ; and I find when again ploughed up, after the crops have been removed, the soil is much deeper, being nearly doubled. With regard to the Sandon correspondent's doubts in having what he terms the pan in gravelly soils broken, formed under the old ploughings, it is by breaking through that very pan where I consider the greatest benefits are derived. 1st. You allow the stagnant water there lodged to escape, which in all cases must be very injurious to all descriptions of plants. Any person at all interested in the growing of plants in pots must have seen the injurious practice of allowing water to remain in the lower pot or saucer after filtering through the soil in the pot where the plant is growing, carrying with it all the excrementitious matter (if I may use such a term) from the roots of the plant ; which, if not drained away, will again be drawn up by the plant, which will in a short time appear yellow and sickly from living on their own filth or excrements. Such is the case in a great measure with all plants living on a gravelly soil, where the pan retains wet. In Brown's work on Rural Affairs he writes :—" The constitutional qualities of gravels, also, point out the propriety of deep ploughing (i. e. subsoiling) ; so that the surface soil may be augmented, and greater room given to the growth of the plants cultivated on them. A shallow ploughed gravel can stand no excess of weather, however enriched by manure. It is burnt up by a day or two of drought, and it is almost equally injured by an excessive fall of rain, unless the pan, or firm bottom which such soils easily gain, be frequently broken through by deep ploughing."

An " Enquirer" requests information on the best method of destroying what he terms "hard-heads," or " hard-tops"—what we in this county (Staffordshire) call " hard-irons." Let " Enquirer" stock his fields (infected with "hard-heads") thickly with sheep up to the middle of June, and I have no doubt but all his "hard-heads" will soon disappear, unless they have harder heads in Herefordshire than any other county. I have tried the above mode, and have always been successful.

If you, sir, think any of the above remarks worth a place in your valuable journal, I shall be obliged. I remain, your obliged servant,
March 10. A Two-years' Subscriber.

THE MURRAIN.

Sir,—A correspondent, who signs himself " A Constant Reader," wishes to know how the murrain is treated with us, both as regards sheep and cattle. I most willingly contribute my mite of information on this score, and if what I advance tends in any measure to the alleviation of that malady, I shall consider myself as amply remunerated. First, then, as regards cattle. The symptoms are with us—considerable prostration of strength; the animal particularly dull and lowering; an ichor issuing from the eyes; a constant flow of saliva from the mouth; the tongue and every part of the mouth ulcerated, and frequently more or less inflammation of the throat; the animal throws up its head wildly, and makes a low, pitiful moan; lameness does sometimes (not always) attend as a concomitant. The mode of treatment is to give doses of Epsom salts, varying from four to sixteen ounces, according to the size of the animal, with a few drachms of nitre, and subsequent doses to be given, varying in quantity as the state of the bowels may require it. Violent purging should be avoided on the one hand, and constipation on the other. To keep the intestines gently acting is the best, and with all doses of opening medicine a few drachms of ginger should be given. A gargle or wash for the mouth should be used, consisting of one pound of chloride of lime (an article cheap, and purchaseable at any druggist's shop) dissolved in six times its weight of water, and with a large paint-brush or a sponge fastened to the end of a short stick to wash the mouth twice or thrice a day, as the severity of the case may require. It is a most powerful antiseptic, and probably the cheapest we have. The walls of the outhouses, and the troughs or mangers of the same, should be daily sprinkled with the same solution, cleanliness in all its departments closely attended to, and the animal kept warm. When lameness occurs, the horn of the hoof should be pared away so far as any division of the parts has taken place, and if any virus has formed, a slight portion of the butyr of antimony should be applied with a feather to the parts, and the animal prevented from placing its feet in any dirt or moisture. Bleeding is seldom or ever necessary; there is generally debility enough without it. The animal should be fed with mashes of bran and split oats in equal proportions; turnips, cut with a sheep cutting machine, if the time of the year will admit of it, may be given, or cabbage, or in fact anything the animal will eat that is not restringent in its properties.

The animal must have all its food so that it can throw it up against its grinders; for the tongue and mouth are so sore from ulceration that it will rather pine than lick up its food. I was fortunate in having a good supply of turnips at hand, and cut them up small with an engine; the animals would get a mouthful, and then, lifting up the head to allow the food to fall into the lower part of the mouth, would by such means feed very well; and I think from the effects of medicine, that they have done better since than before they were affected. As regards the sheep, the treatment is somewhat similar. I bring down to the point of saturation a given quantity of salt, say 14lbs., and then calculate to give every sheep at the rate of one ounce to every animal, and cut all their food. Sheep suffer much more from lameness than do cattle. From some cause or other, probably from something connected with the nature of the disease, there is considerable inflammation in the feet, and when that inflammation subsides, the horn of the hoof is found starting off from the foot on the upper side; sand or dirt gets into the parts—inflammation is the result—suppuration takes place—and nature struggles to throw off the hoof. I perceived this after the disease had apparently run its course, and I immediately assisted her by cutting the horn completely away, and placing the animals in a grass layer for the course of a few weeks, and it was astonishing how speedily they recovered. I have now, sir, given you the general mode of treating this complaint, and if further knowledge is required which I am in possession of, I am ever your humble servant at any future period, and beg to remain Yours, &c.,
S. Gill.

Newstead Plains, Nottinghamshire.

P.S. I would observe that it is always wise to consult the best veterinarian in the neighbourhood, and not to rely too much on your own knowledge.

Reply to " Enquirer," in " Mark Lane Express" of 27th Feb., by Sir Francis A. Mackenzie.

Sir F. winters sheep in all the folds of his farmyard, and finds from several years' experience that they will fatten on one-third less food, and in one-fourth less time than when fed on a field, if exposed to the inclemency of the weather. He has always portable *wooden sheds* for his sheep when feeding on turnips in the field, and it will be found on one trial that all animals—horses, cattle, sheep, and pigs—fatten more speedily and consume less food when not exposed to cold or hardship, than when left without any consideration for their warmth and comfort.

Holfield Grange, Essex, Feb. 28.

Sir,—A gentleman who signs himself " Agricola," is desirous of some information on the now fatal disease in cattle. He says it is not the same that was a year ago. No, certainly it is not the same, but, sir, " Agricola" may be convinced that it is what the late epidemic left lurking in the system. Then he says the veterinary surgeon is lost in this complaint; and well he may be. Now, sir, I have visited a great many cattle under the present fatal disease, and have been at the examination of most that have been killed, and found all of them previously diseased, from the shameful neglect of farmers letting their cattle take their luck, as they term it; and " O do nothing to them, they will get well of themselves," &c. Now, these are the beasts that are now dying all over the country, chiefly with diseased lungs, some the liver, some the kidneys, and all for not having the cattle, in the late epidemic, properly attended to by the veterinary surgeon or farrier, who properly knows how to treat them in the different stages of the complaint; and now the prevailing influenza lays hold of unsound cattle, and they quickly die. Farmers must lay the great loss they have caused to this country to themselves, solely because they let the poor beasts lay from day after day, letting them suffer cruelly to save them the expense of a few shillings, and be the ruin of many others, who are in the habit of buying cattle instead of breeding.

AN OLD SUBSCRIBER.

Park Hill, Feb. 16, 1843.

SIR,—Noticing in your paper of the 13th inst. some remarks from "A Young Farmer," relative to subsoiling, may say that I do not see the justice of them with regard to its effects on light lands. He states, "that by ploughing to a certain depth a pan is formed which much prevents the water soaking lower," the which he appears to consider an evil. Now, I have experienced that by holding the moisture in the surface soil till such time as it can evaporate (such being the principal means of its diminution, owing to the said pan), it not only forms a cement of the angular silicious particles of which light lands chiefly consist, thereby resisting the free action of the atmosphere, but chills the soil to such a degree that the strength and growth of plants are much checked and weakened in hot weather. I have found the heat penetrate even to the pan, though the plough had entered 8 or 9 inches, which of course entirely dispelled every portion of moisture at such times as the 'plants most needed it. Again, I do not consider "deep ploughing" equally advantageous, as it mixes the raw unoxidised subsoil with the mould, which cannot but injure vegetation; whereas, by subsoiling, the under stratum is merely moved, and in time that will become useful mould from the vegetative properties of the surface mould continually soaking into it.

I have been thus led to believe that in most cases the subsoil plough may be used as profitably on light as on the more adhesive and retentive soils.

Yours, truly,

Sandown, Surrey. RESEARCH.

SIR,—In reply to your correspondent "Enquirer," from the best information that I have been able to procure, his object will be most readily obtained by burning the sods and twitch to ashes, which can be done by making piles over a fire of straw and wood, open to the wind, taking care to add more as the fire burns through, so that they may be kept in two or three days.

Sixteen bushels of ashes so obtained, mixed with six bushels common salt, and one cwt. guano or nitrate of soda, would make a valuable fertilizing top-dressing for grass land, or other green crops, at a cheap rate, with the advantage of being *free from seeds of any kind.*

I remain, yours, respectfully,

JOHN CLARENCE, M.R.A.S. of England.

21, *Cullum Street, Feb.* 18, 1843.

TO THE EDITOR OF THE MARK-LANE EXPRESS.

SIR,—In your paper on the 27th of Feb., a Wellingborough correspondent, signing himself "G.G.," wishes for some information respecting the caterpillar which so commonly effects the work of destruction on the gooseberry trees, currant trees, cabbages, &c. The following remarks have only a reference to that species of caterpillar which infest the gooseberry tree.

It appears that your correspondent has formed an idea respecting them which is void of any foundation. He thinks that the larva (as he calls it) lies concealed in the branches and stems of the trees; but I think I shall be able to prove to him in the following lines, that his opinion is not grounded on facts.

The propagator of the above named caterpillar is a kind of a butterfly, called by some the magpie moth; it inhabits the hedges and small bushy trees in the day time; it is not so large as the common butterfly; its body is dark, its wings white, with a streak of black across, and spots of black irregularly scattered over them; its time for flying is at sunset, unless disturbed in the day, when it flies if any one strike at it with a stick or any thing else; if they do not hit it, it will fall to the ground as if it was dead. This destructive fly lays its eggs on the under side of the leaves of the gooseberry tree, all along the ribs of the leaves; the eggs are so small that they can scarcely be discerned, being nearly the same colour as the leaf; when the eggs have remained there for a short time, they hatch into small black caterpillars; as soon as hatched they commence their work of destruction by eating small holes through the leaf on which they are hatched, and by the time they have eaten that, they have acquired sufficient strength to roam over the whole tree, and divest it of its foliage.

The best receipts for destroying them is a strong decoction of foxglove, or strong alum water sprinkled on the leaves when they are dry. Some recommend to take a chaffing-dish with hot cinders, and place it under the bush or tree where the caterpillars are, and throw a small quantity of flour of brimstone on the hot cinders; the vapour of the sulphur will cause them to fall off.

As respects cabbage caterpillars, I am not prepared to give a minute detail with reference to them, not having made any experiments on that subject, but I have seen the following receipt in print:—

"To guard cabbages from caterpillars. If the borders of the ground where cabbages are planted, are sown with hemp, although the neighbourhood be infested with caterpillars, the space included by the hemp will be perfectly free from them.

Yours, respectfully,

J. MOON.

Eccleston, near Chorley, March 9th.

SIR,—If your correspondent who enquires the best mode of feeding horses with Swedish turnips, does it with an *economical motive,* he will give each horse one-and-a-half bushel per day, or six *stone* in weight; and if they work hard, one peck of oats per day with chaff. This is unquestionably the *best* and *cheapest mode* of feeding, with those who have really a regard to economy for horse keeping; as is usually pursued, it is ruinous to farmers. I keep upwards of twenty horses, and they never taste hay. The turnips given in their natural state.

I remain, dear sir, yours, faithfully,

JOHN BROWN.

Norton Hall, near Fakenham, Norfolk, Feb. 22, 1843.

P.S. Seventy to eighty rods of ground ought, if well farmed, to produce sufficient for one horse *thirty weeks* the winter months; and if the land is excellent in quality, sixty rod is sufficient, on the *Northumberland system.*

AGRICULTURAL REPORTS.

SOMERSETSHIRE.

Spring is just commencing, and we can speak of the winter as past, and it may be written down on record as a mild one, less moisture having fallen than is common in a season with so little frost; the late check we have had has been very seasonable, and kept vegetation in about its average forwardness. One consequence of the season has been, as regards stock (especially sheep), that they have done well; never a finer or more successful lambing season; the increase this year is likely to be much greater than an average. There is great complaint in the dairy districts of such a large proportion of the cows proving barren; calves have fallen unusually fine and strong, and there is a good many likely to be weaned. Although (except the very prime) fat cattle have been selling low, and there seems no prospect of high prices, good barreners have sold high, as I consider 12l. to 14l. per head to be, even for the best; but old rough stock sell proportionally low. There is much less apparently done in stocking in for grazing than is usual; the price is not considered low enough, and is by no means abundant. We have had very little complaint of disease among stock, less by far than the two previous winters; but complaint enough of low prices, particularly of mutton, pork, and veal. The present price of mutton is 4d. to 5d., extra down 5¼d.; last year 6d. to 6¼d. Pork, 5s. to 6s.; last year 7s. to 8s. per 20lb. Veal, 2½d. to 3½d.; last year, 4½d. to 6d. Bacon, by the side, last year, 5¼d. to 6d.; this year 3¼d. to 4d. per lb. Surely this is coming down in the meat way. I have not noticed beef, the price of which varies so much, according to quality; but I should say prime was worth 1d. and other sorts full 2d. per lb. less. Cheese from 56s. and 63s. to 46s. and 56s. prime; and from 45s. to 38s. per cwt., and even lower, secondary descriptions, with a large supply at our market. Butter has varied less, being now worth 10d. to 11d. per lb. I must now pass on to the appearance of our corn crops: in some instances the wheat on ground has been attacked by the grub, but the greatest danger is its being too forward; it is thick in plant. Vetches are looking well, and so are our pastures. Beans and peas are mostly put in; and oats and barley are just commenced sowing under very fair prospects, the land working remarkably well for it. Considerable quantity of spring wheat, but not equal to last year, has been put in; and expect there will be more barley than last; of this article the consumption has been very great for grinding, and although less used for malting, expect it will run very near out before the next crop, and the price advance. Do not think the quantity of beans planted is equal to last; there has been a great falling off of the ordinary consumption, but lately, owing to the very low price, they are more used for cattle; the yield was better than expected, but still much under an average crop, and the price lower than I ever remember—from 3s. to 3s. 4d. and 3s. 6d. per bushel, but they are not now so much pressed on the market. Barley, 2s. 9d. to 3s. grinding; and 3s. to 3s. 3d. for malting. Oats, 14s. to 18s. per quarter. Peas, 4s. to 4s. 9d. Vetches, 4s. 6d. to 5s. The supplies of clover seed have been very large; and some very prime secondary and low sorts have been selling at from 32s. to 36s. per cwt.;

middling for this, but very prime for the average of years, 42s. to 46s.; prime and very superior 48s. to 56s.; the last are easily disposed of, but the others are difficult to sell. Prime lots of wheat, white, are scarce, but for those of 64lbs. per bushel 6s. 6d. is hardly obtainable; I should quote 6s. to 6s. 3d., white; 5s. 9d. to 6s., red, 62 to 64lb. per bushel. Flour, 34s. to 35s. per 280lb.; some millers sold at 33s. Some of our large farmers have thrashed and hold in dust. In some districts the stocks have not been lower for years; but in others, although in few hands, there is considerable, except potatoes, the best of which are by no means plenty or very cheap. Few substitutes for bread stuff have been used, and altogether, though not perhaps through the millers and bakers, a fair average consumption has been going on. Labour has been very short; the price given to able-bodied men vary from 6s. to 7s., shepherd and carter 8s., per week; there are some privileges besides, about two quarts of liquor per day to accord with the wages, and much work is done by the piece. The winter has been favourable to out-door labour, and it has not cost much in firewood; this has prevented much suffering which the scarcity of labour produces; but it must be acknowledged that our poor rates are on the increase; whether this arises from the times or the new system may be a question, but I am rather inclined to think the latter has most to do with it. The alteration of the tithe system has been the occasion of a greater quantity of land coming under the plough, and this we might have supposed would have created a demand for labour, and I think it will if the occupier be not drained of his capital, which is the great cause of want of employ; and we are to be made believe this drain would cease, and our labourers would find more employ if the price of wheat was lower still, and that it is possible by lowering rents to sell our wheat at 40s. per quarter, and even less, to meet foreign competition, and pay the direct and indirect taxes which a capital employed in agriculture is subject to, and do better than we have. The Corn League wishes us to believe, and pretend to show us by figures, and they take care to be sure to be right, come what will, as the consequence of the experiment; for if it fails it will be because it was delayed too long. Take off all our import duties; this, if it can be done, will be the free trade we want; but then the public creditor will be minus their interest, and both the manufacturer and agriculturist will lose their best customer. If we were to put our shoulder to the wheel, each interest being willing to sacrifice for the good of the whole, things would work themselves right; but as it has taken time to get out of the way, it will take time to get right.—Street, March 17, 1843.

DURHAM.

The past month commenced with very high winds, which have done considerable damage to the shipping on this coast, and also in unroofing buildings, stacks, and uprooting trees; the temperature was exceedingly low, and a great deal of snow and rain fell during the month; the sharp frosts have materially checked vegetation, and the young wheats that were so luxuriant in January now assume a fallen and withered appearance. We consider this will have rather a beneficial effect than otherwise; we do not observe the plants having that tendency to turn out or loose stock, which we have had frequent occasion to notice after long and severe frosts. An unusual large breadth of wheat is sown, and should Providence favour us with fine and genial seasons a bountiful crop may be fairly anticipated. The last month was very unfavourable for out-door work ; since then we have experienced weather unusually fine for the season. Spring sowing has commenced upon dry soils, but on stronger land it is raw, cold, and damp, and works unkindly. We think it is of the greatest importance to have land in a proper state when the seed is deposited. Clover and seeds are well taken, forward, and promising. The last hay crop was an extreme short one, but we do not apprehend there will be any scarcity ; the open and mild winter has prevented its consumption ; but we have frequently observed that where there exists an impression that there is a scarcity of any crop, it induces the farmer to be as careful as possible, and generally cures itself ; but what does good crops now avail? they are of no value. Sir Robert Peel has ruined and broken down the spirit of the British farmer and pauperised the agricultural labourer. Sir Robert has increased that distress in the same ratio as he has reduced the price of agricultural produce. The farmer has lost all confidence in the present government ; his capital is disappearing every day, and he cannot help it ; there is no redress, no sympathy, no abatement of rent. No, landlords don't like that ; they say, you must exert yourselves, you must drain, subsoil, re-duce your expenditure, and must not stand idly by when your team is in a hole, and call upon Jupiter for help ; and what is the result of all this ? The poor deserving, honest, and peaceable labourer is discharged ; and to go in search of another job, he is only wearing the shoes off his feet and to no purpose. He can have beef at 3d. per lb. and wheat at 5s. per bushel ; but, alas ! he cannot obtain either. Few can contemplate on the present prospect without the greatest anxiety and alarm. Our cattle markets exhibit anything but animation ; graziers have given about a year's keep away ; the money laid out for bones, rape dust, &c. is thrown away ; we cannot go the pace again ; as the old proverb says, " burnt children dread the fire." Large numbers of poor labourers are employed by voluntary subscription, in making roads, footpaths, &c. at one shilling per day, which might all be profitably employed in the cultivation of the soil, to produce provision for our increasing population, and prevent that constant and unnecessary drain of specie sent out of this country to purchase foreign grain, beef, &c. Sir Robert has opened our ports to the foreigners' production, and they have raised their duties on our manufactured goods. The lambing season has partially com-menced ; ewes, poor in condition, and short of milk, consequently lambs appear weak and small. Fat sheep that have been turniped are making 10s. per head less than they did last year. At Darlington, on the first Monday in March, there was a fair at-tendance of buyers. Stock of every description sold at ruinously low prices.—*March* 16*th,* 1843.

AGRICULTURAL REPORT FOR MARCH.

So entirely seasonable was the weather to the end of the third week of the present month, that its effects have been felt throughout the kingdom. A degree of check was maintained by the night frosts, but by the power of a brilliant sun the ground was kept open ; and thus agricultural labours were continuous. Never do we recollect anything more completely propitious throughout ; the crops are strong, and wheat superb—sufficiently verdant, but not gaily luxuriant, and the promise is great.

One circumstance we lament: a gradual atmospheric change was in progress for several days prior to the 21st ; the wind inclined more and more to the south by the east, the mercury receded, and just at the equinoctial period, the fine weather gave way to rain, which fell profusely all the night of the 21st and till 7 a.m. of the 22nd.

This rain in itself is useful, especially as the temperature never was depressed below 45°, and ad-vanced to 53° ; the 22nd day being very fine and sunny. But rain, and a renewed depression of the barometer took place again at night ; and thus, if the equinox is to be regarded as a prognostic, not fre-quently deceptive, we fear there is some cause to anticipate a changeable summer.

All else is cheering, and accounts are nearly con-sentient from every part of the United Kingdom ; even the flocks appear better, and in higher condi-tion than usual. The lambing has been without complaint, and the animals grow and thrive upon the fine turnips, and other good aliment they partake of, with unwonted rapidity.

Perhaps some check may be necessary, yet we would fain hope to see the gathering in of a harvest, which promises to be profuse, perfected without impediment.

We perceive by referring to the letter of Mr. Baker to the editor, that the question of Bekhara clover be-gins to be reagitated ; we thought it had been set at rest, and the plant abandoned, but in fact others it appears, besides Mr. Rodwell, are stirring, for a neighbouring farmer known to us, has just had seeds and directions sent to him. We have grown a little of it, and have observed it elsewhere, but deem it, if not worthless, so much inferior to lucerne, that we should be grieved to see a biennial supersede a crop of vast utility, and of amazing prolificity during seven years. The Bokhara is no clover at all, bo-tanically it is *melilotus leucantha major*, or the great white-flowered Asiatic *melilot* ; and therefore Mr. Baker is right in his conjecture.

If a fine and tried legume—one easy of culture, certain in its qualities, and bountiful to profusion—be required, do let us return to the lucerne, for in it we possess fodder equally good for milch cows, and horses. Well managed, it can be cut over, four, five, six times, between April and November ; and it will stand drought better than any other fodder crop.

The land has turned up in the finest manner; con-sequently amazing breadths of oats, &c. are already deposited therein. Barley will soon be in progress unless wet be profuse ; and potatoes will be begun.

We would suggest early planting, and by all means the introduction of soot where obtainable. This manure contains a quantity of an ammoniacal neutral salt, which manifests itself if the smallest portion of quick lime come in contact with it. Soot remains long in the soil, and is inimical to vermin, and it is carbonaceous matter, chiefly, in its finest form. With that, and farm yard dung, and the proper economising of night soil (sadly overlooked), Britain would soon supply its own fields with all the elements that can be contained in imported ma-nures. Of this fact, a more intimate knowledge of chemical principles would soon convince the en-quiring and liberal minded agriculturist.

March 22*nd.*

GENERAL AGRICULTURAL REPORT FOR MARCH.

This has proved, we have very great pleasure in intimating, one of the finest months, not only for farm labours, but also vegetation in general, almost ever remembered. From the first until about the 20th we were favoured with remarkably fine, and truly vegetative weather, the wind mostly blowing from the southward and westward, accompanied by light showers of rain at night. This state of the atmosphere had, as might be anticipated, a most beneficial influence upon the young wheat plants in all parts of England ; and it is gratifying to ob. serve that the accounts, in respect thereto, which have come to hand, in the course of the month, from the whole of our numerous correspondents in the wheat growing districts, state that though the winter's frosts appear to have somewhat nipped those growing in exposed situations, taking the country through, they are of regular and steady growth, of good colour, and with every prospect of a large forthcoming yield. There is one circum. stance which our farmers ought not to lose sight of during the coming season, viz., the large increase in the breadth of land under wheat culture this year, both as relates to winter and spring sown. That this fact, coupled with a considerable falling off in the consumptive demand at Mark Lane and our leading country markets, cannot fail to have a depressing influence upon prices, no doubt what.. ever can be entertained ; hence, so far as the future prospects of the home producers are concerned, it is but too evident they are of a very gloomy character. It is far, very far from our wish to represent matters worse than they really are, but, as public journalists, we feel it incumbent upon us to lay before our readers such statements as from which they may be the more readily enabled to draw their own in.. ferences to prove as a guide to their future opera. tions. The stocks of wheat now on hand are, we find, tolerably extensive, the time of year considered. But in making this remark it must be observed that we are making allusion, not to those in any parti. cular county, but to England generally, as we are quite aware that in Essex the supplies of wheat are small ; but in Lincolnshire, Cambridgeshire, &c.— as is in part evidenced from the very large shipments which have been, for some time past, made thence to the London market—the quantities on hand are certainly above an average. In warehouse, in the various ports of the United Kingdom, we have still large supplies of free foreign, and for which buyers can with difficulty be found at any price. The latter description of wheat will, in a great measure, have the effect of causing prices to have a down. ward tendency. This at once shows the necessity that exists for the legislature to pass such measures as will positively protect the interests of those who so much require protection in the strictest sense of the word—the British yeomen ; and we are firmly con. vinced that should the present almost-free-trade prin. ciples he suffered to go on in full vigour, that the ruin of that highly-important body will be inevitable. It should therefore be the duty of our ministers—and indeed that of all who have the true interests of their country at heart—to attempt the amelioration of our farmers, who are now suffering to an extent un.. known for some years past. That these are not un. supported statements, we would refer to present prices, not only of corn, but also of stock and other descriptions of farm produce ; and it will be found that they are now fully *thirty per cent.* lower than at

the corresponding period last year ! Here, then, is the necessity for our agriculturists to bestir them-selves in sending up petitions to both Houses of Par. liament, claiming justice at their hands.

It being now well ascertained that a decidedly small quantity of barley has been sown this year, we think there is a probability of an increased value being realised next year for that article ; but not to the extent that can by possibility make up for the actual losses upon wheat and most other grain.

Such has been the activity apparent in the fields, under the auspices of splendid weather, that in some parts the Lent crops have been finished ; and a general conclusion is fully expected to be arrived at by, or very shortly after, the 10th proximo.

The lambing season, notwithstanding the prevail-ing epidemic has committed serious ravages amongst the cattle, has been productive of a fine fall of strong lambs ; and we have very good authority for stating that the quantity of stock in the country is extremely large.

The various corn markets have been tolerably well, but not to say heavily, supplied with wheat, both of home and foreign produce ; but the demand for all descriptions has ruled extremely inactive, and prices in consequence have suffered a decline of from 2s. to 4s. per qr., without effecting scarcely any pro-gress in sales. The barley trade has also ruled dull, and the currencies have given way quite 2s. per qr. In malt no new feature has occurred, and the rates have remained about stationary. On account of the large supplies of oats brought forward, the sale for them has ruled dull, and the rates have fallen 1s. to 2s. per qr. The same observations may be applied to beans and peas ; while flour must be called 2s. per 280lbs. cheaper.

The advices from Ireland and Scotland state that the weather there has been equally favourable as with us. Sowing has gone on with a degree of rapidity almost hitherto unknown, and the grain plants are represented as very promising. The corn trade, however, has been in an unusually depressed state, and the quotations of all grain have fallen from 1s. to 3s., in some instances 4s. per quarter.

Although the supply of turnips has been nearly exhausted, we find that the stock in our grazing districts has fared well, but not without a larger use of cake and other artificial food.

The following is our usual monthly statement of the supplies and prices of fat stock exhibited and sold in Smithfield cattle market. The former have been composed of 11,920 beasts ; 110,215 sheep and lambs ; 1040 calves ; and 2400 pigs ; while the lat-ter have ruled as follow :—Beef, from 2s. 6d. to 4s. ; mutton, 2s. 10d. to 4s. ; lamb, 4s. 8d. to 6s. ; veal, 3s. 10d. to 4s. 8d. ; and pork, 3s. to 4s. per 8lbs., to sink the offals.

As to the trade, this has ruled miserably dull, with comparatively low prices. This state of things is chiefly owing to the supplies of stock in Smithfield, and to the arrivals of slaughtered meat up to New-gate and Leadenhall markets from Scotland and various parts of England being unusually great, and by far more than adequate to meet the wants of the buyers ; upwards of *fifty thousand carcases* having thus come to hand—and so long as such large re-ceipts continue, so long will prices rule low. One of the most important features in Smithfield, in the course of the month, has been the exhibition of about 30 German beasts, which were imported about four months since, and which have been, during that period, fed in a large distillery in the neighbourhood

X

of Brentford, by way of experiment. The beasts in question, when first imported, were worth about 18*l.* per head; but such was the miserable condition in which they were brought to this market, we considered them positively dear at 10*l.* each; while we are given to understand the actual loss upon them was about 8*l.* per head! The only imports since our last statement, have been 24 oxen from Hamburgh, 12 at Hull, and the same number in London.

A STATEMENT and COMPARISON of the SUPPLIES and PRICES of FAT STOCK, exhibited and sold in SMITHFIELD CATTLE MARKET, on Monday, March 28, 1842, and Monday, March 27, 1843.

At per 8lbs. to sink the offals.

	March 28, 1842.		March 27, 1843.	
	s. d.	s. d.	s. d.	s. d.
Coarse & inferior Beasts	3 4	to 3 6	2 8	2 10
Second quality do.	3 8	3 10	3 0	3 4
Prime large Oxen......	4 0	4 2	3 6	3 8
Prime Scots, &c.......	4 4	4 6	3 10	4 0
Coarse & inferior Sheep	3 6	3 8	2 10	3 0
Second quality do.	3 10	4 2	3 2	3 4
Prime coarse woolled do.	4 4	4 8	3 6	3 8
Prime Southdown do.	4 10	5 0	3 10	4 0
Lambs	6 0	7 0	5 0	6 0
Large coarse Calves ..	4 8	5 6	3 6	4 0
Prime small ditto	5 8	5 10	4 2	4 6
Large Hogs...........	4 6	4 10	3 0	3 6
Neat small Porkers ..	5 0	5 2	3 8	4 0

SUPPLIES.

	March 28, 1842.	March 27, 1843.
Beasts............	2,472	2,610
Sheep and Lambs	18,270	23,350
Calves............	42	60
Pigs...............	319	439

The dead markets have been positively glutted with meat, owing to which, the trade has ruled dull, and prices have fallen quite 2d. per 8lbs. Beef has sold at from 2s. 2d. to 3s. 6d.; mutton, 2s. 4d. to 3s. 8d.; lamb, 4s. to 5s. 6d.; veal, 3s. 6d. to 4s. 4d.; and pork, 3s. to 4s. per 8lbs., by the carcase.

APRIL WHEAT.

TO THE EDITOR OF THE MARK LANE EXPRESS.

SIR,—We are desirous of laying before your readers the following brief statement of the valuable properties of the April wheat, which we are now selling for this year's sowing; see advertisement in the present number of the "Mark-lane Express."

The April Wheat, while it may be sown a month or five weeks later than any other wheat, will generally be the first to ripen in harvest. Our correspondents mention having sown it in the last week in April and the first week in May, and even so late as the 20th of May with good success. This wheat is found less liable to blight than any other wheat.

It is very productive, having produced in land of moderate quality 36, 40, and 42 bush. per acre. The quality is good; we have heard of some weighing 64½lbs per bushel. The sample we are now selling weighs 63lbs., and some 64lbs.; and in one instance which has come to our knowledge, it commanded for grinding the highest market price.

The only care required in sowing it is to have the land sufficiently fine; it should be prepared as for barley. The best mode of sowing it is by drill, at the rate of two bushels, or two and a-half bushels per acre.

We are, sir, your obedient servants,
SMYTH & CO.

77, *King William-street, London.*

COMMUTATION OF TITHES— ENGLAND, 1842-43.

The following Report of the Tithe Commissioners in England and Wales to her Majesty's Principal Secretary of State for the Home Department, pursuant to the act 6 and 7 Will. 1V., c. 71, has been presented to both Houses of Parliament by command of her Majesty:

"To SIR JAMES GRAHAM, &c.

"*Tithe Commission Office,* March 6, 1843.

"SIR,—It is our duty to report to you the progress of the commutation of tithes in England and Wales to the close of the year 1842.

"We have received notices that voluntary proceedings have commenced in 9,510 tithe-districts; of these notices 129 were received during the year 1842.

"We have received 6,694 agreements, and confirmed 6,211; of these 346 have been received, and 407 confirmed, during the year 1842.

"3,035 notices for making awards have been issued, of which 857 were issued during the year 1842.

"We have received 2,006 drafts of compulsory awards, and confirmed 1,613; of these 651 have been received and 583 confirmed during the year 1842.

"We have received 6,451 apportionments, and confirmed 5,695; and of these 1,231 have been received and 1,347 confirmed during the year 1842.

"In 7,824 tithe districts, *as will be seen from the above statement, the rent-charges to be hereafter paid have been finally established by confirmed agreements or confirmed awards.*

"We have in our possession *voluntary agreements and drafts of awards,* as yet unconfirmed, which will *include* 876 *additional tithe districts.*

"The proceedings under OUR act are going on regularly, and, *on the whole, very tranquilly.*

"The proportion of compulsory to that of voluntary commutation is increasing, *as must now be expected.*

"Notwithstanding this fact, however, the number of rent-charges established in 1842 slightly exceeds the number established in 1841.

"We have again to regret that the apportionments follow the establishment of rent-charges more slowly than the interests and wishes of some of the parties make it desirable they should.

"We adhere, however, to the opinions expressed in our former reports, that it is prudent to exercise great forbearance in interfering with the privilege of the tithe-payers to apportion the rent-charges by agents of their own selection.

"The power we now have of giving security to the tithe-owner for the payment of unapportioned rent-charges has assisted us in our endeavours to exercise such forbearance.

"In *flagrant* cases of delay, however, *we do not and shall not hesitate to exercise our powers of apportioning compulsorily.*

(Signed)　　"WM. BLAMIRE.
　　　　　　"T. WENTWORTH BULLER.
　　　　　　"RD. JONES."

GUANO.—Attached to this number of the *Farmer's Magazine* will be found a pamphlet on guano, detailing its effects as illustrated by the latest experiments. At a time when the use and advantages of artificial manures, and especially of this fertilizer, are becoming so general, it is highly desirable that agriculturists should be put in possession of all the known facts and experiments bearing on this subject, and we would, therefore, invite a careful perusal of all the statements brought forward in favour of this valuable manure, in order that a correct judgment may be formed as to its merits.

A correspondent, under the signature of a "Colonial Proprietor," enquires—Can you, or any of your readers, inform me if Melvin's Stonehaven Ploughs are to be obtained in London, and if so, where?—March 28.

REVIEW OF THE CORN TRADE

DURING THE MONTH OF MARCH.

Since our last publication the weather has been as favourable to the spring operations of the farmer as could well have been desired. It was dry, and generally frosty; and yet the ice at no period penetrated deep enough into the ground to prevent the preparation of the fields for the reception of the spring seeds of all descriptions. The spring wheats therefore generally, and barley, oats, pulse, and potatoes, are either in a great measure already or speedily will be committed to the ground in most excellent order; and of course, therefore, in so far as the season has at the present time progressed, there exist strong grounds indeed to expect that their produce will in due season be most abundant. But the advantages of this favourable beginning of the spring quarter of the year have not been entirely confined to the preparation of the fields for and to the sowing of them with spring seeds; for they have likewise, in a material degree, been extended to the improvement of the winter wheats themselves. In the beginning of the year the young wheat plants had sprung up much too rapidly, and in many instances they had even assumed that degree of luxuriance which reudered their future fate rather critical. They however, since then, received a most opportune check in their too rapid growth towards maturity by the frosty, yet at the same time mild, weather which occurred in the end of February and in the beginning of last month. They must, from this fortunate event, have now gained that strength at their roots which is necessary to an abundant crop, and in which they were certainly deficient previous to that period. In as far, therefore, as the spring season has advanced, expectations may reasonably be entertained that the ensuing crop will be a large one; but in the present depressed state of the agricultural interest, great doubts may be, and actually are now entertained, whether this circumstance—should it really occur—can be of much benefit to any class of Her Majesty's subjects. Wheat is already considerably cheaper than it can be grown in any part of the United Kingdom; and as an abundant crop this year must still cause a farther material decline in the value of this the most important article produced by our home industry, the farmers must suffer still more severely in their property than as yet they have done, should the wheat crop now in the ground prove, in the event, to be an abundant one. Undoubtedly a farther reduction in its value must be the consequence, and then they may have the privilege of supplying all our markets for a time with cheap wheat; and if, by a further sacrifice of the capital embarked by them in their agricultural operations, even one benefit can be extended to any interest within the British empire, then indeed patriotism may, perhaps, offer some consolation to them for any further sacrifice of property which they may be doomed to make for the public good. But as it is a moral certainty that, in the present state in which British society is constituted, the agricultural interest can neither reap the advantages of prosperity nor undergo the pains of adversity without communicating a full share of their good or of their bad fortune to every class of society within Her Majesty's dominions—to whatever

department of industry their efforts and pursuits may be directed—we entertain strong doubts, indeed, whether an abundant wheat crop, under present circumstances, may not be as fatal to the best interests of the United Kingdom as a really deficient and damaged one most undoubtedly would be. The depressed value of agricultural property at present—which an abundant crop this year must inevitably further increase—must be followed by a more than proportionable decline in the wages of labour; for the amount of labour to be performed would be considerably decreased by the decreased means of the agricultural interest for following out agricultural improvements; and thus must by far the most valuable property in the British dominions—we allude to that of productive labour—be injured very materially by any further depreciation in the value of agricultural produce. This most unnatural state of our internal affairs has been, we may say, entirely created by the illustrations of the doctrines of modern political economy now practised by Her Majesty's Ministers, and supported by the farmers' friends—as the representatives of the farming interest in the Commons House of Parliament lately miscalled themselves. By the unfortunate withdrawing of effective legal protection to home industry, we have transferred a great deal of the best property which any country can possess to foreign states and communities. We now give a considerable portion of the property which our agricultural labourers previously possessed in the production of food for the use of the British people to the field labourers of foreign nations; and we are thus oppressively reducing the wages of at least one-half of our own agricultural workmen, and rapidly driving the other half either into union-houses or that state of life which is so closely allied to destitution and to starvation. It is therefore, we repeat, a subject of considerable doubt whether an abundant crop, in the present internal circumstances of the English empire, would not add to that depression which, for some years now, has been so severely felt by the British people, and which we fear much must continue to be experienced until effective protection be given by law to the products of industry at home, of every description. The wages of labour are already considerably too low in this country for the comfortable living of our workmen, and for the payment of our heavy taxation, and consequently for the real and best interests of the British community. It is from this source alone that we must date a declining revenue, and the collection into few hands of immense sums of unemployed capital. These are the necessary consequences of employing foreign field labourers instead of those of the United Kingdom, in the productive labour of growing food for the consumption of the British people. It is not, however, solely in agricultural matters that this most insane principle is permitted to exist, for it is likewise to be found in various departments of trade. In the fish trade, for instance, the actual value of which has already been deteriorated by the tariff bill upwards of fifty per cent., and from which some of the most eminent factors are about to withdraw that part of their capital which may yet remain to them. Our fishermen have most just reason to complain that even in the London market they find the produce of their labour, and of their dangerous profession, interfered with and undersold, by large supplies of fish of every description, foreign caught, or foreign cured. In the boot trade, in that of hats, in silk goods, and indeed in all the higher grades of manufactured goods, the workmen find themselves also defrauded of their property by the transfer annually now of a considerable portion of their labour to foreign workmen and to foreign artizans. Whilst this ungenerous principle in our foreign trade is permitted to exist, little hope indeed need be entertained of an improving revenue, or of a returning prosperity. The destruction of the only wealth of nations, a productively employed people, must eventually be attended by consequences most prejudicial to the national debt itself, for it may even lead to the necessity of Americanizing the British half-yearly dividends. That reciprocity in trade between the corn-producing districts in Europe and America, and the United Kingdom, cannot exist, is perfectly established by the events which have occurred in our trade with these communities during the last four or five years. Within less than that period we have paid in cash upwards of thirty millions sterling to foreign nations in exchange for foreign grain alone, and at the same time the value of our exports to those nations has annually been on the decrease. This money is now embarked by its now foreign proprietors either in the improvement of foreign agriculture or in extending foreign manufactures, fisheries, and commerce. It is by the means which our liberal system in trade has conferred on them that they are now enabled to supply themselves at home with manufactures which previously were shipped to them from this country, and that they now endeavour to increase their revenues by increasing annually the rates of duty previously imposed on the importation of goods from the United Kingdom. This is a kind of reciprocity which we cannot comprehend, for it is all on one side. In Germany, Russia, and the United States of America, internal industry is now amply protected by law, and the governors of these states display profound wisdom in encouraging their export trade, and limiting as much as possible the amount and value of their import commerce. Had this money which we have remitted abroad during the last five years been retained in this country no commercial complaints would have been made at the present time. It would have continued in circulation at home, encouraging all departments of industry, and our former valuable export trade to the corn-producing districts in Europe and in America would not have suffered any diminution in its amount, in as far as these communities would not have had the means of competing with us in their own markets in manufactures, or indeed in any thing else. The property which our industrious population possesses in labour would not have been deteriorated as it has been latterly, and wages would have been fully supported at their previous rates. Consumption of all articles, either of agriculture or of trade, would have gone on at profitable prices to the producers, and wheat never would have fallen to the miserable prices which are now obtained for it, and which depreciation is entirely occasioned by employing foreigners to do that labour for us which can be well performed by our workmen at home. The farmers cannot at present purchase their usual quantity of manufactured goods, because they do not obtain remunerating prices for their produce. The master manufacturers cannot pay fair wages to their workmen, because the value of the home consumption of goods is reduced by at least one-half, in consequence of the transfer of productive employment from our own countrymen to those of foreign nations, and also because the demand for their products for shipment to foreign grain-growing communities is annually becoming less; the money which we now pay for foreign agricultural produce enabling these states to manufacture for themselves on cheaper terms than we can do. It is because our legislators are labouring under this strange delusion, or rather monomania, respecting free trade, that the British farmers are at present suffering so materially in the capital which they have embarked in the cultivation of our fields at home by the present wretchedly low value of all descriptions of agricultural produce, particularly that of wheat. This important article of agricultural produce has been again gradually on the decline during the greater part of last month ; and at the present moment the farmers' spirits are not cheered by the slightest prospect of any immediate amendment. Even the holders of free foreign wheats are now shewing some anxiety to reduce their stocks in granary, and they permit not any favourable opportunity for making sales to pass from them. Wherever, therefore, the supplies of English wheat have been of late inadequate to the demand, the deficiency has been amply made good by the importers of foreign wheat ; and thus has the late prospect of future improvement vanished—for a time, at all events—from the view of our agricultural interest. To sacrifice the interests of millions of industrious families to those of a dozen of cotton lords is a policy far beyond the general comprehension of mankind ; and it is also an extraordinary circumstance that these gentlemen do not see that all the money which they may have gained by the reduction of wages, they have lost by the severe depression in the home market which low wages chiefly have occasioned. The eyes, however, of the greatest portion of the master manufacturers are now opened to the real causes of the existing general distress ; and the doctrines of the Anti-Corn Law League are becoming, even amongst them, as unpopular as they have always been amongst the manufacturing workmen themselves. Until the agricultural interest in this country, however, be rendered again sound and healthy, that of manufactures cannot generally be expected to improve ; and so long as encouragement is given by British laws to the cultivation of foreign lands, no alteration for the better need be looked for in the general circumstances of the inhabitants of the United Kingdom. We fear much, however, that the time is still distant when proper protection will be again extended to the cultivation of our own fields. Indeed, it is notorious that a bill will, during the present session of parliament, be introduced, and be passed too, under the auspices of her Majesty's present ministers, for the admission of grain of every description from our colonies on the payment of only nominal duties. This prospect is most cheering to our fellow subjects in Canada, from whence our information is to the middle of March. From them it not only opens an almost boundless market for any grain which they can produce above their home consumption ; but the transit grain trade between the United States of America and the United Kingdom must also confer on them advantages of the utmost importance to their future prosperity. The expenses attending the carriage of grain and flour from the most productive banks of the Ohio to Montreal are at least one-third lower than they are from the same districts to New York; and on the payment of 3s. per qr. of duty, their wheat immediately will gain all the advantages which the new act of parliament, to which we now allude, must confer on wheats of colonial growth. This duty is to be applied to the finances of Canada alone, and not one farthing of it will be applied towards the public expenditure of the mother country. We strongly suspect that this proposed alteration in the colonial grain trade is intended by the ministers of the British Crown as only a preliminary measure, either to the entire repeal of the corn laws, or as a step to the imposition of fixed rates of duty on the importation of foreign grain from all quarters. This colonial bill, when passed into a law, as certainly it speedily must be, will not yield in national importance to that corn law which was adopted last year by the Parliament, nor can its consequences be less injurious to the agricultural interests of the United Kingdom. In very few instances, indeed, will the import duty into Canada be paid on the American grain and flour thus introduced, for the vast proportion of it will be smuggled across the lakes. The shores are by far too greatly extended to admit of revenue protection by Customhouse officers, and thus another immense boon will be given to the admirers of freedom in foreign trade, at the farther expense of the British agricultural interest. Our shipping interest will, however, derive some benefit from this trade, in so far as wheat, or any thing else, cannot be imported into this country, unless under the British flag, from any of our colonies. To the agricultural interests in America, however, our new colonial corn bill will be of the deepest importance, inasmuch as it will place before them the British markets for the consumption, duty free, of the produce of by far the finest and largest corn districts within that union. To them it will be advantageous in proportion to the injury which it will inflict on the cultivators of our fields at home; and in our legal export shipments of goods to these States no increase can be made by this further concession to the unintelligible doctrines of freedom of trade, for the American tariff of import duties will be still maintained for the protection of American internal industry. In this field folly and wisdom are arrayed against each other, and it is not difficult to foresee to which the advantage will finally belong. The British farmer's friends in the House of Commons, if such men there be, no doubt will pay due attention to this colonial corn importation bill when it is submitted to the legislature for their sanction, although we very much doubt if their influence now be powerful enough to prevent it from being, during this session of parliament, registered among the laws of the British empire.

From the continent of Europe, the information received since our last publication has generally been in due course of post. In the Baltic ports the prices of wheat have not yet fallen exactly to their level with those in Mark Lane, but it was generally expected that, as the season for activity approached, they would still undergo a farther depreciation. Be this as it may, however, we shall be overwhelmed again with Polish wheat during the next summer and autumnal months; for, should the British merchants decline to purchase Polish wheats abroad, the foreign proprietors of that article will consign it for sale to all the great corn markets within the United Kingdom. At Dantzig the latest nominal price of high-mixed Polish wheats was 30s. per qr.

free on board. Shipping was exceedingly plentiful, and the rates of freight demanded were consequently unusually low. Several foreign ships had been, at that date, chartered for London, at from 3s. to 2s. 6d. per qr.; and the British farmer will before long therefore, by sad experience, discover that, under no circumstances, can our maximum import duty of 20s. per qr. protect his property in the British market from competition with the proprietors of the best descriptions of foreign wheats. Several vessels have likewise been chartered already in Great Britain herself, to proceed to the Baltic for grain; a clear proof that eventually the purchase prices of wheat abroad must assort themselves to the sale ones here. All the markets without the Baltic will also be regulated by the same causes, and therefore, in the face of an abundant growth of grain at home, the cultivators of our fields have but a cheerless prospect before them. From the Mediterranean, and from the southern ports in Europe without that sea, no advices have latterly been received of any importance to British agriculture, excepting that preparations were making in the north of Spain to send us, in great abundance, live cattle, and throughout that peninsula cured provisions were in progress for the consumption of the people in this country. This extreme kindness towards us by foreign nations will last as long as our money does, but not one moment longer.

The value of barley has undergone extremely little variation since our last review of the state and prospects of the corn trade. The distiller's consumption is rather increasing, whilst, on the contrary, the maltster's demand is regularly on the decline, and the one takes off, at present, about the deficiency of the other. Still, however, the distiller's trade is by no means in that healthy state in which the wisdom of our Legislature, if directed into a right channel, might place it. Double the quantity of barley now used would be requisite to an improved system, and no reason whatever can be adduced for not amending one of the most important departments for the consumption of barley, for, improving public morality, and for increasing the national revenue. If the ministers of the crown paid only a little more attention to our excise duties, and a little less to those of the customs, they would far better serve than they now do the best interests of the British empire. To the admission of foreign wines at reduced duties, no person can object; for this article is not, and cannot be produced in this country, but the reduction of the existing duty on foreign spirits is a widely different question. In Portugal and in France various descriptions of wines can be made, the quality of which is so extremely inferior, that consumption for them, neither abroad nor at home, can be found in that character. The object, or at all events the consequence, of the proposed reduction here in the duty at present imposed on foreign spirits, must be the future conversion of these deleterious foreign wines into foreign spirits, for the consumption of the inhabitants of the United Kingdom. The raw material of these spirits, too, is of foreign growth, and the profits of their manufacture will belong to foreign distillers. To suppose that these spirits will be paid for in British commodities of any description, is a stretch of fancy nearly bordering on what is called the insane. Like everything else which we now import from Europe, and from the United States of North America, the precious metals chiefly must be remitted in exchange for any additional quantity of foreign spirits which we may import under the reduced system of duties, and the wages of the workmen engaged in distilling them will be paid to foreigners, and not to the subjects of the British Queen. This policy is not of easy comprehension at a period when nearly every class in British society is complaining of the want of a sufficient quantity of productive employment, and the transfer to foreigners of even the smallest portion of labour which can be accomplished at home, is a positive injury inflicted on the property of the industrious classes in the United Kingdom. To reduce the duty now levied in England on home-made spirits, on the contrary, must be speedily attended by results of a widely different character; it will lead to the entire suppression of the spirit smuggling trade, which is the great root of crime amongst the British people. It will likewise be the means of improving public health, because pure and healthy home-made spirits, drawn from British grain, will afterwards be consumed in England, instead of the foreign spirits now consumed under the present system, and distilled on the worst principles, and to a certain extent from the worst descriptions of foreign spoiled wines, or from inferior qualities of foreign fruits. That our distillers are as scientific as those of Holland, and infinitely more so than those of France, the experience of many years now has very sufficiently established; and that the spirits manufactured by them are better suited to the people of this kingdom, is proved by the higher state of good health which their consumers enjoy, than those do who confine themselves to the use of foreign spirits only, whether they be of French or of Dutch origin. The Chancellor of the Exchequer has the means now within his power of applying an effectual remedy to the imperfections at present exhibited in our distillery and rectifying laws; he has only to equalise the spirit duty throughout the United Kingdom—to raise that now charged in Ireland and Scotland to 5s. per proof gallon, and to reduce the charge in England to the same figure. By a measure of this description he will improve very materially the revenue, in as far as the smuggler's trade must cease, being rendered no longer a profitable one. He will open also a farther channel for the consumption of British grain to the extent of at least half a million of quarters; and he may likewise vastly increase public morality and the public health by the reduced quantity of ardent spirits, of the worst description too, which are now illicitly put into consumption, which the alteration in the duty we now allude to, would inevitably occasion. To increase the growth of barley in this country would be to increase the quantity of the most important tax-paying article in this country, and would, even on that account alone, be an important national advantage. In the malting trade, however, is the great channel for the consumption of an additional quantity of barley to be found; but this too depends mainly on the attention of the legislature being directed to a revision of the excise laws, for the consumption of pure and wholesome beer is now, we may say, in a state of annual decay, and the quantity of barley consumed by the public brewers is, consequently, annually becoming less. Excessive taxation is the sole cause of this effect, so extremely injurious to the agricultural interest, to the public revenue, and to the great body of the English nation. The malt duty is more than one-half too high, and the public taxes paid by the licensed victuallers compel the great majority of that class of society to protect their property invested in their leases at the expence of the consumers' health. It is utterly impossible for the mi-

nor publicans to sell beer at its present price, and to pay, at the same time, the large public expences to which under the present system they are subjected. In this cause originate the numerous conviction, for adulterating beer, which are weekly occurring at the excise office, and the still more numerous cases of the same evil, which meet not the public light. When we say, that by a mixture of coarse sugar and salt, and most frequently of very deleterious ingredients themselves, which we need not here enumerate, two barrels of beer from the public brewer are converted into three by the retailer, we are morally certain that our statement is far within actual bounds, and the finance Minister cannot be better employed than in the immediate application of a remedy to this rapidly increasing evil—indeed, common justice to the people demands that he should do so. It has its origin, we repeat, in heavy taxation, and he alone has the power of removing it; to impose a charge of one shilling per bushel on the raw barley, when sent into the malt house for conversion into malt, instead of the heavy duty now charged on malt itself, would in a few years double the revenue now collected on malt, would triple the quantity of barley now actually converted into malt, and would spread universal satisfaction throughout every part of the British Empire. The benefits, however, of the imposition of a moderate rate of duty on malt, would not be confined to the revenue or to the comforts of the consumers of beer. They would take a far more extended and far more important range even than these are; for they would eventually penetrate into the whole system of British and Irish society. They would render absolutely necessary the cultivation of at least two millions of acres of sandy soil, in addition to the quantity of land now under barley-tillage in this country. This description of land is at present valueless, but by its conversion into utility it would increase the rent of land eventually by as many millions sterling annually. It would proportionably increase the quantity of field-labour now to be done, and thus it would add to the property of the agricultural labourers themselves. Its annual produce and profits also would do far more than pay for the additional expenses which the additional consumption of beer would occasion. It would produce an universal good, unalloyed by one solitary evil; and it would in a short time indeed perfectly prove that within the United Kingdom we have, in great abundance, the means for maintaining our population, were it three times greater than it now is, without transferring to foreign labourers (unless for a few luxuries) even the smallest fraction of work, with the view either of comfortably feeding, or of respectably clothing, the people of this country. On the exorbitant duties, however, now charged on manufactured barley, amounting, as they do, to nearly one quarter of the public expenditure, the members themselves of the Anti-Corn Law League are entirely mute; although their silence on this most important subject expresses far more eloquently than language could do, the real motives by which their conduct heretofore has been, and still is regulated. It is apparently neither to promote the prosperity nor to increase the comforts of the productive labourers, that they at present labour; else the excessive excise duties on manufactured barley would form the leaders in all their addresses to the public. By the total repeal of the corn laws, their silence on the subject of overtaxed barley clearly proves their object not to be the improvement of the condition of the working classes at home, but the increase of the fortunes of a few cotton lords at the sole expense of the multitude. The productive classes, however, now pay little attention to these lecturers on modern political economy. They already repudiate their false principles of philanthropy, and soon—indeed now—will they solicit from the Legislature of the United Kingdom legal protection to home labour, which is their property, and by far the most valuable one too in the British empire, against the interference of foreign labour in all our markets of consumption, whether they be at home, in the colonies, or in any part of our foreign possessions. The real friends to the people at present are those who oppose the modern dogmas of free trade, and who prefer the use of articles of home manufacture, and of home production, to any article of the same description which can be imported from foreign nations. They are the real friends of the British people who employ home labourers in the production of most articles consumed by them, and who purchase from foreign states only those commodities which cannot be grown nor manufactured in the British empire; who confine their annual expenditure as much as possible within the United Kingdom, and who expend not their money on foreign labourers, unless for some luxuries which cannot be produced here; who, in short, are neither Quakers, crusaders against landed property, nor wandering citizens of the world, but who are in the most extensive meaning of the word the true protectors of native industry, talent, and capital. This is the only plan by which prosperity can be restored to the British empire; and by the reduction of the present rates of duty imposed on manufactured barley the Minister will at all events make a good beginning in again leading the people into a rational mode of acting in their future commercial relations with foreign nations.

During the last month no improvement has occurred in the value of oats; but prices previously were so very low, that to cause any additional depression in them would have certainly been an operation of considerable difficulty. The consumption has not in any manner fallen away in its usual amount, and consequently the demand has always cleared away the weekly supplies, which however have not generally been extremely abundant, though still in the value of them no improvement has been the result of this state at all the large oat markets throughout Great Britain; any deficiency in supply which may have at any time existed being amply provided for, under the present liberal system of our corn laws, by oats of foreign growth. This is the low condition into which the cultivators of oats have latterly been placed by the reduction of those import duties by which their capital invested in agricultural operations was previously protected from the interference of foreign oat-growers in all our oat-markets of consumption. To the farmers in the North of England, and throughout the principal counties in Scotland, this circumstance is not now of the same importance which it would have been thirty years ago; because agricultural improvements in those districts have made, during that period, wonderful progress indeed. In Lincolnshire and its neighbouring counties, for instance, the cultivation of wheat has so much superseded that of oats, that instead of supplying the London market, as was formerly the case, with at least one third of the oat consumption there, the same market is this year positively swamped by heavy sup-

plies of north-country wheat and flour. During the last quarter of a century, however, the gradually decreasing supplies of British oats in all our markets for their consumption have been most amply made up by the gradually increasing imports from Ireland. Until this season this circumstance has been the great spur to agricultural improvement in the sister kingdom, and most admirably have the Irish landed interest and their tenantry availed themselves of the road to prosperity thus presented to them for the proper cultivation of their beautiful and prolific country. By the progress made in Ireland in the production of oats in particular, the value of that article has been, comparatively speaking, kept low in Great Britain; whilst the prices obtained for their products have not only remunerated the growers, but also given them the means to pay for still more important improvements. An entire stop, however, is put, for the present at all events, to these most cheering prospects to Irish agriculturists, for at the present average prices of Irish oats in Great Britain this most valuable article cannot be produced by their farmers. Oats cannot be grown on the western coast of Ireland, rent of land and farming expences, preparing them on the kiln to stand a lengthened voyage, and the expense of cartage to and shipment in an Irish port paid, to which likewise must be added freight and sea insurance to London, and the heavy charges made on them in the British markets of sale, if they are for the future to be sold here at from 14s. to 16s. per quarter on the average, as has been the case during the present corn season. If the public generally, or one class in our society, could receive even the slightest benefit from the deterioration in the value of agricultural property which is now in progress, some excuse might exist for the violent alterations made in our former custom-house duties on the importation of foreign agricultural products of all descriptions. But to sacrifice the interests of the multitude to the aggrandisement of a few individuals, to transfer even the smallest portion of the productive labour in growing oats for the consumption of Great Britain from Irish to foreign agricultural labourers, and to permit foreign flags and foreign seamen to participate in the advantages in our oat carrying trade, at the expense of our commercial navy, is a policy which is perfectly unintelligible to common minds, although to those who are gifted with uncommon sense it may be perfectly comprehensible. In the meantime a more favourable month for oat sowing than the last has been, is not in the memory of any living farmer, and the prospect of a large crop towards the close of last month caused a farther decline of 1s. per quarter, which previously was considered to be impossible, in the value of the finest descriptions of this previously too much depressed article of agricultural produce.

COMPARATIVE PRICES of GRAIN.

WEEKLY AVERAGES by the Imp. Quarter, from the Gazette, of Friday last, March 24th, 1843.		AVERAGES from the corresponding Gazette in the last year, Friday, March 25th, 1842.	
	s. d.		s. d.
WHEAT	47 6	WHEAT	58 4
BARLEY	27 11	BARLEY	26 6
OATS	17 4	OATS	18 4
RYE	26 10	RYE	33 5
BEANS	26 8	BEANS	29 9
PEAS	28 6	PEAS	32 0

CURRENCY PER IMP. MEASURE.

MARCH 27.

WHEAT, Essex and Kent, red	42	48	White 46	50	52
Irish	40	42	Do.	40	44
Old, red	—	—	Do.	—	—
RYE, old	32	—	New	32	—
BARLEY, Grinding 21 27 Malting	30	33	Chevalier 30	34	
Irish	21	23	Bere .19	20	22
MALT, Suffolk and Norfolk	56	58	Brown..	50	54
Kingston and Ware	56	60	Chevalier 60	—	
OATS, Yorksh. & Lincolnsh., feed	18	20 22	Potato..	23	24
Youghall and Cork black	15	17	Cork, white 16	19	
Dublin	15	17	Westport 18	19	
Waterford, white	15	17 18	Black ..	15	17
Newry	18	19			
Galway	14	15 16			
Scotch feed	21	—	Potato..	21	24
Clonmel	16	17 18	Limerick 17	18 19	
Londonderry	18	19	Sligo ..	18	19
BEANS, Tick, new	23	26	Old ...	30	32
PEAS, Grey	27	29	Maple ..	26	28
White	30	31	Boilers .	30	32
FLOUR, Town-made 42 45 Suffolk 34 36 pr sk. of 280 lbs.					
Stockton and Norfolk, 34 36					

FOREIGN GRAIN AND FLOUR IN BOND.

WHEAT, Dantzic	—	—
Hamburg	32	34 } nominal.
Rostock	32	35
BARLEY	20	—
OATS, Brew	15	17 Feed... 12 14
BEANS	14	15 19
PEAS	20	22
FLOUR, American, per brl	22	24 Baltic .. — 22

IMPERIAL AVERAGES.

Week ending	Wheat.	Barley.	Oats.	Rye.	Beans.	Peas.
Feb. 11th	47 5	27 1	16 11	30 1	27 5	30 1
18th	47 11	27 1	17 0	27 9	27 0	29 5
25th	48 6	27 2	17 1	28 4	26 11	30 1
March 4th	48 3	27 4	17 3	29 0	26 7	28 6
11th	48 1	27 7	17 2	28 4	26 6	29 4
18th	47 6	27 11	17 4	26 10	26 8	28 6
Aggregate average of the six weeks which regulates the duty	47 11	27 4	17 2	28 5	26 10	29 4
Duties payable in London till Wednesday next inclusive, and at the Outports till the arrival of the mail of that day from London ..	20 0	9 0	8 0	11 6	11 6	11 6
Do. on grain from British possessions out of Europe	5 0	2 0	2 0	1 6	1 0	1 0

Account shewing the Quantities of Corn, Grain, Meal, and Flour, imported into the United Kingdom, in the month ended the 5th Mar., 1843; the Quantities upon which Duties have been paid for Home Consumption during the same month, and the Quantities remaining in Warehouse at the close thereof.

Foreign Grain and Flour.	Quantity imported.	Quantity entered for consumption.	Quantity remaining in warehouse.
	qrs. bush.	qrs. bush.	qrs. bush.
Wheat, from British Possessions	1206 0	1095 3	4443 4
Peas, from do.	1 0	1 0	579 3
Indian Corn, do.	—	55 3	1221 6
Wheat, foreign	8026 4	754 6	221248 6
Barley, do.	10 0	1124 0	51651 0
Oats, do.	822 2	846 2	51683 2
Rye, do.	—	—	1026 6
Peas, do.	533 2	1701 6	20521 0
Beans, do.	0902 2	2598 6	112153 7
Indian Corn, do.	—	203 0	12681 1
Buck Wheat, do. ..	—	—	—
Malt	—	—	—
	cwts. qrs.lbs.	cwts. qrs.lbs.	cwts. qrs.lbs.
Flour and Meal from British Possessions	1489 3 4	14738 1 3	60985 0 21
Flour & Meal, foreign	2125 0 15	38 1 16	42901 3 13

PRICES OF SEEDS.

MARCH 27.

Clover, English, red	42	60	white 44	62 per cwt.
Flemish, pale	44	48	fine.. 52	58
New Hamburg	none		do.. 42	64
Old do.	42	45	do.. none	
French	42	50	do.. none	}
Linseed, English, sowing	48	56		
Baltic	—	—	crushing 42	45 per qr.
Mediter. & Odessa	45	46		
Large, foreign	—	—		
Coriander	10	16	old.... 16	20 per cwt.
Mustard, brown, new	9	11	white.. 9	10s. 6d p.bush
Trefoil, new	18	21	old.... 12	16
Rapeseed, English new.. 32l. 35l. per ton.				
Linseed Cakes, English.. 9l. 10s. to 10l. per 1000				
Do. Foreign.. 5l. 10s. to 6l. per ton.				
Rapeseed Cakes	5l. 5s. to 5l. 10s.			
Hempseed, small	35	38	large .. 40	48 per qr.
Rye Grass, English	30	42	Scotch 18	40 }
Tares, winter	—	—	New 4s 0d 5s 0d p.bush.	
Canary, new	62	63	fine 64	65 per qr.
Carraway, old	—	—	new 42	44

PRICES OF HOPS.

BOROUGH, MONDAY, March 27.

We have a steady demand for Hops of the last year's growth, at last week's prices. The stock on hand has become very limited.

		s.		s.
Pockets, 1842, Wealds		80	to	90 per cwt.
...	East Kent.,	100	—	140 ..
..	Sussex	77	—	84 ..
..	Farnham..	140	—	150 ..
Pockets, 1841, Wealds, good		60	—	70 ..
..	East Kent choice	70	—	80 ..
Bags, 1841,	do.	60	—	60 ..
Pockets, Old olds,	do.	30	—	50 ..

POTATO MARKET.

SOUTHWARK WATERSIDE, March 27.

The supply of Potatoes to the waterside, during the past week, amounts to 3,770 tons, viz.—From Yorkshire, 1,305 tons; Scotland, 1,155; Devons, 440; Kent and Essex, 290; Jersey and Guernsey, 405; Wisbeach, 175. Our sales earlier in the week were dull, owing to the mild weather, but the recent change to cold easterly winds being more beneficial to sales, and preventing fresh arrivals, will no doubt cause the demand to be more active, and a continuance would probably lead to improvement in the price of the best samples.

	Per ton.		Per ton.
	s. s.		s. s.
York Reds	60 to 70	Jersey Blues	— to 50
Scotch do.	40 to 60	Guernsey do.	— to 45
Devons, early	50 to 55	Yorkshire Prince	
Ditto, late	— to 60	Regents	45 to 50
Kent & Essex Whites	45 to 50	Ditto Shaws, for	
Kent Kidneys	— to 55	planting	— to 60
Wisbeach do.	— to 50		

ERRATUM.

TO THE EDITOR OF THE FARMER'S MAGAZINE.

SIR,—On reading the letter in the *Farmer's Magazine* which I addressed to you on the subject of Mr. Smart's essay, I find that you have, by mistake, described the figure as representing the work performed by the "turn-wrist plough", as to represent that performed by the "fixed-wrist plough," and *vice versa*. I would feel obliged by your taking an early opportunity to correct the error.

I have the honour to remain, sir,

Your obedient servant,

HARRY FLOWERDEW.

Suffolk, March 3, 1843.

Printed by Joseph Rogerson, 24, Norfolk-street, Strand, London.

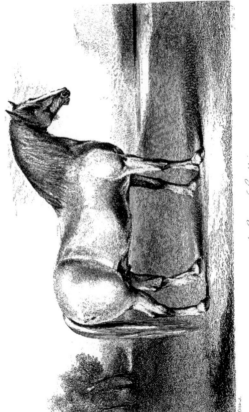

A Cart Stallion.

London Published by Josiah Rogerson, 39, Fleet Side Street, Norwich, May 1, 1848.

Fairway,
A Celebrated Yorkshire
The Property of Mr. John Kilvington, Cottingham, Yorkshire.

London, Published by Joseph Rogerson, 24, Norfolk Street, Strand. May, 1. 1843.

THE FARMER'S MAGAZINE.

MAY, 1843.

No. 5.—Vol. VII.]   [Second Series.

PLATE I.

A Cart Stallion, five years old, the property of C. Neeld, Esq., M.P., of Grittleton, near Chippenham, exhibited at the meeting of the Royal Agricultural Society, held at Bristol, in July last, to which a prize of thirty sovereigns was awarded, as the best horse for agricultural purposes.

PLATE II.

HARKAWAY.

(For Description see page 328.)

ON THE THEORY AND GENERAL, SPECIAL, CHEMICAL, AND PRACTICAL ACTIONS AND USES OF THE WATER OF IRRIGATION; MORE PARTICULARLY AS THEY APPLY TO THE WATER MEADOWS OF ENGLAND.

An intimate acquaintance with, and due appreciation of, the beneficial uses of irrigation we are enabled to trace back to very ancient times. This, like many other primitive practices, must have sprung from an intimate observation of the operations of nature, and her inexhaustible and ever-ready resources for promoting fertility and increase in otherwise hopeless conditions of soil and climate. It is only what might have been expected then, that, among the earliest authentic records of the human race, we find allusions to this practice. In the sacred writings we are told that Egypt was the great storehouse of Asia, and that in times of scarcity and famine the surrounding tribes and nations resorted to her granaries; for even at that period she was distinguished for the cultivation of the arts and sciences, and in a remarkable degree for the perfection of her agriculture—the venerable parent of all art and refinement; and, notwithstanding all the revolutions she has undergone during so many ages, her fertile territory still teems with luxuriant abundance, so deep does agricultural industry strike her vivacious and indestructible root.

But the great resource on which all this fertility

depends is copious irrigation. What a striking example on a mighty scale is afforded, in this luxuriant territory, of the benefit of inundating the parched and thirsty soil! Laden and turbid with his rich burden of mineral and organic wealth, gathered in his lengthened course through central Africa and the luxuriant valleys of Abyssinia, and swollen by the heavy rains poured into his increasing flood by a thousand streams, from a thousand hills and plains, the beneficent Nile rises proudly over his level banks, and scatters wealth and plenty with bounteous and unsparing liberality over the length and breadth of this favoured land. So that the idolatrous natives in their blind and enthusiastic gratitude were fain to become worshippers, and deified the spirit of this mighty stream.

In those years in which the waters of this mighty river did not reach a certain height the *miri*, a tribute, was not exacted—a sufficient evidence of the importance attached to this periodical phenomenon. For before the flooding. Egypt is but a plain of arid dust. On the rising of the river, it assumes the appearance of a boundless lake, and, on the subsidence of the waters, it is

speedily clothed with verdure and bloom, a luxurious paradise of voluptuous beauty and smiling
loveliness.

During the autumnal season the Delta is laid
completely under water; and this is easily accomplished by means of numerous canals, the principal branches supported at the public charge. Rice,
which forms the chief support of the greater proportion of the human race, and which cannot be
cultivated without irrigation, was originally introduced by the Saracens, and is peculiarly adapted
to these low grounds, on which it is sown in June,
after the soil has been softened by the water, so as
to resemble the consistence of mud; and being
laid completely under water, the grain grows luxuriantly in that element, and yields a harvest in
October. None but the courser varieties of grain
produce, such as the *Holcus dhourra*, can, in this
land of sunshine, be cultivated with scanty irrigation. Wheat and barley are grown on the higher
grounds, but, even to these heights, the fertilizing
element is raised by machinery, where at all possible, by the persevering labour of man and brute.
It is clear that without water this productive land
would comparatively and speedily become a
desert.

Let us now look further east, and regard the
magnificent products of Hindostan; and, wherever
water abounds, we are unfailingly refreshed with
evergreen shade and perennial luxuriance. Watered
by copious streams, even with her sandy soil, Hindostan must ever surpass in richness and variety of
vegetation, all the most favoured regions of the
temperate zone. The original covering of sand
with which she is overspread, along the courses of
her mighty rivers and numberless streams, by inundation and culture, has been covered over with a
thin layer of fertile clay; and this is the case in the
rich tract of Bengal, watered by the Ganges and
Burhampooter. The Indus performs a like service
in the west. We have noticed that rice, the great
staple of this favoured land, cannot be cultivated
without irrigation; so that, without a copious
supply of water, India, like Egypt, would comparatively and speedily become a desert.

Let us turn again in the opposite direction to the
naked hordes of central Africa; to those regions
where the plough has never reached—for we cannot much regard the Niger expedition—and we
shall find that by the mere scratching of a hoe, the
only implement of culture, the thankful soil, refreshed by copious, and in some cases but scanty,
irrigation, freely yields the grateful tribute of an
abundant harvest to its rude and unskilful lord
and husbandman. Of the truth of this statement
the ample harvests of rice on many parts of the
banks of the Niger bear ample testimony. We
shall pass over the noble rivers and countless
canals of China in the east; the South American,
Amazon, and Paraguay rivers, with their fertilizing
and sea-like floods; and the Missouri and Missis.
sippi of the northern division of the mighty west.
down to the Sandwich Islander of the Pacific with
the fruitful *Tvro-root*, his chief subsistence, and
the produce of irrigation, and shall content ourselves with stating, preparatory to a consideration
of the beneficial uses and modes of operation of
this fertilizing process in different climates and
different soils, that the art of irrigation is more or
less practised in all the countries of Southern
Europe; and that in Piedmont and the Austro-
Lombardian valley of the Po, containing the magnificent ancient cities of Milan and Venice, this

art is still pursued with surprising energy and success; and that there the moment a spring is discovered, it is appropriated by the lord of the soil,
as would be a precious jewel, and its waters forthwith directed to various distant surfaces in tiny
rills, which are apportioned by the scientific engineer with scrupulous accuracy, and paid for even
by the day, or hour, or quantity, like any other
precious, because familiar and indispensable, commodity of domestic consumption. The gigantic
canals, and aqueducts, and triumphal feats of engineering, for the purposes of extensive irrigation
in this European Paradise, may be still viewed,
amongst all the splendid relics of art, as some of
the most enduring and honourable monuments of
the palmy days of the once mighty Queen of the
Sea—republican Venice.

We have seen then that the art of irrigation is
very ancient; that it is practised in temperate as
well as in tropical regions; and we shall now proceed, step by step, to the scientific consideration
of the subject, as regards its uses, and the various
modes and beneficial principles of its operation.

When the water of irrigation deposits a perceptible sediment, and this by accumulating forms a
distinct layer of rich soil on the surface, we may
at once ascribe its enriching effects in a great measure to this deposit of mixed mineral and organic
matter; making due allowance for the refreshing
coolness and restorative general effect of the presence and contact of the element under a tropical
sun. In our own island in the estuary of the Hum-
ber the brackish water, where the salt and fresh
waters meet, is conducted for miles inland, and
deposits yearly nearly a foot of rich fertilizing sediment, but its beneficial effects, of course, decreasing the further the water flows inland. This
is termed warping, and is practised with great
profit on the Don, the Trent, and the Ouse rivers
in England, and in various other localities of
Europe.

But when the water contains no visible or sensible sedimentary matter, but appears perfectly clear
and limped, it is used with great success for the
purposes of irrigation. In the watered meadows
of England, (Gloucester, Wilts, &c.) it is made to
pass in a continuous and uninterrupted flow over
every part of the surface, and often, having performed its fertilizing office to one surface, it is introduced to another, and finally permitted freely to
escape and be restored to the parent brook, or
river, at a lower level.

In this way the waters of natural springs, and
brooks, and rivers are used in this and other
countries of the temperate zone; and it shall be
our special purpose to enquire how these limpid
waters are enabled to communicate and dispense
with such facility and certainty such wonderful
increase.

In tropical climates, and hot countries generally,
due allowance must be made for the general refreshing influence of the cool current, and indeed in
such circumstances nothing seems necessary but
a copious supply of water everywhere to ensure fertility. But it must be borne in mind, that in warm climates, where every material atom seems instinct with
life—animal, insect, or vegetable, no portion of the soil
is deficient from the death and decay of these countless animated hordes—these constant but epheme-
ral myriads—in a sufficient abundance of the organic elements necessary to support the most luxuriant vegetation.

There are many characteristic points of difference

arising from climatic influence, and these characteristic points of difference, and other attendant circumstances and conditions, peculiar to tropical climates, must ever preserve a marked distinction in the general and specific actions of the practice of irrigation, in producing beneficial results, and as a means of insuring fertility and increase in such climates, to what is observed in the various climates of the temperate zone. Our present object is, however, not to give any particular explanation of these differences of action, but to endeavour to show, on scientific principles, how we are to account for the extraordinary and magic fertility produced by the so frequently perfectly clear and limpid current of the water meadow of England.

In the present state of advancement of the science of agricultural chemistry, it is held to be proved, by satisfactory analysis, that all soils, fertile in grain or herbage, must contain, in some form, sufficient supplies of certain elementary substances, organic and inorganic. It will become necessary, therefore, before proceeding much further, to show what these necessary elementary bodies are believed to be.

The organic parts of plants are composed of four elementary bodies, in various proportions; and these are named carbon, oxygen, hydrogen, and nitrogen; the first compact and solid, the others gaseous, and the last being present in proportionably smaller quantity than the rest. The presence in the soil, therefore, of decomposing organic (animal or vegetable) substances, in sufficient abundance to supply these elements in the necessary proportions, is absolutely indispensable to form a fertile soil; although a considerable proportion of the organic matter of vegetables is believed to be derived from the atmosphere in the form of carbonic acid, &c., the common air we breathe being composed

	By measure.	By weight.
Nitrogen	77·5	77·5
Oxygen	21·0	23·32
Carbonic acid	0·08	0·10
Watery vapour	1·42	1·03
	100 parts.	100 pts.

The portion derived from the atmosphere is obtained by absorption by the leaves direct, and the various combinations formed by the action of the atmospheric influences in promoting the decomposition of the organic matter of the soil, and in aiding recomposition, But, on combustion, all this organic matter disappears, and an ash is left, which, on examination, is found to be composed of various mineral or inorganic elements; the proportions and numbers of these substances present varying in different individuals, according to order, genus, and species, though less considerably the more nearly in relationship the individuals stand to each other. The ordinary mineral substances found in vegetables—either oxygenated, i.e. in combination with oxygen gas, or with one another—are those given in the various tables a little further on; though some others do occur, but so rarely as scarcely to merit notice.

It is natural to conclude, then, that a soil, to be considered fertile, must be capable of supplying all the elementary bodies, in some form, to the vegetation on its surface in healthful abundance; and experience amply confirms the investigations and results of scientific enquiry. It has been proved from careful analysis, that the mineral components cannot vary much, and for a long time, in a plant of a particular species, without producing attenuation, sickliness, and death; and that all the more

valuable products from the most celebrated soils are nearly alike in chemical constitution. That different plants require different soils; and this is proved beyond dispute by the natural distribution of plants over the different formations within the limits of the different zones, and even from their distribution within the small geological circle of our own islands. Without going too far into this subject, but just saying so much as appears to be necessary for our purpose, we shall presently proceed to exhibit, among the tables we have promised, a detailed analysis of a German soil, found particularly favourable to the growth of herbage, and producing a vegetation celebrated for its powers of fattening stock (p. 320). The difference in climate between our islands and this part of Germany can have no very important influence; and, if any, more in degree than in principle.

Having premised so much, we shall proceed to enquire whether it be possible that the clear and crystal-like fluid, with which we are all so familiar, can by possibility supply in its volume any and which of those various substances, or their elements, included in Sprengell's analysis of a fertile grass soil, which will be found a few pages forward; and we may just turn to, and consider it for a moment. (p. 320.)

We shall first proceed, then, with a view to this discovery, with a necessary preliminary enquiry, and endeavour to trace the sources from which the fluid of irrigation, and a supply of water in general, is permanently obtained.

The whole fresh water of our rivers is derived from the immense reservoir of the ocean, which covers three-fifths of the surface of our globe, with the trifling secondary exceptions to be afterwards noticed. This is accomplished by the process of evaporation, which proceeds with greater or less rapidity as the temperature of the atmosphere rises or falls. Pure water consists of the gasses oxygen and hydrogen in chemical combination.

Relative proportions necessary for forming water of the gasses oxygen and hydrogen in 100 parts:

	By measure.			By weight.		
Oxygen	33·34	..	1	88·9	..	8
Hydrogen	66·66	..	2	11·1	..	1
Mixed	100·00	..	3	100·0	..	9
Combined	66·66	..	2	100·0	..	9

Thus we see, that in combining to form water, these gasses contract in bulk.

But, from the relation of its component gasses to heat, water is easily converted into vapour by expansion, and with greater rapidity as the temperature of the atmosphere is increased; and thus, the warmer the air becomes, the more capacity does it acquire for containing moisture. The atmospheric air is composed as follows:

Composition of atmospheric air.

	By measure.		By weight.
Nitrogen	77·5	80	77·5
Oxygen	21·0	20	23·32
Carbonic acid	0·08	—	0·10
Watery vapour	1·42	—	1·03
	100 parts.		100 pts.

And 100 cubic inches of air of the earth's surface, at the temperature 32°, 50°, and 60° Fah., are capable of containing of watery vapour:

Watery vapour, Fah.	32°	0·137 grains
"	50°	0·247 "
"	60°	0·339 "

However, the quantity of vapour may be less at this temperature, though more would be condensed and fall as rain, or the purest natural water. Near the ocean the air has been found to contain a trace of muriatic acid; and near large towns, from the combustion of fuel, sulphurous acid, sulphuric acid, sulphate of ammonia, and even charcoal in suspension, and in the neighbourhood of marshes those pestilential vapours so detrimental to animal existence; but these are merely local and accidental.

But the waters of the ocean, besides the constituents of watery vapour and pure water, which can be procured by the artificial distillatory process alone, are known to hold in solution certain other compounds; and the question arises, what becomes of these, and what are they? The composition of salt water is found to be in the following cases—

By Dr. Murray's examination of the water of the Frith of Forth, it was found to contain, in 10,000 parts, 303 of saline matter in the following proportions:

Common salt .... 220·01
Sulphate of soda .... 33·16
Muriate of magnesia .... 42·08
Muriate of lime .... 7·84

Total quantity of saline matter　303·09

Dr. Marcet found the composition of the waters of the Atlantic to be as follows:

Water .... 478·420 grains, or	480·500ths.	
Common salt .... 13·3	13·	"
Sulphate of soda .. 2·33	2·	"
Muriate of lime .. 0·995	1·	"
Muriate of magnesia 4·955	4·	"
500 grains	500	

Dr. Marcet also found the waters of the lake Asphaltites, or the Dead Sea, to contain in 100 grains:

Sulphate of lime .... 0·054 grains
Muriate of soda .... 10·676 "
Muriate of lime .... 3·800 "
Muriate of magnesia .... 10·100 "

During the process of evaporation all the saline matter is left behind, and the watery vapour—composed of oxygen and hydrogen—ascends in vapour, from the influence of heat and the repulsive principle.

The evaporation goes on also from the surface of all solid bodies as well, which contain water. Thus the watery vapour ascends from the ocean, and is wafted along the atmosphere; and, whenever it encounters a diminished temperature in its progress through the air, it is immediately condensed, and, from its acquired gravity by coudensation, it is precipitated as dew on the surface of objects, or from a greater height as rain, sleet, snow, or hail, according to the precise degree of reduced temperature thus encountered in its ærial flight. As dew it is deposited in sparkling brilliants on the verdant leaf and bud, which in wellknown circumstances part quickly with their acquired heat by radiation. From the surface of the earth thus bedewed, or radiant and sparkling with rain or snow, or hail-clad, the process of evaporation is resumed; so that it is in constant progress from the surface of all bodies which contain water. But this supply, which may be well called secondary in every sense, must be very inconsiderable, even including what is derived from fresh water pools and lakes, when compared with that derived from the vast ocean.

The ocean and other vapours, being condensed in their course through the air and deposited and distributed over the surface of the earth, in the manner and from the causes we have been describing, must necessarily either remain on the surface, or sink below it and disappear.

When they descend, condensed and in the form of rain-water, and remain on the surface, it is of course owing to its being of an impenetrable nature, by which they are prevented from percolating freely through it, and they pass along any convenient descending level, gradually acquiring force as they proceed, until they block up some valley and form a lake, either with or without an outlet, as it may happen, and, if without any outlet, like the Caspian Sea. The surface of the Caspian, which is the largest known lake without an outlet, is 334 feet below the level of the Black Sea; and the Dead Sea of Judæa, also without an outlet, is similarly depressed, its surface level being below that of the Mediterranean in its neighbourhood, and of course much more below the higher level of the Red Sea. Lake Aral, which seems to have been at one time connected with the Caspian—a tract of land of little more than 80 miles intervening, and the ends of these seas being very shallow where they approach each other—is, next to the Caspian, the greatest inland collection of water in western Asia, receiving the two rivers Oxus and Jaxartes, and having no visible outlet. When these lakes have rivers proceeding from them, their waters are quickly restored to the ocean; but when they have none, the evaporation from the surface keeps them at a pretty uniform level, and prevents their overflowing—being made to equal the supply from their tributaries.

When the surface is porous, the rains, as they descend, sink down and re appear either in the form of springs or rivers. When the water, in seeking its way, suddenly meets with an obstruction, it boils up in the form of a spring. Where it meets with a hollow or convenient channel, it is formed into a river—in both cases restoring its comparatively tiny flood to the great source from whence it came. In some cases—in flat situations on the earth's surface, when the descending vapours can find no escape downwards, or a convenient channel and level of escape—their retention and stagnation produce shallow ponds and marshes, exhaling pestilence and death.

The vapour from the sea has, no doubt, sometimes been found to contain a trace of muriatic acid gas, and rain and snow-water sometimes contain a trace of muriate of soda and muriate of lime. But we have shown the precise composition of the atmosphere, and we have mentioned that it often contains foreign accidental substances. From this it may be naturally concluded, that these watery vapours, derived from evaporation from the surface of the ocean, lakes, and from other sources, in passing through the medium of the air to the earth's surface, must be impregnated, in some measure, with any elementary or compound substances with which they have been in contact; and analysis proves the truth of this conclusion.

We find rain and snow-water — the purest quality that can be obtained from natural sources —when procured near towns, containing in solution the various gases and vapours—exhalations from animal and vegetable decomposing substances

—which abound in such situations; and from the roofs of houses, &c., it is always impure, from holding in solution the various substances set free by the combustion of fuel; but even when caught in the country, before it comes in contact with the ground, it is found to be impregnated with the elementary gases of the atmosphere, which we have shown to be oxygen, nitrogen, and carbonic acid. But various other substances—for instance, nitric acid, a most virulent poison—have been detected in rain-water. This substance, of such a deadly and corrosive nature that it immediately decomposes and destroys all animal and vegetable substances with which it comes in contact, and is found in the air during thundery weather, is formed by the atmospheric air being momentarily subjected to the agency of the lightning-flash—to the magic influence of electricity. The air we breathe is by the electric agency instantaneously converted into a virulent poison, and, as rain generally accompanies a thunder-storm, the nitric acid just formed is washed out by the rain and deposited on the ground, where it becomes, by forming various combinations with the elements of the soil, a fertilizing agent, instead of an insatiable destroyer of animal and vegetable life. This wonderful phenomenon—this Protean transmutation—is explained by the fact that the two gases, oxygen and nitrogen, forming almost the whole bulk of the air we breathe, are, in the atmosphere, merely in a state of *mechanical mixture*; but under the influence of the electric spark they become *chemically combined*; and thus simply is the change effected. This is one of the many startling truths which science has disclosed. The vaporous exhalations, too, in very hot weather, when evaporation is very active, are often tainted with traces of the substances which afforded them, and at such seasons have their effect. Thus we find, that before even touching the surface of the earth, the purest natural waters of evaporation become impregnated with foreign substances, and are not in reality by any means so pure as their limpid and sparkling appearance would lead us to suppose.

When talking of rain-water, we may mention, rather as a matter of curiosity than otherwise, in our zone, that the salutary effects of aqueous vapours on vegetation—so necessary indeed to organic existence—are in some situations still further modified by their chemical qualities. In the vicinity of the Caspian Sea we find salt rains and dews, owing to the vapours which are exhaled from the soil, and which are believed in a great measure to contribute to those saline efflorescences which are overspreading the fabled fertility of Persia; and the salt fogs of Jutland, nearer home, are destructive to trees, without doing any injury to the grassy herbage. Substances, approaching nearly to animal and vegetable, have been detected in rain, colouring it variously—sometimes even red like blood. Sometimes sulphur is present, and dry fogs frequently occur which contain no moisture, and, having been observed to occur contemporaneously with volcanic eruptions, have been referred to this cause, and are said to contain the vapours and ashes rejected by these great safety-valves of creation.

But, if this be the case, how very much more impure must water become after it has been brought into contact with the various elementary and compound bodies on the surface of the globe. We shall proceed then to remark, that spring water, which comes from a great depth, and reaches the surface after draining through various strata and dissimilar layers of earth, even in the highest and most rocky situations, where it meets merely with almost insoluble quartz and beds of sand, or granite rock, is never so pure even as rain or snow-water, but contains carbonate of lime or sulphate, a little muriate of lime, sulphates of soda or potassa, a little muriate of soda, or some magnesia. In spring or well water the sulphates and carbonates predominate. The alkalies have been found to be present in larger quantities in river water, and the earths, more particularly lime, in spring water. As carbonate and sulphate of lime abound in nature among the various geological strata, the water rising from any depth must come in contact with some of these calcareous strata; but, though it is undeniable that sulphate of lime is sparingly soluble, and carbonate insoluble in water, unless it should contain carbonic acid, yet, from what we already know of the composition of the atmosphere, we are prepared to answer, that any description of water which has been flowing in contact with the atmosphere, and more particularly if it have drained far through earthy strata, where it would have, of necessity, occasionally met with decomposing animal and vegetable substances, cannot be destitute of carbonic acid, which such vegetable and animal substances in the progress of decomposition give out in abundance; and, thus impregnated, it must therefore be capable of holding the first-mentioned substances in solution, in proportion to the quantity of carbonic acid it contains. We shall presently show that water is capable of absorbing its own bulk of carbonic acid. The most abundant substance brought out by abrasion and solution from the crust of the earth is lime, which is frequently deposited in the form of tuffa, and many excavations observed in limestone masses have originated from this agency and cause; and frequently from the solution and abstraction of gypsum or rock-salt, and other soluble substances from various formations, such considerable changes of interior structure have been wrought, as to occasion subsidences—the superincumbent strata yielding over the subterranean hollows.

We shall now say something of the character and properties of river water. River water is frequently muddy, particularly during and for sometime after floods, containing earthy particles in mechanical suspension. It is stated by Gerard that the annual floods of the Nile had raised the surface of Upper Egypt about 6 feet 4 inches since the commencement of the Christian era, or 4 inches in a century. Where such large rivers enter the sea, triangular pieces of ground are formed called deltas; and these are more perceptible in lakes than even in land-locked seas like the Mediterranean, and more marked in such than in the open ocean, where the continuous progress of the deposition is interrupted by currents. The deltas of the other Mediterranean rivers, the Rhine and the Po, show a yearly perceptible increase; and we need only mention the magnificent ocean delta formations of the Mississippi, the Orinoco, and the Ganges, to illustrate forcibly the surprising transporting power of river currents, and the extraordinary transformations which their increasing agency is silently working on the face of our globe.

But even when flowing over beds of quartz and gravel, it is still found to be more or less impregnated with foreign substances, yet being derived chiefly from melting snow and rain water, it contains less lime than spring or well water. It is thus enabled to dissolve more easily and perfectly common soap; and is thus so far distinguished from spring or well water, which, containing much carbonic acid, is capable of holding in solution, as we have seen, both sulphate and carbonate of lime. River water then is familiarly called soft, from this quality of dissolving soap with facility; spring water hard, as it is deficient in this quality. But numerous springs, we will be told, flow into and partially fill the river channels, and must, in such cases, tend to render the water hard. But it has been ascertained beyond dispute that, when spring water has been flowing for some time in contact with the air, it absorbs a large portion of it, and gradually, at same time, deposits a large proportion of its earthy matter, becoming proportionally soft by the change, as the earthy matter is precipitated. The water of the Clyde in Scotland was found to contain in an imperial pint, weighing 8750 grains, and measuring 34½ cubic inches,

Saline matter .... 1.04 { Muriate of magnesia / Sulphate of soda / Muriate of soda (common salt)

Silica (or earth of flint) 0.1 { Carbonic acid 1-20th / Gases 1-35th of its volume { Common air 19-20ths

The water of marshes and pools or ponds is generally impregnated with the various gases arising from vegetable and even animal decomposition.

Of the following tables, No. I. will show the exact quantities of various gases which water is capable of absorbing at the mean temperature and pressure of the atmosphere. As the temperature of the water is lowered down to freezing, or the pressure increased, the quantities absorbed by an equal bulk of water will be greater from the increased pressure or diminished temperature.

No. II. will show the elementary bodies composing the *organic* substance of all vegetables.

No. III. will show the organic substances found in the soil which are supposed to minister to the growth of vegetables.

No. IV. will show the elementary bodies most frequently met with in vegetables, and forming their *inorganic* substance.

No. V. will show the elements and elementary compounds which enter into the circulation of vegetables, and are afforded by their residue or ash after combustion, with character and properties of elements, and where found in nature.

No. I.

Table of the quantities of a few of the different gases which Water is capable of absorbing at the ordinary temperature and pressure of the atmosphere.

Of ammonia water absorbs .	670	times its own bulk
Muriatic acid..........	500	,,
Sulphurous acid	33	,,
Cyanogen	4½	,,
Chlorine..............	2	,,
Carbonic acid..........	Its own bulk.	
Nitrous oxide..........		,,
Sulphuretted hydrogen..		,,
Clossant gas	1-8th its own bulk.	
Oxygen	1-27th	,,
Nitric oxide	,,	,,
Nitrogen	1-64th	,,
Hydrogen	,,	,,
Carbonic oxide	,,	,,
&c., &c., &c., &c.		

No. II.

Table of elementary bodies composing the organic substance of all vegetables.

Name.	By whom discovered.	When.	Exists in Nature.
Oxygen ..	{ Priestly / Schecle }	1774	{ In air, water, earths, and all organic bodies, most abundant (gaseous).
Hydrogen..	Cavendish	1766	In water, all organic bodies, and some minerals (gaseous).
Nitrogen ..	Rutherford	1772	In air, organic bodies, and some minerals (gaseous).
Carbon ..	{ Known to / ancients. }		{ In organic bodies, air, in union with oxygen in form of carbonic acid, and some minerals (solid).

No. III.

Table of organic substances found in the soil, which are supposed to minister to the growth of vegetables.

NAME.　　　Character and Qualities.

HUMUS—Formed from decomposing vegetable matter.

MILD DITTO—If a soil be washed with water, colours the water brown, but does not sour it; evolves ammonia when headed with caustic potash or lime; and on combustion leaves an ash affording lime and magnesia (favourable to vegetation).

SOUR DITTO—If ditto ditto colours the water brown, and sours it, reddens litmus, a pigment of *parellus* (less favourable to vegetation).

COALY DITTO—If ditto ditto colours water faintly, ash affords little lime; occurs in poor soils, and is corrected by application of an alkali (very unfavourable to vegetation).

HUMIC ACID—Soluble in ammonia, of which water absorbs 670 times its own bulk, and carbonate of potash; on being exposed to air becomes carbonate, and gives out carbonic acid, of which water absorbs its own bulk. A most important element of the food of all vegetables. Composition in 100 parts—carbon 63, hydrogen 6, oxygen 31; and producing humates with various bases.

ULMIC ACID—Ditto, ditto, ditto, and producing ulmates, with ditto; composition—carbon 57, hydrogen 4¾, oxygen 38¼, in 100 parts.

CRENIC DITTO } —If a soil be washed with *hot*
APOCRENIC Do. } water, colours *hot* water brown, and are thus in union with two preceding acids and various bases; and being dried at 230° Fah., ulmates and humates left become insoluble, but crenates and apocrenates soluble in water; contain nitrogen; when they meet with lime in soil, give off ammonia and carbonic acid, water being capable of absorbing 670 times its own bulk of the former, and its own bulk of the latter.

MUDESOUS DITTO—Has a strong affinity for alumina, and in this state easily distributed by water, and very completely as an acid in solution.

N.B. Other acids occur, but it appears unnecessary to specify them.

No. IV.

Table of the elementary bodies most frequently met with in vegetables, and composing their inorganic substance.

Name.	Discovered by	When.	In combination with	And forming
Iodine	Courtois	1812	Metals	Iodides.
Sulphur	Known to ancients		Do.	Sulphurets.
Chlorine	Scheele	1774	Do.	Chlorides.
„			Hydrogen	Sulphuretted hydrogen.
„			Oxygen	Sulphuric acid.
Phosphorus	Brandt	1669	Do.	Phosphoric acid.
Potassium	Davy	1807	Do.	Potash.
„			Chlorine	Chloride of potassium.
Calcium	Do.	„	Do.	Chloride of calcium.
Sodium	Do.	„	Oxygen	Soda.
„			Chlorine	Common salt.
Aluminum	Wöler	1828	Oxygen	Alumina.
Silicium	Brezelius	1824	Do.	Silica.
Magnesium	Bussy	1830	Do.	Magnesia.
Iron	Known to ancients		Do.	Oxides.
Manganese	Guhn and Scheele	1774	Sulphur	Sulphurets.

No. V.

Table of elements and elementary compounds which enter into the circulation of vegetables, and are afforded by their residue or ash on combustion, with character and properties of elements, and where found in nature.

ELEMENT. }
NAME. } Character and Properties, and where found in Nature, and elementary compounds, &c.

IODINE—Solid, lead grey colour, heat converts into violet vapour; Davy found rather to assist vegetation; present in form of iodide of sodium in some salt springs, in water of Mediterranean, in sponges, oysters, and other shell-fish, sea weeds, but has not hitherto been detected in any of the crops of agriculture (slightly soluble in water).

SULPHUR—Native, yellow, solid; in native sulphuric acid, gypsum, heavy spar, alum, alumstone, iron pyrites, green vitriol, sulphurets of arsenic (realgar, orpiment), silver, copper, antimony, lead (galena), zinc (blende), quicksilver (cinnabar), bismuth, cobalt; and in small quantities in other minerals less frequently met with, and in springs; also sparingly in organic bodies, acids of sulphur (see Table II.); sulphurous acid, sulphuric acid, and sulphuretted hydrogen, have a great affinity for water, and are beneficial to clover and pulse, &c., crops (Sprengel, Chemic. ii., p. 355, says, sulphurous waters of irrigation produce luxuriant vegetation). Sulphates used as manures.

CHLORINE—Gas, Greenish yellow colour; in common salt (chloride of sodium), and of course sea water, salt lakes and springs, rock salt, sal ammoniac (muriate of ammonia), horn silver (muriate of silver); muriate of copper, horn quicksilver, and some rare ores of lead, and in animal substances sparingly, in sea weeds, has great affinity for water (see Table I); found by Davy to promote germination of seeds, and favours the growth of plants when it occurs in due proportions in the soil; very frequent in rocks of islands and in land near sea, being deposited by ocean exhalations and deposition of spray by the winds; combines with hydrogen, forming muriatic acid, has a great affinity as we have said for water, dissolving the alkalis and alkaline earths, and those substances which are insoluble, or but sparingly soluble, in water alone.

PHOSPHORUS—Solid, pale yellow, like wax, and burns in common air with pale blue flame visible in dark; in animals chiefly bones, wavellite (phosphate of alumina), apatite (phosphate of lime), bag iron ore, some other ores of iron, some ores of manganese, uranium, copper, lead; exposed to common air is converted into phosphoric acid, has a great affinity for water, and attracts moisture, and dissolves substances insoluble or sparingly soluble in water; unites with alkalis and earths, and forms phosphates, and generally diffused, in some form, through good soils, and necessary to healthful and profitable vegetation.

POTASSIUM—Metal, abundant in land vegetables, and in sea weeds and animals, mica, talc, felspar, chlorite, pumice, obsidian, soapstone, and other components of rocks, nitre, alumstone and soils, chloride, phosphate, nitrate, carbonate and sulphate of potash; very favourable to the growth of plants, and particularly to red clover, lucerne, esparsette, beans, peas, flax, potatoes, &c.; all soluble in water, or organic acids of the soil, and aid water powerfully as a solvent of other substances, and present in most fertile soils.

CALCIUM—Metal; in augite, hornblende, felspar, and other constituents of rocks, slates, clays, earth, earth of lime, marble, limestone, fluer spar, gypsum, apatite, garnet, asbestus, bones and shells of animals, &c., &c.; carbonate of lime present in all fertile soils, and most useful fertiliser known, and the most abundant earth after silica and alumina, and soluble in water containing carbonic acid; chloride and sulphuret of calcium detected in soils; sulphates of lime of general occurrence, and sometimes found free of water, as anhydrites, and soluble in organic acids of soil, and powerful fertilizing agent; nitrate of lime very soluble, and almost deliquescent; phosphate of lime found native masses in England, Bohemia, Spain, and Finland, and important to cruciferous and leguminous plants and others; present in many soils, soluble in water containing carbonic acid slightly, and in the acids of the soil; lime, an oxide of calcium, in the form of carbonate forms one-eighth of the crust of this globe.

Sodium—Metal, in sea weeds, land vegetables, and animals, sodalite, albite, pitchstone, pumice, obsidian, and other components of igneous rocks, nutron, sulphate of soda, nitrate of soda, borax, common salt (chloride of sodium), carbonate, sulphate, phosphate, sulphuret, and chloride, occur in soils, and are important agents in promoting fertility, soluble in water, water containing carbonic acid, or in the organic acids of the soil.

Aluminum—Metal, in corrundum, topaz, sapphire, emery, ruby, garnet, slates, clays, hornblende, asbestos, mica, felspar, chlorite, sulphate of alumina, vavellite (phosphate of alumina), alum, alum-stone, clay, iron ore, and in soils generally, alumina (oxide of aluminum), with silica (oxide of silicon), forms 6-8ths of crust of globe, and is called earth of clays, soluble in caustic potash or soda, and in most acids of soil ; the most abundant earth next to silica, and forming a large proportion of the common soil, and all mineral substances nearly on the face of the earth, sulphate of alumina deliquescent, phosphate of alumina (vavellite) sometimes occurs in soils, but difficult of detection ; alumina always present in considerable proportion in the best agricultural soils.

Silicon—Solid, resembling a metal, in quartz, opal, calcedony, flint, jasper, garnet, topaz, hyacinth, beryl, emerald, augete, felspar, hornblende, mica, soapstone chlorite, a component of the vegetable tissue, in most rocks, earth, and sands, some ores of iron, hot springs as the Geysers of Iceland, the most abundant element next to oxygen, silica (oxide of silicon) in combination with oxide of iron, &c., enters into composition of about 2-3rds of all the earthy minerals, very insoluble unless in combination with an alkali, and afterwards exposed to an acid action ; excessively plenty in rocks and soils, in combination with potash, soda, lime, magnesia, &c., &c., in the form of silicates, and these by the atmospheric action and influences, decompose, and afford silica, &c., in abundance in the soluble state for the wants of vegetables.

Magnesium—Metal, in augite, hornblende, asbestus talc, soapstone, chlorite, bitterspar, magnesian limestone, some clays, mica, carbonate of magnesia, boracite, magnesia in superabundance injurious to vegetation, particularly when free, or in loose combination with acids, and thus in the form of soluble salts, but necessary for the perfection of certain vegetables, particularly grain crops ; the salts of magnesia are very soluble, but carbonate of magnesia requires water containing carbonic acid for its solution ; silica, alumina. lime, magnesia, and oxide of iron, form 19-20ths of the crust of the globe.

Iron—Metal, in union with nickel, in meteoric iron, iron pyrates (sulphate of iron), speenlar iron ore, haematile, &c. (oxides of iron), clay iron ore (carbonate of iron), mixed with many other metallic ores, augite, talc, felspar, mica, hornblende, soapstone, chlorite, and most components of rocks and precious stones, earths in general, and sparingly in animals and vegetables, oxide and peroxide, soluble in water containing the acids of the soil ; the first oxide injuri-ous to vegetation, sulphate of iron very injurious, and corrected by lime and exposure to atmospheric air, carbonate of iron soluble in water containing carbonic acid, and not injurious.

Manganese—Metal ; oxide, sulphuret, sulphate, carbonate and chloride ; oxides, first light green, does not occur in nature, so far as known, unless combined, but second and third oxides present in most soils, insoluble in water, but soluble in organic acids of soil ; oxides and carbonates, however, slowly soluble in these acids, in sufficiency for the wants of vegetables.

When we compare these tables with one another, and consider the great quantity and fertilizing nature of the foreign matter contained in rain or snow, spring or well, or river water, we can easily imagine how powerfully these waters must act, by transporting and depositing, as they pass over the surface of the water meadow, their burden of precipitate. But when the temperature sinks to 32°, or the freezing point, at which water solidifies, the benefit of irrigation temporarily ceases, as the gases are expelled in the process of congelation ; and oxygen, that essential to animal and vegetable life, may often be detected forming little globules in the mass of ice, in which it has been entangled in its escape upwards. On comparing the tables which we have just given of gases and solids, organic and inorganic, elementary and compound, entering into plants, soluble in water, or water containing carbonic acid and the other organic acids of the soil—the results of decomposition constantly in progress in the soil—which might have been extended, with that also given showing the substances detected in the ashes of plants, and the elements, organic and inorganic, of which they are composed, and thereafter the constitution of the celebrated grass soil for fattening stock now to be given, it will be at once apparent how very efficiently the water of irrigation must act in transporting and depositing fresh supplies of fertilizing matter, and preparing rich food for the meadow plants, by bringing the different elementary substances, already present in the soil, into closer contact with each other, and thus disposing them to, and directly promoting various combinations, in which its own elements are frequently absorbed, combined, and lost ; thus performing in succession the several good offices of carrier, chemical agent, and chemical element of composition as required.

Constitution of a pasture soil from the banks of the Weser, near Hoya, from Sprengel's analysis (Die Bodenkunde), and celebrated for fattening stock :—

Silica, quartz, sand, and silicates	71·849
Alumina	9·350
Oxide of iron	5·410
Oxide of manganese	0·925
Lime	0·987
Magnesia	0·245
Potash of soda extracted by water	0·007
Phosphoric acid	0·131
Sulphuric acid	0·174
Chlorine in common salt	0·002
Humic acid	1·270
Insoluble humus	7·550
Organic matters containing nitrogen	2·000
Water	0·100
	100·

Our tables, when carefully studied, distinctly show how the water of irrigation, aided by carbonic acid, the alkalies, and the other organic acids of the soil, is capable of dissolving, holding in suspension, and thus presenting to the absorbents of plants, in the most favourable form for their nourishment, all the substances that occur in this analysis; and thus necessarily, in a rich soil, supplying the only deficiency, the natural menstruum. In a poor soil, the same water of irrigation must operate beneficially in its passage over its surface, by depositing its precipitate, and thus gradually assist in bringing it into a state of fertility.

By means of the water of irrigation, the plant is abundantly nourished and supplied by the selection, absorption, and appropriation of the various substances that constitute its food, through the medium of its leaf and stem pores, at the same time that this same water of irrigation deposits, as we have seen, fresh substances in the form of precipitates, and prepares those raw substances, already existing in the soil, for the easy absorption of the root pores or radical spongioles.

It has been proved beyond dispute that in this climate a great proportion of the carbon contained in the substance of plants has been absorbed by the leaves from the atmosphere, in the form of carbonic acid. A growing healthy plant has been found to absorb the carbonic acid gas from a given quantity of atmospheric air in the sunshine, with more or less rapidity. Carbonic acid gas is very abundantly supplied by the water of irrigation, which is capable of holding a great quantity of this gas in solution, absorbing, as we have seen, as much as its own bulk of carbonic acid, if it meets with organic substances in favourable circumstances for its production in its course to or over the meadow herbage—a proportion of which is ever decaying and aiding in furnishing additional supplies of carbonic acid. So that the water of irrigation, thus impregnated, must be capable of promoting vegetable growth in a very important degree, so much of the organic substance of plants consisting of carbon. This carbonic acid, in ordinary circumstances, is absorbed from the air, and decomposes within the plant by the vital action, aided by the light; and the oxygen is exhaled and returned again to the air, while the carbon is deposited and elaborated into the substance of the growing plant. We have also seen, from the solvent powers of water, that it affords from its own substance, aided by the absorption of atmospheric air alone, all the other elementary gases, constituting, with carbon, the organic substance of all vegetables.

It is unnecessary to dwell on the wonderful effects which are found to be produced by the sowing of soot and other specific soluble manures, in powder, over the damp leaves of young and tender corn, turnip, pulse and clover plants, in a dewy or drizzling morning, when the powder readily adheres, and is dissolved and appropriated; neither need we expatiate on the known efficacy of liquid manures. However, when we consider that water is capable of dissolving almost all the elementary substances constituting these manures, whether liquid or solid—and, in fact, does and must occasionally encounter these constituents in its progress through the various strata to the surface in springs, or in its lengthened course as it passes over the variously-compounded beds and banks of rivers and brooks, acting upon an infinite variety of bodies, organic and inorganic, and selecting liberally from each, how can we regard the water of irrigation in, any other light than as a powerful and important *liquid manure?*

We have seen, then, that water, or water impregnated with carbonic acid—a very plentiful and constantly-occurring substance, is capable of holding in solution and presenting in the form best adapted for the absorption of plants, nearly all the known substances which are believed to be necessary for forming the elements of their abundant and healthful nourishment and sustenance. In fact, that it furnishes wholesome food in abundance, and that food ready prepared in the form best adapted for the immediate satisfaction of their various wants and appetites. But, whatever is wanting in this way is amply supplied by the powerful decomposing action of the various organic acids that occur in most soils, themselves the products of decomposition; for instance, the sulphuric, the nitric, muriatic, fluoric, phosphoric, &c., &c., which supply, without exception, to aid the water, any deficiency in solvent action.

We hope, then, we have made the modes of beneficial action of the waters of irrigation sufficiently clear and intelligible. It operates as a powerful solvent, and in the most comprehensive sense as a *cheap and efficient liquid manure.*

In high situations and latitudes, the process of irrigation will not be so efficient or productive as in lower situations and more genial climates; and in the first place, and more particularly, because the substances presented to the water in its course, such as quartz, sand-beds, and granite, are all very difficult of solution, and contain but sparingly (and frequently not at all) the elements of fertility; and in the next place the influence of a genial climate is indispensable to the full development of the beneficial effects of irrigation.

It must be at once admitted, on a review of all we have said, that in rich soils the water of irrigation, affords the special menstruum provided by nature, alone calculated for holding in solution, and presenting to the absorbents of plants their natural food in the form in which it is believed to be most easily absorbed by them, besides that, it acts in disposing substances to enter into favourable combinations, and in distributing these chemically combined or compound substances, and bringing them within the range of the appropriating energies of the roots of plants.

That, to an infertile soil, on comparing the substances, elementary and compound, capable of solution and absorbtion by water and the organic acids of the soil acting in concert with water, and at the same time considering their constituents—on comparing, we say, these substances with the elementary analysis of a fertile grass soil given above, we can easily see how the water of irrigation acts powerfully in transporting and supplying the means of fertility; and should the soil contain any deleterious substances, it operates powerfully as a solvent and detergent, thus purifying the soil and washing out the noxious impregnations, at the same time that it is constantly adding to the body of the soil an unceasing tribute of wholesome and fertilising matter.

It is absolutely necessary, before applying irrigation to a surface, to ascertain that it either overlies a sufficiently pervious subsoil; or, if the subsoil should be stiff and impervious, to have the portion of meadow thoroughly under-drained, else a very favourable result can scarcely be anticipated. When this is not attended to, the surface has a tendency to become overspread with coarse and comparatively useless subaquatic plants.

It has been stated by Sir Humphrey Davy that water at 40 degrees of temperature (which we know well to be the point of its greatest density) is of greater specific gravity than when at a lower temperature; and that hence when it tends to the freezing point, the warmer portion is next the ground. But what great sensible effect can this difference be expected to produce in a current a few inches in depth? And at any rate the water must be discharged when it nearly approaches the freezing point. We know indeed, when its internal movements are impeded, water is a very slow conductor of heat, and a very imperfect conductor of electricity; whereas, running water has a very different relation to both these principles. So much for the benefit of the current being preserved; but this is only stated by us as subsidiary to the benefits already mentioned.

We may remark too, as of importance, and with some confidence, that on occasions, after the water is let off at intervals from the meadow, the heat of the atmosphere operates powerfully on the surface, and the contained water ascends by capillary attraction, depositing in its passage about the roots of the surface herbage, and the upper stratum generally, and on the surface on some occasions, after the manner of an efflorescence, a rich store of fertilizing matter, which it had held in solution until, in its ascent, it had become disposed to evaporate by more intimate contact with the atmospheric air.

This may in a great measure satisfactorily account for the magical growth which succeeds the temporary discharge of the water from the surface in genial weather, and also tends to establish and confirm, further—if, indeed, it were at all requisite or necessary—the truth of the explanation we have already given of the modes of beneficial operation of the water of irrigation.

THE MANAGEMENT OF FARM YARD MANURE.

By CUTHBERT W. JOHNSON, ESQ., F.R.S.

There is hardly a single operation in the management of a farm which can compare in importance with the preparation of farm-yard manure. And yet it is an operation which is very commonly left to chance rather than systematically carried on with anything like scientific precision. A few facts, which have been collected with much laborious accuracy will perhaps therefore assist the young farmer in arranging his operations. The manure commonly collected in the farm-yard, as I have in another place had occasion to remark, is compounded of a mixture of animal and vegetable substances, chiefly of the straw of various descriptions of grain, mixed with the fæces and urine of cattle, horses, and swine. The mixture of these different substances does not form any new substance, neither by the putrefaction which ensues is anything added to the bulk of the dung; on the contrary, it causes a considerable loss of weight. Neither is the manure produced equal to the amount of food the stock consume. "If," says Dr. Sprengel, we weigh the dry food given the cattle to eat, and also dry and weigh the resulting excrements, we shall find the weight of the latter considerably less than that of the former." Block, who has lately made a great number of experiments

on this circumstance, found that 100lbs. of rye straw yielded only 43lbs. of dried excrement (liquid and solid), while 100lbs. of hay gave 44lbs. Food which contains many watery parts furnished, as may be naturally supposed, a still smaller proportion. Thus, to give one or two instances, 100lbs. of potatoes gave only 14lbs.; 100lbs. of mangel wurzel 6lbs.; and 100lbs. of green clover 6½lbs. of excrement.—*(Journ. Roy. Ag. Soc. Eng., v. 6, p. 460.)*

The dry straw of wheat is composed chiefly of carbon, hydrogen, and water, and about five per cent. of saline and earthy matters. 100 parts of these solid matters usually contain:

Various salts, principally carbonate and sulphate of potash	22½
Phosphate of lime	6 4⁄33
Chalk (carbonate of lime)................	1
Silica (flint)	61½
Metallic oxide (principally iron)..........	1
Foss	7¼

The urine of the cow contains various salts, such as phosphate of lime, the muriates of potash and magnesia, sulphate and carbonate of potash, carbonate of ammonia, and urea, but by far the largest portion is water, of which it contains about 65 per cent. That of the horse, however, contains a still larger proportion of water; a specimen analyzed by M. M. Fourcroy and Vauquelin yielded 94 per cent.; that of the pig contains 92 per cent.; and that of the sheep kept at grass 96 per cent.; and human urine affords nearly as much, some that was examined by M. Berzelius, the great Swedish chemist, yielded 93 per cent. of water.

The fæces of cattle also contain a large aqueous proportion. That of black cattle fed on turnips was found by M. Einhof to contain about 72 per cent. of water.

By good management, and under ordinary circumstances, one ton of dry straw will produce three tons of manure; so that as the common weight of straw per acre is about one ton and a half, the straw grown upon that extent of land should yield about four tons and a half of compost.

The proportion of manure produced by stock, however, necessarily varies with the quantity and quality of the food upon which the animals are fed. In an experiment made at the Cavalry depôt at Maidstone, a horse consumed in a week—of oats 70lbs., hay 84lbs., straw 56lbs.=210lbs. He drank within this time 27 gallons of water. The weight of the dung and litter produced was 327½lbs. In another experiment, on a large-sized Yorkshire milch cow, she consumed in twenty-four hours—of brewer's grains 81lbs.; raw potatoes 50lbs., meadow hay 15lbs. =125lbs., and during that period she drank two pailfuls of water. The urine was allowed to escape, and she had no litter of any kind. The weight of the solid dung she produced was 45lbs. When fed on another day with raw potatoes 170lbs., hay 28lbs. =198lbs., she produced, under the same circumstances, 73lbs. of solid manure.—*(Brit. Husb. v. 1. p. 255).* Taking, therefore, the average produce to be equal to 60lbs. per day, it follows that a cow will make about nine tons of solid manure in the course of the year.

Few operations appear at first sight so simple as the manufacture and collection of farm-yard manure, and yet there are several errors into which the cultivator is very likely to fall without he is ever vigilant to avoid them. Mr. Francis Blakie, in his valuable tract upon the management of farm-yard manure, alludes to several of these: he highly disapproves of the practice "of keeping the dung arising from different descriptions of animals in separate heaps or departments, and applying them to the land without intermixture. It is customary," he observes, "to keep the fattening neat cattle in yards by themselves, and the manure thus procured is of good quality, because the excrement of such cattle is richer than that of lean ones. Fattening cattle are fed with oil cake, corn, Swedish turnips, or some other rich food, and the refuse and waste of such food increase the value of the manure; it also attracts pigs to the yard. These rout the straw and dung about in search of grains of corn, bits of Swedish turnips, and other food, by which means the manure in the yard becomes more intimately mixed, and is proportionately increased in value. The feeding troughs and cribs in the yard should for obvious reasons be shifted frequently." The stable manure should be spread about the yard. "The horse dung," continues Blakie, " is usually thrown out at the stable doors, and there accumulates in large heaps. It is sometimes spread a little about, but more generally not at all, unless when necessary for the convenience of ingress and egress, or perhaps to allow the water to drain away from the stable door. Horse-dung lying in such heaps very soon ferments and heats to an excess, and the centre of the heap is charred or burned to a dry white substance, provincially termed '*fire-fanged.*' Dung in this state loses from 50 to 75 per cent. of its value. The diligent and attentive farmer will guard against such profligate waste of property, by never allowing the dung to accumulate in any considerable quantity at the stable-doors. The dung from the fatting hog-sties should also be carted and spread about the store cattle-yard in the same manner as the horse-dung." *(Blakie on Farm-yard Dung, p. 6.)*

"Some theorists," he adds in another place, " recommend the yards to be so concave as almost to amount to a well shape, giving as a reason in support of their opinion, that the virtues of dung can only be preserved by being saturated in urine, or some other moisture." Others, again, assert that dung yards should be formed convex, and assign as their reason that farm-yard dung should be kept dry. Practical experience points out that a medium between those two extremes is the best; and a yard a little hollowed is the most common shape.

When the dung is sufficiently prepared to be ready to be carted to the compost heap, considerable attention is necessary in its removal and mixture. These observations had not escaped Blakie: he tells us, in a subsequent page of his essay, " When it is found necessary to empty the dungyards early in the season, I recommend that preparation should be made in the usual way for the reception of the dung-heaps in the intended turnip fields, by collecting large heaps of clay, marl, or such other materials. The bottoms of the heaps should not, however, be laid above six or eight inches thick with the earthy material, and a good quantity of it should be placed in rows, on each side of the bottoms, marked out. The dung should then be drawn out of the yards, and placed upon the bottoms, but not in the usual way of throwing it up loosely, to cause fermentation; on the contrary, by drawing the carts with their loads upon the heaps, for the purpose of compressing the dung, and thereby retarding fermentation. One or two men should remain constantly at the heaps, while the teams are at work, on purpose to spread and level the dung regularly, so as to render the

ascent easy for the succeeding teams as they come with their loads. If the dung has not been previously mixed in the yards, it should be so in drawing to the heaps, by taking up a few loads from one yard, and then a few from another alternately —and even from the same yard the loads of dung should be taken from different parts alternately. —for the dung is not of equal quality, nor made with the same regularity, in all parts of the yard.

The coal-ashes, road-scrapings, and all other collections of manure about the farm house, should be also carried to these dung-heaps; and when the heaps are raised as high as convenient for the horses to draw up, several loads should be shot up at the end of the heaps, for the purpose of making them up to the square of the centre; the whole heap should then be completely covered with the marl and clay, or the soil previously collected in rows by the side of the heaps, so as effectually to enclose the dung-heaps in crusts; and they are thenceforth denominated *pies*. In these the dung will be preserved in a very perfect state, with little or no fermentation, and without loss by exhalation or evaporation.

The pies, within ten days or a fortnight of the time the compost is wanted for the turnip land, should be carefully turned over, and the crust, top, bottom, and sides, intimately mixed up with the dung. When the turning is completed, again coat the heaps over with the natural soil around the heaps; the pies will then undergo a gentle fermentation; the earth intermixed with, and covering the dung, will absorb the juices and gaseous matters produced, and the compost come out in a fine state of preparation for using on the turnip lands.

When the dung is taken out of the yards late in the spring, or only a short time before it is required for the turnip ground, the preparation should be somewhat different, because of the compost heaps having less time to incorporate. Thus the dung should not be carted upon the heaps to compress them, and prevent fermentation as in winter; on the contrary, the dung should be thrown up lightly with the fork upon the bottoms, and the side-heaps of earth mixed intimately along with the dung. Turf turned up for a year preceding on wastes, by the sides of roads, makes excellent pie meat. *(Farmers' Encyclopædia.)*

There is no doubt of the advantages of the plan of forming layers under, and of covering compost heaps with earth in the way described by Mr. Blakie; for, by this mode, not only is the fermentation of the dung retarded, but the earth itself is enriched, all the grub and other insects are destroyed, and the seeds of weeds, which commonly abound in the soil, are stimulated into life, and destroyed. This result is produced chiefly by the effect of the gases of putrefaction and the carbonate of ammonia, which, generated in the dung, is volatilized by the heat. To prevent the escape of this, it is a good plan to mix the earth with gypsum (sulphate of lime) in powder, for, by this means, if any carbonate of ammonia is escaping through the soil, it is decomposed by the sulphate of lime, and sulphate of ammonia is formed; this latter salt, not being volatilized by heat, remains in the soil, and when afterwards spread over the fields, is decomposed, and its constituents become the food of the growing crop.

It is very desirable that the farmer should have some ready means of ascertaining when the dunghill is fermenting to an injurious extent, and it fortunately happens that there are one or two easy experiments by which this can be easily determined. If a thermometer, when placed in a dunghill, does not rise above 100°, there is little danger of too much gaseous matter being evolved; if a thermometer is not in the farmer's possession, a piece of rag wetted with spirit of salt (muriatic acid) and held over the dunghill, will pretty accurately determine the state of the fermentation, for if the temperature is too high, dense fumes of ammonia become visible.

In many situations, where the farmer has access to peat, it will be desirable to mix it with the farm yard compost; to this end the peat should be procured in as dry a state as possible, and if it can be placed in situations where it can absorb the drainage matters of the yard, the economy will be the greater. Peat also mixes admirably with night-soil, as is well described by Mr. Dixon, of Hathershaw, in an essay which I commend to the perusal of all those farmers who have access to peat.—*(Jour. Roy. Ag. Soc. v. I., p.* 135).

These precautions, it will be seen upon very slight reflection, tend not only to increase the quantity of the compost of the farm-yard, but to improve its quality, both effects of the highest importance to the farmer—for if he succeeds in attaining these, he can hardly fail of sustaining and increasing the fertility of his land. These, too, were the conclusions of almost the earliest tillers of the soil, for M. Plato, the earliest agricultural writer, whose works we possess, many centuries since told the Italian farmers, in his fourth chapter:—"Study to have a large dunghill, keep your compost carefully, carry it out in the autumn, and when you carry it out, scatter and pulverize it." After an interval of more than eighteen centuries, the observations of Cato still apply as forcibly as ever, and it should be one of the axioms ever borne in mind by the English farmer—"Study to have a large dunghill," and if in attaining this very desirable object, he does not neglect to preserve and improve its quality, he can hardly ever be very far wrong in his tillage.

ON MANURES.

The Stewponey Agricultural Society have published a new edition of their rules and regulations, included in which is the "Essay on Manures," by Mr. Daniel Banton, of Seisdon, a member of the society, which gained the prize at their last anniversary meeting. This essay contains the result of certain experiments tried with various manures in the cultivation of wheat.

"I have used guano and nitrate of soda as manures for wheat and turnips rather extensively this year, the particulars of which, upon wheat, I shall give below, and have only to state here, with regard to turnips, that guano promises to be an effective manure. I have applied it both for common turnips and Swedes, and it appears to answer well in both cases. Part of a field for Swedes had half a dressing in the winter with fold-yard manure, not of the best quality, and ploughed in immediately, before being ridged up. I had sown on the surface scarcely one cwt. of guano per acre; the other part of the field was dressed with butcher's manure. The Swedes are not early, but still growing fast, and promise to be a big crop. The part where the guano was used is quite as good as the other, and perfectly free from mildew. I applied one cwt. of guano upon a plot of spring vetches, but could see no effect.

"The following manures were made trial of in a field of land (in tolerable good condition) situate at Seisdon, within the limits of the Stewponey Agricultural Society, in the county of Stafford. The soil a light sandy loam, commonly called 'turnip and barley land,' subsoil a gravelly sand, based on a red sand stone. This field has a gently sloping aspect to the north-west, a year old clover root, flay-ploughed, and drilled seven inches wide with white wheat, on the 19th of October, 1841, at the rate of 2½ bushels per acre, 38 quarts to the bushel. The plant of wheat was thick and strong through the winter, and at the time of applying the manures, was rather forward for the season. On the 23rd of April six plots of land were accurately measured with a chain, each containing one-eighth of an acre, and manured as under:—

No. 1, with guano, at the rate of 1¾ cwt. per acre.
2, guano and nitrate of soda, equal proportions, 1¼ cwt. per acre together.
3, nitrate of soda, 1¼ cwt. per acre.
4, white caustic lime, at the rate of 4 tons per acre.
5, lime and salt, in proportion of 5 cwt. of salt to 10 cwt. of lime per acre, mixed a week before being applied.
6, had no manure.

"There was no rain for ten days after the manures were applied; the days being hot and the nights generally frosty. Seven days after the first rain a slight difference in colour was visible in plots No. 1, 2, and 3, where the nitrate and guano were applied; and on the 16th of May a striking difference was seen in those plots to the rest of the field, the nitrate assuming the deepest, the nitrate and guano the next shade, and the guano the palest green of the three. There was no visible effects where lime alone, and lime and salt were put. From May, till the wheat shot into the ear, which it did at the same time all over the field, the plots No. 1, 2, and 3, might be distinctly traced by the eye at a considerable distance."

Mr. Banton then proceeds to notice that the red rust, which generally prevailed in the neighbourhood, attacked the plots 1, 2, and 3, particularly that on which the nitrate of soda alone was spread. He considers that white wheat is more subject to rust than red, but though white wheat is yearly more or less attacked by it, the sample or yield is very rarely injured.

"The crop was cut by Welshmen, with hooks, on the 12th of August, and the produce of each plot kept by itself, and so thrashed. The result of which was as under:—

Produce of Wheat per Imp. bushel.			Straw.	Weight of Wheat per Imp. bushel.	Straw per Acre.			Wheat per Acre the Imp. bush.
No.	bush.	pks.	lbs.	lbs.	cwt.	qr.	lb.	bushels.
1,	5	2½	479	62	34	0	24	45
2,	5	2	428	62	30	2	8	44
3,	5	0½	436	62	30	2	16	41
4,	5	1¼	426	62	30	2	6	42½
5,	4	3½	326	62	23	1	4	39
6,	4	3½	326	61½	23	1	5	39

"I have not calculated the tail corn, which was very trifling, not exceeding a quart from each lot. It appears that the lime and salt did not produce any effect, except half a pound per bushel in the weight. It perhaps will appear singular that each lot was the same weight per bushel in the five first, but such was the case. The nitrate and guano were procured direct from the importer, and I believe were genuine. Nitrate 24s. 6d., and the guano 20s. per cwt. The lime 12s., and salt 19s. per ton, exclusive of carriage :—

SUMMARY.

	Cost of Manure per Acre, Including Carriage.	Increased value of Straw per Acre at 2s. 6d. per cwt.	Increased value of Grain per Acre at 7s. per bushel, imperial measure.	Total increase in value of Crop per Acre.	Net Profit per Acre after deducting the expense of manure.	Loss per Acre after deducting cost of manure.
	£ s. d.	£ s. d.	£ s. d.	£ s. d.	£ s. d.	£ s. d.
Guano	1 7 0	0 18 0	1 2 4	2 1 6	1 2 0	
Nitrate and Guano	1 10 3	0 18 2	1 15 2	2 13 9	2 1 1	
Nitrate of Soda alone	1 3 6	0 18 0	1 4 14	2 1 12	11 6	
Lime	0 13 8	0 18 2	None.	2 8		0 1 0
Lime and Salt ..	0 14 0	None.	None.	8 4		14 5 0
						0 4 8

" The foregoing summary, I think, clearly proves that the cost of lime and nitrate of soda, and indeed of most other manures, is at present disproportionately high, compared with the price of grain, and unless considerably reduced cannot long continue to be used for agricultural purposes."

The summary of the results of this clever farmer's experience is, that guano produced the greatest increase in the crop, both of straw and grain, at the smallest cost. We observe he complains that the cost of lime and nitrate of soda, and indeed of most other manures, is disproportionately high : 20s. a cwt. he appears to have paid for the guano employed in the above experiments. It is now regularly quoted at 14s. a cwt., and may be purchased, we are informed, in Worcester at that price, or even lower when a large quantity is taken. Estimating, therefore, guano at 14s. a cwt., the result would be (we make the same allowance for carriage as Mr. Banton, which, we presume, includes the cost of putting it on the land), that 20s. of guano per acre gives six bushels, or two bags an acre, more than the average of No. 6, which had no manure; and eleven tons more straw, or a net profit, after deducting the cost of manure of 2l. 9s. per acre ; the reduction which, we presume, has taken place in the cost of guano making a difference of 7s. 6d. an acre in the cost of applying it. We think it right to state these facts for the information of our agricultural readers.

FORMATION OF FAT.

(From the Annals of Chymistry.)

LIEBIG v. DUMAS.

These two eminent continental chemists are again engaged in a lively dispute concerning a subject of great interest—viz., the formation of fat in the animal body. From observations, which tend to show "that carnivorous animals do not consume any sugar, starch, or gum, with their food ; that therefore these substances are not necessary for nutrition, or, what is the same thing, for the formation of blood ; that they disappear, on the other hand, from the body of herbivorous animals, escaping in the form of carbonic acid and water, and that, therefore, they appear to serve only as means of respiration for the creation of animal heat; that the fat of the animal body disappears, too, in consequence of disease, or increased absorption of oxygen in the form of carbonic acid ; and that, therefore, this azotic substance is, in the animal body, applicable to the same end as sugar, gum, or starch, replacing other azotic substances for the purposes of respiration ; that, further, the flesh of carnivorous animals, although, of all animals, they consume the greatest quantity of fat, does not contain any fat ; whilst it accumulates in the body of herbivorous animals during the process of respiration, the absorption of oxygen being retarded at the same time, Liebig arrived at the inference, that the fat owes its existence to those parts of the food which do not contain azote, the carbon of which remains in the body in the form of fat, provided the oxygen necessary for its transformation into carbonic acid be not present in sufficient quantity. The fat has, therefore, its principal source in those constituents of food not containing azote, although the fat contained in food may tend to increase the amount of fat in the animal body.

Respecting these views of Liebig, the following remarks, by M. Dumas, occur in the *Annales de Chimie et de Physique* :—

M. Liebig is of opinion that herbivorous animals *create* fat, from sugar and starch, whilst Messrs. Dumas and Boussingault state it as a general rule that animals, of whatever kind they may be, do not *create* any fat or other substances than those serving for nutrition, and that they receive their nourishment, be it sugar, starch, or fat, direct from the vegetable kingdom.

" If the supposition of M. Liebig be accurately founded, the views of Messrs. Dumas and Boussingault, stated as a general formula of the chemical equilibrium of both kingdoms, would be erroneous."

The " Commission de la Gelatine," however, has removed any doubt on the point as to whether animals consuming fat are the only ones in the cellular tissue of which fat is observed to accumulate.

The origin of fatty matter in the animal body has thus become a point of dispute, and M. Liebig has developed, in the *Annalen der Chemie und Pharmacie* of January, 1843, the reasons which decided him in attributing to the fatty constituents of the food of herbivorous animals only a slight, if any part at all, in the accumulation of fat in the animal body. It is acknowledged, observes M. L., that those substances which contain a large quantity of starch, sugar, and similar matters, have the greatest influence on the production of fat in the animal body. Thus, for instance, rice, Indian corn, beans, lentils, and peas, potatoes, the marrow of beet-root, &c., are employed in husbandry on a large scale, and with decided success, for the purpose of fattening, that is to say, to secure the accumulation of flesh and fat ; and there is no doubt that animals fed with these different substances, if under certain conditions, as, for instance, abundance of nourishment, absence of motion, high temperature, &c., will, after some time, contain much more fat than before. Now we have several analyses of rice, beans, and peas, by trustworthy chemists. Braconnot found in Carolina rice 0·13⁰⁄₀, in Piedmont rice 0·25⁰⁄₀, and Vogel, in another kind of rice, 1·05⁰⁄₀ of oil ; for every thousand pounds of rice the animal organism then receives 1·3 pounds, or 2·5 pounds, or, according to Vogel, 10½ pounds of fat from every thousand pounds of this food.

Peas contain, according to Braconnot, 1·20⁰⁄₀ of a substance soluble in ether, which he terms chlorophylle ; beans (*Phaseolus vulgaris*), 0·70⁰⁄₀ of a fat soluble in ether ; and Fresenius obtained from peas 2·1⁰⁄₀, and from lentils 1·3⁰⁄₀, of that substance. The organism, then, receives from every thousand pounds of peas 12 pounds, or, according to Fresenius, 21 pounds, of fat, whilst the same quantity of beans yields only 7 pounds.

By further experiments made in the laboratory at Giessen, it has been ascertained that 1,000 parts of dry potatoes furnished 3·05 parts of a substance soluble in ether ; and although these parts possess all the properties of resin or wax, we may admit that potatoes contain ₁₀₀⁄₃₀₀₀ of their weight of fat. Let us, then, compare the effects which a certain quantity of these substances produces on the accumulation of fat in the animal organism.

One thousand pounds of peas and 6,825 pounds of fresh boiled potatoes (corresponding to 1,638 pounds of dried potatoes) are sufficient for perfectly fattening three pigs of one year old in the course of thirteen weeks ; each of them has then increased from 80 to 90 pounds in weight, weighing, on an average, from 160 to 170 pounds, and yielding, after being killed, from 50 to 55 pounds of fat. The three pigs, however, consumed, in the thousand pounds of peas, 21 pounds of fat, and in the 6,825 pounds of fresh potatoes (= to 1,638 of dried), 6 pounds of fat; altogether, then, 27 pounds. Their body, however, contains from 150 to 165 pounds of fat; from 123 to 135 pounds more have been gained than was contained in their food. A pig of one year old weighs from 75 to 80 pounds ; supposing, now, that it contains 18 pounds of fat, there still remain from 69 to 74 pounds of fat, the formation of which in the animal organism cannot be doubted.

Other and still more weighty reasons, in favour of the opinion that fat must be created in the animal body from certain kinds of food, which, not being fat in themselves nor containing fat, are furnished by the observations of the influence of the food of cows on the quantity and elements of their milk, as made by Boussingault, the friend and collaborateur of Dumas.

A cow at Bechelbrunn received for eleven days = 83¾ pounds of potatoes daily ; as food in eleven days, therefore, 921 pounds. Besides this, 8¼ pounds of chopped straw ; in eleven days, therefore, 91 pounds.

During these eleven days she gave 95½ pints of milk, containing 78 ounces 135 grains of butter.

As, now, 921 pounds of fresh potatoes are equal

to 220½ pounds of dry potatoes [potatoes containing, according to M. Boussingault, 76·8 of water and 23·2 of solid substances.—*Annales de Chimie et de Phys.*, 1838, *Avril*, 408] ; further, as 35 ounces 121 grains of potatoes and straw, 0·032⁰⁄₀ of matters soluble in ether (as crystallizable wax), the cow consumed during that period 10 ounces 124 grains + 12 ounces 44 grains = 22 ounces 168 grains of substances soluble in ether. The milk, however, contained 5 pounds 251 grains of fat.

In another instance, when a cow consumed in six days 198½ pounds of fresh (= to 44 pounds of dry) potatoes, and 99 pounds of hay, the milk contained 109 ounces 404 grains of butter. Supposing that these 44 pounds of potatoes contained 2 ounces 51 grains of fat, the remaining 107 ounces 353 grains of butter must have been derived from the 99 pounds af hay; the hay, therefore, should contain nearly 7⁰⁄₀ of fat. This may easily be ascertained by experiment. The best quality of hay of the description consumed by the cow yielded only 1·56⁰⁄₀ of its weight of substances soluble in ether ; and, therefore, not more than 24 ounces 164 grains of butter could be furnished to the animal from 99 pounds of hay. It therefore remains to explain whence the other 103 ounces 189 grains of butter came from,' which M. Boussingault found in milk.

M. Dumas observes, in the *Comptes Rend.* of Oct. 24th, 1842, that "hay in the condition as consumed by a cow contains almost 2⁰⁄₀ of fatty matter," and that he is about to prove, that a fattened ox and milch cow "furnish *less* fatty matter than is contained in the food." This, however, compared with the above facts, may prove a failure.

If, in addition to this, it may be presumed that animals receive the fat contained in their food precisely in the same condition as it is afterwards found in their body, the proof would be completely impossible ; for the question as to whether butter furnished by the cow is contained in the food in the form of butter or not, is easily decided.

Hay digested in ether yields a green liquor, and after the ether has been removed, a green residue of a strong but agreeable odour of hay, not possessing any of the properties characteristic of fatty substances. This green residue consists of several matters, one of which, of a waxy or resinous appearance, is known under the name of chlorophylle (leaf-green.) Another of its elements deposits in the concentrated etherial solution, in the form of fine crystalline laminæ ; it is a crystalline wax, occurring likewise in plums, cherries, the leaves of cabbage, &c. M. Dumas submitted this substance to analysis, but he found its composition and properties entirely differing from those of other known fatty substances, wherefore he termed it by the name of Cerosin.

Straw digested with ether, and the fresh herb of *Fumaria officinalis* digested with alcohol, likewise yielded a crystalline wax very similar to Cerosin.

The chief components of the fat of animals, margaric or stearic acid, occur neither in the seeds of corn nor in such herbs or roots as are used as food. It is therefore evident that if those parts of the food which are soluble in ether can be converted into fat, the margarine and stearine must be formed from wax or chlorophylle. We know, however, that the chlorophylle of fresh green vegetables passes from the body without undergoing scarcely any change : the same presumption applies to wax. In order to remove, then, any doubt concerning this question, the following experiment was made :—The excretions of a cow fed with potatoes and aftermath, were dried and exhausted with ether; they yielded a green solution, which, when concentrated to a certain degree, consolidated to a mass, owing its solidity to a white crystalline and waxy body, surrounded by the dark green mother liquor. This extract, when further condensed by evaporation, evolved an unpleasant odour, and, dried at 212°, left behind 3·119% of the weight of the excretions in fat or similar substances. According to M. Boussingault, stating* that the solid excretions, if dry, amount to $\frac{1}{15}$ of the weight of the dry food, it is evident that these excretions contain very nearly the same quantity of fatty matter as the food consumed. Sixteen and a half pounds of hay contain (at 1·56%) 4 ounces 403 grains of fat; the 33 pounds of potatoes further contained 154 grains; both together, therefore, 5 ounces 120 grains of fat. The solid excretions daily removed weigh 14 ounces 480 grains, containing (at 3·119%) 4 ounces 175 grains of fat. A milch cow who furnishes 109 ounces 404 grains of butter in the course of six days, consumed in the same space of time, in her food, 26 ounces 293 grains of substances soluble in ether; 26 ounces 154 grains of the same substances are removed by excretion; and this leads, therefore, evidently to the inference that those elements in the food had no part in the formation of the 109 ounces 404 grains of butter contained in the milk. It is, then, evident that the fat accumulating in the body of animals whilst they are fattening, as well as that which is daily removed in the form of butter, contained in the milk, cannot be derived from the wax or chlorophylle of the food, but from other elements contained therein.

Another difference of opinion between both chemists concerns the amount of oil contained in Indian corn (maize). Dumas and Boussingault found therein 9% of a yellow oil ; Gorham only 3% of a peculiar substance which he termed *Zein*, but no trace of oil ; Bizio, however, 1·475% of oil ; and Liebig himself 4·67%. These statements differ so considerably, that any inference based on the contents of oil and Indian corn, when used as food for fattening animals, cannot possibly be admitted as general.

[In reducing the above weights, &c., we have made use of imperial weights and measures.—ED. A. C.]

ON THE USE OF LIME.

TO THE EDITOR OF THE FARMER'S MAGAZINE.

Sir,—Having had some experience in the use of lime, I wish to make known to your readers the advantages that may be derived from the judicious application of it as a manure to most soils.

It is not at all my intention to enter into a scientific account of the manner in which lime promotes the decomposition of vegetable substances so as to render them fit food for various plants—a subject on which some of the first chemists have held different opinions—but merely to state to practical men my reasons for concluding this to be one of the beneficial effects it produces.

* Annales de Chim. et de Phys., t. lxxi., p. 322.

Some of the largest and most opulent farmers in this district object to the use of lime on the ground that it is no manure, and therefore is not required for the production of any crops they cultivate ; the error of which must be evident to any one who will be at the trouble of ascertaining that all the plants grown by farmers contain lime in a greater or less degree. In fact, chemists have only found one plant in which they could not trace the presence of lime. Such of your readers as are desirous of obtaining further information on this subject, I refer to the works of Davy, Liebig, and others, on agricultural chemistry, as well as the excellent writings of Cuthbert Johnson.

If it be proved that plants contain lime, it is natural to conclude that they must absorb it from the soil, because the atmosphere does not contain it ; consequently, if the lime taken from the soil be not renewed, the subsequent crops either fail from want of it, or are deficient in some property from the same cause. I have found that wheat is not so liable to be laid by the wind on land that has been limed, and the reapers always say it is harder to cut.

When I first began to cultivate some of the high land in this county, I only grew 12 bushels of wheat to the acre, weighing about 54lbs. the bush., and 20 bush. of barley of a very poor quality. Last year I had 22 bush. of wheat, and 40 bush. of barley per acre. The wheat weighed 62lbs. to the bush., and the barley is a very fair sample. By persevering in a regular course of crops, and liming for wheat, I expect to grow 30 bush. per acre after another year or two. My first crops of clover failed, but since I have taken to the use of lime I have not had a bad piece of clover.

Some of my neighbours who are in the habit of using bone dust do not approve of lime, and are surprised when told that bones contain a very considerable portion of it in chemical combination. Others are talking of trying gypsum on their clover, but object to the use of lime *in toto*. I am well aware that lime is combined with an acid (the phosphoric) in bones, that renders it peculiarly adapted as food for the turnip plant, which pure lime is not ; and therefore I should never recommend any one to drill turnips with lime as the sole manure, because then the crop would most probably fail ; but where the practice of liming for wheat is followed, I think there would be no occasion to use gypsum for the clover—at least it should be tried with caution, not to incur needless expense. In situations where lime can only be procured at a very great expense, and gypsum is found to succeed as a manure for clover, it is invaluable, being so easy of carriage.

There are many cottagers in our neighbourhood who cultivate one or two acres of land, growing potatoes and wheat alternately, with no manure except lime, as long as they consider the crops worth growing ; and then sow oats two or three years running, till no crop of any kind can be produced for some time without a different mode of cultivation. This plan I have known quoted by some large farmers as a proof of the inutility of liming ; but on some of these patches, where, by forming a compost dunghill, they make manure enough for potatoes, with the aid of lime the occupiers succeed in raising good crops on this alternate system ; though it is certainly not a course to be recommended. I have used lime successfully with every kind of crop on land that had not been limed for some time ; but my general plan is to spread the lime on the clover ley about Midsummer, and plough it in hot. This, I consider, promotes the decomposition, or, at any rate, the very minute division of all the vegetable matter on the surface, so as to render it fit food for the wheat plant; at the same time it renders the soil more mellow, and very much facilitates the process of making a good fallow; and I have observed that those farmers who follow the same plan always have the best crops—not only of wheat, but in the whole succeeding rotation.

My land is a poor shallow soil on the mountain or carboniferous limestone, which in many places crops out to the surface, and is obliged to be removed before I can procure sufficient depth of soil to grow anything. As it is situated on a hill, and varies from three to four hundred feet above the level of the sea, I find the five course rotation succeed the best, and always fallow the second year's clover ley for wheat; but on land where ley wheat is generally sown, I should recommend the lime either to be put on for turnips or for barley in the spring.

Lime also appears to have a double kind of mechanical action on the soil. It very much serves to lighten stiff lands, so as to make them work more easily, while it renders light sandy lands firmer; so that by its use wheat may be grown on a soil for which it is not naturally adapted.

When lime is put into headlands, heaps of weeds, &c., it should be covered up immediately; and when slaked, turned up together, so as to mix the lime well through the heap. When put on a ley it should be spread as soon as it is sufficiently slaked, and ploughed in hot. The same should be done when it is used on a fallow, taking care to drag it well in as soon as it is spread. Both these last should always be done in the summer; for when lime is put on the land late in the autumn, and becomes nearly mortar before it can be worked in, I consider it to be worse than useless.

Chepstow April 11.　　　　　　　VERITAS.

HARKAWAY.
PLATE II.

A celebrated roadster, the property of Mr. John Harrison, of Cottingham, Yorkshire. The horse which forms the subject of our second plate, will be recognised by many of our readers as the one which obtained the first prize at the late Agricultural Exhibition which took place at Hull. Harkaway is a strong, vigorous, and active animal, capable from his formation of enduring great fatigue; his body is round and compact, as will be distinctly seen by the engraving, and his limbs are remarkable for their strength. Although the roadster has been greatly neglected of late years, and almost totally superseded by horses of a lighter character, too nearly allied to the race-horse to please us, we cannot help congratulating the Yorkshire Agricultural Society on their spirited exertions to insure improvement in breeding the roadster, which we rejoice to find is again likely to be brought into notice. We do so the more when we consider that Yorkshire, of all other counties in England, stands pre-eminently distinguished for the superiority of its different breeds of horses; and hope to see the same laudable spirit of emulation more general throughout the empire.

The roadster should have good fore and hind legs, feet sound, be even-tempered, and quiet in whatever situation he may be placed; not heavy in hand, and never disposed to stumble. The general notion that the hackney should lift his legs well and he will never come down, is erroneous; the higher the feet are raised the greater the force on coming to the ground, and the greater the danger in case of a stone or other casualty in the road; in addition to which, is the unpleasantness which the rider feels, as well as the battering and wearing of the feet: more dependence is to be placed on the manner in which the horse puts his feet to the ground than on the knee action in raising them up; more on the foot being placed at once flat on the ground, or perhaps the heel coming first in contact with it, than on the highest and most splendid action.

There are some points in forming a judgment of a roadster, that may prove valuable to our readers, and which should be strictly observed :—A horse, whose shoulders are properly formed and placed is not liable to fall; and his soundness chiefly depends upon his legs and feet. The shoulders should not be too upright, but should slope backwards from the shoulder-point to the withers. It is desirable, if the horse is intended to carry a man of much weight, that the shoulders should be rather thick than thin; but it is essential that they should not be too large at the points. A horse whose shoulders are good, stands, when in a natural position, with his fore-legs in a line perpendicular to the ground; it is, therefore, very desirable that the purchaser should see him in the stable, and before he has been moved, for he will then find him in his natural position, in which it may be difficult to place him after he has been once disturbed. Another mode of ascertaining whether the shoulders are properly placed, is by allowing the horse to walk past you, and observing whether he places his fore-foot more forward than the shoulder-point when he puts it on the ground. A horse whose shoulders are properly formed, will always do so; one whose shoulders are upright, cannot. The fore quarters of a horse intended to be used as a hackney, constitute an essential point; his carcase should be round, and his ribs deep. A horse's fore-leg of the proper form should be flat, and as large under the knee as it is just above the fetlock. The pastern should be subjoined to the leg at the fetlock, that the horse should neither turn his feet out nor in; but it is less objectionable that the horse's feet be turned outwards than inwards, providing he hits not his fetlocks.

COMPARATIVE TABLE OF WEIGHTS.

Scores.	Stones, 14lb.			Stones, 8lb.			Hundreds, 112lb.		
	st.	lb.		st.	lb.		cwt.	qrs.	lb.
20 equal	28	8	..	50	0	..	3	2	8
25 —	35	10	..	52	4	..	4	1	24
30 —	42	12	..	75	0	..	5	1	12
35 —	50	0	..	87	4	..	6	1	0
40 —	57	2	..	100	0	..	7	0	16
45 —	64	4	..	112	4	..	8	0	4
50 --	71	6	..	125	0	..	8	3	20
55 —	78	8	..	137	4	..	9	3	8
60 —	85	10	..	150	0	..	10	2	24
65 —	92	12	..	162	4	..	11	2	18
70 —	100	0	..	175	0	..	12	2	0
75 —	107	2	..	187	4	..	13	1	16
80 —	114	4	..	200	0	..	14	1	4

REPORT ON TRIAL WHEATS.

BY MR. W. MILES, M. P.

(From the Journal of the Royal Agricultural Society of England.)

Having been appointed, with Messrs. Handley and Kimberley, to try the four wheats selected for prizes at Liverpool, and a wish having been expressed by some members of the Council that I should drill in several other approved sorts of wheat together with those selected, all subject to precisely similar conditions, in September last I chose for the experiment a one-year-old clover-ley on a sandy loam, gently sloping to the N. N. W. The crop of clover had been very good, nearly 50 cwt. an acre ; from some part of the field I had taken a second crop, feeding the remainder with sheep and young beasts; no visible difference, however, was afterwards apparent in the grain crop, either in quantity or quality, from these distinct modes of treating the second crop of clover.

The field was ploughed on the 20th of September, and, having been laid out in half-acres for the ploughing-match of the Bath and West of England Society, was continued in the same state for the experiment, each half-acre being separated by 27 inches of grass-balk.

The sorts selected for trial were—of white wheats—

From Liverpool, ... No. 1, Belle Vue Talavera.
From ditto, ...No. 2, Chidham.
From Mr. Kimberley, No. 3, Silver-drop.
From Mr. Jones, ... No. 4, a seedling, Jonas's Prolific.
From Lord Ducie, .. No. 5, Sheriff's.
From Mr. Pusey, ...No. 6, Golden Swan.

And of red wheats—

From Liverpool, ...No. 1, Burwell.
From ditto, ...No. 2, Red Champion.
From Lord Ducie, .. No. 3, Britannia.
From Mr. Pusey,.. ..No. 4, Mr. Fisher Hobbs's Red Marigold.
From Wilts, ...No. 5, Old Red Lammas.

To each of these wheats 3 half-acres were allotted, except to Mr. Jonas's seedling, of which I had but sufficient seed for an acre : the quantity sown per acre was 2 bushels and 1 peck. On the 27th of September, previously to breaking up the clover, 10 bushels of ½-inch bones were sown broadcast over the field. On Tuesday the 12th of October, I commenced putting in No. 1 white, with a Suffolk drill, and finished No. 5 red on the Friday following. On Tuesday the 26th, No. 2, white, appeared ; on the following Saturday all the whites were up ; on the 3rd of November the red wheats were partially, but without any apparent priority of germination, showing. The appearances of the white wheats were—No. 1, sixth ; No. 2, first ; No. 3, fourth ; No. 4, third ; No. 5, fifth ; No. 6, second. No. 1 came up very indifferently ; indeed, it seemed, from the incessant rains, which had continued almost without intermission from the time of sowing to this period, to have perished in the ground ; and as this wheat never afterwards improved, but was entirely hoed in again in February, it may be considered as having totally failed with me. Last year, however, in which there were several very sharp frosts and a good deal of catching weather, I reaped a most capital crop of Belle Vue Talavera—nearly 5 qrs. an acre, which had been sown in October, 1840. This wheat, in our climate, I consider essentially a spring wheat, and as such invaluable ; for in the parts of the trial-field this year, where the plant was

very deficient, or had totally failed, I hoed it in from the 6th of February to the beginning of March, and the wheat so sown was ready for the sickle as early as those sown in October. On the 21st of November I found the appearances of the wheats thus noted :—Whites, No. 2, third ; No. 3, fourth ; No. 4, second ; No. 5, fifth ; No. 6, first : Reds, Nos. 1 and 2, first ; No. 3, fourth ; No. 4, second ; No. 5, third. The first fortnight in January was very trying to the plant, as we had alternate sharp frosts and sudden thaws without snow. On the 22nd the wheats were going off terribly, and the wire-worm was general in its ravages : I immediately put the heaviest roller I could get on the field, and rolled it till the surface was as hard as a turnpike-road ; still the damage apparently done was immense, and a neighbouring farmer guessed that the product of the field would not be above 16 bushels per acre ; the rolling, however, stopped the progress of the wireworm. On the 5th of February I began hoeing in Belle Vue Talavera on those spots of the trial-pieces where the plant had nearly disappeared : of the whites the whole of No. 1 was put in afresh ; of No. 5, about two-thirds of an acre : of the reds a little was put in in Nos. 1 and 2 ; nearly all in No. 3 ; and about half an acre in No. 5 : so that of the white wheats, No. 2, 3, 4, and 6, and of the reds, No. 4, were the only wheats which stood the winter for crop as first planted. On the 2nd of April, I find that the wheats on the whole were very bad ; but from the 25th of March until the 23rd of April, not sufficient rain fell at King's Weston to wet the ground, and at this period the wheats began to mend ; their improvement being gradual, but extraordinary. I was absent from home during the blooming, but was informed by my farming-man that very little difference was perceptible between the flowering of the whites, and that the reds came into bloom from a week to ten days after the whites. On my return from London at the end of the first week in July, I found the general improvement still progressing ; the tillering, considering the nature of the soil, had been extraordinary, and the ears were upright and full ; I therefore carried out the experiment as far as practicable, selecting, as had been agreed upon at Liverpool, 16 perches from each variety, cutting it with the scythe, and accurately weighing the grain and straw. On the 2nd August, I marked out, as nearly as my eye could enable me to judge, 16 perches of average equal growth, and occupying relatively similar positions in the field, from Nos. 2, 3, 4, 5, and 6 white ; and from Nos. 1, 2, 4, and 5 red, similar quantities, but, excepting No. 4, not in relative situations to the white wheats ; yet still, had the season been generally favourable, such 16 perches, as I estimated, would have been fair samples of the produce of these wheats. The white wheats, however, throughout appeared better suited to my land than the reds ; and the result of the experiment has convinced me that, in soil and climate, similar to that on and in which I have made the trial, the growth of the former should be encouraged rather than the latter. Before reaping, the appearance of the different wheats was as follows :—Whites, No. 2, third ; No. 3, fourth ; No. 4, first ; No. 5, third ; No. 6, second ; Reds, No. 1, third ; No. 2, second ; No. 4, first ; No. 5, fourth. For the reason before specified, viz. the almost total destruction of the plant of No. 3, no portion of that wheat was measured off for the experiment.

On Friday the 5th of August, I cut with the scythe the whites, on the Monday the reds, and on the following Wednesday and Thursday carted the respec-

z

tive lots. The subjoined table will show you the results of the produce of wheat-straw and flour per acre of each kind, estimated from the product of 16 perches of each. I conceive, however, that, were the whole of the produce of each sort to be thrashed out, none of the crops would come up to this average; but the appearances of Nos. 4 and 6 white, and No. 4 red, were generally good, and the tabular results would not at most give 2 or 3 bushels per acre above their respective produce. Every attempt, however, as far as the season permitted, has been made to carry out the experiment with perfect fairness. I consider for the bulk of straw the yield of grain was extraordinary, and the samples of wheat of each kind can scarcely be surpassed, subjected as they were merely to the usual dressing. The miller declared that he had never ground better flour; but stated that, if he had any preference, he should give it to No. 2 white, and No. 1 red. In the process of converting the flour into bread, better than which I never have tasted, the plan recommended by Col. Le Courteur in vol. I. p. 115 of the Journal, was adopted, viz. "18 lbs. of the flour of each sort was placed to rise or sponge over-night with ¼ a pint of yeast and 2 quarts of water. At nine o'clock the next morning 4 oz. of fine salt were added, together with as much water, milk warm, as each kind would imbibe to fit it for the oven, which was well worked up, *drawn up* (as it were) into strings to expose it to the air as much as possible, in order to render it light, left to rise for 20 minutes or half an hour, baked and weighed next morning." The subjoined tabular statement will, I think, prove the necessity of carrying out all our experiments to the utmost, as otherwise great danger will arise of discarding valuable sorts, merely from their being in one or two instances less productive than others; which may be accounted for from the chances of the season, or other disturbing, but not sufficiently investigated, causes. Of the white breads No. 6 was the whitest, No. 4 the closest, and No. 2 the lighest; of the brown, or rather that made from the reds, No. 5 was the whitest and lighest: the others were much the same in colour and quality.

R. 5	W. 4	W. 6	W. 2	R. 1	Numbers of Wheats.
62	63	64	63	62	lbs. oz. Weight per Bushel.
11	5	5	8	0	
31	32	28	43	32	Head. Bus. lbs. Produce per Acre, estimated
21	8	17	12	20	60 from sixteen perches, cut,
45	22	22	7	0	weighed, and thrashed by
44½	30	60½	43	44	Tail. lbs. hand.
—	—	—	—	—	Tons.
4	4	4	3	2	cwts. Weight of Straw per Acre, si-
6	1	2	6	0	qrs. milarly estimated.
12	14	20	24	0	lbs.
1588	1994	1646	1583		lbs. Weight of best Seconds Flour
1767	1683	1700			per Acre, estimated from two
					bushels of each.
348	439	348	369		lbs. Weight of Gurgeons and Bran,
					ditto, ditto.
16	16	16	16	16	Qts. Quantity of Water imbibed by
					Pints. each sort in working up.
25	24	24	26		lbs. Quantity of Bread from 18 lbs.
8	0	14			oz. of Flour, of each sort.

It will be perceived that No. 4 whet was by far the most productive of the trial wheats, and as Mr. Jonas, when he presented this prolific seedling to me, sent me an account of its origin, I think I cannot do better than insert an extract from his letter, as it may encourage farmers should they accidentally discover amongst their crops ears of corn of extraordinary productiveness, dissimilar to the bulk of the crop, and of apparently new habits, to preserve and cultivate such more generally than they do at present, for the purpose of raising valuable varieties. Mr. Jonas thus wrote in September, 1841:—" You will oblige me by accepting 3 bushels of white wheat, which I have raised from a single ear, and by growing it side by side with the trial-wheats of Liverpool. I have no fear of the result; but should the Liverpool selected wheats be more prolific and valuable than mine, I shall be highly gratified, as I should cease growing the sort I have thus raised, and have some of that which was better. I would thank you not to sow this wheat before the latter part of October, or the beginning of November, as it is inclined to tiller early. I send you the exact quantities grown each year from this single ear, and I do so that you may avail yourself of any opportunity or way you please of showing to my brother-farmers how short a space of time is required to raise a good sort of any grain :—

Years.				Produce.
1838 dibbled in 50 kernels (30 of which only grew) 14¾ oz.
1839	..	..	..	14¾ oz.	.. .. 1 bush. 1 pk.
1840	..	..	..	1 bush. 1 peck	.. 45 bush.
1841	..	..	..	45 bush.	.. .. 537 bush.

And had this wheat not been as much red-gummed as my other sorts, I believe I should this year have had 100 bushels more."

This concludes my report, and it will be for the Council to determine, after the receipt of the reports of Messrs. Handley and Kimberley, whether or no they think the wheats selected at Liverpool for the prizes are so superior to the sorts in general use as to entitle them to the stamp of approbation which the award of the premiums from the Royal English Agricultural Society to either would confer. I consider all the four wheats remarkably good, and well worthy of general attention; and from my tabular results should be inclined to say that, if a premium is to be given to any, it should be the red No. 2, the produce of which was much greater in quantity than from the other reds.

King's Weston, 22nd September, 1842.

SECOND ANNUAL REPORT OF THE RUGELY FARMER'S CLUB.

In reviewing the proceedings of the club your committee regret that from unforeseen circumstances the subjects proposed have not been taken in the order in which they stood on the list; several have been entirely omitted, and these your committee recommend for discussion at an early period in the next year.

The first subject brought forward was—"On the best method of making summer fallows."

The gentleman who proposed it divided the subject in the following order. 1st, the advantage to be derived from a summer fallow; 2nd, the best method of making; 3rd, the expence; and lastly, the abuses to which the system is liable. He observed, if summer fallows were now to be introduced as a new system of fertilizing, and preparing the earth for a crop, they would he thought be rejected on account of the heavy expence of making them; still on very strong land he believed it impracticable to grow wheat extensively without summer fallows.

ON MAKING SUMMER FALLOWS.

First commence by ploughing the land to the full depth in the autumn, opening the furrows so that the water may pass off freely; then reverse the ploughing as early as possible after spring sowing, when diligent use should be made of the scuffle and harrow; cross plough once to a moderate depth, again using the scuffle and harrow. If the weather be favourable, the land will by these operations be freed from weeds. The dung should then be applied and covered immediately; after this no more working should be allowed for some time, until it is drawn into buts ready for sowing. On the expences:—These consist of two years rent, rates, labour, wear and tear, and interest of capital. If these items are fairly calculated they will prove a fallow crop of wheat to be not very profitable.

The abuses of fallowing are, subjecting the land to it more frequently than is necessary, and applying it to a great breadth of land that never ought to be subjected to it. He had often seen farms in the foulest, worst condition where the system is practised to a great extent. The farmer comforts himself for his previous neglect in not cleaning his land by the idea that the fallow year is at hand, when all things will be put straight. He stated, that he considered it the duty of every farmer to think well by what means he might lessen this most ruinously expensive system, and he conceived these were by efficient under draining, by drilling, hoeing, and adopting the best rotation of crops the nature of the farm and circumstances will allow. It was remarked by a member that he was more convinced every day of the necessity of effectually under-draining strong land; and until this was done, and the land pulverized with subsoil ploughing, he despaired of seeing fallows dispensed with.

Several members agreed with the proposer in all his remarks, except the one recommending cross ploughing, because we could never lay the land, even where the furrows had been in the cross ploughing, for some years; and in a wet season this part of the field would be wettest, and of course injure the growing crop. Several members stated they had always been in the habit of cross ploughing their fallows, but should omit it for the future.

The meeting resolved, "that they agreed with the plan proposed of making summer fallows, except that part of it that recommends cross ploughing; this they conceive may be omitted by using the scuffle across the land."

The next subject that occupied the attention of the club was—"The soiling of cattle in lieu of depasturing in the summer." The member introducing the subject stated, that for the purpose of soiling or summer stall feeding, it was desirable to begin in the previous months of August and September to sow a succession of rye, vetches, and rape. These will be fit for use in the spring before the clover and natural grasses are ready. He considered, by always having a regular succession of green crops, that he could keep a greater quantity of stock on an arable farm than he could on that which was

termed a grazing farm, and the quantity of manure he made, amply repaid any extra trouble and expence. That the plan was not only applicable to feeding cows, but also to milking cows. His maxim was, that without green crops few cattle can be kept; without cattle no manure; without manure no corn.

It was stated the system had been tried at Teddesly, by Mr. Bright; and he had had sufficient manure made from the soiled cattle to dress all the clover-leys on that extensive farm intended for wheat.

Very few of the members had tried soiling, but it was the opinion of all present that a portion of the stock on every farm might be soiled with advantage. It was resolved, " It appeared to this meeting, that two benefits arose from soiling—1st, the extra quantity of manure that can be made; 2nd, the saving of food: these they consider are equivalent to the expence, and they recommended a trial of the system at first on a limited scale."

At a subsequent meeting the discussion was— "On the best selection and mode of preparing seed wheat." The member who proposed the subject stated, he considered it one of the most important that could occupy the attention of the club. He first noticed the different species of wheat, their subdivision into varieties, and stated his opinion that these different varieties were frequently produced from a change of soil, climate, and cultivation. He would commence with the selection of seed for the very best strong land; on this he considered it of little consequence what kind of wheat was grown. For the strong clay soils he preferred the old red Lammas, and taking the average of seasons, he thought it would produce more bushels per acre, and of better quality than any other variety, and was also a more hardy plant. For light soils he preferred the different varieties of white wheat; they were equally productive with the red, and generally sold at a higher price. For spring sowing the white Talavera, and though he had heard it said that it was not a productive variety, he had always found it to yield quite as many bushels per acre as he expected. He recommended the selection of the very best sample of wheat for seed, and thought it false economy to sow an inferior article; also, often to change the seed, and always to procure it if possible from land that was earlier than that intended to be sown.

Every member present thought that a frequent change of seed was desirable, but that it was of little consequence where the seed was grown if the sample was clean and good. One advantage of changing seed was, that weeds which grow on light land will not flourish on strong soils, and vice versa.

It was resolved, "that for the strong clay land in this district the old red Lammas wheat is the best variety to cultivate; that the Golden-drop and Salmon are uncertain, and depend much on the season. For the light soils the white wheats are in the opinion of the meeting the most profitable to cultivate." Several members had practised spring sowing; those that had, thought the white Talavera wheat an early variety and equally productive with the other spring varieties.

The second part of the subject—on preparing seed wheat—was afterwards considered. The proposer stated that what was now considered indispensable was first discovered, according to Tull, from accident. A cargo of wheat was sunk near

Bristol, and recovered at the ebb tides ; being unfit for food, it was sold for seed, and at the following harvest all the wheat in that part of England was smutty except the produce of this
brined seed. He thought there was nothing that
required more care and attention than the preparation of the seed previous to sowing, he had for
some years used fermented urine and caustic lime
and his wheat had been free from smut. He had
a strong objection to chemical preparation, from
the great danger of destroying vegetation.

The club at length decided that a preparation
for seed wheat was requisite ; the majority
were in favour of fermented urine and caustic
lime. Several were named, all of which appeared to be efficacious. A wash of lime-water
had been used by some, who had never had
smut since using it, though previously they had
been subject to it.

At the meeting of the 10th of November—
" What is the best rotation of crops for the light
soils of this district ?"—the discussion was proposed by the chairman of the club. He stated
that without the powerful aid of chemistry we
could do little in producing the fruits of the earth ;
that increased fertility was to be mainly attributed
to the liberal but proper use of manure. In detailing on the rotation of crops, he considered the
broadcast system entirely exploded ; that the seed
is never committed to the soil when in a foul or
unfit state to receive it ; that he was fully convinced that a much greater breadth of oats and
barley was grown than was profitable to the
farmer. Wheat was the crop to be debited with
all our liabilities. He never grew what was called
loose or spring corn, but under extraordinary
circumstance ; as, for instance, after having
grazed a field of seeds for two years, and folded
sheep thereon with turnips during the winter ;
such land will be in a condition sufficient to
grow a crop of peas prior to the wheat. The
rotation of crops he recommended was what
was generally known as the four-course system, but sowing a crop of Talavera wheat
in lieu of barley ; thus wheat, turnips, Talavera wheat, and seeds ; or if the seeds had been
treated as be before stated, a crop of peas may be
taken. Many will be inclined to say, this is severe
work. Wheat every second year ; where is the
evil, if the land remain in good heart ? He had
adopted the practice he now recommended on a
field for six years, and in this the sixth year he
had more than 35 bushels per acre. Its last crop
was 41½ bushels, but every one knew that the
wheat plant was this year generally too thin on
the ground. Each crop during the term had been
an abundant one, and the produce was to him a
proof that the land was neither impoverished nor
out of condition. He contended that by applying
those chemical ingredients, in the shape of
manure, which the previous crop of wheat had exhausted, wheat might be grown every alternate
year without impoverishing the fertility of the
soil ; and he also contended that if we had the
knowledge to destroy the offensive excrements
left by plants in the ground, he saw no reason why
wheat or any other corn should not be grown crop
after crop as regularly as in any other rotation.
For the turnip crop, he recommended the manure
to be applied in the autumn. The land intended
for Swedes to be sown with rye, to be eaten off
with sheep in the spring. If for white turnips
with vetches ; the former he found useful for early

eating with ewes and lambs, the latter for mowing
for horses and stock in the yards. The rye is
eaten off by May-day. The land must then be
worked and pulverized, drawn up into ridges, and
the Swedes sown as soon after as possible. It was
contended in the rotation recommended, that the
wheat crop came too often ; and an enquiry was
also made why the proposer of the subject objected
to oats being taken in the rotation. To this the
reply was, that he thought oats an exhausting
crop, and did not for that reason cultivate them.
A member thought that turnips could not be
grown after rye or vetches ; this was decided to be
practicable to some extent. An objection was also
made to the manure being applied for turnips in
the autumn ; but again several members had tried
the plan, and approved of it. After a long discussion, the meeting separated without coming to any
resolution.

At the December meeting, " the best mode of
sowing corn" was proposed. The member who
undertook the subject stated that the remarks he
should offer were the result of his own experience.
He was of opinion that all kinds of grain should
be drilled or sown in rows to admit the sun and
wind to the soil between them. He thought this
method produced a strong stem, a heavy ear, and
a superior quality of grain. The space between
the rows should not be too wide ; seven inches
was sufficient for all white-strawed grain, for the
crop to cover the land, and wide enough for horse
or hand-hoeing. He was in favour of sowing
wheat on light soils when the land was moist ; on
strong soils sowing was more hazardous, and it
should not be delayed till late in the autumn ;
still, he preferred the land being moist, if the
operation could be done early. In conclusion, he
said that, though there are sometimes instances of
crops failing on land well prepared and manured,
which may be attributed to the mode of sowing or
the land being unfit for the growth of the kind of
grain sown, still he thought that many such disappointments might be prevented by a careful observation of facts, by comparing them together, and
reducing them to simple and general rules. Several strong land farmers contended it was the
better system to plough the wheat in on fallows ;
they thought if the crop was drilled the land was
apt to be too fine, and the plant did not tiller so
well in the spring. It was admitted that a very great
advantage was derived from being able to horse
and hand-hoe all crops sown in rows. Some of
the light land farmers preferred using the presser
instead of drilling in the seed, but if the crop was
drilled, it should on light soils always be across
the furrows. The meeting resolved that it is the
opinion of the strong land farmers, that the best
system of sowing wheat on fallows is to plough it
in. Resolved, " that on light soils grain of all kinds
should be drilled or sown after the land has been
pressed, so that the crop may be planted in rows.
The meeting consider the system of drilling and
hoeing all kinds of grain cannot be extended too
far ; that all white-strawed crops should have intervals of from seven to nine inches, beans and
peas from twelve to eighteen inches between each
row ; with these spaces, the horse-hoe may be
used effectually."

Several new members have joined the club
during the year, and an intimation was given at
one of the meetings that Earl Talbot had expressed a wish to be elected a member. Your
committee congratulate the club in having so dis-

tinguished a nobleman and practical farmer enrolled amongst its honorary members. A considerable number of works on agriculture have been purchased for the library during the year, and your committee beg the attention of those members who are in arrear with their subscription to the society of prompt payment, or your committee will be deprived of the means of ordering any new works that may come under their notice, and will also be obliged to curtail the number of the periodicals now taken in. A subscription has been given to the testimonial presented to Wm. Shaw, Esq., a gentleman to whom this club and the farmers of England are indebted for his efforts to improve the cultivation of the soil, and to support the cause of agriculture. One pound has been subscribed and paid to the fund for erecting a monument to the memory of the late Earl of Leicester, the man who did more, during a long life, than any other to improve the poor light lands of this kingdom.

For the Committee, JAMES WYLEY, Jun.,
Secretary.

ON THE PROPOSED REMEDIES FOR THE PRESENT DEPRESSION IN THE AGRICULTURAL AND COMMERCIAL INTERESTS OF THIS COUNTRY.

PAPER I.

BY GEORGE THOMPSON, JUN.

It is undeniable that the present distress, which appears to affect all classes—to be felt in every corner of this great and important kingdom, is calculated to create general alarm, and eventually to produce that lack of energy which must inevitably tend to increase the evil it laments. In such a state of society, at such an important and truly awful period, it is perfectly natural that there should rise up a swarm of conflicting country Premiers—country Secretaries of State—country Chancellors of the Exchequer—in fine, numerous political quacks, who have each of them some favourite nostrum, which they can highly recommend as being calculated to remove the disease under which "John Bull" suffers. Nor is it intended to decry such futile attempts at legislation, since it is obvious that it forms the "hobby" of many undoubtedly well-meaning individuals; and so long as their efforts are confined to literary effusions, no great danger need be apprehended from them; still less, when it is observed what a chaotic mass of mutually correcting "heal-ails" they submit to an enlightened public. But, while on the one hand, we are willing that such *unlicensed* physicians should prescribe, and administer their inoperative medicines, we must claim, on the other hand, a perfect right to apply correctives in such cases where an injurious effect may be produced. Witnessing then, with feelings of poignant sorrow, the too frequent application of the same (apparently remedial, but really) poisonous "lotion," without, of late, the usual correctives, we are constrained by a patriotic impetus to apply a counteracting "blister," which may extract, or rather nullify, the *alcohol-like* influence of a covetous prescription.

Among the numerous schemes broached for the restoration of our long-enjoyed and almost unprecedented prosperity, *the total repeal of our present corn laws* stands most conspicuous. With this project, therefore, we purpose first to deal; not with any pre-existing partiality for one side of the question or the other—not with any determination to make it appear that this or that opinion is the correct one, but solely with a desire to arrive at a correct conclusion, with the fair and honest purpose of affording an answer to the great question—Are our present corn laws beneficial or injurious?

In order that we may discuss the question impartially, we must thoroughly weigh the arguments on each side; and as the propriety of the continuation of the present law naturally became a controverted point from the circumstance of some party having first contended that its repeal would be advantageous, we will first examine the arguments which are adduced to show that the present corn laws should be repealed.

It is contended by the corn law repealers that as the nations on the continent of Europe and America are naturally capable of producing more than sufficient corn for their own consumption, and as we possess natural facilities for manufacturing to a much greater extent than is requisite for the supply of our home markets, as we also produce annually less food than is required for the maintenance of our own population, it is apparent that it would be attended with manifest advantages to allow the free and unrestricted importation of the surplus agricultural produce of other countries in exchange for our own surplus manufactured articles ; that we should find full employment for all classes, from the unlimited demand for our manufactures which would inevitably ensue on this extension of our markets ; that the grain-producing countries would be too eager to exchange their agricultural produce for our manufactures, at an advantage to us ; that, at present, we import uncertain quantities of foreign corn, purely on speculation as to the possibility of selling it in this country, owing to the ever varying nature of our sliding scale of duties, which renders it imperative on us to pay cash for the corn we require ; that this paying cash or bullion to other countries, diminishes our own pecuniary resources, and produces stagnation in our commercial affairs; that the only class the present corn laws can possibly benefit, are the aristocracy and other landed proprietors, by maintaining corn at an extravagant price, and thus enabling them to obtain a greater rent at the cost of the remaining portion of the community : these are the arguments usually urged by the advocates of a repeal.

The supporters of the present corn laws contend, on the contrary, that the British farmer is a member of a community more highly taxed than those foreign nations which would supply us with food, and that the free importation of comparatively untaxed foreign corn must have the effect of driving the home grower out of the market, and of thus depriving the British manufacturer of his best customer.

Such are the strongest arguments broached by each party in favour of their respective views, and such are the arguments we purpose taking into our consideration.

It is undoubtedly correct that the continents of Europe and North America are capable of, and indeed are at this time, producing more than sufficient corn for their own consumption ; it is also unquestionable that Great Britain can produce a much greater quantum of manufactured articles than is necessary for the complete supply of her own markets. We admit also that Great Britain has of late years produced an insufficiency of corn, but we by no means admit that she is incapable of producing more; on the contrary, we shall, in a future letter, endeavour to show that the British Isles may, and will, be made productive of one-half more agricultural produce than they at present afford; indeed, we should imagine that the most staunch supporters of a repeal would readily admit that Great Britain has not yet reached her utmost extent of agricultural productiveness; and if they once admit this, what an argument they supply for checking the introduction of foreign produce, for preserving ourselves as long as possible from a dependency on those nations who look on our supremacy with an envious eye—but more of this in a future letter. It is sufficient for us to know that England is capable of producing a larger quantity of grain than is required for the sustenance of her people.

The next argument of the repealers is, that by a free importation of corn we should extend the markets for our manufactures, and that, Great Britain being a manufacturing country, her legislators should encourage the extension of the markets for her chief productions. This is the principal argument in favour of a repeal, and will therefore require the greater attention.

We observe that the nations from whom our supplies of grain would be chiefly obtained are those contiguous to our shores—nations jealous of our greatness, who, distinctly perceiving that we owe our superiority in a great measure to our manufacturing skill, are of course desirous of imitating our internal policy, and of thus arriving at our enviable position. Germany, Poland, Prussia, and southern Russia, are the countries from which our chief supplies would be drawn. It is contended by many that America would afford our principal supply; but a little consideration must convince such that the European nations would be enabled to afford corn at a much lower rate on our shores, as the cost of transport would be considerably greater from America than from the continent of Europe. Hence, the neighbouring states would afford the chief supply. Now, would they take manufactured articles in return for their corn? We might suppose that the past would answer this question satisfactorily to all, and if it would but be admitted as a lesson by those who advocate a change, we flatter ourselves a repeal of the present corn laws would no longer be advocated, since we find, on reference to unquestionable authorities, that the years in which we imported the greatest quantities of corn were marked by no increase in our exportations—in fact, that they would not take our manufactures in return for their corn. They would have gold. If they wanted our manufactures, they would take them. But what is the fact? They witness —and have long witnessed—our commercial greatness, and they are determined to become manufacturers themselves. If it be true that they require our goods—that they have a desire for our productions, would they not take them in exchange for their corn? If they had any desire to promote reciprocal dealings, would they not have taken the first step towards a system of reciprocity, by allowing our manufactures to enter duty-free? Decidedly they would. But have they done so? They have not. They have invariably taken the opposite course; for in 1823 we repealed

the navigation laws, with a view to satisfy Prussia, and that nation immediately formed the Prusso Germanic League, which imposed a duty on British manufactures, practically amounting to fifty per cent. Many other instances could easily be quoted of concessions made by England, but met by other countries with the imposition of duties calculated to compel their respective populations to manufacture for themselves. Is it rational, then, to suppose that they will adopt a different course with respect to the corn laws? Would it be wisdom on the part of our legislators, with these lessons engraven upon their minds, rashly to repeal the corn laws, when, judging by experience (and experience is the better guide in such cases), it would be followed by the imposition of prohibitory duties on British manufactures? It is of no avail to contend that it would be to their interest to act reciprocally; we have not to legislate as though mankind were disposed to do as they *ought* to do, but we have to legislate with mankind as they *are*. Nor is it surprising to the inquiring mind that such difficulties should present themselves. Unquestionably other nations have as great a right to manufacture as the British—unquestionably observing, as they must, our greatness, they will imitate the means by which we have attained that greatness. It will occur to them, that if they have cheaper provisions, and natural facilities for manufacturing, they need only our mechanical knowledge to compete with us. Being naturally jealous of us, their rulers will assuredly throw every obstacle they can in the way of any encouragement of our trade. *All political experience tends to show that we should not extend our markets by repealing the corn laws.* But, that we may not be accused of coming to a premature conclusion, we will endeavour to show that, supposing we should have a demand for manufactured articles to the value of the corn imported, still that the increase would not be worth so great a sacrifice. We will grant that much of the poorer land in this country would be thrown out of cultivation. The grain which has hitherto been supplied by this poor land would then be grown on richer soils in other countries; hence, so far as this took place, we should merely remove the market for a quota of our manufactures from this country to another; inasmuch as the most violent repealers do not for one moment anticipate that other nations will take more than an equivalent, in manufactured articles, for the corn we import. Consequently, the only increased demand we can fairly expect will be to the amount of the grain we already import, which the repealers expect other nations will then take manufactures for, instead of bullion, as at present. The quantity of wheat (foreign and colonial) which was imported in 1841 was 2,783,602 quarters, the average price of which, in the foreign ports, we may estimate at 35s. per quarter; this will make a gross amount of 4,871,303*l*. 10s., which we will call 6,000,000*l*., by way of including all other importations of grain, &c. Thus, it appears, we would run the risk of obtaining a *less* certain market for our manufactures, for the sake of a foreign demand to the amount of 6,000,000*l*., which is not quite *one-twenty-fourth* of our annual production. Supposing, which we have no rational ground to suppose, that foreign countries would take manufactures in return for their corn, yet the value of that corn would only amount to *one-twenty-fourth* of our annual production in manufactured articles. In order to obtain this, we must sacrifice a large proportion of our home-consumers—those who would be thrown out of employment from the sudden influx of foreign grain consequent on a repeal of the corn laws. And it would be well to bear in mind the fact, that the rich soils of other countries, even if they should grow our corn, would not require such a proportionate number of hands to cultivate them as the poor soils of this country do. Hence, conceding that they would take the same quota of our manufactures per head as the British take, still there would not be the same number of individuals employed in raising one thousand quarters in their rich soils as in our poor ones. By this we must eventually be the losers.

It is maintained by the advocates of a repeal that the grain-producing countries would be too eager to exchange their agricultural produce for our manufactures, at an advantage to us. What are the advantages which are expected to be attained by the free barter of our manufactures for foreign corn? An extended and almost unlimited demand for our productions, with cheaper food for our artisans. We have already endeavoured to show that we should not extend our markets by a repeal of the corn laws; but we will illustrate and confirm this deduction by a farther consideration of simple facts.

If, by the operation of a free trade in corn, ten million quarters of grain were supplied by foreign countries instead of our own, it is obvious to the unprejudiced that we should throw the producers of that quantity of grain in our own country out of employment, and call into existence that number on the continent. Thus we should merely remove the market from home to another land, since no one has yet dared to suppose that other nations will take more, in proportionate value, of our articles, than the corn we import. Indeed, one strong argument of the anti-corn-law party is, that they (foreign nations) have not money to purchase our manufactures, and can only take them to the amount of the corn we import. We must look for the advantages, then, in the reduced price of corn. Now, would corn be reduced in price by a free trade? That it would be so reduced in the outset is undeniable, since vast quantities of foreign grain would rush into the English markets—grain produced on the most fertile soils in the world—on land cultivated by men whose condition is not far removed from that of slaves, and in countries far less burdened with taxation than our own; the consequence of which would be, that for a few years they would sell corn at a less price than our poorest class of wheat soils could be made to produce it, even if they were rent-free. Four or five years of nonremunerative prices would ruin the majority of our farmers. The land would inevitably go out of cultivation. An increasing population would demand increased supplies of grain. An increasing demand for foreign grain would raise the prices, and it is by no means certain that the price of grain would not ultimately be raised above that at which we now purchase it. As our land went out of cultivation, our agriculture would decline, and we must eventually be placed at the mercy of foreign governments. It is not improbable that, under a free trade in corn, Russia would subjugate this country, for the nations which would be our chief resource are those that live under the influence of that power.

But it is argued that we should have abundant employment for all our population in providing manufactured articles for those countries. Bearing in mind that we should only import a sufficient quantity of corn to feed our population, and consequently that we should have a foreign instead of a home market, we will ascertain what proportion of manufactures is consumed per head, per annum, by our own countrymen, and what by our supposed new customers. The returns of the exports in 1836 show that the Russians consumed eight-pence-halfpenny-worth of our manufactures per head, and the Prussians three-pence-halfpenny-worth; whilst the British at the same period consumed *five pounds, thirteen shillings, and eight-pence farthing-worth* per head, of the manufactures of their own country. Even the inhabitants of the United States of America consumed but *seventeen shillings'*-worth each of our manufactures. Would it, then, be consistent to allow the inhabitants of Russia, Prussia, or America, to supply us with corn, when they, none of them, consume *one-sixth* the quantity of our manufactures that those individuals do who now raise corn for us? Yet it will be contended that they would take a much greater proportion if we would take their corn. We already take as much of their corn as we require; but do they take an equal quantity of our productions? If they did, we should not have had such a serious drain upon our currency. Again, are they in that advanced state of civilization to require so great a proportion of our manufactures as we ourselves consume? What occasions the great consumption of our manufactures in the home market? Nothing less than the uninterrupted enjoyment of liberty, wealth, comfort, and education, by our industrious classes, for a long series of ages. And nothing less than the same time, the same liberal laws, the same extension of refinement, will produce the same capacity for the enjoyment of luxuries in the corn-producing people of the continent of Europe. *It appears, therefore, that we should neither extend the demand for our manufactures, nor ultimately be enabled to purchase corn at a less price, by a repeal of the corn laws.*

The next argument we shall consider is, that at present we import uncertain quantities of foreign corn, purely on speculation as to the possibility of selling it in this country, owing to the ever-varying nature of our sliding scale of duties, which renders it imperative on us to pay cash for the corn we require. That this paying cash or bullion to other countries diminishes our own pecuniary resources, and produces stagnation in our commercial affairs. Very good. All this is perfectly correct. But, instead of being an argument against the corn laws, it is one in their favour. We know, or at least ought to know, that the corn-producing countries are more eager for our money than they are for our manufactures. Yet, say the anti-corn-law party, the cause that prevents our goods from entering foreign ports is, that they impose high duties upon them, which would be taken off if we removed the duty on their corn, and that we should then be enabled to effect exchanges, and no longer be subject to the ruinous consequences of an incessant drain on our specie. Again we assert, experience is our best monitor; and what does experience tell us? That our concessions—our attempts at a system of reciprocity—have been invariably met with no similar concession on the part of other countries. We made concessions to Prussia—they were met by a League, who practically prohibited our manufactures. We did the same with Portugal and Belgium—they met us with increased duties on our articles. We have recently lowered the duties on all foreign productions : have they shown the slightest disposition to act reciprocally ? Decidedly the reverse. They show a disposition to impose increased duties on those articles in which we have the advantage of them. Then how absurd—how irrational—for us to imagine that they will adopt a different course for the future. They have abundance of natural power, cheap labour, no combination amongst the lower orders to maintain wages ; and is it probable that they will sacrifice all these manifest advantages to promote our prosperity? Their course is a different one. They distinctly perceive that commercial and manufacturing pursuits are the foundations of national prosperity, and they will steadily but unflinchingly persevere in their efforts to supplant us in those branches. It is most probable that the continental states will continue to prevent, by fiscal regulations, the importation of our manufactures. Even if Russia and Prussia would take our manufactures in return for their corn, still the inhabitants of those countries are not in that state of civilization which would render them so great proportionate consumers as those individuals who now grow corn for us—our own people. Consequently, if our own agricultural population expend the value of five million quarters of grain on our manufactures, the producers of that quantity of grain, even in civilized America, would not expend one million quarters for the same purpose; the remaining five million quarters must therefore be paid for by us, with British money. Hence, as it is obviously the purpose of other countries, at least those countries who are jealous of our power, to rival us in manufacturing—to oppose our commercial prosperity, they will not take our manufactures in return for their corn. Such being the case, as they have abundance of corn and want money, they will undersell, for a time, our home-growers ; we shall thereby lose our best customers, and be compelled to give money for grain, instead of manufactures. The result will be a never-ceasing drain upon our currency. We shall have that commercial embarrassment *perpetuated* amongst us, which we now experience *occasionally*. *A repeal of the corn laws would increase our commercial depression.*

The argument that the only class the present corn laws can possibly benefit are the landed proprietors, by maintaining corn at an extravagant price, and thus enabling them to obtain a greater rent, at the cost of the remaining portion of the community, is as absurd as it is groundless. The introduction of foreign corn would cause a temporary reduction in the price of grain and other agricultural produce, which would probably continue a sufficient length of time to cause the ruin of many British farmers, and the general reduction of rents. When this had taken place, foreign corn would rise in price, and would assuredly become higher than it is, on the average, under the present law. It is needless to state that this would benefit no class. Then, if this did not ensue—if corn remained permanently lower in price, who would be benefited by it ? What advantage would it be to the Manchester operative to purchase corn at five shillings per bushel of the Prussian, who bought threepence-halfpenny-worth of his goods per annum, rather than at seven

shillings of the Englishman, who bought more than five pound's worth? If the labourer could obtain food at a less price, he would be compelled to work for less wages. The price of food regulates the price of wages from ten years to ten years. What would it benefit the manufacturer to lose his best customers? Then who are his best customers ? The following calculation will show : —In 1837 the total value of British manufactures was more than 148,000,000*l.*, but the average exportation for three years ending 1837 was only 48,500,000*l.* We perceive, therefore, that Great Britain consumes more than two-thirds of her own manufactures. And who are her greatest consumers? The aristocracy and landed proprietors. They are the greatest consumers of British manufactures, yet the *repealers* would sacrifice them for the remote chances of a foreign trade. We must conclude, therefore, that the corn laws are for the benefit of all classes—that their benefits are not confined to the aristocracy, but that they are essential to general prosperity.

Our next paper will be devoted to an equally searching investigation of the arguments usually urged in favour of the corn laws.

Lion-Street, Kidderminster,
　　March 20th, 1843.

PRIZE ESSAY ON MANURES,

FOUNDED ON EXPERIENCE OR OBSERVATION ALONE.

AWARDED TO MR. DANIEL BANTON, OF SEISDON, OCTOBER 11TH, 1842.

Experiments with Several Artificial Manures, Applied to Wheat.

It must be gratifying to the friends of agriculture to see the rapid progress it has made of late, now that it has for its patrons most of the noble of the land, and assisted as it is by men in the highest rank of science ; and I hope I may add, gratifying to see also the British Farmer of the present day free from prejudice, and anxious to test, by practice and experience, any theory that he believes likely to lead to beneficial results. The farmer has naturally enough of caution (which by some has been called by a different name) to prevent him straying too far into the field of theory, but courage enough, I trust, to engage in, and assist by his practical knowledge, the discovery of a more sure and certain application of manures ; so as to lead to unerring conclusions as to what is the cheapest, the best, and the most profitable to apply to the different lands and different crops of his country.

I have used guano and nitrate of soda, as manures for wheat and turnips, rather extensively this year ; the particulars of which upon wheat, I shall give below, and have only to state here, with regard to turnips, that guano promises to be an effective manure. I have applied it both for common turnips and Swedes, and it appears to answer well in both cases. Part of a field for Swedes had half a dressing in the winter with fold-yard manure, not of the best quality, and ploughed in. Immediately before being ridged up, I had sown on the surface scarcely one cwt. of guano per acre: the other part of the field was dressed with butcher's manure. The Swedes are not early, but still growing fast, and promise to be a big crop. The part where the guano was used is quite as good as the other, and perfectly free from mildew. I applied one cwt. of guano upon a plot of spring vetches, but could see no effect.

The following manures were made trial of in a field of land (in tolerable good condition) situate at Seisdon, within the limits of the Stewponey Agricultural Society, in the county of Stafford. The soil is a light sandy loam, commonly called "turnip and barley land," subsoil a gravelly sand, based on the red sandstone. The field has a gently sloping aspect to the north-west, a year old clover root, flay-ploughed, and was drilled seven inches wide with white wheat on the 19th of October, 1841, at the rate of 2½ bushels per acre, 38 quarts to the bushel. The plant of wheat was thick and strong through the winter, and at the time of applying the manures was rather forward for the season. On the 23rd of April six plots of land were accurately measured with a chain, each containing one-eighth of an acre, and manured as under:—

No. 1, with guano, at the rate of 1¼ cwt. per acre.
" 2, guano and nitrate of soda, equal proportions, 1¼ cwt. per acre together.
" 3, nitrate of soda, 1¼ cwt. per acre.
" 4, white caustic lime, at the rate of 4 tons per acre.
" 5, lime and salt, in proportion of 5 cwt. of salt to 10 cwt. of lime per acre, mixed a week before being applied.
" 6, had no manure.

There was no rain for ten days after the manures were applied; the days being hot, and the nights generally frosty. Seven days after the first rain, a slight difference in colour was visible in plots No. 1, 2, and 3, where the nitrate and guano were applied; and on the 16th of May a striking difference was seen in those plots to the rest of the field, the nitrate assuming the deepest, the nitrate and guano the next shade, and the guano the palest green of the three. There were no visible effects where lime alone, and lime and salt were put. From May till the wheat shot into the ear, which it did at the same time all over the field, the plots, No. 1, 2, and 3, might be distinctly traced by the eye at a considerable distance. The red rust attacked the wheat pretty generally in this neighbourhood, and I think the white wheat more subject to it than the red, notwithstanding which I have seldom grown red, finding that although the white wheat is yearly more or less attacked by the rust, it rarely injures the sample or yield. I find the produce of the white not inferior to the red upon the same land, and the sample worth more at market.

In passing through the field in question it was perceptible that the rust had attacked the three first plots more than the rest of the field, particularly the plot on which the nitrate of soda alone was spread; and there was also some red gum to be seen in that plot, from which the rest of the field was nearly free.

The crop over the whole field was a fair one, and stood well. It was cut by Welchmen with hooks on the 12th of August, and the produce of each plot kept by itself, and so threshed. The result of which is as follows:—

Produce of Wheat per Imperial Bushel.			Straw.	Weight of Wheat per Imp. Bushel.	Straw per Acre.			Wheat per Acre the Imp. Bushel.
	bush.	pks.	lbs.	lbs.	cwt.	qr.	lb.	bush.
No. 1,	5	2½	479	62	34	0	24	45
" 2,	5	2	428	62	30	2	8	44
" 3,	5	½	436	62	30	2	16	41
" 4,	5	1¼	426	62	30	2	6	42½
" 5,	4	3½	326	62	23	1	4	39
" 6,	4	3½	326	61½	23	1	4	39

I have not calculated the tail corn, which was very trifling, not exceeding a quart from each lot. It appears that the lime and salt did not produce any effect, except half-a-pound per bushel in the weight. It perhaps will appear singular that each lot was exactly the same weight per bushel in the five first, but such was the case. The nitrate and guano were procured direct from the importer, and I believe were genuine. Nitrate 24s. 6d., and the guano 20s. per cwt. The lime 12s., and salt 19s. per ton, exclusive of carriage.

SUMMARY.

	Cost of Manure per Acre, including Carriage.			Increased Value of Straw per acre, at 2s. 6d. per cwt.			Increased Value of Grain per acre, at 7s. per bushel, imperial measure.			Total Increase in value of Crop, per acre.			Net Profit per acre after deducting the expence of Manure.			Loss per acre after deducting cost of Manure.		
	£	s.	d.	£	s.	d.	£	s.	d.	£	s.	d.	£	s.	d.	£	s.	d.
Guano	1	7	6	1	7	0	2	2	0	3	9	0	2	1	6			
Nitrate and Guano ..	1	10	3	0	18	2	1	15	0	2	13	2	1	2	11			
Nitrate of Soda alone	1	18	0	0	18	4	0	14	0	1	12	4				0	0	8
Lime	3	8	0	0	18	2	1	4	6	2	2	8				1	5	4
Lime and Salt	0	14	0	None.			None.									0	14	0

The foregoing summary, I think, clearly proves that the cost of lime and nitrate of soda, and indeed of most other manures, is at present disproportionately high, compared with the price of grain, and unless considerably reduced, cannot long continue to be used for agricultural purposes; as there is but little prospect, I fear, of grain or other agricultural produce taking a higher price for any length of time than it does at present, under the altered corn laws and new tariff.

It is much to be wished that no untoward circumstances may occur to damp the energy of the British farmer, which at present is so manifest throughout the country; and that he may still be enabled to make a living profit, and continue his course of improvement, which cannot fail ultimately to benefit all classes. If a single brother farmer can gain one useful hint from the experiments on manures before recited, it will gratify and well repay the attempt at an essay by the humble writer, A MEMBER OF THE STEWPONEY AGRICULTURAL SOCIETY.

Seisdon, October 1st, 1842.

GLOUCESTER FARMERS' CLUB.

Eleventh Meeting, November 12, 1842.

THE CULTIVATION OF THE POTATO.

Mr. J. B—— said, that owing to the frequent injudicious attempts which had been made to grow potatoes on soils to which they were unsuitable, the cultivation of this plant had become out of repute, nevertheless he could not but think that on loose and friable soils with a porous substratum, to which they were best adapted, it was a crop well deserving the attention of the farmer.

He was in the habit of ploughing the ground on which they were to be planted, in the autumn, and in this state it was left till the dry weather set in the following spring, when after it had been ploughed and worked till it was thoroughly pulverised, deep furrows were struck 27 inches apart with the double mould-board plough, and at the bottom of these furrows the sets were planted 12 inches from each other, and immediately covered with hoes. Whole potatoes were to be preferred for seed, as they were less liable to failure from dry-rot or other causes. As soon as the plants appeared, the rows were cross-hoed, and the horse-hoe followed in the intervals, working as deep as possible, and in this way 10 or 12 inches of mould was obtained. The potatoes were then moulded up by means of a small plough of a peculiar construction, which left the tops of the drills rather flat, and thus retained the moisture for a greater length of time. Great care was taken to perform all these operations, if possible when the ground was quite dry. A friend of his (the late Mr. D——), had been accustomed to plant his potatoes thus—

. . . .
. . . .
. . . .

and thought that by the room given for the extension of the end-roots, a greater produce was obtained, but it appeared to him that the circulation of the air among the plants would be prevented, which must be prejudicial. The potatoes were dug with a three-pronged fork, and the roots collected by women and children, and at the same time those which were small or injured were separated. The heaps were made on level ground of a moderate size, about a waggon load in each: they were covered with straw, and soil dug from round the sides was thrown over them and smoothed down. He recommended the "bread-fruit" as a very valuable variety. "London purples" and "Worcester selks" were also good, but the sort of potato should be adapted to the soil. In planting, it might be taken as a general rule that the larger topped varieties should be grown further apart than those which were less luxuriant. He was not in the habit of manuring for potatoes, as he found the quality of those grown without manure was very superior.

Mr. M—— was accustomed to have his land raftered in the autumn, and during the winter's frost the manure was laid in the hollows, and covered by turning back the furrows upon it. In the spring, the sets (whole potatoes) were planted 24 inches apart, and covered with a breast-plough. He found it useful to harrow the ground after the plants appeared, and they were then weeded and moulded up in the usual way.

Mr. H—— submitted to the meeting the following account of a series of experiments which he had tried upon the cultivation of the potato during the season just ended, and gave in the following tables of the results of his experiments on the growth of potatoes on a light soil (stone brash on the upper oolite), in the parish of Painswick. The produce is given in bags, the weight of each bag being 2½ cwt., or 280lbs. The tubers described as "full sized" were those set apart for the table. The "small sized" were those separated for the pigs, but perhaps rather larger than they would be when such a selection is made for market.

TABLE No. 1.

For 1841.

Sorts.	Sets.	Manure per Acre.	Distance between Rows	Distance between Plants.	Produce per acre. Full-sized Tubers.	Small Tubers.	Total.
			Feet.	Feet.	Bags.	Bags.	Bags.
Welsh kidneys	Whole, middle size	20 bushels soot	3	1	60	25½	85½
Ditto	Ditto ditto	12 tons long dung	3	1	77⅔	10⅓	88
Purples	Cut sets	Ditto	3	1	79½	18	97½
Ditto	Whole, middle size	Ditto	3	1	86¾	25	111¾
Ditto	Ditto ditto	Ditto	4	1	87⅔	26⅔	114⅓
Ditto	Ditto large	Ditto	3	3	97$\frac{1}{7}$	17$\frac{1}{7}$	114$\frac{2}{7}$
Ditto	Ditto ditto	Ditto	4	2	83	19	102

These figures afford four subjects of comparison.

1st. The effect of soot as a manure compared with that of long dung.

Thus that the Welsh kidneys treated with 12 tons of long dung gave a total of 88 bags per acre, but treated with 20 bushels of soot, only 85½. The crop also in the first case was of better quality, for the soot gave not only a less total produce by 2½ bags, but 25½ bags of that produce were under-sized and unfit for the table, while the long dung gave only 10½ small sized.

2nd. The effects of cut sets as compared with whole sets.

The whole sets of the purples of a middle size yielded 13¾ bags an acre more than the cut sets on the gross crop, when both were planted at 3ft. by 1ft., but only 6¾ more of the full sized tubers. When the whole sets were increased in distance to 4ft. by 1ft., and compared with cuts at 3 by 1, the excess in favour of wholes was increased to 16¼ on the total crop, but to only about 8 bags of the full sized. When the plants appeared above ground, not a blank could be observed among the *whole* sets, while several of the cut sets rotted and never came up. During the summer a marked difference in the growth of each was observed, a much less bulk of haulm but a greater profusion of blossoms being produced from the cut than from the whole sets.

3rd. The produce of different sorts compared.

The Welsh kidneys and the purples being treated in every respect similarly, the former gave a "total produce" of 88 bags, but of "full sized tubers" only 77¾, while the latter gave a total of 111¾, and of "large tubers" 86¾. So that this year the purples gave a better yield than the Welsh kidneys on the "total crop" by 23 bags, and on the "full-sized tubers" of 9.

4th. The effect of distances on produce.

The middle sized seed of the purples planted in rows 3 feet apart, each plant being only 1 foot from its neighbour in the row, giving 3 square feet to each plant, yielded a gross crop of 111¾ bags, but when the rows were increased to 4 feet apart, the plants in the rows in each case remaining at 1 foot, giving 4 square feet to each plant, the total produce was increased to 114½ bags, the proportion of small tubers being very nearly the same. So that while the smaller distance took 9 sacks per acre for seed, and the greater took 6¾, there was also an increase in produce at the greater distance of 2⁷⁄₁₂ bags, making in all a gain of 4½ bags an acre; but when the distance of the plant in the row was increased from 1 to 2 feet, although the large and probably more prolific seed was used in the latter case, both rows remaining at 4 feet apart, the crop was reduced from 114 to 102 bags an acre, showing that at this point the increased distance of the plant in the row began to diminish the produce; but which is important, the large seed of the purples planted 3 feet apart every way and hoed up all round, each plant consequently occupying 9 feet superficial of ground gave 114¾ bags, while those in rows at 4 feet apart and plants at 2 feet, each plant occupying only 8 superficial feet, gave only 102 bags, while the loss on the "small sized" is still greater. So that, although 8 square feet are too much for each plant when the rows are 4 feet apart and the plants 2, 9 square feet are not too much when the plants are set three feet apart every way, and hoed all round.

The following table shows the general results of the crop of 1842 :—

TABLE No. 2.

Sorts.	Whole sets.	Distance between Rows.	Distance between Plants.	Produce per Acre.		
				Full-sized Tubers.	Small Tubers.	Total.
		Feet.	Feet.	Bags.	Bags.	Bags.
Purples	Large	3	3	85	11¼	96¼
Ditto	Ditto	3	2	86¾	15¼	101¾
Ditto	Ditto	4	2	70½	16½	87
Ditto	Middle size	4	1	82½	19¼	101¾
Ditto	Ditto	3	1	66½	20½	87
Welsh kidneys	Large	3	3	84	2	86
Ditto	Ditto	3	2	108½	4½	113
Ditto	Ditto	4	2	91½	3¼	94¾
Ditto	Middle size	4	1	85¾	6¾	92½
Ditto	Ditto	3	1	101½	12¼	113¾
Jerseys	Large	3	1 6in.	105	11¾	117½

This year there was no comparison as to the effect of manures, each trial being treated alike in this respect with about 15 tons of rotten dung to the acre, nor was there any further comparison as to cuts and whole sets—the result being in conformity with that generally obtained by others, it was taken for granted that whole sets are more prolific than cuts, and nothing but the former were planted.

The above table, however, offers the two following points of comparison :—

1st. The produce of Welsh kidneys again compared with the purples.

2nd. The produce of both at different distances.

1st. What was the relative proportion of produce from the two sorts?

	Full-sized Tubers.		Small-sized Tubers.		Total Crop.	
	Purples.	Welch Kidneys.	Purples.	Welch Kidneys.	Purples.	Welsh Kidneys.
Large Seed:	Bags.	Bags.	Bags.	Bags.	Bags.	Bags.
Distance 3 by 3 ft.	85	84	11¼	2	96¼	86
3 by 2 ft.	86⅗	108½	15⅕	4½	101⅗	113
4 by 2 ft.	70½	91½	16½	3¼	87	94¾
Middle sized seed:						
Distance 3 by 1 ft.	66½	101½	20½	12¼	87	113¾
4 by 1 ft.	82½	85¾	19¼	6¾	101¾	92½
	390$\frac{9}{10}$	471¼	82$\frac{7}{10}$	28¾	473⅗	500
Average....	78⅕	94¼	16½	5¾	94$\frac{7}{10}$	100

So that at all the distances (except 3 × 3, and there the difference is only one bag in favour of the Purples), the Welsh kidneys were more prolific in "full sized tubers" than the Purples; and upon the average of the crops from the several distances, the proportion in favour of Welsh kidneys was as 94¼ to 78⅕, or 16 bags excess. In three out of the five different distances the "total crop" of Welsh kidneys was the largest, and upon the average of all the distances, the total crop per acre of the Welsh kidneys was to the purples as 100 to 94$\frac{7}{10}$, or an excess of 5$\frac{3}{10}$ bags. The proportions of "small" also among the Welsh kidneys compared with the purples was as 5½ to 16½ bags per acre, thus showing the sample to be much better, while the quantity was greater. This result, however, is at variance with the single instance of comparison for 1841, which gave on the "total crop" 23, and on the "full sized" 9, bags in favour of the purples; a discrepancy which shows how rash it is to draw general conclusions from a single experiment in a particular year, or indeed from any such experiments without repeatedly verifying the facts. Indeed, when it is considered that a very slight difference in the soil, the season, or in the treatment of any of these subjects of comparison, may produce diametrically opposite results, we see at once the use of frequently registering, and recording, and publishing experiments of this sort, in order that at last we may be able, from numbers of similar results, to lay down some general rules. The difference in treatment of the two years in the present case was, that in 1841 both sorts were manured with only 12 tons of long dung, and in 1842 with 15 tons of rotten dung. The inference therefore is, that purples require a less rich soil than the Welsh kidneys.

2nd. The comparison of produce at different distances.

	Full-sized Tubers per Acre.			Small Tubers per Acre.			Total produce per Acre.		
	3 × 3ft.	4 × 2ft.	3 × 2ft.	3 × 3ft.	4 × 2ft.	3 × 2ft.	3 × 3ft.	4 × 2ft.	3 × 2ft.
	Bags.	Bags.	Bags.	Bags.	Bags.	Bags.	Bags.	Bags.	Bags.
Purples, large seed	85	70½	86⅗	11¼	16½	15⅕	96¼	87	101⅗
Welsh kidney ditto	84	91½	108½	2	3¼	4½	86	94¾	113

The result of last year's trial went to show that by increasing the distance of the rows from 3 to 4 feet apart, the plants in each case remaining at 1, there was an increase of crop; but when the distance of the plant was further increased to 2 feet, there was a diminution, showing that the space allotted to each plant cultivated in rows might be increased up to 4 square feet, but that 8 feet was too much.

The experiment of 1842 just quoted shows again that 4 × 2, compared with 3 × 2, is too much—thus the purples at 3 × 2, each plant having 6 square feet, exceeded those at 4 × 2, or 8 square feet to each plant, in "full sized tubers" by 16 bags, and in "total produce" by 14 bags. But the plants 3 × 3, or 9 square feet to each, gave nearly an equal quantity of "full sized tubers" with those at 3 × 2, and 15 bags more than those at 4 × 2, and in "total produce" only 5 bags less than those at 3× 2, and 9 more than those at 4 × 2—showing the sample to be superior.

With the Welsh kidneys the smaller distance in every case gives the greater produce. Those at 3 × 2 giving 17 bags of "full sized tubers," and 19 of "total produce," more than those at 4 × 2; and those at 4 × 2 giving 7 bags "full sized tubers," and 8¾ of "total produce," more than those at 3 × 3, so that in this case the space of 9 square feet to a plant, although hoed up all round, seems considerably too much, leaving the inference that the Welsh kidney, with a richer manure and probably on a richer soil, bears much closer planting than the purples.

The last comparison had reference only to large seed. With middle sized seed the comparison stands thus:—

	Full-sized Tubers per Acre.		Small Tubers per Acre.		Total Produce per Acre.	
	4 × 1ft.	3 × 1ft.	4 × 1ft.	3 × 1ft.	4 × 1ft.	3 × 1ft.
	Bags.	Bags.	Bags.	Bags.	Bags.	Bags.
Purples, middle sized	82½	66½	19¼	20½	101¾	87
Welsh kidneys	85¾	101½	6¾	12¼	92½	113¾

It should be observed that the spaces are now less than in the preceding comparison, and it seems, by reducing the space of the purples from 4 × 1, or 4 square feet to each plant, to 3 × 1, or 3 square feet, that they are brought too close, for the excess of produce in favour of the larger space is considerable. The reverse, however, prevails with the Welsh kidneys, which still bear the closer planting in the richer manure, confirming the observation previously made; for the excess here is 15 bags of "full sized, and 21 of "total produce," in favour of the lesser distance.

Mr. H——— also gave in the following results of similar experiments made by his friend Mr. B———, of Cirencester, in 1842, which afford—1st. A comparison of the produce of different sorts. The soil on which this trial was made was generally a strong stone-brash, but, as it varied in quality, and some parts of the ground were more shaded by trees than others, the experiment is unfortunately deprived in some instances of much of the weight to which it would be otherwise entitled. The ground was cleared of larch the previous winter. No other manure was applied except the ashes of the natural weeds and of the roots of the larch.

Sort. Whole Sets.	Bags per Acre.
Axbridge kidneys	65
Rohan	97
Old purples	98
Prince of Wales.................	101
Welsh kidneys	118
Champion	125

Mr. B—— states the quality of the Axbridge kidney to be the best, but the deficiency of its produce induces him to prefer the Prince of Wales, the quality of which is excellent, and the produce abundant. He recommends it as a second early crop. For winter store he thinks the quality of the Champion as good as the quantity great.

2ndly. A comparison of whole and cut sets.

	Whole. Bags per Acre.	Cut. Bags per Acre.
Old purples........	98	84
Champions	125	102

Exhibiting as usual the great increase of crop derived from planting whole sets.

3rdly. A comparison of the effect of manures. The following trials were made on an orchard which had received no manure for 15 years; the seed used in all the cases was cut sets of Cham-pions, and the result is an average of five trials with malt-dust at the rate of 960lbs. an acre, 8 with guano at the same rate, and 6 with ashes, quantity not given.

	Bags per acre.
Malt-dust	121
Guano......................	117
Ashes......................	106

The details of the above experiment are particularly satisfactory, inasmuch as a comparison being instituted between four alternate rows treated with each manure, all disturbance of the result from the inequality in the soil was avoided. Thus—

		Malt Dust.	Guano.
Row 1	gave	132	
2	....		120
3	....	120	
4	....		126
5	....	123	
6	....		120
7	....	109	
8	....		106
Average.....		121	118

4thly. A comparison of the effect of quantity of manure.

	Bags.
Guano, 960lbs.	117
Ditto, 1920lbs.	100

Showing in a very marked manner the positive mischief of an excess of so strong a manure as guano.

The apparent effect of the guano was that of rendering the haulm a darker green, but the produce, as will be seen, scarcely equalled the malt-dust. The guano and malt-dust were strewed upon the sets when planted. The sets dressed with guano came rather later into leaf, and in the instance in which the double dose was given, some sets were wanting. Salt was tried at the rate of 6lbs. per perch, but with a decidedly injurious effect.

Now, although nothing can be more certain than that in all agricultural experiments such as these, a complicated variety of circumstances may have disturbed the results, no general rules will ever be arrived at but by frequent noting apparent effects, and (without presuming to dogmatize upon them with any certainty) explaining as well as we are able the uniformities or anomalies which present themselves. Thus, it may perhaps be useful to recapitulate shortly some of the general conclusions which these experiments seem to indicate.

1st. The improvidence of the common custom

of planting " cut sets," under the mistaken notion of saving seed, as exemplified by Mr. H——'s experiments, where the gain in the " total produce" upon the "whole," as compared with the " cut sets," varied from 13¾ to 16¼ bags, or from 3l. to 4l. difference in value of the crop per acre, and again still more strongly by Mr. B——'s trials, where the difference in favour of the whole sets was in one instance as high as 23 bags, or perhaps 5l. per acre.

2ndly. The vast advantage not only of selecting a prolific sort, but of ascertaining exactly how that sort should be treated, which the comparison between the purples and Welsh kidneys in the years 1841 and 1842 seems to illustrate ; in one year the purples giving an excess on the " total produce" of 23 bags, and in the next the Welsh kidney exceeding the purples by 26 bags an acre, and making a difference of from 5l. to 6l. in the value of the respective crops, Now it certainly is very possible that the season of the first year may have been more favourable to one sort, and of the next to the other, but still the difference of treatment, viz., 12 tons of long in the one case, and of 15 of rotten dung in the other, seems the more probable cause, and would lead to the inference that the Welsh kidneys give a much larger increase for richer manure, and the purples do better with poorer treatment.

3rdly. The probable advantage of giving more space to each plant than is usually done, and of regulating the distances according to the habits of the particular sort of plant. The usual distance at which the potato is planted is believed to be about 27 inches at the outside between the rows, and 9 inches between the sets ; but it seemed from the trials with the purples that the rows at 4 feet apart were better than at 3, even when the plants were separated a foot from each other, but that this foot could not be increased to 2 when the rows were either 3 or 4 feet apart without considerable loss. But still, that though a space of 6 square feet to each plant thus seemed too much when planted in rows, 9 square feet, when the purples at 3 × 3 were hoed all round, did not give a much less crop. The Welsh kidneys, on the other hand, gave the greatest crop when the distance between the rows was 3 feet, and between the plants 1 ; no less distance being tried, it remains uncertain whether the crop might not be increased by diminishing the distance still more. It seems therefore probable that in richly manured land the Welsh kidney would bear closer planting with profit than the purples ; and generally it may be presumed that the planting at equal distances every way and hoeing up all round is preferable to the common mode of setting in rows. Ploughing with a double-board plough in one direction might economically supersede a part of the hoeing, which being followed by a labourer with the hoe would complete the work. The distance of a yard every way between the plants is probably too great ; 2 ft. 6 in. for plants like purples requiring the wider distances, and 2 ft. 3 in. for such as the Welsh kidney, which bear being closer, would probably be sufficient.

————

TO THE FARMERS OF SUFFOLK.

LETTER VII.

Functions of the Leaf.

GENTLEMEN,—The crude sap introduced at the roots consists of nearly pure water, containing only a very small and variable percentage of certain saline, earthy, and gaseous matters in solution. It is a very common notion, and one upon which most erroneous conclusions are sometimes built by practical men (gardeners and others), that this crude sap is directly employed in the nourishment and development of the various parts of the plant. There is much plausibilty in such an opinion. Every one acquainted with the practice of pruning is aware that by cutting away some parts of a plant, he contrives to throw the rising sap into other parts ; and he finds that in consequence of such treatment, these latter parts are better nourished, and become more developed than they otherwise would have been. But, in spite of so plausible an experiment, the crude sap is not nutritious. We might as well declare that we can receive nourishment ourselves from a weak dose of Epsom salts, or fatten our bodies upon soda water. Living bodies, whether vegetable or animal, can only be nourished and developed by organic matter. Now, crude sap may very possibly not contain a single particle of organic matter. The mystery is explained by the fact, which the science of physiological botany has ascertained, that plants are endowed with the peculiar faculty of preparing organic matter for themselves out of the materials which the crude sap contains. They are mighty agricultural chemists, surpassing Liebig himself in their power of effecting combinations and alterations among the elements of material substances. That justly eminent chemist, and many a one less eminent than he, can now manufacture sugar out of brown paper, and bread out of sawdust ; and they can beat all the ablest conjurors of the good old times, when alchemy and astrology directed the undoubting faith of wondering admirers, by the marvellous extent to which they can carry their transmutations. But not one of all the chemists whom the world has yet seen, has been able to contrive how he might combine the elements of inorganic matter, so as to form out of them a single organic compound. They can change one organic body into another, as starch into sugar ; but they cannot make either starch or sugar directly from the elements of which they consist. It is to the vegetable kingdom alone that this wonderful faculty belongs; and it is by the leaves of plants that the operation is carried on. By certain processes, which I hope to describe to you (so far as they are at present understood), all the leaves of a plant, whilst they are endowed with life, and *stimulated by light*, are enabled to combine three or four out of the fifty-six elements with which chemists are acquainted, into some one or other of the peculiar substances found in its juices, and distinguished as organic compounds. It may be gum, or sugar, or starch, or some other of the numerous vegetable compounds which the leaves prepare in the first instance ; and then, such matters being carried into the system, and undergoing various modifications according to the constitution of different plants, become subservient to their nourishment and development. The crude sap, then, is merely instrumental in supplying the leaves with the materials necessary for the formation of organic matter : it is the " proper juice" (as botanists call it) created by the leaves, and in which such variety of organic matters are dissolved, which forms the real nutritious fluid of the plant, as blood does of the animal. The importance of retaining all the leaves (whilst they are still living) on a plant is sufficiently evident. Not one of them can be abstracted or injured without the plant being deprived of a certain amount of "power" for generating its " proper juice". A man might as well expect to live without lungs, or a fish without gills, as a plant without leaves. It would be ill-timed for me to dwell, in this letter, upon the important relation which the leaf bears to the animal creation, but it may be permitted me to observe how wonderful is the economy of nature—that all the myriad forms of animated beings, from the most minute invisible animalcule to the gigantic whale of 90 feet length, are entirely dependant upon the vegetable kingdom for the organic materials of which their bodies are constructed. Among the various functions of leaves, I propose to direct your attention more especially to the two which are immediately concerned in the organization of brute matter. One of these is termed " exhalation"—a function by which a large portion of the water introduced by the roots, as crude sap, is discharged from the system in a peculiar manner. The other function has been called " respiration" —from an analogy it has been considered to bear to the breathing of animals. Before I can enter satisfactorily upon an explanation of these two functions, so as to render them thoroughly intelligible to those among you who have never turned their attention to these sort of enquiries, I shall beg your permission to say a few words upon one or two of those inorganic substances out of which the leaf prepares the organic matter to which I have alluded. This will oblige me to postpone to another letter the actual discussion of the functions themselves. I think, however, you will find my proposition of greater ultimate advantage than if I proceeded at once to that discussion. I shall, therefore, entitle the remainder of this letter

A digression on the nature of Carbonic acid.

The substance, above all others, with which you should make yourselves well acquainted for rightly understanding the functions of the leaf is carbonic acid. Acquainted, indeed, with it many of you have doubtless long been in a glass of soda-water : the bubbling gas which escapes in that pleasant draught being carbonic acid, which had been forced by artificial pressure into the water, and there retained in solution till the pressure was removed by uncorking the bottle, when the gas again had a struggle for its liberty, and escaped. I mentioned in my fourth letter, how you might cause an escape of carbonic acid to take place from chalk, or marble, or carbonate of ammonia. Carbonic acid always exists as a gas under ordinary circumstances, though chemists, by means of pressure, can cause it to assume a liquid form, and can even, by intense cold, reduce it to a solid state. The gas we call steam is much more manageable in these respects : we all know that it is easily condensed into water, and that water is easily reducible to the state of ice. It may not be impolitic for me to remark here upon a very common popular notion, that certain substances are essentially either gases, or liquids, or solids;

whereas, you are to understand, that every substance may be considered capable, under certain conditions, of assuming each of these three forms. Thus, quicksilver is a liquid at ordinary temperatures : it becomes a solid during the winters of more northern climates : it is readily converted by the heat of a common fire into an invisible gas. I must not dwell upon this subject, but you will find the remark I have made assist you in comprehending how it is that carbonic acid exists as a gas, whilst one of its elements (carbon) appears under a solid form; and that carbonic acid itself when united to lime, forms the solid substance, chalk.

The two elements of which carbonic acid is composed are carbon and oxygen. With the former of these you are well acquainted under the name of charcoal, which is very nearly pure carbon. With the latter you are still more familiar, though some of you may not be aware of it, since every breath of air you inhale is nearly half composed of this element, oxygen. We are all great carbonic acid manufacturers. The oxygen we inhale is fixed in the blood through the instrumentality of the lungs ; it is after a time united with carbon, and the carbonic acid thus formed is discharged from the lungs every time we exhale our breath. There is an easy mode of proving that we are all continually exhaling carbonic acid. Procure some lime-water ; or rather prepare some by putting a few lumps of fresh burnt lime into a bottle of water, and cork it up for a little while, the water will dissolve a portion of the lime, and you will have lime water. Pour some of this, quite clear, into a tumbler, and so place a tube in it (a tobacco pipe will do) that you may breathe through it, whilst the breath can rise in bubbles through the lime-water. As you continue breathing, the lime-water will gradually become milky. This is owing to the carbonic acid in your breath uniting with the lime dissolved in the water, and thus forming carbonate of lime (or chalk). As this substance is not soluble in water, like the lime, it appears in the form of a milky cloud, and gradually falls to the bottom of the tumbler. By the breath of your mouth you may thus call into existence a deposit of chalk.

It may seem strange that a solid black substance like charcoal should form an ingredient in the invisible gas, carbonic acid ; but we may not argue from the condition of one element what will be the condition of a compound body in which it forms a constituent part. Charcoal itself cannot be rendered liquid, much less gaseous, by the most intense heat which chemists can command ; but when carbon combines with oxygen, the new substance, carbonic acid, is gaseous. A chemist could decompose this substance before your eyes, and you would then see the carbon fall down in the form of a black powder, apparently called into existence out of nothing, though in reality coming from an invisible gas—a very striking experiment. The union of carbon and oxygen takes place when charcoal or other substances composed of it are burnt. The charcoal gradually disappears but is not annihilated ; it is now part of the compound which has been formed, (this same important material carbonic acid) and which is invisible to mortal eyes. When woody matter decays and disappears, a similar union of carbon and oxygen takes place, only the process is now effected by very slow degrees, and no heat or light are developed, as in the case of actual combustion.

Your obedient servant,   J. S. HENSLOW.
Hitcham Rectory, February 18th, 1843.

P.S.—Mr. Bree and myself have come to the conclusion that it would be needless to discuss any further the abstruse chemical considerations involved in the fixation of ammonia by gypsum. In a letter from him, he enters, with every appearance of correct inference, into further explanation of his reasons for believing that we shall not be able to fix ammonia in dunghills by means of gypsum. Very possibly he may be perfectly right: we must wait the result of our experiments to know whether he is so. Mr. Bree has also recommended you to try certain experiments for fixing ammonia in liquid manures: and I most cordially second his recommendation. Not that I have much doubt, or any doubt, what will be the result of those experiments. I shall be very much surprised if they fail in fixing the ammonia generated during the putrescence of the urine. I have never scrupled to advise that gypsum should be applied to *liquid* manure for this purpose; for Liebig (as well as other chemists) has spoken so positively on this point, that if there is any error here, the value of his work would indeed be greatly diminished in the eyes of all who may be inclined to trust him. Still I am perfectly agreed with Mr. Bree in thinking that you ought to try these experiments also; and to test for yourselves the value of gypsum or some other substance as a fixer of ammonia in liquid manures. But I have been entirely misunderstood if any one has supposed that I have been advising how manure is to be prepared. This is quite another question from how it may be improved under the form in which it is almost universally prepared in England. Whatever may be the result of the experiment I have proposed, I conceive it will be of value to you. If we find that gypsum can fix ammonia in an open dunghill, then the long approved system of preparing muck in this manner may be continued : but if we find that such is not the case, then it will be a subject of most anxious and serious consideration to you, whether you ought not entirely to change your present system, and prepare your manures in dung-reservoirs, or in some other way in which you may be able to prevent the escape of that important substance, upon the presence of which the amount of produce so much depends. In proposing to try only gypsum, I have endeavoured to confine your attention to one of the simplest forms of experiment which I could devise. Should this substance fail, we must not forget that Liebig has named other substances, as I noticed in my fifth letter, which may serve the purpose—chloride of calcium (bleaching powder), superphosphate of lime, muriatic and sulphuric acid. It may be worth while to have these tried also. If we can only raise our volunteer corps of fifty Suffolk gypsum-powderers, we shall very possibly stimulate fifty or more in each of the neighbouring counties to try one or other of the remaining substances. We may then have a corps of Cambridge bleaching-powderers, an Essex corps of superphosphate-of-limers, and a whole army of Norfolk sulphuric-and-muriatic-acidulators. All may be simultaneously attacking the common fortress—the old dunghill—with one or other of the weapons which Liebig has suggested as most likely to deter the ammonia from attempting its escape; and for retaining it in durance vile to serve a better purpose than merely offending the nostrils of such delicate constitutions as have no particular delight in the pungent odour of fermenting muck.

———

LETTER VIII.

GENTLEMEN,—I must allow the leaves to go on with their exhalations and respirations, without interfering further with these functions for the present, whilst I request your serious attention to a few observations I wish to make on the result of my appeal to you. When I announced my intention of calling for not less than fifty to co operate in the way I have proposed, I found a very decided opinion expressed in all quarters that I should not be able to prevail upon so large a number. I had calculated on the well known spirit and energy of Englishmen, whenever fairly convinced that any particular course is the right course to be adopted : my only fear being that I should not succeed in persuading many of you to see, as clearly as I do myself, what your present course ought to be for securing the speedy improvement of agriculture. I had also witnessed, during the last two years, the great desire expressed by the members of the Hadleigh Farmer's Club for any description of information which might bear directly or indirectly upon your pursuits. I find that I have not miscalculated in the inferences which I drew from these premises. I have received the addresses of forty-three gentlemen who are willing to accept my challenge, and I find from two quarters that I can calculate upon receiving from ten to fifteen more. Before another week has expired I hope I shall have superintended the preparation of the proposed experiment on two or three farms in this parish. I will then print my promised circular, with precise directions how you are to proceed, and with it I will transmit a *Schedule A. (for rotten dunghills!)* containing blank spaces to be filled up by each experimenter. These schedules will be returned to me some months hence, when the results have been obtained.

Now that I consider we are fairly embarked, I must be allowed to speak a little more gravely than I have always found myself inclined to do. I must feel myself quite sure that you correctly understand all that I am aiming at. One point, certainly, is to ascertain whether the addition of gypsum to a common dunghill will improve the quality of the manure—which is putting this question in its simplest agricultural shape, divested of all chemical and theoretical notions. But the decision of this question I hold to be a very subordinate purpose to one of still greater importance which I have had in view. I am chiefly desirous of giving you an example of the manner in which your agricultural experiments ought to be conducted, if you would hope to render them available for scientific purposes. I believe our gypsum experiment to be only one of several which *must* be tried before the question at issue can be fully settled. But every such experiment, thus tried by a numerous body of experimenters, upon a correct principle, will add something so positive to the general stock of knowledge, that it is impossible it should not become of real importance to your interests. The little trouble, or very trifling expense, which each individual experimenter may happen to incur in such cases, is no way increased by his having forty-nine co-operators, whilst the value of his single experiment may possibly be augmented more than fifty-fold. It would be a ridiculonsly trifling tax upon any farmer to perform yearly *one* such experiment. We can all appreciate the advantages which flow from a division of labour ; and many who may not be qualified for suggesting correct methods of experimenting for themselves, might be prevailed upon to act upon the suggestions of others, provided the precise mode of performing an experiment were laid down for them. The old proverb declares that "lazy folk take the most pains," and I almost question whether this proverb was not made prospectively, to apply to the manner in which certain so-called experiments have been conducted in our times. There is no lack of agricultural experimenters. It should seem that we are overstocked with them in England. A gentleman, high in your confidence, writes thus to me:—"The fact is, that whereas farmers were formerly averse to all change, many of them are now ready to try every thing which is recommended, and it is necessary to be cautious not to mislead them into expense." Now, this struck me marvellously as a very lamentable necessity. You are to be restrained in your anxiety to improve, and to be prevented from doing what science has been urging you to do. I have no doubt the remark was just, from the high authority from whence I received it; but it is equally obvious, that the reason it was so, must be because farmers in general have not qualified themselves for experimenting in a safe and judicious manner. Most certainly there have been many experiments of late, conducted in a correct and skilful manner by eminent and practical men, but too many even of these were undertaken with no other than some economical object in view, and not with any scientific aim. The results have mostly been tested by pounds, shillings, and pence, without regard to what might be the real cause of success or failure. Hence no new principles have been worked out. But it is only when these shall have been discovered, that it will be time to test their application to practice by the pocket argument. For instance, the following comparative experiment was lately placed in my hands by an intelligent gentleman of this neighbourhood. It is performed in the approved way of obtaining comparative results; but from want of detail, and from standing single, very little can be inferred from it with respect to the nature of the influence exerted by the nitrate of soda.

Half an acre sown with, and half without the nitrate of soda.

	cb.	bl.	pk.		lbs.
With the nitrate, wheat ..	3	2	3	Straw ..	840
Without ditto	3	1	2	....	746
Increase from nitrate....	0	1	1	....	94

	s.	d.
Cost of nitrate of soda...................	13	6
Value of the 1bl. 1pk. of wheat, at 7s. 6d., 9s. 4½d.; 94lbs. of straw, at 2l. per ton, 1s. 8d.............................	11	0½
Loss on the half acre....... ..	2	5½

Here the balance being against the pocket, no more attempts were made with nitrate of soda. The inspection of the above induced me to ask the experimenter whether he had thought of trying only one-half or one-fourth the nitrate of soda, to see whether the increase might not still be the same. If it should have turned out that such was the case, the pocket would then have pleaded in favour of its application. Before we can expect to understand the precise relation which nitrate of soda or any other salt bears to the effect it produces on a particular crop, there must be many well-digested experiments performed in many parts of the kingdom, and their results registered with a sufficient degree of uniformity to admit of their being compared together. Now, with the ready machinery of your numerous local agricultural societies, and the great central society in London, together with the invaluable advantages offered by the penny postage, you might very easily organize a system of co-operation throughout Great Britain, which I am persuaded would work with a rapidity and an efficiency that would surprise you all. Of course, every one who may be desirous of promoting such a system must be at some trouble, but this will generally not be greater than is required to direct and superintend a labourer for two or three hours, whilst he is trimming a hedge or digging a ditch. The personal trouble to the farmer himself would literally be no greater than that. The intellectual part of these proceedings might be all transacted within the skulls of a few chemists, who would suggest, and within those of the more active members of your various agricultural societies, who might busy themselves in preparing and circulating the different *schedules* to be filled up by the several experimenters. All that is now wanting to the adoption of such a scheme, is to convince the farmers of England generally, that unless they will consent to co-operate, they cannot expect to avail themselves (otherwise than by very slow degrees) of the information which modern science has placed at their disposal. I am no enthusiast in this opinion—I am speaking the words of sobriety. I am only repeating what others, wiser than myself, have continually asserted. I have already referred you in my address to the Hadleigh Club, to the opinion of De Candolle, and I have within these few days met with a similar declaration in an agricultural work in course of publication by Mr. Johnston, of Durham. This gentleman is a chemist of high reputation; and, in his "Lectures on Agricultural Chemistry and Geology," he has suggested several experiments in practical agriculture. In speaking of the effects produced by special manures, either on particular soils or on particular crops, he remarks, " Now, neither of these subjects, which it is so important to investigate, can be determined, either from theory or from experiments devised and executed in the laboratory of a chemist. The aid of the practical farmer, of *many practical farmers*, must be called in. *Numerous* experiments or trials must be made in *various localities*, and by different individuals; all, however, according to the *same rigorous and accurate method*, in order that, from the *comparison of many results*, something like a general principle may be deduced." The whole question, then turns upon this—whether the farmers of Great Britain are prepared to co-operate in making experiments under the guidance of persons qualified for directing their efforts. There is, in fact, an important link yet wanting in the chain which is to connect science with practice; and if science is only permitted to hold the pincers whilst practice plies the blows, that link may be forged and fastened. My hopes are now much strengthened that this will soon take place. I shall in future listen with impatience to any desponding surmises about your not being sufficiently awake to the importance of co-operating for such a purpose. " My own experience (says a valued correspondent) in this neighbourhood (Surrey) is against expecting the present race of adult farmers to become much of readers; and so my hopes rest on their sons." But I conceive it is not necessary, for that description of co-operation which is required of you, that the present race of farmers should become " much of readers." Let them *act* upon the suggestions of others; and then, whilst Liebig is uttering

A A

lamentations over his Germans, and consoling himself by talking of what will be done by a generation to come, the present race of British farmers will have forestalled that generation of foreigners yet to come, and have left the present generation behind. Why should we doubt that the farmers of Great Britain generally would be less prepared to co-operate than the farmers of Suffolk have shown themselves to be? No doubt there are some, and probably not a few, among you, as among every other class of men, who would indolently prefer a shorter road than that which science points out to them. Perhaps it would have been easier for me to have enlisted twice fifty co-operators if I had assured the agricultural world that my past studies in botany had led me to the discovery of a marvellous composition, a certain incomparable vegetable elixir, in which it was merely necessary for the sower to steep his seed, and he would at once be able to double his crops! But to have found more than fifty willing to proceed in the legitimate spirit of philosophy, and without anything promised about reaping an *immediate* return, is an event which I must consider of most excellent omen. From what I have heard since my last letter, I believe a little further delay would have greatly increased our numbers; for I find that several farmers of this neighbourhood have not seen my challenge, and had only heard of it through others. If not more than twenty-five of you had come forward, I should still have asked each man to procure a double, and I make no doubt that we should thus have got our number completed. As it is, I think it will be advisable to increase our numbers, rather for the sake of experimental *instruction*, than for the issue of the experiment; and I shall have a hundred copies of *Schedule A* struck off, that I may be prepared to supply any additional recruits.

Whilst you are performing this experiment, I must call upon you to toss all prejudices and antiquated opinions to the winds; and to proceed as closely as possible upon the instructions with which you will be furnished. There must indeed be a certain latitude allowed, because it may not be convenient for one person to use any but littered straw, or for another to apply it to a particular crop. But the very object of requiring so many as fifty is to merge the inconvenience of such contrarieties as these in the general results obtained. We are not in the position of chemists operating upon weights which it is necessary to test to the tenth of a grain; and we require no costly apparatus for determining our quantities. For the present experiment, your agricultural laboratory need be furnished with no more than the following instruments :—1, A dung-fork. 2, Pair of scales or steelyard. 3, Bushel and quart measures. 4, Sieve. 5, Watering-pot. The gypsum must be finely powdered, and not burnt into plaster of Paris.

Your obedient servant,
J. S. HENSLOW.
Hitcham Rectory, February 25th, 1843.

LETTER IX.

GENTLEMEN,—Since my last letter, I have been present at the preparation of our gypsum experiment on three farms in this parish, where the occupiers had volunteered to try it. I now feel myself a little better prepared than before for giving you precise instructions in the schedule I am about to circulate. I had intended this letter to have served as a comment upon that schedule, and to have been circulated with it. My engagements during the week have unluckily prevented me from putting my memoranda together in time for the editor, under so precise a form as I should wish to see them, and, therefore, I must beg leave to defer communicating them publicly until next week. In the meantime, I hope I shall be able to forward both the instructions and the schedule to those gentlemen who have favoured me with their addresses, which now amount fully to fifty, without some ten or twelve promised from the neighbourhood of Ipswich. I find the experiment even easier to be prepared than I had myself anticipated; and every farmer here to whom I have mentioned the amount of time and material consumed in preparing the three I have superintended, said with surprise, "Is that all?" On a *large* scale, the experiment requires less than two tumbrils of straw, and forty baskets of dung, and not more than twenty pints of gypsum!

I must request those gentlemen who are preserving my letters, as I find some are, to correct two errors which have crept into the seventh. In the *digression on carbonic acid*, I have carelessly stated oxygen to form nearly one-half, instead of one-fifth of the atmosphere; and in the postscript I have supposed that chloride of calcium was the common bleaching powder, having in my eye at the moment the chloride of lime, and forgetting that chloride of calcium was the muriate of lime, by which name it was more familiar to me in my chemical days, I cautioned you, in the end of my third letter, that I should very likely be caught tripping in these sort of details; for my chemistry is very rusty, and though one gentleman, in the *Suffolk Herald*, has been pleased to refer to the *learned leisure* of Hitcham, I can assure him that my opportunities do not always allow me time for turning to a chemical author to ensure perfect accuracy about numbers and component parts, &c. I hope, therefore, that all such slips of pen and memory may be excused. A publisher has informed me that he intends to speculate upon your purchasing copies of my letters, which he proposes to print in the form of a pamphlet, and I hope he will not correct any of the errors of the sort I have just alluded to, further than by adding a little note at the bottom of the page. If he (or any one else) shall acquaint me when he means to reprint them, I will supply him with any critiques of this sort which I may happen to think necessary; and I shall be obliged to any correspondent who will be kind enough to point out such errors.

I have obtained Dr. Daubeny's permission to print the annexed letter from him to me. I think this advisable, as it contains a similar apology to the public for an error of the same class as my own; and it also contains an important caution to the public against an error of a much worse character. Whilst I am in the humour for apologising, let me express a hope that I have given no offence to any one by my seeming, on some occasions, to treat my subject too lightly or too frivolously; and on other occasions, to press it with too much officiousness or censoriousness. There is no body of men of such varied character as those who are engaged in agriculture. From the very subject nearest the throne to many a subject very near the work-house, from every occupation, from every party in the state, from every grade of intellectual cultivation, we have persons who apply their thoughts to enquiries connected with your most important profession; and though these letters have been more especially addressed to the farmers of Suffolk, I have considered the insertion of a few hints which might apply in other quarters, might not be unadvisable. What may possibly have engaged the attention of some may not have been approved by others : but the end has been that our corps of co-operaters has become more than fifty strong. It is with great satisfaction that I find the editor of the widely-circulated *Gardener's Chronicle* taking the same view as myself of the importance of your attending to experimental co-operation. Let your example spread a little further, and let us only see a regular system of co-operation organizing itself through other counties, and I shall be very glad to make my bow as a chemist, and leave it to abler hands to prepare for you schedules B, C, D, &c., &c., to the end of the alphabet. Perhaps I may still be allowed to gratify an itching for discussing some botanico-agricultural question or other, as I may see occasion; but, though I believe it is good practice to concentrate one's fire upon a single point, and never to slacken till the breach is made, I cannot pretend to maintain so rapid a discharge as heretofore, now that the chief outwork has been gained.

Your obedient servant,
J. S. HENSLOW.
Hitcham Rectory, March 3rd, 1843.

TO THE REV. J. S. HENSLOW.

DEAR HENSLOW,—I fear I may have led the public into an error by mentioning, amongst substances that *fix* carbonate of ammonia, common salt.

It is probable indeed, that when this substance in solution is mixed with carbonate of ammonia, also in solution, a partial decomposition of both salts ensues, the acids being divided between the two bases in the ratio of their respective affinities. But I doubt whether this principle can apply in the case of manures, for when the salts become dry, the carbonate of ammonia would volatilize, and then the carbonic acid, united with the soda, would be divided betwixt this base and the ammonia, producing a fresh dose of carbonate of ammonia, which would fly off, and thus cause a repetition of the same process, until the whole of the muriatic acid reverted to the soda, and the whole of the ammonia was dissipated. I do not think, therefore, that any such advantages will be gained by adding muriate of soda as by adding muriate of lime, and the other bodies I had enumerated; and, if you will mix the two salts together, and apply heat, or even dissolve them, and then evaporate, you will find that *carbonate*, and not *muriate* of ammonia will be (at least principally) evolved.

I regret, therefore, that I published this statement in a lecture, which has gained so much publicity through the medium of the Journal of the Royal Agricultural Society. In other respects I see nothing to correct, either in my statements or in your comments upon them ; though, considering that practical men deny the efficacy of gypsum in fixing ammonia, it would be wrong to speak with perfect confidence on the matter, notwithstanding Liebig's authority.

Those, however, who intend to make experiments with a view of settling this question, should recollect that the gypsum must be added, not in lumps, but in fine powder, and that a certain amount of water must be present, in order to bring about the decomposition.

Such hints as these may be considered trite and obvious, but I do not believe them unnecessary, when I find that a chemical manufacturer, who offers to farmers, for manure, an article which he has thought proper to call " Dr. Daubeny's Sulphate of Ammonia," appears to have so mistaken the directions I had given, (which I had conceived to have been plain enough) that, according to the statement of a chemical friend, who has examined this product, it does not contain a particle of ammonia.

Had he consulted me on the subject, before he made free with my name, I should have told him that I had no wish to claim as my own, a process which was nothing more than the application of a well-known chemical process to the case of the ammoniacal liquor obtained at the gas-works ; but I can assure you, that I am quite as little accountable for this, as I am for the ill success that appears to have attended the process, and that I do not even know the name of the maker.

I am, dear Henslow, &c.
Oxford, Feb. 24, 1843. CHARLES DAUBENY.

LETTER X.

GENTLEMEN,—Some persons will consider this letter to be a scene in *Much Ado about Nothing*; but experience had convinced me that I cannot be too minute in pointing out the precise conditions under which our experiment may be carried on ; and, therefore, if I am a little over-circumstantial in recounting to you the mode in which the three experiments referred to in my last letter were performed, I trust you will excuse me ; and I believe you will be the better able to see how very little skill and trouble is necessary for conducting such experiments as these. What is really required of you, is to have a little faith in what chemists and others have declared to you, viz., that such experiments must be tried, if *you wish to help science*, in order that science may be able to return the compliment, and *help you*. Perhaps I may find occasion for saying a few more words on this subject some other time ; but to-day I had better confine myself to an account of the manner in which our three Hitcham Experimenters had fulfilled their parts ; and then proceed to give you a few instructions for the filling up of *Schedule A.* Provided this letter and the schedule are read attentively two or three times over, I think no one can possibly mistake what it is he is required to do ; but if it should appear that I have not sufficiently explained myself, I beg there may be no scruples about applying for further information.

Mr. Hitchcock's Experiment.

I went to the ground accompanied by the experimenter, his brother, and my own gardener; and there found that preparations had been made by shooting down a tumbril load of soil under the name of " good ditch stuff ;" a tumbril load of littered straw ; a tumbril load of clean and fresh horse dung, two pails of house urine, with a ditch full of water to dilute it, and a bushel of gypsum in a sack. Over these materials was presiding a labourer, apparently somewhat puzzled to account for our proceedings. The first step was to mark out two spaces, each five feet square, and upon them to place a bottom of the " good ditch stuff" half a foot thick. It should seem that clean straw is a scarce commodity in Hitcham just at present, and so we were obliged to put up with ch as had been soaking in a cow-yard for two months amidst all the et cetoras of that description of locality. Some sort of rough calculation had been made of the amount of this straw, and also of the horse dung, by weighing a bushel skep of each; but I looked grave at the idea of our being satisfied with any estimate obtained by weighing only a single bushel, and so the steelyards were sent for. It is not necessary to weigh the whole of the materials used, but four or five baskets-full at least should be weighed in order to obtain an average for measuring out the rest. I suppose it is not necessary to remind any one not to forget to deduct the weight of the basket in making his calculations; but I find it is right and just to hint that the weight of a basket-full should not be altered after it has been prepared in order to coax the average. Let each be filled *by guess* as nearly alike as may be, and weighed; and then the whole weight, divided by the number of baskets-full, will give the average for further estimate. Our zeal, however, on the present occasion was sufficient to keep us warm enough for three hours, and through two or three snow storms, until we had weighed out the whole of the materials, and completed our task. We began with the dunghill to be gypsumed, and placed it to the south of the ungypsumed, and finished one first before we began with the other. Two baskets-full of the straw were spread over the bottom, each weighing between 40 and 50 lbs. Then two baskets-full of the horse dung were spread out, each weighing somewhat less than the wetted straw. A pint of gypsum was then sifted over the horse dung; and the coarser particles of the gypsum which did not pass through the hair sieve were preserved, in order that they might be weighed and deducted from the weight of a 'pint of gypsum, for the purpose of ascertaining the exact weight of the gypsum used. A gallon of liquid, half urine and half water, was then poured over this first layer of materials through a rose watering pot. Seven layers were thus prepared in succession, except that the topmost had only two gallons of water, there not having been any urine left. The whole was then covered over with two baskets-full of the wet straw. The other dunghill was then prepared in the same way, except that no gypsum was used—but the amount of materials employed was exactly the same. The two stood now about three feet high, and their appearance was such that it was presumed they would certainly attract any one curious in cucumbers to step out of his way to examine them. The experimenter was also of opinion that they would be objects of curiosity to his cows; and therefore he thought fit to enclose them with hurdles lest these gentle quadrupeds should amuse themselves by poking them into the neighbouring ditch. I think it right to record his precaution here, because it seems a cow is a very inquisitive and experimenting creature. I well remember that a cow once made a tolerably successful attempt at devouring a waistcoat of my own, which I had thrown off in a field whilst I was occupied in chasing the splendid swallow-tail butterflies, which no one with the feelings of a naturalist can ever possibly resist running after in the districts about Cambridge, where they are to be met with. My waistcoat looked very much as if it had visited the cow's first stomach, and required only a little further ruminating to render it sufficiently digestible for being re-swallowed. But, besides the precaution against cows, the experimenter found it necessary a day or two afterwards

to protect our hillocks against the rooks, who had taken a fancy to them, and were doing their best to pull them to pieces. A covering of "good ditch stuff" stopped their proceedings. In this condition, then, the hills are intended to repose until next October, when they are destined to be applied to land reserved for a wheat crop.

Mr. Pilgrim's Experiment.

Here I found two bottoms, each seven feet by five, had been already prepared of fresh turf and mould. There were also on the ground two tumbril loads of very wet litter from the farm-yard, two months old; two tumbril loads of horse dung with a little litter also intermixed; a supply of mixed house urine and much rain water, somewhat high in odour, which had been collected in a tank. Forty lbs. of ready sifted gypsum was an improved mode of bringing this material to the field of action; but only 20 lbs. of it were used. Four large baskets of the wetted straw, averaging 62¼ lbs. each, were spread out as a bottom layer; and upon them were spread four baskets of the horse dung, averaging 57 lbs. each. An improvement was introduced in the mode of applying the gypsum, by continually sifting it over the straw and dung as they were spread out, so that it became more thoroughly incorporated with these materials than in the former instance. Two waterpots of the liquid, each holding ten pints, were then poured over the layer. The two dunghills were proceeding at the same time, as we did not weigh out more than the materials for one layer, and could measure out the rest sufficiently rapidly to allow of this improvement also. Each was composed of five layers like the first, and covered over with a layer of the wetted straw. The experiment occupied about one hour and a half in preparing, under the engineering of five pair of hands. The hills were covered over with turf and earth, and are intended to be applied in June, to land which is to lie fallow till next spring, when it is to be sown with barley.

Mr. Carter's Experiment.

Here we found some clean straw in the barn-loft, and proceeded to tie up two large bundles, each of which weighed 61 lbs. Notwithstanding the very great difference between the weight of this clean straw and that of the wetted litter in the former experiments, we built two hills with it of the same size, or nearly so, as those of Mr. Hitchcock. The bottoms, of five feet square, were prepared with soil taken from a mangel-wurtzel bed. The clean straw proved to be rather an awkward subject to deal with in preparing so small a heap; and the result sadly affronted those notions of propriety which good workmen possess about turning out a job in a workmanlike manner. It may, therefore, be as well in other cases, where clean straw can be got at, to chop it up into three or four lengths to make it more manageable. The straw was spread out into five layers, and on each were placed three bushel baskets of horse dung—the gypsum being continually sifted among the materials as in the last experiment. One waterpot of pure horse urine from a stable tank was poured on each of two of the layers, and two waterpots of much diluted drainings from the farm-yard were poured over each of the other three. The estimate for the whole quantity of dung used was made by weighing out six baskets-full, at 274 lbs., which gives an average of 45¾ lbs. for each basket. The capacity of the watering pot used was ascertained to be nineteen pints. These heaps were hurdled in and covered over with mould, and are to be applied in October for wheat. Although I consider this rough mode of performing the experiment will serve our purpose, I strongly recommend to all who possess the opportunity, to be careful in obtaining the separate materials as pure as possible. Clean straw, as in Mr. Carter's experiment; clean dung and pure urine, as in Mr. Hitchcock's; sifted gypsum previously weighed out, as in Mr. Pilgrim's and Mr. Carter's. Attention to these sort of minutiæ always enhances the value of the experiment; and I dare say that the chemists who are preparing schedules B, C, &c., will be more positive on such points than I have been in this first attempt.

Instructions for filling up Schedule A.

There will be five separate occasions for referring to the schedule as the experiment progresses; and the memoranda have consequently been arranged under five heads. Most of the memoranda under the first head seem to be too simple to need a comment, and a mere reference to the three experiments already detailed will explain them readily.

No. 3 may perhaps seem to be unnecessary; but once for all, I must request that experimenters will be content to submit. The noticing whether A lies to the north, south, east, or west of B, is to avoid any error or doubt that may hereafter arise, as to which of the two dunghills was gypsumed. Some people have very short memories.

No. 11. The whole should be secured of the same quality by mixing in one vessel.

No. 15 will need a little explanation. The chances of fixing the ammonia will be increased in proportion as the gypsum is more finely powdered. That which I have seen is rather coarsely so, and on sifting it through a flour sieve many large particles are left behind. These coarse particles may be thrown into a tank where they will probably be useful. I should very much like to find the experiment has been tried by some persons with gypsum artificially prepared. I have been asked by more than one correspondent whether he could not prepare gypsum for his farm by dissolving chalk in diluted sulphuric acid, which is a very cheap substance; but I have replied that I should conceive there can be very few localities where the native material might not be purchased at a still cheaper rate. It would, however, be very easy to prepare artificially the small quantity required for a dunghill; and I think it would be *well worth while* for some of you to try our experiment with gypsum procured in this way, because the particles would be in a much finer state than we can hope to procure them by mere grinding.

I do not wish it to be supposed that I have been deluding the experimenters to attempt more than I originally proposed; but it has occurred to me that the value of the experiment will be very materially enhanced without much additional labour, by dividing each dunghill into two equal parts, and then proceeding to apply these halves in the manner set forth in the schedule. Nothing further need be done to the two halves of A. But one half of B may be thoroughly mixed up with half as much gypsum as was employed on A, so that we shall be able to compare the effect of applying gypsum (as in half of A) *before* decomposition, with applying it (as in half of B) *after* decomposition. Also there should be six pieces of land marked out

of equal size, to one of which " nothing" should be applied; and whilst one half of A is applied to one piece, the other half of A might be applied through two pieces. Still I do not press this mode of performing the experiment, though I *most strongly* recommend it.

No. 20. The column headed "Nothing" means where nothing has been done to the land. If A and B are not divided into halves, the entries can easily be made to that effect; but if they are, then the length under (A 2) will be twice as much as under any of the others, provided all the pieces of ground are exactly the same shape.

No. 21, 22. The usual terms in which these are expressed in practice is all that is required.

No. 25. It will be better to experiment on a seed crop, if convenient; but still a little variety in this respect is advisable.

No. 27, 28. The columns headed "leaves on" refer to a root crop; which should be given, if possible, both with leaves off (under the first columns) and leaves on.

No. 30, 31. In using the more general term "stalk," I mean it should apply either to the straw of a grain crop, or to the stems of flax, fodder, &c.—Your obedient servant,

Hitcham Rectory, March 9. J. S. HENSLOW.

SCHEDULE A. EXPERIMENTAL CO-OPERATION.

QUERE—THE EFFECT OF GYPSUM ON DUNGHILLS?

* *Preparation of Two Dunghills, one (A) with, and the other (B) without gypsum:*

N.B. Be very careful to make memoranda at the time, and *trust nothing to memory.*

1. Prepared by Mr.[   ] county [   ] parish [   ]
2. Date of preparation, year [184] day [   ]
3. Position of A is to the [   ] of B.
4. Bottom for each is [   ] feet by [   ] feet, and [   ] thick; composed of [   ]
5. Quality of straw [   ]
6. Quantity of straw actually weighed is [   ] lbs., and hence the
7. Weight of straw in each dunghill is estimated at [   ] lbs.
8. Quantity of dung [   ]
9. Quantity of dung actually weighed is [   ] lbs., and hence the
10. Weight of dung in each dunghill is estimated at [   ] lbs.
11. Description of urine [   ]
12. Quantity of urine added to each dunghill [   ]
13. Quantity of water added to each dunghill [   ]
14. If 12 and 13 are uncertain, then state quantity of liquid (described under 11) added to each dunghill [   ]
15. Quality of the gypsum [   ]
16. Quantity sifted among A [   ]
17. The dunghills covered over with [   ]

* * *Manuring the Land.*

18. Date of applying the manure. Year [184] day [   ]
19. State of the muck [   ]
N.B.—If possible (and unless very inconvenient) let each dunghill be now divided into two equal portions, viz., A into A 1, A 2; and B. into B 1, B 2. Let B 2 be thoroughly mixed with half as much gypsum as was applied to A. Let A 2 be applied to a space of land twice as great as A 1 is.

20. Spaces manured

	Nothing done.	A 1—A 2	B 1—B 2
Length			
Breadth			

21. Character of soil [   ]
22. Condition of soil [   ]
23. Previous crop [   ]

* * * *Nature of Crop manured.*

24. Date of sowing year [184] day [   ]

25. Name of seed [ ]
26. Quantity of seed Sown where | Nothing done. | A 1–A 2 | B 1–B 2

* * * * *Results obtained.*

27. Date of gathering the crop. Year [184] day [ ]
28. Quantities actually measured and weighed.

As obtained	Meas.	Wght.	With leaves on Meas.	With leaves on Wght.
from Nothing done				
A 1				
A 2				
B 1				
B 2				

29. Estimate of whole measure and weight.

As obtained				
from Nothing done				
A 1				
A 2				
B 1				
B 2				

30. Quality of crop [ ]
31. Quality of stalk [ ]
32. Average length of stalk [ ]

* * * * * *General Observations.*

33. Any general memoranda may be inserted under this head.

DUTY ON HOPS.

An ACCOUNT of the DUTY on HOPS of the Growth of the Year 1842, distinguishing the Districts, and the Old from the New Duty.

	£	s.	d.
Barnstaple	14	0	8¼
Bedford	113	14	3½
Cambridge	6	5	3½
Canterbury	58,287	18	8
Chester	1	3	9½
Cornwall	7	5	9¼
Derby	508	18	4
Dorset	14	12	11¼
Essex	1,297	12	10
Exeter	1	0	3½
Gloucester	9	5	1½
Grantham	91	7	4
Hants	11,546	10	6¾
Hereford	27,310	7	0½
Hertford	929	18	3½
Isle of Wight	9,675	1	9¾
Lincoln	2,548	2	7
Lynn	43	5	8½
Northampton	3	17	0
Norwich	7	6	7¾
Oxford	77	15	9
Reading	29	9	0¼
Rochester	107,395	19	0
Salisbury	70	10	8
Salop	0	18	0¼
Stourbridge	1,926	6	6½
Suffolk	1,511	9	3¼
Surrey	34	10	2¼
Sussex	79,546	17	5½
Wales, Middle	32	16	8¾
Wellington	48	4	11¼
Worcester	6,932	16	6¾
Total	310,025	8	10¾

	£	s.	d.	
Old Duty, at 1 12-20d per lb.	169,676	6	0¼	12-20
New 0¾ 8-20d "	125,486	14	7½	8-20
Additional Duty of Five per Cent., per 3 Vict., c. 17 ..	14,762	6	2¾	
Total	310,025	8	10¾	

G. A. COTTRELL, Accountant-General.
Excise-office, London, March 10, 1843.

The quantity of British Hops exported from Great Britain to foreign countries, from the 5th of January, 1842, to the 5th of January, 1843, was 662,882 lbs. weight. G. A. COTTRELL, Accountant-General.
Excise-office, London, March 10.

Quantity of Hops exported from Great Britain to foreign countries, in the year ended 5th of January, 1843 (so far as relates to hops of foreign growth.

Nil.

Quantity of Foreign Hops imported into the United Kingdom in the year ended 5th of January, 1843.

Nil.

WILLIAM IRVING,
Inspector General of Imports and Exports.
Inspector-General's Office, Custom House,
London, March 22, 1843.

MALT.

An ACCOUNT of the total number of quarters of MALT made between the 10th day of October, 1840, and the 10th day of October, 1842, in the United Kingdom; distinguishing each year ending the 10th day of October, and the quantity made in each country, and the quantity used by brewers and victuallers, and retail brewers.

YEAR ENDED OCT. 10, 1841.

	Quarters of Malt made.	Qrs. of Malt used. By Brewers and Victuallers.	Qrs. of Malt used. By Retail Brewers.	Total.
England ..	4340873	3099250	395098	3494348
Scotland ..	517564	115016	..	115016
Ireland	156568	132514	..	132514
United Kingdom	5015005	3346780	395098	3741878

YEAR ENDED OCT. 10, 1842.

	Quarters of Malt made.	Qrs. of Malt used. By Brewers and Victuallers.	Qrs. of Malt used. By Retail Brewers.	Total.
England ..	3654850	2976199	382431	3358630
Scotland ..	484778	105715	..	105715
Ireland ...	130297	124139	..	124139
United Kingdom	4262225	3206053	382431	3588484

G. A. COTTRELL, Accountant-General.
Excise-office, London, March 10, 1843.

TORRINGTON FARMERS' CLUB.

The attention of agriculturists is especially invited to the following paper, which was read before the Great Torrington Farmer's Club on Saturday 11th inst., by Mr. Joseph Risdon, of Speccott, near Torrington.

" On the present occasion I shall say but little, and that rather to promote discussion than venture on any particular essay of my own: the fact is, we are living in very precarious times, so that much practical information that would be followed in ordinary occasions, cannot now be proceeded with but with great caution. Politics are very properly excluded by our rules, yet there are questions arising out of the strictures under which we labour that may with great propriety form subjects for free discussion.

"The state of the markets are such at the present time (with the exception of live stock) that the cost of production is greater than the value of the articles produced, a state of things that cannot continue, I repeat that cannot continue, as under existing circumstance, the most fearful calamities must follow. We see before us but little to cheer us as to the future, as all concomitant charges on the land, such as labour, manure, parochial taxes, and almost every other impost, instead of diminishing is on the increase. What then is to be done? Is it possible to cut down the cost of production to the present value of the articles produced? Can the price of labour be reduced? I think not, although I do believe that agricultural labourers in this neighbourhood are generally as well off as they ever were, and in most instances where the husband is industrious and the wife has any just notions of domestic economy, I believe I may say they are better off than they were twenty or thirty years since. It is true we meet with many instances where much distress prevails. Yet I am persuaded they are as I before stated, better off than heretofore, although they are not in circumstances that will enable them to part with the smallest portion of their present hard-earned pittance, so that no relief to agriculture can possibly be looked for from a reduction of wages. The labourer is worthy of his hire, and the humble individual who now addresses you, wishes to see the farm labourer enjoying in his cottage the necessaries of life with the consolations that arise from honest industry, aided by economy and religion, the sure leaders to peace. I am opinion, however, that the agriculturists near this place do not uniformly give the same wages or emoluments to their labourers. I therefore venture to request a free discussion on this head, in order that it may be seen what is most advantageous, not with a view of diminishing the comforts of the labourers, but to make the best plan more generally adopted, and let what will await us, we cannot do without the labourer, nor do I believe any advantage can be taken of him to ameliorate the present agricultural panic.

"We have heard much in the last four or five years of different manures, guano, nitrate of soda, bone-dust, &c., besides lime, and the best method of getting dung from the farm-yard. That expensive manures cannot be successfully used under depressed prices is, I believe, so readily admitted that I need not dwell upon it, and that the land cannot be cultivated to advantage without manure is also well known to every practical man. The best and cheapest manures must therefore be of the greatest consequence to know how to be procured and used to advantage. I believe that much can be done to produce more manure from the farm-yard than is usually done in this neighbourhood, and I recollect a gentleman who I gleaned many useful hints from, telling me in the depressed times, about 1821 and '2, ' that farmers must continue to grow corn, to keep cattle, to make dung—to grow more corn, to keep more cattle, to make *more* dung, to *grow more* and *keep more*, and so on *ad infinitum.*' I confess I never think of this but I feel more strongly upon it, and reflect as it were upon the advantages that must arise in a national point of view if this was more fully carried out: we should not have occasion

under this arrangement to send our working classes to cultivate distant lands, but plenty might be produced at home ; and if our internal arrangements would admit it, we might look downward with prospects of happiness and peace—enough may arise from this to pass off a short time to great advantage, and I trust some of the gentlemen present will favour me and the company with their views upon it.

"I stated at the commencement that parochial taxes and other imposts instead of diminishing were increasing, a fearful sort of contemplation with low prices before us, but this is as I believe the cause of an increase of population, and must increase as we progress—order must be preserved—the indigent must be maintained—the lawless must be punished —the wicked if possible reclaimed—the young taught their duty to God and man—all this must be carried on for the good of the general weal. It is therefore idle to fancy that any material relief to agriculture will be affected by any diminution in this way. I presume you will say if those are your views how will you advise us to act, or under the circumstances act yourself. My answer is, let us be united, and continue to unite more and more for our mutual good ; let us impart to each other that which experience teaches us to be the most likely plan to be pursued with advantage. Increase of productions has enabled us to meet difficulties unknown to our forefathers. Let strict economy be practised without parsimony, and industry without slavery, and let us show all classes that surround us that we are deserving of their confidence and mutual protection, and that the progress we have made and are still making in the advancement of Agriculture does not arise from selfish motives, but from minds properly elevated to the greatest possible good, and that we claim that station in society without prejudice to others, intelligence, wealth, and numbers deserve."

PROBUS FARMERS' CLUB.

On Saturday evening last, a lecture on the "Production of Fat and Muscle," was delivered by Mr. Karkeek, of Truro, to the members of this institution. This is an interesting and important lecture to agriculturists, as may be supposed from the circumstance of the English Agricultural Society having lately offered a premium for an essay on the same subject, explaining the causes which appear to determine the production of fat and muscle, respectively, according to the present state of our knowledge of animal physiology.

Mr. Karkeek stated, at the commencement of his lecture, that some of the physiological views which he had adopted were those of Professor Liebig, they having yielded the most valuable results, in relation to the connection between organic chemistry and dietetics—under which head was comprised the nutritiveness of particular vegetables on the feeding of cattle.

With the view of his lecture being clearly understood, he first directed the attention of his audience to some of the phenomena connected with *growth* and *assimilation*, in vegetables and animals, showing the manner in which the former produce the blood and flesh of the latter; and that man, in consuming animal food, consumed strictly speaking, the vegetable principles which have served for the nutrition of cattle. This part of the lecture was explained in an easy manner by reference to tables containing the analysis of the elementary and proximate principles of the food of herbivorous animals by Boussingault and others, which proved that vegetable fibrin, albumen, and casein—the true nitrogenised principles of their food—were in fact identical in composition with the chief constituents of blood—animal fibrin, which is the fibrin of flesh; animal albumen, from eggs; and animal casein, from milk. He next showed the difference which existed in the aliments of cattle as far as they were concerned in the production of *fat* and *muscle*. This portion of the lecture was clearly explained by reference to Professor Liebig's theory, that one of the effects of respiration was to remove some of the carbon from the blood, by the oxygen of the atmosphere and the forming of carbonic acid gas. In which process a separation of two essential parts of the blood took place—the one being composed of nitrogenised materials, capable of assimilation to the various organs and tissues, muscles, nerves, bones, &c.; the other part being composed of non-nitrogenised materials, which were employed as elements of respiration and in the production of animal heat.

The cow, he said, according to Boussingault, consumed in twenty-four hours 69 oz. of carbon, which were the combustible materials of the food; and she required, in the same period, to inhale 11lb. 10oz. of oxygen, which was the supporter of combustion. But should it happen—as it does in all animals that are stall fed—that a less quantity of oxygen was inspired than was necessary to convert the carbon of the blood into carbonic acid gas, the superabundant carbon was returned into the circulation, and went to the production of fat.

This was a very interesting part of the lecture, as it was clearly shown that all the carbon of the food, not consumed in the lungs, was actually used in producing fat; and that the amount of nourishment required for an animal must be proportioned to the quantity of oxygen taken into the system. And as air was expanded by heat, and contracted by cold, it was evident that equal volumes of hot and cold air must contain unequal weights of oxygen—*ergo*, a larger quantity of food is required when animals were kept cold than when they were warm. This was clearly explained by reference to the voracious appetites of the Arctic savages for train oil, tallow candles, and animal food, compared with that of the Hindoo, living chiefly on rice and vegetable food.

The practical deductions which he drew from these facts were the necessity of keeping animals warm and perfectly quiet whilst in a state of feeding. The effect of exercise being to increase the circulation and quicken the respiration, and the consequent consumption of a greater quantity of food.

He then described the mode of rearing calves for veal in Holland, which was done by keeping them in a small, dark, clean, and dry house, so narrow that they could not turn, and this was said to be very successful.

He also related the method of suckling house lambs, of the early Dorsetshire breed, for the London market. The dams were fed with hay, oil-cake, corn, and cabbage, which is given in an enclosure adjoining the apartments where the lambs are confined. The lambs are excluded from the light, except at intervals, when the shepherd suckles them on the ewes. It was by these means that they speedily fatten, and their flesh became exceedingly white and delicate, and fetch a high price in the London market.

The lecturer produced many other examples, in the feeding of sheep at different temperatures, and under different conditions, clearly showing that by affording animals warmth and shelter, particularly in the winter months, that the saving of food would be very considerable.

The next part of his lecture went to show the manner in which *muscle* or *flesh* was produced. This was also clearly exhibited to the farmers by reference to tables containing analyses of different kinds of food, which proved very satisfactorily that an immense difference existed with reference to some kinds producing fat and others producing muscle.

According to those tables, which were the result of the analyses of Professor Playfair and Boussingault, pease contained fifteen per cent. more of the muscle-forming principle than barley-meal. Barley-meal twelve per cent. more than potatoes, and potatoes one per cent. more than white turnips.

He strongly recommended that barley-meal, when it was cheap enough, as it is at present, should be given to growing stock, particularly to sheep when feeding on white turnips, a pint of barley-meal a day would increase the quantity and quality of the flesh and wool at the same time. It would also tend to prevent scouring—the frequent consequence of so much watery food. For the rearing of breeding animals of all descriptions, he recommended the use of barley-meal or ground oats; and strongly condemned the practice which was frequently pursued of feeding young stock on linseed-cake, which is a very excellent food for producing fat but not flesh. He also condemned the very common practice of tying up the young bull at so early an age as eight or nine months old, and fed at the same time as a calf intended for the butcher. Too much liberty, he considered, could not possibly be given for the first two years as far as was consistent with warmth and shelter in the winter months. Where the pastures were small and convenient, there was no difficulty or danger in allowing the young animal to graze during the second summer; and if not convenient, a large sheltered shed, with a straw yard attached, would answer the purpose, with a comfortable loose box adjoining a straw yard in the winter, in which he might be allowed to range when the weather permitted.

Without exercise, in a moderate way, the young animal could never obtain that proper development of muscle which is required. This, he said, was dependent on an admirable law, that within certain limits, in proportion to the exertion which it is required to make, a part increases in strength, fitness, and size. It was the want of a proper supply of nitrogenised food, and the want of sufficient exercise, that so many of our best bred animals, particularly cattle and pigs, were prevented from breeding at a time when the greatest benefits and profit might be expected by increasing their race. He alluded, more particularly, to the North Devon cattle, those of the improved breed, as well as to a number of the Chinese breed of pigs.

The lecturer then showed that the distinguishing character of a well-bred animal depended not so much on the external as on the internal structure—such as the lungs, liver, spleen, kidneys, stomach, intestines, &c.

Here the lecturer made a singular statement, " that Professor Playfair, in his lecture before the English Agricultural Society, had proved what all butchers knew perfectly well, that an ' ox or sheep having small lungs and small livers, will fatten more readily than those having large lungs and large livers;'" but he, the lecturer, was also convinced, *that in proportion as an animal became fat, did those organs actually diminish in size.* He drew his conclusions, he said, from examining a great number of stall-fed cattle, chiefly of the Devon breed, averaging from 6 cwt. to 10 cwt. of beef. He had seen them slaughtered at all stages of feeding, from four to eight months, and invariably found that according to the amount of fat which they possessed were those organs reduced in size. This was a circumstance never stated before by any author, although the butchers knew this also from frequent experience, and he had gathered his information by visiting their slaughtering-houses.

He explained this by reference to the changes of particles constantly going on in the majority of the tissues of a living body, instancing the effect of exercise on the size of the muscles in that of the arm of a blacksmith, and in the arm of a person unaccustomed to labour. The production of fat he had already shown to be the consequence of the organs of nutrition not performing their natural offices. The lungs, then, of a stall-fed animal adapted their size to the quantity of oxygen consumed, and the liver to the quantity of bile secreted; and it was also a remarkable coincidence, which would account for the diminution of the intestines in a fatted animal, that the fatter it became the less food it consumed.

The lecturer drew some very important practical deductions from these observations, for if they were true, he said, the effect of breeding from fat animals, or from animals disposed quickly to become so, *function* here would *react* on *organisation.* By *reaction,* he meant, when an organ, as the lungs, for instance, became diminished in consequence of the animal becoming fat, from not performing its natural office, its diminished structure in breeding would in some degree be produced in the offspring—hence the *reaction* ; and if the same system be pursued, particularly in breeding from the nearest affinities, at the same time the effect would be more speedily produced. The lecturer here alluded to the improved short and long-horned cattle, the improved Herefords, the improved Devons, as well as the new Leicester sheep, all of which were originally produced by this method of breeding. Alluding to the effect of breeding from fat animals in this manner, he said, that early maturity, which was very desirable to be obtained, was the consequence. But he was of opinion that sometimes it was carried too far, as he believed that extreme early maturity, and the certainty of propagating their kind, were seldom compatible, and he also believed that the loss of a trifling degree of fat, which would be compensated for by an increase of flesh, increase of health, and an increase of strength, with the certainty of propagating their kind, would be excellent substitutes.

At the conclusion of the lecture, which was rather long, occupying an hour and a half in delivery, it was resolved that another evening should be appropriated to the discussion of the various interesting subjects advanced by the lecturer, and accordingly Saturday, the 8th of April, was appointed for this purpose.

CHEPSTOW FARMERS' CLUB.

The committee, in introducing the first annual report, cannot commence better than by expressing their satisfaction at the success which has already attended the establishment of the Chepstow Far-

mers' Club, which has already a list of 78 members, and there is every probability to expect a considerable addition to the number in the course of the ensuing year.

The committee consider it at once, both a pleasure and a duty incumbent upon them to express their gratitude to those gentlemen, who, in becoming honorary members, have so kindly contributed to the separate fund for the encouragement of ploughmen, labourers, &c.

The committee are decidedly of opinion, that nothing can be so conducive to the promotion of good farming in a neighbourhood as periodical discussions among practical agriculturists, whose real knowledge of the subjects must furnish much information in the form of manifold well-founded opinions, necessarily varied, owing to the great diversity of soils and situations; and which will eventually prove of mutual benefit to the members.

The committee, though they refer with pleasure to some very well attended monthly meetings at which subjects of great interest were discussed, still they cannot avoid expressing their regret, that sometimes no discussion took place owing to the insufficient attendance of members.

The committee have now only to lay before the members a concise statement of the proceedings at the monthly meetings during the past year, as well as a short account of the finances of the club ; both of which they hope will prove satisfactory.

At the meeting in December, when the club was established, the time was entirely employed in appointing officers, ordering books, and forming rules for the management of the society.

At the January meeting, the subject entered upon was—" *The breed, management, and best mode of keeping farm horses.*"

After some discussion it was resolved, that a clean-legged cart horse of not less than 15 hands high is the most useful for agricultural purposes in this district; and it is much to be regretted that the Clydesdale breed or the Cleveland is not introduced into this neighbourhood.

Mr. Baker, V.S. stated, " that a heavy cart horse with hairy legs is more subject to disease, such as blindness, farcy, and grease, than the lighter breeds ; and that black horses are more subject to diseases than others."

It was resolved, that cart horses should be kept in a warm shed and open fold-yard, with a sufficiently large manger and no rack, in preference to a stable ; because horses kept in that manner are not so liable to distemper.

The best method of keeping farm horses was stated to be, to cut all their fodder into chaff, which should consist of two-thirds clover or hay and one-third wheat straw, with half a bushel of barley or bean meal and a bushel of bran, with 140lbs. of Swede turnips per week.

At the February meeting, Mr. Baker, V.S. introduced—" *The causes and treatment of the prevailing distemper in cattle and sheep,*" in the following able paper :—

"The subject you have selected for this evening's discussion, although not strictly agricultural, is one of vast importance to the farmer. It is a disease that has made its appearance amongst our horned cattle, sheep, and pigs within the last few years, and has been attended with very serious and fatal consequences: it is commonly called "The Distemper."

"The first thing we have to do is to inquire what is the cause, and if we can remove the cause we shall effect a cure; and I call upon you all for your knowledge and observations, inviting you to a free discussion of the subject.

"I confess it is out of my power to account for it, unless it be produced by more than an ordinary quantity of wet weather which we have had for three or four years past, and other atmospheric changes, which render all animals more susceptible of disease.

"The symptoms of this complaint I need hardly describe, as, I believe, there are but few present who are not acquainted with them, and have not felt their ill effects. If we cannot ascertain the cause we must try to effect a cure; and I think, in most cases, with attention and perseverance this may be done. The best mode of treatment that has come to my knowledge, with horned cattle in good condition, is, to bleed moderately at the first onset of the disease, at the same time giving a laxative drench—not a strong purge—as the latter would tend to debilitate the animal; nor should we bleed after the second or third day if there be much weakness, but depend upon laxative and fever medicine till the bowels are moderately open, giving such food as the beast will take most readily.

"There is one of the effects of this disease which proves very troublesome, that is, the inflammation of the feet and the sloughing of the hoofs. When the beast becomes lame his feet should be searched, and if you find the toes or sole soft, pare them carefully, let out the matter if any has formed, and apply a lintseed meal or turnip poultice, and should any pipes or sinuses be found, dress with a solution of chloride of lime. Now let me caution you against using any hot or caustic applications, as much mischief has been done by ignorant pretenders from applying vitriol, butter of antimony, &c. to the already inflamed parts, which will produce irritation, fever, and death; whereas, if milder means had been employed, nature would have effected a cure. Warmth and cleanliness throughout must be strictly observed.

"The foregoing statement applies to more than ordinary cases, as there are thousands of animals affected, which are ill, and get well, unobserved. The same treatment applies to sheep and pigs as to the ox.

"Should the few remarks I have made in any way contribute to the benefit and advancement of knowledge of this society, and tend to relieve the sufferings of the brute creation, it will afford me much satisfaction."

Owing to the small attendance of members, the discussion was adjourned at the March meeting.

The subject introduced at the April meeting was—"The best system of growing and storing root crops:"—when it was agreed, that

The land intended for turnips should be ploughed immediately after harvest; and, if foul, the ploughing should be shallow, then dragged, harrowed, &c., and the weeds taken off or burned. Before Christmas, as deep a ploughing should be given as the nature of the soil will permit.

If the land be clean, then a deep ploughing should be given at once, and a deep cross ploughing before Christmas, taking care always to have plenty of water furrows, so that the land may lie dry through the winter.

In the spring, the land should be well dragged and scuffled, and, if necessary, ploughed again : should there be any weeds or filth remaining, the land must be cleaned before the turnips are put in.

Swede turnips, mangel wurzel, and the white or Belgian carrot, should always have the best land of the rotation. The wurzel and carrot should be planted the latter end of March or the beginning of April; and if the seed be mixed with sand, by rubbing the seed and sand together, these plants will come up at once, and get the start of the annual weeds. Swedes should be sown from the middle of May to that of June.

It was agreed that the drill system was the best; the drills to be from 24 to 30 inches : the carrot plants to be singled out eight or nine inches apart, and the wurzel and Swedes from ten to fifteen inches.

In the summer the horse-hoe should be freely used, *particularly in dry weather*, so long as the horse can pass between the rows without injuring the plants; the hand-hoe should occasionally be used to cut up any weeds that may escape the horse-hoe.

The discussion then turned upon the best and cheapest manure for root crops. One member stated that he had for the last seven years used one hundred quarters of bones per annum, half dust and half half-inch, and that he considered three quarters per acre (the quantity he uses) was fully equal, if not superior, to 15 two-horse cartloads of good three-quarter rotten dung; and that he had tried both manures in this proportion on the same field, and the crop of Swedes, as well as the after crops of the rotation (barley, clover, and wheat) were by far the best on the land manured with bones. The soil was a good loam resting on limestone. It was unanimously resolved, that 20 bushels of bone manure is equal to 15 solid yards of good farm-yard dung, these being the quantities generally used in this neighbourhood per acre.

A question then arose as to the *value* and advantages as to time in sowing turnips with dung or bone manure, when it was agreed, that with much less labour three times the quantity of land can be put in with bone manure.

At the May meeting, few members attending, the subject of *Storing Root Crops* was adjourned to the next meeting.

The June meeting was entirely taken up in fixing the premiums to be given in October for ploughing, &c., and in agreeing to send a memorial to the Royal Agricultural Society to apply for lecturers. It was also unanimously agreed to recommend that the Chepstow Wool Fair in future shall be held on the 22nd day of June, the present day often interfering with Monmouth and Coleford fairs.

Owing to the harvest, no meeting took place either in July or August.

At the meeting in September, the members were engaged in making arrangements for the ploughing match, and naming the judges for the ploughing, and to award the other premiums.

At the anniversary, October 18th, the ploughing match excited a good deal of interest, and the ploughing, considering the dry and hard state of the ground, was well done under three hours, the quantity being half an acre. The match took place in a field belonging to Mr. R. Philpotts.

After the match, upwards of 40 gentlemen dined together at the George Inn, and spent a very rational and pleasant evening. Mr. S. Matthews, chairman for the year, presided, and Mr. R. W. Purchas (for his son, who was ill) took the vice-chair.

At the October monthly meeting, a discussion took place, "On the best varieties of Wheat for sow-

ing in this district, and the best method of preparing the Seed"

Resolved, that the old red Lammas, and a red wheat called the golden ball, are the best for winter planting; and the golden ball, giant-headed, Scotch white, and Hertfordshire white, are the best for spring planting.

In preparing the seed for planting, many members continue the old practice of wetting the seed with stale urine, and drying with hot lime. Other members make brine with salt strong enough to swim an egg, drying with hot lime. Other members dissolve 2lbs. of blue vitriol in boiling water, and then add sufficient cold water to saturate a quarter of wheat; all of which answer the desired purpose of preventing smut.

At the November meeting, the chairman introduced the subject of *Storing and consuming Root Crops*, by stating his plan to be—to draw the Swedes when *ripe*, and if possible in dry weather, and to put one or two cart-loads in a conical heap, with the roots inside and the tops outside, spreading a bolting of straw on the top to throw off the rain. Supposing the crop to be from 18 to 22 tons, the price paid to store as above is 5s. per acre, labourers' wages being 10s. per week.

It being the day after Christmas-day, so few members attended in December, that it was necessary to adjourn the meeting.

In conclusion, the committee wish to impress on each member, individually, the importance of a regular attendance at the monthly meetings, as it is only by keeping up discussions on subjects of general agricultural utility, that the prosperity of the Chepstow Farmers' Club can be insured.

The committee also consider that the best thanks of the club are due to those members who introduced the various subjects of discussion during the past year. For the Committee,

R. N. PURCHAS, Honorary Secretary.

AGRICULTURAL EXPERIMENTS AND DISTINCTION OF SOILS.

TO THE EDITOR OF THE EXETER FLYING POST.

SIR,—There is probably no means more effective than the periodical press for promoting and accelerating practical improvements. Suggesting experiments as they occur; recording and diffusing the results as they arise; and favouring comparison and discussion; it works like a main-spring upon society at large, and keeps the whole in activity. To the present condition of the farmer it is especially

suited. He needs improvement, and is anxious for it, but has neither means nor time for much study. It is in the agricultural periodicals, and in the weekly newspaper, that he must seek his information of what is going on to his advantage. In these he finds suggestions enough; but, unfortunately, with results so often inconsistent, or even contradictory, that they tend to embarrass and discourage, rather than to help and excite him.

This is due, in great part, to the indiscriminate and indefinite names by which the soils are called in different places; so that it is impossible for the farmer to be sure on what kind of soil the recorded experiment was really made.

Thus, any loose clay is called "Marl" in some parts of England, and "Loam" in others; whilst the latter name is explained by one writer to mean a fat earth, by another a mixture of clay, lime, and sand, without stating proportions; and by others differently again. "On referring to books on husbandry," says Sir G. Sinclair, "we read of a hazel loam, a humid sandy soil, garden mould, &c.; but owing to the perplexity arising out of the want of proper definitions, we find it utterly impracticable to determine what kind of soil is meant; so that of fifty different kinds I have myself examined, in various parts of the kingdom, those under the same name appeared to differ greatly in their respective qualities."

This disheartening confusion may, happily, be obviated without much difficulty, by giving the soils systematic names, according to their properties, and the proportions of their *characteristic* ingredients.

Soils consist chiefly of sand and clay, with more or less of lime and humus (vegetable mould). Sand gives porosity and dryness; clay, compactness and tenacity; humus, attraction for moisture, warmth, and nourishment. Lime corrects excess of the others, and promotes vegetation by decomposing the humus (and other means). On the proportions of these four, therefore, depend the *general* characters of the soil. (The ingredients also present, in minute quantity, were treated of in my last, and do not require further notice here.)

Hence we are supplied with a basis for a tabular arrangement of soils, distinctly intelligible to every one who uses it; and by means of which the results of experiment may be clearly reported, and consistently repeated, from one end of the country to the other. Distributing them into classes and orders, according to their proportions of lime and clay, and subdividing into species, according to the quantity of humus, all the names will acquire definite meanings, descriptive of the qualities of the soil:—

NAMES OF THE DIFFERENT DESCRIPTIONS OF SOIL. PROPORTIONS OF INGREDIENTS IN EVERY 100 PARTS.

Classes.	Orders.	Species.	Clay.	Lime.	Humus.
1. *Argillaceous Soils.* Above 50 per cent. of Clay........	Without Lime.	Poor	Above 50	0	0· to 0·5
		Middling.	ditto	0	0·5 to 1·5
		Rich	ditto	0	1·5 to 5·0
Not more than 5 per cent. of Lime..	With Lime.	Poor	ditto	0·5 to 5·0	0· to 0·5
		Middling.	ditto	0·5 to 5·0	0·5 to 1·5
		Rich	ditto	0·5 to 5·0	1·5 to 5·0
2. *Loamy Soils.* Not more than 50 nor less than 30 per cent. of Clay	Without Lime.	Poor.....	30 to 50	0	0· to 0·5
		Middling.	ditto	0	0·5 to 1·5
		Rich	ditto	0	1·5 to 5·0
Not more than 5 of Lime..........	With Lime.	Poor....	ditto	0·5 to 5·0	0· to 0·5
		Middling.	ditto	0·5 to 5·0	0·5 to 1·5
		Rich	ditto	0·5 to 5·0	1·5 to 5·0

Classes.	Orders.	Species.	Clay.	Lime.	Humus.
3. Sandy Loams. ——— Not more than 30 nor less than 20 per cent. of Clay	Without Lime.	Poor..... Middling. Rich	20 to 30 ditto ditto	0 0 0	0· to 0·5 0·5 to 1·5 1·5 to 5·0
Not more than 5 of Lime..........	With Lime.	Poor .... Middling. Rich	ditto ditto ditto	0·5 5· 0·5 to 5·0 0·5 to 5·0	0· to 0·5 0·5 to 1·5 1·5 to 5·0
4. Loamy Sands. ——— Not more than 20 nor less than 10 per cent. of Clay	Without Lime.	Poor..... Middling. Rich	10 to 20 ditto ditto	0 0 0	0· to 0·5 0·5 to 1·5 1·5 to 5·0
Less than 5 per cent. of Lime......	With Lime.	Poor.... Middling. Rich	ditto ditto ditto	0·5 to 5·0 0·5 to 5·0 0·5 to 5·0	0· to 0·5 0·5 to 1·5 1·5 to 5·0
5. Sandy Soils. ——— Not more than 10 per cent. of Clay..	Without Lime.	Poor..... Middling. Rich	0· to 10 ditto ditto	0 0 0	0· to 0·5 0·5 to 1·5 1·5 to 5·0
Less than 5 per cent. of Lime	With Lime.	Poor.... Middling. Rich	ditto ditto ditto	0·5 to 5· 0·5 to 5·0 0·5 to 5·0	0· to 0·5 0·5 to 1·5 1·5 to 5·0
6. Marly Soils. ———	Argillaceous.	Poor..... Middling. Rich	Above 50 ditto ditto	5 to 20 ditto ditto	0· to 0·5 0·5 to 1·5 1·5 to 5·0
	Loamy.	Poor..... Middling. Rich	30 to 50 ditto ditto	ditto ditto ditto	0· to 0·5 0·5 to 1·5 1·5 to 5·0
	Belonging to the Sandy Loams.	Poor..... Middling. Rich	20 to 30 ditto ditto	ditto ditto ditto	0· to 0·5 0·5 to 1·5 1·5 to 5·0
More than 5, not more than 20 per cent. of Lime.................	Belonging to the Loamy Sands.	Poor..... Middling. Rich	10 to 20 ditto ditto	ditto ditto ditto	0· to 0·5 0·5 to 1·5 1·5 to 5·0
	Humous.	Clayey... Loamy .. Sandy ...	Above 50 30 to 50 20 to 30	ditto ditto ditto	Above 5·0 ditto ditto
7. Calcareous Soils. ———	Argillaceous.	Poor..... Middling. Rich	Above 50 ditto ditto	Above 20 ditto ditto	0· to 0·5 0·5 to 1·5 1·5 to 5·0
	Loamy.	Poor..... Middling. Rich	30 to 50 ditto ditto	ditto ditto ditto	0· to 0·5 0·5 to 1·5 1·5 to 5·0
	Belonging to the Sandy Loams.	Poor..... Middling. Rich	20 to 30 ditto ditto	ditto ditto ditto	0· to 0·5 0·5 to 1·5 1·5 to 5·0
Containing more than 20 per cent. of Lime	Belonging to the Loamy Sands.	Poor..... Middling. Rich	10 to 20 ditto ditto	ditto ditto ditto	0· to 0·5 0·5 to 1·5 1·5 to 5·0
	Sandy.	Poor..... Middling. Rich	0 to 10 ditto ditto	ditto ditto ditto	0· to 0·5 0·5 to 1·5 1·5 to 5·0
	Pure.	Poor..... Middling. Rich	0 0 0	Above 99 " 98 " 94	0· to 0·5 1·5 to 1·5 5·5 to 5·0
	Humous.	Clayey... Loamy... Sandy ...	Above 50 30 to 50 20 to 30	Above 20 " 20 " 20	Above 5·0 ditto ditto

Classes.	Orders.	Species.	Clay.	Lime.	Humus.
8. *Humous Soils.*	Soluble mild Humus.	Clayey ...	Above 50	With or without Lime.	Above 5·0
		Loamy ...	30 to 50		ditto
		Sandy ...	20 to 30		ditto
Containing more than 5 per cent. of Humus	Insoluble carbonized or acid Humus.	Clayey ...	Above 50	With or without Lime.	ditto
		Loamy ...	30 to 50		ditto
		Sandy ...	20 to 30		ditto
	Insoluble fibrous Vegetable Matter.	Bog and Peat Earth.	With Lime. Without Lime.		ditto
					ditto

The remainder of the 100 parts, in each case, is *Sand*.

If this table, which we again owe chiefly to Dr. Daubeny, were in the hands of every intelligent farmer in the kingdom, it would surprisingly obviate the inconsistencies and disappointments, so perplexing in agricultural experiments. To make it clear at first, however, some explanation is requisite.

EXPLANATION OF THE TABLE.

The reader will bear in mind that the general properties of soils depend on the proportions they contain of sand, clay, lime, and humus. The classes and orders are generally regulated according to the lime and clay; the species according to the humus.—(See the table.)

The table begins with those soils which contain little or no lime; at the utmost, less than five per cent.; of which there are five classes, depending on the proportion of *clay* they contain.

Those which possess fifty per cent. of clay are classed under the head of ARGILLACEOUS SOILS, and are distinguished into two orders; the first wholly destitute of lime, the second containing less than five per cent. of that earth. Each of these orders are then subdivided into three *species*, distinguished as rich, poor, and intermediate, according to the proportion of humus or vegetable mould present in them. If the amount of this mould be not more than one-half per cent., the soils are called *poor*, as the fertility of a soil is in all cases greatly influenced by the proportion of this ingredient; if it varies from 0· 5· to 1· 5· per cent. it is called *middling*; if from 1· 5· to 5· 0· per cent. it is distinguished as *rich*.

The second *class* of soils comprehends those which contain from 30 to 50 per cent. of clay, and is denominated LOAMY. These likewise are divided into two orders, the one with, the other without lime; and again into three species, according to the proportion of vegetable mould present in them.

The third class embraces those soils which contain not more than 33 nor less than 20 per cent. of clay. They are called SANDY LOAMS, and are subdivided into orders and species, on the same principle as before.

In the next, or fourth class, under the denomination of LOAMY SANDS, are ranged those soils which contain from 10 to 20 per cent. of clay; the remainder, with the exception of the small per centage of limestone and humus they may contain, consisting of sand.

The fifth class, designated as SANDY, includes all those soils in which the proportion of clay does not exceed 10 per cent.; and here again the same subdivisions are adopted.

Hitherto the amount of calcareous matter present is not supposed to exceed 5 per cent.; but the next two classes are dependent on their contents of *lime*; their orders being determined by the clay.

MARLY soils, the sixth *class*, contains 5 to 20 per cent. of carbonate of lime; and are to be distinguished into five *orders*; of which the first, called *argillaceous*, or clayey, contains above 50 per cent. of clay; the second, *loamy*, from 30 to 50; the third, *sandy loamy*, from 20 to 30; the fourth, *loamy sandy*, from 10 to 20; and the fifth is distinguished by the larger proportion of humus, which exceeds in quantity five per cent. of the whole, and is therefore denoted as *humous* MARL: which last is divided into three species—viz., argillaceous, or *clayey*, which contains above 50 per cent. of clay; *loamy*, which contains from 30 to 50 per cent.; and *sandy*, possessing from 20 to 30 per cent. of the same ingredient.

We next arrive at that class of soils which contains more than 20 per cent. of carbonate of lime, and which is therefore distinguished as calcareous, or limy. These are subdivided *as the marly class*, according to the proportion of clay they may contain. When this earth exists in more than the proportion of 50 per cent. they are to be called argillaceous, or clayey; when it is from 30 to 50, *loamy*; when from 20 to 30, they are said to belong to the *sandy loams* of the calcareous class; when from 10 to 20, to the *loamy sands*; and when either destitute of clay altogether, or containing, at most, only 10 per cent. of it, they are called *sandy*.

Lastly, a calcareous soil, which contains more than five per cent. of vegetable mould, belongs to the *seventh* order; that of *humous* calcareous soils, of which there are three species—viz., the argillaceous, the *loamy*, and the *sandy*—characterised, as before, by the larger or smaller proportion of clay present in them.

A short recapitulation will make all this very clear and simple.

Thus the reader will see that the name *rgillaceous*, or *clayey*, is applied to all soils containing above 50 per cent. clay; *loamy* to all between 30 to 50; *sandy loam* to all between 20 and 30; and so of the others to whichever class they belong.

That the term *marly* applies to all soils containing from 5 to 20 per cent. lime; and *calcareous* or *limy*, to all above 20 per cent. lime.

That the terms *rich, middling*, and *poor*, apply to all soils according to their proportions of humus, under five per cent., and the term *humous* to all above that proportion.

The first five classes being named after the clay they contain, and their orders after the lime.

The sixth and seventh classes, after the *lime* and their orders after the clay, and the species, in each class, (except the 8th) after the *humus*.

There is also a class termed HUMOUS, of which the whole contain above 5 per cent., sometimes a great deal more, and from which they derive their name. This is the eighth and last class, and is distinguished into three orders. The first consists of soluble mild humus, that is of that description of vegetable mould which is in a fit condition to nourish the plants that grow in it; the second of acid humus—viz., containing a free acid, which by its presence is highly destructive to most kinds of vegetation. A third order consists of fibrous vegetable matter, such as peat, which, though not acid, is yet in a condition little fitted for imparting nourishment to plants. These orders are again subdivided into argillaceous, loamy, and sandy, according to the proportion of clay present in them; and lastly, distinguished into two species, the one containing, the other destitute of, calcareous matter.

But the question will now naturally arise—how is the farmer to know the proportions of clay, lime, humus, and sand, in his soils; and of what use is the table to him until he can ascertain them? We must answer this by showing him an easy and simple method of separating them and determining their proportions. Such is the following

Rough and Rapid Analysis.

Take a glass tube three quarters of an inch in internal diameter, and three feet long; fit a cork into one end, and set it upright; fill it half full of pure water; take nearly as much water as has been poured into the tube, and mix with it the portion of soil which is to be examined, in quantity not more than will occupy six inches of the tube (say three-quarters of an ounce,) pour the mixture rapidly into the tube, and let it stand in a corner of the room, or supported upright in any way. In half an hour it may be examined. The earths will have been deposited according to the size and specific gravity of their particles. The portion still suspended in the water may be allowed to settle; and there will appear in the tube layers of sand, clay, and humus, which may be measured by a scale (a common carpenter's rule will do), and thus the proportions nearly ascertained.

See Example at Foot. (1.)

When a farmer is about to hire a farm, of which the quality is not well known to him, he may be much assisted in his judgment by this experiment, if he has no time or opportunity for a more accurate analysis. For the glass tube may be substituted one of tin or zinc, two feet in length, with a piece of glass tube, a foot long, joined to it by means of a brass collar or ferrule, with a screw cut in it, which is cemented to the glass, and screws on the metal tube; and thus the instrument may be made more portable: or still cheaper with sliding joints tightened with twine, like those of a flute, instead of the screw. When the water has been poured off, and the earths only remain, the cork may be taken out, and the contents pushed out on a plate, by means of a rod and plug which fit the internal diameter of the tube. They may thus be more particularly examined.

Thus we have a rough estimate of the proportions of sand, clay, and humus; there remains still to determine the proportion of lime.

For this purpose some of the soil must be dried; spread out thin on a saucer or plate, put over a saucepan of water kept boiling for half an hour, or till the soil loses no more weight: or over a gentle fire, stirring with a chip of wood, which should not be discoloured by the heat. 200 grains of this dry soil (weighed exactly) must be put into a cup

and a little aqua fortis, or muriatic acid, diluted with four times its weight of water, poured on it. A table spoonful of the mixed acid and water will be generally enough for 200 grains. If there is any sensible proportion of lime, there will be an effervescence; and if this is considerable, a little more diluted acid may be added, when it is quiet, and repeated as long as it renews the effervescence; but this will only happen on very limy soils. When all is quiet, the water should still taste sour, to prove there has been acid enough. More water is then to be added, and the solution well washed out of the soil, on a filter. The residue is then to be dried *just as before*, and weighed again. The loss will give the carbonate of lime carried off by the acid. Say 3 grs. = 1½ per cent.—*(See Example at foot.)* (2).

This very simple and easy method is, however, neither very complete nor distinct. As in other cases, practice will give skill and facility: and with practice it may be sufficient for our present infant state of agricultural science.

But for those who have patience and skill to go through with it, I hope to send the details of a more accurate process for your next, or when you have convenient room for it.

Being, Sir, &c.,
J. Prideaux.

Example.

	Depth of	Inches.	Tenths of Inch.	Per Cent.
(1.)	Sand.....	3½	35	58·3
	Clay.....	2⅓	23·3	38·9
	Humus....	⅙	1·7	2·8
			60	100

(2.) Suppose the lime to have come, 1 grain from the sand, and the ½ grain from the clay, the soil will be named and classed in the table, as follows:—

Sand, 57·3.

Clay, 38·4, between 30 and 50—loamy. Class 2.

Lime, 1.5, with lime, Order 1.

Humus 2·8, between 1, 5 and 5 rich, species 3;
and it will be a rich loamy soil, with lime.

THE GYPSUM EXPERIMENT.

TO THE EDITOR OF THE MARK LANE EXPRESS.

Sir,—Allow me to offer one remark on Mr. Bree's letter, respecting "the Gypsum Experiment" which appears in your paper of the 13th inst. He recommends the liquid collected in the tubs to be spread regularly over the land, previous to ploughing in the stable manure. Now, would it not be more beneficial, and its effects more certain, if applied when the crop is somewhat advanced; the decomposition of the ammonia and the assimilation of the nitrogen being perfect only when the plants are in a growing state? Considering the small proportion of nitrogen required by the straw in comparison with that contained in the grain, would not the influence of the weather on the soil so far modify the effects of the sulphate of ammonia as to render it almost useless, if the directions of Mr. Bree were followed?

I am, sir, your very obedient servant,
Hy. Jno. Turner.
Bishopsgate-street, 15th March.

ROYAL AGRICULTURAL SOCIETY OF ENGLAND.

At a weekly Council, held at the Society's House, in Hanover Square, on Wednesday, the 29th of March, present, Thomas Raymond Barker, Esq., in the Chair; Barough Almack, Esq.; David Barclay, Esq., M.P.; W. R. Browne, Esq.; French Burke, Esq.; George Cottam, Esq.; Humphrey Gibbs, Esq.; Sir John Johnstone, Bart., M.P.; John Kinder, Esq.; Sir Francis Mackenzie, Bart.; W. Woods Page, Esq.; Rev. W. G. Rham; Professor Sewell; I. Spencer Stanhope, Esq.; and Colonel Wood, M.P.

Mr. Bullen, Secretary of the Royal Agricultural Improvement Society of Ireland, transmitted to the Society the Prize Sheet of that Society, and informed the Council that the next Cattle Show of the Society would be held in Belfast on Thursday, the 31st of August, on which occasion it was confidently hoped that many members of the Royal Agricultural Society of England would be able to attend as well as to send over some stock to the Meeting; the time of meeting, in order to suit all parties, having been chosen to come after the English and Highland Shows, and the locality such as to be easily reached from all quarters.

Mr. Alexander Nicholl, of the Royal Exchange Court, Glasgow, transmitted to the Council a statement of the peculiar advantages attending the use of the Concrete Furrow Draining of Lord James Hay, of Seaton, in Aberdeenshire.

Mr. Baker, of Cottesmore, transmitted to the Council a collection of facts, illustrated by coloured plans, relative to the capabilities and cultivation of the soil upon the Small Allotment System in Rutlandshire. This communication was referred to the Journal Committee.

The Council then adjourned to Wednesday next the 5th of April.

At a Monthly Council, held at the Society's House in Hanover Square, on Wednesday, the 5th of April, present, Philip Pusey, Esq., M.P., in the chair; Earl of Euston; Thomas William Bramston, Esq., M.P.; French Burke, Esq.; Colonel Challoner; Charles Robert Colvile, Esq., M.P.; Humphrey Gibbs, Esq.; Brandreth Gibbs, Esq.; Stephen Grantham, Esq.; William Goodenough Hayter, Esq., M.P.; William Fisher Hobbs, Esq.; Samuel Jonas, Esq.; John Kinder, Esq.; Sir Francis Mackenzie, Bart.; Sir Robert Price, Bart., M.P.; Rev. W. L. Rham; Johua Rodwell, Esq.; Professor Sewell; and William Shaw, Esq.

FINANCES.

Colonel Challoner presented to the Council the Monthly Report of the Finance Committee, held that day; from which it appeared that the receipts during the month of March had been 1,130l., and the current cash balance in the hands of the Bankers, on the last day of that month, had amounted to the sum of 2,065l.; the Committee accordingly recommending that a further purchase of 1,000l. stock should be made in the New 3½ per Cents, in the name of the Society.

This Report was confirmed by the Council and its recommendation adopted.

PRIZE ESSAY ON STRONG LAND.

Mr. Pusey reported, on the part of the Journal Committee, that the prize of 20l. offered by the Society for the best Essay on the Rotations of Crops for Heavy Lands, had been adjudged to Mr. William Stace, of Berwick, near Lewes, Sussex, for his Essay on that subject, which would appear in the next Part of the Journal.

MEETING AT DERBY.

Colonel Challoner, Vice-Chairman of the General Derby Committee, laid before the Council the Report of the Committee held that day, on the arrangements of the ensuing Meeting, connected with the Show Yard, Dinners, Trial of Implement Field, the free admission of exhibitors to the Yard, the advertisement relating to Certificates, and the Conveyance of Passengers, Stock, and Implements to the Meeting by the various lines of Railway in junction with the Derby Station.

Mr. Colvile, M.P., Chairman of the Derby Local Committee, informed the Council that the Committee of Directors of the Midland Counties Railway, appointed to arrange the Trains and Fares for the Society's Meeting at Derby in July, had decided to supply any number of special trains which might be required on that occasion, requiring only the usual fares for passers, and only half the fares for cattle and farming implements.

These Reports were adopted and confirmed by the Council.

ARREAR OF SUBSCRIPTION.

Mr. Gibbs obtained leave to postpone his motion, on the date at which subscriptions should be considered as in arrear, until the next monthly council.

PUBLICATION OF JOURNAL.

Mr. Pusey, M.P., brought forward his motion on the publication of the Journal, when it was resolved, "That in future the Journal shall be issued in half volumes twice in the year, containing the same amount of matter as heretofore."

ANALYSING CHEMIST.

Mr. Pusey also brought forward his motion, of which due notice had also been given, on the appointment of an Analysing Chemist to the Society, when Dr. Lyon Playfair, of the Royal Institution, Manchester, was unanimously elected to that office. Mr. Pusey informed the Council that Dr. Playfair was at that time engaged in establishing at Manchester a chemical laboratory for the purposes of his scientific investigations, connected with the subject of Agricultural Chemistry, and where he would receive from the Society all enquiries the Council might think proper to make of him, charging all business referred to him by them at the mere cost of manipulation, and replying, without charge, to all their letters of consultation; individual applications of a professional character, being subject, according to the special nature of the enquiry and consequent investigation, to a certain scale of charges, which would be left with the Secretary for the information of the Members.

MODEL FARMS.

The following gentlemen were appointed a Committee to examine into the details of Sir Francis Mackenzie's suggestions for the establishment of Model Farms in England and Wales:—Earl Spencer, Earl of Euston, Earl of Ducie, Mr. Browne, Mr. Burke, Mr. Hobbs, Sir Francis Mackenzie, Rev. Mr. Rham, and Mr. Shaw.

Mr. Sandbach's offer of land for an experimental farm in North Wales was referred to the same committee.

BOKHARA CLOVER AND LUCERNE.

Messrs. Thomas Gibbs and Co. presented specimens of the Bokhara clover, Lucerne, spotted chicory, Pastel, and Swiss chard beet. Mr. H. Gibbs stated that the specimens on the table were intended to illustrate the comparative earliness of Bokhara clover, Lucerne, &c., and had been grown on a sharp mould on a gravelly subsoil, at their Experimental Garden at Brompton: the Lucerne appearing clearly from this trial to be earlier in its growth than the Bokhara clover. He further stated that he had that morning offered some of the fresh Bokhara clover to one of his father's horses, which was at hard work but upon good keep, and that it had refused to eat it. That he then offered to the same horse a portion of the Lucerne, which was taken with avidity. The two being mixed, the horse picked out the Lucerne, and could be made to eat only two small portions of the clover.

COUNTRY MEETING OF 1845.

Mr. S. Brittain, Secretary of the Chester Agricultural Society, communicated to the Council a memorial from the Chairman and Committee of that Society, soliciting the Society to hold its Annual Country Meeting of 1845 in that City.

Alderman Copeland presented, through Mr. Jonas, a sample of Wheat from Lima; Mr. Stokes transmitted the preparation of Hernia with Dr. Lloyd's statement of the peculiarities of the case: Mr. Wills, a communication on the employment of the Poor; Mr. Spencer Stanhope, a statement of the weight of an ox in 1732; Mr. Shaw, a copy of Mr. Hannam's Essay on Rape Dust; Professor Sewell, a copy of the last Number of the Transactions of the Veterinary Association; and the Proprietors, the last No. of the Annals of Chemistry.

The Council having then ordered a completed set of the Society's Journal to be transmitted to the Royal Academy of Sciences at Munich, adjourned over the Easter Recess to Wednesday the 26th of April.

NEW MEMBERS.

The following gentlemen were elected members of the Society:—

The Honourable Colonel E. G. Douglas Pennant, of Penrhyn Castle, near Bangor, North Wales, was elected a Governor.

Abney, William Wootton, Measham Hall, near Ashby-de-la Zouch, Leicestershire
Allsop, Henry, Burton-ou-Trent, Staffordshire
Avery, Thomas, Gloucester
Bainbrigge, Thomas Parker, Derby
Bateman, Thomas Osborne, Stanley, near Derby
Brookes, John, East Halton, near Barton-on-Humber
Chesterfield, The Earl of, Bretby Park, Derbyshire
Copestake, Thomas Goodall, Kirk Langley, Derby
Crewe, Edmund Lewis, Repton Park, near Derby
Dean, Henry, Weston, Petersfield, Hants
Freebody, William Yates, No. 9, Duke-street, Westminster
Fosbroke, Thomas, the Hagg, Stavely, near Chesterfield
Gething, William, St. Julian's, 'Newport, Monmouthshire
Hammond, Thomas, Penshurst, near Tonbridge, Kent
Hodgkinson, John, Hardwick, Derbyshire
Holding, Henry, Shaldon, near Alton, Hants
Jepson, John, Rowthorne, Derbyshire
Jessopp, Francis Johnson, Derby
Knowles, Joshua, Attercliffe, near Sheffield
Llewellyn, William, Court-colman, Bridgend, Glamorganshire
Lloyd, William, Ludlow, Salop
Marsland, Thomas, Henbury Hall, Macclesfield
Mold, Charles John, Makeney, near Derby
Morley, James, Stanton Hall, Stanton-by-Dale, near Derby
Mousley, John, Derby
Palgrave, Charles Frederick, Bedford
Pelham, the Hon. Capt. Dudley, St. Lawrence, Newport, Isle of Wight
Poyser, George, Weston Underwood, near Derby
Rogerson, Joseph, Algerkirk, near Boston, Lincolnsh.
Shaw, William, the Great Hotel, Buxton, Derbyshire
Spencer, John, Odstone Hall, Measham, near Ashby-de la Zouch, Leicestershire.
Spilsbury, The Rev. Francis Ward, Willington, near Derby
Stevens, Henry, Duffield, near Derby
Thornewill, Robert, Burton-upon-Trent, Staffordshire
Turner, William, Derby
Turner, Thomas, Castwood Farm, Rotherham, Yorksh.
Walker, I. Ewart, M.D., 23, Edward-street, Portland-place
Wass, Joseph, Lea, near Matlock Bath, near Wirksworth, Derbyshire
Wheatcroft, David, Buckland Hollow, Derbyshire
Wilmot, the Rev. Richard Coke, Edenson, near Bakewell, Derbyshire
Wyley, William, Vineyard, near Wellington, Salop.

EFFECTS OF PUTRID VEGETABLES, &c., ON THE GROWTH OF PLANTS.

It is well known that in adding decomposing vegetable matter to the soil, we supply to plants those substances which enter into their composition, and which exist in different states of combination. When such matter is to be applied as a manure to plants whose roots are confined in pots or any other given space, it must be made soluble in water; and chemical analysis plainly shows that all plants are resolvable into a certain number of simple bodies, and that these bodies enter readily into combination with water. Water, therefore, is apparently the source through which this nutriment is to be conveyed to the absorbent vessels: and wishing to have ocular proof of the effects of such a liquid, and that too in as economical a way as possible, I had an upright cask, with one end taken out, filled with leaves of cabbage and any other succulent plants; these were pressed down, and rainwater was added until the mass rose level with the surface. In this state putrefaction proceeded quickly, and in three or four weeks it was complete; this, however, depends entirely upon the state of the weather. That I might be the more certain of its fertilizing effects, 500 scarlet Pelargoniums were subjected to an experiment. These had been exposed for the greater part of the year to all the variations of the weather, being pot-bound, having literally nothing to subsist on but what was supplied to them in a fluid state. One-half of them were supplied with the liquid from the cask, the other half with rain-water, and this experiment was carried on for upwards of a month—a sufficient time to prove its usefulness. At the expiration of that period, no one ignorant of their treatment could have believed that they were all of the same age, and had been treated alike in every other respect; the difference was so much in favour of those that had been supplied with vegetable liquid; they had not only grown more vigorously, but their leaves were larger, and of a darker green. However fertilizing this liquid may be of itself, it is made still more so by the addition of animal urine in lieu of rain-water. I also found that the vegetable fibre decomposed with greater facility when acted upon by the urine of cattle in a fresh state, at the same time that the latter forms a liquid, holding in solution all the ingredients that constitute the food of plants, and fitted to supply nutrition in that form in which it can be received by the most minute spongioles. When orange-trees, that had been sickly for some years, were supplied with this liquid, their leaves turned from yellow to green, they bloomed freely, and set their fruit the same year. That this fluid may not receive more than its due, I will subjoin the previous treatment of the above plants. Early in spring, all the earthy matter was washed from their roots; they were repotted in fresh soil, and plunged in a gentle hot-bed, where they made numerous fibres. The liquid was then copiously given; and at no time should this or any other artificial liquid, unless in a very diluted state, be applied to plants where a deficiency of fibres exists. I have supplied this liquid to numerous stove and green-house plants, with very beneficial results, more especially to those with succulent roots, and at no time did it destroy or fail in its effects. Unless sulphuric acid, or some other fixing substance is mixed with it, this liquid cannot be used in any confined apartment, on account of the noxious effluvia that is given off. Where a constant supply is required, two casks or cisterns are necessary, that the contents of one may be putrifying while the other is in use; the portion that remains after the liquid is drawn off, if mixed with light loam, forms an excellent compost.—*R. P. Drummond, foreman, Minto House, Roxburghshire.*

THE CHALLENGE—SCOTCH FARMING.

TO THE EDITOR OF THE HEREFORD TIMES.

SIR,—I observe in your paper a letter headed "Scotch Farming—a Challenge." There are certain facts animadverted upon in that letter, which have often formed the subject of my own observation. Scotch farmers in England have been more remarkable for want of success than otherwise ; and that nearly in proportion as they attempted to introduce Scotch modes. The inhabitants of a district must always know what is best adapted for that district. They are indebted for this knowledge to experience. The farmer who has been trained in one district, therefore, culti- vates land to a disadvantage in another. This observa- tion is applicable to farmers who migrate from one county of England to another, as well as to those who come from Scotland, although in a less degree. But are we to allow error to steal its way into our minds, side by side with truth, and do the greater harm be- cause it keeps such respectable company? Are we, from the undeniable facts stated above, to assume that agriculture has never been benefited by the migration of farmers from one district to another ? or that England has derived no advantage from Scotch farming ? Scot- land lies under similar obligations to England, and they have been to each other as two individuals in so- ciety deriving mutual advantage from an interchange of good offices. Has it never come within Messrs. Winnal and Pierce's own observation, that the success- ful farmer is seldom the introducer of a new improve- ment?—that the experimental farmer (and every stranger is one to a certain extent) has made his experi- ments at his own cost, and to his serious loss?—that he has been laughed at by his neighbours? who, never- less, have profited by his experiments. Let us make a supposition, the opposite of what usually takes place : let us suppose that the English farmer migrates into Scotland ; suppose also he takes with him his two- wheeled plough, his team of four horses or six cattle, and conducts his other operations on a corresponding scale of slow-paced magnificence. Now, do Messrs. Pierce and Winnal suppose that the English farmer will be one whit more successful in Scotland than the Scotch generally are in England ? Will he be better able to contend with a late and precarious climate than the natives themselves are? I am afraid not ; and yet I will venture to assert, that one of those champion agriculturists—those Goliaths who are to stand forth and frighten the armies of Scotch farmers in England, shall not go into Scotland and take a farm, without conferring an advantage upon the district he goes to. Messrs. Pierce and Winnal assert that "we beat them upon the ploughing system, so far as expenses go." Efficiency must always be an element in our cal- culations, in comparing the expenses of two different modes of husbandry. In that view, I will stake 10l., that with four-horse teams they cannot match Scotch ploughing, so far as expenses go. I will farther assert that, in all Herefordshire and Worcestershire both, they will not find ten contiguous parishes so efficiently ploughed with four-horse ploughs as ten I will find in one of the smallest Scotch counties, where no more than two horses have ever been used. I will lay ex- pense out of view in this last instance, and assume alone the test of efficiency, depth, and regularity of furrow.

R.

HIGHLAND AND AGRICULTURAL SOCIETY OF SCOTLAND.

MONTHLY MEETING IN THE MUSEUM.

(FROM THE EDINBURGH EVENING COURANT.)

The monthly meeting was held on Wednesday last, Sir William Jardine, Bart., in the chair.

*　　*　　*　　*　　*

The next paper was a "Report of Experiments on the comparative value of some manures in rais- ing turnips," by John Dudgeon, Esq., Spylan, read by Mr. Stephens. The object of the experiments was to ascertain the value of guano as compared with some other kinds of manure ; and so satisfied is the author with the fertilising powers of that sub- stance, that he has made arrangements to have this season upwards of sixty acres of turnip lands pre- pared with it alone.

The comparative trials were made in three diffe- rent fields, the conditions being varied in each. The first experiment was upon a field lying upon a slope, with a southern exposure, the soil consisting of a good loam upon a retentive subsoil ; the upper part of the field, for about a fourth of its length, gradu- ally becoming shallower in soil, and resting upon a hard muirland pan, so that the value of the lower portion of the field, as compared with the upper, may be estimated at 3 to 1. This field had been but im- perfectly drained. It was dunged in the usual way, immediately before sowing, with well-prepared farm- yard manure, at the rate of about eighteen cubic yards to the acre, with the exception of that portion to which guano was applied. Two ordinary drills for the latter were selected at random, and the guano distri- buted in them by the hand, without any mixture, at the rate of three cwt. per acre ; leaving an interval of three drills, which were manured like the rest of the field. Two other drills were treated with guano at the rate of four cwt. per acre ; and finally, with a similar space intervening, two drills with guano at the rate of fully more than five cwt. per acre. No difference appeared in the turnips (which were the variety named Dale's Hybrid) previous to *singling*, or thinning the plants with the hoe. After that, however, the superiority of the drills with the guano became manifest, and continued to increase with the growth of the turnips, particularly in those drills which received the greatest quantity, till the whole were carted off in October; when the produce (topped and rooted) of the whole six drills was weighed, each two, as differing in the quantity of guano applied, compared with two drills immedi- ately adjoining, on which the farm-yard manure had been used. The following was the result :—

		cwt.	st.
Two drills with guano, 5 cwt. per acre	..	25	5
,, dung, 18 yards ,,	..	18	7
,, guano, 4 cwt ,,	..	22	6
,, dung, 18 yards ,,	..	19	7
,, guano, 3 cwt. ,,	..	20	6
,, dung, 18 yards ,,	..	19	2

In the second experiment a comparative trial was made between guano and bone-dust mixed with coal ashes. The ashes were sifted, and in imately mixed with the bones some days before being applied, in the proportion of sixteen bushels of bones and eight of ashes per acre. The quantity of guano applied was at the rate of three cwt. per acre upon four drills, two and two together, at an interval of eight drills manured with bones and ashes. Then, at a similar interval, followed two drills operated upon

B B

with guano, together with sulphate of soda (glauber salts), at the rate of four cwt. per acre, being the only instance in the course of these experiments in which any foreign substance was used with the guano. The turnips were drawn about the end of November, and on a comparison of the weight of the crop on two of the four drills done with guano alone, with the produce of the average of four drills nearly immediately adjoining, manured with bone-dust and ashes, the result stood thus (the plants being topped and rooted):—

	cwt.	st.
Guano	23	2
Bone-dust, &c.	19	2
Guano and sulphate of soda	23	0

In the third experiment guano was used against bone-dust alone, applied, as is usual in that district, at the rate of 16 bush. per acre. The guano was used at the rate of two cwt. only per acre. The drills manured with the latter showed a very decided superiority, and were ready for the hoe fully eight days earlier than the rest of the field. This more vigorous growth they maintained throughout; and when the turnips (the white stone globe variety) were weighed on the 22nd March, after standing throughout the winter, the result was as follows (the roots and tops being in this instance retained):—

	cwt.	st.
Two drills guano	31	4
" " bone-dust	24	7

Mr. Dudgeon mentions in a subsequent communication, that he has applied guano as a top dressing to winter wheat after potatoes, and that the ridges which were thus treated are now showing a decided superiority to the others; and in contradistinction to that first *rush* of vegetation which follows upon the use of nitrate of soda, it is only of late that the guano has exhibited its effects, though applied with the seed in October. From all that he has seen, Mr. Dudgeon is of opinion that the effects of guano will not be so evanescent as some suppose, but that it will impart a benefit to the soil of considerable permanency. He had the gratification of showing the effects of some of his experiments to Professor Liebig, who seemed much delighted with the style of their operation, and declared that no experiments could be more accurately and fairly performed, even in the laboratory. Dr. Traill made a few remarks on the production and probable endurance of the supply of this valuable manure.

PRODUCTIVENESS OF THE VINE.— Mr. John Mearns, F.H.S., curator of the Leeds Zoological and Botanical Gardens, in a recently published book on the "Pot-Culture of the Grape," says—"I have had berries of the black Tripoli kind frequently above two inches in girth, and perfectly formed. A good sized bunch of some of the best sorts will weigh from one to four pounds; but bunches of the Syrian grape have been grown that have weighed forty pounds, and in this country, from ten to nineteen pounds weight. A single vine in a large pot, or grown as a dwarf standard, in the manner practised in the vineyards in the North of France, generally produces from three to nine bunches; but Mr. Loudon observes, that by superior management in gardens in England, the number of branches is prodigiously increased, and that one plant of the red Hamburgh sort, in the vinery of the royal gardens at Hampton Court, has produced 2200 bunches, averaging one pound each, or in all nearly a ton. That at Valentine's in Essex (*its parent*), has produced 2000 bunches, of nearly the same average weight."

LANDLORDS AND TENANTS.

TO THE EDITOR OF THE NORTHAMPTON HERALD.

SIR,—Through the kindness of a friend, I have had your paper forwarded to me, in which you give (you say at the urgent request of several most respectable farmers,) my remarks on the present unjust system of farm tenure. You have not, however, thought proper to leave your readers to form their own unbiassed opinion, but have gone into some lengthy, but I think rather flimsy arguments, condemnatory of the principle advanced.

Now, sir, as you claim to be regarded as the friend of the farmers, in contra-distinction to "your Anti-Corn and Anti-Agricultural contemporary," you must allow me to test your sincerity and love of fair play, by requesting the insertion of this rejoinder. You say, "it would not be politic to effect the proposed change if possible, nor possible if politic; that it would rouse the indignation of great landlords, and also of little farmers." How little farmers more than great ones, by-the-bye, could be injured by reaping the fruit of their own improvements, I confess I am quite at a loss to divine.

But it will save the reader perplexity to give at once the summary of our proposition. We state fearlessly then, that the statute law of the land, as at present existing, does not hold the scales of justice with equal hand between landlord and tenant. Take an example—let a farmer, being tenant at will, commence the most spirited improvements, first at home, by planting a beautiful orchard, put down a pump where none existed before, add never so many buildings to the farm homestead; and is it not notorious that on leaving, if he were to attempt to touch a particle of them, an action at law would lie against him for injuring the freehold?

But let him also be as spirited in the field as at home—let him employ the whole of the surplus labourers of the neighbourhood in draining the strong land, marling that which was too light, purchase manures on the most extensive scale; and then be unlucky enough to kill an old fat hare, fattened, by-the-bye, on his own Swedish turnips; or be naughty enough to think for himself, and give an adverse vote at an election, and in six short months this tenant may be sent adrift. And where, I ask, is the statute that will award him a single farthing for his improvements? although the farm may be very cheap to his successor at a greatly advanced rent. But even in the absence of any of the above causes, an avaricious man may, under existing circumstances, avail himself of all these meliorations with impunity; as also in the event of a change of proprietors, which is constantly occurring: the tenant is thus often plundered of his property. And all this, sir, it would seem, according to your keen and penetrating perception, is quite right, just as it should be! But, sir, be assured of one thing, that with all the anxiety you may feel to serve your landlord readers—sophisticate the subject as you may—you never will convince the intelligent farmers of Northamptonshire, or the common-sense men of England, that this is a state of things which ought to be allowed to exist another year.

At any rate, sir, you say, "it is a very delicate and dangerous subject to touch; that it would rouse the indignation of great landlords, and they might be tempted to farm their own estates." For my own part I have not the slightest fear of this sort. Rest assured the times are pretty much gone by for landlords to begin to farm very largely, unless it be from necessity. Besides, how many of them could conveniently spare the necessary capital? and I think they would reflect on the matter twice before they would sell one fifth or sixth part of their lands to enable them to farm the remainder.

You say, "that farming is no longer the secret it was." Well, and what now the secret is out? Let any farmer draw his balance-sheet between the close of 1840 and 1842, and a pretty secret he will discover. But to go back to our proposition; what is there in it, I ask, to rouse the indignation of honest landlords? Hold they any moral right, in virtue of their high station, to put into their pockets what in justice belongs to the tenant? and yet for the last thirty years many of them have done so, and are doing so continually. What else has enabled them to keep their rent roll stationary, or even ascendant, ever since the French war, while the price of produce has gone down about one-half? The answer is obvious—the improvements of the tenantry have done it.

But I contend for some modification of the law of landlord and tenant, not merely for the sake of the tenantry, but on public grounds. A great crisis seems near at hand. The men on whom the farmers had relied are going pretty well the "whole hog" in favour of free-trade, and we are to be called upon to grow corn in this highly-taxed country pretty much upon the same terms as in countries where land is about one-tenth of the value. Or else the people are to be fed from thence, although our own sturdy and rapidly increasing sons of agriculture stand looking on, or are cooped up in district workhouses!

Sir, I have been telling the landlords of England that the latter will be the case, so long as the people will bear it, unless they generously meet the difficulty by granting a new Magna Charta to the British farmers. Still it is said, and said by the editor of a country paper, a paper, too, circulating amongst the farmers of England, "that it would be impolitic to impose by law fresh conditions on the letting or quitting of farms." And why? Because, forsooth "bad men would try to evade such laws;" as they do at present by throwing the land-tax and all other burthens possible upon the tenant. But is this argument? Upon this principle there ought to be no law against theft, for every now and then a villain will manage to evade it! I know well, and no one is more ready to make the acknowledgment, that there are many noble-minded and generous landlords, who would not willingly gather into their own garner what strictly belongs to others. And such a man could lose nothing if our proposition was carried into effect to-morrow.

If such a person wish to have his lands improved, and the poor located thereon employed and happy, he has nothing to do but to give a liberal lease, securing to the tenant the benefit of his own improvements, and he is left untouched. If, on the other hand, he prefer a yearly tenure, we take nothing from him; for if he wish to get rid of his tenant, he receives back his land, and the tenant is awarded such improvements only the benefit of which he shall not already have received; and if indisposed to grant that compensation, then he has only to allow the tenant to farm on. To such landlords only could the new law be irksome who wish to hold their tenants in a state of com-

plete vassalage, pocket their improvements, and drive them to the county hustings as the farmer drives his unconscious herd to the fair.

In reprobating my proposal, Mr. Editor, you have cast imputations upon the farmers for their inattention to the moral and religious improvement of their labourers. Now, sir, since you name religion, I will just tell you what I think it is, as appearing in the bible without mystification. The first part of it consists in honouring and loving God; the second in giving that honour to our fellow-man which we should wish to have awarded us in like circumstances.

Upon this latter principle (the principle by which all human laws should be tested) I am quite willing to place my proposal for amending the law of landlord and tenant, more especially as affecting agriculture. To this subject I am committed; to it I shall adhere; and if my brother farmers will only respond to my efforts, feeble though they be, we will be heard in the high places of the land. Sir, however unpalatable that little rough draft of an act of parliament contained in your extract might be to you and some few of your readers, I have no hesitation in saying, let it only become the law of the land, and it would shortly do more for agriculture, and the country at large, than all the societies which have been formed, and all the folio acts of parliament which have been passed for a long series of years!

I can make no apology for this reply, but must rely upon your sense of justice towards the more numerous portion of your readers to give it insertion. I am, Sir, your obedient servant,

THE BEDFORDSHIRE REPORTER.

BURTON FARMERS' CLUB.

"The advantages of growing turnips on strong soils," was the subject which came under the notice of the club at its meeting on Thursday, the 16th March. Mr. Daniel, the proposer, said—

It is very probable, gentlemen, that the subject I have ventured to enter for this evening's discussion has fallen into hands less able to give it effect than are many of the members of this now extensive and effective farmers' club; but I trust the facts I shall relate will lead to an opinion that the growth of Swede turnips, upon the drill system, on strong soils, is of an advantage far exceeding any injury to a succeeding crop of corn, that the most opinionated farmer can adduce. The supposed injury I allude to is the carting over the land in winter, when removing the turnip crop in wet weather, should the soil have become very tender; but to obviate this objection the practice I adopt is early sowing, say between the 25th May and the 10th of June, beyond which period of the year I would not sow Swedes on strong clay soils, unless I meant to let them stand on the ground through the winter for consumption in spring. To cultivate the land effectively for the early sowing above mentioned, the best practice I know of is to begin to prepare it early; that is to say, plough it or scuffle it as soon after harvest as you can; take the most favourable opportunity to pulverize and clean it, and if possible plough it again before winter, laying it in a sound state, and the water-furrows well cleared out; begin with it again as early in spring as other farm business admits. But as I consider a good crop of Swede turnips is often of greater value per acre than a crop of barley or oats, I have on one or two occasions left off sowing spring corn to cultivate and prepare the land intended for Swede turnips rather than be too late with that operation, especially if the latter end of March or the beginning of April should be favourable from its dryness to effect the desired object.

It has been my usual practice to carry out my farm-yard dung as made, on to bottoms of soil already prepared in or near the fields intended for a turnip crop; this, upon heavy soils, cannot be better done than when a frost admits of the cartage being easy, as the land does not then sustain any material injury by the carting over it; and I think it of advantage to the dung-heaps to cover them three to six inches over with soil to keep in the heat, or rather to prevent the evaporation of the essence of the dung, which is too apt to pass off, and the drainage too, unless soil is likewise laid along the sides to suck it up, if I may so term it. A heap thus formed, I turn over and mix altogether but a short time before using it for the turnip crop, and I lay on 10 to 15 Scotch cart-loads per acre, spread out of the carts into drills ploughed 25 to 30 inches apart, which being immediately levelled is ploughed under with as little exposure to the sun's rays as possible, and the seed drilled in under this management. I have succeeded in producing capital and luxuriant turnips, but I have not had sufficient leisure to test the weight of an acre. I did, however, make the attempt by measuring off 30 yards square, which yielded a weight equal to 23 tons 2 cwt. per acre; but beg to observe that my best field of Swedes (grown in 1842) was cleared before I thought of weighing; and I am of opinion that on comparison with my best crop, this would have given 30 tons per acre, as I had the number of turnips counted necessary to fill up the deficient parts in the rows where the 30 square yards were measured off as above stated, which would take 900 turnips, weighing 12½ tons.

Having thus for some years obtained good crops of Swede turnips, another principal object has been to secure them for consumption, which has generally been by a sufficient covering of stubble and straw, having found the turnips heat, and of course become rotten, if covered too soon with soil.

The land having been cleared of my early sown crops of Swedes in October and November, is ploughed and well water-furrowed, to lie till spring, when it is sown without any further ploughing on the stale furrow, the surface made of fine tilth by the scuffler or scarifier, and the harrow.

As the spring crops on this land are usually drilled in at nine inches, I do not sow the grass-seeds till the corn is up sufficiently, so as to admit the horse-hoe, when the sowing immediately follows, and the seeds rolled in. On this plan I have not yet failed to obtain a full plant of grass seeds on the heavy soil I farm. The stock now kept, in consequence of an ample supply of winter food, produced mainly by the management thus brought under your notice, I may safely assert to be one-third more; and this circumstance may, I trust, be a sufficient apology for taking up so much of the time of the club, and rendering my details prolix without adding to its previous knowledge, though, perhaps, not the usual practice.

The extra employment (let me in conclusion, observe) of labour on a farm must of course be considerable where this increased cultivation is in practice; and in my case I feel has been of service in keeping the labourers, their wives, and families independent of parochial aid—a circumstance much to be desired at the present time.

The meeting passed a vote of thanks to the proposer for the able manner in which he had brought forward his subject.

FARMING AND FARM STOCK AT ELLON, ABERDEENSHIRE.

Extracted from No. XLII. of the New Statistical Account of Scotland, just issued, containing the conclusion of the County of Aberdeen.

Rent.—The gross rental is within a trifle of 10,000l. being about seven and a half times the amount of rent paid at the date of the last statistical account in 1792. It must be observed, however, to prevent mistakes in a matter of so much statistical importance, that the augmentation of the rental, though undoubtedly very great, is yet not quite so great as from the above statement it would appear to be. When the last Statistical Account was drawn up, a considerable number of the farms were held on leases, for which, in addition to the annual rent, a premium, or, as it is usually termed, a grassum, had been paid at the period of entry. Still, due allowance being made for the item of grassums, the rental at present cannot be less than four or five times its former amount. Two of the largest farms in the parish are still rented much under the full value,—the old leases by which they are held, and for which grassums were originally paid, having not yet expired. On the expiry of these leases the gross rental will amount to upwards of 10,000l. Some of the land in the immediate neighbourhood of the village is rented at the high rate of upwards of 5l. per Scotch acre; but its actual annual value probably does not much exceed one-half of the rent which is now paid. It is farmed by the villagers in small parcels, less with a view to profit than pleasure and convenience. The average rent of land of the same quality, in more remote parts of the parish, is from 2l. to 2l. 10s. per acre. On the inferior soils, the rent per acre varies from 10s. to 15s. The average rent of arable land for the whole parish will be found, from the data already furnished, to be within a small fraction of 17s. per Scotch acre.

Live-Stock.—The breed of work horses has of late years been much improved. Superior mares have in several instances been brought from Clydesdale and other parts of the west country, celebrated for breeds of horses of good bone and action. Much has been done also for the improvement of the breed of horses by the spirited exertions of the Highland and Agricultural Society. The horses chiefly sought after for agricultural purposes are not those of the largest size, but such as are of good mettle, and easily kept in good condition.

Until of late years almost the only breeds of black-cattle known in this district of country were the Aberdeenshire horned and Angus polled breeds. But what is called the short-horned or Tees-water breed is now prevailing to a considerable extent, and seems, in spite of the opposition which its introduction has encountered from various quarters, to be daily gaining ground. Opinion, however, is still divided between this recent importation and the ancient breeds of the country, and it is not for the writer to presume to determine which party has the right side of the question. One thing is matter of fact, and forces itself upon the attention of even the most ordinary observer, that our farmers now bring their cattle to a much greater weight than in former times, and receive for them a price proportionally more remunerating, Various causes have contributed to bring about this result; one of which, and undoubtedly not the least important is, that much more attention and skill are now applied not only to the feeding off of full-grown stock, but also to the equally important departments of breeding and of keeping the rising cattle in a thriving condition. Had the same attention been formerly given to these important parts of the farmer's occupation, there can be no doubt that cattle even of the ordinary breeds of the country might have been brought to much greater weight than what, under the less perfect mode of management heretofore adopted, they ever attained. Still, as it seems to be admitted on all hands that the short-horns both attain to a greater size, and are capable, from their less active habits, and probably other concurring causes, of being fed off at a much earlier age, it is questionable whether, at least on a good farm, the same amount of profit could be realized by the breeding of cattle of the Angus or Aberdeenshire breeds. The beef of the short-horns is said to be inferior, which is probably the fact. Nevertheless, as no preference seems to be given to the pure Aberdeenshire breed in the London market, an inferiority in the article exposed by him, so long as that inferiority does not affect its exchangeable value, cannot be supposed to have much influence with the Scottish farmer. An apprehension now generally entertained is, that second and third crosses between the Teeswater and Aberdeenshire breeds may be attended with a deterioration of both. Indeed, the most intelligent farmers seem to be of opinion that the two breeds should be kept as distinct and pure as possible, and no intermixture allowed beyond a first cross. Sheep farming is but little pursued in this district of country, and in the parish of Ellon is altogether unknown.

ON MOULD, OR ITS PRINCIPLES, IN THE JUICE OF PLANTS.

(From a Letter of Mr. Hermann, of Moscow.)

I have just made a discovery which will certainly prove to be of great importance in many respects, viz., that the chief part of the extractive components of the juice of plants, and therefore those of officinal extracts of plants likewise, consists of the principles of mould ; and I distinguished in these juices the following substances in particular, as—

Humic acids,
Mould deposit acids,
Apocrenic acids,
Crenic acids, and
Extractive humus.

This discovery will, I hope, decide the question at present so much agitated, on the nourishment of plants, as it is highly improbable that these mouldy substances contained in the juices of plants should not have been absorbed from the mould earth (humus), but formed from carbonic acid, ammonia, and water, by the vital process of the plants.

I request you to give publicity to this notice ; I shall in a short time give a more detailed account. —From *Erdmann's Journ. f. pr. Pharm.*

SUBSOILING.

TO THE EDITOR OF THE MARK-LANE EXPRESS.

Sir,—Noticing in the last number of the "Farmers' Magazine" a letter by "A Two-years' Subscriber," who states therein that subsoiling gravelly soils with a subsoil of gravel is very beneficial, which I questioned in my last upon this subject ; I cannot refrain from offering a few remarks upon his reasons for so thinking. He says, by subsoiling, " you allow the stagnant water there lodged (alluding to a pan which is formed by the plough,) to escape, which in all cases must be very pernicious to all descriptions of plants."

Agreed, if what he has stated be correct, viz., that water stagnates upon this pan, which though I deny. Who ever heard of water stagnating upon a gravelly soil with a subsoil of gravel ? If he means to infer that I considered this to be the case, he is greatly mistaken, as I think a pan only prevents the moisture from sinking with such precipitancy below the roots of plants.

I cannot conceive how water will stagnate upon a gravelly soil ; as it cannot be made of sufficient firmness as to prevent the moisture from soaking through it ; but I can perceive how the moisture may be prevented from sinking so fast into the soil, which is all that we require.

I may make bold to say also, that he never saw plants turn yellow on a gravelly soil, with a subsoil of the same material, from the cause he has stated. I doubt too whether plants will absorb their own excrement, unless they have not a sufficient quantity of sustenance (although then it is a doubtful question), as it is not conformable to nature and reason. The excrementitious matter of one kind of plants is food to another. Subsoiling will allow the water to carry along with it this matter and also manures into the subsoil, and below the reach of the roots of plants, there to remain of no use.

No doubt subsoiling is beneficial to those lands whose subsoil is clay, for the purpose of carrying away the superfluous water, although there is to be taken into the account the loss of manure, which is carried below the reach of the roots of many plants.

Should these few lines be found worthy of a place in your valuable paper, you will oblige,

Your obedient servant,

Santon. A YOUNG FARMER.

We again repeat, that amongst modern inventions calculated to be of essential service to our agricultural readers, in an architectural point of view, are the patent stucco cement and paint, invented by Messrs. Johns and Co., of Plymouth, whose sole agents are Messrs. Mann and Co., of Maiden-lane, London. The former of them is used as a certain preventive to the intrusion of wet through walls and roofs, and the latter as a chaste and ornamental application, as well as being highly preservative in its character ; and the moderate prices at which they can be procured renders them staple articles of consumption. Amongst the number of those who have expressed their high satisfaction with these inventions, we may mention the Hull Dock-yard Commissioners, those of Greenwich Hospital, the Dukes of Newcastle and St. Alban's, the Earl of Essex, Lord Wenlock, and many other influential agriculturists in various parts of the United Kingdom. We therefore conceive it proper to direct the attention of the landed interest to these facts.

THE CURRENCY.

THE PRESENT STATE OF THE CURRENCY —INCREASED ISSUES BY THE BANK OF ENGLAND.

(TO THE EDITOR OF THE MIDLAND COUNTIES HERALD.)

Sir,—The indifference exhibited by Sir Robert Peel in his replies to the Birmingham Chamber of Commerce, and his absolute denial of the correctness of the conclusions of that body with respect to the causes of the prevailing distress, were evidently intended to lead the public to the conviction that the currency question was one of minor importance. Under ordinary circumstances, this might be a proper conclusion upon the remarks of the minister. In the present case, however, Sir Robert Peel appears to have satisfied himself with touching the mere surface of the matter; he avoided grappling with the question. On reading the correspondence, we were certainly more than ever satisfied that circumstances would arise to compel Sir Robert to adopt measures for giving stability to our monetary system ; and that he would find it necessary to take a course exactly opposite to that he has hitherto pursued. We imagined that he might attempt to restore prosperity by an indirect action on the currency—by using the influence of the government upon the bank of England. This is a course by no means unusual ; *and it is now well understood to have been the actual plan resorted to.*

It is probable, however, that this measure, which is always of limited operation, and uncertain in its effects, will be found to be insufficient. It will not restore confidence to the commercial interests, still suffering from the terrific effects of the panic of 1837. The Bank is no more to be relied upon now than it was at the period named. Events not yet foreseen—mercantile changes which may be contemplated by the minister—may lead to results as important as those which followed the attempt of the Bank to replenish her coffers in 1836 and 1837. Sir Robert Peel must therefore apply more vigorous and intelligible measures ; and these we apprehend he will ere long not be unwilling to do, as the necessity of the case will remove all scruples about consistency.

We had hoped that the Chamber of Commerce of Birmingham would continue the discussion of the currency question, after so vigorous and well-timed a commencement. But in this we are disappointed. The matter has been suffered, as on all former occasions, to disappear from before the public. The Chamber, like their friends, allowed the sophisms of the minister and the absurdities of the press to go forth without comment, or at least without that searching examination and exposure which it was their interest to have undertaken.

The Birmingham economists want a currency of a fixed and steady character, and of ample amount ; but they allow their opponents to represent that they seek to establish a currency which would be liable to endless fluctuations. The Chamber of Commerce, and others who have addressed themselves to the question, say to the minister, ' RELIEVE US FROM THE TERRIBLE EVILS CAUSED BY THE FLUCTUATIONS TO WHICH OUR PRESENT MONETARY SYSTEM IS CONSTANTLY LIABLE ;" and their opponents at once charge them with recommending the establishment of a currency which would be subject to great fluctuations, and actually attempt to lead the public to the belief that the present currency possesses that "fixed and steady value indispensibly requisite for the public welfare." This was done by the *Manchester Guardian* during the late discussion, and after we had repeatedly called the attention of that journal to the Manchester Report, in which the evils of the present system are most forcibly detailed.

The Chamber of Commerce assert, and truly, that the Bank of England, in promising to pay her notes in gold, commits a monstrous absurdity. The attempt to keep the coffers of the Bank tolerably well supplied with gold, in order to give a seeming truth to this deception, is, as the Chamber explains, attended with the most grievous results, producing a bad state of trade when all other circumstances are favourable; and even within a few months reducing the country from a state of prosperity to a state of general distress and embarrassment.

Such are the effects of fluctuations. The Chamber at the same time, offer what they are willing to have taken as a test of the soundness of their views as to the advantages of a steady currency. They remark, " experience has shown us that 20,000,000l. of Bank of England paper steadily kept out has been sufficient to maintain the general circulation of the country, and sufficient also to find profitable employment to the labouring classes." We consider this to be a very important sentence ; and it has received additional value since the publication of the correspondence. The Bank, as we have before remarked, under the gentle influences of the government, has increased her issues to the amount named. The return dated March 31, 1843, shows that the institution had notes representing 20,093,000l. in circulation ; and it is known that the circulation of the private and joint stock banks amounted to, at least, the average of the last few years. The Bank, at the date named, had no less than 11,054,000l. of bullion in her vaults. It is clear from this return that the institution is in an easy position. It is also made evident that the "screw" has been relaxed, and that the Bank is prepared to afford such assistance to the commercial interests as would cause a rapid revival of trade, and a rise in prices by no means gradual. The statement made by the Chamber, above quoted, is, we repeat, a test whereby to ascertain the soundness of their views.

The public have consequently the means pointed out of estimating the effects of the currency on general business. In our opinion, there will be no return of general prosperity *until the mercantile classes have some assurance that our monetary system shall not be subject to the fluctuations by which it has hitherto been distinguished.* If this guarantee is not given, low prices of labour and of all manufactured articles must and will continue. The manufacturer will not, by employing capital freely, place himself in a position in which he may suffer all the evils which befel his class in 1837. He will not use his capital in the manufacture of goods which may by an operation of the Bank on the currency be decreased forty per cent. in value, as was the case in 1837.

In the period referred to, we must also bear in mind that the effect of the panic was in some degree lessened (perhaps most materially, especially with reference to Birmingham and Liverpool,) by the assistance which the Bank of England afforded in supporting leading houses by advances upon manufactured and other goods. This was a proceeding which entitles the institution to the highest credit ; yet it might be actually necessary for its own security. It would seem, however, that the bank lost by this well-timed aid to the commercial classes no less than 254,000l. This loss, although, when speaking of the resources of the Bank, of unimportant amount, appears to have been not very patiently endured by the shareholders, one or two of whom at the late meeting were disposed to recommend that the directors should have an eye to the profitable working of the affairs of the institution, without reference to the effects of its measures upon individual interests. Occupying the position which the Bank of England holds, it would have been difficult to have given advice less deserving of attention. *

The publication of the loss sustained by the bank from the advances in 1836-7 will certainly lead to the impression, among mercantile men, that under similar circumstances it would be hardly safe to calculate upon assistance from the same source; and that, in fact, no such assistance would be afforded. Where, then, the currency being left in precisely the same position as it was in 1836 and 1837, and liable to fluctuations from the same causes, are the commercial interests to look for security? How forcible do these considerations show the importance of that steadiness of character for our currency which the Birmingham economists have so long advocated.

Without this fixed character being given to our monetary system, there appears but little hope that the condition of the masses of the people will be permanently improved. On the other hand, were it at once known that the circulation would be kept up to the present amount for the next seven years, and that there would be no sudden change at the end of that period, we venture to affirm that there would be a rapid improvement in every branch of trade, and a greatly increased demand for labour, at higher wages, both in the manufacturing and agricultural districts.† With a fluctuating currency,

* At the meeting referred to, Mr. Blackmore said—He desired to impress upon the proprietors to regard the establishment as a trading company, and not occupy their minds with the visionary idea that the Bank was the great motive power in the affairs of the nation. To look upon the bank as the regulator of the currency, and the manager of all the financial matters of the nation, was, in his opinion, the height of absurdity. He was sure it was not profitable to waste time in the discussion of the policy of the conduct of the directors from such a point of view, and should therefore recommend the proprietors, instead of dealing with the Bank as the regulator of the currency, or with its power to make one man rich and another poor, to confine themselves to the mere mechanical part of the business brought before them.—*Times report.*

† We are disposed to rate perhaps more highly than many persons would do at the present day, the importance, in a national point of view, of applying the capital and labour of the country to increase the produce of the soil. We could show, by many examples, how much the national wealth has been, and may be, increased by these means, but for the present one must suffice. Mr. Pusey, M.P., in the *Journal of the Royal Agricultural Society*, says:—

"The average produce of wheat is stated at 26 bushels per acre: if, by a better selection of seed, we could raise this amount to 27 bushels only, a supposition by no means unlikely, we should by this apparently small improvement have added to the nation's annual income 475,000 quarters of wheat, worth, at 50s., about 1,200,000*l.* yearly, which would be equal to a capital of twenty four millions sterling gained for ever to the country by this trifling increase in the growth of one article alone, and that in England and Wales only. * * * *

"We may consider, in another point of view, the national effect which might result from a general improvement of agriculture: that is, the *additional employment* that would arise from any general effort made on the part of the landowner or the tenant to improve permanently, as by drainage, for instance, the texture itself of the soil: we do not mean of waste

the population must continue in a state of general distress, aggravated by various natural causes over which we have no control, and unrelieved in a perceptible degree by any other changes which may be introduced.

THE AGRICULTURAL INTEREST.

We stated in our first letter that the distress which was then felt by the manufacturing population would soon extend to those engaged in agricultural pursuits. In making this declaration, we did not overlook the many speeches which had been delivered at agricultural meetings, by members of parliament and other landowners, as well as by some practical agriculturists, during the recess. From these addresses the public might be led to the conclusion that low prices of agricultural produce, with high fixed payments, had no effect upon the welfare of the farmer, who was to make up the losses caused by a falling market, by increased energy and by improved systems of cultivation. The Premier, following the example of other landlords, exhibited great zeal for the promotion of agricultural knowledge, recommending the circulation of works treating upon this important branch of national industry, and inviting learned professors from Oxford and Cambridge to discuss with his tenantry the merits of new manures and the advantages of different systems of drainage. All this was most praiseworthy, and calculated to produce the best results. It is surely high time that the discoveries of scientific men should be applied to a branch of industry which, in its most minute details, as well as in its most extensive operations, must depend for success upon unerring principles.

The lectures of scientific men, and the encouraging words of the landlords, appeared for a time to sustain the spirits of the farmer under falling averages. This happy state of delusion was not, however, destined to continue for a long period. Rent-days come round very rapidly, and the landed interest usually expect their tenants to be punctual in their payments. The produce of a farm we need hardly state, (although we question whether even this explanation be not necessary, so absurdly do some people talk,) will not sell for so much money with wheat at 18s. per bag as it will with wheat at 26s. per bag. The low range of prices for agricultural produce which were realized during the half-year ending at Christmas last, was sufficient to justify our opinion as to the inability of the farmer to meet his fixed payments. During the first three months of

ground, but of that which is already, and has been perhaps for centuries, in course of cultivation. If a pound only were thus laid out on each acre, a very moderate supposition, we shall find that, since there are 48 millions of cultivated acres in Great Britain and Ireland, a demand for country labour amounting to 48 millions sterling would thus be created. The assumed outlay, however, of a pound only, for the permanent improvement of each acre, is probably far too low. 3*l.*, 4*l.*, or even 5*l.*, would be scarcely too much. There is much wet land, on which 8*l.*, or perhaps 10*l.* might be laid out to advantage; but at 4*l.* only, the new progressive demand for the villager's only commodity, the work of his hands, would be about 200 millions. So large an outlay as this last must indeed, in part, be necessarily deferred for a long course of years; but in whatever degree it may arise, it has, on the other hand, the further advantage, arising from the nature of the work to be done, that the demand would necessarily take place in the winter months, when labour is most difficult to be obtained, not in the summer, when the crops are in progress, and the labourer finds already sufficient employment."

the present year, prices of every description of produce have been still further reduced ; and at the present time the agriculturists in every part of the country, (except in a few favoured instances,) are carrying on their farms at a serious loss—*a loss which, we believe, we can demonstrate to be considerably more than the gross rental of the land which they are cultivating.* This is a point which can be easily settled, and it is one of vital importance to the landed interest.

Our views of the present position of the landlord and of his tenants are supported by abundant evidence ; and we are enabled to lay before our readers the opinions of a gentleman of great experience, resident in this county, who is himself a landowner. He writes—" With wheat at or about 2*l.* per quarter, or 15s. per bag, in Birmingham market, the rent of three-fourths of the land in England will be annihilated. * * There is no other alternative but to immediately alter the standard ; there is no other course. It is nonsense to offer the working man cheap provisions when he has no money to purchase the cheap food."

How far these opinions are deserving the attention of the landed interest will be further shown by the following extract from the *Circular to Bankers* of the 31st of March. It would appear, that if prices have not already receded to the point named by our correspondent, there is a probability that they will soon be brought still lower.

" What we said last week regarding the measure of letting in flour through Canada was intended to direct attention to it, by alluding to what might happen in extreme cases. The state of the market for Egyptian wheat is one of these cases ; and we have the authority of the best-informed houses in the Canada trade for re-asserting, that under peculiar circumstances like the present, when so little timber is brought from Canada, and when a smaller quantity of British manufactures than even last year—a fact which surprises us—is likely to be sent out to that country, ships might be procured to convey wheat from England to Canada, and back to England, in barrels of flour, at a charge for freight altogether not exceeding six shillings the quarter. We know that this is an unprecedented state of things, and that the freight out and in would ordinarily cost perhaps double that sum. We have no doubt, however, that under the proposed law, when the trade can be carried forward on the basis which it will establish, the cheap ships—the cheaply-worked ships of the northern nations of Europe—will convey wheat from the Baltic to Canada and back to England in the shape of flour, in barrels, at an entire charge of twelve shillings the quarter: then what may happen under that law ? If the price of wheat should come down to the point at which it once stood in the Lower Baltic ports for three successive years, viz., from 16s. to 18s. the quarter—medium price, 17s.—it would be carried to Canada, and let into consumption in England at a lower price than flour made from Canadian and United States' wheat.

"The price of good red wheat may now be bought at Dantzic at 28s. the quarter, free on board. (See *Circular* of 17th of March.) That and the Pomeranian wheat will probably be reduced to 21s. within twelve months, Supposing it to be prepared, as all the Dantzio wheat (as a rule) is prepared—so as to bear long voyages without injury—add 12s. for freight and 4s. for duties, and we shall have foreign wheat laid down in England, in the shape of flour, at a nominal price of 37s. the quarter; but actually lower than this, because the best qualities of their respective kinds will be selected for this purpose ; and wheat of those qualities is worth more than the average wheat of England, of Canada, and the United States, by 3s. or 4s. the quarter. Do the government deliberately intend to bring down the price of wheat in England to 35s. the quarter, or less, and to pass a law which shall prevent it ever rising higher for any length of time than 49s. the quarter ?

If they do, the measure for letting in Canadian flour, produced from wheat of any country, is a good measure for that object."

It appears from the returns of the average price of grain for the years 1841 and 1842, that wheat was 7s. 2d. per qr. cheaper in the latter than in the former year. The averages were 64s. 5d., 1841, against 57s. 3d., 1842. Allowing that the average produce of wheat is twenty-six bushels per acre, the loss sustained in 1842, by the fall in prices on this one description of grain (and all articles were subject to an equal reduction), was at the rate of about 23s. per acre. It further appears, from the returns for the week ending March 31, in the present year, that, as compared with the price of wheat per quarter in the corresponding week of 1842, there had been a fall of no less than 10s. 6d. per quarter ; the average being 57s. 8d. in 1842, and 47s. 2d. in 1843. This would show a diminution in value exceeding 33s. per acre, a sum nearly double the average annual rental per acre of the cultivated land in the United Kingdom.

Some of the landlords at the meetings to which we have referred, generously offered to relieve their tenants of the burthen of the income tax, a payment amounting on the average to about 3½d. per acre. But how absurd it is to exhibit great anxiety about this trifling payment, when a considerable number of the landlords were at the same time obstinately unmindful of the consequences of a bad currency system, owing mainly to the effects of which the produce of the land will be this year reduced in value at least 30s. per acre. If the farmer was not in a position to bear the addition of 3½d. per acre to his yearly rental, we can hardly expect that he was prepared to suffer this serious loss in the value of his products.

We have before observed that as a means of increasing the national wealth it is most desirable that additional capital and labour should be applied to the cultivation of the all-bountiful earth. It may, perhaps, be contended, that if the gross produce of the land were *greatly* increased, the farmer would be enabled to sell that produce at a reduced rate, and still meet his present fixed payments. Allowing this to be the case, it does not follow that this increase could be obtained without the employment of additional labour, and other expenses ; nor could it be effected at once ; the process will be gradual. It is, consequently, clear that any measure which in *one year reduces the value of agricultural produce to an extent exceeding the whole rental of the land* must have a most serious effect upon the capital of the farmer, and tend to a considerable reduction in the wages of labour. Such a reduction in the profits and capital of the farmer, and in the wages of labour, would, have at the same time no really beneficial effect upon the other interests in the country. It is advantageous to all interests that the prices of agricultural produce as well as of manufactured goods should be at a remunerating level. At the present moment *we have cheap food and a starving population;* and the United States, where food is nominally much cheaper than in England, exhibit the same melancholy picture*. The views which we put

---

* The following extracts from a letter on the present condition of the United States, which appeared in the *Manchester Guardian* of the 29th ult., will be read with interest :—

" You have also heard of the abundance and cheapness of provisions here (Cincinnati). This place, in this respect, excels any that I was ever in before. Beef, mutton, and pork, have been regularly selling at

forth last week with respect to the effects of a bad system of currency in the United States are, to a great extent, confirmed by the extracts we have

---

a halfpenny to a penny a pound while I have been here. The beef and mutton are good, the pork excellent. The average price of fine fat hogs during the season, has been one dollar and seventy cents, or about 7s. each hundred pounds ; small and lean hogs have been lower in price. The mutton is not so well flavoured here as the English mutton ; but still it is good. For the choicest pieces of beef you must give three halfpence a pound. Chickens and ducks are fourpence each ; geese, a shilling ; turkeys, one and sixpence each ; butter four to fivepence a pound ; eggs are a halfpenny each, but in the spring they will be live for a penny. Vegetables are very low. Apples (you know what our apples are) have sold last season at fivepence the bushel. Sugar and coffee are at half the price they sell at in England. Flour, eleven shillings the barrel. Wines and spirits are very cheap, but the prevalence of temperance habits has now greatly lessened their use. Fuel, both coal and wood, is very cheap and abundant. Coal is cheaper than with you, and quite as good. House rent is very high, perhaps twice as high as at Manchester. Clothing is also very expensive. Servants wages are high ; say one to two dollars a week. "The land hereabouts is excellent. Farms are on sale in abundance. I saw a list of some, for which forty to forty-five dollars was asked per acre ; improved land, of course, and not very far from this city. At a greater distance it is still cheaper, and in the interior extremely low. Cows, horses, and sheep, are very cheap. Real estates are said to be selling at very reduced prices. Money very scarce, and sometimes loaned at twelve per cent. Real estate, they say, yields six per cent. per annum.

"And yet, amid all this abundance, there is a great amount of distress in this place. Lectures, concerts, &c., are given, with a view to raise money for the relief of the poor ; and in one street here there is a soup kitchen, as there is at Manchester. The farmers are badly off, as you may readily conceive, with produce at such prices. Indeed, I feel much for them, as I see them with hundreds of loaded waggons in the streets, shivering in the cold, and waiting anxiously for those who will kindly become their customers. Sometimes they are heard complaining that they can hardly give their produce away ; and yet there are poor people, not many yards perhaps from those very farmers, who are starving, from the want of such food as can hardly be given away. They cannot have it without money, and money they cannot have without employment, which is very scarce. As to agricultural labourers, the land is too fertile to need many of these ; and why raise produce, if it cannot be sold ? There is too much already. The superabundance of produce is just as great an evil here, as your' over production' is in Manchester. The great fertility of the soil is positively an evil ; for, if it were otherwise, and required many labourers, there would be labour for them, and higher prices for produce. Such is the anomalous state of things hereabouts. As to other places, I read in the papers that in Philadelphia matters are worse. *People there contrive to get into prisons, in order to satisfy the cravings of hunger.* A paper lying before me says, of that city, ' the back gates of our hotels are fairly broken in now-a-days, from morning till night, with a hungry crowd, whose eyes gloat eagerly over, and whose hands fight convulsively for the bits of bread and cold victuals ejected from the kitchen table. Even the slop barrels into which are thrown the scraps and offals, have been the scene of a diurnal siege ; while the little ragged boys and girls, with their thin wan faces, their long bony fingers, and the elder specimens of shivering humanity that cluster with them around the spot, grasping at food from which the rich man's dog would turn away contemptuously, all form a picture of want and wretchedness which makes the heart sick.' This is the state of things in Philadelphia, where provisions are cheap and superabundant. And these evils prevail in a

given below. Similar statements were also made by Lord Ashburton, in a late debate in the House of Lords. It is a circumstance deserving the most serious consideration of every one, that countries having entirely different forms of government—the one possessing unlimited natural resources, and unincumbered with debt ; the other possessing enormous wealth and unlimited means of production, which make even its great national debt a burthen of unimportant amount—should be so long in discovering the means of adequately distributing these blessings amongst their people ; and yet, without this means of distribution being brought into operation, it is clear that there can be no national prosperity or individual security. We have, we believe, satisfactorily shown that a country, whatever its advantages, cannot be truly prosperous under a monetary system subject to fluctuations which affect the value of the whole of its property, reduce the wages of labour, and increase the burthen of its fixed obligations.

There is reason for hoping that the progress of opinion on the currency question is proceeding much more rapidly than has been generally supposed. It is found to be a question affecting in an extraordinary degree the welfare of every class of the community. The advocates of a fixed and stable monetary system have only to persevere in their efforts to furnish the public with accurate information as to the evils of the present system, and a party may be created in the country unequalled for influence and authority, and which would be *supported* and not opposed as at present by the press. The currency question is not a mere abstract question, but one altogether practical ; and its advocates have this advantage—that they have not to deal with opinions and theories, but with facts and figures, which enable them to communicate positive information in every sentence.—We are, Sir, your obedient servants, GEMINI.

Birmingham, April 11, 1843.

---

country where there is no taxation, or scarcely any ; no despotic monarch, no aristocracy, no soldiers to enforce bad laws, and keep the people down ; no blue police ; no hard masters, nobody to ' grind the faces of the poor'. The poor themselves are the masters ; it is a pure democracy, where the lower orders are always the real governors, always can carry the elections : they have things their own way, and have nothing to do but to set to and correct the evils they are suffering ; correct them at once, *if they can.*

"The distresses of this country are occasioned, mainly, by a deranged state of the currency. First, the United States Bank, which had an immense amount of paper afloat, failed some five years ugo. Then other banks were suffered to inundate the country with paper money, which caused a wild system of speculation ; gave to property a false value : people thought that making notes and issuing them, was *making money*—and they made them to their hearts content. At length they found out their mistake : a panic came and hosts of bankers, unable to redeem their issues of paper, failed. Some twenty-three thousand bankruptcies of one kind and another took place. Hence a great stagnation of business, which has caused the present distress. The first remedy to be applied is to regulate the banking system, or the issues of paper money ; but how to do this is the difficulty. One party will have an extensive paper currency ; one will have a moderate one ; and a third party will have none at all, but a currency of hard money. One will have a national bank ; another will not have it. Legislators contend about these matters, and come to no decision. If they do decide, their decision may be rescinded by some other party soon coming into power. Thus are they embarrassed, and business is paralysed in consequence."

THE AGRICULTURAL INTEREST.

DINNER AT WALLINGFORD.

(FROM THE TIMES.)

April 20, being the annual cattle and sheep fair at Wallingford, advantage was taken by the agriculturists of the district to assemble together at the Town-hall, for the purpose of giving expression to their feelings on the present prospects of agriculture; according to the wording of the placard calling the meeting—"the attendance of the farmers and others favourable to the cause of British agriculture, now threatened with absolute ruin, was particularly requested."

Mr. W. S. Blackstone, the member for the borough, took the chair.

About 200 respectable farmers and yeomen of the neighbourhood dined together. There were also present at the Chairman's table, Earl Stanhope, Viscount Barrington, M.P., Mr. B. Cochrane, M.P., Mr. P. Pusey, M.P., the Mayor, the Rev. J. Hillyard, Mr. Q. Dick, M.P., Sir H. Willoughby, Bart., the Rev. J. Dixon, and several other gentlemen of distinction in the neighbourhood.

Judging from the cordial reception of the Chairman and the Conservative gentry who supported him, they had no ground of complaint that the *aura popularis* amongst the sturdy yeomen and substantial farmers by whom they were surrounded was against them.

The dinner was held at the early hour of half-past two o'clock, and after the substantial fare provided had been discussed and the cloth removed,

The CHAIRMAN proposed the health of "Her Most Gracious Majesty Queen Victoria," which was most enthusiastically cheered.

The CHAIRMAN then gave "Her Most Gracious Majesty the Queen Dowager," and "His Royal Highness Prince Albert, Albert Prince of Wales, and the rest of the Royal Family," each of which toasts was drunk with repeated shouts of enthusiastic loyalty.

The CHAIRMAN then said, that being called upon to preside over so numerous and important a meeting as he saw before him, he should claim at their hands some little indulgence in proposing the next toast, not because he feared any want of unanimity amongst them, but because he was aware of the important and critical position of the agricultural interests at this time. (*Cheers*) He approached with the greatest diffidence a subject affecting so materially the interests of so large and important a portion of the community—not a class subject, but one involving the interests of high and low, rich and poor. In proposing to them, therefore, the toast of "Adequate protection to British industry," he did not intend to limit it to the agricultural classes of the community, but to extend it to every person engaged in British enterprise, who ought to be protected by the laws of his country. (*Hear.*) He trusted that, whatever sentiments might be promulgated within that hall, there would be no blinking of the question (*loud cheering*), that it would be fairly discussed; and he was sure that every gentleman would have an opportunity given of stating why British industry ought not to be protected. (*Hear, hear.*) He did not wish to see taken so low a ground as he had seen taken at many agricultural meetings—namely, that the occupiers of the land should be persuaded that it was their duty to employ fewer horses in drawing their ploughs, and that they should turn their minds to a better mode of cultivation of the soil. He was not going to ask their attention to this time if they agreed with him in raising their voice so that it might be heard beyond that Guildhall to recommend any such procedure. But he wished them to show that there was a party, and a strong one, in the country that wished for protection to the industrious classes of the community, and that they should not blindly advocate questions for the employment of capital, when capital would give no return to its employer. (*Loud cheers.*) He must for a short time ask their attention to the proceedings of past years as affecting the interests of agriculture. He would allude now more particularly to a report emanating from a committee of the House of Commons, appointed at a time when it was supposed that the agricultural interest was in a state of depression. They had not at that time reached the point which they afterwards saw of agricultural distress; he alluded to the year 1833, at which time the average price of wheat was 54s. and some few pence. The members who composed that committee had for their chairman the right hon. baronet the Secretary of State for the Home Department, Sir James Graham, and he might mention the names of Sir Robert Peel and of Sir Edward Knatchbull. The report that they drew up was, that "They are duly impressed with the caution which appears to them necessary in drawing any general conclusion, or in offering any positive opinions, where national interests of such vital importance are concerned, where doubts so reasonable exist, and where errors so fatal may be committed; and although it is in the power of the Legislature to do much evil, yet it can do little positive good by frequent interference with agricultural industry. The committee of 1821 expressed a hope' that the great body of the occupiers of the soil, either from the savings of more prosperous times, or from the credit which punctuality commands in this country, possess resources which will enable them to surmount the difficulties under which they now labour.' Your committee with deep regret are bound rather to express a fear that the difficulties alone remain unchanged, but that the savings are either gone or greatly diminished, the credit failing, and the resources being generally exhausted (*hear, hear*); and this opinion is formed, not on the evidence of rent-payers, but of many most respectable witnesses, as well owners of land as surveyors and land-agents. It should, however, be remembered that legislative measures once taken and long established can rarely be abandoned without danger, and that the retreat is occasionally more dangerous than the advance. In conclusion, your committee avow their opinion that hopes of amelioration in the condition of the landed interest rest rather on the cautious forbearance than on the active interposition of Parliament." (*Cheers.*) Such were the sentiments then avowed by a member of the existing Administration; but since that time there had been another declaration from the noble Viscount lately at the head of affairs in this country. Lord Melbourne said that certain attempts were being made to alter the late Corn Law Act of the present Government; but, in his opinion, the agitation of that question would stir society to its foundations. (*Hear, hear.*) But, unfortunately, the late Administration had not acted in accordance with that very sound and wise opinion. They found themselves in a great difficulty. Their strength was daily diminishing; they felt that their hopes of retaining office were very slight unless they could appeal to the country in some way calculated to arouse the passions of the people, and thus give them a chance of recruiting their exhausted forces. Well, the nation was appealed to. The cry of cheap bread was raised throughout the land; and what was the response of the nation? First, turn to the city of London. Lord John Russell was anxious to have the suffrages of the citizens of that great commercial city. The noble lord was returned, certainly, but although at the time of the dissolution of Parliament there were four representatives for London who supported the then Administration, the tables were turned; and although the noble lord was returned, it was by the greatest chance that he obtained even the smallest unit of a majority. (*Cheers.*) Then look to Liverpool, one of the largest commercial cities in the land. At Liverpool the Government candidate was defeated by an immense majority. At Bristol and other great towns there were the same results. That great province of England too, the West Riding of Yorkshire, which contained more than 30,000 inhabitants, also rejected the cry of cheap bread and cheap provisions. And how were the late Ministers received in all the counties of England? Why, was there any supporter of theirs so audacious as even to go to the poll with an avowal of their principles? ("No, not one," and

cheers.) The counties of England rose to a man, the farmers showed their strength, and they placed the present Ministers in the situations they now held. (*Loud cheers.*) Being so placed there, what was the course taken by Sir R. Peel? Why, he took the first opportunity of soliciting the Duke of Buckingham to form one of his Administration—that noble duke who was known at the time to possess the confidence of the farmers of England. (A cry of "Shame on him for deserting us!") For what reason did the Premier then solicit the duke, who was known as "the farmer's friend," to join his Government? Did he think so meanly of his Grace's consistency as to suppose for one moment that he would turn round and support the free trade measures that the Government were about to propose to Parliament? Or did he think it an opportunity to lull and keep quiet the farmers of England until he got so firm in the saddle that he could safely bring forward the measures which he was even then devising? (Cheers.) The farmers of England did exhibit much patience and moderation upon the occasion (*hear*), but that patience might be exhausted. (*Cheers.*) It might happen that the worm would turn upon the heel that trod upon it. (*Loud cheers.*) He (Mr. Blackstone) maintained from that place that the farmer required adequate protection. (*Renewed cheering.*) What was the language of Burke on that head? He said, "It is a perilous thing to try experiments with the farmer, whose capital is more feeble in its nature, whose trade is more subject to risk and losses, whose capital only turns once in a year; in some branches it is three years before the money is repaid." Those were the words of Burke. Why did he quote them? Because they were inserted in that report on agriculture which was made by the committee of which Sir J. Graham was chairman, and of which Sir R. Peel and Sir E. Knatchbull and other members of the Government were members. Those opinions were quoted in that report for the purpose of showing how dangerous it was to interfere with the industry of the British farmer. (*Loud cheers.*) But suppose the people of this country were to agree to abandon the protective duty on agricultural industry, the farmers would have a right to call on those who removed the protection on industry, to make at least an adequate reduction of the burdens to which they were subjected. (*Loud cheers.*) There were many of those burdens. One was the malt tax (*cheers*), a tax of nearly 100 per cent. on the raw article. If that tax were removed it would be a benefit not merely to the grower but to the consumer also. (*Cheers.*) It would increase the consumption. See to what competition the farmer was exposed with the foreigner in fattening his cattle. Remove the tax, and how much cheaper he could fatten them on barley than on oilcake, which he now was obliged to employ. Therefore, he said, give the English farmer the opportunity of fattening his cattle at the cheapest rate. (*Cheers.*) But there was another which he hardly dare call a burden on land, but which was a most important item in the cost of production—he meant the price of labour. He was sure that there was not one gentleman in that room who would accept the boon of cheap provisions if he thought he was to have it on the condition that wages should fall. (*Cheers.*) But when Sir Robert Peel introduced the late corn law he had the candour and honesty to state what were the prices of continental labour, and more especially where the agricultural labourer was supposed to receive more than elsewhere on the continent. He alluded to Belgium. Sir R. Peel said:—
"Additional information has been recently laid upon the table with respect to the condition of the working classes in Belgium. I invite the house to the prices of manual labour as stated in this document. The average prices of labour are—agricultural labourers, 11d.; weavers, 1s.; masons, 1s. 3d.; locksmiths and carpenters, 1s. 3¼d.; operatives working in quarries, mines, &c., 1s. 4d.; jewellers, goldsmiths, and others, 1s. 8d. per diem. That is the rate of wages in Belgium. Now, what is the price of corn in that country? Last year at Ostend wheat was from 51s. 9d. to 53s. per quarter;

at Antwerp it was 51s. to 51s. 2d. a quarter. Taking the general average prices of labour in Belgium, and comparing them with the amount of wages received by the labourers, it does appear to me that notwithstanding the amount of the manufacturing wages, and notwithstanding the amount of the agricultural wages which are received there, it does, I say, clearly appear to me that those wages do not give the labourer there such a command of subsistence as that given him by the rate of wages usual in this country." Now Sir Robert had told them that by his last measure he wished to keep the price of corn between 54s. and 58s. Yet the English farmer was paying 100 per cent. more wages than the farmer in Belgium. (*Hear hear.*) Mr. Brotherton, the wise member for Salford, proposed to have a fixed duty of 4d. a quarter. He knew, he said, that a million of acres of land might be thrown out of cultivation, but he looked to the produce of the fourpenny duty to provide a fund for the labourers who would be thrown out of employment. This was the view of the wise member for Salford. What was it worth? Look to the figures. He had calculated the probable charge. It took about 40s. the acre to cultivate the land, so that to pay the labour thrown out of employ on 1,000,000 acres, 2,000,000*l.* would be required. To effect the object of the member for Salford it would be necessary that 120,000,000 qrs. of wheat should be annually imported. Now the people of this country consume about a quarter of corn a head per annum. Thus the whole consumption of the country would be about 25,000,000 quarters. So that in order to carry out the scheme of Mr. Brotherton, it would be necessary to import 95,000,000 quarters more than there was any demand for. But he would turn from the past measures of the Government to the present state of affairs and the probable future. It could not for a moment be doubted that very general consternation had been produced through the agricultural districts by the announcement that Government intended to allow the importation of wheat from the United States, through Canada, at a nominal duty of about 1s. the qr. Into the subject of that measure he was not going to enter at length, because there were others who would be better able to do so; but he did wish to draw the attention of the meeting to the language used by the Prime Minister on the subject. Sir Robert Peel had tried to state, as significantly as he could (*a laugh*) that it was not his intention to make at present any further alteration in the corn law. On one occasion, a few weeks since, in the House of Commons, he went a step further than even that, and what he then said caused so much satisfaction in his (Mr. Blackstone's) mind, that he could not help rising in his place and expressing his feelings, at the same time adding a hope that Government would not proceed with the threatened measure as to Canadian corn. He did express his thanks to the right hon. baronet on that occasion for an announcement that he knew would gladden the hearts of the farmers of England. (*Hear, hear.*) But great indeed was his disappointment when Sir R. Peel immediately rose to reply to the few observations he made, and altogether repudiated such an interpretation of his sentiments. (*Hear.*) Really after such a proceeding as this he would hardly know how to trust the right hon. baronet's future statements. (*Great cheering.*) From the Ministers, however, he appealed to the farmers of England. He felt assured that they would do their duty—would arouse themselves, and communicate in a marked tone, to advise those to whom they entrusted their interests to look to their safety. (*Hear, hear*, and a cry of "You must not look to Bobby Peel then.") Last year it was said that the farmers of England were contented with the measures proposed by the Government. Except from this county of Berkshire, there was no demonstration to the Government that their measures were not deemed favourable by the agricultural interest, not merely to the farmers of Berkshire, but to the agriculturists throughout the country. On them the blame would rest if they suffered any further steps to be taken to the prejudice of British agriculture. He was glad to perceive that, at the nomination at the East Suffolk election Lord Rendlesham was compelled to state to the electors that he would offer the utmost opposition to the proposed measure of the Government with respect to the importation of Canadian wheat. East Suffolk had done its duty, and he hoped that example would impress on the agriculturists throughout the kingdom, that the blame would rest with them, if they did not speak out their sentiments in a voice of thunder. [Cheering.] He would not further occupy their time. If he felt that the measures about to be proposed by the Government would really relieve the distress of the manufacturing interest, for which no one felt more than he did, then he would not hold this language with regard to them, and he felt that the meeting would sympathize with him in that sentiment. If by lowering the protecting duty on agriculture the great mass of the people could be relieved, then he would not be found saying what he had there said to-day, nor would he refuse to co-operate in Parliament for the attainment of that object. But believing as he did, that in the highly-taxed state of the country, and with a view to the existing arrangements of society throughout the kingdom, it would be found impossible to compete with the low wages of the Continent, he did call on them all to join in the toast with which he would conclude, "Adequate Protection to British Industry."

The toast was drunk amidst the most enthusiastic cheering.

The CHAIRMAN then gave " the County Members."

Two of the members were present. Mr. Palmer was prevented coming in consequence of having long before engaged to lay the foundation-stone of a church in his own parish.

The toast was drunk amidst very general cheering.

Mr. PUSEY rose to acknowledge the toast. He said on ordinary occasions, when he met his constituents at agricultural meetings, they were forbidden, and very properly, by the rules of those societies, from entering on the subject of politics, and this was the first occasion on which he had met a portion of his constituents for the purpose of political discussion. He could assure them he had accepted the invitation to be present at this dinner with much satisfaction, because he felt that in such a critical time for British agriculture [hear, hear] it was necessary for him, whose conduct was in some measure implicated in the recent change in the Corn-law, to show his opinion on this subject. At the last election he had stated to them that he was convinced that any serious innovation on the protection which the British farmers received would be fatal not only to them but to the labourers of the country at large. He adhered to that opinion, and retracted not one word of it, and he had endeavoured to act on that conviction. He had had no wish that the Corn-laws should be altered at all; but he had no part in the government of this country when the plan of the Government had been proposed. He had considered deeply and for many years the working of the Corn law, and it had appeared to him that the present law would not infringe seriously on the protection given to the farmers. That was his individual conviction. They had the declaration of the Government—not only of Sir R. Peel, but sanctioned also by the opinions of old friends of theirs—of the Duke of Wellington, of Lord Stanley, of Sir J. Graham, and of the Duke of Richmond, that the present law would give ample protection, and it had been his opinion that the farmers of England would derive the same amount of protection from it as under the old law. It had been stated by Sir R. Peel, that the new Corn-law would give them an average protection of fifty-six shillings a quarter, and that, as far as he could calculate, had been the average protection given them by the old law. [A cry of " sixty-four shillings."] He then felt it his duty to give his assent to that measure, and they now had a right to call on him for an account why the new law appeared to have produced such very different effects from those which had been anticipated from it. [Hear.] He could only say, that

though he had not so soon expected a fall in the price of corn, he had for years expected that there would be a fall in the price. He had never doubted but that he should see corn at 40s. a quarter under the old law. He did not pretend to any gift of foreseeing future prices, he had only looked to the course of experience under the old law. It had been shown a few years ago by Mr. Wilson, in a pamphlet extensively circulated, that the price of corn rose and flowed in this country as regularly as the ebb and flow of the sea. It therefore required no far-sightedness to calculate that when the price of corn was at the highest it must soon begin to be at its ebb. For a number of years down to 1823 the prices of corn were high, but in 1823 prices fell from 83s. a quarter, which was the flow, down to 44s. a quarter, which was the ebb. The tide of the prices then again rose in 1829, and in 1832 corn was at 66s. a quarter. In 1839 again came the ebb, and corn fell to 39s. a quarter; then, again, the price of corn rose to 64s. According to a statement made by Messrs. Sturge, of Birmingham, in a circular issued by them, dated January, 1840, they stated that " they did not think there would be a permanent fall in the price of corn till the year 1842." But there was in the working of the new corn law a principle which would hasten the fall of prices. In May and June last there had been an expectation of a bad harvest, and at that time 2,000,000 or 3,000,000 of quarters of corn had been introduced into this country. Those who introduced the corn were of course not aware of what would happen; and he had heard that they had been obliged to sell their 3,000,000 of quarters of corn at a very great loss. If this amount of corn had been sold at a profit, with the crop of last year, he should have seen much more cause for alarm. He had been told that those who had introduced this quantity of corn had lost by it about 2,000,000l. sterling; he therefore did not think that what had happened last year would be likely to happen again with regard to the reduction of the price of corn to a similar amount. His belief was that there was also another cause for the price of wheat being lower at this moment—namely, from there being a much larger quantity of land sown with it last autumn, and now growing; and he believed also that the crops were looking remarkably well. He believed that there was another cause which now tended to lower the price of corn, and that the anticipation of a most bounteous harvest kept the price of corn down: He entered into these particulars to justify the vote which he had given. He trusted he was not mistaken as to the effect of the new corn law; nothing would give him so much regret as to find that he had misjudged when the interests of the farmers were concerned; and for his own sake also he wished it to be known that a permanent blight was not inflicted on the country in consequence of the new corn law. When the new tariff had been proposed he could no longer agree with her Majesty's Government, and he had called upon his constituents in many towns in that county to state his reasons to them for opposing it, and had offered to the passing of that measure, he knew, a powerless, but a most sincere opposition. There was another measure which was proposed to be adopted by her Majesty's Ministers, namely, the introduction of corn manufactured into flour from Canada. He had consulted every document to which he could obtain access, and had endeavoured to make up his opinion upon this question; and he assured them that there was the greatest want of information regarding it. He would say at once, that he did not consider that measure to be safe, and, unless he did, nothing should induce him to give his vote in its favour. (Cheers.) There were two views of this question. He was certain that when last year the Government had proposed this question they had not intended indirectly to do any harm to farmers. (Laughter and hisses.) They might not all agree with him, but he knew they would allow him, as an old friend, to say what he thought. (Hear, hear.) He would tell them both sides of the question. On the side of the Government it was said that in order to bring corn into this country from the upper provinces of Canada it would cost 25s. per quarter, and it was also stated, that in order to bring corn from the United States from those places from which it would come it would cost 10s. more, which would be 35s. a quarter. This was one side of the question. On the other side it was stated that new canals would be soon opened, which would greatly reduce the expense of carriage, and that corn might be regularly admitted at almost a free trade price, namely, at a cost of 5s. a quarter, and to a measure which would enable this he should feel bound to give his most decided opposition. He would venture to consider the object for which the meeting was convened, namely, the present state of the agricultural interests, and how the condition of those interests could be ameliorated. His view was, that the salvation of the British farmer depended on two means—first, on maintaining adequate protection; secondly, on an increased growth of corn. Neither of these principles could stand alone. It was impossible that they should maintain protection if population increased at the rate of 2,000,000 every 10 years, unless they were able to grow more corn than they had hitherto done. It was equally impossible that they should adopt improvements in agriculture if they were to have recourse to so reckless a measure as to sweep off at once the present generation of British farmers. How, then, were they to receive protection? He thought it must be done by union (Cheers). He thought they might sometimes learn a lesson from the enemy's camp, and he might say that the main object of the Anti-Corn-Law League at this moment was to sow division amongst the British farmers (Cheers). He would not say anything about the Anti-Corn-Law League which he would not say of them if Mr. Cobden were present, nor so much. He saw it stated, on the one hand, by them, that Sir Robert Peel was desirous to concede free trade in corn, but that the county members would not allow him to do so. On the other hand, he saw it stated that Sir Robert Peel dragged the county members through the dirt wherever he wished them to go. It was evident that these two statements could not be true. He believed that neither was true. Then again it was said—"that the question of the corn laws was a landlord's question only—that it was a mere question of rent—that all the landlords would have to do was to lower their rents, and the farmer with a perfect free trade in corn would then be as well off as ever" (Hear, hear). Others well acquainted with the Scotch system of farming told them of the high rents paid in Scotland—as much as 5l. per acre, and they told them that it was not a landlord's question only, but a farmer's question; that the farmers ought to farm better than they did. Then they were told by Mr. Cobden that they were to have troubles in the south of England amongst the labourers. He (Mr. Pusey) believed that Mr. Cobden was mistaken, and knew nothing of the character of the population of that part of the country. He (Mr. Pusey) believed Mr. Cobden would not succeed in separating the labourers from the farmers any more than he would in separating landlord and tenant. The Anti-Corn Law League had threatened that if any country gentleman should dare to use the argument that the repeal of the corn law would injure the labourer, the League would immediately send down an emissary into his neighbourhood, and examine into the whole state of his property. He (Mr. Pusey) did not wish for any emissary or spy in his neighbourhood, but he would not be deterred from stating what they all knew—that though the price of bread had been much lower last winter than it had been the year before, the agricultural labourer had not been any better off, but, on the contrary, had been much worse off (Hear, hear). His wages had fallen, and by no fault of the farmer; for the farmer had given the utmost that he could give; but wages had fallen, not so much from a failure of wages as from the want of employment [Cheers]. As to the point of increased production by the farmer, he begged to say, that he did not recommend improvement in agriculture from any notion or theory of his own. The rule

he had laid down on this matter was to listen with the utmost attention to the opinions of the farmers, and to consult their views and experience. It was in this manner that he cultivated his own little farm; and his belief was, that Scotch farming, excellent as he believed it was in that country, did not excel the farming of the south of England. The more he saw of the system of farming in the south, the more he was convinced of its excellence. The only thing required was, that the farmers of the different districts should communicate to each other the results of their experience (Hear, hear.) As to the farmers cultivating better, he was sure that they could not afford to make expensive improvements, unless with the help of their landlords (Cheers). It was a common saying in the British army that "there were two kinds of officers, one of which said ' Go along,' and the other ' Come along,' and that the officer who said ' Come along' was generally the most successful" (Cheers and laughter). He said the same of the landlord; he believed it to be the duty of the landlord to lay out money on his farm, and to help his tenants by every means in his power. He believed that the landlord ought to take upon himself the employment of the labourers on his estate for two or three months in the winter; and if two or three wealthy proprietors in each union were to do this, and employ some 50 or 60 labourers each, they would do great good, relieve the farmers from the poor-rates, benefit their farms, and their children would reap the fruits of their well-considered benevolence (Loud cheering). He trusted that they would believe that he had been most anxiously concerned in considering how the prospects of the British farmer and of his labourers could be advanced. He might have been mistaken, but hoped he had not. He could only say it had been his most anxious wish to secure prosperity to the farmer. He thanked them for the attention with which they had heard him, and felt that the kindness with which they had so often received him was an ample reward for any toils which he might have undergone. (Cheers.)

Viscount BARRINGTON, as one of the county members, also rose to acknowledge the toast. He should at all times be most anxious to forward the interests of his constituents, and the moment he found that he could not do so, that moment he would resign his present position. During the first session of the present Parliament he had had very little to do but to drive away from the helm those who at the close of the last election had charge of it, and he believed he had performed this duty to the satisfaction of his constituents, (Cheers and a few hisses.) He did not care the least for a few hisses. It was perfectly impossible in an assembly of that kind, where were many holding a variety of opinions, to give satisfaction to all. It was a great thing for him to have given satisfaction to the majority of his constituents who sent him to Parliament. (Cheers.) He had given no vote in the House of Commons which he had not hoped would be of use to his constituents. There had been during the present Parliament three great measures affecting agriculture, submitted by the Government to the House of Commons. One was an alteration in the corn laws, another was an alteration in the import duty on cattle, and the other measure was—whether it was to be proposed this session or to lie over he could not say—the bill to be introduced on the importation of American wheat through Canada. The first opportunity which had been presented to him and his colleagues of hearing what was the opinion of their constituents on this last measure had been given them by the farmers at a meeting at Reading, and they were generally opposed to it. They had heard complaints of the general distress which existed in this country. He did not hesitate to state that the distress had been caused by the infamous conduct of the late administration. (Cheers.) He had told them that they ought to speak out, and speak out he would, whether with their approbation or disapprobation, because he did not speak from any interested motives. When the affairs of the country had been laid before Parliament, and the great debt we had incurred from the mismanagement of the late ministry had been brought before them, he did not see how it was possible that there should be any great alteration in the commercial tariff of this country, or how the agricultural interest was to be left out of bearing the burden. When the farmer suffered the landlord suffered, for the farmer could not eventually pay his rents. There had been some allusions made to the malt tax and to its repeal. If the country were in a flourishing state he for one should be most happy to vote for the repeal of that tax; but, under all the circumstances, rather than have its repeal, he would have the beer tax again imposed, for, if one thing were better than another for the labouring classes, it was that they should return to those habits of sobriety for which they had formerly been so noted (*hear*). If the labourer could brew his own beer, and brew it good, it would be much more for his advantage than as now (*hear, hear*). He now opposed the repeal of the malt-tax because they were in debt. If that tax, bringing in 4,000,000 of money, was to be repealed, where was the Minister to look to for any thing to supply its place? It might be said, "Make an addition to the income-tax." He doubted whether that would be a very popular measure; and they would recollect that the income-tax was not paid by the people of Ireland, though the malt-tax was, and he thought that they ought to call upon the people of Ireland for a fair proportion of the expenses of this country (*hear, hear*). Considering that the supply of cattle in this country did not keep pace with the increase of population, he was not prepared to resist the importation of foreign cattle under some duty: whether the duty was too low was another thing; but he never could conscientiously say that the people of this country should be debarred from using meat because the supply of cattle did not keep up with the increase of the population. If the proposed bill for regulating the introduction of American corn would tend to injure the farmer, there could be no doubt that it was the duty of those who represented the interests of the British farmer to oppose it. The last question he had heard put in the House of Commons on that subject had been put by Mr. Ewart to Mr. Gladstone, the Vice-President of the Board of Trade, and from his answer it appeared that whatever might be the fate of the provisions of this Canada Bill at present, there was no power to prevent the corn of the United States being imported into this country in the shape of Canada flour. This was no new law—it was as old as the Navigation Act. They were told that whatever was brought from any one of our colonies, which had been there manufactured—and wheat ground into flour was considered as a manufactured article—the colonies had a right to introduce into the mother country; and they were told by the Colonial Secretary, that ample means would be taken by the bill to prevent the smuggling of United States' corn by this means. He could only say with his hon. colleague, that he had no interest on earth that was not bound up with their own, except a small interest in the coal trade. He hoped and trusted that as the prospects of trade revived, their prospects also would revive. No doubt the manufacturers must benefit by it, and the more the great consumers of agricultural produce flourished the more he was satisfied the farmers would flourish. [*Hear, hear.*] He did not look on any duty imposed on corn as a duty for the purposes of revenue, merely conceiving that agriculture was entitled to protection. [*Cheers.*] He begged to thank them for their attention, and should now sit down to hear his noble friend Earl Stanhope address them. [*Loud cheering.*]

The CHAIRMAN then proposed "the health of the Members for the county of Oxford."

Letters were read from Mr. Henley, Lord Norreys, and Mr. Harcourt, explaining the reasons of their absence.

The following is a copy of Mr. Harcourt's letter:—

"Dear Sir,—I was not aware that an Agricultural Association existed at Wallingford, though I have had the pleasure of seeing you sometimes at one of ours in Oxfordshire. Belonging to three in my own county, I should find it very inconvenient to make any exception to the rule on which I have uniformly acted, of declining invitations to public dinners, with that or any other object in adjoining counties, although many of my constituents might attend them. That motive would exist with respect to any public dinners at Reading, where I have canvassed 40 electors. Many of my constituents go to Aylesbury on such occasions, but I have excused myself from joining them. It is solely on this ground that I must beg you to inform the committee of my regret at being obliged to decline their invitation; for if any meeting of an agricultural body took place in Oxfordshire over which Mr. Blackstone should preside, I should be anxious to attend it, although my avowed difference of opinion from him, which is shared entirely by one of my colleagues, and in part by the other, would afford little prospect of unanimity, and therefore I should say of advantage from such meeting.

"Yours faithfully,

"J. Allnatt, Esq."   "G. HARCOURT."

The letter of Lord Norreys was not quite so lengthy. He said—

"Sir,—I am sorry I cannot avail myself of your invitation to dine at Wallingford on Thursday next.

"Yours respectfully,   "NORREYS."

The reading of this laconic epistle caused a general laugh. The toast having been duly honoured,

The CHAIRMAN said, the next toast he should propose was the health of the noble Earl (Stanhope), who had that day honoured them with his presence. He rejoiced that they had received his name with acclamation, for although a stranger to the county, yet they could not but remember that he had the higher claim on their attention of having been an uncompromising champion of protection to British agriculture. He had also a claim from his having so lately presided at that meeting in Buckinghamshire where the farmers unanimously supported resolutions in favour of protection. He was quite sure the toast would be drunk with all the honours. [*Cheers.*]

The toast was then drunk in a very enthusiastic manner.

Earl STANHOPE said, he was inexpressibly gratified by so flattering a mark of their regard, which he valued the more because, as he was unconnected by property or otherwise with the county, he could only attribute it to approbation of his public conduct in defending the rights of the agricultural classes and the producing classes generally. He regarded it as a proof of their concurrence in those principles which he should never cease stedfastly to avow. With regard to the late corn law of the Government, he had not allowed an hour to pass before he protested against it. The report of the debate on the subject reached him by express, and by another express he immediately forwarded a letter to the editor of the *Farmer's Journal*, containing his protest. He was not one of those who invited the farmer to exhibit that patience and forbearance on which the Chairman had so expatiated. He considered that it was in part to that patience and forbearance, which he had never counselled—(*hear*)—which he had never recommended, and which he never would recommend—(*hear*)—that the farmers owed their deplorable, if not destitute condition.—(*Hear, hear.*)—He remembered a story in the *Spectator* of a girl who was asked by a young fellow to take a walk in the evening, to which, as she expected it would end in some love affair, she had no objection—(*Laughter.*)—But the fellow, after taking some innocent liberties with her, ended by picking her pocket.—(*Laughter.*)—He was taken before a magistrate, and she was asked why she did not put a stop to the thing when he first began? "Oh," said she, "I wished to see how far his impudence would carry him."—(*Laughter.*)—Now, that was exactly the case with the farmers. They had waited to see how far the impudence of Sir R. Peel would carry him.—(*Laughter.*) When he first proposed his corn bill to the House of Commons, he evidently had misgivings as to how it would be received. He did not pledge himself to it as a Government measure, but rather seemed to suggest it to the House, when it would be for them to deal with it as they thought fit. If at that time they had had such men in Parliament as Mr. Blackstone and Mr. Cochrane had proved themselves to be, they would have defeated the corn bill, and never heard any thing at all of the tariff.—(*Loud cheers.*) The Chairman had talked about Lord Rendlesham. He (Earl Stanhope) wondered that he had not noticed the ignorance displayed by the noble candidate in that part of his speech where he said that the low price of corn was not altogether attributable to the late measure of the Government. The hon. member for the county (Mr. Pusey) had, to his astonishment, said almost the same thing. Why, the last crop was not on the whole more than an average crop. (Expressions of assent through. out the room.)—In Suffolk, Norfolk, and Essex it was considerably below the average, and he knew that in his own immediate neighbourhood the crop was one-third less than it was the year before. (*Hear.*) Lord Rendlesham told them that there had been a great importation of corn, and Mr. Pusey seemed to him as if he had re-echoed that statement. (A cry of " *Yes, he did.*") Why, the farmers knew that by putting their hands in their pockets. (*Laughter.*) After the passing of the corn bill, no less than 3,000,000 quarters of corn had been imported, 2,000,000 of it in five weeks, at a duty of 8s. Now, would any person venture to contend that there could have been such an importation as that under the old duty? (*Cheers, and a cry of ".No, it never could.*") Then, again, it was argued that the fall in the price of cattle was caused, not by the tariff, but by a panic. He maintained that it was caused solely by the opening of the ports to foreign cattle; but, if it was caused by a panic, pray who gave occasion for the panic itself? (*Cheers and laugh'er.*) If the new tariff had not been proposed, there would have been no panic. And proposed by whom? By the Minister who was placed in office by the agricultural interest, in the belief that he would support their interests. If Sir R. Peel had told the country at Tamworth that he meant to introduce foreign cattle, and lower the protection on corn, could any man doubt that his party would not have been in the ascendant? He (Earl Stanhope) was not a partisan of either faction, but acted on his honest, independent conviction; and if Sir Robert had not been placed in power these measures could never have been carried. He passed from this, however, to entreat them to consider their real situation, which was very imperfectly understood. It was a mistake to suppose that a repeal of the malt tax would restore the farmers to their former prosperity. Another delusion was that put forth by a Agricultural Society, that by new modes of drainage, or by other such means, they could stave off the inroad of free trade opinions that were rapidly destroying them and ruining their families. But by whom was the expense to be paid of these improvements? The tenants were already impoverished, and the landlords would soon be; but would they lay out the money required unless they felt some belief in the permanency of the existing laws? Who could rely on their permanence? Under such circumstances what were they to do? (" *Turn them all out!*") A most excellent suggestion that, but the question was, how were they to do it? (*Cheers and laughter.*) One of the Cabinet Ministers was known to have said, not long since, that the Government must make another plunge into free trade, and that the present corn law would not last another year. The Government did not pretend that there was any difference of principle between them and the Opposition; on the contrary, Sir J. Graham had said, that free trade principles were the principles of common sense, and their adoption was now only a question of time. (*Cheers*) Both he and another Cabinet Minister, in neither of whom could confidence be placed, told the agriculturists, as their only remedy, to take another dose of the draught they had found do better before. (*Hear, hear.*) It was like the case of a man who got drunk, and next morning maintained that all would have been well if he had only taken enough; so, also, the agriculturists were to'd that the only cure for the ruin which free trade principles had brought upon them was for them to gulp down a large dose of them. With regard to the Canada corn bill, which was to be brought in soon after Easter, it was said that it did not alter the present law. Why, the present law certainly admitted wheat at a fluctuating duty of from 5s. t. 7s., but before the corn could be shipped from Canada, there was required a regular certificate that it was the growth of Canada, and not the United States, (A voice, " Flour.") Well, flour; it was all the same thing. What was sauce for the goose was sauce for the gander. They would find what he had stated in the 5th clause, and, moreover, they would also find that where there was no such certificate corn was forfeited to the crown, but by the proposed measure corn might be imported into Canada at 3s. per qr., and re-imported here as flour at a nominal duty. Was not that an infraction of the corn law? The farmers, in fact, had not yet been brought down low enough to suit the Government. Having come down to a state at which rents were for the most part paid out of capital and not out of profits, they were still to be brought down lower. He would not ask now how far this result was owing to the intimidation of the corn law league; but he could tell them what were the private designs of the league, as avowed to a friend of his by a member of the body when he spoke with less reserve than prudence usually imposed upon them. That per-

son said that their real object was to get the land out of the hands of the landlord, and having got possession of it they would re-enact another corn law; they hoped by this means to compensate themselves for the losses they pretended to have suffered through protection; therefore it was that they sought to get the land into their own hands. But they went further; they desired to have retribution, as they called it, on those who had hitherto made the laws. (*Cheers*). The time was come for the farmers to look to themselves. There would be no hope for improvement of prices. He spoke the opinion of a most intelligent and well-informed man, Mr. Joseph Sanders, of Liverpool, who said, when Sir Robert Peel refused to keep the prices between 54s. and 58s., that after a few seasons he expected that the average would be 44s. or 48s. The averages published in the *Gazette* were far above the prices actually received by the grower. He believed that not long hence the prices would be, for corn 38s., for oats 12s., and for barley 18s. He believed that in a short time the public would be made acquainted with information on this subject by Mr. Rolfe, of Beaconsfield. One thing he would show—that on a farm for which no rent was paid on 200 acres, there had been a loss of 50l. per annum. If he were to offer them advice it would be to trust to themselves alone, not to rely on those who conscientiously differed from them in opinion, but to work out their own temporal salvation through their own independent exertions. The Buckinghamshire meeting offered them encouragement. He (Earl Stanhope), unconnected with Buckinghamshire, but standing solely on his avowal of public principle, had succeeded in obtaining the sanction of an overwhelming majority. That was not a packed meeting. It was one of the freeholders and resident inhabitants of the county. He would be glad to see such meetings, not only of counties, but of every town and village; and he hoped, above all, that they would intrust their petitions to persons who would make them heard in Parliament. He would recommend them to ask, not for a diminution of burdens, or for anything of that kind, but for that full protection of British industry to which they were entitled—they should not, indeed, so much ask as demand it. (*Cheers*). Whatever be the result might be, they would have the inestimable satisfaction of knowing that they had discharged their duty to the country at large, a feeling that would sustain them, whatever privations might be in store for them, or whatever calamities might fall upon them. (The noble earl sat down amidst enthusiastic cheering).

Mr. Pusey, in explanation, stated, that he had been misunderstood with regard to the views he entertained as to the proposed measures of the Government. He certainly would not vote for them (*cheers*), unless he saw that it would be for the benefit of the agricultural interest. (*Disapprobation and some hisses*).

Mr. Allnatt rose to propose the next toast. He said he was about to propose the health of two members of Parliament who had honoured them with their company—"Mr. Q. Dick and Mr. B. Cochrane." They were men who had stood by the farmers manfully when so many of their pretended friends had deserted them in order to maintain the unanimity of that great apostate—Sir Robert Peel. (*Loud cheers*). He did not come there to attack their county members on the score of want of sincerity, but he did charge them with a want of consistency. He well remembered what occurred at the last election, and the professions those members then made. Lord Barrington and Mr. Pusey might be very sincere in the professions they then made, and in the course they now pursued, but he would tell them to their faces that if they had dared at the hustings to tell the electors what they intended to do with respect to Government measures they would not now hold the high position they did. As a farmer, he considered that corn law was fatal to the existence of British agriculture. The rent was no longer paid out of profits—it was paid out of capital. Mr. Pusey had told them that the depression of the agriculture of the country was not caused by the new corn law. If it was not caused by that, by what was it caused? The landlords seemed to suppose that the farmers would go on cultivating the country for the mere pleasure of paying the rent, when they were losing their capital. If they did think so, they would soon receive a severe lesson to the contrary. (*Cheers*) After some further remarks of the same character, the speaker concluded by proposing the toast.

Viscount Barrington was then heard in explanation of what the last speaker had said as to his conduct on the hustings. He denied having made any professions which he had not fulfilled. He had declared himself opposed to the principle of a fixed duty.

Mr. Pusey made a short explanation of a similar character.

Mr. Q. Dick then acknowledged the compliment paid to him in a brief speech.

Mr. B. Cochrane next rose to respond to the toast,

and was received with loud cheering. He said he was much flattered at having the opportunity of addressing so influential an assembly, and one met for the purpose of upholding such important interests as those represented by their hon. chairman. (Hear.) Unconnected with their town, unknown to them save as the humble advocate of those interests, he should have hesitated to appear before them, had it not been that the principles which they mutually supported formed a great bond of union between them. (Hear.) Surely, at the present time it were idle to dilate on the importance of such meetings : the most careless observer of the times must perceive that a crisis was at hand, though what that crisis might be, and how it might be best met, must mainly depend upon their own energies and on their own exertions. (Cheers.) It was true that there was an apparent calmness, almost a stagnation of political feeling. To say that this was the calm which preceded the storm was to make use of a trite illustration, instead of an argument ; but it was certain that there were natural causes for a period of delusive tranquillity, while yet the affections of a nation were not entirely alienated, and the great darkness is still gathering in the distance. (Cheers.) If history were indeed philosophy teaching by example, surely the history of all parties would show that the aggressors were ever energetic and vigorous—the defensive careless and indifferent. (Hear, hear.) This, then, was their danger—that they would sacrifice too much to popular clamour, and make concessions which they might hereafter repent of. Let them avail themselves, then, of this opportunity, to invigorate their resolutions and rouse their energies. (Loud cheering.) They would pardon him if he troubled them with a few arguments against further change, not new, indeed, but which, from their truth, would well bear repetition. What was the great strength of all countries ? Was it not national faith ? (Hear, hear.) The Anti-Corn Law League would violate not only the rights of landlords, but the rights of investment and the rights of prescription. When cash payments were resumed after the war, what was the great argument made use of in opposition to Mr. Huskisson ? That the national faith was pledged to the national creditor. Well, but was not the same faith pledged to the landlord ? Had not jointures, mortgages, and settlements been made upon lands, under the full understanding that the principle of the then present laws would be upheld ? (Hear, hear.) The landlord trusted to his land contract as the annuitant trusted to his fund contract. If they repealed the corn laws, did they not increase the income of the annuitant ? (Hear.) Do away with the 30,000,000l. paid annually to the fundholders, and then he believed the landlords would not object to a repeal of the corn laws. (Hear.) It was a sad thing to shake national faith, to teach people that when they said Parliament was omnipotent, they meant to say it had the power of being unjust. (Cheers.) In times of danger, who was the least selfish—the annuitant or the landholder ? He had heard men say, "Oh, but we owe a good deal to circumstances." He also looked to the circumstances of the case, and he knew it required the nicest discrimination to make concessions to circumstances without sacrificing principles. Could they compare the circumstances of this country with those of other countries ? What other country had a debt of 900,000,000l.? What other country subsidized all nations during the war ? What other country had so great a population ? They could no more compare the political features of England and America than they could the Thames and the St. Lawrence. (Loud cheering.) Was this the first time they had heard the cry of cheap bread ? Had it not been raised in Rome and Athens ? They might call for cheap bread, and say the landlords were in fault, and cry for a repeal of the corn laws ; again they would hear the cry of cheap bread, and the aristocracy would be sacrificed, and soon after the monarchy would fall at the cry ; so that bread, which should furnish them with subsistence, would furnish the arguments of their ruin. (Great cheering.) But the first principles upon which these free-traders started were absurd. It was not true that it was desirable that bread should be cheap, if, in order to obtain this cheapness, they reduced the means of purchasing it. (Hear, hear.) Why did not the manufacturers see that their interests were inseparably united with the interests of the landlords ? Take the year 1824. The manufacturers were most prosperous, because the landlords were so. This was not owing to foreign commerce, for in that year the exports fell off 500,000l. But even the Anti-Corn Law League must admit that the landlords were not the only persons who benefited by the corn laws—that the farmers and labourers reaped some advantage, and surely these classes formed no unimportant part of the community. (Great cheering.) A certain supply of corn was wanted ; the question at issue was where it was to be grown ? "Oh, but," their opponents said, "you need not grow corn; trust, like the Israelites, to traffic. Go from the land of Canaan to the land of Goshen with money in your sacks, and buy food; turn the land to pasture." But did they not know that many years must elapse before the pasture would be worth anything ? (Cheers.) Then they said—

"England is a manufacturing country ; she has great facilities : she has her mines, her rivers, her seas ; and she has added to these wide canals which intersect the country, and railroads, which spread the intercourse between man and man." But, he would ask, had England no other features than these ? (Hear, hear.) Who was there who had not seen the traveller, borne rapidly through the country to the great city, point to the rich soil, the luxuriant and yellow crops waving in long ridges to the horizon, to the land studded with happy farms, and felt that this was the great glory of England, and that her tenants were her best bulwark ? (Great cheering.) No one pretended to say that wages must always rise with the price of food ; but what was certain was, that they always fell with it—a fall in prices was almost always associated with diminished demand for labour, and lower wages, (Hear, hear.) Of course it was the interest of all Governments to keep rents as low as possible, for this gave them the power of raising rents by an alteration in the law when they obtained a greater margin for taxation : if farmers could exist when wheat was at 47s., it was evident that when the prices, as in war, rose to 80s., they were apparently well able to bear heavy taxes. One great mistake generally made was, in imagining that the happiness of a country was in proportion to its wealth. Why, the greatest misery existed in Spain at the time Cortes and Pizarro were sending home galleons laden with the spoils of Mexico and Peru. Dr. Smithers had said, "No doubt manufactures add to the apparent wealth of a country, but in a much greater degree they lessen its happiness and security.' And Mr. Huskisson, upon the question of the resumption of cash payments in 1817, said—"It is painful to see, that while public prosperity has increased, and the wealth of the country advanced, the comforts of the labourers have much diminished, the population has kept pace with the circulating medium, and now, though there is increased employment, there are diminished wages." (Hear, hear.) He was not one of those who said that all machines had done harm ; but he did say, its excess was most objectionable. Why, even Mr. Ward had owned this a few days since, when he said, "No doubt the first introduction of machinery into any trade was calculated seriously to injure the workmen." What were the remarks of the Vice-President of the Board of Trade on this subject?—"It is certain that machinery may be some cause of this over-production, by the excess of supply over demand. So long as men labour with their own hands or inert instruments the supply will be in proportion to the demand, but when steam power is applied, which is not a consumer, this proportion must frequently be exceeded." He knew well what advantages the Anti-Corn Law orators possessed in the topics by which they appeal to men's feelings. When they talked of the plains in the far west—of the wide-spread prairies of the Illinois, covered with luxuriant crops—when they spoke of the Mississippi, of the St. Lawrence, rolling down their mighty waters to the ocean, which, no longer a barrier between man and man, had been converted by the genius of a Watt into the highway of commercial industry—when they spoke of all this, and then told them that it was the rude will of the landlord alone which prevented them sharing these advantages, he must express his dissent from such a doctrine. He minded not that the ignorant southern called loudly for justice, but this did not tell them that no advantages could compensate for national industry, and that wealth and prosperity were ill-secured which were dependent on the will of others. They did not tell them that a great nation must have great resources, and that without independence of position there could be no independence of feeling. He remembered a fable of an indolent man, who dreamt of a wealth which he was too idle to pursue. He imagined one night that a vision put a spade into his hand, te ling him to dig in a garden and he would there find wealth. He dug some time, until the latent truth dawned upon him that a man's industry was his wealth, and that the sinews of a nation were the sinews of men. (Cheers.) Need he point out to them how greatly the manufactures of the country affected the feelings and affections of the people ? Did they not know that the social relations, like transplanted flowers, withered away in the atmosphere of crowded cities ? The labourer loved his native village, and he turned from his work in the field to look at its spire. In that spot his forefathers lived— there those he loves were born, and perhaps some he loved best were buried. So even the churchyard, with its narrow path and grassy mound, was to him a pledge of future rest and future hope. (Hear, hear.) When he said that the alterations in the corn law had even now affected the contentment and character of the people, he said that if it were possible they ought to return to the old system ; but vestigia nulla retrorsum, and this should teach them to be careful how they adopted reforms, when return was impossible. He met with a passage in a book written in 1825 singularly applicable to the present time. It said, "The landlords and farmers know not what to trust to ; they exclaim, 'If we sow we know not who shall reap, all improvements are stopped.' The farmer says to the labourer, 'I will not expend a shilling until I know whether I shall be ruined or not. What we fear is, that the Legislature will adopt the wild and mischievous theories of the mob. '" He (Mr. Cochrane) would apply to Sir Robert Peel the same language which the Roman orator applied to Antony: —" Whence comes this great change ? I cannot at'ribute to you any paltry motives. No ; whatever other men may say, this will I not believe. For I have never known in you anything dastard or mean, although high power sometimes debases the understanding ; but I have known your energy, and I wish that you would avoid not only the reproach of having committed a fault, but also the suspicion of evil intention." In conclusion he would say, give us action—

" Rightly to be great
Is not to stir without great argument."

Now, we had the greatest. Let them not underrate the influence of the League, the energy of its leaders. He respected popular passions ; there were some great and noble, some like these to be dreaded, but they could not be despised. It was action which they wanted ; between vague good intentions and fixed, indomitable action, what a difference ! " All action," said the Duke of Wellington, "is attended with risk, but the greatest of all risk is the risk of inaction ;" if men would meet together as they had done that day, the consciousness of strength, the sense of unity, must insure a confidence which would insure success. And, now, having presumed to point out what he considered to be their duty, they would permit him also to show that he understood his own. He was too well aware that while, in some respects, the agriculturists had also been wanting. They knew with what jeers and sarcasm any man was met who presumed to think differently from the majority of his party ; but what they wanted was gallant men like their chairman, who would redeem in the House the pledges of the hustings. (Great cheering.) Ill-judging was that man who entered into politics as a mere abstract speculation, unmindful of all the passions, prejudices, and sympathies which act on men in common life. After all, what were politics? if truly defined—the science of making men happy. Alas !" said Mr. Carlyle, " the beginning of all things is love, and the wise head never was without the generous heart." He (Mr. Cochrane) knew with what taunts any man was met who ventured to limit—some would express it to extend his views—to the sympathies and feelings of more than those for whom he legislated ; but he thought, as a being having to account here and hereafter, it was his duty so to act, and that that Government was most stable which was based upon the affections of the people. That all nations, like all men, must pass away, was most true, but could this be an argument for national any more than it was an argument for individual indifference ? We built up columns, we erected statues, knowing full well that their ruins would one day arrest the footsteps of the stranger. Should we not build up the nei lest of all monuments—our national prosperity, because some convulsion, near or distant, might one day sweep away all classes and all orders in one overwhelming ruin? (Cheers.) The hon. gentleman concluded with these words :—" Sursum corda. Be of good cheer, have strength within yourselves ; but to succeed we must cast off all private interests, luxuries, and pride. In a word, we must forget ourselves. All selfish feelings which are not based on public happiness must be avoided. We must be united ; and united we shall go triply armed to the fight, remembering always, ' That the race is not to the swift, nor the battle to the strong,' but that the victory is to the most enduring. (Loud cheers.)

Several other toasts appropriate to the occasion were afterwards given, and the meeting separated.

CALENDAR OF HORTICULTURE FOR MAY.

The beauty of the early part of April, the warm genial showers, and alternating gleams of sun, produced a stimulus throughout nature, and brought vegetable growth forward with surprising rapidity. A check, of course, followed, and severe night frost occurred about the second week, with considerable quantity of snow in some parts. Every occurrence of this kind indicates caution, and therefore our first advice will be to avoid the full exposure of several choice plants, shrubby and annual, till after the middle of this month. Every geranium and shrub of like habit, which is now employed as the chief ornament of modern gardens, ought to be gradually inured to the open air, in cold pits and frames, or even in open pits of brick or turf, covered at night with straw mats, canvas screens, or common mats ; otherwise, the labour of a winter may perish in a few hours.

THE VEGETABLE GARDEN.

Sow kidney beans on the first warm and sunny day, in drills heated by the sun ; cover the seed three inches deep : repeat the sowing of dwarf French beans about the middle of the month ; and sow, or transplant from pots for a full crop of the runners.

Potato planting of the late winter keepers should be completed. The varieties differ in their habits, and therefore it is impossible to say whether deep or shallow planting should be adopted. Those varieties which work laterally, always below the surface, ought to be planted four inches deep, using two-eyed sets of fine tubers ; on the contrary, the potatoes which raise their tubers above soil must be set rather more shallow, in soft, well pulverized earth, trusting to future mouldings-up for protection from the light.

The "*Irish bread-fruit,*" if we may trust to a specimen just received, promises to gratify every wish ; it is white, extremely hard, and perfectly solid in the pulp. Every country has its favourite, but this is a very fine potato indeed. *Ash-leaved* kidneys are, however, appropriate to every part of the kingdom.

We want to ascertain the effect of autumnal potato planting, for it promises some advantages, which have been asserted by some writers to exist, but which experience is required to establish.

Peas. The imperial and Woodford marrows should be sown, always keeping the rows far apart. The tall growers bear most certainly ; and if the soil be digged, watered, raised in a sort of flat ridge, according to Knight's plan, and the soil saturated with water along the drill prior to sowing, the plant withstands the driest weather. Last summer, when all the dwarf had given in, and become dry, we saw tall rows, all of which had borne in succession from July early to the middle of August. Persons of forethought will act wisely by making a resolute and accurate trial of profuse watering of the ground, prior to sowing or planting almost any kind of crop : surface waterings parch and harden the soil ; but the irrigation now recommended is deep and effectual.

Lettuces, spinach, radish, and every salad vegetable can now be sown in succession ; the first should never be transplanted, excepting the first spring plants from autumnal sowings, because lettuces are almost certain to run to seed if removed ; but the seedlings must be thinned to ample distances.

The whole cabbage family may be propagated : hearting cabbage by transplanting young seedlings ; Cape broccoli, and Brussell's sprouts, borecole, and savoy by seeds ; and a slight sprinkling of early turnip may be made.

Asparagus : yearling plants will yet succeed if planted immediately from the seed-rows into prepared ground, and well watered every warm evening. The same treatment will apply to the rooted suckers of artichoke plants ; but droughty weather is at all times very adverse, to the latter particularly.

Sea-kale of the last cuttings will be backward on account of the extreme winterly weather of mid-April ; therefore, when the crop is taken, the plants may be cut through just below the surface, and the ground levelled: by this treatment, it appears that more laterals are produced, not so apt to run to seed as those which are first developed. We have practised this mode for six years on the same plants.

Every crop should be carefully hoed, and the intermediate ground kept free from weeds. Peas must be sticked when a few inches high; the taller growers will require branchy shorter props, besides those of the full height.

Young growing potatoes are frequently injured by May frost; no mode of protection is equal to trench-planting, because the earth can be applied round the rising shoots, as in celery trenches; but in ordinary cases, the earth must be drawn up as a ridge against the plant, till danger be past; and then the ground between the rows should be either fork-digged, or grubbed with a mattock, to render it light and permeable to the lateral expansion of the roots.

FRUIT DEPARTMENT.

Peach and nectarine trees must be timely disbudded; that is, the supernumerary shoots are to be cut off close to the fruit-bearing wood, leaving one of the lowest for a next year's bearer, another at a point beyond the uppermost fruit, and all those that have fruit at the base. These last may be pinched back, when a few inches long, to within two leaves of their fruit; and all twin fruits should be reduced to one.

Apricot, plum, and cherry trees admit of a somewhat similar regulation, keeping in mind that they bear their fruit upon spurs. No tree, however, should be crowded with growing shoots.

Mulberry trees like the spade, or rather, they prosper by the ground being opened a yard or more round their bole, a few inches deep, when a layer of littery dung may be laid over the earth, and a bucket or two of soap-suds, poured occasionally over that.

Fig-trees should be nailed neatly and regularly to the walls, and the earth lightened and mulched as above directed, for the fig.

The grafts that have succeeded should be examined, and when the shoots advance boldly, the clay may be removed, and the ties loosened to permit the wood to expand. All that have failed ought to be cut back to a well situated bud, which will supply a fresh leader.

FORCING DEPARTMENT.

Examine and keep active the cucumber and melon frames. As the fruit of the former sets, some gardeners stop at that point, others leave two joints. *Melons* must be stopped two or three times from the first shoots to produce a sufficient number of fertile leaders, which are then permitted to run on till they reach the limits of the frames or trellises. Air is indispensable to fertility. No doubt, the farina is conveyed to the female blossoms by the opening of the lights permitting the ingress of flies and bees.

The *fruiting* pine-apples now advance rapidly, and the fruit begins to ripen: 80 degrees is not too hot for this department. *Succession plants* should enjoy an atmosphere of 75°, saturated with watery vapour. Patrick's pits, the linings heaped to the frame with warm dung, mowings of the lawn, &c., are exceedingly appropriate; they are narrow, long, and deep, and in them the plants grow rapidly.

The *early vinery* colours its grapes; and now free air and plenty of sun (but softened by a light canvas covering) are essential. Steam and syringing should be abated. Here a question occurs. Are these appliances useful or detrimental? As to the *flavour* of the fruit, all evidence is in favour of a dry atmosphere; but the *acarus* (called red spider) is generally present, and flourishes. It is the greatest pest of the vine, and the only real and proper remedy is hot vapour. *Sulphur* is offensive, and its efficacy, however applied, becomes more and more questionable.

Peach-house and pits, the fruit of which is expected to ripen about the middle of July, should be assisted by moderate fires and plenty of moist vapour. We have repeatedly proved the great error of early fire heat: *protection* by coverings, and a gentle dung lining during the period of bloom is advisable; but fires, however cautiously managed, are apt to cause the destruction of the blossom. Solar heat, free air, and early closing before sun set, are the safest appliances till the fruit be fairly set, and the storing process advanced. Then, and after the first regulation of the spring shoots, artificial heat with vapour, raised by afternoon syringings over the tree, walls, flue, and paths, aided by pans of water upon the flue, will cause the fruit to enlarge, and accelerate its growth.

FLOWER DEPARTMENT.

We have alluded to cautionary measures, but preparations should be going on by potting off the annuals and perennials intended to bloom in parterres, &c. If *verbenas*, for instance, have been established in the size pot, called sixty, for a month past, and kept under glass, the plants with entire balls can go into the ground after the middle of May, and not a leaf will flag. This remark applies to the endless variety of floral beauties which may be selected.

If persons desire to excel, *fresh soil* in all the small beds is the *sine qua non*. We are acquainted with a gardener who has, by fidelity and skill, maintained his situation for 30 years. He has always adopted this method, and never fails. His lawns are dotted and varied with beds of chaste figure, which sparkle like gems—foliage and bloom being always superior. A fine mellow loam, blended with the manure of expended mushroom-beds, is the staple; the soil of every bed is digged out early, carried to other situations, and renewed prior to bedding out. Common dung, leaf-mould, or heath-soil, are used appropriately, of course; and in the instance of *lobelias*, leaves reduced, not exactly to mould, but to a dark pulpy mass, are used in profusion. Experience must instruct according to local capabilities, but as a general principle, the foregoing statement may be received as undeniable.

Roses, particularly the common China, can be budded with the choicer sorts, and will bloom early. Great care should be taken to remove the caterpillar that infests the rose, otherwise bloom and leaf will be disfigured.

Every department will require assiduous attention. Shrubbery, flower-border, lawn, box-edgings, and gravel walks, all ought to be kept in neat order: slovenliness is the opprobrium of the gardener, and produces ultimate trouble. All mowings of grass are extremely useful, as capping to dung linings; they communicate heat rapidly, and re-excite that decomposing, electro-chemical action which develops heat. Leaves swept up are very useful also : in a word, nothing should be wasted. As to *slugs*, everywhere, we believe, that a very few grains of finely powdered salt, scattered over the soil, would destroy the vermin, or reduce them, and sufficiently salify the earth.

AGRICULTURAL QUERIES.

TO THE EDITOR OF THE FARMER'S MAGAZINE.

SIR,—Some of your numerous and highly respectable correspondents will perhaps inform me of the best plan of keeping milch cows, for the supply of milk in the vicinity of large towns; I imagine that in the great metropolis, where artificial food is dear, there must be great economy in order to afford a livelihood for the cowkeeper. Now, sir, I am only young in the business, and my capital is so small that I have great need to go in a right track without running any risk by trying experiments. My plan is as follows—and if any one will suggest another that will enable me to procure more milk at the same cost, they will confer a lasting obligation upon me :—each cow has one gallon of bran and four pounds of bean meal a day, made into a mash and mixed with chopped hay and straw, and half a bushel of grains per cow if I can procure as many, but it is the want of grains that I am desirous of making out for. This mash forms two feeds, and they have hay twice and turnips or mangel once a day—the cost per head is 8s. 6d. a week, and my cows average eleven quarts each per day, which is now retailed at twopence per quart. Thus you will see when the loss between buying the cows in, and the price out when barren, there is not much left for profit. We have been selling at 2½d. per quart all winter, but do not expect ever to make over 2d. again while provisions are so low. Hay is selling at 6½d. per stone of sixteen pounds, straw 3½d., and turnips were bought in at 15s. a ton.

We must force cows more, or we shall be compelled to give up a trade which has hitherto afforded a comfortable maintenance. But what food to give them to obtain it, I cannot tell ; and I think there are many besides myself that will gladly avail themselves of any practical suggestions thrown out in your excellent journal.

Your humble servant,
A BINGLEY MILKMAN.

TANNERS' BARK.

SIR,—Allow me in your next number to enquire whether any of your readers have tried the ashes of tan (thoroughly burned and sifted,) as a manure, and with what success.

It is generally known that wood ashes are valuable, particularly in combination ; and I am much inclined to think that the ashes produced by burning tan, must be more or less so, and worth the attention of the farmer—if not alone, as an auxiliary.

Your obedient servant,
April 17, 1843. QUERIST.

A correspondent asks—Can any of your numerous readers inform me what is the best and cheapest substance for fixing the ammonia which exists in gas-water, that it may be used or sown out of the hand, in the same manner as grain, upon grass or grain crops?

SIR,—Can you, or any of your numerous readers, inform me if it is too late to sow barley bigg, and how it is cultivated, and where the seed is to be obtained, and the price per qr ? as I believe it answers well in a late situation, being earlier than the other barley, and it answers quite as well for cattle feeding. I remain, yours,
A YORKSHIREMAN.

" A Young Gardener" will be obliged by your horticultural correspondent stating, in your next number, what land is best adapted to the giant asparagus, how the land should be prepared, the best time to plant it, and where the plants can be obtained genuine?

SIR,—Having a friend abroad who is anxious to grow clover-seed extensively, I should feel obliged if you, or any of your readers, would, through the medium of your journal, do me the kindness to inform me whether or not there is a good apparatus for cleaning and shelling clover-seed, and the price of it ? as my friend has not the opportunity of sending it to grist mills, as I believe is frequently the practice in England.

Begging the favour of your inserting this request in your next journal,

I am, sir, your obliged servant,
April 19. A YOUNG SUBSCRIBER.

Would some of the numerous readers of your very interesting and valuable journal give me a little information on the use of salt and lime, as an application for a rough coarse pasture?

I have thought one bushel of salt mixed with two bushels of slacked lime, applied at the rate of 25 to 35 bushels per acre, would be a good dressing. At what time would it be best applied ? An answer to this will much oblige—Yours,
A WARWICKSHIRE SUBSCRIBER.

A correspondent not having sufficient yard manure, wishes to be informed which of the very many artificial manures is best adapted for him to make use of; the soil of his farm is a wet, cold, stiff red clay, and when well drained, with a good season for planting, will produce a good heavy crop of corn.

TO THE EDITOR OF THE FARMER'S MAGAZINE.

SIR,—May I, through the medium of your excellent magazine, enquire whether cart horses of the true *Suffolk breed* are more or less liable to *greasy heels* than those of other breeds, or those of Lincolnshire and the heavy hairy heeled horses of the Midland counties ? And remain, Sir, yours,
April 26. BEDFORDIENSIS.

ANSWERS TO AGRICULTURAL QUERIES.

TO THE EDITOR OF THE FARMER'S MAGAZINE.

SIR,—In the present month's number of your excellent periodical, I observe an enquiry from your correspondent " P." as to the best ingredient for mixing with his charcoal dust, for turnips.

I would recommend the use of some one of the ammoniacal manures, such as guano or sulphate of ammonia, and having used the former for a like purpose myself, with success, I can speak with confidence as to its valuable properties.

Charcoal, it is well known, will absorb and retain fully nine times its own weight of ammonia and fertilizing matter, and is therefore particularly eligible for admixture with ammoniacal manure. I should think from three to four cwt. of guano, mixed with about an equal proportion of charcoal, would be a sufficient dressing for an acre ; and I would advise that the manure should not be drilled with the seed, but should be first deposited in the ridges, which should then be closed, the seed drill following after all. This plan has been successfully adopted on the sand lands of Nottinghamshire, &c., as by this means the seed does not come into immediate contact with the manure, which from its very powerful nature would be apt to destroy the vegetative power.

I am, Sir, very truly yours,
JAMES NAPIER, Jun.
Hackenthorpe, near Sheffield, April 14.

A correspondent, in the last number of your valuable magazine, wishes to be informed where he can procure " the best and cheapest portable one-horse thrashing machine." I have much pleasure in recommending him to Mr. Ferrabee, Phœnix Iron-works, near Stroud, Gloucestershire. I some months since had a machine of the kind from him, which is decidedly the best and cheapest implement I ever had on my farm. It has been tried by several of my neighbours, and gives general satisfaction. It cleans the straw perfectly, without breaking it, and will get over rather more than a quarter of wheat an hour, with one horse, for several days together. I found the average work performed was ten quarters of reaped wheat, or eight quarters of mown. The price of the machine, portable and with the horse-power, is 35*l.*

Your correspondent also wishes a light implement to skim his stubble. I know of none more likely to suit him than the Herefordshire horse breast-plough ; with two horses it will skim from four to five acres a day. I believe it has long been in use in that county, but not to much extent elsewhere. The price is about 4*l.*, and it is very valuable on small farms, from requiring so few horses ; otherwise, I do not consider it possesses any advantages over Earl Ducie's or other cultivators, when worked with their shears fixed.

I consider the introduction of the cultivator one of the greatest of our modern improvements, not only as a saving of horse labour, but in cleaning the land. By using it with the shears, immediately after the crop is taken, all the seeds on the surface will vegetate, and one deep ploughing will destroy them ; after which, working it without the shears will get most descriptions of land into much better tilth, moister, and in every way more suited for the turnip crop, than the old system of repeated ploughings, which (as was often the case) under a scorching sun must be attended with injury to the land.

I remain, truly yours,
EDWARD BOWLY,
Siddington House, near Cirencester.

TO THE EDITOR OF THE MARK LANE EXPRESS.

SIR,—In reply to the question of a " Constant Reader," in your widely-circulating paper of last week, I beg to state that for turnips the urate of the London Manure Company should be applied at the rate of 6½ cwt. per acre, not more than one inch under the seed. Guano is to be applied at the same depth, at the rate of 3 to 4 cwt. per acre ; nitrate of soda, broadcast, 1½ cwt. per acre. Both gypsum and sulphate of ammonia are more adapted for grass and clover than turnips.

I am, Sir, your obedient Servant,
EDWARD PURSER.
40, New Bridge street, March 29.

TO THE EDITOR OF THE MARK LANE EXPRESS.

SIR,—Having perused in your paper of Monday, the 20th of February, a letter from " Grazier," requesting information as to the establishment of a herd of shorthorns ; I beg, through the medium of your valuable journal, to inform him that I have this week returned from a tour amongst the most eminent breeders in the north ; and have been highly gratified with the different herds I inspected, particularly those of Messrs. Bates (Yorkshire), Grofton (Durham), Ridley (Durham), and Watkin (Cumberland). The two latter gentlemen have advertised their stocks for sale by the northern Robins (Mr. Wetherell), very shortly ; and from the healthy character, first-rate blood (combining Colling, Mason, Crofton, &c.), with every appearance of being useful to the dairy, as well as good breeders ; and above all, possessing plenty of hair and a strong robust constitution ; I will venture to recommend " Grazier " to take a trip down to their sales. Their herds appear to have been reared upon ordinary vegetable food ; and as to the outlay he will be better able to form an idea on his return.

I am, Sir, your obedient Servant,
March 25th. A SUBSCRIBER.

TO THE EDITOR OF THE MARK LANE EXPRESS.

SIR,—In the last number of your journal I observe a letter from a correspondent, in which he asks what is the best substance to mix with a quantity of charcoal dust, which he has by him for the purpose of raising Swedish turnips.

I would advise him to mix with his ashes an equal quantity of bone-dust by measure, and by the application of twenty-five bushels per acre of this mixture to land of moderate fertility, I could ensure him a good crop.

I can with confidence recommend the above mixture, as I personally had an opportunity of testing the experiment last season. Part of a field destined for turnips I manured at the rate of twenty bushels of bone-dust per acre ; the remainder of the field received per acre ten bushels of bones and ten bushels of finely-sifted coal-ashes. Upon examining the crop, after the turnips had attained their full growth, I considered that the mixture was quite equal in its effect to the bones used alone.

If any of your correspondents have ever used as a manure any of the lime used in purifying coal-gas, I should be glad to hear from them, if it is attended with any beneficial effect ; and if so, what is the best method of applying it ; and what alteration does the lime undergo after the gas passes through it.

I remain, your obedient servant,
March 30. A SUBSCRIBER.

SIR,—In the *Farmer's Magazine* for this month, a correspondent enquires where he can obtain the best and cheapest one-horse portable thrashing-machine. I have one of that description, which may also be worked by hand (by two men) ; it is by far the best manufactured and efficient article of the kind I have ever seen, and reflects the greatest credit on its maker. It will thrash about ten bushels per hour of wheat or barley, cleaning the straw remarkably well ; and works with so little noise, that at fifty yards off the only sound heard is the humming of the drum. The horse machinery is also very excellent, as may be supposed from its almost-noiseless working.

The chaff-cutting machines, by the same maker, are of a very superior description.

For any further information required, I must beg to refer your correspondent to the manufacturer, Mr. John Ferrabee, of the Phœnix Iron Works, near Stroud, Gloucestershire, whose machinery will, on inspection and use, prove itself to be of the very first order.

I am, sir, your obedient servant,
JOHN B. SMART.
Farnhurst, Haslemere, April 6th.

SIR,—A correspondent wishes to know where he can get the best and cheapest thrashing-machine. I strongly recommend him to Mr. Daniel Haines, machine-maker, Long-street, Devizes. I have had one of his for three years; it is of three-horse power, breaks the straw very little, and cleans it admirably. I can, of our wheat, which yields about twenty-five bushels per acre, thrash twenty quarters a day. The price is now, I believe, about £30.

I wish to fix a bone-mill on to the horse-power: would any body kindly give me their advice—whether it will answer, the expense, and where it might be obtained. Yours, truly,
April 7th. A FARMER.

STRIPPING MANGEL WURZEL.

SIR,—Having read the observations of Professor Henslow on pulling mangel wurzel leaves, I take the liberty of adding the result of my own practical experience on the subject, which was acquired some time ago by superintending a considerable growth of that root in Devonshire for several successive years.

In the same field a part had the leaves pulled three times in the course of the summer; another division had them taken twice, a third portion once, and the leaves were left on the remaining part of the field till the roots were taken up. The result was, the oftener the leaves were taken the smaller were the roots, and the keep obtained was by no means equivalent to the loss of weight in the root, caused by the process of pulling. My own conviction is that the leaves of mangel wurzel should never be removed till the roots are taken up, which should be done as soon as the leaves show signs of approaching decay; when the tops should be twisted, not cut off, and the roots stored.

I also observed that every time the leaves were removed, the plants ceased growing till fresh leaves were produced; and where they were taken three times, the roots never increased in size after the first pulling. Of course the leaves were not stripped off entirely, but only the outside foliage, leaving a cluster at the top of each plant. One great objection I have to stripping mangel wurzel is, it exposes the land to the action of the sun. I observed where the leaves were not removed, and the plants were growing luxuriantly, even in the heat of the day they kept the ground damp between the rows. I am, Sir, your obedient servant,
VERITAS.

AGRICULTURAL REPORTS.

GENERAL AGRICULTURAL REPORT FOR APRIL.

Notwithstanding the temperature of this month has been characterised with considerable variations almost throughout its whole period, it has been not to say unseasonable. However, compared with many previous corresponding months of the year, vegetative progress has certainly been slow, arising from the prevalence, at nights, of cold north and north-easterly winds; yet we have great pleasure in stating that the general tenour of our accounts from the agricultural districts, in relation to the appearance of the wheat and other crops on the ground, is highly satisfactory; and there is every promise of a rich and an abundant harvest.

In our last month's report we took occasion to direct the attention of our readers to the then prevailing heaviness in the demand for most descriptions of agricultural produce, and the consequent decline in their value; urging at the same time the necessity for the legislature to protect the farmers of the country from undue foreign competition. These remarks appear to have caught the eye of the sentimental editor of the *Morning Chronicle,* who, in one of his recent publications, has come forward to refute them. He commences by hashing up a crudity from one of MOLIERE's plays, about "a projector who had a plan for adding enormously to the revenue of France, by making the whole coast into ports, but who forgot the capability of the people to pay for the additional goods that would be thus imported!" and further intimates, *" We are reminded of this mad scheme by the call now made by the agriculturists for legislative aid to keep up*

prices!" The writer of the *Chronicle,* be it observed, is for a *total* repeal of the corn laws, and would, by such a mad scheme, ruin the whole of the agricultural body, by allowing the foreign growers to undersell the former in their own markets. All that our farmers require are fair prices for their corn and cattle; and we see no reason why they should not demand the total repeal of all imposts upon the manufactured commodities, as well as the Anti-corn Law League should require the abolition of the corn laws. The *Chronicle* further tells us that prices are falling, not because foreign food finds its " way into the English markets, but because British consumption is diminishing." This assertion is a direct evidence to our minds, that the party writing such nonsense—evidently concocted to tickle the *humanity-mongers,* for whose *edification* and amusement he is employed—knows nothing, or, at least, pretends so to do, of the subject matter at issue. What! foreign food not finding its way into the English markets! Pshaw! Every school-boy is aware that last year the duty was paid on *upwards of three millions of quarters of foreign wheat alone, of which* MORE THAN TWO MILLIONS AND-A-HALF HAVE GONE AND BEEN ALREADY CONSUMED! Is this an evidence that it does not find its way into consumption here? Is this a proof that consumption is diminishing? Prices, we admit, are still falling, but from what cause? Abundant supplies and unwholesome competition with the foreign grower; for it needs not a philosopher to tell us that the effect would be otherwise with such large quantities of foreign produce thrown upon our markets, and which has passed the customs at almost nominal duties! We do not deny the existence of distress amongst the industrial portion of the community, but we do not find that the aggregate quantity of wheat of either home or foreign growth has, on a comparison with that of former years, in any way decreased during the past quarter, as the returns positively show an increase in the arrivals of wheat up to Mark-lane from our corn-growing districts, over those of the corresponding period in 1842, of net less than *twenty-two thousand quarters!* The heaviness in the demand has, we contend, been almost wholly produced by the immense supplies of foreign pressing upon the market, and which have been the sole cause of the present depressed state of the quotations. Our reason for urging the necessity for protecting the British yeoman, arose from several causes. First, the knowledge we possess of the capabilities of the soil of Great Britain to produce an adequate quantity of corn to meet every demand from the consumers, on an average of years; second, to prevent, as much as possible, the drain upon our stock of the precious metals to satisfy the cravings of the grasping foreigner, who seldom or never allows any portion of them to return to this country; for in no one single instance can it be proved that from those countries whence we have derived the most corn in any stated season, have the exports of our manufactures increased; and we would observe that we make this assertion with a view, if possible, to make those who "do" the *Chronicle*, again enter the lists of controversy, as we shall be always ready and willing to cross hands with them at any time! SIR *Chronicle* says, "the farmers of Scotland, who send so many carcasses of meat to London, cannot have made any great addition to their stocks of cattle in a year or two." Cannot they? What does our friend know about stock, we wonder? Compare the present with the old, and perhaps good system of feeding, and it will be found that the time now required for sending a fat bullock to market, arising from the free use of oil-cake and other artificial food for stock, is fully one-third less than in years gone by; hence arises the rapid increase in the supplies, which are more than keeping pace with that of our population. But the *Chronicle* goes on to state—and mark the absurdity of the doctrine,—that "*the prices of agricultural produce can only be kept up in this country by a successful foreign competition!*" We are confident our readers will pardon us for indulging in a hearty laugh at this balderdash— Foreign competition keep up prices!! We think the best course for our contemporary to have adopted in this matter would have been silence, as he has given publicity to doctrines and statements wholly at variance with facts, in order that his crotchet about the corn laws may not be forgotten.

The state of the corn trade, since our last—if we except the month's commencement, when a slight improvement took place in it—has been that of extreme heaviness, and prices have fallen from 2s. to 4s. per qr. at Mark Lane, as well as most of our provincial markets. This circumstance induces us to refer here to the available stocks of wheat in the hands of our growers, in order that they may be the better enabled to form an accurate opinion as to their future prospects. That they are nearly, or quite, an average for the time of year, we have no hesitation in asserting; and we see but little chance —especially as there are upwards of 800,000 quarters of foreign wheat now in this country—of any important rise in the value of corn during the next three months. Barley, from its limited arrivals, has

been selling at full quotations, and the same remarks may be applied to malt. Extensive supplies of oats have been forwarded, yet the prices have ruled about stationary. Beans, peas, and flour have commanded very little attention.

It is now well ascertained that the whole of the Lent corn has been sown, and we might venture to observe that the period just concluded for that important operation, has been the finest known for a series of years past.

Sheep shearing has been generally proceeded with, and the produce of wool is stated to be very large.

We regret much to observe that the epidemic has committed serious ravages amongst the stock in our grazing districts; indeed, its virulence does not appear to have abated in the least: while the losses sustained by the flock-masters and others have been truly alarming.

By letters received from different parts of Ireland and Scotland, we learn that, with the exception of a few atmospheric visitations in the shape of snow and rain having retarded the progress of the plough, sowing of grain has gone on well, and is now nearly completed. The corn markets have ruled dull, on lower terms.

The following is our usual monthly statement of the supplies and prices of fat stock sold in Smithfield cattle market. The former have consisted of 12,464 beasts; 135,360 sheep and lambs; 1,100 calves; 2,712 pigs; while the latter have ruled as follows:—Beef, from 2s. 6d. to 4s.; mutton, 2s. 10d. to 4s.; lamb, 5s. to 6s.; veal, 3s. 6d. to 4s. 8d.; and pork, 3s. to 4s. per 8lbs. to sink the offals.

The increase which has taken place in the supplies of stock for this market, and the large arrivals of dead meat up to Newgate and Leadenhall, have caused the trade to rule excessively heavy, and prices have declined quite 2d. per 8lbs., and large numbers have been turned out unsold on each market day. Not a single head of foreign stock has been offering, and no imports have taken place in the United Kingdom; but nearly 200 sheep, and a few beasts, have been shipped to France from London and Hull.

A STATEMENT and COMPARISON of the SUPPLIES and PRICES of FAT STOCK, exhibited and sold in SMITHFIELD CATTLE MARKET, on Monday, April 25, 1842, and Monday, April 24, 1843.

At per 8lbs. to sink the offals.

	April 25, 1842.		April 24, 1843.	
	s. d.	s. d.	s. d.	s. d.
Coarse & inferior Beasts	2 10	to 3 0	.. 2 6	2 8
Second quality do.	3 2	3 4	.. 2 10	3 2
Prime large Oxen	3 6	3 8	.. 3 4	3 6
Prime Scots, &c.	3 10	4 0	.. 3 8	3 10
Coarse & inferior Sheep	3 4	3 6	.. 2 10	3 0
Second quality do.	3 8	3 10	.. 3 2	3 4
Prime coarse woolled do.	3 10	4 0	.. 3 4	3 6
Prime Southdown do.	4 2	4 6	.. 3 8	4 0
Lambs	5 8	6 8	.. 5 0	6 0
Large coarse Calves	4 0	4 10	.. 3 6	4 0
Prime small ditto	5 0	5 4	.. 4 2	4 6
Large Hogs	4 4	4 8	.. 3 0	3 6
Neat small Porkers	4 10	5 2	.. 3 8	4 0

SUPPLIES.

	April 25, 1842.	April 24, 1843.
Beasts	2,871	3,022
Sheep and Lambs	23,700	34,680
Calves	68	67
Pigs	312	427

The quality of the Norfolk droves, which have amounted to nearly 6,000 Scots and homebreds, has been by no means first-rate; and the same may be said of those from other quarters. From the Isle of Wight, about 600 lambs have come to hand; and from Scotland, nearly 700 Scots have been received, in but moderate condition.

Newgate and Leadenhall Markets have been liberally supplied with both town and country-killed meat, the receipts of the latter having comprised nearly 18,000 carcasses; while the trade has ruled dull, at the annexed low rates:—Beef, from 2s. 6d. to 3s. 4d.; mutton, 2s. 6d. to 3s. 8d.; lamb, 5s. to 6s.; veal, 3s. 8d. to 4s. 8d.; and pork, 3s. 2d. to 4s. per 8lbs. by the carcass.

AGRICULTURAL REPORT FOR APRIL.

April was introduced with rain, so seasonable, abundant, and fertilising, that nothing could be more benign. During one week were those delightful showers granted; on the 5th the wind became northerly, and the temperature gradually depressed to below the freezing point. Snow also was abundant from the metropolis, westward to, at least, the heart of Somersetshire. As to consequences we may observe that had the registers of the Chiswick garden applied to all localities, some serious damage must have been sustained, for 8 and 10 degrees of frost, with cold piercing wind from the 10th to the 14th days, could hardly be sustained by young juicy vegetables or shoots. However, our own registers are totally at variance, and exhibit no such depression; and the letters of observant practised correspondents are altogether void of complaint. One indeed says that wheat and oats had been a little discoloured, but were rapidly recovering; and that the grass was luxuriant and beautiful. Barley sowing had been propitiously finished in the finest bed imaginable, and the plants were not then in a state to be injured. Northamptonshire and Bucks have advanced their testimony to general luxuriance; our friend in the county last named has no common experience, he is indeed an authority upon the large scale. His report tells us that the agricultural crops were never recollected to be looking so vigorous, and that in fact the frost had operated as a most wholesome check upon rather too rapid a vegetation. Barley sowing was completed at the very period. Beans and peas are observed by all to be healthy and in fine growth. The prospects, in a word, for crops and fruits, and also in respect to the health and abundance of live stock, appear more than encouraging; and as to the spread of science, the land rings with the reports!

In evidence, we beg to cite the neat and unaltered statement of an observant correspondent, residing in a very (naturally) ungenial district of Wilts, north of Chippenham.

"The wheats here (April 8th) are looking remarkably well, in some instances too luxuriant, and the farmers have therefore fed them off with sheep. On one piece of twenty-three perches I have sown sixteen pounds of nitrate of soda (i.e. in about the proportion of one hundred weight per acre), and the effect has been wonderful. Three of our large farmers have this year tried its effects on different tillages—wheat, rye, and grass; on the latter we can distinguish to a foot where the nitrate came; the more mature benefit I will observe, and report to you. We have only a little barley here, and two or three fields show a good and even plant.

"Beans are just appearing, and look well. Our potato pits have this year turned out fewer decayed potatoes than I have ever known; they are selling at 3s. per sack of four bushels."

It would be superfluous to say much more; but in the infancy of our science, it may be urged with propriety, that experiments ought to be perseveringly made to discover the inorganic constituents of all plants, in order to determine the appropriate manures, and in the meantime compound manures ought to be generally adopted, which, by combining all the requisite elements, may furnish each plant with aliment suitable to its own habits.

NORTH EAST OF SCOTLAND.

The past winter has on the whole been an open one in this part of the country. There were, indeed, some days of rather severe frost; but we have not had snow of any depth remaining on the ground for any length of time. Ploughing—the chief out-door business of the winter months—was generally well advanced at an early period of the season, so that the soil was well pulverised and prepared for the action of the barrow by frost. Oats are almost the only grain crop of this district; and the time, therefore, for committing the seed to the ground, in ordinary seasons, is the latter half of March and the beginning of April. Sowing was generally commenced in this district on the 27th ult.; on some of the earlier farms a little had been done before that date, but the business was interrupted by bad weather. Advantage, however, was taken of a week of favourable weather subsequent to the 27th with so much activity that a great proportion of the seed was committed to the ground under rather favourable circumstances. Latterly the weather became very unpropitious; and during the past week we had a severe storm, a strong and biting wind from the north and north-west brought us shower after shower of hail and snow, which on some mornings covered the ground to the depth of inches, though it generally disappeared during the day. The turnip fields are now, however, all that remain to sow in this district. The quantity of grain yielded from last year's crop has been great; but the prices received for it have been so low as to return but a small amount into the hands of the farmer to meet the demands for rent, servants' wages, and other expenses, at next term. Some think that the new corn law has had little, if any, effect in lowering the price, and that the abundance of the produce of last year would have brought the price to the same figure although no alteration of the law had taken place. But this is an opinion which a fair estimate of last year's crop, and a comparison of the price obtained for it, will by no means warrant. The prices generally obtained this season have been 14s. 6d. and 15s. per qr. And the average of Aberdeenshire fiar's prices (the prices annually fixed by the sheriff from evidence given before him) for oats of second quality for the seven years ending with 1837 inclusive, is 18s. 9d. per qr.; and the prices for the subsequent years are as follow:—1838, 24s. 3d.; 1839, 21s.; 1840, 19s. 6d.; and 1841, 17s. Fodder is rather scarce this season, and bears a high price. The quarter's straw has been sold, in some few instances, at so high a price as 14s., which is just about the price that can be obtained for the grain. Turnips are, in general, abundant. That excellent but expensive improvement—thorough draining, has been carried into effect to a greater or less extent on a good many farms in this district; but the subsoil plough is not as yet very generally in requisition. Several artificial manures will be again tried this season, the results obtained from which we shall report at the proper time. Guano will be used to a considerable extent; its efficacy as a manure seems to be pretty well established.—April 15.

AGRICULTURAL INTELLIGENCE, FAIRS, &c.

BAKEWELL EASTER FAIR.—The supply of horned cattle at this fair was great, but the business done was confined to fleshy barreners of feeding qualities and superior new-calved heifers, and those at early note, with appearance of being useful; for other descriptions the sale was dull, and prices had a tendency downwards. In sheep nothing done. Pigs were shown in abundance, and suckers brought from 15s. to 18s. each, strong stores cheaper in proportion. The quantity of cheese pitched was not large; only a few small dairies of second and third wheys, of latter make, in very moderate condition; prices from 45s. to 52s. per cwt., with a fair clearance.

DARLINGTON EASTER MONDAY FAIR.—The show of cattle was limited; sales a little brisker, and prices rather better. The supply of grain was middling and sales better. Red wheat, 11s. to 12s. 3d., white wheat, 12s. to 13s.; Oats, 4s. 4d. to 6s.; Beans, 7s. to 8s.; Barley, 7s. 3d. to 7s. 9d.

AT LINCOLN FORTNIGHT FAIR there was a large supply of both sheep and beasts, and the market was very brisk, better rates being obtained than at several recent fat stock markets.

SLEAFORD EASTER FAIR.—There was a large show of cattle, which fetched good prices. The show of entire horses was unusually good, there being several superb animals exhibited, among which we need only mention Chancellor, Rory O'More, Iago, &c.

GRANTHAM EASTER EVEN FAIR.—A fair show of all descriptions of stock, which were generally sold at advanced prices. Sales were more readily effected than at our great Midland fair. Several pens of sheep were cleared off at an early hour, and altogether a great degree of spirit prevailed amongst purchasers than has lately been manifested.

NOTTINGHAM MAUNDAY THURSDAY FAIR.—At this fair there was an unusually plentiful supply of beasts, which sold very slowly at lower rates. There were not above a dozen fat beasts in the fair which realised former prices. In the horse fair very little was done; the principal part of the supply was of a most inferior description.

HOWDEN SPRING FAIR.—The attendance of farmers and dealers at Howden Spring Fair on the 15th and 17th inst. was numerous and respectable. Amongst them we observed some from London, and others from the midland counties. There was a greater show of horses on Saturday than we have noticed at any previous spring fair; and altogether there was a fair quantity of business done. The best horses were principally sold well at high prices; but inferior ones were not in request, and difficult to dispose of. There was an abundant supply of cattle on Monday, the 17th, and there being a numerous attendance of buyers, a good deal of business was done, at a slight advance in prices. There was a moderate show of sheep. At 12 o'clock, the Howden Agricultural Society held their annual show, when a considerable number of agriculturists were admitted, and were gratified with a most splendid display of 100 head of some of the finest stock in Yorkshire. About 40 stallions (supposed to be the best in the county, and exceeding in number those exhibited at the great county and East-Riding agricultural meetings) were entered and shown for the premiums. The show for all descriptions of horses was excellent, and excited the most close attention; and their general appearance was such as to reflect credit on their several owners. The judges on the occasion were Mr. Sharp, of Weedley; Mr. Thomas Campbell, of Redburn; and Mr. Wiley, jun., of Bransby; who took great pains in

exercising their judgment, and gave general satisfaction. The following is a list of the premiums awarded:—For the best thorough-bred stallion, Mr. John Scholfield, of Faxfleet, for Hunmanby, 5l. For the best coaching stallion, Mr. Tennant, of Osgodby, for Grey Orville, 5l. For the best stallion for roadsters, Mr. James Collins, for Merry Legs, 2l. For the best carting stallion, Mr. Richard Durham, for Nelson, 2l. For the best coaching brood mare, Mr. John Scholfield, of Faxfleet, 2l. For the second best coaching brood mare, Mr. John Scholfield, of Faxfleet, 1l. For the best hunting brood mare, Mr. John Wells, of Armin Pastures, 2l. For the best three years-old coaching gelding, Mr. W. Mitchell, of Yokefleet, 2l. For the best two years-old coaching gelding, Mr. Jonathan Berry, of Holme, 1l. For the best yearling coaching colt, Mr. John Rennison, of Bellasize, 2l. For the best one or two-years-old coaching filly, Mr. Birks, of Eastrington, 1l. For the best yearling colt, by Sancho, given by Mr. Simpson, of Sandholme, Mr. John Hall, Bishopsoil, 3l. For the best yearly filly by Sancho, Mr. Simpson, of Sandholme, 2l. For the best bull of any age, Mr. Henry Smith, of Drax Abbey, for Pilgrim, 5l. For the best bull under two years, the Rev. J. D. Jefferson, of Thicket Priory, 3l. For the best cow in calf or milk, the Rev. J. D. Jefferson, 3l. For the best three-years-old heifer in calf, Mr. Edward Latham, of Wressell, 2l. For the best two-years old heifer, no competition. For the best yearling heifer, the Rev. J. D. Jefferson, 2l. For the best fat cow, heifer, or ox, Mr. Morley, of Eastoft, a ribbond. For the best boar of the large breed, Mr. Wilson, of Barnby, 1l. For the best boar of the small breed, Mr. Henry Smith, of Drax Abbey, 1l. For the best sow, Mr. Penrose, of Barmby, 1l.—The dinner: At 3 o'clock, a respectable company sat down to dinner, at Mr. Bowman's, the Half Moon Inn; Thomas Clarke, Esq., of Knedlington, in the chair. The Judges were on the right and left of the chairman; and many other influential agriculturists were also present. The dinner was sumptuous, and the wines excellent. The customary loyal and other toasts relative to agriculture, with complimentary speeches to the different breeders of stock, were given and drunk with applause, and the company separated in good humour and hilarity, at a late hour in the evening.

DEVIZES SPRING FAIR was, on the whole, very dull and disheartening to the sellers of stock, who, where sales were effected, were obliged to submit to a considerable reduction on the prices of last year. There was less depreciation in the value of fat beef than of any other article; of this there was a moderate supply, which sold pretty freely, at from 9s. to 10s. per score. The supply of sheep was short, the sale was very heavy and lower prices were submitted to. The best cows and calves met a rather better sale than at some of the late fairs. Horses were in large supply; the quality in general was ordinary, and but little business was done; the great indisposition to buy that prevailed prevented a clearance being made.

HEREFORD EASTER FAIR.—The stock in offer was very large. Fresh steers and barrens were in demand, and sustained the full value realised of late, perhaps five per cent. may be quoted as advance in many instances. Cows with calves were abundant, sale dull, and value rather depressed. There was a good deal of business done. Sheep and pigs were in large supply; the demand for ewes with lambs was brisk, but fat sheep moved off heavily. Of fat pigs very few were in offer, and the demand was very dull; stores were numerous, and sold readily. In the horse fair, good roadsters and agricultural draught horses were sought after, and realised a trifling advance in value.

ROMSEY, April 18.—Our Easter fair was fully attended. There was a large supply of all sorts of stock usually brought to fair, and the average amount of business transacted was satisfactory. We have not for many years seen so good a stock as to quality in the cattle market, and there was a brisk demand for barreners and store heifers—a considerable number of the former was purchased early in the morning by a large dealer near Windsor. The sheep pens were well filled, and the neighbouring butchers availed themselves of a good opportunity of purchasing some prime articles at moderate prices. The quantity of cheese pitched was large, but below the average: skim produced from 30s. to 36s.; half coward, 44s. to 48s.; North Wilts and white Somerset, 50s. to 54s.; superior sorts and Chedder, up to 76s. The day being remarkably fine, an unusual number of holiday folks attended. The second day's cheese sale enabled the factors to dispose of a considerable quantity, left unsold on Monday.

WISP CLUB MEETING—PRICES OF STOCK. —The annual meeting of what is called the Wisp Club was held a few days ago at Mosspaul Inn, which is situated on the confines of the counties of Roxburgh and Dumfries. The members of whom this society is composed are, with few exceptions, extensive stock farmers, and the purpose for which it meets is to strike the average prices of all the various kinds of cattle, sheep, lambs, and wool produced in the higher districts of the border counties, and sold the preceding season in the South of Scotland and the North of England markets, and which prices are registered in a club-book kept for that purpose, which now proves a useful record of reference as to the prices of past years, and which has ever been consulted by landlords when about to grant a renewal of leases. There was a numerous attendance of gentlemen, not only from the immediate counties, but also from Selkirk, Peebles, and Lanarkshire. The following is a list of the different kinds of stock, and the prices as they were fixed by a majority of the votes of the whole meeting:—CATTLE.—Shorthorned stirks, 5l.; do. two year olds, 8l. 10s.; Galloway stirks, 3l. 10s.; do. two year olds, 5l. 10s. each. CHEVIOT SHEEP.—Rough wethers, 1l. 0s. 6d.; do. Dinmonts, 15s. 6d.; wether hogs, 12s.; turnip wethers, 1l. 1s.; do. young, or two year old wethers, 16s.; draught ewes, 11s.; black faced draught ewes, 9s. each. LAMBS.—Cheviot top wether lambs, 5s. 3d.; do. mid. wether lambs, 3s. 6d.; do. mid. ewe lambs, 4s. 9d.; black faced top wether lambs, 4s. 6d.; do. mid. wether lambs, 3s. 6d.; do. mid. ewe lambs, 5s. 6d. each. WOOL.—Cheviot tarred wool, of 24lbs. per stone, 13s. 3d.; do. buttered and oiled wool, 3l. 17s. 6d.; do. pure white wool, 1l. 0s. 6d.; black faced tarred washed wool, 7s. 9d.

It may be interesting to the public to compare these prices with those obtained in the years 1839, 1840, and 1841:—

	1839.	1840.	1841.
Short-horned Stirks, each	£7 5 0	£7 15 0	£8 0 0
Ditto two-year-olds, do.	10 5 0	11 5 0	11 5 0
Galloway Stirks, do.	4 15 0	5 10 0	6 0 0
Ditto two-year-olds, do.	7 15 0	8 5 0	9 0 0
Rough Cheviot Wethers, do.	1 6 6	1 8 0	1 6 6
Ditto ditto, Dinmonts, do.	1 2 6	1 3 6	1 1 6
Wether ditto Hogs, do.	0 11 0	0 18 6	0 16 6
Turnip 3 years old Wethers, do.	1 9 0	1 8 6	1 7 6
Ditto two-years old Wethers, do.	1 4 6	1 4 0	1 3 6
Cheviot Draught Ewes, do.	0 16 9	0 17 6	0 18 0
Black-faced Draught Ewes, do.	0 13 6	0 14 0	0 14 0
Cheviot Top Wether Lambs, do.	0 8 9	0 9 6	0 9 0
Ditto Middling Wether Lambs, do.	0 6 6	0 7 0	0 7 0
Ditto Middling Ewe Lambs, do.	0 9 3	0 10 0	0 9 3
Black-faced Top Wether Lambs, do.	0 9 0	0 9 3	0 9 3
Ditto Middling Wether Lambs, do.	0 6 9	0 7 3	0 7 0
Ditto Middling Ewe Lambs, do.	0 9 0	0 9 6	0 8 6
Cheviot Tarred Wool, of 24lb. per stone	0 19 0	0 13 9	0 16 0
Ditto Buttered and Oiled Wool, do.	1 8 0	0 19 6	1 1 6
Ditto pure White Wool, do.	1 10 0	1 2 9	1 4 6
Black-faced Tarred Wshd. Wool, do.	0 14 0	0 7. 9	0 9 6

The following is the average of the prices of the three preceding years as compared with those of last year:—

AVERAGES OF 1839, 1840, AND 1841.	1842.	REDUCTION OF VALUE.
Short-horned Stirks	£7 13 4	£5 0 0	35 per ct.
Ditto two-year-olds	10 18 4	8 10 0	22 ..
Galloway Stirks	5 8 4	3 10 0	35 ..
Ditto two-years olds	8 6 8	5 10 0	34 ..
Rough Wethers	1 7 0	1 1 0	22 ..
Ditto Dinmonts	1 2 6	0 15 0	33 ..
Wether Hogs	0 17 8	0 12 0	32 ..
Turnip three-year old Wethers.	1 8 4	1 1 0	26 ..
Ditto two-year-olds	1 4 0	0 16 0	33 ..
Cheviot Ewes	0 17 5	0 11 0	37 ..
Black-faced Ewes	0 13 10	0 9 0	35 ..
Cheviot Top Lambs	0 9 0	0 5 3	42 ..
Ditto Middling Wethers.	0 6 10	0 3 6	49 ..
Ditto Middling Ewes	0 9 6	0 4 9	50 ..
Black-faced Top Wethers	0 9 2	0 4 6	51 ..
Ditto Middling Wethers	0 7 0	0 3 6	50 ..
Ditto Middling Ewes	0 9 0	0 5 6	39 ..
Cheviot Tarred Wool, 24lbs. per stone	0 16 3	0 13 3	18 ..
Ditto Buttered and Oiled, do.	1 3 0	0 17 6	24 ..
Ditto pure White, do.	1 5 9	1 0 6	20 ..
Black-faced Tarred Washed, do.	0 10 5	0 7 9	26 ..

The above table of prices shews the great depreciation that has taken place within the last year in all kinds of live stock, especially lambs and draught ewes, from which store farmers derive the greatest portion of their revenue.—*Newcastle Journal.*

LONGEVITY OF THE VINE.—The age to which the vine will attain in warm climates is so great as not to be known. It is supposed to be equal, or even to surpass that of the oak. Pliny speaks of a vine which had existed six hundred years; and Bocs says, there are vines in Burgundy upwards of four hundred years of age. In Italy there are vineyards which have been in a flourishing state for upwards of three centuries; and Miller tells us, that a vineyard a hundred years old is reckoned young. The extent of the branches of the vine, in certain situations and circumstances, is commensurate with its produce and age. In the hedges of Italy and woods of America, they are found overtopping the highest elm and poplar trees; and in England, one plant, trained against a row of houses in Northallerton (some years dead), covered a space, in 1585, of one hundred and thirty-seven square yards; it was then about one hundred years old. That at Hampton Court, nearly the same age, occupies above a hundred and sixteen square yards; and that at Valentine's, in Essex, about one hundred and forty-seven square yards. The size to which the trunk or stem sometimes attains, in foreign countries, is so great as to have afforded planks fifteen inches broad, for furniture, and statues; and even in this country, the Northallerton vine above mentioned, in 1785, measured four feet in circumference near the ground; and one branch of the Hampton Court vine measured one hundred and fourteen feet in length. Vine timber is of great durability. It may be remarked that vines regularly pruned and dressed can rarely attain similar magnitudes, nor is it desirable that they should; as in that case all the vigour of the plant would be wasted in making wood.—*Natural History of the Grape Vine, by John Mearns.*

SOWING GARDEN SEEDS.—A celebrated nursery-man, late of Edinburgh, is said to have given the following trite advice to all young gardeners when he sent them out to their "first place." "Sow thickly, thin in time, and keep on good terms with the cook." All kitchen-garden seeds are said by the growers to be in excellent condition this season, with the exception of carrot seed, those plants having been blighted last season, when ripening seed. Carrot-seed must therefore be sown thicker than usual this season; see that the ground for it is in a thoroughly pulverized state. Where the land is stiff, or otherwise uncongenial, it would be a good plan to get two or three barrow-loads of light sifted compost, to cover the seeds with. A careful man should follow the sower with a basketful of the covering, which he could sprinkle along the drills as fast as the seeds were sown.

REVIEW OF THE CORN TRADE

DURING THE MONTH OF APRIL.

Since the close of the last century, the interests of agriculture, and, combined with them, those generally of the only wealth of nations—a productively employed population, have not been placed in a more critical position than they are at the present moment. The value of agricultural products is now much lower than are the necessary expences of their production, and the wages of labour are consequently in a gradual state of reduction, even in a greater proportion, from this unfortunate circumstance. The corn bill, which came into operation in the course of last year, and the reduction made at the same period in our custom-house duties, previously charged on the importation from foreign nations, of almost all articles of general consumption in this country, have deprived the producers at home of similar articles, of that degree of legislative protection which is absolutely necessary to their successful cultivation. Neither wheat nor any article of agricultural produce can be profitably grown in this country at present prices; and consequently our farmers generally are not only unable to pay fair and living wages to their labourers, but they have even in many instances been most reluctantly compelled to reduce very materially the number of workmen previously employed on their agricultural establishments. Unless some amendment therefore should speedily occur in the value of agricultural produce, and the future prospects of our farmers become more cheering, the certain consequence of the existing state of agricultural affairs must be either the transportation to the colonies, at the public expence, of an immense multitude of agricultural labourers, or the final settlement of them in the district union houses. So long as talent, capital, and science, when embarked in agricultural pursuits, were duly protected, upwards of two millions and a half of male labourers obtained their daily bread in this great department of our internal industry; and it was a daring experiment indeed on the part of the farmers' friends in parliament, and of the present ministers of the crown, who obtained their present exalted position solely by the influence of the agricultural interest, and for the protection of their property, to put at hazard that admirable state of society which was conferring most important benefits on every class in the United Kingdom, for the illustration of theories which can never be reduced to practice. When the interests of all classes in our community were legally protected in their industrial pursuits, the British Empire was raised to the highest state of prosperity; and so long as it was not found advisable to pay wages to foreign labourers for doing that work which could be well performed by our workmen at home, complaint was comparatively a stranger to the vast majority of our population. Our commercial system now is however to employ foreign workmen in the production of as many articles as possible; and our humane system is to transport to the colonies those labourers who are rendered idle, because we encourage now the consumption of foreign agricultural products. In the meantime our farmers are called on to sacrifice the money which, under the faith of the late corn law and the former custom-house duties, they had embarked in the tillage and improvement of our own fields, to a one-sided freedom of commerce with foreign nations. Independent of the value of the land and the farming buildings and necessaries of various descriptions expended on it, amounting as it does to upwards of two thousand millions sterling, the farmers' money embarked in the cultivation of their farms is estimated at more than two hundred millions sterling, a sum very considerably exceeding the outlay of the manufacturers in stock and credits. When times are unfavourable the manufacturer can withdraw a great part of his capital from his trade, and wait for better times. Not so however is the case of the farmer; his property is sunk for years in his farm, and he must persevere in his operations, however adverse they may be to his property, so long as he finds one penny in his pocket. The farmers', as we have said above, give productive labour to, and maintain in a certain degree of comfort, upwards of two millions and a half of male workmen with their families and dependents, whilst less than half a million of males are supported by the manufacturing interest. Now it is neither politic nor just to the community to sacrifice four-fifths to one-fifth, even should every one of the latter become a cotton lord. Unless, however, a complete change in our free trade system be soon adopted, this misfortune most certainly awaits us; for the farmers are now sinking their capital, and after it is gone the same amount of money cannot ever again be applied to the tillage of our fields, and to the improvement of agricultural science. So far, however, from hearkening to the dictates of reason and sound policy, her Majesty's ministers have now an act in hand which may consummate their good deeds and good intentions towards the agricultural interest, and towards that only wealth of nations—productive employment at home for the multitude. Even the prospect of this act of Parliament during the last month, has pressed heavily on the value of agricultural produce in all the great markets throughout the United Kingdom; preventing, as it assuredly has done, that material improvement in the prices of British grain which the late small supplies under different circumstances most undoubtedly would have occasioned. The Colonial Grain Importation Bill at nominal duties will, however, soon be registered amongst the free trade and absurd laws of the British empire, and it will be attended by all the injurious consequences to our agricultural interest, which the actual repeal of the present corn-law, in so far as the produce of the United States of North America is concerned, would occasion; for the illicit importation of it into the Canadas could not be prevented, if the whole of our army were converted into custom-house officers for the prevention of smuggling across the American and Canadian frontiers. Abundance of the agricultural produce of the United States will be, as soon as our colonial corn bill becomes the law of Great Britain, smuggled across the Canadian borders, and will pass into this country for consumption at nominal duties, in the character of colonial agricultural produce. The flour and cured provisions of the United States will also be imported here on the payment of colonial duties, which speedily now will be only nominal. No clause in the new colonial grain act, however stringent it may be made, can avert this calamity from the British agricultural, and from the British productive employment interests. Amongst the most virtuous communities, when commercial purposes demand them, false certificates of origin have been, and still may be obtained, at, we may truly say, no expense whatever; and it is not probable that those who repudiate the payment of the half yearly dividends on money borrowed by them, and solely expended by them in cultivating their fields, will feel any qualms of conscience in forging certificates, that their grain was grown in British America, that their flour was manufactured in the Canadas, and that their provisions were cured in the same country. The grain-milling trade is an important one in this country. Much money is embarked in it, and from it thousands of families at present receive their daily bread. Unless it be a part of the ministerial plan to send out to America, at the public expense, those workmen who will be soon deprived of employment by its transfer to the workmen of America, additions must be made to our workhouses and union houses; for this act must eventually reduce to poverty and wretchedness a vast multitude of her Majesty's agricultural subjects. But the inhabitants of the United States of North America are not the only people who will avail themselves of our future colonial corn and provision bill. We well recollect Baltic timber, to save duty, being sent to Halifax, in Nova Scotia, and afterwards delivered into our dockyards at Portsmouth and Plymouth, on the payment of colonial duties. At that time this transaction was perfectly legal, because the Memel timber had been landed, and trans-shipped at Halifax, and consequently had acquired all the privileges of colonial timber. The proposed colonial bill is to grant equal privileges to foreign wheat when imported into any of our colonies, on condition that it be there converted into flour. Under certain circumstances, therefore, Polish, German, and Mediterranean wheats must in future always find their way into our markets. When our prices are remunerating to our own farmers, and when the duty is consequently low, foreign wheats will be imported direct from those countries wherein they were produced; but when our prices pay not the cost of production in this country, and when the import duty is 20s. per qr., it will become a profitable trade to send foreign wheat to any of our colonies, even to Heligoland itself, there to be ground into flour, and afterwards to be introduced into consumption in this country on the payment of colonial, or rather of nominal, duties. Malta likewise may be considered a colony, and so may Gibraltar. To be sure, within themselves, they grow little or rather no grain, but they can import it in the greatest abundance. Mills may be erected in both of these settlements, and eventually we may receive most excellent colonial flour manufactured out of foreign wheats, on the payment of colonial duties from the Mediterranean Sea itself. This colonial act, to be just, must be general; its principles cannot be applied solely to our North American possessions, unless the ministers of the crown intend to grant to them a monopoly, and that too of the worst description. Unless we daily saw, or read about, the most extraordinary pranks which are now practised by the free trade advocates, we could not believe that the ministers seriously contemplated the passing of this colonial corn bill, and much less could we think it possible that the legislature of the United Kingdom

would permit it for a week, after its introduction, to remain amongst the orders of the imperial parliament; but when we almost weekly hear of the exertions of her Majesty's present advisers to conclude commercial treaties with even the most paltry nations and communities, our wonder ceases at the apathy shown by the farmers' friends on this subject; for by them was the present administration brought into office; and we dare say that they confidently believe that their interest will not be willingly sacrificed by their own elected, but that, on the contrary, commercial treaties with foreign nations must eventually increase the value of all descriptions of agricultural products grown in this country. They surely must fancy that the result of the illustration of the principles of free trade must eventually be, that every man in this kingdom will daily boil his fowl or roast his beef, and that in future the London dustman will be clothed in red Italian velvet, else they never would hearken to doctrines so absurd as those are which may be pressed during this session on the representatives in the House of Commons of the agricultural interest. Commercial treaties with foreign nations cannot increase, either in amount or in value, our export trade. Commerce can alone be regulated by the actual wants of those communities to whom our goods and products are forwarded. It cannot be increased by any government regulations beyond the necessary consumption, nor can it be diminished by even the most hostile barrier which may be raised against it. The celebrated decrees of the Emperor Napoleon, issued from Berlin and Milan, when he commanded the continent of Europe, against British commerce, are still fresh in the memories of many London merchants, and they likewise well recollect that our commercial intercourse with Europe was never more flourishing than it was during the existence of those decrees. Commerce, in fact, is like water, and, in finding its level, it bursts through all restrictions which even the most powerful governments may impose on it. No treaties are necessary to render it prosperous, and therefore the policy is short-sighted indeed on the part of our ministers, to sacrifice our landed interest and productive employment at home, with a view to obtain aerial benefits and commercial advantages which, when caught, will be found as valueless as they are impracticable. It is perfectly unworthy of the greatness of the British Empire to solicit commercial treaties with any nation whatever, particularly with governments so extremely insignificant as those of Portugal and the Brazils. The superior quality and lower prices of our manufactures will always force them into consumption everywhere, either by means of moderate import duties, or by the agency of smugglers. To put at hazard the agricultural interest, the productive employment at home of our industrial classes, and the national debt itself, for the possession of a perfect shadow, is, we repeat, a policy which common sense cannot comprehend; and to place this great empire in a position which may hereafter render large crops of grain, grown at home, a curse instead of a blessing to the people, can only be attributed to a certain degree of mental imbecility, which for a period may have taken possession of the minds of many of the farmer's friends who are members of the legislature. A year ago the prime minister himself, in the House of Commons, stated that 54s. to 58s. per quarter was the price necessary to the cultivation of wheat in this country. It is now under 46s., and, calculating the annual growth at from fourteen to sixteen millions of quarters, our farmers have this season sacrificed from seven to eight millions sterling of their farming capital to the illustration of free trade principles, in the article of wheat alone. At this moment, too, the young wheat plants are strong and luxuriant, and as this season a much larger extent of land than usual has been placed under wheat cultivation, it is highly probable that the average price of wheat, at this period in the ensuing year, may be 10s. per quarter under its present value. The present state of the country sufficiently proves, therefore, that, unless when the elements injure our grain crops, we can grow at home abundance of all the necessaries of life for supporting our population, were it doubled ; and for the ideal advantage of adding to the amount and value of our export trade, which no treaties of themselves can do, foreign agricultural produce should not be permitted to interfere with our agricultural pursuits and with our agricultural improvements under such circumstances, nor should productive employment for clothing and feeding the population of the United Kingdom, be transferred from our own labourers to those of foreign nations; for we reduce our workmen to poverty, and enrich the foreign labourers, by this one-sided system of reciprocity in commerce. Bread now is 1¼d. per lb., and butchers' meat is proportionally low in this country; and yet our exports to Europe, and to the United States of North America—from which we have received, during the last twelve months, those supplies of grain and of other articles of foreign agricultural produce, by which their value here has been so materially depressed—are not increased, but on the contrary they have been considerably decreased, during the period in which we have been paying in gold for such immense quantities of their productive labour. Here is a most glaring proof that our export commerce cannot, under any circumstances whatever, be forced beyond those limits which the consumption of the importing nations require, and the futility of commercial treaties for such purposes on our part is rendered perfectly manifest. Germany and the United States of North America are now cultivating the manufacturing arts. In receiving and paying for their agricultural produce, we have afforded them the means of producing goods at home for their own use; and nothing short of superiority in quality and price can hereafter substitute amongst the nations of Europe, at all events, our manufactures for their own.

From the different corn markets in the Mediterranean and Black seas, the letters received are in due course of post. The prices of wheat in all of them were entirely nominal, there existing no export demand from any quarter at those dates ; but when our celebrated colonial corn grinding plan becomes the law of this country, the prices in all these ports will fully justify large shipments being made to our colonies for the conversion of foreign-grown wheats into colonial flour, with the view of the markets in this country for its consumption. In the ports of the Peninsula, and those of France, without the Mediteranean, similar dullness prevails in the corn trade; but from Portugal and the north of Spain, when the season admits, we may expect to receive considerable supplies of live cattle and of cured provisions

—another benefit to be conferred by free trade on our breeders and feeders of stock at home. From all the ports in the north of Europe, and throughout the Baltic Sea, the information received during the last month respecting the state of the corn trade was generally uninteresting to the corn merchants and corn factors in this country. Very few actual sales of wheat for exportation had been effected in any of them up to the latest dates, and prices were consequently nearly nominal. The finest quality of high-mixed Polish wheat could then have been purchased at 30s. per qr., free on board at Dantzic—which, at our present price of the same description, of 56s. per qr., would, after payment of our maximum import duty, do rather more than also pay for the cost price, freight, and for all the usual expenses of importation. Inferior samples were proportionately low, but as the duty and expense of bringing them into this country are the same as the best qualities, of course no shipments of low quality will at present be attempted. At Rostock and Stettin, the best samples of Silician wheat were likewise quoted at about 30s.; but no business to any extent had then been effected in those places.

The leading maltsters have this season ceased their malting operations fully one month earlier than usual ; and this circumstance is the more extraordinary, because the quality of the barleys grown last year has seldom in any previous one been exceeded in fineness, and because till the close nearly of last month the weather was generally cool, and consequently favourable to the manufacture of malt. Those engaged, however, in this department of trade have learned by experience, during the last few years, that the consumption of malt is annually on the decline, and as the heavy duty imposed on it must be paid at fixed times, it is not now for their interest to malt for the succeeding season, however excellent the quality of barley may be ; for the advance of duty would be a greater sacrifice made by them than the probable profit which might arise, from higher prices being afterwards obtained, would justify. This is, however, one of the numerous anomalies arising out of an internal system of taxation ; for whilst foreign goods, and produce any description can be landed under bond, and be detained there without payment of one farthing duty, until the time arrive when they may be profitably introduced into consumption, the malt manufactured and the spirits distilled in England are charged with the duties at stated periods, and in no instance are they permitted to be bonded until markets more favourable to their sale appear. Now this is an act of injustice towards our barley growers which is perfectly unjustifiable, in as far as no duty ought ever to be charged, either on malt or home-made spirits, until the time come for sending them into consumption. To the interests of the English distillers—and this is a most important and valuable department for taxation —the want of permission to bond their spirits is most injurious, for whilst foreign brandies and Geneva are allowed to gain age and softness in bond, our home-made spirits are, in far too many instances, forced into consumption in a very improper state, being deprived frequently of that degree of mildness which age alone can confer on them, and, unless purchased at a great advance in price, being sometimes of that harsh and hot quality which is occasionally so detrimental to the health of their consumers. As it has been completely ascertained, that with proper care in their manufacture, and with the necessary age, British spirits are far more wholesome than either Geneva or brandy are, common sense itself should, we fancy, teach the lords of the British Treasury, that, as the home-made spirit duties eventually would be paid, it is but fair that the English distillers should be permitted to enter their property under her Majesty's lock in the same way as foreign spirits are, until they be in a proper condition to be sent into general consumption, and not till then to be called on for the payment of the duty. In Scotland and also in Ireland, bonding home-made spirits to a certain extent is allowed, and there exists no sound reason why the English distillers should be deprived of the same benefit. If any one of the farmer's real friends in parliament would give himself the trouble to direct the attention of the ministers to our system of excise duties, and prevail on them to restore our Custom-house duties to the same rates which existed about a year ago, the public revenue would be materially improved, and the prosperity of the community at the same time very much increased, if not absolutely restored to its former state, we may truly say, of universal productive employment. It has very frequently been our duty to point out to the attention of our agricultural and commercial readers, the outrageous manner in which barley, when manufactured, is taxed, that it may appear to be repetition again to allude to the same subject; but the advantages of a reduction in the rates of these duties would be so great, that we must continue to point out the grievance until it be amended. To the Treasury, the reduction of the duty now charged on home-made spirits, when consumed in England, would be of the greatest importance, for by the suppression of spirit smuggling, which the imposition of moderate duties in England would occasion, the revenue now collected on spirits of home manufacture would eventually be most materially increased, the expense of the preventive service would also be much reduced, and the morals of the people proportionately improved. Comparing the consumption of home-made spirits in England with that either in Scotland or in Ireland, at least ten to twelve millions of gallons must be illegally introduced into consumption into the former country, of the duties of which the revenue is annually defrauded. This is the necessary consequence of the duty in England being somewhere about four hundred per cent. on the value of barley, when manufactured into spirits within the United Kingdom. There is no good reason why the duties charged in Scotland and in Ireland should be lower than they are in England, for we do not find that the ladies and gentlemen in the Seven Dials, or in Lambeth, are restricted in the amount of their spirit consumption by this extravagant duty. On the contrary, we have undoubted grounds for believing, that the high duty very materially increases the consumption of ardent spirits, of the most pernicious quality too, with which the people are supplied by the illicit trader. To reduce the home-made spirit duty in England to within proper limits, only pure spirits would in future be consumed, and that too in moderation; the health of the people would be improved, and a squalid teetotaller would no longer be seen in the land. Temperance would then be firmly established, and a moderate use of the gifts of Providence would be enjoyed by the inhabitants generally of the United Kingdom. The distillers would use at least half a million of quarters of grain in addition to the quantity they now distil, and the nation would thus reap many signal advantages at the sole expense of the nefarious smuggler of spurious French, or rather Spanish brandies, and of Dutch gin—at the cost of those characters, in short, who are, under the existing system, defrauding the revenue of millions of pounds sterling annually, and who are destroying the property of all the fair and honourable spirit dealers in England. If, however, the excise regulations for the distillery trade be prejudicial to the interests of our barley farmers, those which are applied to the malting trade are more than doubly so; for they not only confine the consumption of malt much under its natural limits, but they likewise are the cause of the very material adulteration in beer which is hourly occurring in the retail trade, but which is so very seldom detected by the officers of her Majesty's excise. The quantity of barley converted into malt is, under the existing system of excise regulations, annually now becoming less and less; of which fact the adulteration of the beer consumed by the great majority of the people is one of the principal causes. It is utterly impossible for the beer retail trade generally to pay their expenses, and to retain the capital which they embark in their licensed houses, at the present retail prices of beer; and adulteration consequently becomes, with a great number of them, not so much a subject for blame as a matter of necessity. When we say that at least one quarter of the beer now in use is spurious, we are not beyond bounds; for the common practice now is, by a mixture of coarse sugar, salt, and several articles of a deleterious quality, to convert two barrels, when received from the brewery, into three barrels to be afterwards sold to the consumers. But even after this adulteration, the value of beer is still much higher in proportion than the wages of labour are amongst millions of the lower classes, and consequently they cannot use any beer under existing circumstances. By a reduction in the duties now levied on malt, government may in part immediately remove the evil, and within a few years afterwards entirely destroy it. To reduce the malt-duty to 1s. per bushel, and to charge this duty on the barley when sent into the malting houses for manufacture, and not on the malt itself, would eventually be one of the most important acts which any administration ever conferred on the British and Irish nations. It would in a few years cause the annual consumption of barley by the maltsters to be more than doubled; it would render adulteration unprofitable, because unnecessary; it would improve the rents of barley lands by from one to two millions sterling annually, because the additional quantity of barley which an alteration of this description would render necessary, would require somewhere about two millions of acres of land at present useless, because unproductive, to be changed into barley fields. The profits arising from the cultivation of this additional quantity of land would much more than pay for the expenses which would arise from the additional consumption of beer; and—a matter of vast importance in the present state of our finances—it would considerably increase the sum now paid annually into the Treasury by the malt-duty collections.

The oat trade has undergone very little alteration since our last publication. The value of this most important article of Irish agricultural produce has certainly not increased during the month of April ; and to have rendered its prices lower than they previously had been, would have been a labour not unattended by difficulty. At the present quotations, oats, like wheat, will not pay the expenses of their cultivation in any part of the United Kingdom; and thus, unless some material alteration eventually occur in the value of oats, further agricultural improvements in the sister island must cease to be attempted. At a time when the complaint in Ireland is *a superabundant population*, an act of the legislature by which this superabundance of population must still be rendered more abundant, by the transfer from them of the productive labour which for years they have been permitted to enjoy in producing oats for consumption in all the great markets in Great Britain, to the foreign cultivators of oats, is a policy far beyond the apprehension of common men, and can only have its origin in that frame of mind which the cupidity of inordinate wealth universally creates amongst reckless characters. The finest quality of foreign oats is generally from 4s. to 6s. per qr. dearer in all our markets of consumption, than is the average value of British oats ; and thus quality in future must go a great way in paying even our maximum import duty. Under the present scale of import duties, therefore, foreign oats, under all circumstances, most probably will interfere with those produced at home in all our markets, and the importers of them, from the opposite coast of Germany and Denmark, will have the advantage of the freights being materially lower than they can be either from Ireland or from Scotland. It will likewise encourage the increase of foreign shipping, and the employment of foreign seamen, at the expense of the British commercial navy ; and it is utterly impossible even to imagine any earthly benefit which we can gain from the transfer of the cultivation of Irish fields to those of foreign nations, and from paying foreign shipowners hereafter freight for the carriage of a considerable portion of our heretofore exclusive coasting trade; by which not only our shipowners must be seriously injured in their property, but thousands of our sailors will be driven out of that service which is the great nursery for manning the royal navy in times of jeopardy and of need. Besides this, however, many millions of acres of land are in a state of nature throughout the United Kingdom, and by the investment of money and the application of labour and science to them, the national wealth may be much increased by their successful cultivation. Without legal protection, however, to agricultural operations, so important as these would be, the tillage of these waste lands cannot be effected without pecuniary loss, and therefore this great advantage to the public wealth must—for the present, at all events —be sacrificed to the unsubstantial doctrines of reciprocity in commerce with all those nations who may be prevailed on to condescend so far as to enter into commercial treaties with the British Empire. The prosperity of our future agricultural operations, and that of the future productive employment of our industrial classes of all denominations, are thus placed at hazard, for shadows from which not one solitary benefit can ever be derived—excepting, perhaps, by about a dozen of cotton-lords, who may acquire princely fortunes at the expense of the multitude. In the meantime the spring grain, seed, pulse, and potatoes have been com-

mitted to the ground in most excellent order. The weather generally continues to be most favourable to vegetation, and therefore most probably, within another short year, it will be ascertained whether an abundant growth of agricultural produce in future be for the interest of the farmers, or be in any manner advantageous to the consumers in general.

CURRENCY PER IMP. MEASURE.

APRIL 24.

WHEAT, Essex and Kent, red	42	48	White 46 50 52	
Irish	40	42	Do. 40 44	
Old, red	—	—	Do. .... — —	
RYE, old	32	—	New.... 32 —	
BARLEY, Grinding 24 28 Malting	30	32	Chevalier 30 34	
Irish....................	21	23	Bere ..19 20 22	
MALT, Suffolk and Norfolk	56	58	Brown.. 50 54	
Kingston and Ware	56	60	Chevalier 60 —	
OATS, Yorksh. & Lincolnsh., feed 18 20 22 Potato.. 23 24
Youghall and Cork black	15	17	Cork, white 16 19	
Dublin	15	17	Westport 18 19	
Waterford, white 15	17	18	Black .. 15 17	
Newry 18	19	20		
Galway 14	15	16		
Scotch feed	21	—	Potato.. 21 24	
Clonmel 16	17	18	Limerick17 18 19	
Londonderry	18	19	Sligo 15 17 18	
BEANS, Tick, new..............	23	26	Old 30 32	
PEAS, Grey................	27	29	Maple.. 26 28	
White	30	31	Boilers . 30 32	
SEED, Rape.... —l. —l. Irish..—l. —l. per last.
Linseed, Baltic....40 46 Odessa 48
English Red Clover.... — — per cwt.
White .... —
Mustard, White 7 10 brown 8 11 per bush.
Tares, old .... 24 28 new 30 34 per qr.
FLOUR, Town-made 42 45 Suffolk 34 36 pr sk. of 280 lbs.
Stockton and Norfolk, 34 36

FOREIGN GRAIN AND FLOUR IN BOND.

WHEAT, Dantzic	— —	
Hamburg	32 34	} nominal.
Rostock	32 35	
BARLEY	20 —	
OATS, Brew..................	15 17	Feed ... 10 14
BEANS.....................14	15 19	
PEAS......................	20 22	
FLOUR, American, per brl......	22 24	Baltic .. — 22

IMPERIAL AVERAGES.

Week ending	Wheat.	Barley.	Oats.	Rye.	Beans.	Peas.
March 11th	48 1	27 7	17 2	28 4	26 6	29 4
18th	47 6	27 11	17 4	26 10	26 8	28 6
25th	47 2	28 4	17 7	29 3	26 3	28 11
April 1st	46 2	28 6	17 4	29 4	26 0	28 5
8th	45 5	28 8	17 2	29 3	26 2	26 11
15th	45 9	28 8	17 1	29 2	25 10	28 1
Aggregate average of the six weeks which regulates the duty	46 8	28 3	17 4	28 8	26 3	28 4
Duties payable in London till Wednesday next inclusive, and at the Outports till the arrival of the mail of that day from London ..	20 0	9 0	8 0	11 6	11 6	11 6
Do. on grain from British possessions out of Europe........	5 0	2 0	2 0	2 6	1 0	1 0

COMPARATIVE PRICES OF GRAIN.

WEEKLY AVERAGES by the Imp. Quarter, from the Gazette, of Friday last, April 21st, 1843.	AVERAGES from the corresponding Gazette in the last year, Friday, April 22nd, 1842.
s. d.	s. d.
WHEAT 45 9	WHEAT 50 7
BARLEY 28 8	BARLEY 27 7
OATS 17 1	OATS 19 3
RYE................ 29 2	RYE............... 32 11
BEANS............. 25 10	BEANS............. 30 0
PEAS 28 1	PEAS 31 2

PRICES OF SEEDS.

APRIL 24.

The operations in the seed market were on a strictly retail scale, and quotations of Cloverseed must now be regarded as quite nominal.

Clover ,English, red	42	60	white 44	62 per cwt.	
Flemish, pale'	44	48	fine.. 52	58	
New Hamburgh	none		do.. 42	64	nominal
Old do.	42	45	do.. none		
French	42	50	do.. none		
Linseed, English, sowing	55	65			
Baltic	—	—	crushing 42	48 per qr.	
Mediter. & Odessa	45	46			
Large, foreign	—	—			
Coriander	10	16	old.... 16	20 per cwt.	
Mustard, brown, new	9	11	white.. 9 10s 6d p.bush		
Trefoil, new	18	21	old.... 12	16	
Rapeseed, English new..	32l.	37l.	per ton.		
Linseed Cakes, English..	9l. 10s. to 10l. per 1000				
Do. Foreign..	5l. 10s. to 8l. per ton.				
Rapeseed Cakes	5l. 5s. to 5l. 10s.				
Hempseed, small	35	38	large.. 46	48 per qr.	
Rye Grass, English	30	42	Scotch 18	40	
Tares, winter	—	—	New 3s 0d 4s 0d p.bush.		
Canary, new	62	63	fine 64	65 per qr.	
Carraway, old	—	—	new 42	44	

WOOL MARKETS.

BRITISH.

LEEDS, April 21.—Sales of both combing and clothing have been rather more extensive this week, and prices are firm at late quotations.

WAKEFIELD, April 21.—We are unable to report any favourable change in the wool market ; the limited demand seems to be chiefly confined to fine combing sorts, such as half-breds and fine Northumberland wools, which are firm in prices at late quotations. Deep combing wools, although light in stock, are neglected, and prices are barely sustained.

LIVERPOOL, April 22.

SCOTCH.—We have no alteration to notice in our demand for laid Highland Wool ; the few transactions are entirely in a retail way for immediate want, at about our quotations. White Highland continues scarce, and not much inquired for. There is some enquiry for good cross, but as this class has all along been in fair request our stock is light. There continues to be a very limited business in Cheviot Wool of all kinds.

PRESENT PRICES:

	s.	d.	s.	d.
Laid Highland Wool, per 24lbs..	6	6 to	7	0
White do. do	8	9	9	9
Laid Crossed do..unwashed..	8	0	9	3
Do. washed do	8	6	10	6
Do. Cheviot unwashed do.	8	3	10	0
Do. washed	11	0	13	0
White do. do.	18	0	21	0

FOREIGN.—The attention of the trade is now almost entirely directed to the aproaching public sales to take place in London next week. There has in consequence been little doing this week in any kind.

FOREIGN.

CITY, April 24.—The imports of Wool into London during the past week were 885 bales ; 706 bales being from Sydney, 45 from Germany, 69 from Odessa, and 65 from Bombay.

The public sales of Wool commence next week, and it is therefore not to be wondered at that business, just now, should be so dull. It is hoped the death of the Duke of Sussex, by bringing on a general mourning, may not check the improvement in trade that every one looks forward to just at this season of the year.

POTATO MARKET.

SOUTHWARK WATERSIDE, April 24.

The arrivals of Potatoes to this market during the past week have been as follows ; viz., from Yorkshire

1295 tons, Scotland 475, Devonshire 220, Kent and Essex 165, Jersey and Guernsey 110, Wisbech 85.—total 2350 tons. Best samples of Reds continue in fair request at our last quotations. The mild weather and the green markets being abundantly supplied with vegetables, cause sales of all other sorts to be heavy.

PRESENT PRICES AS SUBJOINED:—

	Per ton.			Per ton.
	s. s.			s. s.
York Reds	60 to 70	Jersey and Guernsey		
Scotch do.	30 to 50	Blues	— to 50	
Devons, early	— to 50	Yorkshire Prince		
Ditto, late	— to 60	Regents	35 to 40	
Kent & Essex Whites	40 to 45	Ditto Shaws, for		
Kent Kidneys	— to 55	planting	— to 50	
Wisbeach do.	— to 55			

PRICES OF HOPS.

BOROUGH, MONDAY, April 24.

There is nothing doing in Hops, and prices therefore are nominally the same. The young bines are looking healthy, but the wind seems variable, and may check them.

	s.		s.	
Pockets, 1842, Wealds....	80	to	90 per cwt.	
... East Kent..	100	—	140	..
.. Sussex....	77	—	84	..
.. Farnham..	140	—	150	..
Pockets, 1841, Wealds, good	60	—	70	..
.. East Kent choice	70	—	84	..
Bags, 1841, do. ..	60	—	80	..
Pockets, Old olds, do.	30	—	50	..

PRICES OF MANURES.

Subjoined are the present prices of several sorts of manure :—

Hunt's Bone dust, 18s. per qr.
Hunt's Half-inch Bone. 16s. per qr.
Hunt's Artificial Guano, 8l. per ton.
Rape Dust, 7l. to 8l. per ton.
Rape Cake, 6l. 10s. to 7l. per ton.
Rags, 4l. to 4l. 10s. per ton.
Graves, 6l. 10s. per ton.
Gypsum, at the waterside, 32s. 6d. per ton ; landed and housed, 38s. to 42s. per ton, according to quantity.
Agricultural Salt, 34s. per ton.
Lance's Carbon, 12s. per qr.
Ditto Humus, 14s. per qr.
Soap Ashes, 10s. per ton.
Poittevin's Patent Disinfected Manure, 13s. 6d. per qr.
Poittevin's Highly Concentrated Manure, 30s. per qr.
Nitrate of Soda, 18s. to 18s. 6d. (duty paid) per cwt.
Nitrate Potash (saltpetre) 26s. 6d. per cwt.
Petre Salt, 4s. per cwt.
Willey Dust, 4l. 4s. per ton.
The Urate of the London Manure Company, 5l. per ton.
Chie-fou, 21s. per cwt.
Daniell's new Bristol Manure, 8s. per qr.
Hunt's new Fertilizer, 13s. 4d. per qr.
Grimwade's Preparation for Turnip Fly, 10s. 6d. per packet, sufficient for three acres.
Wolverhampton Compost (Alexander's), 12s. per qr., subject to carriage to London, or forwarded from Wolverhampton.
Guano, 10s. to 14s. per cwt., according to quantity.
Potter's Artificial Guano, 15s. per cwt.
Muriate of Ammonia, 24s. per cwt.
Muriate of Lime, 12s. per cwt.
Clarke's Compost, 3l. 12s. 6d. per hhd., sufficient for three acres.
Wright's Alkalies, 28s. and 42s. per cwt.
Soda Ash, 14s. to 16s.
Chloride Lime, 28s. per cwt.
Sulphuric Acid, 2½d. per lb.
Sulphur for Destroying Worm on Turnips, 16s. per cwt.
Sulphate Soda, 7s. 6d. per cwt.
The Liverpool Abattoir Company's Animalised Manuring Powder, 2l. 10s. per ton.

PRICES OF SHARES.

No. of Shares.	Div. per Ann.	IRON RAILWAYS.	Price per Share.
6,300	2l 10s p.c.	Birmingham & Derby ..100l sh pd	40½ a 39½
6,300	13s 4d	Do. Thirds, iss. 8⅓ dis. 33⅓l sh 25l pd	12½
		Do. Eights................1½l pd	
9,500	2l 10s	Do. and Gloucester ...100l sh pd	
10,000	12s 6d	Do. New, iss. 7½ dis. 25l sh 17½l pd	
15,000	4l per ct	Bristol and Exeter..100l sh 70l pd	
7,500	2l 10s	Cheltnm.&G. Westn. 100l sh 80l pd	30 a 2
3,000		Clarence...............100l sh pd	
64,000	2s 9d	Eastern Counties ....25l sh 23l pd	10⅜ a ½
		Ditto Scrip.......... 8l 6s 8d pd	12⅜ a ¼
	3s	Ditto New Registered............	12⅛ a 11¾
64,000		Ditto Debentures .. 8l 6s 8d sh pd	12
12,500	3½l per ct	Glasgow, Paisley, and Ayrshire 50l sh pd	
18,000	5l per ct	Edinburgh & Glasgow .. 50l sh pd	49¼ a ¾
18,000		Ditto New..........12½l sh 7½l pd	
16,000	7s 6d p.sh	Glasgow, Paisley, and Greenock, 27l sh 25l pd	
10,918	10l per ct	Grand Junction........100l sh pd	
11,000	5l per ct	Ditto Half Shares ......50l sh pd	
		Ditto Quarter Shares .. 25l sh pd	
10,000	2½l per ct	Great North of England 100l sh pd	
25,000	4l 5s p sh	Great Western .... 100l sh 65l pd	93¼ a 2
25,000	3l 5s p sh	Ditto New..............50l sh pd	67¾ a 8½
37,500	5s per sh	Ditto Fifths........ 20l sh 12l pd	17½ a ⅝
		Ditto Bonds....1849	
		Ditto Bonds 1850, Letter C	
8,000	1l per sh	Hull and Selby .... 50l sh pd	37½
2,100		Leeds and Selby........100l sh pd	
5,100		Liverpool & Manchester. 100l sh pd	
7,968		Ditto Half Shares......50l sh pd	
11,475		Ditto Quarter Shares ..25l sh pd	
36,000	1l 10s p sh	London and Brighton....50l sh pd	35⅛ a 5
		Ditto Loan Notes....... 10l sh pd	10⅜ a ½
48,000		London & Blackwall Av. 16l 13s 4d	5⅞ a ⅜
43,077	3s	London & Greenwich Av. 12l 15s 4d	
11,136	5l per ct	Preference or Privilege Av. 18l 17s 2d	17½
	5l per ct	Ditto Bonds (183,300)............	
25,000	10l p sh	London & Birmingham 100l sh pd	212 a 10
25,000	2l 10s	Ditto Quarter Shares....25l sh pd	
31,250	3l 4s	Ditto Thirds............ 32l sh pd	
	2l 14s	Ditto New.......... 32l sh 2l pd	37
		Ditto Bonds 1843	
46,200	3l 2s 6d p s	London & South West. Av. 41l 6s 10d	65¼ a ½
		Ditto Bonds 1842	
33,000	13s 4d p s	London & Croydon..Av. 15l 15s 9d	10⅞ a 11
13,000	3l 17s p sh	Manchester & Leeds 100l sh 70l pd	
13,000	1l 13s p sh	Ditto New Shares....50l sh 30l pd	35½ a ¾
	4s	Ditto Quarter Shares........2l pd	
30,000	1l	Manchester & Birming. 70l sh 40l pd	
		Ditto Extension......70l sh 7l pd	
10,000	3l	Midland Counties......100l sh pd	64½
10,000	15s	Do. ¼ Shares, iss. 10 dis. 25l sh 15l pd	
10,000		Ditto Fifths .... 20l sh 2l pd	
		Newcstl.&Darlingt.Junc. 25l sh 6l pd	10½
15,000	3l 5s	North Midland........ 100l sh pd	
15,000	1l 13s 4d	Do. ½ Shares, iss. 10 dis. 50l sh 40l pd	
22,500	1l 1s 8d	Ditto Thirds, iss. at 11l 13s 4d dis. 21l 13s 4d sh pd	
10,256	2l	Northern & Eastern 50l sh 45l pd	
3,136		Do. Scrip..iss. 5 dis. 50l sh 15l pd	
12,208		Do. ½ Shares...12l 10s sh 1l 5s pd	3⅛ a 3
		Paris and Lyons .... 20l sh 2l pd	2¾ a ⅝
72,000		Paris and Rouen ....20l sh 20l pd	27½ a ⅜
40,000		Rouen and Havre.... 20l sh 2l pd	3¾ a ⅝
7,000	5 per ct	Sheffield, Ashton-under-Lyne, and Manchester .... 100l sh 82½l pd	
1,000	1l 15s	Sheffield and Rotherham 25l sh pd	
1,500	15l perct	Stockton and Darlington 100l sh pd	
28,000		South Eastern and Dover 50l sh pd	25¼ a ½
28,000		Ditto New, iss. 25 dis. 25l sh 25l pd	25⅜ a ¾
6,700	10l perct	York & North Midland..50l sh pd	97½ a 7
6,700	10l perct	Ditto New Shares.... 25l sh 20l pd	40½

Shares.	Div.	MINES.	Price.
8,000		Albion Copper ...... 5l sh 3½l pd	
4,000		Alten .... 15l sh 13½l pd	
10,000		Anglo Mexican, iss. 5l p. 100l sh pd	
	1l	Ditto Subscription .... 25l pd	
8,000	1l	Blaenavon Iron & Coal .. 50l sh pd	
2,000		Bolanos .... 150l sh pd	
	3l per ct	Ditto Scrip	4⅜
10,000	17s 6d	Brazilian Imp. iss. 5l p. 35l sh 21l pd	7¼
6,000		Do. Mocaubas & Cocaes United 25l sh pd	
11,000		Do. St. John Del Rey ..20l sh 15l pd	5¾
20,000		British Iron ...... 100l sh 75l pd	
10,000		Cata Branca ....10l sh 6½l pd	
10,000	1l 10s	Candonga .... 20l sh 7½l pd	
		Do. Registered.......... 7½l pd	
12,000		Cobre Copper ....40l pd	
10,000	5l per ct	Comp. Copper Miners in England 100l sh 33l pd	
8,500	15s	Copiapo ....20l sh 13l pd	
10,000		Columbian iss. 5l pm... 55l sh pd	1
1,500		Ditto New ....11l sh pd	
4,000		English ....25l sh 14l pd	
20,000		General Mining ....20l sh pd	
10,000		Hibernian .... 50l sh 10½l pd	
15,000	6l per ct	Imp. Slate Company..10l sh 3l pd	
5,051		Mexican .... 60l sh 59l pd	
20,000	10l perct	Mining Comp. of Ireland 25l sh 7l pd	
11,500		Real del Monte, registered Av. 63l 10s 6d	
		Ditto Ditto unregistered	5⅜ a 4¾
		Ditto Loan Notes .... 150l pd	
10,000	1l	Rhymney Iron .... 50l sh pd	
	10l p sh	Santiago de Cuba .. 25l sh 10l pd	24
6,000		Tin Croft ....10l sh 7l pd	
30,000		United Mexican, iss. 2l p. 40l sh pd	2¼
		Ditto Scrip	
		Ditto New Scrip...........1½l pd	
		MISCELLANEOUS.	
10,000	1l 4s	Anglo Mexican Mint....10l sh pd	
10,000	1l 15s	Australian Agricult. 100l sh 30l pd	
5,473		Australian Trust Comp. 50l sh 35l pd	
8,600	1l	British Rock and Patent Salt 50l sh 35l pd	
6,000		British Ameri. Land 50l sh 25½l pd	
10,000	6l per ct	Canada .... 100l sh 32½l pd	41¼ a 2
10,000	5l per ct	Upper Canada Bonds...........	
	5l per ct	Ditto	
	4l per ct	City Bonds.....................	
1,800	1l 5s	Corn Exchange.... 50l sh 37½l pd	
5,000	5l per ct	General Rever. & Invest. 100l sh pd	
2,700	4l per ct	Equit. Reversionary 100l sh 65l pd	65
20,000	1l 8s and 2s 6d bs	Gen. Steam Navigat. 15l sh 14l pd	
	10l & bs.	Hudson's Bay Stock....100l sh pd	
	1l	London Commercial Sale Rooms Average 75l	
8,000	5l per ct	London Reversionary Int. 50l sh 17l pd	
15,000		Metp. Wood Paving Comp. iss. 1l pm 10l sh 3l pd	
		Mexican & South American 10l sh 7l pd	
20,000		New Brunswick (Land).... 75l pd	
		New Zealand ....25l pd	
		Ditto New .... 25l sh 12½l pd	
6,092	7l per ct	Peninsular & Orien Steam 50l sh pd	51¾
3,200		Ditto ... .50l sh 25l pd	25
15,000		Royal Mail Steam..100l sh 60l pd	
5,387	4½l per ct	Reversionary Int. Soc.. 100l sh pd	100
2,000	8l per ct	St. George's Steam Packet 100l sh pd	
8,000		Ditto ½ Shares........25l sh pd	
14,000	6l per ct	South Australian.... 25l sh 20l pd	
4,000		Thames Tunnel ....50l sh pd	
10,000	6s	Van Dieman's Land..100l sh 20l pd	

Printed by Joseph Rogerson, 24, Norfolk-street, Strand, London.

Three Fat Leicester Wethers.

Bred by Sept of Holme Pierpoint Notts, which obtain'd the first Prize and Gold Medal at the Smithfield Ct

London, Published by Joseph Rogerson, 24 Norfolk Street, Strand, June 1.1843.

THE FARMER'S MAGAZINE.

JUNE, 1843.

No. 6.—Vol. VII.]   [Second Series.

The plate represents Three Fat Leicester Wethers, the property of William Sandy, Esq., of Holme Pierrepoint, Nottinghamshire, which obtained the first Prize and Gold Medal at the Smithfield Club Show, December, 1842.

ON SEED-SOWING.

BY HEWITT DAVIS, ESQ., COMMUNICATED BY C. W. JOHNSON, ESQ., F.R.S.

As in the following paper I shall propose to the cultivators of my country a very considerable reduction in the proportion of seed which they usually employ, it may be well to premise that this recommendation does not emanate from a mere theoretical agriculturist, farming only in his closet and over his books, or from one who follows agriculture merely as an amusing occupation ; but on the contrary, that I am largely engaged as a practical farmer of between seven and eight hundred acres of highly-rented land ; and, moreover, that whatever I am about to recommend, I have not only long and successfully practised, but that I have ever been willing, and am still farther ready to prove these assertions, by showing the crops I in this way produce. And I think that any practical farmer, who witnesses these will readily allow that by the adoption of the system of thin sowing I grow large crops on soils of a very inferior description.

The importance of the enquiry, even in a national point of view, no one will dispute who is made acquainted with the fact, that if my practice of seed saving were general, that the proportion saved would amount to much more than the annual average of the quantity of foreign corn imported into this country during the last fourteen years.*

There are few persons who seriously take into consideration how small a return is commonly realized from the seed sown, and how large a proportion of that return is again swallowed up for seed.

The following calculations, which have been carefully made, and are believed to be accurate, will give the importance to the question which it really merits.

The population of England, Scotland, and Wales, which at the end of the year 1831 amounted to 16,366,011 persons, had increased in 1841 to 18,666,761 persons. For the purpose of calculating, therefore, the consumption of corn during the fourteen years ending with 1841, I consider the population to have averaged 17,000,000 persons. During these fourteen years, the importation of foreign and colonial wheat and flour entered for consumption amounted to 15,875,907 quarters, averaging 1,133,000 quarters per annum.*

Taking the annual consumption of 17,000,000

* And it may be remarked, that this saving is in fact equal to half the rent of the land.

OLD SERIES.]

* The total quantities of wheat and flour *imported* were much more considerable. It was as follows :—

		Qrs.
1828	....	590,929
1829	....	1,725,781
1830	....	1,663,283
1831	....	2,309,970
1832	....	469,902
1833	....	297,565
1834	....	176,321
1835	....	66,905
1836	....	241,743
1837	....	559,942
1838	....	1,371,937
1839	....	2,875,605
1840	....	2,432,765
1841	....	2,783,602

Total.. 17,566,270

persons to be at the ordinary allowance of a quarter of wheat to each person, it will amount to 17,000,000 quarters, and deducting the quantity imported, 1,133,000 quarters, leaves the quantity annually consumed of our own growth 15,867,000 quarters.

Allowing that the average produce per acre of wheat is equal to 20 bushels, and that of these 20 bushels, 17½ bushels are appropriated for food, and 2½ bushels for seed, it follows that about 18,328,518 quarters must have been annually grown, and that to produce this quantity 7,331,407 acres must have been sown with wheat.

Now, to sow 7,331,407 acres at 2½ bushels of seed per acre, which is the ordinary allowance, there would be required 2,291,064 quarters. But to sow 7,351,407 acres at one bushel per acre—the quantity I apply—would require only 916,425 quarters; so that the annual saving of seed would be 1,374,639 quarters. And although I merely take the instance of wheat, I am at the same time proving what may be done with all other corn; for the saving in seed I practise is in equal proportions with other kinds of grain. Having thus proved the magnitude of the national saving capable of being made in seed-corn, and having shown that if my system of thin sowing was universally adopted, there would be no necessity, even with our present enlarged population, for the importation of any foreign corn, and that an actual saving to the farmers of arable land to the extent of half their rent may be made, I will now proceed to detail the course of my own practice.

The consideration of the extraordinary fact that, whilst a single grain of wheat, planted where it has room to tiller out, will produce four hundred-fold, and often much more, and yet that the farmers of England, on an average, only receive back about eight times the seed they sow, first led me to gradually reduce my proportion of seed wheat from three bushels per acre down to about three pecks, which reduction I have accomplished to the evident improvement of my growth of corn. And I have at this time (May, 1843) the finest promise of a crop from this latter quantity, and this, too, after one ploughing of pea and bean stubbles, and upon soils low in the scale of natural fertility, and without any manure having been for some years applied.*

Having, from this brief detail of my practice, shown the success of an extended system of thin sowing, the reader will readily, upon reflection, perceive the explanation of the advantages which I thus derive—why it is that three pecks of seed-wheat per acre must be much nearer the correct quantity than ten pecks.

It is evident that if one grain of wheat, when sown singly, produces four hundred grains, and that one bushel of wheat sown only yields eight bushels (that is, only eight for one, instead of four hundred for one), that ninety-eight grains of seed-wheat are by the ordinary method thrown away.

Again, the produce of an ear of thick-sown wheat yields about forty grains (I say thick-sown,

for thin-sown yields very much more), and therefore the produce of an acre (or twenty bushels the ordinary average) is in reality the growth of the ears from two pecks only (that, too, is allowing only *one* ear from each grain). This being the fact, of what use, I ask, or what becomes of the remaining eight pecks of seed which are commonly sown?

There are, in truth, many disadvantages attendant upon thick sowing. In the early stages of the young plants' growth, when the air and the soil are moist, and the plants small, each vegetating seed, no matter how much seed has been sown, finds sufficient space and food for its support. But as the plants increase in size, a struggle for nourishment commences, which increases in severity, and finally terminates by the destruction of the weaker by the stronger plants, but not until after a contest, which leaves the survivors stinted in their growth, and perhaps diseased.*

That this struggle must take place, is shown by my calculation of the number of straws that can rise into ear, compared with the grains sown. And that this struggle does take place, is very plainly betrayed by the yellow sickly colour of thick-sown corn in the spring, when all other vegetation puts on its greenest tints.

In the early stages, however, of its growth, the appearance of thick-sown corn is much superior to that of the thin-sown. For a *season* its progress is more rapid, the stems rise sooner, the ground appears covered much earlier. This state of things usually continues until about the end of April. But then a change comes over the field—its dark green tints, which shaded it in early spring, change to a yellow sickly colour, and its progress is sensibly arrested. In the meantime, the thin-sown retains its colour, feels the benign influences of spring, tillers out in all directions; and its progress towards harvest is uniformly vigorous, and superior to the thick-sown. It is stouter and more uniform in the height of its straws, and the size of its ears. It is more free from blight, and the weight of the crop is greater.

Nature herself betrays the evils of thick plantations of every description, in dwindling plants, and in the sickly appearance of the crops of all kinds, and the planter and the gardener is ever ready to take warning by the lessons she thus affords. The planter well knows the effect of an over-crowded plantation; the gardener by the full use of his hoe is careful to give ample room to each plant; it is only the farmer who, guided by his eye alone, is pleased in the early stages of his thick-sown crops to see his ground well covered with plants of young corn, without stopping to reason upon the power of the soil to bring them to maturity.†

---

* The soils of Mr. Davis' farms vary very considerably, including stiff clays, sands, poor gravels, and shallow loams resting upon chalk.—C. W. J.

* And when the struggle is over, the injury has not ceased, for instead of a vigorous and unimpaired plant, the vegetation of the survivors is languid and inferior even to the time of harvest.

† I shall be very happy to show any agriculturist, as I have already done to Sir Charles Burrell, Bart., J. A. Smith, Esq., and other eminent agriculturists, my farming, at the Oaks, at Shirley, near Croydon, or at the Selsdon Farm, the property of Mr. G. R. Smith, also near Croydon.

CULTIVATION OF CLOVER.

TO THE EDITOR OF THE FARMER'S MAGAZINE.

SIR,—Having read the Rev. Mr. Thorpe's able article in the last volume of the Royal Agricultural Society's Journal, upon the failure of the red clover, and thinking that the following statement may be of service, as tending to explain in some degree the causes of that failure, I send you a few observations which will go far towards substantiating Mr. Thorpe's opinion. I readily concur with him in thinking that the failure of the clover crop is caused in a great measure by the particles of the surface soil not sufficiently close and cohesive, which renders the plant liable not only to be injured by the frost, but equally as much by the intense heat in hot dry summers.

What I would wish to show is, that the extremes of heat and cold, in other words, *drought* and *frost*, together *with the absence of proper drainage*, are the principal causes of the failure of the clover crop; and that the best remedy against such a loss is to render the surface of the soil as close and cohesive as possible. And although I cannot enter into the minutiæ of the subject, as regards the chemical properties of soils, my observations will be the result of actual experience. Last spring the following fields, which had been sown with wheat, after having been fed off with sheep, were then sown with rye-grass and red clover, in the proportions of six gallons of the former and two gallons of the latter to the acre.

No. 1. Light, sandy soil, greater part dry; the seeds were harrowed and cross-harrowed in, and rolled several times over with two-horse rolls, then rolled over twice with a heavy four-horse stone roll. Remarks.—The clover has stood the winter, is well set, and now looks promising.

No. 2. Light, loamy soil, well drained, but very wet in wet weather; the seeds were harrowed and cross-harrowed in, and rolled several times with two-horse rolls. Remarks —The seeds came up very evenly, but in consequence of the extreme heat last summer, the ground became full of fissures, and at harvest time they all disappeared, with the exception of some on the headlands and the lower and cooler part of the field.

No. 3. Lower part loamy, upper part stiff with sandy subsoil, thoroughly drained, lower part inclined to be wet; the seeds were harrowed and cross-harrowed in, and rolled several times with two-horse rolls. Remarks.—The clover came up very evenly, and looked remarkably healthy. Early in the winter the clover on the lower and loamy part of the field was killed by the frost, but on the remainder of the field has stood well up to the present time, and is still flourishing.

No. 4. Partly loamy, partly stiff clayey, partly sandy soil, sown on winter oats after they had been fed off with sheep; the field is well drained; the seeds were harrowed and cross-harrowed in, and then rolled. The clover came up very weakly, and when the oats were cut, it was all burnt up by the intense heat, with the exception of that on the headlands.

No. 5. Stiff with sandy subsoil, a part of the field drained, the other part very wet; the seeds were lightly rolled, and harrowed in. The clover came up tolerably well, but the field being foul and poor, the plant did not appear strong or healthy. The white frosts in the autumn soon destroyed the clover on the wet part of the field, and on the other part the clover is slight and weakly. The seeds were sown on spring oats.

The heat and extreme dryness of last summer, and almost total absence of rain for many months, had a most injurious effect upon the young clover plant. In Nos. 2 and 4 the ground became full of great fissures, and the clover as soon as it appeared was nearly all scorched up, and after the corn was cut, the little that was then to be seen, having nothing to shade it, entirely disappeared, with the exception of that on the headlands.

In No. 3 one reason of the clover flourishing was, in addition to the field having been well rolled, that the wheat immediately after the seeds were sown grew most luxuriantly, and soon afforded excellent shade and protection to the young plant; and although on the lower portion of the field the clover came up equally as well, and had the same shade, yet the ground lying in a low situation, near a stream, where the frost has most power, it was destroyed by the white frosts in October.

In No. 5, so plain was the line of demarcation between the portions where the clover was living, and where there was none, that a stranger would have thought only a portion of the field had been sown; the total destruction on the one portion can only be attributed to the white frosts and the winter frosts having a most powerful effect upon the wet subsoil.

In No. 1 the clover, as I have said before, came up evenly all over the field, and up to the present moment has continued to promise well. The field is poor, and the soil light and dry; and I can only attribute the present appearance of the clover to the four-horse roll I used, a very heavy one. The field after being rolled appeared like a well trod foot path, and I firmly believe that the surface soil being made so close and cohesive, became a formidable barrier to the drought.

It is worthy of observation that turnips invariably appear first on the headlands of the field, where the surface is most trodden by the horses. It is my usual custom after sowing my turnips to carry some lime into the field, and lay it in several lumps in readiness for spreading on the turnips when they appear; and I have noticed the turnips always show themselves first in the ruts made by the waggons carrying in the lime, which closes the soil, and prevents the attacks of grub and other enemies.

I mention this as I think that turnips, as well as clover, equally require a closely compressed surface soil, drought being a most destructive enemy to both. The turnip and clover plants always appear early in the foot-prints of the horses, or in any part where the ground has been most trodden and closened; and if the clover should in the course of the winter be nearly destroyed, some may always be found on the headlands, the hedges being a great protection from the frost, and the soil being closened by the turning and returning of the horses. Enough has been adduced, I think, to show that frost and drought are alike most destructive to the clover plant; the frost doubly so, in proportion as the soil is wet, and although the ground may be well drained, yet, should it be situated in a cold, damp bottom near a stream, it will be often found to be slightly frozen, when on the higher ground you would not have known there had been the least frost.

I will now conclude with a few remarks upon the remedy for this failure. Believing that the clover plant requires a close surface soil, I would first observe that the seed should be sown upon wheat,

winter barley, or winter oats; the ground sown in
the autumn becomes during the winter firm and
close by the succession of frosts and rain, and is
still more closened in the spring by having sheep
upon it to feed off the wheat, &c.

I would next observe that great attention is necessary when sowing the seed. The following is my
usual method : after having fed off the wheat sufficiently close, and the ground is dry and in good
order, I dredge the field with some bushes in order
to level the nobs of earth and fill up the cracks in
the ground where the seed would be lost. I then
harrow it once or twice, as the state of the ground
requires, then sow the seed with a hand drill, cross
harrow it in, and finish by rolling down the field
either with a light or with a heavy roll. Very much
depends in what state the field is ; if dry, and the
surface hard, it requires more harrowing and rolling
to pulverise the soil. Rolling as a finishing operation ought never to be omitted. I always reap the
wheat in those fields where the clover is sown, as
I think the stubble, which I do not cut until the
spring, keeps off the frost in some measure.

Until the causes of the failure are satisfactorily
ascertained, I would by no means attempt to grow
clover on the same ground more than once in six or
seven years, because during the time it is a clover-
ley, the ground becomes full of wireworm and grub
of every description. The failure of the clover
being so general, and the cultivation of the plant
so important to the farmer, it behoves every one to
pay the greatest attention to the subject, and endeavour to find out every cause of such failure.

I remain, Sir, your obedient servant,

AN AGRICULTURIST.

Goudhurst, Kent, May 8, 1843.

ON MILDEW.

TO THE EDITOR OF THE FARMER'S MAGAZINE.

SIR,—In offering the following remarks to your
notice, it is not trusting in any ability of mine to set
forth any new discovery as to the nature of this destructive disease, but merely to state my opinion
and observations I have made for several years past;
and if you may think them worthy of occupying a
space in your valuable columns, I leave it in your
hands to act as you may think proper.

It is very extraordinary that this disease, the
causes of which have occupied the time of many
learned and scientific men, though their researches
have been made on the best of principles, yet nothing
definite or positive has accrued from such. The
only thing which seemed to set at rest the nature,
cause, and properties of mildew, was an incident
noticed by Sir Joseph Banks, which was the mildew shedding its seed ; and from that it was generally received as an opinion that mildew was propagated by that means; and by the many able
commentators on the subject since, all quote the
above to support their own ideas respecting the
disease. It would, therefore, be too presumptuous
on my part to disannul and do away with this
opinion, supported as it is by so many able and
more experienced persons than myself; but as
it is the duty of every man to exert himself for the
welfare of his country, and as a learned author
said, make the world a little better for their living

in it, to accomplish which object discussions of
all sorts must be entered into to arrive at perfection, and point out the causes of different phenomena of nature; and in my opinion nothing deserves more the notice and observation of an
attentive observer of nature, who exerts himself
in the progress of agriculture, than an enquiry
into the nature and properties of mildew. It is a
disease which we find is more prevalent in one
season than another, consequently must be owing
to an atmospheric influence on vegetation ; to ascertain which it would be necessary, in the first
place, to find out the cause, and trace it through
its different stages, to arrive at a sound conclusion. I shall therefore, in the first place, state
what my opinion is as to the cause, and observations that I have made during my enquiry.

I never could find it congenial to my feelings to
receive and approve of the generally received opinion
that mildew was generated by seed ; and it was
in consequence of my ideas differing so widely
from that, that I endeavoured to search out and
find, if possible, what was the true cause. I consider it is entirely owing to the different variations
of the atmosphere, either from a succession of
heat to cold, or contrarywise. It generally attacks
the plant in the very height of its vegetation,
which is the period when vegetation is more susceptible to the variable changes of the atmosphere
than at other times. Dry gloomy weather at that
time will cause it ; and if a hot sun should succeed
such dry, hazy weather, the corn will be
mildewed in a few days—or rather, rusted,
for mildew seems to be a very inappropriate name for it. It is the same disease
that the Romans called "Ventrigo Red,". owing to
the colour it assumed when in an advanced state.

The rust does not adhere strongly to the blades
of the crop, as a shower will wash a great part off ;
and if a plentiful rain was to follow, the rust disappears and the corn suffers little damage, provided
the weather continues such as to prevent the propagation of it. In clear hot summers we suffer
very little from it ; but when the weather is unsettled, a dry hot atmosphere, succeeded by a
dull, gloomy, hazy one, generally generates mildew ; and as I have sometimes noticed the rust to
be of such a plentiful quantity as to cover the
ground around, I have cut off blades affected by it,
and fresh ones have shot forth and continued free,
owing to the sap having an healthful flow through
that organ. I have also tried to inoculate healthy
ears with that affected by mildew when the rust
has been in an advanced state, and the seeds as
it were flying off, but not with success in any one
instance, having introduced the seeds into the
straw, and profusely dusted the ears with it.
Having now shewn that the cause of mildew is
owing to the state of the atmosphere, I must proceed to point out what would be the effect of such
an influence on vegetation, and how it would
cause the disease to appear. The action of either
the above-mentioned atmospheric influences on the
corn and vegetation generally would be, first to
stop its vegetating powers, consequently throw the
plant into an unhealthy state ; and secondly,
causing the vessels containing the sap to stop
flowing, which, as the plant is in the height of its
vegetation, would be a serious consequence, as it
must cause the escape of the sap by a part which
nature in its healthy state had not intended ; it
would, therefore, stop its usual channel, and cause
the extravasation of its juices from the excretory

vessels of leaves, and stop there in a consistence of what is termed mildew, as it rises in forms of different dimensions, according to the size of the organ from which it proceeds.

When first produced, it is of a whitish colour on corn, but in a few days it turns brown or rusty, and flies off, and is wafted away by the winds—which incident, as I before noticed, was observed by Sir Joseph Banks, and in his opinion was the seeds flying off. I cannot see at present the use of entertaining the slightest idea that such is the case; for those seeds or rust are generated from the extravasation of the juices of plants, not the extravasation from the rust, which must be the case if generated by seed. I therefore consider further, allowing the truth of the extravasation of the nutritive juices of plants, that honey-dew, as it is called, and all other unctious substances found on gramineous plants, are caused by the same atmospheric influence—but of course of different colours, according to the plants from which it proceeds, and the quality and nature of the different substances which they contain—sometimes of an impalpable powder, others of a thick consistence, which is red on garden beans, rusty colour on all kinds of corn, greenish on plumb-tree, yellowish on ash, white on larch, fir, and turnips, and of a honey-like appearance on hops and oak trees.

It is a very serious thing when the mildew attacks the corn when coming into ear, as every corn then affected will be destroyed. At that time the hopes of a farmer are placed on a very critical, uncertain point, as much depends on the weather—whether it is such as to keep the flow of sap in continual motion, and not generate more nor less, but just sufficient to serve all the requiring vessels and keep the plant in a healthy productive state. Turnips are more especially liable to be affected with the mildew in this part of the country—at least, more so than in the northern counties, which allows them to sow much earlier than we can, for with us they are sure to be mildewed if sown before June, and often after that time When I find a piece becoming mildewed, I immediately run the horse and hand-hoe over them, whether there are weeds or not, in order to keep the ground continually moved, and I have often found this answer the required purpose; if not the first time it may the second or third, for I keep it moved at least once a week when attacked by this disease, and I have always experienced the benefit; so that I think one of the best preventives for this destructive disease—as prevention is better than cure—is to keep the ground constantly moved, in order to give the plant the benefit of all the atmospheric and chemical changes caused by a continual absorption of carbonic acid. But if propagated by seeds, why should it stop its ravages, or where are the first seeds to come from? for I have often observed a piece completely covered with it within a few days, and if carefully observed through a microscope, it will appear as the juice or sap of the plant oozing from the excretory organs of the plant, which I think is much more probable than that of its being a growing plant; for persons acquainted with vegetable physiology are well aware of there being all sizes of pores in a leaf or stalk of vegetables, which will account for the different sizes of the consistory substance. Sometimes only patches are affected, the rest of the field free; which spots, if examined, will be found to be of a different nature to the surrounding soil—probably wetter, which, with a hot glaring sun, will cause

it in those spots: this is what may he called a partial mildew.

But a more general mildew is when the whole atmosphere is brought into action. As I have stated before, a hot glaring sun succeeding close, sultry, gloomy weather—when there is no dew—causes it to generate more in the morning than any other part of the day; because at day-break in such weather the atmosphere undergoes a greater change than at another time.

Talavera wheat I have noticed, especially if sown on a cold wet soil, is sooner attacked by the mildew than another sort, owing to its tender nature, and sooner acted upon by the continued variation of an English atmosphere. I have seen it growing in the same field with hedge wheat when it has been very much mildewed, and the other not at all.

But fearful I am trespassing on your valuable time, having gone to much greater lengths than I intended, I must conclude with every sincere wish for the progress of the science of agriculture, and with thanks to you for your kind forbearance in accepting this scribble from

Yours truly,

A HAMPSHIRE FARMER.

ON FEEDING HORSES.

TO THE EDITOR OF THE FARMER'S MAGAZINE.

SIR,—I have been keeper of one horse for several years; my plan of feeding used to be as follows: 60lbs. of crushed oats, 40lbs. of split beans, 20lbs. bran, and 2 cwt. of hay, given whole, per week; but in consequence of being informed by some of my friends that cut hay was better for the horse, and went further, I was resolved to try it cut. So accordingly I bought a machine for the purpose of cutting it, from Mr. Vickers, Manchester, who I was told was the best maker of these machines hereabouts. The first week I gave the cut hay to the horse he did not seem to like it, but on the second week he appeared to relish it very well (I mention this that parties who may wish to try the same plan may not be disheartened if the horse should not take to cut hay all at once); and at the month's end I found I had three trusses, or one and a half cwt. hay left. I now thought there must be some mistake about it, for the quantity saved appeared to me to be too much; but, however, I was determined to try the plan fairly, so I told my man to buy the same quantity of hay as he formerly did when it was not cut, and to lay on one side all that was not eaten, which was done; and at the second month's end I found I had six trusses left, that is, three for each month. I tried the same plan for another month, and at the end of the third month I found I had nine trusses and about half a truss of hay left, which at that time cost 2s. 6d. per truss exactly, so that the saving effected in three months for one horse was 1l. 2s. 6d. It is now two years and one week since I adopted this plan, and I calculate that I have saved 4l., besides the value of the machine, which cost me 5l. 5s., and which to all appearance will last my life out, as there is no sign of it being in the least impaired, except the knives being a little worn. Now if I save 22s. 6d. per month in the keep of one horse alone, is it not clear that all farmers, &c., that keep more horses must be considerable savers by cutting their hay? Since I commenced doing so I have persuaded several of my friends to do so, and they have found the same result as I have. It is a pity this plan is not more extensively known and acted upon, for the saving effected is great.

I was not aware until last week that there was such a publication as your magazine, or I would have sent you the result of my experiment sooner. Hoping you will excuse my trespassing so long on your time and space,

I am, sir, your obedient servant,
  Manchester,   G. JONES.
May 10*th,* 1843.

P.S. I ought to have said that I put a rack full of uncut hay for the horse to pull at in the night.

AGRICULTURAL EXPERIMENTS.

"These experiments, it is true, are not easy; still they are in the power of every thinking husbandman. He who accomplishes but one, of however limited application, and takes care to report it faithfully, advances the science and consequently the practice of agriculture, and acquires thereby a right to the gratitude of his fellows, and of those who come after. To make many such is beyond the power of most individuals, and cannot be expected. The first care of all societies formed for the improvement of our science, should be to prepare the forms of such experiments, and to distribute the execution of these among their members."—*Von Thaër.*

Such is the opinion of one who holds the first rank as a writer on agricultural science, and whose intimate acquaintance both with its theory and practice entitles his opinion to the greatest weight. There are, we doubt not, many of the readers of the *Magazine,* who would be willing to institute a few experiments for the purpose of testing the correctness of the principles which scientific men are now attempting to lay down for the guidance of the practical farmer. Under this impression, the writer of this takes the liberty of calling their attention at this season to some artificial manures which might be tried for turnips and potatoes.

Experiments with various saline and other substances have been made during the last two seasons in the south of Scotland — chiefly at the suggestion of Professor Johnston, of Durham; and the results obtained in many cases are extremely interesting and important, both in a theoretical and practical point of view. These substances, however, have for the most part been applied *singly,* or at least not in such a state of combination as to suit the particular crop for the production of which they were used. But when it is considered that a variety of elements enter into the composition of all our cultivated plants, and that in our common farm-yard manure, which is known to be serviceable for promoting the growth of any of them, a variety of these same elements is also found, it is evident that a combination of several substances, in suitable proportions for the kind of crop to which they are to be applied, is more likely to prove beneficial as a manure than any one of them employed singly. And for our guidance here we feel the need of correct *analyses* of our cultivated plants. Sprengel is at present our chief authority on this subject; and though it is generally allowed that the accuracy of his analyses is not always to be entirely depended upon, yet they are of great value, and give us an indication sufficiently correct for our present purpose. The following is his analysis of turnips :—

The ashes of 10,000lbs. of the bulbs consisted of—avoiding decimals—

	lbs.
Potash	24
Soda...........................	$10\frac{1}{2}$
Lime..........................	$7\frac{1}{2}$
Magnesia......................	$2\frac{1}{4}$
Sulphuric acid................	8
Phosphoric acid................	4
Chlorine	2

with silica, and some alumina and oxide of iron. The same weight of leaves contain all the above substances in much greater quantity.

Looking to the above analysis, we would recommend a manure composed of the following ingredients for turnips :—

	£	s.	d.
200lbs. (about 4 bushels) bones reduced to powder, and then dissolved in half their weight of sulphuric acid (oil of vitriol)	0	18	0
112lbs. sulphate of soda, in the dry state	0	6	0
56lbs. (1 bushel) common salt	0	1	3
56lbs. sulphate of magnesia (Epsom salts)	0	4	0
56lbs. sulphate of ammonia (in pure crystals)...........................	0	8	6
Quantity for one acre—expense....	1	17	9

Potash is omitted in the above, and for two reasons—we have as yet no means of obtaining it at a cheap rate, and it is probable that it is contained in considerable abundance in many of the soils in this island. 35lbs. of pearlash (the quantity necessary to afford 24lbs. of potash for the turnip bulbs) may, however, be added by those who are willing to be at the expense of doing so. Our soils, however, seem to be very generally deficient in phosphoric acid, and a greater quantity of it is therefore given above than would be necessary for both the roots and leaves of a crop of 25 tons (bulbs) of turnips per acre. Sulphuric acid and chlorine are also given in ample quantity. The quantity of magnesia is greatly reduced. 200 or 300lbs. of lime may also be added, if the soil is not known to contain it in considerable abundance. If the bones be not digested in acid, seven bushels will be necessary. It would be interesting to obtain comparative results from an application of the above mixture, with and without the sulphate of ammonia, which affords nitrogen—an element which Liebig affirms that plants may obtain, in considerable quantity, from ammonia contained in the atmosphere.

Suppose the experiment to be tried on one-eighth of an imperial acre, and suppose the drills to be 27 inches in width (the usual size in this part of the country), then one-eighth of the above quantities would have to be put into 806 lineal yards of drill.

For potatoes the following can be recommended with the greatest confidence, as being likely to give such an increase of produce as to afford a profitable return for the money expended in purchasing the manure :—

	Cwt.
A mixture of sulphate of soda, dry ..	1
With sulphate of ammonia, pure	$\frac{1}{2}$
for one acre.	

Or,

A mixture of sulphate of magnesia ..	1
With sulphate of ammonia........	$\frac{1}{2}$
for ditto.	

These manures have already been tried for potatoes, and in every instance with the most marked success.

I would suggest an application of the following mixture as likely to be still more efficacious as a manure for potatoes than either of the above, viz.:—

	Cwt.
Sulphate of soda, dry	½
Sulphate of magnesia	¼
Sulphate of ammonia	¼

Potato tubers contain both soda and magnesia —the former in great quantity; and the tops of the plant contain a large quantity of magnesia with very little soda. Potatoes require also phosphoric acid and lime, and the quality of the roots is likely to be improved by giving a small quantity of bones, along with other manure, at the time of planting. It is perhaps necessary to observe, that, if crystallized sulphate of soda (Glauber salts) be used, double the above quantities will be necessary, as in that state it contains upwards of half its weight of water.

The potatoes having been planted in the common way with a moderate quantity of dung, the above mixtures may be applied with the hand as a top-dressing when the plants are about two inches above ground.

Suppose the experiment to be made on one-fourth of an acre, and the drills to be thirty inches wide, then one-fourth of the above quantities would have to be put over 1,452 lineal yards of drill.

If any person would take the trouble of making comparative experiments on the same field with two of the above mixtures, or with all the three, and reporting the results with exact attention to extent of ground and weight of produce, he would confer a benefit on the agricultural community. To give such experiments their full value, it is necessary that the weight of produce should always be compared with that obtained from an equal extent of the same field unmanured, or manured with a known quantity of common dung.

AGRESTIS.

Ythanside, Aberdeenshire, May, 1843.

ON THE BENEFICIAL EFFECTS OF AMMONIACAL WATER COMPARED WITH OTHER SUBSTANCES, AS A TOP-DRESSING FOR GRASS-LANDS.

BY MR. THOMAS BISHOP,

Land-Steward to Robert Smythe, Esq., of Methven Castle, Perthshire.

(From the Quarterly Journal of Agriculture.)

It having been represented to Mr. Smythe that saltpetre is an excellent stimulant for the production of grass, he desired me to dress an acre of land therewith, and suggested the propriety of giving it a comparative trial along with other substances considered fertilizers. The field selected for the experiment had been three years under grass, the two last pastured with cattle; and consisted of a heavy damp loam, of an irregular surface, which had been *partially drained*, and sown out with a variety of grass and clover seeds.

	£	s.	d.
On the 12th of April a Scotch acre was measured off along one side of the field, and sown with 1 cwt. of the best nitre, which cost..............	1	16	0
A second acre adjoining thereto, with 1½ cwt. of nitrate of soda, at 25s. per cwt.	1	13	6
A third acre, with 5 cwt. rape-dust, at 7l. per ton	1	15	0
A fourth acre, watered with 105 gallons of ammoniacal water, at 4d. per gallon, diluted with five times the quantity of common water..........	1	15	0
And a half acre sown with ⅜ of a cwt. of nitrate of soda (or 74lb.) mixed with 21lb. of common salt	0	18	2

In proportioning the different ingredients experimented with as here stated, regard was had not to exceed in prime cost the expense of the saltpetre applied to the acre.

The apparatus used for distributing the ammoniacal water having become disordered before the dressing was completed, several spaces were left untouched with the liquid, which instantly became apparent from the lighter green tinge that the sward had acquired, where the allotted quantity had been given. To rectify this appearance, two labourers were sent the following morning with watering-pans and about five gallons of the undiluted liquid to make good the deficiencies; but instead of adding thereto five times the quantity of water, they only gave four, and by mid-day the spaces watered with this strength of liquid had all become brown and scorched as with fire.

The acre of ground dressed with the nitrate of soda was the first that shewed its stimulating powers, by the dark green sward which it had acquired in eight days.

The ammoniacal water was the next, and was equally vigorous in twelve days, and soon surpassed all the other dressings for the season, the scorched parts gradually narrowing with borders of luxuriant herbage. The sward, dressed with rape-dust, was the latest that exhibited any benefit from its application, but improved greatly as the season advanced; and from the extra quantity that had been dropped around the bag at the time of sowing it, gave evidence that the proper quantity had not been applied, to shew fully its fertilizing effects, as the produce on this spot was not surpassed by any of the other dressings.

Although the remainder of the field was not in good condition to yield a crop of hay, it was thought expedient, for the sake of testing the experiment, to take hay from the whole field, and afterwards top-dress the hay-stubble on that part of the field which had not been operated upon; and on the 26th of July the crop was cut across both the dressed and undressed parts of the field. The produce in grass from 31 square yards, carefully measured on a crossing line and weighed, was from the acres dressed with nitre, nitrate of soda, and rape-dust, nearly the same, averaging from 98½ to 100lb. The space dressed with nitrate of soda and salt 82lb., and the undressed 55lb.; whilst the produce from the dressing with ammoniacal water weighed 126lb. The produce in hay made from the different parcels of grass, carefully kept separate and weighed on the 2nd of August, in good condition, was similar in proportion. After the dressing with nitre, nitrate of soda, and rape-dust, giving 31, 32, and 30lb., being on the average one pound weight of hay from the square yard; that after the mixture of soda and salt somewhat less, and that from the undressed land only one-half pound; whilst that dressed with ammoniacal water weighed 46lb., or a pound and a half per square yard, equal to 326 stone of hay per imperial, or 410 stones of 22lb. each per Scotch acre. The apparent anomaly of the grass watered with ammonia having lost less weight in being converted into hay than the others did, can only be accounted for by the singular effect that the ammoniacal water had in stimulating the growth of Timothy-grass (*Phleum pratense*) beyond that of any of the other dressings; and it is a peculiarity of this grass to part with fewer of its inherent juices in drying than the greater number of cultivated grasses do, from being furnished with additional joints or valves on the flower-stems. Is not this observation of the effects of ammonia on the roots of Timothy-grass somewhat corroborative of M. Liebig's assertion, that "certain substances are found to exercise a peculiar influence on the development of particular families." (Vide *Art of Culture*). Nor is this the only instance that came under my notice, when examining the effects of the different dressings, particularly in the case where the mixture of salt and nitrate of soda was applied, an excess of hard fescue (*Festuca duriuscula*) became predominant, perfecting more seeds, and raising the flower-stems to a greater height.

After removing the hay crop, the remainder of the field was begun to be top-dressed on the 12th of August with the following substances: and for a farther trial of the effects of gas-ammonia on after grass, I had a present of 110 gallons from the manager of Perth Gas Works, which I reduced with the same quantity of common water as before stated, and applied to another or fifth acre; a sixth acre was dressed with

	£	s.	d.
12 bolls lime-shells, slackened with bog-earth, at 3s. per boll	1	16	0
A seventh, with 12 bushels bone-dust (slightly fermented), at 3s...........	1	16	0
The eighth acre, with cocoa-nut dust, 6 cwt., at 6s........................	1	16	0
The ninth, with 15 cwt. animalized carbon, at 2s. 8d.	2	0	0
And the tenth acre, with 30 bushels bone-refuse or sweepings, at 1s.	1	10	0

In this second experiment with other substances the ammoniacal water shewed a decided superiority, being not only the first to exhibit its stimulating effects, but in keeping up a continuous growth whilst the season permitted; nor did any of the other dressings previously given in the month of April shew an equal luxuriance in the growth of after-grass.

The acre dressed with cocoa-dust was the next that shewed its fertilizing influence, and the two acres with animalized carbon and the refuse of bones the latest. But as this last series of experiments was followed with a long succession of very rainy weather, which greatly impeded the looked for effect of the different dressings, it would only be waste of time to particularize other appearances, farther than to say, that where the ground was perfectly dry, they all seemed to be beneficial, whilst in places saturated with moisture there has been no improvement; and this is a consequence that may, in all cases, be expected as to the effect of manures, where the land has not a complete drainage.

I am aware that some agriculturists and florists in this neighbourhood have suffered loss in the application of ammoniacal water for different purposes, not knowing the proper strength at which it might be profitably used. It is produced at three different strengths in the manufacturing of gas, which could be tested by instruments; but, for the purpose of top-dressing grass-lands, a very safe criterion can be had, by reducing the strength of a small quantity of the liquid by equal portions of water, until its effect, by trial on grass-sward, does not discolour the narrower leaves of grasses, farther than a tinge of lighter green, although it should blacken the broader leaves of ranunculuses, daisies, and others.

BURTON-upon-TRENT FARMERS' CLUB.

At the usual monthly meeting on Thursday, the 13th of April, "The best method of consuming the Straw of the Farm" was the subject of discussion. The proposer, Mr. W. Greaves, read the following paper, which, as the club unanimously appeared of his opinions, elicited but little debate:—

The subject which I am engaged to present to your notice is one which is of great importance to the practical farmer, for no other circumstance perhaps has so much influence on his profits as a judicious mode of consuming the straw of the farm. The straw contains the material of the dung heap; it has value also as fodder. The proportion which he uses for litter or for fodder determines the character of his farming. If he consume it all as litter he is said to farm high; if he use the greater part as fodder he is said to farm low. The opinions of practical men are so various that no rule can be deduced from them. It is the practice of the Flemings to eat up nearly the whole of the straw with cattle; they do not reserve enough to make a dunghill, but collect the urine in tanks, and put it on the land in a liquid state. Many of our best agriculturists, on the contrary, collect an abundance of winter food, and disdaining the small portion of nutriment contained in the straw, convert it all into litter. Others collect no more winter food than is necessary to form with a portion of the straw a diet which will keep the cattle thriving and healthy, and use as much for fodder, and as little for litter as possible. Some, who have strong land farms and cannot conveniently raise root crops, or provide hay for winter food, tread down as much as possible of the straw with cattle fed on green food in the summer. But there is another class similarly circumstanced with the last, who are not careful to mix any other kind of food with the straw, but consume part of it with cattle littered down with the other part. This last is a kind of management which has no advocate among good practical agriculturists of the present day; yet it is a practice which we see frequently pursued. I think an enquiry into the value of straw as food and manure cannot fail to convince every reasonable man that this practice is in every way unprofitable. As to the other various ways of consuming the straw it perhaps depends more on the kind of farm, and consequently on the quantity of winter food which it is profitable to grow, than in the intrinsic value of the straw itself, which of the various methods it is best to pursue. All of them are perhaps equally profitable if they be properly adapted to the circumstances of the farm.

The food which is given to cattle produces no profit to the farmer unless they either grow in size, or lay on fat, or produce milk; and manure is of no value unless it repairs the fertility, of which the corn crops exhaust the soil. Before enquiring into the value of straw for either purpose of fodder or litter, it appears to me necessary to consider generally the nature and uses of the different kinds of food for cattle, and also of the nature and uses of manure. The masterly reviews of the science of chemistry as applied to agriculture and to physiology, which have been lately given to the world by Professor Liebig, make this a comparatively easy task. He has collected and arranged the facts relating to nature of food, and the mode of its assimilation into the living body, and those also relating to the food of plants in such a manner as to give us a tolerably secure hold of the general principles which should be followed, and there are only needed accurate experiments to enable us to apply those principles to the practice of agriculture. It appears that in all kinds of vegetables are contained two different kinds of substances, which are destined and fitted to different purposes in the economy of the animal frame. One of the two kinds of substances resembles—is indeed identical in its chemical constitution with the substance of the animal body itself, and is therefore fitted to supply the materials of its growth. This kind of substance is found under the several forms of vegetable fibrine, albumen, caseine, gluten, &c. The chief difference between it and the other substances contained in vegetables is that it has nitrogen for one of its elements. The quantity of this kind of substance either in vegetables or in the animal frame, may be represented by the quantity of nitrogen which they contain. The other kinds of substance found in vegetables have no nitrogen in their composition, and therefore cannot be assimilated into the animal frame. They appear under the forms of starch, sugar, gum, &c., which differ not at all in the elements of which they consist, but only in the proportion which they contain of each. Their chief ingredient and basis is carbon. Though they cannot form any part of the body itself, except the fat, yet these substances have uses in the animal functions which are not less important. To support the heat of the body seems to be the chief end to which they are destined. But when animals are fed on vegetables which are rich in this kind of substance the excess of them is converted into fat. The facts which the farmer has to bear in mind are, that different kinds of food are required to produce flesh and fat. It is also important to remark that these substances which contain no nitrogen, after fulfilling their office in the animal body, are converted into a gaseous compound, called carbonic acid, and pass off in that form by the lungs, leaving few traces in the body or in the excrements which make the manure heap. The value of any vegetable as an article of food of course depends on the quantity of these nutritious matters which it may contain; and the particular use we should make of it depends in a great measure on the proportion which it contains of one or other of these two different classes of substance.

Besides the two classes of soluble and nutritious substances, vegetables are composed partly of another, which, from its being insoluble, was supposed to be indigestible,—namely, woody fibre. Later enquiries have, however, shown this part of vegetables to be digestible also; and as straw is for the most part made up of this, it is most important to ascertain its value as food. It is like starch and the other carbonaceous compounds, entirely destitute of nitrogen. It is probable that attention to the different composition of vegetable products, and the different uses each is fitted to fulfil in the animal economy, may lead to great improvements in the mode of feeding our cattle. For some uses in the animal body substances rich in nitrogen are required, and for others those compounds in which nitrogen is absent. A young calf which increases its flesh so greatly has furnished to it in the milk a compound containing much of the flesh-making element. A young beast of any age which is growing fast requires in its vegetable food a sufficient quantity of the same kind of compound. The cow which is giving milk must have the materials of the milk supplied in its food, in addition to those which go to supply the daily functions and the daily waste of the body; she must be fed on articles rich in nitrogen. Professor Liebig has shown it to be most probable that muscular force can only be exerted through a change in the substance of the tissue of the animal body. There is required nitrogenous food to supply the waste which the body undergoes from this cause, and hence working horses require such food as corn and hay. But feeding beasts exert no muscular force except that which is necessary to carry on the vital functions; they add nothing to the actual substance of the flesh; they, therefore, need much less of the nitrogenous compounds, and chiefly require an excess of rich carbonaceous food to supply the materials of the fat which forms their only increase. Hence a diet containing a large quantity of starch, sugar, gum, &c., in proportion to the albumen, gluten, casein, &c., is good for feeding beasts. If food containing much of the last substances is given them, part of it is wasted; just the converse of this holds in the case of young stock, milking beasts, and working horses.

We have next to enquire what it is which vegetables require in the soil for their growth, in order that we may find the value of any substance as a manure. The answer is, in the present state of the science of agriculture, not without some difficulty. Yet it seems certain that plants require in the soil substances containing the same elements as they themselves do—precisely in the same way as animals require food of a composition similar to their own bodies. Plants, therefore, as they are made up of the substances we have just now mentioned, together with a certain proportion of salts and earths, require some substances in the soil capable of furnishing them. But they do not require all the materials of their growth in the soil, and it is one of the great problems in the art of agriculture to discover what proportion is required in the soil, and what proportion is gathered from the air and from water. Neither is anything certain known of the form in which plants receive nourishment from the materials in the soil, though Professor Liebig has shown that it is most probable they receive the carbonaceous part in the form of carbonic acid, and the nitrogen in the form of ammonia. Vegetable and animal matters are resolved into these two kinds of compounds in the process of decay, and all our manures are composed of these, or of salines and earths similar to those which they contain. With regard to the proportion of the materials of the growth of plants which it is necessary to furnish in the soil, there is an abundance of facts which enable us to approximate to the truth. By ascertaining the proportion of the produce of the soil which may be removed without diminishing the fertility of the land, we arrive at a knowledge of the quantity of nourishment which is supplied to the plants from other sources. We know very well that if the whole produce is carried off, the land is quickly exhausted of its fertility; but that if the whole produce is left in the soil, as when crops are ploughed in, the fertility of the land is greatly augmented. Then we know that if the corn of the crop be taken away, and all else be returned to the land, yet the soil will lose in fertile power. But if the whole crop be consumed by cattle feeding on the ground, the land improves, though not in the same degree as when the crop is wholly ploughed into the ground. Further, in our climate, and on the average of good fair land, if one crop be consumed with cattle, and the whole of the manure of that and the straw of the succeeding corn crop be returned to the soil, the land will be maintained in a state of equable fertility.

Let us see then what is taken away, and what returned to the soil, in a corn crop carried off and a green crop consumed with cattle. Let us suppose wheat and grass—for the same reasoning will apply to all other corn and cattle crops. On an average wheat will yield a bushel of corn for each cwt. of straw; the corn will therefore be about half the weight of the straw, or a third part of the whole weight. From one-fifth to one-eighth part of the corn is composed of that kind of vegetable substance which contains nitrogen, and if we reckon a crop to produce thirty bushels per acre, there will be contained in it from twenty to thirty pounds of nitrogen. In the thirty cwt. of straw will be contained only about five pounds of nitrogen. Thus in a wheat crop from four-sixths to five-sixths of the nitrogen is carried away in the corn, while two-thirds of all the carbon is returned to the soil in the straw. The corn contains a small portion of phosphates, but all the other saline substances are returned in the straw. The same quality of land which yields thirty bushels of wheat will yield an amount of grass or clover equal to three tons of hay. Good hay is calculated to contain one and a half per cent. of nitrogen; the quantity in three tons would therefore be ninety pounds. If we reckon only one per cent., or if we reckon the produce of an acre something less than three tons in the course of the year, the quantity of nitrogen on an acre will amount at least to sixty pounds, which is double that contained in the corn crop. It is found that one half of the hay is digestible, and that one half the whole weight is returned in the excrements and urine of the cattle. But the important circumstance for us to observe is, that while the greater part of the carbon is breathed out in the form of carbonic acid, the substances containing nitrogen are found in the excrements and urine—all except a small portion which goes to increase the bulk of the animal body, or is yielded as milk. There will, therefore, be returned to the land in the manure of the cattle one half of the whole

carbon of the crop, chiefly in the form of woody fibre, the whole of the salts and earths, and all the nitrogen, except that which we get in the flesh of the animal or the milk. We can form an estimate of the quantity of nitrogen which is carried away by cattle, compared with that which is returned to the land. An ox at his full growth at three years old will weigh ten cwt., and during his growth he will have consumed at least the produce of four acres of pasture, or of other food in equal proportion. Now an animal of 10 cwt. contains in its whole carcase about thirty pounds of nitrogen, while four acres of pasture contain 240 pounds at least; and consequently a beast continuing to grow in size does not carry away more than one-eighth part of the whole nitrogen contained in his food. A beast of full size receives no addition to his frame, and does not take away any of the nitrogenous element of his food, for the fat which he lays on contains none. A milking beast carries off a much larger proportion. According to a recent analysis of Dr. Playfair, there is contained in cow's milk four per cent. of casein. If we reckon a cow's produce of milk to be 600 gallons in the year, it will contain as much nitrogen as twenty-seven cwt of hay; or for every twenty gallons of milk 100 pounds of hay would be required to supply the casein. Swedish turnips contain only one per cent. of azotized matter, and consequently it would take four cwt. to furnish the nitrogen of twenty gallons of milk.

There appears then to be little difference between a crop of corn carried off and a green crop consumed by cattle in regard to the quantity of carbon which they return. The woody fibre of the straw amounts to as much as that of the hay. The great difference consists in the greater portion of matter containing nitrogen which is returned when the crop is eaten by cattle. When, therefore, we would supply the waste of a corn crop by manure from the farm-yard, it is this kind of matter which is required to be added to the straw before it is capable of fertilizing the land; this can only be done by feeding the cattle which are to yield the manure on food which contains nitrogen. We see at once that if they be kept on straw alone the manure cannot contain the necessary quantity of nitrogen.

Except in the case of milking beasts it is seen that no considerable part of the nitrogenized substance in the food is taken from the manure. In the whole year a milking beast yields perhaps nearly one-third of it in her milk, and in the months she is in milk she yields nearly one-half. The growing beast takes away only one-eighth, and the feeding beast very much less. I cannot but think that this view of the matter points out a great error in the practice of some farmers. Green crops ploughed in, malt-dust, bran, &c., and other vegetable matters, rich in food for cattle, are frequently used as manure; but if they were consumed by feeding beasts, we should get the produce of fat they would yield to the cattle, and we should get in the manure of the cattle precisely, or at least very nearly, the same amount of nitrogen as the original substance contained.

It is very material to remark that, of the three ingredients of manure, the woody fibre which is to furnish carbonic acid, the nitrogenized substance which is to furnish ammonia, and the salines which are partly soluble and partly insoluble, all the carbon nearly, and the insoluble salines, and two-thirds of the nitrogen, is found in the dung of the cattle; while the remaining one-third of the nitrogen, and nearly the whole of the soluble salts, are found in the urine. This is the proportion which I find in a table in the appendix of Professor Liebig's last work, which he has taken from Boussingault. The urine of cattle is considerably richer in nitrogen than the dung, if we estimate the quantity contained in an equal weight of each; but the dung of a beast is much more in quantity than the urine. This circumstance, that of the total quantity of nitrogen being found in the dung, seems to be too much overlooked just now by writers in our journals; and consequently the comparative importance of the urine is too much magnified. The value of straw as manure depends greatly in its absorption of the urine of the cattle, and the richness of the urine in nitrogenous matter has consequently a great deal to do with the value of straw used for the purpose of litter.

I do not think that anything satisfactory can be gathered respecting the nutritive properties of straw from the experience of merely practical farmers. Its value depends of course on the quantity and nature of the digestible matter which it contains, and this can only be ascertained by well conducted experiments guided by science. There is a table published in one of the numbers of the Journal of the Royal Agricultural Society which shews the comparative value of the different articles of cattle food. It is compiled by M. Antoine from the experiments of the principal agriculturists of the continent. Hay is adopted as the standard, and the table shews how much of any other kind of food is equal to 100lbs. of it. According to this table:—

	lbs.	
Hay	100	is equal to
Wheat straw	374	
Rye do.	442	
Oat do.	195	
Peas do.	153	
Vetch do.	159	
Bean do.	140	
Buckwheat do.	140	
Wheat, pea, and oat chaff	167	
Rye and barley chaff	179	

In the same table 45 lbs. wheaten corn, 45 of beans, 32 French beans, 308 Swede turnips, 201 potatoes, 504 common turnips are reckoned equal to 100 lbs. hay. It will be evident at first sight that this table does not represent the quantity of digestible substance which each article of food contains, but only its feeding power. It is the different kind of nutritious substance they contain, and not the quantity, which seems to determine the value of each. We know, for instance, that a beast will support life on two cwt. of wheaten straw a week; now this quantity is only equal in the table to about 20 lb. French beans, or 150 lbs. of turnips; and neither of these would furnish the necessary quantity of carbon to support the animal's life. Sir H. Davy thought to discover the quantity of digestible and nutritious matter in vegetables by ascertaining the quantity of matter, soluble in water, which they contained, and according to his experiments the straw of white crops would only yield from four to seven per cent. of nutriment. But, according to Liebig, a cow breathes out from the lungs 70 oz. of carbon, in the form of carbonic acid, daily; and it would therefore require at least 10lbs. of any of the nutritious vegetable substances, sugar, starch, gum, gluten, &c., to furnish this quantity. A more certain method of ascer-

taining the quantity of digestible matter which any substance yields has been followed by other scientific men since Sir H. Davy. In a translation of Sprengel's work on "Animal Manures," in the 6th number of the Journal of the Royal Agricultural Society, the experiments of a German chemist, Bloch, are quoted. According to him 100 lbs. rye straw chopped, given to horses, yields only 42 lbs. of dried excrement; 100lbs. hay, only 45lbs.; 100 lbs. oats, only 51 lbs.; rye 53 lbs. Thus it seems that 60 lbs. of straw is in some way or other digested and assimilated out of 100 lbs. Cattle, it appears, digest rather less, and sheep rather more of any substance than the horse. Sir H. Davy supposed that woody fibre was altogether indigestible, but these experiments prove that it must necessarily be partly digested, and it has been lately explained how it is capable of becoming food. Dr. Daubeny in his lectures on agriculture says, "M. Payen seems to have established that under the name of woody fibre we have confounded at least two distinct substances, one forming the walls of the cells, another deposited on them." "He has succeeded in isolating the two by chemical means, and has found that while the cellular matter has exactly the same composition as starch," and contains 44 per cent. carbon, the incrusting matter or true woody fibre has 53 per cent. of carbon.

It appears that the more soluble kinds of food, such as corn and hay, yield a larger portion of excrement than straw; but this is certainly not because less of them is digested, but because the excrements are richer in animal matters, exclusive of the woody fibre contained in the dung. Nevertheless, if the digestible matter of the straw were equal in nutritive power to that of other articles of food, it would be in a very great degree more valuable than experience proves it to be. The soluble vegetable matters in the straw are capable, perhaps, like those of other articles, of supplying the waste of the animal frame, or increasing its growth; but perhaps the other part, which the digestive process extracts from straw, is only capable of supplying the material for the formation of carbonic acid, and for the support of the animal heat. However this be, it is certain that straw alone will not cause cattle to grow or to get fat, though it will support life.

According to the table which I have quoted, the different kinds of straw of our crops are of very unequal value. The straw of beans and peas and other legumes are much more nutritious than that of the cereal grains, wheat, barley, and oats. The straw of the leguminous crops are also rich in compounds containing nitrogen, as appears by the following table, which I have extracted from a paper of Dr. Daubeny in the Royal Agricultural Society's Journal, and which he takes from Boussingault.

Wheat straw contains	35	parts nitrogen in 10,000	
Oat do.	38	,,	,,
Rye do.	30	,,	,,
Peas do.	231	,,	,,
Clover	206	,,	,,

Thus while bean and pea straw contains rather more of the compounds containing nitrogen than clover or hay, the straw of white crops does not contain more than one-fifth as much. The leguminous seeds themselves are more rich in the nitrogenous substances than the grain of white crops. Beans, for instance, contain, according to

Dr. Playfair, 31 per cent. of this kind of substance, peas 29, and lentils 33, while wheat contains only about 18 per cent., barley 14, and oats 10½. The remainder of the substance of the corn of each kind is composed for the most part of soluble substances, such as starch, &c.

The straw of beans and peas is known to be a good hearty food for cattle, on which they will keep in a thriving condition. In some seasons they are of equal value with hay. They contain everything which is needful for a growing beast, and they should always be consumed as fodder. But the straw of white crops, though in some seasons it is much better than in others, is never so rich in soluble substances as to make cattle grow. It is impossible to get from straw enough nourishment to maintain cattle in health and vigour, much less in a state of profitable growth. We give our cattle food in order that we may increase their value, and whatever food we give without producing some return either in increased size or fatness, or in milk, is entirely wasted. There is thus a necessity for mixing with the straw some food of a more nutritious kind, if we would reap a profit from the stock which consume it. This it is the practice of all good farmers to do. Its value as an article of food is absolutely nothing of itself, for cattle living on it will not yield any return. The question is whether we can extract from it a profitable diet by mixing it with other substances, and whether it does not lose more in value as manure than we gain by consuming it as fodder. If we mix it with a large quantity of nutritious articles, the woody fibre of the straw will not be digested. It will pass away in the excrements, and the animals will be supported wholly by the better food, and the soluble part of the straw. It is useless, therefore, to give straw to feeding beasts. It must be used with a sparing quantity of other, and better food, and consumed by growing cattle. In this way 1½ cwt. of straw with 3 cwt. of turnips will keep a young beast thriving, or 20lbs. of linseed meal per week will have nearly the same effect as the turnips. Seeing that straw is most deficient in the nitrogenous vegetable compounds, it is very probable that one of the articles which contain them in greatest quantity, such as lentils, vetches, beans, or peas, would be the best to form a mixed diet with it. In this way there is no doubt that it may be consumed as fodder to a profit; and the best agriculturists calculate that oat straw so consumed will be worth 20s. per ton when hay is reckoned at 3l. The straw of wheat and barley is not so valuable for this purpose. When the straw is consumed as fodder, therefore, I hold that it should be always mixed with better food.

If we look, on the other hand, to the value of straw in the manure heap, we shall see the same necessity of mixing it with other food if the manure is to be capable of repairing the waste which corn crops occasions. Nothing can come out of straw but what is in it, and as it contains but little nitrogen, and we have seen that this is the chief agent in manure, the dung heap made from cattle feeding wholly on straw would be comparatively of no value.

By eating the straw as fodder one-half of the carbon is dissipated. Professor Liebig considers this element of manure of little value, but it remains to be proved whether his opinion in this respect is in accordance with facts. Then if straw be eaten while litter is wanted to soak up the urine of cattle feeding on better food, the materials of

the growth of plants which the urine contains are lost. We have seen that, except in the case of milking cows, nearly the whole of the nitrogen of the food is transferred to the excrements of the cattle; if, therefore, we know the quantity in the food, we can estimate how much nitrogen there is in the dung and urine. If, for instance, a cow consumes one ton of hay in ten weeks, and we reckon her urine to be 20 gallons, and the excess of moisture in the dung to be half that quantity, and if we reckon that straw will absorb three times its weight of moisture, the cow will wet 1 cwt. of straw in a week. In the ten weeks, therefore, 10 cwt. of straw will contain all the nitrogenous matters in the urine, and we have seen that they amount to about one-third of all contained in the hay. The nitrogen of a ton of hay being 20 to 30 pounds, a ton of straw used as litter for beasts feeding on hay would contain nearly 20lbs. of nitrogen, which is two-thirds of the quantity contained in the corn of a wheat crop. Besides the nitrogen the urine contains the soluble salts of the food. If, therefore, we suffer this valuable liquid to run to waste, we incur a much greater loss than our gain from the straw amounts to when it is eaten as fodder. The urine of horses being much richer in substances containing nitrogen, it is of more consequence to prevent its waste. But in every case the quantity of useful manure in the urine depends upon the proportion of the nitrogen in the food; and, consequently, if cattle be fed poorly, as on straw alone, the urine will be of very little value indeed.

It must clearly be wrong, unless we preserve the urine in tanks, to use any straw as fodder which can be used as litter of animals feeding on good; and rich provender. But if we consume the whole of the straw as fodder, and collect the manure of the cattle in tanks, we have precisely the same ingredients in the liquid manure as we should have had in the solid dung heap, except only that portion of soluble matter which has been extracted from the straw by the cattle. The question, therefore, as to the use of urine tanks is, whether the value of the straw as food is enough to repay the expense of collecting the urine in this manner, instead of our common method of wetting the litter with it. There are other reasons given for preferring the plan of urine tanks. It has been thought the ammonia produced by the decay of the urine is dissipated in the dung heap, and preserved by means of tanks; but it seems doubtful whether the dung heap, well managed, does not preserve the ammonia as well as the other plan. Sprengel shews that unless a large quantity of water is added to the urine in the tanks, the ammonia is partly wasted; and he gives reason to believe that in the mixed mass of vegetable and animal substances contained in the dung heap, the vegetable matters in decaying form an acid, the humic, which is capable of fixing the ammonia formed by the animal substances.

There are inventions for increasing the quantity of nutriment which the cattle are able to extract from straw. By cutting it up small the inward structure is more exposed to the action of the digestive fluid of the stomach. Steaming the straw has the same effect. I question whether either of the two plans will repay the expense in the case of straw. With respect to steaming, as applied to the food of cattle generally, there is not perhaps sufficiently accurate evidence on which to found an opinion. I should suppose that the soluble parts of vegetables are easily capable of digestion without steaming; and that if corn be ground into flour as much of the food would be extracted in the stomach of an animal as it it were steamed. Roots, as potatoes and turnips, are so easily broken up by the teeth of animals that they require no artificial grinding. It is only those kind of substances which contain much woody fibre, mingled with soluble matters, which require steaming. Of these, which consist of straw and the different kinds of hay, the straw of white crops is not valuable enough to pay the cost of the process; but the straw of beans and peas, and vetches, clover, and hay, are of so much value that the saving effected by steaming does perhaps more than repay the cost. An animal can only eat a certain quantity of hay. If that quantity is not enough to promote the growth of fat, or to make it milk largely, we are obliged to add a portion of some other food which contains more nutriment in a given bulk, such as corn, or turnips. But if by steaming the hay a greater portion of nutriment is got from a given quantity, even though it be only woody fibre dissolved, the animal requires no addition of a better kind of food. The dissolved woody fibre, or rather the substance mixed with the woody fibre, perhaps goes to supply the waste of the carbonic acid through the lungs, and the better parts of the hay are reserved for the other uses of the living body.

I have endeavoured to show that these three things are essential in the farm management as regards the straw. First, that if used as fodder, enough of more nutritious food must be mingled with it to support the stock in a growing condition. Secondly, that the manure must contain enough of other matters mixed with the straw, to repair the waste of the fertile power of the soil. Thirdly, that if any part of the urine of cattle fed on good food be wasted by saving the straw for fodder, a greater loss is incurred than the food in the straw is worth. If these things be observed, I believe we get from the straw all the benefit it is capable of yielding. We must ascertain therefore, what proportion of other food is required to form, with straw, a sufficiently nutritious diet for cattle, in the first place; and in the second place, how rich in animal matter the dung heap should be; and in the third place, how we must prevent any waste of the valuable part of the excrements of the cattle.

The richer we require the dung-heap, by so much richer must the diet of the cattle be, and consequently so much the more straw must be used as litter, and less as provender. On a farm where much winter food can profitably be collected, there is a necessity for rich manure to repair the waste of the crops which are carried off; if the urine of the cattle fed on the food be wasted, the manure cannot be rich, and if any of the straw is eaten as fodder there will not be enough to soak up the urine; the whole of the straw must, therefore, be converted into litter, if the quantity of food is sufficient to yield enough urine to wet it all. Reckoning that a full grown beast will convert 1 cwt. of straw into manure in a week, it would require about three tons of hay to make one acre of straw into manure, or it would require twenty tons of turnips to effect the same result. On a strong land farm, therefore, where no turnips or other root crops are grown, it would require that two acres of pasture or seeds should be mown to convert the straw of an acre into manure as litter; and on a lighter turnip farm, on the four-course shift, it would

require an acre of turnips and two acres of pasture or seeds mown for every two acres of straw. This is perhaps a greater proportion than can profitably be mowed on either system, unless in the case where very large pasture farms are joined to very small arable ones. As a general rule, it is more profitable to consume our produce on the ground where it grows, except that kind of produce which is eaten in a green state. In mowing grass and clover for hay, the expense of gathering, the risk of spoiling, and, in the case of pasture, the labour of top-dressing afterwards, make up a sum which is not easily repaid; but as it is evident that when the whole of the salines and the whole of the woody fibre contained in a grass crop are returned to it, we may carry away a part of the matter which contains nitrogen without injuring the fertility of the land, it is undoubtedly profitable to mow our land to this extent, and to apply the excess of nitrogenous matter to increase the fertility of our arable land. If a crop of grass contains twice as much nitrogen as a crop of corn; and if, when consumed on the ground, it will supply the waste of a corn crop and the materials of another crop of grass, at the same time it follows that a third part of the nitrogenous matter may be taken away, and that our pastures might be mown once in three years, if we take care to return to them the salines and woody fibre. We may perhaps reckon that once in four years on an average our pastures may safely be mowed, and the waste of the salines and woody fibre supplied by the very poorest straw manure, while the richer manure may go to the plough land. It appears to me that this is the great advantage of mowing our pastures, and not any fancied necessity for keeping a great quantity of stock in the winter. It is easy so to arrange as to increase or diminish our stock at any period of the year which may suit our convenience; for though there must needs be as much stock in the whole country at all seasons of the year, one kind of farm requires very different proportions at different seasons, and as always one class want to buy what the other class want to sell, matters are so managed that stock pays the same profit for its keep at one part of the year as at another.

It seems then we are not able on many farms to collect winter food enough to convert the whole of the straw into manure, without consuming part of it as provender, but we can on every farm find at least enough other food to convert part of the straw into a sufficient diet for cattle, while the other part is trodden as litter. A full grown beast feeding on turnips alone, will consume from 15 cwt. to 1 ton per week—a quantity equal to 4 cwt. of hay in nutritive value; but the same quantity of turnips with straw will suffice to keep three beasts in a growing condition, or four milking cows in the interval of their milk and calving. A cwt. of good straw and five cwt. of turnips will maintain a beast in good condition, and as the animal will moisten as much litter as though it fed on richer food, it would use as litter the same quantity of straw as it used for food. Suppose the acre of straw to be 30 cwt., and the acre of turnips 20 tons, a beast consuming four tons of turnips would convert an acre of straw into manure. On the four-course shift, therefore, less than half the turnips would in this way use up the whole of the straw; or on a strong land farm, where turnips cannot be grown nor any other green winter crop, it is easy to reserve the straw till the summer, and consume it with a proportion of tares in precisely the same way; or I question if it be not as profitable to consume a part of the straw with corn or oil-cake as with turnips. In many parts of the country the farmers on strong lands pursue such a plan. I am even inclined to think that we pay too dear for our turnips, even on turnip soils, and that the greater use of corn and cake would be profitable on a light land farm. The table of the comparative value of articles of food which I have quoted, makes 300lbs. of Swede turnips equal to 54lbs. of oil-cake or 45lbs. beans. If it were so, there could be no doubt that it would in no case be profitable to substitute corn for turnips; but is the proportionate value of corn and turnips what is set down in the table? Turnips are composed of water nine parts, and solid matter one ; they have ten pounds of solid matter in 100, and of this seven are soluble, and three woody fibre. Now the corn of wheat or beans is nine-tenths composed of soluble nutritious substance, and wheat contains twice, and beans four times as much of that kind of compound which contains nitrogen as turnips do. Though turnips therefore may fatten cattle ·better than corn, I should suppose that they would not be more valuable for growing stock, and I believe practical men find that 20lbs. of meal mixed with straw produces as much effect as three to four cwt. of turnips. I am clear if this be so, that 20lbs. of beans or oil-cake can be procured at less cost than the turnips can be grown on any land, and that it would be the most profitable to consume the straw with it instead of turnips. One would think that no farmer need be reduced to the necessity of keeping his stock gradually growing lean on straw alone, but still the practice continues in too many districts.

If we consume the straw in the manner last mentioned, one acre of straw will contain in the manure made from it only one-fifth of an acre of other food ; and when we consider that at least the produce of one acre should be contained in the manure made from the straw of an acre, in order that the ground may be kept in fertile condition, the manure heap made in this way in very inadequate to fulfil this end. But we must bear in mind that if we do not carry off the clover crop, and if we consume half the turnips on the ground, the land receives from the pasturing of these precisely the same materials which would have gone to the dung heap had we consumed their produce in our yards, and the land cannot want what it has already received. The consideration which is of most importance is, whether there be enough of active soluble matter in the dung heap made of such poor materials to provoke a good fermentation, and to cause the decomposition of the woody fibre of the straw. If a dung-heap were composed only of straw, and the small quantity of other food necessary to convert it into fair diet, it would perhaps be doubtful whether the mixture would be rich enough to ferment healthily ; but on every farm horses make a considerable quantity of manure ; and as it is seldom that some portion of pasture is not mixed with arable land, a part of this is always mowed, and the manure heap is increased in richness in consequence ; so that it is but very seldom that we may reckon less than the produce of half an acre of other land is mixed with the straw of an acre of plough land. A manure heap of this degree of richness will take a sufficient heat, and will be readily decomposed with proper attention to the mixing it well together. The two extremes of richness and poverty in the dung-heap are that made from horses fed with hay and corn, and that made from beasts fed with straw alone. The former has so great a tendency to pass into rapid fermentation, that our cares are directed to prevent its rising too high, while the latter is so sluggish that it requires every assistance of turning, &c. to make it pass into a sufficiently active fermentation. By mixing the two together we improve both, for if the heat rises too high in a dung-heap, great part of the products of the nitrogenous matter may be dissipated in the form of gas. In proportion as there is more or less of animal matter mixed with the straw, and the more or less of the straw which has been used for litter there be, by so much more active or sluggish is the action of the heap. There is no disadvantage in a poor heap except its sluggishness, but in a rich one there is great danger of waste ; so that, perhaps, though the rich heap be more valuable, yet what virtue it has is more likely to be all made available for the fertilizing the soil in a rather poor than a rich dung-heap. If this be so, there is then no reason for any particular way of managing the straw merely on account of the dung-heap, seeing that the least rich which we can have with proper attention to the profitable growth of our cattle is rich enough to secure its decomposition in the earth. Perhaps much of the controversy respecting the advantage of using manure much or little fermented, would be set at rest if the different qualities of manure and of land were always attended to. Poor manure will require the fermentation to be carried further than rich, because the chemical change which has been begun in the heap will not be so actively carried on in the soil. The same manure will decompose more rapidly in light and warm, than in heavy and cold land ; and, therefore, the manure for the former need not be carried so far as for the latter. I have observed, that usually the light land farmers are advocates of new, and the heavy land farmers of old manure. Generally speaking, it will be best to mix together our richer and poorer manure ; but in the case where we mow pasture lands, and wish to give back to them the two parts of the manure—the woody fibre and the salines—and to rob them of a portion of the other, or the nitrogenous part, it may be best to keep the richer for the arable land, and use the poorer for the pasture.

The only case in which it will be argued that there is a necessity for a very rich dung-heap is, where we wish to grow a very abundant crop of turnips. Being a root which will produce in a growth of four or five months an amount of crop sometimes equal to two or three good crops of grass, there is required a great quantity of rich manure, in the immediate neighbourhood of the plants, to secure a green crop. · The argument is, I think, rather specious than solid. Say that we pursue the four-course shift, and mow the seeds, we shall then have in every acre of our straw half an acre of clover, and half an acre of turnips ; and manure of this degree of richness will force a large crop of turnips. But if we consume the seeds on the ground, and part of the turnips on the ground too, and make a poorer dung-heap of the straw, and the other part of the turnips, the ground receives in the course exactly the same amount of the manure of cattle ; and the only difference is, that it receives it gradually instead of at once, and the return in the seeds will in part counterbalance the failure in the turnip crop. Neither is it so certain that the average of our turnip crops will be so much lessened by pursuing this latter course ; for if we manure very largely for the turnip crop, the soil by the time it comes round to that part of the course will be well nigh exhausted, whereas, if we consume on the ground in the other parts of the course, the land is pretty rich, and to grow a crop in a poor soil with manure, though it will succeed in favourable seasons, yet will not, in the average of years, perhaps, produce an average crop so well as to have the land richer, and the manure poorer.

But though it matters not what degree of richness we make our manure, we must take heed lest we put poor manure to an use which rich manure alone can fulfil. It would be ridiculous to expect that manure which is composed of an acre of straw, with half an acre of other produce, should be fit to repair the waste of a course of ploughing. Twelve tons of such manure would not contain the materials necessary for the growth of one corn crop; and yet such manure is frequently used at the end of a long course on strong land. Need we wonder then at the seeds being weak, when we remember that a crop of clover contains in itself twice the quantity of nitrogen which a corn crop requires. If we have not rich manure for our land we must take care that our land do not require it; and if our land require it we must take care to provide it.

The result which I proposed to shew was, that the consumption of the straw did not so much depend on its intrinsic value, either as food or litter, but that its value for either purpose was so nearly balanced that it might depend on other circumstances which of the two ways we preferred. It depends entirely on the kind of farm whether it is convenient to collect much winter food. If much can be collected, I argue that it is best to convert as much of the straw into litter as we can; and that in every case as much should be used for litter as is needed to soak up the whole of the moisture of the cattle, and that the part we consume as provender should always be used with as much other food as will keep the cattle growing. These are the questions which I submit for your discussion, not without great doubt that I have marred some very sound doctrines in the art of agriculture by my imperfect manner of stating them.

PROTECTION TO AGRICULTURE.

(Extracted from *Corn and Currency*, by the Right Hon. Sir James Graham, Bart., now one of her Majesty's principal Secretaries of State.)

".... Politicians and philosophers may talk coldly of the transfer of old family estates—of throwing immense tracts of the inferior soil out of cultivation —of burying for ever the immense capital expended on it—and of the transfusion of an agricultural into a manufacturing population; but let them remember the ties which must be broken, the villages which must be deserted, the gardens to be laid desolate, the second nature of habits which must be altered, the hearts which must sink, and the hands which may rebel under trials such as these." .... "But the ancient landlord's position is still more hopeless; in addition to the public burdens, he is required to meet, with a reduced rental, an increased charge; ruin must be his fate; his tenants and his labourers will sink with him; the former from the weight of their fixed engagements, the latter from want of employment and a fall of wages greater than the reduction of taxation. In such a state of affairs we must come to a tenantry without capital or leases, and to a population eking out existence by potatoes." .... "The clergy and the landowners, the poor and the proprietors, are copartners in the soil; they must stand or fall together on their existing tenures; they may fall indeed, but religion, and mercy, and

justice will fall with them—'and they who are buried in these ruins are happier than they who survive them.'" .... "Let not the landowners lose this great advantage—let them rivet the gratitude of the community to their cause; let them exert all their power, and insist on the revision of Mr. Peel's act of 1819, an act no less fatal to the landowner than to the payer of taxes, an act which from its first introduction goaded the people to insurrection.".... "Here the landowners may with safety make their stand; the position is impregnable; the payers of taxes—the productive classes—are ready to defend it; substantial justice is on our side, and who are they that are against us? The annuitants, the fundholders, and the economists!—a body which the landowners, if true to themselves, and in concert with the people, cannot fail to defeat."...."This is the present fate of the landowners of this country; they are striving in vain against engagements which they cannot meet. Creditors in general receive an undue proportion of earnings, and a sure but destructive revolution is in progress, by which, if it be not arrested, the ancient aristocracy of these realms must ultimately be sacrificed to creditors and annuitants."...." He may sell his estate, indeed; this would be considered only as a transfer of property. But what agony of mind does that word convey? The snapping of a chain, linked, perhaps, by centuries! the destruction of the dearest local attachments, the dissolution of the earliest friendships, the violation of the purest feelings of the heart!".... "What, then, is the alternative which presents itself? Either he must drag out a degraded existence on his paternal estate, exercising no more the hospitality of his ancestors, but gleaning from his tenantry their earnings or their savings, himself the hated steward of the annuitant and the mortgagee, or, unlike the country gentleman of England in a happier day, he must leave his native home, become a wanderer abroad, or a jobber, a sharedealer, a placeman in the metropolis."

GUANO.

DEAR SIR,—As to my experiment with guano, compared with stable yard manure for a turnip crop, I beg to inform you that on 29th November last, I had two rows of equal length taken up from each kind of manure, taking as fair a sample of each as I could, the whole of the tops and tails being carefully cut off. The result was, that the weight of bulbs where stable yard manure was used was 19¾ cwt., and the weight of two rows where guano had been used was 17¼ cwt., but then you will bear in mind that the guano had cost per acre but little more than half as much as the stable yard manure. The cost of dressing one acre with each was as follows: with guano and wood ashes, about 4l. per acre; with stable yard manure (including the cost of setting upon the land), 7l. 10s. per acre.

I think, however, that there was not a sufficient quantity of guano used, for each alternate row was better than the other, and as the field was a little hilly, and the rows were drawn up and down, a greater quantity of manure would be deposited in those rows which were drilled as the horse walked up hill; and those rows, had in every instance, better bulbs than those wherein the manure was deposited as the horse walked down hill, and consequently rather quicker. It yet remains to be shown what difference would arise in the barley crop, and in the seeds; and this I shall not be able to test fairly, a sheep will be folded evenly over the whole field. It is my intention, however, to dress a small field, part with guano at the rate of 6 cwt. per acre, and the remainder with farm yard manure at the rate of 15 tons per acre. I shall draw all the turnips off, and shall not manure either the barley or the seeds, when the comparative merits of the different manures can be then well tested. I have no doubt, however, that for a turnip crop on dry land, guano is one of our best and most economical manures.

I am, dear sir, truly yours,   THOS. DUNN.
Richmond Hill, January 2nd, 1843.
        MR. J. NAPIER.

I have also been favoured with the following testimonial from Mr. Swaffield, Bailiff to his grace the Duke of Devonshire.

DEAR SIR,—The land on which the guano was used being very wet and not calculated for feeding off in spring, I have been drawing off the turnips from the whole field. They are just now finished, and a better crop I never saw on any land. Having been fully engaged lately, I have neglected to ascertain which manure produced the greater weight per acre; but should say, that the part where guano was used, was fully as good if not even better than where the other manure was applied.

I am, dear sir, yours very truly,
Chatsworth, Jan. 4th, 1843.   BENJAMIN SWAFFIELD.
N.B. The cost of the guano was about 25s. 6d. per acre, and the cost of the bones and rape dust was 43s. 6d. per acre.

SIR,—I beg to inform you, that the produce from the guano manure exceeds that of the farm yard manure by fully 1½ ton per acre. The cost of dressing was with guano 3l. 14s. per acre ; with yard manure 7l. per acre.

I am, sir, yours respectfully,
Birley Common Side, Feb. 14, 1843. GEO. WOODHEAD.

FARMING AND FARM STOCK AT ELLON, ABERDEENSHIRE.

Extracted from No. XLII. of the NEW STATISTICAL ACCOUNT of SCOTLAND, just issued, containing the conclusion of the County of Aberdeen.

RENT.—The gross rental is within a trifle of 10,000l. being about seven and a half times the amount of rent paid at the date of the last statistical account in 1792. It must be observed, however, to prevent mistakes in a matter of so much statistical importance, that the augmentation of the rental, though undoubtedly very great, is yet not quite so great as from the above statement it would appear to be. When the last Statistical Account was drawn up, a considerable number of the farms were held on leases, for which, in addition to the annual rent, a premium, or, as it is usually termed, a grassum, had been paid at the period of entry. Still, due allowance being made for the item of grassums, the rental at present cannot be less than four or five times its former amount. Two of the largest farms in the parish are still rented much under the full value,—the old leases by which they are held, and for which grassums were originally paid, having not yet expired. On the expiry of these leases the gross rental will amount to upwards of 10,000l. Some of the land in the immediate neighbourhood of the village is rented at the high rate of upwards of 5l. per Scotch acre ; but its actual annual value probably does not much exceed one-half of the rent

which is now paid. It is farmed by the villagers in small parcels, less with a view to profit than pleasure and convenience. The average rent of land, of the same quality, in more remote parts of the parish, is from 2l. to 2l. 10s. per acre. On the inferior soils, the rent per acre varies from 10s. to 15s. The average rent of arable land for the whole parish will be found, from the data already furnished, to be within a small fraction of 17s. per Scotch acre.

LIVE-STOCK.—The breed of work horses has of late years been much improved. Superior mares have in several instances been brought from Clydesdale and other parts of the west country, celebrated for breeds of horses of good bone and action. Much has been done also for the improvement of the breed of horses by the spirited exertions of the Highland and Agricultural Society. The horses chiefly sought after for agricultural purposes are not those of the largest size, but such as are of good mettle, and easily kept in good condition.

Until of late years almost the only breeds of black-cattle known in this district of country were the Aberdeenshire horned and Angus polled breeds. But what is called the short-horned or Tees-water breed is now prevailing to a considerable extent, and seems, in spite of the opposition which its introduction has encountered from various quarters, to be daily gaining ground. Opinion, however, is still divided between this recent importation and the ancient breeds of the country, and it is not for the writer to presume to determine which party has the right side of the question. One thing is matter of fact, and forces itself upon the attention of even the most ordinary observer, that our farmers now bring their cattle to a much greater weight than in former times, and receive for them a price proportionally more remunerating. Various causes have contributed to bring about this result; one of which, and undoubtedly not the least important is, that much more attention and skill are now applied not only to the feeding off of full-grown stock, but also to the equally important departments of breeding and of keeping the rising cattle in a thriving condition. Had the same attention been formerly given to these important parts of the farmer's occupation, there can be no doubt that cattle even of the ordinary breeds of the country might have been brought to much greater weight than what, under the less perfect mode of management heretofore adopted, they ever attained. Still, as it seems to be admitted on all hands that the short-horns both attain to a greater size, and are capable, from their less active habits, and probably other concurring causes, of being fed off at a much earlier age, it is questionable whether, at least on a good farm, the same amount of profit could be realized by the breeding of cattle of the Angus or Aberdeenshire breeds. The beef of the short-horns is said to be inferior, which is probably the fact. Nevertheless, as no preference seems to be given to the pure Aberdeenshire breed in the London market, an inferiority in the article exposed by him, so long as that inferiority does not affect its exchangeable value, cannot be supposed to have much influence with the Scottish farmer. An apprehension now generally entertained is, that second and third crosses between the Teeswater and Aberdeenshire breeds may be attended with a deterioration of both. Indeed, the most intelligent farmers seem to be of opinion that the two breeds should be kept as distinct and pure as possible, and no intermixture allowed beyond a first cross. Sheep farming is but little pursued in this district of country, and in the parish of Ellon is altogether unknown.

EXPERIMENTS ON CONCENTRATED AND SALINE MANURES, FOR TOP DRESSING AND DRILLING-IN.

" Let us always bear in mind, that while the country grants protection to agriculture, it will expect in return, that the land shall be cultivated in the best and most productive manner."—*Daubeny.*

TO THE EDITOR OF THE EXETER FLYING-POST.

SIR,—Keeping this object constantly in view, whilst the more gradual and costly operations of draining, subsoiling, marling, &c., are in progress or in contemplation, the readiest, cheapest, and simplest method of increasing our crops seems to be, the abundant supply of the indispensable mineral ingredients and the excitement of vegetative action to draw organic elements from the air as well as the soil. And these purposes are well answered by the concentrated and saline manures, applied as top dressings, or drilled in with the seed, for which the season is now at hand.

Those who have time to read and think for themselves, will do well to study Professor Johnstone's *Experiments in Practical Agriculture,* in 1841 and 1842, published by Blackwood, and containing, at about 2s. cost, tables with full explanations and reasoning, of different top dressings, on a great variety of crops and soils ; all conducted on systematic principles and with definite objects.

But to the many who have little time for reading, and still less for reflection and study, I hope to render useful service, in the following abstracts from these tables, inferences from them compared with other experiments, and suggestions for economical and profitable experiments during the present season.

It must be remembered that we have still very much to learn ; that the variety of climate, season, soil, and culture, perhaps even of seed, have made the effects of the same top dressing, on the same crop, very different in different places ; and that, consequently, in profiting by the experiments of others, the farmer can hardly depend, in the present state of our experience, upon similar advantages, until he has tried them on his own ground, and with his own means. But the greater number of these trials we make, on the greater variety of soils and circumstances (provided all these circumstances are attentively recorded) the sooner our uncertainties will be cleared away, and results attained on which we may reckon with confidence.

To begin then with WHEAT. It contains—

In the grain, much phosphoric acid and alkalies, and but little sulphuric acid, lime, or earths. [See down A.]

In the straw, much lime and silica, pretty much phosphoric acid, and but little alkali.

The grain is well known to be improved and increased by nitrogenous manures ; though, if applied in excess, they run it to juicy leaf and straw, rather than ear, and dispose it to lay.

Lime is understood to strengthen the straw, and forward kerning and ripening ; and

Salt appears to fill the grain and increase the weight per bushel.

These may be regarded as something like established principles, founded upon long and extensive practice.

The following are abstracts of Professor Johnstone's Reports above recommended :—

Set of Experiments.	Number of Manures tried.	Best.	Second.	Third.	
Page 24	9	Salt	Nitr. Soda and rape-dust.	Nitrate of soda.	No Guano nor bone tried.
69	11	Rape-dust.	Nitr. Soda and rape-dust.	Salt and rape-dust.	Guano 5th.
70	6	Guano	Rape-dust and sulphate of magnesia.	Sulphate and nitrate of soda.	Bone 6th. (worst of all)
71	8	Sulphate of ammonia and wood ashes with salt.	Sulphate of ammonia and wood ashes with sulphate of soda.	Sulphate of ammonia and wood ashes with nitrate of soda.	Guano 7th. (worst but one)

In comparing these we find rape-dust stand first, and sulphate of ammonia second ; whilst other experimenters have preferred guano and nitrates of soda and potash. Now all these are rich in ammonia or nitrogen, and the guano and rape contain also phosphoric acid and alkalies, corresponding with the ingredients noted above. [A.]

These results will serve as a basis for our further experiments.

But ammonia is most for the money in sulphate of ammonia, and phosphoric acid in bone-dust ; hence, a due mixture of these two (when genuine) may prove the most economical and effective dressing for wheat ; supposing the alkalies to be contained in the soil, or added, the potash in weed and wood ashes, or vegetable manures, and the soda in salt. Near the sea the spray and vapour supply salt enough. But it is possible that rape-dust may have some particular action favourable to wheat—a question which should not be allowed to remain undecided.

Setting out then with that which promises to be most economical and effective, we may try others in competition with it, according to the following table :—

E E

Materials.	Quantities per acre	Cost (a)	Cost per ¼ rood.
		£ s. d.	s. d.
1 { Sulph.Ammo..	¾ cwt.	0 13 6	
Bone-dust (b).	4 cwt.	1 10 0	} 7 9
Weed or Wood ashes	} 3 cwt.	0 18 0?	
2 Rape-dust....	5 cwt.	1 15 0?	4 5
3 Guano...	3 cwt.	1 18 0	5 0
4 Soot........	10 bus.	0 10 0?	1 3
5 { Nitrate of soda	1 cwt.	1 0 0	
Gypsum......	2 cwt.	0 4 0	} 5 10
Bone-dust (b) .	3 cwt.	1 2 6	
6 { Nitr. of potass.	1 cwt.	1 7 0	
Gypsum	2 cwt.	0 4 0	} 6 9
Bone-dust (b).	3 cwt.	1 2 6	

(a) In London : freight, carriage, &c., may be added.

(b) Where the wheat follows boned turnips, the bone-dust will not be needed. It is much more active decomposed by acid, for which directions will be given on TURNIPS.

To each of these may be added common salt, 0 to 5 cwt., according to the distance from the sea, or to shelter (by hills, &c.) from the spray and exhalations.

The intelligent farmer will have other experiments of his own to try, but to be practically beneficial, all must be tried fully and fairly. They should be on one field, of equal quality and preparation throughout ; and its quality, preparation, and condition minutely recorded, as also the state of the plant at the time of dressing, and its subsequent progress, with the changes of the weather. The divisions of the plots should be distinctly marked out ; such experiments having been often frustrated by the loss or removal of the land marks before

harvest. A rood, or half-rood, is quite sufficient for each, if these and any other observations are attentively registered.

OATS.—The proportions of the constituents of oats and wheat, though by no means identical, approach near enough to indicate very similar top dressing. Rape-dust, however, was not beneficial to oats, in the cases recorded last year, but the season was dry, and other top dressings failed equally. Dissolved bones and the alkaline nitrates and sulphates seem to have taken the lead in the production of oats, hence Nos. 5 and 6 may be expected to produce the best results. The other numbers may, however, be worth trying ; even rape-dust, which is reduced in price since the large importations of guano.

Several of these dressings are advantageously applied in a state of solution, as liquid manure, but few of our farmers possess conveniences for that method.

TURNIPS AND POTATOES.

On referring again to the table of Mineral Constituents (a), it will appear that

Turnips contain much phosphoric acid and lime ; much more soda than potass ; much less sulphuric than phosphoric acid ; and a pretty good proportion of chlorine (an element of salt) (a) ; whilst

Potatoes, on the contrary, contain more sulphuric acid than phosphoric ; much more potass than soda ; much less lime, but more magnesia, than turnips ; and but little chlorine (b).

And it will be interesting to observe, in the following abstracts, that accordingly

Turnips thrive best with phosph. lime (bone-dust), nitrate of soda, and salt (a).

Potatoes thrive best with sulphates, nitrate potass, but not much salt or lime (b).

To proceed with turnips.—The experiments reported are numerous and well assorted, supplying a good deal of new information.

TURNIPS.—Table 1.

Set of Experiments.	Number of Manures tried.	Best.	Second.	Third.	Notes.
Page 53	11	Rape-dust and salt.	Guano.	Rape-dust.	No bones tried.
55	23	Guano.	Bone charcoal.	Bones dissolved in muriatic acid.	Rape-dust 19th.
56	18	Guano and wood-ashes.	Nitrate of soda.	Sulphate of ammonia.	Bone dis., &c., 4th ; bone-dust 9th.
57	8	Town-dung and bones.	Rape-dust, bone, peat ashes, and humus.	Yard-dung and bones.	Guano and humus 4th.
58	4	Yard-dung.	Bones and dung.	Bone-dust.	Guano 4th.
59	6	Guano.	Yard-dung and humus.	Dung, humus, and artificial guano.	Dung and bones 4th.

In a general review of these guano takes the lead, and bone follows, both containing phosphate of lime (a), the former in a fine and soft state, very favourable to prompt action. The artificial guanos (b), which contain *dissolved* bones, also produce good crops of turnips. Even bone charcoal (ivory black) answers very well, though it cannot be good *economy* to burn away the animal matter. For

prompt action, the bone should be in as fine powder as possible, or still better decomposed by acid (c).

Rape-dust and nitrate of soda are less certain, especially in dry weather. And there is another consideration relating to turnips, which must precede our suggestions for further experiments. The bulbs are very juicy, containing only from 1-10th to 1-5th of solid, and 4-5ths to 9-10ths water. This is of great consequence; for 30 tons, with 9-10ths water, contain no more solid nourishment than 15 tons with 4-5ths water; so that a juicy crop of 25 tons may be really less worth than a more solid one of 15 tons. The great *practical* importance of this new feature calls for more particulars.—*(See Johnson's Experiments, pp. 56 and 82.).*

Dressed with	Sulphate of ammonia	large, soft, and light.
	Guano & wood-ashes	eminently large.
	Bone-dust	
	Artificial guanos.. (containing bone)	firm and solid, not remarkable in size.
	Potass and lime..	
	Salt and lime....	
	Sulph. of magnesia	small, firm, and solid.
	Nitrate of soda...	

(with "The bulbs were" running vertically beside the middle group)

Hence it would appear, that while ammoniacal manures give large crops, attention must be paid to their solidity and specified gravity, before we decide whether they are profitable. And how far the *ammoniacal* quality of the guano may produce similar effects, is worth investigation, though we may hope otherwise, from the phosphate of lime it also contains.

To proceed now with our suggestions. Sulphate of ammonia, having produced such light juicy bulbs, can hardly be recommended *alone* for *profitable* experiment: but if to ascertain whether it will produce the same effect again, about 28lbs. per root (or 1 cwt. per acre), mixed with earth, may be drilled in under the seed, or sown over the young plant in damp weather, or used half and half each way.

In experimenting on turnips, some of the materials do best drilled in, under the seed, with earth between; others applied as top-dressing to the young plant, in July, avoiding dry weather. In order to distinguish the effect of the top-dressing, it may be applied over only half each drilled plot—that is, supposing, as the annexed table, ½ rood to be *drilled* with guano, then only half of the plot should be top-dressed with gypsum, &c., leaving the other half to the guano alone. *(See plan below.)*

TURNIPS.—Table 2.

For drilling in under the seed.

		Quantity per ¼-rood.	Cost. s. d.
1	Genuine guano	¼ cwt.	6 6
2	Bone-dust	1 cwt.	7 6
3	Bone decomposed by acid	40 lbs.	4 6
	Wood-ashes	3 bush.	1 6
4	Rape-dust	1½ cwt.	10 6

For top-dressing the young plant.
Per ¼-rood.

			s. d.
1	Gypsum (e)	21 lbs.	0 6
2	Nitrate of soda	7 lbs.	1 3
	Gypsum	14 lbs.	0 4
3	Sulphate of ammonia	7 lbs.	1 2
4	Nitrate of soda	7 lbs.	1 3
	Gypsum	14 lbs.	0 4

Adding to each of the top-dressings (e) salt 7lbs. to 21lbs., according to distance from the sea, or to shelter from its spray and vapour.

These dressings are likely to answer best upon dunged land. Some of them were tried against dung in the experiments referred to above, but the distinguishing details would make this letter too long.

POTATOES.

As turnips — Phosph. lime, nitr. *soda*, and salt (a). Sulphates, nitr. of *potass*, and not So potatoes — much salt or lime (b).

In some cases, however, where potass was not deficient, nitrate of soda has been very useful; and nitrate and sulphate of soda, mixed in dung, gave in one case 26 tons (420 bags) per acre. *(Expts., p. 27).*

Potatoes, again, contain variable proportions of water—say 70 to 80 per cent. And we are told by Liebig (p. 127, 2nd edition), that much strong dung makes them *soapy*. Now strong dung is rich in nitrogen, and its effect *may* therefore be, as in the case of turnips above quoted, an enlarged *juicy* growth, rather than increase of nourishment. This is a question for further investigation, and should not be lost sight of in our future experiments. To proceed with the abstracts:—

POTATOES.—Table 3.

Set of Experiments.	Number of Manures tried.	Best.	Second.	Third.	Remarks.
Page 26	4	Nitrate and sulphate of soda.	Nitrate of soda.	Sulphate of soda.	All on thirty tons of yard-dung.
61	26	Guano.	Rape-dust and wood-ashes.	Dissolved bone and wood-ashes.	Bone-dust, gypsum, potass, and lime, all failed.
62	9	Nitrate of soda and sulphate of magnesia.	Sulphates of soda and ammonia.	Nitrate of potass.	Sulphate and nitrate of soda, 4th.
63	7	Silicate of potass.	Sulphate of ammonia.	Nitrate of soda.	Salt injurious.

In these experiments, on dunged land, mixtures of sulphates of magnesia or soda with nitrate of soda, were most successful : and nitrate of *potass* did better than that of soda in the only case tried (p. 62), as might have been expected from the quantity of potass potatoes contain (see up b). The same reason may explain the good effect of silicate of *potass* (p. 63), and their preference of sulphates, particularly that of magnesia, may be referred to the

same principle; the inefficiency of lime and salt, to the converse of it. The experiments thus agreeing with the contents of the plant, in indicating the compounds of *potass*, soda, and *magnesia* with *sulphuric* and *nitric* acids, as the most productive and profitable dressings. On land *without dung*, guano did best ; bones and other compounds of lime failed ; but a cheap compost (d) produced 14 tons of very fine potatoes (224 bags) an acre, upon a *poor soil.* The quantity of potass in this compost is not stated, but must have been small, from the cost; and as potatoes like potass (b), wood or weed-ashes will be better, where convenient, than this indefinite "potass and lime." Sawdust cannot be had gratis every where; but coal tar, on the other hand, may be got at the gas-works, for 2d. per gallon or less, which will leave more than enough to pay for the saw-dust. With these preliminary considerations we may proceed with our suggestions for profitable experiments his season.

TABLE 4.—ON DUNGED LAND.

Materials.	Quantity per acre.	Cost per acre. £. s. d.	Cost per ½ rood. s. d.
1. Nitrate of Potass....	¾ cwt.	1 0 6	
Sulphate of Soda (f)	¾ cwt.	0 7 6	9 0
Magnesia.	¾ cwt.	0 9 0	
2. Nitrate of Potass....	¾ cwt.	1 0 6	
Gypsum (g) }	1 cwt.	0 2 0	
Salt .... }	1 cwt.	0 1 6	4 2
Sulphate of Magnesia	¾ cwt.	0 9 0	
3. Nitrate of Soda....	¾ cwt.	0 16 0	
Gypsum	1 cwt.	0 2 0	
Wood or Weed-ashes	25 bush.	0 12 6	4 2
Salt pan bittern (h)	20 galls.	0 2 6	

These may be applied as top dressings when the plant is five or six inches high; or towards the end of May; avoiding dry weather.

The following, table 5, to be used *without dung*, may be sown on the drills, over the sets, with earth between.

TABLE 5.—WITHOUT DUNG.

	Quantity per acre.	Cost. £. s. d.
1. Guano.................	5 cwt.	3 0 0
2. Cheap Compost (i)		
Salt............ } mixed	cwt.	0 2 3
Old slaked Lime } wet.	5 bus.	0 3 0
Wood or weed-ashes	20 bus.	0 10 0
Sulphates of Soda	½ cwt.	0 5 0
——— of Magnesia....	½ cwt.	0 7 0
——— of Ammonia ..	1 cwt.	0 17 0
Peat or Saw-dust........	1 ton.	0 5 0
Coal Tar	20 gall.	0 3 4

These two last, though they may bring heavy crops of potatoes, can hardly be expected, without dung, to leave the *land* much improved for the following plant. *Green* manuring would probably suit potatoes, and would save dung.

In making experiments of this kind, the ground should be laid out in plots divided by *straight* lines, and well marked, so that there can be no mistakes. And a corresponding plan (see the figure) should be laid down in a memorandum book, with full particulars of the soil, previous culture, manure, seed, weather, &c.; and the progress and appearances of each plot minutely noted from time to time; before, and after the dressings; on changes of weather, &c. All this will require time and attention, but the *expences will be small*; and the experiments will, I hope, repay them with *good profit*.

Drilled under.			
Foreign Guano.	Bone Dust.	Bones decomposed by Acid and Wood-ashes.	Dung only.
Top dressed with			
Gypsum and Salt.	Nitrate of Soda and Gypsum.	Sulphate of Ammonia.	

In conclusion, let me again recommend the attentive study of Professor Johnstone's instructive (and cheap) "Experiments in Practical Agriculture;" from which the above are mostly derived. In compressing their prominent results within newspaper limits, I could not include even summaries of the apt and varied reasoning upon each, nor of the valuable collateral suggestions thereon founded. The most succinct explanations of the principles upon which I have endeavoured to gain a step in advance by taking warning from the failures, has drawn out these letters full long enough for your columns.

Yours, &c.,
J. PRIDEAUX.

(a) See Exeter Flying-Post, Feb. —, 1843.

(b) An excellent substitute for guano may be made in the farm yard, with urine, bone-dust, &c., &c.; for which I hope soon to send you the details.

(c) Bone-dust, sifted fine, and digested with half its weight of sulphuric acid, and as much water (previously mixed together gradually and allowed to cool); or with its own weight of muriatic acid; keeping it three or four days in a soft paste, by adding more water, if necessary, and stirring it well three or four times a day. By this means the bone earth is decomposed, and rendered much more active. It may then be dried up with wood-ashes, or with earth, &c., containing about half as much chalk or slaked lime as the bone dust, to neutralise the acid (mixing the lime with the earth *first*, to prevent clotting). Or the paste may be dissolved in two or three hundred times its weight of water, and applied as liquid manure.

(d) Cheap compost for potatoes, without dung, Johnstone's Experiments, p. 64:—

	Quantities per Acre.	Cost. £. s. d.
Saw-dust..........	40 bush.	0 0 0
Potass and Lime mixed,14 months old	10 bush.	0 7 6
Common Salt	1 cwt. 2 qrs.	0 2 3
Sulphate of Ammonia	1 cwt. 0 qrs.	1 0 0
Sulphate of Soda...	2 qrs.	0 3 6
Sulphate of Magnesia	2 qrs.	0 4 0
Coal Tar	20 galls.	0 10 0
Cost per acre..		2 7 3

This mixture, after being put together, fermented; and was frequently turned, but kept dry. It lay together five weeks, when it was sown in the bottoms of the drills, upon a poor tilly soil.

(e) See Note g.

(f) Sulphate ash from the soap or alkali works.

(g) Gypsum and salt supply sulphuric acid and soda much cheaper than the sulphate of soda; besides the lime and chlorine they contain, which are also useful.

(h) The residual liquor of the salt works; a strong solution of magnesia; and cheap, 1d. to 2d. per gallon.

(i) The salt and old lime should be mixed first, wet; and after a few days, the wood-ashes added dry. Then the sulphates of soda and magnesia.

The coal tar may be mixed in with saw-dust, at the gas works, and the sulphate of ammonia mixed with the saw-dust or peat (or both) before adding to the rest. If old lime is not at hand, new may be used, but then nitrate of potass must be substituted for sulphate of ammonia. They should all ferment together; often turned, but kept in the dry.

ON THE PROPOSED REMEDIES FOR THE PRESENT DEPRESSION IN THE AGRICULTURAL AND COMMERCIAL INTERESTS OF THIS COUNTRY.

Paper II.

BY G. THOMPSON, JUN.

We purpose taking into our consideration in the second paper, the arguments usually urged by the supporters of the present corn laws in their favour. *They contend that the British farmer is a member of a community more highly taxed than those foreign nations which would supply us with food; and that the free importation of comparatively untaxed foreign corn must have the effect of driving the home grower out of the market; and of thus depriving the British manufacturer of his best customer.* The first question that naturally claims our attention in the foregoing argument, is the statement that the British farmer is more highly taxed than the farmer of any other country. We imagine there cannot be the shadow of a doubt as to the correctness of this conclusion; since there is no country on the face of the earth that is burdened with an annual taxation of more than seventy millions sterling, on a population of twenty-six millions, and on an acreage of less than eighty millions, save Great Britain. Nevertheless, it is argued that the British farmers and the British landowners are relieved from the payment of many taxes that assist in raising the revenue; and, indeed, that they pay less in proportion towards the national income than any other class. It is perfectly true that those who own and cultivate the land are relieved from the payment of many imposts which are levied on all other classes. For instance, the farmer pays no auction duty, no horse tax, pays no turnpike toll for haulage of manures; and sundry other advantages are granted by the legislature to him and the land-owner. But we would ask, who pay the chief portion of the poor-rates? Who keep the highways in repair? Who pay the greater share of all county rates? Who support a national church establishment? And the answer must be—the landlord and his tenants. Moreover, we contend

that the amount thus levied from the agricultural portion of the community, far exceeds the amount of those duties, taxes, &c., from which it is freed; and we can with the greatest confidence assert that the agricultural classes, both landlord and tenant, pay more towards the exigencies of the nation than any other; that is to say, more in proportion to the amount of their produce.

If, then, the agriculturist pays more towards the liquidation of the national expenses than any other individual, is it also true than the people of Great Britain are more highly taxed than the people of any other nation? When we state that the amount of taxation in Great Britain is two pounds per head per annum on the total population of the kingdom; and that there is a farther amount of more than twenty millions sterling, which is chiefly raised from the agricultural classes (who are estimated at about one-third of the whole population), as local taxes for the support of the poor, the church, &c.: when we state also that the gross taxation of the country amounts to more than thirty shillings per acre, per annum, upon the *cultivated* land; we feel persuaded that no farther proof is needed, that *the people of Great Britain are more highly taxed than any other people on the face of the earth.* Still, notwithstanding the British farmer is more highly taxed than the foreign farmer, this is no proof that he must be ruined by the competition, inasmuch as the cost of transport may possibly prove a protection in favour of the home grower—a protection exceeding the amount of taxation. And in the *Farmers' Magazine* for March, 1843, is a letter from Mr. W. Rothwell (who states that he was a *rent-paying farmer* from 1813 to 1837), attempting to shew that the whole costs of bringing continental corn into the English markets would be an ample protection to the British farmer. We will see whether such is the case. Mr. R. observes—"I contend that, at the very lowest estimate, the *English landowners* enjoy an advantage of not less than from 16s. to 20s. per quarter over the *landowners of Poland and Russia.* This I contend is quite sufficient to cover the difference of the burdens upon land, and, of course, that we may safely repeal the corn laws." This advantage they possess, he states, in the necessary cost of transport, importer's profits, loss by waste, difference in quality, and other incidental expenses. Now, if it was true that the advantage in favour of the British agriculturist amounted to an average of 18s. per quarter, still it remains to be proved that the well-fed, well-clothed, and well-housed people of Great Britain, can, on similar soils, produce grain at the same price as the half-starved and miserably-clad people of southern Russia. But it is manifestly an error to assert that the British corn grower has an advantage of from 16s. to 20s. per quarter over the corn grower of Poland or Russia. Since the editor of the *Farmer's Magazine,* in his "*Review of the Corn Trade, during the month of March,* 1843," observes that—"At Dantzig the latest nominal price of high-mixed Polish wheats was 30s. per quarter, free on board. Shipping was exceedingly plentiful, and the rates of freight demanded were consequently unusually low. Several foreign ships had been, at that date, chartered for London, at from 3s. to 2s. 6d. per quarter; and the British farmer will before long therefore, by sad experience, discover that, under no circumstances, can our maximum import duty of 20s. per quarter protect his property in the British market from competition with the proprietors of the best descriptions of foreign wheats." We find then that foreign wheat can be imported at 3s. per qr., and as, under a free trade, foreign wheat would find a ready sale, the loss by waste, warehouse rent, &c., would be materially less than it is at present, when the grain is sometimes bonded for months; hence, we may fairly conclude, that 2s. 6d. per quarter would cover all waste, rents, porterage, &c.; moreover, from the circumstance that a free trade would produce a ready and safe sale, the importer would be content with a less profit than heretofore, and 6s. may safely be relied on as ample consideration for merchant's profit and difference in quality, inasmuch as some of the high-mixed Polish wheats are quite equal in quality to our own: thus we have 11s. 6d. per quarter as the *highest* advantage possessed by the home grower over the foreign grower, under a free trade, and supposing that the land was of the same quality in both cases. Even taking Mr. Rothwell's estimate as a correct one—namely, 18s. on the average, as the total cost of bringing foreign wheat into the British market—will he, as a farmer, be bold enough to assert that 48s. per quarter is a remunerative price for the British farmer ? We will go further— would it prove a remunerative price upon the best wheat soils in England ? If Mr. R. be, as he says he is (and which we have no reason to doubt), a practical farmer, he will answer each of the foregoing questions in the negative.

We cannot resist the temptation at this particular stage of our communication, to enter more largely into Mr. Rothwell's letter; and as it would have been more in order in our last paper, we beg to state, as a very conclusive reason why we did not then consider it, that we had not read it. We sincerely hope we shall receive the credit of being impelled by a proper motive, in digressing from the direct course to notice this extraordinary letter. For when agriculturists themselves are so far misled by the growing, but lamentably erroneous opinions of the day, as to advocate, and that ably, the principles which, if adopted, *must ruin British agriculture*; it can be regarded in no other light than as a judicious step, to oppose by all fair and honest means the effects which such apparently impartial conclusions must have upon the wavering. This at least is our purpose, since we fear the consequences of Mr. Rothwell's letter more than all the factious efforts of the notorious League.

If it was true that the British farmer would enjoy an advantage over the foreign farmer, under a free trade, it may still be reasonably questioned if a free trade in foreign corn would not be productive of very serious evils in our currency; but it is an insupportable theory that the difference in value, cost of transport, &c., would prove a protection to the British farmer; and this fact overthrows the greater portion of Mr. Rothwell's arguments; but, as assertion is no proof, we will test the accuracy of the concluding deductions, by weighing their respective merits.

Mr. R. concludes—"First, that we have grown, and shall continue to grow, sufficient for home consumption *in fair average seasons*, and that we can afford wheat in such seasons at from 50s. to 56s., and other grain in proportion."

"Secondly, that the foreign corn-grower cannot produce corn *lower* than this laid down in the manufacturing districts of England, on account of their great distance from this market, the ineffec-

tiveness of their implements of husbandry, their deficiency in skill and that of their labourers, their want of capital, and of good internal communication in the country."

"Thirdly, that these disadvantages are sufficient to counterbalance their *advantages* of lower rents, wages, and taxes."

In consequence of Mr. Rothwell having laid down the theory that the cost of transporting foreign grain to this country would prove a sufficient protection to the home grower, he has fallen into innumerable errors. Having first laid an unsafe foundation the superstructure falls to the ground ; and we are immeasurably astonished that he should have propounded a theory for which he has not adduced a shadow of support. We have already stated, and repeated enquiries have confirmed the truth of our statement, that foreign corn can be brought into this country for less than 12s. per quarter, including a reasonable allowance for the difference in quality. We observe that the price of Polish wheat was 30s.; hence it can be sold in England at 42s. per quarter, and this completely overthrows the argument contained in the second deduction, to the effect that the foreign corn grower cannot produce corn and lay it down in the British corn market at less than from 50s. to 56s. per quarter. And let it be remembered that this contradiction is made from undeniable and existing circumstances. We have not gone back to former times for our quotations, but we have merely stated that which is well known to be correct. We ask then, what would be the consequence if foreign corn could even be brought in at 46s. per quarter ? We fancy the practical man will answer *ruin to the British farmer*. The first deduction of Mr. R.'s we agree with, but it is no argument in favour of a free trade ; it is one against it; since, if we grow sufficient for our own consumption, *in fair average seasons*, why should we allow the introduction of that we do not want, at the imminent risk of reducing to utter ruin numbers of our best customers; nay, more, of driving from the land those who now contribute to the exigencies of the nation, and purchasing our corn of those who would gladly witness the downfall of our empire ?

The second deduction we have disproved from known facts; and the third, of course, falls with it.

We have, "fourthly, that as the principles of the late corn law and the present one are grounded on the idea that the only danger to the British landowners will arise from fair average crops at home ; of course, if my conclusions rest on good grounds, the corn laws may safely be repealed." *Of course, if* his conclusions rested on good grounds, we should be compelled to bring other arguments ; but as his conclusions do not rest on good grounds, *of course*, this deduction is necessarily nugatory.

"Fifthly, we have the declaration that corn laws were never anything but an *injury* to the *tenant farmers and their labourers*." As this is the most serious statement, and particularly as it is the argument with which the *League* has sought to win over the farmers of this country, we shall devote more attention to it than to any other.

Mr. Rothwell states that, "In 1815 wheat got down to the average of 63s. 8d. per quarter, and the landowners considering that with the rents and burdens upon land at that time, it could not be grown for less than 80s., they passed a law prohibiting importation when the price was below that sum. And, under the idea that the general average would be near 80s., landowners, valuers, and farmers, made their valuations and estimates accordingly; and, of course, rents remained at the point which they had gained before the conclusion of the war. Then it was that the ruin of the tenant and the labourer commenced. Then it was that the landowners were receiving 30 per cent. more rent than they ought to have done, &c." Again—"The law of 1823 prohibited importation of wheat when the price was below 70s., with a duty of 17s. per quarter when above. It was again supposed by the farmers and land valuers that the price would average near the above price; of course, rents were still fixed higher than they ought to have been." And—"In 1828 the late law was passed, and has been one of the greatest humbugs that has been enacted of late years. However, the injury it has done the farmers has not been so great as was the case with the two former bills. First, they had had two excellent lessons taught them by the preceding laws, and had not much confidence in any corn laws. Second, what little confidence they had was shaken by the sliding scale, as the price of corn abroad was represented to be so low as to afford the foreign corn merchant to pay almost any amount of duty fixed by the law. They were therefore extremely cautious in their offer of rent; and there had also been a general reduction, to a considerable amount, all over the kingdom, but particularly in the agricultural districts." These are chiefly Mr. Rothwell's reasons for stating that the corn laws have been an injury to tenant farmers and farm labourers, namely, that they have tended to maintain rents at a high rate. Now, how strangely he contradicts facts to serve his own mistaken purposes! If any uninitiated individual should read his letter, they must conclude that land rents in this country have been regulated by what has been considered a remunerative price for wheat; and that the price which the legislature, at stated periods, declared to be a remunerative price, was the groundwork for all calculations respecting the value of land. But the price of wheat has been falling ever since the year 1800, whilst the rent of land has been rising during the same period; and how does this accord with Mr. R.'s theory? He is evidently a very short-sighted politician, or he would know that the rent of land is regulated by the demand, and the degree of improvement in the methods of cultivation.

We have attempted, and we trust successfully, to shew that foreign corn can be sold in the British markets at less than 46s. per quarter. The average rent of our wheat soils certainly does not exceed 35s. per acre, and in many instances 30s. is considered a high rent; all depending, of course, upon the facilities of roads, markets, &c. Now, our best wheat soils produce, on an average, 4½ quarters per acre; hence, allowing that the rent of such soils averages 35s. per acre, we find that the amount of rent to be paid for each quarter of wheat will be nearly 7s. 10d., and as this land is necessarily occasionally unproductive, we will add one-fourth as the quota of rent which must be paid by the wheat crop, making a total of nearly 10s. Mr. Rothwell acknowledges that 56s. per quarter would be a remunerative price. Supposing, then, we reduce the rent to such an amount as will merely liquidate those payments which form a landlord's share towards the national and

local expenses, which is virtually abrogating it, and presenting the land to the tenant free from rent: when we shall have 9s. per quarter to be deducted from 56s., and it should be remembered, that 9s. will be more than the average net income of the British landlord from each quarter of grain produced; this deduction will leave the grain at the price of 47s. per quarter, as a remunerative price to the tenant, when freed from the payment of rent. We have already seen that foreign wheat can be sold in the British market at 46s. per quarter; hence, supposing the British farmer to be liberated from the payment of rent entirely, still he could not compete with the foreign grower under a free trade in corn. Then how fallacious it is to assert that a reduction in rents would enable farmers to prosper under a free trade; and how grievously tenant farmers deceive themselves when they arrive at the conclusion that a free trade in corn would be advantageous to them! We intend entering more extensively into the effects corn laws have upon operative agriculturists, in a review—and we trust a refutation—of a packet of League papers, which has recently been submitted to our inspection; and we will content ourselves for the present, by merely requesting the reader to observe that the only argument adduced by Mr. Rothwell to prove the injurious effects of the corn laws upon operative agriculturists is, that they have maintained rents at an extreme height, by leading the farmer to expect a greater price for his grain than he could ever obtain, and thus inducing him to offer a higher rent than he could afterwards afford to give. In answer to which, we have proved that the corn law price of wheat has had no influence in regulating the value of land, since one has been decreasing, and the other increasing. We would furthermore observe, that we give the farmers of England credit for more judgment than to rely upon any law whatever in making their calculations; and that if experience did not clearly demonstrate that the rent of land was not regulated by the corn laws, still the English farmer would not be guided by the corn laws, but by the average price of wheat in the home market. Mr. Rothwell has therefore failed to prove that the corn laws have injured tenant farmers and farm labourers.

Mr. R. observes—"Sixthly, that all sliding scales are grounded in error; as, however low the duty, when the prices are high here, this will not affect the prices; for as the duty is reduced in England in seasons of scarcity, so the prices will rise in foreign markets, and of course all the advantage will go to the foreign farmer or corn merchant. Common sense will tell any one this, and it only requires facts to be examined to prove its correctness. Sliding scales, however easy and graceful, will lead to uncertainty in the business of corn merchants, but particularly to importers." Observe—"However low the duty, when the prices are high here, this will not affect the prices; for as the duty is reduced in England in seasons of scarcity, so the prices will rise in foreign markets." And yet Mr. Rothwell has previously stated that the corn laws have not benefited the farmer. Is it not obvious to the simplest understanding, that if the effect of the corn laws has been to maintain high prices in seasons of scarcity, that they must have been more beneficial to the farmer than a free trade; under the operation of which, such a quantity of corn would be at all times imported as would perpetuate low prices? When is it the British farmer can afford to sell corn at the cheapest rate? Of course, in seasons of plenty. But is it rational that he should be compelled to sell it at the same low price in seasons of scarcity? Indeed, it is unnecessary for us to ask Mr. Rothwell such questions, as we have only to weigh the merits of his statements. Yet we must beg the reader to observe that Mr. R.'s statement is one of the strongest arguments in favour of corn laws, inasmuch as he acknowledges that by the wholesome regulation of the much abused *sliding scale*, foreign corn is imported when we require it, yet that such importation has not the effect of lowering the prices at the time when the British farmer is least able to bear it.

We have, " Seventhly—that there are other causes than the corn laws for the present depression in trade; for, according to their own statements, when food is *lowest trade is best*, and of course, *trade is best* when there is the *least foreign corn imported*; therefore, corn could not have been taken in exchange for goods." Then why repeal the corn laws? If trade is best when there is the least foreign corn imported, that is, when we grow sufficient for our own consumption, why remove those laws which enable us to grow sufficient, by giving a premium to the advancement of agriculture?

In taking leave of Mr. Rothwell, we will briefly expose a few of his most striking inconsistencies; of which he has so many that it is by no means wonderful his essay should have failed to obtain one of the prizes offered by the League.

Firstly, then, we should not extend our foreign trade by repealing the corn laws. Yet we ought to repeal them!

Secondly—" At present the Germans, Russians, &c., want only *cash*; and while they do this it will be ruin to us to take much of their grain." Therefore we should admit corn duty free!

Thirdly—" Under the corn laws, wheat has been continually getting cheaper, and the quantity produced in this country continually increasing." Still we ought to repeal the corn laws!

Fourthly—" It would not do for England to purchase foreign corn to any extent with *hard cash*. If we must import extensively, so as to injure the British farmer in his own market, wheat must be laid down in the manufacturing districts at a less price than 56s." Therefore we may safely run the risk of repealing the corn laws!

Finally—" As a nation, we can gain nothing by a free trade in corn; but, if foreign growers can undersell us in our markets, we shall be ruined by paying them in cash." Therefore we may *safely* repeal the corn laws!

We trust we have not exhausted the patience of the reader in thus wading through this labyrinth of incongruities; we trust, moreover, that we have not failed to render conspicuous the utter contrariety of the arguments adduced; and reposing calmly in this our confident position, we once more gladly renew our primary course, by testing the strength of the arguments usually and most frequently alleged by the supporters of the corn laws. We have already proved the truth of the argument, *that the British farmer is a member of a community more highly taxed than those foreign nations which would supply us with food.* We have not merely proved this, but we have farther shown that the amount of that taxation,

independent of rent, is more than the disadvantages which the foreign grower labours under.

We have now to see if *the free importation of comparatively untaxed foreign corn must have the effect of driving the home grower out of the market.* In order to sustain this argument we must first prove that other nations can afford us sufficient supplies of corn, at a lower cost than our own growth, to have this effect. We might be content to reason comparatively, and satisfy ourselves by merely showing, that if other nations cannot send us corn, it is useless to admit corn duty free; while, if they can, since we raise sufficient in average seasons, they could only do so by underselling us, and thus driving some of our home-growers out of the market: we might thus argue, and dispose of the question summarily, but that we wish to prove to our readers that other nations would supply us with large quantities of corn, under a free trade.

We have disposed of the ridiculous argument that the foreign corn grower could not undersell us in our own markets; then we have simply to answer the question, can the corn growing countries supply us with larger quantities of that commodity than we have already imported, at the same low price?

When we observe the low rates at which foreign wheats are offered, and when we consider the circumstance that a slight demand in this country invariably causes a superabundant influx, without the least advance in price, we have strong presumptive evidence that we might import a much larger quantity of corn into this country than we do at present. It has been stated that to increase the quantity of foreign corn grown considerable expenses must be incurred; since the corn at present raised is produced on the banks of the rivers, and close to highways well calculated for its transmission at small costs; and that to increase the extent of cultivated ground, new roads, &c., must be constructed, the cost of which must be levied from the produce. This is unquestionably correct to a certain extent; but it behoves us to remember that the formation of *good* roads would be attended with a very trifling increase of expense upon each quarter of corn; and that as money is the thing most wanted, as labour is very low, and as there are extensive tracts of land yet uncultivated which would yield immense crops, the probability is that increasing and almost inexhaustible supplies of corn would be raised at a price sufficiently low to enable the importers to undersell the home-grower. But it signifies little to the substantiation of our argument whether the quantity imported is capable of increase or not, since, under a free trade, foreign corn could be brought into this country at all times, whether our own supplies were sufficient or otherwise; and if the same quantity should be brought in when we produced sufficient as when we did not, the effect must be to reduce the already low price still lower, and thus to drive a portion of the home-growers out of the market. There is no argument so insupportable as that by introducing foreign corn duty free, we should extend the markets for our manufactures; or, in other words, that we could retain our British customers who produce corn, with an extension of our foreign customers whose corn we must then take. The home-growers would be depressed as much as the foreign growers would be encouraged in their operations. The market would not in the end overflow; it would only be competently supplied, and depend in part on foreign instead of domestic industry. If Poland and Russia would produce more for the British manufacturers, Great Britain and Ireland would produce less. Farming to the extent of perhaps six millions of quarters annually would be destroyed in the British Isles, and farming to a similar extent would be called into existence on the banks of the Vistula or the Dnieper. But there could not be any *permanent* increase of the supply over the demand. Foreign competition would do for British agriculture what British manufactures would do, and have often done, when so admitted to foreign manufacturing industry, viz., produce a total destruction of a large part of the deluged branch of industry. We think it indisputable that the introduction of foreign corn duty free, must have the effect of driving a portion of the home-growers out of the market.

We have now to consider an argument arising out of the foregoing, and one which is too often urged in support of the corn laws—viz., that the poor lands of this country cannot compete with the rich soils of foreign nations under the operation of a free trade in corn, even although the cost of transport be added to the price of corn in foreign ports. As *political economists* we are constrained to declare this is one of the most indefensible reasons why we should have a corn law.

No truth is so palpable,—no maxim so generally received, as that *true political economy consists in promoting the welfare of the majority*. Whatever is done by way of upholding the interests of one class to the neglect and injury of those of all others, must inevitably tend to retard the progress of a nation. "Thou shalt do justice and love mercy," was the injunction of the inspired St. Matthew; and we have daily instances of happiness and prosperity attending its application, with as many of misery and ruin following its neglect; affording a striking proof that the same God overlooks the actions and dispenses the portions of men, who ages since was more visibly, though not more effectively, the controller of human events. This decree is equally binding on nations and on individuals, and its neglect equally injurious to both. And the nation which supports the interests of one class in particular is guilty of injustice, which is alike condemned by the laws of God and man. But how frequently we see instances of men, in some particular trade or profession, entertaining and promulgating the opinion that the nation will be ruined, for no other specific reason than that their interests—the interests of an insignificant minority—have been sacrificed for the benefit of the whole nation, perhaps the whole world. This is in a limited degree the case with those agriculturists who oppose the repeal of the corn laws, on the ground that the *poor* lands of this country can never compete with the *rich* lands of foreign countries. Passing over the plea of high rents and other obstacles, we will suppose the land their own, not subject to the payment of rent. Moreover we will reject the excuse, certainly a justifiable one, of more expensive labour. We will suppose the English farmer farming his poorer lands under the same advantages as the foreign cultivator farms his richer soils. Would it even then be just that the whole nation should be compelled by a law to purchase their grain at a higher price of their own countrymen, in order that they may cultivate poor soils, rather than allow them to purchase it at a lower price of another nation? Most assuredly

it would not. And, therefore, the argument is insupportable; for whatever benefits one class to the injury of all others, must eventually injure the nation. Yet, weak as the argument is, it is the chief point urged by many supporters of the corn laws; and by far the greater portion of the writings of the Anti-Corn-Law party have been devoted to the object of overthrowing this particular apology. Many speeches have been made containing no other substantial proposition, than that it is unjust to tax the many for the benefit of a few. Whilst the supporters of the corn laws continue to advocate their existence on the grounds of vested interests and poorer soils, so long will they find a strong opposition to their arguments. *If the corn laws are to be maintained, they can only be maintained on the principle that they are essential to the welfare of the nation at large.*

We have now considered fairly the various arguments of the supporters of the corn laws. We have shown in this paper that the *British farmer is a member of a community more highly taxed than those foreign nations which would supply us with food, and that the free importation of comparatively untaxed foreign corn must have the effect of driving the home grower out of the market;* and, in our last paper, we clearly proved that *this would be depriving the British manufacturer of his best customer.* This conclusion needs no proof, for those who support a repeal of the corn laws declare that foreign nations cannot take our manufactures unless we take their corn, consequently they can only take them to the same amount as we take corn; therefore, as the people who now grow corn for us take our manufactures, by taking foreign corn we shall be merely changing the customers for our manufactured articles, even supposing they will take manufactures for their corn. Now, it is obvious we cannot gain by a repeal, but it is by no means obvious that we shall not lose, as we have already shown in our first paper.

Our next paper will contain conclusions drawn from the foregoing, and applicable to the future.

Lion Street, Kidderminster,
April 26th, 1843.

CHINESE AGRICULTURE.—"I took our cutter the other day, and eight men, and starting from the ship at five o'clock in the morning, went about forty miles up the labyrinth of islands, landing at several places, and going into their villages. The country was beautiful in the extreme—much more so than I ever saw. Fancy the most hilly country that can possibly be, one mountain rising from the foot of another in the most varied manner, and cultivated in the highest degree to the very top! In fact, their farming would not disgrace an English farmer; and I very much doubt whether a man put down here from the clouds would know that he was not in England, but for the circumstance that pieces of land which no Englishman would think of venturing his neck upon, are here in the most beautiful order; indeed, the resemblance between the two countries is in every respect most striking; and I decidedly think that the people I have seen are quite as much civilized, if not more so, than you would find in England in the same situation—they certainly exceed them in politeness. One village I landed in, I sailed the boat up a beautiful creek for some distance, until I was stopped by some large lock-gates, when I landed, and walked up to the houses, alongside quite as good a canal as any I ever saw, with good strong locks on pre-

cisely the same principle as our own. The stone
bridges over it were beautiful, with heads, carved in
stone, of angels and devils, stuck at different places on
the sides. The houses were built of square stones, extremely neatly put together, and roofed with beautiful
red tiles, each ornamented with a different device. The
inside was generally divided into three or four rooms,
all very neat; and there the similarity between them
and Old England, a place they never heard of, became
most ridiculous. There was the plastered floor, the
same shaped tables and chairs, and the closet, with the
cups and saucers (of the most beautiful china, by the
bye); there too, was the kitchen—the wash-house, with
the boiler and sink. In the yard, again, the pig-sties
were very amusing—the identical pig-sty door that they
have at a place you know very well in Yorkshire, opening with a large wooden latch, and a hole to put your
finger through from the outside to lift it up, squeaking
on its hinges when opened or shut, the same to half a
note."—*China as it was.*

AGRICULTURAL TOUR IN DEN-
MARK, SWEDEN, AND RUSSIA.

BY JAMES F. W. JOHNSTON, F.R.S.

I.—DENMARK.

(From the Journal of the Royal Agricultural Society.)

There is confessedly much to be done still for
British agriculture. Many good practices may
still be introduced from other countries, and many
already in use among us may be more widely spread.
Many sound precepts also remain still to be generally diffused—by the application of which we may
reasonably anticipate that the land will be rendered not only more productive on the whole,
but more remunerative also both to the landlord
and to the tenant.

And yet a person moderately skilled in agricultural affairs, who has had the opportunity of previously becoming acquainted with some of our best
cultivated districts, will soon satisfy himself, when
travelling in foreign countries—that in few other
parts of the world is the practical culture of soils
like ours more thoroughly understood than in the
British islands—that in none has so great a breadth
of land been more scientifically and more expen-
sively improved. It may be that to certain parts
of Holland and the Netherlands, and to certain
limited districts in Italy, a general superiority
must be conceded—and that in every country the
traveller visits he will observe something which he
may wish to see imitated at home; yet in few districts of Europe of large extent will he find united
fields so green, hedge-rows so beautiful, stackyards so neat—so little waste and unenclosed land
—so much artificially drained—so much expen-
sively manured—so many improved and profitable
cattle—and, generally, so much visible comfort
and skill pervading every branch of the practice of
husbandry. This much seems to be due to British
agriculture, even from those who see most clearly
its defects, and are most anxious to remove them.

Yet this difference in favour of our own island
is to be ascribed as much to the circumstances in
which it has been placed, as to the superior intelligence and industry of our population. It is easy
to write out a system of practical agriculture, by
which in a given climate the largest amount of
produce of this or that kind may be raised on this
or that variety of soil; but when this abstract system comes to be put in practice in this or that

country, it is interesting to observe how much it
must be altered and modified by the circumstances
of that country—how a very bad system of farming
theoretically, may he the only one which can be
carried on with profit—and may be best suited
consequently to the circumstances of the district.

We ought therefore to criticise leniently, and
with some hesitation, the agricultural methods we
find in operation in other parts of the world. The
nature of the soil—the character of the climate—
the economical condition of the country—the political relations of the several classes of society—
the tenure on which the land is held—the relation
which the number of the people bears to the average production of food—the existence of a more
ready market, either domestic or foreign, for one
or another kind of produce—all have a necessary
and important influence upon the modes of culture.
Hence the candid observer who is in no haste to
condemn, will often, when he becomes acquainted
with all these circumstances, find himself compelled to admit that rude methods and practices,
which are theoretically bad, are, if not the best,
yet the most prudent under all the circumstances
of the place in which he observes them, and such
as he would himself in the like case have adopted.

Of these two truths—the general superiority of
British agriculture and agricultural enterprise, and
the effect of circumstances in modifying the modes
of culture—I observed many illustrations during a
short tour I made in the past summer through part
of Denmark, Sweden, and Russia. As some of the
circumstances I observed were not without interest to myself, I venture to hope that a few notices
of what appeared most worthy of record may not
prove uninteresting to the members of the Royal
Agricultural Society.

As he ascends the Elbe the stock farmer will
not fail to observe on his left how the marshy
lands which skirt the river and stretch for several
miles inland, are everywhere dotted with cattle,
the herds becoming more frequent and more dense
as he ascends, till the pasture is cut off by the
bluffs of Blaukanaes, where the high sandhills
begin to confine the river. To these marshes the
lean cattle of the Jutlands are annually driven to
be fattened.

From the mouth of the Eyder, in the south of
Sleswick, to that of the Elbe, and up the latter
river, narrowing as it ascends, this band of marsh-
land girdles the south-western part of the Danish
territory. That portion which lies on the sea-coast
between the two rivers, a district 30 or 40 miles in
length, forms the Dit-marsh. The Wilster and
Krempe marshes lie on the north shore of the Elbe,
in the neighbourhood of the town of Gluckstadt,
which is generally admired by the stranger as he
ascends the river—and the more so, probably, because the smoothness of the water makes him now
forget the pains of the rough sea, and invites him
upon deck. From these latter marshes the best
oxen are brought to the Hamburg market. These
cattle are fattened entirely upon the natural grasses,
the culture of turnips being almost wholly unknown, and other artificial food seldom had recourse to, except in the neighbourhood of breweries and distilleries.

It is a curious geological fact in regard to the
Wilster and Krempe marshes, on which these
cattle are fattened, that they are known to be gradually sinking in level. Within the last three
hundred years they are said to have sunk about

seven feet, and an area of thirty square miles is now three feet below the level of high water in the Elbe. The whole tract is saved from inundation only by the careful preservation of the embankments. On boring, the cause of this sinking becomes apparent. Ten feet of fertile silty clay rest (float ?) on thirty feet of water; at the bottom of which is the sand of an ancient sea-beach. How this singular arrangement of land upon water has taken place, it is not easy to explain in a satisfactory manner. My friend Professor Forchhammer, of Copenhagen, to whom I am indebted for the fact, suggests that the silt may originally have been deposited upon a bank of sea-weed, and that the slow decay of the latter may have left the vacuity which is now filled with water. However this may be, only long habit, one would suppose, can reconcile people to live without concern on a spot which a sudden inroad of the sea on a stormy night might entirely swallow up.*

During my short stay at Hamburg I visited a dairy-farm at Ham, a few miles from the city, occupied and apparently well farmed by Mr. Hymers. This farm contains 260 scheffels,† a little more than as many acres, of light land, some of it poor and sandy, but which nevertheless grows wheat better than rye. On this extent of land, which is chiefly in grass, are maintained from 120 to 130 cows, all in milk, but they are partly fed on the refuse of a distillery established on the farm. These cattle are milked till the spring, when they are gradually sold off to the butcher, and replaced by others which have newly calved. They are milked during the whole time of fattening; but their beef, as we should expect, is of an inferior quality. In the market it brings only 10 dollars for 100lbs., or one-sixth less than the fat oxen from the marshes. I believe a considerable quantity of this second-rate beef from the numerous dairy-farms is sold in the German markets. The milk and cream produced at Ham are carefully bottled and sealed, and are thus sent to the houses of their customers in Hamburg. The former is sold at 1½d., the latter at 6d. a quart. By this method of bottling, the character of the dairy is maintained, the buyer is secured from fraud, while the milk itself, being less agitated in coming from the country, arrives in a sweeter and sounder state at the house of the consumer.

As good pasture is on this farm of so much consequence, great attention is paid to the top-dressing of the grass land. The liquid manure is conducted from the large and spacious cow-houses into a cistern outside of the buildings, which is arched over and planted with a shrubbery, a square trap-door being left for the insertion of the pump. This cistern is 100 feet long, 14 feet broad, and 8 feet deep, apparently a large size, yet too small still for so numerous a farm-stock. It is capable of containing the produce of three months, which in most cases would appear sufficient, since it is seldom that there is any serious winter before January, so that if the cistern were empty when the cattle are brought in, they would be turned out again to the spring pasture before it was completely full. But such an adjustment of times and quantities cannot always be conveniently made, and a loss, therefore, now and then occurs. The liquid manure (jauche, as it is here called) is applied at almost every season of the year to one field or another, yet it may not always be the most proper time when the cistern is full. Hence the advantage of ample space for a large supply. Upon this conviction Mr. Hymers informed me he was about to erect a second cistern of large dimensions.

English farmers are now, I believe, beginning to understand how very much actual *money* has hitherto been lost in this country by the neglect or waste of the liquid of the stables, cow-houses, and farm-yards. A farmer would not tolerate a servant who wasted the grass or hay intended for his stock, yet *he who wastes liquid manure wastes grass* —diminishing not only his present profits, but his chance of future gains also, for he so far exhausts and injures his landlord's fields. Few are unaware of the benefits derived in many localities from judicious irrigation, and especially where, as in the neighbourhood of Edinburgh and some other large towns, the water of the common sewers can be employed for the purpose. Now the water-cart is only a portable irrigator, and the liquid of the farm-yard is as efficacious as that of the sewers. To collect the former therefore with care, and to apply it to the land whenever the horses are at leisure, would at little additional expense increase both the produce and the general fertility of many of our farms.

Being so near Hamburg, manure is comparatively abundant at Ham. Mr. Hymers therefore manures his land every year, and is allowed to cultivate his arable fields as he pleases. He grows wheat, barley, and potatoes, but no turnips. Wheat yields twelve-fold, and potatoes 6 to 8 tons per acre. Foreign manures are also occasionally applied, such as the fish refuse sometimes brought from Hammerfest in Norway, and, during the last year, the South American guano. About a ton of the latter had recently been applied to the grass-land of this farm; it was then selling in Hamburg at 12l. 5s. the English ton (10 marks courant for 100 Hamburg pounds.)

The rent of land in this part of the country, when at such a distance from Hamburg that milk cannot be readily sent to market, is about 5 or 6 Prussian dollars a scheffel, or 15s. to 18s. an English acre. There is very much of the sandy land in the neighbourhood of Hamburg that cannot be worth half of this rent.

Hamburgh to Kiel, July 5th.—The road from Hamburg to Kiel crosses the southern part of Holstein, and passes through some of the dreariest parts of this extensive duchy. About one-half of Holstein consists of sandy, unproductive tracts of land, and of what are considered by many as irreclaimable heath and moor. Nearly all the flat and level country, with the exception of the marsh-lands, is more or less of this character. Where it undulates and rises into hills, and especially on the northern and eastern portions of the duchy, the soil changes in character;

---

* "In 1421 the sea broke in at Dort, drowned seventy-two villages and 100,000 people, and formed the Zuyder-Zee." This part of Holland, it is supposed, may have originally been in a similar situation with the Wilster Marsh—since it is recorded by an old Dutch writer that in 1420 the proprietor of a farm on the tract of land, which was swallowed up, found *a herring in his well;* and thinking it unsafe to remain where the sea was evidently undermining him, sold his farm, and removed to another part of the country. The following year the catastrophe came.

† *Scheffel* usually denotes a bushel *measure.* It is in this neighbourhood used to express a quantity of land equal to 200 square poles *(ruten).*

the unfruitful gravel and sand giving place to occasional clays, and to clayey loams and marls, productive in corn and rape, fruitful in milk and butter, and bearing a natural growth of magnificent beech.

The existence of so much comparatively worthless land in Holstein is, I believe, contrary to the general impression not among ourselves, but, as I have found, in other countries also. This has arisen, in part, no doubt, from the fame of the rich alluvial pastures of the marsh-lands on its southern and western borders,* and partly from the fact that the east and north of this duchy—the most frequently seen and visited by travellers —can boast of some of the most picturesque and fertile tracts to be met with in the Danish dominions. To satisfy ourselves that the interior of both Sleswick and Holstein is of greatly inferior agricultural value, we have only to cast our eyes upon a recent map of these duchies, when the few names of places which present themselves will indicate at once the thinness of the population and the smallness of the agricultural produce.

The cause of this comparative infertility is to be found in the geological nature of the deposits with which this district is covered. Within the girdle of rich alluvial (marshy) soil that encircles the western coast of South Jutland, Sleswick, and Holstein, stretches a broad band of flat country covered with a white or grey, naturally almost barren sand (the *ahl* formation of Forchhammer), in many places lying waste, but which, like the sands of Norfolk, is capable of being brought into cultivation by the aid of the marl and clay which lie beneath, often at an available depth. This sandy zone, which in South Jutland covers more than half the breadth of the Danish peninsula, narrows towards the south, in Sleswick and Holstein, and terminates in a point on the banks of the Elbe, a few miles below Hamburg.

To the east of this naturally unfruitful band, the remainder of these three duchies, the whole of the Danish islands—with the exception of Bornholm —and a part of the south of Sweden, are covered with a variable thickness of sands, gravels, clays, and marls, in which rolled stones (boulders) of various kinds and sizes abound, and by the presence of which these beds are almost everywhere characterised. In Zealand and Funen, in some of the smaller islands, and on the eastern part of Holstein and Sleswick, this deposit (the boulder formation) forms an undulating country of hill and dale—of rounded hills and basin-shaped hollows. The whole of this undulating tract is rich in clay and marl, and abounds in marl pits. Many of the hollows are filled with peat, or, where this has been much dug out for fuel, as in Zealand, with small sheets of water; and the whole of the drier country bears naturally luxuriant woods of beech, or, when in skilful culture, yields abundant crops of rape and corn. Nearly all that is rich in Danish agriculture is to be seen upon the undulating part of this formation.

---

* The three Danish-German duchies of Sleswick, Holstein, and Lauenburg, have an area of about 340 square German miles—of which the marsh-lands occupy between 60 and 70, or about one-fifth of the whole. (See Mr. Stanley Carr's paper on the Dairy Husbandry of Lauenburg, in the first volume of this Journal, p. 371.) On Professor Forchhammer's geological map of Denmark they appear to occupy a considerably smaller area.

Chemically considered, this boulder formation differs from the sandy *ahl* formation which lies above it by the large proportion of lime it contains. This lime has been derived, as is shown by the many blocks of chalk that are scattered through this formation, from the ancient destruction of some of the chalk rocks which still abound in Denmark, and it is not only deposited in nests and layers of marl—so rich in calcareous matter that it is profitable to dig it up and lay it upon the land—but it is generally disseminated through the sands and clays also in smaller proportion, and thus is a main agent in imparting its natural fertility to a great portion of the country on which this formation rests. But the bottom or lower layers of this same formation consist, where they are best and most extensively seen, of a gravel or sand containing many flints, and in many places *little* lime, and they rest upon dark-coloured beds of a species of clay (belonging to a kind of brown coal formation), which is said to hold out little promise of being useful in improving the flinty layers that lie above it. With this lower sandy and gravelly deposit, containing flints, the *flat* parts of Holstein and Sleswick, which belong to this formation, are covered, and they are in a great measure open heaths and moors, or unenclosed commons. Over such a flat the traveller passes on his way from Hamburg to Kiel. When the heath disappears, the soil is in many places a white and blowing sand.

We left Hamburg at 10 P.M., and reached Neu Minster, about half way, early in the morning. The rye which grew near this place appeared to be perfectly ripe (July 6th), much of it absolutely white; the oats, short, green, and full of wild mustard. The town shepherd, as we changed horses, was blowing his short melancholy cow's-horn, to bring out the cattle for the daily pasture on the common land. The sandy soil with few flints, of the earlier part of our journey, gradually gave place to a gravel, in some places deep and full of flints. It is said that over this wide tract of heathy land the flinty gravel and sand are not more than six inches in depth, and that the nature of the dark bed beneath gives little hope of amelioration from deeper ploughing. It appeared to me, however, that considerable portions of land here and there were capable of being reclaimed, or, where already in crop, rendered much more productive by judicious drainage. In some of the more level parts of the country it might be difficult to find a ready outlet for the water, but otherwise the making of the drains would be attended with little expense. From such drainage I should expect not merely the removal of superfluous moisture, and the gradual amelioration of the climate, but an improvement also in the nature of the subsoil, here said to be unfriendly to vegetation.

The great problem to be solved in many districts, before the soil can be permanently rendered more productive, is the mode of effectually and economically altering the subsoil. This is beyond the reach of ordinary top-dressings and manurings, and even deep ploughing (supposing that by merely bringing it to the surface the quality of the subsoil is materially improved) produces only a partial and temporary change. Draining seems to me to be in general the only way of effectually and permanently altering the subsoil; and this constitutes one of the chief recommendations of its use upon light and sandy soils. The rain, which passes through such soils with comparative ease, washes out from the subsoil those noxious ingredients which are hostile to vegetation, sweetens and salubrifies it to the depth of the drains, and fits it for being brought up to the surface without producing any injurious effect. By such action of the rains upon the thin heathy lands of Holstein, the unwholesome clays beneath might be so far purified as to qualify them for being mixed advantageously with the sands and gravels above, while they would at the same time, where left undisturbed, permit the roots readily to descend into their substance in search of food.

About eight English miles from Kiel the land began to undulate, and at the same time to become more fertile. Though still very light, it produced beautiful crops of oats, barley, rye, and wheat—of each of which kind of grain very extensive fields were seen. The wheat was thick and heavy, and the oats of a peculiarly dark green colour. This soil, as I have already observed, is probably rich in lime, and the natural waste of this substance is supplied from the marl-pits, of which numbers exist at no great distance from the road on the approach to Kiel. Along the skirts of the undulating country also the heath and sandy moor is partially improved, in consequence of the ready access to these deposits of marl.

On some of the otherwise bare slopes of the sandy and gravelly banks by the road-side the *mare's-tail* and the *colt's-foot* abounded, the latter confirming the above opinion as to the presence of lime in the soil, and the former showing its power to yield with ease the abundant supply of silica so necessary to the growth of corn.*

---

* I had no opportunity of enquiring into the mode of cultivation adopted for the *wheat* crops of this neighbourhood, nor whether it differed materially from the improved husbandry of Funen, described in a subsequent page. It appears, however, from the statements of Colonel Le Couteur in his very interesting work " On the Varieties of Wheat" (pp. 39 and 72), that the Kiel wheat (a very productive variety, known by the name of Duck's-bill, and having an exceedingly fine ear) gives a flour which is only fit for making pastry, and is too tenacious for household bread. Now this tenacity is due to the presence of a large quantity of gluten in the flour; and the quantity of gluten is generally supposed to depend upon the quantity of animal or other manure capable of yielding ammonia, which is present in the soil. But we can scarcely, I think, attribute this quality of the Kiel wheat to any high manuring of the land, above the highly farmed districts of our own island. It must depend, then, upon the nature of the soil—upon the large quantity of lime it contains, or which is added to it in the form of marl? This may have some influence, since it is said that in the county Down the wheat grown on soils which rest upon limestone is richer in gluten than the other wheats of the county. If so, this would be an interesting fact in regard to the action of lime, and might help Colonel Le Conteur to the kind of soil on which this variety of wheat may be expected to thrive. It would show also that the proportion of gluten in wheat is not dependent solely on the kind and quantity of manure added to the soil.

But another question still remains. Is the proportion of gluten not dependent upon the *variety* of wheat also, as well as upon the soil or manure?

A railway has been for some time projected between Hamburg and Kiel; and the Danish government has given its sanction to the plan. It would no doubt be a great benefit to the district, though the prospects of a remunerating return to the shareholders are very doubtful. The slender foundation on which the proposers of this line are content to found their hopes was shown by a paragraph in a Hamburg newspaper which caught my eye at Kiel. The projectors of the Altona and Kiel Railway announced that they *now* believed that the return, instead of being only 2½ per cent. on the outlay, might be safely estimated at 2½½ per cent. This happy expectation was founded on the introduction of the new manure *guano*, which was to be carried along the line in such quantities as, besides remunerating the shareholders, to convert also the barren heaths and moors of central Holstein into blooming and productive fields.

Though much corn and rape are grown in the country around Kiel, yet I believe butter is one of the principal articles of export. On some of the farms 200 or 300 cattle are kept, yet on the whole route between Hamburg and Kiel I did not observe a single field-turnip. In Holstein much of the soil is said to be now tired of rape. The cultivator of the land in almost every country is under a strong temptation to raise crop after crop of that kind of produce which finds the readiest sale and yields the largest return. In Great Britain we grow corn as often as we can, and Holstein exhausts herself to supply us with rapeseed, Jamaica to send us sugar, and the United States to give us cotton, tobacco, and rice.

There is a remarkable chemical difference between the straw of the corn-bearing plants and that of rape—the former containing much silica, the latter much potash, soda, and lime.* It is possible, therefore, that a saline manure might ameliorate the soil on which rape has ceased to thrive. Rape straw spread upon the fields and

---

Would, for example, the Duck's-bill, sown alongside of another variety, and under the same circumstances, produce a flour much richer in gluten than that of the other ? This is a very interesting theoretical question ; one not unlikely, I think, to be answered in the affirmative, and which is not unsusceptible of an important practical bearing. Perhaps Colonel Le Conteur could throw some light on this question.

The reader will recollect that the nutritive qualities of wheaten flour are supposed by *some* to be almost directly in proportion to the quantity of gluten it contains.

* Thus 1,000lbs. of ripe wheat and rape straws, though they left respectively nearly the same weight of ash when burned, yet contained the several constituents of the ash in the following very different proportions :—

	Wheat.		Rape.
Potash	0.2	....	8.8
Soda	0.3	....	5.5
Lime	2.4	....	8.1
Magnesia	0.3	....	1.2
Alumina and oxide of iron	0.9	....	0.9
Silica	28.7	....	0.8
Sulphuric acid	0.4	....	5.2
Phosphoric acid	1.7	....	3.8
Chlorine	0.3	....	4.4
	35.2lbs.		38.7lbs.

burned is known greatly to promote the growth of
the succeeding crop. A properly adjusted mixture
of the saline substance of which the rape-ash consists would form a *rape manure*, from which
similar advantages might be anticipated. Even
where husbandry is most carefully practised, and
as much as possible of all the produce is again returned to the corn-fields, there is always an annual
loss of the saline constituents of the soil and
crops, carried away chiefly by the rains and
drains, which must in some way or other be restored to the land, or it will ultimately deteriorate
in quality. A rational practice, therefore, as well
as sound theory, indicates the trial, after previous
marling, of a mixture of common salt with sulphate of soda, wood-ashes, and bone dust, on
lands which have ceased to yield luxuriant crops
of rape.

Kiel to Copenhagen.—The voyage by steam from
Kiel to Copenhagen occupies about twenty-four
hours. The islands which are passed before
reaching the coast of Zealand are Laaland (Low-
land), Falster, and Moen. Except a part of the
island of Moen, where the soil, a calcareous clay,
rests immediately upon chalk, and forms some of
the best wheat land in Denmark, these islands, as
well as Funen and Zealand, are covered by the
same boulder formation which overspreads the
eastern half of Jutland, Sleswick, and Holstein. I
had no opportunity during my recent visit of personally observing the state of agriculture in these
islands, but I was favoured by Mr. Hofman Bang,
of Hofmansgave, near Odensee, one of the most
zealous and intelligent agriculturists in the island,
with much information in regard to the existing
state of farming in Funen. The soil there is generally light and sandy, yet, like the similar soils
in the undulating district of Holstein, it grows
good crops of corn and rape. The custom of
taking three white crops in succession used to be
general. Among the better class of farmers the
course was—fallow with manure, rye, barley, oats,
clover and rye-grass, and then two or three years'
grass ; so that only one-eighth of the arable land
was manured every year. Among the peasants
(small farmers) the artificial grasses are not used ;
and three white crops, followed by two or three
years of grass and a fallow, with manure, is still
the prevailing practice. The improved course introduced more recently on some of the large estates is only a step towards the full measure of
improvement. This is—1st, naked fallow with
manure; 2nd, rye ; 3rd, wheat; 4th, potatoes and
vetches manured ; 5th, barley ; 6th, oats; 7th,
grass, for two or three years. The culture of potatoes is extending, and many are also now grown
in Zealand ; but, though many cattle are kept,
turnips are unknown as a general winter food.
Here and there small experimental patches are occasionally seen ; and Mr. Bang told me that, besides potatoes, he occasionally raises a few
Swedish turnips for fattening his cattle. In
Funen the cattle are kept in the house from the
middle of November to the middle of May, and
are in general fed all the while on straw and hay
only—something of the old Scottish system, now,
fortunately, a matter of history only, or merely
keeping cattle alive till the spring pasture came.
Potatoes with chopped straw are now occasionally
given. Here, as in Jutland, the cattle are seldom
fattened, but are sold lean. In places which are
remote from a market the oats are sometimes used
up in fattening the stock.

As upon the mainland opposite to it, much
butter and cheese are made in Funen, and considerable attention is at present directed to the improvement of the latter article. The refuse milk
is employed in fattening pigs. A mixture of
clover, or nettles or other weeds, with water and
whey, allowed to stand till it is sour, is also much
employed in Holstein and Sleswick in the feeding
of pigs, and is said to fatten wonderfully.

In Funen there exists an agricultural society,
under the name of the Patriotic Society, which
exerts itself in the promotion of a better husbandry. The principal improvements yet effected
have arisen by the introduction of better implements and the encouragement of better ploughing.
The preparation of composts also, through
their exertions, is beginning to be understood
and practised. The meadows are dressed with
town-manure and wood-ashes ; but notwithstanding the wonderful effects it produces in Mecklenburg, a country so near, gypsum has not been
found beneficial in Funen. As the same fact has
been observed also in Holstein, it is probable that
the soils of the boulder formation, which, as I
have said, covers so much of the eastern half of
Denmark, are already sufficiently impregnated
with gypsum or with some other saline sulphates
which act in a similar manner upon vegetation.[*]
If this be so, it affords an illustration of the important practical bearing which an elementary
knowledge of the geological structure of a country
may have upon the operations of the farmer. The
future improvers of Danish agriculture have probably little general benefit to anticipate from the
employment of gypsum, wherever the sand,
gravels, clays, and marls of this formation extend.

That *Danish Agriculture* in general is in an im-

---

[*] It may even be that this supposed richness in
sulphates has been one cause of the known productiveness of the rape crops in these districts, since
the straw of rape is so rich in sulphuric acid (see
previous note, p. 421). The action of the sulphates is no doubt very much owing to the acid
they contain ; and they *all* affect in a similar way
the same kind of plants as the clovers and other
leguminous crops. Yet they act differently also on
certain cultivated plants. Thus Mr. Burnett, of
Gadgirth, near Ayr, informs me that he last year
(1841) dressed two parts of a field of turnips respectively with sulphate of soda and with gypsum.
The former produced no apparent effect, while the
latter *doubled the crop*. At first I fancied that the
land might have been destitute of lime, which the
plant obtained from the gypsum ; but I have since
learned that the land had previously been heavily
limed. Liebig would say that in this experiment
the gypsum had fixed the ammonia of the atmosphere, which the sulphate of soda could not do. I
do not coincide with those who thus explain the
action of gypsum, for reasons which I have elsewhere stated ; but the result of Mr. Burnett is so
very interesting, that I would gladly hear of the
accurate repetition of his experiment.

While this sheet is going through the press, I am
informed by Mr. Campbell, of Craigie House, near
Ayr, only a few miles from Mr. Burnett's, but
nearer the sea, that he has this year (1842) dressed
part of a field of turnips with two hundredweight
of unburned gypsum per acre, *without producing any
apparent effect*. Can the proximity to the sea explain this ?

proving condition, is established by the fact that sixty years ago English flour was imported into Denmark; while at present, notwithstanding the increase of population and the more general use of wheaten bread, flour is exported largely to the Brazils and to Jersey, especially in the form of biscuit.* This increase in the growth of wheat must not be considered merely as an indication that a larger amount of agricultural produce is raised in the country than formerly, but also that produce of a more valuable kind is reaped from the land—that by an improved management soils which formerly grew oats, or perhaps rye, are now enabled to grow wheat. In judging of the advance of agricultural improvement, the quality of the produce, whether in corn or cattle, must be taken into account quite as much as the nominal quantity.

Rye is most largely produced in Denmark, being the principal food of the people; and much of this grain has long been exported to Holland, especially from the province of Jutland. Barley forms, I believe, the largest and most valuable exportable corn produce, as the general lightness of the soil would lead us to expect; and both barley and oats are said to be shipped in considerable quantities to England. The increase of these exports is another proof of the progressive advancement, at least of the arable culture of the country.

During the present century much has been done by the exertions of individual proprietors for the improvement of their own estates or neighbourhoods; and an *Academy of Agriculture* has more recently been instituted at Copenhagen by the Government, but no agricultural schools have yet been established. They are much desired and talked of, however; and when the hampered finances of Denmark admit of it, they will most likely be established. In the mean time, the more zealous agriculturists send their sons to the Prussian or to the new Swedish schools.

The late King of Denmark did more, I believe, for the improvement of the breed of horses than for any other object immediately connected with the agriculture of the country. In 1829 I visited the royal farm at Fredericksborg, in the island of Zealand, and saw the stud, consisting altogether of about seven hundred horses. From this stud stallions were distributed over all Denmark, to the number, I was told, of two hundred, for the purpose of improving the Danish race of horses. In consequence of this encouragement, the export of horses had become considerable; the number taken out of the country in 1828, according to the official returns, being fourteen thousand. Mr. Bang informs me that this crossing of the Danish breed with the English race has not improved the former for agricultural purposes.

The royal farm at Fredericksborg consists of about four thousand English acres, and I found upon it both Merino sheep and improved breeds of cattle; but I am not aware how far the cattle-breeding provinces have availed themselves during the last ten years of the means of improvement thus placed in some measure within their reach.

Agriculture in Jutland.—Jutland supplies the

* Has the alleged glutinous quality of the Danish wheat anything to do with this export of it in the form of biscuit? Can the geological nature of the surface really affect the form in which the corn it produces can be best *cooked*, either for immediate consumption or for distant transport?

greater number of the cattle which are fattened in the marsh-lands of Holstein. I may be excused for inserting a few agricultural notes respecting this province, taken during an excursion I made in this part of Denmark in 1829. The progress of improvement may have effected some changes since that period, but upon the whole I believe the following remarks represent very correctly the several points to which they refer.

Sailing from Elsinore, I landed at Grenae, on the east coast of South Jutland; thence went by the town of Randers to Randrup, an estate about thirty miles north-east from that town. The soil was generally light and undulating—much of it in pasture, and much in the hollows, where the drain would effect great improvements. The estate of Randrup, the property of Mr. Thygesen, consisted of eight hundred tonnen of land (fourteen thousand square ells being one ton of land), and was chiefly in pasture. Like nearly all the land in this district, it was light and sandy, and reposed, at the depth of two or three feet, more or less, on a gravelly sand, with many flints and rounded granite pebbles. The surface therefore rested on the same boulder formation of which I have already spoken, probably on its lower and less fertile part. Much manure was not made except in winter, when the cattle were housed, and this was chiefly applied to the arable land. It was not usual in this neighbourhood to take any measures for the physical improvement of the soil. Mr. Thygesen had lately removed almost an entire hill of a yellow calcareous marl, for the purpose of spreading over his fields, and making the soil more tenacious; but he had not then been imitated by more than one of the neighbouring proprietors. The practice, however, in a country where marl may be expected to abound, will necessarily make its way. Quicklime was never laid upon the land. The rotation upon this improving estate was:—1st, rye, with marl and manure; 2nd, barley; 3rd, rye; 4th, oats, with manure; 5th, rye; 6th, oats; 7th, ryegrass, after which the ground remained five years in grass. This was only six white crops in twelve years, but these six were taken in succession.

Rye is the principal food of the people of all classes; comparatively few potatoes are used, and of these such as are small and waxy are preferred in Denmark generally, as they are in Sweden and in some parts of Germany. The larger potatoes are given to the cattle and pigs. I observed a considerable breadth of buckwheat in some parts of Jutland, especially about Grenae. This grain is much used for puddings, for feeding cattle also, and for distillation.

From the Randers district (Randers Amt) I went north to Gudumlund, in the Aalborg Amt, and near the mouth of the Lyme Fiord. Here also the land was chiefly in pasture, and the character of the soil on the higher grounds was nearly the same as farther south. But in this neighbourhood there is a considerable extent of flat, marshy, or boggy land, on which the soil is a deep black vegetable mould, and which, in the lower unimproved and not naturally drained parts, is covered with an open coppice of birch, intermingled with hazel and oak, and on the drier places with a brushwood of juniper.

On the estate of Höstemark, at the distance of a few miles from Gudumlund, and which was farmed by its owner, Mr. Hvass, the brother of my kind host the local judge, a considerable portion of this low land had been reclaimed and improved. On this farm the rotation on the sandy soils was:—1st, buckwheat, with manure; 2nd, rye; 3rd, rye; 4th, rye-grass, or woolly soft grass (*Holcus lanatus*), and then three years grass, the whole of this sort of land being divided into seven portions to suit this rotation. The light black earth of such of the marshy land as admitted of arable culture was ploughed two or three times when broken up and manured, after which it was cropped with barley, vetches or oats, rye, oats, and then sown down with *Holcus lanatus*, and left four years in pasture. There is a large quantity of this marsh-land, or *moss*, as it is there called, which by good drainage would at once be converted into excellent meadow, while that which already admits of arable culture might by the same means be rendered capable of bearing any crop. It all rests upon a substratum of chalk and flints, so that the means of improvement are at hand. It is possibly the existence of this substratum which makes this marshy surface more naturally productive than the peat-bogs of our own country.

This marshy tract is all new land, gained from the waters, probably of an arm of the sea, within a comparatively recent period. Of this, among other proofs, may be mentioned the muscle and cockle shells found over it all, at a depth of one or two feet—the names of places, such as Skipsted (ship station), Segelflod (sail-stream), which are now far from the sea—as well as the records of sea-fights having taken place where this land now exists. It may be supposed, therefore, that this country of North Jutland partakes in some degree of that elevatory movement by which so much of the opposite land of Sweden and Norway is known to be gradually raised above the level of the sea.

Yet a section observed by Professor Forchhammer on the shores of the Lyme Fiord (at Krabbesbolm near Skiva) would appear to indicate that this district has partaken in historic times of an alternate movement, rather than one of continued elevation. Beneath twelve inches of soil, on which natural oak-wood is growing, he found an oyster-bed eight feet in thickness; and below this, at the sea level, a bed of sand containing deer's-horns and stone axes. It would appear therefore that since the land was inhabited by a people who used stone axes, it had been submerged in the waters of the sea long enough to admit of this large bed of oyster-shells being formed, and afterwards gradually raised again. This inference in regard to the submersion may not be considered as fully justified, since the relics may have been carried down into deep water, but there seems little reason to doubt that the land has actually risen.

The cattle which form so important an article of export from Jutland, are chiefly reared by the peasants, sold by them at the age of two or three years to the large farmers or proprietors, who keep them till they are five or six, when they are sold off to the marsh-lands of Holstein and Sleswick, where another season fattens them. In Jutland they are fed during the winter on hay, chopped straw, and buckwheat. The late maturity of these cattle will enable the stock-farmer to judge both of the value of the breed as raisers of beef, and of the money value of the land on which they are fed. The value of the Danish breed cannot be expected materially to improve until the proprietors become themselves the raisers of stock, and by the growth of green food are enabled to promote

their growth during the winter as well as the summer.

Most of the land in this district is cultivated by the proprietors, who retain inspectors or overseers at a fixed salary. Some is rented out ready stocked, to tenants who pay a fixed rent for land, stock, and implements together. At the expiry of his agreement the tenant leaves every thing as he found it. This system formerly prevailed in certain parts of Scotland. Some of the rents are paid in kind—in corn or butter; and when this is the case the system is similar to the Mezzadria in Italy, only that in Jutland the quantity of produce paid is now fixed; other rents are paid in money. The *Forpagters*, or tenants, are in general so very poor that this method of stocking by the proprietor is a matter of necessity, if he wishes to let his farm at all. In an improving district, however, time may be expected to remove this necessity.

The wages of men-servants are from twenty-six to thirty, and of women from sixteen to twenty dollars a-year (9½ to the pound sterling.) When hired for the summer half-year only, somewhat higher wages is given. In summer they generally have five meals a-day. At four in the morning their *dovre*—beer, bread, and dried or pickled herrings; at eight a *millemad* (mellemmad, middle meal) of bread, butter, cheese, and brandy (to save trouble, a dozen bottles of brandy are generally allowed to each for the summer;) at twelve is *middagsmad*—soup made of flesh and vegetables with the meat, or a pudding of buckwheat or barley with milk, and dried fish or fried bacon, with potatoes and beer; at four or five another *millemad*; and at seven, eight, or nine, always a buckwheat or barley pudding made with milk.

The estimated money-rent of land, together with the taxes, amounts to about five per cent. upon the estimated value of the fee simple—the taxes amounting to nearly one-third of the estimated rental. But the price of land seems to be kept down by the expensive mode of farming it. Thus Mr. Hvass's estate at Höstemark, which consisted of 1400 tonnen of land, of which 600 were wood, 200 meadow, and 500 arable, the rest at present unprofitable was valued at 30,000 dollars, and he would have let it for 1400 dollars, including taxes, or for 1000 dollars, the tenant paying the taxes besides. The direct taxes on this property were then 350 dollars, which certainly appears high, though they were less in proportion to the value than on most of the neighbouring properties, two-thirds of the arable land having been brought into cultivation since the last government valuation by which the amount of tax was regulated. Mr. Hvass was familiar with the works of Von Thaer and Sir John Sinclair, and complained chiefly of want of capital to carry on his improvements more extensively.

On this farm he raised only so much oats as was sufficient for his own horses, and potatoes, buckwheat, and rye for his own establishment, with an excess of 300 or 400 tonnen (worth two Danish dollars a ton) of the latter for exportation. This would barely pay the wages of his servants, of whom in summer, when I visited him, he had no fewer than forty-four. The serfs had been emancipated in his father's time, and since money-wages have been paid it is said that much more work has been obtained from the same number of servants. Yet comparatively little must still be obtained from them, if forty-four servants, male and female, be necessary to perform the work, even in summer, of an estate worth no more in rent and taxes than 150l. a-year.

The farm grazed also 160 oxen, 30 cows, 300 sheep, and 28 horses. The milk, butter, and cheese were all used in his own household, and the horses, I was told, were all employed in the farm, except two or three kept for riding and driving. Some of them, however, were no doubt reared for sale. Although the beer and brandy, as well as the other articles of consumption, were all grown or manufactured upon the estate, yet the large proportion of the produce consumed by so extensive a household must have diminished at once the profits and the marketable value of the land.

In the autumn, when the harvest is over, both the peasants and the proprietors along the coast employ themselves and their servants in taking and salting fish for the winter's consumption. Flat-fish is principally taken, and much of it is dried in the sun. The necessity of having large esta-blishments is further increased by the custom of making and manufacturing, as in former times in our own country, nearly all the ordinary articles of dress and furniture required in the household.

One of the most spirited and persevering im-provers in Jutland was the late Count Schimmel-man, so long minister of finance to his Danish Majesty. At present Count Fries of Friesenburg is one of the most zealous and enterprising. He has imported a skilful inspector from Hanover to arrange the irrigation of his estate, and to pro-mote the extension of a system which is fitted to be of such service in the sandy soils of this part of the kingdom. The government has recently been at the expense of sending four young men into Silesia to learn the method of irrigation practised so extensively in that country.

North of the Lyme Fiord in North Jutland I found the land naked, the soil sandy, often moorish, with tracts of poor pasture, and here and there a few thousand acres in indifferent arable culture. The wind sweeps over this peninsula from the Skager Rack on the west, and from the Cattegat on the east, bearing the salt spray and the drift-sand in some places far inland. Even here, however, the spirit of improvement is not dormant, but capital is wanting. Those who have the desire, the skill, and the ability to improve, have too much of this waste land upon their hands to allow of their speedily bringing the whole into more profitable cultivation.

I made the tour of this district, proceeding from Aalborg, on the Lyme Fiord, to Hiöring, on the west side of the peninsula, and thence to the Skaw, returning by Frederickshavn and Säbye to Hals, at the mouth of the Fiord. We drove through deep sand nearly the whole way—the utmost pace at which a pair of horses could take the driver and myself being usually three miles an hour. I could not help being struck, seeing it then for the first time, with the apparently barren sandy spots on which rye seemed to flourish. Even the drift-sands near the Skaw bore their thin, but I suppose profitable, crops of this grain. The country in general is flat, but through the middle of the eastern half, in a north-westerly direction, runs a long and narrow ridge of sand-hills called the Jutland Aas (pronounced *Ose*), which bears a green pasture, scanty apparently, yet refreshing to the eye amid the sands which present themselves almost without intermission to the eye of the tra-veller, as he proceeds southwards from the town of Säbye. Of such sand-ridges there are many in

Sweden of great length, and called by the same name (sand ascr), which have lately attracted much attention from geologists.

Between this ridge and the sea, towards the towns of Säbye and Hals, there lies much improv-able land, and signs of improvement were visible, especially in the neighbourhood of the former town. *Spurry* is here sown on the sandy soils for feeding the cattle in winter. It is cut when ripe, and dried into hay. In winter, it is given to the cattle two or three times a-day, was much relished by them, as I was informed, and increased the pro-duce of milk.

A plant which springs up spontaneously, and in such quantities in our own corn fields, especially in sandy soils, may well be expected to grow luxu-riantly on such soils when sown as a crop. It is an important principle, in the practical culture of the land, to grow upon it, at least as an occasional crop, that kind of plant—weed it may be—which most delights in or infests it; provided it can be made useful as food for stock, and does not by its roots make the land unclean (plants even which cattle reject, may be in some cases (in many?) profitably raised for ploughing in as a green manure). On this principle is founded the modern practice of sowing land down with natural grasses; it might possibly be applied to the selec-tion and growth of plants of other families hither-to neglected. I shall advert again to this point when I come to speak of Swedish agriculture.

In Brabant the spurry is much cultivated both for pasture and for ploughing in as a green manure. It reaches its full height, about 12 inches, in five or six weeks, may be eaten off or ploughed in and sown again in favourable years three times in a single season, and a rye crop may then be taken without manure. It is said that by sowing two crops of spurry—eating both off with sheep—in one season, and a crop of rye in the following, an alternate husbandry may be kept up without ma-nure, under which sandy soils will improve so as to give on each return of the corn crop a heavier weight of grain.

Von Voght and Schwartz speak of this plant with equal enthusiasm. The former says, " Spurry sown on sandy soils is a better pasture than red or white clover; the cows give more and better milk, and it improves the land in an extra-ordinary degree. If the land is to be several years in pasture, white clover must be sown with it. Sown in the middle of April, it is ripe for pasture by the end of May. Eaten off before the end of June, the land is ploughed flat, and sown a second time, when it gives another beautiful pasture in August and September. If rye be now sown, the land is as much improved as if it had received ten cart loads of manure per acre. The blessing of spurry, *the clover of sandy soils*, is incredible when it is rightly employed. I sow it on the rye and oat-stubble, and I obtain a beautiful pasture and a manuring equal to four or six cart-loads of ma-nure per acre."[*]

Schwartz, in his account of the Belgian hus-bandry (ii., p. 33), says—" Without spurry, the Campine,[†] the best cultivated soil in the world would have been still a desert. A plant this which

* Ueber manche Vortheile der Grüner Dungung, p. 23. In this work Von Voght details the results of many long-continued experiments made upon his own estate at Flottbeck.

† Kempenland, a district in Dutch Brabant.

requires no manure for itself, and which even when mown, by the residue it leaves, gives back more than it takes from the soil—which demands no fixed place in the rotation, but which is satisfied to come in as an after-crop whenever the soil is at liberty—which, except for the seed, requires no preparation—which is satisfied with a soil on which nothing else but rye will grow—which increases the quantity of milk and butter, and improves their qualiy—and which, I am persuaded, may be raised with advantage, even on the best soils, provided only they are somewhat light. A proof of this is the land of Waas (Waesland, in Flanders), the garden of Europe."*

In many parts of Germany Schwartz is regarded as a high authority in practical agriculture, and there is certainly much land in the Jutlands upon which, if its qualities be always such as are above stated, it may be sown with the greatest prospect of advantage. I cannot venture to recommend it to the attention of English farmers in general, because I am aware that it has in former years been so recommended by persons more versant in agricultural practice than. myself, without finding much favour in this country; and yet there may be some desolate and unproductive corners of our island on which its use might prove eminently advantageous. It is sown on the stubble for autumn feed near York; but the soil there is not of the kind I should think for which this crop is most especially adapted.

In the preceding observations upon Danish agriculture, the reader will perceive that there are peculiarities and deficiencies in the culture of the land in that country, compared with English practice; and yet several things will also strike him as satisfactorily accounting for the differences, and in some measure justifying some of the deficiencies. Thus—

1st. Denmark grows with ease more food than her population can consume; and, as markets for the excess of produce are not abundant, corn is necessarily low in price, and does not therefore yield so large a return to the grower, or so highly stimulate the arable culture of the land. Hence the prevalence of pasture in Jutland for the raising of cattle, for which there is a constant demand, and in Holstein for the manufacture of butter, which is readily exported. Hence also the growth of other crops, such as rape, for the seed of which the sale is easy, and which, on soils that suit it, yields a greater profit than any other arable culture yet introduced into these provinces. The same reason justifies in some measure (if want of capital were not in most cases a sufficient reason) the neglect of expensive improvements—such as the draining of the land, which in very many localities would not only increase the absolute quantity of corn produced, but would enable the arable land to grow corn of a more valuable kind.

2nd. But the nature of the soil necessarily causes, in many districts, a different mode of cropping from that which prevails among ourselves. The food of the people is, in most countries, originally determined by the peculiar character of the soil. Large tracts of land have

proved unwilling, by all the forms of persuasion hitherto tried, to grow anything well but rye and buckwheat, and these sometimes but indifferently. On most of the soils of Jutland these kinds of grain used alone to give a sure return: hence it became the object of the farmer to raise the largest quantity of these varieties of corn; and the national produce became, naturally enough, the national food. And now, when an improving agriculture offers to supply other grain in abundance, the national taste remains; and, because the people prefer to live on rye-bread, much rye must still be raised. The produce of the barley and oat, and more rare wheat lands, is in a great measure exported.

Again, the marsh-lands readily indicate their own most profitable employment. How far their value, as rich pastures, is capable of improvement I am unable from personal observation to state. That so much other land is in pasture is owing in part, as I have already said, to the more ready market for live stock and for dairy produce; but in part also to a want of capital, which will probably be long unsupplied.

3rd. In regard to the improvements which might be effected in Denmark—supposing that of supplying better implements to be generally attained, which however is still far from being the case—it will be seen that, in the richer soils, much good might be done by draining; in the dairy districts by improving the quality of the cheese, so that this, as well as butter, might become an article of export, and by the introduction of green crops, by which a rich winter-food might be more readily attained; in the breeding provinces, by the general diffusion of a kind of stock which would come to earlier maturity, so that the price of cattle when fit for the butcher might be lessened by the cost of two or three years' feed; in the flat and gravelly or sandy heaths, by a more extensive marling, and by a trial of the effects of the drain; and on the sandy soils, by irrigation for the dry pastures, and by the use of spurry for the loose and naturally unprofitable arable sands.

The reader who shall hereafter travel in the Danish provinces will probably discover many other improvements which capital and time may effect; yet he will not, I trust, fail to give the Danish people credit for what they have already done. If they are, *in some parts of their country, a century behind our most improved districts,* they are at least as far behind them also in wealth, and in the other means by which improvements are effected.

EXTENSIVE USE OF OXEN.—At the last New-Haven County Agricultural Society's Fair, there were no less than one thousand and twenty-six oxen exhibited upon the ground. They were paraded, in five hundred and thirteen yokes, in the form of a hollow square, in a beautiful green in the shape of a parallelogram of fifty-four by twenty rods, surrounded by double rows of magnificent elms. When thus arranged they covered a space equal to 1¾ mile in length. Such a sight was truly worth seeing, and we think should teach those farmers who use *horses* exclusively for farm purposes that they would find their interest in substituting, in part, oxen or mules in their stead.— *Cont. Farmer., U.S.*

---

* In his later systematic work, however (*Anleitung zum Practischen Ackerbau,* iii., p. 514), while he speaks of spurry in terms almost equally high, he distinctly limits his recommendation to poor, sandy soils, and insists upon its value on such especially as will grow neither clover nor grass.

HINTS to FARMERS' LABOURERS.

"AN HONEST MAN'S THE NOBLEST WORK OF
GOD."

" Ill fares the land, to hastening ills a prey,
Where wealth accumulates and men decay ;
Princes and lords may flourish, or may fade ;
A breath can make them, as a breath has made ;
But a bold peasantry, their country's pride,
When once destroyed, can never be supplied."
Goldsmith's Deserted Village.

THE PEASANTRY OF ENGLAND.

The peasantry of England,
　Who till their native soil—
The loyal, true, and brave are they,
　Although they live to toil ;
For they are England's own true men—
　Her rural sons and free—
To drive the plough or wield the flail,
　Or guard her liberty.

The peasantry of England,
　Whose wealth is their fireside ;
Whose manly sons and daughters fair
　Inspire their breasts with pride ;
Whose only feast " The Harvest Home,"
　Whose only pride "The Fair ;"
Who love the hills and plains to roam,
　Free as their native air.

God bless the English peasantry !
　Blest be their happy home ;
God speed the plough—the loom—the sail—
　A thousand years to come ;
And may the manly pride they boast
　Each gallant breast sustain,
To guard from foes their native coast,
　And England's rights maintain.

　　　　　　　　　　　R. B.

The labour of the husbandman is his wealth.—His
character is his recommendation.—Labour with
character always finds a market.—Labour without character is neglected ;

THEREFORE,

Honesty is the best policy.

Neither steal yourself nor allow others to steal.

Men steal little things, not because they are little,
but the better to avoid detection.

He that will steal a pin will steal a greater thing ;
and he that will steal a pint will steal a bushel.

Lying and dishonesty are next akin.—" Men first
steal, and then lie to conceal."

If you would succeed, neither lie nor steal.—He
that practises either is sure of detection.

" The pitcher that goes oft to the well is sure to
be broken."

Avoid drunkenness, as the parent of all vice, and
as the source of all misery.

Avoid smoking, as it leads to drunkenness.

Avoid drinking on the road when entrusted with
horses.—" Many a little makes a mickle."—Although
you may not intend to get drunk, still you may unconsciously do so.

A drunkard is a pest : he destroys his health—the
peace of his family, and seeks his own destruction.

AS REGARDS YOUR MASTER,

Never divulge your master's secrets.
Never neglect his business in his absence.
Never allow others to rob or injure him.
Never neglect or abuse his cattle or horses.

Never allow live stock to want either food or
water.

Never suffer cattle to break pasture without stopping the gap, or informing your master.

Never allow horses when at work to drink cold
water, until they have first had food.

Never allow horses when heated to stand still
long together.

Never take the halter or bridle from a horse whilst
in shafts.

Never fasten a horse to the manger without a
clog.

Never take a candle from a lantern, or let the lantern door remain open.

Never allow a horse to work on the road without
shoes.

Never turn a pair of horses sharply round at harrows. If harrows are turned over, the horses probably will be both killed.

Never force a key into a lock.

Never meddle with machinery when in motion.

Never borrow or use anything without returning
it.—" There is a place for everything, and everything
should be in its place."

Never use a roller, cart, waggon, or machinery,
that require greasing.

Never allow cattle to refuse food, without informing your master.

Never allow them to remain ill without assistance.
Never suffer rooks or larks to injure crops.
Never suffer pigs to root, without ringing them.
Never beat or correct horses, when angry.
Never drive cows fast from the cowhouse, or on
the road.

Never jump or slide from a loaded waggon or
stack.

Never trust yourself in a cart without reins.
Never ride upon the shafts.
Never give a saucy answer.—" A soft answer
turneth away wrath."

" Waste not, want not."

" Early to bed and early to rise makes a man
healthy, wealthy, and wise."

" For age and want spare whilst you may,
No morning sun lasts a whole day."

A penny saved is a penny got.—He who saves a
penny a day will obtain thirty shillings a year.

" A stitch in time saves nine."

" For want of a nail the shoe was lost,
For want of a shoe the horse was lost,
For want of a horse the rider was lost."

Preserve health as an inestimable blessing ;

TO DO SO,

Never drink to excess.
Never drink strong liquors.
Never drink cold water when heated by labour, or
suffer the body to cool suddenly.
Never sit in a draught of air.
Never cease moving whilst in wet clothes.
Never dry them before the fire whilst on.
Never quarrel or fight.
" Those who in quarrels interpose
Must often wipe a bloody nose."

Remember God seest always ; act as if in his presence. Obey his commands, and above all,

Keep the Sabbath Day Holy.

" The fear of the Lord is the beginning of wisdom." 　　　　　　　　　R. B.

Writtle, January 20th, 1843.

All workmen coming to, or leaving these premises
at morning or night, are desired to do so by the

F F 2

gates nearest the farm-house; and any one detected leaving by the back of the premises will be discharged.

Any workman making application for turnips or other produce will, if his demand be reasonable, have it allowed; but any one detected thieving, however small the thing may be, will be punished.

ST. PETER'S FARMERS' CLUB.

SECOND ANNUAL REPORT.

MAY 24TH.

Subject discussed :—"The best mode of managing a dairy in this neighbourhood in the winter."

Resolved : " It is not in general advantageous to calve the same cows successively for the winter dairy, but to buy in cows as they are wanted. It is advisable to purchase them about four years old, and such as are likely to make good beasts in the early part of the succeeding summer."

The best way of keeping in the winter is on cut fodder, mixing straw with the hay if the latter is good. Also a portion of Swedish turnips and wurzel mixed, but little wurzel the early part of the winter, increasing the proportion as the spring approaches.   We consider carrots to be better than either wurzel or turnips, but we are not prepared to decide whether they are so much better as to pay for the extra expences required in procuring them.   To this food we approve of the addition of two oilcakes per day for each cow, considering the nutritious qualities of this food so great, that the animal will require much less of other, while it will produce an increase of milk, with improvement in condition.   As soon as "green meat" can be obtained, we think it well to mix a small portion with the cut fodder.

Warmth and cleanliness we consider of as much importance to cows as good keep, with a good supply of clear soft water, and as much regularity in the time of milking as possible.   The turnips, wurzel, or carrots, should be given to the cows immediately after milking.   A careful observance of this is necessary, in order to avoid an unpleasant flavour in the milk.

It is not supposed that under this mode of management, or any other, in this neighbourhood, cows can be kept for the purpose of making butter in the winter with any probability of profit. Therefore we do not recommend the keeping a winter dairy to any one who cannot find regular customers for new milk and cream.

SECOND MEETING, JUNE 14TH.

The question respecting the "Management of a summer dairy" was discussed.

Resolved: " That great pains should be taken to obtain good cows, when they are to be kept especially for milking.   The York or Devon breed may be considered to answer our purpose best. But, of whatever breed, we give the preference to a cow possessing the following points—viz., a thin head and neck, broad hipped, clean and short legged, a good skinned udder, but not fleshy, and a good-tempered countenance; and we think that March is the best time for calving.

Taking into consideration the scarcity of grass, and the difficulty of getting a good meadow,

arising from the dryness we are subject to in this neighbourhood in the summer, it is thought best to feed in general on Iucerne.   This produces the greatest quantity of keep, and is very nutritious. We consider it most economical to cut it in a cutting box, and to give it the cows in the stall. When the Iucerne gets old and dry, the food is much improved by mixing with it a little young clover.   We consider stall-feeding preferable the greater part of the summer, as it keeps the cow quieter than any other plan, a consideration of considerable importance in the production of a large quantity of milk.   It is our opinion that in autumn no keep surpasses sanfoin rowin, and that cows may then be taken to the field and kept upon it in the morning and evening with great advantage.

A plentiful supply of good soft water is truly desirable throughout the year, but especially in the summer; and for the purpose of obtaining this, every farm-house should have attached to it a large rain-water tank, and the whole of the buildings should be surrounded by gutters to take the water to this reservoir for the supply of the dairy cows.   If it is necessary to obtain water from the wells at this season of the year, we think it should be exposed to the air two or three days previous to its being given to the cows.

The discussion did not extend to the making of butter, this being a matter of minor importance to a St. Peter's farmer, nearly all the milk our dairies produce being consumed in the neighbouring towns and villages.

THIRD MEETING, JULY 12TH.

The question discussed was respecting the " Best breed of pigs, and the best mode of feeding from the time they are farrowed."

Resolved: "That the best breeds of pigs in this neighbourhood are those which approach nearest the Essex.   That it would be highly advantageous frequently to cross our best sorts.   That it is best to feed a sow, while her pigs are under her, on pollard the first fortnight ; afterwards on pollard with a third part of barley-meal morning and evening, and about half a gallon of beans in the middle of the day.   A plentiful supply of water should be kept by the sow during the whole time her pigs are with her.   That the pigs should be castrated at about five weeks old, and weaned at six weeks old.   That it is best to commence feeding the weaned pigs on soft food, such as sharps or middlings, with a small portion of barley-meal twice a day, and a little whole corn (oats and barley mixed) once a day, for the first fortnight; afterwards grey peas.   That when the pigs get seven or eight weeks old, a greater proportion of barley-meal may be used, with bran (instead of sharps and middlings), and steamed potatoes. The bran is to rectify the too-astringent properties of the barley-meal.   The whole corn now to be dispensed with.

This mode of feeding may be kept up to the last with the gradual increase of the proportion of barley-meal.

Throughout the whole time a good supply of water is essential.

In August and September, owing to the thin attendance of members, no particular discussion was entered upon.

OCTOBER 18TH.

The subject introduced was respecting the " Best mode of preparing wheat for seed."

There were but few points connected with this question in which the members present were of the same opinion. All agreed, however, that there is a tendency in wheat in this neighbourhood to produce collor or smut, and it was pretty generally allowed that if sown without preparation that tendency was greater. Some were disposed to think that collor was produced by the weather; and that, while none may be grown in one year, though the wheat should not be prepared at all, a great quantity may be produced another year, whatever preparations may be used. It was, however, the more general opinion on this point, that in bad years wheat that has been sowed without preparation has been most productive of collor; so that, while in good years it may be of little use to wet, lime, or bluestone the wheat, in bad years it is a very valuable preventive of evil. Some members present were disposed to think, that good seed and a wet season were, in this neighbourhood, all that we wanted to secure us from collor. Others could testify that a field known by them to be good deep land was sown with a most beautiful lot of wheat, brought out of Essex last year, and sown particularly wet, and had produced an abundant crop this year of fine wheat, but more collor amongst it than had been seen any where in the neighbourhood. Some were of opinion, that if there was collor grown amongst the wheat used for seed, it would certainly produce the same again; while others were of an opposite opinion, the latter supposing that the capability of the collor to inoculate the wheat was destroyed in the liming, &c., considered by them of so much importance.

The discussion was carried on with much life and spirit throughout the evening, and as our chairman was absent, it was agreed it should be resumed at the next monthly meeting.

NOVEMBER.—No discussion.

DECEMBER.— The ploughing match of the "Agricultural Association."

JANUARY 3RD.

The subject of "Preparing wheat for seed" was resumed; and after a long discussion, the meeting was unanimous in passing the following resolutions, viz :—

" That it is best in this neighbourhood to obtain our seed wheat from deeper and heavier soils than our own. That it is advisable to sow good stout, healthy-looking grain. That it should be prepared by the application of lime or bluestone."

It is thought best to apply lime in the following way :—Put two gallons of fresh slaked lime into a tub of water that is large enough to receive the seed-basket; stir it well; then dip a basket of wheat, let it remain in the water a few minutes, skim off the corn that swims on the top; then draw out the basket of wheat and shoot it on the floor, and sift over it a small portion of fresh slaked lime (say half a gallon to a bushel of wheat), and mix it up well with the wheat; add occasionally a little fresh lime to your tub of water; and when your quantity for the time is wet, give it a good mixing together, and let it remain in the heap a few hours. Prepared in this way, it will be fit for sowing the next day. If the wheat is to be drilled, it is thought best to use fresh water, and to put more lime in the water, which will render it unnecessary to sift any over the wheat after it is taken out.

The following is the plan recommended for the use of bluestone :—

Dissolve the bluestone in hot water, and mix it with the quantity of water required, at the rate of one pound to every ten gallons of water; and thus throughout, adding one pound of bluestone every time it is found necessary to add ten gallons of water, taking care to skim the light corn and rubbish off the wheat while it is in the water. The wheat under this mode of preparation will be fit either for sowing or drilling on the ensuing day.

JANUARY 31ST.

The " Advantages or disadvantages of keeping sheep in this neighbourhood" were considered.

It was noticed, that we at St. Peter's are very particularly situated with regard to inducements to keep sheep. First, we have scarcely a farm in the parish that has got a sheep-walk, or a meadow of any size, attached to it; and from our exposure to dryness in summer, we have very little inducement to sow grass. Second, we have great facilities for procuring manure, being situated between the towns of Margate and Ramsgate. Still, some were of opinion that sheep would be so great a change to much of our land, that, notwithstanding our facilities of manuring without them, there are still strong inducements to keep them. Those gentlemen who are the principal sheep keepers in the neighbourhood were present, and were found ready to impart their best knowledge for the information of the meeting. It was their opinion, that though in many situations it was most profitable to keep a breeding flock, yet in this neighbourhood (if it was advisable to keep a flock at all) it was better to take in lambs from a respectable breeder at per week, from the middle of September to the middle of April. Some years it might pay better to purchase sheep or lambs, but as our flocks here must be parted with at a certain season of the year, let the price be what it may, it was thought better, in general, to take them to keep for the time we had a supply of food, and then to send them back to the owner. If lambs were kept on this plan, it was most likely to pay on a large scale; at least, it was considered necessary that, to employ a shepherd, not less than 200 should be kept. The following calculations were then made, by which it appears that in our situation, where good meadows are rare and good manure abundant, the inducement to keep sheep or lambs is by no means great.

	£	s.	d.
For keep of 200 lambs 30 weeks, at 50s. per week.....................	75	0	0
20 perches of land folded nightly, 10s. (reckoned equal to 16 sale loads of dung per acre, at 5s. per load, including cartage) 30 weeks	105	0	0
	£180	0	0

	£	s.	d.
12 acres of turnips, at 10l. per acre ..	120	0	0
Cole and grattens	10	0	0
Fodder for 20 weeks, 21s. per week ..	21	0	0
Shepherd's wages, 12s. per week	18	0	0
50 new wattles and stakes annually ...	4	0	0
Sundries.........................	5	0	0
	£178	0	0

Balance in favour of lamb keeping, 2l. per annum.

A crop of turnips was calculated in two ways —first, as to their cost to grow; and secondly, as compared with a crop of potatoes, for which the land is equally suitable, and generally prepared in a similar way; and in either case it appeared that turnips could not be reckoned on an average of years to be worth less or to cost less than ten pounds per acre.

FEBRUARY 7TH.

The subject discussed was respecting a " Rotation of crops."

It was doubted by the club whether it was advisable, in this vicinity, for the farmer to reckon himself bound by any particular system.   It was considered, however, that there are a few general principles with regard to cropping that ought to be always acted on by the club, viz :—First, facilities for procuring manure and opportunities of cleaning the land for green crops being great in this neighbourhood, what are called clear fallows may be entirely dispensed with. Second, that it is desirable as much as possible to plant green crops (such as beans, peas, tares, turnips, radish, and spinach), and white straws alternately ; and while it is allowed that in some cases two white straw crops may be grown in succession, it is pronounced bad farming to attempt the growth of three. And thirdly, it is the unanimous opinion that wheat should not be grown here oftener than twice in eight years.

Observing these principles in the general mode of cropping, the following would be the rotation recommended by the club, as far as their plans can be reduced to system, viz. :—

Beginning with a field of foul wheat gratten, they would by ploughing, scarifying, &c., clear it, and manure it for potatoes or turnips. The second year barley would be sown, and cloverseed ; or, if a part is required for spinach the succeeding year, on that part, of course, the cloverseed is omitted.   The third year the field is clover, or spinach ground. Then, fourth, follows wheat, for which the clover or spinach ground is dunged. Fifth, winter tares may be planted, after which (as they will come off early) the land may be well cleared ; or the field may be well cleared in the autumn and early in the spring, and cropped with peas. Then, sixthly, follows barley ; seventh, radish or beans ; and eighth, wheat.

With this system of cropping, it will be perceived that no provision is made for the growth of canary, oats, sainfoin, or lucerne ; with regard to the two last mentioned, these cannot be grown without throwing the field in which they are planted out of course for a time, and it must be brought in again according to circumstances which it is thought not necessary to mention here, and but slight inconvenience is occasioned thereby ; and as to canary and oats, it is the opinion of the club, that they are not in general so profitable to be grown here as barley, yet not altogether to be dispensed with, as it may be profitable to grow canary where barley would be likely to be too strong, and in some cases it may answer to plant oats after a green crop, and to follow them by another green crop, which will (on that field) throw the second crop of wheat back to the ninth year ; consequently, there is not an opinion in favour of growing oats to a great extent.

As a general principle of manuring, the opinion is, that half the land under tillage should be manured every year, and that the manure should be generally used for wheat, potatoes, and turnips, for barley when the field has not been dunged the preceding year, and for peas.

MARCH 4TH.

Considerable discussion took place respecting the present amount of wages paid to tradesmen.

It has been ascertained that higher prices are paid here than in any other places in the Isle of Thanet. And it was resolved, " that considering the present reduced price of provisions, there ought to be a corresponding reduction in the price of tradesmen's labour ; and that the club is unanimous in determining to bring about this reduction by such means as are in their power."

MINERAL CONSTITUENTS OF VEGETABLES.

" Let us bear always in mind, that while the country grants protection to Agriculture, it will expect in return, that the land shall be cultivated in the best and most productive manner."—Daubeny.

(TO THE EDITOR OF THE WEST BRITON.)

Such, Sir, is the object of manuring ; not just to enable the plant to *live*, but to facilitate and encourage its luxuriant growth, and attain its utmost produce. Such is the farmer's purpose ; and with this in view, he collects and returns to the soil as much as he can of what was drawn from it, as the dung, straw, weeds, &c. And if he could thus return the whole of the produce, the land would go on progressively enriching by organic matter, drawn from the air in vegetation, until it should attain, or even overpass, the utmost limit of fertility that organic matter can confer. But this, in the first place, he cannot do, because he must send more or less of his produce to market ; and next, if he could, there are *other* materials, now well known to be equally necessary to fertility as the organic ingredients, though in much smaller quantity. And agricultural experience has abundantly shown, of late years, that surprising effects have followed the application of small quantities of certain manures, even in some cases when heavy dressings of dung had failed.

In fact, the plant can draw from the air only those elements which exist there in the form of gas and vapour (namely, carbon, oxygen, hydrogen, and nitrogen) ; the rest must be drawn from the soil. And however rich that may be in organic residue, it can produce and bring to perfection no more than it can supply, also, with the others, namely, the mineral ingredients. And hence it is that rich dressing is sometimes less effective than a small quantity of a mineral ingredient, of which the soil happens to be deficient.

To all this the farmer is fully alive. He is trying salt, nitrate of soda, gypsum, bone dust, and other concentrated manures ; sometimes to his great encouragement ; sometimes with disappointment. In the first case he becomes prejudiced in favour of the manure, and will perhaps use and recommend it injudiciously ; in the other he condemns and neglects it, when it might have been serviceable. And how can it be otherwise, until knowing what his respective crops draw from the ground, he has a guide what to restore and supply to it to favour their growth?

The following table will afford, at least, an introduction to such knowledge. It is extracted from a rather more comprehensive one, drawn up by Dr.

Daubeney, and published by the Royal Agricultural Society. And it must be received with this caution; that plants seem to take up rather more of these ingredients where they abound in the soil, and *vice versâ*; as, for example, a turnip crop upon bone dust, would be likely to yield more phosphate of lime than one on yard dung only; and so of others, as seen by the different quantities of fixed (or mineral) ingredients* found by Sprengel and Boussaingault in the same crops.

To establish the best and most productive proportions that the plant will require, a long series of analyses is necessary; but in the meanwhile such as we have, those chiefly of Sprengel, will throw some light upon the farmer's proceedings and results. With this before him, for instance, he would not expect much good from gypsum (sulphuric acid and lime) for a crop of rye or oats; but would try it for clover, where the land did not answer well to other manure:—

MINERAL INGREDIENTS IN 100,000 LBS. EACH OF THE FOLLOWING VEGETABLES.

ACCORDING TO SPRENGEL.	Potass.	Soda.	Lime.	Magnesia.	Alumina.	Oxide of Iron.	Oxide of Manganese.	Silica.	Sulphuric Acid.	Phosphoric Acid.	Chlorine.	Total of fixed ingredients.	ACCORDING TO BOUSSINGAULT. Fixed Ingredients.	Azote.
Wheat............	225	240	96	69	26			400	50	400	10	2157	2430	3510
Wheat Straw.....	28	29	240	32		30	46	2870	57	170	30	3518	6970	350
Barley..........	278	290	106	180	25	14	2	1188	59	210	19	2349		2020
Barley Straw....	180	43	554	76	146	14	2	3356	118	160	72	5244		2020
Oats............	180	132	86	67	6		2	1976	35	160	10	2580	3980	2240
Oat Straw.......	370	2	152	22	2			4583	79	70	5	5740	5090	380
Rye.............	552		122	44	24	42	34	164	23	46	9	1040	2570	1690
Rye Straw.......	32	11	178	18	25/90			2297/84	170	51	17	2793	3680 (3900 dry)	300
Potatoes........	390	234	33	32	5	24		126	54	40	154	814	300	500
Beans...........	415	816	165	138	34		5	490	89	292	41	2136		5130
Bean Straw, dry..	1656	50	624	209	10		3	200	292	226	80	3121		1000
Vetches.........	897	622	160	142	9	9	8	200	50	140	43	2990		500
Straw of Vetches, dry	622	52	1955	324	15			442	182	280	84	5101		2240
Peas...........	1810	739	58	136	20	10		410	53	190	38	2464	3140 (11,000 dry)	1570
Pea Straw, green..	52	58	2730	342	60	8		996	537	190	4	4971		4480
Pea Straw, dry....	810							90	82	240	38	2464		1000
Lucerne, do......	235	166	1504	94	11		7	90	109	353	86	2380		300
Sainfoin, do.....	362	166	1301	69	16			76	82	220	4			300
Red Clover, do...	494	105	527	70	3			94	94	133	76	1571		500
Cabbage, dry.....	419	111	584	202	151		40	589	774	436	518	1671	(7760 dry)	500
Beet Root, dry...	1847	578	1332	139	58			105	123	167	2464	6908		4480
Turnips, fresh...	1481	3178	285	42	20			40	41	73	380	5996	6240 (7580 dry)	1000
Swedes, dry.....	73	110	127	28	8		50	475	890	408	23	558		1660
Carrots, do.....	2651	1164	835	282	40	35	2	40	208	73	266	7046		1668
	2718	709	505	295	30	25	46	105		395	54	5090		2400

* "Fixed" means those which will not burn away—the mineral elements.

From this table he can easily reckon the quantities per acre, according to his produce; say, for instance, that he gets 25 imperial bushels of wheat of 60lbs. each, equal to 1500lbs.; the quantity per acre will be, to that in the table, as 1500 to 100,000; —multiply by 15, and divide by 1,000 or, (which is the same thing) strike off the last three figures, estimating their value. And take the straw at double, say 3,000lbs. :—

POTASS	POTASS.	PER TABLE.
Grain, 225lbs.	Straw, 20lbs.	in 100,000lbs. each.
15	30	

1125	600 straw.
225	3375 grain.

3,375	3,975 or

nearly 4lbs. potass per acre of wheat, and so of the other ingredients.

Another example—Turnips. Say crop 25 tons, or 56,000lbs. per acre. Here the quantity per acre is to that on the table as 56,000 to 100,000. Multiply by 56 and divide by 100, or strike off the last two figures.

Phosphoric acid in the table 73lbs. in 100,000

$$\begin{array}{r} 56 \\ \hline 438 \\ 365 \\ \hline \end{array}$$

Nearly 41lbs. per acre 40·88

And in the same way we may reckon the other contents of a crop or *course* of crops.

Now, the ingredients thus drawn off from the soil must be restored in the manure. If the turnips are eaten on the ground and the straw returned in the dung, the only loss will be in the corn.

But as he cannot get potass and phosphoric acid, in their separate states, at a price to use as manure, he employs other materials containing them : straw and vegetable ashes containing potass ; bone dust and night soil containing phosphoric acid. Therefore, to render his calculations satisfactory, he ought to have also a table of the proportions of these and other ingredients in his manures. Such an one I hope to supply you on a future occasion,

Being, Sir, &c.,

J. PRIDEAUX.

ILLOGAN FARMERS' CLUB.

THIRD ANNUAL REPORT.

Three years have passed away since the formation of the Illogan Farmers' Club, and it is not discreditable that it was the second, in the order of time, which had an existence in the county ; but this would be matter of little gratulation in presenting our third annual report, could we not point at advantages of a much higher order. Our numbers have steadily increased, and we have now from 70 to 80 members, and although in the first year of the club's being established, we had considerably increased the breadth of turnips, and diffused much agricultural information by the monthly discussions and the distribution of books; and the committee hope from the appointment of an assistant-secretary, that a more general and regular delivery will be effected to the diffusion of the science, in connection with the practice of agriculture. The increase of the green crop is highly satisfactory, and we hope soon will generally afford a good and plentiful supply for cattle throughout the circle of the year ; this is one of the greatest instances we know of the intelligence and energy of man overcoming the natural sterility of winter, and making it

equally beneficial to the more fertile and genial summer. Now the farmers' cattle, instead of the few, and those starved and rough, shivering under the hedge in winter, are many, well fed and sleek, in better condition when brought out of the house, than they formerly were at the end of the summer. For this we are mainly indebted to the turnip ; but it is also necessary to have early spring feed, which is found in Italian rye grass, and the new vetch called the " Racer," which will reach three feet high by the 1st of May, an account of which will be found in the third volume of the Journal of the Royal Agricultural Society. We see the Belgian white carrot getting into favour, and we think it will prove a great friend to the farmer ; in a neighbourhood like this, where agriculture generally has long been considered secondary, from the contiguity of the mines, where horse labour was formerly so much required, and which, no doubt, paid better than either feeding or breeding, it is no marvel that it should be comparatively behind ; but from the general intelligence and the loss of the usual employments through machinery and the railway, there is little reason to doubt but the farming of the neighbourhood will soon be abreast with more favoured districts, if not in the fertility of the soil, in the method of cultivation.

The great desideratum of the farmer is manure, and it is scarcely possible on comparatively poor farms, that there can be enough made in the farmyard, although, it must be admitted, that there is no manure so good for all crops—it has the elements of all, and is therefore good for all ; but till enough can be made at home (and the heap may be much increased by sand, ditch and road scrapings, and greatly enriched by throwing over it the liquid manure) we must go abroad for artificial manures ; the best of these are bone and guano. There has been much of quackery in many of the new manures, of which farmers should be aware. The small quantities which will suffice of bone and guano, make these comparatively inexpensive, when carriage and labour are considered. Before quitting manure, we may congratulate the club on the analysis of the sands in the neighbourhood, and which has so clearly shown the great value of the Gwithian and SouthTowan sands, and which appear from former analyses of soils obtained from Professor Phillips to be so essential for this locality ; the carbonate of lime being the ingredient in which the soils are deficient.

It remains now that we record our sense of obligation to our noble patroness, Lady Bassett, through whose generosity we principally attribute our success, and also to our president, John Bassett, Esq., who has kindly made a handsome addition to our library, and whose kindness has always cheered us in any exertions we have made for the club's welfare ; and it would be ingratitude, of which we cannot be guilty, to pass unnoticed our Vice-Chairmen, the Rev. George Treweeke and W. Reynolds, Esq., who, whenever health would permit, winter and summer, were always at their posts in the monthly meetings, and have fostered in every way the Society which involves the prosperity and happiness of a large community.

We proceed to lay before you the minutes of each month.

In April we read our second report, and discussed the subject of " the best rotation of crops as applicable to the neighbourhood," and resolved that for the granite soils, the following rotation was the best :—1st, oats ; 2nd, turnips or potatoes ; 3rd, oats or barley; 4th, grass, to lie unbroken for two or three years. For the clay and heavier soils—1st, wheat or oats; 2nd, turnips; 3rd, barley; 4th, grass; or this rotation—1st, potatoes; 2nd, wheat; 3rd, turnips; 4th, barley or oats; 5th, grass, to lie unbroken for two years.

In May we arranged the prizes, &c., for a ploughing match; and Mr. Peter read his paper on cropping, as applicable to the neighbourhood—the rotations recommended are very much the same as those resolved on in April.

In June the ploughing match took place at Pool, and the work done was of the best description, and was considered highly creditable to the neighbourhood.

The first prize for clean ploughing, without driver, was won by John Skewis, servant of Lady Bassett, Tehidy Park.

Second do., John Clemo, do.

First prize do., with driver, Stephen Rundle, servant of Mr. W. Burgess, Wengore.

Second do., Sampson Baskerfield, servant of Mr. John Teague, Penhillick.

First prize for combing or rib-ploughing, without driver, Thomas Maynard, servant of W. Reynolds, Esq., Trevenson.

Second prize do., with driver, Philip Sings, servant of Mr. Carthew, Tregajorran.

For boys under 16.—First prize for combing, with driver, Samuel Bennetts, jun., son of Mr. Bennetts, Feadon.

Second do., for do., John Davey, jun., son of Mr. Davey, Chigarder.

The club afterwards dined at the Bassett's Arms. The Rev. Geo. Treweeke, V. P., in the chair, and after dinner there was considerable interchange of agricultural information.

In July the subject of "Artificial Manures" was partially discussed, and is to be resumed when some experiments made by the members are completed.

In August, there being no subject of discussion placed on the minutes, the conversation turned on subjects connected with the harvest. It was agreed that oats in very dry weather should be left riper than in wet weather, and the oats were improved by a shower when cut. It was thought a good plan for farmers to assist each other in the cutting down their corn; it would then be down in a day or two, instead of a week or fortnight; there would be less waste, and it would be sooner secured—no trifling advantage in this uncertain climate. It was recommended that farmers should take care that their mowsteads and stackyards should be in order before harvest, that they may not miss the first fitting opportunity for carrying their corn.

In September the prizes for turnips were fixed.

LADY BASSETT'S PRIZES.

FIRST CLASS, HOLDING 40 ACRES AND ABOVE.

	£.	s.	d.
For the best crop of Swedes..	5	0	0
For the best crop of pastures.	2	0	0

SECOND CLASS, HOLDING 10 ACRES, AND NOT MORE THAN 40.

For the best crop of Swedes..	2	0	0
For the best crop of pastures.	1	10	0

The expence of tillage, with the quantity, kind, and value, of the manure used, will be required.

Resolved.—That the Club's prizes for turnips be the same as last year, and that the judges inspect the crops about the middle of November.

In October the most economical mode of winter feeding horses was partially discussed, and is to be resumed at our next meeting.

In November the subject of the most economical mode of keeping horses had further consideration, and it was resolved, that the best was the most economical food; that hay chaffed, and oats bruised, and mixed together, were the best and cheapest for farm and other horses of full work; that about 35lbs. of this mixture was enough for a horse a day; horses with easy work might be kept cheaper on cut straw and steamed Swedes.

Dr. Maddon's paper, on the advantages to practical agriculture of an extended chemical analysis, was read.

In December the annual meeting took place at Pool, when about sixty gentlemen sat down to an excellent dinner; the Rev. Geo. Treweeke, V. P., in the chair. After the usual toasts were drunk, the chairman called upon the judges, Messrs. Rowe and Harris, to state their awards for the green crop, when Mr. Rowe gave a pleasing statement of their inspection of the whole of the parish, the result of which was the following awards:—

FOR THE CLUB.

	£.	s.
Mr. Penpraze, Mount Whistle, 1st. prize for Swedes..........................	3	0
Mr. Hugh Phillips, Forest, 1st prize for pastures	2	0
Mr. John Hickens, Tregea, 2nd prize for Swedes..........................	1	0
Mr. Henry Willoughby, Pool, 2nd prize for pastures	1	0

LADY BASSETT'S PRIZES.

FIRST CLASS.

Mrs. Grace Paull, Highway, 1st prize for Swedes..........................	5	0
Mr. Thomas Davey, Namekuke, 1st prize for pastures	2	10

SECOND CLASS.

Mr. W. Kite, Porth Towan, 1st prize for Swedes..........................	2	0
Mr. S. Bennett, Feadon, 1st prize for pastures...........................	1	10

Mr. Rowe gave a detail of the mode of cultivation and the nature and quantity of manure used. The most esteemed was bone-dust. In the instance of Mr. Penpraze, Mr. Rowe stated that 4l. worth of bone had produced as good a crop as 8l. worth of dung. Mr. Harris corroborated Mr. Rowe's statement, and said the husbandry of the parish was highly creditable.

Mr. James Paull and Mr. John Rosewarne gave their award of Lady Bassett's prize of 5l. for the best cultivated farm, to Mr. Burgess, of Trengove; and that of W. Reynolds, Esq., of 5l., for the farm, of which the buildings, hedges, and gates, were kept in the best order, to Mr. Charles Paull. W. Reynolds, Esq., brought before the meeting the analysis of sands obtained by Mr. Hickens, showing that the sands of Gwithian and Phillack contained 70 per cent. of the carbonate of lime, and that of Porthtowan 48 per cent., both of which are most valuable to this locality, as the soil is deficient of the carbonate of lime, according to an analysis obtained from Professor Phillips.

In January, as there appeared to be some uncertainty respecting the statement of the weight of turnips per acre, it was thought best to institute an enquiry, and it was found that turnips weighing 2lbs. each, in drills of 2 ft. and 1 ft. apart, would give, per acre, 19 tons 8 cwt. 3 qrs. ; do., 3lbs., 29 tons 3 cwt. 1 qr.; do., 4lbs., 38 tons 17 cwt. 3 qrs. ; do., 5lbs., 48 tons 12 cwt. 1 qr. ; do., 6lbs., 58 tons 6 cwt. 3 qrs.

In February there was a revision of the rules, and an assistant secretary was elected, and several regulations respecting the books agreed upon.

In March the subject of " Manures," which was to have been introduced by Mr. M. Harris, was deferred till the next meeting, in consequence of the absence of that gentleman.

It was resolved that the mode of improving land by the folding of sheep, has not been sufficiently noticed or enforced, and that this subject be brought before the club at our next meeting, in connection with the subject on " Manures."

This concludes our year's work, and we may be permitted to hope that the Society has done something by the way of uniting the science and practice of agriculture.—April 15th.

ON LEASES.

TO THE EDITOR OF THE FARMER'S MAGAZINE.

Sir,—As the subject of granting leases is one on which a great deal has been said and written, both for and against, I hope you will not think me trespassing on your kindness in sending the following account of the method of fixing a corn rent on land, which was suggested to me by a very intelligent gentleman, who has farmed well and successfully for some years.

As a preliminary observation, allow me to state that whatever merit there may be in the proposal is entirely due to my friend, as I have only put his ideas on paper, a task he would have fulfilled much better himself, could he have spared the time.

So much has been urged in favour of leases, and so many arguments brought forward by men of the greatest experience to show the risk an annual tenant must incur by investing his capital in the improvement of land on so uncertain a tenure, that I think I may venture to assume a lease is the only security that can justify a farmer in an outlay, for which he can only expect to be remunerated in the course of some years.

Now a lease, taken no more than a twelvemonth ago, at a rent warranted by the value of agricultural produce at that time, should the depression that has since taken place continue a few years, must inevitably ruin the tenant, unless he be a man of independent property, and even then he would see his lease out at a considerable sacrifice ; while by a lease taken at the present low prices, in case of as sudden a favourable change, the landlord would not derive the advantage from his land to which he is justly entitled. It has been fully proved by agricultural writers that a farmer should make three rents, in order to procure a remuneration that would justify him in continuing to hold any land. Taking this for a groundwork on which to fix a corn rent, the average number of bushels, both of wheat and barley, per acre, should be ascertained over the whole farm, the value of one acre of wheat and one acre of barley added together, and one third of the amount will be the rent for four acres. On this principle the intervening green crops are considered as merely preparatory, and therefore are not taken at all into

the valuation. As half the land is under corn on the four field system, the value of the produce of these two acres is the rent of four in fixing a cornrent. Should any other course of crops be followed instead of the proposed system, the valuers would only have to calculate what the land would produce in corn if cultivated on the four field rotation.

My friend, who is an excellent judge of the quality and value of land, first took a hill farm, which we agreed would produce on an average 17 bushels of wheat and 25 bushels of barley per acre, and made the calculation for a corn rent on last year's prices as follows :—

	s.	d.
17 bush. of wheat at 8s..	136	0
25 do. of barley at 4s.....	100	0
3)236	0	three rents.
4)78	8	rent for four acres.
19	8	rent per acre.

Now the land in question has been valued by the best judges with us at about a pound an acre, rather under than over.

We then took a large farm of a better description, and fixed the averages at 25 bushels of wheat and 35 of barley, which gave the value as follows :—

	s.	d.
25 bush. of wheat at 8s..	200	0
35 do. of barley at 4s....	140	0
3)340	0	
4)113	4	rent for four acres.
28	4	value per acre.

which is about the rent paid by the tenant, who has occupied the farm for some years.

If we take these calculations from the average price of corn in this district for the present year, we have

	s.	d.
17 bush. wheat at 6s....	102	0
25 bush. barley at 3s....	75	0
3)177	0	
4)59	0	
14	9	per acre.

And

	s.	d.
25 bush. wheat at 6s....	150	0
35 bush. barley at 3s.....	105	0
3)255	0	
4)85	0	
21	3	per acre.

which would be some reduction in the rent to assist the tenant in meeting the present depression in agricultural produce.

I have only to add, that by this plan of letting a farm out of condition. both the tenant and the landlord would be benefited ; the former, by having his rent fixed at the value of the land when he took possession, would be stimulated to invest capital in the improvement of his farm ; and the latter would have his estate increased in value by the superior manner in which it would be cultivated.

I am, sir, your obedient servant,

Chepstow, May 9th.　　　　Veritas.

EXPERIMENTS WITH GUANO.

[FROM THE WIGTOWNSHIRE FREE PRESS.]

At the recent monthly meeting of the Highland and Agricultural Society of Scotland, held in Edinburgh, several important papers were submitted to the meeting well worthy of public attention. To some of these we shall now shortly advert; and as the season for preparing the ground and manure for turnips is at hand, we allude first to some experiments reported on the subject of guano. Some three weeks ago we gave an excellent article from the *Gardener's Chronicle*, on the general elements of manures, of the mode of making composts, and the effects of each. Since then we have received from Messrs. Gibbs, Bright, and Co., merchants, Liverpool, a copy of their pamphlet on the subject, containing a great mass of experiments made in all quarters with guano, which pamphlet we strongly recommend to our agricultural readers. The experiments, however, to which we mean now more particularly to allude, as reported to the Highland and Agricultural Society, were made by J. Dudgeon, Esq., Spylaw, and were attended with so great success, that this year that gentleman intends to put in sixty acres of turnips with guano. Mr. Dudgeon tested this manure by a trial against common farm-yard dung and bones. In his first experiment he tried the comparative value of dung and guano, used in the following proportions, which show the great advantage and saving of expense of guano :—

	cwt.	st.
Two drills with guano, 5 cwt. per acre	25	5
Do. with dung, 18 yds. per do..	18	7
Do. with guano, 4 cwt. per do.	22	6
Do. with dung, 18 yds. per do.	19	7
Do. with guano, 3 cwt. per do.	20	6
Do. with dung, 18 yds. per do.	19	2

Here, then, with guano, at the rate of 3 cwts. per acre—or say cost of manure, 1*l*. 16s.—a heavier crop was taken up in October than was produced by 18 yds. of good farm-yard dung, costing about 4*l*.—the cost of manure being as two to one in favour of guano.

The next experiment made was with bone-dust *versus* guano. The bones were mixed with ashes some days before being applied, in the proportion of sixteen bushels of bones and eight of ashes per acre. The quantity of guano applied was at the rate of three cwt. per acre upon four drills, two and two together, at an interval of eight drills manured with bones and ashes. Then, at a smaller interval, followed two drills operated upon with guano, together with sulphate of soda (gluber salts), at the rate of four cwt. per acre, being the only instance, in the course of these experiments, in which any foreign substance was used with the guano. The turnips were drawn about the end of November, and on a comparison of the weight of the crop on two or four drills done with guano alone, with the produce of the average of four drills nearly immediately adjoining, manured with bone-dust and ashes, the result stood thus (the plants being topped and rooted) :—

	cwt.	st.
Guano	23	2
Bone-dust, &c.	19	2
Guano and sulphates of soda	23	0

In the third experiment guano was used against bone dust alone, applied, as is usual in that district, at that rate of 16 bushels per acre. The guano was used at the rate of two cwt. only per acre. The drills manured with the latter showed a very early superiority, and were ready for the hoe fully eight days earlier than the rest of the field. This more vigorous growth they maintained throughout, and when the turnips (the white stone globe variety) were weighed on the 22nd March, after standing throughout the winter, the result was as follows (the roots and tops being in this instance retained) :—

	cwt.	st.
2 drills guano	31	4
2 do. bone dust	24	7

The result of this experiment is important. We find guano, costing say 25s. per acre, yielding a larger crop than bones, costing say 35s. per acre—the increase being in the proportion of 31 tons per acre in favour of guano, to 24 tons per acre raised by bone dust, supposing the ground capable of raising such a crop.

Mr. Dudgeon had also used guano in top dressing wheat sown on potato land, and the effect was most promising. Professor Liebig had seen some of these experiments, with which he expressed himself highly pleased.

One word practically as to bones and guano, and of the efficacy of any experiment to be made. The farmer must see that he buys the genuine material. Let him buy from a first-rate dealer, who will warrant the manure genuine, and let him pay a fair value for it, or he need not be surprised if he lose his crop, all his rent, and what money he lays out for the adulterated cheap stuff. We by no means disparage artificial manures. Some of these are very good. But bones have been long tried, and proved to be of substantial benefit in agriculture. Their effect is lasting, and their chemical action, as manure, will, we have no doubt, be greatly felt even in the breaking up of lands which, years before, had been sown down after a turnip crop manured with bones. In this way we think it very unlikely that bones will be entirely given up and guano substituted ; while, however, we have as little doubt that guano will also be extensively and successfully used as a cheap and efficacious manure. Finally, as to guano : it the farmer is resolved to try it, let him see that he pays a fair price—that he gets it from a respectable dealer—and in applying it to the ground with a turnip crop, he ought to have the manure nicely mixed with a certain proportion of ashes, to make it sow more easily ; and, above all, the land should be thoroughly cleaned and pulverized, and the weather and ground dry when the manure is put in and the seed sown.

ANALYSIS OF SOILS.

(From the Annals of Chymistry.)

The analysis of soils is often of great importance to the agriculturist, and in this particular he has frequently to address himself to the chemist. The instructions for undertaking such analysis differ materially from each other. Of themselves they are very simple and easily executed, if a certain plan has been previously laid down for attaining the object in view. This object is two-fold—viz. 1stly, to know how much and what substances of organic origin, (that is to say, how much humus) is contained in the soil : and, 2dly, with what disintegrated minerals the inorganic part of the soil is mixed.

The answer to the first question falls entirely within the compass of organic analysis. The soil is dried in an oil-bath at 266° F.; then treated—in the apparatus figured p. 281 of the Annals—first with ether, then with alcohol, water, and so on consecutively. By this process several different matters are extracted from the soil ; but it is very uncertain if any of them will be distinguished as previously already known. We have not yet sufficiently examined the products of the decomposition of organic bodies, to be able to execute this kind of analysis in such a manner that we can finaly decide what products of decomposition the soil contains. This examination therefore becomes difficult, and yields, even if executed with precision, not very valuable results, until we shall have previously made ourselves acquainted with these products of decomposition by a close examination of them.

Two circumstances respecting humus may be positively ascertained, viz. 1stly, its quantity; which is found out by burning a weighed quantity of soil, after being dried at 266° F., in an open crucible, until all the combustible parts are destroyed, when the loss shows the contents of organic matter: and 2dly, the azote therein contained; which is ascertained by combustion, according to the method of Varrentrapp and Will. The results of these experiments are seldom of much value; since the quality of the humus in soils varies according to the manure added, and as the succeeding crops may absorb the several components of each manure.

The inorganic components of the soil, again, are easily ascertained. An air-dried sample of the soil being disintegrated as much as possible between the hands, is weighed, and sifted through a tinplate sieve, consisting of several plates succeeding each other, with less and lesser holes. The sieve is then shaken, with the cover on, until the mass is divided according to the different size of the holes in the different compartments of the sieve, and each of these quantities is then weighed, in order to give an idea of the different sizes of the various ingredients.

Another air-dried sample is likewise weighed, and then dried in the water-bath, until it ceases to lose weight. A smaller portion of it is then weighed, placed in a glass tube, which has been closed at one extremity by fusion, and heated in the oil-bath to 266° F. until it ceases to lose weight, after which the contents of water are found by calculation. This sample is heated to redness in an open crucible until the whole of the carbon is consumed, and the organic matter of the whole is found by a calculation based thereon.

The greater portion of the sample is likewise exactly weighed, put into a glass vessel, infused in water, and then stirred with a quill. After being left undisturbed for a few moments, all the lighter parts are skimmed off, and the turbid water poured through a muslin sieve into another vessel, where it is allowed to stand for the purpose of depositing. There remain on the sieve fibres of roots, undecomposed portions of straw, stalks, &c. This operation is repeated until the freshly added water no longer becomes turbid by stirring. The finally remaining residue is dried and weighed, but not exposed to a red heat.

This residue is spread on paper, and, if required, examined with the aid of a compound microscope, in case of the parts being very small. The practised eye then detects the grains of those minerals, the *debris* of which form the soil. Grains of transparent quartz, milk-quartz, red and white field-spar, scales of mica, lime, clay-slate, &c. are thus detected, and have been obtained from such minerals as are met with in the neighbourhood; and this easy examination is sufficient to elucidate of what minerals the soil is composed—on which point chemical analysis would not be able to give positive information. In proportion to the more finely pulverized portions contained in soil from the recent formations of mountains, the greater is its fertility, if mixed with the requisite manure. The *debris* of limestones, and different tertiary kinds of aluminous slate, mixed to a certain extent with quartzose or granitic sand, form the best mixtures.

From this residue the carbonate of lime (in case

of the same being contained therein) is extracted by a mixture of one part of nitric acid and 100 parts of water, which are allowed to act on it without heat. When the effervescence has ceased, although the liquor still reddens litmus paper, the liquid is decanted, and the calcareous earth, after being neutralized with caustic ammonia, is precipitated therefrom by oxalate of ammonia. The magnesian earth is then ascertained (if present) by mixing the liquor in excess with carbonate of potassa, and boiling it therewith.

The residue left undissolved by nitric acid is washed, dried, weighed, and treated with concentrated muriatic acid. This solution is then further treated in the way directed for analyzing silicates which are soluble in muriatic acid. The muriatic acid frequently disengages siliceous acid without dissolving it. These are then extracted by boiling the undissolved parts with a ley of carbonate of soda. The undissolved residue is then weighed. It is in general nothing but sand composed of quartz or granite.

We now return to the parts left after being skimmed. That portion which passed through the muslin sieve is a mixture of decomposed organic substances (humus,) clay (alumina,) and extremely fine sand, which frequently contains siliceous shells from infusoria. After being left undisturbed for an hour, the sand and humus have settled; the clay, however, still remains suspended. The water is then decanted from the thick pap of clay, and gradually evaporated to dryness in a weighed basin or a crucible, after which the remaining clay is dried by the application of a rather high degree of heat, *e. g.*, in the oil-bath at 302° F., and weighed.

The deposited mass beneath the pap of clay is placed on a filter previously weighed. The turbid water which passed during the washing of the mass through the filter, together with the clay solution, is exposed to evaporation. The filter, together with all therein contained, is dried at 212° F., weighed, and burnt to ashes; after which the residue is examined under the microscope. It is then further treated in the same way as above stated for the coarser powder.—*Berz Lehr. d. Chemie, vol. x. § 123.*

WENLOCK AGRICULTURAL READING SOCIETY.

EXTRACT FROM THE ADDRESS OF THE COMMITTEE.

"When we reflect on the immense benefits which science has conferred on almost every other branch of the industrial arts, and the tendency which it undoubtedly has to render manufacturers, mechanics, as well as the members of some of the liberal professions, more skilful in their respective avocations, it may reasonably be expected that equal advantages will flow to agriculture from the application to it of the leading principles of science, and that the farmer will be a more successful cultivator of the land, when he becomes acquainted with the composition and qualities of the various soils upon his farm, when he understands the structure and physiology of plants, and the properties of manures, as well as their effects upon the soil, and their influence on vegetation. 'There is no other profession,' says Dr. Liebig, in his valuable work on Agricultural Chemistry, 'in which the application of correct principles is productive of more beneficial effects, or is of greater and more decided influence than that of agriculture. In addition to the general conditions, such as light, heat, and moisture, and the component parts of the atmosphere which are necessary for the growth of all plants, certain substances are found to exercise a peculiar influence on the development of particular families. These substances are already contained in the soil, or are supplied to it in the form of the matters known under the general name of manure. But what does the soil contain, and what are the components of the substances used as manure? Until these points are satisfactorily determined, a rational system of agriculture cannot exist. The power and knowledge of the physiologist, of the agriculturist and chemist, must be united for the complete solution of these questions.' The correctness, gentlemen, of these remarks cannot be called in question; your committee therefore earnestly recommend the attentive perusal of those works on science, vegetable physiology, and other branches of natural history which may be likely to throw some additional light on agriculture, and lead to the establishment in this, as well as in other professions, of general principles for the guidance of the inexperienced farmer. Were the generality of farmers well informed on these subjects, did their knowledge consist more of a few leading principles than a number of isolated facts, agriculture would then become, what it ever should be, a scientific, instead of an empirical art; and the occupation of those who practised it would be the more honourable in proportion to the increase of the skill it required of them.

"There are some who ridicule the idea of applying science to farming, who contend that instead of benefiting the agriculturist, it will only tend to increase his expences. Nothing can be more absurd or untrue than such a proposition, since one of the greatest advantages that will result from science as applied to agriculture is, that it will teach you to farm on certain established principles instead of a system of blind routine, which must of course be uncertain and therefore occasionally deceptive in its results.

"Of the advantages of science to agriculture a better instance cannot be adduced than that of the celebrated French chemist, Lavoiser, who is reported to have cultivated 240 acres of land in La Vendée on chemical principles, in order to set a good example to the farmers; and so successful was his mode of culture, that he obtained a third more of crop than was procured by the usual method, and in nine years his annual produce was doubled.

"When your committee, however, insist on the value of science in reference to agriculture, they must not be supposed to mean every new theory that may emanate from the imaginations of closet speculators, but principles deduced from a judicious and attentive consideration of numerous well established facts, and these principles too afterwards tested by careful and repeated experiments. It is doubtless with this view that the members of the Royal Agricultural Society have been requested to furnish their committee with so many facts relating to the geological formation, the nature of the surface soil and substratum, the elevation, aspect, humidity, &c., of their respective farms; the average quantity and quality of the different crops; nature and prevalence of diseases among their cattle, &c., &c. In themselves such a mass of isolated facts, from the impossibility of generally applying them, would be comparatively useless unless employed as data from which some talented and comprehensive mind may afterwards be enabled to deduce important general principles."

ROYAL AGRICULTURAL SOCIETY OF ENGLAND.

At a weekly council, held at the Society's house in Hanover-square, on Wednesday, the 26th of April, present, Thomas Raymond Barker, Esq., in the chair; Marquis of Downshire, Lord Bridport, Hon. Robert Henry Clive, M.P.; Hon. Captain Hood; John Raymond Barker, Esq.; W. R. Browne, Esq.; Colonel Challoner; F. C. Cherry, Esq.; W. Daniel, Esq.; E. D. Davenport, Esq.; Humphrey Gibbs, Esq.; Brandreth Gibbs, Esq.; C. Hillyard, Esq.; Sir John Johnstone, Bart., M.P.; Sir Francis Lawley, Bart.; William Miles, Esq., M.P.; Joshua Rodwell, Esq.; Professor Sewell, and J. Spencer Stanhope, Esq.

BOKHARA CLOVER.

Mr. Rodwell, of Alderton Hall, near Woodbridge, Suffolk, communicated to the Council the following explanation of the specimens of Bokhara he had presented to the Society, and the results of his experience in the garden cultivation of this plant.

"SPECIMEN No. 1, alba altissima. The growth of 1841. Seed sown, April 21. The plant the growth of 138 days. First year's produce. Length 8 feet 11 inches.

"SPECIMEN No. 2, alba altissima. The growth of 1842. Second year's produce from the roots of the former year. Pressed when in blossom. Growth of 125 days. Length 11 feet 4 inches.

"SPECIMEN No. 3, alba altissima. Growth of 1842. Second year's produce from the roots of the former year. Pressed when in seed. Growth of 189 weeks. Length 12 feet 10 inches.

The specific name of this plant has not been hitherto quite decided, to my knowledge, it having been designated Melilotus arborea, Melilotus gigantea, alba altissima, and by other distinctive names that are unimportant excepting to the scientific or the botanist. The seed from which the specimens now exhibited in the Council Room of the Society was obtained through the kindness of S. Taylor, Esq., of Stoke Ferry, who received it from Bokhara, a district in Persia.

"1841, April 21.—Seed sown in drills about 18 inches apart, each seed having a space of 6 inches in the drills. The soil a rich loamy mould, deep and dry. The subsoil, loamy craig, about 4 feet from land springs. Preparation, deep digging and manuring after a crop of potatoes. Cultivation in May; hoeing and weeding in the usual manner. In June, its rapid growth (at the rate of an inch in 24 hours), and its disposition to throw out lateral shoots, requiring great care and attention in giving it support during some of the genial days in this month. In July, the same attention as in the preceding month. In September, the specimen No. 1 was gathered and dried when in full bloom; In October, the produce was carefully cut down, and applied for fodder to cattle. Horses not fond of it; cows and pigs prefer other food. Some specimens of the fibre and stalks of this year's produce were enclosed to Mr. Buckingham of Lopham, a hemp manufacturer, for the purpose of his testing their properties in reference to manufacturing objects, in reply to which communication he says, 'I can find no available matter in them for manufacturing purposes.'

"1842. Early in the spring of this year the plants which had been carefully cut down in the autumn, began to exhibit their spring shoots as soon as the severity of the winter would permit them, long before the lucerne shoots were visible; thus establishing two important points—early vegetation and great hardiness; the rapidity and great luxuriousness of the growth of these shoots, as the spring advanced, exciting the surprise of all who witnessed them. The plant now required great care and attention in supporting the lateral branches, so as to prevent them falling. Early in June the blossoms began to make their appearance, and continued to make fresh bloom during the months of July and August, forming not only an ornamental but a very fragrant garden plant. In this state, the specimen No. 2 was taken as an average growth. In August and September the seed-pods were formed and began to ripen; and the seed gathered at the end of September, yielding eight pounds to the square rod. The specimen No. 3 was gathered at the same time.

"Upon the usefulness of this plant, I am at present unable to give any very favourable report, its properties for feeding cattle having no great recommendation, as it was found that a preference was always given to any other food, either in its green or dried state. It has shown itself with my mode of treatment a biennial plant, no vegetation having appeared during the present year; this, however, may possibly not be its characteristic with repeated cuttings in a green state; a point which I have not at present ascertained by trial."

Mr. Rodwell having stated to the Council that he had placed at the disposal of Messrs. Thomas Gibbs & Co. the whole of the seed of the Bokhara Clover obtained from this cultivation of it, Mr. H. Gibbs corroborated Mr. Rodwell's remarks, as to the unwillingness of animals to eat the plant when lucerne could be had by them; and stated, that when his father first introduced the plant, the seed was grown in some quantities for him by the late Mr. Arthur Young, the editor of the "Annals of Agriculture." Mr. Gibbs's idea was, to cut and stack the clover in alternate layers with oat straw, and afterwards cut the two into chaff for use; also, to mix it with grass in haymaking, when there was the chance of damage from wet weather, so as to impart a good smell to the hay, and thereby give it the character of hay well got up.

ANNUAL COUNTRY MEETING OF 1845.

The Hon. Robert H. Clive, M.P. gave notice that he should propose, at the next monthly meeting of the Council, that the annual country meeting of the Society should be held at Shrewsbury in the year 1845.

MANGOLD WURZEL AND SWEDISH TURNIPS.

Mr. Hillyard informed the Council, that he had had six small Hereford oxen, all of one person's breed, and divided as equally as possible, fed for sixteen weeks in his stalls; three of them on mangold wurzel and three on Swedish turnips, a bushel and a half each daily, with a bushel and a half of cut hay, mixed with one quart of boiled linseed, and three quarts of barley meal, for the purpose of testing the comparative feeding qualities of these roots. The oxen slaughtered by Mr. Giblett, of New Bond-street, would be exhibited to members of the Society, and the public generally, at his shop, on Monday, the 1st of May, and the three following days.

The Council adjourned to Wednesday next, the 3rd of May.

A monthly council was held at the Society's house, in Hanover-square, on Wednesday, the 3rd of May, present, the Earl of Hardwicke, President, in the chair; Marquis of Downshire; Earl of Euston; Earl Spencer; Earl of Ducie; Lord Bridport; Hon. Robert H. Clive, M.P.; Hon. George H. Cavendish, M.P.; Hon. W. Bingham Baring, M.P.; Col. Austen; Thomas Raymond Barker, Esq.; John Raymond Barker, Esq.; T. J. M. Bartlett, Esq.; John Benett, Esq., M.P.; French Burke, Esq.; Col. Challoner; F. C. Cherry, Esq.; C. R. Colvile, Esq., M.P.; E. D. Davenport, Esq.; James Dean, Esq.; Humphrey Gibbs, Esq.; Stephen Grantham, Esq.; Rev. Daniel

Gwilt; W. Goodenough Hayter, Esq., M.P.; C. Hillyard, Esq.; W. Fisher Hobbs, Esq.; Sir Hungerford Hoskyns, Bart.; Sir John V. B. Johnstone, Bart., M.P.; Samuel Jonas, Esq.; Geo. Kimberley, Esq.; John Kinder, Esq.; Sir Francis Lawley, Bart.; Sir Charles Lemon, Bart., M.P.; Sir Francis A. Mackenzie, Bart.; Townshend Mainwaring, Esq., M.P.; William Miles, Esq., M.P.; E. W. W. Pendarves, Esq., M.P.; S. Peploe, Esq.; E. S. Chandos Pole, Esq.; Philip Pusey, Esq., M.P.; Rev. W. L. Rham; E. Ayshford Sanford, Esq.; Professor Sewell; William Shaw, Esq.; J. Spencer Stanhope, Esq.; W. R. Crompton Stansfield, Esq., M.P.; Charles Stokes, Esq., and Colonel Wood, M.P.

Mr. Raymond Barker, Chairman of the Finance Committee, reported to the Council that agreeably with the order of the Council, the Committee had purchased 1,000l. in the New 3½ per Cents. in the name of the Trustees of the Society; the total amount of the Society's Stock in the funds now amounting to 7,700l., with a current cash balance at the Bankers, at the end of the previous month, of 1,204l.

Agreeably with recommendation of the Committee a new form of Election Letter was adopted by the Council, and the names of 49 Members, whose subscription was in arrear, ordered to be expunged from the List of the Society.

PRIZE ESSAY ON DRAINAGE.

The Journal Committee reported to the Council that the Judges of the essays sent in to compete for the Society's prize of fifty sovereigns for the best essay on the drainage of land, had unanimously adjudged the prize to the essay of Mr. Thomas Arkell, of Pen Hill Farm, Cold Harbour, near Swindon, Wiltshire.

MEETING AT DERBY.

Colonel Challoner, vice-chairman of the General Derby Committee, presented to the Council the report of the proceedings of the General Derby Committee, as well as of the Local Derby Committee, transmitted by Mr. Colvile, M.P., and the progress of the various arrangements for the meeting in July, especially in reference to the land for the trial of implements, and the best and most convenient mode for the exhibition, to the members of the practical working of stationary agricultural machinery to be tried on the occasion; the classification and arrangement of the implements in the show-yard; the preparation of the catalogue: the publication of the programme of proceedings; the nomination and direction of the requisite police force; the registration of lodgings; the issue of advertisements for tenders of contract for the council and pavilion dinners, &c. This report was received and adopted by the Council, and its recommendation that the exhibition of implements should be open for admission to the public (at the same rate as in former years) on the Tuesday, as well as on the Wednesday preceding the general day of the show, confirmed.

MODEL FARMS.

The Model Farm Committee laid before the Council their final report, which was received and read.

ANNUAL COUNTRY MEETING OF 1844.

The Council then proceeded to the consideration of the question of the place of the Society's Annual Country Meeting of 1844; which, agreeably with the established routine in the succession of districts, must, for that year, be selected from the district formed of the following counties:—Middlesex, Surrey, Kent, Sussex, and Hampshire, including the Isle of Wight and the Channel islands of Jersey, Guernsey, &c.

Deputations from Maidstone, Southampton, and Winchester, had successively an interview with the Council, for the purpose of advocating the claims of the towns which they respectively represented.

Deputation from Maidstone: Viscount Torrington and Viscount Marsham, M.P.

Deputation from Southampton: The Mayor of Southampton (E. Mayes, Esq.), Lord Charles Wellesley, M.P., H. C. Compton, Esq., M.P., H. St. John Mildmay, Esq., M.P., C. Gater, Esq., and G. W. Johnson, Esq. (secretary to the committee).

Deputation from Winchester: The Mayor of Winchester, the Hon. W. Bingham Baring, M.P., Sir William Heathcote, Bart., M.P., Sir Thomas Baring, Bart., W. W. Bulpett, Esq. (Chairman of the Committee), T. B. East, Esq., M.P., B. Escott, Esq., M.P., J. N. Hughes, Esq., Cuthbert W. Johnson, Esq., W. Simonds, Esq., and Thomas Woodham, Esq.

These deputations were received with every mark of respect and attention by the Council; and the liberal terms in which they placed at their entire disposal, and free of every expense, whatever local advantages they respectively possessed, in reference to the holding of the annual country meeting of 1844, evinced the strong interest felt by the friends of agricultural improvement in the south-eastern counties of the kingdom, and their zealous desire to promote the national objects of the Society.

The members of each deputation laid before the Council the replies to the official queries transmitted to them on their original application, and required by the resolutions of the Council to be satisfactorily answered prior to the selection of any town as the place of the annual country meeting of any year, accompanied with plans of the various sites proposed by them, for the purposes of the Council and pavilion dinners, the cattle and implement show-yard, the land for the trial of implements, and the rooms for the transaction of the official business of the Society; and they also gave the Council detailed information in reference to the communication of each place by railways, coaches, waggons, and steamboats, with the surrounding district, as well as the additional accommodation that would be provided by the various companies to meet the increased demand of traffic; and stated that no less than 100,000 visitors could be accommodated on the occasion by any one of the three proposed towns and its immediate vicinity. The directors of the South-western Railway, following the example of the directors of the Midland Counties Railway at Derby, and on the representation of Mr. Etwall, M.P. for Andover, on Friday last, also decided " to convey to and from Southampton *all the show-cattle at half fares*, and further pledged themselves to give every facility for quick conveyance, and not to charge any additional fares for passengers."—(*Hampshire Independent*, May 6.)

On the motion of Earl Spencer, the President was requested to direct a special council to be summoned for Thursday, the 11th of May, and the following committee was appointed to report to the Council on that occasion: The Earl of Hardwicke, the Duke of Richmond, Earl Spencer, Mr. Benett, M.P., Mr. Burke, Mr. Childers, M.P., Mr. Dean, Mr. Hobbs, and Mr. Pusey, M.P.

PRIZE-SHEET OF 1844.

Agreeably with the standing regulations of the Society, the Council ordered that a preliminary impression of the Prize-Sheet for next year should be prepared, and laid before the Members, at the ensuing Anniversary Meeting on the 22nd of May, for their revision and suggestions, previously to its final adoption and confirmation by the Council; on which occasion Mr. Charles Stokes gave notice that he should propose the first prizes in each class of Bulls to be raised from 30*l.* to 50*l.*

A letter was read from Mr. Barugh Almack, suggesting the adoption of an open and unconditional prize, to be awarded under the direction of the Journal Committee, of a similar nature to that of the prize for " any implement" already in the Prize-List of the Society; in order to collect all the really useful information on every branch of practical farming, for the purpose of making it generally known through the medium of the Journal: many valuable practices being at present only locally known, and confined in many instances to the knowledge of parties who would be incapable of writing on these subjects. This communication was referred to the Journal Committee.

ARREAR OF SUBSCRIPTION.

Mr. Gibbs then brought forward his motion on the subject of the date at which subscriptions shall be considered to become in arrear, which was seconded by Earl Spencer, and carried unanimously, namely:— " That all members shall be considered to be in arrear, whose subscriptions, due in advance for each year on the first of January, remain unpaid by the first of June ensuing."

ANNUAL COUNTRY MEETING OF 1845.

The Hon. Robert Henry Clive, M.P. presented to the Council the following documents, in favour of Shrewsbury as the place of the Society's Annual Country Meeting of 1845, to be held in the North Wales district, comprised of the counties of Anglesey, Carnarvonshire, Merionethshire, Montgomeryshire, Denbighshire, Flintshire, Cheshire, Shropshire, and Staffordshire.

1.—Replies to the official queries of the Society, signed by the town-clerk of Shrewsbury.
2.—A plan of Shrewsbury, showing the various local sites offered to the Society.
3. The memorial of the corporation of Shrewsbury, signed by the town clerk, and bearing the great seal of the borough affixed to the document, inviting the President and Council of the Royal Agricultural Society of England to hold the annual country meeting of the Society for the North Wales district, at Shrewsbury, in the year 1845.
4. The memorial of the inhabitants of the town of Shrewsbury, signed by Edward Haycock, Esq. (mayor), and ninety-five of the principal inhabitants, pledging themselves, should their ancient town of Shrewsbury be selected as the place of meeting, to use their best exertions to provide upon the most liberal terms every requisite accommodation for the members and other visitors attending on that occasion, and to promote the interests of the Society by every endeavour in their power.
5. The memorial of the Shropshire Practical Farmers' Society, signed by Viscount Hill, their President, detailing the several advantages possessed by Shrewsbury, in an agricultural point of view, for the purposes of the meeting, strongly stating the peculiar merits of the localities proposed for the show-yard, pavilion, and trial of implement ground; explaining in detail the lines of communication from Shrewsbury to every part of the north and west of England.

Mr. Clive then informed the Council that the Race Course, at the distance of about half a mile from the town, offered a most suitable site for the show-yard and the trial of implements, the whole extent of the course comprising 20 acres, of which 19 acres were peculiarly eligible, and there was a good supply of water, free of cost; and the whole guaranteed by the Corporation free of any charge to the Society, either by owner or occupier. That there was an excellent room in the centre of the town capable of dining 500 persons, which was also freely offered to the Society 'without any charge, as well as the requisite rooms for the transaction of the official business of the Society. The unrivalled public grounds called " The Quarry," and immediately adjoining the town, presented a most inviting and eligible spot for the erection of a Pavilion for the great dinner of the Society, whatever might be its required magnitude. Mr. Clive stated that every arrangement was making in Shrewsbury to anticipate the wishes of the Society and its members, should the inhabitants be so fortunate as to succeed in their present application, by establishing a maximum rate for lodgings and the conveyance of passengers and stock to and from the town, and thus at once practically evince the desire felt by the town and county of Salop at large to promote the objects of the meeting, and the comfort and advantage of the visitors. Mr. Clive concluded by announcing that a subscription to defray every expense of the meeting was in progress ; but such was the feeling of the members in that neighbourhood, that they alone would guarantee a subscription to any amount that might be required for the purposes of the meeting ; all being anxious to show their respect to the society, and he himself had thus participated in the general feeling, and discharged an agreeable duty in bringing this subject before the Council.

Mr. Brittain, secretary of the Chester Agricultural Society, transmitted to the Council a statement of the proceedings in progress in that city for replying satisfactorily to the official queries transmitted to it.

The Council then directed these documents to be registered and reserved for consideration at the date when the question of deciding upon a place for the meeting of the Society in the North Wales district should be brought before the Council for final decision.

Dr. Playfair returned thanks to the Council for his appointment as " Consulting Chemist " to the Society. Mrs. Davies Gilbert presented specimens of Bokhara clover, and a statement of the progress of the Willingdon schools ; the Rev. J. M. King presented a copy of his translation of Virgil's Georgics ; Professor Henslow, a copy of his Letters to the Farmers of Suffolk ; Dr. Tilley, the numbers of his Agricultural Chemistry ; Mr. R. Green, an account of his Under-Draining Plough ; and Mr. Evans, copies of the Farmer's Herald. The Marquis Mazzarosa informed the Council of the meeting this year of the Italian Scientific Association at Lucca during the two last weeks of September.

The Council then adjourned to Wednesday next, the 10th of May.

A weekly Council was held at the Society's House in Hanover Square, on Wednesday, the 10th of May, present—The Hon. Robert Henry Clive, M.P., in the Chair, Marquis of Downshire, Earl Spencer, R. W. Baker, Esq., Thos. Raymond Barker, Esq., W. R. Browne, Esq., F. Burke, Esq., F. C. Cherry, Esq., E.D. Davenport, Esq., Alexander Davidson, Esq., Sir John Guise, Bart., Sir Francis Lawley, Bart., E. S. Chandos Pole, Esq. ; W. R. C. Stansfield, Esq., M.P., and George Wilbraham, Esq.   Count Cavoure, from Piedmont, and Professor De la Rive, of Geneva, were also present at the Meeting.

POITTEVIN'S MANURE.

Mr. Poittevin presented to the Society a bag of each of his two manures, and informed the Council that he was now capable of supplying any quantity, of either kind, at a very short notice.

GUANO EXPERIMENTS.

Mr. Davenport communicated to the Council the following results of trials made last year with guano, on his farm at Capesthorne, in Cheshire:—

" *On Meadow.*—One acre sown with 3 cwt. of guano and 3 cwt. of gypsum ; crops, when ready to stack, 2 tons 18 cwt.

One acre sown with 2 cwt. of guano and 2 cwt. of gypsum—2 tons 8 cwt.

One acre sown with 2 cwt. of guano only—2 tons.

Turnips.—One acre of turnips, 4 cwt. of guano and 4 cwt. of gypsum—30 tons produce.

One acre of turnips, 2 cwt. of guano and 2 cwt. of gypsum—27 tons.

The difference between an unmanured acre, and one manured with 3 cwt. of guano and the same quantity of gypsum, was 27 cwt. of hay additional. The guano was of the best kind, sold by Myers, of Liverpool, last year, at 15l., and this year at 10l. the ton. Its effects on greenhouse plants, when sufficiently dilated, is great ; but it is easy to do mischief by excess. Water is the best vehicle. When sown, it should be in showery weather. Altogether it appears to be

the cheapest manure known, and strong soils suit it best.—E. D. DAVENPORT."

SIMPLE AND ECONOMICAL PLOUGH.

Mr. Henry Wilson, of Stowlangtoft Hall, near Ixworth, Suffolk, presented to the Society a model of Rouse's Improved Plough.

This plough is the invention of William Rouse, a wheelwright, residing at Barton, near Bury St. Edmund's, and the principal points of advantage ascribed to it, as communicated by Mr. Wilson, are the following :— " That the share may be deepened, or *fleetened*, to or from the land in an instant without stopping the horses, or the ploughman's hand being taken off the plough ; that it will go with or without a ground, with or without wheels, with a wood breast for turnip and summer land, and with any shaped iron breast that may be required or preferred ; that it requires no sledge for its removal from place to place : that the coulter may be moved six ways, by a movement effected in an instant, and so firm that no horse can move it ; that the furrow can be taken any width and any depth, up hill or down hill with equal facility ; that it will be less expensive to the farmer and more easy to the labourer than any plough yet made, the whole construction being so simple as to be kept in repair at less cost than other ploughs." The communication of Mr. Wilson stated that the plough had received the approbation of Mr. Allan Ransome, and had undergone the test of practical trial on various kinds of land in Suffolk.

Mr. Arthur Hall presented the First Annual Report of the Chepstow Farmer's Club, and Mr. S. Taylor, the Third Annual Report of the Stoke-Ferry Farmer's Club.   Mr. Munn presented to the Society the bar and frame Bee-hive of his invention, with an account of its peculiar advantages over the common hives—for which the thanks of the Society were ordered.

SPECIAL COUNCIL.

A Special Council was held on Thursday last, the 11th of May, present—The Earl of Hardwicke, President, in the Chair, Duke of Sutherland, Marquis of Downshire, Earl Spencer, Hon. Captain Spencer, Hon. R. H. Clive, M.P., Sir Thomas D. Acland, Bart., M.P., R. W. Baker, Esq., Thomas Raymond Barker, Esq., John Benett, Esq., M.P., Thomas William Bramston, Esq., M.P., Edward Buller, Esq., M.P., Frenche Burke, Esq., Colonel Challoner, F. C. Cherry, Esq., John Walbanke Childers, Esq., M.P., James Dean, Esq., Humphrey Gibbs, Esq., Brandreth Gibbs, Esq., William Fisher Hobbs, Esq., Sir John Johnstone, Bart., M.P., George Kimberley, Esq., Sir Charles Lemon, Bart., M.P., William Miles, Esq., M.P., Joseph Neeld, Esq., M.P., E. W. W. Pendarves, Esq., M.P., Philip Pusey, Esq., M.P., William Shaw, Esq., Professor Sewell, W. R. C. Stansfield, Esq., M.P., Thomas Weall, Esq., George Wilbraham, Esq., and Colonel Wood, M.P.

Henry Colman, Esq., Agricultural Commissioner of the State of Massachusetts, was also present, and took his seat as an Honorary Member.

ANNUAL COUNTRY MEETING OF 1844.

Earl Spencer read to the Council the Report of the Special Committee of enquiry appointed on the 3rd of May, and the President detailed in succession the various points of advantage presented by each locality proposed to the Society for the next year's Meeting, when the final decision of the question was made, and Southampton duly chosen as the place of the Annual Country Meeting of 1844, agreeably with the memorial and other documents presented to the Council in favour of that town.

MAYOR OF DERBY.

The Mayor of Derby (John Bell Crompton, Esq., of Milford House) invited the Council to a public dinner to be given to them by him, in his municipal capacity, on Tuesday, the 11th of July, at the Royal Hotel in that Borough, and the invitation was unanimously accepted, with the thanks of the Council.

GENERAL DERBY COMMITTEE.

The Hon. Geo. Henry Cavendish, M.P., of Ashford Hall, Bakewell, Derbyshire, was elected a Member of the General Derby Committee.

PRIZE ESSAYS.

The Journal Committee reported the adjudication of the Prize of Ten Sovereigns, for the best Essay on the comparative advantages in the employment of Horses and Oxen in Farming work, to JAMES COWIE, of the Mains of Haulbrerton, Laurencekirk, Kincardineshire, Scotland; and the Prize of Twenty Sovereigns for the best explanation of the causes which appear to determine the production of Fat and Muscle respectively, according to the present state of our knowledge of Animal Physiology, to W. F. KARKEEK, of Truro, Cornwall; both of these gentlemen being Veterinary Surgeons, and pupils formerly under Professor Sewell at the Royal Veterinary College, London.

ELECTION OF COUNCIL.

Mr. Childers gave notice that he should move at the next Monthly Council, " that of the 25 Members of Council who go out by rotation, the 10 who have attended the fewest times during the year shall not be recommended by the Council for re-election."

The Council then adjourned.

A weekly Council was held at the Society's House, in Hanover-square, on Wednesday, the 17th of May, present, The Marquis of Downshire, in the Chair, Earl Spencer, Hon. Robert Henry Clive, M.P., Col. Austen, Thomas Raymond Barker, Esq., George Raymond Barker, Esq., T. J. M. Bartlett, Esq., W. R. Browne, Esq., French Burke, Esq., Colonel Challoner, F. C. Cherry, Esq., John Walbanke Childers, Esq., M.P., Henry Colman, Esq., E. D. Davenport, Esq., Alexander Davidson, Esq., A. E. Fuller, Esq., M.P., Humphrey Gibbs, Esq., Brandreth Gibbs, Esq., Sir John V. B. Johnstone, Bart., M.P., Henry R. Sandbach, Esq., Professor Sewell, and Dr. Whitlaw.

The Marquis of Downshire gave notice that he should call the attention of the Council at their next Monthly Meeting to the question of taking into consideration the propriety of the Society's recommending a course of public Lectures to be given in London by Mr. Smith of Deanston on the subject of Thorough-Draining and Subsoil-Ploughing, similar to those he had recently delivered with so much success in Ireland.

A letter was read from Mr. Kerr on the subject of grated tiles to prevent the entrance of vermin into drains; and a specimen of the mode of preparing tiles for a similar purpose suggested by Mr. Barton of Threxton, was exhibited to the Meeting.

Mr. Clive expressed his intention of exhibiting at the Derby Meeting a cheap fire-engine of simple construction, throwing 25 gallons of water each minute. Mr. Davenport informed the Council that he had formed a fire-engine on Merewether's construction very cheap and effective; and Colonel Challoner stated that Mr. Sherborne, of Bedfont, employed a single-actioned engine with fly-wheel to prepare his manure with water in the summer.

The Marquis of Downshire presented the yearly Report of the Royal Agricultural Improvement Society of Ireland; and Mr. Butsford, of Portland-place, a specimen of the Guinea-Grass from seed sown last spring at Hampton Lodge, near Farnham, in Surrey, Mr. Butsford stating that this grass in Jamaica grows to the height of five feet, and is considered as unrivalled for cattle.

Mr. Whitlaw having offered some remarks on the distemper among stock, the Council adjourned.

The ANNIVERSARY MEETING, agreeably with the date established by the Charter, was held at the Society's House, No. 12, Hanover Square, London, on Monday, the 22nd of May, present—the Right

Hon. Earl Spencer, in the Chair; Geo. Kimberley, Surrey; John Warsop, Huntingdon; C. Hillyard, Northampton; Henry Boys, Kent; Samuel Druce, Oxon; W. G. Freebody, Middlesex; Philip Pusey, M. P., Berks; H. S. Northcote, Somerset; Thomas Raymond Barker, Oxon; Sir Hungerford Hoskyns, Bart., Heref.; Rev. J. R. Smythies, Heref.; Colonel Challoner, Surrey; Colonel Wood, M.P., Brecon; Edwin East, Surrey; Humphrey Gibbs, Beds; H. S. Thompson, Yorks; J. W. Childers, M.P., Yorks; W. B. Wingate, Linc.; John Houghton, Berks; George Johnstone, Middlesex; Stephen Grantham, Sussex; John Hercy, Berks; Henry Strafford, Middlesex; John Read, Essex; William Smart, Kent; Hon. Captain Spencer, Northampton; B. T. Brandreth Gibbs, Middlesex; John Kinder, Herts; John Ellman, Sussex; Jackson Gunniss, Linc.; C. Whitlaw, Middlesex; Colonel Digby, Middlesex; Professor Pryme, Cambridge; Geo. Burrard, Hants; James Beadel, Essex; W. Fisher Hobbs, Essex; Sir John V. B. Johnstone, Bart., M.P., Yorks.; Henry Blanshard, Essex; William Shaw, Middlesex; W. Penn Gaskell, Glouc.; French Burke, Middlesex; Rev. T. S. Turnbull, Cambridge; W. R. Brown, Wilts; Edward Tull, Berks; Henry Colman, America; Rev. George Rous, Somerset; John Hibbart, jun., Middlesex; C. Wren Hoskyns, Warwickshire; Sir R.P. Joddrell, Bart., Derbyshire; John Benett, M.P., Wilts; George Emery, Somerset; Lt. Colonel Scudamore, Heref.; Henry R. Sandbach, Denbigh; Sir Charles Burrell, Bart., M.P., Sussex; Jonas Webb, Cambridgeshire; T. Bush Saunders, Middlesex; Thomas Knight, Middlesex; Lord Worsley, M.P., Linc.; F. C. Cherry, Surrey; Lord Sondes, Norfolk; R. A. Slaney, Salop; Professor Sewell, Middlesex; Rev. R. H. Leeke, Salop; A. Elliot Fuller, M.P., Sussex; O. F. Meyrick, Anglesea; Barugh Almack, Middlesex; George Wilbraham, M.P., Cheshire; Henry Knight, Hants; Andrew Lawson, M.P., Yorks; J. C. Somerville, Somerset; E. M. Mundy, M.P., Derbyshire; Colonel Vaughan, Middlesex; Thomas Tweed, Kent; J. V. Shelley, Sussex; R. Archbold, M.P., Kildare; Sir M. W. Ridley, Bart., Northumberland; E. W. W. Pendarves, M.P., Cornwall; Samuel Jonas, Cambridgeshire; A. F. Campbell, Norfolk; J. T. Cantrell, Middlesex; Lt. Colonel Elwood, Sussex; Henry Price, Kent; J. H. H. Foley, Worcestershire; C. Mostyn, Monmouthshire; L. W. Buck, M.P., Devon; James Wood, Sussex; M. Fothergill, Middlesex; F. W. Etheredge, Hants; Douglas Grantham, Sussex; Colonel Hulse, Wilts; Rev. Leyson Penoyre, Heref.; Sir John W. Guise, Bart., Glouc.; W. Allen, Yorks; W. W. Farr, Hants; George Crundwell, Kent; Rev. Charles Griffith, Brecon; Sir Robert Price, Bart., Heref.; Rev. T. Cator, Yorks; Alex. Davidson, Middlesex; Charles Eyston, Berks; Layton Cooke, Surrey; Walter H. Coyney, Staffs; Rev. John Vane, Surrey; R. G. Welford, Herts; M. Bass, Staffs; A. Bass, Staffs; S. Tremenheere, Middlesex; Edward Holland, Worcestershire; William Marden, Essex; Thomas Wakeley, Kent; Captain Ord, Kent.

ELECTIONS.

The following elections were made unanimously:—

PRESIDENT.—The Right Honourable Earl Spencer: on the motion of Colonel Challoner, seconded by Mr. Grantham.

TRUSTEES.— Sir Thomas Acland, Bart., M.P.; Hon R. H. Clive, M.P.; Marquis of Downshire; Duke of Grafton; Right Hon. Sir James Gra-

G G

ham, Bart., M.P.; Henry Handley; Sir Francis Lawley, Bart.; Joseph Neeld, M.P.; Duke of Richmond; Duke of Rutland; Earl Spencer; Duke of Sutherland.

VICE-PRESIDENTS.—Duke of Buckingham; Earl of Chichester; Earl of Ducie; Marquis of Exeter; Earl Fitzwilliam; Sir Thomas Gooch, Bart.; Sir Charles Morgan, Bart.; Duke of Northumberland; Lord Portman; Earl Talbot; Duke of Wellington; Lord Worsley, M.P.

GENERAL MEMBERS OF COUNCIL.—I. *Members remaining from last year's Council.*—David Barclay, M.P.; Thomas Raymond Barker; French Burke; Henry Blanshard; Hon. George Henry Cavendish, M.P.; John Ellman; Stephen Grantham; George Webb Hall; W. Goodenough Hayter, M.P.; C. Hillyard; W. Fisher Hobbs; Sir Hungerford Hoskyns, Bart.; Samuel Jonas; George Kimberley; John Kinder; Sir Charles Lemon, Bart., M.P.; W. Woods Page; E. S. Chandos Pole; Professor Sewell; William Shaw; Hon. Captain Spencer; Charles Stokes; Henry Stephen Thompson; George Wilbraham; Col. Thomas Wood, M.P. II.—*Members re-elected from last year's Council.* — Col. Thomas Austen; Hon. Wm. Bingham Baring, M.P.; John Benett, M.P.; Thomas William Bramston, M.P.; Edward Buller, M.P.; Colonel Challoner; John Walbanke Childers, M.P.; Humphrey Gibbs; Sir John V. B. Johnstone, Bart., M.P.; William Miles, M.P.; E. W. W. Pendarves, M.P.; Sir Robert Price, Bart., M.P.; Philip Pusey, M.P.; Francis Pym; Rev. W. L. Rham; John Villiers Shelley; T. H. S. Sotheron, M.P.; W. R. Crompton Stansfield, M.P.; Henry Wilson. III.—*New Members of Council.*—Samuel Bennett, Beds.; Edward Fellowes, M.P., Huntingdon; Lord Hatherton, Staffs.; W .H. Hyett, Glouc.; W. Fielder King, Hants.; Edward Ayshford Sanford, Somerset.

REPORT OF THE COUNCIL.

The Noble CHAIRMAN then directed Mr. HUDSON, the Secretary of the Society, to read the following Report from the Council:—

The Council have the satisfaction of reporting to the members, at their Fifth Anniversary Meeting, the uninterrupted progress of the Society in the accomplishment of the objects for which it was originally founded.

The number of its members now amounts to upwards of 7,000, no less than 1436 having been elected during the past year.

This extension of the Society, by the accession of new Members from every part of the kingdom, affords a striking proof of the interest with which its objects are regarded by the friends of agricultural improvement, and the increased amount of subscription has added considerably to the annual income of the Society.

The Finance Committee have laid before the Council a highly satisfactory statement of the funds of the Society, and the result of their inquiry connected with the general receipt of subscription. Not only has every claim against the Society been discharged, and bills amounting to upwards of 1,000*l.*, for the work executed by estimate and contract in preparing the present House for the reception of the Society and the transaction of business, been duly paid, but a further investment of capital has also been effected by the purchase of 1,000*l.* Stock in the New 3½ per Cents.; the total amount of the Society's funded property now amounting to 7,700*l.*,

and the current cash balance in the Banker's hands to 1,200*l.*

The Council steadily maintain their firm conviction, that the permanency and usefulness of the Society are dependent, in a great measure, upon the possession of such a fixed amount of reserved capital as will carry on, at all times, and under every circumstance, the current machinery of the establishment; and they therefore not only receive with great satisfaction the result of the Finance Committee's care and attention in thus husbanding the resources of the Society, and increasing annually its permanent investments, but they are also strongly convinced of the absolute necessity of abstaining from embarking the Society's funds in any doubtful speculations, and of strictly confining them to immediate objects of legitimate and undoubted importance.

With respect to the best mode of collecting the subscriptions, the Council have confirmed the recommendation of the Finance Committee, that while those friends of the Society in various counties, who would undertake the trouble, should be requested to favour the Society with their inspection of the list of such subscriptions as might be outstanding and unpaid in their respective neighbourhoods, and communicate at their discretion with the parties whose names had been transmitted to them, the remittance of subscriptions by means of Post Office Orders, should be generally recommended by the Society to its Members as the most direct, practicable, and secure; this system of payment having been found perfectly successful and satisfactory to all parties who have adopted it, and each Member of the Society having been enabled by its means to remit to the Secretary, as it has become due, and from every part of the country, however remote, the subscription of the year, and to obtain by immediate return of post an official notification of the reception and registration of his money. It has been chiefly by this means that no less a sum than 1,097*l.* has been received since last Christmas, on account of arrears alone.

The Council have decided that in future all subscriptions due in advance on the first of January in each year, shall be considered as in arrear on the 1st of June ensuing.

The Council, on mature deliberation, have resolved to strike out from the list of the Society the names of those members who, previously to the date of the Charter, attended the early country meetings, and paid the subscription of the then current year, for the temporary purpose solely of enjoying the privileges of membership on those occasions, but without any intention of becoming continued members, or being aware of their liability to be called upon for the subscriptions of subsequent years. The cancelling of these claims will greatly diminish the amount of what has hitherto been viewed in the light of arrears, while, at the same time, no inconvenient precedent will be established.

In the official department of the Society, the rapid increase in the amount of correspondence with so large a number of members, and the reception and accumulation of documents of every kind in the various branches of the current business of the Society, along with the multiplicity of accounts and numerous details requiring daily attention and great exactness, have rendered further aid indispensable to enable the Secretary to meet and discharge, satisfactorily to himself and to the members, the increasing duties and responsibilities of his office; and in consequence of the Finance

Committee's report, the Council have made a permanent addition of two clerks to be placed under his control; suitable arrangements having also been effected in the convenient adaptation of the offices to the purposes of the daily transaction of business.

The Council have obtained, on reasonable conditions, a lease of the Society's present House, for a term of ninety-nine years, at an annual rent of 330*l.*, the counterpart of which has been duly executed, and the common seal of the Society affixed, in the presence of the Council, agreeably with the powers of the Charter.

The Bristol Balance Sheet has been laid before the Council, and the sum of 573*l.* ordered to be paid out of the funds of the Society to meet the deficiency to that amount, occasioned by the excess of the expenditure over the receipts at that meeting.

The General Derby Committee have nearly completed their arrangements for the meeting to be held at that town in July; and the Local Committee have reported the resolution of the Directors of the Midland Counties' Railway, to undertake the supply of any number of special trains that may be required on the occasion, liberally proposing to receive only half fares for the conveyance of Cattle and Farming Implements, and no advance on the usual fares for passengers.

The Council have decided on Southampton as the place of the Annual Country Meeting of 1844; and have every reason to believe, that the selection they have thus made will be found advantageous both to the members of the Society at large, and to the agricultural population residing within the district, in the amount of accommodation to visitors, which the town itself and its immediate neighbourhood are capable of affording, and in the facility of communication with every part of the kingdom.

In order to diminish the expense attending the distribution of the Journal, the Council have confirmed the recommendation of the Journal Committee, that the publication shall in future take place in half-yearly parts, the first half-volume to appear in the Spring, and the second in the Autumn of each year; the whole volume for the year containing the same amount of matter as heretofore: and the first half-volume for the present year will accordingly be issued in a few days, agreeably with this new regulation.

Dr. Playfair having resolved to devote his attention exclusively to the study and practice of agricultural chemistry, and to establish at the Royal Institution at Manchester a laboratory for the pursuit and investigation of this subject, the Council have gladly availed themselves of the opportunity of appointing him the consulting chemist to the Society; an honorary designation, in virtue of which the Society will at all times be favoured with Dr. Playfair's gratuitous opinion on any question in that science submitted to him by the Council, while Members who wish to obtain analyses of soils or other substances, may at any time, by applying to the Secretary, obtain the scale of Dr. Playfair's charges.

The Journal Committee have reported the following adjudications of Prizes for Essays :—

To WILLIAM STACE, of Berwick, near Lewes, Sussex, the prize of Twenty sovereigns, for the best Essay on the rotations of crops suited for heavy lands.

To THOMAS ARKELL, of Pen Hill Farm, near Cold Harbour, by Swindon, Wiltshire, the prize of Fifty sovereigns for an account of the best mode of under-draining land, regard being had to variety of soil, subsoil, and other local circumstances.

To JAMES COWIE, of the Mains of Haulkerton, Laurencekirk, Scotland, the prize of Ten sovereigns for the best Essay on the comparative advantages in the employment of horses and oxen in farming work.

To W. F. KARKEEK, of Truro, Cornwall, the prize of Twenty sovereigns for the best explanation of the causes which appear to determine the production of fat and muscle respectively, according to the present state of our knowledge of animal physiology.

The Essays on the construction of Cottages, on the Management of Farm yard Manure, and artificial Manures or Hand Tillages, are still under the consideration of the Judges.

The Journal Committee have also reported the following Prizes and subjects of the Essays, for 1844, the conditions of which will be given in the ensuing half-volume of the Journal.

1. For the best account of the comparative value of water meadows and uplands generally, for cattle, sheep, and horses, but especially for milch cows.—Twenty sovereigns.
2. For the best Essay on the influence of climate upon cultivation within the limits of Great Britain and Ireland.—Thirty sovereigns.
3. For the best Essay on the indications which are practical guides in judging of, the fertility or barrenness of the soil.—Fifty sovereigns.
4. For the best report of the present state of the agriculture of the county of Norfolk.—Fifty sovereigns.
5. For the best report of the present state of the agriculture of the county of Chester.—Fifty sovereigns.
6. For the best report of the present state of the agriculture of the county of Essex.—Fifty sovereigns.
7. For the best report of the present state of the agriculture of the county of Wilts.—Fifty sovereigns.
8. For the best account of improvements made by artificial deposits of soil from the sea or tide-rivers, and the subsequent cultivation of the land.—Twenty sovereigns.
9. For the best account of the cheapest way of keeping farm horses in good condition, both in winter and summer.—Twenty sovereigns.
10. For the best essay on any agricultural subject.—Twenty sovereigns.

By order of the Council,   JAMES HUDSON,
London, May 22, 1843.   Secretary.

CENSUS OF MEMBERS.

Mr. Raymond Barker, Chairman of the Finance Committee, laid before the Meeting the following Census of Members, and abstract of accounts :—

Life Governors	101
Annual Governors	206
Life Members	399
Annual Members	6551
Honorary Members	13
	7270

HALF-YEARLY ABSTRACT OF ACCOUNTS.

RECEIPTS.

	£.	s.	d.
Balance in the hands of the Bankers, July 1, 1842	1587	12	1
Balance in the hands of the Secretary, July 1, 1842	12	19	2
Half-year's Dividend (less income tax) on 5711l. 7s. 7d. Stock in the New 3½ per Cents., to July 5, 1842	97	0	8
Do. on 1000l. Stock in the 3½ per Cent. Red. Ann., to Oct. 10, 1842	16	19	10
Amount of Subscriptions and Compositions	2607	2	0
Sale of Journals	40	9	0
Sale of Cottage Tracts	27	18	11
Sir Charles Morgan's Prize for Glamorgan Cattle	15	15	0
Receipts on account of Bristol Meeting	35	18	4
	4441	15	0

(Signed) SPENCER, Trustee.
THOMAS RAYMOND BARKER, Chairman of the Finance Committee.
C. B. CHALLONER.
THOMAS AUSTEN.
HENRY BLANSHARD.
J. W. CHILDERS.

PAYMENTS.

	£.	s.	d.
Permanent Charges	8	14	6
Establishment	888	14	1
Expences of Journal	871	15	10
Postage and Carriage	58	17	3½
Prizes given by the Society	1262	0	0
Prizes given by Sir Charles Morgan	15	15	0
Advertisements and Miscellaneous payments	62	8	0½
Payments on account of the Bristol Meeting	590	14	7
Balance in the hands of the Bankers, Dec. 31, 1842	656	3	4
Balance in the hands of the Secretary, Dec. 31, 1842	26	12	4
	4441	15	0

(Signed) C. H. TURNER.
THOS. KNIGHT.
CHARLES TAWNEY.
Auditors on the part of the Society.

BRISTOL BALANCE SHEET.

Colonel Challoner then reported the final close of the Bristol accounts on the 1st of March, 1843, and read to the Meeting the various items of receipt and expenditure incurred on account of that meeting, and detailed in the General Bristol Balance Sheet, he then submitted to the Members.

This balance-sheet shewed the total receipts of the meeting to have been 4,201l. 14s. 5d., and the total payments 4,775l. 1s. 8d.; a balance of 573l. 7s. 3d. being thus left chargeable on the funds of the Society, and which the Council had ordered to be paid.

Colonel Challoner explained to the meeting that, at the end of 1842, the date to which the half-yearly statement of the accounts just read by the Chairman of the Finance Committee had been audited, only 35l. 18s. 4d. had been received, and 590l. 14s. 7d. paid, at Messrs. Drummond's, on the general account of the society; and consequently only 554l. 16s. 3d. of the deficiency then paid out of the funds of the society, the Bristol accounts not having been finally closed till three months after that time, when the further and remaining sum of 18l. 11s. was paid.

Colonel Challoner also explained that, as the greater part of the receipts and payments had been made at the Bristol Bank, there only came into the hands of Messrs. Drummond, in London, a small transfer, not required at Bristol, in consequence of the remaining payments having been paid by cheque in London, the final balance of the whole agreeing with the balance then shown on the Bristol balance-sheet he then read to the meeting.

AUDITORS.

Mr. Hampden Turner, of Rook's Nest, Godstone, Surrey; Mr. Knight, of Edmonton; and Mr. Alderman Tawney, of Oxford, were declared duly elected as auditors on the part of the Society for the ensuing year.

PRIZE-SHEET FOR 1844.

The noble Chairman announced that the preliminary prize-sheet for next year had been printed (in proof), for the inspection and suggestion of members prior to its consideration and adoption at the Council on the last Wednesday in June.

COUNTY REPORTS.

Mr. SLANEY wished to know whether the premiums to be given for the essays on the counties would come out of the funds of the society, or were offered by individuals.

The noble CHAIRMAN had no doubt gentlemen recollected that during the existence of the board of agriculture, reports were made of the state of agriculture in every county in England. The Council of the society were desirous of ascertaining whether any improvement had been made in the counties since that time, 40 years, as they were of opinion that if their published reports showing—if such turned out to be the case—that some counties had made improvements and others had not, since the time of the board of agriculture, but that they actually remained in the state they then were, the latter would be ashamed of their want of energy and enterprise, and be induced to make exertions to rival the improvements of their brother farmers. (Hear.) The society, by offering these prizes, might get good reports, and could subsequently obtain reports upon the state of agriculture in every county. He did not see that anything was better calculated to improve agriculture than the publication of such reports. (Hear, hear.) The prizes would be given out of the funds of the society.

VOTE OF THANKS.

The report having been adopted, a vote of thanks, on the motion of Mr. Raymond Barker, chairman of the Finance Committee, seconded by Sir Hungerford Hoskyns, Bart., was passed to the Secretary, Mr. Hudson, for the zeal and ability with which he had conducted the affairs of the society.

AMERICAN AGRICULTURE.

Mr. HENRY COLMAN, agricultural commissioner of the state of Massachusetts, and deputed to make a report of the progress of agriculture in this country, addressed the meeting, thanking them for having made him an honorary member of the society, and expressing his conviction that the prizes for the best essays on the state of our counties would lead to most beneficial results.

CULTIVATION OF WASTE LANDS.

Mr. HOUGHTON wished to see the Society encouraging some practical measure to benefit the suffering population. His desire was that they should see if something could not be done with the waste lands of the country. He had had considerable experience with such lands, and had proved most satisfactorily that much could be done with them. For twenty years this matter had engaged his attention, and he would observe that he had occupied almost the largest quantity of land of any man in the kingdom. The plan that he would propose was that 3,000 acres of waste land should be divided into thirty parts, and a premium given to him who should best prove the capabilities of the soil. He should be happy to contribute £50 towards the expense of the experiment.

The Noble CHAIRMAN said a discussion of Mr. Houghton's proposition would involve a great many details, and it could therefore be entered upon only before the Council.

VOTE OF THANKS.

A vote of thanks was then, upon the motion of Lord WORSLEY, given to Earl Spencer, who returned thanks and the meeting broke up.

A WEEKLY COUNCIL was held at the Society's House, in Hanover-square, on Wednesday, the 24th of May, present, the Right Hon. Earl Spencer, in the chair, W. R. Browne, Esq., Edward Buller, Esq., M.P., Colonel Challoner, F. C. Cherry, Esq., E. D. Davenport, Esq., J. H. Hodgetts Foley, Esq., Humphrey Gibbs, Esq., Brandreth Gibbs, Esq., W. Goodenough Hayter, Esq., M.P., C. Hillyard, Esq., Sir John V. B. Johnstone, Bart., M.P., Professor Sewell, Rev. T. S. Turnbull, Sir Charles Lemon, Bart., M.P., and T. Tweed, Esq.

AMERICAN AGRICULTURAL LITERATURE.

Henry Colman, Esq., presented to the Council the following works for the Library of the Society:—
1. Professor Hitchcock's Final Report on the Geology of Massachusetts, 2 vols. 4to., with numerous plates
2. Mr. Colman's Second Report of the Agriculture of Massachusetts, embracing the county of Berkshire
3. Mr. Colman's Third Report, embracing principally the subjects of Wheat and Silk
4. Mr. Colman's Fourth Report, comprising the counties of Franklin and Middlesex
5. The Report of the Commissioner of Patents of the United States, for 1842 : On the Agriculture of the United States
6. The First Annual Report of the Munroe County Agricultural Society

The best thanks of the Council were ordered to be returned to Mr. Colman for these valuable presents.

Dr. Mease, Vice-President of the Philadelphia Society for promoting Agriculture, transmitted at the same time, through Mr. Colman, the last volume of the Memoirs of that Society, with an intention of forwarding, at a subsequent opportunity, the previous volumes of those Transactions : for which the Council also ordered their best thanks to be returned.

DRAINAGE.

Mr. Bailey Denton, of Southampton, expressed his intention of exhibiting, at the Derby Meeting, a model three feet square, representing a map in relief of a district, with instruments, invented by himself; similar to the one in possession of the Society, and presented by him at a former council. The model is constructed of plaster, or electrotyped in copper, to a true scale; any height or distance being obtained by the aid of an instrument accompanying it. Mr. Denton considered that the use of this invention as a complete guide to draining was evident; while the properties of an undulatory surface were made apparent by pouring water upon the map thus modelled, which flowing to the lowest levels exhibited the mode in which the waters of the higher lands might be profitably applied.

Mr. Read transmitted a plan for improvements in the making and burning of tiles, which was referred to the Journal Committee.

DERBY MEETING.

Mr. Colvile, M.P., Chairman of the Derby Local Committee, has announced to the Society the same liberal concession, on the part of the Birmingham and Derby Railway Company as already made by the Midland Counties' Company, in favour of exhibitors attending the Meeting, or sending Stock or Implements; namely, to require only half fares for Stock and Agricultural Implements, and the usual fares for passengers; putting on such additional and special trains as may be considered most conducive to the general accommodation of the Members and public on the occasion.

Mr. Gibbs presented the prize-sheet of the ensuing Smithfield Club Show, to be held in London on the 6th, 7th, 8th, and 9th of December next; Sir Charles Morgan, the prize-sheet of his Annual Show of Stock at Court-y-bella, Newport, on the 13th of December; Mr. Beeton, the prize-sheet of the West-Suffolk Show, at Bury St. Edmunds, on the 9th of June; and the Secretary, the prize-sheet of the Barnstaple Show on the 31st of May.

NEW MEMBERS.

The following gentlemen were elected members of the Society:—

Viscount Torrington ; John Bell Crompton, Esq., Mayor of Derby ; and Charles Hampden Turner, Esq., F.R.S., of Bruton-street, Berkeley-square, London, and Rook's Nest, near Godstone, Surrey, were elected Governors.

Adams, Captain George, Ross, Herefordshire
Aglionby, H.A., M.P., 5, Brick-court, Temple
Allen, Thomas, jun., Upton Cottage, Macclesfield
Arkell, Thomas, Pen Hill Farm, Cold Harbor, Swindon, Wilts
Arkwright, John, Reck House, near Matlock, Derbyshire
Arkwright, Godfrey H., Sutton Chesterfield, Derbyshire
Barton, Henry, Rangemoor House, near Burton-upon-Trent
Bearcroft, Edward, Meer Hall, Droitwich, Worcestershire
Beecham, William Payne, Hawkhurst, Kent
Bell, William, Park-row, Nottingham
Bennett, William, Standon, Puckeridge, Herts.
Berners, John, Holbrook, Suffolk
Bextall, James, Snibstone, near Ashby-de-la-Zouche
Brown, Thomas, Bowling Green Farm, Ewell, Surrey
Bostock, Ellis, 41, Hunter-street, Brunswick-square
Burrell, Hon. Lindsey, Stoke Park, Ipswich
Burroughs, Thomas, Derby
Buxton, the Rev. German, Sutton-on-the-Hill, Derby
Calvert, Thomas, Dove Bank, Uttoxeter, Staffordshire
Carver, William, Ingersby, Leicestershire
Champion, John, Carrington, near Nottingham
Champion, George Harding, Well-place, Penshurst, near Tonbridge, Kent
Chawner, Richard, Sudbury, Uttoxeter, Staffordshire
Chawner, Henry, Houndshill, Uttoxeter, Staffordshire
Cheffins, Henry, Little Easton Manor, near Dunmow, Essex
Cheney, Robert Henry, Badger Hall, near Shiffnall, Salop
Chetwynd, Major William Fawkner, Brockton Hall, near Stafford
Childe, Richard Beaumont, Melbourne, near Derby
Cooke, John, the Chase, Ross, Herefordshire
Cox, George Henry Richardson, Spondon, near Derby
Cox, William Thomas, Spondon, near Derby
Cox, Samuel Walter, Breadsall, near Derby
Coppard, Thomas, Horsham, Sussex

Corbet, Sir Andrew Vincent, Bart., 88, Eaton Square
Corfield, — Berwick, Shrewsbury
Cresswell, Richard Edward, Ravenstone, near Ashby-de-la-Zouche
Crewe, Sir George, Bart., Calke Abbey, near Derby
Crossley, John, Scaithcliffe, near Todmorden, Lancashire
Darton, Thomas Harwood, King's Walden, Hitchin, Herts
Davidson, Alexander, 25, Portman-place, Maida-hill
Denham, William, Siddall's-lane, Derby
Derry, Charles, Gedney, Lincolnshire
Dewes, William, Secretary of the Ashby-de-la-Zouche Agricultural Society
Dighton, Francis, Northallerton, Yorkshire
Draper, George, Melbourn, near Derby
Earp, John, Toton, near Nottingham
Earle, Henry Francis, 18, Henrietta-st., Cavendish-sq.
Everard, Thomas, Hoefields, Thurlston, Leicestershire
Every, Simon Frederick, Quarndon, near Derby
Evinson, Thomas, Angel Inn, Chesterfield, Derbyshire
Fearn, Samuel Wright, Derby
Fenton, Kirkby, One Barrow Lodge, Loughborough
Field, William, the Vale, Chesham, Bucks
Flint, William, Hemmington, near Kegworth, Leicestershire
Forester, the Rev. R. F., Elinley Lodge, Droitwitch, Worcestershire
Foster, Richard, Castle, near Lostwithiel, Cornwall
Foster, William, Brackenboro' House, near Lincoln
Fox, Samuel, St. Leonards-on-the-Sea, Sussex
Frean, Benjamin, Derby
Gardner, John, King-street, Snow-hill, London
Garnett, William, Lark Hill, Manchester
Gisborne, Thomas, jun., M.P., Korwick House, Buxton, Derbyshire
Gibbon, N. Walker, Summeries, Luten, Bedfordshire
Goodall, John, jun., Normanton, Derby
Goodwin, William, Kedleston, near Derby
Grazebrook, Thomas Worrall Smith, Dallicot House, Wolverhampton
Grime, Thomas, Ticknall, Derbyshire
Hall, William, Tempe, Ashby-de-la-Zouche
Hall, the Rev. Henry Banks, Risby, near Derby
Hall, Captain William Haghurst, R.N., Risby Hall, Risby, near Derby
Hammond, George, Horsmonden, Lamberhust, Kent
Hardy, T. Edmund, Mason street, Edge Hill, Liverpool
Harrison, John, Snelston Hall, near Ashbourne, Derbyshire
Harrison, John, jun., Snelston Hall, near Ashbourne, Derbyshire
Hassell, John, Shelford Manor, Nottingham
Hearsey, Henry, Greatham, near Petersfield, Hampshire
Higgins, John, Alford, Lincolnshire
Hincks, Richard Robinson, Hackleton, near Northampton
Holbrook, Charles, Alvaston, near Derby
Hollier, Walter, Walton, near Burton-on-Trent, Staffordshire
Holder, John, Cubberley, near Ross, Herefordshire
Holmes, Hon. William A'Court, Westover, Newport, Isle of Wight
Howitt, William, Somerhall, Uttoxeter, Staffordshire
Hudson, John, Derby
Hunt, William, Leicester
Hurst, William, Doncaster
Hurt, Francis, jun., Duffield, near Derby
Hurt, Richard, Wirksworth, Derbyshire
Kendall, Nicholas, Pelyn, near Lostwithiel, Cornwall.
Kitloe, Thomas, Linkinghorne, Liskeard, Cornwall
Knight, Henry, Llwynderw, near Swansea
Knollis, J. E., Penn Parsonage, Beaconsfield, Buckinghamshire
Landor, Thomas, Burton-on-Trent, Staffordshire
Lejeune, William Rickman, Southampton
Lowrey, William, Barmoor, near Berwick-on-Tweed
Mackrell, William, Collingbourn, Kingston, Wilts

Manclarke, Richard B., Warslow Hall, near Ashborne, Derbyshire
Marshall, Thomas John, Spondon, near Derby.
Mather, Joseph, Bull Bridge, near Alfreton, Derbyshire
Matson, Henry, Rodmersham, Sittingbourne, Kent
Melville, the Hon. Alexander Leslie, Branston Hall, near Lincoln
Meux, Sir Henry, Bart., Theobald's Park, Waltham Cross
Middleton, Marmaduke, Hopton Hall, near Wirksworth, Derbyshire
Miller, T. B., Thorpe Villa, Loughborough
Morley, William Bateman, Mugginton, near Derby
Mosley, Thomas, Edensor, near Bakewell, Derbyshire
Mostyn, Sir Pyers, Bart., Talacre, Holywell, Flintshire
Murphy, James Brabazon, Derby
Nainby, Richard, Barnolly-le-Beck, near Grimsby, Lincolnshire
Nevill, John, Packington, Lichfield
Newman, Thomas, Mamhead, Devonshire
Norman, George, Goadby, Marwood, near Melton-Mowbray
Ogilvie, George, Calne, Wiltshire
Oldknow, Henry, Draycott, near Derby
Orton, F., Bottisford, near Grantham, Lincolnshire
Osbond, Joseph, Spondon, near Derby
Owen, John, Field House, Mantington, near Uttoxeter
Parker, Capt. Windsor, Clopton Hall, Woolpit, Suffolk
Pipon, Major Thomas, 19, Charles-street, St. James's
Pollen, the Rev. George Pollen Boileau, rector of Little Bookham, near Leatherhead, Surrey.
Potter, Thomas, jun., Swancer Field, Nottinghamshire
Preston, Captain, R. N., Borde Hill, near Cuckfield, Sussex
Ray, the Rev. George Henry, Hanor Hall, near Derby
Raworth, B. C., Quorndon-place, Leicestershire
Richardson, John, Burton-upon-Trent, Staffordshire
Richardson, Joseph, Burton-upon-Trent, Staffordshire
Richardson, James, Burton-upon-Trent, Staffordshire
Robe, Charles, Draycott, near Derby
Robinson, Dixon, Clitheroe Castle, Clitheroe, Lancashire.
Robinson, Samuel, The Shaw House, Melbourne, Derbyshire
Royston, J. C., Codnor Park, near Derby
Royston, James Christopher, jun., Codnor Park, Alfreton, Derbyshire
Rudkin, John Charles, Derby
Russell, David, York
Sale, R., Barrow, near Derby
Sanders, Joseph, Liverpool
Sewell, The Reverend Thomas, Nether Broughton Rectory, Melton Mowbray, Leicestershire
Shaw, Richard, Newhaven House, near Ashbourne, Derbyshire
Simpson, William, M.D., Hilton Cottage, near Derby
Smalley, Francis, Toton, near Nottingham
Smallpiece, John, Leith Hill-place, near Dorking, Surrey
Smith, Rev. John Tetley, Repton, near Derby
Smith, Richard, Foremarck Park, near Derby
Spencer, William, Derby
Standly, George, Swinfen, near Lichfield
Stanley, Sir William Massey, Bart., Hooton, near Chester
Statham, William, Derby
Staunton, the Rev. Dr., Staunton Hall, near Birmingham
Stevenson, William, Derby
Strutt, John, Bridge-hill, Belper, Derbyshire
Straton, The Reverend George W., Somersal Rectory, Uttoxeter, Staffordshire
Streets, John, jun., Spring Farm, Sandiacre, near Derby
Sutton, James, Shardlow Hall, near Derby
Swettenham, James Oldham, Belper, Derbyshire
Timm, William, Wickersly, near Rotherham, Yorkshire
Tingey, John, Scoulton, Hingham, Norfolk

Tunnard, Thomas, Frampton, Boston, Lincolnshire
Tunaley, Thomas, Derby
Thompson, Edmund, Legh Lodge, Ardwick, near Manchester
Thornewill, Edward, Park Hill, Derby
Vernon, Hon. and Rev. John V., Kirkby, Mansfield, Nottinghamshire
Walters, John, Derby
Watson, G., Daybreak, near Nottingham
Wayte, George, Stenson, near Derby
Wayte, Henry Smith, Milton, near Derby
Webb, The Reverend John Moss, Swarkstone, Derbyshire
Whiston, William, Derby
Wild, S. B., Costock, near Loughborough, Leicestershire
Williams, Rev. Charles, Gedling Rectory, near Nottingham
Williamson, William, Little-over, near Derby
Wilmot, Francis Scheverell, Stanton-by Dale, near Derby
Willson, Thomas, Knaptoft, Leicestershire
Wood, Willoughby, Campsall Hall, Doncaster
Woodward, George, Thorndon, near Eye, Suffolk
Worsop, John Arthur, Sandford House, Salisbury
Yates, Trevor, Sapperton, Derbyshire

TO THE FARMERS OF SUFFOLK.

LETTER XI.

GENTLEMEN,—There being no very direct communication between Hitcham and the rest of the world, the arrival of the packet of Schedules, from Bury, has been accidentally delayed beyond the time when I had proposed to have circulated them; and I must beg to apologise, in the name of our unmacadamized bye-roads and tardigrade carriers'-horses, for so long trespassing upon your patience. I trust, however, before this letter appears in print, that each of the *sixty-nine* gentlemen who have already favoured me with their addresses, will have received his copy; and I shall be ready to distribute the rest of the hundred among those who may repent of their previous determination to have nothing to do with us. Mr. Potter, a practical chemist, in London, whose letters in the *Gardeners' Chronicle* prove him to be equal to the task he has offered to undertake for you, has publicly expressed himself so anxious that our experiment should have a fair trial, that he is willing to test every sample of gypsum, in order that you may be quite sure the material you are using is of the right quality. You are doubtless aware that this is a very liberal offer on the part of Mr. Potter, whose time is *professionally* occupied in performing chemical analyses. I have not the pleasure of knowing him, otherwise than by correspondence; but I feel obliged to him for the interest he has shown in volunteering his services. I shall, therefore, request every one who receives a schedule, to send me as much of the gypsum he is about to use as can be conveyed in a penny letter; and I will then forward all the samples to Mr. Potter for his opinion of them. These samples should be labelled with the addresses of the persons who send them; and this will also serve me for an acknowledgment that the Schedule has been duly received.

I do not know why it is that I cannot proceed a step in these endeavours to point out to you the necessity of experimental co-operation for the advance of agriculture, without being met (I won't say obstructed) by sundry hints and surmises that my task is a hopeless one. I had thought the simple fact of your having accepted my challenge (and that in greater numbers than I had called for) would have been sufficient to have silenced all disputers about your readiness to co-operate, and all doubters about your being willing to bring our experiment to a proper issue. But I find I am now assailed with a fresh insinuation, that it is not likely many of those who have engaged to co-operate will be *able* to fill up the Schedule in a satisfactory manner. Old proverbs are somewhat musty in these days of super-refinement, but I like them nevertheless, and so I say, I suppose these fresh doubtings imply that "I may lead a horse to the pond, but that I cannot make him drink." Certainly, if the horse is unwilling, and the pond somewhat muddy, I should not imagine that he would drink—but if the horse is thirsty, and the pond clear, he will need no persuasion, and nature has supplied him with ability. I have mislaid a letter from a gentleman who lives at a distance, and who has expressed himself desirous of having a Schedule to put into the hands of his bailiff. I had intended to have quoted to you his unfavourable opinion of the capabilities of practical men, in a declaration he makes to me, "that he never yet knew a farmer who could correctly fill up a schedule of any sort!" I can only believe him to be very unfortunately placed. His estates are not in Suffolk! I am determined not to be a doubter, and I shall hope on till I see my hopes fulfilled, because I feel assured they will be. Of course I expect to find errors and inaccuracies in several of the returns; but still I am confident that the great majority of the schedules will be as fully and fairly filled up as may be necessary for our purpose. Let any farmer only look attentively through the schedule, and say whether it contains a single question which he is not likely to be able to answer with perfect ease, and far more readily (I suspect) than he found himself able to fill up certain schedules which he received from the parish assessor a few months back. Should any one feel himself doubtful about the meaning of any of the questions in our Schedule A, I would suggest that he should first apply to the parish assessor for his advice, and if, after all the training which that individual has so lately received in filling up schedules, he cannot satisfy the inquirer, I shall then advise that he will inform me of his doubts, and I will endeavour to remove them. The plea of idleness, of unwillingness, or of indifference, I can easily comprehend, but any plea of *incompetency* is to me incomprehensible. I am much more apprehensive lest another suggestion of evil surmise should prove partially true, and I must beg leave to be a little particular upon this subject. It has been suggested to me, that if our experiment should *fail*, such a result would produce a bad effect, by shaking whatever confidence you may at present be disposed to place in the recommendations of scientific men. "I hope it will succeed," said a gentleman who first suggested this possible contingency to me. Now really, Farmers of Suffolk, I am half inclined to say that I hope that it may not succeed, if I am so little likely to be understood, that you have supposed I have formed any decided opinion about its success or failure. If I had wished to play the conjuror, or had cared to count upon your applause by foretelling success, I dare say I could have contrived some experiment in which success could have been secured, or at least not left very doubtful. Perhaps some of you might then have been persuaded to consider me an agricultural Solomon, and would have allowed me to dictate to you any wild schemes or plans for agricultural improvements, without any attention to common prudence or circumspection on your parts. But I hate all such manœuverings and under plots, as I would detest the pious lures and frauds put forth to prop or propagate an unstable faith. Look back through my letters, and you will see that the object and end which I have proposed to myself has been the suggesting to you the necessity of " experimental cooperation," and that all I aim at in our present experiment is, to show you how " experimental cooperations" should be carried on. It would be very presumptuous and very unphilosophical in me to say beforehand, that I am positive of what will be the result of our experiment; but I do say that I am positive the experiment *cannot fail* in producing some good result; and that is all that a wise and cautious philosophy would have us look to. Let us first see what the result may be, and then let us speculate afterwards upon what that result may teach us. With this determination the experiment *cannot fail*—it must teach us something. And so of every experiment conducted on correct principles—it never fails. However it may fail in producing that particular effect which the experimenter may *desire*, or fancy he can secure, yet, even if he should be completely baulked in his expectations, the experiment has assisted him in discovering *the truth*; and it will, in consequence, teach him either to cleave to the " old ways," or to turn to the " new ways," according as he finds that the one or the other practice will best serve his purpose. This discussion is not unnecessary; for I find that some persons have already been purchasing gypsum, and strewing it over their dunghills, just as if it were a settled point that such a practice *must* be correct. We shall never get on if we allow such hasty inferences to influence our determinations. I will quote to you three or four sentences from Sir John Herschel's *Discourse on Natural Philosophy*, and his word is worth a score of letters from me on such a subject. "To experience we refer as the only ground of all physical inquiry. But before experience itself can be used with advantage, there is one preliminary step to make, which depends wholly on ourselves: it is the absolute dismissal, and clearing the mind, of all prejudice, from whatever source arising; and the determination to stand and fall by the result of a direct appeal to facts in the first instance, and of strict logical deduction from them afterwards." " Not that we are so unreasonable as to demand of the inquirer, an instant and peremptory dismission of all his former opinions and judgments; all we require is, that he will hold them without bigotry, retain till he shall see reason to question them, and be ready to resign them when fairly proved untenable, and to doubt them when the weight of probability is shown to lie against them. If he refuse this, he is incapable of science." " With respect to our record of observations, it should not only be circumstantial but *faithful*; by which we mean that it should contain all we did observe, and nothing else. Without any intention of falsifying our record, we may do so unperceived by ourselves, owing to a mixture of the views and language of an erroneous theory with that of simple fact; there is no greater fault (short of positive fraud) which can be committed by an observer." I have one passing word for the consideration of those worthy and excellent men, my seniors in years, who have lived and prospered under that system of farming into which they were initiated somewhere between fifty and ninety years ago. Some of them, I hear, think me a meddling fellow, and they laugh pretty loudly at the notion of my being able to advise them in anything worthy their attention. But will they tell me whether they have any idea how it is that an astronomer is able to measure the distances of the planets from the sun, and to obtain an accurate estimate of their bulk and weight, or how it is that he can foretell to a fraction of a second when particular celestial phenomena are to recur after the lapse of long periods of time? Now the mariner is indebted to this very astronomer (who perhaps never felt the discomfort of sea-sickness, or possibly never saw a ship) for those nautical tables and calculations by help of which he can fearlessly traverse the broad ocean by night as by day, and tell exactly where he may be in the wide world after sailing for weeks together out of sight of land. I do not say that the science of chemistry has yet attained to the same degree of excellency as the science of astronomy; but it has made, and is still rapidly making, very decided progress towards perfection. It is even now capable of lending great assistance to those who plough the land, though it may not as yet be quite so great assistance as that which astronomy can offer to those who plough the sea. If then some of our worthy seniors do not like to be put out of their old ways, at least let me advise our active juniors not to be daunted or discouraged by any of their pleasant banterings. Let these happy boys of the old school enjoy their humours, as long as they are good humours, and they will be amused (I doubt not), whilst I quote for their edification the account which a Roman poet, who lived more than eighteen hundred years ago, has given us of the hapless old heathens of A.D. 1, so different from the hopeful old Christians of A.D. 1843! I will try whether I cannot roughly translate his verses for the sake of those who have forgotten their Horace, or possibly may never have known anything about him.

" Multa senem circumveniunt incommoda; vel quod
   Quærit, et inventis miser abstinet, ac timet uti;
   Vel quod res omnis timide gelideque ministrat;
   Dilator, spe lentus, iners, pavidusque futuri;
   Difficilis, querulus, laudator temporis acti
   Se puero, castigator, censorque minorum."

" Many are the disadvantages under which an old man labours; either he is niggard and timid about making use of whatever he has acquired by dint of his own exertions: or else, if he does venture to act, he sets about everything with cold and hesitating caution. He is full of delays, of very faint hope, inactive, a professed alarmist, hard to please, a determined grumbler, ever praising the good olden time when he was himself a lad; always correcting and scolding his juniors."

Whilst the active members of a rising generation continue to pay all due respect to grey hairs and old prejudices, and are ready to allow " that there is nothing new (that is worth knowing) under the sun," they may still be trusting to their own judgment, and be striving to keep pace with others in all matters relating to their own times, and to their own affairs.

Now that I consider our gypsum adventure is fairly afloat, it will probably not be requisite that I should refer to it again for many months to come. May it prosper to the improvement of your judgment, and tend to assist you in discerning what is most requisite for hastening the progress of agriculture! I shall hope to resume and carry on our discussion of the "Functions of the Leaf" through another letter or two; and by that time I shall be called to duties in Cambridge, which will occupy me too closely for a few weeks to allow of my troubling you any further, for the present, with a continuation of these letters.

Your obedient servant,
J. S. HENSLOW.
Hitcham Rectory, March 9th, 1843.

LETTER XII.

Function of Exhalation.

GENTLEMEN,—Every farm house in Suffolk can doubtless furnish forth half-a-dozen clean tumblers; and we shall need no other apparatus for illustrating one of the two functions of the leaf to which I alluded in my 6th and 7th letters. I have just been trying three little comparative experiments in a very simple form, and find they will be sufficient for our purpose. Let us call the three experiments A, B, C, respectively. Each will require two tumblers, one of which is to be filled about two-thirds with water, and the other to be left empty. Place a card over each of the three tumblers which contain the water, and large enough to completely cover it: and then place an empty tumbler, mouth downwards, upon the card. You might use a piece of stiff paper (as I did,) varnished with a solution of shell-lac in rectified spirits of wine, which will prevent its imbibing moisture, and more effectually cut off all communication between the two tumblers. Now make a cap to one of the tumblers (say B) by rolling round it in two or three folds a piece of thick paper, sufficient to prevent the light from penetrating: and by giving it a twist above it may be kept rolled up. Lastly, drill a small hole in the middle of each card, just large enough to admit the stalk of a leaf—I used large ivy leaves. The stalks of three leaves are to be passed through the three cards respectively, and the apparatus must be so adjusted that we shall have the bottom of each stalk dipping into the water in the lower tumbler, whilst the blade (or limb of the leaf, as botanists term it) is enclosed under the inverted empty tumbler: the card cutting off the communication between the two tumblers in each experiment. Place A and B in the direct rays of the sun; B with its cap on. Place C in clear day-light, but removed from the influence of the direct rays of the sun. In less than five minutes the empty tumbler of A will have become coated on the inside with a cloud of dew; but on lifting up the cap from the empty tumbler of B it will be seen that no dew has been deposited; neither, as yet, will any be found in the empty tumbler of C. If B be closed over again with the cap, and matters left as before, for a little time longer, the dew will be seen to increase rapidly in A, and after some time a little will also be found deposited in C. In B none will be found, except that, *occasionally*, there may be seen a deposit on the side of the empty tumbler, opposite to the side on which the sun has been shining. I proceed to explain the causes of these results. The rapid formation of the dew in A arises from the strong "exhalation" of steam, proceeding from the leaf when exposed to the direct rays of the sun—a continued supply being kept up by the water in the lower tumbler imbibed by the leaf-stalk. This exhalation of steam is not kept up very rapidly in C, exposed only to ordinary daylight; and in the dark, in B, it ceases altogether. The dew which makes its appearance on one side of

the tumbler in B arises from another cause. We all know that a wet or moist substance gradually becomes dry by exposure to warmth and a dry atmosphere. Now a fresh leaf is a moist body, and the evaporation of its juices will gradually take place until it becomes thoroughly dried. The warmer the surrounding atmosphere the more rapidly does this evaporation take place. The very card also between the tumblers contains some moisture, which will be given off when the experiment is placed in the warmth of the sun-beam, and will rise in steam into the empty tumbler. The side towards the sun being the warmest, and the opposite side the coldest, the steam in the tumbler becomes condensed on the colder side only; in short, the appearance is strikingly different from what we witness in A. The little moisture in B has arisen merely from the effect of common evaporation, and subsequent condensation. You will find the very same effect taking place in the upper part of the lower tumbler immediately over the water; the steam which rises there condenses on the side opposite the sun, which is kept cool by being shaded by the card above it. In A the moisture continues to accumulate over the whole inner surface of the tumbler; and is occasioned, not by the heat, but by the light of the sun, exciting or stimulating the leaf to the performance of that vital function which is termed "exhalation." Even in C the same action is carried on by the stimulus of common daylight; but so feebly, that it is scarcely rendered apparent by our mode of conducting the experiment. With proper apparatus, an exact estimate may be obtained of the quantity of moisture absorbed and exhaled by a plant; and it has been ascertained that a sunflower, three feet high, will absorb as much as 30 ozs. and exhale 20 ozs. in the course of a day. When the first rays of the morning sun rouse the dormant energies of the leaf, they set it off exhaling at a rapid rate; but at that time of day the temperature of the air is so cool that the steam condenses as fast as it is discharged from the myriads of untaxed stills which are there manufacturing a more healthy beverage than gin or whiskey. I dare say that many a sportsman, who at an early hour has been wading through a field of coleseed, never thought of attributing the ducking he received to this "exhaling" power of the leaves, but has concluded that it all arose from the ordinary effect of common dew precipitated from the moisture in the atmosphere. If a plant be completely excluded from light it soon becomes dropsical, because the roots continue slowly to absorb moisture, but the leaves have no power to exhale it, and it therefore accumulates unduly. Perhaps I cannot make you perfectly understand the nature of that contrivance by which the function of exhalation is carried on, because it requires you should first take a peep into that hidden world which is exposed to us only by the microscope; but I think that you may obtain a good general notion of it, by fancying you can see the skin on both sides of the leaf perforated by minute pores. Through these invisible pores the steam is exhaled, much in the same way that the insensible perspiration is continually escaping from the surface of our bodies, and which is often rendered uncomfortably demonstrable to persons who encase themselves in Macintosh coverings. Imagine these invisible pores to be formed by means of a pair of invisible sausage-shaped bladders, filled with vegetable juices; these bladders lying side by side, and attached only at the two ends. By pressing the ends towards the middle the bladders would curve outwards, and thus an opening, like a slit or pore, would be formed between them. We may consider this description of apparatus forming the pores as so many invisible floodgates, which can be opened or shut at the command of the sun, that the steam may be exhaled or retained accordingly. Now 1 do not pretend to assert that this is precisely the way in which the function is carried on by the mechanism I have described; because some of my physiological acquaintances may possibly have better notions about the manner in which glandular structures perform their functions; but I think this is perhaps the most popular and plausible manner in which I may hope to give you some general idea of the subject. Under the microscope we may distinctly see these peculiar arrangements by which the pores are closed and opened ; and they are studded over both surfaces of the leaf; more especially on the under surface. The beauty and regularity in the texture of the skin (or *epidermis*) of a leaf, as much excels those of the most delicate web that can be wrought by human skill, as the gorgeous clothing of the lily surpasses the most glorious array of Solomon. The number, disposition, and form of these pores (to which botanists have given the name of *stomata*, or " little mouths'') vary greatly in different species of plants; succulent plants, or those which have very juicy leaves and stems, have very few pores on their surface. Such plants might seem, on first thoughts, to require a larger supply of moisture than others, but the very reverse is the case. They are destined to occupy dry and barren spots, imbibing the little moisture which the night dews may convey to them ; and husbanding their resources, they refuse to part with it even in the scorching heats of a sandy desert. It has been ascertained, that the amount of water distilled by exhalation is about two-thirds of the quantity imbibed by the roots ; and consequently that one-third remains fixed in the plant. The conditions under which it is fixed will be more particularly detailed when I come to speak of the other functions of the leaf, which I hope to describe in my next letter. There is another result to be noticed, which has been obtained by the exhalation of this two-thirds of the water imbibed. Whatever matters the water may have held in solution—salts, earths, or metallic oxides —these have all been retained in the plant. Thus we may understand how such substances may be gradually accumulated in considerable quantities, though they may be present in the soil in too minute proportion to admit of the chemist detecting them. The plant may have been exhaling off ounces after ounces of water before it has been able to retain a single grain of a particular substance essential to its health, and consequently essential to its successful cultivation. To give you an example, noticed by Liebig, of the patient perseverance of common seaweeds, which accumulate an element named Iodine, which is furnished to them in such sparing proportions that it does not form so much as one millionth part of the weight of a given quantity of sea-water. Yet they collect it from this storehouse in sufficient abundance for the chemist to extract it from them as an article of commerce.

Your obedient servant,
J. S. Henslow.

Hitcham Rectory, March 23rd, 1843.

P.S.—More than one person have expressed to me a desire that I would myself re-publish and edit my letters to you, under the form of a pamphlet. The following considerations have determined me to do so. Although I believe I have not allowed the in-

terest I have felt in this correspondence very materially to trespass upon my attention, to the exclusion of any of the more important duties attached to my position as a parish priest; yet it is evident that whatever of thought, time, or money I have allotted to this subject during the past three months, might have been otherwise devoted in some way advantageous to my parish. It seems to me, then, that I may possibly be able to make some *amends* for such deficiencies by appropriating to some parochial utility or other, whatever may accrue from the re-publication of these letters. I have, therefore, no very delicate scruples about requesting any of you to promote their circulation, if you think them calculated to excite the farmers of other counties to co-operate, after the example of the farmers of Suffolk. I see no reason why we should not have *at least* 100 distinct experiments performed every year ; and each carried on by between thirty and fifty practical men, whilst each man need not be called upon for more than a single experiment annually. I propose inserting in this pamphlet my address to the Hadleigh Club, and to add a few explanatory notes, or some sort of commentary and glossary, which may give them a more general character, and enable them to serve as a *precursor* for inducing the farmers of other counties to listen to any future suggestions which may possibly (and will probably) be made to them, for organizing a complete system of experimental co-operation throughout England. My hopes that such will be the case are greatly strengthened now that I find it publicly asserted by a superior authority that he considers such a scheme both *advisable and practicable.*

Letter XIII.

Function of Respiration.

Gentlemen,—I shall be obliged to draw a little more deeply upon your faith than was necessary in my last letter, whilst I endeavour to explain to you that function of the leaf which has been named "respiration." Still I do hope to be able to set before you two or three very simple experiments, which may serve to convince you that botanists are not very far wrong in what they have asserted concerning this function. The function may be thus expressed —" that leaves decompose carbonic acid under the stimulus of light, the oxygen of this substance being discharged from the plant into the atmosphere, and the carbon fixed as an ingredient of that ' proper juice' by which all parts of the plant are nourished and developed." I shall first ask you to try a little experiment which may serve to remove a cause of error that might otherwise warp our judgment in estimating the actual effects produced by the function we are about to consider.

Preliminary Experiment.

Place a tumbler full of spring or pond water before a fire, and another in the direct rays of the sun. As the water becomes warm, you will find a number of little bubbles will collect on the bottom and sides of the tumblers; and if you place in the tumblers a piece of stick or metal, or other substance, bubbles will also collect upon these. If you place several tumblers of water in the direct rays of the sun, and put into them differently coloured substances, you will find that bubbles will first make their appearance in those tumblers which have the darkest coloured substances in them ; because the darker the substance the more rapidly it will become heated, and so heat the water sooner. It is very evident that these air-bubbles have made their appearance in consequence of the heating of the water. But from whence do these bubbles proceed? They are derived from air which we may describe as being *dissolved* in the water, just as we find a piece of salt or sugar may be dissolved in water, and thus rendered invisible. When we boil water, all the air which is thus dissolved in it is driven off; and upon allowing it to stand exposed to the air it will again dissolve a certain quantity. Various gases, besides common air, may thus be dissolved in water—as carbonic acid, &c.; and many springs upon issuing from their subterranean courses give off into the atmosphere a portion of the gases which are dissolved in their waters, and which are retained in them so long as they remain underground. Whoever has been to Harrowgate is acquainted with the offensive odour of the mineral waters of that place of public resort; and whoever wishes to have a good idea of it without going there need only smell at a rotten egg, or wash out a recently discharged gun-barrel into a tumbler and apply his nose to it. I have already observed in my seventh letter that common soda-water contains a large quantity of carbonic acid. I have used the term *dissolved* in these cases in rather an improper sense, but it will possibly serve to convey a general idea of what takes place. Carbonic acid is thus dissolved in all waters, and is also present everywhere in the atmosphere. Supposing, therefore, that leaves can act upon it, and decompose it under both circumstances, we may then be able to exhibit the result of their action upon that which is dissolved in water, even though we might not be able to do so upon that which is dispersed in the air; because, in the former case, the oxygen which is set free would rise through the water in bubbles, and we shall see these, whereas, in the latter case, it would be discharged as an invisible gas into the air. Let us try whether we can make this clearer by a simple experiment.

Illustration of the Function of Respiration.

Fill two or three tumblers with pond or spring water, which will be sure, in either case, to hold some carbonic acid in solution. Place a leaf or two under the water in each tumbler. I find that common laurel leaves are well adapted to experiments of this sort, only from their size they require large glass jars, instead of tumblers, unless we cut them in halves. In order to place the leaves conveniently under the water, I make use of a split shot, or small piece of lead, with which I nip the edge of the leaf and leave it fixed there. This causes it to sink and yet retain a vertical position. Place one tumbler in common daylight, and the others in the direct light of the sun. In the former you will observe no effect produced; but in the latter you will soon find numerous little bubbles making their appearance upon the surface of the leaves. I suspect these bubbles have not unfrequently been considered to be oxygen which is escaping through the pores of the leaf, upon the decomposition of the carbonic acid contained in the water; but I now feel satisfied that we must ascribe them to the separation of the dissolved air, by the heating process as described above. Still I do hope to shew you a partial effect produced by the decomposition of carbonic acid by the leaf. Arm yourselves with a little of that gift of patience, so essential to all farmers and experimenters; and of

course doubly essential when farmers become experimenters. In due time (perhaps in less than half an hour) you will be able to distinguish certain bubbles, which will make their appearance at the cut end of the leaf, or else here and there upon its surface. These will increase in size more rapidly than the rest, and at length rise to the surface. After one has risen, another will immediately begin to make its appearance at the same spot. A little attention will soon convince you that these bubbles have proceeded from the interior of the leaf, and we may, I think, allow them to be the oxygen which the leaf has separated from the carbonic acid introduced into it. The interior of the leaf is composed of little invisible bladders filled with fluid; and these bladders are so packed together as only to touch each other here and there, and thus to leave open spaces between them, which are filled with air or some other sort of gass. Especially in the under part of the leaf the bladders are so loosely packed that a very large portion of air or gass is retained there. This is the cause why the under surface of leaves is generally the palest; but if the air is expelled, as I shall presently describe how it may be, and water be allowed to enter, the under surface will then become as dark as the upper. Plunge a leaf into hot water, and the air which it contains will escape in bubbles from the cut end, and also from a few points on its surface. Sometimes a bubble thus driven out will be seen to adhere to the surface for a few seconds, and then be suddenly re-absorbed into the leaf. When we place leaves in water, under an air-pump, the air they contain escapes in bubbles with great rapidity, from the cut end of the leaf-stalk. If you allow the leaves to soak for a few hours in the tumblers, the water will gradually insinuate itself, either through the cut end of the leaf, or through the part pinched by the split shot, or through some accidental rupture in the skin. The water will thus displace the air, and the under surface will first appear to be blotched with dark spots, wherever it has penetrated, and at length the whole will become uniformly dark coloured. I refer especially to laurel leaves. It is after these leaves have been soaking for two or three days that I have witnessed the stimulating effects of light in exciting the function of respiration in the most illustrative and convincing manner. The oxygen will often issue in a continued stream of little bubbles, even with a distinct noise, from the cut end of the leaf, or from some point or other upon its surface. If the hand or any solid substance be interposed between it and the sun, so as to cast a shadow over the leaf, the effect ceases; but it is immediately renewed upon the removal of the obstacle. Even whilst the leaf continues to be shaded, the stream of bubbles may be caused to issue afresh by throwing a gleam of *reflected* light upon it from a looking glass. When we happen to get a leaf into such good humour for these experiments, they become very amusing and instructive; indeed, the information you may thus draw from a common tumbler is far more satisfying and enduring than any fleeting gratification that could be afforded you by the best shilling's-worth of brandy and water which it ever yet held. Only *try these simple experiments, and think* a little about them, and the knowledge you will thus acquire will wonderfully assist your conceptions of the manner in which these functions of the leaf are carried on. When the leaf has become thoroughly saturated with water, it is very curious to see the under surface gradually recovering its pale tint as soon as the tumbler is placed in the light of the sun. When I wish to give the water a good dose of carbonic acid, I fill a vial with this gas, twist a piece of lead round its neck, and let it float in the tumbler or glass jar, with its mouth downwards. In a few hours the water will have taken up all the carbonic acid ; a large portion of which will, however, soon escape from the water into the air ; still there will be enough of it retained to cause the function to be renewed with fresh vigour, after it had ceased from want of fresh supply. I have had a little aquatic plant growing in a glass jar full of water for the last six months, on the table of my study, and whenever the sun falls upon it, up rise several little streams of bubbles of oxygen from the edges of some of the leaves which happen to be torn ; but I do not perceive that any oxygen can be detected escaping from the surface of the sound leaves.

I feel a little sceptical about the manner in which it is commonly asserted that carbonic acid is admitted within the leaf. That some portion of carbonic acid must be introduced with the moisture imbibed by the roots seems to be undeniable ; but that other portions are introduced through the very pores by which the stream is exhaled, and the oxygen discharged, appears to me to be still open to further enquiry. This, however, is a subject for botanists to look into, and one that is not suited to these letters : only you will observe that what I have said in illustration of the functions of respiration is no way affected by this part of the theory. It is usual to treat the effects we have described to " exhalation" and " respiration" as the results of a two-fold action, both excited by the same stimulus of light : but I question whether it would not be preferable to consider them as the common effect of a single function, which might be appropriately termed the " function of organization." What we really observe is the simultaneous discharge of water and oxygen from the leaf. This effect is attended by the fixation of the elements of water, oxygen, and hydrogen, with carbon, in the form of organic matter. But I must suppress an inclination I feel to discuss the subject more fully. I have before noticed the fact, and I cannot resist again alluding to it, that plants are engines or laboratories employed by the Creator in the great work of combining a few elements into a nutritious material, which is to serve for the development of the whole animal creation. I am not acquainted with any natural law which impresses me with a greater sense of wonder than this "function of organization." Here we see mere crude matter brought under subjection to the ruling principle. It is wonderful to view the effects of gravity retaining the planets in their orbits ! it is wonderful to witness the magic changes which chemical affinity can work in compounding and decomposing a variety of mineral substances ! but to me it seems far more wonderful that man, and all other animals, are entirely dependant upon the leaves of plants for manufacturing materials for those bodies of corruption in which, for a little while, they are destined to live and move and have their being. As the hopes of the agriculturist are so much dependant upon the healthy performance of this important function, surely he ought to know at least as much about it as the present ignorance of science may be able to teach him, if he would expect to be able to shape his practice in accordance with the laws of nature, and not

needlessly to set himself in hopeless opposition to them. He will ever find nature a kind hand-maid, and ready to minister to his wants whilst he woos her skilfully ; but a very termagant whenever he resists her rudely. I have perhaps been dwelling too minutely through the last two letters upon these functions of the leaf, but I have not had time to condense my materials into smaller compass. I have still a few observations to make with respect to their practical bearing on some points of agricultural interest, but I shall have the Editor looking more gravely than yourselves at the length of my letter if I prolong it any further. I must therefore reserve for next week what I have yet to say upon this subject.   Your obedient servant,
                               J. S. HENSLOW.
Hitcham Rectory, March 31, 1843.

AGRICULTURAL QUERIES.

A correspondent enquires where he can obtain the best hand machine for grinding rapecake for drilling as manure, and whether the same machine might not be used for pulverizing guano. Also, what is the price of the machine.

A Correspondent asks—" Can you, or any of your numerous readers, inform me, through the medium of your valuable Journal, whether or not wheat vitrioled for planting, twelve months since, would now contain any injurious properties, relative to giving it to pigs, mixed with barley ? Such information will greatly oblige.

ANSWERS TO AGRICULTURAL QUERIES.

SIR,—In answer to your correspondent, " A Warwickshire Subscriber," relative to salt and lime as a manure for meadow land, I beg to say, that I have found great benefit from sowing *two* bushels of lime mixed with *one* of salt, at the rate of *twelve* bushels per acre. If more is sown it has a bad effect; in fact, it would destroy rather than improve the quality of the herbage. I have always found my given quantity very effectual in enriching as well as increasing the quantity.

Another subscriber, who signs himself " Bedfordiensis," wants to know if the *true Suffolk breed* of cart horses are more subject to *grease* in their heels than other breeds. My answer is, *certainly not ;* but I consider all horses having coarse heels more subject than the Suffolk breed. A pure Suffolk cart horse has little more hair about his legs than a thorough-bred animal ; and therefore his legs are sooner dry in wet weather, and always clean ; which causes (with neglect) are the ones I assign for grease.   I am, sir, your obedient servant,
May 4, 1843.   A SUFFOLK YEOMAN.

In the *Express* of April 17th, " A Subscriber" asks if any correspondent has tried " the lime used in purifying coal gas." It *has* been tried as a manure on young clover, and found to answer as well or better than coal-ashes. The latter was uniformly applied in the neighbourhood where the other was experimented upon, now more than 20 years ago. The gas in its primary gross state is passed, at the manufactory, through the lime, to get rid of its volatilized carbon, and some oil or bitumen, which it retains, and is beneficial as a fertilizer. A portion of sulphurous vapour, which substance is more or less in all coal and its distillations, also stays in the lime, as may be proved by the effluvium it conveys, and from which the gas is purified when properly refined.

TO THE EDITOR OF THE MARK LANE EXPRESS.

SIR,—Seeing an enquiry in your *Express* of the 24th inst., of a "Young Subscriber," wishing to know who is a maker of seed drawing machines, we beg to inform you that we have made a great many that answer the purpose most effectually; and if the gentleman will favour us with his address, shall be most happy to correspond with him on the subject.

We remain, Sir, your most obedient servants,
RICHARD GARRETT AND SON.
Leiston Works, Saxmundham, Suffolk.
April 26, 1843.

CALENDAR OF HORTICULTURE FOR JUNE.

The month of May, to the period when we commence this article, has been altogether at variance, as respects the weather, from any of its predecessors for a great number of years—cold, wet, and windy. If we are to attach credence to the prognostic of the old " saw," our farmers may hope to find their barns filled to repletion ; at all events, come when they may, a few warm days will produce an effect in the gardens which must be astonishing. In the meanwhile, we may observe that vegetables are, and long have been, abundant, and superior in quality ; those of the brassica tribe have surpassed anything which the late arid parching springs could produce. Potatoes rise well, their young foliage verdant and healthy. Peas are excellent, though not early, the first sowings having been roughly dealt with by the snow-storms of February and April. Of fruit, we hear complaints concerning the setting of apricots, and the more delicate pears. The peach-trees in some localities we know to be well-fruited ; cherries are more or less deficient ; but the bloom of the apple-trees is quite superior. Upon the whole, the promise is very fine.

VEGETABLE DEPARTMENT.

Sow in the first week *cucumbers* for open ridges over dung : thin out, and lead carefully the runners of plants sown in May ; plant also on prepared ridges, young rooted cuttings raised in pots, turning them out with entire balls.

Gourd-seeds, and best sorts of vegetable marrow, or rather having raised plants in pots, transplant them in rich beds prepared in the following manner. Choose a warm sunny situation. Dig a hole a yard wide, every way, two feet deep ; place therein a barrow or two of strong warm manure, return the earth if really good, or cover the dung with rich turfy loam, to nearly a foot above it, scattering the old removed soil so as to form a sloping bank on every side. Plant out two or three vegetable marrows, and cover them with a hand glass for a time, shading during hot sun. If the weather be warm a rapid growth will soon

take place, and by tilting the glasses with four bricks, the advancing vines may be led out, and trained in regular order (a circumstance of some moment) across the sloping ground.

Sow early the last crop of tall marrow peas, and another of the earliest " May" or Warwick ; these do well as an autumn pea. As the season is so dripping, peas will not require watered ridges as suggested by Mr. Knight ; otherwise, a thorough saturation of the soil at the time of sowing secures the crop.

Beans for the latest supply ; some recommend the white-flowered. Kidney beans of both kinds, in the first week, and finally about the 20th or an earlier day of the month. Stick the scarlet runners of earlier sowings, after moving the earth near the roots.

In the second and third weeks sow early horn carrot ; onions for drawing ; young white and yellow Dutch turnip, for autumnal supply ; endive at the end of the month.

Plant slips of hyssop, lavender, rosemary, savory, sage, and other aromatic herbs, in a shady spot, and give water frequently.

Transplant, at the latter end of the month, seedling cabbage, brocoli, borecole, Brussells sprouts, savoy—chiefly for nursery rows and beds. Celery into deep, richly-manured trenches. In doing this work remove every offset, then fix each plant firmly in its hole, seven inches apart, and water copiously ; success depends mainly on the regular supply of water.

Leeks must be set in good ground, or manured trenches, fixing the root only in a little fine manure at the bottom of the hole ; fill that with soft water, but let the soil remain undisturbed, to form a kind of open sheath for the plant.

Loosen the earth between rows of peas ; draw it to a sort of shallow ridge near the stems, then stick the peas. Destroy weeds everywhere among the crops. Clear away cabbage-stalks, decayed leaves, and litter of every kind. A mere pint of finely-powdered dry salt, sprinkled on the moved ground, will destroy hundreds of slugs. Powdered quicklime, with a tenth part of coal-soot, scattered early in the morning, and again late at night, will also tend to clear the ground.

Collect balm, sage, mint, savory, and other fragrant herbs, for drying. All aromatic herbs are in their highest condition just before flowering. Cut them in dry weather, tie them in loose bundles, and dry them in a shaded, airy shed.

FRUIT GARDEN.

Look over the peaches, nectarines, and apricots, to remove foreright and redundant growths, and to give regularity and figure to the trees ; yet prune but little now. Take off double fruit, leaving one—the best situated.

Apples and pears, as dwarf or espalier, may be regulated at the end of the month, when the spring growth has become somewhat ripe. " Spur pruning" may be commenced then, but experience must determine the exact time, it being the object to cut back every projecting shoot to within a few eyes of its origin, in order to induce those eyes to enlarge. It will be manifest to the experienced naturalist, that if a shoot be thus shortened while the plant is in full activity, a number of secondadaries will be emitted ; therefore the work should be deferred till the sap be rather tranquil, and the wood firm.

Vines are in rapid progress, and must be regu-

lated weekly. If the main branches be sufficiently distant, it will be easy to lay in the bearing laterals orderly, without crowding. All useless wood should be removed.

Fig-trees require close, even training, in order
to expose their tender fruit to the sun.

Some cut away the superfluous shoots of gooseberry and currant bushes, but perhaps without
reason ; no ground suckers ought, however, to
remain on the trees

Strawberry plants should be divested of runners,
unless it be an object to obtain new plants. The
sorts wanted for forcing might be raised by plung-
ing the smallest pot at a part where a strong
runner plant could reach it, and then, by filling
with soft loam, and laying a stone on the string to
keep the plant on the earth, it would soon take
root.

Examine the fresh grafted trees, and tie up the
advancing shoots; when thus secured, ease the
bandages, to enable the united parts to enlarge
with freedom.

Keep all the spaces about fruit-trees, and in
plots of bearing shrubs, clean and free from weeds.
Hoe the soil, and use the rake, but never dig the
ground, unless it be to remove intrusive suckers.

Hothouse and Pits.

Look to the pine-apples. Those succession
plants which require shifting, having filled their
pots, may now be fresh potted. A free-working
turfy loam, or the earth of good reduced couch
roots, with one-third of sheep's or deer's dung,
pretty rotten, will suit this plant. Cut off no roots,
but strike the ball smartly against the potting-
bench, to detach some of the old earth, and in a
degree liberate the external coil of roots : then,
with the hand, draw off a portion of the top soil,
and place the plant in the new pot upon so much
of the fresh soil as will permit deep potting. A
strong moist warmth (not active bottom heat) of
75°, in closed pits, will bring the plants into active
work in a very short time. The potting earth
ought to be just so moist as to work freely, and
no more ; nor ought water to be given till growth
is established. Some shading is good.

The fruiting house should be kept at 80° by
day, with some air, and at 70° by night.

The vinery may require a little fire if the nights
be cold, but none by day. Air during sun, and a
transparent covering, are excellent appliances ;
the former confers flavour and colour, the latter
defends from the scalding power of a hot sun.

Melons, while setting, require much air.
Sprinkling in the afternoon of sunny days, with
immediate closing of the sashes, promotes a salubrious, warm vapour, and repels the red spider.

Flower Garden.

We may now notice in well-ordered gardens the
following approved plants in bloom ; they cannot
be surpassed, though the list appeared several
years since in the " Domestic Gardener's Manual."
Thousands, however, have been since introduced
by the laudable efforts of our collectors.

Deciduous shrubs.—Roses of many sorts—deciduous, and the China *azaleas*, six or more hardy
species : *spiræa*, three or four species ; the guelder
rose *(viburnum opulus)*; Carolina allspice *(caly-
canthus)*; shrubby potentilla, an extremely pretty
yellow flowering shrub ; the fringe tree *(chionan-
thus)* ; and all the scarlet pelargonia.

Evergreen shrubs.—Rock-rose, *cistus* and *helian-*

themum, ten or twelve sorts ; *rhododendron*, numerous species ; *vaccinium* and *ericæ*, or heaths,
three or four natives.

Herbaceous plants. — Indian , pink, *dianthus
sinensis*, and many other species of *dianthus*, including sweet William ; larkspurs—*delphinium ;*
the *superbum* presents blue of tint so rich, as
hardly to admit of a rival ; yellow *mimulus;*
mignionette ; marvel of Peru *(mirabilis)* ; rose
campion, &c.

Bulbous Roots.—Atamasco lily *(Amaryllis ata-
maso)* ; yellow dog's tooth *(Eyrythronium luteum);*
ranunculus anemone, great variety ; and of British
Orchideæ ; *orchis ustulata*, conopsia, maculata,
militaris, latifolia, and *ophrys apifera*, or bee
ophrys.

Miscellaneous Operations.

Continue to sow the approved annuals in patches
for succession. Plant layers and pipings of pinks,
cloves, picotees, and carnations ; this tribe delights
in calcareous road sand. Transplant orchises from
the woods and downs, always remembering to raise
the tubers perfect, and just when the flower is fully
formed and near expansion ; also plant balsams,
tricolors, cockscombs, and globe amaranths. Numbers of frame and green-house plants of modern introduction may go into prepared beds, borders, and
parterres.

The Indian azalias, Rhodendron Hirsutum, Kal-
mias ledums, acacia armata, Daphne cneorum, and
the like, do well in select plots, the soil of which
consists of heath-mould, decayed earth of leaves,
and pit-sand ; *loam* is a term which includes so vast
a variety of constituents, that we dare not generalize—local experience must direct its availability.

Geraniums, not only the horse-shoe and scarlets,
but many of the once famous prize varieties of Pelargonia, adorn the parterres, therefore may be introduced very early in June.

The Greenhouse

may now contain, chiefly, balsams, capsicums,
cockscombs, and similar tender annuals, with the
choicer geraniums. A house with an eastern or
even north exposure, is required for the camellias,
epacrises, heaths, and tender azalias. All such
plants like heath mould as their staple earth, and
this ought never to become quite dry ; half the injuries which the delicate hair-rooted plants sustain,
arise from the irregular use of water—sometimes it
is given in deluge, at others so restricted as to render the ball of earth dry at the centre ; a free medium temperament, as to moisture, with little sun,
and plenty of dry air, are the essentials in the management of the beautiful hard-wooded tribes.

Note.—The wet weather appears confirmed in
this third week of May, and we begin to be soli-
citons.

PLUMPTON SALE OF SHORT HORNS took
place on Tuesday, April 25th, and although the day
was extremely unfavourable, yet upwards of twelve
hundred gentlemen assembled, amongst which were
breeders from various parts of England, as well as from
Ireland and Scotland. Precisely at 12 o'clock upwards
of four hundred gentlemen sat down to a most sumptuous luncheon, provided by Mr. Watkin ; the chair was
taken by Mr. James Parkin of Skiregill, whose urbanity
of manners and gentlemanly conduct on all occasions
so eminently befit him for the situation. After the
health of the Queen, Prince Albert, the rest of the
Royal Family, the Navy and Army, the Earl of

Lonsdale, the peasantry of England, the health of Mr. Watkin and a good sale to him, was drunk with three times three, after which the company proceeded to the place of sale, where Mr. Wetherell made a few pertinent remarks on the good blood and qualities of the hero he was about to offer, and concluded by stating that t he highest credit was due to Mr. Watkin for selecting both males and females, from which he had been able to breed so fine a herd, and observed he could give them no greater proof of their excellence than, since 1836, Mr. Watkin had, at the following societies; viz., the Highland and Agricultural Society of Scotland, the Northumberland, the county of Durham, and the Carlisle and Penrith, obtained no less than 136 prizes. He then apologized for having so long detained the company, and proceeded with the sale. The following are the prices and the purchasers' names:—

Lot		Guineas.
1	Wallflower, roan, calved in 1829, got by Staintor (2695), &c. &c.	17
2	Whiteface, had a misfortune, not offered for sale: dead	
3	White-stockings, red and white, calved in 1838, got by Majesty (2250)	20
4	Westernbelle, roan, calved in 1838, got by do.	23
5	Wellington, roan do. do., got by Captain.	24
6	Countess, roan do. 1839, by Gainford (2040)	21
7	Whiteface, roan do. 1838, by Chorister, (725)	20
8	Wildflower, roan do. 1834, by Monitor (2330)	20
9	Woodburn, roan do. 1838, by Majesty (2250)	23
10	Wear, roan do. 1834, by Harlsey, (2091)	31
11	Picottee, do. do. 1835, by Prince Paul, (730)	22
12	Western Gaiety, do. do. 1836, by Easthorpe (1947)	34
13	Fair Helen, red and white, do. 1840, by Chorister, (725)	34
14	Wallflower, 2nd white, do. 1836, by Emperor, (1974)	35
15	Windermere, roan do. 1834, by do. (do.)	38
16	White Lilly, do. do. 1836, by Sir William (2836)	41
17	Whitefoot, do. do. 1838, by Herrington (2121)	40
18	Wallflower, 4th do. do. 1840, by St. Helena.	80
19	Princess Royal, do. do. 1841, by Chorister (725)	38
20	Weardale, red and white, do. 1840, by St. Helena	80
21	Adelaide, red and white, do. 1841, by Plumpton (2440)	38
22	Ganeforth, roan do. 1840, by Rockingham (2550)	21
23	Waverly, red, do. 1840, by Cæsar, dam by Newton, (2367)	24
24	Woodnote, do. do. 1840, by Rains Colonel (11)	40
25	Westminster, roan do. 1840, by Antonio (724)	16

YEARLING HEIFERS.

26	Woodlass, red & white, do. 1841, by Bloomsbury	32

Lot		Guineas.
27	Winston, white, do. 1841, by Lord Mayor	13
28	Wyville, roan do. 1841	9
29	Desdemona, red and white, do. 1841, by Wallace	not offered
30	Waterloo, roan do. 1841, by Charles 12th	19
31	Wortley, do. do. 1841, by Majesty	not offered
32	Welfare, do. do. 1841, by Charles 12th	28
33	White Lady, white, do. 1841, by do.	63
34	Webb, roan do. 1841, by Pickwick	36
35	Dorothy Gwyn, do. do. 1842, by Prime Minister (2456)	32
36	Wild Planet, do. do. 1842, by Melbourne.	15

HEIFER CALVES.

37	Waxy, roan, calved in May, 1842, by Melbourne	20
38	Wedlock, do. July, 1842, by Gainford 2nd	24
39	Wharton Lady, do. August, 1842, by do.	17
40	Wearmouth, do. March, 1842, by Melbourne.	30
41	Wallflower, 5th, do. August, 1842, by the Earl	21
42	Weardale Lass, do. February, 1843, by Eden.	15

BULLS.

43	The Duke of St. Albans, roan, 1840, by Chorister	20
44	Conservative, roan, calved in 1840, by Prime Minister (2456)	not offered
45	The Prince of Wales, red and white, do. 1841, by Chorister	80
46	St. Thomas, roan do. 1841, by Pickwick	35
47	Mr. Squeers, white, do. 1841, by do.	27
48	Coronation, do. do. 1841, by Monarch	18
49	Thalberg, do. do. 1842, by Violin	21
50	Tory, do. do. 1841, by Charles 12th	18
51	Prince, red and white, do. do. 1842, by do.	15
52	The Farmer's Friend, do. 1842, by The Earl	20
53	Mungo Park, do. do. 1842, by Lillywhite	22
54	Liverpool, do. do. 1842, by Melbourne	20
55	Voltaire, white, do. 1842, by Charles 12th	13
56	Lammas, do. do. 1842, by The Earl	18
57	A British Yeoman, do. do. 1842, by Sir Harry	35
58	The Duke of Wellington, red and white, do. do. 1842, by the Earl (lost au eye)	5
59	Sir Robert Peel, red and white, do. 1843, by Conservative	16

Guineas 1534

55 Cattle brought 1,534 guineas—£1,610 14s.; auctioneer, £40 5s.; total for the 55 cattle, £1,650 19s., or about £30 each.

At Plumpton, near Penrith, Mr. Watkins 55 shorthorns averaged about £30 each.

AGRICULTURAL REPORTS.

YORKSHIRE.

Six weeks of almost incessant rains precede the date of this report; that is, there has scarcely been the intermission of one day of more or less rain; still there have often been drying winds, and occasionally warm sun, so that the apparent excess of water, especially on the surface even on strong clay lands, has by no means been great; still the amount of wet and cold, and especially the severe occasional frosts which intervened, particularly on two nights, have contributed to make sad havoc of vegetation. On the extreme light lands the wheat has suffered most materially. It is spiry and yellow, and does not, though springing for shooting, cover the interstices between the drills. On the extreme wet and heavy lands, too, this plant, although once very vigorous and promising, has sickened, and dwindled into the bare furrow appearance of a very severe winter, and the weed was never so amazingly abundant. Upon the whole the prospects for wheat, notwithstanding the extremely large breadth sown,

are by no means very promising. Still nothing has yet been done to prevent an average supply of quarters of wheat, as an unusual number of acres is under that grain. Barley is overset with wet, and dwindles before the cold nights and eastern winds. Cloverseeds seem to be nearly annihilated by the frosts. Oats, which have acquired a little more strength, seem to be more promising, and beans are tolerably good of plant. Tares, though backward, are looking thriving and well. The pastures, though neither long nor very grassy, are well set, and the grass appears good. The stock are starved, and not doing very much good. Some farmers have taken the wool off their holding sheep, but the weather has prevented many from clipping. Wool seems to be rallying in price; we have heard of 11d. per lb. being bid on the sheep's back; 1s. was asked, but no bargain was made. If the prospects of a foreign trade be realised now that our home employment is so surely, though somewhat slowly advancing, it will sell well. The season makes the fallows for turnips not only difficult to clean, but really in a backward state, and but few Swedes are put in. The few that are sown have remained long in the ground, and have had to sustain a season of wet and cold, which too often arrests their early growth, and often impairs their progress for some weeks, as well as gives the weed a very unpropitious advance of the turnips. Potatoes for the same reason are by no means in the ground generally ; the ground is yet in many cases quite unfit to receive them, and most of them have been planted very late. If fine weather should now take place farmers will be exceedingly busy. Prices during the month have improved only a shade—not to pay interest of capital, nor even for the waste of keeping corn. Beef has rallied a little, but mutton is still very low.—*May 26.*

EAST CUMBERLAND.

The early part of the spring—that is, during the months of February and March—passed over without any rain, comparatively speaking ; the land indeed never got a thorough wetting till the month of April, and the winter being generally mild and open, enabled the farmers to make great progress with their out-door work ; it was consequently in a very forward state by the beginning of April, and though a considerable quantity of rain fell at intervals during that month, yet it was not such as greatly to retard field labour, consequently the operations of agriculture were probably never in a more forward state at the commencement of May. Much of the land intended for potatoes and turnips turned out very foul, in consequence of having been laid down for grass during some of the late very wet seasons ; but the weather being not altogether unfavourable hitherto for the operation of cleaning, it has generally been got into good order for the reception of the seed. Potato planting has been brought to a close, the great bulk having been put in some time ago, but a few patches were not finished till within the last two or three days. They have been put in under circumstances very favourable to their growing, except a few days which were very dry, with a cold, withering east wind. There are partial complaints made of seed going in the dry rot, but this is not likely to be so general as to materially affect the crop. A considerable quantity of Swede turnips has been sown ; it is considered rather early yet for the later sorts, especially those for winter use. Wheat is generally looking remarkably well upon dry land ; upon clays and wet retentive sub-soils, much of it has, for some time back, assumed a yellow, sickly hue, owing in a great degree to the cold and wet occasionally experienced during the last six weeks. East wind has lately been very prevalent, and with it a very low temperature. Last week the mornings were generally frosty, succeeded during the day by a nipping east wind. Rain set in on Sunday morning, which continued almost without intermission throughout the day, the following night, and Monday morning, with the wind still in the east. A heavy rain again commenced yesterday (Wednesday) evening, and continues to-day, consequently the land has got a complete soaking. The wind has veered round to the west, and the temperature has risen, but should much more rain fall it must necessarily have a bad effect. Warm, dry weather is now necessary for wheat, to stiffen the straw, prevent its getting too long, and to enable it to get well into ear, and fill without lodging. It came up, and still is so very thick upon the ground, and looks so gross on dry land, that it must

suffer seriously from too much wet. Barley and oats came up well, and so far are very promising. There are few complaints of wire-worm and grub, and though the effect of their labour is here and there visible, it is more partial and limited in extent than has commonly been the case. Owing to the open winter and mild temperature in the early part of the spring, grass was forward, and plentiful at a more early period than usual, but the late cold easterly winds will have their natural effect, especially on sown grasses, and will cause the hay to be a lighter crop than it would otherwise have been : the meadows, being later, will, from the recent rains, have a chance of producing an abundant crop. Notwithstanding the appearance of the grass fields, cattle does not sell as might have been expected ; there is certainly some demand, but at a very low figure. For milch cows the price is somewhat better, and fat stock is a shade higher, but still very low. Grain markets have been a little better for two or three weeks back. Wheat and barley at an advance of from four-pence to six-pence an imp. bush., and oats about three-pence. There are very few stacks to be seen in the country ; fodder being scarce caused people to thrash freely for the use of the cattle ; and the grain being generally sent to market as soon as thrashed, makes it pretty certain that there are only small stocks in the hands of the farmers. The deficiency in quantity of the hay and straw of last year's growth, had the natural effect of producing small dunghills ; but there seems a prevailing disposition amongst the farmers to make up for this by the use of artificial manure. Large quantities of Guano have been taken to manure with, and experiments with it are in progress ; the results of which, when ascertained, may be expected to be useful guides in future. There seems a general opinion that, can the article be depended on as free from adulteration, and had at a cheaper rate, it would become of very general use. It is thought that, as it will cost little or nothing where it is procured, it would pay the shipper well at a much less price than is now sought for it.—*May 25th.*

AGRICULTURAL REPORT FOR MAY.

We do not remember to have witnessed, during the course of forty-four years, so wet a month of May. They, however, who can retrace the tremendous year 1799, will bear in mind that after a very frosty, early spring—so cold throughout, that the hawthorn-bushes and elm-trees had scarcely protruded a leaf on the 1st of May—the rain then set in, and continued, with extremely small intervals of fine weather, till October, when the destruction of the crops was consummated.

Thunder has recently been frequent, and this electric meteor mainly contributed to establish that season of profuse rain which the magnetic phenomena about the period of the vernal equinox introduced. The temperature, which was very low till the 18th, began then to meliorate, and we now observe 50 or 52 degrees by night, and 60 to 66 degrees in the shade, as a maximum. The barometer has never been much depressed, but then the mercury (as usual in similar seasons) has fluctuated between 29 in. 40 c. and 29 in. 80 c., or thereabout.

We know one farmer, whose experience and fears justify the remarks contained in the first part of the Mark-lane Review, col. 1, May 22 :—"On cold wet lands the colour of the blade has already, in many instances, changed from a healthy green to a sickly yellow." But the farm in question affords the only example within our ken ; and here be it stated that a great portion of the land is hilly, rising ground, in every way favourable to good and effectual draining ; yet it remains untouched, as nature left it, and stagnant water abounds at a small depth below the surface.

Our crops generally are magnificent—tall, of course, but close and thick on the ground. The yellow tinting of the wheat originated with the snow and keen frost of April 10-13th, by which some of the more advanced foliage and the upper superficial roots being paralysed, a torpor was created, perhaps a partial death, the effects of which still remain visible. The rain may soon produce its own peculiar effects, but as respects the past, it is equally certain that the oats and barley—particularly those sown late—are exceedingly verdant. We also can testify, from observation in several counties, that to the end of the third week of May the promise was very cheering.

The turmoil that involves the nation at the present time originates in misconception. This is ably, pointedly, incontrovertibly exposed in the letter upon the "Corn Laws—Transition from War Prices," which appeared in the last *Express*, p. 2, col. iii., *et seq.* The exposition of causes, and the arguments founded thereon, are equally clear and powerful : as an observer of facts, recollecting in detail the whole course of the French war and the introduction of the abominable corn law of 1815, we feel the truth of that *exposé.* In fact, it is perfectly surprising that farmers should take the least degree of interest in legislative measures of protection, when " he that runs may learn," as one would think all persons of sense must have learned, that *prices of grain have varied through the entire range, from the greatest depression of 6s. the single bushel of fine flour to the enormous charge of 13s., or 65s. per sack, during the operation of the selfsame bill.*

This bill, or any arrangement whatever upon the sliding scale, has it, we ask, any other tendency than to keep up rents and to foster most vicious speculation ? Answer who can in the negative, but it will not be in the voice of truth and candour.

The real remedy for all the evils of the land will be found in the improvement of agriculture—not in the miserable restrictions, which tend only to high rents and the starvation of the millions. England has doubled, and can re-double its produce ; and if peace continue to extend free and harmonious intercourse, a reciprocity exactly suitable to the wants of the whole world will be the blessed result.

The crops of all kinds now growing on the earth are measureless ; we only tremble for the ingathering. The grass is heavy ; lucerne, sainfoin, and tares super-luxuriant ; potatoes highly promising, but the prognostic of weather is unfavourable. Still it is *spring ;* and a dripping spring is frequently the precursor of fine harvest weather.

May 24.

GENERAL AGRICULTURAL REPORT FOR MAY.

This has been, perhaps, one of the wettest months recollected at any previous corresponding period of the year since 1826. From the 1st up to the 24th, not a single day passed without our being visited in almost all parts of England with heavy rains, which, as might have been expected, flooded the lowlands, but we are happy to state that the damage sustained has been very trifling : yet much inconvenience has been experienced from the saturated condition of the soil. Since the date last above mentioned, the weather has been comparatively fine, and vegetation, from the prevailing warm and genial temperature, has made considerable progress. The accounts that have reached us relative to the general appearance of the young wheat and other grain plants are for the most part satisfactory. The spring crops are described as unusually regular, of full average growth, and of a fine healthy colour, with every indication of a good forthcoming yield.

The early fruit trees exhibit a good promise for an abundant supply of most descriptions of fruit, especially apples and pears, the cold nights having prevented the ravages of the insects amongst the young buds.

The low prices at which all descriptions of agricultural produce have been selling for some time past, have naturally excited no little degree of inquiry as to the probable time any improvement will take place in them ; hence we purpose, on the present occasion, throwing out a few hints, which will, we trust, prove useful to those more immediately interested. Prospectively speaking, a gloom hangs over the welfare of our agriculturists, which will, we much fear, have the effect of producing results anything but satisfactory. The trite but correct adage, that " supply and demand are the great regulators of price," is being fully exemplified at this period, and the observations which we have from time to time penned on this head are being borne out by facts. The question, then, for our consideration is, when will matters improve ? Putting it upon the basis of the above quotation, we candidly confess the period when any permanent or beneficial alteration will take place is extremely problematical. If we refer to the stocks of wheat of last years' growth, in the hands of our farmers, it will be found that they are—notwithstanding the partial deficiencies in the crop—more than an average for the time of year, while the quality is unusually fine. That these circumstances, combined with the supplies of free and bonded foreign grain being on the increase—upwards of 700,000 quarters of wheat, on which duty has been paid, being still in warehouse in the various parts of the United Kingdom—cannot fail to have a depressing influence upon prices, we are quite convinced. Hence the serious attention of those chiefly interested should now be drawn to these facts. In offering these remarks, we beg to observe that we do so from the necessity we conceive exists for setting matters on a correct footing, and for allowing all parties to have an opportunity of forming their own opinions. In taking a glance at the political horizon, we find the free-trade phalanx as clamorous as ever to obtain their object, and our ministers so far favouring it as to lay before the Commons a bill for the admission of flour from our Canadian possessions at a much lower rate of duty than is at present levied upon that article. Sir Robert Peel gravely tells us that the proposed measure will not have an injurious effect upon the growers here; but it does not, we consider, require much discernment to prove that the large supplies of flour which will reach us from Canada during the present year, and by which our farmers will be much undersold in their own markets, will cause the value of English qualities to fall below what can possibly be considered even the most moderate profit, and

H H

eventually cause a ruinous loss to those in this country. This bill, then, we deem nothing more nor less than a premium on smuggling, and as such ought to be generally discountenanced. It is well-known that, for many years past, immense supplies of wheat and flour have found their way from the United States into Canada, and thence shipped here as the produce of that colony, without having paid any duty on the frontier. This is fully evidenced by the large quantities which are at this time under bond in London and elsewhere.

In the early part of the month, an improved demand sprung up for wheat, and an advance of from 1s. to 2s. per quarter was obtained for the finest qualities of both red and white. Since about the 15th, however, the enquiry has become much less active, yet the above advance has been mostly supported, although the quantities on offer have been on a liberal scale. Some few speculative purchases have been effected in bonded wheat, but at very low prices. Very little barley has been brought forward, yet the sale for it has ruled inactive, at barely previous currencies.

The malt trade has again ruled inactive, and we have no variation whatever to report in the ruling prices. Oats have come forward rather slowly, yet the supplies have proved quite adequate to meet the wants of the dealers. Beans and peas have been in very limited supply, at full prices. In flour we have no alteration to notice.

The importations of live cattle under the new tariff have been confined this month to 49 oxen from Germany, at Hull. These beasts have been purchased on speculation and sent into Lincolnshire to graze the London market. Having had an opportunity of inspecting them, we find that instead of feeding well and increasing in bulk and weight, the very reverse is the case; and we consider them from 2l. to 3l. per head less in value than when they were first landed. This fully bears out the truth of the remarks we offered on this head some time since —while we are confident that in almost every instance the grazing of foreign stock in this country will be attended with serious losses.

From our Scotch advices we learn that considerable quantities of rain have fallen, yet the crops are looking tolerably well. The supplies of grain on offer in the different markets have been only to a moderate extent, while the general demand has ruled steady, without any material alteration in prices.

The accounts from Ireland are satisfactory. The wheats are looking remarkably well, and the fine rains have materially improved them. The supplies of wheat offering in the principal markets have been extremely small, and prices in consequence have kept up, but without much business passing. Oats and most other corn have somewhat improved in value.

The following is our usual monthly statement of the supplies and prices of fat stock exhibited and sold in Smithfield cattle market. The former have comprised 11,200 beasts; 117,429 sheep and lambs; 1341 calves; and 1294 pigs; while the latter have ranged as follow :—Beef, from 2s. 6d. to 4s. ; mutton, 2s. 10d. to 4s. ; lamb, 4s. 8d. to 5s. 8d. ; veal, 3s. 4d. to 4s. 4d. ; and pork, 3s. to 3s. 10d. per 8lbs. to sink the offal.

During the whole of the month, the general demand has been of an extremely varied character,

yet, on the whole, the quotations have been supported, arising, in a great measure, from the falling off observed in the receipts of country-killed meat up to Newgate and Leadenhall markets, compared with those reported in the previous month. Notwithstanding the numbers of store cows, barrens, heifers, &c., have been far from extensive, scarcely any sales have been effected in them, and the rates have ruled miserably low. As to the quality of the fat stock, this has, on the whole, proved good, but by no means so prime as we have noticed at many previous corresponding periods of the year. As is invariably the case in May, the strength of the bullock supplies has been derived from Norfolk, whence about 6,200 Scots and home-breds have been received ; and a fair number—or about 1700 Scots—have reached us, by sea, from Aberdeen, Dundee, and Perth; with nearly 200, via Liverpool, from Dublin. The condition of both beasts and sheep has, we regret to observe, been anything but satisfactory—a large portion of them being much affected with the prevailing epidemic, and from the effects of which disease, great losses have been sustained on the roads. The lambs, however, have proved in much better condition than many parties might be prepared to expect, particularly as relates to those from Kent, Sussex, and Surrey, including those from the Isle of Wight, per railway—the latter numbering about 1300.

Some surprise has been expressed at the non-arrival of any quantity of foreign stock—the only import having been that of 49 oxen at Hull, from Aalborg—for our markets ; but it appears very evident that, so long as prices rule at their present miserably low level, it will never answer the purposes of speculators to purchase largely.

A STATEMENT and COMPARISON of the SUP-PLIES and PRICES of FAT STOCK, exhibited and sold in SMITHFIELD CATTLE MARKET, on Monday, May 30, 1842, and Monday, May 29, 1843.

At per 8lbs. to sink the offals.

	May 30, 1842.		May 29, 1843.	
	s. d.	s. d.	s. d.	s. d.
Coarse & inferior Beasts	3 2 to	3 4	.. 2 4	2 6
Second quality do.	3 6	3 8	.. 2 8	3 0
Prime large Oxen......	3 10	4 0	.. 3 2	3 6
Prime Scots, &c.......	4 2	4 4	.. 3 8	3 10
Coarse & inferior Sheep	3 6	3 8	.. 3 0	3 2
Second quality do.	3 10	4 0	. 3 4	3 6
Prime coarse woolled do.	4 0	4 2	. 3 6	3 8
Prime Southdown do..	4 4	4 6	.. 3 10	4 0
Lambs	5 4	6 4	.. 4 4	5 4
Large coarse Calves ..	4 6	5 0	.. 3 4	4 0
Prime small ditto	5 2	5 4	.. 4 2	4 4
Large Hogs...........	4 0	4 6	.. 3 0	3 6
Neat small Porkers ..	4 8	5 0	.. 3 8	3 10

SUPPLIES.

	May 30, 1842.	May 29, 1843.
Beasts	2,680	2,952
Sheep and Lambs	26,294	30,140
Calves	130	176
Pigs	320	324

Up to Newgate and Leadenhall markets, about 11,000 carcasses of various kinds of slaughtered meat have been received, while the demand has ruled heavy, at the following quotations :—Beef, from 2s. 10d. to 3s. 8d. ; mutton, 2s. 6d. to 3s. 8d. ; lamb, 4s. 6d. to 5s. 6d. ; veal, 3s. 4d. to 4s. 4d. ; and pork, 3s. to 3s. 10d. per 8lbs. by the carcase.— May 30.

REVIEW OF THE CORN TRADE

DURING THE MONTH OF MAY.

Nothing occurred, during the month of May, in any manner calculated to clear away the gloom which has been suspended over the heads of the agricultural interest since that most unfortunate alteration in the corn laws, and in our import duties on various articles of agricultural products, which was effected during the last session of Parliament. On the contrary, not one cheering circumstance has presented itself either to the landowners, to the tenant, or to the labourers generally, throughout the United Kingdom, since our last review of the existing state and future prospects of the corn trade. A trifling advance in the value of wheat no doubt occurred during the month, but this is a natural consequence of the period of the season, and on this occasion it has been much smaller than in former years we have been accustomed to report. The average value of wheat is still nearly 10s. per qr. under the estimated price by the present prime minister of the Crown, at which it can be grown in this country; and taking our annual production of wheat at betwixt fourteen and sixteen millions of quarters, the loss entailed on our farmers by these unwise measures in the short period of eight or nine months, is immense; nor, under the new system of political economy now practised, need any immediate, or even distant, hope be entertained of any amendment taking place sufficiently extensive for extricating the landed interest, and the productive classes of all denominations, from the difficulties with which they are at present surrounded. The Anti-Corn-law Leaguers have had the assurance, since our last publication, to recommend to the farmers to pass at once into the lowest scale of adversity into which, under any circumstances, they can be driven. In fact, Mr. Cobden advises them to sink the money which they have embarked in the cultivation of their farms, with the view of compelling a reduction in the rents, and afterwards to trust to their own agricultural science for future prosperity, instead of continuing to place confidence in experience, capital, and in legal protection to their agricultural products. The same orator declares, that the manufacturers require no legislative protection whatever to their labour; and his opinion of the intellects of his hearers must be low indeed, when he ventures to make such broad and unfounded assertions. There are three or four departments in manufacture which are now suffering severely from the late alterations made in our Custom-house import duties, on articles of the same description as those which they produce in this country. There is one class, for instance, in this country which heretofore has been accustomed to supply our entire population, of upwards of twenty-six millions of human beings, with boots and shoes, and which, we should fancy, requires legal protection, at the present moment, to their labour. The masters in this department of industry, no doubt, have not yet reached that point in science which enables them to work by steam. They pay, however, three men for one, who receive their daily bread from the cotton manufacturers by steam; and whether Mr. Cobden thinks so or not, it is their opinion that the law should protect them and their workmen from foreign labourers in the same line of business. There are likewise glove manufacturers, fishermen, and hatters, and various other descrip-

tions of useful labourers in this country, who are, in every respect, as respectable as Mr. Cobden is, and who are most justly complaining, and loudly too, of the losses to which they are subjected by the interference in our markets by foreigners in the same line of business. By this illustration of the principles of free trade, the master hatters, shoe makers, glovers, British straw bonnet makers, fishermen, and others, have within the last twelve months been compelled either to reduce the wages of, or to discharge one-half of their workmen, in order that foreigners in the same lines of business may be employed instead of her Majesty's subjects in supplying this empire with these necessary articles of consumption, and in order also that foreigners may be enabled to purchase Mr. Cobden's steam-printed goods with money which ought to be now giving food and dress to our workmen at home. That foreign hats, foreign boots and shoes, foreign gloves, foreign straw bonnets, and foreign fish, since the alteration in our Custom-house duties, are inundating all our markets of consumption, and reducing to poverty multitudes of valuable British labourers, must be obvious to all. But should the Anti-Corn-Law lecturers require this fact to be proved, they have only attentively to direct their attention to the present state of our finances, and to discover, if they can, any better causes for the dangerous deficiency which now exists in our public revenue, than the violent alterations in the circumstances of our agricultural interest, and in the wages universally of our productive labourers, which have been solely the consequences of the attempts now in progress, of illustrating what are falsely called free trade principles; we mean that description of foreign trade of which foreigners reap all the advantages, and by which our industrious classes are defrauded of the sacred property! which they hold in productive employment at home. To transfer finally the healthy labours of the fields from British and Irish agricultural workmen to Russian slaves and Polish serfs, to German boors and to American helps, most assuredly must, within a very few years, be the result of the total repeal of the corn laws; and not one interest in the empire can reap the smallest advantage from a policy not more anti-British than it is positively insane. Without the wages of labour at home be maintained, the revenue cannot be collected; and to fill the union houses with idle men, and to transport thousands of valuable agricultural workmen to the colonies, is certainly a most extraordinary plan for increasing national wealth. The interest on our heavy public debt can never be paid by reducing the wages of labour to starving rates; and yet this misfortune is now rapidly in progress, not only amongst our agricultural labourers, but also universally amongst the manufacturers of leather, of hats, of straw, and most particularly amongst our fishermen; in fact there is no department in our industrial pursuits wherein this evil is not at present steadily gaining ground. To reduce the means to pay for tax-paying articles, amongst the great body of consumers, is not the best plan possible for increasing the malt, tobacco, spirit, and sugar duties; and the greater the quantities of foreign agricultural products and of foreign manual labour which may be consumed in this country, the greater hereafter must be the increase of poverty here, and the annual revenue of the empire must decrease proportionally to the decrease in the means of the consumers to pay for articles from which the public income is derived. In fact we are paying money to foreign nations to an immense amount annually for agricultural products, and for various articles which can be in the greatest abundance pro. duced in this country. During the last corn season, for instance, we have remitted abroad in the precious metals upwards of five millions sterling in payment for foreign wheat alone, and we have thus given to foreign communities the means to raise manufactures and to make goods within themselves fully equal to their own wants. Our legal shipments of British goods to Europe and to the United States of America, have annually been less during the last four or five years, for which no more satisfactory reason can be given than that it is the certain consequence of the encouragement now given to foreign agriculture on the ruin of our agricultural interest at home. Never certainly did a better opportunity exist for the establishment of reciprocity in trade amongst friendly nations than we have witnessed for several years past, for we have taken and paid to foreign nations most liberally for their products; but they have found no occasion to reciprocate; thus proving that barter trade, in the present state of society, is impracticable, and only suited to Utopian principles, which the altered condition of the human mind however may, centuries hence, find it necessary to illustrate. In the meantime the British empire is loaded with a heavy national debt, and her wealth and resources are annually tending towards decay. How the evil can be remedied by placing the agricultural interest in the gap, and by sacrificing the landed proprietors and the farmers to the groundless complaints of a dozen or two of our cotton lords, is far beyond the common comprehensions of common minds; for heretofore a productively employed population has generally been considered not only as the best, but as the only wealth of nations; but the new commercial philosophy, it appears, sanctions not these old fashioned prejudices. Had we encouraged agriculture at home, even during the last year, the rates of the wages of labour would probably, in all departments of industry, have been fairly maintained; there would have then been no falling away in the consumption of taxed articles, the public revenue would now have been in a flourishing condition, and no complaints of distress would have been heard of amongst those who are industriously disposed. The money sent abroad for these articles of consumption would have been embarked in public and private improvements at home, more particularly in the cultivation of land at present in a state of perfect uselessness to the people, but many millions of acres of which may, within a short period, be rendered equal to the best producing lands in the United Kingdom. Each of these acres is well able to support at least two men, and calculating the whole at only fifteen millions of acres, in this channel alone have we the means in abundance of supporting an additional population of thirty millions of males, with their families and connections. The power and greatness of the British empire can only be maintained by productively employing the entire population, and any system which would compel the most valuable part of it to e migrate to the colonies, or would drive them into the union workhouses, is not the real way to promote the public wealth, or to increase the public happiness. Most certainly by reducing the number of productive labourers at home, and by reducing

the wages of those who may be fortunate enough to obtain labour, is not the most legitimate way to raise a public income annually of upwards of fifty millions sterling; indeed such an amount of taxation can never be obtained, unless proper employment and adequate wages be given to every able labourer at home. The law should prevent the employment of foreign workmen in the production of any article which can be grown or manufactured within the United Kingdom, else annually in future must the malt and home spirit duties decline in productiveness, and so also must those charged on sugar, tea, coffee, tobacco, and numerous other articles of which the multitude are the great consumers, and consequently the principal payers of the immense amount of revenue latterly collected on them. In the meantime we have the prospect, at all events, of another abundant crop of grain in this country, but whether it will be a blessing to the people or not, is, under existing circumstances, more than doubtful. Bread is already to be obtained in London, of wholesome quality, at 1¼d. per lb., and in Ireland potatoes have been selling as low as 1d. per stone. These prices are ruinous to the farming interest, and another large crop can only tend to the increase of this ruin. The certain consequences of another large crop therefore must be a correspondent reduction of wages, an addition to the multitude of unemployed and destitute human beings, and an increase in our, at present, great financial difficulties. In Mark-lane, and in all the great markets of consumption throughout the United Kingdom, the utmost dulness has prevailed in the wheat trade during the last month. The millers only purchased wheat in proportion to their consumption, and although the finest samples were a trifle dearer, yet this circumstance, being occasioned solely by the chance of flour—unless manufactured from the finest wheats—heating during the summer months, cannot be considered any actual improvement in the wheat trade since our last publication; for the sale of inferior qualities is always difficult at this season of the year, and when forced a larger reduction in their value must be submitted to than is the improvement in the finest samples. The markets generally have also lately been labouring under the influence of supplies, both of wheat and flour—for they too throw their shadows before them—expected to arrive from our North American possessions in the course of the present and next month. Several ships, it is known, have been already dispatched to the river St. Lawrence for this purpose, and the quantity will probably be considerable. The importers will be sufficiently remunerated by our present prices, even should they pay the existing Colonial duties; and in this manner is this bantling, this infant colony, to be raised into prosperity at the sole expense of the landed interest throughout the United Kingdom. This is liberality, however, perfectly on a par with those changes in our customhouse duties which are at present inflicting such severe and heavy injuries on all classes within the United Kingdom. This system is the cause of a deficient revenue, and the Prime Minister must either retrace his steps, and restore those institutions to the empire on which her greatness and prosperity formerly were mainly founded, else, to use a common expression, he must go the whole hog, and that speedily too, for he cannot maintain himself in a middle position with any safety to the state. The destruction of the farmer's capital, and of the wages of the agricultural labourer, must soon be followed by the ruin of the trade of those manufacturers themselves who are now so loud in demanding unrestricted freedom in foreign commerce, in order that they may be able to reduce the wages of those workmen by whose exertions they are at present making fortunes of more than princely magnitude. The home consumption of manufactured goods is by far the most valuable market which these would-be cotton lords now possess; and their fortunes and property must suffer in a much more serious manner than they at present suppose, should the home market disappear before them. This event also would speedily render their intercourse with foreigners unimportant.

The letters received from the United States, and from our North American possessions, since our last publication, are dated in the middle of last month; and the information which is communicated by them is important in the present agricultural state of this country. Anxiety was felt in every quarter for the passing of our promised Colonial Corn and Provision Bill—the future increase of agricultural prosperity throughout the United States depending at present on this act for a regular future market for the consumption of all descriptions of their agricultural produce. In the great western states of the republic, and in even a part of that of New York itself, the beneficial effects of the promised bill were universally admitted, opening as it must do the British markets at all times to their agricultural products. The idea of transit duties was ridiculed everywhere, because their collection was known to be impossible. From Ohio and other western states, the most productive districts in the American Union, the water distance to Montreal is considerably shorter than is that to the city of New York, and the expense of transit through the lakes Huron, Erie, and Ontario, now, we may say, rendered one by means of the Great Welland Canal, constructed at an enormous expense to the United Kingdom, is, in comparison, much cheaper than to any port of shipment within the United States. These western states are intersected by canal and river navigation, and ships under the British flag, whether it be actually so or not, after the passing of our free trade Colonial Corn and Provision Bill, will load in their own ports American wheat, flour, and cured provisions, and will proceed with these cargoes direct to the ports in the St. Lawrence, with well-authenticated certificates on board that the wheat was grown in Canada, that the flour was ground, and the provisions cured in the same quarter. The geographical position of the two countries renders the detection of fraud entirely impossible; and the corn merchants themselves in Montreal and Quebec will not spoil a profitable commission trade by any exposure of its illegality. Even to the state of New York this bill will be of immense consequence, for the agricultural produce will likewise be passed to the St. Lawrence at a trifling expense, and be transformed into wheat, the growth of our American possessions, without the payment of any duty whatever. From Quebec and Montreal it will be shipped to this country at a freight certainly not 1s. per quarter higher than the charge would be from any port within the United States; and it will be admitted into consumption, throughout the United Kingdom, on the payment of nominal duties. Let it not be supposed that these supplies can, under any circumstances, ever be insignificant. We know that in Upper Canada, where labour is dear, wheat was worth no more than 18s. to 20s. per quarter lately, and it must still have been lower at the same period in the western states of America, because labourers there are more plentiful, and wages are consequently

more moderate. The means for increased production are boundless, and the quality of the wheat in particular is extremely fine, being fully equal to the best grown in Essex itself. American pork likewise is superior to any which even Wiltshire can produce, for it is fed on Indian corn, wild nuts, &c. and consequently cures better than any grown either in Ireland or Great Britain. Her Majesty's ministers, however, are acting only on a most benevolent principle, their object being to encourage and assist our infant and late rebellious Canadian colonies. In these benevolent attempts, however, we firmly believe that they will fail in giving satisfaction to our fellow subjects in America, although, no doubt, to the citizens of the United States they may for a time be of considerable consequence. Circumstances, however, may occur, and that too within a shorter period than is at present calculated on, which may render our corn trade with the United States a direct one—chiefly, however, under the American, and not exclusively under the British flag, to which the proposed Colonial Corn Bill must confine it. We now allude to a commercial treaty between this country and the United States, which in the beginning of the last month it was confidently asserted, in all the American trading cities, was under negociation, and which it was thought would speedily have a successful termination. If the terms of this treaty be as liberal as we have heard them reported to be, we shall before long have a partial experiment of a corn trade under fixed rates of duties; for into this system, it would appear, our prime minister is inclined to slide. It is reported that the American government, on the part of the United States, is prepared very materially to reduce the heavy duties now levied on the legal importation of British-manufactured goods into that Union. In making this concession, however, the American government makes no sacrifice whatever; for, since these exorbitant import duties were placed on British goods, the smuggler has enjoyed a most profitable trade by supplying the American people with that quantity of British manufactures which their wants actually demanded, and the American treasury has been the only sufferer by the late vain and absurd attempt to impose limits on our commercial enterprise. In consideration for this concession on the part of our friend Jonathan, rumour proceeded in the American ports, and at the time to which we are now alluding, to state that on our part American agricultural produce of all descriptions is to be admitted, for home consumption here, on the payment of fixed and moderate rates of duty. We dare say that commercial treaties with foreign nations may be of some advantage to the inhabitants of the British empire; but still, if the terms of the proposed commercial treaty with the United States of America be correctly given, we are morally persuaded that the alteration will again inflict another heavy blow on our agricultural interest at home, and be of little advantage indeed to our manufactures—for commerce is like water, it will find its level, and it will burst through every hostile obstacle which human laws can oppose to it. No American enactments can prevent smuggling; but by heavy duties it can be materially assisted. The farmers' friends in Parliament—if any such characters now exist—will, we trust, closely watch the progress of all treaties having commercial affairs for their foundation; for undoubtedly the farming interest must suffer by their conclusions eventually. Even under the existing Canadian Corn Act, however, in a short time we shall receive a considerable quantity of wheat and flour at prices sufficiently low to remunerate the importers at the present London quotations. At Montreal alone forty-five thousand barrels of flour were ready to be shipped as soon as the weather permitted ; and at Quebec also, some quantity must be exported either to this country or to some of our West India colonies. The freight from Montreal to London was under 3s. per barrel, and shipping was plentiful. This is an admirable commentary on that part of Lord Stanley's speech delivered in the House of Commons on the 19th ult., wherein he stated that Canada grows not a sufficient quantity of wheat for the consumption of its inhabitants, and that our agricultural interest has nothing to fear from the new Canadian Corn Bill. Our colonial secretary knows most imperfectly the capabilities of our American possessions and of the United States to produce grain and provisions of all descriptions, else he would never have uttered such random assertions as he did at the time to which we now allude, for his purpose could never have been to lull the British farmers into a state of false security. A few years' experience, however, of a free trade in grain with America, or even of one at fixed rates of duties, must dispel these false ideas, if they do exist at all ; for since the present corn bill became the law of this country, we have repeatedly warned our agricultural readers against its injurious consequences, as we now entreat them not to be deceived by the ministerial special pleading in favour of the colonial one. We universally have stated that the maximum duty on wheat would, under no circumstances, prohibit the importation of the finest qualities, nor prevent them from passing into consumption. Our predictions on this subject have been amply accomplished, for considerable quantities of the best qualities of Polish and Silesian wheats have already arrived, and greater quantities are on the passage from different places in the Baltic to the river Thames, where, according to contract, these wheats are to be delivered, *in good order* and *free from expense,* at from 30s. to 34s. per quarter. These wheats are now worth here from 54s. to 58s. per quarter ; and, although they leave little or no profit, after the payment of 20s. per quarter of duty, the London metage, and the corn factor's commission, still the speculation is not attended by any sacrifice of money, and the introduction of ∫foreign wheat at present into our markets of consumption, when the average price of home grown wheat is little above 46s., or 10s. per quarter under the expense of its production, according to Sir R. Peel's acknowledgment, is an act of unmitigated cruelty to the farmers of the United Kingdom. The next importation of Polish and Silesian wheats into London, will be at prices lower than those which we have now mentioned, and during the entire season all our markets will be abundantly supplied with wheats of similar descriptions, and then the agricultural interest will have most ample proof placed practically before them, that the present corn laws protect neither their capital invested in the cultivation of the fields, nor the produce of their agricultural operations ; and those ministers who were raised into office for the protection, as well of agricultural property as of the wages of productive employment generally, may therefore speedily see good reason to retrace their liberal commercial steps, and again to place the industrial classes of this country into their former position of positive prosperity. The proposed colonial corn and provision act, if permitted ever to disgrace the statute book of the United Kingdom, will

press even more heavily on the interests of British and Irish agriculture than the existing law does ; for by the latter, at all events, an increase may be made to our public revenue, but from the operation of the proposed colonial bill no revenue can be received equal to the expences of its collection, and, so far from increasing the consumption of British manufactured goods throughout the United States of North America, its consequences will be the reverse, for within a few years it will furnish the American people with capital for raising at home manufactures quite equal to their home consumption. Under existing circumstances the Americans require considerable quantities of our goods, and these goods they must have, either by smuggling or by direct importation under moderate duties. Our legislature should leave well alone. They should restore fair and adequate protection to agriculture at home, and every effort should be also made to maintain the value of wages, else we feel a moral conviction that the public revenue of fifty millions sterling cannot be annually collected.

The barley trade has not improved in any manner during the last month ; on the contrary, the value of it has been on the decline, some quantity of foreign barley having been admitted into consumption on the payment of a duty of nine shillings per quarter. After the liquidation of this duty, of freight, and of all importation expenses, the speculation has not been an unprofitable one, and farther supplies may therefore be reckoned on from the same foreign quarters during the progress of the present corn season. We had prepared the readers of the " Farmer's Magazine"—by many preceding articles published under this head—for a material deficiency in the quantity of malt manufactured last season; but we must candidly confess that the defalcation in the malt duty for the season closing in the beginning of April last is far greater than we could possibly have conceived, and affords an admirable illustration of the injurious consequences to our agricultural interest, resulting from the outrageous manner in which manufactured barleys are taxed in this country. But the land proprietor, the farmer, and the agricultural labourer are not the only sufferers by this most unpopular tax, for the beer consumers generally reap their full share of the evil. In it originates the nefarious custom of beer adulteration, as detrimental to the health of the people as it is injurious to the public revenue and to the property of the barley farmer. At least one-third part of the beer now consumed is manufactured from coarse sugar, salt, and many deleterious articles ; for two barrels from the licensed brewer are regularly now converted into three by a mixture of ingredients of the above description, and by such means is the honest beer consumer defrauded of the article for which his money is paid, and his health materially injured by the substitution of spurious for pure beer. The minor retail publicans cannot be blamed for this adulteration. They have heavy licenses to pay for permission to retail beer, and also heavy house expenses : and unless the price of beer be low, they would lose their custom, and with it the property embarked by them in their licenses. It is the system which creates the evil ; and the opposition made by our excise laws to the modification of this system renders its continuation, we had almost said, perpetual. It cannot, however, last longer than the Chancellor of the Exchequer pleases; for, by the reduction of the malt duty to 1s. per bushel on the quantity of barley applied to this purpose, he can not only remedy the evils complained of, but he has it likewise in his power to double the sum at present paid into the Treasury by the malt duties. But should the Anti-Corn-Law Leaguers prevail with her Majesty's ministers, and induce them to slide either into fixed rates of duties on the importation of foreign grain, or into the liberal system of no protection whatever to British agriculture against that of our colonies and of foreign nations, it will be only an act of common justice en the part of the advisers of the crown to repeal the duties altogether now chargeable on manufactured barley. Unless some change in the present system, however, be immediately effected—unless the duty on malt be reduced to 1s. per bushel, and unless 5s. per gallon, at most, be the duty on English-made spirits—the public revenue must annually decay. This season the principal maltsters ceased working at least a month earlier than they did last year, and therefore it requires no soothsayer to predict that, reduced as the malt duty has been last year, it will be still less on the 1st of April, 1844. These disheartening prospects to our farmers have caused less barley than usual to be sown during this spring, but the young plants are strong in the ground; and, in as far as any opinion can be formed at this early period of the season, they are in a healthy and in a sufficiently forward state. Still, under the present system of liberal laws, strong doubts may be, and actually are, entertained whether an excellent barley-crop can be considered a national benefit, or whether it may not add to the difficulties under which the British empire at present labours; for to this state have the doctrines of theorists reduced the inhabitants of the United Kingdom. These internal evils must annually increase in magnitude.

Since our last little improvement has occurred in the value of oats; and to say that the trade now is worse than it then was would be an assumption of considerable difficulty to prove, bordering, as it would be, on the impossible. In the meantime this deplorable state of the oat-trade is operating on the property of the oat-growers very injuriously, more particularly throughout Ireland; and the people there have just reason to complain of the detrimental consequences to their interests universally, of the late alterations in the corn laws, and more particularly of the reduced duties at which all descriptions of foreign agricultural produce are now admitted into all our markets of consumption. The Irish population has been in many instances thrown entirely out of employment from this cause alone, and in all instances the small pittance which they had previously received for their labour is now daily becoming more petty. *Paddy* now has not the means to pay for potatoes, even at one penny per stone; because the low value of grain, of live stock, and of cured provisions, prevents the farmers from paying any thing like living wages even to the poor and now distressed Irishmen. Discontent at existing matters is now rearing itself into even dangerous eminence; and the new liberal principles as practised in our foreign commerce, and neither religious nor political feelings, are the only grounds for this discontent. Before these relaxations were made in our foreign-import commerce the agricultural products of Ireland found remunerating prices in the British market, and at the same time the value of all descriptions of them was kept sufficiently moderate for the best interests of the great body of the consumers. Until the late most uncalled-for change was effected, the improvements in Ireland were in a gradual state of extension; the workmen at home

received wages adequate to their few wants, and contentment and order were daily gaining ground amongst them. Less than one year's experience of the principles and workings of the new system of political economy—that one-sided system of foreign trade which gives away many advantages, and which receives not one—has totally altered the previously advancing prosperity of Ireland; but of what consequence is the happiness of Irishmen when placed in the scale against the interests of Messrs. Bright, (quaker) and Co. ?—of those of the inhabitants of foreign nations, and more particularly of those of our infant colony of Canada? But Ireland is not the only sufferer by the present state of the oat-trade; for wherever this article has been cultivated during the last year, it has been attended by much loss of property to its cultivators. In another year the shipping interest will likewise be considerably affected by the present system of liberality towards foreign land proprietors and foreign commerce; for a great portion of the grain and provision-carrying trade betwixt Ireland and the east coast of Great Britain will be entirely lost. Foreign flags in future will supply us with oats grown in foreign states, and shipped in foreign harbours and rivers; and for these oats we must exchange the precious metals so long as any wealth of this description remains within the United Kingdom. Like wheat and barley, even the maximum duty hereafter to be levied on the importation of foreign oats for our home use, can be no preventive to the importation of the finest qualities grown abroad. For the coming oat-crop the weather during the last month has been uncommonly favourable, and the young plants are now looking as well as the farmers could possibly require; but, unless the prices next corn season be sufficiently high to pay wages to the farmer's workmen and rent to the farmer's landlord, a large crop cannot be of the smallest benefit to him. The potato crop now in the ground likewise is looking as favourably as could be desired at this season of the year, and the quality of the last crop of this article continues to be of an excellent description, the price remaining moderate, and fortunately so; for the scanty means of the great majority of the consumers would scarcely be found sufficient even for the purchase of potatoes, was their value now more remunerating to the grower than it is at the present time. Indeed in Ireland the means of the vast body of the consumers to pay for this article are already nearly exhausted.

CURRENCY PER IMP. MEASURE.

MAY 29.

WHEAT, Essex and Kent, red	48	52	white 52 56 58		
Irish	48	—	Do. 48 54		
Old, red	—	—	Do. ..... — —		
RYE, old	32	—	New.... 32 —		
BARLEY, Grinding 26 29 Malting	30	33	Chevalier 32 35		
Irish....................	24	28	Bere ... 22 26		
MALT, Suffolk and Norfolk	56	58	Brown.. 50 54		
Kingston and Ware	56	60	Chevalier 60 —		
OATS, Yorksh. & Lincolnsh., feed	20	22	Potato.. 23 26		
Youghall and Cork black	—	17	Cork, white 17 19		
Dublin	17	18	Westport 19 20		
waterford, white 15	17	18	Black .. 17 18		
Newry 19	20	21			
Galway	15	16			
Scotch feed	21	—	Potato.. 21 24		
Clonmel	17	18	Limerick18 19 21		
Londonderry	18	19	Sligo 17 18 19		
BEANS, Tick, new..............	23	27	Old 30 32		
PEAS, Grey....................	27	29	Maple... 26 28		
white	30	31	Boilers . 30 32		
FLOUR, Town-made 42 43 Suffolk 35 36 pr sk. of 280 lbs.					
Stockton and Norfolk, 35 36					

COMPARATIVE PRICES of GRAIN.

WEEKLY AVERAGES by the Imp. Quarter, from the Gazette, of Friday last, May 26th, 1843.		AVERAGES from the corresponding Gazette in the last year, Friday, May 27th, 1842.	
	s. d.		s. d.
WHEAT	47 2	WHEAT	61 10
BARLEY	27 0	BARLEY	25 11
OATS	17 5	OATS	19 7
RYE	29 2	RYE	33 7
BEANS	26 10	BEANS	32 1
PEAS	28 2	PEAS	30 11

IMPERIAL AVERAGES.

week ending	Wheat.	Barley.	Oats.	Rye.	Beans.	Peas.
April 15th	45 9	28 8	17 1	29 2	25 10	28 1
22nd	46 7	28 5	17 4	28 7	25 11	27 5
29th	47 0	28 7	17 6	29 3	26 3	28 3
May 6th......	46 4	28 2	17 2	27 7	26 4	28 1
13th	46 2	28 1	17 3	29 2	26 8	28 9
20th	47 2	27 0	17 5	29 2	26 10	28 2
Aggregate average of the six weeks which regulates the duty	46 6	28 3	17 4	29 10	26 4	28 1
Duties payable in London till Wednesday next inclusive, and at the Outports till the arrival of the mail of that day from London ..	20 0	9 0	8 0	11 6	11 6	11 6
Do. on grain from British possessions out of Europe........	5 0	2 0	2 0	2 6	1 0	1 0

STOCK OF GRAIN, &c., IN BOND, IN THE PORT OF LONDON, ON THE 5th MAY.

wheat.	Barley.	Oats.	Beans.	Peas.	Rye.	Flour.
qrs.	qrs.	qrs.	qrs.	qrs.	qrs.	cwts.
107,287	6,648	18,814	44,402	5,551	—	29,614

Cloverseed, 12,735 cwts.

Account shewing the Quantities of Corn, Grain, Meal, and Flour, imported into the United Kingdom, in the month ended the 5th May, 1843 ; the Quantities upon which Duties have been paid for Home Consumption during the same month, and the Quantities remaining in Warehouse at the close thereof.

Foreign Grain and Flour.	Quantity imported.		Quantity entered for consumption.		Quantity remaining in warehouse.	
	qrs.	bush.	qrs.	bush.	qrs.	bush.
Wheat, from British Possessions	166	0	925	0	4184	7
Peas, from do......	22	6	145	6	390	3
Indian Corn, do....	442	0	412	0	1214	5
Wheat, foreign	14243	2	2415	2	223055	2
Barley, do........	14609	6	14725	6	40392	1
Oats, do........	4146	5	81	2	44146	6
Rye, do.	—		—		57	6
Peas, do.	82	1	382	3	24005	0
Beans, do.	5989	6	2141	0	112317	0
Indian Corn, do....	1	6	180	7	9981	4
Buck Wheat, do. ..	—		—		—	
Malt	—		—		—	
	cwts.	qrs.lbs.	cwts.	qrs.lbs.	cwts.	qrs.lbs.
Flour and Meal from British Possessions	711	1 15	21880	3 13	35152	0 20
Flour & Meal, foreign	10	0 13	41	0 3	43205	3 4

PRICES OF SEEDS.

MAY 29.

Linseed, English, sowing 55	65		
Baltic	—	—	crushing 42 48 per qr.
Mediter. & Odessa 45	46		
Large, foreign....	—		
Coriander............	10	16	old.... 16 20 per cwt.
Mustard, brown, new ..	9	11	white.. 9 10s 6d p.bush
Trefoil, new............	18	21	old.... 12 16

Rapeseed, English new.. 32l. 37l. per ton.
Linseed Cakes, English.. 9l. 10s. to 10l. per 1000
Do. Foreign.. 5l. 10s. to 6l. per ton.
Rapeseed Cakes........ 5l. 5s. to 5l. 10s.

Hempseed, small........	35	38	large ..	46	48 per qr.
Rye Grass, English......	30	42	Scotch	18	40
Tares, winter	—	—	New 3s 0d 4s 0d p.bush.		
Canary, new............	73	74	fine	75	76 per qr.
Carraway, old	—	—	new	42	44

PRICES OF HOPS.

BOROUGH, MONDAY, May 29.

We continue to experience a good demand for Hops, which are scarce ; and it will be seen from the prices annexed that there has been a decided advance since this day week in all the parcels of last year's growth. The dealers manage now to bring out supplies, but only at the advanced rates. The wet weather, it is believed, will clear off any fly that may have appeared.

		s.	s.
Pockets, 1842, Wealds....		102 to 115	per cwt.
...	East Kent..	120 — 140	..
..	Mid. Kent.	115 — 130	..
..	Sussex....	100 — 108	..
Pockets, 1841, Wealds, good		70 — 80	..
..	East Kent choice	84 — 100	..
	Mid. Kent.	80 — 95	..
	Sussex	70 — 80	..

POTATO MARKET.

BOROUGH AND SPITALFIELDS MARKET.

Full average supplies of Potatoes have arrived in the Pool since our last statement, yet the demand for them may be considered firm, on the following terms:—

	Per ton.		Per ton.
	s.		s.
Scotch Reds........	55 to 70	Jersey and Guernsey	
York do........	80to100	Blues .... 50 to 55	
Devons,..........	65 to 75	Yorkshire Prince	
Kent & Essex Whites	45 to 50	Regents .... 30 to 50	
Kent Kidneys......	55 to 60	Ditto Shaws, for	
Wisbeach do.	50 to 55	planting .... — to —	

PRICES OF MANURES.

Subjoined are the present prices of several sorts of manure :—

Hunt's Bone dust, 18s. per qr.
Hunt's Half-inch Bone, 16s. per qr.
Hunt's Artificial Guano, 8l. per ton.
Rape Dust, 7l. to 8l. per ton.
Rape Cake, 6l. 10s. to 7l. per ton.
Rags, 4l. to 4l. 10s. per ton.
Graves, 6l. 10s. per ton.
Gypsum, at the waterside, 32s. 6d. per ton ; landed and housed, 38s. to 42s. per ton, according to quantity.
Agricultural Salt, 34s. per ton.
Lance's Carbon, 12s. per qr.
Ditto Humus, 14s. per qr.
Soap Ashes, 10s. per ton.
Poittevin's Patent Disinfected Manure, 13s. 6d. per qr.
Poittevin's Highly Concentrated Manure, 30s. per qr.
Nitrate of Soda, 18s. to 18s. 6d. (duty paid) per cwt.
Nitrate Potash (saltpetre) 26s. 6d. per cwt.
Petre Salt, 4s. per cwt.
Willey Dust, 4l. 4s. per ton.
The Urate of the London Manure Company, 5l. per ton.
Chie-fou, 21s. per cwt.
Daniell's new Bristol Manure, 8s. per qr.
Hunt's new Fertilizer, 13s. 4d. per qr.
Grimwade's Preparation for Turnip Fly, 10s. 6d. per packet, sufficient for three acres.
Wolverhampton Compost (Alexander's), 12s. per qr., subject to carriage to London, or forwarded from Wolverhampton.

END OF VOLUME XVIII.

Printed by Joseph Rogerson, 24, Norfolk-street, Strand, London.

INDEX TO THE SEVENTH VOLUME.

(SECOND SERIES.)

Printed by Joseph Rogerson, 24, Norfolk Street, Strand, London.

Lightning Source UK Ltd.
Milton Keynes UK
UKHW022306210219
337726UK00009B/973/P